MANAGING CHANGE
Cases and Concepts

MANAGING CHANGE
Cases and Concepts

Todd D. Jick
Harvard Business School

IRWIN

Burr Ridge, Illinois
Boston, Massachusetts
Sydney, Australia

© RICHARD D. IRWIN, INC., 1993

Senior sponsoring editor:	Kurt L. Strand
Editorial assistant:	Lisa Brennan
Marketing manager:	Kurt Messersmith
Project editor:	Karen J. Nelson
Production manager:	Mary Jo Parke
Cover designer:	Teresa Oeffinger
Art coordinator:	Mark Malloy
Compositor:	ParaGRAPH Design Studio
Typeface:	10/12 Times Roman
Printer:	R. R. Donnelley & Sons Company

Library of Congress Cataloging-in-Publication Data

Jick, Todd
    Managing change : cases and concepts / Todd D. Jick.
      p.   cm.
    Includes index.
    ISBN 0-256-11231-2
    1. Organization change. 2. Organization change—Case studies.
    I. Title.
    HD58.8.J53 1993
    658.4'06—dc20   92-24166

Printed in the United States of America
      4 5 6 7 8 9 0 DOC 9 8 7 6 5

To Rose, Zoe, and Adina

Preface

During the last 15 years, a wide variety of management topics have interested me, such as: how organizations merge and how they downsize, how individuals handle the stress of organizational life, and how leaders can help organizations through challenging crisis conditions and revitalize. I taught a course about how the quality of organizational life can be improved and another course about the realities of power and politics, focusing on how managers try to influence people in their day-to-day behavior.

What increasingly became clear to me about my interests, research, and teaching was the common thread of CHANGE. In everything I did, and everything I was observing about managers, someone or something was changing. The management challenge was always to figure out a way to create that change or to ease the burden of change, or both.

Moreover, students taking my courses came with dreams and aspirations, and with a burning question: "How can I help organizations to change—for the better?" And, increasingly, another question also emerged as the pace and complexity of change evidenced in daily newspaper stories became overwhelming: "How well will I cope with all the change happening in today's organizations?"

I, thus, decided that it was time for a course, and ultimately this textbook, which addressed the issue of managing and adapting to change. In 1986, I set out to develop ideas, cases, videos, and a logic that would bring the subject of managing change "live and in color" to students facing the daunting challenges of the 1990s and the new century ahead. I originated the Managing Change course at the Harvard Business School in 1988, and over 600 students had taken the course by 1991 and helped me to refine the materials contained in this textbook.

Indeed, over the years, I have dedicated myself to making this subject of managing change a very personal matter. Introducing change in an organization is an exciting and yet formidable venture, and adventure. The lives and well-being of many are affected, including those who are at the cutting edge of driving change. Careers are made and sometimes broken as a result of major organizational change efforts. Managing change taxes the talent, skill, and conviction of an individual. It tests one's ability to understand the complexity of organizations, of corporate culture and politics, and of human psychology. And, inevitably, it hits up against ethical questions and choices.

This book attempts to give you a firsthand look and feel of how organizations change and how you can become a proactive participant in the many changes occurring in organizations today. It is designed to be a realistic preview of the difficulties and the pitfalls, while also suggesting the more successful paths for significant change in large complex organizations.

To achieve these objectives, materials had to be assembled with great care and with an unyielding focus on managerial situations that would be exciting change "puzzles" to try to solve. The cases and the readings contained herein will challenge your imagination and managerial aspirations, provoke you to discover and test your personal values and assumptions, and allow some fun along the way.

I had lots of help in putting all this together. First and foremost, I had the intellectual partnership and creativity of my editor, Barbara Feinberg, who stuck with me from the days of a blank syllabus through the final completion of this book. Barbara gave me, and now gives you, an impeccable eye to what make a case "sing" and how to link a series of cases that build more and more "sophistication," as she would call it. She also gave me every bit of confidence and support that an author and teacher would want.

The cases were written and crafted with the help of three research associates over the years. Each of them was subjected to the same ambiguities of weaving a story from a ragtag amalgam of facts and opinions—and from the same burden of dealing with me. The cases in this volume attest to their many skills in helping me to tell fascinating stories and in a well-written way. Their names are on their respective cases, but I want to thank each one individually.

My gratitude goes out to Susan Rosegrant who weathered the last two years of an accelerated, frantic pace; to Lori Ann MacIssac, who went right from Wellesley College into the offices of CEOs with amazing ease; and to Mary Gentile, my first research associate, who set a very high standard for writing, sensitivity, and humility.

Academic colleagues and friends challenged my ideas and offered suggestions throughout the development of the Managing Change course. Harvard colleagues included Chris Argyris, whose timely and insightful feedback were always intellectually challenging; Mike Beer, with whom I collaborated for a number of years in teaching executives the subject of organizational effectiveness and change; Jack Gabarro, who was a personal role model of what teaching and cases can be; Rosabeth Moss Kanter, who helped me see the relationship of my ideas to the "field," and with whom I collaborated on another book about change, *The Challenge of Organizational Change*; John Kotter, whose instincts and pithy comments about my work were always on the mark; and, finally, Len Schlesinger, who not only helped to bring me to Harvard initially but who also gave me the inspiration to "think big" always.

Others who, through no fault of their own, were subjected to my intellectual quandaries and who often used my cases and found new richness in them: Peter Frost (UBC), Paul Goodman (Carnegie Mellon), Vic Murray (York University), Noel Tichy (University of Michigan), Mike Tushman (Columbia University), and Dave Ulrich (University of Michigan). I also received support and counsel from the Brookline Group, a group that claims responsibility for no one, but which is nurturing to all of us that meet monthly to discuss personal and professional issues. Thanks to all of its members: Lee Bolman, Dave Brown, Tim Hall, Bill Kahn, Phil Mirvis, and Barry Oshry.

Last to thank, but hardly least, is my wife, Rose, who is a dedicated and skillful teacher from whom I have learned, and who is a wonderful spouse from whom I have learned much as well. By chance, the birth of our first child, Zoe, coincided with the birth of the Managing Change course and the arrival of our second child, Adina, coincides with the birth of this textbook. Rose is almost as proud of my course and textbook as she is of our daughters, and that is saying a lot, more than I and the book surely deserve.

The course has "grown up" since its inception and I think has developed nicely. I trust you will agree, and, if you do, all the people listed here deserve some of the credit.

Todd D. Jick

Contents

Introduction

Change is not made without inconvenience, even from worse to better.

Richard Hooker, 1554–1600

An adventure is only an inconvenience rightly understood. An inconvenience is only an adventure wrongly understood.

G. K. Chesterton, 1874–1936

In the 1990s when business and political leaders—indeed, entire governments—assert their dedication to change, and when "change agent" is a title many proudly claim, it seems propitious to write a textbook on how to deal with the phenomenon. It is hardly a new topic, of course; human beings have been commenting on change for millennia. These comments, moreover, consistently fall into two broad camps: it's good, it's bad! It is also inevitable, and in recent years has been very much in the forefront of the business world's agenda.

Management guru Tom Peters's blunt formula, "change or die," has been the bottom line for countless U.S. firms since at least the mid-1970s, as competitive onslaughts ravaged industry after industry. It is hard to over estimate this shock to so many companies, whether they should or should not have been prepared for it, whether they deserved it or not. And, to their credit, many firms chose not to die, but embarked on tremendously ambitious change efforts, some of which are chronicled in this book. There may be much to criticize about many of these efforts, but that criticism should be directed toward doing it better, not denigrating those who pioneered.

Doing it better is the goal of this text. Unfortunately, there is no singular *best* that can be shared. There are no sure-fire instructions which, when scrupulously followed, make change succeed, much less eliminate or solve the problems accompanying any change process. Changing is inherently messy, confusing, and loaded with unpredictability, and no one escapes this fact. At the outset, then, it's important to keep a sense of proportion about change. As an example, a Harvard Business School case was recently being written about a Fortune 100 company in the middle of a major revamping of one division—a soup-to-nuts change effort. It was not a pretty picture and the firm's public relations chief was extremely nervous about the image being portrayed in the case. The head of the change effort saw it differently. "This is cutting edge," he exclaimed. "This is what cutting edge looks like!"

Just because change is inherently difficult does not mean that attempts to put order on it haven't been made. The dream of coming up with a never-fail change process that will work across the board has captivated many. Organizational change must be originally conceived of; it must be implemented, which means some kind of procedures need to be put in place; and to succeed, the change must be accepted (i.e., those who have to change do so). Traditionally, these three elements have been arrayed as phases or steps, with hierarchical roles assigned responsibilities for tasks within each. A composite of this process flow looks like this:

Change strategists, leaders, visionaries, etc., are concerned about the connection between the organization and its environment (i.e., industry, market, competition). They provide a vision of how to close the gap they perceive between the two and a strategic design of varying degrees of specificity for implementing it. Yet, change is not always labeled as such: "We need to be more customer-focused" is not change per se. It is the implication of that statement which constitutes the change: to be more customer-focused usually necessitates an overhaul of how things are done. Change strategists are clearly the initiators of change and traditionally have represented the top leader(s) of the firm.

Change implementors, agents, champions, etc., are responsible for the micro-dynamics of the (by now) change effort, its internal organizational structure, and coordination of elements. This role is traditionally associated with the *middles*—the middle level of the organization and the middle of the change process. As such, implementation involves project management and execution rather than conception.

Change recipients, "changees," etc., traditionally are those, as a group, most strongly affected by the change. Since, typically, they have not participated in either the conception or implementation of the change, they feel its effects undiluted. Further, there are more recipients, as the change effort so far has been confined to upper and middle organizational ranks. Nonetheless, recipients' actions or reactions crucially determine a change's success, yet their role emerges toward the end of a change process, at least as the end is officially described.

Needless to say, no change program has ever rolled out with the ease implied by such a three-phased process. This book richly explores how (many) things can go awry no matter how thorough the planning, how careful the implementation, and regardless of everyone's good intentions. Some of these difficulties are related to the change model itself; others are connected to the itself-changing environment to which it is applied.

When a change process is conceived as a sequence of steps with certain tasks assigned to each and performed by different ranks in the organization, it is tempting to think of the change as a thing passed along, and when it finally hits bottom, change will happen. People don't consciously make this formulation, but considering change as a series of discrete activities encourages a possible detachment. A corollary to this possibility is that "they" do the changing and "we" will tell them how. Of course, "they" might resist, but even in the absence of resistance (which is admittedly rare), when the change is welcomed or at least perceived as an improvement, implementing on people invites problems. At a minimum it invites *avoidable* problems. No implementation plan ever covered all contingencies and the further away the implementors are from those who will operationalize the change, the greater the potential for predictable problems to appear.

One case in this text, for example, describes the introduction of a new computing system, plans for which had been meticulously drawn up by middle management and intended to be operationalized the day it was set up. Naturally, all sorts of unforeseen problems arose related to the computers themselves, but one huge snag related to the workers and was completely avoidable. Workers placed leftover work from the previous day in various "corners" to pick up and begin first thing the next day.

Unaware of this, implementors had arranged the new system differently, the workers could not find their leftover orders, the system became immediately clogged, work piled up, was done out of sequence, customers grew irate, and the whole mess went into a free fall. Even if the workers had been involved in every aspect of the implementation surely problems would still have arisen, but because they were not involved in any part of the plan those problems compounded.

A related danger in thinking of implementation as separate from operationalization is that it may be hard to change the change plan itself. The more people are intensely involved in drawing up the plan, as opposed to focusing on the change, the more reluctant they may be to alter it, even when it patently isn't working. So much time and energy have been invested in the effort, it may be tempting to try to make the people fit the plan rather than the reverse. Implementation planning can take on a life of its own; moreover, as is well known, planning something can be easier and more enjoyable than actually doing it.

Finally, a top-down sequencing change model may conflict with the goals of a change program itself. Many firms are making concerted efforts to flatten their hierarchies, empower their workers, and radically reconfigure how work is done. These elements are sometimes combined into a single change program, for example, General Electric's Workout program, subject of a case in this book. Or they may be part of another effort, perhaps a quality program. In either event, if the change process is conceived as top-down driven, but change is encouraged as bottom-up participation, there is a conflict between process and intended results.

The restructuring of organizational roles and responsibilities is emblematic of the new landscape change programs are being planted in and the new challenges they face. Given that a change must be decided on, implemented, and accepted to succeed, who is now responsible for these elements? If a firm is intentionally thinning its middle management ranks, who now does implementation? If line workers are to come up with their own improvements, are they now implementing on themselves? Are they even envisioning the change they will implement on themselves? Quite possibly, they are, under the traditional change model.

In addition, the new change landscape contains many changes efforts occurring simultaneously. There may be the ongoing quality push, now in its final year of roll-out. The customer-first program, four years old, is now reaching down to the next to last group for implementation. The globalization effort is gearing up, and the teams-now! reorganization is hot off the press. Thus, one employee could be in the following situation. As a member of a newly formed cross-functional team (part of the teams-now! drive), she is envisioning a radically different product development process with major ramifications for R&D, engineering, and operations. As a functional manager, she is simultaneously drawing up Implementation plans for the globalization change program. She is also participating in the customer-first effort by intensifying her interactions with key clients. And, she has just learned that, as part of a dramatic shift in strategy, the CEO intends to sell off her division, she may soon be redundant, but she must nonetheless inform her direct reports of their fate. Looking at this person's overall work, we can say her *job* is managing change, not enacting pieces of change programs.

This is precisely the point of "Managing Change": how to manage change overall, not how to become a particular player in the change program. The learning from this book appears when envisioning, implementing, and receiving change are seen as fundamentally *interrelated* activities.

Thus, the materials—cases and readings—have been chosen and arranged to introduce change as an integrated process. There are modules dedicated to envisioning, implementing, and receiving change, but these are provided to look at specific issues each entails, not to present them as separate activities. Indeed, it is impossible to determine when "rolling out the vision" ends and implementing it begins.

Cases in the text represent a wide variety of change situations. Companies range from a few hundred employees to hundreds of thousands. Industries span from bottle caps to international airlines. Some change programs are intended to be introduced over a weekend, while others are to be phased in over years. There are stunning successes, dismal failures, and a lot in between.

Every case reveals turbulence, confusion, and not a little pain as organizations wittingly or unwittingly makes choices and trade-offs.

Accompanying many cases are readings, likewise chosen to reflect a broad range of issues. Some readings provide theoretical underpinnings for a case, supporting the action; others challenge the action with alternative viewpoints. This material comes from popular business magazines as well as from professional journals. Beyond demonstrating the range of opinions on the topic of change, they reinforce how pervasive the issue has become.

Each module contains a summary of the major points the cases and readings explore, and three modules contain practical and highly realistic activities. You are challenged to come up with a vision for a company just formed from two competitors. In the next module, as part of a team, you must implement a major change in a firm, choosing and sequencing various approaches to get the troops on board. Finally, you must decide the best way to proceed with a massive downsizing for another organization.

The people whom you meet throughout the cases in this book are themselves learning how to manage change; in that sense, each situation is really a work-in-progress. They are your guides through the messy change terrain and will teach you much if you let them. That is, if you allow yourself to experience change as you approach this book, you will discover at the end, that although you have not discerned *the* answer to managing change, you can pose the four questions that count:

1. What is to be changed?
2. How is it to be done?
3. Who is affected?
4. What are the consequences so far?

Those who are managing change with some degree of success—for themselves and for others—recognize that they must continually ask these questions and listen to the answers, then transfer that learning to continually modify their efforts. In fact, this all adds up to the following, as many wise people have noted: managing change well means, quite simply, managing well.

Outline of the Book

The first module of the course, *The Challenge of Change,* examines the forces that create change, as well as the forces that can inhibit change. This represents an eternal tension that managers must manage, and cases will address the basic conditions under which change may be successfully introduced. It also underscores the book's focus on large-scale change efforts that are directed at transforming an organization's fundamental way of operating and the mindset and behavioral change commensurate with that.

A foundation for any change process is a vision of what will be changed or different. The second module of the course, *Envisioning Change,* highlights the criticality and difficulty of crafting a vision to direct and shape the change effort. The "vision thing" is often all too mushy and abstract, and it fails to motivate an organization to change or help to sustain change beyond the "program-of-the-month" mentality prevailing in many companies. However, all major changes we have observed in an organization have included at least the beginnings of a vision of what will and must change.

The third module, *Implementing Change,* is the bread-and-butter section of the book. It is the "how" that everyone seeks to understand. What managers most often bemoan is their frustration with how long it takes to make change happen, with how to overcome the resistance they encounter, with how to communicate information about the change, and so on. The lengthy list of issues to consider in how to get an organization to change are sampled in this module. And while there are no quick and easy formulas for addressing all of these succesfully, you will be able to develop some rules of thumb: some do's and don'ts for dealing with a myriad of choices around how change gets implemented.

Before you can be successful, however, at managing change, you must deepen your sensitivity and understanding about how people respond to change. How do people typically react? Is there really a "typical" reaction or is it different for each person? How can managers make it easier for people to cope with change? And what can an individual do to prepare and respond better to life in organizations that will be subject to continuing change? These questions, among others, must be considered before one can be successful as an agent of long-lasting change.

And, thus, the final module of the course is an upfront and personal look at what it means to be a *Change Agent.* By developing an understanding of the challenges of change, the use of a vision to target change, and the ways to implement change and sustain it by managing successfully the recipients, you will have strengthened your cognitive abilities to take on this critical managerial task. However, "being" a change agent is a hefty emotional and personal challenge. This module offers some insights into the frustrations and the joys of being a change agent, from a personal standpoint.

Thus, we begin and end the course with greater appreciation of the challenges—organizational and personal—about managing change. After all, it is the challenge itself that has brought out the best in many managers. How about you?

The Challenge of Change

INTRODUCTION

This module explores what drives change; what kinds of changes organizations pursue; when change is to be introduced, and what factors "enable" that introduction; and what reactions change evokes. Underlying this exploration is the assumption, a hopeful one, that change can be managed. But before it is to be managed, its ramifications must be appreciated.

FORCES FOR CHANGE

"Change," in its broadest sense, is a planned or unplanned response to pressures and forces. Hence, there is nothing new about change or the need for it. Technological, economic, social, regulatory, political, and competitive forces have caused organizations to modify for decades—if not centuries. Change is such a potent issue these days, however, because simultaneous, unpredictable, and turbulent pressures have become the norm. When this is broadened to a global scale, the forces multiply, some might argue, exponentially. Competition intensifies, more complex relations with other firms are established, strategic choices increase, adaptation is needed for survival.

It would be unrealistic to suggest that there is universal agreement on the magnitude, the time frame, and the implications of these forces. One part of an organization might perceive reasons for change, while another may not; different parts of the organization might find different forces driving change as well. Furthermore, the forces for change can be considered a two-edged sword. To illustrate, one response to the increased pressure for change is to say that change had better be managed perfectly the first time around—or else; there is no margin for error. On the other hand, it can be argued that a willingness to accept mistakes as part of the managing change process is actually a competitive plus: the organization can learn from its mistakes, thus increasing its flexibility and perhaps leading to longer-term success.

Ultimately, the pressures that provoke change can be considered obstacles or challenges, threats or opportunities. They can elicit despair or mobilize energy. The reactions depend on how an organization interprets the forces surrounding it, and what it does with them.

TYPES OF ORGANIZATIONAL CHANGE

The previous section began with a broad definition of change—a planned or unplanned response to pressure—and surveyed the "pressure." Here we explore

FIGURE 1   Three Perspectives on Change

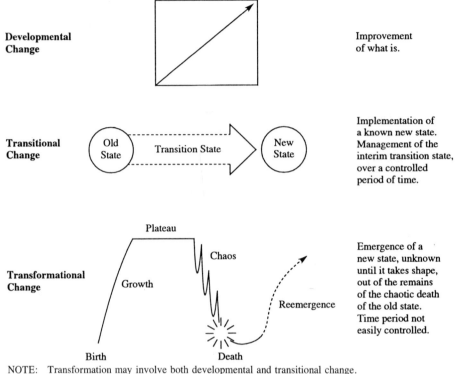

**Developmental
Change**

Improvement
of what is.

**Transitional
Change**

Old State   Transition State   New State

Implementation of
a known new state.
Management of the
interim transition state,
over a controlled
period of time.

**Transformational
Change**

Plateau

Chaos

Growth

Reemergence

Birth   Death

Emergence of a
new state, unknown
until it takes shape,
out of the remains
of the chaotic death
of the old state.
Time period not
easily controlled.

NOTE: Transformation may involve both developmental and transitional change.
Transitional change may involve developmental change.
Transformational change in an organization may be managed as a series of transitional changes.

© Linda S. Ackerman, Inc., 1984. (Now Linda Ackerman Anderson, Being First, Inc., Berkeley, California.)

"planned response." Linda Ackerman[1] provides a useful way of categorizing changes
common in organizations, each of which varies in scope and depth (see Figure 1).

The first type Ackerman suggests is *developmental* change: "The improvement
of a skill, method or condition that for some reason does not measure up to current
expectation . . . [thus] 'to do better than' or 'do more of' what already exists."[2] This
might be considered fine tuning—helping an organization stretch and, thereby, change.
The next two categories Ackerman proposes are those that we are principally
concerned with; they are more far-reaching, potentially wrenching, and, therefore,
most in need of managing.

Transitional change is introduced to have an organization evolve slowly. Current

---

[1] Linda Ackerman, "Development, Transition or Transformation: The Question of Change in Organizations," *OD Practitioner*, December 1986, pp. 1–8.

[2] Ibid., p. 1.

ways of doing things are replaced by something new—for example, reorganizations; mergers; introducing new services, processes, systems, technologies, and the like. This kind of change involves many transition steps, during which the organization is neither what it once was nor what it aims to become. Such steps include temporary arrangements, pilots, phased-in operations. The firm eases into a new picture of itself.

The most radical change Ackerman suggests is *transformational*:

> It is catalyzed by a change in belief and awareness about what is possible and necessary for the organization. . . . It is something akin to letting go of one trapeze in mid-air before a new one swings into view. . . . Unlike transitional change, the new state is usually unknown until it begins to take shape. . . . Most of the variables are not to be controlled, rushed, or short-circuited.[3]

Transformational change does require a leap of faith for the organization, although often it is initiated when other options appear to have failed. It is typified by a radical reconceptualization of the organization's mission, culture, critical success factors, form, leadership, and the like. Transformational changes occurred in the automobile and steel industries in the 1980s, for example. Other industries, and the companies within them, undoubtedly will require such change in this decade.

Determining what kind of change an organization requires is clearly vital, for the depth and complexity of implementation grow significantly from developmental (much skill-building training) to transitional (setting up temporary positions, structures) to transformational (developing new beliefs, systems, gaining organizationwide commitment). The level of investment grows accordingly.

A way of assessing the kind of change an organization needs is to ponder the following questions. Given that the organization is under pressure to change its current way of doing things:

1. How far do we want to go? Is that too far—not far enough?
2. Are we contemplating the "path of least resistance," or a direction that is truly needed?
3. What kind of results do we want—short term, longer term?
4. Do we want permanent change—or will that risk inflexibility, making future change more difficult?
5. How much change can the organization absorb? At once? Cumulatively?
6. Can the changes contemplated be presented positively? If not, why not?
7. What happens if we don't change at all?

Woven into the determination of what changes an organization needs is envisioning the future "look and feel" of the organization. The vision may embrace only improvements of what already exists; it may depict a new look that gradually materializes; or it may be a fuzzier image—not clearly distinguishable for the moment but resembling nothing like the current organizational "shape."

---

[3] Ibid., p. 2.

WHEN TO CHANGE

Given the pressures and the types of changes possible to institute, when is the decision made to pull the lever, "Let's change now"? Basically, an organization can institute change when things are going well, when results are mixed, or when a full-fledged crisis is upon it.

An organization can anticipate pressures down the road. Considering making changes proactively can be partly a matter of foresight and preparation; but it also can entail the belief that, if the organization is not routinely changing itself, it risks complacency and stagnation.

Or, an organization can encounter a problem, not necessarily life-threatening but one deserving attention, and, thus, feel the need to introduce change. It might, for example, consider a reorganization in response to a competitor's new product introduction; it might consider creating a quality program after receiving disturbing results about its own product or service quality.

Alternatively, an organization faced with a definite threat—alarmingly deteriorating results, the withdrawal of a major account—most probably will institute change, acutely recognizing the need to do so.

Given these general "times" for introducing change, one might assume that the process is easier when the organization is in crisis: the situation is clear to all, survival is on the line; everyone recognizes that the way things have been done won't work anymore. But the very fact of the crisis suggests that at best there has been inattentiveness to its origins; there may be deep organizational problems that deter introducing changes to confront the situation. Thus, one might say, changes really should be made in anticipation of difficulties. But, paradoxically, making changes before "the event" is equally difficult—how can an organization be energized to make changes when the need for them is not universally perceived? How *far* down the road is down the road?

Some argue that a way around this paradox is to manufacture a sense of crisis, rather than wait for the "real" one to appear. This crafting of urgency presumably elicits a responsiveness to change while not placing the organization at risk. The danger of this approach is in crying wolf. Claim too many times that survival is at stake, and the organization will greet you with "This, too, shall pass."

When to change, thus, involves an exquisite sense of timing: have we waited too long or have we started too soon? The challenge is to choose the time when the organization both should make changes and can do so. However, those two dimensions don't always come together—hence, the challenge.

ENABLING CHANGE   → can think about when analysing cases ie how fast? scope?

Beyond the issues of what kind of change is needed and when it should be introduced, an organization considers how to enable the change to be effective. This is not strictly an implementation matter; rather, it involves yet another group of strategic choices to be contemplated before actual (tactical) implementation occurs.

The first enabling issue is *pace*. How long will it take to design the change plan/program? How quickly should the change unfold? How much accommodation should be made for trial-and-error learning? Is it easier for the organization if the change is introduced quickly or over a period? But how much time does the organization have, given customer needs, competitive demands (i.e., the forces that are driving the change in the first place)?

Related to pace is *scope*. Obviously, this issue stems in large measure from the vision of what change is needed, but there are still choices to be made. Should the change start small and grow, or should it start big? If it is to be piloted—where and with whom? Should the pilot run in an area "loaded for success"? Where is the best climate for experimentation? Where is it more generalizable to the rest of the organization?

If the decision is to start big, issues of *depth* arise. How many changes can be introduced in any one area? The high risk/high reward approach is to simultaneously blitz an organization with a large number of consistent changes to ensure maximum impact. But there is probably a limit to how much change can be absorbed before resistance is mobilized—actively or, possibly, positively or negatively.

And related to scope is *publicity*: how loud, how long, and to whom should the organization announce change is on the way? There is, on the one hand, the hype approach. Out come the speeches, the binders, the newsletters, the banners/buttons/ T-shirts. The rationale is that to enable an organization to change there must be many clear reinforcements and motivational cues: everybody has to be excited and committed at the outset.

On the other hand, of course, this approach raises expectations (which may be too high already) and makes the change highly visible and, thus, a target for snipers and naysayers (and legitimate critics as well). Little room for flexible adjustments of the change plan may be left. Thus, there is an argument for a quiet, understated introduction, which controls resistance, allows for mistakes in learning, and moderates expectations. In either approach the issue is publicity, not communication, which is essential, although the degree of explicit information and to whom it is given may vary. (Communicating change will be discussed in greater detail subsequently.)

Another enabling change issue is *supporting structures*. What mechanisms does an organization have, or put in place, to further the change effort? Decisions here clearly are linked to pace and scope; but regardless of choices in those areas, some care and nurturing of the change will be needed. How much should be done through normal management processes and how much should be specially created?

Going through routine channels enables the change to be considered part of the normal and expected organizational activities. The risk, of course, is that it might not be perceived as sufficiently important to get adequate attention and dedication. All too many change projects die early because they become too routinized. However, bringing in too many consultants and having too many task forces or off-site gatherings risks making the change effort the only organizational preoccupation.

The final enabling issue is deciding who *drives* the change. The classic approach has a senior staff person or a CEO develop a vision, which in turn is endorsed by top management, and then assigned to middle management to implement. Clearly, this approach depends on gaining top management commitment, but it underplays the need for middle- or bottom-level ownership. A second classic approach is the reverse: the need for change is envisioned from deep down in the organization to implement. A third approach uses an outside consultant as an implementer/facilitator.

What seems clear, given the complexities that the challenge of change involves, is that the selection of the change team is pivotal. All too often people are chosen on the basis of their availability, rather than on their ability to comprehend the full ramifications of introducing change.

REACTING TO CHANGE

Perhaps the greatest challenge of all comes with the awareness that managing change *includes* managing the reactions to that change. Unfortunately, change frequently is introduced without considering its psychological effect on others in the organization—particularly those who have not been part of the decision to make the change: those who arrive on Monday to learn "from now on, it's all different." Further, when reactions are taken into account, they often are lumped under "resistance" to change, a pejorative phrase that conjures up stubbornness, obduracy, traditionalists, "just saying no." It seems fair to state, however, that, if the reactions to change are not anticipated—and managed—the change process will be needlessly painful and perhaps be unsuccessful.

Traditionally grouped under resistance to change are inertia, habit, and comfort with the known. For most people, change isn't actively sought; some level of routine is preferred. But routine is preferred because it enables some control. Given that change, at its onset at least, involves some ambiguity if not outright confusion, this control is threatened. That is, resistance is frequently a reaction to a loss of control, not necessarily to the change itself. The further away a person is from knowing the rationale for the change and the implications of the change and how the change is to be operationalized, the greater the threat to that person's control over his or her environment. Quite simply, contemplating change in the abstract *can* evoke fear.

Other forces also may serve to dampen change. Collective interests to preserve the status quo can emerge to mobilize political roadblocks, and a conservative culture may prevent an organization from appreciating the gravity of a problem, the up side of an opportunity, and the creative boldness of a major change.

Change also may be perceived as an indictment of previous decisions and actions. It is difficult for people to change when they have been part of creating the conditions that precipitated the change. Or change can be resisted when there are barriers to being able to respond adequately.

Finally, people are simply more alert. Given "streamlining," "downsizing," and "restructuring"—all euphemisms for layoffs (itself a euphemism for being fired)—people are more wary of change because of its inferred adverse consequences.

For all these reasons, employees at all levels in organizations psychologically defend against change, and reactions can be both more hostile and less predictable than the phrase "resistance to change" might imply.

Reactions to change are not always in the psychological realm, of course. Legitimate philosophical differences of opinion may exist. The change solution that is designed to treat one problem can create difficulties elsewhere: many changes for the good have led to changes for the worse. People who say, "Wait a minute, maybe we shouldn't" aren't always hopeless reactionaries.

One final point about reacting to change. There are limits to the stress that organizations can absorb—either at a given moment or cumulatively. Organizations, like individuals, can become saturated and, thereby, be either unwilling or unable to integrate new and deeper changes, even if these are acknowledged to be needed.

For one theorist, Herbert Kaufman,[4] there is a predictable pattern to managing change that encompasses resistance. He argues that (1) organizations require change to survive; (2) yet they always face considerable forces of resistance; (3) nevertheless, they do change; (4) but that change is always "dampened" later, with the original inertia and status quo overtaking the change—leading back to (1), when organizations face the need to change once again. This somewhat dispirited assessment of a change process underscores the difficulty of instituting and institutionalizing *permanent* change.

Other organizational theorists are more sanguine that substantial change can indeed be created:

> Change must become the norm, not cause for alarm. The bottom line: if you can't point to something specific that's being done differently from the way it was done when you came to work this morning, you have not "lived," for all intents and purposes: you surely have not earned your paycheck by any stretch of the imagination. Furthermore, the incremental changes of today must almost unfailingly be in support of nonincremental change—that is, a bold goal to be achieved in record time.[5]

OVERVIEW OF CASES AND READINGS

The challenge of change is, perhaps more than anything, that of managing paradoxes, tensions, trade-offs, and, as the first case shows, company politics. "John Smithers: Change Agent" is the case about a young middle manager in a high-tech firm who was asked to co-lead a quality program that may require considerable changes to the company's operations. Everything goes wrong, however, and Smithers moves from enthusiasm to cynicism over the eight months the case covers. This change "failure" illuminates the quandary of attempting to change when all the ingredients for its success are not neatly in place, which means it's a typical situation, if not in the particulars.

The accompanying reading, "Managing the Challenges of Trigger Events: The Mindsets Governing Adaptation to Change," introduces four "mindsets associated with the process of change that provide the mental maps through which individuals make sense of the events." The author traces how one company dealt with circumstances roughly similar to those facing Smithers: new ownership, flagging competitiveness, and the introduction of a quality program. The article, however,

---

[4] Herbert Kaufman, *Limits of Organizational Change* (University, Ala.: University of Alabama Press, 1971).

[5] Tom Peters, *Thriving on Chaos* (New York: Alfred A. Knopf, 1988), p. 464.

takes the perspective of those "receiving" change and, thus, is an interesting counterpoint to the case, which takes the "doing" point of view.

The lens of change challenges widens with the next case, "The 36-Hour Work Day (A)," to include a much broader and varied group of stakeholders. The case describes a highly publicized death of a young woman in a major New York City teaching hospital. A grand jury investigation has concluded that long work hours of the interns (as many as 36 in a row) contributed to the woman's death. An advisory group formed by the state health commissioner must decide whether to make any changes to the medical/educational system, what those changes would be, and their implications. Because the landscape in this case is so complex, and any implementation task so daunting, the need for change itself is a highly charged issue that brings both practical and ethical arguments to the fore. Yet environments like this will have to be understood if large-scale change, such as those with which governments increasingly wrestle, is ever to be attempted.

A striking example of a large, complex—and successful—change is found in the final case in this module, "Changing the Culture at British Airways." During a decade, the airline went from "bloody awful" to "bloody awesome," with stunning statistics to back up that assessment. All the issues that will be examined in depth throughout subsequent modules are here: what "vision" drove the changes, how it was implemented, sustained, modified, how people responded, and what it faces in the future. The accompanying reading, "Re-Energizing the Mature Organization," reinforces the case substantially as well as presents more generic recommendations for established firms.

Though "the future" is raised as a concern at the end of the BA case, the issue needs to be incorporated in thinking about a change process. What BA will "do as an encore" is a profound matter, which is probably the ultimate challenge of change.

CASE

JOHN SMITHERS: CHANGE AGENT

It was a few days before Christmas 1988, and a light snow had covered the New England town where John Smithers

This case was prepared by Research Associate Susan Rosegrant (under the direction of Professor Todd D. Jick).

Copyright © 1990 by the President and Fellows of Harvard College. Harvard Business School case N9-491-035.

lived with his wife and two young children. But instead of planning surprises and wrapping presents, the 37-year-old Smithers was working on his résumé. He had already warned his wife that within weeks he expected to be fired by his employer of three years. His boss and mentor had just been demoted to what appeared to be an extraneous position. Now, he figured, it was just a matter of time until his job was taken, too.

Eight months earlier, things had looked very different. Then, Smithers' boss, Andrew Cross, had selected him for what appeared to be a challenging and potentially rewarding opportunity: to become one of two site instructors for a Total Quality program soon to be launched at Sigtek, the telecommunications company where he worked. Not only was Smithers excited at the chance to apply some of the management tenets he believed in so fervently, he also felt that this program could be the key to setting Sigtek on a path toward much needed change.

Founded in the early 1960s by three Western Electric veterans, Sigtek manufactured printed circuit boards for signal handling, which it sold primarily to AT&T. Although the company was sold in the late 1970s, the parent corporation maintained a hands-off management style and left Sigtek to its own devices. Sigtek was small, but it faced few competitors in its niche, and grew steadily, particularly in 1985 following the breakup of AT&T. With the telecommunications industry in turmoil, both the newly formed Baby Bells and the distributors that served them stockpiled products, including the signal-handling equipment that Sigtek made. As a result, Sigtek's sales in 1985 shot up to more than $60 million, its work force topped 1,000, and prospects seemed very bright. Many within the company predicted that, by 1990, Sigtek would be a $100 million company.

But Sigtek's growth spurt was short-lived. Because of the industry stockpiling in 1985, sales the following year were artificially depressed. Moreover, for the first time, Sigtek began to face serious competition in its marketplace. As the company's printed circuit boards became

more of a commodity product, customers began to base their buying decisions less on quality and more on price and delivery time. On top of that, the company's first attempt to incorporate software into a computer system for signal handling was falling abysmally behind schedule. By 1987, Sigtek's sales had tumbled to about $40 million, and it had trimmed its work force to 800.

Other changes were in the air. In 1987, another company bought Sigtek. But unlike its former corporate parent, its new owner, Telwork, a $500 million European telecommunications joint venture, made it clear in the first year that it planned to be seen *and* heard. In November of that year, Telwork began formulating a Total Quality program, based on a highly acclaimed model, which it intended to bring to all its subsidiaries. The goal of the program was not only to improve product quality and encourage better management practices, but also to gather all of the scattered and diverse companies which Telwork had acquired under a single corporate umbrella. By April 1988, Telwork was ready to begin training instructors from each of its facilities in the Total Quality program.

Smithers Makes a Choice

When Andrew Cross, Sigtek's vice president of engineering, asked Smithers to become one of two site instructors for the Total Quality program, in many ways he seemed a natural choice (see Exhibit 1). Smithers looked up to Cross as a mentor, and the two men had similar ideas about the best way to manage people. Although Sigtek's management style overall could be characterized as autocratic and largely unresponsive to worker concerns, both Smithers and Cross had been working within the engineering side of the business

EXHIBIT 1   Sigtek Organizational Chart

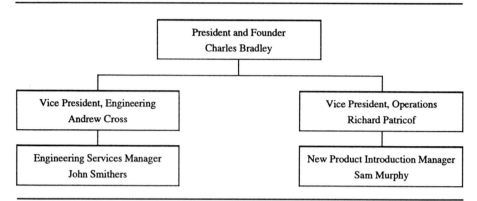

to encourage problem solving and open communication, and to enlist worker participation.

Moreover, Smithers already had shown an uncanny ability to identify problems within a specific department at Sigtek, and to come up with effective strategies for resolving them. Less than a year earlier, Cross had promoted Smithers to head up engineering services, the group responsible for doing product design work and documentation for manufacturing, and one of Sigtek's more troubled units. As engineering services manager, Smithers was faced with redefining a haphazard design process, correcting inadequate documentation, and cutting the highest employee turnover rate in the company.

Relying on readings, as well as his own managerial experience at a series of computer startups, Smithers set to work. First, he made some personnel changes, removing or reassigning a few managers who were particularly resistant to change. Next, he gathered group input on how to better define the design process, designed and implemented a new computer integration strategy, and reoriented the group to focus on customer-satisfaction goals. After just a few months, the results

already had been impressive: the company's design process had become more responsive to customer needs; the designs themselves had fewer errors; the time it took to complete a design had been cut in half, and Smithers had eliminated the former high attrition rate.

In addition, Smithers had an infectious enthusiasm, which had made him a popular leader. His easy, egalitarian manner with both his immediate peers and subordinates, as well as the typically middle-aged women who worked on the line assembling printed circuit boards, made him a good choice as a teacher.

Finally, Cross was determined to get a strong representative in the Total Quality program. Although many companies experience a natural split between their engineering groups and the rest of their operations, at Sigtek the split was carried to an extreme. In fact, the corporate culture was best characterized by the extreme polarity that existed between the two sides of the organization. Sigtek's engineering staff was isolated in its own building, separated from the rest of the operations by a long hallway, and this physical separation seemed symbolic of the deep

peit bet
divisions are
plus, heads are
very different

organizational gulf which divided the two sides.

This antipathy between engineering and operations had existed for many years. But the current heads of the two groups—Cross, and his counterpart in operations, Richard Patricof—seemed particularly ill-matched. While Cross was committed to bringing in new blood and new management practices, Smithers characterized Patricof as leaning more toward style and less toward substantive results—a manager who rewarded those who parroted his beliefs, and who rarely questioned the status quo.

Since both Cross and Patricof were responsible for selecting one instructor for the program, Cross felt strongly that he needed to put forward one of his best managers for the job. Charles Bradley, Sigtek's largely absentee president and the last remaining member of its founding team, had chosen Patricof as the company's representative on the corporate Quality Improvement Team, the advisory group for the Total Quality program made up of representatives from corporate headquarters as well as each of Telwork's subsidiaries. As Cross saw it, this already had given Patricof an unfair opportunity to use the quality program for his own advancement. Smithers, he felt, would bring some important balance to the process.

When Cross asked him, Smithers said yes. But his answer betrayed his ambivalence. "When I first started, I said to him, 'I will do it if I don't have to lie' " Smithers recalled. " 'If I lie, I stop doing it.' I was skeptical about our ability to effect change."

A number of factors lay behind Smithers' uneasiness. For one thing, he was afraid that a program of this sort might raise workers' expectations too high. He had seen evidence already of how resistant the organization's culture might be to change. In particular, he feared that the company's marked polarity would present a formidable barrier to *any* change program which intended to rally and unite the entire organization behind a single cause.

Although he had succeeded at encouraging cooperation within his own engineering design department, Smithers already had had personal experience with the frustrations of attempting this kind of cooperation on a companywide scale. Several months earlier, when first working to upgrade the engineering design process, Smithers had tried to create an effective cross-functional team to iron out ways in which his group could better serve and work with Sigtek's other operations. But the "team" concept had fizzled out when his peers from other areas either came to meetings reluctantly or simply didn't bother to attend.

Another drawback of the teaching post was that Smithers was to be paired as an instructor with Sam Murphy, a "fire fighter type manager" from the operations side with whom he had already had run-ins, and for whom he had very little respect. "It was a joke," Smithers laughed. "It was like they were saying oil and water have been chosen to do this training together."

But despite these fears, Smithers retained some of his enthusiasm. Secretly, he hoped that the quality program would prove to be the pivotal change which Sigtek needed. "I saw it as the last possible opportunity to alter the organization in a way that I had been trying to do in my own engineering services group," he explained. "I told my own people to just wait. If I can get this quality stuff going, we will all have a common battle cry."

In fact, Smithers was becoming increasingly convinced that, unless Sigtek embraced some kind of change program, its days would be numbered. The antagonism between engineering and operations which had flourished under the weak leadership of Bradley was not only making it impossible for the organization to operate in an efficient and effective way, it was literally threatening to tear the organization in two. "There was one operations manager there who told me right before he resigned that he just wished the fight between Cross and Patricof would end," Smithers confided. "Then at least we would know who had won and what to do."

The Process Begins

During May and June, Smithers and Murphy joined 10 other instructors from Telwork's other facilities for three weeks of training, designed to familiarize them with the Total Quality materials and to teach them communication and presentation skills. Although there were still reminders of the obstacles he faced—Smithers and Murphy tried to get seats apart from each other when they flew to these off-site sessions, for example—Smithers felt encouraged by the caliber of the program. "I was impressed with the materials," he recalled. "Because I had been doing a lot of reading already, this incorporated most of the stuff I had figured out."

Specifically, the program focused on raising employee awareness of the following six Total Quality Goals:

1. To provide product and service quality better than all competitors.
2. To be the lowest-cost quality producer.
3. To relentlessly pursue quality improvement.

4. To manage through leadership.
5. To personally involve all employees through participative activity.
6. To be comprised of employees who approach the job fearlessly.

With these goals in place, the program literature promised, Telwork would be well on its way to becoming the market leader in the telecommunications industry.

These concepts were not new to Smithers. But apparently they were new to Richard Patricof, Sigtek's representative to the corporate Quality Improvement Team, who had attended some of the same meetings. "When I came back from my first introduction to this stuff, Patricof said, 'Boy, that was great. You learn a lot of new stuff,'" Smithers recounted. "Because I had heard most of it before, I said, 'No, I didn't really learn a lot of new things, I learned some new terminology. And it was very exciting to learn the terminology that goes along with the management style I have been trying to practice.'"

Smithers and Murphy weren't due to start training at Sigtek until September. In the meantime, Telwork sent a team of corporate trainers to Sigtek in July to present the Total Quality module to the company's senior and middle managers. Altogether, about 25 managers attended the two-day, 16-hour program—the same program which Smithers and Murphy would later be presenting to the rest of the organization. "There were two purposes here," Smithers explained. "To help make our job as instructors easier, and to give management time to think about the magnitude of the change that would be happening after we started to give it to the ranks."

But for Smithers, at least, the response to the program was deeply disturbing. He still remembered the uneasy sensation which gripped him as the presentation to managers ended. "This was the first time our entire senior management had seen the program," he recalled, "and there were no questions during the entire presentation. What scared me the most was thinking that nobody cares. Or that nobody comprehends. Or that they are scared out of their boots." He added: "They had told us in class that, when we presented the material, we would have first, our champions; second, our people we could convert; and third, our 'no-sales.' What I realized as I looked around is that there were a couple of champions and possibly no converts."

Before starting the general training, Smithers and his cohort, Murphy, tried to lay the groundwork necessary to support the ambitious program they were about to present. They met with the site Quality Improvement Team, a cross-functional group of managers largely hand-picked by Patricof, which was intended to serve as a sort of steering committee—establishing guidelines and in other ways helping to implement the Total Quality program. In addition, they struggled to pull together their presentations. During this time, the two instructors' mutual respect began to grow. Both of them were committed to the program, Smithers said he realized, and they tried to put their differences aside for the good of the company.

But as the quality program took more and more time, Smithers' own department was starting to suffer from his frequent absences. There were personnel issues to resolve, for example. As his attention was pulled in two directions at once, both he and Murphy agreed that they needed an extra week to be ready for the September launch of the program. But

when they asked Patricof, as the corporate quality representative, for a one-week extension, he turned them down. "I'm not even going to judge whether it was Patricof not wanting to wait," Smithers said, "or corporate telling him to get moving."

Total Quality Training Begins

With a little scrambling, Smithers and Murphy got the training underway. In September, they together presented three two-day classes to groups of about 25 employees who were usually all at the same hierarchical level. "According to me, what they were supposed to get out of this was a belief in a new system of management and a new work environment," Smithers said. "We laid out specific things that people could do, and things they should see happening."

Doing the sessions revived some of Smithers' hope and optimism. For one thing, he liked the materials he was using. The format was not entirely rigid and allowed the instructors to emphasize the points they found most relevant. Moreover, the program's mix of workshops, videos, and other multimedia presentations was entertaining, both for the instructors and the audience. "I felt I had the tools I needed," Smithers mused. "I felt I could make the glaring deficiencies of the organization apparent to everybody."

But even better than that, the line workers who attended the programs were buying into the Total Quality concept wholeheartedly. According to Smithers, employees were coming to the workshops with lists of examples of how things weren't working according to a Total Quality plan, and with ideas about how to fix them. "What was intriguing was the ability of the line workers to understand what we were talking about and the inability of most of those above them to understand,'' he exclaimed. ''These were people who in some cases did not have a full high school education, but they picked it up in a snap. For them, what it came down to was common sense and just treating people right.'' He added: ''If I could have taken 95 percent of those line workers and gone off and started another company that day, in terms of problem solving, in terms of productivity, and in terms of motivation, we would have been in good shape.''

The Unraveling Begins

It wasn't long, however, before Smithers' burst of optimism began to fade. Within weeks of the training kickoff, his original fear of being put in the position of disseminating lies began to weigh heavily on his mind. ''I am pretty good at pumping up a crowd,'' he explained, ''and I could see that, with these tools and with my enthusiasm for it, the first thing you are going to do is heighten expectations way beyond reality. The workers would go back to their real world and, not only would nothing be changed, they'd see that they *couldn't* change them.''

In fact, Smithers claimed, this is exactly what began to happen. One of the ''easily fixable'' problems which a worker had submitted at one of the first quality workshops was the dilemma of the ''bouncing boards.'' Specifically, the way the assembly process was set up, workers would place small components on a printed circuit board, stack the boards on carts, and then wheel them across the room to where other workers would solder the components in place. But because many of the carts had hard metal wheels, when they rolled across cracks in the floors the

boards would bounce and send the unsoldered components flying like pieces of popcorn.

This was just the sort of manageable problem Smithers wanted to attack. He led the workshop participants in finding acceptable solutions—either to have the maintenance people build new carts out of spare parts or to order new ones with soft rubber wheels—and encouraged them to take the ideas back to the floor supervisors for action. But the problem didn't go away. ''Three or four weeks would go by and I'd have a new class,'' Smithers recounted. ''I'd say, 'Give me an example of something that can be fixed,' and they'd say, 'Bouncing boards!' I was incredulous.'' He added: ''At some point, the people coming in knew it had been a topic in the past, and I was losing credibility.''

Smithers finally asked Murphy to look into the situation, since it was on the operations side of the business, just as new carts arrived. But even though the problem was eventually resolved, Smithers never forgave the damage done to his credibility by the long waiting period. ''Patricof was always telling us to get known wins—to go for the easy wins,'' he griped. ''Yet this was the simplest problem, and it wasn't getting fixed. I didn't see it as a success, because I saw the bureaucratic structure and the value system behind it all.'' He added: ''Management just had this attitude like, 'I'm working on problems that are more serious than the components bouncing out of the boards.' ''

There were other disturbing interactions. One woman in an early workshop complained that for years she had been banging her knee on a metal plug receptacle which stuck out from the wall under her particular work station. After coaching her in how to raise this issue at her group's weekly quality meeting, the woman left happy. But when Smithers went out on the floor the following week to touch bases with the workshop participants, he recalled, the woman hissed at him, "John Smithers, you speak with a forked tongue." Not only had she been unable to air her complaint with her floor supervisor, the woman told him, the supervisor had peremptorily declared that she had no time and no budget for weekly meetings.

Smithers, unable to resolve the matter with either the supervisor or her boss, finally appealed to accounting, determined that the meeting—a supposed "corporate mandate" of the quality program—would take place. "I went over to accounting and I said, 'I want to charge an hour meeting to my group because that group over in operations can't pay for it, and those people are going to have a meeting!'" he recounted. "The person in accounting liked me, and she understood what I was trying to do, but she told me she could not do it that way." He added: "It must have taken a month for that meeting to happen, and another month for that socket to get fixed. That was a success, but look at the effort."

Such incidents left Smithers doubting whether any of the company's senior managers, including Patricof, Sigtek's quality liaison to corporate, were committed to the changes they were preaching. Although the training manual stressed the importance of encouraging worker participation and input, employees who asked for changes—like the woman who complained about the plug receptacle—usually were ignored or, worse yet, viewed as troublemakers. "Senior management knew how to do *everything* better than the person working on the floor," Smithers grumbled. "There was a very healthy Theory X

environment, especially in manufacturing. I kept hearing things along the lines, of 'Gee, John, real men don't manage that way.'"

In addition, Smithers said, some managers began trying to push through their own agendas by cloaking them in the mantle of the new quality program. "People would say, 'Well, I'm trying to do Total Quality,'" he said, "'and if you don't agree with me, you're not for Total Quality.'"

As Smithers and Murphy continued training people on into October, their sense of operating in a vacuum deepened. The site Quality Improvement Team, for example, which was supposed to coordinate and facilitate Total Quality efforts at the facility, was so quiet that most people were unaware of its existence. "There was no visibility," Smithers contended. "No memos, no newsletters. They made promises to us about meeting with people throughout the company but did not keep them."

According to Smithers, instead of getting actively involved in the implementation of the program, the team wasted its time on inconsequential bureaucratic decisions. "The guy in charge of the reward and recognition program spent months trying to write a formula for how many 'atta boys' it takes to get a key chain, and how many for a coffee mug," he exclaimed. "All that these people knew about management was how to fill out time cards. That's the way Sigtek had trained them—it wasn't their fault."

As obstacles to the quality program continued to mount, Smithers voiced his frustrations not only to his boss, Cross, but also to his staff of five and to a number of other direct reports. Although publicly he kept up a facade of optimism, behind closed doors he confessed his doubts in the

[handwritten margin note: ? Driver to be... seems to be a desire to please HQ; not to be a better worker]

program and his misgivings about Patricof. "I'm a pretty open person," Smithers explained. "Perhaps I wasn't as good a buffer as I could have been. But that's what makes me credible." He added: "I am lucky, because, as a person, I can manage in a way that is consistent with my personality and get things done while treating people nicely. Richard Patricof wanted to be the same kind of person, but in my estimation, the required results were missing. He spent so much energy on style that things like the trucks in manufacturing wouldn't get fixed."

Pulling Back

By early November, Smithers was ready to put the Total Quality training process on hold. It wasn't that he felt the program had been completely futile. "I could still really get my energy level up there and believe during those classes that we were effecting change, because I couldn't have gotten up in the morning if I didn't," he reflected. "If I could change those bouncing carts in three months, versus them never being changed, I could do something."

Nevertheless, Smithers said, he felt that the visible successes had been far too small. In order to build the commitment and enthusiasm necessary to mobilize the work force, he needed some big wins— examples of real changes that the Total Quality program had achieved. Not only had there been no such big wins, company morale was dipping lower than ever. Sigtek appeared to be headed for its first loss. Moreover, in the seven months since Smithers had first agreed to be a quality instructor, there had been four rounds of layoffs at the company, each more severe than the last.

Convinced of the need for a reassess-ment, Smithers and Murphy asked for a temporary break in the classes. But, once again, Patricof refused their request. "This was clearly not an option with Patricof," Smithers said. "He was obviously thinking, 'Corporate has a schedule, and we will not be the slowest ones.' It was all keeping face."

Smithers kept teaching, but his dissatisfaction grew. The Total Quality program, itself, which had seemed so impressive and thorough at first, now began to seem inflated and overambitious for Sigtek's needs. "Instead of being too little, too late, it was way too much, too late," he declared. "The more I dealt with it, the more I realized it was a cookie-cutter program, it was dogmatic, and it was way too much."

Smithers also began to question Telwork's motives in imposing such a program on all of its divisions, regardless of their businesses and needs. Word was going around the plant that Telwork was expecting the same inventory practices and turns from Sigtek that it did from its fiber optic cable companies—businesses that made a straight commodity product. In addition, Telwork didn't seem to understand that a major corporate change typically takes years. "Corporate was giving us such a mixed message," he complained. "They put all this money into a Total Quality program and in the end, all Patricof was supposed to give them was weekly numbers, and I don't mean quality numbers." He added: "The joke was that short-term planning under Telwork is one week, and long-term planning is two weeks. The kinds of numbers we were supposed to give them were physically impossible."

In the midst of all these doubts, Telwork orchestrated a major management change which, to Smithers, at least, formalized a power structure which had already existed in practice for months. Charles Bradley, the founder and president, was terminated, and Patricof—who in Smithers' eyes embodied all that was wrong with Sigtek's leadership—was named the new general manager.

Once at the helm, Patricof immediately took steps to consolidate his power, according to Smithers. First, he told the two quality instructors that they should no longer attend the site Quality Improvement Team meetings, since these were his responsibility. And in December, Patricof, in effect, demoted Smithers' boss and mentor, Cross, by naming a second director of engineering and putting Cross in charge of a single faltering product line.

At this point, Smithers said, the writing was on the wall. "I was lying," he stated bluntly, referring back to his early fear that the teaching job might force him to offer false hopes and expectations to employees. "I asked to stop teaching. My public justification was that my job needed me full time." Smithers made this decision even though he knew it threatened his career. "I realized I was committing suicide," he recalled. "As soon as I got off that teaching schedule, they could lay me off any time." But despite the palpable dislike which existed between Smithers and Patricof, the new general manager told him to keep teaching. "He told me I was too valuable and had too many followers to lose," Smithers recounted. "I had him in a position he didn't want to be in because, to some people, I was even more credible than he was."

On the surface, Patricof's request might have seemed like an endorsement. To Smithers, however, the end appeared to be in sight. "By Christmas, there were no knowns," he lamented. "Bradley was gone. Patricof had won. I started doing my résumé."

As he looked back over the preceding eight months, he was filled with a sense of profound regret. "I got into an organization where I thought I could accomplish something; I found a good mentor, but it didn't work," he remembered thinking. "Could I have done something different? That's still a hard question for me to answer."

READING

MANAGING THE CHALLENGES OF TRIGGER EVENTS: THE MINDSETS GOVERNING ADAPTATION TO CHANGE

Lynn A. Isabella

Associate Professor of Business Administration,
Darden Business School,
University of Virginia

More and more companies are challenged by trigger events—that is, large system changes are precipitating new behaviors and thoughts on the part of managers and subordinates. This article discusses the four mindsets associated with the process of change that provide the mental maps through which individuals make sense of the events. These mindsets direct attention to managing the puzzle, managing comparisons and analogies, managing symbols, and managing the conclusions and learnings as key challenges faced in trigger events.

Mergers and acquisitions, corporate relocations, new chief executives, and corporate restructurings are changes with major consequences for companies and their managers. What makes these events so significant is that they are "trigger events"—that is, events that precipitate new behaviors and new thoughts by managers and others as they try to understand what's happening. These events challenge managers to manage into the future as well as in the present. Not only must managers orchestrate and cope with the day-to-day operational changes, they also must use those events as opportunities to position the company for attaining future goals and

objectives. Thus, for example, as General Motors embarks on its corporate downsizing plan, more is involved than simply closing plants and laying off workers. The future success of GM and its position in the automotive industry are at stake. For those who must manage such large system change, the challenges are neither easy nor uncomplicated.

Consider the following. During the 1970s, FSI was a family owned, medium-sized financial services company in the Southwest. Gross sales were in the $100 million range and the company was quite successful, having carved out a very specific, profitable, yet limited growth market niche. By the mid-1980s, however, the financial services environment and general economic condition were resulting in deteriorating performance and an imperative to rethink previously successful strategies. Concomitantly, this company was challenged by a number of potential trigger events, which occurred at the rate of about one per year beginning around 1980. The once family owned company was sold, and a new president from outside the company was brought in as chief executive officer. This CEO and his executive staff instituted a corporatewide quality program, introduced new products to expand markets, relocated corporate

SOURCE: *Business Horizons* (to be published in 1992).

headquarters, and reorganized the company along geographic lines.

How the management of this firm confronted these events, as well as helped and occasionally hindered others in the company through the chaos, can demonstrate to others the managerial challenges posed by trigger events. For this company and others like it, the consequences of not meeting these challenges are substantial. At a minimum, the company experienced increased turnover, decreased productivity, low morale, and counter-productive behavior. At a maximum, the company's ability to meet market demands, service customers, and maintain a competitive level of quality and professional service was compromised or threatened. This one company's survival depended upon its ability to positively meet the challenges. Managing the challenges of trigger events is what this article is all about.

The Nature of Trigger Events

Common trigger events can include such changes as the following: mergers or acquisitions; corporate relocations; new top managements (especially new presidents and CEOs); major reorganizations or restructurings; downsizings or retrenchments; layoffs; unanticipated crises; or new strategic initiatives. They are so named because their magnitude and potential for organizational, as well as personal, impact set in motion a series of mental shifts as individuals strive to understand and redefine the situation. By their very nature, they unbalance established routines and evoke conscious thought on the part of organizational members. They stir up feelings and emotions that come to affect people's reactions to the change. In short, trigger events bring people's mindsets into the arena of change.

Mindsets are an under-recognized aspect of change. As a change unfolds, managers and others are interpreting actions and observations, and they're using those interpretations to inform their decisions and behaviors. They are actively constructing a series of mental maps along the way that are instrumental to making sense of the experience, to guiding behavior and actions, and, ultimately, to creating the success of the transition itself. Tom Peters (1978) went so far as to state that these mental maps are tools that "may be the most effective change vehicle available in today's environment."

The Mindsets of Change

My research (Isabella, 1990) identified the four different mindsets operational as a trigger event unfolds and the mechanisms at work that encourage mindsets to change. (Table 1 describes the research study in more depth.) In anticipation of a trigger event, an "assembly" mindset draws together rumors and tidbits of information. Once the event is confirmed as about to occur, a "conventional" mindset focuses attention on routine explanations and comparisons to past events. Once culminated, an "amended" mindset focuses people on conditions before and after the trigger event as they search for symbolic meaning. Afterward, an "evaluative" mindset causes managers and others to review the consequences of the event for overall conclusions and perspectives. Mindsets change when the event becomes "personalized" and real—that is, when the event touches individuals' sense of who they are, their job, or their future. (See Figure 1)

These mindsets transcend the particular

TABLE 1   Research Design

This research, which was published in the *Academy of Management Journal*, investigated how managers view key organizational events and how those events were linked to the change process. To explore these questions, I interviewed 40 managers across three different levels within an urban financial services company. I spoke with all members of the top management team, and a sample of managers at middle and lower organizational levels.

Prior to the interviews, preliminary discussions had identified five critical events. They were:

1. Acquisition by a leading European financial giant.
2. New president from outside the company (first in its history).
3. Relocation of corporate headquarters.
4. Corporatewide quality program.
5. Major reorganization.

Each of these events was presented to executives during the interviews, and they were asked to talk about the events in terms of what happened, when, and what various occurrences meant to them along the way. Interviews were transcribed, then systematically analyzed for themes and trends that captured all the data involved. This analysis identified four stages, each with a different reality, a set of interpretive tasks, and a predominant frame of reference. The analysis also revealed that these stages paralleled the process of change.

---

type of event. That is, whether the event in question is an acquisition, or a new president, or a new corporatewide program, individuals will bring to the change similar points of view at different times. (See Figure 2) What follows are snapshots into the mindsets of one organization, the questions managers asked, and the mental maps that guide their answers.

FIGURE 1   Unfolding of a Change

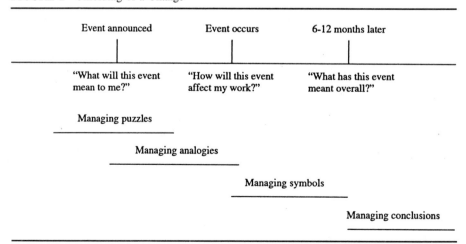

Snapshot into the Mindset of FSI: The New President

Just prior to the acquisition, FSI was in the hands of the founder's grandson, M, a debonair bachelor whose antics were the subjects of considerable hallway conversation. Although the acquiring company decided to retain M as president, soon after the transfer, stories began to fly. M spent a lot of money refurbishing the company plane, taking trips, mountain climbing in South Africa, and redecorating the family estate that was owned by the corporation. The costs of a single bathroom were the subject of considerable debate. Most individuals reported that M was rarely around and, when he was, his mind never seemed to be on business. Neither were the minds of others. Managers estimated that people spent a good 40 percent of their time musing over the latest M story. To say that productivity suffered is an understatement.

An Assembly Mindset

Most large-scale changes in organizations do not occur totally by surprise. There is often an anticipatory stage during which countless rumors, hunches, suspicions, and scattered bits of information pepper organizational thoughts and conversations. For example, prior to each of the events I studied, a prolific rumor mill supplied speculative information about possible upcoming occurrences. There were rumors about possible acquirors, possible sites for a new corporate headquarters, and possible structural changes designed to deal with declining services. There was also heavy speculation about potential candidates, both internal and external, for the presidency. These fragments are analogous to randomly arranged pieces of a puzzle for which managers possess neither a final picture as a construction guide nor a specific indication of whether the final picture will contain some, all, or none of the pieces.

FIGURE 2   Mindsets at Work during Change

Change Time Frame	People Concerned about	Cognitive Tasks	Managers Need to
Pre-event	Rumors, tidbits of information.	Assemble a reasonable cognitive understanding.	Manage puzzles.
Event confirmed	Other similar events; their own organizational history.	Employ conventional explanations.	Manage analogies/ comparisons.
Event occurs	Old versus new. Loss of familiar patterns. Heightened symbolic impact.	Amend understandings.	Manage symbols.
After some time	Winners and losers. Strengths and weaknesses.	Evaluate. Draw overall conclusions.	Manage overall learnings.

What people are trying to do during this phase of change is to assemble a reasonable picture of understanding. Rumors and informational appetizers structure an otherwise uncertain environment by providing clues around which to build viable interpretations. Though never complete, and always tenuous, such a picture begins to prepare individuals for the eventuality of the change. Thinking about the possibilities allows people to speculate about the probabilities.

Snapshot into the Mindset of FSI: The Acquisition

While the announcement of the acquisition put to rest the rumors and innuendos of what was happening, a new set of thoughts began to emerge. People began to gather information about the acquiror and especially began to swap stories about the acquisitions they had been through or had heard about from others. Uncertainty and anxiety ran high. Although the top managers had knowledge of the "hands-off" policy on the part of the new parent, many people were either unaware of this fact or perplexed because it didn't fit the "common wisdom" of what happens post acquisition. The question on everyone's mind was: "What will this event mean to me personally?"

A Conventional Mindset

When there is confirmation that an event will occur—that is, a new president is selected, an acquiror identified, a site picked, or a reorganization announced—managers and employees become concerned less about rumors (though there will continue to be rumors) and more about the nascent reality. Propelling individuals' thoughts is the question of what the event will mean to them personally.

At this time, understandings are no longer tenuous or uncertain; they are conventional. Conventional understandings are presumptions of what will be—based upon what happened in a similar situation or "what always happens in cases like these." For example, conventional explanations might describe how an acquiring company completely alters the character of an acquired company, how a new president brings in favored staff to replace previous personnel, or how reorganizations inevitably bring job loss.

What people are trying to do is create a standard picture that explains the event about to occur by turning to their own history or the history of others for analogous situations. Conventional mindsets reduce uncertainty, because people have a script in which they can locate themselves, can "read ahead" to future dialogue and interactions, and, more important, can know how the story ends.

Snapshot into the Mindset of FSI: The Corporate Relocation

After months of preparation, and in the midst of considerable fanfare, FSI relocated in its new headquarters, which was a large, modern building on the fringes of the city's downtown section owned by the new parent company. Compared with the previous offices, these were grand. FSI, once cramped into three floors, was spread out over eight. Individuals were assigned office space by rank, with each rank having associated with it a location in the building, specific equipment, and setup. While careful planning went into these decisions, certain anomalies were visible. The company boarded up a window because it was adjacent to the work station of someone whose rank did not "get" a window. They placed individual coffee rooms on each floor, thereby eliminating the very popular central cafeteria/breakroom. Finally, a number of employees, receiving the requisite rank equipment, did not have the room or equipment to do their job adequately. The question on everyone's mind was: How will this relocation affect my job or my ability to do my work?

An Amended Mindset

Once the event occurs—that is, when the new president comes on board or corporate headquarters relocates—individuals become primarily concerned with the question of what changes will mean for their job. Focus is on "double exposures": the juxtaposition of the old versus the new. Managers often express a sense of confusion about the old not working or a feeling of being perplexed about new behaviors replacing old ones. In my study, people were confused by what was required under the new structure that had been created by the quality program; they were perplexed by actions of the new president, which appeared to violate old chains of command or other priorities; they reminded themselves of the loss of familiar patterns occasioned by the move into the new building. At this time they amend their view of an event and reconstruct frames of reference based upon the day-to-day experiencing of changes in organizational life and procedures. Hands-on experimentation, testing, and learning by doing are key. And, the mundane has more power than many executives realize.

What people are trying to do is actively reconstruct their environment: deciding what to retain and what to alter. Reference to symbols and the symbolism in certain actions, gestures, and decisions is pervasive, which is why the window-boarding episode described earlier had so much impact. More than ever, there are varied and multiple individual mindsets and di-

vergent interpretations. Symbols are critical at this time, because they signal appropriate views, and they make multiple realities seem less divergent and more as interconnected parts of the whole. As these divergent perspectives become shared among managers and employees, individuals build a community identity.

Snapshot into the Mindset of FSI: The Quality Program

The quality program began from the top, with managers going off in groups of 10 to 15 to attend the training workshops. The purpose of these workshops was to educate managers in the program's goals and to begin action planning for the changes required. The intent was to cascade the changes through the organization over a two-year period, in that it would take two years to put all managers through the training. Within six months, however, as a result of the first group of managers' changes, people began to evaluate the information. A task force was established to formally study the changes, but its purpose was suspect. Many believed that its charge was only to rubber stamp top management's opinions. The question most on people's minds at this time was: What has this quality program meant overall?

An Evaluative Mindset

As time passes, a series of little events begin to signal what the event has meant overall to individuals and to the corporation. There is a growing concrete realization of the permanent changes wrought and of the consequences that those changes and the event itself have had for the organization and its members. The mindset is an evaluative one. Knowing winners and losers and knowing precisely what each group won or lost dominates individuals' thoughts. People search for consequences, actively seek and are receptive to the strengths and weaknesses of changes wrought by the event, and, whenever possible, reassert certainty.

What people are trying to do at this time is to draw overall conclusions and learnings of the event and, thus, put the event in perspective. This is a critical cognitive stage, because the mindsets formed now are likely to be the standard and conventional interpretations that will frame the next similar event. Thus, now paramount becomes managing the conclusions and learnings and making sure that employees and managers are drawing evaluations and conclusions consistent with the organization's mission and strategy.

What Managers Can Do

Because people bring different mindsets to understanding change, and because these mindsets occur at different points in the change process, a manager's focus and actions vary as a change unfolds. Initially, managers need to manage puzzles. As the event becomes more certain, attention turns to managing analogies. Once the event occurs, managing symbols becomes the critical focus. And, finally, as the event wanes, managers need to attend to the conclusions and learning resulting from the trigger event. The following section, summarized in Figure 3, describes these roles and suggests ways in which managers can fulfill them.

Pre-Event: Managing the Puzzle

Before the event, when speculative information and prolific rumor mills abound, the actions of the manager focus on the puzzle. Because individuals are wrestling with assembling puzzle pieces, managers must be alert to their own con-

fusion as well as the confusion of others during this period. Therefore, managers will want to:

1. *Be aggressive in terms of hearing and addressing rumors.* Rumors will occur. Thus, rather than stopping rumors, it is critical for managers to manage the anticipatory grapevine. Those who have studied rumors (Rosnow and Fine, 1976) and their management (Simmons, 1986) suggest that it is critical to identify types of rumors (e.g., fantasy, bogies, or aggressive rumors), as well as their content. Fantasy rumors are those expressing unfulfilled or desired wishes. Bogies are rumors expressing fear and anxiety; while aggressive rumors are malicious stories intended to harm. Bogies and fantasies can be managed by well-informed and straightforward communication. Aggressive rumors require swift and direct statements of the truth, even if the truth hurts. While anxiety and fear cannot be stopped, giving people as much complete information as possible can help, rather than hinder, their adjustment.

2. *Provide information, even if speculative or incomplete.* If one does not know, then say so. Even no information can be critical for people struggling to gain a cognitive perspective on the change. For example, although top managers involved in delicate lease negotiations could not disclose exact relocation sites, they could and did make statements reiterating the company's intent to relocation within city lines, not county lines. (One major rumor was the company's relocation to a particular suburban location, which would have made continued employment almost impossible for those who relied on public transportation.)

FIGURE 3   Managing Trigger Events

To Manage	Managers Need to
Rumors	Be aggressive in terms of hearing and responding to rumors.
	Provide positive information, even if speculative or incomplete.
	Anticipate rumors and be ready with replies.
	Provide the puzzle box picture.
Comparisons	Manage the announcement of the change.
	Provide the analogies.
	Use positive past history or reframe negative history.
	Introduce people, whenever possible, to the new environment.
Symbols	Orchestrate the transition carefully and with ceremony.
	Communicate the vision, the strategy, and what the organization will become as a result of this change.
	Turn ordinary actions into symbolic communications.
	Make changes from the beginning.
	Specify new works rules and procedures carefully, concisely, and with rationale.
Conclusions and learnings	Create events that signal consequences of the change.
	Communicate in very concrete terms what the event has meant.
	Admit errors and state new strategies to turn those around.

3. *Anticipate rumors and be ready with replies.* Employees are very cognizant of almost every little nuance and detail during times of emotional uncertainty. Thus, they have their antennae out for informational crumbs. No commander in the Gulf War went into a press briefing without anticipating press questions and formulating possi-ble answers. No manager dealing with change should fail to anticipate possible scenarios and develop well-thought-out responses.

4. *Provide the puzzle box picture.* The cognitive energy expended to figure out how the pieces of the puzzle will fit can be constructively harnessed

by providing preliminary fits or, in the least, suggesting the boundaries in which the puzzle can be constructed. For example, prior to the quality program, the company's senior executives were particularly informative on the strategic direction of the company, and what the company was hoping to accomplish, and, thus, how a quality program and focus on quality fit into that plan.

Confirmation of the Event: Managing Analogies and Comparisons

Because this stage is fought with comparisons to past similar events or past organizational history, this is a critical stage for reframing history or selecting the historical precedents to be used. While individuals naturally will use evidence of the past as indications of the future, the manager can actively manage comparisons by suggesting alternative analogies and comparison points. Thus, during this cognitive stage, managers must:

1. *Manage the announcement of the change.* How individuals find out about the change directly affects how they respond to the question of what the event means to them personally. For those who were informed either personally or part of an announcement made to the larger employee audience which was the procedure for the quality program, feelings of inclusion and positive reactions were high. However, in the case of the acquisition, there was very little forthcoming information and most people found out from the customers and suppliers, thus fueling "disaster" speculations.

2. *Provide the analogies.* Managers can use the fact that the individuals look to similar events by suggesting to

the individuals the standard of comparison either hypothetically or in actuality. For example, as the new quality program was being announced, the executives at the company constantly made reference to the success and benefits that this program had brought at their sister company. In this way, they actively tried to counter the alternative explanation of people losing jobs. According to John Sculley, in his book *Odyssey* (Sculley, 1987: 406) analogy is an under-utilized method for "seeing new points of view and explaining them in ways that add depth and clarity."

3. *Use positive past history or reframe negative history.* Let people know this event will be similar to one in the past, or let people know that it will not be like a more disastrous event. During the recent Gulf War, there were continuous comments of this confrontation being another Viet Nam. Much was done by the military and the media to constantly remind people that this war was different. Specific differences were cited to concretize those differences.

4. *Introduce people, whenever possible, to the new environment.* This can be accomplished by pointing out the similarities that the new will have with the old. Just before the reorganization, when people were especially sensitive to their new job responsibilities under the new structure, the company I studied held informal sessions to describe the changes in terms of the similarities to the current work environment. Similarly, before the relocation the organization researched and published a list of eateries and stores similar to ones being left behind. The message here is not to wait until the event occurs to

begin to acquaint organizational members with the new environment and upcoming changes.

Occurrence of the Event: Managing Symbols

Once the event occurs, managers, particularly senior managers, are likely to focus their attention onto the next strategic initiative. This is, however, a most critical time for the employees and lower managers, because, as the event takes hold, they begin to actually experience changed routines and rules. Because symbols and their meanings become particularly critical, managers need to:

1. *Orchestrate the transition carefully and with ceremony.* The rituals and ceremonies that accompany the culmination of a trigger event provide a lasting cognitive snapshot for members of the corporation. For some events, in which the message is business as usual, no added ceremony is required. For those trigger events, however, for which the purpose is a cultural or value change, orchestrating the transition is a first step to signaling new values or cultural norms. For example, in the relocation, the top managers arranged a ribbon-cutting ceremony, complete with formal dinner and tour of the new facilities. This was a gala event at which the top managers began to reinforce the vision and values in the "new" corporation.

2. *Communicate the vision, the strategy, and what the organization will become as a result of this new change.* Emphasize the process as well as the intended outcome. Let people know what they need to do to contribute to the process as well as the outcome. Many times before and dur-

ing the quality program, top managers reiterated that they wanted the organization to appear more professional and customer responsive. They talked about why this was important to the future health of the organization and pointed out ways in which customer and agent frustrations were negatively affecting business. The organization used both formal meetings, such as quarterly meetings, informal seminars, and the company newsletter to promote the strategic rationale.

3. *Turn ordinary actions into symbolic communications.* According to Tom Peters (1978), there are symbolic messages in everyday settings and actions. When the new president came on board, he made it a point of having coffee with all members of the organization. One group was particularly impressed because he greeted them when they arrived for work at 7 A.M. and, as one employee stated, "He even brought the doughnuts." This simple gesture communicated symbolically that this new president did, in fact, care about his employees.

In another situation, the new president realized after a short elevator ride that he had failed to acknowledge the hellos of an employee. Concerned that this would communicate "being snubbed," he took a few minutes to jot a personal hello and apology. That note is framed on the desk of the employee. As one theorist has said: "The most important decisions are often the least apparent."

4. *Make changes from the beginning.* Because people are at an adjustment stage, it often is easier to introduce and gain acceptance of new ways of doing business. Changing routines once established is more difficult. For

example, after several weeks in their new headquarters, the company I studied announced a ''no-eating, no-drinking at your desk'' policy. This policy was met with considerable resistance because people had already established new routines and were not prepared to change again.

5. *Specify new work rules and procedures clearly, concisely, and with rationale.*   Many of the managers I studied often expressed a sense of confusion about the old not working or a feeling of being perplexed about new behaviors replacing old ones. For example, people were confused by what was required under the new structure dictated by the quality program. Having a timetable to new procedures, and hot lines to call with questions, eased the transition.

As Time Passes: Managing Conclusions and Learnings

As individuals spend time with the changes, they begin naturally to evaluate the rightness or wrongness of the changes for them and for the organization. This is a time when managers need to manage the conclusions and learnings that are extracted. To do so, managers must:

1. *Create events to evaluate the change.*   There are many opportunities that managers can use to facilitate the learnings resulting from the change. Task forces, studies, or more informal surveys are all mechanisms to begin the evaluation process. For the quality program, the company established an interfunctional task force to examine the consequences of the new initiatives. Their findings were used by management to reinforce or realign.

2. *Communicate in very concrete terms what the event has meant overall.*   Managers need not wait for organizational members to formulate their own conclusions. They can suggest conclusions and meanings for the consideration of others. This has been particularly true in the recent Gulf War. After the cessation of hostilities, the news media and official announcements were filled with references to what the war meant and, in particular, who won and who lost.

3. *Admit failures and state new strategies to turn those around.*   Not all changes will proceed as planned, and the best strategies may result in unanticipated and less than desirable outcomes. Rather than ignore failures, the company should consider hitting them head on. For example, although the organization had stated that no one would lose their job as a result of the quality program, many people did, in fact, lose their jobs. The company had underestimated the skill base of its employees and their general flexibility to change skill sets. Rather than focus on this miscalculation, the company put energy into broadcasting what this event taught it about managing subsequent changes in the future.

Conclusion

Getting people to adjust quickly and positively to trigger events is crucial. In so doing, the organization begins to maximize worker productivity, and it avoids the downtime that turns focus away from business as usual. However, managers often are confused by the change themselves and by the questions being expressed. Understanding those adjustments, anticipating the relevant and timely queries, and responding to the mindset at work is instrumental to effectively managing trigger events for one's self and for others in the company. While some management decisions and actions during the various trigger events in the organization I studied were positive, others, in fact, caused considerable problems. But, the company's management did recognize one valuable lesson. As a senior level manager stated: "We got into trouble whenever we miscalculated, underestimated, or simply failed to take into consideration what was on people's minds during these events." The suggestion to other companies confronted by trigger events: Meet the challenges of trigger events by understanding and working with, not against, the mindsets that govern adaptation to change.

References

1. L. Isabella, "Evolving Interpretations as a Change Unfolds: How Managers Interpret Key Organizational Events," *Academy of Management Journal* 33 (1990), pp. 7–41.
2. T. Peters, "Symbols, Patterns and Settings," *Organizational Dynamics*, 1978, pp. 3–23.
3. R. Rosnow and G. Fine, *Rumor and Gossip: The Social Psychology of Hearsay*, New York: Elsevier, 1976.
4. J. Sculley, *Odyssey*. New York: Harper & Row, 1987.
5. D. Simmons, "How Does Your Grapevine Grow?" *Management World* 15 (1986), pp. 16–18.

CASE

THE 36-HOUR WORK DAY (A)

In June of 1987, David Axelrod, New York State health commissioner, convened a group of nine distinguished physicians to advise him on one of the most difficult challenges facing the medical profession. Three years earlier, an 18-year-old college student entered a prestigious New York teaching hospital late at night with an ear infection and died during the next morning's shift. A New York grand jury subsequently blamed the medical profession's practice of training its interns and residents through 36-hour shifts for the young woman's death. In the ensuing months, Axelrod's Ad Hoc Advisory Committee on Emergency Services would now debate the issue of medical training and other hospital practices in New York State. These topics, of initial concern to the medical community, as well as the general public, would now receive an official government response.

The Case of Libby Zion

On March 5, 1984, 18-year-old Libby Zion died at the New York Hospital, eight hours after she had been admitted through

This case was prepared by Research Associate Lori Ann Levaggi (under the direction of Professor Todd D. Jick).

the emergency room. The resident, who had assumed treatment for Libby while in her 18th consecutive hour on duty, reported that she had done everything possible to get her temperature down, even putting her on ice. Zion's father, an attorney and writer for the *New York Times*, claimed that his daughter had received inadequate care at the hands of overworked and undersupervised residents. Mr. Sidney Zion summoned New York County district attorney Robert Morgenthau to begin a grand jury investigation into her death.

New York Hospital attorneys asserted that Libby Zion's care had been appropriate and that her death was no fault of the resident on staff. However, in December of 1986, the New York grand jury submitted a subsequent report saying that "the most serious patients should not be cared for by the most inexperienced doctors and that interns and residents should be better supervised and their long hours limited."

Although the grand jury issued no criminal indictments against the New York Hospital or its physicians, it found fault with the system of residency training and physician staffing. According to the *New England Journal of Medicine*, "the grand jury's report was, in effect, an indictment of American graduate medical education."[1]

Grand Jury Recommendations

The grand jury's nonbinding report listed five circumstances that it believed contributed to Zion's death and recommended corrective measures be made in five corresponding aspects of hospital-

care. Three of the five proposed recommendations concerned the issue of fatigued and undersupervised residents. (The other two issues related to the use of physical restraints and the lack of a system to check for contraindicated combinations of drugs.)[2]

The First Recommendation. This recommendation stated that "State Department of Health regulations mandate that all level one[3] hospitals staff their emergency rooms with physicians who have completed at least three years of postgraduate training, called senior residents, and who are specifically trained to evaluate and care for patients on an emergency basis." Libby Zion had been initially evaluated in the emergency room by a junior (second-year) resident who had only discussed her care over the telephone with the referring attending physician (a patient's private physician). Ms. Zion had not been examined in the emergency room by an attending physician.

The Second Recommendation. Ms. Zion had been admitted to the medical service under the immediate care of an intern and a junior medical resident. The grand jury recommended that "State Department of Health regulations should insure that interns and junior residents in teaching hospitals be supervised contemporaneously and in person by attending physicians or senior residents who have

---

[1] *New England Journal of Medicine* 318, No. 2 (March 24, 1988), p. 772.

[2] Drugs are considered to be contraindicated to each other when their joint administration will have adverse or undesirable effects.

[3] Level one hospitals are hospitals that provide "comprehensive" emergency services, in which the emergency department is open 24 hours a day with at least one "experienced" emergency physician on duty at all times.

completed at least a three-year post-graduate residency program.''

The Third Recommendation. Ms. Zion had been admitted to the medical service at 2 A.M., when the intern and junior resident caring for her had been at work for 18 hours. The grand jury recommended that ''the State Department of Health institute regulations to limit consecutive working hours for interns and junior residents in teaching hospitals.''

The New York grand jury attributed Libby Zion's death to neglectful treatment by tired and undersupervised young residents.

Medical Education and Training

When asked how the young medical student makes the difficult transition from student to doctor, many will answer ''very quickly.'' One intern reflected:

> One moment you are a medical student; the next a doctor. One moment you are in the cocoon, protected from most real responsibilities; the next, you are a physician fully hatched, charged with the protection of the living world. For four years you have been primarily a bookish creature, valued more for your scholarship than for your grasp of the practical side of patient care. Then one day you are pronounced a physician. Suddenly you find yourself husband to a team of patients. You grin queerly, like a groom before an altar, waiting for the momentous change to descend. But it never does. Your new life simply begins.[4]

After four years of medical school, the graduate entered the second phase of medical education, internship and residency, at a teaching hospital like New York Hospital, one of more than 5,500 accredited residency training programs in the United States. By the mid-1980s, the state of New York alone trained more than 14 percent of the nation's physicians of 13,000 annually. The first year of the three-year residency program was called the *internship*, and the remaining two years was the *residency*. Although there is no required number of hours a resident must work to complete the program, there is a specified number of cases and clinical experiences which must be encountered. The physician, called an *intern* for the first year, became a *junior resident* in the second year and a *senior resident* in the third year. After this program, residents moved into their chosen specialties and received more training and clinical experience, which could last anywhere from one to two years for internal medicine to five years for neurosurgery.

Throughout the program at the teaching hospital, the intern or resident delivered patient care as part of a medical team consisting of attending physicians or wards, other residents, and interns and nurses, with the attending physician ultimately responsible. (See Exhibit 1) In this team, residents were supervised by other residents one year their senior, and established physicians,[5] gradually accumulating responsibility and being given increasing latitude to make decisions and treat patients. The guiding principle of supervision was graded responsibility: those with more education and experience

---

[4] Stephen A. Hoffmann, *Under the Ether Dome: A Physician's Apprenticeship at Massachusetts General Hospital* (New York: Charles Scribner's Sons, 1986), p. 31.

[5] An established physician is someone who has completed the training and licensing procedures required by the state and the accrediting board.

EXHIBIT 1   The 36-Hour Work Day (Hierarchy of medical team)

Ward Attending

• Oversees delivery of care. Primary responsibility to patient.

Senior Resident

• Supervises junior residents.
• Expedites delivery of care: follows up with consultants, reviews lab and radiologic data, teaches interns and students.

Junior Resident

• Supervises interns.
• Expedites delivery of patient care: follows up with consultants, reviews lab and radiologic data, teaches interns and students.

Intern

• Assists medical students, performs "scut work," or writing orders and seeing patients.

supervised those with less. Whether the senior staff intervened to assist a second-year resident depended, however, on whether the latter understood the graded responsibility principle, knew when to call for help, and did so. Inexperienced residents might lack the judgment or knowledge that they needed help, and they might be reluctant to bother senior colleagues. Senior staff might also interpret a call for help as meaning the resident was unable or unwilling to make independent decisions.

Most residents claimed that they did not hesitate to call on their senior colleagues for help, but others have admitted that

"pride can get in the way." One resident said, "It's a real step to take—you have to wake someone up. People feel like I should be able to figure this out on my own. It is a macho thing not to call."[6]

First-year residents (interns) typically spent four to eight weeks in a particular unit of a hospital, then moved to another area. This first year usually entailed the most extreme pressures and longest hours. A typical schedule consisted of at least five day a week, a minimum of 16 hours a day,

---

[6] *Brookline Tab*, June 28, 1988, p. 32.

EXHIBIT 2   The 36–Hour Work Day (A typical resident's day)

7 A.M.	*Work rounds*	Junior and senior residents teach interns and medical students.
9 A.M.–10 A.M.	*Resident report*	One hour each day to discuss interesting cases with various subspecialists.
10:30 A.M.–12:30 P.M.	*Attending rounds*	Teaching done by the ward attending.
	Grand rounds	One hour per week—outside speaker on a special topic.

• Occasional noontime conferences.
• Remainder of day is spent in the operating room, checking on patients, writing orders, and admitting patients.

Total Hours Worked per Week by Program Specialty

	First Year		All	
Program Specialty	*Average*	*90th Percentile**	*Average*	*90th Percentile**
Family practice	82.3	110.0	70.6	101.0
Internal medicine	90.3	116.9	74.6	107.0
Surgery	98.0	125.0	87.0	122.0
Pediatrics	93.6	120.0	79.2	107.2
Obstetrics/gynecology	93.9	120.2	89.1	117.3
Radiology	51.0	71.2	50.1	71.0
Psychiatry	66.5	96.0	52.6	74.7
Anesthesiology	81.4	121.2	76.0	102.0
Pathology	54.2	78.4	48.0	75.1
Other	87.0	112.0	70.6	102.0

* 90th percentile—90 percent of respondents reported a value less than the 90th percentile.

SOURCE: 1987 Survey of Resident Physicians, American Medical Association Center for Health Policy.

and being "on call" in the hospital every third night, in a unit such as the intensive care unit, and every fourth night on a ward. In a large city institution like New York Hospital, being on call could mean 36 hours of work without sleep. After two more years of residency, the trained doctors would choose an area of specialization and then devote their remaining required years to mastering it.

The majority of a resident's instruction occurred during "attending rounds." This daily event lasted two hours, during which time the ward attending, or most senior physician, instructs the residents. Once a week "grand rounds" occurred, hosting an outside speaker to discuss a special topic for the residents. "Resident Report" was a more informal gathering of residents, for one hour each day, to discuss interesting cases with subspecialists. The more commonly known ritual of "work rounds" took place every morning when residents traveled the wards to visit all of their patients, taught less-experienced doctors, and documented their progress. (See Exhibit 2) .

A Change from the Past

The work and intensity of medical education and training had dramatically changed since the 1960s. The knowledge base that residents commanded was far greater than that of the past—whole new fields had arisen, and new technology, procedures, and equipment had to be learned. Moreover, hospital patients in the mid-1980s tended to be sicker than in the past; very ill patients lived much longer, thanks to sophisticated procedures and drugs; the population was aging, so a larger percentage of people was vulnerable to more serious diseases. In addition, because of skyrocketing medical costs and new Medicare rules, patients tended to be released earlier (by 1987, a patient's average hospital stay was 40 percent shorter than it had been in 1985). Thus, nearly every hospital bed was occupied by a very sick person.

Many procedures that residents performed in the past had been taken over by technicians and nurses. The "scut" work of 20 years ago included performing laboratory tests, starting intravenous lines, or drawing blood—activities that involved patient contact. By the mid-1980s, a resident's "scut" work entailed clerical responsibilities, coordinating consultants, dictating complicated discharge summaries, and scheduling various procedures. Residents spent far more time on administrative matters, in part a result of what was called the *medical-legal* environment that reflected increased numbers of malpractice suits and soaring malpractice insurance rates. Malpractice insurance premiums of all physicians rose significantly, from an average of $5,800 in 1982 to $8,400 in 1984. These figures ranged from $4,600 in general practice to $18,000 for obstetrics and gynecology. A serious nursing shortage also contributed to increasing residents' responsibilities.

Additionally, since hospital patients were sicker in the 1980s, their care was more expensive. Since the health care industry became increasingly complex, because the number of health service suppliers that reimbursed hospitals had grown, increasing costs were being borne by an increasing number of people and institutions, further complicating the system. Therefore, the modern health care industry, made up of numerous providers of care and suppliers of funds (private, third-party, or government-financed), became a complex matrix of doctors and hospitals providing health care, and insurance institutions and government agencies paying for it, all within constrained budgets and increasing costs. (See Exhibits 3 and 4)

Moreover, in an era of high-tech, high-volume medicine, hospitals themselves drew criticism. The head of New York Hospital commented: "Hospitals have improved so much in diagnostics and treatment that expectations are much higher. When I was an intern, you held the hand of a dying patient. Now, bulbs go off and people rush in to save the patient, so if they die, something must have gone wrong."[7]

As of 1987, there were no state restrictions on how long an intern or resident could be required to work; their weekly hours ranged from 90 to 100, with shifts often lasting 36 hours or longer. In 1987, the average resident was paid less than $30,000 a year.

---

[7] *New York Times Magazine*, January 1988, p. 20.

EXHIBIT 3   Cost of Health Care

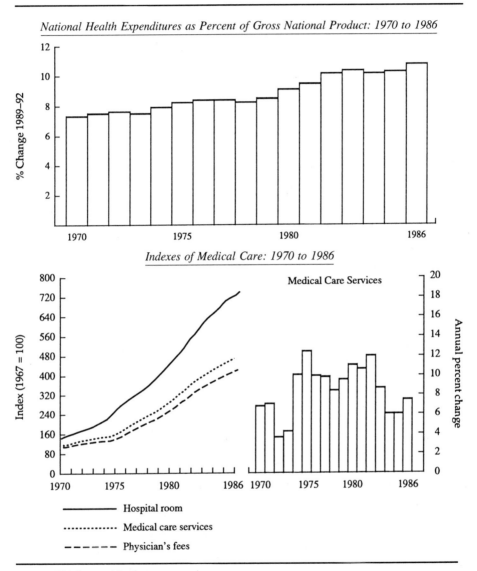

National Health Expenditures as Percent of Gross National Product: 1970 to 1986

Indexes of Medical Care: 1970 to 1986

—————— Hospital room

············· Medical care services

— — — — — Physician's fees

The Experience of the Residents

On July 1, 1982, the Essentials of Accredited Residencies in Graduate Medical Education, adopted by the Accreditation-Council for Graduate Medical Education (ACGME), were established. Among these "essentials" enacted was the right of residents to participate in policy development and review of the training program. A second essential stated that there must be institutional and program policies and procedures ensuring that all residents

EXHIBIT 4 The Rising Cost of Health Care

Indexes of Medical Care Prices: 1970 to 1986

Year	Index, Total	Medical Care Services				Medical Care Commodities‡	Annual Percent Change					Medical Care Commodities‡
		Professional Services			Hospital Room		Total	Medical Care Services			Hospital Room	
		Total*	Physicians	Dental				Total*	Physicians	Dental		
1970	120.6	119.7	121.4	119.4	145.4	103.6	6.3†	7.1†	7.5†	5.8†	12.9†	2.3†
1971	128.4	127.5	129.8	127.0	163.1	105.4	6.5	7.3	6.9	6.4	12.2	1.7
1972	132.5	132.1	133.8	132.3	173.9	105.6	3.2	3.7	3.1	4.2	6.6	0.2
1973	137.7	136.4	138.2	136.4	182.1	105.9	3.9	4.4	3.3	3.1	4.7	0.3
1974	150.5	148.2	150.9	146.8	201.5	109.8	9.3	10.3	9.2	7.8	10.7	3.5
1975	166.6	164.5	169.4	161.9	236.1	116.6	12.0	12.6	12.3	10.3	17.2	8.4
1976	184.7	179.4	188.5	172.2	268.6	126.0	9.5	10.1	11.3	6.4	13.6	6.1
1977	202.4	194.1	206.0	185.1	299.5	134.1	9.6	9.9	9.3	7.5	11.5	6.4
1978	219.4	208.8	223.1	198.1	332.4	143.5	6.4	6.6	6.3	7.0	11.0	7.0
1979	239.7	226.8	243.6	214.8	370.3	153.6	9.3	9.7	9.2	8.4	11.4	7.2
1980	265.9	252.0	269.3	240.2	418.9	168.1	10.9	11.3	10.6	11.8	13.1	9.3
1981	294.5	277.9	299.0	263.3	461.1	186.5	10.8	10.7	11.0	9.6	14.8	10.9
1982	328.7	301.5	327.1	283.6	556.7	205.7	11.6	11.9	9.4	7.7	15.7	10.3
1983	357.3	323.0	352.3	302.7	619.7	223.3	6.7	6.7	7.7	6.7	11.3	8.6
1984	379.5	346.1	376.8	327.3	670.9	239.7	6.2	6.0	7.0	6.1	8.3	7.3
1985	403.1	367.3	398.8	347.9	710.5	258.7	6.2	6.0	5.8	6.3	5.9	7.1
1986	433.5	390.9	427.7	367.3	753.1	273.6	7.5	7.7	7.2	5.6	6.0	6.6

(Index, Total column values: 1970 124.2; 1971 133.3; 1972 138.2; 1973 144.3; 1974 150.1; 1975 179.1; 1976 197.1; 1977 216.7; 1978 235.4; 1979 258.3; 1980 267.4; 1981 318.2; 1982 356.0; 1983 387.0; 1984 410.3; 1985 435.1; 1986 468.6)

* Includes other services, not shown separately.

† Prior to 1976, covers drugs and prescriptions only.

‡ Change from 1969.

SOURCE: U.S. Bureau of Labor Statistics, *CPI Detailed Report*, January issues.

EXHIBIT 4 *(concluded)*

National Health Expenditures, by Object: 1970 to 198

Object of Expenditure	Expenditure (dollars in billions)									Percent		
	1970	1975	1980	1981	1982	1983	1984	1985	1986	1970	1980	1986
Total	$75.0	$132.7	$248.1	$267.0	$323.6	$357.2	$391.1	$422.6	$458.2	100.0%	100.0%	100.0%
Spent by—												
Consumers	43.4	71.3	135.6	157.0	178.3	196.4	219.9	235.4	258.9	57.6	54.7	56.0
Government	27.6	56.3	105.2	121.2	135.3	147.5	159.7	176.0	189.7	37.0	42.4	41.4
Philanthropy and industry	3.9	5.1	7.3	6.7	10.1	11.3	11.5	11.2	11.7	5.1	2.9	2.5
Spent for—												
Health services and supplies	69.6	124.3	236.2	273.6	309.4	341.6	375.4	407.2	442.0	92.6	95.2	96.5
Personal health care expenses	65.4	117.1	219.7	254.7	266.5	314.7	341.9	371.3	404.0	86.1	88.6	68.2
Hospital care	26.0	52.4	101.6	119.1	135.2	146.8	156.3	167.2	179.6	37.3	41.0	39.2
Physicians' services	14.3	24.9	46.6	54.6	61.8	64.8	75.4	82.8	82.0	19.1	18.9	20.1
Dentists' services	4.7	6.2	15.4	17.3	19.5	21.7	24.6	27.1	29.6	6.3	6.2	6.5
Other professional services*	1.6	2.6	5.7	6.8	6.0	9.3	10.9	12.4	14.1	2.1	2.3	3.1
Drugs and sundries	6.0	11.9	16.6	20.7	22.1	24.5	26.5	26.7	30.6	10.7	7.6	6.7
Eyeglasses and appliances†	1.9	3.2	5.1	5.3	5.8	6.2	7.0	7.5	8.2	2.6	2.0	1.8
Nursing home care	4.7	10.1	20.4	23.9	26.7	29.4	31.7	35.0	36.1	6.3	6.2	6.3
Other health services	2.1	3.6	5.9	6.6	7.4	8.3	9.4	10.6	11.9	2.8	2.4	2.6
Net cost of insurance and administration‡	2.6	4.0	9.2	10.6	13.5	17.1	22.6	23.6	24.5	3.6	3.7	5.4
Government public health activities	1.4	3.2	7.3	8.5	9.3	9.9	11.0	12.3	13.4	1.9	2.9	2.9
Medical research	2.0	3.3	5.4	5.6	5.9	6.2	6.6	7.4	8.2	2.6	2.2	1.8
Medical facilities construction	3.4	5.1	6.5	7.6	8.4	9.2	8.9	6.1	8.0	4.6	2.6	1.8

* Includes services of registered and practical nurses in private duty, visiting nurses, podiatrists, physical therapists, clinical psychologists, chiropractors, neuropaths, and Christian Science practitioners.

† Includes fees of optometrists and expenditures for hearing aids, orthopedic appliances, artificial limbs, crutches, wheelchairs, and so on.

‡ Includes administrative expenses of federally financed health programs.

SOURCE: U.S. Health Care Financing Administration, *Health Care Financing Review*, Summer 1967.

are supervised in carrying out their patient care responsibilities. The level and method of supervision had to be consistent with the special requirements for each program. The ACGME also called for adequate counseling for residents, stating that graduate medical education placed increasing responsibilities on residents and required sustained intellectual and physical efforts; for some residents, according to the ACGME, these demands would, at times, cause physical or emotional stress.

The long hours residents experienced and the enormous responsibilities they shouldered took their toll on many residents. One admitted, "I was tired enough that I nodded off at the surgery table once." Recalling his entire first year as an intern, he added, "I don't remember too many nights when I got more than three or four hours of sleep." A resident at New York City Hospital reported that a colleague had been on duty for nearly 24 hours and had just enough energy to oversee safely the birth of a baby at 4 A.M. When he emerged from the delivery room, he literally collapsed. The early morning hours nearing the end of a shift are seen as the "danger zone" for patients. According to the New York City Hospital resident, "When it is 5 A.M. and the case doesn't appear to be life-threatening, the next thing you want to know is can it wait until 7 A.M., because that is when the next resident comes in."

Moreover, the long hours have been seen to dehumanize residents, as reflected in their attitudes toward patients. Some have described patients as "slimeballs," referring to intravenous drug users who come to the emergency room looking for more drugs, or "trainwrecks," referring to terminal patients with multiple medical problems.[8]

Established physicians believed that the stressful existence of students in medical education included decreased social interaction, excessively long hours, sleep deprivation, and lack of emotional support. A 1985 study revealed that physicians were more likely than others in the same socioeconomic group to have marital and substance abuse problems as well as a strong aversion to seeking help. The conclusion drawn: "There is the possibility that medical training reinforces proclivities toward self-deprivation and avoidance of requests for emotional assistance."[9]

Other studies supported the claims that sleep loss was detrimental to the work of a resident. When interns and residents were examined at New York's various teaching hospitals, after 31–36 hours without sleep, it was found that "the threshold for fatigue varies from person to person but it is likely that only a limited amount of sleep loss can be sustained by an intern or resident before emotional and intellectual functioning deteriorates." Summing up the results, one of the interns in the study remarked: "I am so tired I forget what name is on the chart I am writing in. As a result I write progress notes in the wrong charts and try to correct myself in the morning."

Moreover, the medical community realized that the potential negative effects of residency training did not end with graduation but pervaded future practice and life-style. Two common problems of medical education were deemed most likely to characterize the physician's later life: the "overwork syndrome" and sleep deprivation. It was suggested that 6 out of 10

[8] *Brookline Tab*, June 28, 1988, p. 32.
[9] Hawkins et al., "Sleep and Nutritional Deprivation and Performance of House Officers," *Journal of Medical Education* 60 (1985), pp. 530–35.

practicing physicians in the United States had or would have severe problems with alcoholism, drug dependence, depression, suicidal tendencies, and anxiety. It also was reported that "physicians are destroying themselves at twice the rate of the population they want to keep healthy."[10]

Other external pressures affecting the life of a resident resulted from the individual's inevitable role change from student to physician. Accompanying this major transition were the increased responsibility of the new multiple roles most residents played, including husband/wife and father/mother. Finally, it has been shown that financial problems and responsibilities, as well as a lack of emotional support in their work, increase the potential for friction and stress.[11] Commented one resident: "People deteriorate. Your goal is to survive the day." (See Exhibit 5)

A Different Perspective

The debate over the grand jury's recommendations concerning Libby Zion's death was the subject of the Focus Section of the *New England Journal of Medicine* (3/24/88). One of the contributors was Dr. Norman Levinsky, for the past 20 years chief of medicine in a municipal hospital and a university teaching hospital. Dr. Levinsky discussed the issues of residents' schedules, fatigue, and the difficulties limiting the schedules implied.

> Residents do work hard and they make mistakes, but it is unclear how often there is a causal connection between these two facts. Studies indicate that prolonged sleep deprivation reduces

speed and accuracy in performing mental tasks, but there is no evidence that fatigue itself has similar effect in the absence of sleep deprivation. Common sense suggests that it may and that exhaustion is not conducive to learning. On these humanitarian grounds, we should take steps to reduce residents' fatigue. Fatigue results not only from long shifts and work weeks but also from the intensity of the workload. This in turn depends on many factors: how sick the patients are, how many patients the resident cares for, how many he or she must admit each shift, how many hours must be spent in performing surgery or other procedures, and how much help is available.

> Residents work many fewer hours now than they did 20 or 30 years ago, when shifts every other night and the weekend were the rule. Yet there is a widespread perception that fatigue has not changed or is worse than in the past. This is probably because of the increase in the severity of illness of patients admitted to major teaching hospitals. Cost-control measures demand that even for these very sick patients the length of stay be reduced. The work of patient care is compressed. These factors increase the wear and tear on residents, offsetting the relief afforded by shorter work schedules. What can be done to decrease fatigue? The principal recommendation is to set limits on the number of hours that residents may work.

Levinsky then considered two alternatives to simply limiting the number of hours that residents may work.

> If residents spend less time caring for patients, who will assume that task? In some programs responsibilities can be redistributed from junior residents to more senior residents, who now may have fewer scheduled hours of direct patient care. However, the ability to

---

[10] Asken and Raham, "Resident Performance and Sleep Deprivation: A Review," *Journal of Medical Education* 58 (1983), pp. 382–87.

[11] Ibid.

EXHIBIT 5   The 36-Hour Work Day

Diary of an Intern

To an intern, personal time is always reckoned in minuses. It is the time remaining when workups, conferences, dictations, and clinic sessions are taken away, or it equals the time left over after work, sleep, and errand running are subtracted from a day. Fatigue by whatever means, personal time often seems like a sum that is unaccounted for, the small amount that balances the ledger of hours. And in the tallying of hourly expenditures that every intern makes, it lies on the debit side. Personal time is still owed. . . .

Infatuated with being an intern and preoccupied with work, I hardly cared about my life outside the hospital. I was perfectly content to think of my apartment as a place in which to camp out between shifts and to consider my private time as only time in which to recuperate and run occasional errands.

With time, of course, my attitude changed. The intoxicating sense of novelty I experienced at the beginning of the year began to wear off, and as it did so, my infatuation with the job began to fade. I also grew more confident in my abilities as an intern and was no longer so absorbed by having to prove myself every day. Less fulfilled and less obsessed by work, I began to want more from my personal life. What I found, three or four months into the year, however, was just how difficult it was to do any of the things I wanted to do with my free time.

One problem was simply finding the time. I was on-call every third night, during which I seldom managed to sneak in more than one or two hours of sleep (if any); so on the following night, when I returned home, I would usually be too exhausted to do much of anything. Only on the third night would I have any time to speak of; and even then, truly personal time was hard to come by. For one thing, I had errands to attend to. There was laundry to do, bills to pay, food to buy. For another, I couldn't help but be preoccupied by the impending day and night on-call, and I would need to prepare myself both psychologically and physically for the stresses I would face.

Time was a domineering presence in my life as an intern. I learned to live by a different calendar, a calendar with only three days—the day on-call, the day after being on-call, and the day before being on-call—and telling the time became an obsession. My calendar dominated my mind's life. It insinuated itself in my thoughts at unexpected times, surfacing in the midst of dealing with a patient's cardiac arrest, creeping in during dinner with a group of friends, or competing with the plot as I turned the pages of a book. Even on vacation I found myself slipping unconsciously into the intern mode of telling time, as if I had sensed a pull from far away. The circadian rhythms of the on-call schedule, which stretch not over 24 but over 72 hours, are what govern an intern's biological and psychological lives. Unable to ever lose sight of the time, I allowed my life to become tyrannized by my awareness of nights and days.

If my schedule as an intern threatened personal time, so did a condition closely related to the hours I kept—fatigue. It only took one or two months for me to grow hopelessly sleep-deprived; and exhaustion, I soon discovered, made everything I did during my off-hours more difficult. Like a physical impediment, it was a disability I had to work around. I learned that dim rooms and dark places were to be avoided like the plague, since the urge to sleep could be overpowering. I had to give up going to a favorite restaurant of mine (which was quiet and had subdued lighting) because my chin had a couple of close scrapes with the soup. I learned to fortify myself with a bracing cup of coffee before going to a concert and went to the movie theaters only at my own great peril. I also learned to stay, as much as possible, in constant motion. I hesitated to make plans that would oblige me to stand in line, whether at a restaurant or box office, since, it often required a tremendous investment of energy to keep awake. Even taking the T was a challenge.

EXHIBIT 5   *(concluded)*

Having missed my stop more than once, I made it a firm policy never to sit down on the subway.

If fatigue made it hard for me to engage in almost any activity, it also made it difficult for me to keep track of my commitments. I learned to distrust my memory, once something I had prided myself on. I forgot engagements and promises, and arrived late to friends' homes, having misremembered the time for which I had been invited. To avoid embarrassment, I eventually resolved to write every appointment and invitation down.

Worse still, I forgot entire conversations. If I awoke to answer the phone at night, I might have a long and perfectly lucid conversation but have no recollection of it come morning. This even happened with my sister once. Only after she reminded me of her call did I remember our having spoken and even then, I at first drew a blank, privately doubting that the conversation had actually taken place. . . .

Although I missed having much of a personal life as an intern, I felt guilty at acknowledging that I wanted one. Much as a part of me cried out bitterly for what I could no longer do or had difficulty doing as a doctor, another part of me refused to admit that I could want more out of life than only medicine. Somewhere along the way I acquired the idea that being a doctor should be sufficient to fulfill me. What could be more satisfying than a life of ministering to people's needs, a life of constant giving? Admitting that I could want something more from my life seemed to incriminate me. It made me appear selfish in my own estimation, a failure.

The more I felt my own needs, the harder I worked at trying to overcome them. If I found myself looking forward to leaving the hospital, I would force myself to stay late, and if I came home after a long day of work, I would not allow myself to flick on the TV or read a magazine, but made myself study instead. How could I not study when what I learn might contribute to saving a life? If I did give in, however briefly, to whatever it was I really wanted to do—say reading a book—it was as if I were giving in to baser instincts and turning my back on someone in need. In the contest between medicine and personal life, personal life always seemed to exert the weaker claim. Like a bastard brother, it seemed forever tainted with illegitimacy, always to reek of unseemliness.

But as internship wore on, I could not ignore the truth: I, too, had needs, and the more I pretended to disavow them the more acute they became. I wanted time for myself. I wanted someone to love me. I, who professed to want to be everything to everybody in need, wanted also to be taken care of.

SOURCE: Stephen A. Hoffmann, M.D., *Under the Ether Dome: A Physician's Apprenticeship at Massachusetts General Hospital.*

compensate for mandated reductions in working hours by making such adjustments is limited. Given the decreasing-number of graduates of American medical schools, adding residents is not a viable solution.

It seems likely that one or both of two methods will be used to compensate for the decrease in patient care due to residents' working fewer hours. The first is that not as many residents will be on call at any time but that each will be responsible for more patients when on duty. That means, of course, that fatigue from an increased workload per shift will probably replace fatigue from working long hours as a potential cause of medical error. Moreover, the need for more frequent transfers of information among residents will add to the potential for errors due to faulty transfer of information. My own experience in staffing our intensive care unit both in the traditional manner (with interns working every third night) and with a "night float" [a resident who works only at night] suggests that errors due to faulty transfer of information are at least as frequent as those due to fatigue from being on call overnight.

The second alternative is that fewer patients will be admitted to teaching services. On nonteaching services, attending physicians are called when nurses consider it necessary. There is no reason to believe that a nurse can judge the need to involve an attending physician better than a resident can. Nor is it likely that a nurse will call an attending physician at the office or at home as readily as she or he will call a resident at the hospital. Thus, the quality and amount of physicians' participation in the care of patients shunted to nonteaching services will probably not improve. Ironically, attending doctors involved in patient care at night are not prohibited by the proposed rules from maintaining a full schedule in the office or operating room the next day. There is little reason to believe that a tired attending physician working for 36 consecutive hours is less prone to error than a tired resident.

Finally, Levinsky commented on what he felt could be done but cautioned that there were other factors to be considered, such as moonlighting by residents and the great diversity of hospital settings and training programs:

There is no evidence—despite dramatic cases—that inadequate supervision and long work weeks are major causes of poor patient care. I doubt that these factors are nearly as important as nursing shortages or the appointment of poorly trained graduates from foreign medical schools as residents. It makes sense, however, to use the momentum gener-

ated by the media's attention to residents' fatigue and need for supervision to improve medical care and education on teaching services. . . .

Given the great diversity of the hospital settings and training programs, it is impossible for states to specify detailed schedules and supervisory programs suitable for all teaching services. Each program director should be responsible for using the available resources to implement the mechanisms most likely to succeed in the context of the specific program. States can monitor compliance by estimating review committees. The public, the government, and the administrators of teaching services all have the common goal of optimal patient care. Rigid regulations not tailored to local circumstances are as likely to affect care adversely as to improve it. Governments, like medical practitioners, should at least do no harm.

Other Physicians' Opinions

Medicine is a demanding mistress . . . any doctor or student who is unable to make the commitment necessary to care for the patient whenever he is needed is better off in some other field of endeavor.

Established Physician

The issue of reducing the number of hours residents work has threatened to "introduce a shift mentality" to medicine, according to some established physicians, as it was "generally inconsistent with the delivery of high-quality patient care." Other doctors asserted that, since medicine was not practiced according to rigid hourly shifts, residents should not be taught in that framework.

Moreover, many doctors insisted that the long hours of residency were a critical part of medical education. "Illness knows no shift," explained Dr. Robert

Petersdorf, president of the Association of American Medical Colleges. It was argued that, since some ailments, such as diabetic coma or toxic shock, could progress over 36 hours, a physician had to follow the history of the particular illness. Others asserted that, if shifts were significantly shortened, residencies might have to be lengthened to ensure that residents got enough experience. Since medical residencies in some specializations already lasted up to eight years, many residents might not welcome the prospect of longer study.

The medical establishment and some of the trainees themselves said the intense schedule of the resident was necessary: It gave young doctors extensive experience in a relatively short period, allowed them to see disease at all stages, prepared them for late-night calls from patients in later years. Defenders of the current system indicated there was no danger to patients because help from more experienced doctors was always only a phone call away.

Established physicians recalling their years of training often espoused the attitude, "If I went through it so can you." Many believed the training and experience had been dramatic and character-building; the ritualistic meaning and the tradition-steeped institution of the residency generally provoked positive memories. One doctor revealed that "the intensity of experiences is remembered favorably, and the fatigue and self-neglect seem to have been unimportant, making it difficult to generate much enthusiasm for change."

Although most people in the profession viewed the residency years as intensive training for the difficult predicaments the physicians would encounter indefinitely in the field, a study showed that practitioners rarely encountered the crises that residents often face daily, and most practitioners

had more time and resources to deal with them. Jack D. McCue, M.D., who conducted this study, asserted that:

> Responsible, conscientious behavior on the part of physicians is more likely to be taught by example than by requiring long hours and frequent night call, with limited faculty supervision, and the knowledge needed to respond effectively to crises can be taught at any time, not just at night. In fact, because physicians function poorly when fatigued and deprived of sleep, we may actually be teaching residents to tolerate and rationalize unnecessary errors and lower standards of patient care.

The Administrator's Point of View

The issues of changing the work schedules, long hours, and scant supervision of medical interns and residents were not new. Long before the case of Libby Zion, informed and concerned parties both in and out of the medical profession examined the great costs of working medical students incessantly, as well as the seemingly comparable costs of changing this established system. Hospital administrators responded negatively to proposals, such as those made by the New York grand jury, asserting that changing the hours and responsibilities of residents would change the way doctors were trained and, in turn, wreak havoc on the staffing of teaching hospitals, which "depend on the cheap labor of residents."[12]

The Example of New York Hospital

In the past, fine administrators, really spiritual leaders, ran this hospital, at a time when this institution had unlimited resources. But things have changed.

---

[12] *Time*, September 31, 1987, p. 54.

This is a "real world" place now, not a gentleman's place, not the place where beds were made by stern German ladies from Yorkville or where you could hire 14 more people if the emergency room was dirty. It needs management.

New York Hospital Physician

Founded in 1771, New York Hospital, a not-for-profit institution, was one of the largest teaching hospitals in the country, with more than 6,000 full-time employees. Affiliated with Cornell Medical College, New York Hospital housed 1,421 staff physicians, over 400 of whom were interns or residents, 1,700 nurses, 1,462 beds, over 300 volunteers, and admitted 980 patients daily, or more than 40,000 patients annually. In 1987, like most hospitals, New York Hospital had a 15 percent nursing vacancy rate and a continual shortage of support services. Its annual revenues in 1987 were $353.4 million and its annual expenses for the same year were $375.9 million, $219 million of which was paid out as salaries, wages, and benefits. New York Hospital's enormous expenses reflected the nationwide trend of rising expenditures on hospital care, rising from $101.6 billion in 1980 to $179.6 billion in 1986. In 1979, the New York Hospital joined the 911 Emergency Medical Service system; before then, fewer than 10 percent of its patients arrived through the emergency room. By 1988, close to 20 percent were admitted this way.

By the mid-1980s New York Hospital experienced various problems that some have called "endemic," namely, a weak administrative apparatus, nurses delivering care of uneven quality, and inefficient, half-century-old quarters for patients. The hospital's occupancy rate fell from 89.2 percent in 1985 to 83.9 percent in 1987— below that of most other teaching hospitals

in New York City.[13] As a major teaching hospital, New York Hospital has received its share of complaints referred to the state health department.

Yet the administration of New York Hospital remained firm regarding the quality of care it provided. Since the end of 1987, New York Hospital required that an attending physician—not a resident— approve all admissions and discharges and "accept responsibility for medical care," a move previously taken by other academic medical centers. The new head of the hospital remarked: "Being a teaching hospital does not excuse poor patient care. The nature of a teaching hospital is that there are teachers as well as students, and the teachers are supposed to run it."[14]

Problems With Changing the System

According to the Greater New York Hospital Association (GNYHA), there were numerous problems with changing the system of medical education in the United States, particularly the ability to realistically implement a limit on the number of hours residents worked:

> It is unrealistic to expect nurse clinicians and physicians' assistants to fill gaps, given the present shortages of these personnel. Thus, the only realistic possible options for covering any gaps include hiring new physicians or relying more heavily on existing attending physicians. The former may not be easily accomplished particularly for evening, night, and weekend coverage, and the latter needs considerable further research to determine its feasibility in

---

[13] *New York Times Magazine*, January 1988, p. 50.

[14] Ibid., p. 51.

light of existing commitments and work schedules.[15]

Concerning the issue of increased supervision of residents, the president of the Association of American Medical Colleges representing all 127 U.S. medical schools and more than 450 major teaching hospitals, Robert G. Petersdorf, M.D., claimed that his organization was not against supervision of residents but rather against overly fatigued residents. However, he explained that the current practices of medical education had a long history and tradition and, furthermore, resulted in well-trained physicians who were able to make critical decisions about seriously ill patients. Dr. Petersdorf also pointed out that, if residents worked fewer hours, additional personnel would have to be hired, necessitating the revision of present reimbursement policies and the increase of payments.

Most administrative groups, including the Association of American Medical Colleges, the Accreditation Council for Graduate Medical Education, the Committee of Interns and Residents, and the American Medical Association generally agreed that limiting the number of hours a resident worked in the emergency room made sound medical sense. However, most of these groups disagreed with the grand jury recommendation to limit the number of hours residents might work in an in-hospital setting, for largely similar reasons, which, articulated by Dr. Petersdorf, included:

1. Limiting resident hours would necessitate the training of more residents.
2. Limiting resident hours had no relationship to the needs of patients for

services. Therefore, unless these needs were addressed, limiting resident hours might simultaneously limit patient access to care.
3. Residency programs should be developed primarily for the education of the trainee and only secondarily to render patient services. If the programs were restructured, important educational consequences would have to be addressed. For example, formal effort at recordkeeping would have to be developed to ensure that residents accumulated clinical experience with multiple patients, where in the past they used to gather their clinical experience over time with one patient.
4. Increasing resident supervision will alter the activities that faculty undertake. If more hours are required for resident supervision, fewer hours remain for student teaching, research, and administration.
5. There would be a need for sufficient flexibility in the residency program. For example, limiting resident availability without actively addressing the problem of nursing recruitment, retention, and satisfaction was unrealistic.

The president of the Committee of Interns and Residents, Janet Freedman, M.D., expressed a few other concerns regarding the proposed recommendations. She asserted that limiting resident hours would introduce a "time clock mentality" to training physicians, giving them license to "walk off the job" after the specified number of hours. In the current system, although the next "shift" of residents arrived, the residents on duty would not leave but remained to finish the day's work—afternoon rounds, checking outstanding laboratory results, or completing paperwork. The presence of the new on-call team served to protect the old team

---

[15] Final Report of the New York State Ad Hoc Committee on Emergency Services, October 1987.

from new work. She commented further:

> I do not see any reason to believe that this attitude would change. Resident physicians do not view their work hours as rigidly set, but some reasonable limits must exist. There must be some protection from the 32–48 hour shifts residents now routinely work.

Another common concern of most administrators was that limiting resident hours would jeopardize the vital educational concept of continuity of care. According to Dr. Frank Spencer, professor and chairman of the Department of Surgery at the New York University School of Medicine, continuity of care means "knowing the patient, including diagnosis, treatment, recent events, and frequent examination. This knowledge of all facts, especially recent ones, is essential in decision making with a complex illness."[16] In response to this concern, the American College of Physicians revealed that:

> In learning the meaning of continuing responsibility, physicians have a lot in common with parents: we all understand and applaud the dedication of parents when they stay up with fragile or needy offspring for many days and nights. It would be unrealistic to expect residents to absorb the realities of caring for their equally fragile and needy patients if their working hours were fixed according to an arbitrary schedule, however well-intended.[17]

A final and controversial concern of the medical profession, which the American College of Physicians called "their real issue," was the ability and right of an outside authority to impose regulations on other professions. The American Medical Association (AMA) believed that "the establishment of rigid requirements for working hours by administrative regulations or by legislation at the state or national level was improper and had the potential to interfere with the provision of medical care of high quality and with the education process in teaching hospitals."[18] The American College of Physicians asserted that their mere existence as a medical organization is predicated on the principle of self-improvement, analysis, and regulation:

> Regulations concerning matters of graduate medical education . . . however well-intended and intrinsically reasonable, strip those within the profession *responsible* for crucial areas of graduate medical education of the *authority* to make decisions in those areas.[19]

The Committee Heard Testimony

The committee convened by Axelrod in June heard testimony over the course of the summer from many concerned and informed parties, including: the Accreditation Council for Graduate Medical Education, the American College of Physicians, the American Medical Association, and the Greater New York Hospital Association. Much of the testimony centered on the potential effects of implementing the grand jury recommendations, especially their impact on graduate medical education, hospital staffing, malpractice litigation, and health care financing. During the course of the Ad Hoc Advisory Committee hearings, the Greater New York Hospital Association offered a detailed analysis that estimated the cost of

---

[16] Final Report of the New York State Ad Hoc Committee.
[17] Ibid.

[18] Ibid.
[19] Ibid.

changing shift hours in its 50 New York City hospitals. The analysis indicated that, if the shifts were rearranged to limit residents to 12 hours in emergency service, 16 hours out of emergency care, with at least 8 hours off between shifts, this would require an additional 2,045 full-time equivalent attending physicians and 974 full-time equivalent ancillary personnel, for an annual cost of $203,955,000.

CASE

CHANGING THE CULTURE AT BRITISH AIRWAYS

I remember going to parties in the late 1970s, and, if you wanted to have a civilized conversation, you didn't actually say that you worked for British Airways, because it got you talking about people's last travel experience, which was usually an unpleasant one. It's staggering how much the airline's image has changed since then, and, in comparison, how proud staff are of working for BA today.

British Airways employee, Spring 1990

I recently flew business class on British Airways for the first time in about 10 years. What has happened over that time is amazing. I can't tell you how my memory of British Airways as a company and the experience I had 10 years ago contrasts with today. The improvement in service is truly remarkable.

British Airways customer, Fall 1989

In June of 1990, British Airways reported its third consecutive year of record profits, £345 million before taxes, firmly establishing the rejuvenated carrier as one of the world's most profitable airlines. The impressive financial results were one indication that BA had convincingly shed its historic "bloody awful" image. In October of 1989, one respected American publication referred to them as "bloody awesome,"[1] a description most would not have thought possible after pre-tax losses totalling more than £240 million in the years 1981 and 1982. Productivity had risen more than 67 percent over the course of the 1980s.[2] Passengers reacted highly favorably to the changes. After suffering through years of poor market perception during the 1970s and before,

---

This case was prepared by Research Associate James Leahey (under the direction of Professor John P. Kotter).

Copyright © 1990 by the President and Fellows of Harvard College. Harvard Business School case N9-491-009.

---

[1] "From 'Bloody Awful' to 'Bloody Awesome,'" *Business Week*, October 9, 1989, p. 97.

[2] As measured by available ton-kilometers per employee, or the payload capacity of BA's aircraft multiplied by kms flown, the industry standard for productivity. BA's ATKs per employee were 145,000 in 1980 and 243,000 in 1989.

BA garnered four Airline of the Year awards during the 1980s, as voted by the readers of *First Executive Travel*. In 1990, the leading American aviation magazine, *Air Transport World*, selected BA as the winner of its Passenger Service award. In the span of a decade, British Airways had radically improved its financial strength, convinced its work force of the paramount importance of customer service, and dramatically improved its perception in the market. Culminating in the privatization of 1987, the carrier had undergone fundamental change through a series of important messages and events. With unprecedented success under its belt, management faced an increasingly perplexing problem: how to maintain momentum and recapture the focus that would allow them to meet new challenges.

Crisis of 1981

Record profits must have seemed distant in 1981. On September 10 of that year, then chief executive Roy Watts issued a special bulletin to British Airways staff:

> British Airways is facing the worst crisis in its history . . . unless we take swift and remedial action we are heading for a loss of at least £100 million in the present financial year. We face the prospect that by next April we shall have piled up losses of close to £250 million in two years. Even as I write to you, our money is draining at the rate of nearly £200 a minute.
>
> No business can survive losses on this scale. Unless we take decisive action now, there is a real possibility that British Airways will go out of business for lack of money. We have to cut our costs sharply, and we have to cut

them fast. We have no more choice, and no more time.[3]

Just two years earlier, an optimistic British government had announced its plan to privatize British Airways through a sale of shares to the investing public. Although airline management recognized that the 58,000 staff was too large, they expected increased passenger volumes and improved staff productivity to help them avoid complicated and costly employee reductions. While the 1978–79 plan forecasted passenger traffic growth at 8 to 10 percent, an unexpected recession left BA struggling to survive on volumes which, instead, decreased by more that 4 percent. A diverse and aging fleet, increased fuel costs, and the high staffing costs forced the government and BA to put privatization on hold indefinitely. With the airline technically bankrupt, BA management and the government would have to wait before the public would be ready to embrace the ailing airline. (See Exhibit 1)

The BA Culture, 1960–1980

British Airways stumbled into its 1979 state of inefficiency in large part because of its history and culture. In August 1971, the Civil Aviation Act became law, setting the stage for the British Airways Board to assume control of two state-run airlines, British European Airways (BEA) and British Overseas Airways Corporation (BOAC), under the name British Airways. In theory, the board was to control policy over British Airways; but, in practice, BEA and BOAC remained autonomous, each with its own chairman, board, and chief executive. In 1974, BOAC and BEA

---

[3] Alison Corke, *British Airways: Path to Profitability* (London: Pan Books, Ltd., 1986), p. 82.

EXHIBIT 1 British Airways' Results, 1977-1990

	1977	1978	1979	1980	1981	1982	1983	1984	1985	1986	1987	1988	1989	1990
						Year-End March 31								
Turnover (revenues) in £ billions	1.25	1.36	1.64	1.92	2.06	2.24	2.50	2.51	2.94	3.15	3.26	3.76	4.26	4.84
Operating profits in £ millions (airline only)	96	57	76	17	(102)	5	169	274	303	205	183	241	340	402
Pretax profit in £ millions	96	54	90	20	(140)	(114)	74	185	191	195	162	228	268	345
Net profit in £ millions	35	52	77	11	(145)	(545)	89	216	174	181	152	151	175	245
Revenue per passenger kilometer (pence)	2.98	3.24	3.28	3.35	3.74	4.20	4.89	5.57	5.87	5.80	6.00	5.82	5.96	6.37
Number of employees (000s)	54	55	56	56	54	48	40	36	37	39	40	43	49	50
ATK per employee (000s)	121	123	135	145	154	158	182	199	213	221	222	236	243	247

finally issued one consolidated financial report. In 1976, Sir Frank (later Lord) McFadzean replaced the group division with a structure based on functional divisions to officially integrate the divisions into one airline. Still, a distinct split within British Airways persisted throughout the 1970s and into the mid-1980s.

After the Second World War, BEA helped pioneer European civil aviation. As a pioneer, it concerned itself more with building an airline infrastructure than it did with profit. As a 20-year veteran and company director noted: "The BEA culture was very much driven by building something that did not exist. They had built that in 15 years, up until 1960. Almost single-handedly they opened up air transport in Europe after the war. That had been about getting the thing established. The marketplace was taking care of itself. They wanted to get the network to work, to get stations opened up."

BOAC had also done its share of pioneering, making history on May 2, 1952, by sending its first jet airliner on a trip from London to Johannesburg, officially initiating jet passenger service. Such innovation was not without cost, however, and BOAC found itself mired in financial woes throughout the two decades following the war. As chairman Sir Matthew Slattery explained in 1962: "The Corporation has had to pay a heavy price for pioneering advanced technologies."[4]

Success to most involved with BEA and BOAC in the 1950s and 1960s had less to do with net income and more to do with "flying the British flag." Having inherited numerous war veterans, both airlines had been injected with a military mentality. These values combined with the years

BEA and BOAC existed as government agencies to shape the way British Airways would view profit through the 1970s. As former director of human resources Nick Georgiades said of the military and civil service history: "Put those two together and you had an organization that believed its job was simply to get an aircraft into the air on time and to get it down on time."[5]

While government support reinforced the operational culture, a deceiving string of profitable years in the 1970s made it even easier for British Airways to neglect its increasing inefficiencies. Between 1972 and 1980, BA earned a profit before interest and tax in each year except for one. "This was significant, not least because as long as the airline was returning profits, it was not easy to persuade the workforce, or the management for that matter, the fundamental changes were vital."[6] Minimizing cost to the state became the standard by which BA measured itself. As one senior manager noted: "Productivity was not an issue. People were operating effectively, not necessarily efficiently. There were a lot of people doing other people's jobs, and there were a lot of people checking on people doing other people's jobs . . . ." As a civil service agency, the airline was allowed to become inefficient because the thinking in state-run operations was, "If you're providing service at no cost to the taxpayer, then you're doing quite well."

A lack of economies of scale and strong residual loyalties upon the merger further complicated the historical disregard for efficiency by BEA and BOAC. Until Sir Frank McFadzean's reorganization in 1976, British Airways had labored under

---

[4] Corke, p. 39.

[5] Ibid., p. 116.
[6] Company document, p. 2.

several separate organizations (BOAC; BEA European, Regional, Scottish, and Channel) so the desired benefits of consolidation had been squandered. Despite operating under the same banner, the organization consisted more or less of separate airlines carrying the associated costs of such a structure. Even after the reorganization, divisional loyalties prevented the carrier from attaining a common focus. "The 1974 amalgamation of BOAC with the domestic and European divisions of BEA had produced a hybrid racked with management demarcation squabbles. The competitive advantages sought through the merger had been hopelessly defeated by the lack of a unifying corporate culture."[7] A BA director summed up how distracting the merger proved: "There wasn't enough management time devoted to managing the changing environment because it was all focused inwardly on resolving industrial relations problems, on resolving organizational conflicts. How do you bring these very, very different cultures together?"

Productivity at BA in the 1970s was strikingly bad, especially in contrast to other leading foreign airlines. BA's productivity[8] for the three years ending March 31, 1974, 1975, and 1976 had never exceeded 59 percent of that of the average of the other eight foreign airline leaders. Service suffered as well. One human resources senior manager recalled the "awful" service during her early years in passenger services: "I remember 10 years ago standing at the gate handing out boxes of food to people as they got on

the aircraft. That's how we dealt with service." With increasing competition and rising costs of labor in Britain in the late 1970s, the lack of productivity and poor service was becoming increasingly harmful. By the summer of 1979, the number of employees had climbed to a peak of 58,000. The problems became dangerous when Britain's worst recession in 50 years reduced passenger numbers and raised fuel costs substantially.

Lord King Takes the Reins

Sir John (later Lord) King was appointed chairman in February of 1981, just a half-year before Roy Watts's unambiguously grim assessment of BA's financial state. King brought to British Airways a successful history of business ventures and strong ties to both the government and business communities. Despite having no formal engineering qualifications, King formed Ferrybridge Industries in 1945, a company which found an unexploited niche in the ball-bearing industry. Later renamed the Pollard Ball and Roller Bearing Company, Ltd., King's company was highly successful until he sold it in 1969. In 1970, he joined Babcock International and as chairman led it through a successful restructuring during the 1970s. King's connections were legendary. Hand-picked by Margaret Thatcher to run BA, King's close friends included Lord Hanson of Hanson Trust and the Princess of Wales's family. He also knew personally Presidents Reagan and Carter. King's respect and connections proved helpful both in recruiting and in his dealings with the British government.

One director spoke of the significance of King's appointment: "British Airways needed a chairman who didn't need a job. We needed someone who could see that

---

[7] Duncan Campbell-Smith, *The British Airways Story: Struggle for Take-Off* (London: Coronet, 1986), p. 10.

[8] In terms of available ton-kilometers per employee, taken from annual reports.

the only way to do this sort of thing was radically, and who would be aware enough of how you bring that about.''

In his first annual report, King predicted hard times for the troubled carrier. ''I would have been comforted by the thought that the worst was behind us. There is no certainty that this is so.''

Upon Watts's announcement in September of 1981, he and King launched their Survival plan—''tough, unpalatable and immediate measures'' to stem the spiraling losses and save the airline from bankruptcy. The radical steps included reducing staff numbers from 52,000 to 43,000, or 20 percent, in just nine months; freezing pay increases for a year; and closing 16 routes, eight on-line stations, and two engineering bases. It also dictated halting cargo-only services and selling the fleet, and inflicting massive cuts upon offices, administrative services, and staff clubs.

In June of 1982, BA management appended the Survival plan to accommodate the reduction of another 7,000 staff, which would eventually bring the total employees down from about 42,000 to nearly 35,000. BA accomplished its reductions through voluntary measures, offering such generous severance that they ended up with more volunteers than necessary. In total, the airline dished out some £150 million in severance pay. Between 1981 and 1983, BA reduced its staff by about a quarter.

About the time of the Survival plan revision, King brought in Gordon Dunlop, a Scottish accountant described by one journalist as ''imaginative, dynamic, and extremely hardworking,'' euphemistically known on Fleet Street as ''forceful,'' and considered by King as simply ''outstanding.''[9] As CFO, Dunlop's contribution to the recovery

years was significant. When the results for the year ending March 31, 1982, were announced in October, he and the board ensured 1982 would be a watershed year in BA's turnaround. Using creative financing, Dunlop wrote down £100 million for redundancy costs, £208 million for the value of the fleet (which would ease depreciation in future years), even an additional £98 million for the 7,000 redundancies which had yet to be effected. For the year, the loss before taxes amounted to £114 million. After taxes and extraordinary items, it totalled a staggering £545 million.

Even King might have admitted that the worst was behind them after such a report. The chairman immediately turned his attention to changing the airline's image and further building his turnaround team. On September 13, 1982, King relieved Foote, Cone & Belding of its 36-year-old advertising account with BA, replacing it with Saatchi & Saatchi. One of the biggest account changes in British history, it was King's way of making a clear statement that the BA direction had changed. In April of 1983, British Airways launched its ''Manhattan Landing'' campaign. King and his staff sent BA management personal invitations to gather employees and tune in to the inaugural six-minute commercial. Overseas, each BA office was sent a copy of the commercial on videocassette, and many held cocktail parties to celebrate the new thrust. ''Manhattan Landing'' dramatically portrayed the whole island of Manhattan being lifted from North America and whirled over the Atlantic before awestruck witnesses in the U.K. After the initial airing, a massive campaign was run with a 90-second ver-

---

[9] Campbell-Smith, p. 46.

sion of the commercial. The ad marked the beginning of a broader campaign, "The World's Favourite Airline," reflective of BA's status as carrier of the most passengers internationally. With the financial picture finally brightening, BA raised its advertising budget for 1983–84 to £31 million, compared with £19 million the previous year, signalling a clear commitment to changing the corporate image.

Colin Marshall Becomes Chief Executive

In the midst of the Saatchi & Saatchi launch, King recruited Mr. (later Sir) Colin Marshall, who proved to be perhaps the single most important person in the changes at British Airways. Appointed chief executive in February 1983, Marshall brought to the airline a unique résumé. He began his career as a management trainee with Hertz in the United States. After working his way up the Hertz hierarchy in North America, Marshall accepted a job in 1964 to run rival Avis's operations in Europe. By 1976, the British-born businessman had risen to chief executive of Avis. In 1981, he returned to the U.K. as deputy chief executive and board member of Sears Holdings. Fulfilling one of his ultimate career ambitions, he took over as chief executive of British Airways in early 1983. Although having no direct experience in airline management, Marshall brought with him two tremendous advantages. First, he understood customer service, and second, he had worked with a set of customers quite similar to the airline travel segment during his car rental days.

Marshall made customer service a personal crusade from the day he entered BA. One executive reported: "It was really Marshall focusing almost on nothing else.

The one thing that had overriding attention the first three years he was here was customer service, customer service, customer service—nothing else. That was the only thing he was interested in, and it's not an exaggeration to say that was his exclusive focus." Another senior manager added: "He has certainly put an enabling culture in place to allow customer service to come out, where, rather than people waiting to be told what to do to do things better, it's an environment where people feel they can actually come out with ideas, that they will be listened to, and feel they are much more a part of the success of the company." Not just a strong verbal communicator, Marshall became an active role model in the terminals, spending time with staff during morning and evenings. He combined these actions with a number of important events to drive home the customer service message.

Corporate Celebrations, 1983–1987

If Marshall was the most important player in emphasizing customer service, then the Putting People First (PPF) program was the most important event. BA introduced PPF to the front-line staff in December of 1983 and continued it through June of 1984. Run by the Danish firm Time Manager International, each program cycle lasted two days and included 150 participants. The program was so warmly received that the non-front-line employees eventually asked to be included, and a one-day "PPF II" program facilitated the participation of all BA employees through June 1985. Approximately 40,000 BA employees went through the PPF programs. The program urged participants to examine their interactions with other people, including family, friends, and, by association, customers. Its acceptance and impact was extraordinary, due primarily to the honesty of its message, the excellence of its delivery, and the strong support of management.

Employees agreed almost unanimously that the program's message was sincere and free from manipulation, due in some measure to the fact that BA separated itself from the program's design. The program emphasized positive relations with people in general, focusing in large part on non-work-related relationships. Implied in the positive relationship message was an emphasis on customer service, but the program was careful to aim for the benefit of employees as individuals first.

Employees expressed their pleasure on being treated with respect and relief that change was on the horizon. As one frontline ticket agent veteran said: "I found it fascinating, very, very enjoyable. I thought it was very good for British Airways. It made people aware. I don't think people give enough thought to people's reaction to each other. . . . It was hardhitting. It was made something really special. When you were there, you were treated extremely well. You were treated as a VIP, and people really enjoyed that. It was reverse roles, really, to the job we do." A senior manager spoke of the confidence it promoted in the changes: "It was quite a revelation, and I thought it was absolutely wonderful. I couldn't believe BA had finally woken and realized where its bread was buttered. There were a lot of cynics at the time, but for people like myself it was really great to suddenly realize you were working for an airline that had the guts to change, and that it's probably somewhere where you want to stay."

Although occasionally an employee felt uncomfortable with the "rah-rah" nature of the program, feeling it perhaps "too

American," in general, PPF managed to eliminate cynicism. The excellence in presentation helped signify a sincerity to the message. One senior manager expressed the consistency: "There was a match between the message and the delivery. You can't get away with saying putting people first is important, if in the process of delivering that message you don't put people first." Employees were sent personal invitations, thousands were flown in from around the world, and a strong effort was made to prepare tasteful meals and treat everyone with respect. Just as important, BA released every employee for the program, and expected everyone to attend. Grade differences became irrelevant during PPF, as managers and staff members were treated equally and interacted freely. Moreover, a senior director came to conclude every single PPF session with a question and answer session. Colin Marshall himself frequently attended these closing sessions, answering employee concerns in a manner most felt to be extraordinarily frank. The commitment shown by management helped BA avoid the fate suffered by British Rail in its subsequent attempt at a similar program. The British Railway program suffered a limited budget, a lack of commitment by management and interest by staff, and a high degree of cynicism. Reports surfaced that employees felt the program was a public relations exercise for the outside world, rather than a learning experience for staff.

About the time PPF concluded, in 1985, BA launched a program for managers only called, appropriately, Managing People First (MPF). A five-day residential program for 25 managers at a time, MPF stressed the importance of, among other topics, trust, leadership, vision, and feedback. On a smaller scale, MPF stirred up issues long neglected at BA. One senior manager of engineering summarized his experience: "It was almost as if I were touched on the head. ...I don't think I even considered culture before MPF. Afterwards I began to think about what makes people tick. Why do people do what they do? Why do people come to work? Why do people do things for some people that they won't do for others?" Some participants claimed the course led them to put more emphasis on feedback. One reported initiating regular meetings with staff every two weeks, in contrast to before the program when he met with staff members only as problems arose.

As Marshall and his team challenged the way people thought at BA, they also encouraged changes in more visible ways. In December 1984, BA unveiled its new fleet livery at Heathrow airport. Preparations for the show were carefully planned and elaborate. The plane was delivered to the hangar-turned-theater under secrecy of night, after which hired audio and video technicians put together a dramatic presentation. On the first night of the show, a darkened coach brought guests from an off-site hotel to an undisclosed part of the city and through a tunnel. The guests, including dignitaries, high-ranking travel executives, and trade union representatives, were left uninformed of their whereabouts. To their surprise, as the show began an aircraft moved through the fog and laser lights decorating the stage and turned, revealing the new look of the British Airways fleet. A similar presentation continued four times a day for eight weeks for all staff to see. On its heels, in May of 1985, British Airways unveiled its new uniforms, designed by Roland Klein. With new leadership, strong communication from the top, increased acceptance by the public, and a new physical image, few

on the BA staff could deny in 1985 that his or her working life had turned a new leaf from its condition in 1980.

Management attempted to maintain the momentum of its successful programs. Following PPF and MPF, it put on a fairly successful corporatewide program in 1985 called "A Day in the Life" and another less significant program in 1987 called "To Be the Best." Inevitably, interest diminished and cynicism grew with successive programs. BA also implemented an "Awards for Excellence" program to encourage employee input. Colin Marshall regularly communicated to staff through video. While the programs enjoyed some success, not many employees felt "touched on the head" by any successor program to PPF and MPF.

Privatization

The financial crisis of 1981 rendered the 1979 announcement of privatization by the British government irrelevant until the return to profitability in 1983. Unfortunately for BA, a number of complicated events delayed the selling of shares to the public for almost four more years. On April 1, 1984, the government passed legislation which made BA a public limited company. Still, the minister maintained control of the shares. Before a public sale, BA first had to weather an antitrust suit against it and a number of other airlines by the out-of-business Laker airline chief Freddie Laker. BA also was confronted by complicated diplomatic difficulties with the United States concerning U.K.-U.S.A. flight regulations, and increased fears of terrorism. Finally, the airline faced a challenge at home by British Caledonian over routes, a challenge that ironically turned out to be the final ingredient in the cultural revolution.

In 1984, British Caledonian management persuaded some influential regulators, civil servants, and ministers that the
government should award the smaller airline some of BA's routes for the sake of
competition. In July, the Civil Aviation
Authority (CAA) produced its report recommending the changes. Arguing that
substitution was a poor excuse for competition, Lord King led BA into a fierce
political battle. Against the odds, King
managed to extract a nonthreatening compromise. Called "The White Paper," the
October report recommended increased
competition but rejected forced transfers
from BA to British Caledonian. Instead, it
approved of a mutually agreed transfer
between BA and BCal by which BCal
attained BA's Saudi Arabia routes and BA
attained BCal's South American routes.
Perhaps just as important as the results,
King led BA through a battle which both
bound staff together and identified their
cause with his board. Over 26,000 British
Airways employees signed a petition
against the route transfers. Thousands sent
letters to their MPs and ministers. King's
battle may have been the final stake in the
heart of the lingering divisions which existed from the BEA and BOAC merger
from more than a decade prior. The organization had been offered a uniting motive and leader with whom to identify. As
BA's legal director offered, King "took
his jacket off, and he had a most fantastic
punchout with [the government] about
keeping the route rights. He got the whole
of this organization behind him because
they could see that he was fighting for
them."

With its CAA review, diplomatic concerns with the United States, and with the
Freddie Laker legal battle finally resolved, BA was ready for privatization in
1986. In September of that year, newly

appointed Secretary of State for Transport
John Moore announced the intention to
sell shares to the public in early 1987. With
the offer 11 times oversubscribed, the
public clearly displayed its approval of the
changed British Airways.

After privatization, King and Marshall
made globalization a major thrust. In
1987, BA took a 26 percent stake in Ga-
lileo, an advanced computer reservation
system also supported by KLM Dutch
Airlines and Swissair. That same year, BA
arranged a partnership with United Airlines, allowing each carrier to extend its
route coverage without stretching its resources. In early 1988, British Airways
finally outmuscled Scandinavian Airlines
System (SAS) to acquire British Caledonian. Finally, in December 1989, BA
concluded a deal with Sabena World Airlines through which it secured a 20 percent
stake in the Belgian carrier. Combined,
the steps bolstered British Airways global
power and prepared it for what analysts
expected to be a post-1992 European
marketplace in which only the strongest
carriers survive. They also put an exclamation point on an evolving shift from a
strongly British, engineering, and operationally driven culture to one which
emphasized global marketing through
customer service.

Reaction at BA

Although not unanimously, by 1990
staff and management at BA felt that the
culture at the airline changed for the better
since the 1970s. There was near complete
agreement on the positive feelings generated by success.

Senior Manager, Marketing

The general atmosphere of the company
is a much more positive one. There is

an attitude of "we can change things, we are better than our competition. . . . " I'm not certain if there's a relationship which is that a good culture leads to a successful company, but there is certainly the converse of that, that a successful company leads to a better culture. We are a more successful company now, and as a result of that it's easier to have a positive culture.

Senior Manager, formerly of Cabin Services

I think the core difference is that when I joined this was a transport business. And I now work for a service industry.

Senior Manager, Engineering

You start to think not just as an engineering department, where all my concerns are just about airplanes and the technical aspects. My concerns have developed into what the operation requires of me, and the operation is flight crew, cabin crew operations, ground operations. . . . What do I need to do to help British Airways to compete aggressively against all the other operators?

Veteran Engineer

Fifteen years ago, you just did one thing, and only went so far with the job, and the next bloke would do his bit. Now, I can go and do the lot, whatever I need to do. I don't call someone else to do the job. Now, you just get on with it. A job that could have taken eight hours is done in two hours.

Ticketing Supervisor

In the late 1970s, it was very controlled, a lot of rules and regulations. It stifled initiative. . . . We've become very free, and that's nice. There's not so much personal restriction. You can now talk to your boss. When I first started, it was definitely officers and rank. Now you've got more access to managers.

Executive, Human Resources

In terms of both its superficial identity, its self-confidence, and also the basic service and product, there's an enormous difference to 10 or 11 years ago. Its management is perceived as more professional, and its business is perceived to be more competent and effective.

Challenges for the 1990s

Despite the enormous change in the culture over the 1980s, BA still faced huge challenges. Management and staff agreed that, while the new culture fostered a strong commitment to service and a much higher morale and a better market image, certain pockets within BA still needed to institutionalize change.

Veteran Engineer

I like it much better now, but I think it's still got a long way to go. . . . The trust and the belief in this organization is not quite there. We can see the problems, but we still don't have any input. . . . We waste so much time waiting for spares, waiting for airplanes. . . . We still think of ourselves as little areas. The five shifts here are five little outfits. We still don't quite think of ourselves as British Airways.

Executive, Human Resources

I don't think the culture change by any means has taken place as much as the public perceives. I think a lot has been done, but I don't feel it has become the norm. There is in places a lack of recognition of emotional labor, and the management and leadership requirements of emotional labor. I suspect we've gone a long way compared to many organizations, but it would be very easy to lose it. Eight years is a relatively short period of time to establish that, particularly when the economic pressure comes back on.

Veteran Engineer

If you all pull together, then you get more out of it. The problem is getting everyone pulling together. You never get 100 percent, obviously, but I suppose if you get 80 percent pulling together, then you're not doing too bad. There will always be a percentage that won't be pulling together.

Ironically, attacking those pockets was more difficult because of the strong impact of the 1983–85 corporate celebrations. Employees as a group were changed by those celebrations, and to some degree by successive programs, but excessive repetition risked rebellion. Management had to make a judgment of whether the communication programs of the 1980s were worn out.

Senior Manager, Passenger Services

I think that the fundamental message has not changed over the last decade. We're restating old values. When the message was first heard, people did listen and read and absorb, because it was new, and it was radically different from the previous decade. So they had an incentive. The difference is there is no longer the incentive. First, because it's old news. Second, because there is a degree of cynicism about the sincerity.

Veteran Ticket Agent

You go on a million courses to see how wonderful you are and how wonderful

British Airways is, and you get back to work and nothing changes. ... The larger you are, it has to be more and more impersonal. You are always going to find that the lower levels feel so far removed from the upper levels that pulling together is almost an impossibility.

Executive, Marketing and Operations

You can't go on selling the same old socks. In terms of messages and themes and something to focus the company around, it's a bit difficult to repackage in another way, and put all the sort of support mechanisms around it that we did in the 80s, and do it all again in a way that captures the imagination in the 1990s.

Increasing costs complicated the effort to fine-tune the cultural changes. In the middle and late 1980s there was a grade drift toward higher ratings and higher pay scales. Added to that was an increase in sheer numbers, due to the 1987 merger with British Caledonian and the loss of focus.

Ticket Supervisor

When this all started five years ago, the idea was to cut out levels of management, and they did one night—that night of the long knives, they called it. Forty managers, hundreds of years of experience were chopped. We've doubled those managers now.

Executive, Marketing and Operations

We're trying to get our cost base down. We're trying to find out why it is that, as we try to grow, somehow or other our costs rise faster than our revenue generation. How do you manage all those issues, get them under control, as well as keeping the people in the business focused upon delivering quality consistently over time?

BA also faced both a loss of focus and a contradictory new message. The apparent contradiction between cutting costs and driving customer service may have been the most difficult challenge of all.

Executive, Internal Business Consulting

During the early and mid-1980 period, there were some specific challenges for us to overcome, and they are less obvious now than they have been in the past.

Executive, Human Resources

The real challenge in a people culture and a service culture is when the pressure's on. How do you manage change which requires you to get more productivity or more cost-efficiency or whatever, but still maintain a degree of trust, a respect for the individual, which I still think underpins service?

Executive, Marketing and Operations

Today, there is the unrelenting almost fanaticism about being able to deliver customer service. It's the thing staff remember above all else. And the frustra-tion they talk about now is in terms of their ability to deliver that customer service and some of the difficulties that we as a company are having in trading off still needing consistent customer service, but also needing to do it at a cost. We're struggling with a way of putting that message across to the work force that doesn't some way get returned to us as "you don't care about service anymore" because we've generated that single focus over the last seven or eight years.

In less than 10 years, British Airways had lifted itself out of bankruptcy to become one of the world's most respected airlines. The financial crisis of 1981 and the drive to ready itself for privatization had given the people of BA a focus which led to many changes. Still, there were obviously parts of the organization in which new beliefs were not institutionalized by the tornado of change. And in looking for a new focus, management dealt with the seemingly unattractive alternative of trying to get staff to identify with an issue as glamorless as cost-cutting. Yet, without increasing the value the culture placed on productivity and profits, while maintaining or increasing the value placed on customer service, King and Marshall could not guarantee BA's continual success in an increasingly competitive global marketplace.

READING

RE-ENERGIZING THE MATURE ORGANIZATION

Richard W. Beatty

*Professor of industrial relations and human resources in the
Institute of Management and Labor Relations at Rutgers University*

David O. Ulrich

Professor on the faculty of the School of Business at the University of Michigan

Globalization, reduced technology cycles, shifting demographics, changing expectations among workers and customers, and restructuring of capital markets made the 1980s a "white water decade," rapidly introducing changes for both public and private organizations.

The greater the forces for change, the greater the competitive pressure, the greater the demand for change. This seemingly endless cycle of competition-change can become a vicious circle if executives cannot discover novel ways to compete.

Traditional ways of competing have reached a level of parity in which businesses cannot easily distinguish themselves solely on the basis of technology, products, or price. The ability of an organization to conceptualize and manage change—to compete from the inside out by increasing its capacity for change—may represent that novel way to compete. The universal challenge of change is to learn how organizations and employees can change faster than changing business conditions to become more competitive. That is, to change faster on the inside than the organization is changing on the outside.

This need to understand and manage change is salient, particularly for mature firms where the long-established norms of stability and security must be replaced with new values, such as speed, simplicity, unparalleled customer service, and a self-confident, empowered work force. The purpose of this article is to explore how mature firms can be re-energized. To do this, we will describe the unique challenges of creating change in mature firms, detail principles that can be used to guide change, and identify leadership and work activities required to accomplish change.

The Challenge of Change and Organization Life-Cycle

Organizations evolve through a life-cycle, with each evolving stage raising change challenges. We shall use an hourglass to portray the process of organizational life-cycles and change challenges.

As illustrated in Figure 1, organizations in their entrepreneurial stage focus on the definition and development of new products and markets. During this life-stage, the change challenge is primarily one of defining and learning how to penetrate a market or niche. Managers who translate ideas into customer value overcome this *niche challenge* and proceed to the growth stage.

FIGURE 1   Organization Life Cycle and Change Challenges

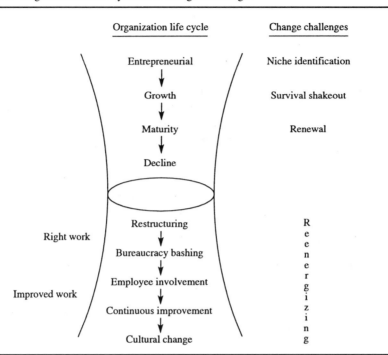

In the laundry equipment industry, for example, the entrepreneurial stage developed in the early 1900s, when over 60 appliance makers entered the market to provide more automated equipment for doing laundry. These autonomous (and often small) appliance makers served local markets with their specialized machines.

During the growth stage, businesses proliferate. This evolutionary stage could become corporate nirvana—if it persists. Unfortunately, as more firms enter a market, meeting the change challenge becomes necessary for survival. Over time, small firms frequently join together to form large firms; firms that cannot compete either merge or go out of business. Between 1960 and 1985, a major shakeout occurred in the North American appliance market. From over 60 major appliance

makers, the market shrank to five major companies that, together, held over 80 percent of the market. Each of these five major appliance makers faced and overcame the shakeout change challenge.

As organizations overcome the niche and shakeout challenges, they develop standard operating procedures. This third evolutionary stage is maturity. Organizations in the mature stage face a significant renewal change challenge. The presence of established norms that once helped accomplish past success may lead to complacency, and managers may become too dependent on these for future success. These calcified norms then become irrevocable patterns of behavior that eventually lead to structural inertia, as would be evidenced in the way they affect structure, systems, and processes. Not only do they create inertia but the insulation they provide leads to an avoidance of challenges that can lead to success.

In the appliance industry in the late 1980s, renewal became a major agenda. For example, Whirlpool changed its century-old functional organization into business units and formed a joint venture with Phillips to enter markets outside North America. General Electric spent over $1 billion refurbishing plants, technologies, and management systems. These efforts at renewal, still under way, will predict which firms will emerge as winners in the next century. Organizations that fail the renewal change challenge enter a period of decline, during which they slowly lose market share to firms that have renewed.

In many ways, the renewal change challenge is more onerous than the niche identification or shakeout challenges. To overcome the niche and shakeout challenges, managers in successful organizations were able to focus on customers and develop products and technologies to meet customer needs. During the maturity phase, product and technological parity is likely to emerge. Competitors offer customers similar product features at comparable costs. Given a technological and financial parity, managers facing a renewal challenge must identify additional capabilities to meet customer needs. They must learn to compete through competencies; they must develop the ability to compete from the inside out—to build internal organizational processes that meet external customer requirements.

Organizational Mindsets and Life-Cycles

Perhaps the greatest effort involved in overcoming the renewal challenge is to change the mindset of employees at all levels of an organization. The mindset represents a shared way of thinking and behaving within an organization. Mindsets are reflected in "accepted behaviors and attitudes"—customer service at Nordstrom, quality at Ford, and speed, simplicity, and self-confidence at General Electric. Mindsets are often institutionalized in vision, value, and mission.

It takes time for mindsets to be instilled. By the time an organization becomes mature, it has likely established a relatively fixed mindset. Employees self-select into the organization because of its particular set of norms. They are rewarded by promotions, salary increases, and enhanced job responsibility when they embody the mindset. Mindsets become very powerful means of gaining unity and focus. Students of Japanese service organizations have argued that this unity of mindset becomes a means of gaining competitiveness. The mindset provides a common focus and, therefore, increases the intensity of work done.

In mature organizations, a shared mindset can be a liability, and its intensity may hinder the ability to change. Since employees come to accept, adopt, and associate with the mindset of a mature company, the renewal process requires letting go. To accomplish renewal, traditional control measures must be replaced with an empowered work force that is more self-directed, self-managed, and self-controlled, thus reducing the need not only for strong competencies in managerial control but for large numbers of managers and supervisors as well. Thus, a truly empowered work force is one that acts out of commitment to purpose without the traditional boundaries and narrow mindsets of mature organizations. In Figure 1, the more open end of the hourglass represents the more open and flexible organizations; the closed end of the hourglass represents the constraints of mature organizations. The hourglass analogy shows this movement from more open and flexible (top of hourglass) to closed and inflexible (center). In this model, renewal becomes the change challenge that allows a firm to go through the ''neck'' of the hourglass and rediscover a vitality and energy that move the mature firm out of the decline trap and into a revived state of activity.

Principles of Renewal

Responding to the renewal challenge is difficult at best and unlikely in most cases. Few organizations successfully accomplish renewal from within. Rather than renew, organizations that perpetuate outmoded mindsets become prey to consolidations, acquisitions, or mergers— external pressures that *impose* renewal. We propose that the probability of renewal of mature organizations increases if four principles are understood and practiced. If managers recognize these principles, they may be able to help overcome the renewal challenge.

1. Mature organizations renew by instilling a customer perspective and focusing on customer demands. To begin to overcome the renewal challenge, a company and all its employees must be completely devoted to gaining a sustained competitive advantage. Competitive advantage comes from understanding and meeting customer needs in unique ways.

One of the most difficult challenges of renewal is the ability to recognize whether existing mindsets and practices are inconsistent with current customer require-

ments. When the mindset within an organization becomes a way of life, embedded in employee work habits, it is even more difficult to acknowledge or change. By examining the organization from a customer perspective, employees may better understand the internal processes and practices that reinforce existing mindsets. Hewlett-Packard, one of the first organizations to adopt such a practice as a part of its renewal effort, did this by incorporating internal and external customer satisfaction into its performance appraisal system.

A more detailed example of this practice is provided by a company that, in working through the renewal challenge, experienced at first mixed results. While employees enjoyed participating in innovative self-managed work teams and preparing vision statements, over a period each new activity that appeared promising fizzled, and employees went back to business as usual. To encourage and advance renewal, a workshop was held in which the employees were asked to examine their organization and four of its major competitors, pretending they were buyers of the product. As customers, they talked about why they would pick one supplier over another. They explored the images each of the five companies communicated and examined reasons why customers picked one competitor over another. After performing this analysis, they were able to articulate, from a customer's perspective, the perceived mindsets residing within each of the five competing organizations.

Having done this customer assessment of the competitors, the employees were able to decipher and enunciate the mindset within their own company and distinguish how their company's mindset differed from those of their competitors.

Becoming devoted to customers comes

from employees spending less time thinking about internal company policies and practices and more time interacting with and worrying about their next customers. Companies that compete through service seek creative and extensive ways to involve customers in all activities. Customers may become involved in product design, in reviewing vision statements, in attending and making presentations at training and development sessions, and in doing employee reviews. The more interaction there is between customers and employees, the more a customer perspective is instilled within the organization. By taking an active role in meeting customer needs, employees in mature organizations may begin the conquest of the renewal change challenge. They can in effect change their performance expectations from meeting demands vertically dictated, to focusing horizontally on the process requirements in order to meet internal and external customer requirements. When meeting customer needs becomes more important to the organization than preserving political boundaries, employees will be more willing to renew themselves and their company. There are several reasons for this, including the freedom from autocratic directions by giving autonomy to those whose services are dependent upon it.

Mature companies seeking to renew have engaged in a variety of activities to ensure customer commitment. At Hewlett-Packard, engineers who design products spend months meeting with customers in focus groups, in laboratories, and in application settings to ensure that new products meet customer requirements. When the mini-van was first announced at Chrysler, several senior executives were not supportive of

the concept. They believed the vehicle was neither a truck nor a passenger car and would have no market. However, after extensive meetings with customers, the executives became convinced that this vehicle created an entire new niche.

At an oil service company, sales personnel were trained to interview and work with customers to identify their needs, rather than sell products. As these sales personnel spent time with customers and became aware of their current and future needs, the oil service company experienced dramatic market share growth.

The principle of customer-centered activity is consistent with the extensive work on quality done by a number of management researchers over the years. It encourages employees to define their value as a function of customer requirements, rather than personal gain. It replaces old practices with new ones that add value to customers. It refocuses attention outside to change inside—that is, toward the ultimate and the next customer.

2. Mature organizations renew by increasing their capacity for change. Most individuals have internal clocks, or biorhythms, that determine when we wake up, when we need to eat, and how quickly we make decisions. Like individuals, most organizations have internal clocks that determine how quickly decisions are made and activities are completed. These internal clocks affect how long it takes organizations to move from idea to definition, to action. It has been argued that a major challenge for organizations is to reduce their cycle time, which means to change the internal clock and timing on how decisions are made. For mature organizations to experience renewal, their internal clocks must be adjusted.

Cycle lengths must be reduced and the capacity for change increased.

Typically, the internal clocks of mature organizations have not been calibrated for changing erratic and unpredictable business conditions. To enact and increase a capacity for change, managers need to work on alignment, symbiosis, and reflexiveness.

"Alignment" refers to the extent to which different organization activities are focused on common goals. When organizations have a sense of alignment, their strategy, structure, and systems can move more readily toward consistent and shared goals.

Aligned organizations have a greater capacity for change, because less time is spent building commitment, and more energy and time are spent accomplishing work. To calibrate alignment, a number of organizations have sponsored "congruence" workshops where the degree of congruence between organizational activities is assessed.

"Symbiosis" refers to the extent to which organizations are able to remove boundaries inside and outside an organization.

General Electric CEO Jack Welch describes any organizational boundary as a "toll-gate." Any time individuals or products must cross a boundary, an economic, emotional, and time toll is paid. When organizations have extensive boundaries, tolls can be direct and indirect expenses. Direct boundary costs result in higher prices to customers, because of extra costs in producing the product. Indirect boundary costs occur from each boundary increasing the time required to accomplish tasks. Boundaries, and the tolls required for crossing, set an organization's internal clock and impair capacity

for change. Increasing cycle time and creating symbiosis mean reducing boundaries and increasing capacity for change and action. The Ford Taurus has become a classic example of reducing boundaries and increasing capacity for change. By forming and assigning a cross-functional team responsible for the complete design and delivery of the Taurus, boundaries were removed between departments. The time from concept to production for the Taurus was 50 percent less than established internal clocks.

To ensure that a capacity for change continues over time, individuals must become reflexive and have the ability to continue to learn and adapt over time. "Reflexiveness" is the ability to learn from previous actions. Organizations increase their capacity for change when time is spent reflecting on past activities and learning from them.

The capacity for change principle expedites renewal. When individuals and systems inside an organization can so change their internal clocks that decisions move quicker from concept to action, renewal occurs more frequently. In this way, organizational cycles differ from individual biorhythms: Cycle times are not genetic and intractable but learned and adjustable. By adjusting cycles, the capacity for change increases, which may lead to renewal of mature organizations.

3. Mature organizations renew by altering both the hardware and software within the organization. Management activities within an organization may be dissected into hardware and software. Management hardware represents issues, such as strategy, structure, and systems. These domains of activity are malleable and measurable and can be heralded with high visibility—for example, timely announcements about new strategies, structures, or systems. Also, like computer hardware, unless they are connected to appropriate software they are useless. In the organization, software represents employee behavior and mindset. These less visible domains of organizational activity are difficult to adjust or measure, but they often determine the extent to which renewal occurs.

Most renewal efforts begin by changing hardware—putting in a new strategy, structure, or system. These hardware efforts help mature organizations to turn around or change economic indicators. They do not, however, assure transformation; this comes only when new hardware is supported by appropriate software. Organizational renewal efforts that focus extensively or exclusively on strategy, structure, and systems engage in numerous discussions and debates. These discussions are necessary but are not sufficient to make any difference. At times, in fact, these discussions consume so much energy and resources that too few resources are left to make sure that employee behavior and mindset match the changes. Just as many companies have storage rooms filled with unused hardware, many organizations have binders of strategy, structure, and system changes that were never implemented.

For renewal in mature organizations, changing strategy and structure is not enough. Adjusting and encouraging individual employee behavior and working on changing the mindset are also critical. In one organization attempting to examine and modify software, the focus was not on strategy, structure, and systems but on work activities. Groups of employees met

in audit workshops to identify work activities as done by suppliers for customers, then to examine each set of work activities to eliminate whatever did not add value to customers and to improve whatever did. The key to the success of these work audit workshops was that participants would leave with work inspected and modified in a positive manner. As a result of the workshops, participants have changed some of the existing behaviors and beliefs within the business.

For organizations seeking to increase the probability of renewal, new mindsets must be created that will be shared by all employees, customers, and suppliers. For suppliers, this commonly is a shared perspective that leverages competitive advantage. Xerox, between 1980 and 1988, reduced its number of suppliers from over 3,000 to 300. By focusing attention and certifying qualified suppliers, Xerox has built a shared mindset among its supplier network. Ford Motor Company has done similar work with suppliers. A team of Ford executives must accredit each Ford supplier on a number of dimensions of quality, delivery, and service. Without passing the accreditation test, the supplier cannot work with Ford. By maintaining this policy, Ford builds its vision and values into its supplier network, and Ford suppliers mesh their vision and values with Ford. These types of activities build the software that reinforces the hardware, or system changes that eventually lead to renewal.

4. Mature organizations renew by creating empowered employees who act as leaders at all levels of the organization. Shared leadership implies that individuals have responsibility and accountability for activities within their domain. Individuals become leaders by having influence and control over the factors that affect their work performance.

Organizations that renew have leaders stationed throughout the hierarchy regardless of position or title. Employees are trusted and empowered to act on issues that affect their work performance. Leaders have the obligation of articulating and stating a vision and of ensuring that the vision will be implemented. Leadership can come either from bringing new leaders into the organization or building competencies into existing leadership positions.

When Michael Blumenthal became chairman of Burroughs, he changed 23 of the top 24 managers within his first year. His assessment was that the current leadership team was so weighed down with traditional vision and values that they could not develop a new leadership capability, capacity for change, and competitiveness. Blumenthal could change the top echelon of his organization, but he could not replace the 1,000 secondary leaders throughout the organization. These leaders needed to be developed to induce a renewal within the company.

Primary and secondary leaders must be able to communicate the new mindset, articulating the vision and values in ways that are not only readily understandable and acceptable to all employees but that are inspirational, also. In other words, the employees must believe that it is worth giving extraordinary effort to make the vision a reality.

In addition to communication, leaders are expected to possess the competencies members perceive as necessary to lead the organization to the heights of its vision. Although some of these competencies may be functional, others are clearly the management of human resources, especially the effective use of measures both positive and negative following the actions of all employees. While the use of alternative reward strategies has become extremely popular in the last few years, leaders should be able to confront employees who are unwilling to perform at levels necessary for making a substantive contribution to competitive advantage.

Finally, leaders must be credible. Members must be able to trust in the word of their leaders; if they cannot, they will be unwilling to accept the vision or the values—and certainly unwilling to marshal the level of energy necessary to accomplish higher and higher levels of performance. The credibility of leadership cannot be overestimated when trying to energize the organization's human resource.

In brief, we have proposed four principles that can increase the probability of renewal for a mature organization. By understanding these four principles, managers may engage in a series of activities that make this renewal possible.

Leadership and Work Activities

Having identified a need for mature organizations to overcome a renewal challenge, and a set of principles on which renewal is based, we can identify specific leadership and work activities which accomplish this effort. Generally, the process for re-energizing mature organizations follows the five steps shown in Figure 2, although these may not always be in sequence as some steps may occur simultaneously.

Stage 1: Restructuring. Organizational renewal generally begins with a turnaround effort focused on restructuring by downsizing or delayering, or

FIGURE 2   A Process For Re-Energizing Mature Organizations

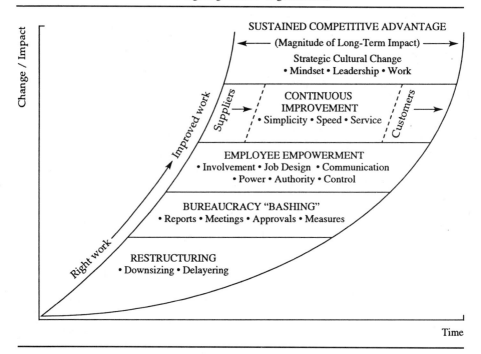

both. Through head-count reduction, organizations attempt to become "lean and mean," recognizing that they had become "fat" by not strategically managing performance at all levels. Organizations continue to improve global measures of productivity (sales or other measures of performance per employee) by reducing the number of employees.

At General Electric, staff reductions removed approximately 25 percent of the work force between 1982 and 1988. This reduction came from retirements, reorganizations, consolidations, plant closings, and greater spans of control. Such a head-count reduction can save organizations billions of dollars and initiate renewal. At J. I. Case, the implement manufacturer, well over 90 percent of the top management group was replaced as the organiza-

tion faced a substantial change in how it was to do business in a highly competitive global environment.

The leadership requirement during restructuring is clear: Have courage to make difficult decisions fairly and boldly. No one likes to take away jobs. It will not lead to great popularity or emotional attachment of employees. However, leaders who face a renewal change challenge must act. They must implement a process that ensures equity and due cause to employees. By so doing, leaders start the renewal process by turning around an organization through restructuring.

Stage 2: Bureaucracy Bashing. "Bureaucracy bashing" follows restructuring. In this stage, attempts are made to get rid of unnecessary reports, approvals, meeting, measures, policies, procedures, or other work activities that create backlogs. By focusing on bureaucracy reduction, employees throughout the organization experience changes in how they do their work. Often, sources of employee work frustration come from being constrained by bureaucratic procedures and not being able to see or feel the impact of their work. Bureaucratic policies and processes that consume energy and build frustration may have been developed in older work settings, causing more harm than good; these need to be examined and replaced.

In the restructuring stage, mindsets of corporate loyalty are shattered. Employees who believed in lifelong employment and job security may be angered by restructuring activities. Many companies that go through the restructuring phase eliminate corporate loyalty but fail to replace the employee contract with the firm. As a result, employees feel that their contract with the firm is one-way and short-term. They are giving their psychological commitment to the firm, but only for short term monetary gains. To resolve this imbalance, employees may reduce their commitment. Executives must learn to sustain employee commitment by replacing loyalty with some other means of employee attachment.

In one company, employee contracts based on loyalty were replaced with opportunity. The chief executive of this company was honest with employees. He told them that there were no guarantees. Job loyalty, as known in stable work settings, could no longer be an economically viable alternative. However, he promised each employee that loyalty would be replaced by opportunity. He personally promised each employee that the organization would guarantee that each of them had the opportunity to develop his or her talents, to participate in key management actions,

and to feel that they belonged to a part of a winning team. To guarantee this opportunity, bureaucracy had to be removed. Employees were able to identify the bureaucratic blockages in their jobs, to discuss these blockages with their bosses and peers, and to suggest how they could be removed. By so doing, employees could feel and see the value of opportunity in their work.

The bureaucracy bashing stage is necessary because, even though the head-count may have reduced costs, the workload still remains, and adjustments must be made to meet the work volume requirements with the reduced head count.

At General Electric, Jack Welch has talked about reducing the work force by 25 percent but not reducing work. As a result, employees are faced with the burden of doing 25 percent more work, which over a period may lead to malaise and lower productivity. Unnecessary, non-value-added work must be removed to gain parity between employees and their workload.

To get rid of bureaucracy requires getting rid of work that adds little value to customers. Continuous improvement programs that focus on meeting needs of internal and external customers may be desired to yield higher quality, speed, and greater simplicity in how all suppliers service the organization.

A process developed by one of the authors and shown in Figure 3 focuses on bureaucracy "busting." A work audit is conducted using two questions: (1) To what extent does this work activity add value to customers? and (2) To what extent are these activities performed as effectively as possible?

The first question is answered by inviting customers to share their views on the value added by work activities performed

FIGURE 3   Developing A Customer Focus In Bureaucracy Bashing

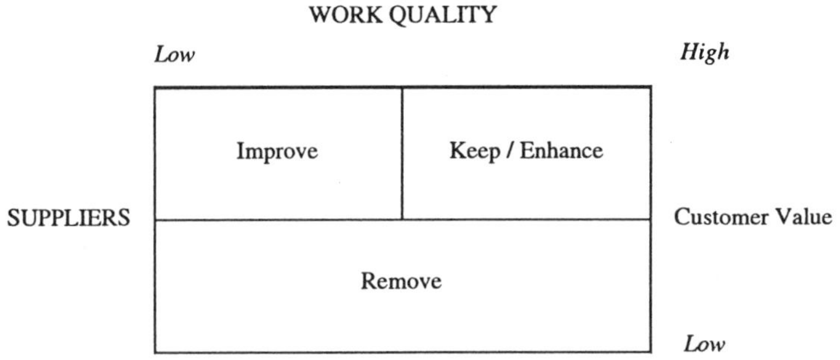

WORK QUALITY

Low   High

Improve	Keep / Enhance

SUPPLIERS   Customer Value

Remove

Low

by the supplier. This dialogue between suppliers and customers may occur exclusively within a company (internal supplier/customer discussions) or between a firm and its external customers. One company began inviting customers to training programs in an effort to understand customer needs and to ensure that work activities proposed within the company met customer requirements. Activities which add little value to customers were removed. This two-step process attempts to determine the "right" of the organization to leverage its competitive advantage and that of its customers.

Activities that add great value to customers become subject to the second question. This question is answered by developing an improved process to perform the work. Auditing work processes encourages specific analysis to ensure that quality in work activities is improved.

However, leaders must first model the bureaucracy busting they advocate. They must be willing to let go of work systems that were implemented but that have added little or no value to the processes' next or ultimate customer. Reports or procedures that may be seen as bureaucratic blockages to employees must be identified, and leaders must be willing to concede their pet

projects for the sake of removing these blockages. Leaders must demonstrate flexibility and listen to all reasonable requests (as long as they add value to customers and fall within legal and ethical boundaries). Finally, leaders need to encourage and reinforce risk taking among employees who initiate bureaucracy busting activities. A single equation predicts the propensity for risk taking. We see risk taking as a function of the will to win, divided by fear of failure. If the numerator is high, by selecting and developing committed employees, then leaders have the responsibility of reducing the fear of failure quotient.

Stage 3: Employee Empowerment Stage.   Bureaucracies empower top managers. Bureaucracy busting empowers employees. Removing barriers between employees and managers builds openness and dialogue in ongoing management processes and begins to change the nature of the organization. Self-directed work teams, employee involvement processes, and dialogue should be built into the fabric of the organization. Without employee involvement and a fundamental new approach to management, costs may be reduced, productivity increased, and bureaucracy eliminated—but the results will not be long lasting if employees are not empowered for organizational improvement.

Many work activities encourage employee involvement. In a Japanese firm, newer professional employees have the opportunity and obligation to make the first drafts of important business proposals. By asking new employees to make these first drafts, the employees learn more about the overall business, feel empowered to have an impact on the business, and build relationships with colleagues in preparing the proposals. PepsiCo has involved and empowered all employees by announcing profit sharing for all. Federal Express has institutionalized employee involvement by guaranteeing employees access to the senior management meeting held each Wednesday. Employee complaints may be directed to this forum by employees without fear of any retributions by their immediate bosses. IBM assures employee involvement by allowing employees to work through a corporate ombudsman, who can represent the employees' views to management without fear of reprisal or having to undergo subordinate appraisals. Amoco has initiated an extensive employee involvement program, where employees are formed into teams to discuss ways to improve work and to get subordinate appraisals of their managers. These examples of employee involvement mark a fundamental change from the traditional work contract of hierarchical mature organizations to a more fluid, flexible, mutual work environment.

Traditional models of power and authority came from position and status. Power and authority in a renewing organization should come from relationships, trust, and expertise. Empowerment is a movement away from leader and expert problem solving to a system where everyone is continuously involved in improving the organization in order to leverage its competitive advantage through speed, simplicity, and service. Leaders must learn that sharing power builds a capacity to change, commitment, and competitiveness.

Stage 4: Continuous Improvements. Employee empowerment builds employee commitment. This initial commitment must be translated into long-term processes so employee involvement is not tied to any one individual but is part of a system.

Continuous improvement efforts began in mature companies by focusing on error detection and error prevention. In these efforts, statistical tools—for example, flow charting, Pareto analysis, histograms, studies of variance, and operational definitions—were used to ensure that errors could be taken out of work procedures.

The continuous improvement required for this stage includes, but also goes beyond, this error focus. Continuous improvement is changing not only the technical tools of management but also the fundamental approaches to management. The continuous improvement philosophy overcomes the practice. The focus on continuous improvement must be upon the "right" work that was identified through restructuring and bureaucracy bashing. The philosophy must be one of service to customers through speed and simplicity in work processes. As this philosophy is understood throughout an organization, it becomes the rallying cry, ensuring an ongoing commitment to improve work processes.

Generating this philosophy becomes the major leadership requirement at this stage. The leader must manage through principles. The leader must articulate and communicate the principles that will govern the organization. These principles must be sensitive to each of the previous stages—restructuring for productivity, bureaucracy busting for flexibility, and employee involvement for empowerment. By instilling a philosophy of management that can then be practiced according to the specific needs of the business, leaders are able to set a direction, motivate, and steer a company through renewal.

Stage 5: Cultural Change. The final stage of renewal is really an outgrowth of the other four. Fundamental cultural change means that employees' mindset—the way they think about their work—is shifted. Employees do not feel part of a "mature" company, but they see themselves as having faced and overcome the renewal change challenge. They feel the enthusiasm and commitment of trying new approaches to work and, as a result, they bring more desirable changes into the organization.

We would agree with many others who have studied these issues that accomplishing cultural change takes many years. Our rule of thumb is that, for mature organizations, the cycle time for creating fundamental cultural change is twice the cycle time it takes for introducing a new technology. Some technologies change more rapidly than others—say, for example, genetic engineering as opposed to utilities. In more rapidly changing technologies, there is more receptivity to cultural change. These organizations seem to have a more external focus. In industries with slow changing technologies, the cycle time for cultural change is extended, since these industries probably have a greater structural inertia. The latter are more internally and vertically focused.

In the re-energized organization, every leader would be judged by his ability to persevere, and how strong an advocate he is of the new culture. But it is also necessary that he exhibits tolerance since culture changes require time to take effect. More importantly a leader must constantly and demonstratively be a model and a cheerleader of the culture he hopes to implement.

At General Electric, Jack Welch has committed the entire company to a cultural change. He constantly talks about his commitment—to financial analysts, to investors, to shareholders, to employees, and to public forums. He has defined a set of principles and has frequently asked managers to spend time implementing these principles. Welch also has asked his manager to provide him with feedback on his personal behavior. At GE he has become the nucleus of encouraging employees to commit energy and time to understanding and adopting the new work culture.

In short, the five stages in Figure 2 indicate a sequence for adopting changes to re-energize a mature organization. By first defining the right work to do, then finding ways to improve that work, companies may make simple, short-term changes that can have major, long-term impact. These five stages are based on the four principles we have identified.

Making It Happen

We have put forward a very simple argument in this paper: Mature organizations must face and overcome the renewal change challenge; they must change; they must redefine how work is done and re-create work cultures consistent with changing customer demands.

How do we anticipate that these changes will occur? It will happen because organizations and leaders at all levels have developed a new vision of strategy and culture. Organizations are becoming far more strategic, far more purposeful, and far more customer oriented. It will happen also because of new tools that are focusing more and more closely upon performance and that are raising difficult questions about the value of work and of the customer requirements within the organization.

Most mature organizations will sooner or later have to face the renewal change challenge. They will then have to find ways to change their culture; their vision will have to actually be translated into specific actions, and managers must be prepared to help employees improve, to observe their progress, and to give them feedback. Employees also must seek responsibilities, strive for continuous improvement, and change the organization's culture by making each effort add value to its customers and investors strategically and continuously.

The role of the leader is to challenge the value of each process for its contribution to customers and investors, encourage a shared vision and values, and enable employees to act by encouraging greater customer and cost consciousness, adaptability, initiative, accountability, and teamwork. To accomplish these goals, managers must model the way and immediately recognize the contributions of employees as they take risks in changing established work habits and attempt to continuously improve and enhance their contributions.

If the renewal change challenge can be overcome, an organization may move through the neck of the hourglass (see Figure 1). At the other side of the hourglass is the ability to become re-energized and meet customer needs through innovative, resourceful, and bold customer-focused initiatives.

Selected Bibliography

Several pieces have appeared recently that explore the broad range of activities and values of interest to us. One is "Why Change Programs Don't Produce Change" by Michael Beer, Russell Eisenstadt, and Burt Spector in *Harvard Business Review*, November–December 1990. It demonstrates how most change programs fail because they are guided by a fundamentally flawed theory of change. The authors claim that many change programs assume that change is a conversion experience that requires an attitude change. We agree that real change requires a change in attitude and in the fundamental roles, responsibilities, and relationships that should provide the alignment of the appropriate behaviors. However, our major focus is that change occurs because work and work relationships have been redesigned to leverage the organization's human resource competitive advantage.

Another piece that is consistent with our approach is Randy Myer's "Suppliers Manage Your Customers," in *Harvard Business Review*, November–December 1989. He points out that "customer-backed" organizations are successful, because, to satisfy the next and ultimate customers, you must be provided by suppliers who treat you as important customers.

A significant piece on the leader's role appeared in the *Sloan Management Review* in 1990. The article by Peter M. Senge was entitled "The Leader's New Work: Building Learning Organizations." This is a major piece that focuses on the leadership role in transforming organizations. It recognizes that becoming heuristic is essential to successful transformation—that is, an organization must learn and build the internal capability that enables it to return to viability, regardless of the level of environmental turbulence. The article stresses two leadership styles that have emerged over the years: traditional (plan, organize, and control) and transformational (vision, alignment, motivation). But a third type of leader, the leader of the future, is one who is a designer of work, a teacher, and a supporter of change—in essence, the ultimate change agent that companies have been alluding to for years but is seldom seen represented.

Finally, a corollary piece appeared in *Harvard Business Review* in January–February 1991 by Robert G. Eccles, entitled "The Performance Measurement Manifesto." It suggests performance measurement is an essential missing element from many organizational change efforts and certainly from discussions on re-energizing mature organizations. Identifying the right work is essential but so is measuring the right work. Clearly, if organizations are to survive, customers need to be prioritized and processes need to be clarified. Both require measures to assess their effectiveness and to test whether they are aligned with organizational goals and objectives.

Envisioning Change

INTRODUCTION

"Visions," "visionaries," "envisioning" are concepts everyone agrees to be essential to change; indeed, common sense tells us that a change must be "seen," its direction in some way charted, before anything happens. Someone or a group of people must be authorized explicitly or implicitly to come up with that vision. Put another way, in the words of Dennis Hightower, the protagonist of a case appearing later in this text, "If you don't know where you're going, any road will take you there."

At the same time, vision is a vexing idea, frustratingly difficult to pin down. Noted one CEO in a study mentioned below, "I've come to believe that we need a vision to guide us, but I can't seem to get my hands on what 'vision' is" (Collin and Porras, 1991:31). This is hardly surprising. "Vision" in the non-business world reverberates with contradictions, denoting at the same time dreams, impracticability, as well as unusual competence in discernment or perception. Definitions of vision within the business environment also are elusive, as the following examples show:

> Visions are the product of the head and heart working together. As such, vision is much more than a mental image, and visioning is more than a mental process. Visions are rooted in reality but focused on the future. Visions enable us to explore possibilities. They are desired realities. (Parker, 1990:2)
>
> The guiding philosophy is where vision begins . . . [the philosophy] is a system of fundamental motivating assumptions, principles, values, and tenets . . . [it] comes from the early leaders who originally shape the organization . . . [and] serves as the organization's "genetic code"—in the background, but always present as a shaping force. (Collins and Porras, 1991:33–34)

The first definition comes from an international consultant who spearheaded the turnaround of Norway's largest industrial group. Working with people in such areas as petrochemicals, biomedicine, agriculture, and oil and gas that constitute the group, she helped them to come up with the image of a *garden*, "to diagnose and visualize complex organizational interrelationships and thereby think more systemically about the organization and dynamics" (Parker 1990:21).

The second definition reflects research results. Collins and Porras investigated "visionary" organizations and concluded that "vision is an overarching concept under which a variety of concepts are subsumed." They divided vision into two components, guiding philosophy (sketched above) and tangible image. "Guiding philosophy is deep and serene; tangible image is bold, exciting, and emotionally charged" (Collins and Porras, 1991:32, 42).

Other attempts to define *vision* appear throughout the cases and readings in this module, yet none provides a "nice" concrete synonym; in fact, in neither of the two quotations above is the word actually defined!

Not surprisingly, the difficulties encountered in defining vision do not end at that point. Some researchers and practitioners insist that visions are captured in documents: vision statements. Others argue that the minute a vision is written, it loses its power and sinks into the category of mission statements, goals, slogans. Speeches are another vehicle for visions, the most famous being Dr. Martin Luther King, Jr.'s aptly named "I Have a Dream" speech. Who "does" visions is further point of disagreement. Richards and Engle, in the reading accompanying the first case in this module, flatly state: "Creating a vision statement is the responsibility of the highest level of management in an organization . . . [they] are best written by one person—the senior person in the organization." For their part, Collins and Porras (1991) claim: "Is vision setting only for CEOs? We don't think so. Vision setting should take place at all levels of an organization, and each group should set its own vision—consistent, of course, with the overall vision of the corporation" (p. 32).

Given all this imprecision, the cases and readings in the module do not assume one model or framework for visioning but, instead, present various cuts on the concepts. The readings in particular have been chosen to introduce the terrain that vision occupies, even if the authors enter it from different paths. The three case series ("Alpha and Omega"/"Merger Case"/ and "Motorola") present the most pressing vision challenges of change today: At the outset of a merger, when the fate of the joined company depends on a change direction, and at a mature organization, which risks bureaucracy and failing competitiveness if it doesn't change its approach.

OVERVIEW OF CASES AND READINGS

The module begins with two brief cases—joined as "Texocom and Falcon"—which describe attempts to get employee buy-in of vision statements; the accompanying reading, "After the Vision: Suggestions to Corporate Visionaries and Vision Champions," discusses in detail a procedure for effectively gaining such commitment. The point of these cases and reading is that a vision is simply an exercise in "what if" without being supported and acted upon. Yet gaining such support is no easy matter, and Falcon, especially, shows that skepticism is an ever-present issue to overcome.

How to begin to deal with skepticism and more negative concerns is the task presented in "Alpha and Omega," a brief sketch of an actual merger. Using the information, you are to prepare a 10-minute "vision" speech to deliver to the first official meeting of Alpha and Omega top officers. On the surface, a vision seems obvious in this situation: the merger is just "beginning." Yet there is considerable baggage around. Three readings (a *Fortune* article, an excerpt from General Electric chairman Jack Welch's statement included in the company's 1991 annual report, and an Op–Ed piece from *The Wall Street Journal*) discuss some of the newer ideas being captured in visions. At the end of the "Alpha and Omega" session, you will receive the case that reveals the actual situation, what the CEO did, and what happened to the merged companies in their first year.

"Bob Galvin and Motorola, Inc. (A)" takes visioning into the territory of renewing (revitalizing, re-energizing) a company; this is frequently called "revisioning." Galvin's challenge, among others, is one raised in the previous module: *when* change should be initiated. Motorola, at the time of the case, is performing well, and, as a consequence, the need for change, particularly of the sort Galvin considers, is not apparent. Thus, unlike "Alpha and Omega," when a vision seems at least appropriate because something is beginning, in this case, the role of visioning is murkier. In a provocative accompanying reading, "From Bogged Down to Fired Up: Inspiring Organizational Change," the author argues for a concept he calls "diffusing satisfaction" as a way to prepare an organization for change. And *The Wall Street Journal* article, "Akers to IBM Employees: Wake Up!" describes IBM's chairman as being thoroughly unhappy with his organization's performance. A question that can be asked when contemplating Galvin's situation, however, is: How does one *inspire dissatisfaction?*

The final case in this module, "Bob Galvin and Motorola, Inc. (C)," follows Motorola for two years after Galvin's speech. Thus, we return to the issues squarely raised in the opening case: is the company buying-in, to what Galvin indicated was needed? Was there a vision? The "Vision Thing" readings are useful to this discussion. The first, by Jick, synthesizes various research and other ideas on vision; the second, from *The Economist*, describes in greater detail the Collins and Porras study mentioned in the introduction to this module.

One more point that the Motorola (C) case raises, and which threads through this module, is: When is a firm "rolling out the vision" (the phrase Texocom uses) and when is it implementing change? These two characterizations occupy the same domain as they both involve shifting from awareness to action.

References

Collins, James C., and Jerry I. Porras. "Organizational Vision and Visionary Organizations." *California Management Review*, Fall 1991.

Parker, Marjorie. *Creating Shared Vision*. Clarendon Hills, Ill.: Dialogue International, Ltd., 1990.

CASE

TEXOCOM AND FALCON: TRANSLATING A VISION INTO REALITY

TEXOCOM[1]

In November 1986, Contel Texocom's executive management group, consisting of the president and all his direct reports, participated in a team-building session. One of the outcomes of that session was a corporate vision, a collective statement that was the product of many personal visions of the executive management group members. It read as follows:

> We are a world class team of inspired professionals committed to creating a challenging and rewarding environment. Our culture is characterized by openness, integrity, and the willingness to resolve tough issues. Quality and attention to the needs of our customers are paramount.

Having crafted an uplifting vision statement of which the entire executive management group felt proud, Texocom now faced the issue of how to disseminate the statement in such a way that each and every Texocom employee would be enrolled in the vision. The result of its efforts was a design for a plenary session of all Texocom managers, a process of one-by-one enrollment utilizing sponsors, and a series of physical emblems of enrollment highlighted by a large canvas banner.

---

[1] From Paul Graves and Jack Rosenblum, "Rolling Out the Vision." Reprinted with the special permission of *OD Practitioner*, December 1987.
   Copyright © 1987 OD Network.
   Harvard Business School case 8-491-085.

They came to refer to all these activities under the generic description, "rolling out the vision."

The Plenary Session

A meeting of all Texocom managers, a group of 25 people, was held with the president presiding. By way of creating a context for the meeting, the group received a briefing on the concept of visionary leadership, the function of a vision statement, and the process by which Texocom's vision statement had been created. Then the other members of the executive management team stood up and gave personal testimony on what the vision statement meant to each of them. Upon concluding, each team member went to the canvas banner and formally enrolled in the vision by signing the banner. When all the executive management team members had spoken and signed the banner, the other Texocom managers were told that they were not required to sign the banner; enrollment would occur only when (and if) they could see their desired future in the statement. A number of managers responded by offering spontaneous testimony regarding their alignment with the vision. After the managers' meeting, each signee then became eligible to sponsor others who were interested in enrolling.

The Enrollment Process

The plenary session of managers created a pool of potential sponsors, who had *what happens if you don't sign?*

do the actions of those who've signed change?

formally enrolled in the vision by signing the canvas banner. The enrollment process continued from that point. Anyone interested in enrolling or even in exploring the possibility of enrolling was required to meet with a sponsor to discuss this vision statement. Employees could select anyone whose name already appeared on the banner, other than their direct supervisor.

This requirement of a conversation between potential enrollee and sponsor had a salutary effect: it encouraged people to share their personal visions with each other; as they did so, they were attracted to elements of each other's vision and alignment occured. Naturally, people had varying degrees of attraction to the company vision statement and even different interpretations of some of the actual words. But it turned out that by far the most significant result of these sponsorship conversations has been the developing commitments toward the high ideals expressed in the vision statement.

The role of sponsor is carefully defined. First, it is hierarchy-free—that is, salary, grades, or titles play no role in determining who might sponsor whom. To be someone's sponsor requires only that your name appear on the canvas banner and that you be selected by the potential enrollee. Second, once you are sought out as a sponsor by an interested party, it is your responsibility to arrange a time and place to discuss the vision. Third, once the person has formally enrolled, the sponsor notifies Human Resources so an enrollment package (described below) can be prepared.

The sponsorship system, in addition to producing lots of enrollees and authentic alignment within the organization, had an additional benefit. It carried the meta-message to individual employees that they are important members of the Texocom team, that their feelings about the vision and their enrollment in it are important. The system worked to increase the self-esteem of employees and to enhance their feeling of belonging to a community in which they are valued and respected.

Physical Emblems of Enrollment

In addition to having their name inscribed on the canvas banner along with those of the president, the executive management team, and all previous enrollees, the new enrollees also receive a package of physical emblems. The purpose of the emblems is to acknowledge them for their commitment to the vision and to allow them, if they wish, to display the emblems as a public declaration of their alignment with the vision.

The package consists of the following items: (1) a badge with the words "Be TEXOCOM Good"—this is the 1987 vision theme; (2) an 8×10 certificate of enrollment and 8×10 copy (both suitable for framing); and (3) a wallet-sized laminated copy of the vision statement.

As the final act of sponsorship, the package of emblems is forwarded to the sponsor who then bestows it in a small but appropriate ritual upon the new enrollee.

Other Explicit Uses of the Vision

Beyond the enrollment process, the vision statement has been used as the cornerstone for an "Employee of the Month" program. In this program, a person who has lived the ideals expressed in the vision statement may either self-nominate or be nominated by a peer, supervisor, or customer. Employees selected are recognized at monthly, companywide employee meetings and are awarded cash and non-cash awards. The vision statement is also prominently featured in internal communication efforts as a way of understanding and explaining the company's direction and positions on key policy issues.

* * *

FALCON[2]

A few years ago, I worked for 15 months at a company I will call "Falcon Computer," a manufacturer of micro-computers located in the heart of Silicon Valley. While I was there, the company quintupled in size until it had over 250 employees. It was featured on the covers of important trade publications, and even *Time* singled out Falcon as one of the rising young stars of Silicon Valley—possibly another Apple.

Although I did not join Falcon to do research, my training led me to keep accurate notes of what went on. At meetings, I offered to take the minutes, and I made it a point to memorize interesting conversations, recording them in my journal later the same day.

Shortly after joining the company, I was told by one of the managers that the vice presidents and the president met periodically in closed session to develop "Falcon culture," and that they had hired a management consulting firm to help them define it. One goal, the manager said, was to preserve the free and open atmosphere of a "start-up" even after Falcon became a big company. The manager referred to these sessions as "culture meetings," but later on they were officially designated "values meetings."

[2] From Peter C. Reynolds, "Imposing a Corporate Culture." Reprinted with the special permission of *Psychology Today*, March 1987. Copyright © 1987 American Psychological Association.

With middle management and everyone else excluded from their deliberations, the president and his executive staff created a document called "Falcon Values" that supposedly expressed the culture of the company. They then distributed the document to middle managers who met, again in closed session, to further discuss and refine it.

By this time, I had been made a manager myself, which gave me a front-row seat on all subsequent deliberations. At one meeting, the president of the company and most members of the executive staff were present, so I was able to observe their cultural deliberations as well. In fact, since the tables at culture meetings were always arranged in a circle—unlike all other meetings, in which the top people were at the front of the room or the head of the table—my vantage point on this issue was as good as the president's.

The "Falcon Values" document is two pages long. It summarizes such things as the proper attitude toward customers and colleagues, the preferred style of social communication and decision making, and the working environment the company wanted to achieve. For example, under "customer orientation," we read, "Attention to detail is our trademark; our goal is to do it right the first time. We intend to deliver defect-free products and services to out customers on time."

Yet, even as this policy was being adopted in executive session, computers known to be defective were being shipped to customers. Two people told me that this decision had been made at the highest level to squelch growing rumors that Falcon would miss its announced release date for shipment of the new computer. This is secondhand evidence, but I was able to confirm the product's deficiencies for myself when I borrowed several computers from the shipping room to use in a training class. These were brand-new units, already packed in their printed cartons for shipment to customers. But only two of the four machines started up correctly when the disk was inserted, and I only got them running because I had a technician on my staff.

Consider another statement in the values document: "Managing by personal contact is part of the [Falcon] way. While we recognize the importance of group sessions, we encourage open, direct person-to-person communication as part of our daily routine." "Open communication" was a buzzword at Falcon, often used by software engineers to pry information out of management. But the corporate culture document itself was created in secret, strictly following the chain of command. The executive staff developed the initial draft without consulting middle management; middle managers were asked to approve the document under the guise of "discussing" it; and rank-and-file employees were only told about it and its affirmation of open communication after "Falcon Values" had already been adopted by the company.

The "Falcon Values" document did not fool very many employees into thinking they would get promoted by espousing open communication or blowing the whistle on defective products. For example, one of the vice presidents who seemed genuinely interested in the concept of open communication circulated an initial draft of the values document to all of the people on his staff, asking for their comments and suggestions. Many programmers took the opportunity to compare Falcon to other companies where they had worked. Some of these written replies, shown to me after the company went bankrupt, reveal an undisguised skepticism about the possibility of legislating a culture. One engineer said it explicitly: "You can't create values." Another responded, "The way 'culture' is used at [Falcon] is pretty simple-minded, compared to, say, anthropology." A third likened the values document to another archetypal example of corporate stupidity in Silicon Valley—an executive, known as Mr. Clean, who was charged with keeping desks neat.

Almost everyone knew that the operative values at Falcon were hierarchy, secrecy, and expediency, regardless of what the official document said. My journal preserves a number of statement about social relations that present a very different picture from that given by the values document: "Make sure that training does not become a gating item for the software," a marketing manager told me shortly after my promotion. (Translation: Make sure that delays in software development cannot be attributed to delays in the training program.) "I've seen this before. Bill [a fictional name for a VP of engineering] is going to kick the ball upstairs and try to get himself off the hook by saying that Sam's group and marketing are not ready."

In computer companies, the sales department will normally tell customers what they want to hear or try to sell them products that do not exist; engineering is expected to hold the line on truth. But at Falcon, one manager reflected over lunch: "There is a curious role reversal in this company: Sales is the conscience, while engineering is living on fantasies."

The "Falcon Values" document was so at variance with what people saw every day that few of them took it seriously. Even some official communications seemed to contain ironic humor. For example, the vice president of finance and administration used the principals of

Falcon culture to justify the use of employee badges. Although badges are commonplace in the computer industry, they are presented as security measures, rather than as examples of open communication. Yet, at Falcon, the directive about security badges pointed out that they would contain only first names, "in keeping with our casual culture."

Even members of the executive staff noted the employee skepticism. In one case, a vice president reported to the executive values meeting on an informal survey of how his own staff perceived Falcon values. There were, he said, three main categories of responses:

- It's all motherhood and apple pie.
- So what?
- Boy! Is this company becoming bureaucratic.

In reviewing my journal entries, I have come to the conclusion that the people at Falcon did, in the main, believe in defect-free products and democratic decision making. Among themselves, employees were not shy about evaluating the company by their own standards when corporate behavior was perceived as unjust. For example, a software engineer told me: "Basically, if some people have to work the Labor Day weekend, then everyone should. Since the software has to be ready on the sixth, then everyone should work one weekend, or the last three weekends in August—everyone in the company."

As the company's fortunes began to decline, the disparity between the values meetings and the everyday culture became even more grotesque. While the public relations department was claiming "volume shipments of product to key accounts," the manufacturing division was producing what were essentially hand-crafted machines. The mother board on the Falcon computer, the circuit board containing the central processor and other important logic elements, had a design flaw that made it necessary to hand-solder jumper wires during manufacturing. These hand-fixes absorbed all the economics provided by mass manufacturing and were so time consuming that production slowed to a trickle.

At this point in the company's history, when the manufacturing line was turning out handicrafts, when the mother board would take a minimum of six months to redesign, when a manager at Procter & Gamble reportedly shouted that he never wanted to see a Falcon computer again, and when financial reserves were disappearing at the rate of $2 million a month, people turned to cynical humor to express the disparity between the actual and the official cultures. The manufacturing division was dubbed "Research and Development," and one manager told me: "We do have a zero-defect program: Don't test the product and you'll find zero defects." Another manager gestured at the closed doors of the marketing conference room: "The sales meeting is taking so long," he explained, "because they're trying to get the regional sales managers to agree to the impossible, to sell the product as it exists."

The values meetings, however, plunged on, gathering steam even as the company itself was slowing down. Personnel asked all departments to begin a series of regular meetings to discuss the values document and devise plans to implement it. Vice presidents, and sometimes the president himself, attended these values meetings, which led to a series of roundtable discussions that were just starting when the first big layoffs reduced the staff by a third.

The executive staff, looking for a scapegoat, fired the vice president of marketing in the middle of the night, broke up his department, and allocated his staff among themselves. The next morning, the company was abuzz with stories, in spite of the official blackout imposed by the advocates of open communication. When one of the department secretaries asked me what I thought about the events of the night before, I told her I thought it was sleazy even by Falcon standards. She nodded, and then said, angrily, "It makes you realize what bullshit Falcon values are."

READING

AFTER THE VISION: SUGGESTIONS TO CORPORATE VISIONARIES AND VISION CHAMPIONS

Dick Richards
Sara Engle

It was as if a great bell called to me, far away, a light to the faraway lights in the marsh, saying, "follow" . . . *and I know that the truth, the real truth, is there, there, just beyond my grasp, if only I can follow it and find it there and tear away that veil which shrouds it* . . . *it is there if only I can reach it.*

Lancelot

What organization does not want its people, like Lancelot, to reach for something great that lies just beyond their grasp, to seek the "faraway lights" (Bradley, 1984)? What organization does not wish to challenge its people to pursue the best in themselves and the best possible future?

Today, in some of our most successful companies, a few visionary leaders truly are looking to the future and defining new realities. These leaders have discovered a powerful tool for capturing the spirit and energy of their organizations: the vision statement.

A vision statement is a document describing the way things could be. It is a declaration of the organization's most desirable future; it describes the faraway lights, and invites the organization on a quest to reach them.

The trend toward writing vision statements has been ignited by a widespread rediscovery of the centrality of human values in the conduct of business, and has been fueled by the publication and popularity of many books, especially Peters and Waterman's *In Search of Excellence* (1982), which struck a chord in the hearts of many executives and managers by affirming the significance

Reprinted with permission from *Transforming Leadership*, John D. Adams, Ph.D., General Editor. (Published by Miles River Press, 1009 Duke Street, Alexandria, VA 22314.)

of vision and values to corporate success.

Creating a vision statement is the responsibility of the highest level of management in an organization. The most successful visions seem to be those that come from the visionary's heart. They come from executives who say things like, "I want to leave something here that I can be proud of," or, "I'd like this to be a place I'd be happy to have my kids work in," or, "I know this company could be great if we all put our energy in the same direction." It is no simple task, this writing of a corporate vision; it requires a deep understanding of the organization and of oneself, considered judgment about what will be best for the organization in the future, and an ability to articulate that understanding and judgment in a way that is energizing, uplifting, simple, and direct.

A vision statement is a document around which an organization can build its culture, as American culture is built around the Declaration of Independence and the Bill of Rights. Edgar Schein (1984) has written that an organization's culture can be understood at several different levels. The first level is visible artifacts, like technology, patterns of behavior and dress, or documents. The second level is values, which is what people say are the reasons for what they do. The third, and deepest, level is its basic paradigm or framework for looking at the world and its people; its underlying assumptions about human nature, relationships, the nature of business, or the relationship between man and his environment. If it is to serve as the stimulus and centerpiece of an organization's culture, a vision statement must address values and underlying assumptions.

One executive whom we helped to write a vision statement believed teamwork to be important to his company's future. Teamwork is an artifact, a pattern of behavior. When we asked him, "Why teamwork?" he replied that he thought teamwork stimulated creativity. Creativity is a value, one level deeper in his understanding of the kind of culture he hoped to build. When we asked, "Why creativity?" he replied that he believed that to create was in the nature of people, and that without creation, life was meaningless. For him, creating was a reason for being. This then is the level of underlying assumptions, the kind of belief around which cultures are organized and visions ought to be written.

Vision statements frequently contain abstract terms like *trust, creativity,* or *freedom;* and sometimes more concrete terms, like *lowest cost producer,* or *100 percent on-time delivery.* Sometimes they contain statements about artifacts, like teamwork or communication. Some vision statements are quite brief, describing only a set of ideals and values. Some are longer, including perhaps a historical perspective, a summary of where the organization is at present, statements about the marketplace or the world at large, and guidelines for how people in the organization ought to work and be valued. Almost always a vision statement will include two things: a description of the organization's most desirable future, and a declaration of what the organizations needs to care about most to reach that future. Often there is an accompanying slogan or logo that captures the essence of the message and becomes an important reference: "We feel good when you feel good"; "The customer comes first"; "Technology is our business"; "Partners in making dreams come true."

Vision statements are best written by one person—the senior person in the organization who should seek input from allies, from others who might be key players in implementing the vision, and from people outside the organization who might offer a fresh perspective. Involvement of allies and key players will increase their commitment to the vision and help in its initial implementation.

After the vision is written, a visionary must be prepared to spend considerable time, thought, and energy helping to make it happen. One corporate visionary told us, "When you are looking at a long-range vision, you can't really delegate it to a few people and expect it to happen. We are all in this together—the entire organization. The prime reason for me to be heavily involved is that there is a certain weight to my support that can't come from anyone else. If I don't keep the momentum going, who will?" Also, the role of the visionary may change dramatically after the vision. The same person also said, "I am spending considerably more time on creating the environment that will make people more productive and will make the vision happen, and far less time managing issues and problems, and monitoring the specifics of the business as closely as I used to."

Our experience indicates at least three situations in which companies can benefit from a vision statement. First is the *emerging* company, which is growing so quickly that things sometimes seem to be out of control. Often the founder is struggling to define a new role; he or she is no longer able to maintain daily contact with all employees, is beginning to think about installing personnel systems, and is worrying about how to preserve the values that marked the company's beginnings.

Second is the *retrenched* company, which has successfully completed some kind of downsizing effort, has felt the pain of coming to grips with its limits, needs to recapture the energy inherent in moving toward a desirable future, and has restated its mission.

Third is the *refocusing* company, which, because of increased competition, mergers, varying customer demands, new opportunities, or a host of other reasons, needs to consider seriously and communicate clearly what the company is about and what it must do to remain successful. For example, following the publication of *In Search of Excellence*, which demonstrated the importance of customer service, many companies are refocusing on a "close to the customer" orientation.

These three kinds of companies have in common a need to articulate what they wish to become—to define their best possible future. And that is the function of a vision statement.

Many difficult questions arise after a vision statement is completed and the quest begins: How will the vision be communicated? Will people be energized and excited? How can others be included in the process of creating the future? Publishing a vision seems to be an excellent means for stimulating an organization, yet there is little information about how to create the environment most likely to support useful and innovative actions leading toward realizing the vision. Perhaps we all have too little experience of quests.

While facilitating visions in large companies, we uncovered four processes involved in gaining an organization's commitment to a vision—*communication, boundary testing, sign-on,* and *celebration*. Visionaries, and others who are helping to facilitate organizational commitment to a vision, will have to give considerable attention to these processes.

Communication

The first after-the-vision process is *communication*—the presentation of the vision to the organization by the creators or by people designated by them, who we will call "champions of the vision."

Initial communication is most often accomplished by distributing printed copies of the vision, holding meetings to talk about the vision, showing videos of the vision-maker introducing the vision, and discussing the vision at training events or seminars. The following suggestions and ideas about communicating a vision are based on our experiences during this first phase.

Education. The concept of "leadership by vision" may be new to the people hearing the vision, and education about the visionary leadership process can be helpful to gaining commitment. When people experience something new, they try to fit it into their past experience as a way of understanding it and figuring out how to deal with it. If their existing experience is full of "management by objective," "directives from management," "short-term goals," and "stewardship reports," they will tend to see the vision as just another set of objectives, directives, or goals, and something that will require formal stewardship. This can easily result in the vision being trivialized, discounted, and dismissed. It is important to tell people who are experiencing a visionary approach to leadership for the first time that the approach is different from their past experience, and how it is different.

There are at least three ways in which visionary leadership differs from what many organizations are used to. First, it focuses on hopes for the future, rather than on the problems of the present.

Second, it deals in human values and assumptions about the nature of people as well as strategies and business objectives. Third, it involves the entire organization in the process of creating the future, pushing responsibility and authority downward within the organization.

There are many mechanisms to help people understand visionary leadership, ranging from simple explanations to in-depth training in visionary leadership for key people in the organization. For many organizations the process is so far outside the boundaries of their experience that constant reminders are required. In these situations individuals must feel free to challenge one another when they spot activities that are inconsistent with the new process.

Creating the Environment. After the vision is written, a visionary must be prepared to spend a considerable amount of time, thought, and energy helping to create the appropriate environment for the organization to progress steadily toward the vision. This begins during the communication phase, when as many people as possible should have the opportunity to interact with the visionary or a primary champion. People will want first of all to test the sincerity and commitment of the visionary. Sincerity and commitment are far more easily communicated in person, and a face-to-face interaction gives a more realistic picture of the visionary and the vision.

In large decentralized organizations, where face-to-face contact between the visionary and all members of the organization is not possible, videotaped messages from the visionary are useful. These messages should be presented by champions of the vision, who can provide the essential two-way communication with the audience, demonstrate their own commitment to the vision, and testify to their experience of the leader's sincerity and commitment. Printed material used to stimulate discussion is also effective.

Face-to-face contact also helps mitigate against the inevitable process whereby an organization places its leaders under a microscope, expecting them to be superhuman. During the early stages of communicating a vision, this process is accelerated, and leaders are expected never to behave in any way that might be seen as inconsistent with the vision, and, furthermore, never to have behaved inconsistently in the past. We do tend to expect too much from our leaders.

During these face-to-face sessions, it is helpful for first-time visionary leaders to acknowledge that the process is new to them, that they expect to make some mistakes, and that they expect to be challenged when they do. Also, there are many times when actions that in the minds of organizational leaders are perfectly consistent with the vision also seem perfectly inconsistent to others. It is imperative that visionaries explain the link between such actions and the vision. In one instance, a large corporation sold one of its many plants. The sale was, for many reasons, an action that fostered attainment of the vision. However, it was not perceived as such by many members of the organization until after the leaders were challenged and explained the link between the sale and the vision.

Producing Miracles. People will want a "sign." You know, like a burning bush; or an old man with a long white beard, wearing a robe and sandals, stalking the corporate corridors carrying stone tablets inscribed with the vision; or a flood that wipes out half the auditors. History tells us it's probably a good idea to give them one—and one that is credible. In organizations where people are cynical and distrusting about the effectiveness of managers and leaders, it is particularly important for leaders to show the force of their intent and commitment by challenging "sacred cows," by changing the things that people believe impede the vision and by doing away with those things the vision renders irrelevant. Sacred cows might include rigid norms for how meetings are held, how presentations are given, how performance is appraised, how people greet one another, how competitive or collaborative people are within the organization, how managers relate to subordinates, and so on. Changing ingrained patterns that impede the vision is often experienced by the organization as a miracle, and witnessing a miracle can move people a long way toward supporting a vision.

Ambiguity. It is useful to remember that a vision statement is a leading-edge document. If it weren't on the leading edge, it wouldn't be a vision; and because it is on the leading edge, it can't be totally and satisfactorily explained at the beginning. This will be a problem in organizations where ambiguity is not tolerated, and leaders and champions will have to continually assure people that not knowing all the answers is OK. There are many questions about how a vision will be translated into action that ought to be answered with "I don't know." And "I don't know" ought to be followed by "Let's find out."

Consistency. The process of sharing the vision must be consistent with the

Falcor

content of the vision. If the vision talks about two-way communication, there had better be lots of two-way communication about the vision, or the visionary and champions will soon be packing up the handouts and video equipment and retiring to their offices to dream about what might have been. If the vision speaks about change, creating an environment to discuss the vision that is recognizably different from the organization's typical meeting environment will give a signal that change is accepted and, in fact, happening.

One divisional manager believed that the largest impediment to realizing his organization's vision was an excess of formality and an overly critical attitude in his group that destroyed energy, creativity, and dialogue. He held a three-day meeting to communicate the vision, to translate it into actions within his group, and to begin changing unproductive norms around formality and criticism. Ordinarily, these meetings were characterized by formal agendas with hour-by-hour schedules, ritualized presentations, vu-graph projectors, copious handouts, and a lengthy meeting evaluation form. He began this meeting by inviting his people to join him in a ceremony, held on a beachfront, during which they burned a pile of agendas, handouts, and evaluation forms. In this way he clearly demonstrated his willingness to try something new, and their meeting was said to be "The best we've ever had."

Accepting Criticism. Visionary leaders and vision champions must be sensitive to how others react to the vision, and sensitive in how they deal with those reactions.

It seems important to encourage people to express their negative thoughts and feelings about the vision. A vision is not truth, but hope, and people have fears attached to hopes, fears that often need to be aired, recognized, and responded to.

It is much too easy for visionaries, excited and energized by their vision, to overlook the reactions and fears of others about the vision; too easy to discount them, shut them off, discourage people from airing them. These reactions are often inquisitive, sometimes doubtful or skeptical, and frequently emotional. Such comments as, "This is obvious and it's about time somebody said it"; or, "Sounds good, let's see if they can pull it off"; or, "Just another directive from management" are sometimes unpleasant or threatening for the visionary to hear, but, without airing and discussing these reaction and fears, it is doubtful that any true commitment to a vision can be achieved.

Inevitably, some people will remain silent, hoping the vision will suffer a quiet death. The best a visionary or champion can do is pay careful attention to those who are sincerely raising their concerns, encourage others to do the same, and get on with the job of implementing the vision in the hope that enough people will support it and breathe life into it.

A vision can be seen as a stimulus to creativity, where a creative response is expected from the system in which the vision exists. A vision is somewhat like a half-formed idea waiting to be filled in. While it is important to hear people's concerns and fears, the best way to stimulate creative responses to a half-formed idea seems to be to encourage people to say what they like about it as well as what they don't like about it.

In organizations that reward analytical

and critical skills, it may be too much to hope that people will embrace a vision without a good deal of analysis and criticism. However, a vision is as much about stirring people's hearts as it is about challenging their minds; discussions of a vision ought to focus on both.

It is particularly important that people explore the meaning of values expressed in the vision. What is the meaning of "integrity," "trust," or "cooperation?" One effective technique for stimulating such an exploration is to ask groups of people to decide on the opposites of those values. Concepts can be defined by their opposites, and talking about the opposite of integrity forces us to clarify what we mean by integrity. For example, in one organization, a discussion of the opposite of trust, yielded "suspicion" (we did not allow mistrust as an answer), and stimulated a discussion of how and why people in the group were suspicious of one another, and what they need to do to become more trusting.

Focus on the Future. Discussions about the vision should focus on the future, not on the present or the past. This is not to say that the past is unimportant and shouldn't be discussed, only that when talking about where we are going, it serves little purpose to talk about how bad things are or have been, or even about how good things are or have been. It is less helpful to look at what was wrong in the past and try to fix it, than to look forward to the future and see what is needed to achieve a desired result. Besides, people can get testy if they think they are being told they are ineffective, and visions are not about criticism; they are not a strategy for giving feedback to an organization

about how bad it has been—at least they shouldn't be.

Visions Create Problems. A vision statement describes a different reality, not necessarily one that people will view as better. People will tend to look at a vision expecting it to solve some problem they face on a day-to-day basis. The truth is that a vision will probably create as many problems as it solves. For example, one organization that included the words "the customer comes first" in its vision statement found it then had to change the way many decisions were made, change aspects of how performance was appraised, discourage internal competition that caused delays in processing customer orders and complaints, and solve a whole host of other problems. That vision moved the organization in a positive direction, yet created many new problems along the way.

Networking. The most important communication problem, after initial publication and discussion of a vision, is how to build the critical mass—how to advertise evidence of change and build networks to promote change. Networking can be a powerful tool for building the critical mass. Networking strategies might include newsletters dedicated to publicizing evidence of the vision in action, computer conferencing among champions of the vision, and meetings of those who are working toward the vision, with no other agenda except talking about how that effort is proceeding and celebrating one another's successes.

Boundary Testing

If the visionary is serious about his or her commitment to the vision, and the vision doesn't fade away, communication of the vision will be quickly followed by *boundary testing*, which essentially means asking, "How will things be different?" Many boundaries will be questions: the boundaries of leadership in the organization, as well as the boundaries of individual jobs, roles, influence, relationships, and so forth.

There are elements of organizational life that appear to be opposites, such as visionary leadership and rational management, efficiency and creativity, individual effort and teamwork. For all of these pairs of organizational elements, the more you have of one, the less you have of the other. Boundary testing should result in the best balance among contradictory elements. What is the best proportion of visionary leadership to rational management, of efficiency to creativity, of individual effort to teamwork? Boundary testing efforts will answer those questions.

Boundary testing is also a critical component of gaining organizational commitment to a vision, for people will want permission to step outside the existing boundaries, to break long-standing patterns of belief and behavior, to try new things, and they will be sensitive to the reactions of others, particularly those of the visionary and other people in authority.

Boundary testing is the second process to which visionaries must attend after the vision. Here are some ideas and suggestions for facilitating boundary testing.

Challenging Norms. Norms are the unwritten rules of an organization that govern how people are supposed to behave and what they are supposed to believe. These behaviors and beliefs come to be considered by the organization's people as "normal." Often the norms need to be challenged and changed or they will inhibit achieving a vision. However, because they are considered so "normal," people in the organization are frequently not aware of them; thus, they have no sense of how they might inhibit the vision and little sense of how to change them.

It is often useful in involve an outsider who has skill in identifying norms and assessing their impact. We once consulted with an executive group whose vision included "utilizing the creative potential in all of us." Their meetings were held in a formal room, around a long table, with formal portraits of the company founder peering over their shoulders. Each person entered the room without speaking to anyone else, sat at the table, and took a yellow lined pad from a stack provided. Each person spoke politely in turn, and everybody wrote down everything that was said. These were the norms for meetings in the company for as long as anybody could remember. They were surely not conducive to creativity.

Encouraging Leadership. The publication of a vision raises questions about the nature of leadership in the organization, especially if the vision is the first for that organization. One question that often arises is, "What is the difference between leadership and management?" In our view, management is mostly concerned with control, allocating resources, and solving problems. Leadership is about articulating visions, embodying values, and creating the environment within which things can be accomplished. Leadership is spiritual and emotional, characterized by uncertainty and ambiguity. Management is more focused on today, leadership on tomorrow. An effective balance between the two is essential.

During the early phases of a vision, it seems important that more time be given to leadership activities. These include ensuring acceptance and acceptability of the vision, creating common values, creating value-related opportunities, developing an environment that supports innovation and productivity, defining a global perspective, postponing closure on new ideas, nurturing the good ones, looking for "win-win" opportunities—rather than "win-lose"—being visible, and creating celebrations.

Flexibility. Recognize that the steps to implementing a vision cannot be planned in advance—but after people understand and sign on to the vision, initial steps are usually obvious. After initial steps are taken, the next steps should be equally obvious if they are truly guided by the vision. Occasional midcourse corrections are recommended, and, if these yield a slight change in direction, that should be considered a successful outcome. There should be sufficient flexibility in achieving a vision to make room for the needs of the people charged with achieving it.

Risk. Since the outcome of a vision statement is unpredictable, and vision will require boundary testing, risk is an integral part of the vision-making process. This is further exacerbated if "taking more risks" is part of the vision. It is no easy undertaking to change an organization from a low-risk environment, where outcomes are fairly predictable, to one in which risk-taking is acceptable and outcomes are less predictable. Reward structures must be examined to discover how they discourage or encourage risk-taking, and managers who say they want their people to take more risks had best start examining

their own risk-taking behavior and become aware of new options and limits. A clear understanding of what constitutes a risk—and the differences among personal risk, career risk, and business risk—and some clarity about the kinds of risks required to achieve the vision are essential.

Also, it can be very helpful for managers to ask themselves, just after having made some decision, "What is the next biggest risk I might take?" If managers begin to calibrate risks—perhaps on a scale that reads "safe–risky–riskier–riskiest"—it will help them understand their own risk-taking, be aware of the limits of their commitment to the vision, and perhaps produce more creative solutions.

Momentum. Another important issue is how to keep the momentum going—how to publicize evidence of commitment to the vision and to encourage as much networking as possible. After the vision has been communicated and understood, the visionary must devote time and energy to keeping up the momentum while the concepts in the vision are being integrated and the critical mass is building. This might involve discussions with champions on how to make things happen, defining changes in roles, exploring system or structural changes to move systems toward consistency with the vision, monitoring progress in new and creative ways, and helping to set new boundaries and ease the transition. A prospective visionary who simply sets the vision in front of people, and expects them to carry it out without his or her very active participation, is doomed to fail.

Training. One effective means for introducing people to the vision and exploring new boundaries utilizes training sessions in which people are encouraged to explore the vision and are supported in reacting to it, as well as in sorting out what it means or might mean for them. Such programs will reflect the organization's degree of commitment to the vision. Do not expect to hold a few one-hour meetings and have people believe that there is great commitment; rather, be prepared to demonstrate commitment by allocating resources to helping people get on board.

Meetings and Stories. Perhaps the most difficult tasks for champions who are anxious to have the vision concepts implemented in their part of the organization are preparing for a "vision meeting" and engaging in the follow-up needed to make the vision happen. In preparation for these steps, the champion must develop a clear understanding of his or her limits for change and risk, must anticipate as far as possible the inevitable gap between what he or she intends and what actually results, must be comfortable with the behavior needed to support people and make things happen, and must be open to subordinates' feedback, reactions, and fears. Further, the champion must be willing to walk the fine line between being committed and being involved and providing support on the one hand, and destroying creativity and enthusiasm with excessive control and interference on the other.

During vision meetings it seems useful to recognize actions that are consistent with the vision. One plant manager held a meeting in which he talked about his vision; then he invited people to tell stories of recent happenings that were consistent with the vision. He sprinkled his response to the stories with a lot of,

"That's exactly what I'm looking for." His "laying on" of the vision was extremely gentle, which seemed to give people a chance to understand and integrate it. His sincere, "atta-boys" were energizing; people discovered what was expected of them; the process of hero-making, story-telling, and myth-making began; he encouraged breaking unproductive norms and setting new, productive ones; and new boundaries were established for "how we do things around here."

The telling and retelling of "stories" in support of the vision are essential. Alan Wilkins (1984), writing about organizational culture says, "Stories are powerful vehicles for transmitting values because they give concrete context to abstract values. They also provide scripts about how to get things done and what to expect in organizations."

Champions who are interpreting the vision within their own part of the organization also need to redefine limits and direction in an open manner to their group. However, people are less likely to respond well to broad statements of openness than they are to clear statements about what the new rules are; a great deal of time can be saved if these rules are developed and articulated up front. About the worst thing a manager can do after a vision is published is to lead people to believe that they can have or do things that he or she fully believes to be out of the question and therefore will not be able to support.

Experimentation. Experiments are good methods to test new ideas and new ways of doing things. Creating an opportunity for individuals and small groups with common interests to design an in-depth experiment with fixed parameters to try out something new is an excellent way to generate energy and test boundaries. The experiments should represent a departure from previous ways of doing things, be within the control of the experimenters, have some elements of risk, and, most important, be exciting to the experimenters. There should be no taint of failure attached to experiments that don't work out as planned; these should be viewed as learning and testing experiences, and rewarded as "a good try." And remember that consistency with the vision is a key criterion for the success of an experiment.

Task Groups. Task forces are an inevitable part of the culture of most organizations, and it is essential that task groups emerging after the vision are consistent in both content and process with that vision. If the vision speaks about cooperation and flexibility, then task forces must work cooperatively and have flexible boundaries and membership. Sufficient time and resources must be available for task forces to get on with their tasks.

One creative use of task groups is using them to implement the vision concepts in the same way they are used to solving organizational problems. Here are some ideas for using task forces for vision follow-up:

1. Set up task forces around key concepts or values expressed in the vision: a task force on "participation," one on "cooperation," one on "reaching our individual potential."

2. Set up task forces to explore how the vision might affect different people, roles, or organizational processes: a task force on "the supervisor of the future," one on "getting close to

the customer," one on "how our performance appraisal system impedes and facilitates the vision."

3. Provide each task force leader with a process consultant, a peer of the leader, who is chosen by the leader but is not a task force member, and who is responsible for consulting with the task force about its consistency with the vision. The process consultant, who should be a champion of the vision, monitors the task force's process and product.

4. Have task force leaders meet to apply the test of consistency with the vision to the entire task force process, to how task forces make recommendations, to the limits of task force authority, and so on.

5. Select members of functional task forces with the vision concepts and values as well as the task in mind. This would mean, for example, that, if the vision included a "close to the customer" orientation, employees who work in personnel and auditing functions would be included on task forces dealing with customer problems. They might not have the technical expertise the problem seems to require, their functional specialties might at first glance seem irrelevant to the problem, but, if the organization wants everybody to understand what "close to the customer" means, then everybody needs the opportunity to be "close to the customer."

Initiative. In multilevel hierarchical organizations, people will normally look to the levels above themselves for initiatives in support of the vision. Unless the vision specifically calls for that to continue, it is important to help people at all levels find areas within their control wherein they can form their own initiatives, take self-responsible action, and test the boundaries of their upward influence.

Facilitating boundary testing might be the most significant leadership challenge after the vision. Writing and communicating a vision are in the realm of words and ideas; boundary testing is in the realm of actions, where we encounter resistance from long-established ways of doing things, where our commitment becomes concrete, and where we test whether our ideas are credible. It is in boundary testing where visionaries and champions discover the real meaning behind the ideas and words of their visions.

Sign-On

The third process that must be considered in order to gain organizational commitment is a *sign-on* by members of the organization. By sign-on we mean an individual's commitment to the vision. The kind of commitment needed to truly enact a vision cannot be coerced; it is a self-responsible acceptance of the invitation to the party. In order to make such a choice, one must feel free to make the opposite choice—not to come to the party—or one is likely to have a terrible time, be a bore, and maybe ruin the party.

Sign-on happens within individual members of the organization, and there is little else that a visionary can do to produce it except communicate well, facilitate boundary testing, and provide celebration for actions leading toward the vision. Here, however, are a few ideas, suggestions, and things to keep in mind while attempting to get committed sign-on.

Action.   The best indicator that someone has signed on is some personal action to carry out the vision, or some kind of missionary activity: preaching or teaching the vision, spreading the word, telling the stories, networking with others who support the vision, and promoting and supporting changes that facilitate the vision. Visionaries and champions can help this process by providing formats within which these personal actions can occur: meetings, training events, reward ceremonies, and networking processes like newsletters and computer conferencing.

Visions and More Visions.   A critical step to sign-on occurs when each subset of the organization establishes its own set of values within the framework of the vision. By each *subset* we mean each division, department, or group, and, especially important, each person.

After establishing their own set of values, the next question for each organizational subset to ask is, "How will we (or I) put these into practice?"

A useful question to ask of organizational subsets that are preparing their own visions is, "What do you want to be like in the future?" This question—as opposed to, "What do you want to be doing?" or, "How do you want to work?"—encourages thought and discussion of values, purposes, and organizational climate.

Personal Visioning.   An effective way of getting people to internalize the organization's vision, and indeed the concept of visioning, is to have them develop their own personal vision of where they might like to be in the future. This involves collecting personal data about successes, interests, career and life stages, values, and the like, and creating a personal statement of "who I am" and "who I want to be in the future." The process of personal transformation or change is analogous to organizational change, and encouraging people to engage in their own personal vision process, while exploring how the organization's vision is linked to their own, goes a long way toward obtaining a committed sign-on.

Asking people to create their own personal visions also can raise significant issues around the company's vision. One plant manager, after publishing his vision and getting sign-on from his management committee, sponsored a five-day program for his key managers to examine the vision and their role in implementing it. During the program, as an aid to writing a personal vision, each person was asked to select from a long list of values those which he or she held as most important. None of the 12 participants listed "helpfulness to others" as among their most important values. Yet the company vision statement called for "helping each person maximize his or her potential." This important discrepancy led to much discussion about the meaning of the vision and re-examination of personal values. Each person came away with a stronger commitment to the vision and deeper understanding of his or her own role as a facilitator of the vision.

Patience. Visionaries can too easily forget that preparing their vision required soul-searching, study, risk, and time. Because their vision seems so obvious and right to them, they can come to expect it will be equally obvious and right to others and that sign-on will be automatic. It won't be, at least for most people seeing or hearing about the vision for the first time. Visionaries and champions must allow others the

same opportunity for soul-searching, study, risk, and time that produced the vision. And they should be skeptical of sign-on that comes too easily, because easy sign-on often reflects shallow understanding of the vision, or shallow motives for signing on, and produces shallow commitment. More than anything, perhaps, visionaries must practice patience.

Symbols and Ceremonies. A personalized symbol that reflects an individual's commitment to the vision can be a powerful aid to sign-on. During one meeting, where a group of managers were digesting and interpreting their organization's vision statement, each manager was asked to decide on his or her own personal slogan, a short statement that reflected a personal commitment to the vision. An engraver was brought to the meeting to make desk nameplates for each person; their slogans were engraved on the backs of the name plates. During another meeting, managers were asked to visit a nearby shopping district to purchase their own personal vision sign-on symbol.

A formal sign-on process, involving some tangible recognition of having signed on might be useful—a kind of baptismal ceremony, or a talisman of some sort.

Bringing It Home. In many organizations people look upward within the organization for solutions to problems. A sign-on process requires that people look to themselves, asking, "What can I do to make it happen?" One visionary told his people, "You have to be comfortable that the overview is right, that the vision is correct, then the specifics have to come from you."

Celebration

The fourth process that visionaries and champions of a vision will need to pay attention to after the vision has been written is *celebration* of actions that foster the vision. We prefer to talk about celebration, rather than rewards, because the latter is a narrower term and because celebration connotes ceremony, acclaim, and festivity.

Why Celebrate? There are two reasons why celebration is important after the vision. First, to reward and enjoy success. This is especially important where organizational systems and norms, such as performance appraisal systems, might impede the vision because they do not reward actions that foster the vision. Second, celebrations send clear signals to the organization about the kind of actions that support the vision, and are, in that sense, an aspect of continuing to communicate the vision.

Accentuate the Positive. Whenever a vision is published, part of the organization will sign on quickly, part will resist, and part will adopt a wait-and-see attitude. Wait-and-see is usually the largest category. In many organizations, especially those that view managers as problem solvers, a great deal of time and energy will be spent trying to get those who resist on board; they pose a problem to be solved. In the meantime, those who have signed on and those who wait and see can easily become disenchanted and cynical. Celebrations are effective ways to focus attention and energy on those who have signed on, rather than on those who resist, and give those who wait and see something positive to see.

Variety. Celebration means commem-orating an event with a ceremony. Celebrations can be large or small, planned or spontaneous. They can occur at formal or informal meetings, seminars, or training programs. Visionaries and champions must be certain that celebration ceremonies fit the tone and style of the vision. Ways to celebrate include ovations, letters from top executives, weekend trips, dinners out with a spouse, flowers, lunch with an executive, a cheese and wine party during a training session about the vision, awards ceremonies, plaques, balloons, and cash awards. Often a handshake, smile, and "atta-boy" are enough. Hoopla is not required, though it seems important to many people. Be creative.

During the initial stages of communicating the vision, it is very useful to celebrate the aspects of the vision that already exist. If the vision talks about teamwork, celebrate the outstanding teamwork that the organization has had in the recent past; if it talks about customer service, celebrate recent examples of good customer service.

Positive Reinforcement. Celebration is positive reinforcement. In *In Search of Excellence*, Peters and Waterman wrote that the most important output of management is getting others to shift attention in desirable directions, and that positive reinforcement is a potent tool for doing that. Such reinforcements tend to have more impact when they happen on-the-spot, when they contain as much information about exactly what is being reinforced as possible, when they are not easily achievable, when they are unpredictable and intermittent, and when the substance of the reward is largely intangible.

Frequent sincere celebration of the

vision will provide an upbeat atmosphere around the vision, and will also—let us not overlook this—provide visionaries and champions with much-needed reasons to celebrate as well.

A Few Final Words

Eight months after the publication of a vision for his company, a corporate president told us that he had three pieces of advice for others who would take a visionary approach to change in their organizations. We think it is sound advice, and worth repeating. First, he said, "Go from the general to the specific, from values and broad statements to actions, as quickly as possible without short-circuiting communication." When a visionary is sure that someone or some group in his organization is clear about the vision and ready to act, often a simple statement is enough to get things moving. The statement probably ought to be, "Do it," or, "Why are you asking me?" or, "What do you need from me?"

The second piece of advice our visionary gave is, "Focus not on the problems of the past or the present but on what will be different in the future." This is not as easy as it sounds, particularly because people trained as managers often view themselves as problem solvers and are happiest solving the immediate problem. It takes courage to hold fast to the long-range view and delegate the day-to-day issues—courage and trust in subordinates.

Finally, our visionary said, "The whole organization must be involved in creating what we all want. The top of the organization should do the minimum to get results, focusing instead on publicizing the vision and creating the environment in which things will get done."

It can be quite a jolt for first-time visionaries when they shift from focusing on results to focusing on the vision and the climate of the organization. Success takes no less than a redefinition of the role of the senior people in the organization; they become less "producers of results" and more "keepers of the vision and values."

In this article, we have given some suggestions and ideas to visionaries and champions of a vision who are seeking an organization's commitment about the processes we believe will claim a great deal of attention after a vision is written—communication, boundary testing, sign-on, and celebration—and we know what we have written is not enough. The after-the-vision process is fragile and complex. It involves a total organization and a total human response—thoughts, feelings, and actions. It involves visionaries who must be visible, consistent, courageous, and creative; champions who must be innovative in publicizing the vision, sensitive in responding to the reactions of others, thoughtful in setting new boundaries, and ingenious in navigating the labyrinth of change; and finally, it involves the people who make up the organization, who must be willing to take risks, able to make commitments, and ready to experiment with themselves.

At the beginning of this paper we referred to the after-the-vision process as a quest, a reaching for the "faraway lights." We like the metaphor because the notion of quest calls to mind adventure, achievement, creativity, challenge, and leadership—qualities that we believe to elicit the best in all of us. It is our hope that more and more of our organizations will call more and more of their people to such a quest.

CASE

ALPHA AND OMEGA

It is the end of May, and the chairman and CEO of Alpha Corporation has just taken control of Omega Corporation, which is in the same industry. He had attempted a friendly merger one year earlier and had been rebuffed. Alpha and Omega are similar in product and market penetration, yet customer overlap is minimal. Each company's customer bases are, however, large and loyal. Alpha's and Omega's technologies are comparable, but their products are incompatible.

Alpha Corporation employs about 56,000 people; its global sales and marketing forces are geographically organized, except for its largest division. Omega Corporation, with 65,000 employees, has primarily a "line of business" structure in its sales and marketing organization. Both companies have different and conflicting distribution systems, both order entry and billing, yet, combined, the nearly 122,000 employees will operate in all 50 U.S. states and in more than 100 countries.

This case was prepared by Research Associate Lori Ann Levaggi (under the direction of Professor Todd D. Jick).

Copyright © 1988 by the President and Fellows of Harvard College. Harvard Business School case 9-488-003.

The more-centralized Alpha Corporation has a top-down, performance-based culture that is bottom-line oriented. The "entrepreneurial" Omega Corporation puts a premium on creativity and close-knit relationships within the firm. Having been pioneers in the industry, both firms have histories and traditions dating back a century or more. Both companies are proud of their cultures and have unflattering—if not derisive—opinions of the other's.

Although the merger makes the new company the second largest in its industry worldwide, financial and industry analysts are skeptical that these two "also-rans" with substantial differences can together challenge the overwhelming industry leader in a highly competitive environment. Nonetheless, Alpha's chief has pledged that earnings will be tripled within the next 18 months. He is determined to unify the two companies, to strengthen the new firm's overall marketing position, and to maintain and revitalize both companies' product lines—all by year-end.

Memorial Day weekend seemed a good time, after months of dizzying negotiations, to begin developing a vision for the merged company. His challenge was to sketch the shape and the spirit of this new organization.

READING

A NEW AGE FOR BUSINESS?

Frank Rose

Are American corporations ready for the New Age? Michael Murphy, founder of the Esalen Institute, thinks so. Next year Murphy, 60, hopes to start luring business groups to Esalen, the Big Sur spa where the human-potential movement was born nearly three decades ago. Laurance Rockefeller has given $250,000 to convert the Big House, the clifftop Victorian built by Murphy's grandparents, into a corporate retreat. George Leonard, an Esalen trustee, will offer a set of exercises based on aikido, the Japanese martial art that seeks harmony rather than dominance. Conferees will be able to select from a menu of other Esalen techniques promising everything from stress reduction to creativity enhancement.

A few years back, all this might have seemed strange. Not anymore. Now companies like AT&T, Procter & Gamble, and Du Pont are offering employees personal-growth experiences of their own, hoping to spur creativity, encourage learning, and promote "ownership" of the company's results. A handful of visionary leaders—General Electric chairman Jack Welch chief among them—are going beyond training seminars to a fundamental reordering of managerial priorities. Meanwhile, a small network of consultants, thinkers, and academics are working to transform business. Propelled by a belief that the world is undergoing major change, they call for a new paradigm—a whole new framework for seeing and understanding business—that will carry humankind beyond the industrial age.

The result is a curious convergence: executives seeking ways to reverse America's fall from dominance sharing common ground with freethinkers drawn to business as the most powerful institution in a global society. "In the 60s, these people would have slit their wrists before walking into any institution of corporate America," says Harriet Rubin, a business books editor at Doubleday. "Now corporations are seen as a sort of living laboratory for their ideas." As for the business side—well, Rubin's best-selling title is *Leadership Is An Art*, an inspirational tome by Herman Miller chairman Max DePree that includes chapters like "Intimacy" and "Tribal Storytelling" and is packaged with the ethereal look once reserved for the poetry of Kahlil Gibran.

What next? Crystals on the assembly line? Channeling in the boardroom? Not likely. "The whole Shirley MacLaine approach makes me ill," says Stewart Brand, creator of the *Whole Earth Catalog* and now a co-founder (with former Royal Dutch Shell planning chief Peter Schwartz) of the Global Business Network, an on-line ganglion of thinkers underwritten by the likes of AT&T, Volvo, Nissan, and Inland Steel.

The new paradigm might be described as New Age without the glazed eyes. The word ''paradigm'' comes from the Greek for ''pattern,'' and the new paradigm is just that: a new pattern of behavior that stems from a new way of looking at the world. The old world view—Newtonian, mechanistic, analytical—is present in everything from the Constitution, with its clockwork system of checks and balances, to the rectilinear street plans of Washington, D.C., and San Francisco, to the assembly lines devised by Henry Ford. The new paradigm takes ideas from quantum physics, cybernetics, chaos theory, cognitive science, and Eastern and Western spiritual traditions to form a world view in which everything is interconnected, in which reality is not absolute but a by-product of human consciousness. Nobody is promising universal enlightenment next week, however. ''What we're talking about here is not a search for nirvana,'' says Michael Ray, 51, holder of the BancOne chair in creativity at the Stanford business school. ''It's an attempt to deal with a very difficult time.''

So far, what has emerged is a host of management theories and practices befitting an age of global enterprise, instantaneous communication, and ecological limits. Some are familiar: hierarchical organizations being replaced by more flexible networks; workers being ''empowered'' to make decisions on their own; organizations developing a capacity for group learning instead of waiting for wisdom from above; national horizons giving way to global thinking. Others may still seem a little far-out: creativity and intuition joining numerical analysis as aids to decision making; love and caring being recognized as motivators in the workplace; even the primacy of the profit motive being questioned by those who argue

that the real goal of enterprise is the mental and spiritual enrichment of those who take part in it.

Individually, each of these developments is just one manifestation of progressive management thought. Together, they suggest the possibility of a fundamental shift. Applied to business, the old paradigm held that numbers are all-important, that professional managers can handle any enterprise, that control can and should be held at the top. The new paradigm puts people—customers and employees—at the center of the universe and replaces the rigid hierarchies of the industrial age with a network structure that emphasizes interconnectedness.

Why would companies want to embrace a new paradigm? ''Because the old paradigm isn't working,'' says Ray. He argues that the decline of American business from its postwar apogee is like a scientific anomaly—a situation the old theories fail to explain. Just as a new paradigm emerges in science when old theories stop working, the new paradigm in business began to take form when the old by-the-numbers school of management started to founder during the 70s. The surprise success of *In Search of Excellence*, with its explicit attack on the old model, signaled the beginnings of a new perspective.

Several factors since have encouraged the trend. Perhaps the most visible is the faltering performance that has fed the vogue for Japanese management techniques and the quest for ''excellence.'' But the driving force is the need for speed: The spread of computers and telecommunications and the rise of global markets have rendered bureaucracies hopelessly unwieldy. At the same time, a series of wrenching changes—deregulation, corporate takeovers, the demise of the Soviet bloc—has made the extraordinary seem commonplace. The sudden backlash against the money mania of the 80s—combined, some say, with the gradual rise to power of the 60s generation—has put idealism back on the agenda. The result is a vague but growing sense that business has to be conducted differently.

"The current world economy clearly will not work for the planet," warns Willis Harman, 72, head of the Institute of Noetic Sciences, a Sausalito, California, organization founded by Apollo astronaut Edgar Mitchell. "It's going to change somehow. The question is how. Do we make it through this smoothly, or do we go through real chaos—economic depression, people starving, conflict with the Third World? When society goes through a deep shift like this, we've got to hold the whole thing together or a lot of human misery will result. That's why the business sector is so important."

Though their eye is on the future, experts like Harman Ray are actually building on work that began in the 40s with the socio-tech movement in Britain and the study of group dynamics in the United States. While the socio-tech thinkers at London's Tavistock Institute tried to get people and technology to work together smoothly in factories and coal mines, the group-dynamics crowd centered at MIT was inventing the T-group—the T stands for sensitivity training—in a series of free-wheeling experiments in leadership and decision making at the National Training Labs in Bethel, Maine. In the 50s, West Coast psychologists began shifting their focus to personal growth. Meanwhile, MIT's Douglas McGregor developed his famous Theory X and Theory Y, opposing styles of management based on opposing views of human nature—that people are lazy and have to be whipped into shape, or

that they're responsible and need only to be encouraged.

The split between the West Coast and East Coast—between those mainly interested in personal growth and those more concerned with the health of the organization—persists to this day. While the personal-growth faction yielded Esalen and the human-potential movement, MIT spawned the organizational development network—consultants and academics who advocated management with a humanistic bent.

Until a few years ago, when guru-entrepreneurs like Werner Erhard with his Transformational Technologies won lucrative personnel-training contracts from such major corporations as TRW and Ford, the West Coast human-potential crowd was considered too far-out for the business world. Organizational development, or OD, was more influential, but it faltered during the 70s, the victim of its own naiveté: Not only did things not always get better once everybody learned to communicate freely, they sometimes got worse.

OD flourished in the military, however, under the name organizational effectiveness. A round of post-Vietnam soul-searching culminated in the establishment of Task Force Delta, a cadre of army officers whose mission was to scan for new ideas. One of their slogans was "Be all you can be," a human-potential message that eventually found its way into the Army's recruitment campaign. Organizational effectiveness flamed out in the early 80s, just as the OD network was yielding a spinoff called "organizational transformation," composed of people concerned less with communication and team building than with deeper issues like myth, ritual, and spirit.

Among Task Force Delta's livelier

members was Lieutenant Colonel Jim Channon, 50, now retired from the military and working as an OD consultant to such organizations as AT&T, Du Pont, and Whirlpool. He specializes in helping managers express their vision by creating a picture that makes corporate goals tangible against a starry universe or earthscape background. But at heart he sees himself as a shaman. "Three things are missing from almost every organization I've been through," he says. "A sincere desire to love each other in a brotherly way, an ability to incorporate spiritual values in their work, and an ability to do something physical together." On all three counts he thinks modern corporations could learn from tribal cultures: "Just because those guys can't make toasters doesn't mean that singing together, dancing together, and telling stories around a fire isn't a damn good thing to do."

This kind of thinking can be carried only so far: "If people stop buying your toothpaste," says Richard Beckard, a retired professor from MIT's Sloan School, "you can love each other all over the place and you're still out of the toothpaste business." But after the excesses of the greed-is-good crowd, who knows what a little altruism could do?

"Let's say you accept Milton Friedman's idea that the only business of business is profit," says Robert Adams, a former executive vice president of Xerox. "It's really a combination of altruism and self-interest to want to do the best for your employees, and it's only common sense to want to treat your customers well. Why we have to learn those things from the Japanese, Lord knows."

In a recent speech before San Francisco's Commonwealth Club, Levi Strauss chairman Robert Haas, 48, sketched his idea of the corporation of the future: a global enterprise relying on employees who "are able to tap their fullest potential" and managers who act not as authority figures but as "coaches, facilitators, and role models." Levi Strauss is striving to transform itself along those lines because it needs creative thinking and rapid response to satisfy a fashion-conscious public. "This company isn't turning into a group of Moonies for some Platonic management good," observes chief counsel Tom Bauch, 47. "It's a way of promoting our own success."

Presumably Levi Strauss won't be turning into a bunch of Moonies at all. The point of the new paradigm is not to get people to "om" out in front of some guru but to encourage them to think for themselves. Ideally, this yields an organization that functions like a rugby team. "Rugby is a flow sport," says Noel Tichy of the University of Michigan Business School. "It looks chaotic, but it requires tremendous communication, continuous adjustment to an uncertain environment, and problem solving without using a hierarchy." American business has been conducted more like football, with every play a call from the sidelines.

One man who's ready to play rugby is Jack Welch of GE. Having streamlined GE organizationally with a flurry of sales, acquisitions, and plant closings, Welch has now turned to the culture. "Productivity is the key," says GE's head of management development, James Baughman, a former Harvard Business School professor charged with effecting much of the change. "You can only get so much more productivity out of reorganization and automation. Where you really get productivity leaps is in the minds and hearts of people."

Tichy, who used to work for Baughman, views the changes there as simply common sense: "It's just treating people with dignity and making them feel part of a team. If that qualifies as a new paradigm, so be it." But GE's moves bear the twin hallmarks of new-paradigm thinking: the systems view—seeing everything as interconnected—and the focus on people. Welch's goal is fast turnaround, and to get it he intends to create what he calls the "boundaryless organization"—no hierarchical boundaries vertically, no functional boundaries horizontally. For Baughman, this means radical changes at GE's Management Development Institute in Crotonville, New York.

Crotonville was one place where the old-paradigm approach to business—the scientific, rationalist world view—was perfected in the years after World War II. A vast team of experts (Peter Drucker among them) codified modern management practices there in an eight-volume "blue book" that served as the manual for American business. By 1981, GE had grown an elaborate, multitiered, wedding cake bureaucracy that Welch is now blasting apart. "We wrote the book on bureaucracy," says Baughman. "Now there aren't any books, just real people talking about problems face to face, sweating it out and grunting through. It's a revolution, nothing less, from control to let-'er-rip. Historians will tell us in the 21st century if we were crazy."

Not every company has to wait so long. Pacific Bell miscalculated badly when it hired two associates of Charles Krone, a reclusive Californian who has developed an elaborate training methodology out of a melange of systems theory, socio-tech thinking, Sufi mysticism, and the writings of G. I. Gurdjieff. Krone's work is supposed to teach people to think more precisely, but it is jargon-laden and off-

putting, and when enthusiastic Pac Bell managers tried to give it to their 62,000 workers, they discovered some people didn't want to be told how to think—especially by their employer. While attendance at the "Krone sessions" was supposedly voluntary, those who resisted were left with the impression their careers would be jeopardized. After employee allegations of mind control sparked a public investigation, which uncovered huge expenditures on the training, the program was canceled abruptly. Pac Bell has since undertaken a more mainstream total-quality program, so far avoiding controversy.

Must change come from the top to be effective? Many proponents thought so, until the Pac Bell debacle. The experience of Procter & Gamble indicates that consistent attention from on high isn't always necessary. The giant packaged goods company began testing socio-tech ideas in its manufacturing plants more than 20 years ago, moving from the hierarchical command-and-control model to a team approach with workers largely managing themselves. Company officials rarely talked about this in public: P&G's management style was considered part of its competitive edge and was as tightly guarded as its toothpaste formulas. Managers were even careful how they discussed it internally, since corporate headquarters in Cincinnati was focused on marketing and not particularly interested in new organizational ideas. To avoid trouble, one division manager, worried about disturbing his management experiment, decreed that no one from elsewhere in the company could visit a plant without going through him.

Charles Krone, 61, whose esoteric theories would later fare so badly at Pacific Bell, was an internal organization specialist in P&G's soap division, for which he set up a detergent plant in Lima, Ohio, that outperformed every other soap plant in the company. A counterpart, Herb Stokes— now a corporate consultant and cattle rancher in Abilene, Texas—led a similarly successful effort at a P&G paper products plant he organized in Albany, Georgia. But while a number of factories like these have resisted the rigid thinking and abject boss-pleasing once labeled "bureausis," decades of running battles within P&G suggest that what's needed is some combination of support from the top and enthusiasm in the ranks.

That's what a former Boise Cascade senior vice president named George McCown, 55, is trying to achieve. Besides serving as chairman of the World Business Academy, a group of business people and thinkers devoted to propagating the new paradigm, he heads McCown De Leeuw, a California investment firm that specializes in doing LBOs. He and his New York City-based partner, David De Leeuw, a former vice president of Citibank, target well-positioned but underperforming businesses and restructure them to stress empowerment of employees, creativity, and openness. Last December they joined former baseball commissioner Peter Ueberroth in his purchase of troubled Hawaiian Airlines, which Chairman Tom Talbot, a Ueberroth associate, is now trying to pull out of a "plantation mentality" by involving people at every level in an overhaul of operations.

One of McCown De Leeuw's early buyouts was Coast Gas of Watsonville, California, a propane distribution company that has tripled in size in four years to revenues of about $100 million. While borrowing fueled much of the expansion, CEO Keith Baxter has achieved much of the company's growth by instituting new practices that range from the mundane (a budget system) to the innovative. Having taken over a notoriously rigid organization (sample rule: No more than two employees could converse at one time), he literally tore down the walls to transform it to one in which everybody understands the business and its problems.

Helping Baxter reshape the culture at Coast Gas is Michael Blondell, a Carmel, California, consultant who works with a number of McCown De Leeuw businesses. Unlike many self-styled "change agents," whose promises of weekend transformation are worthy of weight-loss products, Blondell works with companies on a long-term basis. "I look at spirituality, at the way people live their life," he says. "What is their motivation? Do they want things to be better? Do they want to be open and honest? But I don't think we're really teaching anything new. I think we're going back to basic, fundamental values—issues of trust, respect, dignity, commitment, integrity, and accountability. The world is crying out for these things to become more important."

Is anything really new about the new paradigm? Well, yes and no. "I can argue both sides," says Noel Tichy. "No one element is new, but the attention to soft issues is new to American multinationals."

Seventeen years ago sociologist Daniel Bell wrote that, for most of human history, reality was nature; then it became technology; and now, in the postindustrial age of knowledge work and information science, it's the "web of consciousness." That is what's genuinely new about the new paradigm: this focus on human consciousness—not on capital or machinery, but on people. It has challenging implications. "If consciousness is important, then money and profit are no longer that important," argues Michael Ray of Stanford. "They're a way to keep score; but, if you don't have any vision, you're not going to be successful in the long run. If you go for money and that's all, when you get it, there's nothing there."

So what's the alternative? Business as a spiritual pursuit? Don't laugh. Jack Welch recently remarked that he wants people at GE to feel rewarded "in both the pocket-book and the soul." This is the lesson of the new paradigm: If people are your resource and creativity the key to success, then business results cannot be divorced from personal fulfillment. Which is why many executives may discover, as they arise from the hot tubs at Esalen, that when you eliminate the charlatans and strip away the bull, business and human potential are the same thing.

READING

A "BALANCE BETWEEN VALUES AND NUMBERS"*

Following is an excerpt from a statement by John F. Welch, Jr., General Electric's chairman and chief executive, and Edward E. Hood, Jr., vice chairman and executive officer, in the company's 1991 annual report:

Over the past several years we've wrestled at all levels of this company with the question of what we are and what we want to be. Out of these discussions, and through our experiences, we've agreed upon a set of values we believe we will need to take this company forward, rapidly, through the 1990s and beyond.

In our view, leaders, whether on the shop floor or at the tops of our businesses, can be characterized in at least four ways:

The first is one who delivers on commitments—financial or otherwise—and shares the values of our company. His or her future is an easy call. Onward and upward.

The second type of leader is one who does not meet commitments and does not share our values. Not as pleasant a call, but equally easy.

The third is one who misses commitments but shares the values. He or she usually gets a second chance, preferably in a different environment.

Then there is the fourth type—the most difficult for many of us to deal with. That leader delivers on commitments, makes all the numbers, but doesn't share the values we must have. This is the individual who typically forces performance out of people, rather than inspires it: the autocrat, the big shot, the tyrant. Too often, all of us have looked the other way—tolerated these "Type 4" managers because "they always deliver"—at least in the short term.

And perhaps this type was more acceptable in easier times; but in an environment where we must have every good idea from every man and woman in the organization, we cannot afford management styles that suppress and intimidate. Whether we can convince and help these managers to change—recognizing how difficult that can be—or part company with them if they cannot, will be the ultimate test of our commitment to the transformation of this company and will determine the future of the mutual trust and respect we are building. In 1991, we continued to improve our personnel management to achieve much better balance between values and "numbers." That balance will change further in 1992 and beyond, because we know that without leaders who "walk the talk," all of our plans, promises, and dreams for the future are just that—talk.

READING

EMPLOYEE ALIGNMENT?
MAYBE JUST A BRAKE JOB WOULD DO

Jack Gordon

Mr. Gordon is editor of Training: The Magazine of Human Resources Development (published by Lakewood Publications of Minneapolis), from which this article was adapted.

On the Top 40 chart of management buzzwords, "alignment" is rising fast. If your company hasn't begun trying to align you yet, it will soon, so you might as well have some idea what you're in for:

A car's wheels are in alignment if they are so adjusted that the car travels straight and smoothly in the direction it is steered. An organization is in alignment if everyone who works there accepts a common set of overriding goals or a single vision of what the organization is trying to accomplish. You are in alignment with your job to the degree that the work you do—and the way you do it, and the way you interact with other people while doing it—is personally satisfying to you and pleasing your employer. It's every bit as simple as that.

From *The Wall Street Journal*, February 13, 1989.

Alignment is tied to the popular concepts of leadership, vision, teamwork, and change. ("Change" in the management training world ranks right up there with "excellence" and "feedback." But that's another story.) Aligners come in two varieties, one decidedly more vociferous than the other. Both aligners (with a small "a") and Aligners (with a capital "A") are likely to speak of "empowering" you; but an aligner will be trying to enlist your support for a change in the organization, while an Aligner will be talking about changing *you* to suit the organization.

If your boss is of the big "A" variety, it's easy for him to get carried away. First thing you know, he'll have some consultant splashing around in your psyche, trying to dredge up your Oedipal resentments and "re-parent" you: the CEO as Robert Young; the employees as Princess, Kitten, and Bud.

It's like this. Say I'm the new chairman of the Democratic Party. I have a dream. The national anthem will be changed to "America the Beautiful," and only Ray Charles will be allowed to sing it. If Ray can't make it to a particular football game or Olympic medal ceremony, they'll have to play a tape of his stirring rendition. Never again will Americans live in fear that, at any given sporting event, Pia Zadora may show up and try to sing "The Star-Spangled Banner." The Democratic Party will make this proposed law the centerpiece of its campaign for the presidency.

You'd think that would produce all the alignment we'd need. Everything else should be a straightforward matter of logistics: planning, organizing, recruiting candidates to carry our banner. By the 1992 presidential election, Democrats should be positioned to hang Pia Zadora around George Bush's neck and pay him back for that Pledge-of-Allegiance number he ran on poor Mike Dukakis.

Sadly, aligning my organization around this new vision won't be that simple. The Democratic Party is sluggish, splintered, and set in its ways. It has the inertia of a continental land mass. It is rife with factionalism—hundreds of little interest groups, each with its own agenda. In short, it's a lot like your company.

Intel Corporation Chairman Andrew Grove observed in his latest book, *One on One with Andy Grove*, that, if management wants to introduce a major change to the organization, it must focus on middle managers. High-level managers should communicate their vision "directly and in depth" with large numbers of them, since middle managers are the ones whose control is direct enough and manageable enough to produce lasting changes. It will take a long time and

there are no shortcuts. Mr. Grove doesn't use the word "alignment" here, but that's what he's talking about.

Tom Peters doesn't use the word either, but alignment is what he's getting at in "Thriving on Chaos," when he urges corporate leaders to "develop and live an enabling and empowering vision. . . . Work with colleagues, work with customers, work with everyone to instill such a philosophy and vision."

So, if I want to align (small "a") all of you Democrats behind my vision, I must somehow enlist your support for the anthem switch as our central theme and the touchstone for all decisions we make. Whenever you are unsure about a course of action, I want you to stop and ask: Does this or does it not advance the cause of Ray vs. Pia? It won't be easy, but, to the extent that I can persuade you to do that, we have achieved alignment.

But suppose I find you insufficiently committed to the vision. Here's where Alignment will rear its head. It's not enough for me that you be entrepreneurial change-masters with a passion for excellence, whose renewal factors allow you to thrive on chaos while you reinvent this new corporation of ours. No. As your leader, I want to know you're really behind me on this Ray Charles thing. We can't get bogged down in the petty squabbling that arises when individuals with different personalities and outlooks try to accomplish something together. When I say we'll work as a team, it's not baseball I have in mind; it's the pairs competition of synchronized swimming. I want us to function as an organic whole—one brain with many hands. I want absolute dedication.

Of course, it's not as if my own sense of self-importance has anything to do with this. But I am, after all, the leader here. It's my vision we're supposed to follow. You can't very well expect me to leave it to chance that your idea of personal fulfillment will mesh exactly with my idea of how we're all going to walk and talk and dress and act and feel and think. In order to get each of you Aligned to your job, to your work team and to the overall team effort, I'm going to have to make some changes. In you. Surely you're not afraid of a little change, eh?

You'll be needing a positive, can-do attitude (like mine), so I'll require you to participate in my favorite personal-growth experience, which happens to be a fire-walking seminar. Beckoning you onward from the far end to the glowing pit will be that big poster of Ray and me.

And so on. You may think you resent some of this, but I know better. You're just "experiencing some natural discomfort with the change process." Pretty soon you'll be transformed. Happier. More productive. Brimming with team spirit. Aligned. Just like me. Sure you will.

CASE

BOB GALVIN AND MOTOROLA, INC. (A)

On April 24, 1983, the biennial meeting of Motorola, Inc.'s top 153 officers was drawing to a close, and Bob Galvin, chairman and chief executive officer of the $4 billion company, was about to offer his concluding comments. The theme of the two-day session had been "Managing Change," an appropriate topic, since the 55-year-old producer of electronics equipment had experienced a year of 15 percent growth—or half a billion dollars between 1982 and 1983. Galvin knew that the message he had in mind was surprising in light of the company's apparent success.

Increasingly as he "walked the halls"

This case was prepared by Research Associate Mary Gentile (under the direction of Professor Todd D. Jick).

of the corporation, Galvin had heard more and more complaints. Managers were upset by longer product development cycles, by too many layers in the management structure, and by ponderous, inflexible decision-approval processes. Galvin interpreted these frequently heard complaints in the context of a rapidly changing competitive environment. He recognized the growing threat from Japanese manufacturers to key Motorola products, such as cellular telephones and semiconductors. And much to the annoyance of his senior managers, he often asserted "we haven't even begun to compete internationally yet."

Galvin believed that the firm's current inability to respond quickly and flexibly to the changing needs of the customer could prove fatal in the coming global competitive crisis. Still, he kept asking himself if he, as chief executive officer, could make the kinds of changes Motorola needed. If he did nothing else in his last years before retirement, he wanted to reposition Motorola on the path toward renewed competitiveness. He knew this would be all the more difficult because many of his managers did not recognize the problems he saw. As he approached the speaker's podium, Galvin reflected that "I suppose I've been preparing for this speech for the last 45 years."

Motorola, Inc.

Galvin Manufacturing Company was founded by Paul V. Galvin, Bob Galvin's father, in 1928. The Chicago-based firm's earliest products were alternating electrical current converters and automobile radios. Paul Galvin dubbed the car radio he developed the "Motorola"—from motor and Victrola—and in 1947, this became the company's name as well.

From their firm's modest beginning with less than $1,500 in working capital and equipment, Paul Galvin and his brother, Joe, tried to create a humane and democratic work environment for their employees; everyone, from Paul Galvin himself to the newest production line employee, was addressed on a first-name basis; the Galvins had replaced the typical time clock in the plant with an employee honor system; and, by 1947, Paul Galvin established a profit-sharing program for the 2,000 workers the firm then employed. As a result of such efforts, Motorola remained union free.

Over the years, Motorola extended its product base to include home radios, phonographs, televisions, and transistors and semiconductor components. By 1983, however, under Bob Galvin's leadership, the firm had sold many of its consumer electronic businesses and developed other markets based on new technology. By then, the firm was composed of five geographically dispersed sectors or groups:

1. **The Semiconductor Products Sector**, with 1982 net sales of $1.3 billion, produced such products as microprocessors, memory chips, and integrated circuits.

2. **The Communications Sector**, with 1982 net sales of $1.5 billion, produced such products as two-way radios, paging devices, and cellular telephones.

3. **The Information Systems Group (ISG)**, with 1982 net sales of $485 million, produced an integrated line of data transmission and distributed data processing systems.

4. **The Automotive and Industrial Electronics Group (AIEG)** and **the Government Electronics Group (GEG)** had combined 1982 net sales of $564 million. AIEG produced such products as fuel-injection systems, electronic engine controls and instrumentation, and electronic appliance controls. GEG conducted research in satellite communications technology.

This product-focused organizational structure grew out of Paul and Bob Galvin's emphasis on the customers' interests and their concern that a large, centralized organization might not be responsive enough to those interests. Over the years, Motorola had gradually decentralized. In the 1950s, Paul Galvin formed divisions; in the early 1960s, Bob Galvin established product lines with product managers, who managed specific marketing and engineering areas, but who purchased the centralized manufacturing and sales functions. By the 1980s, the groups and sectors structure was in place, along with a multilayered matrix system of management. At the close of 1982, Motorola had approximately 75,000 employees, with operations in 15 foreign countries as well as the United States.

Bob Galvin

Bob Galvin joined the firm as a stock clerk in 1944, without completing his college degree. He worked in a variety of positions until 1948 when he became executive vice president. He became president in 1956, and chairman/chief executive officer in 1964.

Galvin was an equitable and accessible manager. His leadership style was rooted in humility and an abiding respect for his father's values. He often quoted Paul Galvin when explaining a decision he had made; and in assessing his own influence at Motorola, he pointed to the "privilege" of his long service with the firm, as well as to the "mantle" he had received from his father: "I am fortunate to carry some of his reputation, in addition to what I've earned myself." He was a serious and thoughtful man who defined his role as "leading the institution: I try to be a good listener, to look for the unattended, the void, the exception that my associates are too busy to see."

Over the years he had championed not only various reorganizational efforts and product/market shifts but a variety of participatory management, executive education, and strategic planning programs. For example, in the late 1960s, Motorola developed a technology innovation planning process—the Technology Roadmap—which involved the periodic projection of future technological developments and the subsequent planning and reviewing of the

firm's progress against that projection.

In the 1970s, Motorola developed the Participative Management Program (PMP) as a means to enhance productivity and employee involvement in the firm. PMP divided employees into small groups that met to discuss problems and potential improvements in their area of responsibility. Each group sent one member to report its ideas to the group one level up, which thereby enhanced communication in all directions. PMP efforts were also tied to a bonus incentive program.

Galvin's style and the Motorola culture were clearly people oriented. High value was placed on senior service and, in fact, no employee with more than 10 years' service could be fired without approval from Galvin himself. John Mitchell, Motorola's president, commented: "Bob *is* the culture here."

Some Motorola managers, however, criticized Motorola's "low demand environment," a tone set by Galvin himself. He devoted significant attention to the development of a strong managerial succession at Motorola and consequently was quite confident in Motorola's senior managers—his "family," as he called them. He felt convinced that, if he but pointed out a problem to his officers, they would certainly be motivated and capable of resolving it appropriately. From time to time he gave a speech on leadership as he perceived it (see Exhibit 1), including the following excerpt:

> Again we see the paradox of the leader—a finite person with an apparent infinite influence.
>
> A leader is decisive, is called on to make many critical choices, and can thrive on the power and the attention of that decision-making role. Yet the leader of leaders moves progressively away from that role.

EXHIBIT 1   Bob Galvin and Motorola, Inc. (A)

***

Speech by Bob Galvin on Leadership

I would like to share with you a special selective view of leadership. It finds its expression in a series of paradoxes.

We know so much about leadership, yet we know too little. We can define it in general, but find it hard to particularize. We recognize it when obvious, but it is not always obvious why. We practice leadership, which implies we are still preparing for the real thing.

It is neither necessary to impress on you an elaborate definition of leadership nor is this an appropriate time to characterize its many styles. Let it suffice that we acknowledge that no leader is worthy of the title absent creative and judgmental intelligence, courage, heart, spirit, integrity and vision applied to the accomplishment of a purposeful result through the efforts of followers and the leader. Rather, I elect to share with you some observations on a further series of paradoxes that reveal themselves as we analyze leadership.

When one is vested with the role of the leader, he inherits more freedom. The power of leadership endows him with rights to a greater range of self-determination of his own destiny. It is he who may determine the what or the how and the when or the where of important events.

Yet, as with all rights, there is a commensurate, balancing group of responsibilities that impose upon his freedom. The leader cannot avoid the act of determining the what or the who or the where. He cannot avoid being prepared to make these determinations. He cannot avoid being prepared to make these terminations. He cannot avoid seeing to their implementation. He cannot avoid living with the consequences of his decision on others and the demands these consequences impose on him. Only time will prove the merit of his stewardship. Because he is driven to pass this test of time, he will be obliged often to serve others more than himself. This obligation will more and more circumscribe his destiny. So those who assume true leadership will wonder from time to time if the apparent freedom of the leader adds a greater measure of independence, or whether the dependence of others on him restricts his own freedom.

For one to lead implies that others follow. But, is the leader a breed apart, or is he, rather, the better follower? Leadership casts the leader in many such roles:

- Observer—of the work his associates perform.
- Sensor—of attitudes, feelings, and trends.
- Listener—to ideas, suggestions, and complaints.
- Student—of advisors, inside and out of his situation.
- Product of experience—both his and others'.
- Mimic—of other leaders who have earned his respect.

Is he not the better follower, as he learns more quickly and surely from the past, selects the correct advice and trends, chooses the simpler work patterns and combines the best of other leaders? Is it not good leadership to know when not to follow an aimless path?

The paradox again: To lead well presumes the ability to follow smartly.

Because a leader is human and fallible, his leadership is in one sense finite—constrained by mortality and human imperfections. In another sense, the leader's influence is almost limitless.

He can spread hope, lend courage, kindle confidence, impart knowledge, give heart, instill spirit, elevate standards, display vision, set direction, and call for action today and each tomorrow.

The frequency with which one can perform these leadership functions seems without measure. His effectiveness and personal resources, rather than attenuating with use, amplify as he reuses and extends his skills.

EXHIBIT 1   (concluded)

Like the tree whose shadow falls where the tree is not, the consequence of the leader's act radiates beyond his fondest perception.

Again, we see the paradox of the leader—a finite person with an apparent infinite influence.

A leader is decisive—is called on to make many critical choices, and can thrive on the power and attention of that decision-making role. Yet, the leader of leaders moves progressively away from that role.

Yes, he or she can be decisive and command as required. Yet that leader's prime responsibility is not to decide or direct, but to create and maintain an evocative situation, stimulating an atmosphere of objective participation, keeping the goal in sight, recognizing valid consensus, inviting unequivocal recommendation, and finally vesting increasingly in others the privilege to learn through their own decision.

A wiser man puts it thus:

> We measure the effectiveness of the true leader, not in terms of the leadership he exercises, but in terms of the leadership he evokes; not in terms of his power over others but in terms of the power he releases in others; not in terms of the goals he sets and the direction he gives, but in terms of the plans of action others work out for themselves with his help; not in terms of decisions made, events completed, and the inevitable success and growth that follow such released energy, but in terms of growth in competence, sense of responsibility, and in personal satisfactions among many participants.
>
> Under this kind of leadership it may not always be clear at any given moment just who is leading. Nor is this important. What is important is that others are learning to lead well.

The complement to that paradox is that the growth that such leadership stimulates generates an ever-growing institution and an ever-increasing number of critical choices, more than enough of which fall squarely back on the shoulders of the leader who trained and willingly shared decision making with others.

And there are others which, if not paradoxes, at least are incongruities. Have we not witnessed some who have claimed leadership yet never fully achieved it? Have we not observed others who have shunned leadership only to have it thrust upon them?

Each of us here is at once part leader and part follower as we play our roles in life. Fortunately, there is a spark of leadership quality in many men and women, and, most fortunately, the flame of future leadership burns brightly in many who matriculate here. It is this wellspring from which we will draw and which gives us confidence for the continued advance of society.

On this day, you may feel a sense of relief that you have borne your final test. Walter Lippman, for one, would not long have let you cherish this illusion. He once observed:

> The final test of a leader is that he leaves behind in others the conviction and will to carry on.

This, for a few of the best of you here who would be leaders, may by the most personal paradox and crucial test of all.

Yes, he or she can be decisive and command as required. Yet that leader's prime responsibility is not to decide or direct but to create and maintain an evocative situation, stimulating an atmosphere of objective participation, keeping the goal in sight, recognizing valid consensus, inviting unequivocal recommendation, and finally vesting increasingly in others the privilege to learn through their own decisions.

Galvin hoped to encourage this "privilege" through the variety of innovative programs that Motorola adopted.

Motorola in 1983

Galvin believed, in the spring of 1983, that Motorola was poised on the edge of a new competitive era. The company had just come through a recession in the semiconductor industry, which had caused an 8 percent downturn in earnings between 1980 and 1982. Difficult as that period had been, however, Motorola's losses had been far less severe than those of competitors like Texas Instruments and Intel. "Motorola did see their profits slip by 6 percent during the worst year of the recession. But their arch-rivals, TI and Intel, experienced a 49 percent and 72 percent drop, respectively."[1] (See Exhibit 2.) And Galvin wanted to build on Motorola's strengths at a time when performance was beginning to look strong again. Although the first quarter was a bit slow, sales seemed to be on the upswing as Motorola faced the summer of 1983, and Galvin saw the national economy and his firm gearing up for rapid growth in the next few years. He recognized this growth as a blessing and a threat.

Increases in sales and earnings were welcome, of course, as was the accompanying confidence within the firm. However, rapid expansion brought new structural and managerial challenges and

exacerbated existing deficiencies. In addition, confidence could engender a dangerous complacency that made change all the more difficult. And finally, Galvin was all too cognizant of the cyclical nature of the semiconductor and computer industries and the growing threat of Japanese competition in both the communications and the semiconductor sectors of the business.

Galvin was also looking internally. One of Galvin's favored management techniques was walking the halls of the organization, listening to the ideas and the complaints of Motorola's employees, especially the middle managers. Galvin believed these managers were in touch with "real world" implementation issues that higher-level managers might miss because of their need to oversee so many different functions and systems. Galvin was a strong believer in open communications, and he encouraged employees at all levels to sit down with him in the company cafeteria at lunch, or to catch him in the halls of the firm to share their ideas and their criticisms.

Structural Issues

The issues he heard about in spring 1983 were disturbingly consistent with concerns that had been building throughout the 1970s. Galvin identified them as "structural concerns." Employees complained of the problems engendered by the sheer size and complexity of Motorola's matrix organization. Objective and methodology conflicts routinely developed between Motorola's customer-oriented functional managers (in sales or distribution, for example) and their product line managers. Although traditionally Galvin had always stressed the importance of staying close to the customer and the

[1] James O'Toole, "Second Annual NM Vanguard Award," *New Management* 3, no. 2 (Fall 1985), p. 5.

EXHIBIT 2   Bob Galvin and Motorola, Inc. (A)   (Motorola financial information, 1979–1982)

Four-Year Financial Summary
(Motorola, Inc., and consolidated subsidiaries, years ended December 31)

	Operating Results (in millions of dollars)			
	1982	1981	1980	1979
Net sales	$3,786	$3,570	$3,284	$2,879
Manufacturing and other administrative costs of sales	2,269	2,066	1,895	1,672
Selling, general, and administrative expenses	1,013	985	877	756
Depreciation and amortization of plant and equipment	244	205	173	132
Interest expense, net	48	35	43	27
Special charge	—	—	13	10
Total costs and other expenses	3,574	3,311	3,002	2,597
Earnings before income taxes and extraordinary gain	212	259	282	282
Income taxes	42	77	90	111
Net earnings before extraordinary gain	170	182	192	171
Net earnings as a percent of sales	4.5%	5.1%	5.8%	5.9%
Extraordinary gain	8	—	—	—
Net earnings	$ 178	$ 182	$ 192	$ 171

Sector Performance
(1979–1982)

Information by Industry Segment and Geographic Region: Information about the Company's operations in different industry segments for the years ended December 31 is summarized below (in millions of dollars).

	Net Sales				Operating Profit			
	1979	1980	1981	1982	1979	1980	1981	1982
Semiconductor products	$ 992	$1,222	$1,278	$1,298	$170	$186	$131	
Communications products	1,272	1,252	1,422	1,527	139	144	162	$ 97
Information systems products	NA	279	358	485	NA	34	42	31
Other products	7,655	683	718	564	14	26	50	44
Adjustments and eliminations	(61)	(60)	(82)	(88)	(3)	2	(4)	(7)
Industry totals	2,713	3,098	3,335	3,786	259	274	251	307

customer's needs, the complexity of the firm's products often caused product line managers to be more technology-driven than market-driven in their planning and managing processes.

No single manager was clearly responsible for a particular project through all its cycles, from its origin in customer discussions through design, development, testing, production, and into sales. Consequently, project deadlines set by engineers carried little weight with the production staff, and the needs of the sales and distribution managers were poorly integrated into the realities of the manu-facturing area. Galvin was alarmed by the ever-lengthening product development cycles.

Motorola's lines of authority were as often dotted as solid and spans of control were narrow. As the company grew and its products multiplied (see Exhibit 3), man-agement layers increased as well. One company study, completed in 1983, re-ported 9 to 12 layers between first-line managers and the executive level, with an average span of control over five people or fewer. Thirty percent managed three or fewer people. Individuals were struggling to preserve their turf and budget and main-tain internal performance standards. Long-term competitive strategy and cus-tomer needs were obscured by short-term incentives, and employees felt both over-managed and underdirected.

Top management's efforts to energize the firm and to enhance creative cooper-ation translated into programs like the periodic technology review and PMP, with their step-by-step procedures and committee-based processes. Such pro-grams involved employees at all levels and kept critical issues before them, but some managers worried that their format was too mechanistic and that they enabled em-ployees to comply with the letter, rather than the spirit, of the programs.

Finally, Motorola's chief executive of-fice was structured as a triumvirate, with Bob Galvin as chairman, William Weisz as vice chairman, and John Mitchell as president. Galvin defined their respective responsibilities as follows: "John Mitch-ell is running the business; Bill Weisz is managing the company; and my job is to lead the institution. And in a way, they are all the same thing." Mitchell elaborated: "Bill Weisz and I share the COO position. I handle the Communications Sector, the

Automotive and Industrial Electronic Group, and Japan; Bill handles the Semi-conductor Products Sector, the Informa-tion Systems Group, and the Government Electronics Group." Galvin saw the chief executive office as a model of democratic practice and open communications for the firm.

However, this tripartite structure was one of the other complaints that circulated among Motorola's managers. Mitchell ex-plained: "They call us the three bears and they ask 'why can't you be single in voice, style, and direction?' "

Galvin reviewed the concerns he had gathered from Motorola's managers; from his son, Chris, who worked in the Communications Sector; and from his own observations. Taken alone, he be-lieved they were cause for concern. When he also considered the rapid growth Mo-torola appeared to face as the economy emerged from the last two years of reces-sion, and the growing competitive threat from Japan, Galvin became convinced that it was time for action.

Japanese Competition

Motorola was one of the world's lead-ing producers of two-way radios, cellular telephone systems, semiconductors, and microprocessor chips, and Japan was competing in and threatening each of these markets. The firm faced Japanese market practices, such as "dumping" (selling product at less than "fair value" as a way to increase market share quickly) and "tar-geting" (the cooperative efforts of a group of Japanese firms, supported by Japanese law, to break into and capture a particular international market, such as computer memory chips). In response to these chal-lenges, Galvin worked with federal for-eign relations and trade committees,

EXHIBIT 3   Bob Galvin and Motorola, Inc. (A)

Motorola Products

Semiconductor Products Sector
Bubble memories
Custom and semicustom semiconductors
Fiber optic active components
Field effect transistors
Interface circuits
Microcomputer board-level products
Microcomputer systems
Microprocessors
Microwave devices
MOS and bipolar anolog ICs
MOS and bipolar digital ICs
MOS and bipolar memories
MPU develop system hardware
    and software
Operational amplifiers
Optoelectronics components
Power supply circuits
Pressure and temperature sensors
Rectifiers
RF modules
RF power and small signal transistors
Telecommunication circuits
Thyristors
Triggers
VLSI macrocell arrays
Voltage regulator circuits
Zener and tuning diodes

Communications Sector
Base stations
Car telephone systems
Closed-circuit television systems
Communications control centers
Component products
Digital voice-protection systems
Electronic command and control systems
Health care communications systems
Information-display systems
Microwave communications systems
Mobile and portable FM two-way
    radio communications systems
Portable data terminals
Radio paging systems
Signaling and remote control systems
Test equipment

Information Systems Group
Communications processors
Data network analyzers/emulators
Digital service/channel service units
Electronic data switches
Intelligent terminals
Leased-line modems
Limited distance modems
Local area networks
Modems
Multifunction computer systems for
    distributed information processing and
    office automation applicances
Multiplexers
Network and management systems
OEM modem cards
Software for data entry, word processing,
    office management
Switched network modems
System processors
Technical control facilities
Video operator stations

Automotive and Industrial Electronics Group
Alternator charging systems
Automotive and industrial digital
    instrumentation (tachometers, speedometers,
    odometers, hourmeters), and electronic
    instrument clusters
Automotive and industrial digital monitoring
    systems
Automotive and industrial sensors
CRT display monitors, color and
    monochrome (5'' to 23'')
Data and graphics terminals and subsystems
Electronic appliance controls
Electronic engine and powertrain controls
Electronic engine governors
Electronic fuel-handling systems
Electronic ignition systems
Electronic motor controls
Electronic regulators
Electronic transmission controls
Engine management systems
Telecommunications equipment
Vehicle monitoring and recording systems
Wireless systems and devices

EXHIBIT 3   (concluded)

Motorola Products

Government Electronics Group
Countermeasures systems
Drone command and control systems
Electronic fuse systems
Electronic positioning and tracking
    systems
Fixed and satellite communications
    systems
Intelligent display terminals and systems

Missile and aircraft instrumentation
Missile guidance systems
Satellite survey and positioning systems
Secure communications
Surveillance radar systems
Tracking and command transponder systems
Video processing systems and products

attempting to fight "unfair" trade practices and protectionism:

> Testifying before the Senate Foreign Relations Committee last September [1982], he said U.S. policy on trade in high-technology products should make it clear that this country "will not accept a situation where foreign national industrial policies, based on nonmarket mechanisms and unreasonable trade practices, enable any country to disrupt U.S. markets, prevent reasonable access to its home markets, or give unjustified advantage to its firms in pursuing Third World markets."[2]

Galvin also knew, however, that he had to make changes closer to home, within Motorola. His success in obtaining an order from Nippon Telegraph & Telephone Public Corporation for paging devices in early 1982 was a result both of pressure from the United States government and Motorola's efforts to produce 100 percent defect-free product. And even during the difficult recession years of 1981–82, Motorola continued to invest in research and development, in order to

position itself competitively for the market growth it believed would follow. Galvin thought that effective competition with the Japanese meant not only modifications in federal trade regulations but Motorola's investment in R&D, enhanced productivity, and quality control. And he believed the means to this end were through the company's employees. This was consistent with the kind of thinking behind PMP, 10 years earlier.

As Galvin considered his company's current condition and challenges, he felt a great sense of personal urgency. He was 61 years old, nearing retirement, and he wanted to leave a strong and healthy company to his family of managers. And although he wasn't certain how to implement a process of "renewal" at Motorola, he was quite confident of the need. He remembered his father's advice to "just get in motion" when action was required, confident that he would find his way.

Motorola Biennial Officer's Meeting: April 1983

Galvin came to the officers' meeting[3]

---

[2] Grover Herman, "Competing with the Japanese," *Nation's Business*, November 1982, p. 48.

[3] "Officers" refer to both business officers and officers of the corporation (appointed and elected

with his mind full of a recent trip to Japan. He had been impressed by the commitment of the industry employees he saw there and with the cutting-edge production technology the Japanese firms utilized. On the long plane ride back to the United States, Galvin had been reading the current management best-seller, *In Search of Excellence*. Its authors, Peters and Waterman, advocated simpler organizational structures with direct ties to the consumer.

With all these observations, conclusions, and influences in his mind, Galvin felt an uncanny, undeniable immediacy in his senior officers' discussion of their efforts to manage change. Every time an individual complained of too many layers of command, Galvin winced—"There it is again." Each time an officer mentioned the absence of realistic and convincing deadlines that made sense across departments, Galvin sighed—"There it is again." He knew he needed no more evidence. He was sure of his message and of its significance.

As the meeting drew to a close, his staff expected Galvin's usual clear, concise, concluding summary. Instead he stood up and issued a challenge. He called upon his senior managers to take a fresh look at their organizations and to consider structural changes—smaller, more focused business units. He wanted to decrease the many layers of management and to bring management closer to the product and the market. Galvin spoke with ease and conviction: "My message was spontaneous in tone and mood, but it had been building out of years of experience. I had been hearing this mes-

sage from my middle managers and I'm a good listener."

In his speech, Galvin stressed Motorola's

> ... constant thrust for renewal. Renewal is the most driving word in this corporation for me, the continual search for ways to get things done better.
>
> As I walk the halls, I keep my ears open and I keep picking up signals. A middle manager might tell me that he can't understand how the business did because we keep aggregating our results into one big number. Or another might tell me he thinks he has a good idea but he can't get the authority to get it done.
>
> I see a welling up of the evidence of need, and today I think the window is open. So I decided to express my concern and my conviction to you, confident that you share my insights and that together we will find our way to an organized effort of change. When we come together in two years, we will report and share the changes made and the lessons learned.

Galvin had not discussed this presentation with Weisz or Mitchell beforehand. Nor had he explicitly addressed with his human resources staff the issue of structural reorganization as the key method of a change at Motorola. He was confident that he knew his audience, his "constituency," and that they would welcome his challenge.

As Galvin concluded, however, and managers stood and began to move out of the room, the buzzing conversations were colored more by surprise and confusion than eagerness. Suddenly the firm's rising sales were a problem. Was this just another PMP pep talk? Was Galvin serious about restructuring the organization? Who would be responsible for this? Even Galvin's wife, Mary, turned to him later

---

VPs). Elected officers are elected by the board of directors, and appointed officers must be approved by the chief executive officer.

that evening and asked: "What exactly did you have in mind, Bob?"

That was Friday evening. On Monday morning, the calls started coming in to Galvin's office, to Joe Miraglia, corporate vice president and director of human resources, and passed back and forth between the various senior managers. Rumors were spreading: people wanted to know what had Galvin been reading, and with whom had he been talking? One senior manager jested that perhaps Galvin was miffed that Motorola had not been mentioned enough by the authors of *In Search of Excellence*. But everyone wanted to know: what did Galvin mean and was he serious?

Responses to Galvin's Challenge

The Chief Executive Office. Responses to Galvin's surprise speech varied according to each individual's position and to the implications of this challenge for his or her responsibilities. William Weisz, vice chairman, and John Mitchell, president, for example, did not expect the timing and form of Galvin's presentation. The message itself, however, felt familiar. It coincided with both a long-term trend in Motorola toward decentralization and with Galvin's constant concern for the customer's needs. Mitchell commented:

> Bob Galvin's style is to make strong statements like "the implied solution to the problems of the matrix is to divide the company into small businesses." This took people aback. It sounded simplistic and it sounded like it would start right away.

Both Mitchell and Weisz could place Galvin's comments into a context, knowing and trusting the CEO as they did, and although they may not have chosen the timing and the particular solution Galvin

proposed, they agreed with his diagnosis of Motorola's ills. As Galvin explained: "The vice chairman came on board with me on this issue in the spirit of faith and of insight. The president was preoccupied with running the business, but he came on as well."

Operating Officers. For many of the top sector and group officers at Motorola there was an initial hesitancy about Galvin's unexpected spontaneous challenge, according to Robert Schaffer, an external consultant who interviewed these officers. Although they recognized that Galvin was earnest, they asked themselves some questions before considering what their response would be and how serious an effort was involved. Was this another in a string of innovations that arose from the visionary Galvin? Was this a commitment by all three chief executive officers or something Galvin alone would pursue as a reflection of his frustration? Would the head of any unit take this as a commitment to action? Did Galvin already have answers or was he willing and ready to open up the issue for questions?

Many of the firm's top officers did not share Galvin's sense of urgency about Motorola's competitive position. The company had a tradition of market strength and of technological leadership. Employees felt secure there; the culture placed a premium on commitment and length of service. And in the spring of 1983, the outlook looked particularly good for semiconductor products. For despite the threat posed by Japanese competitors, the company had grown by half a billion dollars in the last year and it was still moving. One vice president in the Semiconductor Products Sector explained that Galvin's biggest problem in selling his change agenda was the "status quo: Managers here are scientists. They see themselves and the sector as renegades on the leading edge of technology; but when it comes to management and productivity measures, they stick with 'what worked before.' " Even in the Communications Sector, where Japanese competition was posing a very serious threat to the pager business and to the just burgeoning cellular telephone business, much of the blame was placed on "unfair" Japanese trade practices.

Perhaps managerial resistance to Galvin's challenge was all the more prevalent because no one was quite sure what he was proposing. Was this a major and radical call to action or only a proposal for new executive training? Many believed it was the latter and, thus, even those managers who shared Galvin's concern for Motorola's competitive position were doubtful that more educational programs would make a difference. If, on the other hand, Galvin was ordering a concrete structural change (an action that would be uncharacteristically directive), then he needed to be more precise. In the meantime, many managers simply waited for the thing to blow over.

Human Resources. In the ensuing days, while top management struggled to understand what Galvin had meant in his speech and what implications it had for them, Galvin himself met with Joe Miraglia, vice president of human resources at Motorola, whom he considered his "professional pivot point" within the organization; Galvin took the human resources function very seriously. The two promptly set about developing the vision the chief executive officer had introduced. Although Miraglia did not question Galvin's identification of problems in the organization, he commented:

Bob's idea was to create smaller business units more functionally integrated at lower levels. We in human resources disagreed; structure was not the sole answer. We didn't want this to be seen as just a structural solution imposed from above by "those who know better."

Miraglia believed Galvin's vision had to be developed and that his influence had to be focused more clearly.

Nevertheless, Miraglia and his staff within the sectors supported Galvin's basic assumptions. Phil Nienstedt, manager of Human Resources Programs for Semiconductor Products, explained:

Business had been good in 1983, but it was something of a false prosperity as the company came off the leaner recession years. The company was growing with little control or discipline. Galvin was hitting some hot buttons in the officers' meeting when he said we needed to focus on the customer, to develop flexibility, smaller business entities, wider spans, less levels, fewer inefficiencies. The human resources staff had discussed these issues with Joe Miraglia before. But Bob Galvin was vague and unclear as to what he wanted to do about these things. I think he did this intentionally, to be provocative, to get people thinking and wondering. The problem with this kind of change, however, is that short-term objectives, like getting the work out the door, get in the way of addressing this kind of long-term problem.

Dick Wintermantel, director of Organization and Human Resources in the Semiconductor Products Sector, pointed to another inhibitor to change:

It's difficult for managers to make changes at Motorola, and many times this difficulty relates to core cultural values that served the company well on its way *up* the growth curve, but which may be dysfunctional now. For example, respect for senior service may run counter to competitive staffing needs. Once you have 10 years of service, you're treated with employment *and* job security. We are constrained to redeploy people even if there are strategic and competitive reasons to do so.

Always responding to the customer's request for new products can result in thousands of products and no coherent and efficient organization. A mentality of "we can do it ourselves" runs counter to the alliances necessary for penetrating offshore markets and resources. And, finally, a mistrust of "systems" and "bureaucracy" can obstruct the development of necessary cost reduction systems or worldwide communications systems.

Although the HR team shared Galvin's sense of urgency and his belief in the necessity for change, they questioned both his structural focus and some aspects of the culture he had built. Miraglia explained: "Bob Galvin is confident that, if his senior line managers agree with him, they will be able to assemble the infrastructure necessary to make change happen." The HR staff believed that neither managerial agreement nor an effective change process would be easy to come by.

READING

FROM BOGGED DOWN TO FIRED UP: INSPIRING ORGANIZATIONAL CHANGE

Bert A. Spector
Northeastern University

My point is simply this—managing organizational change is a topic American business needs to examine and understand because fundamental change will be the order of the day for the foreseeable future. [1]

The statement above, made by the president of Southwestern Bell, reflects a growing consensus among U.S. business leaders concerning the demands that will be placed upon them and their organizations in the coming decades. That consensus has two distinct dimensions:

• Massive organizational change is inevitable given the volatile nature of our competitive environment.

• Adaptable, flexible organizations will enjoy a distinct competitive advantage over rigid, static ones.

Scholars, too, have been paying attention to the dynamics of large-scale organizational change. How do organizations change? More specifically, how can our understanding of organizational change inform the actions of managers who want

From *Sloan Management Review*, Summer 1989.

to transform their own organizations?

A key question for scholars concerns the initial stage of the change effort; that is, how do managers create a state of organizational *readiness* for change? Organizations are bureaucracies, and as such, Renato Mazzolini says, they tend almost naturally to resist change.[2] Barry Shaw explains at least some components of that resistance less in terms of bureaucratic organizational structure than in terms of individual behavior. Organizational members become committed to a course of action and then escalate that commitment out of a sense of self-justification.[3] In order to overcome such resistance to change, extraordinary pressures must be brought to bear on organizations and individuals.

The need for this pressure has long been recognized by students of organizational change. Michael Beer, for instance, notes that organizational arrangements experience pressure to change only when they no longer allow the organization to respond to new competitive or environmental conditions.[4] Dissatisfaction with the status quo, in other words, fuels organizational change.

But the literature on change tends to focus exclusively on how such pressures are experienced and acted upon by top managers or unit leaders. "*Top management* [emphasis added] seems to be groping for a solution to its problems," writes Larry Greiner of the opening stages of organizational change.[5] Wendell French and Cecil Bell agree: "Initially, in successful organization development efforts, there is strong pressure for improvement, at least on *top management* [emphasis added] of an organization or one of its subunits, from both inside and outside the organization."[6] Noel Tichy and Dave Ulrich elaborate on this view: "The *dom-*

inant group [emphasis added] in the organization must experience a dissatisfaction with the status quo."[7] Those dissatisfied leaders, in turn, mobilize commitment to a new vision and translate that vision into practice by institutionalizing reinforcements for a new organizational culture.

A recent study of organizational change and revitalization conducted by the author with colleagues Michael Beer and Russell Eisenstadt suggests that the dissatisfaction of top leaders may well be *necessary* in order to initiate an organizationwide change process, but that dissatisfaction alone is hardly *sufficient* to bring about and sustain real change.

Changing Organizations

Our study targeted six companies engaged in a process of organizational revitalization; these firms were attempting to fundamentally redefine the relationship between individual employees and the corporation in order to make the organization more competitive. We selected six companies that would provide a range of organizational forms—centralized and decentralized—as well as of industries—smokestack manufacturing, financial services, consumer electronics, and information systems.

The research methodology included extensive field interviews and observations conducted over a four-year period. We spent five to six weeks, and in some instances longer, in each company. We started by interviewing human resource executives and then visited various plants, branches, and divisions. In all locations, we interviewed key line managers, employees at all levels, human resource, staff, union leaders if there were any, and consultants. Finally, we interviewed top corporate executives. Later we made follow-up visits to get longitudinal data on the change process.

When the fieldwork was completed, we ranked the six companies on an effectiveness dimension: how innovative were their changes, and to what extent had innovations permeated the organization? We ranked each individual unit visited, as well as the corporations as a whole. Data from the questionnaires distributed to organizational members after the field research was factored into the judgments of effectiveness.

What became clear to us was that organizational leaders do not change organizations. What they do is to oversee and orchestrate a process in which line managers up and down the organization attempt to change their own operating units. Plant managers seek increased worker commitment to enhance productivity and quality as well as shopfloor flexibility. Divisional leaders encourage general managers to do more collaboration and problem solving. Unit leaders try to instill employees with more aggressiveness and responsiveness. While leaders may be convinced of the need for change based on their own dissatisfaction with the status quo, that dissatisfaction is not enough. They must find ways of sharing it with the members of the organization who will actually institute new ways of thinking and acting.

This distinction between a dissatisfied leader and a leader who *diffuses dissatisfaction throughout the organization* is more than a simple refinement of the existing theory of organizational change. Overlooking the diffusion step can be (and often is) profoundly debilitating. When leaders jump directly from being dissatisfied to imposing new operating models, they fail to generate any real commitment

to change. Employees greet new organizational and behavioral models with resistance or, at best, half-hearted compliance. Change programs get bogged down, and leaders become frustrated by employees' failure to perceive the dire and seemingly obvious need for change.

Strategies for Diffusing Dissatisfaction

In the successful change efforts that we observed, the top leader's desire for change was inevitably followed by interventions that diffused his or her dissatisfaction. The interventions can be sorted into four generic types.

- Sharing competitive information.
- Pointing to shortcomings in individual, on-the-job behaviors.
- Offering models that suggest not just where the company ought to be headed but also how far it is from that goal.
- Mandating dissatisfaction.

Sharing Competitive Information. The most common method for diffusing dissatisfaction was the dissemination of information. Usually the information consisted of details about the company or unit's competitive position. For the most part, this information had previously been available *only* to top management.

Information sharing of this kind is a symbolic way of equalizing power, overcoming conflict, and building trust.[8] It also spreads dissatisfaction. The case of Scranton Steel's Youngstown plant illustrates this use of information sharing.[9]

As the competitive crisis within the steel industry in general and at Scranton Steel in particular mounted, plant manager Fred Howard started sharing competitive information throughout the plant. "If you look at the newsletters we're sending out now," he said, "quite frankly there's information in there that in the past wouldn't have been given to all our employees. On a case-by-case basis, we've given departments actual profit information on their products. Ten years ago, this wouldn't even have been considered."[10]

And what was the impact of this information sharing? One of the key stakeholders was the local United Steelworkers' union. Because of the existing contract, little change could occur in the way work was organized on the shop-floor without the union's okay. The local union president *did* support Howard's call to change, reporting that Howard's willingness to share information—"to open the books to the union"—convinced him that the plant faced a severe competitive crisis. The information made union leaders, as well as rank-and-file workers, aware that maintaining the status quo would result in extensive layoffs, if not a plant closing. Thus, as dissatisfaction spread beyond the plant manager's office into the union hall, union leaders and the employees they represented began working closely with management on a wide variety of labor innovations.

The information sharing we observed was sometimes less rooted in specific competitive data than was the case at Youngstown. When Hugh Dorsey assumed control of the Fairweather Corporation, he presented not competitive data but an organizational diagnosis, and not by quietly disseminating information throughout the organization—he took his blunt, prodding diagnosis to the press. Dorsey talked freely to national and local reporters about his belief that poor management had undermined Fairweather's competitive position.

Similarly, when Henry Lester became president of US Financial, he frequently used the press as a platform. Almost immediately after becoming president, he announced on the pages of a national business magazine his intention of turning US Financial's "cautious and conservative style into a more streamlined and venturesome enterprise that stresses a market-oriented strategy and strategic planning." His use of the press as a bully pulpit from which to spread his message through the ranks of the organization continued throughout his tenure; he later used *Business Week* to complain about the risk-averse, noninnovative culture that he claimed permeated upper management.

Based on our research, these two approaches to information sharing are not equally effective. Most managers at Fairweather and US Financial reported being aware that their leaders' public statements indicated a high level of dissatisfaction. But they also reported feeling resentful toward these highly public and extremely critical comments. "These are matters that should not be aired in public," stated one of Dorsey's direct reports. Said another, "Dorsey talks about 'tough love' when he makes these statements. Well, as far as I can see, there's no 'love' here. Just a lot of 'tough.' " These managers and others like them remained in the organization, but top management's approach may well have caused them to resist or to comply only minimally with proposed changes.

Creating Behavioral Dissatisfaction. Sharing competitive information is intended to unfreeze attitudes and shake up the status quo. But organizational change has a micro as well as a macro perspective; it also focuses on individual managers' on-the-job behaviors and styles.

The field of organizational development has long recognized and employed such individually oriented interventions, ranging from T-groups and team building to more systematic ways of analyzing, categorizing, and transforming managerial behavior. Half the companies in our study used specific strategies to change individual behavior; interventions were designed to create dissatisfaction with the way managers were currently behaving.

Shortly after becoming president of US Financial, for instance, Henry Lester introduced attitude surveys that would be given regularly throughout the organization. The main tool was an employee opinion survey administered annually to about half the company's employees. It included a core group of about fifty questions designed to elicit a "general satisfaction level"; each division could add its own questions to meet specific needs. The results were broken down by units and given to unit managers, who were expected to conduct feedback sessions with employees and "contract" for some specific actions to address issues raised by the survey.

Both Scranton Steel and Fairweather relied heavily on team building as part of their change process. At Scranton Steel, it occurred at the plant level as a follow-up to local union-management agreements. Immediately following an agreement to work toward improved quality of worklife and productivity, there was an off-site session attended by top plant management and local union leadership. Specifics of the change process were worked out at that session, but participants from both union and management reported that the meeting was more important from the perspective of team development. External faciliators

helped participants from both sides confront behavioral impediments to future collaboration. Said Howard, "If I could isolate one important step in getting us on the right footing, it would be the off-site. To me, that was a major turning point. When the meeting ended, it was clear to me just how similar our goals and ends really were. The process of getting away was an absolutely necessary step."

Fairweather's experience with team building was not nearly as successful. Immediately after assuming the presidency, Hugh Dorsey adopted an explicit strategy for building dissatisfaction with managerial behavior. He arranged for his managers to be taken off-site in groups of 25 to 30; for five days they were put through a rigorous behavioral workshop that included self-assessment, lectures, team-building exercises, role playing, skits, and outdoor "survival" exercises all designed to point out shortcomings in current behavior and foster the new behaviors desired by Dorsey.

The actual impact of this behavioral intervention was evidently somewhat limited. Participants openly wondered about its relevance to their work lives. Organizers worried that they had never successfully followed up on the insights and commitments made at the off-site sessions. And Dorsey himself, although still a supporter of this type of intervention, conceded that the resulting change had been too small and had occurred too slowly to help save the company from its declining competitive position.

How can we account for the apparently significant differences in the impact of interventions aimed at creating dissatisfaction with behaviors? The key variable in the examples here seems to be the degree to which the dissatisfaction resulted from actual on-the-job behaviors or was imposed upon managers by the leader. US Financial's use of attitude surveys did seem to have some immediate impact. The company's own internal research could formally track improved attitudes and informally point to improved bottom-line performance in divisions that used the surveys rigorously. And the dissatisfaction reported in those surveys was produced, at least indirectly, by how managers actually behaved on the job. However, the positive impact proved to be transitory. Little evidence could be found regarding any real long-term changes in on-the-job behaviors.

Scranton Steel's team building proved more successful. Remember, though, that it occurred in this context: managers *had* to behave in new ways as they began working with union representatives to solve real business problems. The literature on plant-level change where unions are involved indicates that Youngstown's example is far from unique.[11] When managers work with unions in new ways, some training mechanism is required to confront, indeed change, traditional modes of behavior.

Fairweather's experience with team building was the least successful intervention. Whereas US Financial's attitude survey related directly to performance behaviors, and team building at Scranton Steel followed up union-management agreements that require changing old patterns of adversarial behavior, Dorsey's intervention seemed (to many participants) to be rooted less concretely in the needs of the business. The off-site sessions followed Dorsey's own assessment that his company needed to foster more collaboration among employees if they were to compete more successfully. Partici-

pants were not so sure. Some used words like "weird" and "crazy," while others dismissed the whole exercise as brainwashing. "You guys are trying to——with our minds" was the blunt assessment of one disgruntled participant. A key organizer admitted that participants found it difficult to take what they had learned back to their day-to-day work situation.

The changes promoted at Fairweather's off-site sessions, in other words, seemed to meet the needs of one individual—Hugh Dorsey—rather than to address the demands of the business. Thus, they could easily be dismissed.

Using Models to Produce Dissatisfaction.   Scholars and managers alike stress that successful models encourage change to occur. They provide a vision of the future, and they can also help spread dissatisfaction with the status quo.[12]

Scranton Steel, for instance, used internal subunit models to build dissatisfaction. Almost immediately after a union contract made collaborative quality-of-worklife efforts possible, Scranton Steel's head of labor relations began working with consultants on a process to ensure successful implementation. The consultants suggested using a survey to identify plants where implementation was most likely to succeed. These plants would already be close to the new model: a high level of union-management cooperation, managers whose problem-solving style had already become more participative, and generally positive working conditions.

The survey identified two possible plants, but the process had a more far-reaching impact than that. Information about these sites got back to the nondesignated plants; as managers at the firm's two largest plants realized, they had not even been considered, and, as word spread that the new chairman had endorsed joint union-management efforts in the strongest possible terms, anxieties began to arise. A member of the task force created to oversee implementation recalled, "Plant managers were saying to us, 'If we're not ready, what do we need to do to get ready?' " Key line managers began to demand a process that would move them toward revitalization. Holding some plants up as models of readiness, in other words, created dissatisfaction in many of the organization's other plants.

Mandating Dissatisfaction. When Don Singer, the newly named chairman of Scranton Steel, announced at an executive meeting what changes he considered necessary, one member of his management team objected. "You're talking about participative management—about collaborating with the union, information sharing, cooperative problem solving. But it won't be so easy. There's a lot of history to overcome." Singer listened while the executive finished this cautionary speech. He then pointed his finger directly at the executive and said, "Things are going to change around here. This is a way of life. And if things don't change," he added, "I won't be the first to go." Hugh Dorsey delivered virtually the same message: you must change according to my diagnosis of what needs to be done or leave the organization.

It would be difficult to pinpoint the precise impact of such a threat. In both cases, it was used only once. (This may be a case of "once is enough," since intimidating messages spread quickly.) Nevertheless, judging from the reports of managers, these mandates seemed to create compliance more than commitment. At Scranton Steel, the manager to whom the warning was delivered reacted by repressing any further public objections and reluctantly going along with the effort. He never agreed to an interview for the research project, so I cannot offer any direct insight into his thought processes. But subordinates and superiors alike agreed about his lack of enthusiasm and commitment. The chairman took to referring to the individual as his "internal resister."

Occasionally, the individuals to whom warnings were issued were replaced at a later stage of the change process. But while they were with the company, they almost never wholeheartedly accepted the leader's diagnosis. Top-down commands and threats violate the notion of free choice; doubters don't feel they "own" the choice to adopt new patterns of behavior.

At least one mandate proved much more effective. Duluth Products, the most successful "change" company in our sample, used models designed to create dissatisfaction, as well as a kind of threat, though not one aimed directly at individuals. After some early successes at job restructuring, participative management, and gain-sharing plans in small, relatively isolated plants, chief operating officer John Watson simply mandated dissatisfaction with the status quo throughout the organization. He made no explicit threats to job security. Instead, he announced that future corporate investments would go only to plants that undertook similar innovations. If plant managers did not yet share Watson's dissatisfaction with the status quo, Watson would provide them with a new source of dissatisfaction: you will lose corporate investment and support if you maintain the status quo.

TABLE 1   Dissatisfaction Diffusion Interventions

Company	Sharing Competitive Information	Pointing to Individual Behavior	Using Original Models	Mandating Dissatisfaction
Leading Company (Duluth Products)	X		X	X
Middle Company (Scranton Steel)	X	X	X	X
Lagging Company (US Financial)	X	X		

Diffusing Dissatisfaction—A Key Concern

While this article has identified four distinct strategies for diffusing dissatisfaction, it is clear that not all applications of those strategies are equally effective in promoting change. Table 1 lays out the intervention strategies employed by three of the companies in our research sample: the leading change company (Duluth Products), the lagging company (US Financial), and a middle-level company (Scranton Steel). Although overall success in transforming organizations rests on far more than the initial intervention strategy, the evidence is nonetheless revealing on several points:

- First, no single intervention alone is sufficient to diffuse dissatisfaction properly.

- Second, pointing to individual behaviors early in the change process is not necessarily associated with success. Successful transformations aim to change the organizational context in which individual behaviors occur, rather than the behaviors themselves. Individual behavioral changes result from contextual interventions, not from direct assaults on those behaviors.

- Third, consistent with much previous literature on organizational change, models can show both where the organization is headed and how great a gap exists between the reality and the goal. The use of models seems to be a key element in diffusion strategies.

- Fourth, some sort of forcing strategy also seems to be a key element, although, as noted earlier, some forcing strategies are more effective than others.

It is commonplace to see dissatisfied leaders who attempt to impose change on organizational members who are not ready—and yet this pattern is inevitably disastrous. Of our six case studies, five started with a dissatisfied leader who imposed change programs. In each instance, little real change occurred. We need to add a new step to our understanding of how change unfolds: the leader with a "felt need" for change must diffuse dissatisfaction before lasting change can occur.

References

1. Z. E. Barnes. "Change in the Bell System." *Academy of Management Executive* 1 (February 1987), p. 43.

2. R. Mazzolini. "Strategy: A Bureaucratic and Political Process," in *Competitive Strategic Management,* ed. R. B. Lamb. Englewood Cliffs, N.J.: Prentice Hall, 1984.
3. B. M. Shaw. "The Escalation of Commitment to a Course of Action." *Academy of Management Review* 6 (1981), pp. 577–87.
4. M. Beer. *Organization Change and Development: A Systems View.* New York: Scott, Foresman, 1980.
5. L. E. Greiner. "Patterns of Organization Change." *Harvard Business Review,* May–June 1967, p. 122.
6. W. L. France and C. H. Bell, Jr. *Organization Development,* 3rd ed. Englewood Cliffs, N.J.: Prentice Hall, 1984, p. 216.
7. N. Tichy and D. Ulrich "Revitalizing Organizations: The Leadership Role" in *Managing Organizational Transitions,* ed. J. R. Kimberly and R. E. Quinn,

Homewood, Ill.: Richard D. Irwin, 1984, p. 245.
8. This use of information sharing as opposed to information hoarding has been discussed in: R. R. Blake et al., *Managing Intergroup Conflict in Industry.* Houston, Tex.: Gulf, 1964; and in R. E. Walton and R. McKersie, *A Behavioral Theory of Labor Negotiations.* New York: McGraw-Hill, 1965.
9. Company names were disguised.
10. Unless otherwise noted, all quotes were collected as part of the field research.
11. See, for example: J. M. Rosow, *Teamwork: Joint Labor Management Teams in America,* ed. New York: Pergamon Press, 1986.
12. See, for example: Beer (1980); Tichy and Ulrich (1984); and G. Barczak et al., "Managing Large-Scale Organizational Change," *Organizational Dynamics,* Autumn 1987, pp. 22–35.

READING

AKERS TO IBM EMPLOYEES: WAKE UP!

Paul B. Carroll
Staff Reporter of The Wall Street Journal

International Business Machines Corporation Chairman John F. Akers is fed up.

Although IBM may publicly blame its problems on a slow economy, Mr. Akers is saying the real problem goes far deeper. He is telling IBM managers that IBM has been steadily losing market share to competitors—and that he's tired of it. He is complaining that the quality of IBM products is inadequate. In addition, he is

telling managers to fire far more marginal employees.

While bits and pieces of Mr. Akers's message have made their way outside IBM's walls over the past few months, the most detailed and sternest version yet has surfaced in the form of notes that an IBM manager took at a small group seminar Mr. Akers addressed a month ago. The manager, Brent Henderson, who wasn't available for comment, apparently thought he was circulating the notes just to people in his area. But, through the

---

From *The Wall Street Journal*, May 29, 1991.

magic of IBM's extensive electronic mail network, the word quickly spread through the company.

"We won't rip the IBM Company up in a bad economic cycle . . . but after six years with one approach . . . it's time to try another," the notes quote Mr. Akers as saying.

Mr. Akers's pique and dismay are surfacing at a time when IBM's reputation for leadership in the computer industry, a key technology for American industrial success in the 21st century, is under broad re-examination. IBM's overall market share worldwide has slipped to about 23 percent from 37 percent as recently as 1983, according to the Gartner Group, Inc., market research firm. The company's reputation as a stock market leader and growth stock that always rebounds from adversity is also losing currency.

All of that frustrates Mr. Akers, who has been straining to rejuvenate the company since its earnings hit their peak in 1984 but has only managed to stem the speed at which competitors have eroded IBM's proud tradition. Mr. Akers is 3 . 5 years away from IBM's mandatory retirement age of 60 and is starting to talk in terms of what he hopes will be his legacy, so there seems to be a heightened sense of urgency in his statements.

Much of what Mr. Akers described would consist simply in communicating that urgency to employees. "The fact that we're losing market share makes me goddam mad. I used to think my job as a [sales] rep was at risk if I lost a sale. Tell them theirs is at risk if they lose one," Mr. Akers is quoted as saying.

"I'm sick and tired of visiting plants to hear nothing but great things about quality and cycle time—and then to visit customers who tell me of problems. If the

people in labs and plants miss deadlines . . . tell them their job is on the line, too.

"The tension level is not high enough in business—everyone is too damn comfortable at a time when the business is in crisis."

An IBM spokesman, while confirming the basic validity of the notes, cautioned that the notes aren't a verbatim transcript of the meeting. He added that Mr. Akers and others have been delivering stern messages internally for months now. He said the executives aren't merely reacting to the problems IBM disclosed late in the first quarter—problems that meant IBM's operating earnings fell 50 percent in the quarter and that led securities analysts to expect them to fall about 30 percent for the full year.

The spokesman said the tough messages don't change IBM's position that the company's prospects will improve once the worldwide economy turns around. He said the messages merely mean that IBM is tired of the loss of market share that has been gradually going on for several years now and feels the need to accelerate its restructuring.

"They're intended to be long-term messages that are meant to improve the business, but they're not meant to improve the business next month," the spokesman said.

Still, many industry executives see IBM's problems continuing, and some analysts say the latest round of restructuring is the start of something major.

"There is a fundamental rethinking of the business going on," says Steve Cohen, a securities analyst at SoundView Financial Group, Inc., who has been negative on the company for almost a year. "IBM's cost structure presupposes premium pricing." But computer hardware has become so standardized and

Causes of the IBM Chairman's Concern

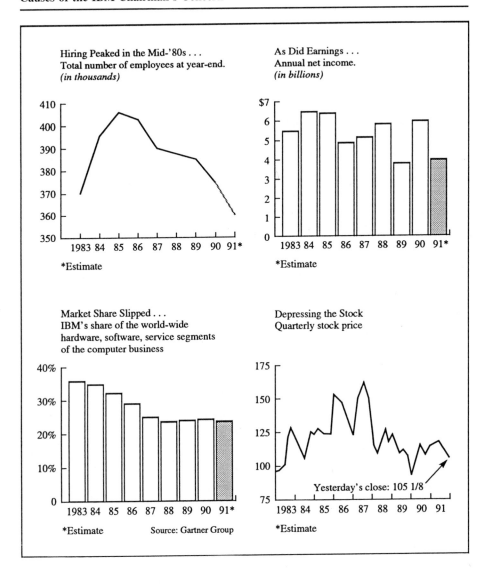

Hiring Peaked in the Mid-'80s . . .
Total number of employees at year-end.
(in thousands)

*Estimate

As Did Earnings . . .
Annual net income.
(in billions)

*Estimate

Market Share Slipped . . .
IBM's share of the world-wide
hardware, software, service segments
of the computer business

*Estimate   Source: Gartner Group

Depressing the Stock
Quarterly stock price

Yesterday's close: 105 1/8

*Estimate

price wars so severe that "IBM won't be able to get premium prices for who knows how long," Mr. Cohen says. "If that's the case, then the fundamental business model is wrong, and you have to do something about it."

In addition, IBM's room to maneuver seems to be getting smaller, simply because it has already done so much. By the end of this year, IBM will have cut its work force to fewer than 360,000, down 47,000 from five years ago. It has moved so many people into new jobs, often in new locations, that two years ago a book on IBM's personnel practices described the IBM restructuring as the biggest movement of people since the troops came home after World War II.

While IBM announced another job-reduction program in March and hinted that more might be coming, most of its recent moves have just been fine-tuning. It announced a change to its U.S. pension plan that gives employees modest incentives to retire early. It said it would close most of its U.S. headquarters operations the week of July 4 so it could save money on air-conditioning, cafeteria costs, and so forth. It told employees they had to start taking the vacation they used to carry over from year to year, so the company can cut the payments it has to make for deferred vacation when people retire. (One side effect of the increased vacation-taking is that IBM has found it can't schedule big meetings on Mondays or Fridays. A consultant who works with IBM has complained that has made life tough because executives at the company are tied up in meetings all day Tuesday, Wednesday, and Thursday.)

Mr. Akers is quoted as saying at the April seminar that he doesn't see room for major asset sales, given that IBM in March completed the sale of its type-writer, laser-printer, and office-products businesses.

The one way Mr. Akers might be able to cut employment sharply is through firing—known as MIA, or management-initiated attrition, in IBM-speak. That is a delicate issue at IBM, because of its no-layoff tradition and because the distinction between layoffs and extensive firings can be thin, even if the company fires only those it considers to be marginal performers.

While it's not yet clear how much firing will pick up, Mr. Akers is quoted as saying at the seminar that "our people have to be competitive, and if they can't change fast enough, as fast as our industry . . . good-bye."

He is quoted as saying that only one of every 200 people at an IBM lab was fired last year and as advocating "a forced march on the MIA problem."

Not everyone, of course, sees things the way Mr. Akers does. One IBMer, reacting on an internal network to the seminar notes, wrote: "I think it is time the people at the top accepted some part of the responsibility for our present problems." He added: "I don't see any sign of that happening." Another complained of the "arthritic bureaucracy" and said his attempts to circumvent the process were discouraged.

Mr. Akers singled out parts of the world where IBM was doing much worse than he expected—managing to cover most of the world in the process, according to the notes.

He is quoted as saying that four years ago a U.S. sales force of 20,000 delivered $26 billion of revenue, while in 1990, 25,000 people produced just $27 billion. "Where's my return for the extra 5,000 people?" he is quoted as asking.

Mr. Akers is quoted as saying that IBM has been losing market share in Japan for two years and that first-quarter results were "disastrous" in that country. He is quoted as noting that the European economy is stronger than the U.S. economy and that indigenous European computer makers are faring poorly. "The business benefits should therefore accrue" to IBM, he is quoted as saying. "Where are they?"

The notes quote Mr. Akers as saying that "share loss in any sector of the business would not be tolerated."

The notes begin with Mr. Akers complaining that his messages gets filtered as soon as listeners leave the room. That, Mr. Henderson explains, is why "I left the room with a real sense of obligation to spread the word."

The IBM spokesman said that effort was laudable but, with word circulating so widely, added that Mr. Akers might have preferred that his message be communicated "in a more controlled manner."

CASE

BOB GALVIN AND MOTOROLA, INC. (C)

The Organization Effectiveness Process

If the focus of phase one of the change process was information gathering, phase two focused on "Initial Implementation," or, more specifically, on communication of the 1983 research results, action planning, and pilot projects. In 1984, for example, the Galvin initiative received its name, the Organizational Effectiveness Process (OEP). Although a clear label facilitated communication and lent the project a certain tangibility and validity, many managers wondered if this new OEP would become simply another acronym in

This case was prepared by Research Associate Mary Gentile (under the direction of Professor Todd D. Jick).

Copyright © 1987 by the President and Fellows of Harvard College. Harvard Business School case 9-487-064.

the "alphabet soup" of programs at Motorola.

In February of 1984, the Policy Committee heard the results of the HR team's survey of managers and of Schaffer's interviews with senior staff. The HR survey results were clearly consistent with Galvin's diagnosis of Motorola's management problems. Galvin was not at all surprised by this, for he had based much of his thinking on reports he had previously heard from middle managers throughout the corporation. For a CEO, he was remarkably well-connected to lower levels in the management structure. Schaffer's report on the Policy Committee interviews also showed considerable agreement with Galvin's diagnosis and concluded that: "While enthusiasm, commitment, and perceptions are varied, there is enough consensus—and respect for Galvin's perspective—to get the change process going now."

Despite these research results, senior officers were, for the most part, still uncertain of what was being asked of them, especially since each one was pursuing improvements in their own areas to the best of their ability. Schaffer explained: "Everybody professed not to understand what Galvin was up to and reacted . . . as if they were merely observers or critics and not key players."

Schaffer's report to the Policy Committee also included recommendations for further actions and suggested "assignments" for the committee members to take back to their respective groups. For instance, each officer was asked to share the latest draft of the OEP guidelines paper with his teams, in an effort both to refine the document and to spread the concept. This paper went through numerous revisions in this way and, in all, was the subject of several Policy Committee meetings.

Policy Committee members were also asked to identify a few key areas, or "breakthrough" projects, where they could begin to apply the OEP thinking and concepts in their own work. Such an assignment was still somewhat vague for many officers. They had been working with the OEP guidelines, to be sure, but even in its so-called finished form (October 1984), this paper was still 16 pages long and proceeded to raise questions (48 of them), rather than give directions. The Policy Committee guidelines focused to a large extent upon organizational structure, the assignment of managerial authority and accountability, and finally on management systems. But there was plenty of room for managers to "customize" projects to suit their particular needs. Galvin was determined not to offer a single "cookbook" solution to the varied problems of a complex organization. He wanted his managers to adopt the spirit, rather than the letter, of his program. This decision left OEP open to interpretations, however.

Policy Committee members were asked to identify key OEP projects in their own area of the business, to establish task forces and completion timetables, and to report back to the Policy Committee on their plans and their results. Some officers took this assignment as an opportunity for free rein to try some new and innovative management experiments. Some accelerated change efforts already in process, and some simply re-labeled existing efforts to satisfy their assignments. These steps began in the spring of 1984.

Over the summer, reports were made to the Policy Committee meetings. The general managers of the different sectors would give presentations, assisted by their own HR team, that detailed the OEP efforts they were pursuing. Galvin was pleased with the reports, but Miraglia was not satisfied:

> I believed Galvin was being offered a smokescreen by some of our businesses. I thought he was hearing what was already going on, without enough major breakthroughs in the OEP spirit. I checked with my Human Resources staff in the field on this and they agreed. The senior managers were *institutionalizing* OEP—creating organizational goals—rather than *internalizing* and really believing in it as a new way of looking at problems.
>
> I discussed this with Bill Weisz, vice chairman and chief operating officer, and at the next meeting of the chief executive officers, with me present, he said: "Joe thinks the managers are not being completely accurate about the amount of energy being spent on this

issue." A frank discussion followed out of which came the decision by Bob that he needed to use his influence more actively.

Subsequently Galvin set up a series of one-on-one meetings with the general managers. These were lengthy conversations. Galvin listened closely to each manager and tried to communicate how serious he was about OEP. He immediately wrote up detailed notes on each conversation and sent a copy to both the general manager and to Joe Miraglia.

By this time—the summer and fall of 1984—a general "Action Framework" and suggested "implementation steps" were given to Motorola officers (see Exhibit 1), and they all knew they were expected to report on their results in public review meetings before the close of the year.

The Semiconductor Sector

Gary Tooker, general manager of the Semiconductor Products Sector, had mixed reactions to Galvin's initiation of the OEP. In general, he agreed that managers had to begin looking at the business in a global context, that the business had to move from a more technical orientation to a competitive business focus, that management layers should be reduced and spans of authority increased, and that management and incentive systems should be brought into line with strategic goals. For example, Tooker explained that his sector's financial reporting systems (the P&Ls) were too focused on regional business and not tied into the global competitive context. Thus financial incentives were unfortunately determined by short-term, narrowly focused objectives. In fact, Tooker was already at work on a number of compatible initiatives when Galvin

raised the subject of OEP. However, he was concerned that:

> Whenever you focus on a mechanical project or talk about it in capital letters, you have to be careful it doesn't become the "program of the month." I'm not so sure I want managers to be signed up in OEP so much as I want them to be thinking about what makes them successful—to personalize it. I see OEP as a model process we can use to break inertia and to continue doing what we know we have to do. It never hurts to have the CEO interested, but it's unhealthy to just spring this on the organization. Wintermantel and Miraglia have to work with Galvin to channel this idea.

Although Tooker did not want to diffuse the energy of his efforts already underway before OEP, he encouraged operating managers to use a workshop designed by human resources to find new opportunities to improve effectiveness. Moreover, Tooker challenged HR to come up with a way to convey that OEP was more than a matter of organizational structure alone. And he was supportive of conducting surveys with his management group, initiated by HR, which would identify strategic and structural deficiencies. All along, however, he continued to focus more on the major organizational changes he was introducing than on OEP, per se.

Wintermantel described the sector's challenges in 1983 as follows:

> Coming off a two-year slump in the semiconductor business, there was a great deal of perceived growth. But customers were actually double and triple ordering to ensure delivery; there were lots of cancellations. Still, the sector wanted to believe this growth would last. In addition, as old technologies merged and new ones developed, our structure became inefficient.

EXHIBIT 1 Bob Galvin and Motorola, Inc. (C)

Action Framework for the Organizational Effectiveness Process

I. Better Strategy Formulations
- Anticipation
- Selection
- Commitment

II. Modify Organization Structures
- Focus Authority and Accountability

III. Improve Processes
- Systems, Policies, Staffing

IV. Improve Performance
- Execution to Strategy

1. Doing Better Job of Business Strategy
- Anticipation—Selection—Commitment
  Including:
  — Asking the right questions.
  — Surveying comprehensively the opportunities and risks.
  — Assessing them against the mission of the business.
  — Making clear-cut decisions.
  — Committing the resources.
  — Defining the actions necessary for success.

2. Move Aggressively to Modify Organization Structures
   In order:
   — To focus authority and responsibility.
   — Improve coordination between functions and businesses.
   — To carve out "independent businesses."
   — Integrate basic functions lower in the business (deaggregate).
   — To eliminate complexity and redundancy.
   — To simplify decision making and cut layers.

3. Modifying and Strengthening Processes
   — Systems, policies, staffing.
   — Styles, skills (infrastructure to make strategy and structure work).

4. Doing a Better Job of Improving Performance through "Execution to Strategy"
   Including:
   — New product development.
   — Product introductions.
   — Cost competitiveness.
   — Market and customer responsiveness.
   — Facilities planning and construction.

In fact, earlier that year, we brought in an expert from MIT to discuss strategy and structure with the top 40 managers. We discussed a reorganization around product groups and markets rather than technologies, resulting in more, smaller groups who were more oriented to the different customers' criteria.

When Galvin presented his ideas, some

in the sector were concerned that he would want to break their organization down into even smaller units than their own internally proposed reorganization required. They believed small business units were impractical because of the heavy front-end investment in equipment. They felt threatened by Galvin's promise that: "In two years, this will be a different Motorola."

But Wintermantel urged Tooker to use OEP as an incentive to implement his original reorganization plan, "to make *that* our OEP project." He worked with Tooker to define and customize OEP to fit the concerns of the sector's particular business and its current high-growth state. This apparent growth, however, both obscured any sense of urgency to reorganize and also kept Tooker and his staff fully occupied with day-to-day operations. As one sector vice president commented: "The 40 percent growth in 1983–84 let us cover up a lot of inefficiencies." Nevertheless, the reorganization did occur, and it was Tooker who reported on it both to the Policy Committee and to the annual November Executive Conference review meetings with the chief executive officers. OEP, it seems, had been a catalyst to change the structure and to review strategic and operational priorities.

The Communications Sector

Ray Farmer, general manager in the Communications Sector, explained that he and his manager needed no convincing that they had problems. The year, 1983, had been a difficult one because they had taken the brunt of Japanese "dumping" practices in the pager business. Furthermore, operating profits had declined due to investments in new product technology and factory automation, while R&D

spending rose 24 percent. An HR survey in 1983 revealed a consensus among the sector's top 100 managers on the need for change. Schaffer, the consultant, also noted that Farmer's sector "was more ready for help," so he began to develop relationships there and to propose OEP projects.

Although Farmer recognized the need for improvement, he was at first suspicious of OEP. Schaffer noted that Farmer believed his sector's performance problems were only indirectly caused by organizational structure and, since he initially identified OEP as reorganization into smaller units, he was not enthusiastic. But when he saw that he could adapt OEP to what he thought were more urgent sector matters, he became more enthusiastic and teamed up with George Fisher, the new assistant general manager. Schaffer worked with Farmer, Fisher, and Craig Mudge, the HR director for the sector.

Fisher was a young, aggressive manager who had risen quickly, moving from divisional to sectorwide responsibilities in April 1984. Fisher himself stated:

> For Ray to bring me into this position was a rather unorthodox move, and it communicated that nothing is certain. I was brought in with the expectation that I make changes, and I have the advantage of having been fairly low in the organization fairly recently. This means I know the inhibitors to change and the systemic problems, and I also understand the real need to do something. This understanding doesn't come easily when you're the premier business of your kind in the world.

Schaffer explained that Farmer and Fisher utilized OEP as a means to address their own agenda: to accelerate the product development cycle, to increase the likelihood of meeting business and product plans, to establish management and system controls, and to make more demands of the organization overall. Farmer noted that it was sometimes "frustrating to have to determine if our initiatives actually fit into Galvin's plan; but we had frequent review meetings with him when he would assure us that 'Yes, that's what I mean.' " Eventually Farmer concluded that, for him, OEP was a "vehicle to pull together diverse issues and to create an atmosphere conductive to constructive change."

By spring 1984, Farmer and Fisher decided to stop talking and to start acting. They used their weekly Monday morning staff meetings for 10–12 managers to "try to get them past agonizing over what OEP *was* and into an action mode," remarked Farmer. They presented the four-part OEP Action Framework (see Exhibit 1). Each manager was required to initiate work on a project that addressed some aspect of that framework. Some of them were simplistic; others were impractical. But some were genuine breakthrough projects. Farmer explained:

> We were looking for projects where our operational needs coincided with divisional managers' authority. We looked for projects with the credibility to convince other managers, and we found receptive ones, such as the Mobile Division general manager in Ft. Worth, Texas.
>
> We also looked at the sector level and made some significant changes. For example, Direct Sales for the United States was organized functionally for the entire sector, and it was a very successful area. However, the customer needs and specifics of the Cellular Radio service were unique, so we decided to split this sales group off and have them report directly to the appropriate business managers. This was rev-

olutionary and it meant messing with a very workable and successful formula.

> Again, at the sector level, we took some smaller growth-oriented groups and had them report directly to us, at the sector general manager level. We were getting away from the classic organizational chart with boxes all the same size. We were conveying that size is not the only criterion for structure.

The Mobile Division in Ft. Worth turned out to be a model of active experimentation. R. H. Schaffer & Associates sent a consulting team down to work with the on-site managers of this mobile radio products group. Senior management clearly communicated its support and specific new product development goals were identified, with each project assigned a champion or manager with ultimate responsibility. Temporary "project teams" with explicit accountabilities were established. Detailed project work plans with *real* deadlines for intermediate and final goals and with clearly monitored milestones were written. Finally, everyone had to commit to and sign off on the plan before initiating the work. These team efforts resulted not only in accelerated product development cycles but in the introduction of an effective model for demand-making and team management.

The initial success of these efforts in 1984 led to their extension into 1985. A number of new product development projects that had been lagging were accelerated, and, most notably, a new product (European Land Mobile radio) championed by John Mitchell, Motorola president, was developed in 18 months. Farmer expected that, without the OEP effort, this project would have taken three years and would have cost one and a half times as much as it did. Schaffer saw this as a monumental breakthrough project, because this project, combined with others, "showed that doing things differently, they were capable of far more than what they considered 'normal.'" And Mudge of HR agreed:

> It helped redefine the standards of good performance in product development. Furthermore, it was achieved by a team spread out over three locations on two continents, which shows that complexity can be managed.

In addition, this effort stimulated the creation of entirely new businesses headed by entrepreneurial managers in the spirit that Galvin was urging.

OEP: Phase Three

As the Organizational Effectiveness Process entered its third year in 1985, its focus was "institutionalization" of the process, which meant communicating its successes to date and incorporating OEP into the ongoing management systems and reviews at Motorola, in an effort to "cascade the program to lower levels of management."

Each division general manager in the Communications Sector reported on the results of his or her OEP project to the sector officers and to Bob Galvin personally at a review meeting in September 1985. In addition, each manager developed an OEP Plan Book for the next year, working from a set of guidelines from Farmer, Fisher, and Mudge. This plan book was to be submitted in November, at the same time as they submitted their one-year financial plans and their quality plans. These plans would be reviewed, feedback given, and the managers would be evaluated on their results the following year. Craig Mudge was also at work on various efforts to share the success stories from the preceding

year with a group of perhaps 30–40 managers via the circulation project reports among the top two or three layers of the sector management.

In the Semiconductor Products Sector, Gary Tooker and other officers presented the results of their various OEP projects to the chief executive officers and other senior managers at the annual Executive Conference meeting in November 1985. Dick Wintermantel was at work developing a "7S" model for implementation of OEP and a series of OEP workshops for communicating the OEP objectives and this model to larger groups of managers (see Exhibit 2).

In addition, a two-day, corporatewide Awareness Program was being planned by the Motorola training and HR team for perhaps 2,000 managers in the United States, Europe, and Asia, to be held in early 1986. This training program was being designed to build an awareness of competitive urgency and a global outlook, with particular emphasis on the Asia challenge. The program was to include workshops that would encourage creativity and provide specific tools to enable managers to see how they could "make a difference" for Motorola.

Joe Miraglia was developing a 1986 Goal Work Plan for OEP, which covered 1986–88. This would be revised with both Galvin's input and that of the Policy Committee. This plan would present the next objectives for the program and propose a new implementation tool—"benchmarking." Benchmarking meant finding the best competitors in any particular area and then identifying characteristics, or "benchmarks," that Motorola would need either to remain competitive or overtake them. Miraglia hoped that particular models and tools like these would facilitate the goals of

EXHIBIT 2   Bob Galvin and Motorola, Inc. (C)

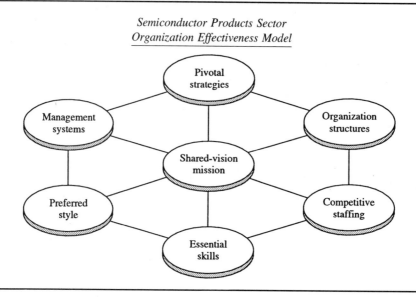

Semiconductor Products Sector
Organization Effectiveness Model

training thousands of managers in the next phases of OEP.

Other measures taken in 1985 included the incorporation of OEP evaluation measures into the Motorola Executive Incentive Plan (MEIP) and the further integration of OEP into various Motorola training programs.

The 1985 assembly of the biennial Motorola Officers' Meeting provided an opportunity to review OEP's progress to date, two years after Bob Galvin's surprising initiation of the process, and to lay out the future objectives. At the meeting, Joe Miraglia gave a presentation wherein he examined the first three phases of OEP and discussed the establishment of a new "Top 10 Corporate Goal." When Motorola decided to endorse an existing initiative, it would develop a corporate goal and appoint a "champion" of that goal who would represent and promote it. Bob Galvin was named the champion of this new OEP corporate goal, which read:

In support of our stated strategies, top 10 corporate goal no. 6 states: "Refine the processes, structures, and assignments of authority and accountability for each business and function, so that well-qualified managers can most competitively anticipate, commit, and perform more profitably to each and all customers' needs."

Miraglia then went on to discuss an "Action Framework" for implementing this goal, which included suggested objectives and questions surrounding the four OEP foci: strategy, structure, process, and performance.

Despite Human Resource Staff efforts and those of many managers at the corporate and the sector level, Miraglia had many concerns about the OEP in the summer and fall of 1985, midway through its third year. He believed that 1986 was to be a key year for the program, when its goals and strategies must begin to involve thousands of middle managers. Although

OEP's successes were dramatic—George Fisher commented that "more has happened in one year in the Communications Sector than in the previous five"— Miraglia was concerned about the effort:

> I've been concerned about the pace of change, although Schaffer assures me that it's not been unusual for an organization this size. I think we could have moved further, more quickly if the first documents had been more clear and precise. I think we should have communicated more to more managers in all areas earlier in the process. We probably should have pushed our senior management to be even more demanding in this area. More than one senior manager has come to me to ask: "Is this just Bob's idea?" And we should have done more thinking earlier on how to fit OEP into other ongoing efforts at Motorola, especially the Participative Management Program.

Many managers shared Miraglia's concerns and criticisms of the effort. Several, at both the sector levels and on the HR team, complained that it was hard to tie OEP efforts to short-term, quantifiable kinds of results and this made these efforts difficult to evaluate and difficult to sell. Some HR representatives felt, even in 1985, that the process was too ambiguous, while others praised its customizability. Almost all were concerned that, without Galvin and the HR team, the process would not persevere. As George Fisher commented: "Craig, our HR manager, is the continuity here. He keeps the subject of OEP at the forefront. Ray and I are very busy and we need the continual presence of a staff person who feels this is his most compelling assignment."

Third Quarter, 1985

As Motorola faced the fourth quarter of 1985 and the close of OEP's third phase, the company was experiencing a severe downturn in profits, particularly in the Semiconductor Products Sector. A press release issued on October 11, 1985 reported:

> Motorola, Inc., today reported that sales in the third quarter declined 6 percent to $1.30 billion from $1.38 billion in the 1984 third quarter. Nine-month sales totaled $4.00 billion, compared with $4.05 billion in 1984.
>
> The company had a loss in the third quarter of $39 million, or 33 cents per share, compared with earnings of $86 million, or 73 cents per share, in the third quarter of 1984. Nine-month earnings were $28 million, or 24 cents per share, vs. $262 million, or $2.21 per share a year ago.

Reflecting on the severe slump in the semiconductor products industry and on the increasing toll that Japanese competition was taking on the firm, Bob Galvin said:

> When I introduced the concept behind OEP, I was trying to anticipate this sort of crisis and to say, "Let's make changes while we are enjoying reasonably good business, instead of waiting until this third quarter of 1985." It's a bad time to start changing when you're already in bad shape. OEP was a purposeful revolution. Because of it, the Communications Sector developed new products in 1984, which give us pockets of strength to offset the current recession.

Galvin was optimistic that the OEP, having had almost three years to establish itself, would help the company through this crisis.

Galvin still believed that the OEP objectives could provide the momentum and the process to pull Motorola through its present difficulties. Its effectiveness, however, would depend on his officers' ability to get thousands of middle managers committed. Joe Miraglia reported that in January he asked a training group of two dozen director-level managers if they had heard of OEP and one responded affirmatively. Nine months later, 50 percent of a similar group reported recognition. This was progress, but was it fast enough? Miraglia feared that, in its third year, OEP might have been "one of the better kept secrets at Motorola."

READING

THE VISION THING (A)

The "vision thing" has become a major preoccupation in the past decade in both the corporate and the political areas. Arguably, this demand for "a vision" from our leaders has served to overwork and trivialize—perhaps even distort— what real visions are and why they are necessary. It is true that the concept of vision is elusive; there are many definitions, none of which is precise. It is, in fact, almost easier to say what a vision isn't. Despite this imprecision, however, a vision is considered fundamental for helping a firm, quite literally, *visualize* its future.

When that future includes change, particularly of the transformational sort, having a vision of the new direction in advance of actually making the changes is indispensable. According to one study, "We found that no effort to produce strategic change was successful without a new vision."[1]

But visions are difficult to craft and often remain paper exercises. All too few achieve their purpose of helping an organization to meet its goals and to stimulate change. What is a "good" vision? How do effective visions get created? What do successful visionary leaders do? And how can those without formal authority influence the conceptualizing of an organization's vision? In addressing these questions, this note will help managers think about the use of vision and envisioning in the change process.

What Is a Vision?

A vision is an attempt to *articulate* what a desired future for a company would look like. It can be likened to "... an organizational dream—it stretches the imagination and motivates people to rethink what is possible."[2] Martin Luther King, Jr.'s,

This reading was prepared by Professor Todd D. Jick.

Copyright © 1989 by the President and Fellows of Harvard College. Harvard Business School case N9-490-019.

[1] L.A. Bennigson and H. Swartz, "The CEO's Change Agenda," *Planning Review* 15, no. 3 (May/June 1987), p. 13.
[2] W. P. Belgard, K. K. Fisher, and S. R. Rayner, "Vision, Opportunity, and Tenacity: Three Informal Process That Influence Transformation," in *Corporate Transformation*, R. Kilmann and T. Covin, eds. (San Francisco: Jossey-Bass, 1988), p. 135.

most famous speech is literally labeled "I Have a Dream," because he elucidated his vision of a nonracist America.

Visions are *big* pictures. They are new terrains, descriptions of a time and place that are happy and successful. In that sense, they are idyllic, perhaps even "impossible dreams." But when the time and place are understandable (e.g., "one happy family") people can and do respond. We know some of the things that one happy family implies: we don't beat up on each other, we try to cooperate, and so on.

According to one observer, a vision has two fundamental elements:

> One is to provide a conceptual framework for understanding the organization's purpose—the vision includes a roadmap. The second important element is the emotional appeal: the part of the vision that has a motivational pull with which people can identify.[3]

A vision is not the same as a mission, which is a brief explanation of the organization's purpose. A vision is not the same as strategic objectives, the specific measurable performance goals. A vision is not the same as a philosophy, the values and belief system underlying a company. Yet, a vision must be consistent with mission, strategy, and philosophy. A vision is both much more than and much less than these elements. It is much less than these elements because visions tend to be evocative, rather than precise. And yet in its simplicity and evocativeness, a vision can have a more profound influence on real behavior than binders full of strategic plans with detailed documentation.

[3] N. Tichy and M. Devanna, *The Transformational Leader* (New York: John Wiley & Sons, 1986), p. 130.

Indeed, the true value of a vision is to guide behavior. Tom Peters tells the story of the Raychem worker on the night shift who notices something amiss with the packing labels on the last few boxes going onto a truck. No supervisor is around. No one else seems to have noticed and, in fact, senior employees have already passed on the order "as is." The worker could just let it go, and no one would have known about the problem.

But he stopped the line! With the company's vision of zero defects and the best quality products ringing in his consciousness, the worker took the initiative to catch the problem. He could have let things go by, with no negative personal consequences. But he didn't because the dream and spirit of Raychem's vision led him to make a different calculus and a different choice. Behavior was changing at Raychem on account of a new vision.

How does this happen? When are visions effective? Why did this employee change his habitual behavior? Many characteristics of good visions can be identified. Good visions are:

- Clear, concise, easily understandable.
- Memorable.
- Exciting and inspiring.
- Challenging.
- Excellence-centered.
- Stable, but flexible.
- Implementable and tangible.

Consider the following example:

> Liza Foley has an ideal and unique image of the future for the organization she leads. Foley is the president and chief executive officer of Canon Industrial Corporation of Canton, Illinois [which] occupies the old International

Harvester facility that was shut down in 1984, putting 250 people out of work in a town with a population of 14,000 in the guts of the rust belt. . . .

[Bought with private funds and the help of the city] there were 42 people working initially there. A year and a half later there were 200. It was also the only publicly held, women-owned, and operated manufacturing facility in the United States. We asked Foley what motivated her to buy the company and take such a risk, she replied: "I saw what closing a plant did to the community. And I also saw that there was a great deal of desire. People were anxious to get to work. And that was challenging. . . . I have a clear sense of purpose and vision of where I want to go.

. . . For the organization, I want to take this to a $100 million company in less than five years. I want to make acquisitions. . . that will allow us to service some of our key customers from several locations. I want to make Canton, Illinois, the mailbox capital of the world. I can see a little sign as you enter the town: Welcome to Canton, the Mailbox Capital of the World. . . . I'd like to think that we are starting the resurgence of the rust belt.[4]

This particular example seems to meet many of the criteria above. It inspired people, it elicited an image of excellence, and it challenged people to new heights.

A vision is sometimes even captured by a slogan, although this is very risky because of the shallowness of such sloganeering. But the following seems to have been a successful use of a slogan to symbolize and embody a vision of creativity and innovation:

A software company executive replaced the firm's slogan, "We Can Do Anything," with one he thought better typified his vision, "The Technical Edge." . . . As he mulled over phrases that might recapture the old vision in fresh language, he considered, "Think Young," but then he realized that the phrase might offend some older employees. Then it struck him: "Outrageous Thinking." He might have to fine-tune it, but it did express what he wanted from his people. . . . A week after his meditation, the software executive pinned a button to his jacket: "Outrageous Thinking Keeps Us Ahead." Soon, the slogan fired up even the senior staff, who seemed to enjoy this call to youthful exuberance.[5]

A slogan, thus, sometimes becomes the vehicle for communicating and symbolizing a new vision. And yet, there is always a fine line between an empty slogan and an inspirational vision and guide. This particular embodiment of a vision seemed to work; many others fail.

What is it about a vision that grabs people? First, people like to feel proud that they are part of something larger than their career or family, and the corporate vision tends to mobilize this source of personal motivation. Second, having a vision of the future highlights the contrast with today's reality. This creates a structural tension between today and tomorrow that seeks a resolution.

Another reason why visions have become so important is because, with increasing turbulence in organizations, people are seeking some sort of anchor or certainty as a mooring. In providing a

---

[4] J. Kouzes and B. Posner, *The Leadership Challenge* (San Francisco: Jossey-Bass, 1988), pp. 92–93.

[5] C. Hickman and M. A. Silva, *Creating Excellence* (New York: New American Library, 1984), p. 167.

direction and a focus, an organization can more easily converge on the necessary actions. For example, when Johnson & Johnson experienced the Tylenol poisonings, it responded very quickly and with consensus because its long-standing credo, which clearly placed the needs of the customer above all else, served as a worldwide guide for action.

Vision statements tend to incorporate four elements: (1) customer orientation, (2) employee focus, (3) organizational competencies, and (4) standards of excellence. These elements help the organization do the "right thing." They specify the key success factors in satisfying the customer (e.g., service, quality, delivery); the values and principles that employees stand for and rally behind; the organizational capabilities that have distinguished its performance in the past and provide a foundation for the future; and finally, a demanding standard of excellence that appeals to the pride and desire of all associated with the organization. Thus, visions always seem to include such superlatives as world class, lowest cost, fastest.

How Visions Are Created: The Visioning Process

Visions have been created in organizations in very different ways. Some are very personal experiences of creativity and inspiration. Some are products of elaborate information-gathering processes. Some are developed at a workshop or off-site with key players. Some are even wordsmithed by public relations or advertising staff. The most typical are: (*a*) CEO/leader developed, (*b*) CEO–senior team developed, and (*c*) bottom-up vision development.

CEO/Leader Developed

A study by Warren Bennis of 90 top leaders highlighted the central role they played in developing visions for their organizations.[6] Although obviously this is never purely a solo endeavor, the impression is that these leaders all had compelling visions and dreams about their companies. The classic examples are Steve Jobs at Apple, Harry Gray at United Technologies, Mitch Kapor at Lotus, and Jack Welch at General Electric. These people are typically described as self-styled visionaries. Bennis concluded that the successful visionary CEO does the following:

- Searches for ideas, concepts, and ways of thinking until clear vision crystallizes.

- Articulates the vision into an easy-to-grasp philosophy that integrates strategic direction and cultural values.

- Motivates company employees to embrace the vision through constant persuasion and by setting an example of hard work.

- Makes contact with employees at all levels in the organization, attempting to understand their concerns and the impact the vision has on them.

- Acts in a warm, supportive, expressive way, always communicating that "We're all in this together, like a family."

- Translates the vision into a reason for being for each employee by continually relating the vision to individual cares, concerns, and work.

---

[6] Ibid., pp. 160–61.

- Concentrates on the major strengths within the organization that will ensure the success of the vision.
- Remains at the center of the action, positioned as the prime shaper of the vision.
- Looks for ways to improve, augment, or further develop the vision by carefully observing changes inside and outside the organization.
- Measures the ultimate success of the organization in terms of its ability to fulfill the vision.

These various actions place the visionary leader in a very visible and powerful position in the development of a vision. It assumes that this leadership is *the* key. Indeed, inspiring a shared vision is often listed as a key leadership success factor.

Yet, managers say that inspiration is most difficult to apply and only 10 percent think of themselves as inspiring.[7] Maybe managers are selling themselves short, or glorifying those enviable individuals who have that certain something called "charisma." Managers who are successful in providing a vision, however, do some very simple things, which more than 10 percent are certainly capable of doing: they (1) appeal to a common purpose, (2) communicate expressively, and (3) sincerely believe in what they are saying.[8]

Other leaders view the process in much more collaborative fashion and, thus, craft an immediate partnership with their senior staff. They view vision creation as less inspiration and more perspiration.

Leader–Senior Team Visioning

This collaborative vision process is one described and epitomized by Michael Blumenthal, former CEO of Unisys. When he was chairman of Burroughs, he recalled how he went about shaping a vision for that company:

> I gathered six or eight people around me and we talked about everything, and were very open. I'm very open and I listened to them, and I traveled around and talked to a lot of people, and then eventually I tried to enunciate what it was that we learned and I suggested this is what we are going to do. And then people reacted to it and at the end I said, okay.[9]

This informal gathering of thoughts and testing for reaction is one approach in building a vision with a senior management team. But there are more and more companies that do this in a more structured and systematic format—using the help of inside or outside facilitators.

For example, after Contel Texocom's executive management team drew up a vision statement, it had the statement inscribed on a banner, which each team member signed. Next, the executive group met with the company's entire management, with members explaining what the statement meant to them. Managers were invited to sign the banner as well. Anyone who decided to sign the banner became a "sponsor." That is, potential "enrollees" could select any name appearing on the banner (other than direct supervisor) and arrange a one-on-one meeting with that person, during which the vision and its meaning would be discussed. That process was voluntary and nonhierarchical.

Bottom-Up Visioning

Finally, the third prototype involves

---

[7] Kouzes and Posner, p. 109.
[8] Ibid., p. 113.
[9] Tichy and Devanna, p. 137.

more bottom-up or middle-up involvement. It can be done again through formal channels or through informal influence processes.

For example, there are various techniques used with middle managers to stimulate them to "dream" a vision of the future. In one design, managers are asked to write an article about their company that they would like to see in an issue of *Business Week* five years hence. What would they like to be able to read about their company? How would the company be described in ways different than it was today? Then the articles are read to each other and commonalities and differences are discussed. Ultimately, the group might agree on one scenario, or a few, which would then be presented to senior management.

With this bottom-up approach, visions are only effective insofar as they are meaningful and motivating to those that have to implement them. Thus, it is better to solicit or be responsive to those in the middle particularly. Otherwise, there will be resistance or apathy, and the vision will be an unrealized dream or an empty slogan.

However, those who are neither the leader nor in an organization that formally structures an opportunity are not doomed to passive acceptance. It is possible to participate as a "vision influencer," rather than a "vision driver." These influencers are typically persons with limited hierarchical power (e.g., lower-level managers and staff) but they can influence key executives. They not only can generate ideas but also can gather support for a future transformation through their ability to influence still other people.[10]

What do effective influencers do? One study describes their actions:

They create a vision of the potential future state of the transformed organization, they take advantage of every opportunity to discuss their vision, and they tenaciously support processes that facilitate the implementation of the vision while discouraging processes that inhibit it.[11]

Thus, change influencers can develop their own vision and opportunistically find occasions to discuss and gain support for it, whether through formal meetings or chance water cooler encounters. With a vision and opportunity comes one other key element, tenacity. Influencers must be dogged and dedicated, willing to make their case as strongly as possible, personally modeling the behaviors they are promoting, and being flexible and politically astute wherever needed. Specific actions might include: conversations in parking lots, informal networking and lobbying, phone calls, and occasional blank stares.

The premise of this kind of approach is that those down in the organization may have a better "feel" for what is needed to revitalize, reshape, or transform an organization. After all, they are the ones closest to the customers, the products, and the services.

Indeed, those without the formal authority to create or authorize a vision are often the most frustrated. They constantly complain that the top-down visions are unclear, inadequate, or misguided. They become weary from trying to figure it out or unsuccessfully challenging the top people, and they yearn for the empowerment that would give them an easier say in the visioning process.

---

[10] Belgard, Fisher, and Rayner, p. 133.
[11] Ibid.

Having Visions That "Take"

Whichever approach is used, certain steps must be taken. A vision ultimately must be deemed strategically sound. It certainly must have widespread support to be made real and translatable into behavior. It continually must be reinforced through words, symbols, and actions or else it will be viewed as temporary or insincere. Respected individuals, wherever they reside in an organization, must personally embody the vision by how they spend their time, whom they surround themselves with, and, of course, what they say.

The creation of a compelling vision that guides behavior and change is never easy. Perhaps no complaint is more common in today's fast-moving and turbulent environment than "We just don't have a clear vision of where we're headed." In part, this is common because the path to the future, much less the "best" future, has become increasingly less obvious. But it's also true that managers have not given enough attention to the *process* of crafting and gaining commitment to a vision. It's not just having a vision—the "right" one, of course—that counts, but also one that is well accepted and can be translated into an actual behavior.

Many organizations may find themselves in a situation similar to one I recently observed. A large international unit of a major Fortune 500 company brought together its top 25 managers to ponder their strategy and direction. Their vision, established three years earlier, focused on their global impact, the rekindling of some of the basics of their business, and the dedication of longstanding employees. They captured this in a well-communicated phrase, which seemed simple and compelling enough: "Redirect the Ship."

In their discussion about the current state of the business, everyone nodded when the phrase was used. It seemed like it continued to serve as a guide to decisions and behavior. But then, one manager suggested it was time for a new vision because the ship had been redirected. The business had moved in the new strategic direction and the new behaviors were well in evidence. Another manager, however, disagreed and argued that the ship indeed had not yet been redirected enough. And then a third voiced emerged quizzically and stated, "I don't even know what 'redirecting the ship' means!" Sure enough, the group was split in thirds. Was it time for new vision, a reaffirmation of the old vision, or clarifying what the vision meant anyway?

The "vision thing" had reared its ugly head again. The organization would have to grapple with all the issues raised in this note. Ultimately, this crossroads would test how well the vision had been created in the first place, how well it was adhered to, and how an organization can use a vision to provide direction when change is needed again.

READING

THE VISION THING (B)

What is the point of Apple, the Californian maker of personal computers? As far back as 1980, Steve Jobs, the company's co-founder, had no doubt: it was "to make a contribution to the world by making tools for the mind that advance humankind." Tautological humbug? In advanced computing, the only profitable tools will be those that advance humankind. Perhaps, but the idea that such visionary zeal can be helpful is undeniable. More and more company bosses look enviously at the likes of Britain's Body Shop, Japan's Sony, Italy's Benetton, Switzerland's Swatch, and America's Wal-Mart and Merck. Vision—a sense of purpose, a reason for being, a guiding philosophy, call it what you like—feels especially useful to global, decentralized firms, and ones that have long grown out of their entrepreneurial origins. A shared vision can help motivate and unite a large, scattered work force.

If, that is, the company gets it right. Understanding what constitutes "corporate vision" is notoriously difficult. Many vision-seeking firms simply end up writing themselves a "mission statement"—a paragraph or two displayed prominently in each year's annual report. But the problem with most mission statements is that they are little more than a bland description of what the company does, with the odd inspirational word thrown in. Far from grabbing and galvanizing,

they usually provoke the reaction "So what?"

Does that mean would-be corporate visionaries should give up, unless they have an inspiring, entrepreneurial founder? James Collins and Jerry Porras, two academics at Stanford University's Graduate School of Business, think not. In a new study,[1] they argue that visionary companies can be created without the help of a visionary leader. To help bosses and managers kick-start this process, they have developed a simple framework for thinking about what vision actually is.

To become visionary, claim the Stanford duo, firms need two things: a guiding philosophy and a challenging, shorter-term goal, or mission. Together, these should combine to form a clear image that the company's employees can identify with. The trouble is that most firms find it hard to distinguish philosophy from mission. To clear up the confusion, says Mr. Porras, companies must follow a set of rules which define the differing roles of the two characteristics.

MANAGEMENT FOCUS

Mission is the easiest to define. First, it should have a finish line—you need to be able to know when you have achieved the goal. Second, it should be risky—attainable, but only with effort. Third, it helps to have a time limit, which should be short enough to be within reach of present

---

[1] "Organizational Vision and Visionary Organizations," Research paper 1159, Stanford GSB.

employees—say, five years or so. A good role model is President Kennedy's mission for NASA, defined in 1962, of "achieving the goal, before this decade is out, of landing a man on the moon and returning him safely to earth." A quarter of a century later, Bob Miller, chief executive of America's MIPS Computer, mimicked that model when he described his firm's mission: "To make the MIPS microprocessor architecture the most pervasive in the world by the mid-1990s."

A mission's goals do not have to be "internal." Some of the most effective are directed outside the company, on competitors. PepsiCo's mission has long simply to "Beat Coke!", a goal it has yet to achieve. Honda, faced with the prospect of Yamaha dethroning it as the world's leading motorcycle maker, penned the memorable mission, "We will crush, squash, slaughter Yamaha!" It did.

In isolation, however, missions can be self-destructive. Concentrating single-mindedly on their mission, many firms lose their way when the strived-for goal is achieved. Having landed a man on the moon, NASA drifted. It has yet to find a new mission as compelling as its first one. Missions aimed at rivals suffer similar difficulties: when the war is won, what next? Nike lost its sense of purpose after it beat Adidas in the sports-shoe market. The company regained its vitality only when it was itself overtaken by Reebok.

But framing a mission is a good way for firms to start thinking about the more esoteric business of creating a guiding philosophy. The mission defines what a company's practical goals are; the guiding philosophy must take those goals and try to put into words *why* the firm is bothering to pursue them—instead of, say, selling off its assets and shutting up shop.

Fine in theory. In practice, directors and managers tend to be disingenuous when they try to examine the purpose underlying a firm's existence. The question "What values and beliefs do we hold?" often becomes "What values and beliefs *should* we hold?" Rhetoric, rather than reality, makes for a worthless guiding philosophy. "Purpose," claim the Stanford academics, "is in the woodwork of the organization, and is not set or created as much as it is recognized or discovered." Ask honest questions about why our company does what it does, and you will uncover its underlying philosophy; try to be too idealistic, and you will fail.

How to articulate what you uncover? A "vision statement" has to be everything a mission statement is not. It should have no finish line, so employees will strive toward it after short-lived missions are attained. It should set its sights high, for much the same reason. And it should have no time limit; any corporate vision worth its salt should last for at least a century, thinks Mr. Porras.

The "Statement of Corporate Purpose" of Merck, a big American healthcare group, fits the mold: "We are in the business of preserving and improving human life. All of our actions must be measured by our success in achieving this." But a company does not have to be in a "caring" industry to come up with a motivating vision: Disney's, for instance, is simply "To make people happy."

Do such expressions of corporate philosophy and mission motivate employees and make a firm more competitive—or are they, as cynics claim, just motherhood and apple PR? To find out, Messrs. Collins and Porras asked 170 American bosses to identify the 20 companies they thought were the most visionary. A dollar was then "invested" in shares of each of the firms in the mid-1920s. If any of the companies did not exist at that time, the dollar was left in an interest-bearing account until the firm was born; it was then invested. On average, over the period, the visionary firms outperformed Wall Street by a factor of 50. Fascinating—but not conclusive. "Visionary" may simply remain a synonym for successful, not an identifiable cause of success.

MODULE 3

Implementing Change

INTRODUCTION

Implementation is the "how" of the change process. It is the initial "How do we get the organization to change?" It is the "Here is how we will go about changing." It is the monitoring question "How are we doing?" And that involves "How are people responding to the change?" These four hows should continually interrelate.

How to get an organization to change entails choosing among a range of techniques, most of which are familiar and used for other purposes: speeches, seminars, off-sites, training, newsletters, and the like. What transforms these into change vehicles is the message they carry: With these devices, here is how we will go about changing. Recall the OEP situation in "Motorola (C)." At first it was unclear what OEP was—perhaps another ingredient in the firm's "alphabet soup." It would have to be made clear that the program would be used as a "model for change."

Crucial to such a message is its consistency, which runs from perception to reality. The former may arise, usually in its negative inconsistency, when one group believes that it is doing all the changing, and business as usual occurs elsewhere. This may be an artifact of the implementation processes, whereby certain changes are made in one area before another. Real consistency is more difficult to achieve, and again this can be illustrated negatively. Cross-functional teams are increasingly being used as change vehicles, charged in many cases to design and implement processes with large ramifications to a company. Yet all too often functional (and other) constraints inhibit their work. The message and the ability to enact are inconsistent and, unchecked, will derail the change effort.

Discovering such problems means that the change process must be monitored; monitoring, of course, also means determining what is going *right*. Monitoring, however, is not the same as measuring concrete results.

Change programs intended to improve productivity, increase quality, speed up product development, and so on, which is to say most efforts explored in this text include numerical goals—a 20 percent increase in X by Y time. Such goals are essential. Change efforts are expensive, either in direct resource outlay or in the time and productivity loss associated with disrupted routines, particularly at the outset. Measuring progress in concrete terms helps justify this expense and encourages those enacting the change. But there is often a tendency, or at least the temptation, to confound achieving the numerical goal with making the deeper and inherently less measurable changes in thinking and behavior that most change efforts intend.

A manufacturing quality effort, for example, invariably includes statistical standards for ultimately producing defect-free products. Progress toward achieving these standards can be measured, and increments toward reaching them are to be celebrated along the way. But while this progress is being made, competitors may be redefining or expanding the *concept* of quality to include total customer satisfaction— one *component* of which is (ultimately) defect-free products. If a firm is not paying attention to how its employees are understanding quality per se, and, if the focus has been only on achieving a numerical goal, it can end up in the unhappy position of winning a battle and losing the war. (This point is embedded in the readings on "Change Agents" in the fifth and final module of the book.)

Monitoring a change effort, while it includes tracking concrete goal achievement, entails asking broader questions and listening to the answers—How are we doing? How are people responding to the effort?—beyond the numbers. Depending on factors like the size of the organization, this can be an informal process or a formal one; Xerox, for example, a case in this module, employed a companywide survey. To be effective, however, monitoring must be perceived as helping the effort, not as an implied threat like looking over employees' shoulders to see if things are being done right. And most important, built into any monitoring process must be the willingness to revisit the first two hows: how to get the organization to change and how to convey the change message within those methods. As such, what is built into any overall implementation effort that hopes to succeed is the potential of changing the change program itself.

CASES AND READINGS

The module opens with the "First National City Bank Operating Group (A) and (B)" cases, which describe the origin, implementation, and results (two years later) of a new control system in the bank's operating group. The series looks at the effort from various perspectives, revealing that what is perceived as a strength from one constituency is greeted with more ambiguity from another. Another important point appears: the "how" to get the group to change is intertwined in an assessment of what the group is. That is, the role of the operating group, it is decided, is a factor. Everything in the change effort is predicated on that assumption and, as such, is consistent.

The next case, "Peter Browning and Continental White Cap (A)," introduces new elements into the implementation challenge, which can be summed up as: where to begin? In this case, the decision to "push for real, measurable change in the division's (White Cap) culture and performance" comes from the corporate level; at the same time, however, nothing is to be done to disrupt that culture's "tradition of employee loyalty," which is a direct result of the family-style culture itself. Leading the change effort is Browning, who not only comes from another part of the organization but has, in his previous assignment, instituted a "drastic and accelerated change program," which he called "radical surgery." Finally, since the division has led its market for 50 years and is deemed a "jewel" by corporate, it, not surprisingly, does not perceive the need for real, measurable change in its culture and performance!

From the implementation process that unfolded at City Bank's Operating Group, with its 8,000 employees, and Peter Browning's challenge at White Cap and its 1,450 employees, the focus shifts to Xerox, with 105,000 employees. Implementation issues on this scale are a whole other order of magnitude (as previewed in the reading by Todd Jick on "Implementing Change"). "Xerox Corporation: Leadership through Quality (A)" details the drawing up of a companywide program that the CEO calls "a revolution in the company." In addition to the scale of the change and its "revolutionary" aspects, the program is planned to unfold over five years, each year having its own set of goals. The (B) case in this series, which is handed out at the end of the (A) discussion, explores the final phase of the plan. "Organizational Frame Bending: Principles of Managing Reorientation," the reading accompanying the Xerox (B) case, goes deeply into the distinct challenges of managing large-scale planned change and the difficulties inherent in sustaining the effort when the implementation process was intended to be long.

To provide a hands-on grasp of implementation dilemmas, which is the next part of this module, is an activity called the "Organizational Change Game." The task is straightforward: in the role of a consultant and as part of a team, persuade as many managers as possible, within a two-year period, to adopt an organizational "innovation." A variety of tactics and strategies are available, and as important as the choice of a tactic is the sequencing of them all. Although the activity is a competition (the team getting the most managers on board in the least time wins), the dynamics within each team are powerful and can hint at what struggles must be made to get people to change.

In the final case in the module,"Jacobs Suchard: The Reorganization for 1992," instead of an individual persuasion task, change was addressed through organizational restructuring that included dramatic alteration in incentive programs and other procedures. The Swiss-based firm contemplating the 1992 Common Market changes in Europe thus faces implementation challenges across borders and the local/global dilemmas increasingly prevalent.

Accompanying this case is the provocatively titled article, "Why Change Programs Don't Produce Change." Arguing for bottom-up, grass-roots change and "task alignment," the authors assert that "the most effective way to change behavior . . . is to put people into a new organizational context." The case and the reading, therefore, form an interesting overview of this approach—and an effective lead-in to a module devoted to understanding what it is like to receive change.

CASE

FIRST NATIONAL CITY BANK OPERATING GROUP (A)

John Reed paced along the vast glass walls of his midtown Manhattan office, hardly noticing the panorama of rooftops spread out below him. One of 41 senior vice presidents of the First National City Bank, Reed, at 31, was the youngest man in the bank's history to reach this management level. He headed the bank's Operating Group (OPG)—the back office, which performed the physical work of processing Citibank's business transactions and designing its computer systems, as well as managing the bank's real estate and internal building services. Today, musing about the forthcoming 1971 operating year and his plans for the next five years, John Reed was both concerned and angry.

He was concerned that his recent reorganization of the Operating Group, though widely recognized as a success, was not sufficient. His area still followed the traditional working procedures of the banking business, and OPG was still seen by the rest of the bank as a necessary evil which, tolerated by its more intelligent brethren, should muddle along as it always had. After a year with OPG and five months as its head, he still had few concrete measures of its performance. But most of all, John Reed was concerned

that his initial concept of what OPG needed—massive new computerized systems for coping with a growing mountain of paper-based transactions—might be both impractical and irrelevant. Reed's new staff assistant, Bob White, had been pushing hard for a change in management approach, to emphasize budgets, costs, and production efficiency instead of system development.

And, uncharacteristically, John Reed was angry. He looked again at the management report he had received the day before. Only now, in September, had he learned that his manpower had grown by 400 people in July and August. Maybe Bob White really had something in his stress on control and management.

First National City Bank

The Operating Group was one of the six major divisions established in a reorganization of Citibank at the end of 1968. The five market-oriented divisions, shown in the organization chart in Exhibit 1, generated varying demands for OPG services; all of them were looking forward to continued growth in 1971, and all were pressing for improved performance by the Operating Group.

Citibank's Personal Banking Group (PBG), with 181 branches and 6,000 employees, provided a full range of services to consumers and small businesses in the metropolitan New York area. As the area's leading retail bank, PBG projected a 3 percent annual growth in checking account balances, and a 2 percent annual

This case was prepared by John A. Seeger (under the direction of Professor Jay W. Lorsch and Associate Professor Cyrus F. Gibson).

EXHIBIT 1   Institutional Organization—1970

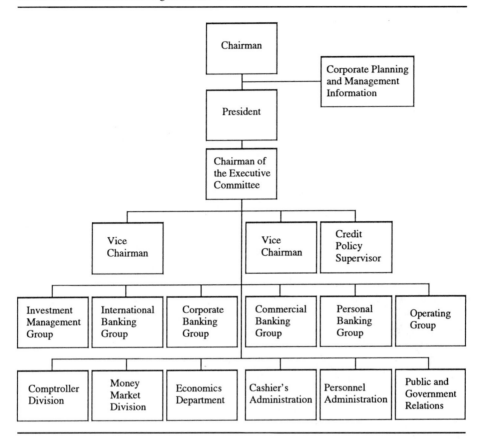

growth in savings accounts over the next several years; in addition to an increase in number of accounts, PBG anticipated continuation of the recent trend toward more activity per account.

The Investment Management Group, with 1,700 employees, managed assets for personal and institutional investors, and provided full banking services to wealthy individuals. In the latter category, the group currently carried some 7,000 accounts, and it hoped to increase this figure by 25 percent in the next four years.

The Corporate Banking Group (CBG),

itself subdivided into six industry-specialist divisions, served big business (generally, companies with more than $20 million in annual sales), financial institutions, and government accounts within the United States. CBG aimed at an annual growth rate over 5 percent, but qualified its ambitions: in order to gain market share in the increasingly competitive world of the major corporations, the bank would have to improve both its pricing structures and the quality of its services. Operating Group errors, CBG said, had irritated many major accounts, and OPG's reputation for slow, inaccurate service made expansion of market share very difficult.

The Commercial Banking Group operated 16 regional centers in the New York area to serve medium-sized companies, most of which did not employ their own professional finance executives and, thus, relied upon the bank for money advice as well as banking services. The fastest growing group of the bank, Commercial Banking, projected an annual growth rate of about 10 percent.

The International Banking Group (IBG) operated some 300 overseas branches, in addition to managing several First National City Corporation subsidiary units concerned with foreign investments, services, and leasing. Although IBG conducted its own transaction processing at its overseas centers, still its rapid growth would nevertheless present new demands on the Operating Group in Manhattan. All business originating in New York was handled by Reed's people, and the IBG complement of 160 New York-based staff officers was expected to double in five years.

Worldwide, First National City Corporation had shown assets of $23 billion in its financial statement of December 31, 1969. Earnings had been $131 million after taxes (but before losses on securities traded). The corporation employed 34,000 people, having doubled its staff in the previous 10 years, while tripling its assets. Citibank's published goals for financial performance presented another source of pressure for improvement in OPG: Board Chairman Walter B. Wriston had recently committed the bank to an annual growth rate of 15 percent in earnings per share of common stock. President William Spencer had made it clear to Reed that OPG was

expected to contribute to this gain in earnings.

The Operating Group's Functions

As the bank had grown, so had its back office. Increases in services offered, in customers, in volume per customer, and in staff all meant added transactions to be processed by OPG. As the volume of paper flowing through the bank increased, so did the staff and budget of the back office. In 1970, John Reed had some 8,000 people on his group payroll, and he would spend $105 million on the direct production of the bank's paperwork. For several years, transaction volume had increased at an annual rate of 5 percent; OPG's total expenditures had grown faster, however, at an average of 17.9 percent per year since 1962.

OPG headquarters was a 25-story building at 111 Wall Street, several miles south of the bank's head offices at 399 Park Avenue. The volume and variety of work flowing through this building were impressive; in a typical day, OPG would:

- Transfer $5 billion between domestic and foreign customers and banks.
- Process $2 billion worth of checks— between 1.5 million and 2 million individual items.
- Start and complete 900 jobs in the data processing center, printing five million lines of statements, checks, and other reports.
- Process $100 million worth of bill and tax payments for major corporations and government agencies. (During the 16 weeks between February 1 and May 30, the group also processed 50,000 income tax returns per day for the city of New York.)

- Handle 102,000 incoming and outgoing telephone calls and 7,000 telegrams and cables.
- Mail out 30,000 checking account statements and 25,000 other items, requiring postage expenditures of $10,000 a day.

Operating Group Organization

In 1969, John Reed transferred into OPG from the International Banking Group to become a vice president of the bank and to set up a task force pointed toward reorganization of the group. He had assembled a team of young, technically oriented managers (most of them relatively new to OPG) to analyze and rearrange the basic functions of the group. Systematically, this task force had examined the structure and function of each OPG subdepartment, working with the line managers to question where the subgroups fit in the organization; to whom their managers reported and why; what processes and technologies they shared with other groups; and how the physical output of each group affected the operation of the next sequential processing step. The result of this study was a complete realignment of reporting responsibilities, pulling together all those groups doing similar work, and placing them under unified management.

A leading member of OPG's systems management team during this reorganization effort was Larry Small, who had followed Reed from the planning staff at the IBG in 1969. Small, a 1964 graduate of Brown University (with a degree in Spanish literature), set the keynote for the task force approach with his concept of basic management principles:

Managing simply means understanding, in detail—in *meticulous* detail—where

you are now, where you have to go, and how you will get there. To know where they are now, managers must measure the important features of their systems. To know where they are going, managers must agree on their objectives, and on the specific desired values of all those measured factors. And to know how to get there, managers must understand the processes which produce their results. Significant change demands the participation of the people involved, in order to gain the widespread understanding required for success. Management is essentially binary; all change efforts will be seen as either successes or failures. Success follows from understanding.

Few major changes in equipment or physical space were required by the new organization, and the approach characterized by Small's statement made the transition an easy one. By late 1969, OPG was running smoothly under a four-area structure as shown in Exhibit 2.

Area I was the operating part of the Operating Group; it included the people who processed the transactions that constituted the bank's business. Area I operated the computer systems, processed checks for collection from other banks, posted the accounts for Citibank's customers, transferred funds from one customer to another, and prepared customers' bank statements.

Area II encompassed system design and software for computer operations; it was the intellectual side of OPG, developing new computer systems for the use of Area I. The subgroups in charge of operations analysis, management information systems, and data control also belonged to Area II, as did the programming group in charge of ALTAPS, a new automated loan and time payment processing system.

Area III, quite removed from OPG's paper-oriented processing groups, was a

EXHIBIT 2   Basic Organization—Operating Group

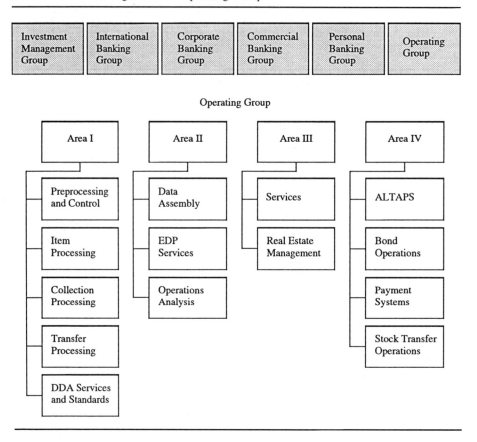

freestanding organization in charge of Citibank's real estate, physical facilities, and building services. (When he was not concerned about processing transactions in the back office, Reed could worry about the quality of cafeteria food and the cleanliness of the bathrooms.)

Area IV was composed of the relatively low-volume, high-value transaction processing departments—stock transfer, corporate bonds, corporate cash management, mutual funds, and government services.

In addition to the routine day-to-day operations, Reed was responsible for the long-range development of both hardware and software systems. For several years, a subsidiary of the bank—with operations in Cambridge, Massachusetts, and California—had been working on the kind of on-line systems and terminals that would be required to support the checkless society which the financial community expected would some day replace paper-based record processing. Reed had decided to maintain the separation of this advanced research and development activity from OPG. "Let's face it," he said, "the computer systems we have now will never evolve into the systems needed for point-of-sale transaction processing. When those new systems come, they'll come as a revolution—a total replacement of existing technology. We should develop the new systems, sure. But we shouldn't let them screw up the systems we need today and tomorrow in the meantime."

In September 1970, John Reed, feeling comfortable with the overall structure of OPG but impatient with its lack of measured progress, had assigned Small to head Area IV. Small's demonstrated skills in management of change held out the promise that this highly sensitive area, where any errors could cause major problems for the bank's most important customers, would soon be under more effective control. Now Reed was considering the future course of Area I, where even more people and dollars were involved.

Area I: The Demand Deposit Accounting System. The largest single job performed by OPG was demand deposit accounting (DDA), the complex process of handling the physical flow of paper and communications, posting transactions, distributing processed items, and producing the bank's daily statement of operating condition. Some 2,000 employees in Area I performed this work. The process was composed of three parts: the "front end," which received, encoded, and read transactions onto magnetic computer tapes; the data center, which sorted the data and printed statements; and the "back end," which microfilmed and filed the checks of Citibank's own customers, prepared and mailed their statements, and handled accounting exceptions.

Around the clock, mail sacks containing checks, deposit slips, traveler's checks, transfer vouchers, credit memos, and other paper transaction records arrived in the eighth-floor receiving room at 111 Wall Street to enter the front end of the demand deposit accounting system. The first step of that process was to weigh the bags, gauging the volume of work coming in: one pound of mail equaled about 300 items to be processed.

Each incoming mailbag contained a control sheet, listing the various bundles of checks and the aggregate total of the bundles. Contents were checked against control sheets to ensure that all bundles listed were actually received. From this point onward in the DDA system, each batch of material was signed for whenever it moved from one area of responsibility to another. The records of these transfers, together with any changes in batch totals, as discrepancies were discovered or generated, were accumulated by a proof clerk on each operating shift. The following morning, these proof worksheets were consolidated into the bank's daily report of its operating condition, as required by the Federal Reserve System.

Materials arriving from other banks and check clearinghouses were already partly processed; but items from domestic Citibank branches, the head office, mail deposits, and lockboxes had to be encoded with machine-readable information. These papers were distributed to one of the 150 magnetic-ink encoding machines, where operators would key the dollar amounts into a keyboard. The machines would print these amounts on the checks, accumulating batch totals for each 300 checks processed. Some machines had several pockets and sorted the work into different pockets for different kinds of media, adding up separate control totals for each pocket. As the pockets filled, the paper was unloaded into conveyor trays, to be transported to the next operation, where the checks were read by machines and sorted by their destination, while the information from the checks was recorded on computer tape.

Encoder operators were generally women, who worked on an incentive pay arrangement and processed 800 to 1,100 items per hour. No direct record of keypunching accuracy was kept, and operators were not penalized for errors. About 600,000 checks each day entered the back end of Citibank's process, where they were microfilmed, screened for exceptions, and filed by customer for rendition and mailing of statements.

At the read/sort machines, on the floor above, the paper media were sorted into two major classifications. "On-us" checks—those written against the accounts of Citibank's own customers—were directed to the back end of the DDA system; "transit" checks, written on other banks, were directed to the various check clearinghouses and exchanges. Firm deadlines held for these exchanges. For example, the major Manhattan banks met at 10 A.M. each morning to trade checks with each other and to settle the differences between the checks paid and collected for other banks. This meeting had been a New York tradition for well over a hundred years; banks were not late for the exchange.

Overdrafts, stop payment orders, and "no-post" items were listed by the computer and referred to exception clerks, who searched through the incoming paper for the offending items, in order to route them to the proper offices for special handling. No-posts were especially troublesome; about 1,300 items per day, with an average value of $1,000 each, would flow into the back end, destined for accounts that had been closed, or were burdened by attachments, or had invalid numbers, or belonged to recently deceased owners, or were suspected of fraudulent activity. On a typical day, the exception clerks would fail to find between 50 and 100 of these checks, and the cases would be referred to the investigation unit.

In the filing and signature-checking section, women worked at 158 large filing machines, where each operator was responsible for 5,000 to 7,000 accounts. In addition to simply filing the day's flow of checks, each operator handled telephoned check-cashing authorizations; reconciled "full sheets" (the first pages of multi-page monthly statements); compiled the daily activity of medium-volume accounts (between 25 and 125 items per day) into so-called SMUT listings;[1] and ruled off the accounts scheduled for next-day statement rendition.

Nine clerks in the breakdown section received the checks for the next day's statements from the filing clerks, collated them with the statements arriving from the computer printer, and prepared the work for the rendition group for the following day. The 60 women in rendition confirmed the count of checks to go with each statement, observed special mailing instructions, and sorted the outgoing mail into heavy, medium, and light weight classifications.

Throughout the DDA process, errors could be generated in a variety of ways.

---

[1] The Citibank executives interviewed for this background material were generally young men who had served with OPG for only two or three years. They did not know the antecedents of the acronym SMUT.

If out of adjustment, any of the machines could eat a check. Multipocket encoders could add a check into the total for one pocket, but sort the paper into a different pocket, creating a shortage in one batch of material and a corresponding overage in another. Conveyor trays could be spilled, and loose paper could be stored in desk drawers, or shoved under furniture, or swept out in the trash. The bank's proofing system recorded variances in all the processing steps, and accumulated the errors in the "difference and fine" account—commonly called the "D&F."[2]

The Operating Group Staff. By tradition, OPG was a service function to the customer-contact divisions of the bank. Citibank's top management attention was directed outward—toward the market. OPG was expected to respond to change as generated and interpreted by the customer-contact offices. As a consequence, tradition held that the career path to the top in banking led through line assignments in the market-oriented divisions. "The phrase 'back office' is commonly assumed to mean 'backwater,'" said Reed. "Operations is a secure haven for the people who have grown up in it; it's a place of exile for people in the other divisions."

In 1970, most of OPG's management was made up of career employees who had spent 15 to 25 years with the group, often beginning their service with several years of clerical-level work before advancing to supervisory jobs. Through years of contact with "their" outside divisions of the bank, managers had

built up rich personal acquaintance with the people they served. Frequent telephone contacts reinforced these relationships. Dick Freund, OPG's vice president for administration and a veteran of 42 years' service with the group, commented on the close interaction between OPG people and the customer-contact offices:

> Problem solving here is typically done on a person-to-person basis. For example, an account officer in International Banking, faced with tracing some amendment to a letter of credit, would know that Jerry Cole, an assistant vice president on the 22nd floor, could find the answer. He'd call Jerry, and yes, Jerry would get him an answer. Whatever else Jerry was doing in the Letter of Credit Departments could wait; when a customer needs an answer, our men jump. They're proud of the service they can give.

Recruits for the managerial ranks of the bank typically came directly from the college campus. Freund described the process:

> We hire people straight out of college—most of them without business experience—and shuttle them around in a series of low-level jobs while they learn the bank. The Yale and Princeton and Harvard types eventually settle in the customer-contact offices; the Fordham and St. John's and NYU types come to Operating Group. We don't have the glamorous jobs that IBG and Corporate can offer, but even so there's a lot of prestige to working for First National City, and the security we offer means a lot to some of these people. I know one officer who bases his whole employment interview on security. "You come to work for us," he says, "and put in a good day's work, and you'll never have to worry about your job. Never."

---

[2] The source of the name "D&F" for the variance account was obscure—one manager thought that a monetary fine once may have been levied against the bank that failed to balance its accounts perfectly.

Management Succession and the Changing Role of the Operating Group. Freund traced the recent succession of top managers at OPG:

> From 1964 to 1968, when he retired, we had a top man who convinced the Policy Committee that our operating capabilities were becoming more and more important—that we simply couldn't afford to take them for granted. There was a tidal wave of paperwork coming—the same wave that swamped so many brokerage houses in 1968—and we had to pay attention. Until 1968, nobody cared much.
>
> The first clear signals that management attitudes toward the Operating Group were changing came in 1968, when Bill Spencer was appointed executive vice president in charge of Operations. Mr. Spencer was generally regarded as a prime candidate for the bank's presidency. It was plain that his appointment wasn't some form of punishment. He had to be here for a reason, and the reason had to be that Operations was, after all, an important part of the corporation.

It was Spencer who recruited John Reed to move from the International Banking Group to Operations, and who promoted Reed to senior vice president, in 1969. "And that was another sign that things were changing," Reed said. "For one thing, nobody my age had ever made SVP before. But more important, I wasn't a 'banker' in the traditional sense. Most of Operations' management had been in the group for 15 to 30 years; I'd only been with Citibank for 5 and none of that was with OPG."

Reed's undergraduate training had been in American literature and physical metallurgy. After a brief job with Goodyear Tire and Rubber and a tour in the Army, he had taken a master's degree in management at Massachusetts Institute of Technology, and then joined the IBG planning staff, where he applied systems concepts to the international banking field with impressive results. His rise in the organization was not at all the usual pattern of career development, as the experience of other bank officers suggests. For example, a gray-haired senior vice president from the Corporate Banking Group reported: "I've spent all my life in the bank. I was trained by assignment to different departments every two years; then, when I went into a line position, I had enough experience to correct something by doing it myself. At the very worst, I always knew people in the other departments who could straighten out any problem."

A PBG vice president said: "I started with Citibank as a night clerk in Personal Banking. It was 10 years before I reached supervisory ranks, and by then I'd had a lot of experience in credit and in operations as well."

A newly appointed assistant vice president in the Operating Group added: "I joined the bank as a naive liberal arts graduate and spent three years in clerical work before making first-line supervision. After eight years as a supervisor, you get a pretty good feeling for what's happening around you."

In May 1970, to the surprise of no one, William Spencer was named president of First National City Corporation. Reed—youth, nonbanking background, and all—was selected to head the Operating Group.

Operating Group Costs. By tradition, the method of meeting increased work loads in banking was to increase staff. If an operation could be done at the rate of 800 transactions per day, and the load increased by 800 pieces per day, then the manager in charge of that operation would hire another person; it was taken for granted. Financial reports would follow, showing in the next month-end statement that expenses had risen, and explaining the rise through the increased volume of work processed.

But in the late 1960s, the work load began to rise faster than the hiring rate could keep up; moreover, operator productivity decreased. Backlogs of work to be done would pile up in one OPG department or another, and they could not be cleared away without overtime. Even with extensive reassignment of people and with major overtime efforts, some departments would periodically fall behind by two or even three weeks, generating substantial numbers of complaints from customers. Three or four times a year, special task forces would be recruited from other branches of the bank to break the bottlenecks of these problem departments. Trainees, secretaries, junior officers, and clerks would be drafted for evening and weekend work, at overtime pay rates. "The task force approach is inefficient, annoying, and expensive, but it gets us out of the hole," said Freund. "A lot of these people don't *want* to work these hours, but it has to be done." In 1970, OPG spent $1,983,000 on overtime pay.

There were other sources of expense in the Operating Group that did not show up on financial reports. Reed described a major area of hidden costs:

If we have cashed a $1,000 check drawn on the Bank of America in California, we are going to be out $1,000 until we send them the check. If we miss sending the check out today, it will wait until tomorrow's dispatches to the West Coast, and we'll wait a day a longer for that $1,000. There are rigid deadlines for each of the clearinghouses; even a relatively small number of checks missing these deadlines can cost us a great deal of money. If each day only 3 percent of the $2 billion we handle is held over, then we will lose the interest on $60 million for one day. That turns out to be something like $3 million a year in lost earnings. We call it "lost availability."

That's a big number. Yet, until a few months ago we were making no effort to reduce it, or even to measure it. No one had thought of it as a cost. Check processing has always been treated as a straight-line operation, with bags of checks going through the line as they were received. Whatever wasn't processed at the end of the day was held over, and cleaned up the following day. It was just another clerical operation.

In 1970, lost availability amounted not to 3 percent of the value of checks processed, but to 4 percent.

Operating Group Quality. "Quality is something we really can't measure," said Freund. "But we can get perceptions that the level of service we're providing isn't acceptable. For all our outlay of expenses, it seems we are not improving, or even maintaining, our performance."

Indications of poor service came to OPG in the form of customer complaints, usually voiced through account officers from the market-contact divisions of the bank. Failures could take many forms, including loss of checks after they had been posted, late mailing of statements, miscoding of checks, payment of checks over stop orders, misposting of transfer, and, on occasion, loss of whole statements. Since any kind of error could cause inconvenience to the customer, the people in direct touch with the market were highly sensitive to quality. These account officers frequently assumed the role of problem solvers on the customer's behalf, traveling to the Wall Street office to work directly with OPG staff to remedy specific errors affecting their accounts. A separate section had been set up to analyze and correct errors in customer accounts; its backlog of unsolved inquiries was a major indicator to management of OPG's quality level. In the fall of 1970, this investigations department faced a backlog of 36,000 unsolved cases.

The importance of error-free operation to the customer-contact officers was pointed out by several officers from outside of OPG. A vice president from Corporate Banking Group said:

> Sure, I know the volume of paper has gone up. I know we have 750,000 accounts, and most of them are handled for years without a mistake. But Operations has to perform at 100 percent, not at 99 percent. Errors can be terribly embarrassing to the customer; repeated errors can lose customers for us. I have 600 checks missing from last month's statement for a major government account . . . and there were 400 missing from the previous month's statement. Now how can I sell additional services to that account, when we can't even produce a correct monthly statement for him?

An assistant vice president from Personal Banking added:

> We tell the customer that his canceled check is his legal receipt, and then we lose the check. What am I supposed to tell the man then? I can get him a microfilmed copy of the check, but that's not very useful as a legal document, is it?

An account officer in the International Banking Group said:

> Just getting a simple transfer through the books can generate a whole family of problems. Here's a typical case. A translator at 111 Wall Street miscodes the original transaction (it was written in Portuguese), and the transfer goes to the wrong account. When that customer inquires, we trace the error and reverse it. But before the correction goes through, a follow-up request comes in from Brazil; it's a duplicate of the first request, and our people don't catch the fact it's a follow-up, so they put through another transfer. Now the same item has gone through twice. Where does it all end? My customer is tired of writing letters about it.

And a CBG vice president sighed: "If our operations were perfect, we'd have a tremendous tool to go out and sell against the competition."

The Technological Fix. An important issue for DPG was the extent to which its problems could be remedied through technology. Reed explained:

> The customer-contact side of the bank, and to some extent the top management group, shows a natural tendency to press in the direction of great, massive, new, total computer systems—bringing the ultimate promise of technology into instant availability. It has been natural for all of us to blame mistakes and daily operating problems on inadequate systems; after all, if the systems were perfect, those mistakes would be impossible. But maybe we've all been brainwashed. Maybe we expect too much.

Fifteen years before, Citibank had acquired its first computer—a desk-sized Burroughs machine used to calculate interest on installment loans. Over the next four years, OPG had cooperated in an extensive research program on automated check processing, based on equipment developed by ITT to encode and sort mail in European post offices. This experimental system had progressed to the point of pilot use on the accounts of First National City's own employees when, in 1959, the American Banking Association adopted Magnetic Ink Character Recognition (MICR) as an industrywide standard approach to check processing. Citibank immediately dropped the ITT system and installed MICR equipment.

Although the computer facilities had grown immensely in the ensuing decade, the basic process performed by OPG remained the same. "For example," said Reed, "people used to verify names and addresses against account numbers by looking them up in paper records. Now they sit at cathode-ray tubes instead, but they're still doing the same operation."

Reed's computer people had reported to him that Citibank's use of machines was already highly efficient. The Operating Group was—and had been for several years—at the state-of-the-art level of computer use. A new survey by the American Bankers Association seemed to verify this conclusion: whereas the average large bank spent over 30 percent of its back-office budget on machine capacity, OPG spent less than 20 percent.

Reed paused beside his corner window and said:

Think about this for a minute. We've been running this operation as if it were a computer center. We've been hoping for some Great Mother of a software system to come along and pull the family together. Well, she's slow. None of us children has heard one word from her. Maybe she's not coming. What if it's *not* a computer center we have here? What other point of view could we take that would result in running the

Operating Group differently? Better? What if it's a *factory* we've got here?

The Factory Concept. Through much of August 1970, Reed had worked with Small and White to develop the implications of viewing OPG as a high-speed, continuous-process production operation. White, working without an official title, had just joined Reed's staff after six years with Ford Motor Company, most recently as manager of engineering financial analysis for Ford's product development group. At the age of 35, with an Ohio State bachelor of science degree and an MBA from the University of Florida behind him, White brought a firm conviction to OPG that the McNamara philosophy of budgets, measurements, and controls was the only way to run a production operation.

Now, in early September, Reed was trying some of these ideas on Freund to get a sense of their impact on the traditional banker. Freund, with more than four decades in the organization, was serving as a sounding board; Reed had almost decided to carry a new program to the Policy Committee of the bank, and he wanted to anticipate their reactions:

We know where we want the Operating Group to be in five years' time. For 1971 and 1972, we want to hold expenses flat; in spite of the rising transaction volumes we'll keep the same $150 million expense level as this year, and after that we'll let costs rise by no more than 6 percent a year. By 1975, that will mean a $70 million annual saving compared to uncontrolled growth at 15 percent. At the same time, we want to improve service and eliminate our bottlenecks and backlogs, like the jam-up in investigations.

To accomplish those goals, though,

we will have to put over a fundamental change in outlook. We must recognize the Operating Group for what it is—a factory—and we must continually apply the principles of production management to make that factory operate more efficiently.

It is not important for the people in the factory to understand banking. We'll take the institutional objectives and restate them in terms of management plans and tasks that are quite independent of banking. The plain fact is that the language and values we need for success are not derived from banking, and we couldn't achieve what we want in terms of systems development and operations if they were.

To control costs, we must think in terms of costs. That means bringing in management people trained in production management—tough-minded, experienced people who know what it is to manage by the numbers and to measure performance against a meaningful budget. We have to infuse our management with a new kind of production-oriented philosophy, and the process has to start with new, outside points of view. Good production people in here can provide a seed crystal and the present management staff can grow around the seed. Some of them will make it; others won't. Our headhunters can find the top factory management people to start the reaction. From there on, it's up to us.

Our costs are out of control because we don't know what they are, let alone what they should be. Our quality is criticized when we don't have any idea what quality really is, or how to measure what we're already doing. Our processes run out of control and build up backlogs because our efforts are aimed at coping with transactions instead of understanding what made them pile up in the first place.

I'm not talking about turning Operating Group *into* a factory. I'm talking about recognizing that it *is* a factory, and always has been. The function isn't going to change, but the way we look at it and manage it must.

Reed turned to Freund, who had been listening intently, and said: "What will they say to that, Dick?"

Freund smiled and his eyes sparkled:

They'll go for the stable budget idea, and in spite of skepticism they will hope you can do it. They'll love the idea of improved service, but they'll know you can't pull that one off if you're holding costs down. And the factory management idea?

There's one other bit of history you should know, John. The first engineer we ever hired came to work here in 1957, the year after we bought our first little computer. He was an eager guy, really impressed by the challenge of managing back-office operations. He poked around for a few days and then came back to the head office to declare that this wasn't a bank at all. It was a factory, he said. Nothing but a goddamn paperwork factory. That was after just two weeks on the job. It was his last day on the job, too.

Reed grinned broadly and turned to face White. "Are you ready to move out of the office, Bob? This concept is going to fly, and we're going to need someone down at Wall Street who can make it happen. Why don't you get yourself ready to take over Area I?"

CASE

FIRST NATIONAL CITY BANK OPERATING GROUP (B)

Picture a high-pressure pipeline, five feet in diameter, carrying money to dozens of different distribution pipelines. Your job is to make a lot of plumbing changes in the pipes, but you can't shut off the flow of money while you work. If anything goes wrong and the pipe breaks, all those dollars are going to spill out on the floor. In a week's time, you'll be wading around in 10 billion dollars. You'll be up to your eyebrows in money. Other people's money.

John Reed, one of six executive vice presidents of Citibank and the officer in charge of the bank's Operating Group (OPG), was reflecting on the process of change in a continuous-process, high-volume production operation. It was January 1973, and Reed was reviewing the accomplishments of the past two and a half years. On the surface, it was easy to document progress; OPG had numbers to show for its efforts. But Reed was anticipating criticism, too, as he prepared for the policy committee meeting at the end of the month. After all, the group's performance hadn't been perfect; the money pipeline had broken down for the second time only four months ago. Several customer-contact divisions still complained that service and quality levels in OPG were going downhill, in spite of numeric measurements that showed substantial improvement. And Reed's fellow EVPs and division heads on the policy committee had tenacious memories.

This case was prepared by John A. Seeger, research associate (under the direction of Professor Jay W. Lorsch and Associate Professor Cyrus F. Gibson).

Copyright © 1975 by the President and Fellows of Harvard College. Harvard Business School case 474-166.

Added to his other concerns was a new situation, highly visible to the bank as a whole. Organizers for the Office and Professional Workers Union (OPWU) were handing out thousands of leaflets to workers at 111 Wall Street, OPG's office building. Citibank's pay scales were competitive with other Manhattan employers' rates, but there were some indications of dissatisfaction in the work force. The previous year, for example, 125 women had walked off the job with a list of grievances; bringing the situation back to normal had required four months' full-time effort by one of OPG's most experienced assistant vice presidents. There was little feeling among top management that unionization was an immediate threat, but still the OPWU leaflets could not be ignored.

How, Reed wondered, could changes in the bank's back office be evaluated in terms of their impact on the rest of the institution? How could the new nonbanking approach of the Operating Group be made meaningful to the traditional bankers from the market-oriented divisions? For that matter, how could Reed himself picture the full impact of his changes on OPG and on the bank?

He stood at the window of his Manhattan office, high above the early morning traffic on Park Avenue. Behind him on his huge desk lay the two documents he had studied the night before. One was a draft of a speech that Robert White, senior vice president in charge of the production areas of OPG, would soon deliver to the American Bankers Association (ABA). The speech outlined the management approaches Citibank had applied to its back-office operations over the previous two years. Citibank's success in gaining control of its paperwork had attracted industrywide attention; in 1971 and 1972, OPG had handled substantial increases in volume of work, while reducing its expenditures below the 1970 level. The chairman of the First National City Corporation had been widely quoted as crediting the Operating Group for a major share of the bank's increased earnings. Judging by the numbers, John Reed had few reasons for concern.

The second document on his desk, however, seemed to tell a different story. It was a consultant's report, which Reed had commissioned in order to hear an outside viewpoint on the effects of the changes he and his colleagues had engineered in the past two years. The report was based largely on interviews the consultants had conducted with some 70 officers of the bank, both inside OPG and in the market-contact divisions; it focused sharply on some undesirable side effects of OPG's changes. The imposition of tight control policies, the report suggested, could lead to anxiety and insecurity in middle management. These fears could lead, in turn, to the establishment of unrealistic goals (as an effort to please the new bosses), and to increased resistance to change (as middle management's effort to protect itself). The consequence of these two factors could be poor performance, seen as missed deadlines and crises, and as a

sensed need by top management for still tighter controls. It was a classic vicious circle.

Placed side by side, the two documents made interesting reading. Reed wondered how OPG could learn from the comparison—how it could avoid unanticipated consequences of change in the future.

Change in the Operating Group, 1970–1972

Soon after his promotion to head OPG in May 1970, Reed had faced the question of defining just what OPG was. Was it, as banking tradition dictated, simply a mechanical support group for the customer-contact offices of the bank? Or could it be seen as an independent, high-volume production operation—a factory—which designed and controlled its own processes and products in the style of a manufacturing organization?

Reed decided that OPG was a factory. As such, it badly needed managers who knew how to run factories—people skilled in planning and controlling mass production processes. Dick Freund, OPG's vice president for administration and a veteran of 45 years' service with the bank, described the group's first effort to recruit professional production management:

> What industries do you think of when you want examples of outstanding factory management? Well, automotives have to be close to the top of the heap. And what companies do you think of? The winners: General Motors and Ford. The first head-hunter Reed turned loose on the job happened to have his foot in the door at Ford. You should have seen the first man who came to interview; we really went all the way to impress him. Reed had the fellow out to his home to talk, and so did Spencer (the bank's president). The guy was obviously impressed, and went back to

Detroit to think it over. Then he told us "no." His family was well established in their present home, and he didn't want to bring them to New York. His kids had put on a very convincing flip-chart presentation, he told us. Can you imagine it? Reed and Spencer were just incredulous—couldn't believe it. Here's a really top guy, and he lets his kids decide what he's going to do! We were flabbergasted.

Succeeding efforts at recruiting production-oriented executives were more fruitful, and OPG began to fill its management ranks with young, aggressive talent. One of the early arrivals was Bob White, who left Ford Motor Company to work as John Reed's assistant. For several months, the two men worked intensively to build a specific action framework around the 1971 goals of OPG. Then White, supported by other newly recruited executives—three of them from Ford—moved into the line organization to take charge of the transaction-processing responsibilities of OPG's Area I. (See "First National City Bank Operating Group (A)," HBS case 474-165, for the basic organization of the Operating Group.)

Top-Down Management

The draft of Bob White's speech for the ABA explained how the change process began with a fundamental look at the group's whole philosophy of management:

In general terms, we can say that "administering" connotes a passive mode, while "managing" bespeaks an active mode. An administrator is, in a sense, a bystander, keeping watch on a process, explaining it if it goes awry. But managing means understanding your present world, deciding what you would like it to be, and making your desired results happen. A manager is an agent of the future, of change.

The fact is that, traditionally, banking operations are not really managed at all. In a sense, the people in charge are running alongside the processing line, instead of being on top of it pressing the process levers. All you can do in such a situation is react. At Citicorp, we decided that this was unacceptable. We wanted to manage our back office, not administer it.

There are two critical prerequisites for this: conviction and orientation toward results. Each manager must be absolutely convinced that he can control all factors relevant to his operation. That conviction must begin at the top, and must carry with it a willingness to spend for results. I am talking about spending in terms of change to the organization, its structure, its fabric—about the amount of top management time and energy expended, and about the type of people you are willing to accept in your culture.

To ensure an environment that will foster the kind of dedication and commitment we need, we use a pass/fail system as a management incentive. A manager passes or fails in terms of result objectives he himself has set within the top-down framework. He is rewarded or not rewarded accordingly. No excuses or rationalization of events "beyond one's control" are accepted.

"I've been treated better in the past three years than in all of the previous nine years."[1]

---

[1] Italicized quotations used throughout this case are representative comments of other managers who were involved in or affected by the OPG reorganization, as reported to the consultants whom Reed had hired. These quotations, of course, did not appear in the ABA speech.

"Reed has been very fair with everybody who has produced, in a salary sense."

"The feeling was we should do things, especially make or beat budget, and that if we didn't we should expect to be out."

The ABA speech continued:

The style of management we sought was top-down management. Each manager sets his own objectives for his own level in translating objectives set from above. Although people felt initially constrained by a top-down approach, I am fully convinced that it is the *only* approach. Each manager is not only free to exercise his vision—he is expected to do so. He is unfettered by what is traditional, by what is the norm. Nothing is sacred. The real problem is that the top-down system *strains* people, but it does not *constrain* them. Good people thrive in such an environment.

"This job is exciting, like working for a glamour company, almost like having your own company. I really like being a 'maverick.'"

"I like the opportunity to work for change, and to have responsibility for it. What I don't like is the incompetence of those who resist."

"I work 10 to 12 hours a day. I guess Reed works 24 hours."

"OPG has lived in crisis for the past six years, but it's worse now, especially the hours and pressure that everyone is under. I spent the whole summer working six days a week and never saw the kids. Finally got up the courage to tell my wife I was working Labor Day weekend. She put it to me; well, I called and said I wasn't coming in. The guys I used to work with say to me now, 'Congratulations,' even though my new job isn't a promotion. They see me as being better off, just to be out of that place."

White's speech continued:

If you start your management process with the first-line supervisors and accumulate upward, you are assuming that the smartest people and the strategic direction for the business come from the bottom of the management pyramid. If this is true, we need to reverse the present salary structure so that the first-line people are paid the most money. It is not a question of brightness or ability, it is rather that top management has a better view of the overall organization, its direction, goals, strengths, weaknesses, and so forth.

The speech went on to outline the basic management theories that OPG had formalized and applied to its functions in the past three years. "Management 101," it was called, and it was simply stated as "knowing *where we are, where we want to be, and how we plan to get there.*" Responsible managers were expected to know, in formal terms, the current state of their world and all the processes that were producing their current results; the *desired* state of their area and the processes that would produce *those* results; and finally the changes they would make in today's processes to turn them into tomorrow's processes. "It is not results we are managing, but processes that achieve results." After defining the 1970 situation of the Operating Group and its three goals for 1971 (flat costs, improved service, and elimination of the investigations backlog), the speech proceeded:

What was left was to design the action plan—the processes that would get us to the results we wanted. (See Figure A, which reproduces a slide shown to the audience at this point in the speech.)

We planned to build a strong management team, to hire managers who had the conviction and motivation to control

FIGURE A   Phase I Action Plan, November 1970–June 1971

- Hire the right "Top Management" people to build up a new style of management team.
- Squeeze out the "Fat."
- Implement major new computer systems.
- Develop a Financial Control System that forecasts:
  - People and annual salary rates.
  - Overtime.
  - Lost availability.
  - Inventory.
- Define the "Rock" cleanup process.
  - Separate backlog from current work.
  - Do today's work today.

---

their own operations with management skills as opposed to administrative skills.

We planned in 1971 to cut out all the fat accumulated during the prior 10 years of 18 percent annual cost rises—at that rate we knew there was some fat.

We planned to develop and install a financial control system, emphasizing simplicity and the major cost elements: (1) people, (2) overtime, (3) process float, or lost availability, and (4) equipment and computers.

We planned to define a process for cleaning up "rocks," such as the 36,000 backlogged investigations, so that we could come out from under the crisis environment and get control of our processing. This meant designing the techniques to separate rocks out from current work so that we could both dissolve the rock and do today's work today so that the rock would not grow.

In fact, the real significance of the Phase I action plan was that it enabled us to get a handle on the operating environment. With this program, we started to get on top of the back office so as to control and manage it.

"The whole management team was brought in cold, predominantly from Ford. So you had this whole new team applying industrial concepts to paper flow. It has worked. But people took affront that these bright young stars were coming along and changing the whole new world."

"The number of people actually severed from the bank was actually very small for the organization—only 179— but the image is very negative."

"The fear of a cut—a layoff—wasn't a very realistic one. In fact, there have been very few—but the perception of it was the important thing."

"The key issue in the bank today is job security."

"There was a language problem. The buzz words used by the new guys differed from the language the old managers used and understood."

"Lots of people close to retirement retired early. People at the AVP level are running scared."

"The bank no longer offers security to old-timers. My chance to become a VP is almost nil, regardless of performance; I just don't have the right background."

"People have really put out in this place, some of them have really worked. But when some old-timers were pushed out, it hurt a lot of us. We said, 'Is that what's in store for us if we keep going here?' Also, when the old-timers who knew other parts of the bank left, we lost a way to get a lot of contacts with the other groups."

To gain control of costs, it was necessary to forecast what our expenditures would be *before* we were committed. We developed a one-page expense summary report based on forecast, rather than on history. (See Exhibit 1) The manager is in control of all his variables. We do not recognize any type of expense as uncontrollable or institutional. Forecasts are updated monthly and are met.

"We have a tendency now to try to meet due dates at all costs."

"Due dates for changes are, in most cases, absurd. Time commitments are ridiculous, and the consequences of not meeting due dates aren't made known beforehand."

"People try to be optimistic to please the boss. When they miss the milestones, they get screwed."

But when we set about implementing new computer-based systems, we learned a very important lesson: We hadn't gone back to basics enough. We found we did not really understand the present processes completely.

And so a second action plan, Phase II, was devised in June of 1971. We called it the Performance Criteria System, PCS. What we were aiming at was breaking up the operations into manageable, controllable, understandable pieces. These were the key approaches to defining the back-office dynamics.

1. Define the products/services as recognized by the customer.

2. Develop a customer-to-customer flowchart and procedures for processing each product/service.
3. Develop the organization to match and support the product definition and process flow on a customer-to-customer basis.
4. Develop our physical layout into a closed-room/one-floor layout that matched the flows, procedures, and organization so as to enhance control and minimize movement.
5. Decentralize all peripheral equipment.
6. Incorporate support functions into the responsible line organization.

Our processing had always been conceived of in functions, rather than in system processes. All the work flowed into one pipeline of processing functions; for example: preprocessing, encoding, read-to-tape, sorting, reconcilement, repair, and dispatch. You can visualize the functions along a vertical axis, and the people and time frame along the horizontal axis (see Exhibit 2), giving us a very wide pipe carrying 2 to 3 million transactions per day. If the one pipe breaks, all the work in the pipe before the break stops or spills out. That shouldn't happen often, but when it does, the whole operation stops.

We aimed to break down that pipeline into several smaller lines, each carrying a different product and each supervised by a single manager who controlled every aspect of his process, from the time a customer originates a transaction all the way through a straight line until we dispatch the results back to the customer. (For an example of this straight-line flow, see Exhibit 3.)

We began by breaking the operations out on the basis of six separate input streams: two flows from our domestic branches, separate domestic and international mail deposit flows, one flow from our head office department, and one from incoming exchanges. Each of

EXHIBIT 1 1973 Expense Forecast (dollars in thousands)

AREA	DIVISION	DATE	EXHIBIT
AREA 1			

DOA RECAP

	MONTH OF JANUARY			MONTH OF FEBRUARY			MARCH–DECEMBER			FULL YEAR 1973		
	ACTUAL BUDGET	ACTUAL (O)/U BUDGET	ACTUAL (O)/U 1972	FORECAST	FORECAST (O)/U BUDGET	FORECAST (O)/U 1972	FORECAST	FORECAST (O)/U BUDGET	FORECAST (O)/U 1972	FORECAST	FORECAST (O)/U BUDGET	FORECAST (O)/U 1972
	ACTUAL	FORECAST	ACTUAL			ACTUAL			ACTUAL			ACTUAL
SALARIES												
Official and nonofficial												
Part-time												
Fringe benefits												
Overtime												
Temporaries												
Severance												
Subtotal salaries												
OTHER OPERATING (incl. 799's)												
Education & training												
Computer time—outside vendors												
Consultants												
Computers												
Furniture & equipment												
Insurance & legal												
Postage												
Stationery & supplies												
Telephone, telegrams, & cables												
Travel, membs. & subs.												
Business prom. & ent.												
Food												
Operating losses & losses not insured												
Difference & fine												
Lost availability												
Rent												
Rental Income												
OPC occupancy expense												
Real estate taxes												
Building depreciation												
Utilities												
Freight & cartage												
Other												
1972 related expense												
Provisions												
Subtotal other operating												
Total expense												

EXHIBIT 2   Functional Organization Pipelines

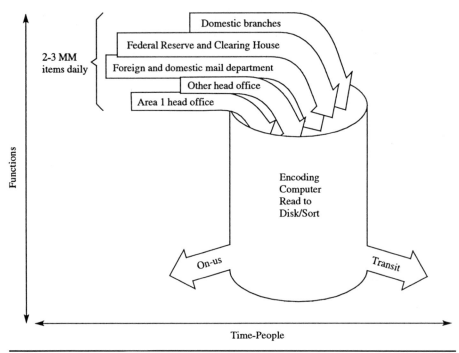

these became a separate processing line (see Exhibit 4). These flows are not mere theory; they exist in documented fact.

"In came flowcharting and the product-line concept. We had a flowchart that stretched across the room and back. White had an incredible ability to understand the whole thing—to point to something and just ask the critical question about how something worked, or why it was part of our activity and not somewhere else. The result was a definition of 11 different products and a full reorganization in one month. It's the only way to run a bank."

"Changes were viewed differently by different people. People started flowcharting everything, and Bob White was going over everything, step-by-step. But lots of people got the feeling that they

didn't know what to do. They didn't fit in this new environment."

The Blowup: September 1971

In August of 1971, White decided it was time to act on the new organization of Area I. "We had been talking a lot about reorganizing the flow," he said, "but nothing was actually happening. We had spent months with people, talking about implementation, and we thought they understood. It was time to move."

On a hot September Friday evening, when the regular work shift went home, equipment crews began the job of rearranging the facilities at 111 Wall Street. By Monday morning the physical layout was set up for six separate lines, each with

EXHIBIT 3 Straight-Line Organization

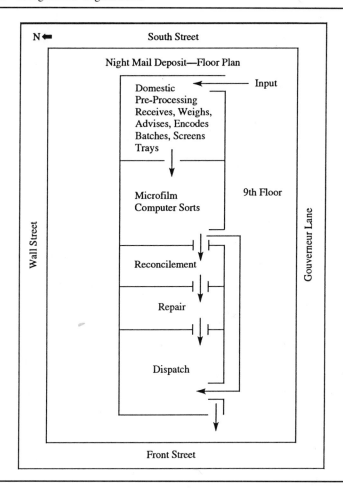

its own full complement of peripheral equipment, ready to begin work. And soon after the work force reported on Monday, it became clear that the Demand Deposit Accounting (DDA) system had problems. Equipment had been moved and connected, but technicians had not had time to check operations before it went back into service; some of the machines refused to operate at all. Machine operators, informed on Friday that they would still have their same machines but in different locations on Monday, arrived at work with questions and there were not enough supervisors to answer them. Leftover work from Friday's processing, tucked away in accustomed corners by machine operators, was nowhere to be found; the customary corners were gone.

The money pipeline creaked and groaned under the strain.

As the week wore on, new problems

EXHIBIT 4 Product/Process Organization Pipelines

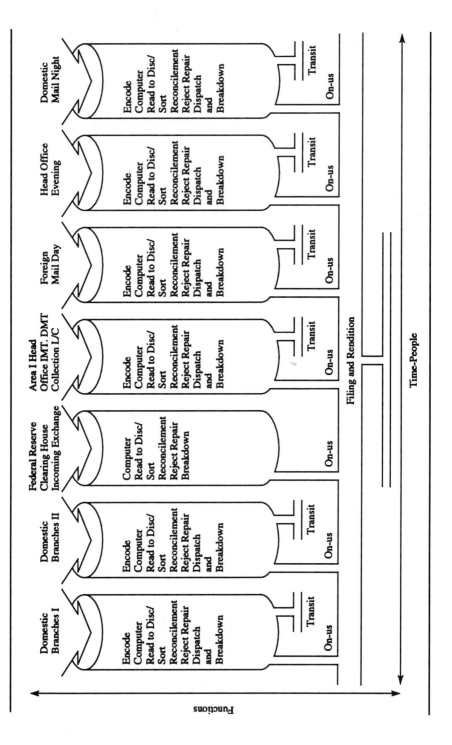

came to light. The three proofing clerks, who had handled three shifts of consolidated front-end operations, could not keep up with the load generated by decentralized work streams. With new people in charge of new areas, proof clerks did not know whom to call to resolve apparent discrepancies; the "Difference & Fine" (D&F) account of accumulated variances began to grow alarmingly. By the end of the week, it was apparent that Citibank's problems were greater than just debugging a new system. OPG's managers were inventing new systems on the spot, attempting to recover. By the second weekend of September, the disturbance had grown to tidal wave proportions. The D&F account hit $1.5 billion on each side of the ledger before heroic weekend work by the group's middle managers brought it back down to $130 million. First National City Bank failed to meet the other New York bankers at the 10 A.M. exchange, and it failed to file its Federal Reserve reports.

The money pipeline had burst.

Geoffrey MacAdams, the grey-haired head of the proofing operation, walked into the computer room, waving his hands in the air. "Stop the machines." he said haltingly to the computer operations head. "Stop the machines. It's out of control."

"I remember walking through the area and finding a pile of work, out on a desk-top, with a note on the top saying, 'This is out by a million, and I'm just too sleepy to find it,' " said one manager. "There was maybe 20 or 30 million dollars in the stack. At least the girl was good enough to put a note on it. We were learning, the hard way, not to put papers like that into desk drawers."

Larry Stoiber, operations head for four of the six processing lines, looked up slowly one morning when White greeted him, and he delayed several seconds before showing signs of recognition. Stoiber had been at work for 55 hours without a break. White sent him home in a Citibank car, with instructions not to let him back into the bank until he was coherent.

In two weeks' time the new production processes began to work. Within a month of the change, routine operations once more ran routinely (note the difference between White's memo of August 30 and the status report of October 8 on lost availability, included as Exhibits 5 and 6). But it was five months before the backlog of work and problems generated by the DDA blowup were resolved.

In early October, as the DDA system began to return to normal, and its managers turned their attention to the problems of cleaning up the side effects of the blowup, Reed visited the Wall Street building to talk to Small and White. "I wanted to be the first to tell you this news," he said. "The promotions committee met this morning. You have both been named Senior Vice Presidents of the bank." He smiled broadly. "Congratulations."

"The design for change from the top just cannot anticipate all the problems that are going to arise at the first-line supervisor level; those people have to know more than just the before and after job description."

"I'll tell you why people didn't protest the change, or question their instructions. We were scared—afraid of losing our jobs if we didn't seem to understand automatically."

"The changes were accompanied by a great fear that people would get fired. Most lower managers and clerical workers felt management—that's AVP level and above—was highly insensitive to people."

EXHIBIT 5 White's Memorandum of August 30, 1971

MEMORANDUM TO:
J. Cavaiuolo, Operations Head
L. Stoiber, Operations Head
F. Whelan, Operations Head

Effective Tuesday, August 31, I would like a report (attached) from each of you showing lost availability and deferred debits and credits for each of your operations:

- Branch—Whelan
- Domestic Mail—Stoiber
- Foreign Mail—Stoiber
- Head Office—Stoiber
- Lock Box—Stoiber
- Exchanges—Cavaiuolo

The first lost availability report should cover the period from the first city-country deadline on Monday to the New York–New Jersey deadline on Tuesday. The deferred debits and credits report should be based on one DDA update to the next.

The report should be completed and on my desk by 1:45 P.M. daily. Initially the report will be in addition to the regular lost availability daily report—I assume you will insure the report will tie. You are now each *personally* responsible for insuring that all lost availability is measured. I would rather not *ever* find any more "undiscovered" lost availability.

If you have any questions or any problems in meeting this deadline, see me today. If not, I will expect the first report at 1:45 P.M. on Tuesday.

Robert B. White
Vice President

August 30, 1971

"Reed and White and the new guys know what they're doing; they're good at setting up cost and quality measures and conceptualizing the system. But at the practical level, things haven't worked. In the past, new instructions would be questioned and worked through until they were either understood, or the designer was convinced there was a problem. For example, if I go out there and tell Mary to start writing upside down and backwards on what she is doing, she'll look at me and say 'Why?' because she knows me and to her it doesn't make sense. If one of the new guys tells her to write upside down and backwards, she'll do it and not say a word. If anything a little unusual starts to happen, she won't know why it's important, and she won't say a word about it. When the 'Ford kids' say do it, people do it. But they're scared.*"

"It hurt us, credibilitywise, with the rest of the bank. The sharks smelled blood in the water and came at us from all directions. But things are better now—an order of magnitude better."

Just a year later, in September 1972, the demand deposit accounting system

EXHIBIT 6   Excerpt from October 8, 1971, Internal Report on the Status of "Rocks" in the Demand Deposit Accounting System

Float

Float statistics for the month of September were not available due to incomplete data as a result of procedural changes caused by the recent reorganization. A data-capturing network has now been developed and implemented; and reliable and complete data were reported on October 1 and thereafter, indicating an average 3.2 percent lost availability for the three-day period October 1–5.

Lost Availability as a Percent of Potential

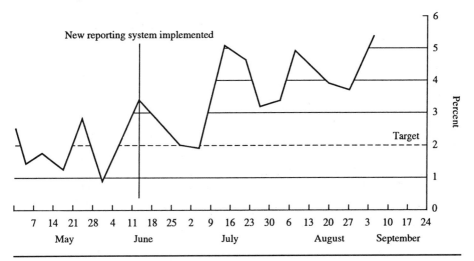

blew up again, this time centered in the back end of the process, where the filing and telephone authorization process was being changed to anticipate the installation of computer voice answer-back equipment. The changes altered the way accounts were ruled off in preparation for statement rendition, making it impossible for the file clerks to select the proper checks to match with the computer-printed last pages of customers' statements. Unlike the 1971 crisis, this blowup affected customers directly and immediately. "The problem looked critical to the branch people, who had customers standing in line at the tellers'

windows waiting for answers that never came. And it seemed critical to account officers in corporate banking, who couldn't get statements for their customers. But it was actually much less serious than the 1971 episode, because it didn't involve the proofing system," said White. "We were able to react much more quickly, and we were pretty much recovered from it within a month and a half."

Achievements in the Operating Group

The draft speech for the American Bankers Association summarized the results of Operating Group's improvement

EXHIBIT 7   Summary Expense Forecast

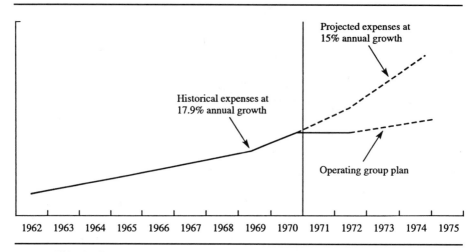

SOURCE: Slide taken from ABA speech.

efforts in two charts reproduced as full-color slides (see Exhibits 7 and 8). By the end of 1973, according to the forecast, personnel in the group would be reduced by 30 percent from 1970 levels; overtime would be down by 71 percent; lost availability would be down by 75 percent; and the backlog of investigations would be shrunk from 36,000 to 500 cases—one day's load. The speech elaborated:

The real achievement here, though, is that we forecasted what we would achieve and then made it happen. More-over, we *did* put together the kind of management team we wanted, and we *did* get hold of the processes within our shop. At the same time, we developed a control system to measure the two fac-ets of service to our customers: quality and timeliness. Quality measures error rate; it is the number of errors as a per-centage of the total work processed on a daily basis.

EXHIBIT 8   Results

Year	Headcount		Overtime		Lost Availability	
	Number of employees	Cumulative % decrease from 1970	$ (000)	Cumulative % decrease from 1970	$ (MMs)	% of potential
1970	7,975	—	1,983	—	56.4	4.0%
1971	6,610	17%	1,272	35%	32.8	2.0%
1972	5,870	26%	845	57%	26.5	1.8%
1973	5,528	30%	564	71%	14.2	0.5%

SOURCE: Slide taken from ABA speech.

We currently measure 69 different quality indicators, and we are meeting the standards 87 percent of the time. When a given indicator is met or beaten consistently, we tighten the standard; we expect to continue this process indefinitely.

Timeliness is the percentage of work processed in a given time period—generally a 24-hour time period. At the moment, we have defined 129 different standards for timeliness, and we expect that number to continue to grow. Today, we are meeting 85 percent of these standards. Moreover, we also continually tighten these standards as soon as we prove they can be consistently met. I think it is fair to say that our service performance has improved greatly since we began to hold costs flat—if for no other reason than that we now *really* know what we are doing.

"In order to make progress, we had to be firm with the other divisions of the bank. We used to interrupt anything in order to handle a special request. No more. We're consciously shutting them out, so we could work on the basic processes here. Now we have no people wandering in here to distract our clerks."

Changes were also evident from outside of OPG. Three officers from the customer-contact divisions commented as follows:

"My frustration is I wish there were more old-time bankers in there and fewer systems and organization types. There is a huge loss of old guys I can turn to for help in getting things done, people who know banking. Maybe they should keep just a few. Some. A few cents a share might well be worth it."

"People over here say that if those guys are so good, why do they keep screwing up? You'd think they'd learn something in two years."

"In the old days, when the old guys were running things, you knew who to go to. Now we don't know. Even if we find somebody, he's faced with a process where he couldn't give special service even if he wanted to."

White's speech concluded: "These, then, were the achievements of two years of fundamental change. They are, I think, substantial, and they provide us with the solid base we need to focus in on the future."

"One of John Reed's magazine articles that came around said something about people being replaceable, like machines. That hurt. You lose solidarity."

"Somebody asked me once if I liked it that we were working in what Reed called a factory. That really struck home. So, maybe it is like a factory. Why do they have to say it?"

CASE

PETER BROWNING AND CONTINENTAL WHITE CAP (A)

On April 1, 1984, Peter Browning assumed the position of vice president and operating officer of Continental White Cap, a Chicago-based division of the Continental Group, Inc. Having completed a successful five-year turnaround of Continental's troubled Bondware Division, Browning found this new assignment at White Cap to be a very different type of challenge. He was taking over the most successful of Continental's nine divisions—"the jewel in the Continental crown," as one Continental executive described it. White Cap was the market leader in the production and distribution of vacuum-sealed metal closures for glass jars.

Browning's charge, though, was to revitalize and reposition the division to remain preeminent in the face of threatened, but not yet fully realized, changes in the competitive environment. Sales were stable and costs were up. Recent years had brought changes in the market: one competitor in particular was utilizing price cuts for the first time to build market share, and the introduction of plastic packaging to many of White Cap's traditional customers threatened sales. White Cap had not yet developed a plastic closure or the ability to seal plastic containers. After more than 50 years of

_____

This case was prepared by Research Associate Mary Gentile (under the direction of Professor Todd D. Jick).

Copyright © 1986 by the President and Fellows of Harvard College. Harvard Business School case 9-486-090.

traditional management and close control by White Cap's founding family, corporate headquarters decided it was time to bring in a proven, enthusiastic, young manager to push the business toward a leaner, more efficient, and more flexible operation—one capable of responding to the evolving market conditions.

From the very start, Browning recognized two major obstacles that he would have to address. First, few managers or employees at White Cap acknowledged the need for change. Business results for more than 50 years had been quite impressive and, when dips were experienced, they were perceived as cyclical and transient. Second, White Cap had a family-style culture characterized by long-term loyalty from its employees, long-standing traditions of job security, liberal benefits, and paternalistic management. Attempts to alter these traditions would not be welcome.

Reflecting on his new assignment at White Cap, Browning recalled that at Bondware he had walked into a failing business where he "had nothing to lose." Now he was entering "a successful business with absolutely everything to lose." One White Cap manager observed: "White Cap will be the testing period for Peter Browning in the eyes of Continental." Browning's success in reframing the business would be critical for his future in corporate leadership there. Browning thought about the stern words of caution he had received from his boss, Dick Hofmann, executive vice president of the

Continental Group: "White Cap needs changes, but just don't break it while you're trying to fix it. Continental can't afford to lose White Cap."

White Cap Background

In 1926, William P. White ("old W.P.") and his two brothers started the White Cap Company in an old box factory on Goose Island, located in the Chicago River. From the beginning, the White Cap Company was active in many areas: in closure production and distribution, in new product development, and in the design of cap-making and capping machinery. Thus, White Cap promoted itself as not only a source of quality closures but also providers of a "Total System" of engineering and R&D support and service to the food industry. It claimed the latest in closure technology—for example, in 1954, White Cap pioneered the twist-off style of closure, and, in the late 1960s, it developed the popular "P.T." (press-on/twist-off) style of cap. It also took pride in its capping equipment and field operations service. White Cap's customers were producers of ketchup, juices, baby foods, preserves, pickles, and other perishable foods.

In 1956, the Continental Can Company bought White Cap, and, in 1984, the Continental Group, Inc., went from public to private as it was merged into KMI Continental, Inc., a subsidiary of Peter Kiewit Sons, a private construction company. The White Cap Company became Continental White Cap, the most profitable of the parent firm's nine divisions—each of which produced different types of containers and packaging.

Despite the sale of White Cap in 1956, the White family continued to manage the organization, and its traditional company culture persisted. As the manager of human resources at the Chicago plants expressed it: "I really think that many employees felt that White Cap bought Continental Can, instead of the other way around." W. P. White, the company founder, and later his son, Bob, inspired and encouraged a strong sense of family among their employees, many of whom lived in the Polish community immediately surrounding the main plant. Once hired, employees tended to remain and to bring in their friends and relatives as well. At the two Chicago plants in 1985, 51.2 percent of the employees were over 40 years old and 30 percent were over 50.

The Whites themselves acted as patrons, or father figures. Legends recounted their willingness to lend money to an hourly worker with unexpected medical bills, or their insistence, in a bad financial year, on borrowing the money for Christmas bonuses. In exchange for hard work and commitment, employees received good salaries, job security, and the feeling that they were part of a "winner." In an area as heavily unionized as Chicago, these rewards were potent enough to keep White Cap nearly union-free. Only the lithographers—a small and relatively autonomous group—were unionized.

White Cap was rife with rituals, ceremonies, and traditions. In the early days of the company, Mrs. W. P. White would prepare and serve lunch every day for the company employees in the Goose Island facility. Over the years, White Cap continued to provide a free family-style hot lunch for all salaried employees and free soup, beverage, and ice cream for the hourly workers.

A press department manager, a White Capper for 28 years, explained:

For work in a manufacturing setting, you couldn't do better than White Cap. White Cap isn't the real world; when the economy is hurting, White Cap isn't. White Cap always lived up to the ideal that "our people are important to us." They sponsored a huge family picnic every year for all White Cappers and friends. When they first instituted the second shift in the factory, they lined up cabs to take late workers home after their shift. They sponsored golf outings and an "old-timers' softball team." People generally felt that nothing's going to happen to us as long as we've got a White there.

But in 1982, Bob White stepped down and turned the management over to Art Lawson, who became vice president and executive officer. Lawson, 63 years old, was an old-time White Capper, and many saw him as simply a proxy for the Whites. Even Lawson would say that he saw himself as a caretaker manager, maintaining things as they had always been.

At about this time, price competition began to heat up in the closure industry. White Cap had been the market leader for over 50 years, but customers were beginning to take the Total System for granted. There were by then 5 significant manufacturers in the national marketplace and 70 worldwide who offered the twist-off cap. Competitors like National Can Company were beginning to slash prices, aware that the very advantage White Cap had maintained in the market (i.e., its R&D and full service) made it difficult for it to compete effectively with drastic price cutting.

Just at this time, plastic containers—requiring plastic closures—began to be available (see Exhibit 1). In 1982, the Food and Drug Administration had approved the use of a particular plastic substance as an appropriate oxygen-

barrier for food containers. Subsequently, the American Can Company's Gamma™ bottle, a squeezable plastic container, was adopted by the Heinz Company for its ketchup and by Hunt for its barbecue sauce. (White Cap had held 100 percent of the ketchup business worldwide.) Welch's jams and jellies also adopted this new technology, and the reasons were typical:

> Welch's expects the new packaging to help revitalize a relatively flat product category, having conducted research indicating that their customers are willing to pay more for the convenience of the squeezable plastic bottle.[1]

Another major White Cap account had announced plans to introduce a new juice line in plastic containers for the spring of 1986, as well. Without a competitive plastic closure, White Cap would continue to lose customers. Senior White Cap management, however, had been reluctant to allow R&D to commercialize plastics developments because such plastics threats in the past had never materialized.

In 1984, two years after Bob White had left, Peter Browning was named vice president and operating officer, reporting to Art Lawson. He took over a division with $175 million in gross sales, 1,450 employees (of whom 480 were salaried), 12 sales offices, and 4 plants (2 in Chicago, Illinois, 1 in Hayward, California, and 1 in Hazleton, Pennsylvania).

Peter Browning's Background

I'm Peter Browning and I'm 43 years of age. I have four children—three girls, 20, 16, and 12, and a 7-year-old son.

---

[1] Melissa Larson, "Dispensing Closures Revitalize Flat Markets," *Packaging*, August 1985, p. 25.

EXHIBIT 1   *Changes in the Container Industry*

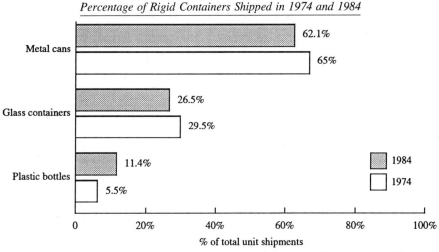

Percentage of Rigid Containers Shipped in 1974 and 1984

SOURCES: Bureau of the Census, Can Manufacturers' Institute, International Trade Association, and *U.S. Industrial Outlook 1985.*

Shipments of Plastic Bottles for Food

	Market Year			
	1978	1982	1983	1984 (estimated)
Millions of units	260	697	798	900

SOURCES: Bureau of the Census, International Trade Administration, and *U.S. Industrial Outlook 1985.*

My undergraduate degree is in history, and, while at White Cap, I earned my MBA through the Executive Program at the University of Chicago. I have been with Continental for 20 years.

This was Peter Browning's characteristic opening each time he presented himself and his ideas to a new audience. On first impression, Browning appeared youthful, charming, and intellectually and socially curious. Various employees and managers described him alternately as "Mr. Energy," "ambitious," "direct," "the most powerful boss I've had," "the quintessential old-time politician, shaking hands and kissing babies." His speeches to management and staff were peppered with inspirational aphorisms and historical, often military, metaphors, repeated as refrains and rallying cries.

In spring 1985, the Continental Group arranged for each of the nine divisional managers to be interviewed by industrial psychologists. The psychologist's report on Browning stated:

His intellectual ability is in the very superior range. . . . He is a hard-driving individual for whom success in an organization is extremely important. . . . Further, he is completely open in communicating the strategy he has conceived, the goals he has chosen, and the ongoing success of the organization against those goals. He cares about people, is sensitive to them, and makes every effort to motivate them. . . . His own values and beliefs are so strong and well-defined that his primary means of motivation is the instilling of enthusiasm and energy in others to think and believe as he does. By and large he is successful at this, but there are those who have to be motivated from their own values and beliefs, which may be different but which may nonetheless lead to productive action. These people are apt to be confused, overwhelmed, and left behind by his style.[2]

Browning's career began with White Cap and Continental Can in 1964 when he took a position as sales representative in Detroit. He continued in marketing with White Cap for nine years and then in other Continental divisions until 1979. At that time, he returned to Chicago to become vice president and general manager of Continental's Bondware Division. Once in the area again, Browning was able to touch base with old contacts from White Cap and to observe firsthand the challenges they faced.

At Bondware (producers of waxed paper cups for hot and cold beverages and food), Browning took over a business that had lost $24 million in five years (1975 to 1979) and that Continental could not even sell. Browning adopted a drastic and accelerated change program, employing what he called "radical surgery" to reduce employees by half (from 1,200 to 600), to eliminate an entire product line, to close four out of six manufacturing sites, and to turn the business around in five years.

---

[2] Alexander B. Platt, Platt & Associates, Inc., May 2, 1985.

Browning Is Reassigned

Early in 1984, Browning received his reassignment orders from the executive officers of the Continental Group (Stamford, Connecticut). They wanted definite changes in the way the White Cap Division did business, and they believed Browning—fresh from his success with Bondware and a veteran of White Cap himself—was surely the person to make those changes.

Continental's executive officers had several major concerns about White Cap. First of all, they saw competitive onslaught brewing that they believed White Cap's managers did not recognize. They believed the business instincts of White Cap's management had been dulled by a tradition of uncontested market leadership. The majority of White Cap's managers had been with the firm for over 25 years, and most of them had little intention of moving beyond White Cap, or even beyond their current positions. They were accustomed to Bob White's multilayered, formal, and restrained management style—a style that inhibited cross-communication and that one manager dubbed "management without confrontation." Some of them were startled, even offended, by the price-slashing tactics practiced by White Cap's most recent competitors, and they spoke wistfully of an earlier, more "gentlemanly" market style.

Continental's executive officers were also concerned that White Cap's longtime success, coupled with the benevolent paternalism of the White family management, had led to a padded administrative staff. They instructed Browning to communicate a sense of impending crisis and urgency to the White Cap staff, even as he reduced the salary and administrative costs which Continental perceived as inflated. Furthermore, he was to do all this without threatening White Cap's image in the marketplace or its tradition of employee loyalty.

Browning recognized that corporate attitudes toward White Cap were colored by a history of less than open and cooperative relations with Bob White:

> Bob White engendered and preserved the image of White Cap as an enigma, a mystery. He had an obsession with keeping Continental at arm's length, and he used the leverage of his stock and his years of experience to preserve his independence from corporate headquarters. After all, Bob never wanted to leave White Cap or go further.

This kind of mystery, coupled with White Cap's continued success, engendered doubts and envy and misconceptions at the corporate level.

A former Continental Group manager elaborated:

> White Cap has always been seen as a prima donna by the Continental Group. I'm not convinced that there aren't some in Connecticut who might want to see White Cap stumble. They have always looked at the salary and administrative costs at 13 percent of net sales, compared with a 3–4 percent ratio in other divisions, and concluded that White Cap was fat.

Perhaps the demand for cost cuts was fueled by the fact that the Continental Group was going through its own period of "radical surgery" at this time. Since 1984, when Peter Kiewit Sons acquired the company, corporate headquarters had "sold off $1.6 billion worth of insurance, paper products businesses, gas pipelines, and oil and gas reserves" and had cut corporate staff from 500 to 40.[3] The corporate climate was calling for swift, effective action.

Taking Charge

In the first month of his new position, Browning turned his attention to three issues. To begin, he felt he had to make some gesture or take some stand with regard to Bob White. White was very much alive in the hearts and minds of White Cap's employees, and, although retired, he still lived in the Chicago area. Although White represented many of the values and the style that Browning hoped to change, he was also a key to the White Cap pride and morale that Browning had to preserve.

In addition, Bob White's successor, Art Lawson, was another link to White Cap's past, and his strong presence in the marketplace represented continuity in White Cap's customer relations. Since corporate headquarters was determined to maintain an untroubled public image throughout White Cap's transition, they brought Browning in reporting to Lawson—the division's vice president and executive officer and a person Browning had known for over 20 years (see Exhibit 2). Browning knew he had to give some strong messages about new directions if he was to shake up the comfortable division, but he had to do this from below Lawson and in spite of White's heritage.

A second challenge facing Browning was White Cap's marketing department. At a time when major, long-term customers in mature markets were faced with the attraction of an emerging plastic-packaging technology and were beginning to take the White Cap Total System for

---

[3] Allan Dodds Frank, "More Takeover Carnage?" *Forbes*, August 12, 1985, p. 40.

EXHIBIT 2   Organization Chart, April 1984

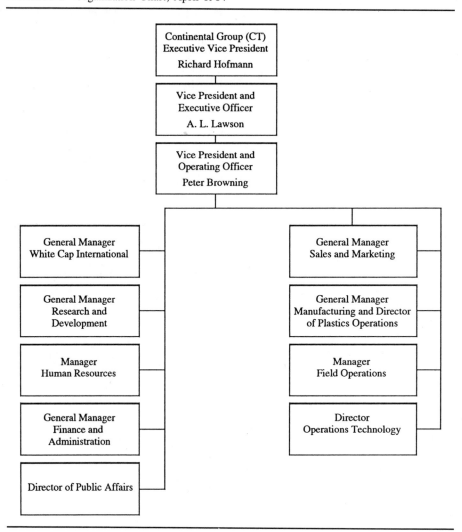

granted, Browning found a marketing and sales organization that, according to him, "simply administered existing programs." It was not spending constructive time with the customers who had built the business, nor was it aggressively addressing new competitive issues.

Jim Stark had been the director of marketing for the previous five years. He had a fine track record with White Cap customers and, as an individual, maintained many strong relationships in the field. Customers knew him well and relied on him. He had been with the company for 30 years and had been a regional sales manager before his transfer to marketing.

In this prior position, Stark's strength had clearly been his ability to deal with the customers, as opposed to his people-managing skills. Despite his strong outside presentation and selling ability, his internal relationships with his marketing staff and with the field sales force had apparently soured over the years. Team spirit was not in evidence. Stark complained that he didn't receive the support he needed to make changes in marketing.

Stark's boss, the general manager for sales and marketing and a highly competent sales professional, urged Browning to avoid any sudden personnel changes and "to give Stark a chance." Moreover, relieving a manager of his responsibilities would be unprecedented at White Cap. Yet, for some, Stark was like "a baseball coach who has been with the team through some slow seasons and was no longer able to turn around his image."

Browning also inherited a manager of human resources, Tom Green, whose role and capabilities he began to question. Browning had always been a proponent of a strong human resources function. He met with Tom Green and asked him to help identify and evaluate key personnel throughout the division in terms of promotion and reassignment decisions. Green was a veteran White Capper, with 20 years' seniority and 5 years in his current position. Older managers were very comfortable with him and he was well-liked. He offered few surprises to employees and helped maintain all the traditional and popular benefit policies and practices that they had come to expect from White Cap.

Browning soon recognized a problem with Green:

> In reviewing the personnel files with Green, I found he had few constructive ideas to offer. He seemed to do a lot of delegating and to spend a lot of time reading *The Wall Street Journal*. And a lot of managers seemed to work around him. I found myself getting involved in decisions that he should have been taking care of, such as deciding whether a departing secretary in another department needed to be replaced or not.
>
> One possibility was to replace Green with the human resources manager from Bondware who had helped me with the changes I had made there. But Green was also a valuable information source and someone who could be a nonthreatening conduit to and from White Cap employees.

Peter Browning pondered these initial choices and decisions carefully. He wanted to rejuvenate White Cap and yet not demoralize its loyal work force and management. Browning knew that Dick Hofmann, his boss, expected him to push for real, measurable change in the division's culture and performance. What was less clear was how far he should push—and how fast—in order to succeed. Even Hofmann acknowledged that Browning's assignment put him "smack dab between a rock and a hard place."

READING

IMPLEMENTING CHANGE

When people think about change, they often picture designing a bold new change strategy—complete with stirring vision—that will lead an organization into a brave new future. And, in fact, this crafting of a visionary strategy is a pivotal part of the process of change. But even more challenging—and harder to get a grasp on—is what follows the strategy and the vision: the implementation process itself. When it comes to the daily, nitty-gritty, tactical, and operational decision making of change, the implementor is the one who makes or breaks the program's success.

Of course, the implementor doesn't act alone. Change succeeds when an entire organization participates in the effort. An organization can be divided into three broad action roles: *change strategists, change implementors,* and *change recipients,* and each of these roles plays a different key part in the change process. Change strategists, simply put, are responsible for the early work: identifying the need for change, creating a vision of the desired outcome, deciding what change is feasible, and choosing who should sponsor and defend it. And change recipients represent the largest group of people that must adopt, and adapt to, the change. These are the institutionalizers, and

This note was written by Professor Todd D. Jick.
Copyright © 1991 by the President and Fellows of Harvard College. Harvard Business School case N9-491-114.

their behavior determines whether a change will stick.

But change implementors are the ones who "make it happen," managing the day-to-day process of change. The implementors' task is to help shape, enable, orchestrate, and facilitate successful progress. Depending on the extent of the "vision" they are given, they can develop the implementation plan, or shepherd through programs handed down to them. Simultaneously, they must respond to demands from above while attempting to win the cooperation of those below.

What is the experience of implementing change really like? Here is how the chief executive officer of a major U.S. airline describes managing multiple changes during the tempestuous period of the late 1980s:

> It beat any Indiana Jones movie! It started out with a real nice beginning. Then suddenly we got one disaster after another. The boulder just missed us, and we got the snake in the cockpit of the airplane—that's what it's all about! You've got to be down in the mud and the blood and the beer.

This vivid description captures a sense of the drama involved in wrestling with complex, real-time issues day after day in a changing environment. Because today's companies are composed of and affected by so many different individuals and constituencies—each with their own hopes, dreams, and fears—and because these companies operate in a global environment—with all the regulations, competition, and complexity that implies—implementing change may, indeed, require the dexterity, alertness, and agility of an Indiana Jones.

It sounds exciting, but is it doable? As this brief description implies, implementors face a daunting task. They often feel they have insufficient authority to make change happen entirely on their own, and that they fail to receive the support from above to move forward. At the same time, the more the "recipients" balk at the decisions implementors make, the more frustrating the task becomes. This middle role in the change process is a challenging one, indeed.

Common Pitfalls of Implementation

Real-life stories of corporate change rarely measure up to the tidy experiences related in books. The echo of well intentioned and enthusiastic advice fades as the hard work of change begins. No matter how much effort companies invest in preparation and workshops—not to mention pep rallies, banners, and pins—organizations are invariably insufficiently prepared for the difficulties of implementing change. The responsibility for this situation lies in several areas.

Both the popular press and academic literature tend to consider organizational change as a step-by-step process leading to success. Although recent writings have grown more sophisticated, many treatises on organizational change fail to concede that difficulties lie along the way.

This unrealistic portrayal of the change process can be dangerous. Already organizations are inclined to push faster, spend less, and stop earlier than the process requires. Such inclinations are further strengthened by an illusion of control that,

in fact, does not exist. By making change seem like a bounded, defined, and discrete process with guidelines for success, many authors mislead managers, who find that the reality is far more daunting than they expected. They feel deceived; instead of a controllable process, they discover chaos.

This kind of frustration is part of the terrain of change. In fact, while the literature often portrays an organization's quest for change like a brisk march along a well-marked path, those in the middle of change are more likely to describe their journey as a laborious crawl toward an elusive, flickering goal, with many wrong turns and missed opportunities along the way. Only rarely does a company know exactly where it's going or how it should get there.

Those who make change must also grapple with unexpected forces both inside and outside the organization. No matter how carefully these implementors prepare for change, and no matter how realistic and committed they are, there will always be factors outside of their control which may have a profound impact on the success of the change process. These external, uncontrollable, and powerful forces are not to be underestimated, and they are one reason why some have questioned the manageability of change at all. Shift in government regulations, union activism, competitive assaults, product delays, mergers and acquisitions, and political and international crises are all a reality of corporate life today, and managers cannot expect to implement their plans free of such interruptions.

Studies examining the most common pitfalls of implementation document just these kinds of frustration. In one study of strategic business units in 93 medium- and large-sized firms, respondents were asked to reflect on the implementation of a recent strategic decision.[1] The survey results showed seven implementation problems that occurred in at least 60 percent of the responding firms, as follows:

1. Implementation took more time than originally allocated (76 percent).
2. Major problems surfaced during implementation that had not been identified beforehand (74 percent).
3. Coordination of implementation activities (e.g., by task force, committees, superiors) was not effective enough (66 percent).
4. Competing activities and crises distracted attention from implementing this strategic decision (64 percent).
5. Capabilities (skills and abilities) of employees involved with the implementation were not sufficient (63 percent).
6. Training and instruction given to lower-level employees were not adequate (62 percent).
7. Uncontrollable factors in the external environment (e.g., competitive, economic, governmental) had an adverse impact on implementation (60 percent).

While these seven points are undoubtedly among the most pervasive problems, the list goes on and on. Other frequent implementation shortcomings include failing to win adequate support for change; failing to define expectations and goals clearly; neglecting to involve all those who will be affected by change; and dismissing complaints outright, instead of taking the time to judge their possible validity.

Tactical Implementation Steps

In order to avoid such pitfalls, students and managers frequently call for a checklist for implementing change—a list of do's and don'ts that will guide them on their way.

Unfortunately, managing change does not adhere to a simple, step-by-step process. There is no ironclad list or easy recipe for implementation success. In fact, the more we have studied change, and the more we brush up against its effects, the more humble we have become about dictating the ''best'' way to do it. Behavioral scientists, themselves, disagree on a number of fundamental implementation issues. A recent book attempting to pull together the best in practice recognized discord among its contributors on such basic questions as whether there is a logical sequence to the change process; whether change ''agents'' can lead an organization through a process that cannot be explained ahead of time; even whether change can be planned at all.[2]

But even though there are no easy answers, students and managers can still learn from the experiences of others. Over the last two decades, the growing body of work examining the change process has produced a number of implementation checklists. Although the following list is my own, it embraces many of the major prescriptions contained in the planned change literature—a kind of Ten Commandments for implementing successful organizational change (see Figure 1).

As already mentioned, no guidelines provide a recipe for success, and this list

[1] Larry Alexander, ''Successfully Implementing Strategic Decisions,'' *Long Range Planning* 18, no. 3 (1985), pp. 91-97.

[2] Allan Mohrmann, S. Mohrmann, G. Ledford, T. Cummings, and E. Lawler (eds.), *Large-Scale Organizational Change* (San Francisco: Jossey-Bass, 1989).

FIGURE 1   The 10 Commandments of Implementing Change

The Ten Commandments

1. Analyze the organization and its need for change.
2. Create a shared vision and common direction.
3. Separate from the past.
4. Create a sense of urgency.
5. Support a strong leader role.
6. Line up political sponsorship.
7. Craft an implementation plan.
8. Develop enabling structures.
9. Communicate, involve people, and be honest.
10. Reinforce and institutionalize change.

is no different. Instead, managers and students should view these commandments as an inventory of ingredients at their disposal. Through a conscientious process of testing, adjusting, and testing again, implementors may find the right combination of ingredients in the right proportion to fit the change needs of their particular organizations.

10 Commandments for Implementing Change

1. Analyze the Organization and Its Need for Change. Change strategists and implementors should understand an organization's operations, how it functions in its environment, what its strengths and weaknesses are, and how it will be affected by proposed changes to craft an effective implementation plan. If this initial analysis is not sound, no amount of implementation knowhow will help the organization achieve its goals.

As part of this process, changemakers also should study the company's history of change. While failures in the past do not doom later change efforts, one observer suggests that companies with historic barriers to change are likely to continue this pattern of resistance.[3] If a company already has a track record of opposing change, more care should be taken to design a gradual nonthreatening and, preferably, participative implementation process, including the following tactics:

- Explain change plans fully.
- Skillfully present plans.
- Make information readily available.
- Make sure plans include benefits for end users and for the corporation.
- Spend extra time talking.
- Ask for additional feedback from the work force.
- Start small and simple.

___

[3] Murray M. Dalziel and Stephen C. Schoonover, *Changing Ways: A Practical Tool for Implementing Change within Organizations* (New York: American Management Association, 1988).

FIGURE 2

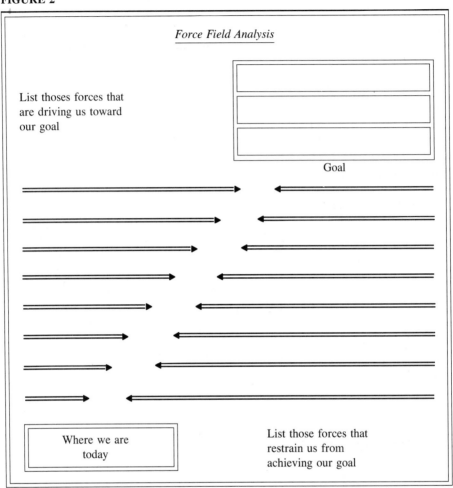

Force Field Analysis

List thoses forces that
are driving us toward
our goal

Goal

Where we are
today

List those forces that
restrain us from
achieving our goal

- Arrange for a quick, positive, visible payoff.
- Publicize successes.

At this early stage of the change process, implementors may also want to systematically examine the forces for and against change (see Figure 2). Change will not occur unless the forces driving it are stronger than those resisting it. By lifting these forces, managers have a way to determine their organizations' readiness for change. If the forces against change appear dominant, implementors should consider what additional forces they can muster—for example, in the form of committed followers, or of better proof of the need for change—before launching a change plan.

2. Create a Shared Vision and Common Direction. One of the first steps in engineering change is to unite an organization behind a central vision. This vision should reflect the philosophy and values of the organization, and should help it to articulate what it hopes to become. A successful vision serves to guide behavior, and to aid an organization in achieving its goals.

While the crafting of the vision is a classic strategists' task, the way that this vision is presented to an organization also can have a strong impact on its implementation. Employees at all levels of the organization will want to know the business rationale behind the vision, the expected organizational benefits, and the personal ramifications—whether positive or negative. In particular, implementors should "translate" the vision so all employees will understand its implications for their own jobs.

3. Separate from the Past. Disengaging from the past is critical to awakening to a new reality. It is difficult for an organization to embrace a new vision of the future until it has isolated the structures and routines that no longer work, and vowed to move beyond them.

However, while it is unquestionably important to make a break from the past in order to change, it is also important to hang on to and reinforce those aspects of the organization that bring value to the new vision. That is, some sort of stability—heritage, tradition, or anchor—is needed to provide continuity amidst change. As the changes at many companies multiply, arguably this past-within-the-future becomes even more essential.

4. Create a Sense of Urgency. Convincing an organization that change is necessary isn't that difficult when a company is teetering on the brink of bankruptcy, or foundering in the marketplace. But when the need for action is not generally understood, a change leader should generate a sense of urgency without appearing to be fabricating an emergency, or crying wolf. This sense of urgency is essential to rallying an organization behind change.

From an implementation standpoint, this commandment requires a deft touch. While strategists may see very real threats that require deep and rapid action, implementors—usually middle managers—may see something else, in two senses. This group may believe that the need isn't as drastic as strategists think, and that, instead of deep change, perhaps more modest alterations will work. Alternatively, implementors may see, from their perspective, that the situation is even worse than the strategists have described. In either case, implementors may be forced to adopt a pace of change that is either faster or slower than they believe necessary. The best protection against this is direct and frequent communication between implementors and strategists.

5. Support a Strong Leader Role. An organization should not undertake something as challenging as large-scale change without a leader to guide, drive, and inspire it. This change advocate plays a critical role in creating a company vision, motivating company employees to embrace that vision, and crafting an organizational structure that consistently rewards those who strive toward the realization of the vision.

It should be noted, however, that this leadership role may not be held by one person alone. As the environments in which companies are changing become increasingly complex, and as the implementation of change becomes more demanding, many organizations are now turning to change leader teams. Such teams can have the advantage of combining multiple skills; for example, pairing a charismatic visionary with someone skilled at designing a strong and effective implementation plan.

6. Line up Political Sponsorship. Leadership, alone, cannot bring about large-scale change. To succeed, a change effort must have broad-based support throughout an organization. This support should include not only the managers or change implementors but also the recipients, whose acceptance of any change is necessary for its success.

One way for strategists and implementors to begin winning support for change is to actively seek the backing of the informal leaders of the organization—beginning with those who are most receptive. In addition, they should demonstrate strong personal support for the change effort, and make it clear that the program is a high priority by allocating ample resources to do the job.

In winning sponsorship, it is not necessary to get unanimous support: participation can be representative, not universal. Of more importance is determining precisely whose sponsorship is critical to the change program's success. To help do this, one behavioral scientist suggests that implementors develop a ''commitment plan'' encompassing the following elements:[4]

- Identify target individuals or groups whose commitment is needed.

- Define the critical mass needed to ensure the effectiveness of the change.
- Develop a plan for getting the commitment of the critical mass.
- Create a monitoring system to assess the progress.

As part of this overall strategy, implementors may want to plot a commitment chart to help secure the minimum level of support necessary for a change program to proceed (see Figure 3).

7. Craft an Implementation Plan. While a vision may guide and inspire during the change process, an organization also needs more nuts-and-bolts advice on what to do and when and how to do it. This change plan maps out the effort, specifying everything from where the first meetings should be held to the date by which the company hopes to achieve its change goals.

In most cases, this implementation plan is best kept simple: an overly ambitious or too detailed plan can be more demoralizing than it is helpful. This is also the time to consider how many changes an organization can tackle at once. Because the risk of employee burnout is so real during major transformations, the change should be broken into staggered steps in order not to overburden workers with multiple demands.

At the same time, the plan should include specific goals and should detail clear responsibilities for each of the various roles—strategists, implementors, and recipients. Input from all levels of

---

[4] Richard Beckhard and Reuben T. Harris, *Organizational Transitions*, 2nd ed. (Reading, Mass.: Addison-Wesley, 1987).

FIGURE 3 Commitment Charting

To make a commitment chart, list all the members or groups who are part of the critical mass—those whose commitment is absolutely essential—on the vertical axis of the chart. Across the top, list the degrees of commitment: "No Commitment," "Let It Happen," "Help It Happen," and "Make It Happen," and draw vertical lines to make columns.

For each member or group in the left-hand column, place an "O" in the box that indicates the minimum commitment you must have for the change to occur. Do not try to get as much as you can; settle for the least you need.

Then study each of the people and groups as they are *now* and, using your best judgement, put an "X" in the box that represents their *present* degree of commitment.

Where the "O" and "X" are in the same box, circle them and breathe a sigh of relief; no work to do to get the necessary commitment.

Where the "O" and "X" are *not* in the same box, draw an arrow connecting them. This gives you a map of the work to be done (though not how to do it) to get the necessary commitment.

Sample Commitment Chart

Key Players	No Commitment	Let It Happen	Help It Happen	Make It Happen
1.		X ————	———————→	O
2.		X ————	—→ O	
3.		X ————	———————→	O
4.		O ←	—— X	
5.			XO	
6.	X ———	—→ O		
7.		X ————	———————→	O
8.		XO		
9.	X ———	———→ O		
10.			O ←	—— X

SOURCE: This information appears in Richard Bechard and Richard T. Harris, *Organization Transitions,* 2nd ed. (Reading Mass.: Addison-Wesley, 1987), pp. 94–95.

the organization will help to achieve this "role-oriented" focus. A plan devised solely by strategists is far less likely to reflect the realities of what the organization can accomplish than one which involves all three action roles from the start.

As with most other aspects of the change process, the implementation plan also should be kept flexible; a kind of "living" document that is open to revision. Too much and too rigid planning can lead to paralysis, indecision, and collapse. Organizations that are locked in a rigid change "schedule" of planned goals and events may find themselves following a path that no longer meets their evolving needs, much less those of the world around them.

8. Develop Enabling Structures. Altering the status quo and creating new mechanisms for implementing change can be a critical precursor to any organizational transformation. These mechanisms may be part of the existing corporate structure or may be established as a free standing organization. Enabling structures designed to facilitate and spotlight change range from the practical—such as setting up pilot tests, off-site workshops, training programs, and new reward systems—to the symbolic—such as rearranging the organization's physical space.

The more complex and large-scale the change, the more important it becomes that these enabling interventions be well thought out and consistent with each other. A series of choices among tactical options is thereby needed. This includes whether to use a pilot test or to go pan-organization; whether to be as participative throughout the process as the goals might warrant; whether to change certain systems sequentially or simultaneously; whether to reject the old or accentuate the new; whether to use a "programmatic approach" or to have each unit develop its own interpretation; and whether to drive change bottom-up or top-down.

9. Communicate, Involve People, and Be Honest. When possible, change leaders should communicate openly and seek out the involvement and trust of people throughout their organizations. Full involvement, communication, and disclosure are not called for in every change situation; but these approaches can be potent tools for overcoming resistance and giving employees a personal stake in the outcome of a transformation.

Effective communication is critical from the very start. Even the way in which the change program is first introduced to the work force can set the stage for either cooperation or rejection. The following list describes some criteria designed to increase an organization's understanding and commitment to change, reduce confusion and resistance, and prepare employees for both the positive and negative effects of change.[5]

In general, a constructive change announcement:

- Is brief and concise.

- Describes where the organization is now, where it needs to go, and how it will get to the desired state.

- Identifies who will implement and who will be affected by the change.

- Addresses timing and pacing issues regarding implementation.

- Explains the change's success criteria, the intended evaluation procedures, and the related rewards.

- Identifies key things that will not be changing.

- Predicts some of the negative aspects that targets should anticipate.

- Conveys the sponsor's commitment to the change.

- Explains how people will be kept informed throughout the change process.

- Is presented in such a manner that it capitalizes on the diversity of the communication styles of the audience.

Too often, "communication" translates into a unilateral directive. But real

---

[5] O.D. Resources, Inc., *Change Announcement Planning Guide*, Atlanta, 1985.

communication requires a dialogue among the different change roles. By listening and responding to concerns, resistance, and feedback from all levels, implementors gain a broader understanding of what the change means to different parts of the organization and how it will affect them.

10. Reinforce and Institutionalize the Change. Throughout the pursuit of change, managers and leaders should make it a top priority to prove their commitment to the transformation process, to reward risk-taking, and to incorporate new behaviors into the day-to-day operations of the organization. By reinforcing the new culture, they affirm its importance and hasten its acceptance.

This final commandment is made even more demanding by the fact that what many organizations are seeking today is not a single, discrete change but a continuous process of change. Given this reality, to speak of ''institutionalizing'' the change may be partially missing the point. Instead, what many companies really want is to institutionalize the *journey*, rather than the change. In other words, instead of achieving one specific change, organizations hope to create cultures and environments that recognize and thrive on the continuing necessity of change.

Both a Science and an Art

As already mentioned, these commandments are not the only tactics that the planned change literature has advocated. But they do provide a useful blueprint for organizations embarking on change, as well as a way to evaluate a change effort in progress. By going through this list, students and managers can begin to put together their own strategies for implementing change.

But no list is enough. Implementation is also a process of asking questions like these: Are we addressing the real needs of the company, or taking the easy way out? How shared is the vision? How do we preserve anchors to the past while moving to the future? Does everyone need to feel the same sense of urgency? Can change recipients, particularly those far down in the hierarchy, have an impact? How do we handle those who oppose the change? When should progress be visible? How do we integrate special projects to mainstream operations? When is it wise/best to share bad news? And now that we've gotten this far, is this the direction we still want to go?

Questions like these help to keep an organization focused and flexible, and to remind managers that implementing change is an ongoing process of discovery.

In addition, it is, perhaps, most important for students and managers to remember that implementation is a mix of art and science. *How* a manager implements change can be almost as important as *what* the change is. In fact, implementation has less to do with obeying ''commandments'' and more to do with responding to the various ''voices'' within the organization, to the requirements of a particular situation, and to the reality that change may never be a discrete phenomenon or a closed book.

CASE

XEROX CORPORATION: LEADERSHIP THROUGH QUALITY (A)

Xerox is clearly in a period of transition. We are no longer the company we once were, and we are not yet the company that we must be. If we are to successfully complete the transition and continue our record of success, every individual in the corporation will have to work toward our common goals.

With this statement addressed to Xerox employees late in 1983, (CEO) David Kearns described the new "Leadership through Quality" strategy for bringing about "the company that we must be."[1] To Xerox managers, aware of scattered efforts since 1980 to achieve some quality improvements in the company, Kearns's announcement came as no surprise. The detailed, companywide strategy being launched in 1983 had taken months to design and would take years to implement. Its objective was to create a new culture in which quality of goods and services would improve while costs declined, thereby enabling Xerox to become an effective competitor in an increasingly competitive marketplace.

Background

During the 1960s, Xerox had experienced explosive growth in a market when its product held a virtual monopoly. The first viable xerographic office copier had been introduced in 1959 by the old Haloid Corporation—renamed Xerox in 1961. Shielded from direct competition by several hundred patents, Haloid (and then Xerox) was able to take full advantage of the market. Demand for Xerox products skyrocketed. One executive recalled that:

> My first day as a salesman, back in the 60s, I walked out of the office and looked at all the buildings around me and thought, "Every one of those offices wants what I have to sell."

With no competitors to compare results with, the company, as it grew, relied entirely on internal standards and internal competition to measure its own performance.[2] One Xerox executive described the monopoly culture with an example from its billing center, which had just undergone a major change. The new procedure required that the name of the copier shipped to the customer be printed on the invoice, rather than just the product code. "The firm had gotten so internally oriented," he remarked, "that our programmers didn't bother with the copier name, just the product code, which of

---

This case was prepared by Amy B. Johnson and Lori Ann MacIsaac (under the direction of Professors Len Schlesinger and Todd D. Jick).

Copyright © 1989 by the President and Fellows of Harvard College. Harvard Business School case N9-490-008.

[1] *Xerox World* 2, no. 3, Fall 1983.

[2] See "Xerox Corporation Background Note," Harvard Business School Publishing Division No. 675-002, and "Note on the World Copier Industry," Harvard Business School Publishing Division No. 384-152.

course does not tell our customers if they received the copier they ordered.''

Xerox entered international markets by way of joint ventures. In 1956, the company joined with the Rank Organization, Ltd., of Great Britain to form Rank Xerox. This subsidiary manufactured and marketed copiers in Europe and Africa. In 1962, Rank Xerox and the Japanese firm Fuji Photo formed Fuji Xerox to cover the Far East.

Xerox introduced faster machines with more features aiming at the high-volume market occupied by offset duplicators.[3] Sales effort was concentrated on this and the middle-volume market, which had high profit margins, leaving the very low-end business to manufacturers of less-sophisticated copiers requiring coated paper. Protected by its patents and cushioned by a steady income of lease revenues, Xerox enjoyed remarkable success during the 60s.

Competition and Quality

In 1973, the Federal Trade Commission filed a monopoly complaint against Xerox. After two years of negotiation, Xerox agreed to license its copier patents to other manufacturers and dropped its legal actions against competitors' prior patent infringements. Between 1971 and 1978, 77 different plain paper copiers were introduced in the United States. From 1978–80 another 70 entered the domestic marketplace. Xerox market share dropped

---

[3] The high-volume segment was defined as customers making over 10,000 copies per month on one machine. High-volume copiers/duplicators could make 40 to 90 copies per minute and ranged in price from $20,000 to $130,000. Low-volume copiers were used to make fewer than 500 copies per month.

from nearly 100 percent in the 1960s to below 50 percent in 1980.

IBM and Eastman Kodak entered the copier market in 1970 and 1975, respectively, challenging Xerox in the medium- and high-volume segments. The IBM Copier II introduced in 1972 featured such attractions as document feed, image reduction, automatic collation, and two-sided copying. The Kodak Ektaprint 100 Copier/Duplicator was the first to use a microcomputer to monitor performance.

An even bigger challenge came from Japanese manufacturers in the mid-1970s. They entered the relatively neglected low-volume market with unanticipated zeal. Xerox found itself with no competitive products of its own in a rapidly growing market.

Having established a strong position in the low-volume market, the Japanese set their sights on the more lucrative medium- and high-volume segments. Canon made the first move here, introducing a line of middle-volume copiers in 1981. The Japanese were their major potential threat in the profitable high-volume arena. Japanese machine designs were simpler and used some interchangeable parts, which made service simpler and allowed the machine to make more copies between breakdowns, resulting in significantly fewer service hours required per machine.

Diversification

Xerox's first venture in information technology was the acquisition in 1969 for $967 million of Scientific Data Systems (SDS), a mainframe manufacturer. The strategy of moving into larger products backfired when minicomputers took off, and Xerox lost $1.4 billion before selling SDS in 1975. The $84.4 million write-off for that sale resulted in Xerox's first quarterly decline in profit growth in 17 years.

Despite this disappointment, Xerox continued to forge ahead with additions to its information systems business. In the early 1970s, the corporation acquired Diablo Systems, creators of the daisy wheel printer, and Century Data Systems, makers of computer memories. Acquisitions continued after an office products division was formed in 1975. Xerox introduced the Series 800 word processing systems and the Star Work Station, but, despite high expectations for both, the former was quickly outdated and the latter was too expensive for many customers. In 1979, the division launched Ethernet, a local area network capable of linking computers and peripherals through an entire building. In the early 1980s, Xerox brought out the memory writer, a successful line of electronic typewriters. With 20 percent of the U.S. electronic typewriter market, Xerox was first in market share in 1984.

Xerox also developed a new electronic printing technology using lasers and xerography. This technology, developed by the Xerox Palo Alto Research Center, was incorporated in a range of Xerox electronic printers that followed the copier market pattern of high-volume, mid-volume, and low-volume. Xerox quickly established a strong leading position in electronic printing.

In January 1983, Xerox acquired Crum and Forster, a property/casualty insurance company for about $1.6 billion in cash and stock, a move that received a mixed response from analysts. A year later, Xerox acquired the investment firm Van Kampen Merritt and created a financial services organization. Management expected financial services to produce one third of all Xerox profits over the next few years.

Xerox in the 1980s

The work of the 1980s for Xerox was to rise to the challenges of the 1970s to meet increased competition, sustain growth and profitability, control costs, and improve quality. These were the priorities for David T. Kearns, a former IBM executive who joined Xerox in 1971, became president in 1977, and was named CEO in 1982 by the chairman of the board, C. Peter McColough.

One of Kearns's most formidable tasks as president had been to reduce Xerox's swollen work force of 125,000. By 1983, lay-offs, divestitures, and early retirements brought the number of Xerox employees down to 104,000 worldwide.

The company also began to emphasize cost reduction efforts in manufacturing. This led to the setting of competitive benchmark targets and plans to achieve them.

Competitive Benchmarking

The increased emphasis on quality and customer requirements prompted some Xerox managers to reevaluate their notions of competition. The monopoly environment that Xerox grew up in had fostered internal competitiveness. It had been company practice to measure the quality of one Xerox machine by the standards of other Xerox machines, to compare sales results with the previous year's, and so forth. In the face of outside competition, this was no longer realistic. A consultant to Xerox described the situation as follows:

> The monopoly focus for setting goals and standards is internal. We say we'll do 10 percent better than last year, and so forth. But that may be irrelevant if competitors are doing something completely different.

EXHIBIT 1   Competitive Benchmarking

The competitive benchmarking process is outlined in five phases: (1) planning, where it is determined which activity will be benchmarked and who the best competitor is, and the data collected; (2) analysis, where the competitor's strengths are assessed against Xerox performance; (3) integration, where the data and analysis are used to develop plans for improvement; (4) action, where these plans are implemented; and (5) maturity, where competitive benchmarking has brought Xerox to a leadership position on that particular activity.

Xerox documented a number of competitive benchmarking projects, including the following:

Reprographic Manufacturing Group: Working with Fuji Xerox, the group benchmarked itself against its Japanese competitors. It projected the assessment out to 1985 and set its goals on an incremental basis. It also established periodic updating milestones to assess its productivity progress, and that of its competition, during the same period. These periodic assessments allowed RMG to make the proper adjustments to its long-range plans on an ongoing basis.

Information Products Division: In electronic typing—a new business for Xerox—competitive benchmarking was used to help Xerox successfully enter a new market. The obvious benchmark was IBM. Xerox entered the market in late 1981 and, by 1983, it had succeeded in capturing a market share of 20 percent and establishing Xerox as a market leader.

Reprographics Business Group: Competitive benchmarking enabled Xerox to determine the cost, quality, and reliability performance needed to reestablish market leadership. The result was the highly successful 10 Series of copiers. By all accounts, these copiers are the most successful Xerox has ever introduced and are now the standard in the industry.

Electronic Printing Division: Xerox places more electronic printers than all of its competitors combined, and is using competitive benchmarking to help maintain its leadership position.

Xerox had to look outside in particular functions to identify the best competitors and how they did certain things, be it cost, quality, or product reliability. It is a pain-creation mechanism, to get people to take a different frame of reference—customer-oriented, competitor-oriented, rather than internally oriented.

Reprographics had led the way in 1979 by setting up a system for evaluating competitors and using them as a standard for improvement. In 1980, all Xerox organizations became involved in competitive benchmarking and achieved significant improvements throughout the organization as a result of these efforts. Competitive benchmarking was defined by Xerox as:

. . . the continuous process of measuring our products, services, and practices against our toughest competitors of those companies renowned as leaders.

Our goal is superiority in all areas—quality, product reliability, and cost.

Exhibit 1 shows some examples of the uses of competitive benchmarking.

Employee Involvement

In the late 1970s, Peter McColough became interested in the quality circle activity he observed in visits to Japan. In 1978, he chartered a task force in personnel to study the application of quality of work life at General Motors and other U.S. manufacturers, as well as the Japanese model, and concluded that there was a place for employee involvement at Xerox. The task force recommended that an Employee Involvement function be established at the corporate level. Dr. Harold (Hal) J. Tragash, manager of personnel research, was brought from Rochester in 1979 to head the new Organizational Effectiveness office, which would foster employee involvement.

As Xerox was getting started in employee involvement, the first competitive benchmarking activity studying competing Japanese products was completed. The study recommended the use of employee involvement to help Xerox achieve the changes required to bring costs closer to the competition's. This provided an early opportunity to put employee involvement to use.

The earliest widespread use of employee involvement was in the North American Manufacturing Division. By 1980, the "new build" (as opposed to refurbishing) operation had an extensive training strategy involving nearly 30 percent of their work force. By 1982, the accomplishments of nearly 100 Employee Involvement groups had made a visible contribution to cost reduction, employee satisfaction, and product quality. Tragash said:

> That was the real business indicator to the rest of the organization that employee involvement was here to stay, that you can make meaning and make money out of it. Then it began to ripple out.

Business Effectiveness

In August 1980, David Kearns appointed Dwight F. Ryan to head a new function, Business Effectiveness. The Business Effectiveness office was charged with improving productivity, cost effectiveness, and customer satisfaction. Ryan also was responsible for working with a McKinsey & Company task force studying the Xerox structure. Over the follow-

ing year, while Ryan and the task force worked on restructuring the organization, operating units worked on the three objectives of business effectiveness. Different groups took different approaches, and some, like Reprographics Manufacturing, made substantial progress, while others made little.

It was soon apparent that making effective use of competitive benchmarking data often required the cooperation of the union and employees. Hal Tragash's work with employee involvement thus became part of the Business Effectiveness function to be used as a tool in conjunction with competitive benchmarking.

In July 1981, at the conclusion of the McKinsey study, Xerox announced a major restructuring of its businesses into strategic business units. A Business Equipment Group, led by Executive Vice President William F. Glavin, was organized along product lines, with the Business Systems Group handling all sales and service. Shortly thereafter, Dwight Ryan took over as group vice president of Business Systems.

September marked a new focus for Business Effectiveness. In a meeting that month with roughly 50 top managers, David Kearns announced that it was time to relaunch Business Effectiveness, with a focus on the two pillars of employee involvement and competitive benchmarking. Norman E. Rickard (Norm), vice president of planning and finance for the Reprographics Manufacturing Group (RMG), was named the new director of Business Effectiveness.

Between October 1981 and February 1982, Kearns, Rickard, and Tragash visited each operating unit of Xerox. With the top executive of each unit, they toured the facilities and reviewed business effectiveness plans. In Rickard's words, "Kearns' shadow began to fall" on business effectiveness. His personal attention and physical presence signaled the seriousness with which he viewed the three goals of productivity, cost effectiveness, and customer satisfaction. Furthermore, he told executives that progress on business effectiveness would figure into the compensation plan for 1982. With the focus of business effectiveness on employee involvement and competitive benchmarking, Rickard and Tragash continued to work closely together.

Total Quality Control at Fuji Xerox

The 1970s had been a difficult time for Xerox in Japan as well as in the United States. Although Fuji Xerox had always been managed by a Japanese president and Japanese senior management team, in the early and mid-1970s Fuji Xerox was totally reliant on Xerox for product designs. This became a problem for Fuji Xerox when Japanese competitors began to develop plain paper copiers and launched them first in the Japanese market. Fuji Xerox felt the punch of Japanese competition more acutely than the rest of the company, and its business results began to suffer. Fuji Xerox management took quick, dramatic action beginning in 1976 with a program of total quality control called "The New Xerox Movement." The thrust was to work together to improve quality by doing the job right in the first place and meeting customer requirements. The New Xerox Movement resulted in a dramatic turnaround in results and, in 1980, Fuji Xerox won the prestigious Deming Award for quality.

David Kearns made several trips to Japan in the months following the Deming Award, trying to understand what impli-cations Fuji Xerox's experience might have for the rest of Xerox, and how Fuji Xerox was successfully combating in Japan what had become formidable competition with the United States and Europe. One senior manager recalled that Kearns faced a different culture within Xerox:

> There was always a big difference between Fuji Xerox and Xerox. When the head of Fuji Xerox said, "This is the way we are going to go," everyone got in line quickly. And with nearby-Japan competitors eating their lunch, they knew there was a crisis. At Xerox, when Kearns would say, "We have to go do this," everyone said, "Why?" Maybe at the very highest level there was a sense of crisis, but not if you looked down through the company.

[handwritten note in right margin: no sense of crisis in the ranks]

Total quality control, which fully encompassed a commitment to the customer, was the direction Kearns wanted for Xerox. And, thus, the business effectiveness area—with its focus on productivity, cost effectiveness, and quality—seemed the logical place to begin. The business effectiveness staff had been encouraging managers to use competitive benchmarking and employee involvement hand-in-hand; using benchmarking to set goals that employee involvement groups could start working on. The movement toward quality was seen as being consistent with this work. Through the winter and spring of 1982, Tragash, Rickard, and their staffs worked on a business effectiveness strategy for Xerox, benchmarking other companies, particularly Fuji Xerox, and studying quality experts. One member of this group talked about the results of their work:

> There was agreement that, yes, Xerox should pursue a total quality approach,

yes, there was absolutely a need; that what we were suggesting was broader than what anyone else was doing, so we couldn't just "lift" someone else's plan. We also came up with the conclusion that we probably could not follow any one of the "gurus," but rather we wanted pieces of all of them, tailoring it to Xerox.

These conclusions were the basis for a meeting with David Kearns on July 28, 1982, where the quality strategy, called "Pursuit of Excellence," was discussed. The Business Effectiveness group used the meeting as a work session to further develop the strategy with Kearns. Together they decided to form a task force, including members from the Reprographics Business Group (some of whom had helped develop "Pursuit of Excellence") and members from the Business Systems Group. The task force was to work with senior managers on further developing the strategy and an implementation plan. If they could create a clear enough vision of Xerox's future, they believed key managers would become involved in the process of developing a strategy, and feel a sense of ownership and an obligation to carry it through. One participant explained: "It was hard to sign people up for a long trip—not just short-term quality improvement. We felt we had to do something *big* to change the whole deal."

Kearns and the task force agreed to follow the Fuji-Xerox model of working with an outside consultant. David Nadler, of the Delta Consulting Group, was retained in October of 1982, to work as an advisor to Kearns and as the eleventh member of the task force.

The Blue Book

Kearns scheduled a meeting of the Corporate Management Committee and operating unit heads for February 1983. In the months before that meeting, the task force worked on a briefing document (the "Blue Book") intended as a starting point for the development of a corporatewide quality strategy. Task force members met with each one of the 25 executives who would be attending the meeting to get their input for the Blue Book. One task force member remembers:

> Anybody who was going to the meeting in February had a sit-down meeting with Tragash, Rickard, or Nadler sometime during December or January. For the most part, it was to share with them what was coming. The idea was to avoid surprises: if there were any objections or concerns or issues, the idea was to get them out before the meeting so they could either be dealt with in the book, or, if it was too late for that, could somehow be reflected in the agenda for the meeting itself.

They distributed articles about quality and invited quality experts like Phil Crosby and Edward Deming to speak at their meetings. "No announcement would be made," one team member explained, "but every time they turned around, there was some meeting or article about quality."

Furthermore, the Blue Book, the first draft of the Xerox quality strategy, expounded its basic philosophies:

> Quality improvement is the key priority for long-term business success.

EXHIBIT 2   Discussion Questions at Leesburg Off-Site, February 1983

1. Is there agreement on the principles, tools, and management actions on which the definition of Leadership through Quality is based?
2. Is there agreement on the proposed definition of the total quality process and its implications for the way in which Xerox people accomplish their work?
3. By what name should Xerox's total quality strategy be known?
4. Is the proposed problem-solving process accepted as basic to the concept and part of its definition?
5. Is the description of the mature state complete, and are these expectations appropriate?
6. Do we believe that five years is a realistic time period to achieve this state?
7. Do we believe that the activities described will result in the improved business results (e.g., increased market share and customer satisfaction, improved profits, and increased employee job satisfaction)?
8. How specific should the expectation levels be for 1987? Should the Quality Implementation Team be asked to develop more specific expectations for the operating units as part of the unit implementation plans?
9. Is the time required for planning the implementation and for training senior executives really necessary before launching quality improvement? Or should we start sooner?
10. Should all operating units begin at the same time, or should efforts be concentrated on the major units with the others selecting the pace based upon need and capacity?
11. Is there agreement on the need to train *all* employees on Leadership through Quality?
12. Is there affirmation of the top-down training implementation?
13. Is there support for the "family group" approach to training?
14. Is there concurrence with the recommended training objectives?
15. Is the training task force an appropriate vehicle to develop Leadership through Quality training?
16. What is the process called?
17. Will the process be titled identically throughout the Corporation?
18. Will Corporate develop communications guidelines? Will the operating units develop their own strategies?
19. Will Corporate preannounce the process?
20. When will the process be announced?
21. Will the process for incorporating quality into the management process be established as proposed?
22. Given that competitive benchmarking and customer satisfaction surveys are underway, should new methods be utilized to define external customer requirements (e.g., a more formal process for collecting customer visit information by executives, tech reps, and marketing reps)?
23. Should guidelines for a process to establish internal customer requirements be developed by the Quality Implementation Team?
24. Should a Quality Policy be established?
25. How should units develop the cost of quality? Annually? What level of precision?

EXHIBIT 2 *(concluded)*

26. How will quality be incorporated into the management process? For example, for these:
    a. *The objective setting process.*
    b. *Management MBOs.*
    c. *Ensuring all employees know their roles in improving quality.*
    d. *The planning (Operating Plan and Business Plan) process.*
    e. *Operations reviews.*
    f. *All decision-making processes.*
    g. *The quarterly CMC quality reviews.*
    h. *Any others?*
27. Are the proposed principles appropriate?
28. What actions will senior management take to demonstrate its involvement and support of a quality rewards and recognition system?
29. When should this system be in place and functioning?
30. To what extent is there agreement on the proposed implementation and structure for quality?
31. Is there agreement on the need for consistent and sustained effort on the part of senior management to assure the successful implementation of Commitment to Excellence?
32. Is there agreement and commitment on the "Guidelines for Quality Management" regarding the managerial behavior needed to make/help/let it happen?
33. Is there approval for periodic survey research to monitor and evaluate managerial practices required to sustain the Leadership through Quality over time?
34. Is there support for focusing on our own teamwork to better understand the quality of our team management process (how well we work together) as a critical ingredient in the success of our Leadership through Quality?

Quality is determined by the customer, whether external or internal.

Quality improvement comes from doing the right things and doing them well.

It recommended that problem solving and quality training be introduced at all levels of management at Xerox, that senior management take initiative in personally modeling desired behaviors and fostering a quality environment, and that the reward system be revised to recognize employees using quality tools. The Blue Book also emphasized the concept that every function has a customer, internal, or external, and that the customer defines quality.

Leadership through Quality

In February 1983, David Kearns chaired the first Leesburg meeting (so named for its location at the Xerox off-site training facility in Leesburg, Virginia) of the company's top 25 executives who would become responsible for the quality strategy. Describing the content of the meeting, one participant stated:

> We understood from the very beginning that we would have to change the culture of the company. ... There was real discussion about the issue of doing it faster, even Fuji Xerox felt that we were going too slow. Kearns's answer to that was that quality means doing it right the first time and we are going to do this one right the first time. Doing it

EXHIBIT 3   Definition of Leadership Through Quality

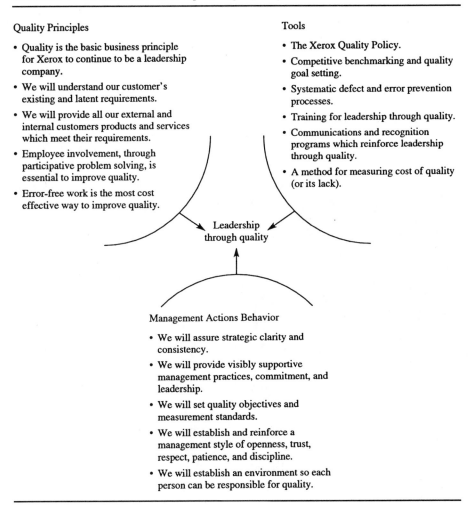

Quality Principles

- Quality is the basic business principle for Xerox to continue to be a leadership company.
- We will understand our customer's existing and latent requirements.
- We will provide all our external and internal customers products and services which meet their requirements.
- Employee involvement, through participative problem solving, is essential to improve quality.
- Error-free work is the most cost effective way to improve quality.

Tools

- The Xerox Quality Policy.
- Competitive benchmarking and quality goal setting.
- Systematic defect and error prevention processes.
- Training for leadership through quality.
- Communications and recognition programs which reinforce leadership through quality.
- A method for measuring cost of quality (or its lack).

Leadership through quality

Management Actions Behavior

- We will assure strategic clarity and consistency.
- We will provide visibly supportive management practices, commitment, and leadership.
- We will set quality objectives and measurement standards.
- We will establish and reinforce a management style of openness, trust, respect, patience, and discipline.
- We will establish an environment so each person can be responsible for quality.

slowly was one of the very few firm decisions Kearns made, other than to do it at all.

The Blue Book was used for briefing and discussion, rather than being presented as a finished product. The executives spent two and a half days at Leesburg in small groups, working on different aspects of the strategy. (See Exhibit 2 for topics discussed.) The subgroups formulated the vision, defined the broad strategy, and created the policy; the sessions were spirited and debates intense. Ownership and commitment to the result came from involvement, not from intellectual acceptance. For example, one group worked on the communication piece of the strategy, while another worked on reward

EXHIBIT 4 The Xerox "Fishbone"

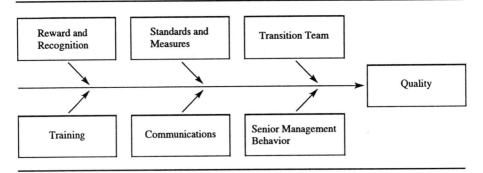

and recognition. The strategy was given its formal name, "Leadership through Quality," and the Xerox quality policy statement was formulated:

> Xerox is a quality company. Quality is the basic business principle for Xerox. Quality means providing our external and internal customers with innovative products and services that fully satisfy their requirements. Quality improvement is the job of every Xerox employee.

The group also defined the broad principles of the strategy, which appear under the headings: Quality, Principles, Quality Tools, and Management Actions/Behavior (see Exhibit 3).

Finally, the participants devised a uniform description of quality and the strategy for achieving it:

> *Quality* is meeting the customer's existing and latent requirements.
> *Improving quality* means understanding and working to satisfy the customer's requirements.
> Business Effectiveness, encompassing Competitive Benchmarking and Employee Involvement, continues to be an integral part of the process.
> All-pervasive quality—preventing errors, satisfying our external and internal customers in all our business activities, and continuously improving or innovating

our work and products—is the key to maintaining and increasing our market leadership and making our work life more satisfying.

Kearns was the last to address the meeting:

> This is a revolution in the company and we have to overthrow the old regime. The quality transition team is the junta in place to run things on a temporary basis. The standards and measures equate to the laws of the land and of the company. The reward and recognition system is the gaining of control of the banks and economic systems. The training is capturing control of the universities. Communications is the seizing of control of the press, and the senior management behavior is putting your own people in place to reflect the revolution. All of these elements are needed to change a culture. So let's go out and do just that, change the culture at Xerox to one of a total quality company!

With that, the Leesburg meeting was adjourned. Xerox was poised for the next step in the quality process. Now that senior management had actively helped create Leadership through Quality and made a visible commitment to it, the work of spreading the total quality process throughout the company began.

In the months following (April–August), a "fishbone" chart was developed, which summarized the building blocks of how Xerox would become a total quality company. (See Exhibit 4)

Corporate Quality Office

The first step was the creation of the corporate quality office, announced March 29, 1983. Fred B. Henderson was named vice president of quality and elected a corporate officer by the board of directors. He reported to Paul Allaire, chief staff officer. Henderson had a long history of success with Xerox and had been senior vice president of customer service in the Business Systems Group before moving to the quality office.

The internal announcement of the new quality office, addressed to Xerox managers, emphasized employee involvement and competitive benchmarking as key tools for pursuing the "overriding goal of achieving leadership through quality." Henderson stressed that Xerox managers should not expect quick fixes or a plethora of short-term slogans and solutions.

The announcement went on to quote Henderson:

> Like competitive benchmarking and employee involvement, we plan to implement this process slowly and deliberately so that it becomes a permanent part of our behavior at Xerox. It will take shape in different parts of the corporation at different paces. We want to make certain that we learn to walk before we try to run.

Henderson talked privately about some of his feelings on accepting his new role:

> I was concerned. American business culture makes it difficult to stick with a behavior or performance-change strategy for very long. These changes that

don't have immediate impact on the numbers traditionally come and go.

On the other hand, employee involvement started at the lowest levels and consistently gained momentum. It never became a buzzword for senior managers. It was just the way of getting the work done. The same was true of competitive benchmarking. So the real test was, does this just become another motivated theme song, or does it become the way we do work.

According to John Kelsch, named director of quality:

> We looked at quality at Xerox as a business strategy, plain and simple. When you talk about managing change, it is important to understand that the change we were managing was our fundamental business strategy and the way we manage the company; it was more essential than our product strategy.

Quality Implementation Team

With the creation of the corporate quality office, a companywide quality implementation team (QIT) was formed. Executives of each business group selected a representative to the QIT. Nine QIT members came from the field and six, including Tragash and Rickard, came from corporate staff. (Financial Services and Diversified Businesses were not represented.) The strategy was to focus on the core of the business first before spreading to the rest of the organization. One QIT member described the composition of the team:

> We were a group of people with a great deal of seniority within the corporation and we had all been successful in our operating units. We believed in Xerox, and we believed certain changes had to be brought about if the corporation was

going to make this transition, so we were committed.

Selection of successful, well-regarded, upwardly mobile managers just one level below business group presidents for the QIT was intended to signal top management's commitment to Leadership through Quality. Each was named vice president of quality, reporting directly to the president of his business group. Most were long-term employees and were seen to have the respect of their peers as well as the regard of top management.

In April 1983, the QIT met in Stamford, Connecticut, Xerox corporate headquarters, to start a six-month effort to fully develop the strategy and detailed implementation guidelines from which the operating units and business units would create their implementation plans. One QIT member later described his feelings as they embarked on the project:

> We went through all the questions, "Why me? What is this all about? Is the corporation going to stick with it?"— the whole credibility issue. There's a view in this company, like others, that we take off on a program or a strategic change, get all excited about it for the initial period and, if they don't get relatively quick results, they abandon that thrust for the next "strategic" thought.

Another was concerned about the time frame:

> We all had a lot of difficulty thinking in terms of a long-term strategy, something that dealt with changing the way we do business, cultural change, and the amount of time that it takes to put a process in place and actually change the way the organization functions. . . . It's very difficult because we come from a culture that is very short-term–oriented. With my background, marketing at Xerox, my ori-

entation was that I had to make a plan every 30 days, or 60 days, or maybe 90 days, and that was long term.

One QIT member was all too aware of the programs he had seen come and go in the past:

> We would have a great idea and build a program around it. There would be special forms and three-ring binders of instructions and reports and special meetings. Soon there was so much busywork, it overshadowed the original intent. Things became so bureaucratic that they died of their own weight.

The first few weeks were spent learning about quality and problem solving and working out how the group was going to function.

> Initially it was slow to start, and before long we had personality clashes, some of which perhaps most of us do not want to remember, because we put up with it. We were mature enough to realize that the final goal was far more important than some petty frictions that develop around people when they are in tight quarters. And we were in tight quarters.

Soon after the QIT began its work on the implementation, a quality training task force (QTTF) was put in place. This group also took up residence in Stamford and worked parallel to the QIT. When the QIT finished work on one aspect of the action plan, they turned it over to the QTTF to design the training. In this way, the training was ready for use at almost the same time as the action plan was completed.

The work of the QIT was punctuated by visits from David Kearns and other executives. One member remarked:

> We challenged senior management. We went back to Kearns and we went back to the Corporate Management Committee

and I to my boss and so on, and said, "Do you really know what you're getting into?" Because, as we started understanding what this meant for Xerox in terms of change, we had to challenge senior management and say, "Hey, do you really know what the hell you are getting into?" And they said, "Yes," and then we went back and said, "But do you really, really know? Are you willing to make these changes personally, to be the role models; do you really know what you're signing up for?" And every time we went to them they came back and the answer was, "Yes, we know; yes, we know; yes, we know."

The general feeling toward senior management behavior and its role in the process was described by one executive as: "The most critical element of all. They have to 'walk like they talk.' And people must see their local managers acting in a way that supports the process."

The QIT was stationed in Stamford for six months, with a series of brief visits back to the home offices to discuss their progress with group presidents, to share ideas and get input, and to establish the home office's stake in the process.

By August 1983, the team had produced a second Blue Book, a corporate implementation plan for total quality process in Xerox. The 25 executives who had met in February reconvened in Leesburg to work through the Blue Book and ratify the Leadership through Quality strategy. This meeting resulted in the issuance of the completed strategic plan, now called the Green Book.

The Green Book emphasized the difference between the long-term Leadership through Quality strategy and other short-lived thematic programs by defining it as:

> First, a goal, because we have yet to attain it.

> Second, a strategy, because we will achieve a competitive edge and attain leadership in our chosen business through the continuous pursuit of quality improvement.

> Third, a way of working or process, because in Xerox quality is the fundamental business principle upon which our management and work processes will be based.

The bulk of the 92-page document concentrated on guidelines for implementation. It listed aspects of the culture that would be required to successfully implement Leadership through Quality. (See Exhibit 5) It defined the cost of quality (Exhibit 6). It outlined a quality improvement process (Exhibit 7) and a problem-solving process already in use by many employee involvement teams (Exhibit 8), as well as several statistical problem-solving tools. It described competitive benchmarking as a key tool for evaluating Xerox success in meeting customer requirements. Finally, it set out an implementation timetable in the form of goals for each year from 1983 to 1987. (See Exhibit 9)

One of the innovations of the strategy was the quality training plan. Training was to be done in "family groups," consisting of a manager and his or her direct reports. The manager, assisted by a professional trainer, conducted week-long problem-solving and quality-improvement training. During the course of the week, the group was to select a problem or project for application of the quality processes and tools. After training, the manager guided the family group in the use of the quality processes and inspected progress on their selected project. Once the project was underway, members of the family group then worked with a professional trainer to deliver the week-long training to their own

EXHIBIT 5 Desired Behaviors in New Xerox Culture

Use of a systematic approach to understand and satisfy both internal and external customer requirements.

A shift from a predominantly short-term orientation to the deliberate balance of long-term goals with successive short-term objectives.

Striving for continuous improvement in meeting customer requirements, rather than accepting a certain margin of error. Doing things right the first time.

Participative and disciplined problem solving and decision making using a common approach.

An open style with clear and consistent objectives which encourages problem solving and group-derived solutions.

subordinates, who then chose their own application project. This method of training top managers first and having them participate in the training of their subordinates was called a training "cascade." The "learning by doing" approach was called the LUTI process ("learn-use-teach-inspect") (see Exhibit 10).

EXHIBIT 6 The Six Elements of the Cost of Quality

1. *Cost of Prevention*—These are the costs of activities that keep failure from happening. Examples include training employees to use the Quality Improvement Process and time spent by managers, facilitators, and other employees on quality circle activities.
2. *Cost of Appraisal*—These are the costs incurred to determine conformance with quality standards. Examples include inspection of incoming work, verifying final inspection, and auditing results.
3. *Cost of Internal Failure*—These are the costs of correcting products or services that do not meet quality standards prior to delivery to the customer. Examples include engineering design changes after product introduction and correction prior to mailing of invoices that were not done right the first time.
4. *Cost of External Failure*—These are the costs incurred to correct products or services after delivery to the customer. Examples include installation of retrofits, like-for-like machine replacements, customer invoice adjustments, and sales commission adjustments.
5. *Cost of Exceeding Requirements*—These are the costs incurred to provide information or service that are unnecessary or unimportant, or for which no known requirement has been established. Examples include reports that are excessively long or unread by the recipients, detailed analytical effort when a scoped estimate was requested, and sales calls that have no purpose and which annoy the customer.
6. *Cost of Lost Opportunities*—These are the lost revenues resulting from purchase of competitive products and services or from cancellations of Xerox products and services due to not meeting customer expectations. Examples include cancellations due to inadequate service response at critical demand times, as well as ordering of competitive products because the customer was previously sold equipment or services that were inadequate or excessive to their needs.

EXHIBIT 7   Standards and Measurements Nine-Step Quality Improvement Process

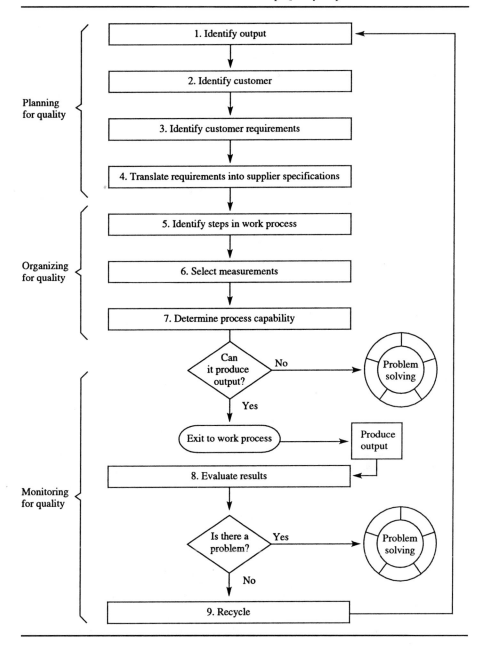

EXHIBIT 8 Problem-Solving Process

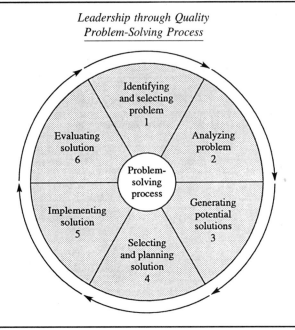

Leadership through Quality
Problem-Solving Process

Early Implementation

After the second Leesburg meeting, David Kearns told Xerox employees:

> The plan we approved may very well be the most significant strategy that Xerox has ever embarked on. It is aimed at fundamentally changing the culture of Xerox over the next several years. . . . It will require rigorous attention to detail in its implementation by all Xerox people. Without your active endorsement and total commitment, it will fail. With your active endorsement and total commitment, it will be the powerful lever that helps us accomplish our ambitious but achievable goals for the remainder of this decade and into the 1990s.

With the initial work of the QIT completed, the participants returned to their business groups. Except for those from the corporate office, each was named vice president for quality, reporting directly to the president of each business group. These new vice presidents were charged with developing and enacting implementation plans for their groups. Armed with the Green Book, the training program, and support from the corporate quality office, they were to make Leadership through Quality the Xerox way of doing business. Since most of the group presidents had received the quality training as members of executive vice president William Glavin's family group, and several had participated in the original Leesburg group, they were familiar with the strategy. Even so, the new quality vice presidents realized they faced many challenges:

> We may have been overly zealous in presenting Leadership through Quality

EXHIBIT 9   1983 Summary of Annual Strategic Goals by Year through 1987

1983   **Start-Up Activities**

- Training piloted and validated.
- Operating unit quality organization structures established and staffed.
- Management bonus objectives for 1984 adjusted with a weighting for Leadership through Quality training and implementation.

1984   **Year of Awareness and Understanding**

- All employees to receive Leadership through Quality orientation.
- Corporate and local communications to emphasize Leadership through Quality.
- Recognition and reward systems modified to promote Leadership through Quality.
- Approximately 4,000 senior and middle managers to be trained.
- All Xerox people beginning to understand the dimension and scope of Leadership through Quality.

1985   **Year of Transition and Transformation**

- Most Xerox managers and approximately 40–50 percent of individual workers to have been trained.
- All managers to have quality improvement goals included in their objectives.
- Managers begin to exhibit team leadership and use of the problem-solving and quality-improvement process.
- The results of quality improvement become evident in business results and in the motivation and morale of Xerox people.

1986   **Year of Significant Results**

- Training completed for all Xerox employees.
- Objectives and plans for quality improvement become a normal and natural part of the planning, management, and work processes.
- An internal "Deming-type" award program announced at the corporate level.
- Improving trends in Xerox market share, revenues, profit, and return on assets become evident.

1987   **Year of Approaching Maturity**

- Implentation of Leadership through Quality is completed.
- Xerox people worldwide are applying the quality processes as part of their normal work in striving to meet internal and external customer requirements.
- The results of Leadership through Quality actions have made significant contributions toward the achievement of our long-term corporate objectives.

EXHIBIT 10   Family Group Managers Training Approach

In the learning cascade, subordinates in Family Group A *learn* the quality process in a week of training led by their manager and a professional trainer. After training, they *use* the process on an application project. They *teach* their own subordinates (Group B) as family group manager, working with a trainer, and *inspect* their use of the quality process.

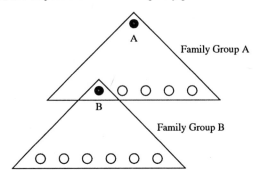

Learn-Use-Train-Inspect Approach to Training Cascade

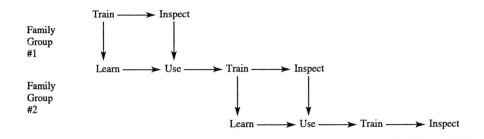

as a solution to Xerox's problems. By itself, it's not going to do anything at all. If we don't have good product development people, good engineering people, with vision and understanding of their business, if we don't have good salespeople, service people . . . we've got to have all those things to be successful.

Kearns is committed to it, but I worry about it being a one-man strategy. Are the other senior managers really interested in making the change? Will they really lead the way?

People at my level, the group level, may someday find themselves having to say, "Hey boss, you're not following the process." Can we say that to our bosses?

Even if you accept the basic idea, it doesn't become easy to use the tools. A simple idea can have complex applications or be difficult to implement. Everyone understands and agrees with quality, but when we sit down to work with it, it is very foreign.

What is my chance of personal success? Where does my career go next?

EXHIBIT 11 Evolution of Leadership through Quality

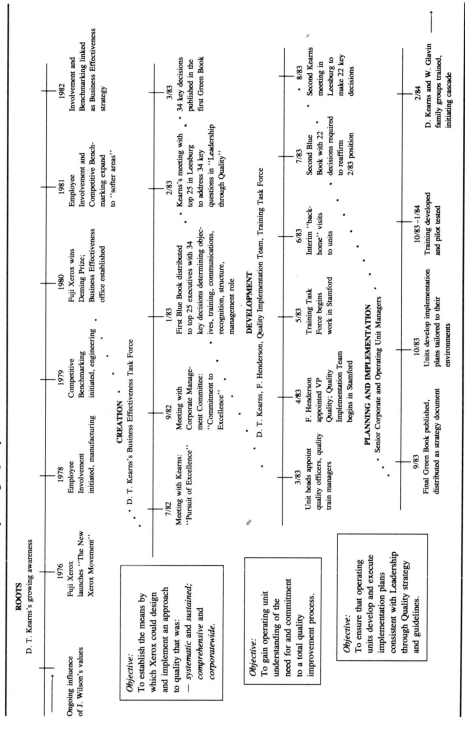

The Strategic Assessment

By 1985, "the year of transition and transformation," all middle and senior managers had been trained. In 1986, Paul Allaire became the new president and one of his early actions was to take stock of how the Leadership through Quality was faring at Xerox. He thought about its evolution (summarized in Exhibit 11). He conducted operational reviews with heads of the unions. He also directed that interviews be conducted across functional organizational levels, with 120 managers in all. Data from annual surveys of management behavior (see Exhibit 12—this questionnaire had been given out since the fall of 1984) were then combined with findings from the interviews and analyzed.

EXHIBIT 12   Xerox Corporation: Leadership through Quality (A)

Evolution: Management Behavior Survey—1986

Part A. BACKGROUND

1. How long have you been working
   for Xerox?
   (check one)

   _____ Less than 2 years

   _____ 2 to 10 years

   _____ More than 10 years

2. How many people report directly to you?
   (check one)

   _____ None

   _____ 1 to 5

   _____ 6 to 10

   _____ More than 10

Part B. *LEADERSHIP THROUGH QUALITY* TRAINING AND APPLICATION

1. When did you complete Leadership through Quality training? (check one)

   _____ Haven't completed this training yet

   _____ Less than 6 months ago

   _____ 6 to 12 months ago

   _____ More than 12 months ago

2. Since completing training, have you participated in a Quality Improvement Project/Problem-
   Solving Project? (check one)

   _____ No, I have not yet participated in a project

   _____ Yes, we are working on the first project

   _____ Yes, we have completed at least one project

3. How comfortable are you with using each of the concepts, skills, or processes listed below?
   How frequently do you apply each of these in your work?

Leadership through Quality Concepts, Skills, and Processes	*Degree of Comfort* (check one)			*Frequency of Use* (check one)		
	Not very comfortable	Fairly comfortable	Very comfortable	Never	Occasional	Often
Problem solving	☐	☐	☐	☐	☐	☐
Quality improvement process	☐	☐	☐	☐	☐	☐
Competitive benchmarking	☐	☐	☐	☐	☐	☐
Interactive skills	☐	☐	☐	☐	☐	☐
Cost of quality	☐	☐	☐	☐	☐	☐

EXHIBIT 12   (concluded)

Part C. MANAGEMENT BEHAVIORS
How frequently does your manager do each of the following? Please circle the response that best describes your manager's behavior.

My Manager	Very Infrequently	Infrequently	Sometimes	Frequently	Very Frequently
1. Provides me with honest feedback on my performance	1	2	3	4	5
2. Encourages me to monitor my own efforts	1	2	3	4	5
3. Encourages me to make suggestions	1	2	3	4	5
4. Provides me with an environment conducive to teamwork	1	2	3	4	5
5. Gives me the information I need to do my job	1	2	3	4	5
6. Clearly defines what he/she requires of me	1	2	3	4	5
7. Acts as a positive role model for Leadership through Quality	1	2	3	4	5
8. Openly recognizes work well done	1	2	3	4	5
9. Listens to me before making decisions affecting my area	1	2	3	4	5
10. Makes an effort to solve my work-related problems	1	2	3	4	5
11. Encourages all of us to work as a team	1	2	3	4	5
12. Informs me regularly about the state of the business	1	2	3	4	5
13. Displays an understanding of Xerox objectives and strategic directions	1	2	3	4	5
14. Summarizes progress during meetings to seek understanding and agreement	1	2	3	4	5
15. Encourages me to ask questions	1	2	3	4	5
16. Ask questions to ensure understanding	1	2	3	4	5
17. Encourages an environment of openness and trust	1	2	3	4	5
18. Behaves in ways which demonstrate respect for others	1	2	3	4	5
19. Makes an effort to locate and remove barriers that reduce efficiency	1	2	3	4	5
20. Ensures regularly scheduled reviews of progress toward goals	1	2	3	4	5
21. Monitors the Quality Improvement Process	1	2	3	4	5
22. Monitors department progress through competitive benchmarks	1	2	3	4	5
23. Rewards those who clearly use the Quality Improvement Process	1	2	3	4	5
24. Sets objectives based on customer requirements	1	2	3	4	5
25. Uses the Quality Improvement Process	1	2	3	4	5
26. Uses the problem-solving process in order to solve problems	1	2	3	4	5
27. Treats Leadership through Quality as the basic Xerox business principle	1	2	3	4	5

READING

ORGANIZATIONAL FRAME BENDING: PRINCIPLES FOR MANAGING REORIENTATION

David A. Nadler
Delta Consulting Group, New York

Michael L. Tushman
Graduate School of Business, Columbia University

One of the hallmarks of American business in the past decade has been the attempts by large organizations to manage large-scale planned change. In some cases—AT&T, Chrysler, and Apple, for example—the efforts have been dramatic and have captured public attention. Other cases, such as Corning Glass, Xerox, Citicorp, and GTE, have received less attention, but the changes have been no less profound.

The concept of planned organizational change is not new; but this most recent generation of changes is somewhat different from what has gone before. First, they typically are initiated by the leaders of organizations, rather than consultants or human resource specialists (although they have played significant roles in some cases). Second, they are closely linked to strategic business issues, not just questions of organizational process or style. Third, most of the changes can be traced directly to external factors, such as new sources of competition, new technology, deregulation or legal initiatives, maturation of product sets, changes in owner

ship, or shifts in fundamental market structure. Fourth, these changes affect the entire organization (whether it be a corporation or a business unit), rather than individual SBUs (strategic business units) or departments. Fifth, they are profound for the organization and it members because they usually influence organizational values regarding employees, customers, competition, or products. As a result of the past decade's changes, there are now more large visible examples than ever before of successful planned organizational change.

Our work has brought us into contact with a number of examples of these changes.[1] In general, they have been changes that encompass the whole organization, have occurred over a number of years, and have involved fundamental shifts in the way the organization thinks about its business, itself, and how it is managed. Our experience has included changes that both internal and external observers rate as successes, some that have been described as failures, and some that are still going on.

Our purpose in this article is to share some insights, generalizations, and hunches about large-scale organizational changes, working from our perspective of

EXHIBIT 1   Organization Model

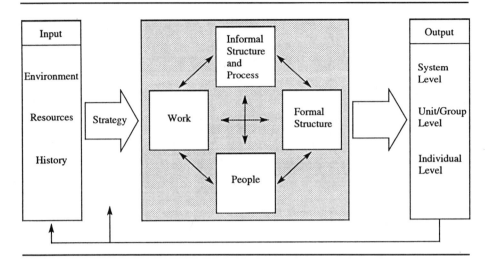

close observations. We begin by reviewing some basic concepts of organization and change that have shaped the way we think about and observe these events. Next, we briefly describe an approach to differentiating among various types of organization change. Finally, we devote the rest of the article to our concept of "frame bending"—a particular kind of large-scale change found in complex organizations.

Basic Concepts of Organization and Change

Thinking about Organizations. We view organizations as complex systems that, in the context of an environment, an available set of resources, and a history, produce output. To illustrate, we have developed a model that consists of two major elements (see Exhibit 1). The first is *strategy*, the pattern of decisions that emerges over time about how resources will be deployed in response to environmental opportunities and threats. The second is *organization*, the-

mechanism that is developed to turn strategy into output. Organization includes four core components: work, people, formal structures and processes, and informal structures and processes. The fundamental dynamic is *congruence* among these elements. Effectiveness is greatest when a firm's strategy is consistent with environmental conditions and there is internal consistency, or fit, among the four organizational components. Our model emphasizes that there is no one best way to organize. Rather, the most effective way of organizing is determined by the nature of the strategy as well as the work, the individuals who are members of the organization, and the informal processes and structures (including culture) that have grown up over time.[2]

While our model implies that congruence of organizational components is a desirable state, it is, in fact, a double-edged sword. In the short term, congruence seems to be related to effectiveness and performance. A system with high congruence, however, can be resistant to change. It develops ways of insulating itself from outside influences and may be unable to respond to new situations.[3]

Organizational Change. From time to time, organizations are faced with the need to modify themselves. The change may involve one or more elements of the organizational system, or it may involve a realignment of the whole system, affecting all of the key elements—strategy, work, people, and formal and informal processes and structures. A central problem is how to maintain congruence in the system while implementing change, or how to help the organization move to a whole new configuration and a whole new definition of congruence. Critical issues in managing such changes include (1) managing the political dynamics associated with the change, (2) motivating constructive behavior in the face of the anxiety created by the change, and (3) actively managing the transition state.[4]

While these approaches have been useful for managers and implementors of organizational change, they have limitations when applied to large-scale, complex organizational changes. Specifically, these larger-scale changes entail at least some of the following characteristics:

- *Multiple transitions.* Rather than being confined to one transition, complex changes often involve many different transitions. Some may be explicitly related; others are not.
- *Incomplete transitions.* Many of the transitions that are initiated do not get completed. Events overtake them, or subsequent changes subsume them.
- *Uncertain future states.* It is difficult to predict or define exactly what a future state will be; there are

many unknowns that limit the ability to describe it. Even when a future state can be described, there is a high probability that events will change the nature of that state before it is achieved.

- *Transitions over long periods.* Many large-scale organization changes take long periods to implement—in some cases, as much as three to seven years. The dynamics of managing change over this period of time are different from those of managing a quick change with a discrete beginning and end.

All these factors lead to the conclusion that the basic concepts of transition management must be extended to deal with the additional issues posed by large-scale changes.[5]

Types of Organizational Change

As a first step toward understanding large-scale organizational change, we have developed a way of thinking about the different types of change that organizations face. Change can be considered in two dimensions. The first is the scope of the change—that is, subsystems of the organization versus the entire system. Changes that focus on individual components, with the goal of maintaining or regaining congruence, are *incremental* changes. For example, adapting reward systems to changing labor market conditions is an incremental, systems-enhancing change. Changes that address the whole organization, including strategy, are *strategic* changes. These changes frequently involve breaking out of a current pattern of congruence and helping an organization develop a completely new configuration. Incremental changes are made within the context, or frame, of the current

EXHIBIT 2   Types of Organizational Change

	Incremental	Strategic
Anticipatory	Tuning	Reorientation
Reactive	Adaptation	Re-creation

set of organizational strategies and components. They do not address fundamental changes in the definition of the business, shifts of power, alterations in culture, and similar issues. Strategic changes change that frame, either reshaping it, bending it, or, in extreme cases, breaking it. For example, when John Sculley took the reins from Steven Jobs at Apple Computer, or when Lee Iacocca took over a Chrysler, systemwide changes followed.

The second dimension of change concerns the positioning of the change in relation to key external events. Some changes are clearly in response to an event or series of events. These are called *relative* changes. Other changes are initiated, not in response to events but in anticipation of external events that may occur. These are called *anticipatory* changes. (The relationship between the dimensions can best be described using the illustrations shown in Exhibit 2.) Four classes of change are the result:

- *Tuning*. This is incremental change made in anticipation of future events. It seeks ways to increase efficiency but does not occur in response to any immediate problem.

- *Adaptation*. This is incremental change that is made in response to external events. Actions of a competitor, changes in market needs, new technology, and so on, require a

response from an organization, but not one that involves fundamental change throughout the organization.

- *Reorientation*. This is strategic change, made with the luxury of time afforded by having anticipated the external events that may ultimately require change. These changes do involve fundamental redirection of the organization and are frequently put in terms that emphasize continuity with the past (particularly values of the past). Because the emphasis is on bringing about major change without a sharp break with the existing organization frame, we describe these as frame-bending changes. For example, the sweeping changes initiated by Paul O'Neil and Fred Federholf at ALCOA are frame-bending changes in that they are not driven by performance crisis (i.e., they are proactive) and they build on ALCOA's past, even though they involve widespread organization change.

- *Re-creation*. This is strategic change necessitated by external events, usually ones that threaten the very existence of the organization. Such changes require a radical departure from the past and include shifts in senior leadership, values, strategy, culture, and so forth. Consequently, we call these *frame-breaking* changes. Examples of these reactive, systemwide changes abound, and include those at National Cash Register, U.S. Steel, AT&T, GM, ICI, and SAS.

Building on this classification scheme, these different types of change can be described in terms of their intensity (Exhibit 3). Intensity relates to the severity of the change and, in particular, the degree of

EXHIBIT 3 Relative Intensity of Different Types of Change

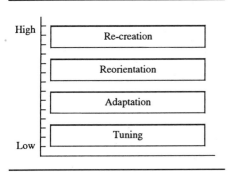

shock, trauma, or discontinuity created throughout the organization. Strategic changes are obviously more intense than incremental changes, which can frequently be implemented without altering an organization's basic management processes. Reactive changes are more intense than anticipatory changes, because of the necessity of packing substantial activity into a short time without the opportunity to prepare people to deal with the trauma. There is also less room for error and correction.

Relative intensity is further affected by organizational complexity. Organizations become more difficult to change as they increase in complexity—complexity determined by (1) the size of the organization in terms of employees and (2) the diversity of the organization in terms of the number of different businesses, geographic dispersion, and so on. Smaller organizations with a few highly related businesses are easier places in which to implement changes than are larger, highly diverse organizations.

If we put these concepts together, we get a map of the difficulty of organizational change (see Exhibit 4). The least difficult changes are those that are low

intensity and take place in fairly noncomplex settings. The most difficult changes are those that are high intensity (strategic) and take place in highly complex settings. Our focus is on strategic organizational change. Re-creations are the most risky and traumatic form of change, and our assumption is that managers would rather avoid the costs and risks associated with them. The challenge, then, is to effectively initiate and implement reorientations, or frame-bending change, in complex organizations.

Observations of Effective Organizational Frame Bending

In the last section, we identified the activities and elements that characterize effective organizational re-creation. The principles have been organized into four clusters for discussion purposes, and we will refer to them as *principles of effective frame bending*. First, there are those principles associated with initiating change. Next, there is a set of principles having to do with how the reorientation is defined, or the *content of change*, and another set having to do with *leading change*. Finally, there are principles associated with *achieving change*, relating to the activities that are required to implement, sustain, and complete reorientations over long periods. The clusters and principles are displayed in Exhibit 5.

The Diagnosis Principle. Managing organizational reorientation involves managing the *what* as well as the *how*. The *what* concerns the content of the change: what strategies and elements of organization will have to be changed to enable the organization effectively to anticipate, respond to, and even shape the challenges to come. While much of the focus of this perspective is on process of managing

EXHIBIT 4   Types of Change Management

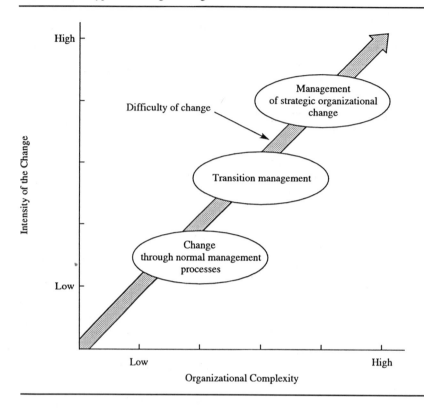

reorientations, the content is neverthe-less critically important.

Identification of the appropriate strate-gic and organizational changes comes from diagnostic thinking—analyzing the organization in its environment, under-standing its strengths and weaknesses, and analyzing the implication of antici-pated changes. Diagnosis typically in-volves the collection, integration, and analysis of data about the organization and its environment. It involves assess-ment of the organization usually based on some underlying model of organizational effectiveness.

Effective reorientations are character-ized by solid diagnostic thinking. In

these cases, managers have spent time understanding the potential *environmen-tal challenges and forces*, be they tech-nological, regulatory, competitive, or otherwise. They have worked to identify the *critical success factors* associated with achieving effective anticipation or response. They have looked hard at the *organizational strengths and weak-nesses*, thus gaining a systematic view on what has to change and why.

In contrast, the less effective reorien-tation suffers from a lack of diagnosis and the quick adoption of ''solutions in search of problems,'' which often comes about through *organizational mimicry*. In these cases, the senior

EXHIBIT 5   Principles of Effective Frame Bending

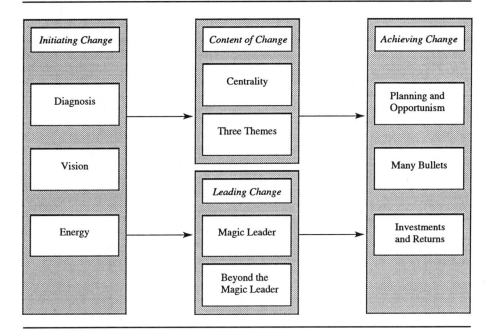

management of one organization observes how "model" organizations (the referents vary—they could be industry leaders, generally respected companies, and so on) are responding to or anticipating change and they then copy what the model is doing. What they fail to grasp is that the model organization typically has done diagnostic work and has identified a set of changes unique to its own conditions. Because the management of the model organization has participated in the diagnostic work, it has both the understanding and the commitment that results from the process. Thus, mimicking organizations not only adopt strategies that are not designed for the problems or challenges they face, but do so in a manner that leads to low commitment to change. Little wonder that they tend to fail.[6]

The Vision Principle. An effective reorientation involves movement from one state to another. The most effective reorientations include a fully developed description of the desired future state. Since the nature of the change is usually both very broad and profound, this description is more than a statement of objectives or goals; it is a *vision* of what the organization hopes to be once it achieves the reorientation. This vision may range from a set of principles or values all the way to detailed papers outlining specific strategic objectives, operating modes, organizational structures, and so on. In most cases, it addresses values as well as performance. Overall, most visions touch in some way on each of the following points:

- *Rationale*. A description of why the vision is needed, or why the change is required.

- *Stakeholders*. A discussion of the organization's stakeholders and what it seeks to provide for them.

- *Values*. A description of the core values and/or beliefs that drive the organization of the change.

- *Performance objectives*. A definition of what will characterize effective performance of the organization (and in some cases individuals) once the change has been achieved.

- *Organizational structure or processes*. How the organization will be structured or will work to achieve the vision.

- *Operating style*. A discussion of some of the specific elements of how people in the organization (particularly managers) will operate and interact with each other. In some cases, this is an attempt to describe the required culture in operational terms.

Visions are developed for a number of different purposes. They are directional, signaling where the reorientation is headed. They are symbolic, providing a point for rallying and identification. They are educational, helping individuals to understand the events around them. Finally, they are energizing.

In this context, effective visions seem to be ones that are credible, responsive to the current (or anticipated) problems, and provide a balance of specificity and ambiguity. Effective visions also have a balance of new and old or sustaining ideas, values, or perspectives. In contrast to recreations (in which a break with the past is often necessary and appropriate), effective visions for reorientations often are crafted to have "resonance"—to meld with themes from the organization's past.

Effective reorientations tend to have visions that are responsive to the issues raised in diagnosis and meet many of the criteria listed above. Less effective reorientations either have no vision or have visions that are flawed, are the result of mimicry, or have been developed in a way that does not facilitate the creation of understanding and/or commitment.[7]

A final note on vision. The question of whether or not to make a vision public has been faced in a number of reorientations. While the issue is important, no definitive answer has yet been identified. Clearly, the vision needs to be made public at some point. The directional, energizing, and educational goals of the vision cannot be met if it is kept secret. On the other hand, there are many cases of premature articulation of vision leading to negative consequences. In what some have called the "rush to plexiglass," certain companies have developed vision statements and immediately distributed them throughout the company, using posters, documents, plaques, pins, plexiglass "tombstones," and so on. When the vision is poorly thought out, when it is not clear how the vision will be achieved, or (perhaps most importantly) when the vision is very much at odds with current management behavior, employees tend to greet such statements with justified skepticism; the net result is a loss of management credibility. In some cases, this problem has been dealt with by clearly positioning the vision as aspirational and recognizing that this is not the way the organization functions today.

The Energy Principle. One of the

great strengths of organizations is that they contain tremendous forces for stability. They are able to withstand threats and challenges to the established order. The flip side of this characteristic is that organizations (and particularly successful ones) can be inherently resistant to change, particularly change that undermines strongly held values and beliefs. Energy must be created to get change initiated and executed.

Organizational reorientation presents a particular dilemma. In a crisis situation (e.g., the Tylenol poisoning case, the Union Carbide disaster at Bhopal, or deregulation at AT&T) the clear, present danger of organizational failure creates the energy needed to make change happen. Reorientation, by definition, is different because it involves changes in anticipation of the events that may make it necessary. The need for change may be apparent only to a small number of people. For the majority of people in the organization—and sometimes this includes much of senior management—the need for change is often not clear.[8]

Effective reorientations seem to be initiated by specific efforts to create energy. Most often this involves some effort—usually by leaders—to create a *sense of urgency*, and somehow to communicate and convey that sense of urgency throughout the organization. In some cases, a sense of urgency can be created by presenting information that shatters widespread assumptions about the current situation. But this tactic addresses the intellectual inertia. Urgency and energy are emotional issues, and experience indicates that people and organizations develop the energy to change when faced with real *pain*.

The larger and more intense the change, the more extreme the pain needed to mobilize individuals to consider doing things differently. There are a number of different ways in which pain can be created. Most of them involve employees participating in the process of data collection, discovery, and comparison of their organization against accepted benchmarks (frequently competitors). Some reorientations have been started by getting senior managers to spend time with customers, use competitive products or services, or visit companies that are competitive analogs (the now familiar "trip to Japan"). Since individuals have a unique capacity for denial, multiple intense exposures may be necessary to create the required depth of emotional reaction.

The problem is that pain can create energy that is counterproductive. The consequences of pain can be dysfunctional behavior as well as functionally directed action. Negative information can lead to certain defensive reactions, such as denial, flight, or withdrawal. To the extent that the organization is characterized by pathology, the creation of pain or urgency may stimulate maladaptive responses. Therefore, the challenge is to develop methods of creating pain that will create energy and catalyze action.

Successful reorientations involve the creation of a sense of urgency right at the limits of tolerance—just at the point where responses border on defensive. At the same time, efforts are made to track dysfunctional or pathological responses and find ways to redirect the energy in positive ways. In many less-effective reorientations, sufficient energy has not been generated early or broadly enough. This is particularly true in very large organizations that have the capacity to absorb or buffer pain.

The next two principles assume that change has been initiated, and focus on the content of the change. These will be followed by two principles regarding the role of leadership in reorientation.

The Centrality Principle. For a change to engage the entire organization, it must be clearly and obviously linked to the core strategic issues of the firm. The positioning and labeling of the reorientation are critical. Successful long-term changes are positioned as strategic imperatives that are compelling to members of the organization. Usually, the connection is so clear and has so much validity that the relationship of the change to company health and survival is obvious. For example, the emphasis on quality and customer service at Xerox and ALCOA were clearly linked to their enhanced competitiveness. Where changes are not seen as central to the survival, health, or growth of the organization, they tend to be transient, existing only so long as the perceived interest of senior management lasts. For a change to "catch," employees have to see a clear connection with core organizational and individual imperatives.

To the degree the change is central, it raises another dilemma. If the organization has been successful and has built some degree of congruence over the years, employees may resist wholesale changes. In many successful long-term changes, managers worked to make sure that the core themes of the change (and the vision) had organizational resonance—that is, that they seemed related to and consistent with some of the historical core values of the organization.

But how can one find themes with strategic centrality in an organization of great diversity? It appears to be more difficult to find such themes across widely diverse businesses in large organizations. Success comes most often when generic themes, such as quality, competitiveness, or innovation, can be positioned across the businesses and then related with specificity to each particular operation's situation.[9]

The Three-Theme Principle. While a strategic change may involve a large number of specific activities, most managers of change find it necessary to identify *themes* to communicate and conceptualize the changes. Themes provide a language through which employees can understand and find patterns in what is happening around them. At the same time, however, they seem to be capable of integrating only a limited number of themes in the midst of all of the other transactions that make up daily life. Employees are bombarded with programs, messages, and directives. In many situations, individuals cope by figuring out which messages they can safely ignore. Usually, more are ignored than not. Successful long-term changes are characterized by a careful self-discipline that limits the number of major themes an organization gives its employees. As a general rule, managers of a change can only initiate and sustain approximately three key themes during any particular period of time.

The challenge in this area is to create enough themes to get people truly energized, while limiting the total number of themes. The toughest part is having to decide not to initiate a new program— which by itself has great merit—because of the risk of diluting the other themes.

Most successful reorientations are characterized by consistency of themes over time. It is consistency that appears to be most significant in getting people to believe that a theme is credible. The problem then, is how to maintain consistency while simultaneously shaping themes to match changing conditions.[10]

The Magic Leader Principle. Another important component of a successful reorientation is an individual leader who serves as a focal point for the change, whose presence has some special "feel" or "magic." Large-scale organizational change requires active and visible leadership to help articulate the change and to capture and mobilize the hearts and minds of the people in the organization. This kind of leadership relies on special effects created throughout the organization by the individual leader and, thus, this type of individual can be thought of as a *magic leader*. These leaders display the following characteristics:

• *Distinctive behaviors*. Magic leaders engage in three distinctive types of behavior that encourage employees to act in ways consistent with the desired change. The first is *envisioning*—creating an engaging and inspirational vision of a future state. Next is *energizing*—creating or stimulating energy through personal demonstration, rewards, and punishments, and setting high standards. Finally, there is *enabling*—helping to create the processes, resources, or structures that enable employees to do the things they have been motivated to do. The most successful large-scale change leaders exhibit elements of all three of these types of behavior.

• *Ability to create a sense of urgency*. The magic leader seems to be critical in creating a sense of urgency so essential to organizational changes. The leader is a key player in the creation and management of pain.

• *Guardianship of themes*. The leader is the guardian of the themes of the change. He or she is the one individual who can make sure the themes survive. Successful change managers exhibit great tenacity (or even stubbornness) in the articulation of themes over a period of years, in both good times and bad.

• *A mix of styles*. Magic leaders also display an interesting mix of management styles. On one hand, they appear to be directive and uncompromising in furthering their objectives for change. On the other hand, they seem to welcome participation and spend time getting people involved in shaping the change process. This combination of autocratic and democratic tendencies appears to be critical to their effectiveness.

The dilemma here is that, while the individual magic leader is essential to successful reorientation, continued dependence on him or her can lead to disaster. The change can become too personalized; nothing happens unless that individual assumes personal sponsorship, and the next levels of management may become disenfranchised. Furthermore, when the leader makes mistakes (as he or she inevitably does) the magic may fade. The magic leader finds it difficult to live up to the fantasies that subordinates create. Thus, the challenge is to fulfill the need for the leader at the very time when the organization needs to grow beyond the leader.[11]

The Leadership-Is-Not-Enough Principle. While magic leadership is necessary, it cannot, by itself, sustain a large-scale change. Success depends on a broader base of support built with other individuals who act first as followers, second as helpers, and finally as co-owners of the change.

The expansion of the leadership of change beyond the magic leader requires efforts in two directions. The first complements the magic leader with leadership that focuses on the necessary elements of management control, or instrumental leadership.

The second broadens the base of leadership beyond one or two individuals. The most common way to achieve this is through the executive team of the organization. Successful changes are characterized by a large investment in the executive team, both as individuals and as a group. This team needs to share and own the vision, to become over time more visible as champions, and to come to grips collectively with the task of managing today's business while also managing the chance to position tomorrow's business. In addition to the executive team, leadership can be expanded through the development and involvement of senior management and by efforts to develop leadership throughout the organization.[12]

The first seven principles have focused on how to initiate change, how to define the content of change, and the role of leadership. The final three principles have to do with the problem of sustaining change and achieving reorientation over time.

The Planning-and-Opportunism Principle. Profound organizational reorientation does not occur by accident. Rather, it is the result of intensive planning. On the other hand, it is naive to believe that reorientation in the face of uncertainty can occur by mechanistically executing a detailed operating plan. Successful reorientations involve a mix of planning and unplanned opportunistic action.

The argument for planning flows naturally out of many of the principles that have already been articulated. Diagnosis, the development of vision, the creation of energy, and the crafting of the content of the change all require in-depth thinking and planning. The system's nature and complexity of organizations also require that significant changes with multiple components be sequenced and linked together. A number of successful reorientations have involved six months to two years of planning prior to any public action.

At the same time, there is a valid argument for the inherent limitations of planning. By definition, reorientations involve planning in the face of uncertainty. The architect of change does not know for sure what will occur environmentally in the future. Typically, unforeseen events—both positive and negative—will occur and have a profound impact on the reorientation. Some of these events are themselves consequences of the reorientation efforts—products of its success or failure at different stages. Each event may present an opportunity; to ignore them because "they are not in the plan" would be foolish.

As a consequence, effective reorientations seem to be guided by a process of iterative planning; that is, the plans are revised frequently as new events and opportunities present themselves. This reflects the fact that planned organizational change involves a good deal of learning and that this learning can and should shape the development of the vision and reorientation itself. Thus the planned sequence of activity is balanced with what might be called *bounded opportunism*. However, it does not make sense nor is it effective to respond to every problem, event, or opportunity. Some potential courses of action may simply be inconsistent with the intent of the change or may drain energy from the core effort. It is within certain boundaries, then, that the effective architect of reorientation is opportunistic and modifies plans over time.[13]

The Many-Bullets Principle. The nature of organizational stability and resistance to change was discussed earlier. It clearly has implications for initiating change, but it also has ramifications for achieving change.

Organizations are typically resistant to change. Changes in one component of a system that do not "fit" are frequently isolated and stamped out, much as the human body fights a foreign organism. In these cases, the forces for congruence are forces that work for stability. Similarly, individual behavior in organizations is frequently overdetermined. If an individual's patterns of activity were examined, one would see that there are multiple forces shaping it—for example, the design of the work, the activities of supervisors, the immediate social system, the rewards, the organizational structure, the selection system that attracted and chose the individual, and the physical setting. Indeed, there are frequently more factors reinforcing a pattern of behavior than are necessary. As a result, changing those patterns will require more than a modification of a single element of the environment.

Effective reorientations recognize the intractability of organizational and individual behavior and, thus, make use of many "bullets"—as many different devices to change behavior as possible, incorporating intentionally redundant activities. They thus involve planned changes in strategy, the definition of work, structure, informal process, and individual skills—along with attitudes and perceptions.

In effective reorientations, managers use all available points of leverage to bring about change. Underlying the Many-Bullets Principle is the assumption that the organization ultimately must come to grips with the need to adjust its infrastructure to be consistent with, and supportive of, the change. As all the other work is being done, there is the less glamorous but still critical work of building the structures to enable and reinforce the changes. This is tough, detailed, and sometimes tedious work, but it is crucial. Things that need to be addressed include:

- Standards and measures of performance.

- Rewards and incentives.

- Planning processes.

- Budgeting and resource allocation methods.

- Information systems.

The problem here is one of timing. The work cannot get too far ahead of the change, yet it cannot lag too far behind. Successful managers make skillful use of these levers to support and in some cases drive the change over time.[14]

The Investment-and-Returns Principle. The final principle concerns the amount of effort and resources that are required to achieve a truly effective reorientation as well as the long time span that is usually required to realize the results of those efforts. There are two subpoints to this principle—one concerning investments (the *no-free-lunch* hypothesis) and one concerning returns (the *check-is-in-the-mail* hypothesis).

The *No-Free-Lunch Hypothesis.* Large-scale, significant organizational change requires significant investment of time, effort, and dollars. While change may yield significant positive results, it is not without its costs.

Successful changes are characterized by a willingness on the part of the changers to invest significant resources. The most scarce resource appears to be senior management time. Organizations engaging in large-scale change find it necessary to get senior managers involved in a range of activities—senior team meetings, presentations, attendance at special events, education, and training—all of which are necessary to perform the functions of leadership in the change. This broadening of ownership also requires a significant investment of time, particularly of the senior team. Less successful changes often prove to be those in which the investments of time were delayed or avoided because senior managers felt so overloaded with change activity that they could not do their work. In successful reorientations, senior managers saw change as an integral part of their work.

The dilemma here is that while the senior team's investment of time is essential, it may also cut into time that the team needs to spend being leaders for the rest of the organization. This could lead to charges that the senior team is too insular, too absorbed in its own process. The challenge is to manage the balance of these two demands.

The *Check-Is-in-the-Mail Hypothesis.* Organizational reorientation takes time. In particular, as the complexity of the organization increases, so does the time required for change. Each level of the organization engaged in the change takes its own time to understand, accept, integrate, and subsequently own and lead change. In many changes, it becomes important to sell and resell the change throughout many levels of the organization. Each level has to go through its own process of comprehending the change and coming to terms with it.

Organizations go through predictable states as they deal with a change and a set of themes:

- *Awareness.* People within the organization first become aware of the need to change and the dimensions of the change. They work to come to grips with this need and to understand what the change is all about.

- *Experimentations.* Small-scale efforts are made to experiment with the changes in a bounded and manageable setting. Efforts are made to see whether the change will really work in "our unique setting."

- *Understanding.* The experimentation leads to increased understanding of the change, its consequences and implications. At this point, employees begin to realize the scope of the change and what it may involve.

- *Commitment.* The leadership faces up to the decisions to change and makes a significant and visible commitment to take action.

- *Education.* Employees spend time acquiring the skills and information needed to implement the change. This may involve training or other transfers of skills.

• *Application to leveraged issues*. The new approach, perspective, and skills are applied to key issues or specific situations where there is leverage. This is done consciously, and even a bit awkwardly.

• *Integration into ongoing behavior*. The new changed behavior starts to become a way of life. Employees naturally (and unconsciously) are working in new ways.

Obviously, a change rarely follows the steps exactly as described above. Moreover, different levels of the organization may go through the stages at their own pace. But at some time, each part of the organization must come to grips with each of these issues in some way.

As a result, experience indicates that large-scale reorientations generally take from three to seven years in complex organizations. The efforts may entail false starts, derailments, and the necessity to start over in some places. In addition, significant payoffs may not be seen for at least two years. Again, there is a dilemma. People need to be persuaded to invest personally in the change before there is any evidence that it will pay off, either for the organization or for them personally. Their motivation is essential to success, but proven success is essential to their motivation. The challenge is to demonstrate (through experiments, personal example, or through "face validity") that the change will ultimately pay off.[15]

Conclusion

This article has focused on the factors that characterize the most successful attempts at frame bending—large-scale, long-term organizational reorientation. But it would be a mistake to conclude without commenting on the very important, critical, and central aspects of organizational life and how these affect change.

Two elements are tightly intertwined with the implementation of organizational change—*power politics* and *pathology*. All organizations are political systems, and changes occur within the context of both individual and group aspirations. Thus, strategic changes become enmeshed in issues that are ideological ("What type of company should we be?") as well as issues that are personal ("What's going to be the impact on my career?"). These are not aberrations; they are a normal part of organizational life. However, they will be magnified by and indeed may "play themselves out" through the change. It is difficult to provide general guidance for dealing with this, since the issues vary greatly. However, the successful change manager works at understanding these dynamics, predicting their impact on the change and vice versa, and shaping the situation to make constructive use of them.[16]

Not all organizational life is adaptive. Organizations, like people, have their dark sides—their destructive or maladaptive responses to situations. Organizations develop stylized responses to problems and situations. These responses may be elicited by the intensity of a strategic change. An organization that engages in collective despair may become more despairing. Again, it is the leader who must understand the organizational pathology and confront it.

We have attempted here to share some initial views on a particular subset of organizational change—reorientations. Our belief is that reorientations are a particularly significant kind of change. While reorientations require sustained senior management attention, they are more likely to succeed than re-creations.

More and more organizations face the need for such change as competitive pressures increase. This article is a further step in trying to understand this need and to provide guidance to those who are called upon to lead these organizations.

Endnotes

1. This article is based on observations of approximately 25 organizations in which we have done work over the past five years, and specifically our very close work with the most senior levels of management in planning and implementing significant, multiyear strategic-level changes in six particular organizations.

2. See D. A. Nadler and M. L. Tushman, "A Diagnostic Model for Organization Behavior," in E. E. Lawler and L. W. Porter (eds.), *Perspectives on Behavior in Organizations* (New York: McGraw-Hill, 1977); and D. A. Nadler and M. L. Tushman, "A Model for Organizational Diagnosis," *Organizational Dynamics*, Autumn 1980.

3. See M. L. Tushman, W. Newman, and E. Romanelli, "Convergence and Upheaval: Managing the Unsteady Pace of Organizational Evolution," *California Management Review*, Fall 1986, pp. 29–44. Also see M. L. Tushman and E. Romanelli, "Organizational Evolution: A Metamorphosis Model of Convergence and Reorientation," in B. L. Staw and L. L. Cummings (eds.), *Research and Organizational Behavior* (Greenwich, Conn.: JAI Press, 1985), p. 17.

4. R. Beckhard and R. Harris, *Organizational Transitions* (Reading, Mass.: Addison-Wesley, 1977); K. Lewin, "Frontiers in Group Dynamics," *Human Relations* 1 (1947), pp. 5–41; and D. A. Nadler, "Managing Organizational Change: An Integrative Perspective,"

Journal of Applied Behavioral Science 17, (1981), pp. 191–211.

5. See Beckhard and Harris, endnote 4; and W. G. Bennis, K. D. Benne, and R. Chin, *The Planning of Change* (New York: Holt, Rinehart & Winston, 1961); and W. G. Bennis and B. Nanus, *Leadership: The Strategies for Taking Charge* (New York: Harper & Row, 1985).

6. See P. A. Goodman and Associates, *Change in Organizations: New Perspectives on Theory, Research, and Practice* (San Francisco: Jossey-Bass, 1982); and E. E. Lawler, D. A. Nadler, and C. Cammann, *Organizational Assessment* (New York: John Wiley & Sons, 1980).

7. J. M. Burns, *Leadership* (New York: Harper & Row, 1978); and Goodman et al., endnote 6.

8. See Bennis et al., endnote 5; Lewin, endnote 4; and J. M. Pennings & Associates, *Organizational Strategy and Change* (San Francisco: Jossey-Bass, 1985).

9. See M. Kets de Vries and D. Miller, "Neurotic Style and Organizational Pathology," *Strategic Management Journal* 5 (1984), pp. 35–55; and N. M. Tichy and M. A. Devanna, *The Transformational Leader* (New York: John Wiley & Sons, 1986).

10. See D. A. Nadler and M. L. Tushman, *Strategic Organization Design* (Glenview, Ill.: Scott, Foresman, 1988); J. B. Quinn, *Strategies for Change: Logical Incrementalism* (Homewood, Ill.: Richard D. Irwin, 1980); and J. B. Quinn and K. Cameron (eds.), *Paradox and Transformation*, (Cambridge, Mass.: Ballinger, 1988).

11. See D. A. Nadler and M. L. Tushman, *Beyond the Charismatic Leader: Leadership and Organizational Change* (New York: Delta Consulting Group, 1987); and Tichy and Devanna, endnote 9.

12. D. A. Nadler and M. L. Tushman, *Managing Strategic Organizational Change* (New York: Delta Consulting Group, 1986); and Nadler and Tushman, endnote 11.

13. See Quinn, endnote 10; and Tushman et al., endnote 3.
14. See Nadler and Tushman, endnote 10; and Pennings et al., endnote 8.
15. See Quinn, endnote 10; Quinn and Cam-
eron, endnote 10; and Tichy and Devanna, endnote 9.
16. See M. Kets de Vries and Miller, endnote 9; and Tichy and Devanna, endnote 9.

SIMULATION

ORGANIZATIONAL CHANGE GAME

Janet P. Near

Participant's Guide

You should refer to the following guide as you play the OC Game; your performance will be better if you also read it before the game.

Your Task. You are getting ready to participate in a game called the Organizational Change Game, or OC Game for short. You are to play the role of a specialist in an organizational change. You have been hired by corporate headquarters of the company to act as a consultant to the management level personnel in their Northwest Division. You will be working with other people as a consultant team. Your charge as consultants at Northwest Division is to persuade as many management people as possible to adopt an innovation called management by objectives (MBO).

The Game Setting. You have been given two years to implement the MBO plan. You must convince management of the value of the plan and persuade managers to adopt it. Corporate head-

quarters has given no directives, instructions, or advice to Northwest Division management concerning the merits of MBO. The innovation adoption techniques from which you are to choose are listed on a sheet called the Organization Change (OC) Tactics/Strategies Guide Sheet (see Appendix A). There are 17 techniques from which you may select. As in life, each technique that you use costs time. Depending on the technique selected, you will be assessed one or more weeks to be deducted from your two-year time period of 104 weeks. Your goal will be to get as many MBO adopters as possible before you have used up your 104 weeks. You will record the cost in weeks on the guide sheet.

Of the 24 persons listed on Northwest Division's organizational chart, 22 are potential adopters. The names of all 24 persons are listed on a score sheet called the MBO Adopter Check Sheet (see Appendix B). You will record on this sheet during each round of play your progress in moving persons toward the MBO adopter status. For each round of play you will choose from a list of 17 possible OC tactics or strategies the one method you believe to be most effective for that round. Assisting your team during play will be a person called a facilitator. His or her job will be to give you a response for each action you initiate during the game. You should record a summary of each transaction on the OC Tactics/Strategies Log Sheet (see Appendix C). The log sheet is a kind of diary and should be helpful to you in remembering what worked and what didn't. This probably sounds rather confusing now, but it should become clear once play begins.

The Adoption Process. Adoption of change moves in a series of well-defined stages. The first stage is AWARENESS, in which the individual is alerted to the existence of something new. Next is the INTEREST stage, in which the individual gathers information and an aroused level of curiosity. This is followed by the APPRAISAL/TRIAL stage, in which the new idea is tried out in a trial operation. The final stage is ADOPTION, in which the individual incorporates the innovation as a part of the resources he or she uses on the job. It is an orderly process through which all individuals must pass who become adopters. This scheme is used in structuring the MBO Adopter Check Sheet.

People vary in terms of the speed with which they move through the stages and MBO. As you play the game and plan your moves, you will want to match the technique you select against what you know about the characteristics of the person whom you are trying to

influence and where that person is in the adoption process. Development of these skills is at the heart of your role as a change agent.

Playing the Game. Your team has in front of it a game board showing the organizational structure of Northwest Division. In consultation with other team members you will plan your strategies using the OC Tactics/Strategies Guide Sheet. After you have selected your first technique, record it on the log sheet and show this sheet to your facilitator. Your facilitator, using a carefully designed set of algorithmic instruments, will respond to you with some printed information. You will use this information to complete portions of the guide sheet, the adopter's sheet and the log sheet and to plan your next move in the game. In this fashion you will continue play until you either have achieved 22 adopters or your two years are up.

Take time to think about what you are doing. Try to develop a sound change adoption program. Enjoy the game!

References

Beckhard, R., and R. T. Harris. *Organizational Transitions* and *Managing Complex Change*. Reading, Mass.: Addison-Wesley, 1978.

French, W. L., and C. H. Bell. *Organization Development*. 2nd ed. Englewood Cliffs, N. J.: Prentice-Hall, 1973.

Rogers, E. M., and F. F. Shoemaker. *Communication of Innovations: A Cross-Cultural Approach*. New York: Free Press, 1971.

Appendix A

OC TACTICS/STRATEGIES GUIDE SHEET

ASK HELP: Request help or advice about an OC strategy from any one staff
  member of Northwest Division.   1

BACKGROUND: Obtain background information on any 3 employees.   1

COMMITTEES: Find out who are members of the various committees set up in
  the division.   1

COMPANY NEWSLETTER: Arrange to have a brief article in the company
  newsletter/magazine about MBO at Northwest.   2

COMPULSION: Persuade the VP to issue a bulletin directing all directors and
  managers to institute MBO immediately.   6

CONFRONTATION: Work behind the scenes with a group of managers who want
  to take some action to improve productivity in the division. At your suggestion,
  they meet the VP to lobby for the use of MBO as one method toward this goal.   6

EXECUTIVE DEVELOPMENT: Arrange for any 5 employees to attend an
  executive development program on MBO. Specify the 5.   4

INTERDEPARTMENTAL UNIT MEETING: Arrange for several director/
  managers to meet to discuss MBO.   3

INTERNAL WORKSHOP: Have a particular manager/director lead a session
  on creative uses of MBO.   5

INTERVIEW: Set up a meeting and informally interview 1 person.   1

LUNCHMATES: Observe who lunches with whom.   3

MEMO: Send a brief report describing the advantages of MBO to any 5 persons.
  Specify the 5.   1

PILOT TEST: Attempt to influence 1 director/manager by asking to let you
  implement MBO in a short-term project.   3

PRESENTATION: Get on the agenda of a regularly scheduled staff meeting to
  explain MBO and encourage discussion about it.   3

SAMPLE SURVEY: Send a survey to several directors/managers to gather
  information about interest in setting up an MBO program.   2

SEMINAR: Arrange to have Professor Peter Brucker speak on "MBO: Its
  Role in Increasing Productivity."   4

SOCIAL: Observe the social patterns to learn who plays golf together,
  racket ball, etc.   3

1st Year

	Jan.	Feb.	Mar.	Apr.	May	June
Start—	□□□□	□□□□	□□□□	□□□□	□□□□	□□□□
	July	Aug.	Sept.	Oct.	Nov.	Dec.
	□□□□	□□□□	□□□□	□□□□	□□□□	□□□□

2nd Year

	Jan.	Feb.	Mar.	Apr.	May	June
Start—	□□□□	□□□□	□□□□	□□□□	□□□□	□□□□
	July	Aug.	Sept.	Oct.	Nov.	Dec.
	□□□□	□□□□	□□□□	□□□□	□□□□	□□□□

Appendix B

MBO ADOPTER CHECK SHEET

Feedback cards will tell you what influence you are having on management. Check off boxes from left to right as you move persons toward MBO adoption. When all boxes from AWARENESS through APPRAISAL/TRIAL have been checked, you have an MBO adopter. Mark the ADOPTION box.

		AWARENESS	INTEREST	APPRAISAL/TRIAL	ADOPTION
Vice president	A	□	□□□□□	□□□□□	□
Comptroller	B	□	□□□□		
Secretary	C	□	□□□□		
DIRECTORS					
Production	D	□	□□□□□	□□□□□	□
Marketing	E	□	□□□□□□	□□□□□□□	□
R&D	F	□	□□□	□□□	□
Personnel	G	□	□□	□□	□
Finance	H	□	□□□□□	□□□□□	□
MANAGERS: Production					
Plant A	I	□	□□□□□	□□□□□	□
Plant B	J	□	□□□□□	□□□□□	□
Plant C	K	□	□□□□□□□	□□□□□□	□
MANAGERS: Sales					
Advertising	L	□	□□	□□	□
Sales	M	□	□□□□	□□□□	□
Market research	N	□	□□□□	□□□□	□
MANAGERS: R&D					
Research	O	□	□□□	□□□□□	□
Product development	P	□	□□	□□	□
Liaison production	Q	□	□□□	□□□	□
MANAGERS: Personnel					
Employee	R	□	□□□□□□□	□□□□□□□	□
Industrial	S	□	□□□□	□□□□	□
Organizational Development	T	□	□□□□□□	□□□□□□□	□
Physical plant	U	□	□□□□□	□□□□□	□
MANAGERS: Finance					
Budget plan	V	□	□□□□	□□□□	□
Purchasing	W	□	□□□	□□□	□
Accounting	X	□	□□□	□□□	□

Appendix C

OC TACTICS/STRATEGIES LOG SHEET

Player names _____

_____

_____

Round	OC Tactic/Strategy Selected	Results
1.		
2.		
3.		
4.		
5.		
6.		
7.		
8.		
9.		
10.		
11.		
12.		
13.		
14.		
15.		
16.		
17.		
18.		
19.		
20.		

21. _____

22. _____

23. _____

24. _____

25. _____

26. _____

27. _____

28. _____

29. _____

30. _____

31. _____

32. _____

33. _____

34. _____

35. _____

36. _____

37. _____

38. _____

39. _____

40. _____

CASE

JACOBS SUCHARD: THE REORGANIZATION FOR 1992

Klaus J. Jacobs, chairman and CEO of Jacobs Suchard, had presided over much change in the past year. Now it was April 1989, and more change was still to come.

The main impetus to change had come from the European Economic Community's plan to "bring down the frontiers" by 1992, freeing the flow of goods, people, and capital across the 12 country borders. It meant for Jacobs Suchard, the Swiss-based producer of coffee and chocolate, that no longer would it be facing an EEC of 12 unique and independent markets, each serviced by autonomous business units, producing and selling for their own countries; now the EEC would be unified, and the company could eliminate some factories, take advantage of the larger scale, and market its products more globally.

Since chocolate was already more "global" across Europe in taste than was coffee, Jacobs had been able to move faster in making organization changes and in eliminating factories in chocolate. People in different countries preferred different coffee blends, so there was less immediate opportunity to produce and sell one brand for all countries. (The coffee business, under Charles Gebhard, however, was preparing to launch one new global brand, called Night & Day.)

Gerhard Zinser managed the chocolate

business. In preparing for the coming common market, Jacobs and the CEO office had already appointed "global brand sponsors" within his organization, to begin struggling with how to market his five basic brands across Europe, rather than independently in each country. Jacobs also had moved the manufacturing functions from Zinser to Hermann Pohl, the new corporate manufacturing and logistics manager reporting to Jacobs. Thus, much had already been done.

Yet, there was still more to do in organizing and setting new measurements and procedures. One proposal, made by a team that had attended Harvard's Managing Change program, called for further reorganization, breaking up the independent country organizations even further. But the proposal was very controversial and few supported it. Still, the question remained: What more had to be done?

Jacobs Suchard

Jacobs Suchard was a Swiss-based producer and marketer of coffee and chocolate products. Klaus Jacobs, chairman and CEO, was the majority shareholder. The company's 1988 revenues of 6.4B SFr were divided between its three businesses: coffee (2.7B SFr); confectionery (2.9B SFr); and trading, industrial, and finance (0.8B SFr). (See Exhibit 1 for the company's financial performance.) In 1971, Suchard had purchased Tobler, to form the Interfood company, and, in 1982, Jacobs, the coffee manufacturer, purchased Interfood to combine the two popular

This case was prepared by Philip Holland under the direction of Professor Robert G. Eccles.

EXHIBIT 1   Jacobs Suchard: The Reorganization for 1992

Consolidated Financial Statements of the Group
Important Corporate Data (five-year summary)
(million francs, except per share data)

	1988	1987	1986	1985	1984
Sales	6,382	6,104	5,236	5,382	5,111
Operating profit	476	471	338	265	244
Income on ordinary activities	307[a]	265	191	150	120
Cash flow (net income and depreciation of buildings and plant)	441[a]	394	294	243	205
Income as percentage of average shareholder's equity (%)	19.7[a]	20.5	13.6	14.1	16.6
Income as percentage of sales (%)	4.8[a]	4.3	3.6	2.8	2.4
Current assets	3,556	2,206	2,920	2,008	1,390
Fixed assets	1,024	886	832	674	666
Shareholder's equity	1,980	1,143	1,450	1,352	776
Total assets	4,580	3,092	3,753	2,682	2,056
Capital expenditure	211	158	85	100	153
Employees	16,799	16,053	10,063	9,260	10,632
Income per bearer share[b]	503.-[a]	503.-	414.-	353.-	351.-
Dividend per bearer share	165.-[c]	165.-	160.-	155.-	150.-
Dividend as percentage of net income (%)	33[c]	31	35	39	34

[a] Excluding the extraordinary income of 36.4 million Fr.

[b] Adjusted figures.

[c] Board of directors' proposal before considering the extraordinary income of 36.4 million Fr. and the proposed bonus of 50 Fr.

products. To further expand its markets, the company in 1986 purchased the Van Houten Group, a German-based confectionery manufacturer, and, in 1987, E. J. Brach, the confectionery manufacturer based in Chicago, and Cote d'Or, the Belgian chocolate manufacturer. Jacobs Suchard employed roughly 16,800 worldwide, 76 percent of whom were in the confectionery business.

Its basic chocolate products included the famous Milka line, with the recent additions of Lila Pause and Nussini (bars), I Love Milka (filled chocolates), Knusperzauber (a chocolate bar for children), and Milka Drink (chocolate powder). The other main products were Tobler and Toblerone, popular worldwide, and the Suchard assortments. Jacobs Suchard led all its competitors in chocolate sales across the EEC, the largest competitors being Nestlé, Mars, and Lindt. The company had offices in Switzerland, Germany, Austria, France, Italy, Denmark, Belgium, the Netherlands, Great Britain, Spain, Greece, North and South America,

Japan, and Australia, as well as principal licensees in Portugal, Africa, Asia, and Latin America.

A Company of Entrepreneurs

"Jacobs Suchard is an enterprise of entrepreneurs." So reads the opening statement of the company's 1987 annual report. It had been the company's basic philosophy since its three founders began their respective ventures: Philippe Suchard, in 1825, and Johann Jakob Tobler, in 1867, with their confectionery shops; and Johann Jacobs, in 1895, with his coffee shop.

The principle of entrepreneurship meant for the modern Jacobs Suchard corporation a great degree of decentralization, including a small corporate staff. Klaus Jacobs reaffirmed this principle in 1986 when he approved a new organization structure, with one person heading each core business (coffee and chocolate), to whom would report independent business unit general managers, with clear profit responsibility for the country each managed. For chocolate, the manager was Gerhard Zinser, to whom 13 general managers reported. (See Exhibit 2 for his organization chart.) This restructuring cut two levels of management between Jacobs and the general managers. In a letter sent to his top executives, Jacobs said of the new organization:

> We want to have as flat an organization as possible; personal relationships are what make this organization work and not hierarchical reporting relationships.
>
> Our type of business succeeds—or fails—at the front line; our money is made or lost at the business unit level depending on how effectively we run the business and at the very top man-

agement level where we set global strategies, allocate resources, and plan and execute strategic alliances.

> Any organization layers between these two levels must be justified on the basis of their value to the business units; most of our headquarters units are the servants, not the masters, of the business units.
>
> No cost centers; but we should be striving for profit centers in all areas, including administrative activities.

"Entrepreneurial," said Zinser, "means that people make their own decisions. It's a 6 billion SFr company with only 60 people in the corporate office." Said Rudy Fischer, manager of corporate management development, "Here we have fast decision making. Often major decisions are made in 10 minutes! The worst thing in this company is if you don't do anything." Decentralization also meant that the management typically used task forces to make the highest-level decisions. They appointed managers from across countries and functions, thus trying to achieve a bottom-up solution to problems.

Aside from how flat the organization was, top management also sought to rotate people around frequently, to avoid letting people fall into routines and to build the informal links, rather than the formal structure, that Jacobs wanted to rely on. As Fischer put it, "The structure is there just to solve conflicts."

The General Manager

The key position in the decentralized structure of Jacobs Suchard was the general manager of a business unit. Typically, the general manager was responsible for the activities of a core business in one country. So, for example, there was a

EXHIBIT 2 Jacobs Suchard: The Reorganization for 1992

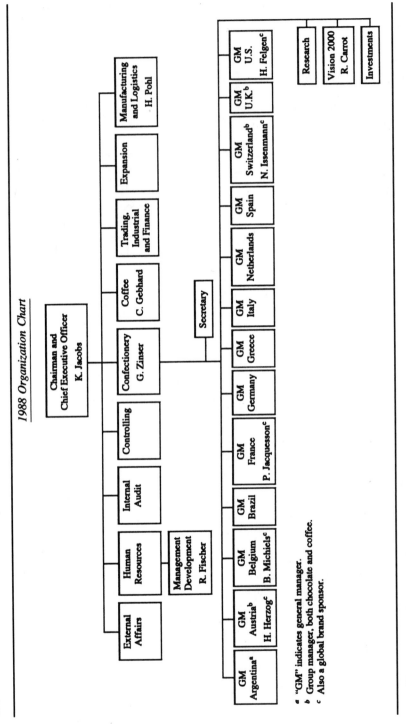

1988 Organization Chart

Chairman and Chief Executive Officer
K. Jacobs

- External Affairs
- Human Resources
  - Management Development
    R. Fischer
- Internal Audit
- Controlling
- Confectionery
  G. Zinser
- Coffee
  C. Gebhard
- Trading, Industrial and Finance
- Expansion
- Manufacturing and Logistics
  H. Pohl

Secretary

- GM Argentina[a]
- GM Austria[b]
  H. Herzog[c]
- GM Belgium
  B. Michiels[c]
- GM Brazil
- GM France
  P. Jacquesson[c]
- GM Germany
- GM Greece
- GM Italy
- GM Netherlands
- GM Spain
- GM Switzerland[b]
  N. Issenmann[c]
- GM U.K.[b]
- GM U.S.
  H. Felgen[c]

- Research
- Vision 2000
  R. Carrot
- Investments

[a] "GM" indicates general manager.
[b] Group manager, both chocolate and coffee.
[c] Also a global brand sponsor.

EXHIBIT 3   Jacobs Suchard: The Reorganization for 1992

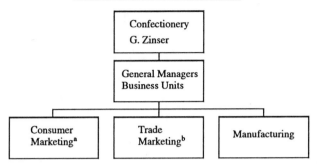

*Typical General Manager Organization (Partial) with Measurements
Prior to Changes for Globalization*

Measurements

• General manager: profit (profit after tax [PAT], return on total assets [ROTA]).

Note: Only marketing, sales, and manufacturing are shown, to contrast with later organization changes. Other functions include raw materials, logistics, quality assurance (later moved to IMCs) and other shared support functions.

[a] The equivalent of what might normally be referred to as "marketing."

[b] The equivalent of "sales."

SOURCE: Company records.

general manager of confectionery in France, coffee in Germany, and so on. In a few cases, such as with Switzerland, the general manager managed both the coffee and chocolate businesses.

The general managers had total profit responsibility for their business. They had trade marketing (sales), consumer marketing (marketing), and manufacturing functions reporting directly to them. They sold to their own local market, and they produced what that market demanded. (See Exhibit 3 for the organization chart for a typical general manager of a business unit, prior to any changes for the Common Market.) They made almost every decision pertaining to their business. Zinser described the position as "a man in his own market acting as an entrepreneur, making share-

and profit in his own business."

A general manager could receive a bonus of up to 100 percent of base salary; the average bonus was 50 percent, and nearly all fell within the range of 20 to 80 percent. The bonus was calculated by weighting the general manager's performance in three areas: corporate profit after tax (PAT) and return on total assets (ROTA); business unit PAT and ROTA; and personal MBO objectives—where the weights were: corporate performance, 20 percent (10 percent each for PAT and ROTA), business unit performance, 40 percent (20 percent each for PAT and ROTA), and personal objectives (40 percent). Within each area, the general manager was measured on a nine-point scale versus budget, one being the lowest score, five being "on target," and nine being "outstanding." The scale was calibrated as follows:

Score	Percent of Target	Bonus
1	< 90%	0%
3	90 – 100	30
5	100 – 105	50
7	105 – 120	70
9	>120	100

For example, a general manager could earn a "5" in corporate PAT (bonus = 50 percent) and a "7" in corporate ROTA (bonus = 70 percent), a "1" in business unit PAT (bonus = 0 percent) and a "5" in business unit ROTA (bonus = 50 percent), and finally a "5" in personal objectives (bonus = 50 percent). Thus, the general manager's annual bonus would be:

(10% weight)/(50% bonus) + (10%)/ (70%) + (20%)(0%) +(20%)(50%) + (40%)(50%) = 42% of salary.

The general managers' direct reports (those immediately under the general managers and perhaps one more level below them, depending on the size of the country) also could receive bonuses, though without the tie to corporate performance. For these managers, half the bonus came from business unit performance (PAT and ROTA) and half from performance against personal objectives.

To be a general manager was the career goal of many within the business units— they would move up the hierarchy of a particular function—and many general managers did not want to move any higher in the organization. To many, it was *the* position. One general manager, Pierre Jacquesson (France, confectionery), when asked why he thought general managers stayed in their positions, said: "They *are* the position. They think, 'It's my results, my people, my company.'

They feel they are the owners.''

European Economic Community, 1992

On March 25, 1957, representatives of six European countries—Belgium, France, the Federal Republic of Germany, Italy, Luxembourg, and the Netherlands— signed the famous "Treaty of Rome," thereby establishing the European Economic Community. In 1973, three more countries joined—Denmark, Ireland, and the United Kingdom; Greece joined in 1981. And with the addition of Spain and Portugal in 1986, the total in the community became 12.

Then, in February 1986, the 12 took their greatest step toward creating a common market: they signed the "Single European Act," its major objective being "for the citizens of the European community to wake up on the morning of 1 January 1993 in a frontierless Europe." The commission set out more than 300 measures to be adopted in removing the border obstacles, about a quarter of which had already been implemented by April 1989. According to Lord Cockfield, the program's architect, in discussing the EEC's lagging economic performance:

> The fragmentation of the European markets into 12 penny packets is not the only reason for this indifferent performance but it is one of the major reasons. It means that we impose on ourselves quite unnecessary costs in complying with frontiers and frontier controls; we deny ourselves the economies of scale that would flow from being able to manufacture and market on the basis of a market of 320 million consumers.

There are three types of barriers between borders: physical, technical, and fiscal. *Physical barriers* are the customs, frontier controls, and restrictions on the importation of certain products. It is common for transport vehicles to spend days trying to cross certain borders. *Technical barriers* are the mass of different standards and regulations that producers must conform to in each country. For example, most countries have limits on the amount of vegetable fat permitted in chocolate and ice cream. By 1992, these would all be eliminated. Finally, *fiscal barriers* are the value-added and excise taxes levied on products crossing borders. In 1989, they varied greatly from country to country. By 1992, though not eliminated, they would be harmonized.

Perhaps the slowest to change in building the common market would be the different tastes of the countries' consumers. But as people began to travel more freely across Europe to live and work where they chose, even these were likely to become more uniform.

For countries not in the EEC, such as the EFTA (European Free Trade Association) countries—Switzerland, Sweden, Norway, Iceland, Finland, and Austria—what was happening in EEC was still a call to action. Some of these countries, like Austria, might try to join the EEC; others, like Switzerland, might try to negotiate for reduced external barriers to the EEC.

Changing for the Common Market

Because of tariffs, duties, and poor transportation between countries, when the original Suchard company began to expand, it decided to set up independent offices and factories in the countries it entered outside Switzerland. Tobler had pursued a similar strategy, though on a smaller scale. This strategy, combined with Suchard's—and later, Jacobs Suchard's—acquisitions strategy, left the company with 19 different confectionery manufacturing plants across Europe.

Each country became autonomous, producing everything it needed to serve its local market. It produced all brands and all combinations of forms: fillings (hard, crunchy, and layered); baked (wafers, cookies, and crusts); molded (chocolate poured into a mold); and enrobed (chocolate dripped over a solid filling). Furthermore, each country produced its own cocoa liquor (from roasting and grinding the cocoa beans) and chocolate mass (from adding cocoa butter and sugar to the liquor), as well as handled all the end packaging, of which there were three different types: flowpacks (vacuum sealed), folded (wrapped flat around a chocolate bar), and twisted (sealed in a wrapper by twisting one or two ends). Thus, the countries had to be able to handle a wide range of products with limited volumes of each type, which hurt productivity.

What was happening in the EEC meant new possibilities—immediately, for the chocolate business, and, in the future, for the coffee business. No longer were 19 small, low-volume factories needed; now Zinser could take advantage of greater economies of scale by producing in fewer, larger factories, and then shipping the products across Europe to the markets. And no longer would he have to produce the same brand with different recipes and packaging for each country, but could reduce the variations of the products. Even advertising and pricing would become more global.

To prepare for these changes, Jacobs and his manager began to plan how they would reorganize. Now there would be "global brands," and someone would have to coordinate this work. Now, too, there would not be a factory in every country, reporting to a general manager, but fewer factories, servicing many general managers. Someone would have to coordinate this work, as well. Globalization became the top issue for the company. It was featured in the 1988 annual report and was the chosen theme for the first year of the Marbach Center of Communication, Jacobs Suchard's brand-new management development center.

Global Brand Sponsors

In taking a first step toward shifting the chocolate business away from a purely local to a more global focus, the CEO office, in early 1987, began appointing "global brand sponsors" for the five major confectionery brands. Each sponsor was also a general manager of a business unit, who now would be responsible both for the local business and for coordinating the strategy and implementation of the global brand. The following were the five managers appointed, the countries they already managed, and the brands they were assigned:

Hartmut Felgen
  (United States)   Sugus (Brach)
Hans Herzog (Austria)   Suchard
Nico Issenmann
  (Switzerland)   Tobler/Toblerone
Pierre Jacquesson (France)   Milka
Baudoin Michiels (Belgium)   Cote d'Or

Neither the CEO office nor Zinser specified what the job would involve. Essentially, the managers were told that they were responsible for the global brand. Each manager got a separate budget to cover this new activity, but no additional people.

Creating the International Manufacturing Centers

Some of the most difficult changes would come with trying to close down many of the small country-oriented factories and building up others to handle global volumes for certain products or forms—difficult both because factories were being closed down and because the independent country organizations would lose their manufacturing responsibilities. The general managers, who had seen themselves as the heads of their own self-sufficient businesses, would now be dependent on an outside organization for a central function.

Vision 2000. Even before the EEC had voted to create a "frontierless" Europe, Jacobs had seen the need to reduce the number of his manufacturing plants, to take advantage of economies of scale. Thus, he hired consultants from McKinsey to study which plants to eliminate. The name of the study, the implementation of which was later coordinated within the company by Robert Carrot, manager of the Strassburg factory, became Vision 2000.

The goal of the study was to make manufacturing a low-cost producer. Not only were there 19 factories, all producing a similar set of products, but each factory was using different processes to produce the same product, in order to satisfy local laws that required different processing temperatures or durations. So, for example, one factory might roast the cocoa beans or "conch" (final mixing) the chocolate differently from another.

Jacobs reviewed the Vision 2000 recommendations in December 1987, then appointed Robert Carrot to coordinate the implementation. The primary recommendation was to cut the number of factories to six. These factories would then be expanded, retooled for automation, and loaded with certain products to be shipped throughout Europe. Two of the factories would be new. Each would produce from between 80,000 to

100,000 tons of chocolate a year, whereas some of the old plants produced only 5,000 tons a year. The six factories would be:

Berlin, Germany (new)	Countlines and Milka Lila Pause
Bern, Switzerland	Toblerone
Halle, Belgium (new)	Cote d'Or
Herentals, Belgium	Wafer products (e.g., Nussini)
Lorrach, Germany	Milka tablets and bars
Strassburg, France	Pralines (boxed chocolates)

The six new factories would be called "International Manufacturing Centers" (IMCs). They represented a significant change from the old organization structure, where each general manager was directly responsible for a manufacturing plant. Given the company's entrepreneurial philosophy and decentralized decision making, how to organize and delegate authority for this new organization would be a great challenge.

The Issenmann Task Force. Jacobs kicked off a task force in March 1988, to be chaired by Nico Issenmann, country manager of Switzerland, responsible for both the chocolate and coffee businesses. Six other managers joined Issenmann on the task force; one from headquarters in Zurich, the others being either general managers, factory managers, or finance managers from Switzerland, Germany, and France. The plant closings begun after Vision 2000 had led to questions of pricing and delivery procedures, so the goal of the task force was to define the roles of the international manufacturing centers, the general managers, the global brand sponsors, and the rules by which the three should interact. The task force focused on the chocolate business, but suggested that its recommendations could also apply ultimately to the coffee business as well. The team published its recommendations in August 1988.

Organizationally, the group recommended the appointment of a "manufacturing center sponsor" to manage the six new manufacturing centers. They suggested the following responsibilities for the different managers:

- General Manager Business Unit: Brand penetration and business development in countries (i.e., business units).

- Global Brand Sponsor: Brand, product, pricing harmonization, standardization, and inspiring new product and sub-brand development in all countries/business units and, thus, on a global basis.

- Manufacturing Center Sponsor: Optimization of manufacturing economies of scale by concentrating on standardized "global product" production in few large-scale manufacturing centers, allowing for competition and entrepreneurial production of new/test products at the same time.

Under this organization, the general managers would keep trade marketing and consumer marketing, and lose manufacturing. Five of the general managers would become global brand sponsors as well. The manufacturing center sponsor would be an independent manager, reporting to Zinser, manager of the confectionery division. (See Exhibit 4 for the proposed structure.) The task force went on to elaborate on the above roles, on how each manager should be measured, and on how the transfer pricing—or, the "intercompany business regulations"—between

EXHIBIT 4   Jacobs Suchard: The Reorganization for 1992

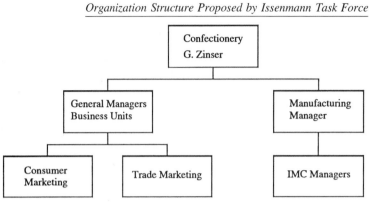

Organization Structure Proposed by Issenmann Task Force

Measurements

- General manager: Profit (Revenue – Cost of goods sold from IMCs) and ROTA (current assets).
- Manufacturing manager: COGS, productivity, ROTA.

[a] Five of whom are also global brand sponsors.

SOURCE: Company records.

the IMCs and general managers should take place.

General managers. Measuring the general managers would be similar to when they had also been responsible for manufacturing: their performance depended on PAT and ROTA. (Profits were calculated by subtracting total costs from revenues for the country, net of taxes.) However, now the cost that went into determining profits was the cost of goods sold incurred at the IMCs and charged to the general managers. In addition, now ROTA would be based on current assets, such as inventory and accounts receivable, rather than the previous total assets, since the fixed assets now belonged to the IMCs.

Regarding the general managers' role, the task force said: The "focus lies on consumer marketing, trade marketing (sales), and economic affairs (finance),

based on agreed strategies with relevant global brand sponsor and (core business manager).'' In other words, the general managers would still be responsible for consumer marketing and trade marketing, though now under the coordination of the global brand sponsors.

Global brand sponsors. Being also a general manager, the global brand sponsors had a lot to do. As the task force put it: They "have responsibility for a rather vast area of activities they cannot handle all by themselves. The individual sponsor is, therefore, encouraged to form a team of people from his own and other sister units.''

The global brand sponsors would have to "develop and safeguard the financial well-being and share growth of (their brands) on a global basis.'' They would develop and get agreement from the gen eral managers regarding the following:

- Actions to be taken to increase the importance and share of the global brand in terms of tons or sales units and return on sales.
- International advertising strategies for the global brands, helping the general managers with the implementation.
- Standardized sales units packaging for international usage.
- Activities together with the general managers and corporate R&D to introduce new products for the global brands.
- Activities together with the manufacturing center sponsor to use existing capacities to a maximum and to facilitate and make less complex intercompany relations and logistics.

The task force did not specify how the global brand sponsors should be measured, beyond their measurements as general managers of business units.

Global manufacturing sponsor. The global manufacturing sponsor, who was to report to Zinser, and to whom the six IMC managers would report, had the responsibility to ensure that all manufacturing sites were state of the art, and that capacity was shared between the global brands based on the demand statements from the general managers. The global manufacturing sponsor was to allocate where each product was to be manufactured and for which countries, taking into account capacity, productivity, logistics, and duties (if any).

The task force recommended that the appropriate performance measurements should be: productivity (both in terms of sales units per man-hour and tons per man-hour), maximization of raw materials usage, and ROTA for the total corporation.

International manufacturing centers (IMCs). In the past, the managers of the manufacturing plants had reported directly to the general managers and for the most part served only them. Now, however, the IMC managers would report to the global manufacturing sponsor and "provide the business units only with products prior agreed to by the manufacturing sponsor and the responsible global brand sponsor." Based on the sales plans prepared by the local business units, each IMC would consolidate its orders and, in turn, provide delivery plans for each business unit.

One of the most difficult steps for manufacturing in terms of the variability of the product line was packaging. In the past, each country had used different labels (largely because of language difference) and packages of different sizes; for example, three versus six bars to a package. Now the IMCs would have to get their packaging instructions from the global brand sponsors, who would try to eliminate much of the variability by standardizing the products. The IMC managers would be measured on productivity and maximization of raw materials usage, and would add to their prices a ROTA charge of 4 to 5 percent, to ensure that they were generating enough capital for reinvestment.

Harvard and Managing Change

In August 1988, Fischer, Carrot, and Christian Bridoux went to Harvard to attend the Managing Change program. The team's mission was to take another look at how to organize marketing and manufacturing for Europe 1992. Carrot had been a member of the Issenmann task force.

EXHIBIT 5   Jacobs Suchard: The Reorganization for 1992

Organization Structure Proposed by Harvard Managing Change Team

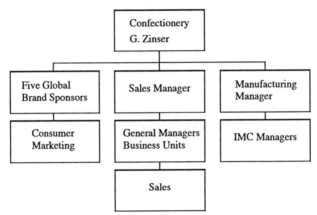

Measurements

• Global brand sponsors: profit (based on revenues and costs from all functions).
• Sales manager: total volume and volume/brand.
• Manufacturing manager: cost of goods sold.

Note: In actual organization announced February 1989, H. Pohl named manager of IMCs reporting directly to K. Jacobs, not G. Zinser.

SOURCE: Company records.

They recommended the following for the Confectionery Division, which might later be followed by the Coffee Division:

1.   Establish each global brand as a clear-cut profit center. The five profit centers' executives report directly to the executive vice president (EVP) of the Confectionery Division.

2.   Change the current business units to sales units, reporting directly to one European sales executive, who reports to the EVP Confectionery Division. The performance of the sales units are measured on total volume and on volume per brand. In this structure the global brand executive and the sales unit general manager will be two different people.

3.   Establish independent core factories reporting directly to one manufacturing executive. This manufacturing executive will report to the EVP, Confectionery Division. There is no organizational link between the core factory managers and the sales unit. The cost of goods sold of the core factories are to be charged to the Global Brands.

(See Exhibit 5 for the proposed organization structure.) The team believed that the global brand managers should get profit responsibility; otherwise, "the gap between the authority and responsibility will be too wide." In addition, unlike what the Issenmann task force had proposed, they thought that the global brand managers and the sales unit manager had to be different people: a single person doing both jobs, they felt, could get into conflicts over global strategy and local sales unit profits.

The old business units would now be called sales units, because consumer marketing would be moved from them to the global brand managers. The business units would also lose manufacturing, which would be independent of both the global brands and the sales units. The team also recommended having regular meetings between the global brand managers, the manufacturing and sales managers, and the confectionery EVP. Summing up their proposal, the members wrote:

> The above sketched model allows us to stay as close as possible to the competitive attitude which characterizes Jacobs Suchard. Many sources of conflict are reduced since there are always direct line responsibilities to only one superior. For example, consumer marketing reports directly and only to the global brand executive and the sales unit general managers directly to the sales executive, etc. However, the level of potential conflicts will still be substantially higher than in the present organization, for intensive negotiations between the centralized manufacturing, centralized consumer marketing, and the local sales units have to take place.

The Announcement of Hermann Pohl, IMC Manager and Follow-On Task Forces

The Issenmann task force dealt broadly with the issues of roles and responsibilities, and many specifics still had to be worked out for implementation. So in March 1989, five new task forces began meeting to address the following issues: transfer pricing, ordering and delivery procedures, how the IMCs would report to

the business units, information services support, and the need for a new cost accounting system. Each task force had from four to eight members, representing different countries and areas of responsibility.

In February 1989, Jacobs announced that he was appointing Hermann Pohl as head of corporate manufacturing and logistics. Pohl reported directly to Jacobs, and the six IMCs reported to Pohl. Thus, Zinser no longer had responsibility for manufacturing, even though both the Issenmann task force recommendation and the Harvard team's recommendation had been to keep the global manufacturing sponsor under the core business unit manager. Pohl, who had previously reported to Jacobs as manager of corporate economic affairs, had been working on the implementation of Vision 2000 and the issues of structure, pricing, and complexity reduction. He had seen the need for one person to coordinate this work and to give it high-level influence, and, since he was already a member of the head office management, Jacobs gave him this new responsibility. According to Pohl, it might be possible to phase out his position in two to three years.

April 1989: Status of the New Organization

By April 1989, the organization changes were complete and many of the 19 old factories had been closed. What remained was to work out the implementation of the follow-on task force items and to further reduce the product and packaging variability so the brands became truly global. Whether the organization at the general manager level should be further changed was still in debate also, although most people believed that they should not go as far as the Harvard team had recommended; that is, to make the global brand sponsors separate from the general managers and to give them consumer marketing, leaving the general managers with trade marketing. Some thought that such an organization might be possible in the far future; others thought that it should never be done, because the general managers had to remain the key position in the company.

Global Brand Sponsors.   With no clear direction about how they were to carry out their new assignments, the global brand sponsors began experimenting with how to work with the general managers to devise and implement global brand strategies. Themselves general managers, the global brand sponsors knew the strong incentives that moved their peers to maximize profits for the business units, incentives that would make the general managers balk at a change that would standardize a product for the global market but hurt local sales. Since the global brand sponsors had no consumer marketing or trade marketing support of their own—all the consumer marketing and trade marketing managers belonged to the local business unit general managers—the challenge for the global brand sponsors was to get the general managers, as Issenmann put it, to "think globally and act locally."

Zinser saw the relationship working this way. The global brand sponsors would have to make all strategies in cooperation with the general managers, and then the general managers would have to take the strategy and try to develop it in the local market. He said:

> For example, Italy is developing a Milka sponge product and Belgium is developing a marshmallow Milka. Both will be tested in the local markets for global possibilities. Who will pay for this development? The local managers. Why would they? One, because they benefit; and two, it's fun to contribute to the global business. A general manager knows that success with a product will get global attention.

The same idea applied to research and development, which resided both in the business units and at the corporate level. To promote entrepreneurship and decentralization and to keep the bottom-up decision-making process, Zinser expected the business units to come up with new product ideas and develop them locally for ultimate distribution on the global market.

The relationship between the global brand sponsors and general managers was informal, and the effectiveness of that relationship depended a great deal on how much both parties respected and trusted each other. Many of the rules that would govern the relationship were still being worked out in the task forces, and the global brand sponsors were still groping for how to unify the different countries' objectives. Jacquesson, general manager of French chocolate and global brand sponsor for Milka, began by holding formal meetings with the consumer marketing managers from the different countries, to discuss global consumer marketing strategy, but quit after six months. The country consumer marketing managers couldn't make decisions, because the general managers to whom they reported always changed those decisions later. Then he tried holding regular meetings with 15 general managers, but couldn't get agreement on anything. Finally, he set up a steering committee of four of the general managers with the largest markets— Germany,   Belgium,   England,   and

France—and asked them to meet every two months. This system, at least, produced some recommendations that the others felt some pressure to accept. Jacquesson characterized his role as "nearly an impossible mission." What did he think were the conditions for success? "The ability to fight, to be fair, to be open—to be young!"

Inevitably, there were conflicts—every day, according to Zinser. What the global brand sponsors wanted often clashed with what the local general managers wanted. There were conflicts over packaging sizes, what language to put on packages, how to advertise, who would pay for international media, which factory to source from (there were still options, and some general managers preferred certain factories), who pays for investments—and many others. Sometimes a global brand sponsor and the general manager would agree on a European advertising strategy; but when it came time to share the costs, a few general managers would refuse. In such cases, the global brand sponsor would be stuck with the cost in his own local budget, thereby hurting his own profits and would have to go to Zinser to get the general managers to pay. Sometimes general managers would just refuse to go along with a global advertising strategy. Cultural differences affected the content of local advertising, such as the hair color of the people in the advertisement; the general managers, therefore, saw global advertising as a threat.

Jacquesson explained how he handled such conflicts. If a general manager refused to implement the global strategy, "I listen to the facts," he said, "and if he makes a strong enough case, maybe I'll let him do what he wants. If he just says he doesn't feel the strategy will work, I won't accept that. Much of the conflict has to do with personalities. I try to be fair, and to take into account what they're concerned about."

When a global brand sponsor and a general manager reached an impasse, then the global brand sponsor could go to Zinser for resolution. This was a last resort, however, because Zinser had such a large span of control and so couldn't get involved in every difference of opinion. And a few people believed that Zinser often supported the local country management, anyway, fearing that otherwise he would hurt profits.

Despite the conflicts, however, Zinser, Issenmann, and Jacquesson all believed that, contrary to what the Harvard team had proposed, the global brand sponsors had to be general managers themselves, as well. They believed that not only would a separate global brand sponsor have no credibility with the general managers—the general managers would not want to take orders from someone who did not also have to take the same risks with a local business—but also that setting up a separate global brand sponsor might threaten the independence of the general managers, who still had *the* position. Said Issenmann: "A purely global manager would become like a staff member and would just get frustrated, trying to deal with the line managers." Jacquesson gave an example of when he had needed that credibility. He had had to launch a new product globally, Lila Pause, and so had to decide on a package size. He insisted on six-packs, which was different from the traditional three-packs. When he tried it in his own country, he got 2.4 times the expected sales, which then made it possible for him to convince Germany to use the six-packs. Otherwise, he thought, Germany never would have gone along.

Yet, if they agreed that a global brand

sponsor also had to be a general manager, they also agreed that the workload to do this was excessive. "We can't do it all," said Issenmann, "but it's the best way to do it." Said Jacquesson, simply: "The workload is too much."

Regarding measurements and bonuses, the global brand sponsors were measured the same as general managers, with the personal objectives part of the bonus formula reflecting the additional duties. Typically, the global brand sponsors were expected to complete projects associated with globalization, such as launching advertising campaigns, and were measured according to the number of projects and their effectiveness. The rest of the general managers, those who were not global sponsors, were not measured on how much they contributed to the globalization projects.

The International Manufacturing Centers

By April 1989, the chocolate business had moved about 80 percent toward concentrated production in the six IMCs. By October, all the extra factories would be closed.

Like the relationship between the general managers and global brand sponsors, the relationship between the general managers and IMC managers was also fraught with conflict. Where the IMCs sought standardization of a product line to maximize volumes and reduce costs, the general managers sought distinctive packaging and other requirements to serve their local markets.

Having Pohl as their new manager, with direct access to the head office and Jacobs, the IMC managers had gained a new independence. Prior to Pohl, when they were still reporting to the general manag-

ers, the IMC managers had had to follow what the general manager wanted. They could not act against the general manager's profit goals, even if they thought it was in the best interests of globalization. Now, however, they reported only indirectly to the general managers.

The general managers had not liked losing manufacturing, but, according to Pohl, most now saw the benefits. The key was the change process. "People realize," he said, "that, when the top guys get involved with change, it's serious. Plus, they know they'll be involved. We have to involve them in how we do it." Pohl always sought agreement from the general managers on what he was trying to do. On some issues, getting this agreement took a long time; on the issue of standardized pricing, for example, it took four months.

The general managers still were responsible for profit in their countries, and so, when the IMCs wanted to do something that would affect their bottom line, the general managers fought it. For example, the first fully international product, I Love Milka—it had one recipe and one box—would soon be produced solely in Strassburg, France, to be sold across Europe. Currently, it was mainly marketed in Germany. Nevertheless, before the Strassburg line was even completed for I Love Milka, Germany was already developing four new recipes, which would greatly expand the need for space and capacity at the factory. Whether or not Strassburg would respond to what Germany wanted depended on the agreed-upon global strategy. Said Carrot, now IMC manager of Strassburg: "We are awaiting a decision from the global brand sponsor on this. What's holding them up? Consumer marketing is still independent and local." Consumer marketing managers still reported to the general managers, and they did not always have the incentives to follow what the global sponsors wanted.

Pohl described another standard conflict:

> We wanted to have one Milka language wrapper for all of Europe, but people screamed, because we couldn't fit all the languages on the package. So, to compromise, we decided on three different packaging versions: one for Greece, one for the German-speaking countries, and one for the others. I agreed to this for now, because I needed the full commitment of all the general managers. It's the only way to get movement.

Jacquesson thought that many of the problems would not exist if there was a clear financial structure, outlining who had to pay for what. "The IMCs have good ideas, but they don't care where the profit is," he said.

> The unwritten rule is, "Help yourself." There's no formal decision structure. It's conflict management by design— which is very tough! For example, I wanted Germany to pay for the start-up of a product made in France for Germany, but they originally said no. Sometimes I need to bring in Zurich as an arbitrator. Case by case, issue by issue, we are trying to establish a philosophy for dealing with these cases, to build rules.

For Pohl, the most important issue to be dealt with was product complexity. Before standardization had begun, there were about 1,500 stock-keeping units (SKUs) for chocolate, considering all the variations of flavors, sizes, and language. Pohl didn't want to begin centralizing manufacturing with this "chaos." So he began task forces with the consumer marketing managers to try to reduce the SKUs, twice

getting nowhere, because no one could get beyond the issue of language. The third time, Pohl took language off the discussion table and simply asked the teams for a big reduction, wanting to let them recommend that was to be done. When they were finished, it looked as though they could cut the number from 1,500 down to 750.

Beyond this issue, how the IMCs should be measured and compensated, and how the IMCs should charge the general managers—the issue of intercompany business regulations—was still open. Should the IMCs charge by standard costs, and, if so, who would cover the risk of the volatile swings in the commodity prices of cocoa beans and cocoa butter, as well as swings in currencies? There were a number of related issues here, still to be worked out in the task forces. Once the task forces were done, they would have to present their recommendations to all the general managers for acceptance, and then to Jacobs.

How Far to Go?

Was the present organization sufficient to create the incentives and priorities for a successful launch of the global brands, or did the company need to follow the recommendation of the Harvard team and break out the responsibilities of the global brands and local business units? Jacobs hadn't said no to the idea, but neither did he think the organization was ready. And, could the company maintain its decentralized structure and entrepreneurial spirit, while trying to deal with products and markets that seemed to require more centralization? As Fischer put it, "We are trying to both centralize *and* keep a small staff." Finally, what was the future of the general manager? Many were already upset at losing functions; most would quit without profit responsibility. In a truly global business, it wasn't clear precisely what the role of the general managers might be. What further complicated the problem was the fact that there would always be local products. These were some of the questions that faced Jacobs as he looked ahead to EEC 1992, which was fast approaching.

READING

WHY CHANGE PROGRAMS DON'T PRODUCE CHANGE

Michael Beer
Russell A. Eisenstat
Bert Spector

Michael Beer and Russell A. Eisenstat are, respectively, professor and assistant professor of organizational behavior and human resource management at the Harvard Business School. Bert Spector is associate professor of organizational behavior and human resource management at Northeastern University's College of Business Administration.

In the mid-1980s, the new CEO of a major international bank—call it U.S. Financial—announced a companywide change effort. Deregulation was posing serious competitive challenges—challenges to which the bank's traditional hierarchical organization was ill-suited to respond. The only solution was to change fundamentally how the company operated. And the place to begin was at the top.

The CEO held a retreat with his top 15 executives, where they painstakingly reviewed the bank's purpose and culture. He published a mission statement and hired a new vice president for human resources from a company well known for its excellence in managing people. And in a quick succession of moves, he established

From *Harvard Business Review*, November–December 1990, pp. 158–66.

companywide programs to push change down through the organization: a new organizational structure, a performance appraisal system, a pay-for-performance compensation plan, training programs to turn managers into "change agents," and quarterly attitude surveys to chart the progress of the change effort.

As much as these steps sound like a textbook case in organizational transformation, there was one big problem: two years after the CEO launched the change program, virtually nothing in the way of actual changes in organizational behavior had occurred. What had gone wrong?

The answer is "everything." Every one of the assumptions the CEO made—about who should lead the change effort, what needed changing, and how to go about doing it—was wrong.

U.S. Financial's story reflects a common problem. Faced with changing markets and increased competition, more and more companies are struggling to reestablish their dominance, regain market share, and, in some cases, ensure their survival. Many have come to understand that the key to competitive success is to transform the way they function. They are reducing reliance on managerial authority, formal rules and procedures, and narrow divisions of work. And they are creating teams, sharing information, and delegating responsibility and accountability far down the hierarchy. In effect, companies are moving from the hierarchical and bureaucratic model of organization that has characterized corporations since Work War II to what we call the "task-driven organization," where what has to be done governs who works with whom and who leads.

But while senior managers understand the necessity of change to cope with new competitive realities, they often misunderstand what it takes to bring it about. They tend to share two assumptions with the CEO of U.S. Financial: that promulgating companywide programs—mission statements, "corporate culture" programs, training courses, quality circles, and new pay-for-performance systems—will transform organizations, and that employee behavior is changed by altering a company's formal structure and systems.

In a four-year study of organizational change at six large corporations (see the boxed insert, "Tracking Corporate Change"; the names are fictitious), we found that exactly the opposite is true: the greatest obstacle to revitalization is the idea that it comes about through companywide change programs, particularly when a corporate staff group, such as human resources, sponsors them. We call this "the fallacy of programmatic change." Just as important, formal organization structure and systems cannot lead a corporate renewal process.

While in some companies, wave after wave of programs rolled across the landscape with little positive impact, in others, more successful transformations did take place. They usually started at the periphery of the corporation in a few plants and divisions far from corporate headquarters. And they were led by the general managers of those units, not by the CEO or corporate staff people.

The general managers did not focus on formal structures and systems; they created ad hoc organizational arrangements to solve concrete business problems. By aligning employee roles, responsibilities, and relationships to address the organization's most important competitive task—a process we call "task alignment"—they focused energy for change on the work itself, not on abstractions such as "participation" or "culture." Unlike the CEO at U.S. Financial, they didn't employ massive training programs or rely on speeches and mission statements. Instead, we say that general managers carefully developed the change process through a sequence of six basic managerial interventions.

Once general managers understand the logic of this sequence, they don't have to wait for senior management to start a process of organizational revitalization. There is a lot they can do even without support from the top. Of course, having a CEO or other senior managers who are committed to change does make a difference—and when it comes to changing an entire organization, such support is essential. But top management's role in the change process is very different from that which the CEO played at U.S. Financial.

Grass-roots change presents senior

Tracking Corporate Change

Which strategies for corporate change work, and which do not? We sought the answers in a comprehensive study of 12 large companies where top management was attempting to revitalize the corporation. Based on preliminary research, we identified six for in-depth analysis: five manufacturing companies and one large international bank. All had revenues between $4 billion and $10 billion. We studied 26 plants and divisions in these six companies and conducted hundreds of interviews with human resource managers; line managers engaged in change efforts at plants, branches, or business units; workers and union leaders; and, finally, top management.

Based on this material, we ranked the six companies according to the success with which they had managed the revitalization effort. Were there significant improvements in interfunctional coordination, decision making, work organization, and concern for people? Research has shown that in the long term, the quality of these four factors will influence performance. We did not define success in terms of improved financial performance because, in the short run, corporate financial performance is influenced by many situational factors unrelated to the change process.

To corroborate our rankings of the companies, we also administered a standardized questionnaire in each company to understand how employees viewed the unfolding change process. Respondents rated their companies on a scale of 1 to 5. A score of 3 meant that no change had taken place; a score below 3 meant that, in the employee's judgment, the organization had actually gotten worse. As the table suggests, with one exception—the company we call Livingston Electronics—employees' perceptions of how much their companies had changed were identical to ours. And Livingston's relatively high standard of deviation (which measures the degree of consensus among employees about the outcome of the change effort) indicates that within the company there was considerable disagreement as to just how successful revitalization had been.

Researchers and Employees—Similar Conclusions

Company	Ranked by Researchers	Rated by Employees Average	Standard Deviation
General Products	1	4.04	0.35
Fairweather	2	3.58	0.45
Livingston Electronics	3	3.61	0.76
Scranton Steel	4	3.30	0.65
Continental Glass	5	2.96	0.83
U.S. Financial	6	2.78	1.07

Extent of Revitalization

managers with a paradox: directing a "nondirective" change process. The most effective senior managers in our study recognized their limited power to mandate corporate renewal from the top. Instead, they defined their roles as creating a climate for change, then spreading the lessons of both successes and failures. Put another way, they specified the general direction in which the company should move without insisting on specific solutions.

In the early phases of a companywide change process, any senior manager can play this role. Once grass-roots change reaches a critical mass, however, the CEO has to be ready to transform his or her own work unit as well—the top team composed of key business heads and corporate staff heads. At this point, the company's structure and system must be put into alignment with the new management practices that have developed at the periphery. Otherwise, the tension between dynamic units and static top management will cause the change process to break down.

We believe that an approach to change based on task alignment, starting at the periphery and moving steadily toward the corporate core, is the most effective way to achieve enduring organizational change. This is not to say that change can *never* start at the top, but it is uncommon and too risky as a deliberate strategy. Change is about learning. It is a rare CEO who knows in advance the fine-grained details of organizational change that the many diverse units of a large corporation demand. Moreover, most of today's senior executives developed in an era in which top-down hierarchy was the primary means for organizing and managing. They must learn from innovative approaches coming from younger unit managers closer to the action.

The Fallacy of Programmatic Change

Most change programs don't work because they are guided by a theory of change that is fundamentally flawed. The common belief is that the place to begin is with the knowledge and attitudes of individuals. Changes in attitudes, the theory goes, lead to changes in individual behavior. And changes in individual behavior, repeated by many people, will result in organizational change. According to this model, change is like a conversion experience. Once people "get religion," changes in their behavior will surely follow.

This theory gets the change process exactly backward. In fact, individual behavior is powerfully shaped by the organizational roles that people play. The most effective way to change behavior, therefore, is to put people into a new organizational context, which imposes new roles, responsibilities, and relationships on them. This creates a situation that, in a sense, "forces" new attitudes and behaviors on people. (See the table, "Contrasting Assumptions about Change.")

One way to think about this challenge is in terms of three interrelated factors required for corporate revitalization. *Coordination* or teamwork is especially important if an organization is to discover and act on cost, quality, and product development opportunities. The production and sale of innovative, high-quality, low-cost products (or services) depend on close coordination among marketing, product design, and manufacturing departments, as well as between labor and management. High levels of *commitment* are essential for the effort, initiative, and cooperation that coordinated action demands. New *competencies*, such as knowledge of the business as a whole,

Contrasting Assumptions about Change

Programmatic Change	Task Alignment
Problems in behavior are a function of individual knowledge, attitudes, and beliefs.	Individual knowledge, attitudes, and beliefs are shaped by recurring patterns of behavioral interactions.
The primary target of renewal should be the content of attitudes and ideas; actual behavior should be secondary.	The primary target of renewal should be behavior; attitudes and ideas should be secondary.
Behavior can be isolated and changed individually.	Problems in behavior come from a circular pattern, but the effects of the organizational system on the individual are greater than those of the individual on the system.
The target for renewal should be at the individual level.	The target for renewal should be at the level of roles, responsibilities, and relationships.

analytical skills, and interpersonal skills, are necessary if people are to identify and solve problems as a team. If any of these elements are missing, the change process will break down.

The problem with most companywide change programs is that they address only one or, at best, two of these factors. Just because a company issues a philosophy statement about teamwork doesn't mean its employees necessarily know what teams to form or how to function within them to improve coordination. A corporate reorganization may change the boxes on a formal organization chart but not provide the necessary attitudes and skills to make the new structure work. A pay-for-performance system may force managers to differentiate better performers from poorer ones, but it doesn't help them internalize new standards by which to judge subordinates' performances. Nor does it teach them how to deal effectively with performance problems. Such programs cannot provide the cultural context (role

models from whom to learn) that people need to develop new competencies, so ultimately they fail to create organizational change.

Similarly, training programs may target competence, but rarely do they change a company's patterns of coordination. Indeed, the excitement engendered in a good corporate training program frequently leads to increased frustration when employees get back on the job only to see their new skills go unused in an organization in which nothing else has changed. People end up seeing training as a waste of time, which undermines whatever commitment to change a program may have roused in the first place.

When one program doesn't work, senior managers, like the CEO at U.S. Financial, often try another, instituting a rapid progression of programs. But this only exacerbates the problem. Because they are designed to cover everyone and everything, programs end up covering nobody and nothing particularly well. They are so general and standardized that they don't speak to the day-to-day realities of particular units. Buzzwords like "quality," "participation," "excellence," "empowerment," and "leadership" become a substitute for a detailed understanding of the business.

And all these change programs also undermine the credibility of the change effort. Even when managers accept the potential value of a particular program for others—quality circles, for example, to solve a manufacturing problem—they may be confronted with another, more pressing business problem, such as new product development. One-size-fits-all change programs take energy *away* from efforts to solve key business problems—which explains why so many general managers don't support programs, even when they acknowledge that their underlying principles may be useful.

This is not to state that training, changes in pay systems or organizational structure, or a new corporate philosophy are always inappropriate. All can play valuable roles in supporting an integrated change effort. The problems come when such programs are used in isolation as a kind of "magic bullet" to spread organizational change rapidly through the entire corporation. At their best, change programs of this sort are irrelevant. At their worst, they actually inhibit change. By promoting skepticism and cynicism, programmatic change can inoculate companies against the real thing.

Six Steps to Effective Change

Companies avoid the shortcomings of programmatic change by concentrating on "task alignment"—reorganizing employee roles, responsibilities, and relationships to solve specific business problems. Task alignment is easiest in small units—a plant, department, or business unit—where goals and tasks are clearly defined. Thus, the chief problem for corporate change is how to promote task-aligned change across many diverse units.

We saw that general managers at the business unit or plant level can achieve task alignment through a sequence of six overlapping but distinctive steps, which we call the *critical path*. This path develops a self-reinforcing cycle of commitment, coordination, and competence. The sequence of steps is important because activities appropriate at one time are often counterproductive if started too early. Timing is everything in the management of change.

1. *Mobilize commitment to change through joint diagnosis of business problems.* As the term *task alignment* suggests, the starting point of any effective change effort is a clearly defined business problem. By helping people develop a shared diagnosis of what is wrong in an organization and what can and must be improved, a general manager mobilizes the initial commitment that is necessary to begin the change process.

Consider the case of a division we call Navigation Devices, a business unit of about 600 people set up by a large corporation to commercialize a product originally designed for the military market. When the new general manager took over, the division had been in operation for several years without ever making a profit. It had never been able to design and produce a high-quality, cost-competitive product. This was due largely to an organization in which decisions were made at the top, without proper involvement of or coordination with other functions.

The first step the new general manager took was to initiate a broad review of the business. Where the previous general manager had set strategy with the unit's marketing director alone, the new general manager included his entire management team. He also brought in outside consultants to help him and his managers function more effectively as a group.

Next, he formed a 20-person task force representing all the stakeholders in the organization—managers, engineers, production workers, and union officials. The group visited a number of successful manufacturing organizations in an attempt to identify what Navigation Devices might do to organize more effectively. One high-performance manufacturing plant in the task force's own company made a particularly strong impression. Not only did it highlight the problems at Navigation Devices but it also offered an alternative organizational model, based on teams, that captured the group's imagination. Seeing a different way of working helped strengthen the group's commitment to change.

The Navigation Devices task force didn't learn new facts from this process of joint diagnosis; everyone already knew the unit was losing money. But the group came to see clearly the organizational roots of the unit's inability to compete and, even more important, came to share a common understanding of the problem. The group also identified a potential organizational solution: to redesign the way it worked, using ad hoc teams to integrate the organization around the competitive task.

2. *Develop a shared vision of how to organize and manage for competi-*

tiveness. Once a core group of people is committed to a particular analysis of the problem, the general manager can lead employees toward a task-aligned vision of the organization that defines new roles and responsibilities. These new arrangements will coordinate the flow of information and work across interdependent functions at all levels of the organization. But since they do not change formal structures and systems like titles or compensation, they encounter less resistance.

At Navigation Devices, the 20-person task force became the vehicle for this second stage. The group came up with a model of the organization in which cross-functional teams would accomplish all work, particularly new product development. A business-management team composed of the general manager and his staff would set the unit's strategic direction and review the work of lower-level teams. Business-area teams would develop plans for specific markets. Product-development teams would manage new products from initial design to production. Production-process teams composed of engineers and production workers would identify and solve quality and cost problems in the plant. Finally, engineering-process teams would examine engineering methods and equipment. The teams got to the root of the unit's problems—functional and hierarchical barriers to sharing information and solving problems.

To create a consensus around the new vision, the general manager commissioned a still larger task force of about 90 employees from different levels and functions, including union and management, to refine the vision and obtain everyone's commitment to it. On a retreat away from the workplace, the group further refined the new organizational model and drafted a values statement, which it presented later to the entire Navigation Devices work force. The vision and the values statement made sense to Navigation Devices employees in a way many corporate mission statements never do—because it grew out of the organization's own analysis of real business problems. And it was built on a model for solving those problems that key stakeholders believed would work.

3. *Foster consensus for the new vision, competence to enact it, and cohesion to move it along.* Simply letting employees help develop a new vision is not enough to overcome resistance to change—or to foster the skills needed to make the new organization work. Not everyone can help in the design, and even those who do participate often do not fully appreciate what renewal will require until the new organization is actually in place. This is when strong leadership from the general manager is crucial. Commitment to change is always uneven. Some managers are enthusiastic; others are neutral or even antagonistic. At Navigation Devices, the general manager used what his subordinates termed the "velvet glove." He made it clear that the division was going to encourage employee involvement and the team approach. To managers who wanted to help him, he offered support. To those who did not, he offered outplacement and counseling.

Once an organization has defined new roles and responsibilities, people need to develop the competencies to make the new setup work. Actually, the very existence of the teams with their new goals and accountabilities will force learning. The changes in roles, responsibilities, and relationships foster new skills and attitudes. Changed patterns of coordination will also increase employee participation, collaboration, and information sharing.

But management also has to provide the right supports. At Navigation Devices, six resource people—three from the corporate headquarters—worked on the change project. Each team was assigned one internal consultant, who attended every meeting, to help people be effective team members. Once employees could see exactly what kinds of new skills they needed, they asked for formal training programs to develop those skills further. Since these courses grew directly out of the employee's own experiences, they were far more focused and useful than traditional training programs.

Some people, of course, just cannot or will not change, despite all the direction and support in the world. Step 3 is the appropriate time to replace those managers who cannot function in the new organization—after they have had a chance to prove themselves. Such decisions are rarely easy, and sometimes those people who have difficulty working in a participatory organization have extremely valuable specialized skills. Replacing them early in the change process, before they have worked in the new organization, is not only unfair to individuals, it can be demoralizing to the entire organization and can disrupt the change process. People's understanding of what kind of manager and worker the new organization demands grows slowly and only from the experience of seeing some individuals succeed and others fail.

Once employees have bought into a vision of what's necessary and have some understanding of what the new organization requires, they can accept the necessity of replacing or moving people who don't make the transition to the new way of working. Sometimes people are transferred to other parts of the company where technical expertise, rather than the new competencies, is the main requirement. When no alternatives exist, sometimes they leave the company through early retirement programs, for example. The act of replacing people can actually reinforce the organization's commitment to change by visibly demonstrating the general manager's commitment to the new way.

Some of the managers replaced at Navigation Devices were high up in the organization—for example, the vice president of operations, who oversaw the engineering and manufacturing departments. The new head of manufacturing was far more committed to change and skilled in leading a critical path change process. The result was speedier change throughout the manufacturing function.

4. *Spread revitalization to all departments without pushing it from the top.* With the new ad hoc organization for the unit in place, it is time to turn to the functional and staff departments that must interact with it. Members of teams cannot be effective unless the department from which they come is organized and managed in a way that supports their roles as full-fledged par-

ticipants in team decisions. What this often means is that these departments will have to rethink their roles and authority in the organization.

At Navigation Devices, this process was seen most clearly in the engineering department. Production department managers were the most enthusiastic about the change effort; engineering managers were more hesitant. Engineering had always been king at Navigation Devices; engineers designed products to the military's specifications without much concern about whether manufacturing could easily build them or not. Once the new team structure was in place, however, engineers had to participate on product-development teams with production workers. This required them to reexamine their roles and rethink their approaches to organizing and managing their own department.

The impulse of many general managers faced with such a situation would be to force the issue—to announce, for example, that now all parts of the organization must manage by teams. The temptation to force newfound insights on the rest of the organization can be great, particularly when rapid change is needed, but it would be the same mistake that senior managers make when they try to push programmatic change throughout a company. It short-circuits the change process.

It's better to let each department "reinvent the wheel"—that is, to find its own way to the new organization. At Navigation Devices, each department was allowed to take the general concepts of coordination and teamwork and apply them to its particular situation. Engineering spent nearly a year agonizing over how to implement the team concept. The department conducted two surveys, held off- site meetings, and proposed, rejected, then accepted a matrix management structure before it finally got on board. Engineering's decision to move to matrix management was not surprising; but because it was its own choice, people committed themselves to learning the necessary new skills and attitudes.

5. *Institutionalize revitalization through formal policies, systems and structures.* There comes a point where general managers have to consider how to institutionalize change so the process continues even after they've moved on to other responsibilities. Step 5 is the time: the new approach has become entrenched, the right people are in place, and the team organization is up and running. Enacting changes in structures and systems any earlier tends to backfire. Take information systems. Creating a team structure means new information requirements. Why not have the MIS department create new systems that cut across traditional functional and departmental lines early in the change process? The problem is that, without a well-developed understanding of information requirements, which can best be obtained by placing people on task-aligned teams, managers are likely to resist new systems as an imposition by the MIS department. Newly formed teams can often pull together enough information to get their work done without fancy new systems. It's better to hold off until everyone understands what the team's information needs are.

What's true for information sys-

tems is even more true for other formal structures and systems. Any formal system is going to have some disadvantages; none is perfect. These imperfections can be minimized, however, once people have worked in an ad hoc team structure and learned what interdependencies are necessary. Then employees will commit to them, too.

Again, Navigation Devices is a good example. The revitalization of the unit was highly successful. Employees changed how they saw their roles and responsibilities and became convinced that change could actually make a difference. As a result, there were dramatic improvements in value added per employee, scrap reduction, quality, customer service, gross inventory per employee, and profits. And all this happened with almost no formal changes in reporting relationships, information systems, evaluation procedures, compensation, or control systems.

When the opportunity arose, the general manager eventually did make some changes in the formal organization. For example, when he moved the vice president of operations out of the organization, he eliminated the position altogether. Engineering and manufacturing reported directly to him from that point on. For the most part, however, the changes in performance at Navigation Devices were sustained by the general manger's expectations and the new norms for behavior.

6. *Monitor and adjust strategies in response to problems in the revitalization process.* The purpose of change is to create an asset that did not exist before—a learning organization capable of adapting to a changing competitive environment. The organization

has to know how to continually monitor its behavior—in effect, to learn how to learn.

Some might say that this is the general manager's responsibility. But monitoring the change process needs to be shared just as analyzing the organization's key business problem does.

At Navigation Devices, the general manager introduced several mechanisms to allow key constituents to help monitor the revitalization. An oversight team—composed of some crucial managers, a union leader, a secretary, an engineer, and an analyst from finance—kept continual watch over the process. Regular employee attitude surveys monitored behavior patterns. Planning teams were formed and reformed in response to new challenges. All these mechanisms created a long-term capacity for continual adaptation and learning.

The six-step process provides a way to elicit renewal without imposing it. When stakeholders become committed to a vision, they are willing to accept a new pattern of management—here the ad hoc team structure—that demands changes in their behavior. And as the employees discover that the new approach is more effective (which will happen only if the vision aligns with the core task), they have to grapple with personal and organizational changes they might otherwise resist. Finally, as improved coordination helps solve relevant problems, it will reinforce team behavior and produce a desire to learn new skills. This learning enhances effectiveness even further and results in an even stronger commitment to change. This mutually reinforcing cycle of improvements in commitment, coordination, and competence creates a growing sense

of efficacy. It can continue as long as the ad hoc team structure is allowed to expand its role in running the business.

The Role of Top Management

To change an entire corporation, the change process we have described must be applied over and over again in many plants, branches, departments, and divisions. Orchestrating this companywide change process is the first responsibility of senior management. Doing so successfully requires a delicate balance. Without explicit efforts by top management to promote conditions for change in individual units, only a few plants or divisions will attempt change, and those that do will remain isolated. The best senior manager leaders we studied held their subordinates responsible for starting a change process without specifying a particular approach.

Create a market for change. The most effective approach is to set demanding standards for all operations and then hold managers accountable to them. At our best-practice company, which we call General Products, senior managers developed ambitious product and operating standards. General managers unable to meet these product standards by a certain date had to scrap their products and take a sharp hit to their bottom lines. As long as managers understand that high standards are not arbitrary but are dictated by competitive forces, standards can generate enormous pressure for better performance, a key ingredient in mobilizing energy for change.

But merely increasing demands is not enough. Under pressure, most managers will seek to improve business performance by doing more of what they have always done—overmanage—rather than alter the fundamental way they organize. So, while senior managers increase demands, they should also hold managers accountable for fundamental changes in the way they use human resources.

For example, when plant managers at General Products complained about the impossibility of meeting new business standards, senior managers pointed them to the corporate organization-development department within human resources and emphasized that the plant managers would be held accountable for moving revitalization along. Thus, top management had created a demand system for help with the new way of managing, and the human resource staff could support change without appearing to push a program.

Use successfully revitalized units as organizational models for the entire company. Another important strategy is to focus the company's attention on plants and divisions that have already begun experimenting with management innovations. These units become developmental laboratories for further innovation.

There are two ground rules for identifying such models. First, innovative units need support. They need the best managers to lead them, and they need adequate resources—for instance, skilled human resource people and external consultants. In the most successful companies that we studied, senior managers saw it as their responsibility to make resources available to leading-edge units. They did not leave it to the human resource function.

Second, because resources are always limited and the costs of failure high, it is crucial to identify those units with the likeliest chance of success. Successful management innovations can appear to be failures when the bottom line is devastated by environmental factors beyond the unit's control. The best models are in healthy markets.

Obviously, organizational models can serve as catalysts for change only if others are aware of their existence and are encouraged to learn from them. Many of our worst-practice companies had plants and divisions that were making substantial changes. The problem was, nobody knew about them. Corporate management had never bothered to highlight them as examples to follow. In the leading companies, visits, conferences, and educational programs facilitated learning from model units.

Develop career paths that encourage leadership development. Without strong leaders, units cannot make the necessary organizational changes, yet the scarcest resource available for revitalizing corporations is leadership. Corporate renewal depends as much on developing effective change leaders as it does on developing effective organizations. The personal learning associated with leadership development—or the realization by higher management that a manager does not have this capacity—cannot occur in the classroom. It only happens in an organization where the teamwork, high commitment, and new competencies we have discussed are already the norm.

The only way to develop the kind of leaders a changing organization needs is to make leadership an important criterion for promotion, and then manage people's careers to develop it. At our best-practice companies, managers were moved from job to job and from organization to organization based on their learning needs, not on their position in the hierarchy. Successful leaders were assigned to units that had been targeted for change. People who needed to sharpen their leadership skills were moved into the company's model units, where those skills would be demanded and, therefore, learned. In effect, top management used leading-edge units as hothouses to develop revitalization leaders.

But what about the top management team itself? How important is it for the CEO and his or her direct reports to practice what they preach? It is not surprising—indeed, it's predictable—that, in the early years of a corporate change effort, top managers' actions are often not consistent with their words. Such inconsistencies don't pose a major barrier to corporate change in the beginning, though consistency is obviously desirable. Senior managers can create a climate for grass-roots change without paying much attention to how they themselves operate and manage. And unit managers will tolerate this inconsistency so long as they can freely make changes in their own units in order to compete more effectively.

There comes a point, however, when addressing the inconsistencies becomes crucial. As the change process spreads, general managers in the ever-growing circle of revitalized units eventually demand changes from corporate staff groups and top management. As they discover how to manage differently in their own units, they bump up against constraints of policies and practices that corporate staff and top management have created. They also begin to see opportunities for better coordination between themselves and other parts of the company over which they have little control. At this point, corporate organization must be aligned with corporate strategy, and coordination between related but hitherto independent businesses improved for the benefit of the whole corporation.

None of the companies we studied had reached this "moment of truth." Even when corporate leaders intellectually understood the direction of change, they were just beginning to struggle with how they would change themselves and the company as a whole for a total corporate revitalization.

This last step in the process of corporate renewal is probably the most important. If the CEO and his or her management team do not ultimately apply to themselves what they have been encouraging their general managers to do, then the whole process can break down. The time to tackle the tough challenge of transforming companywide systems and structures comes finally at the end of the corporate change process.

At this point, senior managers must make an effort to adopt the team behavior, attitudes, and skills that they have demanded of others in earlier phases of change. Their struggle with behavior change will help sustain corporate renewal in three ways. It will promote the attitudes and behavior needed to coordinate diverse activities in the company; it will lend credibility to top management's continued espousal of change; and it will help the CEO identify and develop a successor who is capable of learning the new behaviors. Only such a manager can lead a corporation that can renew itself continually as competitive forces change.

Companies need a particular mindset for managing change: one that emphasizes process over specific content, recognizes organization change as a unit-by-unit learning process, rather than a series of programs, and acknowledges the payoffs that result from persistence over a long time as opposed to quick fixes. This mindset is difficult to maintain in an environment that presses for quarterly earnings, but we believe it is the only approach that will bring about successful renewal.

The Recipients of Change

INTRODUCTION

No one can predict the ultimate effect of this past decade's massive overhaul in U.S. manufacturing that left millions of people temporarily or long-term unemployed—receiving change in its most powerful form, at least in the individual's work life. This restructuring now is beginning to take hold in the service sector, portending more dislocation for tens of thousands of people. Whether these downsizings will lead to a new kind of contract between company and employee; whether even more people will attempt to survive as independent workers or found their own firms; whether the two "sides" will view each other with increased hostility and suspicion, with loyalty becoming a quaint concept of the past—one thing is clear: the ramifications of change are profound. Thus, this module shifts the focus from designing and implementing change programs to what it is like to be on the receiving end. By looking squarely at the impact of change on individuals and their social arena—work environment, families, communities—we gain a better appreciation of what both sides can do to mitigate, in some way, the extremes of experiencing change.

One aim of this module, then, is to consider how change can be introduced, given an understanding of its effects. Can an organization learn from its mistakes? its successes? Likewise, can a recipient of change in one situation use that experience positively? Or is the once-burned-twice-shy adage inevitable?

The second aim of the material is to provoke discussion of what obligations exist between company and employee. What "right" has an organization to either demand change or superimpose it on a person or a group? But has the individual or group the right to threaten the organization's viability by refusing the change?

CASES AND READINGS

The module opens with a controversial article from *The Wall Street Journal* and its responding Letters to the Editor that both support and criticize its validity. The article, for which the author won a Pulitzer prize, describes the aftermath of the 1986 leveraged buy-out of Safeway Stores and emphasizes the human toll. Critics of the article claim that the author failed to stress sufficiently the competitive gains that Safeway achieved through the LBO, and, instead, seemed to imply through dramatic vignettes that the company's action "caused" such horrors as the suicide of a longtime employee.

The Safeway case, "The Reckoning: Safeway LBO Yields Vast Profits but Exacts Heavy Human Toll," leads off this module not to encourage debate about the appropriateness of LBOs as business strategy but to force attention on receiving change in its most dramatic form—being fired. As such, the viewpoint could be that of the workers in the 19 "old factories" that were closed as part of the Jacobs Suchard reorganization, discussed in the previous case.

Not only is being fired a change at its extreme, being fired as part of a large-scale downsizing effort is particularly difficult. The motivation behind the business decision to downsize is almost never the actions of an individual worker. It is not, from the company's perspective, a series of individual firings that together constitute downsizing. Yet, at the individual level, the reactions are intensely personal, reflecting, especially for the longtime employee, a sense of betrayal in a relationship. "How could they do this to me?" is a typical cry.

The accompanying reading grew out of a classroom discussion of the Safeway story. In class, a Harvard MBA student briefly described his ethical turmoil about the business-exigencies versus individual-consequences dilemma as they were played out within his own family. He subsequently agreed to explain the situation more fully, and that appears in the reading "A Conversation about LBOs."

The Safeway discussion explored the point when change collided with recipients. In the next situation, the change hasn't happened yet. In "Donna Dubinsky and Apple Computer, Inc. (A)," Dubinsky confronts a possible reorganization of the firm's distribution system, which she built essentially from scratch and currently manages. She is, however, in a position to influence whether this change will take place. What this case introduces to the subject of receiving change is reactions to the *anticipated* change—in particular, how those reactions are stirred when the change threatens someone's direct, personal contribution to the organization.

At the end of the Dubinsky session, another Apple case is distributed, in which the same situation that Dubinsky faced is examined from someone else's perspective. This person, too, was shaken by the possible change—interestingly, both protagonists used the same phrase: "Sheer misery"—but in somewhat different ways. The reading, "The Recipients of Change," accompanies this second Apple case. This note introduces the *process* of reacting to change: the initial impact, the stages of coming to terms with being changed, and gradual acceptance. It also suggests some approaches for both the "changee" and implementor that may lessen the difficulties in receiving change and shorten the process of acceptance.

The two Apple cases and the reading underscore that organizations which fail to appreciate the dynamics of reacting to change at a minimum waste an appalling amount of time, as people nurse their wounds. That is, when there is no acknowledgment, explicit or implicit, of what people are experiencing, recipients are hindered from getting through their psychological and very "normal" responses. Moreover, when these recipients must (or should) be carrying their everyday responsibilities as well as deal with a potential change to those responsibilities, if there is no support for dealing with the latter, the former will surely suffer.

The next case series, "Rick Miller (A) and (B)," introduces another employee who discovers that his company has been sold, unbeknownst to him; in fact, it happens twice in a row. But this protagonist is not a minimum-wage employee at Safeway. In the first instance he was CFO of RCA, and, in the second, he was head of General Electric's $2.2 billion consumer electronics business. Strikingly, his response to these changes in his life is nearly identical to that found in the Safeway article. Thus, one point this series makes is the near universality of reactions to change, particularly abrupt change, that one has had no part in deciding.

But the Rick Miller series injects a new theme. Miller finds himself simultaneously reacting to a change and having to announce the same change to his hand-picked management team. This is by no means an unusual situation today: people who have experienced change will be called upon, sooner or later, to implement change themselves. "Sooner," because within an organization many change efforts may be underway—someone can simultaneously receive one change and implement another. And "later," because many people have survived changes in one organization, only to discover that they must enact them in another. The question is what is done with that experience of receiving change. Is it shared, and, if so, how?

The final segment of this module, "Apex Manufacturing," is a similation exercise. A company is preparing to notify its employees of an across-the-board massive downsizing and is contemplating a variety of approaches it can take. These must be assessed according to importance and timing—from "do this immediately," to "don't do it all." Like the "Organizational Change Game" in Module 3, this exercise entails choice and sequencing; but in this situation, the aim is not to introduce an "innovation"—rather, it is to tell thousands of people that they have lost their jobs. As such, it is also implementing change, but now draws upon a deeper understanding of receiving it.

CASE

THE RECKONING: SAFEWAY LBO YIELDS VAST PROFITS BUT EXACTS HEAVY HUMAN TOLL

Susan C. Faludi
Staff Reporter of The Wall Street Journal

Oakland, Calif.—On the eve of the 1986 leveraged buy-out of Safeway Stores, Inc., the board of directors sat down to a last supper. Peter Magowan, the boyish-looking chairman and chief executive of the world's largest supermarket chain rose to offer a toast to the deal that had fended off a hostile takeover by the corporate raiders Herbert and Robert Haft.

"Through your efforts, a true disaster was averted," the 44-year-old Mr. Magowan told the other directors. By selling

From *The Wall Street Journal*, May 16, 1990.

the publicly held company to a group headed by buy-out specialists Kohlberg Kravis Roberts & Company and members of Safeway management, "you have saved literally thousands of jobs in our work force," Mr. Magowan said. "All of us—employees, customers, share-holders—have a great deal to be thankful for."

Nearly four years later, Mr. Magowan and KKR group can indeed count their blessings. While they borrowed heavily to buy Safeway from the shareholders, last month they sold 10 percent of the company (but none of their own shares) back to the public—at a price that values their own collective stake at more than $800 million, more than four times their cash investment.

Employees, on the other hand, have considerably less reason to celebrate. Mr. Magowan's toast notwithstanding, 63,000 managers and workers were cut loose from Safeway, through store sales or lay-offs. While the majority were reemployed by their new store owners, this was largely at lower wages, and many thousands of Safeway people would end up either unemployed or forced into the part-time work force. A survey of former Safeway employees in Dallas found that nearly 60 percent still hadn't found full-time employment more than a year after the layoff.

James White, a Safeway trucker for nearly 30 years in Dallas, was among the 60 percent. In 1988, he marked the one-year anniversary of his last shift at Safeway this way: First he told his wife he loved her, then he locked the bathroom door, loaded his .22-caliber hunting rifle, and blew his brains out.

"Safeway was James's whole life," says his widow, Helen. "He'd near stand up and salute whenever one of those

trucks went by." When Safeway dismissed him, she says, "it was like he turned into a piece of stone."

Eighties Fad

Few financial maneuvers have drawn more controversy than the leveraged buy-out, or LBO, a relatively old money-making tactic that was dusted off and put to extensive use in the 1980s, thanks largely to the rise of junk-bond financing.

In a leveraged buy-out, a small group of investors that generally includes senior management borrows heavily to buy a company from public shareholders and takes it private. The debt is to be rapidly repaid from the company's own cash flow or from sales of its assets.

The returns on some such highly leveraged investments have been astronomical, enriching such financiers as Henry Kravis, Ronald Perelman, and Nelson Peltz to a degree unheard of since the days of the Robber Barons. Proponents of LBOs argue that they are good for business and good for America, triggering long-overdue crash weight-loss programs for flabby corporations. By placing ownership in the hands of a small group of investors and managers with a powerful debt-driven incentive to improve productivity, the argument goes, companies can't help but shape up.

Success Story

The Safeway LBO is often cited as one of the most successful in this regard. It brought shareholders a substantial premium at the outset, and since then the company has raised productivity and operating profits and produced riches for the new investors and top management. "We could not have done what we did do without going through the incredible trauma and pressure of the LBO,'' Mr. Magowan said in late 1988.

But while much has been written about the putative benefits of LBOs, little has been said about the hundreds of thousands of people directly affected by the past decade's buy-out binge: employees of the bought-out corporations. In the case of Safeway, a two-month investigation of the buy-out reveals enormous human costs and unintended side effects. The company dropped tens of thousands of employees from its payroll, suppliers and other dependent industries laid off hundreds more, and communities lost the civic contributions of a firm whose first store had been opened by a clergyman who wanted to help his parishioners save money.

When Safeway itself selected a group of its employees to speak to this newspaper on behalf of the company, not one of those interviewed praised the buy-out. ''I think LBOs are very ugly,'' said Carl Adkins, an inventory control clerk who described himself as happy with his job. ''I think they are harmful to individual working people. I think they honestly stink.''

Moreover, the evidence doesn't entirely support the argument that the LBO made Safeway a healthier institution. The supermarket chain cut plenty of muscle with the fat, both from its holdings and from its labor force, and deferred capital improvements in favor of the all-consuming debt. Many employees find the post-LBO working environment more difficult—as a company legendary for job security and fairness resorts to hardball labor policies and high-pressure quota systems.

Just before the Safeway deal was struck in 1986, Mr. Magowan's mother grew worried about the employees. The supermarket dowager wanted to be sure the LBO wouldn't damage Safeway's long-standing reputation as a benevolent employer.

Will anyone get hurt? Mrs. Magowan pressed her son at the time, according to company staff members. Will anyone lose his job?

No, Mom, Mr. Magowan promised, according to the staffers' account. No one will get hurt.

''Yes, I was greatly concerned about the people,'' Mrs. Magowan recalls today, in her mansion overlooking the San Francisco Bay. She declines to comment further.

Mr. Magowan's recollection: ''Well, I don't ever remember such a conversation ever occurred. ...I might have said things like, 'We're going to do the best we can for our employees and I'm hopeful that we are going to be able to keep the vast majority with the new owners.' ''

In any event, before that summer was out, Mrs. Magowan's son had begun firing Safeway employees. Not long after, Safeway replaced its longtime motto, ''Safeway Offers Security.'' The new corporate statement, displayed on a plague in the lobby at corporate headquarters, reads in part: ''Targeted Returns on Current Investment.''

* * *

Before the LBO, Safeway was hardly a prime example of the sluggish, out-of-shape sort of company that LBO proponents like to target. Founded in 1926, it had grown under Magowan family leadership to encompass more that 2,000 stores in 29 states and in England, Australia, Canada, and Mexico. Mr. Magowan's father, Robert, had largely built Safeway, and his mother, Doris Merrill Magowan, is the daughter of a founder of Merrill Lynch & Company, which helped finance Safeway's growth.

Many companies, including Safeway, had allowed their payrolls to become bloated in certain underperforming divisions, and layoffs were common throughout large American companies during the last decade.

But Safeway was already doing—albeit at a slower pace—many of the things LBO experts advocate. It was remodeling its stores and creating the upscale "superstores" that have now proved such a big success. It was experimenting with employee productivity teams, phasing out money-losing divisions, and thinning its work force with a program that included some layoffs but generally relied on less painful methods like attrition.

All these changes produced earnings that more than doubled in the first four years of the 1980s, to a record $231 million in 1985. The stock price tripled in three years, and dividends climbed four years in a row.

But all that wasn't enough for takeover-crazed Wall Street, where virtually no company was invulnerable to cash-rich corporate raiders. When the deep-pocketed Hafts began buying Safeway shares in the open market and then offered to buy the company for as much as $64 a share, management felt it had to take defensive action. Selling to the Hafts might have cost chairman Magowan his job and, he felt, ultimately might have brought a breakup of the company.

Safeway considered and rejected a plan to fend off the Hafts through a so-called recapitalization. This was a move that its supermarket-industry competitor, Kroger Company, would use two years later to keep the same raiders at bay while allowing shareholders to realize a big one-time gain.

The decision to sell to KKR instead brought immediate benefits to some.

Shareholders got $67.50 a share—82 percent more than the stock was trading at three months before—plus warrants that give them a 5.6 percent stake in the ongoing company. Employees owned roughly 10 percent of Safeway shares at the time of the buy-out.

Mr. Magowan and other directors and top executives received $28 million for their shares, $5.7 million of which went to Mr. Magowan. He and about 60 other top executives also got options to buy a total of 10 percent of the new Safeway at only $2 a share; those options are now valued at more than $100 million, or $12.125 a share.

The Hafts made $100 million by selling the Safeway shares they had accumulated to KKR, and, as a consolation prize, they were also given options to buy a 20 percent stake in the new Safeway. The Hafts sold that option back to KKR 2.5 months later for an additional $59 million.

The three investment banks that worked on the deal made a total of $65 million. Law and accounting firms shared another $25 million.

And then there are Henry Kravis, George Roberts, about a dozen other KKR employees, and the 70 investors KKR brought into the buy-out. KKR itself charged Safeway $60 million in fees just to put the deal together. The five KKR partners then put up a small fraction of the equity funding—1.1 percent or roughly $2 million—and received a 20 percent share of the eventual profits from any sale of Safeway.

KKR's investor group, half of which consists of state pension funds and which also includes banks, insurance companies, and even Harvard University, got most of the rest.

Mr. Roberts rebuts the notion that too few people really benefit in an LBO. He says that some of "our 70 limited partners represent retired teachers, sanitation workers, and firemen, and 80 percent of our profits go to them."

But at the largest of those investors, Oregon's public-employee pension fund, LBO investments make up only a tiny portion of investments and, thus, haven't had a "a significant impact" on retirees' benefits to date, according to Bob Andrews, fund manager.

*   *   *

The immediate gains for some triggered immediate costs for others. The first employees to be fired shortly after the buyout's completion were more than 300 staffers from Oakland corporate headquarters and a nearby division in Walnut Creek, California. The following spring, the entire Dallas-area division was shut down, and nearly 9,000 more employees were dismissed—employees with an average length of service of 17 years.

"This is going to kill people," transportation manager Richard Quigley says he told his boss when he learned that layoffs would take place.

On the Friday afternoon before the dismissals went into effect, Patricia Vasquez, a 14-year systems analyst, heard that her name was on the list. That evening, Mrs. Vasquez, a Safeway devotee famous for her refusal to take lunch hours, packed her service citations in a cardboard box and left looking pale and drawn. The next morning her two young children found their single mother on the bathroom floor, dead of a heart attack.

That Monday, Mr. Quigley came home with the news that he, himself, would be fired. His worried wife's blood pressure began to rise. A diabetic who had been in good health for years, she was hospital-

ized by Labor Day weekend—and dead by September 5. Rightly or wrongly, Mr. Quigley blames his wife's death on his Safeway layoff: "She was very traumatized by it."

Told of these deaths and several suicides that family members and friends attribute to the Safeway layoffs, Mr. Magowan says: "I never heard of this before. If it's true, I'm obviously sorry about such a tragic thing, but any attempt to associate this directly with the LBO shows a disposition to want to believe the worst of LBOs."

For many at Safeway, firing day was only the first in a long series of financial and emotional body blows.

"The dominoes began to tumble and they crashed for a long time to come," says Ron Morrison, a former corporate systems manager. When Mr. Morrison lost his 14-year job, his fiancée announced she couldn't marry an unemployed man.

He found work as a transportation analyst at Del Monte, but then KKR bought that company, too—and he was laid off again, just before Thanksgiving. By the time 1990 rolled around, Mr. Morrison had not only gone through two KKR-led LBOs, he had lost his second home and was unemployed again.

"Right now I pretty much live in a cocoon," Mr. Morrison says. "You begin to pull in your tentacles because you can't afford to have any more cut off."

While at Safeway, Mr. Morrison says, he helped conduct a transportation study that trimmed millions from the company transit budget. And he wasn't the only fired employee at headquarters whose work had brought the company big savings. Refrigeration engineer Mikhail Vaynberg, a Soviet émigré, says he invented a new cooling system for the stores that cut energy costs 35 percent, saved

$1.6 million a year, and was copied by many suppliers. (A Safeway spokesman says the company doesn't contest these cost-saving claims.)

After he was fired, Mr. Vaynberg couldn't find work in his field and, like many other employees fired at headquarters, says he couldn't get a current letter of recommendation from Safeway; he says his boss told him he wasn't allowed to supply a written reference because "you might use it to sue the company." (A Safeway spokesman says it is company policy not to grant reference letters for "good, sound legal reasons," but maintains that managers were allowed to make exceptions for employees laid off in the 1986 firings at headquarters.)

Mr. Vaynberg says his greatest blow came a few weeks after the layoff, when his only son dropped out of engineering school weeks shy of graduation: "The country doesn't want engineers: Look what happened to you," he told his father. Now Mr. Vaynberg, still unemployed, spends his days in a painfully clean living room, prowls the halls at night, and avoids old friends and neighbors. "I am ashamed," he says, staring at his big empty hands. "I am like an old thrown-out mop."

Safeway fired its corporate employees with no notice, cut off their medical insurance in as little as two weeks, and provided severance pay of one week's salary for every year of service, to a maximum of just eight weeks. And to get the pay, many employees say they were told to sign a letter waiving their right to contest the severance package later. (A company spokesman says the letter wasn't a waiver but simply an "acknowledgment" that they understood the terms.)

Mr. Magowan concedes that many of the people fired at headquarters in the summer of 1986 were "very good" employees. The cuts were made in a hurry, as he said later in a court deposition, so as "to put this whole unpleasant matter behind us as soon as possible." For such haste, Safeway would wind up paying $8.2 million to settle a wrongful termination class-action suit and $750,000 to settle a separate suit for age discrimination.

One executive who left headquarters voluntarily was accorded much better treatment. Safeway president James Rowland was granted a $1 million bonus when he retired a few months after the buy-out.

Mr. Rowland advised Mr. Magowan in a memo to approve the bonus privately and divide the amount into smaller portions with labels like "paid consultant." The reason, as Mr. Rowland wrote: "Peter, I do not want to put you in an embarrassing situation."

(Mr. Rowland, reached at his Arkansas home, says he never got a "million-dollar bonus. I got my regular bonus. I just don't recall what it was. I'm not going to go back and rehash all that." He then hangs up. Mr. Magowan says Mr. Rowland wasn't paid a lump sum of $1 million. He was paid his previous year's bonus, which he had earned, plus an advance on consulting work he would do for Safeway. Mr. Magowan says, "It wouldn't have been some side deal under the table between Jim Rowland and me that nobody knew about. That's not my style.")

* * *

"I wouldn't be surprised if 11,000 jobs were created out of" the roughly 9,000 jobs lost, Mr. Magowan announced to the press after he closed the Dallas division. He says he assumed that other grocery chains would expand to fill the Safeway vacuum. "What I'm talking about here is a theory of mine," he says later. "I will get right up front and say I don't have facts to support it.'' Mr. Magowan says he has not been back to Dallas since the closure.

When the Dallas division shut down, the state unemployment office had to open on the weekend—for the first time ever–just to accommodate the Safeway crowds. The Dallas employees had a thin financial pallet to cushion the blow. Their severance pay was half a week's pay for each year of service, up to a maximum of eight weeks.

And their severance checks didn't start arriving until July 1987, three months after the shutdown. Russell Webb, a 12-year produce clerk and single father with three children, didn't get his severance check for eight months. Vacation pay arrived even more slowly: First the union had to go to arbitration to get it; then, the company didn't start mailing the checks until February 1989. Safeway says the severance and other checks arrived late because they weren't part of the union contract and, thus, ''had to be negotiated.''

In addition to Mr. White's suicide, at least two others tried to kill themselves. One was Bill Mayfield, Jr., a mechanic in the Safeway dairy since it opened in 1973, who slashed his wrists, then shot himself in the stomach; the bullet just missed his vital organs and he survived.

''I would say [the layoff] devastated about 80 percent of the people in the division,'' says Gary Jones, president of Safeway's credit union in Dallas, which eventually had to write off $4 million in loans. ''Overnight we turned from a lending institution into a collection agency.'' At one point, more than 250 repossessed cars were sitting in his parking lot.

KKR and Safeway blame organized labor for the fall of the Dallas division. Once the leading grocer in the area, Safe-way had seen its market share fall by nearly half in the 80s. KKR and Safeway officials say the company was paying too much in wages, some 30 percent more than rivals, thus preventing it from cutting prices, remodeling stores, and the like.

But rival Kroger was also a union shop, and it found a way to prosper and expand in Dallas by renovating stores and negotiating lower wages with the union. Its market share was on the rise. The Kroger case suggests that the Safeway layoffs might have been necessitated as much by mismanagement as by labor costs. Some company officials concede that Safeway had other problems besides wages in Dallas: Its stores were too small, too old, and poorly designed.

While grocery competitors in Dallas eventually bought more than half the 141 Safeway stores, they were less eager to pick up the unionized workers. According to a state-funded survey of the displaced workers, stores under new management typically recalled no more than a half a dozen of the 40 to 60 former Safeway employees who staffed each outlet.

And wages fell sharply, no matter where the workers landed: In 1988, according to the survey, ex-Safeway employees reported that their average pay had dropped to $6.50 from $12.09 an hour.

Cindy Hale, an 11-year Safeway employee, saw her wages fall to $4 an hour when she took an identical grocery clerk's job with the AppleTree Markets, at an old Safeway store. Her new employer would only hire part-time, so Ms. Hale, a single mother, lost her medical benefits. She eventually lost her house, too, and had to send her son to live with her parents.

''But it really wasn't as bad for me as the others,'' says Ms. Hale.

For Dallas employees, working for

Safeway had often been a total family experience, and many households lost more than one income after the buy-out. The Seabolts lost three: Husband, wife, and daughter all got their pink slips on the same day. Ron Seabolt, who worked in the company's distribution center for 17 years, searched for months before taking a job as a janitor. Now he works at the post office.

Kay Seabolt, a human resources supervisor at Safeway and a 17-year company veteran, counseled ex-employees for a year under a state job-placement retraining program. The program's counselors sometimes fished into their own pockets to buy groceries for those who streamed through the counseling center, an abandoned Safeway office. When Safeway sold it, the new owners evicted them.

Seared into Mrs. Seabolt's memory is the day one tattered man arrived at the office. A long-timer in the Safeway bread plant, the middle-aged baker made his way to her desk with a slow, wincing limp. He apologized for his appearance, explaining that he had just walked six miles from the temporary labor pools: His car had been repossessed. He was living in a homeless shelter. "I gave him a few job leads," she recalls, "but he was pretty shabby and I didn't hold out much hope." Before he left, she slipped him some money for bus fare. She says, "I never saw him again."

When the layoff rumors first began circulating, Clara Sanchez took to praying in the parking lot of Store No. 677. Her silent pleas went unanswered. On April 24, 1987, she and her husband, Jesse, lost their jobs. She had been a checker for 12 years; he had been an order filler in the warehouse for 18 years.

Clara could find no work, and is still unemployed; Jesse searched for eight months before the city hired him to cut grass for $3.55 an hour. Then he washed cars for $4.50 an hour. Two months later, he was laid off. Finally, with $14,000 in unpaid bills, the Sanchezes filed for bankruptcy.

The church sent canned goods, and Mr. and Mrs. Sanchez skipped supper some evenings so their children could eat better. After a while, Mr. Sanchez was too depressed to eat anyway. "I wasn't a man; I wasn't worth anything as far as I was concerned," he says. "Why live if I can't support my kids?" One Friday night, Mr. Sanchez told his wife he was going to watch a wrestling match, but went to a friend's house instead with a business proposition. "I told him I would pay him $100 to take my life. I didn't own a gun or I would've done it myself." The friend put his gun out of reach and sent Mr. Sanchez home.

When Safeway pulled out of Dallas, the shock waves didn't stop at the supermarket doors. The shutdown led to secondary layoffs at almost all the big food and beverage vendors in town, and some construction businesses suffered. For Harry W. Parks Co., a general contractor, Safeway represented 85 percent of annual revenues; Mr. Parks had dropped most of his other clients to assist Safeway in its big remodeling program in the early 80s. After the pull-out, his company nearly folded, all but three employees were laid off, and Mr. Parks had a heart attack and died.

"Safeway was his whole world," says his son, Harry, Jr. "That's all he cared about for 30 years. When they pulled out, it was like his whole family died."

The North Texas Food Bank suffered, too. It lost a founding member and its leading contributor; Safeway used to donate 600,000 pounds of food a year.

"The bottom line," food-bank director Lori Palmer says, "is fewer people ate."

* * *

The layoffs in Oakland, Dallas, and elsewhere were just one part of KKR's broad-based plan to cut costs, boost profitability, and meet the stiff interest and principal deadlines set by the company's lenders and debt-holders. About 1,000 of the company's stores were sold, as were 45 plants and other facilities.

Safeway put whole divisions in Kansas, Oklahoma, Arkansas, and Utah among others on the auction block. They were sold to a few grocery chains, many other LBO investors, and, in some cases, real estate investors.

The real estate investors didn't rehire any Safeway workers: They converted the properties to video shops, thrift stores, and in one case, a bingo parlor. Some were boarded up.

While grocery chains bought some Safeway stores just to shut them down and reduce competition, other chains bought whole Safeway divisions and kept most of the workers; the British and Oklahoma divisions are examples of this. In other cases, new owners retained only selected workers. In virtually all cases, though, new ownership meant pay cuts.

In what seemed at first the best deal for employees, the grocery chain Borman's, Inc., bought the entire Safeway Utah division and hired virtually all the workers. But nine months later, these 3,000 employees lost their jobs when Borman sold the division, piece by piece, to local competitors and investors. Only a few of the stores in the Salt Lake City area still operate as supermarkets.

Don Schanche, a Safeway meatcutter in Salt Lake City for 25 years, spiraled downward from his $12.33 hourly pay at Safeway to a reduced wage scale at Borman's "Farmer Jack" outlet, to an unsuccessful appeal for any minimum-wage employment at the same store, which had been bought by his old manager. Now, Mr. Schanche drives by a "for lease" sign in front of the store, which is empty, having gone belly-up. Mr. Schanche is making a living as a "job coach" in a state-funded displaced-workers program—where he is currently counseling other ex-grocery store employees following an LBO involving their employer, Alpha-Beta.

Mr. Magowan, as Safeway's CEO but no longer the man with final decision-making authority, was at first opposed to the extent of the divestiture program, people familiar with the situation say. He liked being the head of the world's largest supermarket chain. But KKR officals gave him little choice if he wanted to stay on board, these people say.

Mr. Magowan himself says that "no one twisted my arm" over the restructuring. Still, he says he "regrets" selling promising divisions, mentioning in particular Los Angeles, El Paso, Tulsa, and Little Rock.

Still others point with regret to the loss of the company's 132-store British division—a top-performer known in-house as the "jewel" of the Safeway collection—and the sale of Safeway's successful discount chain of liquor stores, Liquor Barn, which under its new owners (Majestic Wine Warehouses, Ltd.) filed for Chapter 11 bankruptcy protection in 1988.

Despite such regrets, however, Mr. Magowan is now a self-professed believer in the LBO concept. For one thing, his own performance has been rewarded under KKR, which has increased his annual compensation by about 40 percent to $1.2 million including bonus. His bonus potential has climbed to 110 percent of base pay from 40 percent before the buy-out, and he has earned the highest possible bonus every year.

Many things have gone well for the buy-out group. The sale of the British division alone brought $929 million, part of the $2.4 billion that KKR got from asset sales—or 40 percent more than KKR officials say they had projected.

Thanks to sales of some money-losing operations, Safeway's basic business could earn more without raising prices. The company's stores are now No. 1 or 2 in most of its markets. By 1989, operating profit per employee was up 62 percent from 1985, and operating margins had increased by nearly half. The company is producing nealy twice as much annual cash flow as it needs to cover yearly interest payments. As a result, Safeway has been able to pay bank lenders ahead of schedule and negotiate lower interest rates.

Finally, KKR and Safeway officials also credit a new combination of incentives and quotas that they say make workers more entrepreneurial and at the same time more accountable.

Mr. Magowan says that employees are thriving in this post-LBO culture: "I am convinced that today's typical Safeway employee feels better about the company than he or she has at any point since the buy-out." Store managers, he says, "genuinely enjoy this extra responsibility" of meeting new quotas.

Not every part of the new Safeway picture is as rosy as Mr. Magowan portrays it, however.

The public offering completed recently didn't quite go as planned. The offering's underwriters knocked the price down to $11.25 from the $20 a share envisioned last summer. Mr. Magowan himself con-

cedes, "I think if we had known right at the start that this was the price that we would've gotten, we probably wouldn't have come out with our offering." He blames the much-publicized problems of other leveraged companies for unjustly tainting Safeway's offering and driving away stock shoppers.

But some potential investors say that it was Safeway's own financial condition that turned them off.

The company labors under an interest bill of about $400 million a year, a negative net worth of $389 million, and a remaining $3.1 billion in debt. The company's net income was only $2.5 million last year (after accounting for nonrecurring expenses), down from $31 million the year before. Safeway lost a whopping $488 million in 1987, the first year of the LBO.

A large amount of capital improvement has been postponed, with such annual spending falling from an average $600 million to $700 million in the three years before the buy-out to an average of $300 million in the years since. The company estimates it must spend $3.2 billion on store remodeling and openings over the next five years. And Safeway now has few assets left that it can justify jettisoning.

* * *

When Mr. Magowan in 1988 sat down with a group of specially selected employees to tell them the story of "our growing success," the workers had a different story to tell him, as chronicled by the company's own magazine, *Safeway Today*.

"The morale in Richmond [California] right now is rock bottom," Vince Macias, a 25-year trucker, told the boss. He added that drivers were forced to pull as much as 16-hour shifts and were so overworked

The Leveraged Buy-Out Game

Buying a company or a division with a small amount of equity and a large amount of debt is the hallmark of the LBO. The debt is repaid out of the company's cash flow. Below, the top LBOs ranked by dollar value.

Date Announced	Target Name	Acquiror Name	Amount (in billions)
10/21/88	RJR Nabisco	Kohlberg Kravis Roberts	$29.57
1/24/88	Federated Department Stores	Campeau Corp.	7.42
10/16/85	Beatrice Co. Inc.	Kohlberg Kravis Roberts	6.20
7/27/86	Safeway Stores Inc.	Acquisition group led by Kohlberg Kravis Roberts	5.65
7/3/87	Southland Corp.	Acquisition group	5.10
9/15/88	Hospital Corp. of America	Acquisition group led by management	4.91
4/12/87	Borg Warner Corp.	Acquiring group led by Merrill Lynch	4.23
3/7/88	Montgomery Ward (Mobil Corp.)	Acquisition group led by management	3.80
10/21/85	RH Macy & Co. Inc.	Acquisition group led by management	3.71
6/19/89	NWA Inc.	Wings Holdings Inc.	3.65
12/11/86	Owens Illinois Inc.	Kohlberg Kravis Roberts	3.64
6/22/88	Fort Howard Paper Co.	Acquiring group led by Morgan Stanley	3.58
9/4/86	Allied Stores Corp.	Campeau Corp.	3.47
7/5/89	Elders IXL Ltd.	Acquisition group led by management	3.37
5/21/84	Esmark Inc.	Beatrice Foods Co.	2.71
5/21/87	Burlington Industries Inc.	Acquiring group led by Morgan Stanley	2.63
3/17/88	American Standard Inc.	Kelso & Co. Inc.	2.51

SOURCE: I.D.D. Information Services, Inc.

they were "dangerous" on the highways.

"The morale is so bad in some of our stores," Christie Mills, a San Jose employee, told him, that it's driving away customers.

"There aren't many of us, and hours are cut so much, " said Cheryl Deniz, a bakery clerk. "I don't let the customer see it, but inside I'm miserable. . . . I want to be happy when I wait on them. . . . I try my best, but sometimes I'm so overloaded. It's unfair to the customer, and it's unfair to the employee. . . . And some of you feel the same way."

Mr. Magowan looked around the room. "I see everybody nodding their heads to what you are saying," he told her. Then he added: "I've heard this before."

(A Safeway spokesman says the company immediately followed up on the workers' complaints and that Mr. Magowan personally wrote letters to those employees who voiced concerns.)

Certainly, many employees have emerged unscathed from the LBO and feel comfortable working under the new regime. A good number of them even applaud the company for its rapid surfacing from the debt depths.

But among a group of workers that Safeway supplies to this newspaper as a sampler of "happy employees," no one interviewed is praising the LBO.

"We've recovered well," says Jim Ratto, a Safeway liquor merchandiser. "But personally, I think Safeway would have been better off if we had never gone through the leveraged buy-out. It definitely added some problems, and the company would have been farther ahead now if it had never happened."

"Safeway's made a beautiful comeback, we're getting on our feet again, and I have no complaints," says George Voronin, an affable wine steward who says "I always try to look on the positive side." But even Mr. Voronin adds, "When someone comes in and takes all your funds and sells your stores, isn't that what we in the United States call dishonest?"

The new espirit de corps trumpeted in the executive suite is less apparent in the grocery aisles, where store employees say the KKR-inspired quotas—based on complex return on market value formulas—create anxiety as well as productivity. And the pressure mounts as one goes down the chain from manager to checker.

While Safeway executives call the quota program an "incentive" plan, some store managers refer to it as "the punishment system." That's because store managers say, if they don't make the week's

quota, they can be penalized. In some divisions they report that they must work a seven-day week as penance. Working a month without a day off isn't unusual, managers in the Washington and California divisions say. In some stores managers who miss quota say they have to pull 6 A.M. to 6 P.M. shifts.

Mr. Magowan says corporate headquarters sets no such penalties. "I have never heard of any such program, " he says. "I simply do not believe for one second that this is any widespread activity." A company spokesman says that at least 50 percent of store managers are meeting their quota.

Even among the list of satisfied employees that Safeway provides, many aren't profiting from the incentive plan. Either they are too low on the totem pole to get a bonus (with a few exceptions, only department heads and higher qualify), or their departments aren't generating enough sales volume to meet the demanding quotas. Mr. Voronin, whose wine department has been on the incentive plan for two years, has yet to get a bonus. Mary Wise is head of the floral department, but the company hasn't yet cut her into the plan. She says she doesn't mind: "I leave feeling good, knowing I did the job right, and for me that's my bonus." She adds, "But I'm one of those people you look at and say, 'Oh, why is she always so happy?' "

In Seattle, only one of more than a dozen store managers in one district expects to meet quota this year, managers say. Last year, none made more than 20 percent of their bonus potential, the store heads say. A Safeway spokesman says most managers in that region are making their quota.

On Safeway's home turf in the San Francisco area, managers are "stepping down'' and becoming checkers. Some have been forced to turn in their manager badges when they didn't meet quota; others say they are voluntarily taking lower status and pay—out of exhaustion.

"A number of store managers have stepped down, this year particularly," a company spokesman acknowledges. "In recent years, the job has gotten tougher."

In the wake of the LBO, the company was able to squeeze labor concessions from the unions, using the Dallas shutdown as an object lesson of what can happen when labor costs are deemed too high. With the debt hovering overhead, you could "get the labor concessions you deserve," Mr. Magowan says.

"It was like coming to the table with a gun at our heads," recalls Ed Hardy, a United Food and Commercial Workers negotiator. While the company's average hourly wage has risen slightly in the last three years—the exact amount is confidential, Safeway says—the small increase trails the inflation rate.

The strategy of catering to the upscale at many stores has also enabled KKR to cut service workers' wages even further. To staff trendy specialty departments, Safeway has hired "general merchandise clerks," a classification that pays as little as half the wages of food clerks.

This disparity troubles even the upbeat floral manager Mary Wise. "Gosh, you can barely live on what they are paying them," she says. She broached the subject with Mr. Magowan at the 1988 meeting. These specialty clerks are performing a job that requires training and skill, she said, and "Safeway should pay them accordingly."

Mr. Magowan's response, as quoted in the company's magazine: "The problem, Mary, is this. The reason we got the lower GMC [general merchandising clerk] rate was to allow our labor costs to be competitive." But he reassured her that the company was taking steps to make up for the low pay. "What I've suggested from time to time is saying, 'Do you like weekends off? Do you like to work 8 to 5? . . . We'll give you the lower rate but a better schedule.' That might make them very happy."

* * *

In one division, Safeway has extended the incentive program beyond the department manager level in an experiment aimed at letting all workers benefit in the enhanced productivity they are generating. Employees in the Denver division took a 14 percent pay cut, but were assured that, on average, the new profit-sharing plan would more than make up the difference. The company acknowledges this hasn't happened in nearly half the cases; the union estimates that even fewer increased their earnings.

Store employees in Denver also complained about the way the incentive system was linked—as it is throughout the company—to grievances and work-related medical claims. "Managers have been saying to people, don't file workman's comp because it will hurt the bonus," says Charles Mercer, president of the Denver local of the United Food and Commercial Workers. Mr. Magowan concedes that the Denver bonus plan is "not very popular."

Mr. Magowan's assertion that Safeway's culture is more collegial now also doesn't always square with the view from the retail floor. In stores around the country, employees report that management is pushing out older, skilled, and well-paid employees, turning to cheap part-time help (who don't get medical insurance and other benefits) and piling extra work on the remaining staff. Union officials estimate that the average age of the stores' work force has dropped 10 years since the buy-out; a company spokesman disputes this, but says Safeway doesn't track age.

"Safeway used to be one of the best-places to work of the retail grocers," says Rowena Schoos, a middle-aged Safeway meatcutter in Oregon for five years. "But after the buy-out, they started cutting hours to the nitty-gritty, the store managers went into mass panic, and Safeway just turned into a burnout company."

Ms. Schoos herself recently left, after she was cut back to 16 hours a week and lost her medical benefits. Like many of the older and well-paid meatcutters, she says, she was relegated to the "extra board," a tour of duty that can require driving more than 100 miles a day to different stores to fill in where needed.

For the older butchers, many of whom suffer physical injuries from the years of toting and carving, the assignment is the final shove out the door. Ms. Schoos, for example, has two herniated discs, which she attributes to years of lugging 100-pound carcasses.

A Safeway spokesman responds, "That's just another case of an isolated situation. She was just not performing the job adequately," and, thus, her hours were cut.

The company also says that meatcutters' numbers have been reduced primarily because a gradual shift to prepackaged goods in meat processing has lessened the need. Employees in the meat department argue that even with the changes, much of the work still requires a butcher's expertise and that the cutbacks have been too severe.

While on the extra-board circuit, Ms. Schoos had the opportunity to observe the LBO-fallout at many stores. "It was the same thing everywhere I went," she re-calls. "The managers were desperate to meet quota and the older people always got it the worst. They'd bust them back to lower positions. One produce manager was told he had a 'choice'—go back to being a checker or get fired. One lady asked for a break, and the manager cut her from 40 to eight hours."

In response, Mr. Magowan produces a recent employee survey conducted in the Portland, Oregon, division that finds that more the 80 percent of employees feel Safeway offers advancement opportunity and other advantages. "These would be good scores to decertify the union should we ever wish to do so," Mr. Magowan says, adding, "which we have no intention of doing, whatsoever."

Closer to headquarters, at the Market Street store in San Francisco, employees report a grind of tension and overwork. Some say they are shouldering as many as nine different jobs.

In the meat department, the butchers' numbers have been cut back sharply and inexperienced clerks take up the slack. "Everyone is burned out," says another employee, who points to a counter where overripe meat is on display, the result of a hasty stocking effort. "It's a whole new ballgame and everyone's discontented."

In the Market Street store, employees complain that clipboard-toting managers patrol the floors, closely monitoring performance, and filing a blizzard of disciplinary reports. A company spokesman disputes these accounts: "There is no ROMV [return on market value] police."

Last month, at the Market Street store, food clerk Steve Dolinka lost his job after 25 years of service. His malfeasance: He says he forgot to pay for the cup of soup and toast he ate at the deli on his lunch hour. Mr. Dolinka apologized, shelled out the few dollars that his food cost, and

Before and After the LBO

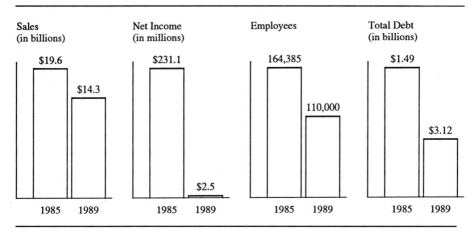

Sales (in billions): 1985 $19.6, 1989 $14.3
Net Income (in millions): 1985 $231.1, 1989 $2.5
Employees: 1985 164,385, 1989 110,000
Total Debt (in billions): 1985 $1.49, 1989 $3.12

explained why he was so distracted—his mind was on a murder trial that had ended few weeks earlier. A gas-station robber was before the court charged with slitting the throat of Mr. Dolinka's 15-year-old son in 1982 in an assault that the investigating detective called "the most brutal in my experience."

"My wife says I've been forgetting things a lot lately," Mr. Dolinka says.

"In our business, employee theft is a serious problem," a company spokesman says of Mr. Dolinka's expulsion. "And every employee is treated the same way."

Mr. Dolinka says he doesn't blame his manager for the firing. "The way it works here, I don't think any of the managers have the freedom to make these decisions. It's all coming down from company policy, and they have got to follow it like their bible."

To all such reports from the store front, Mr. Magowan says he's skeptical: "Our productivity is up, " he points out. Employees are donating more to Easter Seals, and workers' compensation claims are down, he says. And when the earthquake hit, "our employees stayed up all night cleaning up their stores."

"Are these acts of a disgruntled work force?" he asks. "I don't think so."

George Roberts, one of KKR's two principal partners, notes that workers at many corporations are being asked to do more, whether an LBO is involved or not. Employees "are now being held accountable," Mr. Roberts says. "They have to produce up to plan, if they are going to be competitive with the rest of the world. It's high time we did that."

Facing Raiders, Kroger Took Another Path

Susan C. Faludi
Staff Reporter of The Wall Street Journal

CINCINNATI—"Kroger Is Gone, Analysts Predict," was the dire headline in the *Cincinnati Post*. Hostile bidders, the Hafts and KKR, had descended on the nation's second largest grocery chain.

When the September 1988 story came out, "people were crying in the hall," says Joseph Pichler, Kroger's president. " 'Make this go away,' they told me. I said, 'I wish I could.' "

He did. Faced with much the same threat to its independence as rival Safeway faced two years earlier, Kroger chose a very different path. Instead of going private in a KKR-led LBO, Kroger officials countered by offering shareholders a hefty dividend and employees a significant ownership stake in what remains a public company.

While Kroger had to take on $4.1 billion in debt and it had to cut costs, it sold far fewer assets than Safeway did and reduced its work force by about 3 percent, while Safeway reduced its by about a third. Yet today Kroger has about the same operating profit per employee as Safeway.

In some ways, Kroger's story undermines two LBO articles of faith: That a company under attack from raiders has to go private to ward them off, and that, after an LBO, labor forces have to be cut severely to support the resulting interest burden.

This isn't to suggest, however, that an LBO can't be structured to share ownership more broadly or to cut costs in a less severe manner than Safeway, or that recapitalizations are panaceas. Harcourt Brace Jovanovich plunged into crisis after its recapitalization when it couldn't sell assets for enough cash to pay down its huge debt.

But the recap seems to have worked so far for Kroger. "We kept asking ourselves the question, if it's so good for an outside group of investors to come in, leverage up a company, peel off underperforming assets, pay down debt, and walk off with the equity themselves, why shouldn't it be equally good for our existing shareholders to benefit from exactly the same transaction?" Mr. Pichler recalls.

Safeway says it looked at the same question two years earlier but chose to do an LBO because it would free the company from having to please shareholders with short-term profits and from future takeover threats. Certain tax breaks since rescinded also made the LBO option more attractive in 1986 than in later years.

For Kroger, the call to action came when the Hafts offered $55 a share for a "business combination." The KKR made an unsolicited bid—despite its reputation as a "white knight"—to buy out the company for $58.50 a share. When Kroger turned a cold shoulder, KKR upped its offer to $64.

Kroger quickly unfurled its plan: Shareholders would get a $40 a share cash dividend, plus an $8 junior subordinated debenture, and a remaining interest in the company, called stub stock. The package was valued by Kroger at $57 to $61 a share. The recap plan also liberalized stock options so that all employees, rather than a thin slice at the top, could increase their ownership: Employees could go from owning 6 percent to more than 25 percent of Kroger's shares; corporate officers' ownership, on the other hand, could rise only from 1 to 3 percent.

The recap lagged by at least 5 to 10 percent behind KKR's $64 final bid. Even so, the board approved the recap on September 23 and the company remained public. Investors and employees reacted favorably to the offer. The value of the stub stock initially more than doubled but has since slipped to $14, still well above the initial offering price of $9.13. And Kroger workers took ample advantage of the new stock options. By 1990, Kroger increased employee ownership even more, to 35 percent.

The recap yielded them tens of millions of dollars for senior managers. Lyle Everingham, the chairman, got an estimated $10.5 million in cash and another $2.3 million in debentures. Mr. Pichler got $3.5 million in cash and $763,000 in debentures. And Goldman, Sachs & Company made $25 million for advising Kroger.

In the aftermath, Kroger, too, was faced with a multibillion-dollar debt. It laid off 314 people from headquarters, and, with the subsequent asset sales, purged more than 4,000 employees from the payroll.

But the Kroger severance package was more generous than Safeway's. Fired employees received a month's salary for every year of service to a maximum of nine months, compared with a maximum of eight weeks' salary at Safeway. They also got medical benefits for one year, while Safeway employees lost their benefits in as little as two weeks.

Kroger's generosity shouldn't be overstated, though: Kroger cut costs by cutting average hourly salaries of $8.12 (or $11.39 with fringe benefits) in 1985 to $7.07 (or $9.84 with benefits) in 1989. Kroger, like Safeway, saved money by paying its specialty department workers a lower rate. And Kroger has also negotiated two-tier pay scales and raised eligibility requirements for medical benefits.

In selling assets, Kroger sold less-prized properties and a total of 100 stores, only 10 percent of its operations. Safeway, on the other hand, sold 1,100 of its 2,325 stores. Kroger also turned to employees who generated thousands of cost-saving steps.

Like Safeway, Kroger has adopted an incentive bonus plan, but it appears to be more democratic than its Oakland rival's. Kroger's new bonus system extends to secretaries and the plan adjusts for factors beyond employees' control—such as working in a store in a high-crime neighborhood.

"We're fairly excited about Kroger's bonus plan," says Ed Hardy, a national negotiator for the United Food and Commercial Workers Union. "It's more of a gain-sharing plan than a bonus based on profits."

While Kroger has improved its profit-sharing plan, Safeway stopped contributing to its plan in 1987. At the same time, Safeway also tried unsuccessfully to raid surplus funds in its employee retirement account, which provides retirees with an average pension of less than $400 a month. Retirees retained counsel to halt the raid, and Robert Van Gemert, retired Safeway general counsel, did some research and discovered that the original Safeway pension charter in fact grants the surplus to the retirees.

So far, Kroger seems to be faring competitively at least as well as Safeway. In fiscal year 1989, its first year after restructuring, Kroger's cash flow rose 22 percent—better than the 16 percent gain the company originally forecast at the time it restructured. Kroger, like Safeway, hasn't raised prices—and in some markets has lowered them. And Kroger, like Safeway, managed to refinance its bank-credit agreement and lower interest expenses.

But Kroger also now supports 60,000 more workers than Safeway, while maintaining a similar operating profit as a percentage of sales.

Kroger also has increased its charitable cash contributions since the recap to $3.6 million last year from $2.1 million in 1987, while Safeway trimmed its corporate cash giving to $2.7 million last year from $3.2 million in 1986.

Thanks to the massive debt, Kroger operated at a net loss of $72.7 million in

1989; Safeway's net loss was $488 million its first year after the buy-out. (The two chains are fairly comparable in number of stores and in sales.) By the first quarter of 1990, Kroger's net loss had shrunk to $10 million, a 46 percent improvement from the same period a year earlier. And analysts are estimating earnings for next year.

"Kroger is an extremely strong company today, with very strong cash flow and very strong markets," says Debra Levin, a retail analyst who follows Kroger for Salomon Brothers. "If they had been taken over (in an LBO), they might not look all that different from the way they look today, but I don't know that they would have gotten that same motivation level from their employees."

CASE

LETTERS TO THE EDITOR

Safeway's CEO Disputes Portrayal

I don't recall ever having seen a more one-sided story in the Journal than the Safeway article on page one May 16. Your thesis in the article that the Safeway LBO is responsible for or the primary cause of a whole host of "human cost" that otherwise would not have occurred is both distorted and unsound. Safeway is a smaller but better company than it was in 1986. Its employees have more security as part of a growing and profitable company. This could not be without the actions that have taken place over the past three years.

A brief look at a summary of supposed consequences of the LBO reveals it to be a ludicrous insult to common sense. You imply or directly state that the Safeway LBO is responsible for the following:

Killing people, heart attacks, suicides and attempted suicides, a broken marriage engagement, a college dropout, and a nationwide shortage of engineers, car

From *The Wall Street Journal*, June 15 and 20, 1990.

repossessions, age discrimination, quotas, homelessness, sweatshop conditions, a seven-day-week wage discrimination, cuts in charitable contributions, and mortgage foreclosures.

That's some powerful, heartless financing technique.

The indictment is wrong. Safeway employs more than 100,000 men and women. When you employ that many people, there are naturally going to be events in their lives that are unhappy and tragic, no matter what happens at the company. But to assert or imply that an economic transaction is the primary cause or factor in a tragic event like a heart attack or suicide is to betray a bias that is so sharp and so deep that it defies reasonable discussion, not to mention demonstrating a total misunderstanding of the human heart. We discussed all these matters with you over a period of three months.

Most important, you never confronted the real question: the costs of change versus the costs of no change. Never once did you mention the primary reason for most of the changes that took place at Safeway: labor costs that were out of line, the consequences, long and short term, of those costs, and the absolute business necessity in a low-margin, highly competitive industry for parity of labor costs. Safeway had to confront its major business problem—labor costs that were so out of line with its nonunion competition that they caused a situation where 66 percent of the company was either making no money or losing money.

It was this that caused the pressures for and the need for change at Safeway. And it was this business problem, LBO or not, that had to be solved. The bleeding had to stop. The most important effect of the LBO was to highlight this need and provide the urgency and incentive to act quickly.

The consequences of choosing to act are sometimes hard, and sometimes they do not fall equally across the board. But your portrait is a reflection of this in a fun-house mirror. In the case of the Safeway corporate staff, that staff had to be cut to match the smaller size of the company. There was no alternative. Staff cuts have taken place at other major companies, all over America, to reflect their business realities. If you write about the consequences of such cuts, why confine yourself to LBOs? Or perhaps only LBO staff cuts cause "a heavy human toll."

Unions faced a hard choice: Either they and their members accepted the fact that they would have to adjust their wage demands to make them more competitive with the labor forces Safeway and they were competing with, or the management of Safeway would either quickly sell or close the stores. Regardless of the LBO, that problem had to be faced. It is to the great credit of the union officials with whom we bargained that after the sale of our Dallas division they recognized the

dilemma forced on us by the Hafts and were willing to work with us to minimize the impact.

Many companies faced the same problems that Safeway did. It is the history of the grocery business in the 80s that wage parity was being requested everywhere. Yet Safeway dealt with its problems not perfectly, but in as humane a manner as it could, and it came through. We believe that if you were to ask international union officials, they would confirm that Safeway worked very hard and in good faith to ensure that people buying our divisions would also hire our employees. The consequences to all of the company's constituents would have been far worse if we had ignored those problems. The facts are that the overwhelming majority of our employees are working at higher wage rates and with more benefits than was the case at the time of the buy-out. By focusing solely on selected, individual, anecdotal portraits of the purported individual costs of change, you ignored the larger business and human reality.

The financial success of the company is "kissed off" in one or two paragraphs stating that the company has "raised productivity and operating profits." Among the things that did not appear in your lengthy article:

- Operating profit in 1989 was higher ($462 million) on $14 billion of sales than it used to be in 1986 on $20 billion of sales. That is no small achievement.

- Our 1989 operating profit margin of 3.2 percent ranked Safeway third of the top 10 food chains.

- Our operating cash flow of 5.2 percent of sales in 1989 ranked us first of the five leading food chains.

• Our debt has been reduced from $5.7 billion to $3.1 billion.

To not include these key aspects of our financial performance is misleading to say the least—especially when you do include, "The company's net income was only $2.5 million last year, down from $31 million the year before."

The good news for Safeway's customers wasn't mentioned at all. Safeway's prices are more competitive than any time in the past 10 years. We have more service in our stores (39 percent more employee hours per store than in 1985). Our service is not only better, it is friendlier. We remodeled 200 stores in the past few years to add all the specialty departments our customers want.

A balanced portrait of what happened at Safeway would have explained what happened and why.

Finally, I believe your article seeks to establish a new measure by which corporate behavior should be evaluated— providing guaranteed lifetime employment. It judges the success of corporate behavior primarily on that criterion regardless of other business or financial consequences. As such, I feel it is the most anti-investor-biased article imaginable. It implicitly tells corporate management and investors: Don't do the right thing by taking the painful measures you know are necessary to ensure the health of the business in the future, and forget about shareholder value if it requires tough action. Don't do it because *The Wall Street Journal* will be there to impose its own "reckoning."

Readers may well ask themselves: Who pays the ultimate price to be extracted for investing according to the new standard you are imposing?

PETER A. MAGOWAN
Chief Executive Officer
Safeway Stores, Inc.
Oakland, California

Pillaging to Enrich the Few or Courageous Turnaround?

I applaud your willingness to print the Safeway LBO article. I am president of a moderate-sized business and have been forced to downsize the company, so I have great empathy for the workers and a fair understanding of business pressures.

It is plain to me that KKR and its predecessor in this deal care little for the fabric that bonds employees to a company. Mr. Magowan and senior management have earned economic windfalls at great expense to the average, dedicated employee. Why must such a cadre of wealthy executives stick it to the employees working in their stores?

George Roberts pontificates that quotas and pressure to perform are facts of life in today's world of global competition. Most surely they are. Yet, while he roams the world as a wealthy man delivering this message, his employees are scraping by at lower than pre-buy-out wages. Their families will never forget his arrogance or the policies that stretched out severance payments over months to those who can least afford it. It is simply revolting.

Business can be tough, but it should establish a standard by which it will be judged within the society. Although KKR, Mr. Magowan, and a handful of executives will continue to reap financial rewards, it has been done in a most shameful way.

ROBERT C. MCNALLY
President,
Landex Corporation
Parsippany, N.J.

* * *

Your article is not only the single best I've read in your paper, but also the single best argument that unions are necessary to keep management humane.

Your reporting is as telling as those photographs in textbooks of 10-year-olds who worked 12-hour days in the Lowell textile mills earlier in our century.

What employees today trust management to be loyal to them? Very few, I'm afraid, and if so, they are naive or fools.

WARREN OWENS
Bethel, Connecticut

* * *

It must be remembered that Safeway was originally jeopardized by uninvited corporate predators. The defensive actions that followed were then necessary and appropriate, in my opinion.

Our relationship with Safeway officials both before and after the LBO shows no change in their always high regard for other humans. Their responsibilities following the LBO were difficult. From our vantage point, they went about their task with integrity and sensitivity.

Suicide, heart attack, and diabetes result from lifetime proclivities. Your effort to attribute the sole cause to Safeway is uncommonly cruel.

R. L. HANLIN
President
Sunkist Growers, Inc.
Van Nuys, California

* * *

Your article presents a grim picture. It stands in sharp contrast to our experience with the management buy-out of Safeway's Oklahoma division. The division wasn't acquired by a grocery chain.

A company formed by Clayton & Dubilier, along with 33 local managers, purchased the division in 1987, keeping all 5,624 employees and 106 stores. What we found when we bought Homeland was a small, neglected part of a larger corporate bureaucracy, starved for capital, and losing market share.

With an ownership interest in the company conferred on full-time employees through a stock appreciation rights program, Homeland has developed a new entrepreneurial spirit. In addition to growing faster and becoming more productive since the buy-out, Homeland has added more than 1,200 new jobs, expanded advertising expenditures 25 percent, and, over the past two years, invested $60 million in new stores and store remodels compared with the $3.6 million invested by Safeway the year before the buy-out.

The lesson of the Safeway buy-out is not the unbalanced portrait of despair that we were left with in your article; it is equally a story of the remarkable benefits achievable through the organization innovation represented by Homeland and many similar divestiture LBOs. We have seen it many times. Free from big-company constraints, managers and employees who become owners of enterprises are capable of great feats. And this is something American business sorely needs to remain globally competitive.

MARTIN H. DUBILIER
Chairman
Clayton & Dubilier, Inc.
New York

* * *

Messrs. Haft, Kravis, Magowan et al. inflicted more suffering than if they had ridden through town on horseback pillaging and plundering, as their spiritual forebears once did. We see our society as more civilized now, but some of us still regard material gain as more valuable than human life.

The deal-makers care little that the costs

of this transaction greatly outweigh the rewards; they have kept the gains while passing on the costs to others. Their lack of conscience permits them to talk of "efficiency" and "profitability" to justify dumping thousands of loyal employees, with pitifully meager severance pay, and to treat the remainder like overworked pack animals, driven by the fear of their own dismissal.

KELLY M. RANSON
San Antonio, Texas

* * *

A sound that I could not identify kept me awake last night. Perhaps it was Herbert Haft and his son laughing over the Safeway LBO on their way to the bank.

You are to be commended on your article on Safeway. It is good that this legalized piracy is exposed to the light of day, with its shocking loss of employment and even human lives.

ALAN MCFARLANE
Aberdeen, S. D.

* * *

Your story confirms to me once again that when thugs like Kravis and Roberts loot a business it's somehow considered legitimate. Yet, when the Mafia does the same thing, it's a crime.

The article also confirms how LBOs, with their crushing debt burdens, turn industry leaders into also-rans with appalling consequences for employees.

JOHN J. DIETSCH
Washington

* * *

I was appalled and disgusted to read that Steve Dolinka, a 25-year Safeway employee, was fired for "theft" after he forgot to pay for soup and toast he ate at the deli. Given the circumstances of the man's loss of a teen-age son in a brutal murder, no trivial oversight by him on the job in any way justifies his dismissal. Business may be business, but when simple human compassion is lost to this shocking degree in any firm, the organization and its managers deserve to fail miserably.

Have you no shame, Mr. Magowan? The man whom you fired even accepted the rationale for his dismissal! I extend my belated condolences to Mr. Dolinka on the terrible loss of his son.

JOSEPH A. LAZZARO
New Britain, Conn.

* * *

For years, I worked as a competitor of the Safeway Food Stores. To respect them as an industry leader was prudent. This was prior to the LBO. I left the industry for a time and returned as a vendor, supplying services to companies like Safeway. I am an outsider. The respect I held for the firm in earlier years has grown significantly and I am proud to be associated with such a fine organization. The "monsters" you attempt to portray exist only within your misguided thought process.

If the same manner of exposé were foisted upon any other major company in America, the names would change but the story would read the same. The 80s were tough on all of us. I know. Twice in my career I have faced a pink slip. Once due to an LBO. But, you know, life does go on.

PATRICK R. CRONIN
President
Service Village
Wyckoff, N. J.

* * *

Your exhaustively researched and documented (but oh so depressing) story could serve as a textbook on how the capitalist system ought not to work. A well-managed and prosperous business that produces and sells real goods is basically sold as real estate to the great profit of the paper-pushing deal-makers. Loyal, productive employees are fired by the thousands and those remaining (except at the very top) are required to do much more for much less. In the affected communities, competition is reduced as market share becomes concentrated in fewer hands. For the consumer, price increases are accompanied by service declines as fewer workers staff the operating units.

The incentive for employees in this atmosphere (''you get to keep your job'') is akin to the employee-motivation methods used in Stalinist Russia (''you get to continue breathing''). The results are about the same: a lot of poor people, a few suicides, and an army of nine-to-fivers whose chief concern is making quota.

JAMES P. STRAIN
San Diego

* * *

You do a masterful job describing how an LBO can enrich a few at the expense of many and, in the process, threaten the long-term viability of an enterprise that has been a leader in its field.

In 1889 my grandfather founded a chain of grocery stores in San Diego that Charlie Merrill purchased in 1929 and that became one of Safeway's most successful divisions. About 100 years later, Charlie's grandson Peter Magowan found it necessary to sell the San Diego operation in order to support the LBO.

MILTON F. HELLER, JR.
New Canaan, Conn.

* * *

Any jerk in CEO's clothing—or president's clothing or plant manager's

clothing—can make an operation look suddenly efficient by firing a quarter of the employees, reducing benefits, deferring maintenance, and the rest. Pay the people for a 40-hour week but arrange it so they really have to work 50 hours and the money rolls in like never before.

However, except for the CEO or president, practitioners of this art know you must have yourself promoted away from this kind of highly successful operation because after two or three years the best people will begin having heart attacks, employees divorces will increase, and employee unhappiness will become an unrecognized, unquantified drag on profits.

ROBERT G. WORMAN
Seminole, Fla.

* * *

In March of this year, Safeway and Safeway's employees presented the second-largest check ever given on the National Easter Seal Telethon—a check for $4.1 million, which was an increase of $2.5 million over 1989. A company without a heart, a company with disgruntled and unhappy employees could hardly be expected to perform such a miracle.

Safeway also remains one of the major contributors to food banks and feeding programs around the country, and its corporate office and division offices provide tremendous support to charitable groups in the communities where they operate.

You unfairly attacked and misrepresented a good company and its great employees.

WALTER A. SPENCER, JR.
Chairman
National Easter Seal Society
Chicago

* * *

First, it was Nordstrom. Next came Safeway. Who's next? Disneyland?

A thoughtless, left-wing attack on two great American companies on the pages of *The Wall Street Journal?* Has Pravda bought the Journal?

HOWARD R. SCOUTEN
Safeway Employee
Pittsburg, Calif.

* * *

You tell of the former Safeway trucker who you say "blew his brains out." The man went into the bathroom and used his .22-caliber rifle on himself after a year of depression over his lost job.

I am offended not only by the choice of words used, but also by the lack of sensitivity for the victims in your story. How do you think the widow is going to feel when she remembers that devastating time by reading such lurid details. As a former reader, I question your integrity.

DIANE MURPHY
Edmonds, Wash.

* * *

I was struck that this entire affair was one of excess: Employee and unions overreached and asked too high a wage; management and stockholders wanted too great a profit; the banks, investment houses, and deal-makers eschewed reasonable fees and exacted egregious levies. Hence, any merit this LBO might claim is overshadowed by the embarassment of riches enjoyed by some and the tragic losses endured by others.

Some restraint on the part of all would have won big for all. A concern for ethics and morality (there is a place for these in the business world) might have tempered the attitudes, resulting in a happier outcome. As it was, the conduct and consequences seem more like war than diplomacy, the tools used more like chain saws than pruning shears.

JON A. HOLLOWAY, M.D.
Spokane, Wash.

* * *

I read the article with fascinated horror. All I could think of was the story of Coriolanus, the Roman patrician who so hated the common people that he even opposed the free distribution of corn when the city was in the grip of a terrible famine. Not surprisingly, he was expelled from Rome. He retaliated by gathering up an army of Rome's enemies and marching on the city.

The women of Rome appealed to his aged mother, Veturia, to intercede. Supported by her daughter-in-law and grandsons, she walked out the city gates to the enemy camp. The historian Livy describes how seeing his mother, Coriolanus ran forward and "would have embraced her had he not been checked by her sudden turn to anger. 'I would know,' she said, 'before I accept your kiss, whether I have come to an enemy or a son.' " She then upbraided him in no uncertain terms for his treachery to his own people. Weeping, he fell at her feet and begged forgiveness.

It hardly takes effort to see Coriolanus in Mr. Magowan. But if only his mother bore some resemblance to Veturia! Alas, what might have been a triumphant story is destined for Greek tragedy.

HALLIE BLACK
Faculty
Hopkins Grammar Day
Prospect Hill School
New Haven, Conn.

* * *

We have been a major supplier to Safeway Stores for more than 50 years. We have always worked closely with Safeway, particularly during the time when it went through its LBO.

There is no question in our minds that Mr. Magowan and his associates have been able to accomplish a complete turnaround for the Safeway organization. In our judgment, Safeway would not have made it through the 1980s if it had not restructured its organization in order to address its competitive position in the marketplace. Today, Safeway is alive and well and a leader in the industry on a number of key financial measurements. This is indeed a remarkable success story and a company where 100,000 people are still productively employed.

Our free-enterprise system does not work without pain, and we all know that from time to time difficult decisions must be made to stay competitive in a fast-changing market. Safeway made those decisions in the late 1980s and, as a result, is a strong viable competitor in the retail-grocery business.

W.E. LAMOTHE
Chairman and CEO
Kellogg Company
Battle Creek, Mich.

"Painful Measures": A Matter of Timing

Peter Magowan's response (Letters, June 15) to the Journal's May 16 article on Safeway made very interesting reading. There is one point on which I would very much like to hear from Mr. Magowan. He was the chief executive of the company for many years prior to the leveraged buyout, during which time, according to his letter, labor costs were out of line. Mr. Magowan justifies his action after the LBO as "taking the painful measures you know are necessary to ensure the health of the business in the future," and on behalf of "shareholder value." Why did it take the Hafts and an LBO to enable the chief

executive of the company to address its most critical problem? If he had taken those actions while the company was publicly owned, other shareholders would have derived the value.

This is an underlying question and argument that has bedeviled the LBO picture generally. Perhaps Mr. Magowan can help clarify the matter.

HAROLD M. WILLIAMS
President and CEO
J. Paul Getty Trust
Chairman
Securities and Exchange Commission
1977–81
Los Angeles

* * *

Your article contains false assertions and misquotes that I consider to be most serious.

The writer indicates that my son Peter, chairman of Safeway, was "pressed" by me in 1986: "Will anyone get hurt? Will anyone lose his job?" in the process of Safeway's LBO. The story stated that I expressed concern that the company's long-standing reputation as a benevolent employer not be damaged by the LBO. Both of these statements are untrue. Peter and I had no such conversation, and I highly resent having been quoted in this fashion.

In the changing economic climate of the past decade, hostile takeovers have been commonplace. When the Haft family announced its intention to buy up Safeway, many serious and long-reaching decisions had to be made by management in a short period of time.

In any takeover situation, it is a given that jobs will be lost. Every effort was made to minimize this effect.

In addition, I extremely resent the intrusion of your reporter into my home. She telephoned me requesting an interview "about the good old days at Safeway," and was told a day or two later by my assistant that as policy I do not meet with the press. Disregarding this, she showed up at my home uninvited. As I had no intention of speaking with her, it was necessary to ask her to leave my home. I very much resent her disrespect for my wishes and privacy, as well as her inac-

curate portrayal of a conversation between my son and me.

Peter is a man of high moral character, integrity, sincerity, and honesty. He and the management team have consistently attempted to preserve as much of the "old" Safeway as possible under very trying and altered circumstances.

DORIS MERRILL MAGOWAN
San Francisco

READING

A CONVERSATION ABOUT LBOs[1]

A Second-Year Harvard Business School Student

I graduated from Columbia with a degree in economics in 1986 and took a job in a two-year program as an analyst at a New York investment banking firm. I was 22. After a seven-month period I decided to join the merchant banking group, which had $1.5 billion to invest in leveraged buy-outs. We only did so-called friendly deals, friendly to the management in power at the time. So we would not combine ourselves with a hostile takeover artist like an Icahn to take over a company. But in a lot of ways we were doing

the same thing, except with the management of the company. And often it was in defense of a raider that was coming after them. All of a sudden these managers decide, "Oh no, we've got to offer more money for the company. And then since we're taking on all this debt, there are a number of things we're going to have to do to be able to pay the interest."

So I was very much involved working with the financial people from the company to put together a budget, and to get to a new cash flow number based on cost savings and increases in productivity and efficiencies, in order to cover the tremendous amount of debt they would take on in a transaction. As you ran a transaction you were trying to beat one or more competitive bidders. If their price got higher than yours and you could no longer cover the interest, then you would look for more cost savings. Almost always that meant headcount reductions. Not in terms of individual names on my part, though.

In 1991, during a class discussion of leveraged buy-outs, a second-year student at the Harvard Business School spoke up about his own experiences with LBOs. This student later agreed to be interviewed in more depth about his thoughts and observations. This case is a slightly edited version of that conversation.

The management was just coming to me and saying, "We're going to reduce headcount by so many. The average salary is $30,000 a year, plus add on the benefits and you have $40,000 a year." I would just take the headcount and multiply it by that amount of money to get the aggregate savings, and I would add a line in the model titled "Cost Savings."

In the beginning, I couldn't even begin to think about these different ethical decisions that you're making just by *not* thinking about it. But I also didn't understand the transactions fully. I had very specific tasks that I did. I downloaded all the numbers, and I would incorporate them into the financial model that had the new capital structure, just to see if they could pay debt, to see if the returns were there for our investors.

I came to understand it much more when they started actually sending me to the companies to do due diligence. You go there and basically make sure that what the company represents as far as the plants and their operations is true, and also to look around and see if actual cost savings can be realized. In other words, is there really excess headcount? Is there really inefficiency that can be improved? Because some companies are not capable of undergoing that kind of dramatic change. My primary reason for being there was to be the note taker, the facilitator, and to record and incorporate the numbers into my model. That was in my second year, and that was when I started thinking really hard about what I was doing. I was 23 at the time.

The fewer people who went, the better, because the employees became suspicious. We would either tell people we were consultants, or we would tell them that this is just general corporate finance business that we would be doing for them. We obviously would never tell people why we were there, both at the request of management, and because as a public company their stock could be affected. Even so, that's when you first start to wonder a little bit. Whenever you can't be open about what you're doing, you always wonder if what you're doing is right. And then also for the first time I saw faces. In the deals we did they were usually trimming down middle management, so you see a lot of middle managers who, you know—just from experience—will not be there if the transaction goes through. People whom you may even request information from. You may say, "I need information from your department," and the exact reason you're asking him is to answer, do we need him? Do we need his department? Can it be done by someone else? That's where the realization really comes over you a lot.

Your salary goes up very fast. I started at $29,000 and they gave me a $5,000 bonus. They raised my salary to $33,000 the next year and gave me a $15,000 bonus. I was promoted from analyst after the two-year program to associate, and, when I left after four years, my salary was $60,000 and my bonus was $120,000. Some of the bonuses that I received later on were simply a result of almost a surreal period in investment banking. In my opinion, there wasn't a very good relationship between bonuses and the actual work that you did.

Let me explain now how this all relates to my dad. My father worked for a family-owned grocery store chain in the Southwest. A number of things had happened to my dad that I, as a son, felt were unfair. He went to high school, but he never graduated and did not choose education as a route. But he worked as a bag boy for this chain even in high school.

The owner knew by dad personally, and my dad always felt that, if he put in his time, he would move up in the store. And actually he did. He became a produce manager in a store, and then he even became a store manager when I was in high school.

Then the family that owned the chain sold out to somebody, and they fired my father, although he had worked for the firm at that time for about 20 years. He couldn't find any work, and just did odd jobs and stuff. For me it had a profound effect. First of all, my dad wouldn't tell us that he was fired. He told us that he quit. My mom told us that he got fired, and that was later on. According to her, he was just embarrassed. He didn't want to tell his kids. I was 16. So it was tough. They were sending me to a private Catholic high school and they were getting ready to send my brother there. And when my dad lost his job, my mom—who wasn't working at the time—got a job as a secretary.

Finally, in two years, he got a job back as a produce manager in a store that didn't even deal with groceries much. His job was wrapping vegetables in plastic; he absolutely hated it. But as things didn't work out with that company, he was laid off. Now he's in his 50s, and this is when I'm in college. He's having trouble finding a job. People just don't want to hire a guy who was a grocery store manager, then didn't work for two years, then worked as a produce manager for a store that's not even really a grocery store.

He still knew some people at the grocery store chain where he had worked for so long, and somehow he got a job back there. They decided my dad was too old to be a produce manager, too much lifting and stuff, and they sent him to the central buying area. That was the last job that he had there. When I was at the investment banking firm in 1987, Kroger, which owned the grocery chain at the time, was being hostilely attacked by the Dart Group. They did a friendly deal—the same kind of deals that we did—with another firm to fend off the raiders. As a result, they dramatically cut down the warehouse operations and my dad was laid off.

At the same time, I'm typing in cost savings numbers, and, even though I saw the faces before, it was much easier to rationalize that these people would be able to find other jobs; that this was better for the company on the whole; that this was for the long-term survivability of the company; that it fulfilled the responsibilities to the owners of the company, who were the shareholders, by giving them the most amount of money, since they had latent value that was being eaten up by too much overhead, and those people were part of the problem. But then when it's your father, and you know the difficulty that you dad will have finding a job. . . . Even though economically it may be right to lay people off when they're not needed, there is a tremendous amount of pain that is inflicted that maybe should be weighed more. Perhaps, instead of just looking at dollars and cents, you need to look at the amount of pain that you cause to the people involved.

This is where I found myself sometimes almost nauseated by the things that I would think. There was even a point where I said, "Well, I make a lot more than my father does, so it makes more sense for him to lose his job than for me to say something and lose my job." Now I thought that, and immediately when I thought it, I couldn't have felt worse. But you think of it. You do think of it. That's something I struggled with the rest of the time I was there.

In 1987, he lost his job the last time. He could not—he absolutely could not find work. I visited him that summer. They were doing all right financially because the kids were through school now. I was working, my brother was working, my mom was working as a secretary, so money really wasn't the problem. The problem was my father's self-esteem. Because my brother and I had done so well in school—all of which had obviously been handed to us on a silver platter by my parents—he didn't realize that he was the one who really did it for us. He felt as though he had let us down by getting fired. He didn't want us to know. He wanted us to think that our dad was a good person and also a success. It's funny, but when I looked at other people around me in investment banks who were literally millionaires, I knew that my dad was every bit as smart as they were.

But anyway, my dad just couldn't find work, and I guess in the end that's worked out well. My mom and dad had bought a house for $13,000 and it was now worth $80,000, and they took a huge risk and they sold the house and took the money and opened up their own business. My mom really was the person who pushed him into it because my dad is very risk-averse; but my mom decided that my dad couldn't work for anyone else anymore, because he was just a broken man. The whole six or seven months when he was unemployed he just flipped the TV channels and watched TV day in and day out. And he used to say things, like, "Sometimes I just don't think life is worth it," and these kinds of things that make you worry a hell of a lot. It really hit home with me at the time, because I knew that the exact same thing that cost my dad the job, I was someway involved in, also.

But they opened up their carpet store and are still there today and doing fairly well, considering the economy. My dad now looks at people that he used to work with at the grocery store and he pities the people whom he liked, and he loves it when bad things happen to the people who he felt did him wrong.

When I was in college I used to talk about business quite a bit. I was driven to get out of college and get a very good job that paid a lot of money. And my dad, when I would talk in college about getting out and making a lot of money, would say to me, "Son, I've never had any money, my parents have never had any money, and I'm afraid it will be the same for you." It was easy for him to be depressed, because you start with a young man who really thought that just through hard work he could achieve a lot in an organization, and then, through things that were totally out of his control, and not really based on his performance, he ended up with nothing to show for it at all.

I never told my dad what I did at work. I'm not sure he knew it was any different from commercial banking, making loans to people. I also felt I could never tell my dad what I was making because I felt it was unjust. Usually the reason investment bankers give for making as much money as they do is the number of hours they work. Well, my dad was a store manager, responsible for a whole store. If the freezer went out Sunday night at 3 A.M., he was there. He was in charge of that store, and he put in easily 75 to 80 hours a week, which is similar to investment banking. He was lucky if he brought home $200–$300 a week. When I first got the job, and I told him that I was starting at $29,000, and that I would get a $5,000 bonus, he said, "That's nice, son, but I'm sure you misunderstood them, that must be for the whole two-year program.'' My dad just couldn't conceive that someone at 22 years of age with no experience could actually lock in a job for above $30,000. Because my dad had worked all his life and probably never made $30,000.

I might return to the investment bank in essentially the same capacity. It's an issue I've never resolved, unfortunately. I fight with it all the time. There's a million ways you can think about it. One is that whether or not I'm there, leveraged buyouts are going to happen. And I do believe there is some basis to the economic arguments. I've actually seen times when I feel like we've done

great things for companies. We've done ESOP buy-outs where the employees will actually own the company when we're done, and we like doing those. Everyone feels better about those, even the senior bankers. To me it's the same kind of complex situation as when people talk about free trade with Mexico, where perhaps it's the most efficient way, but, meanwhile, how many Americans are going to lose their jobs? There's no way to measure the pain and suffering that it inflicts on society. And that's my problem. I don't know how to measure that. And I continue to fight with it and wrestle with it.

CASE

DONNA DUBINSKY AND APPLE COMPUTER, INC. (A)

At 7 A.M. on Friday, April 19, 1985, Donna Dubinsky placed an urgent phone call to her boss's boss, Bill Campbell, executive vice president for sales and marketing at Apple Computer, Inc. Dubinsky, director of distribution and sales administration, was attending a management leadership seminar located more than two hours away. Her words were crisp and to the point: "Bill, I really need to talk to you. Will you wait for me today? I'll be back at the office around 5."

This case was prepared by Research Associate Mary Gentile (under the direction of Professor Todd D. Jick).

Copyright © 1986 by the President and Fellows of Harvard College. Harvard Business School case 9-486-083.

"Absolutely, I'll be here," Campbell replied, although he knew nothing about the purpose of her call.

Dubinsky inhaled a deep, anxious breath. She felt the time had come to "bet her Apple career" on the ultimatum she was going to deliver to Campbell at the head office in Cupertino, California.

Still, she could hardly believe it had come to this. Her first three years at Apple, from July 1981 through the fall of 1984, were ones of continuous success with increasing authority and recognition. She had refined and formalized much of the Apple product distribution policy, and she worked closely with the six distribution centers across the country.

Unexpectedly, however, in early 1985, Steve Jobs, Apple's chairman of the board and general manager of the Macintosh

Division, had proposed that the existing distribution system be dismantled and replaced by the "just-in-time" method. Jobs's proposal would not only place all of Apple's distribution activities under the supervision of the directors of manufacturing within the two product divisions, Macintosh and Apple II, but would also establish direct relationships between the dealer and the plant—essentially eliminating the need for the six distribution centers. Jobs claimed that this change would result in significant savings for the company by shrinking the product pipeline and reducing inventory, an especially attractive promise since Apple's market share was declining steadily. Dubinsky cited her experience and track record with distribution, however, and argued that the new method was infeasible. In the past four months, despite Dubinsky's criticisms, Jobs's proposal had gathered momentum and support throughout the company.

Upon leaving the leadership seminar and driving to Cupertino for her meeting with Campbell, Dubinsky reflected on the effect this distribution proposal would have on her job and on the company. She believed that it spelled catastrophe for both and that it was time to take a stand.

Donna Dubinsky

Dubinsky, a Yale graduate, had worked for two years in commercial banking before entering the MBA program at the Harvard Business School. While job hunting just before her graduation, Dubinsky decided that Apple was the kind of cutting-edge technology firm that interested her, and she further decided that, despite her financial background, she wanted a position close to the customers. Apple had few MBAs at that time, and their Harvard

recruiters were looking for technical backgrounds. Nevertheless, Dubinsky pushed hard for interviews and finally received an offer after pointing out that they would probably never find another Harvard MBA who wanted to work in customer service.

In July 1981, she started as customer support liaison in a department of one, reporting to Roy Weaver, the new head of the distribution, service, and support group. Over the next three years, Weaver continued to expand her responsibilities until April 1985, when she became director of distribution and sales administration with 80 employees and a $10 million budget. (This promotion had been approved in December 1984. See Table A.) Weaver had concluded early on that the best way to retain a talented manager like Dubinsky was to continually reward and challenge her. His strategy worked so well that, when Jobs himself tried to hire Dubinsky for his Macintosh indroduction in 1983, she chose to stay put. Dubinsky commented:

> Roy has been the best mentor I could have asked for. He always gave me just enough rope, yet was available whenever I needed his advice and guidance. He was continually looking for opportunities to give me visibility as well as more responsibility.

Although Dubinsky rarely fought for her own career progress, she willingly and ably fought for her subordinates—her "people" as she called them—and for the Apple dealers and customers. When asked to describe her management style, Dubinsky focused primarily on her caring and honest relationships with her subordinates. One of Dubinsky's subordinates commented:

> Donna Dubinsky is very direct. She says what she thinks. And she fights for

TABLE A   Dubinsky's Career at Apple

July 1981 — Joined firm as Customer Support Liaison
July 1982 — Customer Support Program Manager
               Add first direct report and Field Management responsibility (six dotted-line managers)
Oct. 1982 — Add Customer Relations
Dec. 1982 — Add Direct Sales Administration Group
Jan. 1984 — Distribution manager
               Add Product Distribution Group
               Add warehousing
June 1984 — Add Field Communications
               Add AppleLink Operations (computerized communication with the field)
Oct. 1984 — Add Teacher Buy (special distribution project)
Jan. 1985 — Add Traffic
               Add Developer Relations
Apr. 1985 — Director, Distribution and Sales
               Administration (promotion approved December 1984)

               Add Forecasting

her issues. If she feels she's right and she loses her issue, she goes down fighting. She always presents an image of confidence. She doesn't let peer pressure sway her mind. She's not intimidated by upper management. But that's not to say that she won't change her mind.

And she'll always support a company decision even if she doesn't agree with it. That's an important quality for a "support" organization. She always has the company's interests at heart.

She's extremely intelligent. She has a great sense of humor. . . . I learned a great deal from her about taking risks and about when to really hold a hard line on an issue.

If you look at where she was three years ago and where she is now, it's phenomenal. It really is. And she can grow a lot more.

Dubinsky characterized herself as thick-skinned and nondefensive. One human resource manager commented: "Dubinsky projects a lot of confidence and conviction in her beliefs. You defi-nitely know where she stands. She is not a political animal at all."

Commenting on her direct style and willingness to take certain risks, Dubinsky explained:

As a middle manager, I often was put in the position of making decisions beyond my authority, or at least within the gray area of unstated authority levels. In a more seasoned company, making that decision on my own could cause serious organizational repercussions. At Apple, the middle manager had to presume the boss's agreement and was comfortable that she or he was allowed to make mistakes.

Weaver, her first and longest-term supervisor, valued her clear, precise thinking; her presentation skills and voice command; and the power of her presence.

Campbell, Weaver's boss, described Dubinsky's contribution:

What we had was this unbelievable plethora of ideas in the product divisions that came down to a marketing

EXHIBIT 1   Apple Financial Performance and Market Share, 1980–1985

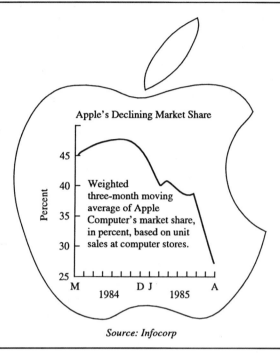

Apple's Declining Market Share

Weighted three-month moving average of Apple Computer's market share, in percent, based on unit sales at computer stores.

Source: Infocorp

SOURCE: *New York Times*, September 22, 1985. Copyright © 1985 by the New York Times Company. Reprinted with permission.

execution funnel. We didn't have the systems in place that would enable us to execute, and Donna was the only one who understood that and who understood what we could do in terms of execution. Donna was a battler for procedure before we ever thought procedure was important.

He added, however:

> But I've told her many times, "You've got to work the halls and sell your ideas. You can't expect things to happen by fiat."

Company Background

Apple's inception and meteoric rise received frequent press coverage and became well known from the time of its founding in 1976 through its entry in the

Fortune 500 six years later. The easy-to-use Apple II, a home and educational computer, appeared in 1977 and, in its various enhanced forms, remained the major-selling product of the Cupertino, California–based company through 1985.

In 1983, Apple and its cofounder, Steve Jobs, lured John Sculley from his position as president of PepsiCo to take on the presidency at Apple. His challenge was to bring new organization and marketing discipline to Apple, without sacrificing creativity and spirit. He also faced IBM's 28 percent market share in 1983 as compared with Apple's 24 percent, down from Apple's 40 percent share in 1981 (see Exhibit 1).

The Macintosh was introduced in early

EXHIBIT 1 *(concluded)*

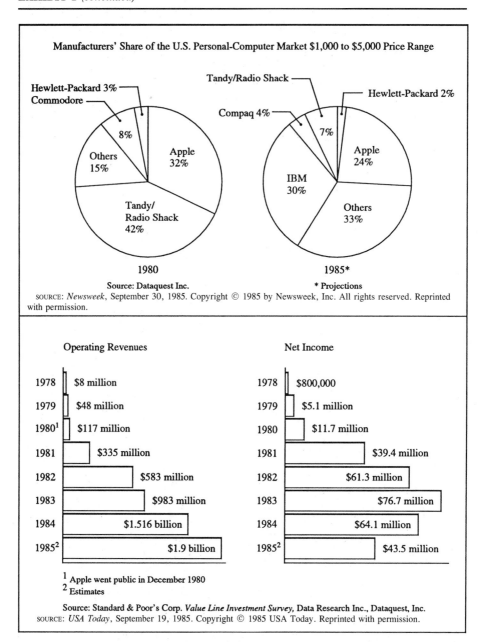

Manufacturers' Share of the U.S. Personal-Computer Market $1,000 to $5,000 Price Range

1980

Hewlett-Packard 3%
Commodore
8%
Others 15%
Apple 32%
Tandy/Radio Shack 42%

Source: Dataquest Inc.

1985*

Tandy/Radio Shack
Compaq 4%
Hewlett-Packard 2%
7%
Apple 24%
IBM 30%
Others 33%

* Projections

Operating Revenues

1978	$8 million
1979	$48 million
1980[1]	$117 million
1981	$335 million
1982	$583 million
1983	$983 million
1984	$1.516 billion
1985[2]	$1.9 billion

Net Income

1978	$800,000
1979	$5.1 million
1980	$11.7 million
1981	$39.4 million
1982	$61.3 million
1983	$76.7 million
1984	$64.1 million
1985[2]	$43.5 million

[1] Apple went public in December 1980
[2] Estimates

Source: Standard & Poor's Corp. *Value Line Investment Survey,* Data Research Inc., Dataquest, Inc.

1984 and, although its sales never matched Apple's projections, they were still impressive in that first year. Although actual Mac profits were lowered by high market-entry costs, Apple II sales carried the firm through a record Christmas quarter. By 1985, however, sales failed to reach projected planning levels, causing profitability problems, since expenses had been based on the higher revenue figures. Tensions were mounting between the Apple II Division, which felt its contribution to the firm was undervalued, and the Macintosh Division, whose general manager, Jobs, saw it as the technological vanguard within Apple. Previously, Jobs had split his division off from the rest of the firm, dubbing them "pirates," whose creativity would be unfettered by rules and bureaucracy. By 1985, Jobs and Sculley were beginning to feel the strains in a hitherto remarkably close and interdependent relationship.

Apple's early rapid growth meant a constant influx of new employees. Apple attempted to create and solidify a sense of identity by developing a statement of basic values (see Exhibit 2). For a long time organizational charts were not printed at Apple since they changed too quickly. Frequent reorganizations reflected the conflict between product organization and functional organization. When Apple began, it had only one product and, therefore, its structure was largely functional. As new products began to develop, each team formed its own division, modeled on the original Apple, each with its own marketing, its own engineering, and so forth.

When Sculley joined the firm, he simplified its structure with a compromise format, centralizing product development and product marketing in just two divisions—the Apple II and the Macintosh—with U.S. sales and marketing services centralized in a third division. Nevertheless, this revised format still reflected a mix of functional, product, and geographic organizations. Seven divisions reported directly to Sculley (see Figure A).

He believed that a coordinated sales and marketing approach was necessary for the firm to present a clear message to dealers and to compete with IBM's highly trained sales force and other firms with larger resource bases and well-established marketing relations and procedures.

Product Distribution at Apple

In January 1984, Dubinsky became U.S. distribution manager for all of Apple, with dotted-line responsibility for the six field warehouses and direct responsibility for sales administration, inventory control, and customer relations. Organizationally, she was situated within U.S. sales and marketing, although she required ongoing contact with the product divisions.

Apple's product appealed mainly to the home and educational markets whose seasonal and sometimes fickle purchasing patterns placed a strain on physical distribution. Predicting sales patterns was difficult, but it was also imperative that the product be available when requested. In addition, Dubinsky's group maintained relationships with Apple's dealers, a critical factor in the competitive battle for limited dealer shelf space; neither Apple nor any of its competitors could afford to own their dealers. Most dealers started as mom-and-pop organizations and were often undercapitalized, particularly given the growth in the market. Finally, since Apple's operation was primarily design and assembly (rather than fabrication), inventory and warehousing control for parts, works-in-process, and finished goods were potentially costly and critical to Apple's profits and responsiveness to the market.

The distribution group took all Apple products from their respective manufacturing sites (or from their ports of entry for

EXHIBIT 2 Apple Values

Achieving our goal is important to us. But we're equally concerned with the WAY we reach it. These are the values that govern our business conduct.

Empathy for Customers/Users: We offer superior products that fill real needs and provide lasting value. We deal fairly with competitors and meet customers and vendors more than halfway. We are genuinely interested in solving customer problems and will not compromise our ethics or integrity in the name of profit.

Achievement/Aggressiveness: We set aggressive goals and drive ourselves hard to achieve them. We recognize that this is a unique time when our product will change the way people work and live. It's an adventure, and we're in it together.

Positive Social Contribution: As a corporate citizen, we wish to be an economic, intellectual, and social asset in communities where we operate. But beyond that, we expect to make this world a better place to live in. We build products that extend human capability, freeing people from drudgery and helping them achieve more than they could alone.

Innovation/Vision: We build our company on innovation, providing products that are new and needed. We accept the risks inherent in following our vision and work to develop leadership products which command the profit margins we strive for.

Individual Performance: We expect individual commitment and performance above the standard for our industry. Only thus will we make the profits that permit us to seek our other corporate objectives. Each employee can and must make a difference; for in the final analysis, INDIVIDUALS determine the character and strength of Apple.

Team Spirit: Teamwork is essential to Apple's success, for the job is too big to be done by any one person. Individuals are encouraged to interact with all levels of management, sharing ideas and suggestions to improve Apple's effectiveness and quality of life. It takes all of us to win. We support each other and share the victories and rewards together. We're enthusiastic about what we do.

Quality/Excellence: We care about what we do. We build into Apple products a level of quality, performance, and value that will earn the respect and loyalty of our customers.

Individual Rewards: We recognize each person's contribution to Apple's success, and we share the financial rewards that flow from high performance. We recognize also that rewards must be psychological as well as financial and strive for an atmosphere where each individual can share the adventure and excitement of working at Apple.

Good Management: The attitudes of managers toward their people are of primary importance. Employees should be able to trust the motives and integrity of their supervisors. It is the responsibility of management to create a productive environment where Apple values flourish.

---

products imported from overseas vendors) to the dealers. For example, Macintosh computers were assembled at the facility in Fremont, California. Based on monthly sales forecasts, the distribution group allocated a specific number of those computers to each of the six distribution sites: Sunnyvale, California; Irvine, California; Chicago, Illinois; Dallas, Texas; Boston, Massachusetts; and Charlotte, North Carolina. Each of these sites was actually a customer support center that provided warehousing, customer service, credit, repair service, order entry, and a technical group to assist dealers. Individual dealers called in orders to their area support center

FIGURE A Apple Organization Chart, October 1984

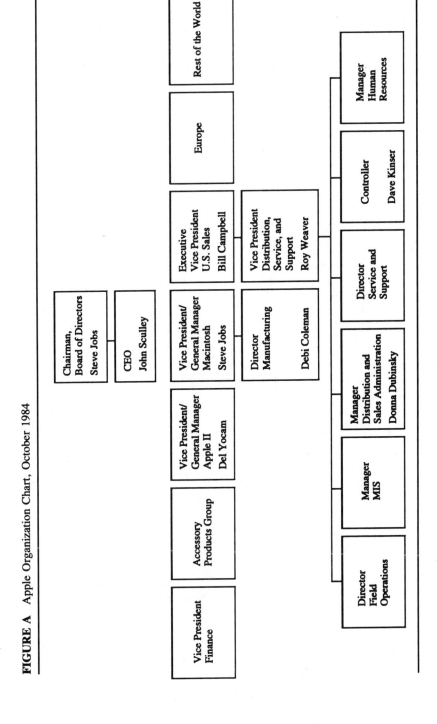

representative, who arranged to have the requested product sent out. Employees of the distribution group took pride in this system's efficiency and simplicity, although forecasting mistakes often caused shortages or excesses of individual products.

Planning and analysis were luxuries for product distribution as Apple grew. Dubinsky recalled:

> I might also mention what was not done: analytical overkill. One incident stands out. My boss needed to request funds from the president to build a warehouse in Boston. He showed me his notes; he merely was going to tell the president the amount of yearly lease cost. As a newly minted MBA, the idea of approaching the president without a full-blown, discounted cash flow analysis was beyond belief, so I offered to prepare one, an offer instantly accepted. After several hours of work, I produced a VisiCalc model that would have been attacked for its simplicity by my B-School classmates, but seemed adequate under the circumstances. When my boss returned from the meeting, he told me that the president had glanced for several minutes at my neatly laid-out analysis, looked up, and asked one question; "What is the yearly lease cost?" After hearing the response he said, "OK. Let's do it." No time for analysis.

The Distribution Conflict: September to December, 1984

The conflict over Apple's distribution strategy began in September 1984, when Dubinsky and her boss, Weaver, presented the distribution, service, and support group's 1985 business plan to the Apple executive staff for review. Both Dubinsky and Weaver had presented their plan confidently because of this group's strong performance record. The plan held no real surprises, but it did call for a long-term distribution strategy review to be conducted throughout the coming year, particularly concerning the development of additional distribution centers.

Jobs challenged the plan, however, complaining that he had not received a good explanation for the current distribution, service, and support cost levels and structure. Dubinsky and Weaver were taken aback by Jobs's criticism. Cost had never been a problem in the distribution area. In a firm that devoted most of its energy and interest to new product development, Dubinsky and Weaver were proud that distribution had never caused a delay in product delivery, and they believed that the absence of complaints was probably their highest praise. In addition, they had just shipped out goods for a record quarter by over 60 percent, without missing a beat.

A few weeks later, however, Jobs had dinner with Fred Smith, founder and CEO of Federal Express. The two dynamic entrepreneurs found much in common, and Jobs was particularly interested in Smith's discussion of IBM's just-in-time distribution of selected computer components. Jobs saw a potential for reducing costs in this process, which would eliminate the need for Apple's warehouses, carrying costs, and extensive inventory. An Apple dealer would report an order as it was placed, triggering manufacturing's immediate assembly of the requested product. Upon assembly, the product would be shipped overnight, by Federal Express, to its dealer/customer destination.

Jobs and his director of manufacturing, Debi Coleman, investigated this concept, certain that their plant could efficiently incorporate the distribution function. Jobs was proud of the Macintosh Division's fully automated manufacturing facility and confident in the ability of Coleman, a Stanford MBA who was quoted as boldly stating:

> I didn't walk into this job with all the credentials. They picked me because I will grow the fastest with it. I want to be the best in the world—there's no doubt about it. [1]

And the project was all the more attractive to Jobs because Macintosh sales were down. One manager later observed: "In order to defend themselves, they [the Macintosh Division] went on the attack."

Dubinsky, however, believed the change proposed by Jobs was a mistake. As distribution manager, she was confident that she held the most pertinent perspective; and she suspected the Macintosh manufacturing's motives. The flaws in a distribution plan as radical as Jobs and Coleman's seemed obvious to her:

> We were an off-the-shelf business. You've got to have inventory. The dealers couldn't stock the inventory because they didn't have the cash resources to do it, so we essentially played a role as distributor, creating a buffer for them that we could afford and that they couldn't afford. [Jobs and Coleman's idea] was a total nonrecognition of our business as far as I was concerned. It was a manufacturing/logistics/cost-control point of view that had no value in the real world.

Dubinsky was further confused by the rumored interest expressed by Sculley and the rest of the executive staff in Jobs's idea.

Weaver was similarly confused. The fall of 1984 was a difficult time for him,

both personally and professionally. In particular, he felt unsure of his relationship with his new boss, Campbell. (Campbell had been personally recruited in July 1983 by Sculley from Eastman Kodak for his teaching ability and marketing leadership. He had previously worked at the advertising firm of J. Walter Thompson after serving six seasons as the popular head football coach at Columbia University.) Shortly after the September business plan review meeting, Campbell's responsibilities had been shifted to include Weaver's group. Weaver had previously reported directly to Sculley. The unexpected distribution issue focused on one of the areas Weaver was most proud of and threatened to remove it from his and Dubinsky's control; thus, Weaver's objections appeared to management as more defensive than well reasoned.

Both Dubinsky and Weaver had difficulty taking this new distribution idea seriously. To a certain extent they chalked it up to Jobs's penchant for "big, elegant things," like a single automated manufacturing/warehouseing facility, and to Coleman's personal style. One human resources manager described Coleman as "very aggressive, very intimidating, very bright, and having little finesse." Nevertheless, responding to Jobs's challenges, Campbell and Sculley called for a strategy review and recommended improvements from the distribution group by mid-December.

Meanwhile, Dubinsky began hearing reports of an elaborate presentation, a book-length Distribution Strategy Proposal, which Coleman and her staff were preparing. More and more people were learning about the proposal; furthermore, Dubinsky could see her boss, Weaver, growing more unsure, more certain he could not win. At one point, Weaver

---

[1] *USA Today*, August 29, 1985.

decided to try to talk with Sculley himself, but Weaver's boss, Campbell, discouraged him, explaining that Weaver would only appear to be defensive. Dubinsky commented:

> I had always looked to Roy for advice before on how to handle any difficult situation; he always had a refreshing, honest point of view. At this point, however, he was becoming paralyzed by the situation, and I found it harder to turn to him.

As distribution was Dubinsky's responsibility, the task of preparing a strategy review fell to her. The more she heard about the presentation Coleman was preparing, the more sure Dubinsky became of her own position. She worked with Dave Kinser, controller for the distribution, service, and support group on a research project intended to defend the existing distribution system. Since this was the Christmas season—a very busy time for distribution—Dubinsky was unable to allocate an extensive number of hours or people to the project. Still, she thought, distribution was her area and she knew it best; surely her judgment and past record of effectiveness would carry more weight than Coleman's untested and radical proposal. But, as the mid-December strategy review deadline set by Sculley in September drew near, Dubinsky realized that she was not prepared to defend her area against the sophisticated presentation that Coleman had reportedly prepared, and Dubinsky finally requested an extension.

The Distribution Task Force: January to April, 1985

The conflict sharpened when, unexpectedly, on a Monday evening in early January 1985, Weaver called Dubinsky at her home, the first time he had ever done

so. He anxiously explained that he had just learned from Campbell that Coleman would be presenting her distribution proposal at a three-day executive meeting, scheduled for Wednesday, Thursday, and Friday of that same week. The meeting would be held off-site at Pajaro Dunes, the regular Apple retreat, and it was originally planned as an opportunity to evaluate new product developments. Only executive staff, division heads, and one engineer from each of the Apple II and Macintosh teams were supposed to attend. Dubinsky could not understand why Coleman's presentation on the distribution issue was even on the agenda, and, if this issue was to be discussed, she felt that as distribution manager, she should be the one to address the topic.

Weaver had just learned of the agenda change from Campbell, who explained that Sculley had heard Coleman's presentation recently and had asked Campbell if she could be included in the Pajaro meeting. Weaver thought Campbell should have refused since distribution fell within the authority of Campbell, Weaver, and Dubinsky, but Campbell had agreed to Sculley's request.

Weaver called that evening asking Dubinsky to drop everything and put together a counter-proposal, an overview that he would deliver at Wednesday's meeting. Dubinsky agreed and, in one day, completed a presentation that was hand-delivered to Weaver in time for the executive conference.

She learned later that Coleman's and Weaver's presentations triggered an emotional and very difficult discussion that day. The vice president for human resources, Jay Elliot, criticized the executive meeting process, pointing out that, counter to Apple values, this was an all-too-familiar instance of top management stepping around its own middle managers and engaging in top-down management. Why was Coleman presenting to Sculley instead of to Weaver, and why was Coleman instead of Dubinsky presenting the distribution issue at Pajaro? Coming at a time when Jobs and Sculley were facing growing disagreements and when Jobs was pressuring Sculley to accept Coleman's proposal, the executive staff took this criticism to heart.

It was resolved to entrust the distribution problem to a task force composed of the parties involved and a few "neutral" individuals. The task force would report to Campbell, and, as a demonstration of its confidence and commitment to the Apple team, the executive staff pledged to accept the task force's recommendations.

The Distribution Task Force included Dubinsky, Dave Kinser (controller), and Weaver; all of the distribution service and support group; Coleman and Jim Bean, from Macintosh and Apple II manufacturing respectively, and both supporters of the just-in-time proposal; and Jay Elliot, Joe Graziano (vice president of finance), and Phil Dixon (management information systems) as the "neutral players."

Most of those at the Pajaro meeting applauded this task force solution. Campbell, who was dissatisfied and embarrassed by the presentation his group had mounted, saw it as a way to force analysis. He thought his group "hadn't done its homework" and that its presentation did not reflect a thorough reexamination of the distribution process. For Weaver, it was a kind of reprieve.

But Dubinsky was angry and disappointed:

I didn't know why there should be a task force at all. Distribution's our job. . . . I couldn't get out of this mentality that what we had was working so well. The thing had never broken down. . . . Now I was supposed to go back and do this strategy, and I couldn't figure out what problem I was solving.

She had always assumed that she would continue to gather ideas from the field for suggested improvements in the existing system. But Coleman's proposal was much more than simply suggested improvements; in fact, Dubinsky thought, it was more than a new distribution system. It was a total change in distribution and manufacturing strategy, taking Apple from supply-driven to demand-driven procedures, and reducing the distribution and warehouse centers from six to zero.

The longer Dubinsky, Weaver, and Kinser thought about it, the more problems they found in Coleman's proposal. As the task force began and continued over the next four months, weekly at first and then less frequently, the members raised objections: for example, the proposal failed to consider the more than 50 percent of Apple products that were manufactured off-shore; it focused only on central processing units, ignoring Apple's other products; there was no provision for customer complaints and product returns; multiple product line orders would be inconvenient for dealers who would be required to split their request between the two product divisions and their respective directors of manufacturing.

Coleman consistently stressed the point that her proposal would save money, because it got inventory out of the pipeline, thereby eliminating storage costs and inventory obsolescence. Dubinsky tried to reframe the issue, explaining that the inefficiencies were not in the warehousing and the physical distribution but rather in the forecasting process. She also pointed out discrepancies in Coleman's figures and assumptions.

The task force meetings continued to hit stalemate after stalemate: Coleman made proposals; Dubinsky raised objections. The distribution issue had taken on enormous proportions because top management had seized on it as an opportunity to demonstrate its faith in middle management decision-making ability; but middle management could reach no consensus. Campbell was frustrated because he knew that Jobs was pushing Sculley to accept Coleman's plan, and Campbell had no alternative plan from his group to offer Sculley; Weaver was weary, and Dubinsky, who had never understood why the reins had been taken from her hands in the first place and given to a task force, was beginning to consider jobs in other companies.

She also found that the meetings and counter-meetings were taking all her time; she spent less time with her own staff. The task force, in still one more attempt to find some middle ground, finally reported its agreement to Campbell that the just-in-time concept was the best direction for Apple to pursue, but it had not agreed on a feasible implementation plan. Dubinsky recalled:

> It was like a dripping faucet. There was all this pressure to agree. You wanted to agree so you found a ground to agree on. . . . But you know what? I never really believed it.

During the final task force meeting, Campbell restated this conclusion for the final time, saying: "So you all agree that this is what we should work toward?" And Dubinsky, despite herself, could not choke back her late but very definite "No." Campbell ended the meeting an-

grily and Dubinsky, thoroughly depressed, was ready to just walk away from it all.

The "Leadership Experience" Seminar: April 17–19, 1985

In April 1985, Dubinsky was asked to attend an Apple "Leadership Experience" meeting, scheduled for three days at Pajaro Dunes for a group of 40 upper-middle managers. Its purpose was to break down barriers, to encourage communication and creativity, and to challenge participants to find new perspectives and new solutions for old problems. At this point, Dubinsky was at her emotional nadir, and, being skeptical of such programs, she went merely to be out of the office for a few days. As she put it, "I had no intention of getting anything out of it."

The program was fast paced and imaginatively designed. Many of the exercises required participants to break into preassigned small groups, and, much to Dubinsky's surprise, Coleman showed up in almost all of these groups. To Dubinsky it seemed that Coleman was using the three-day workshop to lobby for her cause, while Dubinsky herself "felt destroyed and was questioning [her] own judgment."

To Dubinsky, the whole "Leadership Experience" seemed ill fated. She wondered how she could be self-reflective and thoughtful when she felt incapable of expressing feelings to anyone without being totally negative. How could she design an action plan for her group, as one exercise required, when she did not even know if the distribution group would still exist?

As the seminar progressed, however, Dubinsky recognized that everyone felt confused, demoralized, and critical of the company. She saw the morale problems as fallout from the Macintosh/Apple II rivalry. During one exercise, for example, participants were asked to draw pictures that reflected their perceptions of Apple. One manager drew a picture of two men (Jobs and Sculley) both trying to steer a single boat, but one man (Sculley) appeared to be totally controlled by the other. Someone else sketched a caricature of Jobs with two hats—one as operating manager and one as chairman of the board, and he had to choose between them. A third participant drew a picture of the manager of the Apple II Division, out at sea, alone on a wind surfer, looking to see which way the wind was blowing. Dubinsky began to feel less isolated with her frustration, and she began to see the distribution issue as part of a much larger problem.

On the second day of the workshop, Sculley spoke to the group. He talked generally of Apple's goals, stressing the need for both individual contribution and team effort, likening the Apple mission to the building of a cathedral. Dubinsky raised her hand and charged that Apple employees could not build that cathedral when they were not receiving any direction from him. She was beyond caution at that point, and she proceeded to question the contradictions she heard in his speech, issue by issue. Sculley responded angrily, charging that it was Dubinsky's job to make decisions, that executive staff could not hand them out on a silver platter. Before other managers could speak to the issue, time ran out. Many people ran up to Dubinsky immediately after the session and praised her for having the nerve to say what needed to be said. But somehow Dubinsky felt as if she was "alone on the boat as it pulled out, as my friends and colleagues waved from the shore."

Later that day at lunch, Dubinsky sat beside Del Yocam, executive vice president of the Apple II Division. She respected Yocam as a manager—he was one of the few seasoned executives around—and she decided to confide in him, hoping to get a reality check on the whole distribution issue. She could no longer get such a perspective from Weaver because of his closeness to the situation. She hoped that Yocam's distance might provide a clearer view. Dubinsky asked him whether he thought the just-in-time strategy was appropriate for Apple. Yocam responded that, from his standpoint, he could not judge; that Dubinsky was in the position to know what impact this strategy change could have on Apple; and that if she truly believed it was wrong, she had better stop it. He also added sharply that he would hold her responsible if she failed.

Something clicked in Dubinsky's head as she listened to Yocam. He was so serious, and he looked at this issue not as a turf or charter battle or as a question of who was right. He saw it as a question of Apple's fate. Dubinsky recalled:

I truly believed the proposed distribution strategy to be so radical that it would shut the company down. Yocam's reaction really brought home to me the high stakes involved in the issue.

She had critiqued and reacted to Coleman's proposals, detail by detail, but she had gone no further. This was Thursday afternoon, April 18, 1985.

The Ultimatum, April 19, 1985

After her 7 A.M. call to Campbell the next day, Dubinsky awaited the completion of the Pajaro Dunes seminar before returning to Cupertino to meet with him. Driving back to the office, Dubinsky flashed upon a memorable piece of advice that she had received from one of her Harvard Business School professors almost six years earlier. He had told students that the first thing to do after graduating was to start pulling together their "go-to-hell money." Dubinsky took that to mean that she should never put herself in a situation from which she could not walk away. Dubinsky had followed that advice, and now she had her savings stored away and no prohibitive obligations. The time had come to test her independence.

Campbell and Dubinsky met for two intense hours late that afternoon. In their meeting, Dubinsky acknowledged her previous blind spots. She asked for an additional 30 days to get her own distribution strategy presentation together. "But," she added, "distribution is my area, and I will evaluate it myself, without the interference of an outside task force."

Campbell demanded: "Why can't you defend what you're doing to others if you think it's right?" But Dubinsky snapped back that she did not have to if it was really her job. They wrestled on over this point until Dubinsky finally took her stand and delivered her ultimatum: If Campbell did not agree to her terms, she would leave Apple. Campbell promised to talk with Sculley and to let her know Monday.

Over the weekend, Dubinsky wrote her letter of resignation. On Monday morning she told Weaver about the ultimatum that she had delivered to his boss the preceding Friday. She then waited for Campbell's call.

READING

THE RECIPIENTS OF CHANGE

It's tough for people who have done real well to feel pushed out the door. Tough for the ego, like cutting out a big piece of yourself. Especially, when you've been there for a while, you're rooted. . . . It's who you were, part of who you are.

The comment above was made by someone in a company that was "downsized." But as the statement indicates, the person himself was downsized in a way—losing a "big piece" of himself. This image is by no means unusual; people in the throes of change often speak in terms of being

diminished. They also use words like anger, betrayal, shock—in short, they describe dramatic emotions that rarely encompass the positive. They experience being unappreciated, anxious, at a minimum, confused.

In contrast, much has been written about the need to embrace change with enthusiasm. We are to "foster hardiness" and be flexible; change is a challenge to confront, an adventure; we must "thrive on chaos." What accounts for this difference between actual reactions to change

This case was prepared by Professor Todd D. Jick

Copyright © 1990 by the President and Fellows of Harvard College. Harvard Business School case N9-491-039.

and what we are supposed to feel? Can this gap be bridged? Not easily.

No organization can institute change if its employees will not, at the very least, accept the change. No change will "work" if employees don't help in the effort. And, change is not possible without people changing themselves. Any organization that believes change can take hold without considering how people will react to it is in deep delusion. Change can be "managed" externally by those who decide when it is needed and how it-"should" be implemented. But it *will* be implemented only when employees accept change—and the specific change—internally.

This case explores how people, in general, react to change, why they do so, and how they may be able to understand their reactions better. The perspective is that of the "changee," or recipient, but the ideas are helpful to change agents as well. By grasping more firmly the experience of being changed, those managing the process can gain a broader understanding of the effects— intended and unintended—of the changes they are instituting.

One point must be stressed at the outset. For some people, any interference with routine provokes strong reaction. These folks we call "set in their ways"—or worse! At the other extreme are those for whom the next mountain is always to be attacked with ferocity. These are the daredevils among us. Most people fall between these two poles, and it is with them that we are concerned. Further, the "change" we address is more than minor disruption in ways of operation; we are dealing with the kinds of change that are experienced as transformational.

Reactions to Change

The typical employee spends at least eight hours a day at the workplace, doing, in general, fairly regular and predictable tasks. Indeed, most companies have orientation programs that emphasize the company "culture," which implies some stability. Employees usually have some sort of job description, performance appraisals that are linked to that description, and job planning and reviews, all of which tacitly indicate that there is a quid pro quo. The employee does X, and if that is done well, on time, and so on, the employee receives Y in compensation.

In addition to this external contract is a psychological one: belonging to the organization, fitting into the work and social patterns that exist in the company. There is a political dimension here as well. For those seeking advancement in the organization there are written and unwritten "rules" of the game. "The way we do things around here" is something that career-minded employees attend to.

But what happens when the rules are changed in the middle of the game, as in the following:

> So this morning we get a memo addressed to "all staff." It says the policy of year-end cash performance bonuses is discontinued. Just like that—30 percent of my salary! And after all the long hours I've put in during the last months.

What would we suppose this accountant might feel? In fact, one could argue that almost any reaction she has is normal and "justifiable." She has experienced a trauma.

But the "loss" a change implies need not be as definitive as the bonus situation above. A loss can be imaginary, as, for example, what a change in job description may entail. This may be a perceived loss in turf, a perceived diminution in status, in identity, or self-meaning in general. Everything that someone has built is con-

EXHIBIT 1   Frameworks to Explain Reactions to Change

Transition Stages	Change Stages (Risk Taking)
1. *Ending phase*—Letting go of the previous situation (disengagement, disidentification, disenchantment).	1. *Shock*—Perceived threat, immobilization, no risk taking.
2. *Neutral zone*—Completing endings and building energy for beginnings (disorientation, disintegration, discovery).	2. *Defensive retreat*—Anger, holding on, risking still unsafe.
3. *New beginnings*—New possibilities or alignment with a vision.	3. *Acknowledgment*—Mourning, letting go, growing potential for risk taking.
	4. *Adaptation and change*—Comfort with change, energy for risk taking.

sidered threatened: even if the change is a promotion people can react with anxiety; in fact, people often try to perform the new job and the old one simultaneously so as not to experience the (imaginary) loss.

For most people, the negative reaction to change is related to *control*—over their influence, their surroundings, their source of pride, how they have grown accustomed to living and working. When these factors appear threatened, security is in jeopardy. And considerable energy is needed to understand, absorb, and process one's reactions. Not only do I have to deal with the change per se, I have to deal with my reactions to it! Even if the change is embraced intellectually ("things were really going bad here"), immediate acceptance is not usually forthcoming. Instead, most feel fatigued; we need *time* to adapt.

The Evolution of Change Reactions

Most people, of course, do adapt to change, but not before passing through some other psychological gates. Two "maps" (below) describe the complex psychological process of passing through difficult, often conflicting, emotions. Each of these approaches emphasizes aprogression through stages or phases,

which occurs over time and, essentially, cannot be accelerated (Exhibit 1). To speed up the process is to risk carrying unfinished psychological "baggage" from one phase to the next.

One way to think about the reaction pattern relates to a theory based on risk taking.[1] Change, they assert, requires people to perform or perceive in unfamiliar ways, which implies taking risks, particularly those associated with self-esteem—loss of face, appearing incompetent, seemingly unable or unwilling to learn, and so on. People move from discomfort with risks to acceptance, in four stages: shock, defensive retreat, acknowledgment, adaptation and change. This can be likened to bereavement reactions.

In the *shock* phase, one is threatened by anticipated change, even denying its existence: "This isn't happening." The psychological shock resembles the physiological—people become immobilized and "shut down" to protect themselves; yet at the same time, they deny the situation is occurring. As a result of this conflict, productivity is understandably low: people

---

[1] Harry Woodward and Steve Bucholz, *Aftershock* (New York: John Wiley & Sons, 1987).

feel unsafe, timid, and unable to take action, much less risks.

We move from shock to *defensive retreat* (i.e., we get mad). We simultaneously lash out at what has been done to us and hold on to accustomed ways of doing things. Thus, we are both keeping a grip on the past while decrying the fact that it's changed. This conflict also precludes taking risks, for we are uncomfortable and feel unsafe.

Eventually, we cease denying the fact of change, we acknowledge that we have lost something, and we mourn. The psychological dynamics include both grief and liberation. Thus, one can feel like a pawn in a game while being able to take some distance from the game, viewing it with some objectivity. At this point, experimenting with taking risks becomes possible; we begin exploring the pros and cons of the new situation. Each "risk" that succeeds builds confidence, and we are ready for the final "gate."

Ideally, most people *adapt and change* themselves. The change becomes internalized, we move on, and help others to do so; we see ourselves "before and after" the change; and, even if it's a grudging acknowledgment, we consider the change "all for the best." In some cases, people actively advocate what they recently denied.

Another approach to how people come to terms with change also is based on phases, in this case three: letting go, existing in a neutral zone, making new beginnings.[2]

Ending and letting go means relinquishing the old prechange situation, a process

that involves dramatic emotions: pain, confusion, and terror. That is, we first experience a sharp break with what has been taken for granted; included in this pain is a loss of the identity we had invested in the old situation. This situational "unplugging" and loss of identity lead to a sense of disenchantment—things fail to make sense. People feel deceived, betrayed.

Such feelings lead into a second psychological phase called a *neutral zone:* a "wilderness that lies between the past reality and the one that . . . is just around the corner." People feel adrift and confused; the previous orientation no longer exists, yet the new one seems unclear. In this period of "full of nothing," we grow increasingly unproductive and ineffective. But psychologically, the neutral period is essentially for mustering the energy to go on. It is the time between ending something and beginning something else. When someone is "lost enough to find oneself" and when the past becomes put in perspective, the emotions have been experienced and dealt with and put aside—then there is "mental room" to reorient and discover the new. The third phase is the seeking out of new possibilities: *beginning* to align our actions with the change.

Organizations often are tempted to push people into the "beginning" phase, not recognizing—or not accepting — the need to complete the psychological work (and it *is* work) of the two previous phases. But jumping into a flurry of "beginning-type" activity—planning, pep rallies, firing up the troops—only increases people's discomfort of change. Only if sufficient attention had been paid to letting go and dwelling in the neutral zone—only if the old has been properly buried—can the new appear. People then can draw from the past and not be mired in it; they can be

---

[2] William Bridges, "Managing Organizational Transitions," *Organizational Dynamics*, Summer 1986, pp. 24–33.

eager to embrace new possibilities.

These basically optimistic theories about how people eventually embrace change, while psychologically accurate, are somewhat simplistic. Most people will work through the emotional phases they delineate; some will do so more quickly than others. But others will get stuck, often in the first stages, which encompass the most keen and jagged emotions. The catch-all word "resistance" is used to describe these people: they are destructive (internally or even externally), and they won't move forward.

People get stuck for two basic—and obvious—reasons: "change" is not some monolithic event that has neat and tidy beginnings and ends; and people's subjective experiences of change vary considerably as a result of individual circumstance.

Thus, frameworks that presume periods of psychological sorting out while the change is being digested are somewhat flimsy in helping us deal with multiple changes. How are we to be in "defensive retreat" with one change, in the "neutral zone" with another, while adapting to a third? If these changes are also rapid-fire, a fairly common situation in these unheaving days in the political and economic arenas, it becomes clearer why some people "resist." For example, changes involving significant personal redirection, like job restructuring, often are accompanied by changes in a firm's ownership, leadership, and policies. All coming at once (or in rapid sequence), they can severely stress or even undo chief anchor points of meaning. These affect the previously agreed-upon ways of doing one's work, one's affiliations, skills, and self-concept. When these anchor points come under siege, most of us are likely to be immobilized and even obdurate. In a worst-case scenario, the individual going through this siege at the office is simultaneously experiencing major change at home, a divorce, for example.

People do not always easily pass through the phases described above because, notwithstanding the psychological validity of the progression of emotions, not everyone interprets "change" in the same way; thus, experiences of "change" vary. Other personality issues must be considered as well. People who are fragile emotionally will have much greater difficulty swimming through feelings of loss; they may continually see themselves as victims. Such obscuring emotions will hinder their ability to move on. Instead, they may cycle back to shock-like or defensive behavior, never breaking out of the early phases.

Organizational Responses

As indicated, many firms attempt to accelerate employees' adaptation to change, for understandable reasons. Employees who are preoccupied with their internal processes are less likely to be fully productive; indeed, as the description of patterns of change reveal, people in the early phases of reacting to change often are unable to do much at all. Thus, it makes good "business sense" to help people cope, with a minimum of dysfunctional consequences.

Unfortunately, from the recipient's perspective, such good intentions often are considered as controlling, even autocratic. If the change is hyped too much—too many pep rallies, too many "it's really good for you and all for the best"—those of us who feel no such thing can grow increasingly isolated and resentful. How can they say everything is rosy when I feel so miserable?

Consider the following list of typical advice presented, in one form or another, for dealing with change:

- Keep your cool in dealing with others.
- Handle pressure smoothly and effectively.
- Respond nondefensively when others disagree with you.
- Develop creative and innovative solutions to problems.
- Be willing to take risks and try out new ideas.
- Be willing to adjust priorities to changing conditions.
- Demonstrate enthusiasm for and commitment to long-term goals.
- Be open and candid when dealing with others.
- Participate actively in the change process.
- Make clear-cut decisions as needed.

Seemingly straightforward and commonsensical, this advice is eminently rational and usually presented in good faith. But as we now understand, such directives —for that is what they are—fail to take into account that psychological needs must be addressed. Most people are aware of the wisdom of taking responsibility for dealing with change themselves; they recognize the importance of the "right attitude." Americans in particular pride themselves on pioneer spirit, challenges, adventure—the can-do philosophy.

It appears, however, that most people do not want this shoved down their throats, especially when they are first grappling with the magnitude, or their perception of it, of a change's effect on them. Rather, most of us prefer some empathy, some understanding of what we are experiencing—not just advice for getting on with it.

The next two sections of this case explore ways in which people facing change can help themselves experience the change less painfully, and some guidelines their managers can use to help their employees (and themselves) cope with difficult parts of the change process. While these ideas are simple, even commonplace, they look at the experience of change in it totality; they acknowledge that "change" is not merely doing A on Monday and B on Tuesday. There is a transition between the two, and if that is ignored—by either the recipient or those instituting the change—full adaptation to, and embracing of, the change itself is jeopardized.

Individual Coping with Change

Given the strong emotional responses that most of us feel at the onset of a change—anger, depression, shock—and that often these are "unacceptable" emotions either to ourselves or at the workplace, we need to console ourselves that these are indeed natural reactions. People need to give themselves permission to feel what they are feeling; change always implies a loss of some kind, and that must be mourned: a job, colleagues, a role, even one's identity as it has been wrapped up in the prechange situation. Accepting and focusing on our negative reactions is not the same as wallowing in them, of course.

It has already been pointed out that dealing with change takes energy. Even more energy is required in fighting negative reactions. Thus, to accept, at the outset, that strong emotions are part and parcel of the change process is at least to avoid wasting some energy; we are better able to reduce the added strain of constantly keeping feelings at bay. In fact, one's strength is increased by letting what is natural take its course.

A corollary to accepting strong reactions to change is patience—that time is needed to come to grips with a situation, and that moving through various constellations of emotions is not done in an instant. Whereas most people experience the range of emotions described earlier, there is no timeclock that works for everyone. The adaptation process involves an unsettled and ambiguous period for most of us,[3] and, if we accept that, at the least we can function superficially—if not at our peak—until we strengthen and begin to act more meaningfully.

A major reaction to change is a feeling of losing control; what was assumed to be the norm now isn't, and we are in an unknown land. A valuable antidote to feeling powerless is to establish a sense of personal control in other areas of our lives, and avoid as much as possible taking on other efforts that sap energy. Thus, if one accepts that adapting to change will be arduous, one husbands one's resources. This means maintaining our physical well-being and nourishing our psyches.

It is no coincidence that a new field called "managing stress" has arisen during a period of major and pervasive organizational restructuring. And the recommendations that practitioners in this area make, while simple, are useful: get enough sleep; pay attention to diet and exercise; take occasional breaks at the office; relax with friends; engage in hobbies. Making such efforts is not escapism or distracting oneself from "reality."

Rather, they are ways of exerting control over one's life during a period of uncertainty.

Accepting strong emotions and acknowledging the importance of patience in dealing with change are vital; but so is developing a sense of objectivity about what is happening. We do have choices in how we perceive change, and we are able to develop the capacity to see benefits, not just losses, in new situations. Coming to accept and adapt to change is in fact a process of balancing; what have I lost, what am I gaining? Different from the "look on the bright side" exhortations frequently espoused by those who ignore the powerful emotions a change can evoke inventorying personal losses and gains is a real step toward gathering the strength to move on.

Related to such inventorying is "diversified emotional investing." The individual balances the emotional investment in essential work-related anchor points of meaning—how work is done, affiliations, skills, self-concept in relation to the work—with emotional investments in other areas of life—family, friends, civic, religious activities. Thus, when one or more anchor points at the workplace is threatened, the person can remain steadier through the transition to adaptation.

Admittedly, such inventorying and "diversified emotional investing" are difficult when in the throes of strong emotions. Perhaps the best mechanism for coping with change, then, is anticipating it. No one escapes the effects of change, in the workplace or elsewhere; and those who recognize that its impact will be powerful, that the process of adaptation and change takes time, and that we all have other sources of strength, are in much better shape than those who delude themselves into thinking "it can never happen to me."

---

[3] Leonard Greenhalgh and Todd Jick, "Survivor Sense Making and Reactions to Organizational Decline," *Management Communications Quarterly* 2, no. 3 (February 1989), pp. 305–27.

EXHIBIT 2   Strategies for Coping with Change

Individuals	*Managers*
1. *Accepting feelings as natural:* Permission to feel and mourn. Taking time to work through feelings. Tolerating ambiguity.	1. *Rethinking resistance:* As natural as self-protection. As a positive step toward change. As energy to work with. As information critical to the change process. As other than a roadblock.
2. *Managing stress:* Maintaining physical well-being. Seeking information about the change. Limiting extraneous stressors. Taking regular breaks. Seeking support.	2. *Giving first aid:* Accepting emotions. Listening. Providing safety. Marking endings. Providing resources and support.

3. *Exercising responsibility:*
Identifying options and gains.
Learning from losses.
Participating in the change.
Inventorying strengths.
Learning new skills.
Diversifying emotional investing.
	3. *Creating capability for change:*
	Making organizational
	    support of risks clear.
	Continuing safety net.
	Emphasizing continuities,
	    gains of change.
	Helping employees explore
	    risks, options.
	Suspending judgment.
	Involving people in
	    decision making.
	Teamwork.
	Providing opportunities
	    for individual growth.

Managing the Recipients of Change

Obviously, the manager who has experienced change personally is potentially more effective in helping others work through their adaptation processes. But beyond recalling their own experiences, managers should consider three areas that are essential for easing their employees' difficulties: rethinking resistance, giving "first aid," and creating capability for change. (See Exhibit 2)

Rethinking Resistance

Resistance to change, as mentioned earlier, is a catch-all phrase; it describes anyone who doesn't change as fast as we do, as well as people who seemingly refuse to budge. As such, resistance per se is considered an obstacle, something to be overcome at all costs. Those labeled resistant are deemed people with poor attitudes, lacking in team spirit. Not surprisingly, treating "resistance" this way serves only to intensify real resistance, thereby thwarting or at least sidetracking possibilities of change.

As the discussion of patterns of change has revealed, however, resistance is a part of the natural process of adapting to change; it is a normal response of those who have a strong vested interest in maintaining their perception of the current state and guarding themselves against loss. Why should I give up what has successfully made meaning for me? What do I get in its place? Resistance, at the outset of the change process, is far more complicated than "I won't." It is much more of a painful "why should I?"

When resistance is considered a natural reaction, part of a process, it can thus be seen as a first step toward adaptation. At the very minimum, resistance denotes energy—energy that can be worked with and redirected. The strength of resistance, moreover, indicates the degree to which change has touched on something valuable to individuals and the organization. Discovering what that valuable something is can be of important use in fashioning the change effort organizationally. One theorist puts it this way:

> First, they ["resistors"] are the ones most apt to perceive and point out real threats, if such exist, to the well-being of the system which may be the unanticipated consequences of projected changes.
>
> Second, they are especially apt to react against any change that might reduce the integrity of the system.
>
> Third, they are sensitive to any indication that those seeking to produce change fail to understand or identify with the core values of the system they seek to influence.

Because "resistance to change" is such an amorphous phrase, many attitudes labeled resistant are not that at all. Depending on the change involved, people may be required to learn new and difficult skills, for example. Their frustration in doing so may cause them to nay-say the effort. Calling the nay-saying resistance is a genuine error: if the effort to change is in fact being made, it should be encouraged. Further, listening to the criticism may provide clues that the training is ineffective.

There are also entirely rational reasons for resistance. By no means are all change agendas perfect, as the quote above indicates. The organization that assumes it can superimpose "change" on its employees and then labels any negative reaction "resistance" is guaranteeing that change, if it occurs at all, will hardly accomplish the purpose for which it was intended:

> One of the common mistakes made by managers when they encounter resistance is to become angry, frustrated, impatient or exasperated. . . . The problem with an emotional reaction is that it increases the probability that the resistance will intensify. . . . Remember that anger directed toward others is likely to make them afraid and angry in return.[4]

In sum, rethinking resistance to change means seeing it as a normal part of adaptation, something most of us do to protect our self-integrity. It is a potential source of energy, as well as information about the change effort and direction. Instead of assuming that all "resistance" is an obstacle, managers should look carefully to see if real resistance is present, over time (i.e., there are always people who won't change and who will complain all the while). In general, however, going with the "resistance," not condemning it but

---

[4] Ken Hultman, *The Path of Least Resistance* (Austin, Tex.: Learning Concepts, 1979).

trying to understand its sources, motives, and possible affirmative core, can open up possibilities for realizing change. Writes one expert on the subject:

> Without it [resistance], we are skeptical of real change occurring. Without real questioning, skepticism, and even outright resistance, it is unlikely that the organization will successfully move on to the productive stage of learning how to make the new structure effective and useful.[5]

Giving "First Aid"

Many managers find that addressing straightforward technical issues in the change effort—such as the new department layout, who gets what training—iscomparatively easy. But consciously or not, they ignore the more complex and often unpredictable concerns of people being changed. The rationale can be a business one: we don't have time for that, we're here to make money. Or it can be emotional: I don't want to get involved in messy feelings; that's not my job.

For whatever reason, not allowing employees opportunities to vent feelings is overlooking a powerfully effective coping strategy. Administering emotional first aid, particularly in the early and most difficult stages of change, validates recipients in their terms and doesn't leave them in an emotional pressure cooker. We have already seen that a major coping mechanism for the individual is acknowledging that his or her reactions are natural; when this is combined with external validation, the result is profoundly effective. Indeed when management provides opportunity for grievances and frustrations to be aired

constructively, employee bitterness and frustration may be diminished.

As the above implies, first aid, in its most powerful form, is simply listening. Nonjudgmental listening. The dominant attitude of the nonjudgmental listener is respect for what the individual is experiencing; this in turn is predicated on accepting that everyone needs time to absorb change, and that complicated and even contradictory emotions belong to the early stage of the process.

First aid also means providing safety by delineating expectations and establishing informal and formal rewards for those experiencing change. It also involves identifying and clarifying what is not changing—and probing to uncover why. Where do people feel they will be taking the biggest risks? It is in these areas, as we have seen, that the most powerful concerns—and resistance—lie.

Finally, first aid means providing resources to help people through their greatest difficulties—ongoing information about the change, support, and counseling where needed, particularly forums in which employees can help each other. These resources are especially critical when someone has bid farewell to the old but has yet to become attached to the new.

Listening, accepting, and supporting may seem like simple, almost basic, advice for the manager of changees. Unfortunately, all too often they are missing from the manager's toolkit for change. Such essential human interaction tends to get lost in the maze of plans, committees, and reports typically accompanying major change efforts. For the recipients to adapt fully to their new circumstances requires more than the passive response of managers, however; managers need to help changees become more capable of change.

---

[5] Ibid.

Creating the Capability for Change

Creating the capability for change is undertaken after the "bleeding" has stopped and the need for first aid lessens. The manager's dual task is to help people move into the current change and encourage them to feel confident about accepting subsequent changes.

Providing safety and rewards, a part of first aid, also is essential to creating a climate in which people will take risks. (This is similar to what good parenting is all about!) In the workplace, managers who expect their employees to change— and particularly if the change is in fact multiple changes—need to make clear how the organization is willing to support their efforts. What differentiates this effort from first aid is its continuance. First aid is *first;* it is the effort that eases the pain, but it does not cure the disease much less help prevent its occurrence.

Safety in creating the capability for change goes deeper into risk taking. Perhaps a nonevaluative period can be declared, one in which income, rank or other aspects of job security are put on hold, as employees test the waters. Having employees evaluate themselves vis-à-vis the change is another approach; in all cases, the more involvement people have in the changes that surround them the better. It is a fundamental tenet of participative management that employees are more likely to support what they help create. Cooperation, negotiation, and compromise are critical to the implementation of any change; it is difficult to *get* cooperation, negotiation, and compromise from people who are effectively ordered to change, never listened to or supported, and then faulted if they fail to change as expected.

Rewards, in creating capabilities for change, often are implicit. Consider the popularity of programs like Outward Bound. The "rewards" in these arenas are the pride of accomplishment and the cheers from one's co-participants. Encouraging employees to take similarly difficult, albeit in many cases psychological, risks means creating environments in which they can shine, not necessarily the standard rewards of money and promotion. Creative managers who truly wish their employees to grow, who recognize the difficulties inherent in the challenge of change, and who support efforts to make change, are patient along the way; their reward, in turn, is the trust of their employees—and a potentially more flexible organization.

Is Continuous Change "Good" for Us?

> I hear change is coming, and it no longer sends shivers up my spine. I have to trust it won't clobber me. There's not really anything I can do but learn to survive and help others through it.

This case has treated "change" and its effects on employees as a first-time event: the company, having done its thing for about 50 years, suddenly throws the cards in the air and everyone picks up from there. It is, of course, increasingly rare to find such situations. Most people are more or less continually facing major changes in their work environments, from the rapid-fire of new technology and processes to new owners, perhaps foreign, to an increasing emphasis on change itself as essential. The ability to change rapidly and frequently seems to be a critical mechanism for survival, many argue.

Obviously, an organization that encourages constant change hardly has the time to do first aid, and all the rest; everyone is moving around, and no one—neither the changee nor the manager—has time to examine the psychological ramifications, much less get into support. Two questions need answering in the face of such constant change: Does experience with change help people cope with it better? What are the longer-term implications of constant change for individuals and organizations?

Some evidence exists that an "inoculation effect" takes hold after confronting continuous change; people do react to the same situation, when it recurs, differently. Hurricane victims, for example, exhibit a "confidence curve" as a result of repeated experiences with the phenomenon. Those who have been through a hurricane once are most stressed; they become hyperwatchful and overprepare on even the faintest signal of a hurricane warning. They become gun-shy to the prospect of another similar event. In contrast, those who have had repeated exposure to hurricanes come to view the approach of an impending storm with more equanimity.

If this analogy is transferable, then recipients—in the face of continuous change—may exhibit a learning curve. At first, they will be hypersensitive but later will become more "matter of fact" and psychologically more ready for change. However, we haven't enough evidence yet to be certain of this. And some fear that the opposite effects could occur, instead, whereby recipients will become more vulnerable, more resistant, and less equipped as more and more change unfolds. More-over, if someone experiences constant change, has she or he ever completely dealt with the first one completely?

Perhaps the answer revolves around expectations. In some companies today, people are routinely moved in and out of projects and positions: it is the nature of the work requirements in that organization. But this is understood by all from the beginning. As such, employees harbor the expectation that there will be constant change. Indeed, some are attracted to the company because of that. If people know at the outset that frequent change, in positions, responsibilities, and the like, is in fact their job, we can suppose that a kind of self-selection takes place; those who wish that kind of experience will seek out jobs in the company, and, in turn, the company will hire those who can accept that kind of mobility. With more and more companies now exhibiting continuous change, people may come to expect it and be more inured to it.

The notion of continuous change as the ideal organizational state is fairly recent, so many of its effects in the long term on individuals within such environments are not known precisely. But we all—change agents and change recipients—must develop the strength and the capability to cope with the emotions and the demands that come with this new territory. The individual and the organization share the responsibility and obligation. When both make "good faith efforts," the results can be buoying.

CASE

RICK MILLER (A)

The spring of 1970 marked the beginning of a career of change and challenge for Richard (Rick) W. Miller. After two years at Harvard Business School, Miller now faced the reality of finding a job that satisfied his appetite for a challenging and somewhat unusual work environment. Having followed the plight of Penn Central Railroad, an ailing company on the brink of bankruptcy, Miller felt he might find an interesting challenge there. He wrote a letter to the CFO of Penn Central, traveled to Philadelphia to meet the people of the firm, and later received an offer to work for the troubled railroad. Miller accepted this job offer to work on a special financial projects team for $19,000 a year, the lowest he received; other firms offered him up to $35,000 a year, or more.

Penn Central

Deliberately choosing risk and uncertainty, Miller recalled his selection of Penn Central with affection, believing that it turned out to be a fantastic experience: "It was a perfect time for me to take risk. I was still growing and I felt I wanted to be in a situation where maybe I could make a difference, no matter how high the mountain was to climb."

This case was prepared by Research Associate Lori Ann Levaggi (under the direction of Professor Todd D. Jick).

In late May of 1970, Miller, his wife, and their newborn daughter moved to Philadelphia and lived in a rented apartment. After only three days on the job, Miller came home and told his wife, "Don't buy any drapes!" He said he always knew they were going into uncertainty but only after working a few days did he realize to what extreme degree. On June 21, 1970, 20 days after Miller began with Penn Central, the company filed for bankruptcy, the largest in U.S. history.

During the bankruptcy reorganization, Miller worked on corporate restructuring. He then became the in-house expert on Arvida, a real estate company in Florida of which Penn Central owned 58 percent. Miller wrote a report that explained the value of the company and stated that, if Penn Central was not going to change the operations of the business, Arvida should be sold. Penn Central's board decided that Miller should be the one to initiate the change at Arvida, and soon Miller found himself in the real estate business in Florida. Thinking back on the experience, Miller said, "If anyone had asked me earlier if I would ever be in the real estate business in Florida only a year and a half out of HBS, I would have thought they were crazy!"

In 1972, Miller moved to Florida and remained there with Arvida until 1979. He began this venture as CFO and, 18 months later, at the age of 32, Miller became a vice president of operations, eventually overseeing almost all of Arvida's real estate development and resort/hotel management operations. A new president with real estate experience was recruited, and, together, he and Miller took Arvida from breakeven point in 1972 to earnings of $30 million in 1978.

In the fall of 1978, Penn Central came out of bankruptcy. After a power struggle, Richard Dicker became chairman of the new company. In 1979, Dicker asked Miller to come back to the parent company as its CFO. Miller built a strong financial team and worked closely with Dicker on numerous acquisitions, growing Penn Central from sales of $600 million to $3.3 billion in just three years. By 1982, Penn Central had begun to attract the interest of some takeover investors, which made Miller uneasy. He felt their presence would only "complicate my life as CFO since I sensed that their values were not closely aligned with mine, as their reputations had indicated." In short, Miller did not want to take apart a company that he had just helped put together.

A Move to RCA

While Miller was still pondering the CFO spot at Penn Central, Thornton Bradshaw, newly named CEO of a troubled RCA, telephoned Miller and explained that he needed a capable, experienced CFO to help RCA out of financial trouble. In January 1982, the two men met for lunch, a meeting that lasted five hours. At its conclusion, Miller felt he understood what needed to be done at RCA and he liked Bradshaw personally. In March 1982, Miller joined RCA as its new CFO.

At the time, RCA had over $700 million of short-term commercial paper funding its operations. The firm had tried to fund itself using long-term debt a year earlier, but its ratings were downgraded and the offering was canceled. The stock price was depressed at $16 a share and the company needed cash to fulfill its short-term debt obligations. Although RCA was a larger, more established blue-chip company than was Penn Central, Miller felt he had done similar financial restructuring and organization-building before and knew what was needed.

Miller recalled his first day on the job as "challenging, to say the least." It was Monday, and Bradshaw told him that on Wednesday, only two days away, they had to make a recommendation to the board on what dividend should be declared that quarter. Bradshaw told Miller that they would meet for lunch that day, Monday, at noon, and Miller was to have his dividend recommendation ready at that time.

Miller retreated to his office, and, after a brief introduction to the people who worked for him, he immediately went to work. At the time, RCA was paying $1.80 per share as a dividend, which Miller knew was quite high for a company with negative cash flow and negative earnings. After some careful consideration, Miller chose to recommend cutting the dividend in half, to $0.90 per share. He explained: "It was more symbolic than financial, since the firm had to show the creditors that it was serious about conserving cash and, at the same time, show the equity markets that they were important to RCA in the future." The board approved the recommendation.

During the next three years, Miller replaced much of RCA's financial organization, and he worked very closely with Bradshaw. The two also disposed of some large nonstrategic businesses that RCA had bought over the years and refocused the company's resources on its strategic elements, namely electronics, communications, and entertainment.

In early 1985, Robert Frederick, who was brought in as president in late 1982, became the new CEO of RCA, as Bradshaw was stepping down. Both Frederick and Bradshaw wanted Miller to get some line management experience, for this was the only area of the organization where Miller had not spent any time. Miller himself felt that this operating experience was crucial, because he knew that he could be the next CEO of RCA but needed this "notch on his belt" to secure the position. In the spring of 1985, Miller took an operating job, executive vice president–Consumer Products and Entertainment, responsible for almost $4 billion of RCA's $10 billion in sales. By this time, RCA's stock price had risen to $50 a share.

The Surprise

As 1985 came to a close, Miller sensed that something strange was happening at the firm; the staff officers he had worked with for over three years were avoiding him. When Miller asked what was going on, one individual replied, "I can't tell you." Miller immediately called Bradshaw, who told him that the firm was having discussions with General Electric about the possibility of a sale, but nothing had been decided yet. Miller offered to get involved, but he was never given the opportunity. The following day the board met and decided to finalize a deal that took Miller by surprise.

In late December of 1985, RCA announced that it was being sold to the General Electric Company, for $6.4 billion, in the largest merger of non-oil companies in history. In his position as a line manager, Miller was not asked to participate in the negotiations. Miller described his initial reaction to the news as shocked. He elaborated:

> I was furious. It was awful; I was bitter and very upset. I felt that I had been betrayed. I felt there wasn't any need for this to happen—I knew the finances of the company as well as anyone, and we had recently fended off some potential suitors. Our profits were at an all-time high, as was our stock price. I just never bought the idea that RCA had to be sold.

Miller admitted, however, that RCA was not without its problems, especially in its consumer electronics division. The future of that difficult competitive business remained to be seen, but Miller thought that RCA was working toward improving those prospects. In Miller's opinion, he was working hard to put a good management team in place, the business generated cash for the first time in years and helped to raise the stock price steadily. And then, without notice or reason, as Miller put it, "the company got sold."

Just before the board had voted to sell the firm, Bradshaw called a meeting with top management to tell them what was about to happen. Everyone was stunned at the news. Miller, having some advance warning, was the only one to speak up, posing two questions for Bradshaw and Frederick: "How many people from outside the GE company in mid-career have gone on to hold high positions in the GE company?" Miller challenged, and then continued angrily, "If you are going to sell the company, why are you selling it too cheaply?" In a flood of emotion, Miller then proposed: "If this is what you really want, then I can sell it for more money!"

More tactical than serious about his second remark, Miller was stalling. He felt that he needed time to convey any glimmer of a hope to stop the sale process, not to find a better deal. Miller's questions were answered, but not sufficiently in his opinion. Bradshaw said that he had assurance from Jack Welch, the CEO of GE, that RCA people would be taken care of and that contracts would be designed to give them further protection. The answer to the second question was that the investment bankers involved in the deal said that they were willing to give a fairness opinion to RCA's directors saying it was a fair price. With that, the meeting was over and the deal was done.

To Stay or Not To Stay

Miller now had to face his own decision about remaining at the company under GE. Although on paper he looked like quite an adaptable person, having been at different companies in his career, he had some old-fashioned values. Miller said, "I usually develop a great sense of pride and loyalty to the institution that I am a part of. I have to, that is my psyche." He further remarked:

> I don't consider myself to be a hired gun or a vagabond that moves from situation to situation without any emotional attachment. I am not like a bounty hunter who does what needs to be done and collects for it. I have developed a great emotional attachment to the businesses and the people that I have been a part of. At RCA, I felt we had resurrected a great old American name and institution and I was looking forward to continuing it.

A Meeting of the Minds

In late January of 1986, RCA held its last annual management meeting in Boca Raton, Florida. GE's chairman, Jack Welch, and the four top people at GE were also invited. Miller had never met Welch and during the course of the meeting, Welch singled him out and asked him to sit at his table for dinner that night. Miller accepted.

At dinner, the conversation between Miller and Welch lasted about two hours. Miller asked Welch "if theoretically he knew that most mergers don't work and all big mergers don't work." Relating stories from his past, Miller recalled his days at Penn Central where the concept of "red hats" and "green hats"—fiercely competing cultures after a merger—became all too apparent to him. The two talked candidly about potential weakness in the GE strategy and organization. Miller pointed out that, if GE was number one or number two in each of its industries, that the firm might not teach its people how to deal with serious business adversity. Miller and Welch got along well and met again later that month in New York to further discuss each other's business philosophy and strategy. Miller stated: "I liked Welch. I thought he was an outstanding leader and the best CEO I had ever seen. He and I didn't agree on everything, but I really respected the guy."

A New Role for Miller?

As mid-year 1986 approached, Miller and Welch discussed potential roles that Miller might play in GE. Since the announced sale of RCA six months earlier, Miller had devoted all of his time to a smooth transition of his people and their operations into the GE organization. Miller felt a strong commitment to his people. Miller revealed that, in January 1986, he would "have bet his kids" that he would not go to work for General Electric; he had never said this to anyone because he felt a strong obligation that his people should make their own choice, as he, too, would eventually have to do.

Miller, therefore, resolved to encourage his team to keep working hard until the merger was completed by June of 1986, because at that time new jobs would be available to them. Instructing his people not to make emotional decisions about their future, Miller encouraged them to contain their bitterness and anger so these feelings would not adversely affect their ability to perform or to make wise decisions. Miller felt that, if he allowed people to mentally quit or take a holiday, they would not have a chance of surviving in the new organization, because a new owner would have every right and reason to replace them quickly and get on with running the business. Miller further explained that "some companies get turned on and some companies get turned off" at tough times like these. Those that "turn off," he said, leave their people with no choices; those that "turn on," and keep showing how good they are, at least leave their people with an option later, whether to continue there or to go somewhere else.

Moreover, Miller chose the turn-on route for his people from RCA and, thus, sought to be a positive role model for them. He explained that, in a merger, people are disappointed, hurt, and don't know how to behave. They, therefore, will look to their leader, and, "if he is jumping ship or saying the hell with it, then the place falls apart." However, if the leader acknowledges feelings openly and does not try to pretend there is no disappointment, Miller believed, the people will follow that lead. Based on that philosophy, Miller remained at the new firm helping his people adjust smoothly to their new environment.

Although signing his people up for the "GE team," Miller told Welch that he was not sure he wanted to join GE. Miller explained that he was 45 years old and had been on his way to running a major U.S. corporation at RCA and he doubted he could ever run GE. He felt maybe he

should get on with his career elsewhere. Miller would finish helping GE with the transition and move on. Welch objected to Miller's conclusion. He told Miller that he wanted him to stay at GE and the two discussed several job options.

In late June, Welch asked Miller to run the combined firm's consumer electronics business. The two had discussed this option before, but Miller felt that GE was not really committed to the business and consumer electronics would be an orphan. Miller expressed that he did not want to run what was perceived as an unwanted appendage of the GE company.

Nevertheless, Welch made Miller an offer that was impossible to refuse. Miller would report directly to him, the chairman, and would have an office on the same floor, right down the hall. Welch explained that he wanted Miller to establish a base of operations at GE headquarters in Fairfield, Connecticut, and he wanted him to get exposure to the entire GE company. By this time, Miller trusted Welch and liked the offer, so he accepted it.

Miller's Charge

As head of the consumer electronics business, Miller had the job of merging RCA's $2.2 billion operation with GE's $1.0 billion operation, and creating both a new organization and strategy for the new unit. According to Miller, "Welch gave me carte blanche to recruit talent from all over the GE company for the consumer electronics business." Miller did just that by putting a new team in place, with strong people from many areas of GE closing factories, and moving forward with a business plan for 1987.

Backed by Welch's clout, Miller cut both manufacturing and administrative costs drastically to boost profits. He compressed the management layers in the TV factories from nine to five and planned to reduce the number of salaried employees by one fourth and close the consumer electronics business in up to 8 of the 23 plants—all by 1988. During the first half of 1987, GE spent $20 million to modernize the production lines in RCA's former flagship plant in Bloomington, Indiana, to show its commitment to its new division.

According to Miller, Welch lived up to all of his promises throughout the year. Miller received a broad exposure to GE, because he was involved in much more than the consumer electronics business. He liked being a Welch confidante and respected business partner and enjoyed the freedom and responsibility he possessed to do his job. "Consumer electronics was my business, no doubt about it," Miller had said.

Welch had publicly stated that GE would give the consumer electronics business two to three years to make its mark at GE by earning a 15 percent ROI or more annually, based on an estimated $1 billion of GE's assets in the business. However, consumer electronics was not a part of the mainstream business of GE. Before the RCA acquisition, GE had failed on its own in the consumer electronics industry and had moved the business out of the three strategic circles of GE, meaning that it must be fixed or sold quickly. Miller, a senior vice president of the GE company by now, was happy with his freedom to do his job and to learn about the GE company. He recalled, "I think I was earning my stripes at the GE company. Who knows where it was leading me, but I was traveling on a path I was comfortable with!" By the end of the second quarter of 1987, GE reported that its earnings had risen 16 percent because of

its 1986 RCA acquisition and strong results from other businesses.

Still Another Change in Ownership?

In late June 1987, Welch returned from a two-week trip to Europe, where he had visited Alain Gomez, the chairman and CEO of Thomson S.A., the French government-owned electronics company. Upon his return, Welch entered Miller's office in Fairfield, on a Thursday morning, closed the door and sat down. Welch's almost sorrowful glance across his desk caused Miller's mind to race. "What could he have to say now?" Miller wondered to himself. "Our division did so well last quarter, and it has only been established for nine months!" There was a long, hollow silence. Welch than began, "Rick, I've got a bomb for you. I know I've given you a few before, but this is the biggest."

Welch related that he had a conversation with Gomez, Thomson's chairman, about trying to acquire its medical operations. Unexpectedly, for Welch, Gomez said that he would like to trade for GE–RCA's consumer electronics business and he pressed the issue with enthusiasm. Welch became intrigued and told Gomez he would think about it, giving him some encouragement regarding the possibility of a deal being worked out.

After a brief pause to allow Miller to digest the news, Welch went on to say that he wanted to tell Miller as soon as possible about this important development. As Welch continued talking about his next scheduled meeting with Gomez and other details, Miller was only half listening. He knew that he would have to respond to Welch in a few minutes, and his prior similar experiences told him the importance of his immediate response in determining the future course of events and his involvement.

Miller's Reaction

While Welch talked, Miller's mind raced ahead. In some ways he was numb, but many thoughts ran through his head:

> I haven't even had the chance to prove myself at GE and Jack, you went ahead and sold me and my division just when we were turning the corner! How could you do that to me? But how can I be angry at Welch for being untrue to me when I think of how things happened at RCA? There, no one came to talk to me and the deal was done behind my back! At least Welch had the decency to tell me right to my face and early in the process!
>
> I wonder what I would have done if I were in Welch's shoes ... maybe I would have done the same thing. GE never really wanted a consumer electronics division, given the intensity of foreign competition in the industry; it might just drain their profits. Strategically, I guess the deal with Thomson makes sense. ... But he told me I had two to three years to prove myself, and it has only been nine months! Maybe this is just a case where an offer too good to refuse came along. ... I know Welch was not out peddling the business which I have tried so hard to build. ... Welch is honest and forthcoming. ... I really don't think he went into Gomez's office asking him if he'd like to buy the consumer electronics business. It all seems so sudden. ... I can't believe this is happening to me again.
>
> If the deal goes through, where would I go? What will I tell my people, whom I've spent so much time encouraging and training to be the best consumer electronics business in America, not in France! How could I get them excited about working for the French

government when I am quite uncomfortable with the idea myself? Part of me feels it is important to maintain my old-fashioned values and work to make a small contribution to the improvement of U.S. competitiveness ... that is what I have always tried to do. ... How does Thomson fit into that philosophy? I don't even speak French. I don't even know the French national anthem! ... But if Thomson buys us, we will still be making American products, employing American workers and managers, and using American brands ... but answering to the French government? Yet, I guess all that would really change is ownership, mostly capital ... so maybe I could decide to join Thomson ... or perhaps I should wait.

> But what about my people? I cannot wait to handle them. ... How should they be involved if the deal becomes a reality? I know how hard it is being a part of a business that is sold to another company ... you can get sucked into the negotiations and it is an awful position to be in ... you constantly ask yourself, "Whose side am I on? Do I work for the new owner and against the GE company ... or do I work for the GE company, my old loyal partner and against the new owner, and with what risks?" I have seen too many deals before where the people who are being sold get involved and many relationships are damaged. ... I can't let that happen here. ... I have a responsibility to keep my people protected now and for the future.

The Personal Decision

After Welch had talked for about 20 minutes, Miller gathered his thoughts and began:

> I am disappointed, Jack. I would have liked to have had the chance to prove myself with consumer electronics at

GE, although I don't know how it would have all played out. If I could sit here today and guarantee that I was going to make this into a real business, that truly deserved to be a part of the GE company, I would try hard to talk you out of the sale. But I cannot guarantee you that, which doesn't mean I think we are going to fail; but you know as well as I do how tough the business is. I cannot be sure we have a winner, so I can't tell you not to do this.

Miller stopped to gather his additional thoughts and then proceeded:

I see my obligations as twofold. First, I'll help you do the deal. I think you have reached a logical, strategic decision for GE and I will help you get the deal done. Second, I am going to take care of my people. I have an obligation to them. I have recruited many of them, from other parts of the GE company; people took career risks and I am not going to let them get run off the plantation. They are good managers. I want to work with you and Thomson to put things in place to protect my people.

In accepting Miller's proposal, Welch asked what Miller personally planned to do. Miller replied, "I make no promises. I do not believe in shotgun weddings and I'll decide later what I am going to do. That decision is just between you and me." After the two agreed that no one in Miller's division could know anything about the deal until it was finalized, Miller bid Welch good-bye and went home.

Driving home, Miller kept thinking about what was happening:

What if the deal doesn't go through? Would I be content staying at GE yet knowing I could never run it? I liked GE . . . every company had its bad points, but I liked working there a lot. . . . I had a lot of fun. However, what if the deal does go through? Should I back away or get on board? If I get on board, I would be saying I was joining a team that I was not truly sure I wanted to join. . . . But if I jumped ship, I would be abandoning my people whom I had recruited, trained, and befriended over the last 10 months. I guess both choices have their drawbacks and trade-offs . . . but I have to decide what to do, because if it goes through, as is likely, the time is drawing near when my people will have to be told and all eyes will be on me.

Miller entered his home that night quite confused and distressed and told his wife the news. He realized that he was truly disappointed, not so much with Welch but with the circumstances that had transpired. "I am tired of being sold," he thought. "My wife and children are mad: they are tired of my getting sold, too."

CASE

RICK MILLER (B)

For the next four weeks, Miller continued to work with his people in a business-as-usual fashion. The deal with Thomson had been agreed on but not actually finalized, legally and financially. Miller struggled with his conscience daily as he tried to accept the reality of the situation and face his unsuspecting people, knowing that their organization had been sold to a foreign company.

Miller met with Gomez in France in July, before the deal was finalized. There, Miller repeated what he had said to Welch concerning his obligations and commitments, as well as his own uncertainty about his future. Although Gomez, too, wanted a stronger commitment from Miller about his future status, Miller stood his ground and replied, "I said I will stay for the transition, maybe 6, 9, or 12 months, however long it takes for a smooth transition and then we can have a chat. In the meantime, we can get to know each other." Gomez had to be satisfied with that, as he desperately needed Miller's managerial expertise, not to mention his highly talented people.

The Deal Is Finalized

By the end of July, the deal was agreed on. Thomson would receive the GE–RCA

This case was prepared by Research Associate Lori Ann Levaggi (under the direction of Professor Todd D. Jick).

Copyright © 1988 by the President and Fellows of Harvard College. Harvard Business School case 9-489-002.

division, which designed and manufactured U.S.-made televisions and sold VCRs, tape decks, and other Far East-made goods; in return, Thomson sold GE its medical equipment business and paid an estimated $800 million in cash.

GE had not yet made a public announcement of its sale of the GE–RCA division. Miller had struggled over the past four weeks to make peace with himself about how he would proceed concerning his people. As he had made explicit in his initial meeting with Welch, Miller worked to protect his people. He had spent the past two weeks negotiating contracts for the top 25 people in the consumer electronics division. The contracts guaranteed employment for two years and provided a bonus at the end of that time merely for staying with Thomson. Miller felt satisfied that this was the best and most fair arrangement he could make; he had pushed hard to obtain such benefits from both sides.

Let the Truth Be Known

On Thursday morning, July 23, 1987, the deal was finalized. Welch had phoned Miller in Indianapolis the night before. He told Miller that the deal would be announced publicly to the entire company on Friday, July 24, at 10 A.M. and that Miller should notify his top people before this time. Welch offered to help Miller in any way that he saw fit and was willing to come to Indianapolis to meet with Miller's people.

Again, Miller's mind raced as it had

when he had first heard about the negotiations with Thomson. "How will I tell my people? Will they lose all faith in me as their credible leader? What can I say to make them understand that I am on their side . . . yet I have pledged to help do the deal . . . won't they think I am betraying them?" Miller spent the day in his office pondering these questions and trying to devise a palatable solution.

READING

DOWNSIZING/SURVIVING

David O. Heenan

David O. Heenan is chairman and chief executive officer of Theo. H. Davies & Company, Ltd., Honolulu, Hawaii.

The Right Way to Downsize

As U.S. industry copes with the recession, chief executives are reintroducing the remedy of the 1980s: downsizing. In a recent survey of 250 top corporate officials, Louis Harris & Associates predicted that further cutbacks in the central staff are all but certain. The pollsters found overwhelming agreement on the need to "give serious thought to fewer levels of management to shorten decision-making time."

The taboos against "downsizing" (slashing away at the corporate staff) and "delayering" (eliminating unnecessary levels of management) have been broken permanently. So-called minimalist strategies are now "an ongoing corporate activity without regard to a company's economic performance," says Eric Greenberg, editor of the American Management Association's research reports.

He claims that a previously downsized firm is six times more likely to downsize again as the process becomes one of constant refinement.

Corporate America's shift to smaller, sleeker command centers is a story of good news/bad news. On the positive side, the minimalist approaches of the 1980s enabled the United States to fend off, at least partially, the competitive onslaught of Japan, West Germany, and other industrialized nations. These approaches have not come without substantial costs, however.

Downsizing unnerved many working Americans. For a generation raised on Kellogg's Corn Flakes and "Ozzie and Harriet," the concept of lifetime employment became a thing of the past. Fear and anxiety set in as employees sensed that traditional work values—dedication and company loyalty—no longer mattered.

A *Time*/CNN poll of Americans conducted by Yankelovich Clancy Schuman reports a sharp decline in perceptions of corporate loyalty as well as expectations

From *The Journal of Business Strategy*, September/October 1991.

of future job hopping. Among those surveyed, 57 percent said companies are less loyal to employees today than they were a decade ago, while 63 percent said workers are less loyal to their firms. Asked whether they trust their employers to keep their promises to workers, 48 percent said "only somewhat." While 60 percent of the workers said that they would prefer to stay on the job they have now, 50 percent said they expected to change jobs within the next five years.

"The most important thing to remember is that these people are going through an unbelievable culture shock," says Daniel J. Valentino, president of United Research, a New Jersey consulting firm that works on human relations issues. Culture shock, in turn, has flamed widespread resentment across the country. "The Cynical Americans," Donald C. Kanter and Philip H. Mirvis call us, in their similarly titled best-seller.

Their research reveals that one out of four members of the U.S. work force disbelieves management; less than a third described management as trustworthy; and nearly 30 percent are dissatisfied with their places of work.

"It's no fun any more—it's just a job," is a frequent complaint today. As a result of continued downsizing, America's cynical and shell-shocked workers are withdrawing their commitment from the enterprise. Looking after number one continues to take precedence. "Call it the middle-management malaise or the leaner-and-meaner blues," says *Fortune*'s Anne B. Fisher. "Managers are joining a union called 'Me-First.' "

America's integrative institutions are also losing ground. The death of compulsory military service, shrinking church membership, declining summer camp enrollments, and the rising divorce rate are but a few examples. At times, the United States seems unable to sustain, let alone build, the cultural or organizational conduits needed to synthesize an increasingly heterogeneous society. One wonders: Would "My Country, 'tis of *Me*" be more appropriate lyrics to the well-known song?

A Nation in Transition

The glib solution to the problem of coping with a business world viewed as increasingly cold, uncaring, and hypocritical is to withdraw from it. Although a segment of today's younger-to-middle-aged generation is dropping out, a more popular career choice is self-employment. "Running your own business means controlling your own destiny," says David L. Birch, president of Cognetics Inc., a Cambridge-based consulting firm.

While starting a company is rarely easy and takes great effort, it can promise greater satisfaction, flexible working conditions, and control over one's life-style. Nevertheless, U.S. industry need not suffer the hemorrhaging of talented dropouts and prospective entrepreneurs from the traditional work force.

If corporate America is to regain the hearts and minds of people, it must reestablish values of trust and caring. However, time is running out. Business's renewed preoccupation with tough-minded downsizing comes at a time when our global competitors (most notably, the Japanese) are demonstrating the power of pulling together.

Besides the challenge of foreign competition, the forces of demography also demand quick action. For one thing, America's baby boomers are hitting middle age. For the rest of the decade, most of the boomers—those born between 1946 and 1964—will move through their forties, years perfect for introspection and reexamination. Already, "fortysomething" issues are beginning to affect these aging Americans. They want to pursue new, less frantic careers. Community, family, security, and meaning are distinctly more important to them today, and this trend will continue.

The seeds of change are taking root. We are seeing the emergence of important trends that will influence our lives well into the 21st century. Life-style concerns are beginning to outweigh the drive for material success. Working to live is becoming more important than living to work. In large part, credit for this new credo goes to activist women in business.

Working women, who now account for 45 percent of the labor force, will comprise 63 percent by the end of the century. Moreover, working mothers are the fastest-growing segment of the work force. By the year 2000, the Department of Labor estimates that 84 percent of all females of child-bearing age will be working.

Men and women alike desperately want business's support in balancing corporate and human needs. Nor are these concerns likely to evaporate. "People have no choice but to bring these problems to the workplace," says Dana Friedman, co-president of the New York-based Families and Work Institute. Employers must respond or lose any hope of regaining the trust and loyalty of their workers.

Then there is the added challenge of the shrinking labor pool. Because of lower birth rates, an average of only 1.3 million people will enter the labor force every year of the decade, down from 3 million in the 1970s. The growth rate of the labor force during the 1990s is projected at only 1.2 percent—virtually half of the 2.2 percent growth rate between 1972 and 1986. By the year 2000, the Bureau of Labor Statistics predicts, there will be a shortage of 23 million workers. Hence, firms today must deal with a labor market that is no longer a buyer's market.

These demographics are revolutionizing the work force. Americans of every age, sex, and race are insisting on corporate policies that enable them to act more responsibly toward their families, friends, and the community at large and still satisfy their professional ambitions. "Balance," therefore, is the current watchword of the times.

Paternalism Redux

Enlightened companies are restyling themselves to accommodate these changes in values. They recognize that employees are attracted to their organizations because they offer them flexible employment opportunities along with meeting their personal and financial needs. Farsighted firms are drafting a new social contract that better balances work and family responsibilities.

Despite the downside of downsizing, the quest for minimalist strategies is permanent—and we should not forget it. U.S. enterprise must be fast and footloose if it is to compete in the global industrial system. "Companies want fewer obligations to their employees, not more," argues Michael J. Piore, an economist at MIT.

Working people, for their part, are equally intent on keeping their options open. Having witnessed the severe cutbacks of the 1980s, the present generation treasures its freedom and independence. "Flexibility will continue to spread, partly because people want it and partly because employers need it," says *BusinessWeek*. "We are moving irresistibly in the direction of a more and more flexible society.''

Nevertheless, employers and employees both want more stability than ever before. U.S. industry needs a well-trained semipermanent cadre of highly committed workers in order to blunt the steady advance of foreign competition. By the same token, the country's aging and shrinking work force is prepared to sacrifice some of its freedom for those employers that truly care for them, their families, and the community at large.

The challenge of the decade, therefore, is to forge a new kind of corporate culture—one that combines elements of independence (or flexibility) with those of interdependence (or community). This kind of conceptual framework might best be likened to a two-story house. The foundation or ground floor consists of collective values: egalitarianism, teamwork, participation, and caring. The second floor embodies the need for individual and organizational freedom. Corporate America's new home is the sleek, highly decentralized organization that fosters a greater sense of "family."

In our company's opinion, the cultural revolution that is unfolding is leading to a decidedly paternalistic environment, one that should not, however, be likened to the bygone era of the company town. Gone are the days when a supposedly benevolent employer could dominate every aspect of employee life—from shopping at the infamous company store to living in substandard company housing. The "neo-paternalism" of the 1990s and beyond will be less intrusive. It will redefine the proper balance between work, family, and community needs, while regaining the trust and confidence of a downsized work force.

The Upside of Downsizing

The furniture industry's two leading performers, Herman Miller, Inc., and Steelcase, Inc., are demonstrating the way to downsize with a friendly face.

Office furniture orders softened considerably during the past year as firms slashed budgets in the face of the recession and as the weakened commercial real estate market curtailed new office building construction. Rather than indiscriminately prune their staffs, Herman Miller and Steelcase turned to voluntary layoff programs to cut expenses.

According to Jacqueline Mitchell of *The Wall Street Journal*, 200 Miller employees are on voluntary leaves of up to several weeks at its Zeeland, Michigan, headquarters. Steelcase, on the other hand, asked 250 to 3,000 of its 6,500 hourly employees in nearby Grand Rapids to take up to 60 days' leave of absence at reduced pay. Both furniture makers remain convinced that targeted voluntary leaves are a better option than forced layoffs.

The actions of Herman Miller and Steelcase should come as no surprise. Words such as love, warmth, and respect are embodied in the Miller culture, and its chairman, Max DePree, is not embarrassed to use them. Workplace intimacy, he says, "directly affects our accountability and personal authenticity at the work process. And a key component of intimacy is passion.''

Passion and soul are critical values to DePree. He has little time for the hordes of antiseptic analysts who have trimmed corporate America to the bone. "Managers who have no beliefs but only understand methodology and quantification are modern-day eunuchs,'' he contends.

"They can never engender competence or confidence."

Always the philosopher, the 66-year-old DePree proves that compassionate cutbacks are possible. "If every company in America were managed like Herman Miller, we would not be concerned with the Japanese right now," argues the University of Southern California's James O'Toole, author of *Vanguard Management*.

Neopaternalism, Steelcase-style, means treating employees as extended family and recognizing their need for external support even in tough times. "We have families of products, families of dealers, and many of us have family working alongside us in our offices and plants," explains Frank Merlotti, a corporate director and head of Steelcase's executive committee. "We work at being fair to employees and keeping the benefit levels as high as we can, and sharing—whether it's profit sharing or information or just good feelings."

Softies? Forget it. "Don't get the idea that [we're] easy," argues Merlotti.

"You've got to work your ass off when you get here." Steelcase insists on strict accountability at all levels and constantly creates pressure to work harder—especially in tough times. Benevolence blended with firmness has helped make Steelcase number one in the furniture industry.

By almost any standard, Herman Miller, Steelcase, and many other companies demonstrate that *downsizing* and *success* are not contradictory terms. Corporate America could benefit greatly from their soulful passion. Sharing and caring transcend the fixation on the fast buck. Neopaternalistic firms view their employees and the community as family. In tough times, they never lose touch with their constituencies.

The trend today is toward creating corporate cultures in which cooperation is in everyone's best interest. The prevailing winds are in the direction of greater togetherness, and companies like Herman Miller and Steelcase have captured this trend. They deserve widespread emulation.

SIMULATION

APEX MANUFACTURING

Background

You work for Apex Manufacturing, a 4,000-employee firm that used to be the world's foremost company in its field: small, specialized gasoline motors. Together with two domestic competitors, which had been founded by alumni from your company, Apex made most of the world's supply of such motors—in 1980, it alone make 52 percent of the motors produced.

Since 1980, however, two Asian firms and one German company have entered the field, and one of the American competitors has invested huge amounts of money in new plants and equipment. To make matters more difficult, new governmental noise abatement standards have forced Apex to redesign the motors' exhaust systems. Somehow, your competitors foresaw these new standards and built them into new designs. You didn't and had to make costly modifications. By the end of the 80s, you had only 43 percent of the world's market, and the figure was falling.

There have been rumors of impending plant consolidations and staff layoffs for some time, but only a week ago the CEO was quoted in a *Wall Street Journal* article as saying that Apex would be able to do its trimming by attrition alone and that he expected sales figures to increase significantly by the end of the year. "We're just caught in one of those cycles," he said. "We'll have 50 percent of the world market again within two years."

Yesterday morning you received an E-mail message from the vice president of personnel asking you to come to a noontime meeting in her office. When you got there, you saw a dozen of the company's most respected managers—everyone from supervisors to directors. The VP told you briefly that several decisions had been made by the leadership team.

First, two of the company's five plants will be closed, affecting 900 nonexempt workers and 100 exempts, about a third of the company's manufacturing group. The situation will be complicated by several factors. The two plants made one of the company's more modern and successful lines of motors. The locations of the plants raised costs and led to their being pegged for closure. The plants must continue producing motors for at least eight more months while other plants are readied to take over their production.

Second, there is to be a 20 percent reduction in the level of employment at the company—800 jobs. All departments are to make cuts, though specific targets for different groups have not yet been set. Neither have the provisions of a possible early retirement plan. It has not even been decided how many of the terminated employees will be from among the 1,000 extra manufacturing employees. Many of them were long-term employees whom the VP of manufacturing wanted to reassign to one of the other plants or to some other part of the company.

"There are still a lot of questions," the personnel VP said. "But you are being called together as a transition management advisory group. The leadership team made the decision as to *what* will be necessary—downsizing and consolidation. We're asking you to help us work out *how* we should do it. Specifically, you are being asked to come up with a scenario for announcing and implementing the closure and for working out a plan for handling the reductions in the work force.

"We're going to meet together all day tomorrow," she continued, "and I want you to clear your calendars. We have to get a tentative plan back to the leadership team within 10 days. It doesn't have to be detailed, but it does have to sketch out the issues we need to be ready to deal with and give us some ideas for dealing with them. We want it to advise us on communications, training, and any new policies or arrangements we need to have in place to get people through the transition.''

Then she handed out a sheet on which she had listed some of her own concerns:

Transition Management Concerns

1. Apex has not had a layoff in the past 20 years. During most of that time it was growing.
2. The 1,000 workers from the two plants to be closed include some highly talented people that the organization would hate to lose.
3. There is a strong sentiment among the leadership team for an across-the-board cut in employment levels (''It would be fairer''), but the personnel VP and some others share a concern that some parts of the company are already dangerously lean while others are ''fatter.''
4. There is a perception among rank-and-file employees that the senior managers, whose pay has always been generous, are not bearing enough of the brunt of the difficulties of the company they led.
5. The basic announcement of the decisions is scheduled to go out tomorrow in a memo to all employees. A copy is attached:

> TO: All Apex Employees
> FROM: R. E. Owens, President and CEO
> REGARDING: Measures Needed to Restore Profitability
>
> In order to recover ground lost to foreign competitors, who have been able to dump their government-subsidized products on the American market, the executive team has decided to consolidate all manufacturing into the plants at Worthington, San Jose, and Little Rock. The plants in Stevens Mills and Grandview will be phased out over the next eight or nine months.
>
> During the same period, employment levels in the company, which have recently risen past the 4,000 mark, will be readjusted to a level around 3,200. At that level we will be able to maintain profitability if we can contain other costs. In the latter regard, all employees are asked to refrain from ordering supplies and equipment unless it has been personally approved by a member of the senior management team.
>
> Apex has a noble tradition, but in recent years too many of our employees have forgotten that we must make a profit for our stockholders. If, however, we can tighten our belts and do more with less, we'll not only climb back into the black, but we'll also recover the market share that slipped through our fingers when we let ourselves get too comfortable.
>
> I will be back in touch with you when the details of the plant closures and layoffs have been determined. In the meantime, I am sure that I can count on your continued hard work and loyalty.
>
> R. E. Owens
> President and CEO

''We're in a tight spot,'' the VP concluded. ''Frankly, I'm not sure all the senior managers realize how tight it is. I'm looking to you folks to help me make the case for handling the human side of this whole mess with some care. And I'm looking to you to help me show that there is, in fact, a way to do it that doesn't just drop everything on the people like a bomb and then leave them to take care of their own wounded.''

''I'd suggest that you go back to your units and arrange to free up the next couple of days.

Then I'd like you to look over the following list of suggestions that were made by different members of the senior management team and rate them on a scale of one to five."

"We'll compare reactions in the morning and come up with some first steps."

You go back to your office, get the secretary to postpone and cancel your meetings, and start to work on the list of suggestions. (*Do that now. Write a number to the left of each item on the list. Finish doing so before you continue.*)

1 = Very important. Do this at once.

2 = Worth doing, but takes more time. Start planning it.

3 = Yes and no. Depends on how it's done.

4 = Not very important. May even be a waste of effort.

5 = No! Don't do this.

____ Cancel the memo and don't distribute any communications until firm plans have been made for the details of the layoffs and plant closures.

____ Rewrite the memo to convey more sensitivity to the impact on the company's employees.

____ Set up a "manufacturing restructuring task force" to recommend the best way to consolidate operations and how to determine the disposition of the 1,000 excess workers from the plants at Stevens Mills and Grandview.

____ Set up a "downsizing suggestion plan" through which everyone can have input into how the downsizing will be carried out.

____ Sell the problem that forced the changes.

____ Fire the CEO.

____ Bring in all site managers and directors for an extensive briefing. Hold a frank question-and-answer session. Don't let them leave until they're all satisfied that there is no better way to handle the situation.

____ Make a video explaining the problem and the response to it. Hold all-hands meetings at each company site, where the site manager takes and answers all questions.

____ Set up a hot line to give employees current, reliable information.

____ Get the senior management team to agree to a one-year 20 percent cut in their own salaries.

____ Order an across-the-board 20 percent budget cut throughout the company.

____ Institute a program of rewards for cost-saving suggestions from employees.

____ Plan closure ceremonies for the two plants.

____ Use time to redesign the whole business: strategy, employment, policies, and structure.

____ Get the CEO to make a public statement acknowledging the tardiness of the company's response to the realities of the marketplace.

____ Make it clear up front that the company is headed into a protracted period of change.

____ Explain the purpose, picture, plan, and the parts people will be playing in the announced changes.

____ Circulate an upbeat news release saying that this plan has been in the works for two years, that it isn't a sign of weakness, that its payoff will occur within a year, and so on. In all communications, accentuate the positive.

_____ Allay fears by assuring workers that the two plant closures are the only big changes that will take place.

_____ Develop or find career-planning seminars to help people whose jobs are being threatened or lost because of the changes.

_____ Immediately set new, higher production targets for the next quarter so people have something clear to shoot for and so that by aiming high, they will ensure adequate output even if they fail to reach the goals.

_____ Make a video in which the CEO gives a fiery "we gotta get lean and mean" speech.

_____ Analyze who stands to lose what in the changes.

_____ Redo the compensation structure to reward compliance with the new system.

_____ Help the CEO put together a statement about organizational transition and what it does to an organization. The result should be empathetic and concerned about people.

_____ Set up transition monitoring teams in the Stevens Mills and Grandview plants, as well as in other units that are significantly affected by the changes.

_____ Appoint a "change manager" to be responsible for seeing that the changes go smoothly.

_____ Give everyone at Apex a "We're Number One!" badge.

_____ Put all managers through a quality improvement seminar.

_____ Reorganize the leadership team and redefine the CEO's job as a team coordinator.

_____ Give all managers a two-hour seminar on the emotional impacts of change.

_____ Plan some all-hands social events in each company location—picnics, outings, dinners.

_____ Launch a plan to buy the smallest of Apex's domestic competitors to gain market share and a strong research and development group.

_____ Find ways to "normalize" and to redefine in terms that have more benefit to both the organization and its employees.

SOURCE: William Bridges, *Managing Transitions: Making the Most of Change* (Reading, Mass.: Addison-Wesley, 1991), pp. 105–10.

MODULE 5

Change Agents

INTRODUCTION

Just as organizational structures and practices have undergone profound transformations, so has the role of change agent. When the term became popularized in the 1960s, it typically denoted an outside consultant, often an academician, who came into an organization to assess its need for change. Armed with the best theories of the time and charged by upper management to "fix" some specified problem, these visiting consultants typically would interview workers and managers, draw up an action plan, and leave its implementation to the discretion of senior management.

During the 1970s, this outsider role was gradually supplemented and partially replaced by inside "consultants," usually drawn from human resources groups that focused on "people" issues, such as bettering employee/management relations and individual career development. Although now embraced as an internal function, change programs, led by internal change agents, were still seen as directed toward precisely targeted efforts.

The change arena drastically expanded in the 1980s, along with the change agent's role and responsibilities. As corporate chieftans watched eroding competitiveness and simultaneous demands for "maximizing shareholder value," and as they embarked on new kinds of relationships—joint ventures, for example—they determined that vast changes were needed just to survive. Entire "cultures" were to be thrown out and "old" ways to be rejuvenated. This went beyond tinkering with employee policies and called for a more visible and high-powered effort. CEOs themselves would be called change agents on occasion.

Outside consultants still are involved; in fact, the 1980s saw an explosion in business, as the need for change penetrated whole sectors of the U.S. economy and newly founded and established consulting firms rushed in. Even consulting groups traditionally associated with other areas, like accounting and auditing, climbed aboard the bandwagon, adding entire divisions to concentrate on "change." Moreover, unlike their more detached predecessors, these consultants typically guide the process of change from conception through implementation.

Meanwhile, the concept of change agent continues to evolve, along with the concept of change. As change effort succeeds change effort (or more usually overlaps the preceding one), and as "continuous change" becomes the rallying cry for organizations, companies are experimenting with new forms of change agents. Change agents can be teams, they can be "empowered" workers; they play all the parts—

envisioning, implementing, as well as receiving, for many times they are implementing their own change as well as others'.

It is this last point that is the focus of this module on change agents: because they are called on to play all the change roles, they are the most susceptible to change themselves. Whether this susceptibility takes the form of discouragement, as we saw with John Smithers at the outset of this book, or the form of adventure, as will be seen in the ensuing cases, depends on coming to grips with some potent issues:

Resistance. Change agents will face resistance, no matter how needed a change effort may be, and no matter how close they are to the process and the people they are dealing with; resistance can come from anywhere, even the same level as the agents themselves. The Dallas Works case, later in this module, makes this point vividly. Moreover, given the complexity of change agendas, resistance may arise from the diverse needs of multiple constituencies, all experiencing other challenges simultaneously.

Frustration. As has been made abundantly clear in the cases and readings so far, change almost always takes longer than is expected, events always intrude, and the process inherently encompasses ups and downs, and, probably more frustrating, plateaus. In the middle of the process, trying to do change can feel like wading through a muddy stream against the current. It can be hard to tell whether any progress is being made, even if everyone is still heading in the right direction.

Loneliness. By the nature of their role, change agents are "out in front" on their own, covering rough or unfamiliar terrain with little sense of whether those whom they are trying to reach are with them or straggling behind. This awareness can leave change agents with a sense of isolation from the rest of the organization. If it is not acknowledged, however, it can turn, paradoxically, into a sense of elitism.

Pain. Allied to loneliness is the double-barreled problem of recognizing that change agents bring change, rarely enthusiastically embraced, and, when that change involves layoffs, demotions, and wholesale firings, people are devastated. Even if they are not responsible for the decision to implement such changes, they are the messengers and accordingly blamed. Conscientious change agents in these situations feel double pain—by being blamed and by being aware that in some sense they "caused" the situation, if only by introducing it.

Despite this dispiriting list of "be carefuls," being a change agent, alone or part of a group, can produce almost euphoria. In the middle of a long change program described in this module, one change agent exclaims: "[it was like] I've died and gone to heaven. I don't want this to end." What they don't want to end, typically, is the sense of gratification and excitement that can accompany a change effort. The list of negative emotions experienced by change agents often are interspersed with positive emotions that make for a veritable roller coaster ride. These include the following:

Challenge. There is a real adrenalin feeling from taking on the challenges that are well represented in change efforts. Transforming all the pieces of an organization can be experienced as if putting a puzzle together.

Teamwork.   Since change requires collaboration, there can be a very positive affect created in working closely with others on a common challenge. New friendships and new ways of working can be the natural by-products.

Personal Growth.   Although loneliness may occur, there is also a strong likelihood that change agents will grow and develop their talents, skills, and resourcefulness. "Digging deep down" and utilizing a range of skills can be very revealing to an individual about hidden strengths. And all change agents report that they learned a lot about themselves. As one noted: "I wouldn't have given it up for the world. It definitely changed the way I look at life and business, and how I handle myself."

Gratification.   Finally, despite a large number of setbacks and frustrations often encountered, change agents can find their efforts highly gratifying at times. Change never occurs in one step, or, to use a football analogy, "from the large bomb." Rather, it is a series of small steps, "three yards and a cloud of dust." But those small steps can be rewarding and gratifying in and of themselves. And, as change agents step back from the dust over time, they discover that indeed the cumulative gains have been substantial.

Change agents, then, live in a world of incompletion—constantly. As they look at their organizations, they almost always discover that the organization is "neither what it once was, nor what it needed to become." As change agents dwell on where the organization should be, they may experience some of the negative emotions. However, as they observe the incremental steps of progress, and, as they reflect on the journey itself, more positive emotions arise. In summary, change agents live in a world of conflicting emotions, which are more intensely felt than most people experience.

The people introduced in this module represent well-known companies: Disney, Northwest Airlines, Honeywell, AT&T, General Electric. They also range from the individual to the group, all designated as change agents. The challenges they face are those increasingly associated with what might be termed dilemmas for change agents of the future. Therefore, these are people who might respond to a question, "Is being a change agent a dreadfully lonely, frustrating experience, or a great adventure?" by saying, "yes."

OVERVIEW OF CASES AND READINGS

Dennis Hightower, in the opening case of this module, "Dennis Hightower and the Walt Disney Company in Europe," faces, at least on the surface, an ideal situation for a change agent. He is given a broad mandate to "do something different." He is supported in various ways by the Disney organization. His job, which is to bring a new management structure to the firm's European affiliates, has been agreed to by those directly affected by this change, and this field of change is small—only a hundred or so are employed by Disney in Europe overall. Yet, on closer examination, particularly in conjunction with the accompanying reading, "A Cross-Cultural Perspective on Organizational Change," the situation begins to take on some complexity. Hightower is the ultimate "conflated" change agent: he must develop a vision, secure approval of it, begin with its implementation—all while he is surely experiencing great changes in his own life, and *having* to be changed if he hopes that he will succeed. As the reading points out, "different change strategies are likely to be needed in different cultural environments."

From the challenges facing a single agent, the next case introduces a change agent duo, in "Northwest Airlines Confronts Change." CEO Steve Rothmeier hires Dr. Ken Myers to be "a general's aide," and the two embark on an attempt to transform Northwest's culture. Like British Air, Northwest recognizes that its survival depends on becoming more service/customer-driven in a brutally competitive industry. How Rothmeier and Myers conceived of their roles and how they worked together and apart is as interesting as what they accomplished; this case raises important issues about "insiders" and "outsiders" as effective change agents. Thus, while CEO Rothmeier is a change agent, he also makes a critically important business decision—buying a rival airline that doubles the work force literally overnight—that profoundly impacts the change agenda he and Dr. Myers have charted. Survival and change are vividly etched over the three years the case covers, a period Rothmeier likens to an "Indiana Jones movie."

A somewhat more placid change arena is found in the next case, "Three in the Middle: The Experience of Making Change at Micro Switch." The change agents here are three middle managers who individually reflect on the "pleasures and pain" of their roles. Micro Switch, a division of Honeywell located in a small Midwest town, and a market leader for decades, faces the usual suspects that lead to change effort: intensifying competition, complexifying technology, and so on. The focus of the case, however, is less the introduction of the change effort than what it is like to be in the middle of it: as middle managers and about half-way through the planned change process. Whereas each manager brings an individual perspective, together their stories underscore the kinds of energy needed to manage change over time, the stress that entails, and the self-monitoring the experience provokes.

This "middle space" is explored in an accompanying reading, "Converting Middle Powerlessness to Middle Power: A Systems Approach." The middle manager's middle position has never been simple, argues the author, because it means being a conduit between the top and bottom of an organization. At a time when firms are stripping their middle management ranks to the bone and simultaneously requiring more from those who remain—not the least of which is implementing change efforts—the author's suggestions about converting middle space to "potentially powerful space" are salient. They also are interesting to contemplate in light of the experiences chronicled at Micro Switch.

A fascinating experiment in new forms of change agents unfolds in the next two cases, "AT&T: The Dallas Works (A) and (B)." Here, the change agents were a team of shop-floor workers and supervisors, none of whom even knew each other before being given a year to "go out and find problems and fix them." The problems were not difficult to locate: waves of layoffs had recently reduced the work force by two thirds, leaving worker/management relationships in disarray; the manufacturing process was in bad shape; the Works's status had just been changed to that of a strategic business unit, and new operations and personnel were shortly to be transferred to the facility; yet, at the same time, rumors persisted that Dallas would either be closed or production moved to Mexico.

A new plant manager brought in to deal with this situation conceived of the idea of this team, to spearhead a broader change program that encompassed more traditional components—action teams, training programs, and the like. The group was given something close to a free rein in its efforts; in particular, to be free from the cumbersome red tape that had strangled change efforts in the past.

In addition to providing a close look at how this team set about its work, at the obstacles it faced, and at how it surmounted some of them, the case raises important points touched on elsewhere in this book. On the one hand, the transformation of the Works, and the team's role in that effort, was deemed a "stunning success"; on the other hand, deep problems remained. As change agents, in their sphere of influence the team was energetic; but that energy dissipated when the group was disbanded. This is an issue for any "form" of change agent. What happens when the individual, the duo, the trio, or the team stops—people leave companies or are transferred to other assignments; their work even may be declared "done" by others within the organization. How dependent is "change" on the change agent? And that raises the question, What exactly are change agents supposed to do?

A current answer to that question is empowerment—people are given the authority to make change, and the goal is that they internalize that authority; they do not have to be continually told, they take initiative. The Dallas team, in fact, was empowered and showed the strength of the concept. Several empowerment issues, however, remained at the end of the case, including whether the empowerment had provided that a group like the change team would be accorded others, and whether others would accept it.

The next case, "Nigel Andrews and General Electric Plastics (A)," raises empowerment issues another notch: What happens when the empowered folks, using their power, come up with something that conflicts with other exigencies? GE has embarked on a highly publicized and massive change program called Workout (which is described in full in the accompanying reading). The case looks at a series of Workout sessions and at a decision that participants reached, which hits a major snag before it is even made operational. In working out the resolution of this problem, all the issues of managing change come into play: what is to be changed, who is to be changed, how is this to be done—and can everyone live with the consequences?

A systemic change program like Workout intends a new organizational structure, one that spurs flexibility, swiftness, and creativity/innovation; such characteristics depend pivotally on an ability to manage change. Like "quality," managing change is becoming less of a goal in itself and more of a given. No player on the global stage today can be competitive without quality built into its products and, increasingly, its services. Similarly, no organization will be successful if it cannot, collectively and at the individual level, manage change. Thus, ultimately, people are being called on to be change agents, acting on others as well as themselves. In that sense, the change agent of the future is everyone. If this were not daunting in itself, companies also are increasingly interweaving themselves with their suppliers and customers, which means that the change terrain is even broader and involves a complex linking of constituencies.

The three final readings in this book explore in their own ways this terrain. "The Leader's New Work: Building Learning Organizations" introduces the idea of generative learning, which emphasizes expanding capabilities; this is contrasted to adaptive learning, which stresses coping, not creating. Learning organizations, by their nature, absorb and use new ideas from internal exchanges and interaction with other organizations. This involvement with others is a point raised in the next reading, "Customers Drive a Technology-Driven Company: An Interview with George Fisher." Fisher, CEO of Motorola, details the challenges of a company being involved intimately with its customers. And interestingly, the author of the previous article and Fisher come to the same conclusion about these evolving customer relationships. The former indicates that being able to "see" what customers might truly value but never experienced or would never think to ask for is connected to generative learning, a new "way of looking at the world." Fisher notes: "We marry our technology developments with a deep understanding of our customers' business needs . . . we can develop products and systems they can't even imagine—but that are immensely valuable to them."

The flexibility to be able to anticipate what customers need or want transcends the notion of managing change as being either a discrete goal or an achievable skill. Rather, the ability to manage change is considered interwoven with individual growth and improvement and an environment that encourages those characteristics to flourish. A second reading on Motorola, "Motorola U: When Training Becomes an Education," describes that company's effort to provide such an environment. In 1979, the firm established a training plan to upgrade its employees skills; 10 years later, this had evolved into a "university" that also included "students" from suppliers and customers, that was actively involved in education efforts as part of an outreach program, and that conceived of its mission to make "our education relevant to the corporation, to the job, and to the individual."

For the short term, change agents in whatever form will still be needed to help wrench organizations out of sclerotic patterns—there is plenty of work available! But, if innovative organizations like Motorola are heralds of the future then, "managing change" may be more associated with fostering creativity, and "change agent" may be recalled as an interesting occupation that many courageous people pursued in the past.

CASE

DENNIS HIGHTOWER AND THE WALT DISNEY COMPANY IN EUROPE

"Go out and grow the business. Do something different from what has been done in the past. Develop a strategy and bring it back to us in three months." This was the challenge Frank Wells, president and COO of the Walt Disney Company, presented to Dennis Hightower, newly hired vice president of Consumer Products for Europe and (subsequently) the Middle East. The time was June 1987.

The Disney Organization in Europe, 1938–1987

Europe was the first area outside the United States for the marketing of other Disney consumer products than films. In 1938, Walt Disney personally visited Italy to initiate a licensing business with a major Italian publishing company. After the war, Walt Disney hired his first country manager, for France; the French manager hired all subsequent country managers. By 1987, there were eight wholly owned business subsidiaries: Denmark (Copenhagen), the United Kingdom (London), Belgium (Brussels), Spain (Madrid), France (Paris), West Germany (Frankfurt), Portugal (Lisbon) and Italy (Milan). These subsidiaries operated in 26 different markets and together employed about 102 people. In addition,

there were independent marketing licensees in Greece (Athens), Egypt (Cairo), and Israel (Tel Aviv). Approximately half of these licensees' business was Disney-related. Each subsidiary and marketing licensees' representative reported individually to Barton K. (Bo) Boyd in Burbank, California, Disney's world headquarters; country managers submitted budgets and indicated their expected profits.

The Country Managers

By 1987, all eight country managers had spent substantial time in their positions. The French manager, personally hired by Walt Disney, was 70 and had been in his role for nearly 40 years. He was considered a "living legend," being credited with having essentially built Disney's European business since World War II. He was also considered the titular head of Europe, although this status had never been formally acknowledged by Burbank.

The Danish country manager was 61 and had worked for Disney for 24 years; the German country manager, also in his 60s, had held his position for 30 years. The Belgian country manager, 60, had held his job for 35 years; and the Italian manager, also 60, for 26 years. The three youngest country managers, the Spanish at 44, the Portuguese at 41, and the United Kingdom at 41, had been in their positions for 16, 10, and 15 years, respectively.

All the longer-tenured country managers knew the Disney family personally. Most had known Walt, along with his

This case was prepared by Barbara Feinberg (under the direction of Professor Todd D. Jick).

Copyright © 1989 by the President and Fellows of Harvard College. Harvard Business School case 9-490-010.

brother, Roy Disney, Sr. The Disney children were regularly sent to Europe on vacation, where they would stay with the various country managers at their homes. Roy Disney, Jr., the company's current vice chairman, "learned the business" from the French and German country managers when he became active in the company nearly three decades earlier.

Perceived as "senior senators," the country managers for all practical purposes *were* Disney in Europe. They were proudly independent, having effectively built a level of awareness of the company that was critical throughout Western Europe.

Book and magazine publishing and a full range of merchandise licensing of apparel, toys, housewares, and stationery, and the like had all been developed. Special events related to the Disney characters' birthdays and animated film releases were also staged. As a licensing-driven business, little investment had been made in hard assets. Hence, it was an extremely high-margin enterprise, with the rate structure based on the properties involved or the product categories. It was also a very profitable enterprise.

Preparing for 1992

In late 1986, the Disney organization was negotiating to build a Euro-Disneyland; an agreement was ultimately reached with the French government to build the theme park outside Paris, to be opened in 1992. The recognition that both the park and the European markets were scheduled to "open" in 1992 was a catalyst for rethinking Disney's European operations. Opportunities would undoubtedly be tremendous. It also was felt that European market penetration had lagged behind the United States penetration, due

to a lack of coordination among the country subsidiaries.

As a first step toward taking advantage of perceived marketing opportunities, Disney management decided to establish a European headquarters, in Paris. A newly created position, vice president of consumer products for Europe and the Middle East, would head the office; duties would include profit and loss responsibility, marketing and business development, responsibility for salaries and bonuses, and instituting performance measures. The country managers had been consulted on this decision. The sentiment was that the new European head should not be a European; the notion of an American who could "relate" to the studio (as the Burbank headquarters was called) and build credibility locally was much more appealing.

Once the decision to establish the Paris office was made, it was announced worldwide: throughout the entire Disney organization and to Disney affiliates and licensees. Everything concerning the eight-country subsidiaries that had previously been managed by Burbank would now be run by Paris.

The New Position Is Filled

The search firm of Russell Reynolds was hired to find candidates for the new European vice president job; Dennis Hightower, head of Russell Reynolds' Los Angeles office, was in charge of the search. Hightower and Bo Boyd spent three weeks in Europe interviewing prospective candidates and discussing with each country manager to get a sense of both the business issues confronting each group and what kind of person would generate confidence, respect, and trust for that group. Many candidates were put forth for the role but, in the end, very much to his surprise, Hightower himself was offered the job. He had joined the company in June 1987. Before he had been approached, however, Boyd called the three most senior country managers (Italy, Germany, and France) to share the decision with them. Would there be any problems? Later, once Hightower accepted the position, Boyd told him of these conversations and assured him that the three managers had approved of the choice.

Dennis Hightower, 45, brought a varied background to his new job. After college, he served eight years as an intelligence officer in the Army, with assignments in southeast Asia and a specialty in Eastern Europe. Subsequently, he earned his MBA at Harvard and worked at McKinsey during four years. He then joined GE, becoming a country manager in Mexico. Recruited by Mattel as the vice president of corporate planning, he was involved in that company's expansion in Europe. Three years later, he joined Russell Reynolds, where he worked primarily with international clients.

Accepting the Challenge

As Hightower contemplated his newly created job, he thought wryly to himself, "If you don't know where you are going, any road will take you there!" His task was to figure out where Disney would be in 1992. What role should Disney play in Europe? What changes would that entail? He mused:

> These European managers have been running themselves for years. They have been very successful; it is a very profitable business for Disney. It could have been more profitable, but things were fine just the way they were.
>
> So what do I bring to the party? Not only am I an outsider, I am a boss they never had before and probably don't want—no matter how much they may intellectually agree to the need for one.
>
> How am I going to develop a strategy that will unify Europe, grow the business beyond any one individual area, and introduce critical thinking and creative approaches—all in three months? Where do I begin?

READING

A CROSS-CULTURAL PERSPECTIVE ON ORGANIZATIONAL CHANGE

André Laurent

If the concept of organizational culture is

Excerpt from *Human Resource Management in International Firms*, pp. 91–93.

relatively new, the concept of national culture has been around for quite a while. National cultures represent an important element of an organization's context, from which the firm draws its resources and with which it transacts. In spite of its obvious impact and in spite of the attention of the organizational literature to environments, this national culture context has been grossly overlooked for many years. Unconscious parochialism and unfounded universalistic claims have marked the field of management and organization (Hofstede, 1980b). Approaches to organizational change have suffered from the same ethnocentric pathology (Faucheux et al., 1982). Strategies for organizational change that were developed in one particular national culture continue to be viewed by many as perfectly appropriate for any other culture (Kreacic and Marsh, 1986). Management and organizational theorists persist in entertaining the comfortable assumption that their object of study, their observations, and their concepts are culture-free.

Yet comparative research has demonstrated that different national cultures hold different conceptions and assumptions about organizations and their management (Hofstede, 1980a; Laurent, 1983). Managers from different national cultures hold different assumptions about the nature of management, authority, structure, and organizational relationships. These assumptions shape different value systems and get translated into different management practices, which in turn reinforce the original assumptions.

For example, national cultures can be positioned on a continuum from those holding an instrumental view of organizations to those with a social view. In the first case, more typical of North America, the organization is perceived primarily as a set of tasks to be achieved through a problem-solving hierarchy, where positions are defined in terms of tasks and functions and where authority is functionally based. According to the social view, found particularly in Latin cultures, the organization is primarily conceived of as a collectivity of people to be managed through a formal hierarchy, where positions are defined in terms of levels of authority and status, and where authority is attached more to individuals than to their offices or functions (Inzerilli and Laurent, 1983).

The instrumental view looks at authority as a means to achieve tasks; relationships are instrumental to task achievement. The social view looks at tasks as means to establish authority; tasks are instrumental to the development of relationships (Amado and Laurent, 1983). Whereas the instrumentally oriented manager is primarily interested in finding out who is responsible for what, the socially oriented manager is more inclined to consider who has authority over whom. While these represent ideal types, there is some evidence that different cultures approximate such types to differing degrees.

In the same way that it has taken some time and the help of the Japanese mirror for American management writers to identify what is American in American management (Schein, 1981), so it has been difficult to recognize the cultural values that have inspired various approaches to organizational change. Such movements as "organization development" (OD) in North America, "industrial democracy" in Northern Europe, "institutional analysis" in France, and "quality control circles" in Japan are obviously not independent of the cultural context in which they have emerged. It should come as no surprise that the United States was the home of OD, with its instrumental focus on organizational processes as tools to be improved, while the Latin countries favored institutional approaches that tried to deal with the social intricacies of human collectivities (Faucheux et al., 1982). Nor should we be surprised that the OD movement has traditionally downplayed the importance of power issues in organizations, while institutional analysis has been obsessed by such issues.

If organizations reflect their social context (Maurice et al., 1980), strategies for changing organizations obviously cannot ignore this. Different change strategies are likely to be needed in different cultural environments. A contingent approach to organizational change needs to be developed that takes national culture as a major parameter.

When a majority of German managers perceive their organizations as a coordinated network of individuals taking rational decisions based on their professional knowledge and competence, any process of planned organizational change in Germany will have to take this into consideration. When a majority of British managers view their organization primarily as a network of interpersonal relationships between individuals who get things done by influencing and negotiating with each other, a different approach to organizational change may be needed in England. When a majority of French managers look at their organizations as an authority network where the power to organize and control the actors stems from their positioning in the hierarchy, another change model may be called for in France.

These national caricatures, while based on comparative research in managerial assumptions (Laurent, 1986), are obviously oversimplistic, like any other caricature. They are intended to highlight the challenges of managing change that are faced by organizations operating across national boundaries.

Research indicates that the corporate culture and policies of long-established multinational companies do not reduce national differences in management conceptions (Laurent, 1983). While the corporate culture may lead to significant behavioral adjustment, it seems to leave intact the deep-seated assumptions of the various nationals.

What are the implications of such findings for the management of change in multinational organizations? If the cultural change of organizations has to do with the creation of new meanings, how can this process be managed when different sets of meanings exist in the various national organizations that constitute the multinational enterprise?

In order better to frame this issue, we need to return to a number of points made earlier in this book. If we look at organizational change as a process of transformation of state A into state B, the easiest part of the management task may be to specify what state B ought to be. Most organizations do not encounter too many problems at this stage. Few organizations would be explicitly against the development of a total quality concept, against paying more attention to customers and personnel, against the improvement of competitive performance. Gospels on the corporate values distributed by companies to their personnel show more similarities than differences. Reaching consensus on such overarching corporate goals may not be too difficult, even in large multinational firms that have a high degree of cultural diversity.

Cross-national difficulties start at another level. Different national organizations are likely to favor different means in order to implement the desired changes, reflecting cultural differences in the art of managing and organizing. This may also reflect a completely different assessment of state *A*—that is, a different assessment of what needs to be transformed in the first place. Effective strategic organizational change, at a minimum, requires the integrative management of a decentralized process if it wishes to avoid the pitfalls of ethnocentrism.

If the corporation is truly "multinational," it may actually try to learn from its culturally different constituencies, so as to transfer and adapt change know-how from these subsidiaries to headquarters, and between subsidiaries. In this way,

learning and cultural synergy can be heightened. The international firm progressively acquires a true multinational identity through the deliberate use of its cultural diversity. However, this cannot be the result of a rational management decision. It requires an evolution in ways of thinking from a parochial and ethnocentric conception of management and organization to a world view. This may be one of the most important challenges in the strategic change of multinational organizations.

CASE

NORTHWEST AIRLINES CONFRONTS CHANGE

I thought it would beat any Indiana Jones movie. The change effort starts out with a real nice beginning, and then suddenly you get one disaster after another: The boulder just misses you, and you get the snake in the cockpit of the airplane. That's what it's all about. You've got to be down in the blood and the mud and the beer.

Steve Rothmeier
Former CEO of Northwest Airlines

I happen to believe that a service organization operates with and through its people. The quality of customer service is in large part determined by the quality of human resources, and the kind of climate and culture you bring to bear.

Dr. Ken Myers
Former vice president, organization services, at Northwest Airlines

When Steve Rothmeier took over as CEO of Northwest Airlines in January 1985

This case was prepared by Research Associate Susan Rosegrant (under the direction of Professor Todd D. Jick).

Copyright © 1990 by the President and Fellows of Harvard College. Harvard Business School case 9-491-036.

and brought on Ken Myers to be his partner in transforming the carrier into a more service-oriented organization, the two set to work in an environment which seemed under continual fire—both from within and from without.

Since Congress's deregulation of the airline industry in 1978, there had been a steady stream of almost yearly challenges which had forced carriers to react as nimbly as possible in order to stay aloft. In 1979, a growing fuel shortage, and the temporary grounding of the popular DC10 aircraft because of safety concerns, played havoc with airlines' schedules and routes. The 1981 air traffic controllers' strike significantly reduced available air space, forcing another round of route and schedule negotiations. In addition, People Express and a slew of other low-cost airlines which started up in the early 1980s added a new competitive twist—forcing cross-industry fare cuts and stirring up union-management acrimony, as established carriers looked to recoup lost passenger dollars by lowering wages and revising work rules.

This onslaught of changing conditions and increased competition took a heavy toll. Although 20 new carriers had taken wing from the time of deregulation up to the end of 1984, a full dozen jet airlines had filed for bankruptcy protection during the same period.

Northwest Airlines was by no means immune to the pressures which accompanied deregulation. First under the tutelage of Donald W. Nyrop, chief executive from 1954 until 1979, and then under M. Joseph Lapensky, from 1979 to 1985, the Minneapolis/St. Paul-based carrier had become known both for its conservative financial controls and for its hard-line labor relations policies. Although the airline's financial savvy had given it a strong balance sheet, the antagonistic stance taken toward labor had saddled the airline with a track record of union dissent. Just during the decade of the 1970s, Northwest endured four separate strikes.

Perhaps the greatest challenge that Rothmeier faced as he took over in 1985, however, was to transform Northwest into a more responsive, customer-driven service organization capable of competing in the new era. For, despite the fact that six years had passed since deregulation, Northwest still displayed neither the technological capabilities—such as sophisticated travel agent computer reservation systems—nor the people skills that were being honed at such major competitors as American Airlines, United, and Delta.

Rothmeier was intimately familiar with Northwest's strengths and weaknesses: Except for a brief stint in marketing at General Mills, the Minneapolis-based food products company, Rothmeier had spent his entire professional career at the airline. Armed with a marketing degree from Notre Dame and an MBA from the University of Chicago, Rothmeier joined Northwest in 1973 as a financial analyst, and soon became Nyrop's protégé. Ten years later he was named president and chief operating officer; and, in 1985, at the age of 38, he became the youngest chief executive officer of any major U.S. airline.

Rothmeier knew he wanted to make some major changes in the airline's culture right away. But he didn't take the conventional route of hiring an outside consulting firm, or of implementing a tried-and-true change program model. Instead, to spearhead the change effort, he chose outsider Ken Myers, a consultant and professor of strategic management, introduced to him in late 1984 by Northwest's vice president of personnel after Myers ran some training programs at Northwest.

Like Rothmeier, Myers—or "Dr. Ken," as he came to be called—took up the task with impressive credentials. While serving in the Navy as a chief petty officer and earning his undergraduate degree in psychology at the University of Hawaii in the early 1970s, Dr. Ken participated in a major human resources management program that the Navy instituted under Admiral Elmo Zumwalt, Jr. After earning his PhD in organizational behavior from Case Western Reserve, Dr. Ken went on to become an assistant professor at the University of Minnesota and to head the school's executive development center.

For Rothmeier, Dr. Ken appeared to be the agent who might be able to woo employees into a more conciliatory relationship with management and to lay the groundwork for a more service-oriented operation. And for the 45-year-old professor, Northwest—although a potentially hostile environment—represented an opportunity to practice his change-implementing skills on a grand scale. Together, the two set out to create change at Northwest.

Rothmeier's Story: Part I

When Rothmeier took over at Northwest, he saw the faithfulness and pride of its employees as one of the airline's greatest assets. "There is a tremendous loyalty here," he declared. "We went through a 93-day pilots' strike in 1972, and a 103-day pilots' strike in 1978. Everybody came back to work. Nobody left Northwest. They could complain and moan about it, but everybody came back to work, and there was a deep-seated pride that was really remarkable."

But if loyalty was the airline's greatest asset, in Rothmeier's estimation, the unions were its greatest liability and were at the heart of many of the problems he was trying to change. With 95 percent of its employees belonging to a union, the carrier was the most highly unionized

airline in the world, Rothmeier declared. "We had to drive a wedge between union leadership and union membership," he asserted. "Instead of creating an environment where union employees went to a shop steward to solve a problem, I wanted them to come to their managers to solve that problem. I wanted them to be part of the team."

Specifically, Rothmeier believed that it would be next to impossible for employees to embrace the importance of such concepts as emphasizing customer service and participating in management decisions as long as they were wedded first to the union cause. Moreover, while the airline might have been able to prosper against a backdrop of labor/management hostility in the past, Rothmeier was convinced that such acrimony could prove fatal in the new era of deregulation.

"The world has changed," he recalled saying. "I used to go tell the union members, 'Every carrier's expanding at double digit numbers. Everybody's growing at enormous rates, but guess what? The pie isn't really that big. The appetites are growing larger than the pie is. And that means that you can take all this fraternal stuff and stick it right up your nose, because, if United Airlines does it better than we do, that union guy over there is going to get your job.' "

Rothmeier saw Dr. Ken as just the person for taking this message to the masses. "Ken was to come in," he explained, "to make sure the organization could become a big service company, and to bring the employees into the process." Specifically, Dr. Ken's initial charter called for him, among other things, to launch training programs to improve skills and morale, and to prepare supervisors and managers for taking a more participative role.

The fact that Dr. Ken—a bearded academic—looked unlike the typical Northwest manager fit perfectly with Rothmeier's design. "What better way to prove to the troops that you are a serious agent of change," he said, "than to bring in Dr. Weird Beard, who goes out with them after their second shift and has a beer, or sits down with them on the ramp and says, 'What the hell do we have to do differently? The boss wants to know.' And he could tell them, 'I'm not a 30-year Northwest guy. I'm not even an airline guy. Your boss brought me in from outside. You know why? Because your boss wants to make some changes and he thinks I can help do that.' "

Similarly, Rothmeier said he purposefully did not give Dr. Ken a top-ranking title because he did not want employees to view him as a management tool. Instead, he said, Dr. Ken was like "a general's aide"—reporting directly to the top and wielding a great deal of influence behind the scenes. In fact, Rothmeier confided, this was how he, himself, had garnered power and influence when he first joined the airline. "When Nyrop was running the airline and I was director, I had more conversations with Mr. Nyrop about policy issues than some of his VPs did," he mused. "I find that process very comfortable."

Rothmeier had one additional role in mind for Dr. Ken. As he explained to his staff, Dr. Ken would be in an ideal position to read the pulse of the working people. "I told them, 'I don't care if you like Ken. That's not the real issue. The fact is, Ken can handle the people that we want him to handle. He can address them, he can communicate with them, he can get the message across, and, you will find out, very quickly, that he will have more intelligence available for us than anybody

could imagine, because the employees are going to see this guy as totally bizarre in this company.' " He added: "We had to have someone who understood organization, who understood motivation, who could handle the foreman, who could handle the blue-collar worker, and that's what Ken was."

Northwest, in many respects, was in a reasonably strong position when Rothmeier took over: The airline was the dominant U.S. carrier in the Pacific, and it had a particularly strong domestic presence in its Twin Cities hub. As a result, Rothmeier and Dr. Ken had to carefully craft a change rationale that would acknowledge the airline's strengths, yet still push for substantial improvements. "You've got to slant the message to something that will grab people," Rothmeier explained.

To accomplish this, Rothmeier said, he focused less on issues of survival and, instead, tried to stress the difficulties Northwest would face in hanging on to its "championship" status. "We all know that it's tougher to repeat as national champion than it is to get there the first time," he asserted. "We'd tell them, 'We're in a knock-down, drag-em-out fight, and there is nothing un-American about going home every night with perspiration on your brow. There's nothing un-American about getting paid eight hours of pay for eight hours of work each day.' That's what you need to defend the national championship."

Dr. Ken's efforts began to have an impact at the airline within months, Rothmeier contended. But reaching all the participants of Northwest's geographically diverse and mobile organization proved extremely difficult. "The most frustrating thing was the amount of time it took to change a large organization," he recalled. "In the airline business, pilots and flight attendants are away all the time. You can't get them in one room. You can't get them in 10 rooms! So you have an incredible communications problem, because the rumor mill works better than anything else." He added: "Rumors travel instantly. But facts weren't so easy to relay."

To help reach all the airline's employees, Rothmeier filmed a series of videotapes explaining Northwest's mission and how the organization was trying to change. But this medium, also, was limited in its usefulness. "You've got a 30-minute video, the pilots and flight attendants watch it, and then they're off to catch a flight, and the whole rumor mill starts all over again," he complained. "'The boss said this.' Well, the boss didn't say that, but that's what they thought they heard the boss say. That was the biggest frustration. The communications process was so unwieldy."

At the same time that he was meeting with Dr. Ken to discuss these and other change issues, Rothmeier was also facing the troubling question of how Northwest could survive against the growing dominance of such "megacarriers" as American and United. In January 1986, one year after he became CEO, Rothmeier announced that Northwest would acquire long-time archrival and fellow Minneapolis/St. Paul-based carrier, Republic Airlines (see Exhibit 1).

For the next nine months, until the acquisition became effective in October, Rothmeier's energies were largely focused on the merger. Still, looking back, he felt pleased with the progress of the change effort to date. "We were making tremendous strides in improving the morale of the troops, and we had moved out of the middle of the pack and were up as high as fourth in customer service," he

said. "These things were very threatening to union leadership, because you didn't have some guy that was 65 years old trying to kick the hell out of the employees. You had Dr. Ken telling the rank-and-file employees that they were going to have a role to play in decision making. And, God forbid, he was taking the foreman and training him in human relations skills and management skills. And he was motivating them." He added: "There were some very strong signs of change. We felt it was moving along very nicely."

Dr. Ken's Story: Part I

Dr. Ken didn't mince words when he described the company and the culture he was faced with changing when he joined Northwest as director of organization services in January 1985. "Very quickly, I said, 'Jesus Christ, there's nothing here!' " he recalled. "What a marvelous opportunity."

Specifically, Dr. Ken said he discovered an organization which had never invested significantly in marketing, operations, or human services. "The infrastructure was from the 1940s and 1950s," he complained. "You couldn't get information from one place to another efficiently. There was no marketing, just sales. And the personnel system was driven by punitive, negative, human relations policies. In short, there was nothing that speaks to the airline of the 1990s."

According to Dr. Ken, Rothmeier gave him very little direction when he first arrived, other than to suggest that he might do some training. "I was coming out there to do my magic," he recounted. "I was given no charter." To Dr. Ken's dismay, he also was not given the title or the budget that he had requested. "If you don't have

EXHIBIT 1 Excerpt from NWA, Inc., 1985 Annual Report Describing Planned
Republic Acquisition

The planned $884 million acquisition of Republic Airlines by NWA, Inc., represents a logical
and positive development from practically any business standpoint. Through this proposed
combination of two medium-sized carriers with complementary route systems and fleets,
Northwest will gain the economic mass necessary to compete more effectively and efficiently in
this intensely competitive industry. When this transaction is approved by Republic's shareholders
and the federal government—as it is expected to be—the new Northwest will be the nation's third
largest carrier in terms of revenue passenger-miles. Northwest will operate more than 300
aircraft, employ over 30,000 people, and serve more than 130 cities worldwide.

The rapid expansion of carriers, such as American and United, since the beginning of airline
deregulation has resulted in these airlines becoming "megacarriers." To compete effectively
against these carriers over the long term, Northwest needs a domestic system of a certain threshold
size. Northwest was building toward this critical mass by expanding internally, but it became
apparent that a more rapid expansion was needed to achieve a stronger market presence.

Northwest has historically had one major domestic hub, located at Minneapolis/St. Paul.
Republic, in addition to serving the Twin Cities, also has developed significant hub and spoke
systems at Detroit and Memphis. By combining the operations of the two airlines, Northwest will
become the largest carrier at these three major airports and will greatly increase domestic on-line
traffic.

The strong domestic system resulting from a Republic/Northwest combination will allow
Northwest to greatly expand the feeder traffic to the airline's eight international gateways. This
will enable Northwest to offer more single-carrier service to the Orient and Europe. In short,
acquiring Republic will permit Northwest to attain a key objective in today's highly competitive
environment: to keep passengers flying on a single airline—in this case, Northwest—for all or
most of their trips.

Northwest's and Republic's fleets are excellent matches in terms of operational capabilities.
Republic's smaller aircraft, which average 102 seats, are ideal for building and serving domestic
hub and spoke systems. Northwest's larger aircraft, averaging 228 seats, are well-suited for
longer hauls, including transcontinental and international service. The combined fleet will
facilitate further development of a strong domestic system linking most areas of the United States
with both the Orient and Europe.

the organizational trappings to be one of
the power brokers, you're not going to get
done many of the things you want to
accomplish," he asserted. "I didn't get
power or resources."

Although he felt hampered by his lack
of resources and status, Dr. Ken quickly
went to work. "The purpose of that first
six to eight months was to build myself
into the system, and to build some knowledge and credibility," he explained. To do
that, Dr. Ken set out to establish a spot for

himself in the corporate hierarchy. "I
began studying the structure of the organization to help me look more like an
insider," he recounted. "In short, I
played the role of a politician running
for office. In the first six months, Steve
got a continuous stream of information
that I was good for the organization,
and that I was professionally sound."
He added: "Very early on in the evolution of change, it's real easy to stub
your toe. You have to build as large a

political constituency as you can, as rapidly as you can.''

Simultaneously, Dr. Ken immersed himself in the problems and concerns of Northwest's workers. In doing this, he didn't limit himself to the airline's Twin Cities hub but traveled widely, visiting 41 of the carrier's then 49 line stations. Gaining the trust and cooperation of employees would be particularly important to the change effort in this case, he believed, because the unionized setting gave employees the ability to strongly influence the organization—whether for better or for worse. "There was a great deal of pent up hostility, emotion, and frustration, and no one had ever listened," he marveled. "I said, 'I'm new. I'm trying to learn things, tell me what's going on.' I got permission from the unions to actually do the work, so I learned the vagaries of the system first hand." Among the jobs Dr. Ken undertook was to load bags on and off airplanes for a day, providing a "a real lesson in how hard this work could be."

Finally, Dr. Ken devoted himself to becoming indispensible to Rothmeier. During the first six months, he established a pattern of meeting with Rothmeier about once every two to three weeks to share his ideas about the changes needed at Northwest and to discuss the best ways to pursue them. "Over that series of interviews, we established a fairly personal relationship," Dr. Ken stated. "He had a lot of people out there who knew him and trusted him and fed him pretty straight information, but he didn't have anybody like me who could interpret and put patterns to it, and that's what he appreciated."

At the end of six months, Dr. Ken reached an agreement with Rothmeier on what his charter should be: to analyze and start to shift the culture to a more customer-responsive and people-oriented culture; to build a new sense of esprit, professionalism, and pride in the corporation; to design and conduct the training that would support these goals; and to alter the processes that were the antitheses of the desired change.

As a first step, Dr. Ken searched for a low-cost way to send the message that the organization was changing, and to establish himself as a legitimate and pivotal figure in that change process. In addition, he said, he wanted to alter the oft-accepted image of Rothmeier as someone who "doesn't care about people." With $10,000 from Rothmeier's contingency fund, Dr. Ken launched an internal motivational campaign known as "People, Pride, Performance." Starting with a kickoff celebration, and announcements in the company newsletter, Dr. Ken began distributing cloth patches and buttons sporting the "People, Pride, Performance" logo to all uniformed employees. "The idea that you pay attention to people, have a lot of pride and, therefore, have a sterling performance wasn't new to me, but it's worth repeating," he said. "It was the best thing I could think of to force the organization to look in the mirror. And it was the first that people heard of Dr. Ken."

This "mostly smoke and mirrors" program was fortified by a more practical professional leadership training program which Dr. Ken conducted for first-line supervisors—first with the maintenance and engineering groups and later with ground services. The three-day sessions, held in on-site facilities in Minneapolis, stressed such basic leadership skills as communication and behavioral techniques. "I had to start somewhere where I could have an impact," explained Dr. Ken. "The important part was not the content but the fact that it was deliberately designed to bring in a cross-level and cross-functional mix of managers and supervisors, and to be a sounding board and mixing pot for all these people who had never talked to each other before.'' He added: ''I got a big bump out of that. Many of Rothmeier's Deep Throats went back and reported, 'Jesus Christ, what is this guy? He's a miracle worker!' So that got me more resources.''

One other highly symbolic change which Dr. Ken pushed through in the first year was the revision of the PD-146, an employee performance report card for noting both good and bad behavior that, he said, ''had been used so hard and so long and so frequently as a kick in the butt that it was genuinely feared and hated throughout the system.'' Dr. Ken assembled a group of 36 employees, ranging from flight attendants to senior managers, and, in two days, they designed a new form—the PD-292—as well as an administrative manual entry on how to use it. ''We said that a leader's responsibility is to go out and catch people doing something right!'' he exclaimed. ''Here's the form and here's how to do it.''

Although the act of revising a form might not seem significant, Dr. Ken said the gesture sent shock waves throughout the airline. ''These 36 employees went back to their constituencies absolutely raving about this process,'' he recalled, ''not only what we did, but how we did it.''

But despite these small successes, Dr. Ken frequently felt frustrated. Although Rothmeier seemed pleased with his progress, he still wasn't providing the financial backing which Dr. Ken felt was necessary. Dr. Ken even remembered one case where the vice chairman responsible for personnel refused his request to buy an overhead projector for use in training. ''I didn't have the critical mass to bring these

changes about,'' he complained. ''Steve—like us all—learned a lot, and grew a lot. But I was always pushing harder than he was willing to go, and faster than he was willing to go.''

The announced acquisition of Republic raised some more troubling issues, Dr. Ken recalled. Three days after the announcement, he gave Rothmeier a position paper discussing the opportunities and problems inherent in merging the human side of two very diverse organizations; and, about two months before the actual merger, he gave soon-to-be president John Horn a proposal detailing a ''a bare minimum'' of simple and inexpensive action steps he felt Northwest should take (see Exhibit 2). But although Rothmeier bought the idea that the deal should be called a merger, rather than an acquisition, he did not institute many of Dr. Ken's other suggestions concerning the importance of team-building and pre-merger planning between the two airlines. Although Dr. Ken, himself, began trying to build relationships with Republic employees, he saw little evidence of reaching out on the part of the rest of the airline. ''They didn't do adequate planning for the information systems merger, the operations merger, or the customer service issues,'' he complained, ''let alone what it would take to integrate two disparate cultures—one moving toward a much more service-oriented culture and the other our old militaristic culture.''

Overall, as the autumn date of the actual merger approached, Dr. Ken remembered feeling that the change effort had barely started. ''We'd built a springboard,'' he reflected. ''We had done enough training that some people were starting to use some of the tools, and to talk about the fact that there could be a new culture. But it was more in the hope stage than anything else.''

EXHIBIT 2   Ken Myers's Proposal to John Horn Suggesting Premerger Action Steps

Confidential

John F. Horn, Executive Vice President   08-08-86
Integrating the New Northwest

Background: Integrating similar size companies is an organizational as well as financial/ marketing and operational challenge. The evidence is clear that *People* must be actively integrated or expected synergy and marketplace performance will not be achieved. Active integration requires three considerations: (1) indoctrination, (2) socialization, and (3) organization building.

Indoctrination means providing employees with the early and basic knowledge they need to reduce change anxiety, take care of personal and professional needs, identify with the company, and get work done. This includes information on position, pay, privileges, reporting relationships, the organization and its future, policies, and the like.

Socialization simply means providing continuing information, symbols, company spirit-building activities, training, and equitable rules. This allows the individual and the underlying informal organization to build company allegiance and deflect outside agitation (such as from the disgruntled or the unions).

Organization building is actively building individual and work team relationships where change and new players have disrupted the existing status quo. It means providing role clarification, clear goals, interpersonal agility, reducing potential conflict, and helping work team/units oil their workings with better communication and problem-solving skills. Organization building means active steps to speed up the slower natural processes.

Action Steps: The following action steps would be important to take:

Indoctrination

- A short (1/2 hour) indoctrination session for all new NWA (old Republic) employees conducted at their existing workplace by an existing manager. An information packet consisting of an indoctrination booklet (who handles records, where to ask questions, pass policy, and so on), welcoming letter, safety and security note, and other timely information would be handed out. As well, an easily developed modification to the eight-minute "You are Northwest" videotape would be put together and shown. It would feature a three- to four-minute introduction by S. G. Rothmeier to the new Northwest. Managers might be given a briefing instruction book and a set of expected questions/answers.

- A series of get-acquainted "coffee hours" or "town meetings" in each city or region in which employees are gathered, cross-function and cross-organization, welcomed to the new Northwest, and given an opportunity to meet and interact with each other. These meetings would be one to two hours long and perhaps run by the sales department. Some details of this are noted in my enclosure, but could simply involve a brief introduction by an attending NWA officer, director, or manager. Promotion and indoctrination materials would be available.

- A three- to six-month-long "we get questions" bulletin process. The bulletin would include any basic information personnel (et al.) wanted to get out and answers to general questions coming into a published address.

- Officer visits to selected key field sites to answer questions and walk around getting to know the troops and the operation.

- A "buddy" system where NWA personnel are assigned to get to know a peer, assist in getting information, technical assistance, and so on. "Know Your Buddy," or "Be a Buddy."

EXHIBIT 2   *(concluded)*

Socialization

- Come out smoking with the "People, Pride, Performance," Professional Team Symbol. I have buttons for every Republic employee. Get the posters (I have) up and get the patches retrofitted to Republic uniforms (available).
- Mix Republic and Northwest people in every possible ongoing training activity.
- Get all new Northwest managers participating together in our Northwest Management Club.
- Hold G.O. and Main Base open houses for employees and families.
- Get an upbeat company paper going every two weeks.
- Get each level of management to hold periodic *short* updates for their troops on unfolding events, work progress, etc.

Organization Building

- I will be working with Finance, Maintenance and Engineering, and Ground Services on unit meetings where layers of management get together, meet (even socialize) with each other and follow a guided (by me) process to work successfully together on clarifying roles, responsibilities, and tasks ahead. This "process" will be the *oil* which lubricates later effectiveness. This "team-building" can be done with others including the officers if I can get the resources.
- Get the management salary project moving with a focus on the *process* of interactive information gathering/negotiation on the positions. This project can be dynamite if layers of employees interact about the job dimensions. It is this communication that will breed further understanding about work relationships and expected performance in addition to the salary restructuring.
- If I can get some resources to do basic management skill-building training programs . . . their interactive design will also build strong cross-function/organization work relationships. I can even get them drinking beer with each other and oiling the informal system. I can produce a basic three- to five-day program and the staff to run it on short notice. Ben Lightfoot and Terry Rendleman can attest to the relationship building possible through what I call "process training." This is similar to the Professional Leadership Program recently conducted.

I would be prepared to discuss specifics at your convenience.

Ken W. Myers

The Republic Merger

On October 1, 1986, Northwest Airlines completed its $884 million buy-out of Republic Airlines—the largest merger in the airline industry to date. The merger, which nearly doubled the carrier's size to almost 33,500 employees, made Northwest the fifth largest airline company. Most industry observers applauded the move, claiming that it positioned Northwest strongly to compete through the second half of the 1980s and beyond. Within hours of the merger, Northwest's Twin Cities operations had come to a virtual standstill.

Rothmeier's Story: Part II

When Northwest's systems balked following the merger, Rothmeier wasn't altogether surprised. Because of Department of Transportation antitrust regulations, Northwest and Republic were prohibited from engaging in detailed scheduling, pricing, and marketing discussions prior to the merger's final approval, he said. Moreover, after giving the acquisition careful thought, he concluded that most of the integration glitches would have to be worked out after the two airlines' systems had already been combined. "From my understanding of the airline business, if you didn't put all the departments and their divisions together at once, you would be solving problems that would just create more problems," he explained. "You had to find out how these two computer systems really interfaced. You had to find out how the crew scheduling worked. It's a very, very complex business."

What did surprise Rothmeier, though, was the speed of the collapse. "When we did it, I said: 'In 48 hours, we'll know every problem we have in the system, and then we'll have to work our way out of it,' " he recalled. "It didn't take 48 hours. It took about two hours. And we had every problem and 400 more that we never dreamed of."

In the early days following the acquisition, most of the difficulties Northwest experienced were simply the result of trying to merge two highly disparate operations. Flight delays, double-booking of passengers, and lost luggage were all too frequent occurrences. But even worse, Rothmeier recalled, was the unexpected intensity of the union discord which followed the merger.

Because the unions representing Republic were, for the most part, different than those representing Northwest, there was a tremendous uproar as the rival unions fought to win employee backing for the right to represent the combined organization. At one point, Rothmeier said, he was dealing with almost 20 different negotiating units. Moreover, union leaders made the most of the fact that some Republic employees were paid less than their counterparts at Northwest, having accepted wage cuts a few years earlier in an attempt to salvage their struggling airline. "We knew we were going to be in bad shape for 18 months or so after the merger," Rothmeier recounted. "What we didn't count on was that we'd get the opposition from the unions. We really believed that they had more sense of what was necessary for long-term survival."

Rothmeier found it particularly difficult to deal with the former Republic union leaders, who were making the most of the differences between the two carriers' cultures. "What better way for them to fight for representation than to paint the big competitor across the street that took strikes in 1962, 1964, 1970, 1972, 1975, 1978, and 1982 as this great big ogre who had no respect for its people, and who kicked the crap out of them all the time," he fumed. "They came to negotiate with management with a list of demands that would have bankrupted the carrier, and they knew it, but they also knew that they could go back then and just stir up the operation. They had a planned program to try and destroy the service levels of the airline and bring the company to its knees."

As he struggled to repair and improve the airline's beleaguered postmerger operations, as well as to counter escalating union demands, Rothmeier said, he still hadn't lost sight of Dr. Ken's efforts to encourage a new, more participative culture at Northwest. But, by necessity, the change effort had taken a backseat to the logistical problem of resolving the daily confrontations which now typified his job. "At that point it was just like combat," Rothmeier explained. "You're in the fight now, and guess what? There are more tanks on the other side than you thought, they've got heavier artillery, and you're up to your butt in alligators." He added: "Your plan is still there to try to change the culture, but one of the things you find out is that the company you just acquired probably isn't going to buy into the program. You're planning to give them a new chance in life, and they don't believe that."

To make matters worse, as one of Minneapolis' largest employers, Rothmeier's every move was being scrutinized by the press, who often characterized him as cold or ruthless. Yet, Rothmeier insisted that throughout the ordeal, his relationship with workers overall was excellent. "The union always came back through the media and portrayed me as a guy who sat in the office and never talked to the troops," he exclaimed. "They knew that was absolute bullshit. That was all part of the propaganda by the union leadership to try to portray me differently than I was, to try and drive that wedge between management and the employees."

Although he had a "very capable" team of executive vice presidents who helped him chart a course through those difficult times, Rothmeier often felt alone in the spotlight. "There isn't anybody that's going to help you at that point," he reflected. "I did talk to a lot of other CEOs who had been through similar processes, but it was never magnified by the media.

To get away, I went down to my exercise room and lifted weights."

Looking back on the strife which followed the merger, Rothmeier claimed that if he had to do it over again, he would follow his instincts and impose more controls on the whole process. "I think we were way too participative in the early stages," he said. "We spent too much time trying to satisfy the newcomers and trying to educate them, instead of saying, 'You've got a choice. This was an acquisition, fellows, either do it our way or go do something else.' "

Moreover, although he believed there was value in eventually working toward a more participative culture, Rothmeier contended that there would always be a limit to how much freedom employees should be allowed in an airline environment. People Express's failure, he asserted, was indicative of what could happen if management gave up too much control. "In order to have a safe airline, you've got to have procedures, you've got to have discipline, and you've got to have structure," he explained. "You can't manage by seance."

In the months following the acquisition, Northwest rapidly put in new systems and practices to accommodate the combined operation. But although many of the technical snafus were solved, the relationship between labor and management just grew uglier. By the summer of 1987, Rothmeier said, mechanics and baggage handlers were conducting an unofficial slowdown; the carrier had topped the government's list of passenger complaints; there had been a few instances of antiunion employees being beaten up; and Rothmeier, himself, had received death threats.

But Rothmeier didn't have much time to worry about the threats: his attention was soon pulled elsewhere. As he lifted weights in his suburban home one hot August night, he got a phone call telling him that a Northwest flight had crashed on takeoff from Detroit.

Dr. Ken's Story: Part II

Dr. Ken never questioned the wisdom of acquiring Republic Airlines. The merger, he contended, was a stroke of genius on Rothmeier's part. But when it came to putting the two airlines together, the process was "farcical," he declared. "At least 50 percent of the glitches could have been taken care of by appropriate preplanning," he asserted. "Republic had been through this once before, and many of their people were telling me privately, 'Listen, this thing is going to come apart.'"

Dr. Ken faulted the premerger process on several fronts and made his feelings clear to Rothmeier, who had appointed an "old guard" vice chairman to orchestrate the acquisition. Northwest didn't do enough groundwork to lay out how the two physical operations should be combined, he felt. The airline failed to prepare workers adequately for the ways in which their jobs and responsibilities would change. And, perhaps worst of all, from a human resources standpoint, Northwest laid off 400 employees just after the merger. "That absolutely sandbagged everything we'd been saying about how they had to trust us," Dr. Ken exclaimed. "Morale skidded. It literally came unglued in every worst way—just as I had warned—and suddenly I was the 'prophet.' Then I started getting invited up by [president and chief operating officer] John Horn, Rothmeier, and others."

Walking around the Minneapolis hub on the day of the merger, Dr. Ken re-

called, was like visiting a battle zone. "Did you ever go to 83 gates looking for a plane?" he asked. "The pilots were sitting on the tarmac wondering which gate to pull in to, and the passengers were wondering on the other side where to go. It didn't take a behavioral scientist to tell people this thing had gone down."

Minneapolis was not the only city affected. In Memphis and Detroit, former Republic strongholds, baggage piled up in the corridors as employees wrestled to integrate the operations. Not surprisingly, Dr. Ken said, the turmoil sparked strong resentment on the part of many workers. "There was a story that, after the merger, the people in Detroit shut down the sewage system by simultaneously flushing all of their 'People, Pride, Performance' buttons down the toilets," he recounted. "I don't know if the story is true, but I do know that for several months, the buttons disappeared."

In the days following the merger, as the system shuddered to a virtual halt, Dr. Ken began to receive calls from frantic workers, both at work and at home. "Ten days into this, I got a call from one of the ramp chiefs that I had worked with, and he said, 'Dr. Ken, we're being killed over here, and nobody's listening,'" he recounted. That Saturday, Dr. Ken brought president John Horn—one of his strongest allies in the top echelon—together with six employees, who risked the union's wrath by sharing their concerns with these management representatives. "That's when the purse strings opened," Dr. Ken recalled. "John went back and started signing the checks and throwing people and equipment into the process in an attempt to stop the hemorrhage." He added: "That story went through the ranks like wildfire, first, that Horn really listened, and second, that Dr. Ken facilitated all that. That was the positive effect.''

In fact, Dr. Ken had found an unexpected silver lining to the adversity he found himself managing. For the first time since joining Northwest, he felt that his efforts were really appreciated. ''The lowest point for me were the months prior to the merger when I saw us fiddling while Rome burned,'' he remembered. ''The most exciting was when this thing went in the tank, because I knew we were finally going to get some resources.''

Unquestionably, something needed to be done. The Northwest and Republic factions—known as ''red tails'' and ''green tails,'' respectively, for the color of their companies' planes,—were not mixing. And despite the money that Horn was pumping in to improve the system, Northwest was suffering. ''The service operation was dead,'' Dr. Ken proclaimed. ''The relationship between the union and management was so antagonistic you practically had to take a whip out there to get people moving.''

In order both to bring Northwest and former Republic workers closer together, and to begin to heal the wounds opened in the labor/management relationship, Dr. Ken devised an initiative aimed at first-line supervisors—a group which he felt could have the greatest and speediest impact on employee morale. Three months after the merger, with the help of one staff member and one consultant, he launched the Crew Chief and Supervisor Academies. ''A lot of people thought this was good old leadership training,'' he chuckled. ''What they didn't understand is that its real purpose was to get the first-line supervisors to take responsibility for making service happen out there.''

The week-long off-site sessions, typically attended by 36 supervisors at a shot, consisted primarily of ''heavy behavioral stuff,'' which gave the participants some skills, while building an awareness of their importance to the organization. At the end of the first session, with ''thirty of the most hard-nosed people you'd ever want to see,'' Dr. Ken invited John Horn in to hear the group's reactions. ''The first guy to talk was a veteran crew chief,'' Dr. Ken recalled. ''He stood up with a tear in his eye and said, 'Mr. Horn, I've been with this company for 39 years, and this is the finest week I've spent with the airline.' '' He added: ''From then on, John would always come in at the end of the meetings for feedback and two-way dialogue with people. It really opened up the organization, perhaps more than any other thing we did.''

Despite the academies' success with many participants, however, union turmoil at Northwest continued. In a few instances, there were even acts of vandalism. Although the aircraft, themselves, were not threatened, Dr. Ken recalled, there were cases where acid was poured on managers' cars and sugar was put in the gas tanks of ground equipment. Dr. Ken found these events particularly frustrating because he believed the union antagonism could have been avoided. ''There could have been a much broader and deeper set of planning and integration meetings before the merger to bring the unions into this process in at least a nominal role, if not as co-equal partners,'' he declared. ''Those who feel they have a part in the process, rather than being surprised by events, more traditionally help rather than hinder.''

When he first joined Northwest, Dr. Ken had made a point of trying to build relationships with some union leaders. But when labor relations worsened after the merger, Rothmeier told him to stay away from those contacts. "He had no model for cooperation in that organization," Dr. Ken mused. "Rothmeier felt anything he gave up to the union leaders was giving them power, and that later came back to haunt him." He added: "If you kick the union, by extension you kick the employees, and guess what happens? They kick the customer. In a service organization, every piece of turbulence in the company/union relationship ultimately shows itself in a direct interaction with the customer. There's simply no way around that."

As he pondered what more could be done to break the union/management deadlock, Dr. Ken heard that a Northwest plane had crashed and rushed in to headquarters to begin to assess the damage.

The Crash

On August 16, 1987, Northwest Flight 255 crashed after takeoff from Detroit, killing 156 people. The accident was later attributed to pilot error. It was the second-worst disaster in American aviation history, and the worst disaster by far in Northwest's 61 years.

Rothmeier's Story: Part III

Rothmeier didn't go to Detroit immediately after the crash in part because he feared the media would exploit the situation and use it for its own purposes. But within two weeks, Rothmeier held sessions at the Detroit, Memphis, and Twin Cities airports to meet with every one of the employees involved in the accident. "I explained, first of all, how much we appreciated what they did and how difficult it was," he recounted. "I had spent one year in Vietnam picking up killed-in-actions and shipping them home, so I knew what the hell was going on in Detroit." He added: "I talked with them and told them what my experiences were and shared some of this. We did more with our employees after the crash than any airline had ever done in history."

As he worked to piece things back together in the weeks after the accident, Rothmeier was struck by how the disaster affected people. For the flying public, he said, it seemed to serve as a lightening rod for complaints and criticism. "You have to recall that service in general in the airline industry was bad at that point, and we stunk," he explained, "but the reaction by the public was absolutely unbelievable. We had complaints about incidents that never even happened and about flights that were nonexistent. That's when we spiked the 47 complaints per 100,000 passengers, the worst in the industry at that time."

But if the traveling public was vitriolic, within Northwest, itself, the crash had an oddly cathartic effect. According to Rothmeier, the combination of union intimidation, passenger antagonism, and, finally, the crash, forced many employees to realize that things had to change. "The cards and letters and the phone calls I got said, 'Boss, you've got to do something about this now,' " he recalled. " 'Why do we have people sabotaging the operation? Why do we have people tearing off baggage tags and making customers mad, who then come back and vent it at me?' Everybody focused on the fact that we've got to live differently, or we're going to go right down the dumper."

A few months after the crash, Rothmeier approved a more far-reaching effort than the airline had ever attempted before. Dubbed Operation Breakthrough, the program included a range of initiatives, from Town Hall Meetings—employee forums chaired by Rothmeier or Horn, which were designed to encourage two-way dialogue; to Station Action Teams—groups based at outlying stations, made up of union, employee, and management representatives, which were given the autonomy to handle a range of issues without corporate involvement. "We basically quadrupled the size of the change program we had at Northwest, made it for the whole airline, and were far more explicit," Rothmeier stated. "We stood up and said, 'What don't you like? Tell us right now.' They could get up and pour hot tea on us if they wanted to."

With Operation Breakthrough, Rothmeier felt that Dr. Ken had really come into his own. "He started out down on the ramp, with whomever would come talk to him," he noted, "but by the end he had built up to a formal program where he and a staff of three or four professionals were running these academies, and he was performing to standing ovations and getting acclamation from the troops that was just unbelievable."

Yet, even as Operation Breakthough began to break down some of the barriers between labor and management through 1988, Rothmeier felt that a barrier was going up between Dr. Ken and himself. In September 1987, Rothmeier finally approved Dr. Ken's request to become a staff vice president. The results of this, Rothmeier contended, were threefold: (1) because Dr. Ken was now an official representative of management, he lost his link to the rank-and-file employee; (2) because Dr. Ken was now part of the senior echelon, he had to follow standard hierarchical procedures and lost his "general's aide" status; and (3) Rothmeier began to feel that Dr. Ken occasionally was overstepping his bounds. "He wanted to get more into how the organization should work from the CEO down to the senior people," he recalled. "He wasn't going to do that in my organization, because that's what I do."

None of this seemed to affect the pace of Northwest's turnaround, however. With Operation Breakthrough in place, 1988 proved to be a banner year for Northwest, according to Rothmeier. The efforts to efficiently combine Northwest's and Republic's operations were finally bearing fruit in record profits (see Exhibit 3). One by one, Rothmeier was reaching contract agreements with the same unions he had been fighting one year before. And by early 1989, Northwest had achieved the second best on-time record of the major airlines and had reduced passenger complaints to the point where its service was rivaling industry leaders.

But even as Rothmeier seemed poised to enjoy a stretch of relative peace and prosperity at the airline, his calm was shattered once again. In March 1989, outside investors—including Pan Am Corporation and billionaire Marvin Davis—began a bidding war for Northwest, which culminated in the friendly buy-out of the airline in August by Wings Holdings, Inc., a Los Angeles-based investor group headed by Alfred Checchi. At the end of September, Rothmeier and four other top executives, including John Horn, abruptly announced their resignations from the airline.

"We told the union back when they were doing all those disruptive things that they were risking their own jobs," Rothmeier asserted. "Had we not had a disruption of the magnitude we had in 1987, we would have produced higher earnings a half year earlier, and with a normal airline price/earnings multiple on our stock, we'd never have been taken over."

Even with all the turmoil, however, Rothmeier left Northwest satisfied that he

EXHIBIT 3 NWA, Inc., Five-Year Summary (dollars in thousands except per-share figures—unaudited)

	1988	1987	1986	1985	1984
Operating revenues:					
Passenger	$ 4,815,771	$ 4,371,624	$ 2,920,458	$ 2,154,394	$ 1,984,999
Freight	495,788	453,160	406,726	328,400	355,336
Mail	94,333	101,393	87,459	80,126	58,339
Charter and other transportation	89,355	69,589	78,110	55,959	38,559
Other	155,156	146,458	96,421	36,612	7,741
Total operating revenues	5,650,403	5,142,224	3,589,174	2,655,491	2,444,974
Operating expenses:					
Depreciation and amortization	335,966	340,338	242,213	182,563	167,203
Other	5,109,278	4,605,756	3,180,316	2,395,841	2,181,495
Total operating expenses	5,445,244	4,946,094	3,422,529	2,578,404	2,348,698
Operating income (loss)	205,159	196,130	166,645	77,087	96,276
Interest expense = net	(50,497)	(105,005)	(76,537)	(19,873)	(4,268)
Other income (expense) = net	59,020	85,232	12,133	7,529	25,380
Earnings (loss) before taxes and extraordinary item	213,682	176,357	102,241	64,743	117,388
Income tax expense (credit)	78,584	73,346	25,300	(8,376)	30,521
Net earnings	$ 135,098	$ 103,011	$ 76,941	$ 73,119	$ 55,964*
Net earnings per share	$ 4.63	$ 3.59	$ 3.26	$ 3.18	$ 2.44*
Cash dividends	26,207	25,487	19,645	19,586	17,933
Dividends per share	0.90	0.90	0.90	0.90	0.825
Stockholder's equity	1,633,670	1,523,126	1,105,916	947,001	892,923
Number of shares outstanding at year end	29,128,475†	29,110,325†	23,890,095	21,774,251	21,749,667
Book value per share at year end	56.09	52.32	46.29	43.49	41.05

EXHIBIT 3 *(concluded)*

	1988	1987	1986	1985	1984
Assets and long-term debt:					
Flight equipment at cost	$ 4,214,142	$ 4,130,052	$ 4,109,553	$ 2,784,553	$ 2,356,048
Flight equipment at net book value	2,331,178	2,369,058	2,593,393	1,427,114	1,151,930
Total assets	4,372,001	4,268,812	4,322,854	2,320,006	1,754,233
Long-term debt and capital lease obligations	915,821	949,059	1,386,232	494,093	100,000
Statistics = scheduled services:					
Revenue plane miles ('000)	352,713	356,142	246,711	159,337	143,410
Revenue passenger miles ('000)	40,148,343	39,549,501	28,814,957	22,341,334	19,772,355
Available seat miles ('000)	61,275,077	61,420,541	48,408,440	37,148,562	32,663,660
Passenger load factor	65.5%	64.4%	59.5%	60.1%	60.5%
Passengers	35,783,704	37,246,682	23,167,120	14,538,744	13,215,907
Freight ton miles ('000)	1,476,060	1,219,456	1,022,864	886,355	965,868
Passenger and cargo revenue ton miles ('000)	5,708,755	5,397,405	4,135,343	3,334,257	3,103,799
Yield per revenue passenger mile	11.99¢	11.05¢	10.14¢	9.64¢	10.04¢
Statistics = total operations:					
Revenue plane miles ('000)	354,746	357,047	249,168	161,186	144,568
Available ton miles ('000)	10,152,321	9,882,269	8,123,450	6,450,509	5,837,972
Operating expenses per available ton mile	52.8¢	49.1¢	41.2¢	39.8¢	40.2¢
Number of employees at year end	35,532	33,724	33,427	16,864	15,185

* After extraordinary loss of $30,903 or $1.30 per share resulting from the settlement of a lawsuit.
† Excludes 1 million shares held in treasury.

had accomplished what he set out to achieve. "We took care of the customer, we took care of the employees, we took care of management, and we took care of the shareholder like the shareholder had never been taken care of before," he declared. "We won this one, and we got paid off to do it, too."

Dr. Ken's Story: Part III

As critical as Dr. Ken had been of Northwest's handling of the Republic merger, he could hardly say enough good things about the airline's behavior in the aftermath of the crash. "As tough and as antagonistic and as punitive as this old place could be, it handled its employees with the absolute tenderest of care," he marveled. "Everyone joined together in this. The way Northwest handled this was a model for how airlines ought to do it."

Probably in part because the airline managed the incident with so much sensitivity, Dr. Ken believed, the crash served to unite the company, rather than to tear it apart. "It certainly was a catastrophe, but it was also such an all-consuming event for the total company that people put aside their differences," he explained. "In fact, the crash, probably more than any other single event, speeded up the integration."

But although the crash may have put employees in a more cooperative frame of mind, Dr. Ken said, the airline was still desperately in need of a more comprehensive change program. Rothmeier was getting heavy pressure from the board to launch some sort of initiative, he reported, and John Horn was in danger of being fired if he couldn't turn the opposition around. Together with Horn and a few outside consultants, Dr. Ken devised the Operation Breakthrough program. In addition to instituting the Town Hall Meetings and Station Action Teams, Operation Breakthrough expanded the Crew Chief and Supervisor Academies; introduced a program called On-the-Line, bringing vice presidents out to visit the various line stations; created the first training program at Northwest aimed at managers; and instituted employee fairs, traveling road shows featuring presentations by both Rothmeier and Horn to introduce the overall change program to employees and their families.

Looking back, Dr. Ken saw Operation Breakthrough as his greatest success. "In the space of nine months, we took that thing from the worst performer in the industry—literally on fire—to the point where we had the fire out and were making real substantial progress," he declared.

Yet, even with this success in hand, Dr. Ken still often felt discouraged. Like Rothmeier, he believed that the contact between the two of them had begun to slip. As takeover rumors began to surface at the end of 1988 and early in 1989, and as Rothmeier tried to fend off the unwanted acquisition, he became even more absorbed with strategic issues and less available for discussions about change. But perhaps most frustrating, after briefly building to a peak budget of $1.75 million in 1988, Dr. Ken said, "at the first squeeze," that budget was cut in half. "It was a matter of priorities, and mine looked the softest," he concluded. "There needs to be a definitive kind of culture in order to sponsor a quality service organization, and you have to fund it with the same tenacity you put into fleet planning or any other operational expense."

When Rothmeier announced that Northwest was to be acquired, Dr. Ken assumed that his days at the airline would be numbered. After Wings Holdings' $3.65 billion takeover was completed, he stayed on for almost a year. But he never "bonded" with the new regime, he said, and his eventual resignation was expected by all.

When Dr. Ken left the airline, he believed that his efforts had made it a better, more functional organization. But to the end, he was never satisfied with the resources or the commitment which Northwest put into the change process. "They spent $125 million on each new 747, and I had a budget of only $1.75 million at the peak, " he complained. "Yet, there was such a reservoir of goodwill at Northwest if only people would pay attention to it." He added: "Service comes from the heart. It's what people do when management isn't looking. We did a marvelous job of cooling the mobs, but that's all that happened. We just got things settled to a low roar."

CASE

THREE IN THE MIDDLE: THE EXPERIENCE OF MAKING CHANGE AT MICRO SWITCH

As a change agent, some days you're going to be a star, and some days you're going to be a turkey; but if you're true to what you think is right, you'll end up OK. And, hell, if they fire you for doing the right thing, then you didn't want to work for that company anyway.

Rick Rowe, Director, Materials

People are struggling so much because they're trying to understand what this desired state is. I have been told I'm supposed to do this, this, this, and this—well, which one do I tackle first, and with what kind of focus, and what's the time frame?

Deb Massof, Director, Aerospace, Ordnance, and Marine Marketing

Now is the time for determination and just grunting it out. And that's where we're going to start seeing folks say, "Ah, baloney, I'm not cut out for this amount of frustration. I'm tired of trying to balance all this." It's not for the fainthearted right now.

Ellis Stewart, Director, Fabricating Operations

Prologue

It was mid-summer 1990, and Micro Switch was changing. In fact, the manufacturer of switches and sensors, a division of Honeywell, Inc., was embroiled in

---

This case was prepared by Research Associate Susan Rosegrant (under the direction of Professor Todd D. Jick).

EXHIBIT 1   Micro Switch Organizational Chart

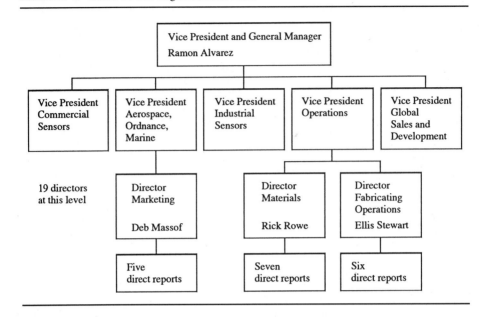

change. For the last three years, the Freeport-based company, in the rural northern corner of Illinois, had been striving to transform itself from a mature provincial business into a more dynamic customer-driven, global operation capable of surviving into the 21st century. Indeed, most of the division's managers believed that without profound changes, Micro Switch's days would be numbered.

Recently, the responsibility for shepherding this change effort had begun to fall more and more on the shoulders of the company's directors—a group of 19 middle managers who reported directly to the vice presidents under the division's general manager (see Exhibit 1). In order to form a more cohesive and skilled "change agent team," both the vice presidents and the directors had begun attending a series of formal offsite team-building and training sessions

beginning in November 1989. Rick Rowe, Deb Massof, and Ellis Stewart all had been active participants in these "Eagle Ridge" sessions, named for the meeting site.

After the second of the Eagle Ridge sessions in March 1990, Rowe, Massof, and Stewart each had tried to describe in their own words how it felt to be a change agent in the middle of the process—detailing both the pleasures and pains of making change. Four months later, each of the three directors had sat down and revisited many of the same subjects again. The second time, however, their comments were colored by changing circumstances. It was becoming clearer by the day that most of the "easy" changes had already been accomplished, they claimed. Moreover, a stubborn business slump facing both Honeywell and Micro Switch, as well as many other U.S. manufacturers, threatened to sap both the energy and the resources necessary to keep the change effort moving.

Rowe, Massof, and Stewart all had declared their dedication to change, no matter how rocky that road might prove to be. Yet after they each finished talking, a final unspoken question seemed to be on all of their minds: Had something gone wrong, or was this the way a successful change process was supposed to feel?

Change at Micro Switch: 1987-1990

Founded in 1937 and acquired by Honeywell in 1950, Micro Switch in its early years had established a solid reputation as an industry leader in switches, sensors, and manual controls, making thousands of products ranging from simple lawnmower switches to sophisticated controls for NASA's first manned orbit around the earth in 1962. The company had also established itself as a reliable source of profits for Honeywell. But as aggressive and international competitors attacked Micro Switch's traditional markets with less-expensive products in the late 1970s and early 1980s, and as switching technology began shifting from electro-mechanical to electronic and solid-state, the division's performance began to suffer. Honeywell, the Minneapolis-based company offering products and services in information processing, automation, and controls, did not release figures for its divisions. But Micro Switch's operating profits began a downward tumble in 1985, which put its corporate overseers on red alert (see Exhibit 2).

To make certain Micro Switch regained its competitive spirit, Honeywell recruited Ramon Alvarez, a 49-year-old company veteran who had already helped turn around two other divisions. Arriving in September 1987, with the corporate charge to do what was necessary to revitalize Micro Switch, Alvarez set in motion a wide-ranging mix of change actions (see Exhibit 3). First, Alvarez and his staff crafted a three-year plan for the company, put together a mission statement, and created a new vision for Micro Switch— "Growth through quality solutions to customer needs." Next, Alvarez initiated a rigorous annual strategic planning process, to make the company more competitive, responsive, and financially savvy. And, finally, Alvarez instituted a broad communication, recognition, and quality program known as APEX—an acronym for Achieve Performance Excellence.

In its first year, APEX was designed to convince Micro Switch's more than 4,000-member work force that change was necessary and to give each employee specific ways to help strive for excellence. The program included an employee suggestion system and awards for meeting performance objectives.

By its third year, APEX had become more sophisticated. At the heart of the 1990 program was a network of committees and councils, dubbed Building Block Councils, to encourage divisionwide involvement in six key strategic areas: a customer satisfaction council, to set standards for products and customer relationships and to create practices to meet those standards; a quality council, to establish and help achieve overall quality standards for satisfying customers; a goals council, to find appropriate ways to measure progress in reaching divisions goals; an awareness council, to promote awareness of quality issues throughout the division; a training council, to ensure employees get the training they need to improve quality and customer satisfaction; and a recogni-

EXHIBIT 2   Honeywell Micro Switch Division—Sales

Sales by year

Honeywell Micro Switch Division—Operating Profit

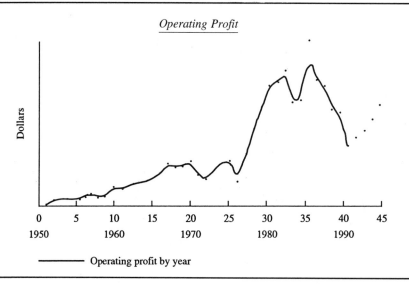

Operating profit by year

tion council, to develop and oversee an effective recognition policy. Rowe, Massof, and Stewart each chaired one of the councils.

In addition, Alvarez had put a number of key "platforms"—or change-building steps—in place, ranging from efficiency-boosting improvements such as installing a network of personal computers to process-oriented programs such as Barrier Removals, in which each group within the division identified specific barriers to

EXHIBIT 3   Summary of Change Efforts: 1987–1990

9/87:	Alvarez joins Micro Switch.
10/87:	Immediate target set: improved on-time product delivery. Weekly meetings instituted for one year attended by production, controls, and materials managers; within three months, on-time delivery boosted from 75% to above 90%.
Fall–Winter 1987:	Management team restructured; mission statement and vision crafted; vice presidents and directors required to attend Honeywell management training courses.
1/88:	APEX kick-off: Overall goals: 10% revenue growth; 10% improvement in quality, productivity, and delivery; communicate need to revitalize; teach importance of recognition; earn revitalization funds.
	Program features: employee suggestion boxes; award stamps to win prizes; monthly APEX management meetings for managers and supervisors.
Spring 1988:	First strategic planning process: individual business units wrote mission statements; did detailed market analysis, including assessment of customers, markets, competitors, and strategic issues; proposed key strategies and actions; and presented results.
Mid-1988:	Midyear APEX reassessment.
1/89:	APEX 1989: 1988 overview: exceeded 10% delivery improvement; achieved 10% revenue growth; fell short on productivity and quality goals; overall improvement in communication, recognition, and customer responsiveness.
	Overall goals: 25% organizational productivity improvement by January 1991; 10% revenue growth; time-to-market improvement; focus on becoming world-class company, making incremental improvements.
	Programs: employee suggestions; award stamps; monthly meetings; quarterly video updates by Alvarez summarizing APEX achievements and challenges.
Spring 1989:	Second annual strategic planning process.
Mid-1989:	Economic downturn felt as several major U.S. markets soften.
11/89:	First Eagle Ridge off-site management training session (see Exhibit 5).
12/89:	Barrier removals (under the APEX program): focus on identifying and removing obstacles blocking employees from achieving performance excellence.
1/90:	APEX 1990: 1989 overview: coped with difficult economy; disappointing financial performance; operating profits reached only 69% of 1989 level; nevertheless, strong improvements in responsiveness, global orientation, and strategic focus.

EXHIBIT 3   *(concluded)*

	Overall goals: qualifying for Malcolm Baldrige National Quality Award by 1992; using Barrier Removals program and Building Block Councils to help achieve world-class status; moving from three-year APEX program to a way of life.
	Programs: employee suggestions; monthly APEX meetings; video updates; Building Block Council meetings; Barrier Removals departmental meetings.
3/90:	Second Eagle Ridge off-site management training session (see Exhibit 5).
Spring 1990:	Third annual strategic planning process.
Mid-1990:	Overall goals modified due to investment limitations: have Total Quality Management System that meets Malcolm Baldrige criteria by mid-1992; reach sustained performance of Total Quality Management System by mid-1995; achieve highest level of perceived quality in all markets by mid-1995.

quality which they could attack and remove (see Exhibit 4). As these platforms began to yield improvements, they reinforced the value of the more difficult organizational and attitudinal changes which still lay ahead.

With these efforts in place, Alvarez had activated a final critical component in his plan to revitalize Micro Switch—the systematic training of a change agent team. Beginning with the first Eagle Ridge session in November 1989 (see Exhibit 5), Alvarez had begun to focus more and more on Rowe, Massof, Stewart, and the rest of the division's directors. "We have spent the past two years putting this team into position, conditioning it, and preparing it for the 1990s," Alvarez had declared in his opening speech at the first Eagle Ridge session. "While we all have a fear of the unknown, I think we have with us tonight a team that has made enormous changes over the past two years, and welcomes the opportunity to anticipate the future and manage it." With

the conclusion of the second Eagle Ridge, the time had come for the team of young change agents to assume a larger role.

Rick Rowe

It was late March 1990. Rick Rowe had returned to the office from the second Eagle Ridge session a few days earlier, and, just like after the first session, Rowe was charged up and ready to go. He had already run a one-day "mini Eagle Ridge" for about 30 of his extended staff. Now the 40-year-old Rowe was still pondering many of the issues raised at Eagle Ridge—such as empowering the work force and changing established behaviors—and wondering how to bring them alive for the lower ranks of the organization. "We've gotten where we got to on the backs of the people," he declared, "and now what we have to do is transform them. How do we take the people of Micro Switch to a different place."

EXHIBIT 4   Micro Switch Approach

• Implementing "platforms" while carefully creating "healthy dissatisfaction with the current state."

APEX	Metal Forming Reconfiguration
Barrier removals	Laser & CNC Machining Centers
Process mapping	"V" Switch Focused Factory
Time-to-market	Mars Hill Focused Factory
DOE	CAD/CAM/DNC—Plant 1
Concurrent engineering	Supervisory Performance Standards
Procurement quality assurance	Mfg. Engineering Performance Standards
CAD/CAM/CIE	SPC/PPM
CAD mold design system	Process Simulation
FMEA	SCM/CFM/JIT
Finite element analysis	CEDAC
Personal computers	Operator Training & Certification
CAT/CAI	APEX College
Engineering data/change management system	Preventive Maintenance System
Health, safety, and environment	Apprenticeship Program

A few months before, Alvarez had named Rowe to chair the Building Block Council on Recognition. Rowe's initial charter was to ferret out the best ways to recognize, motivate, and reward employees in an effort to reinforce the beliefs and behaviors—emphasizing quality and customer satisfaction—that Micro Switch now sought from its work force. In addition, the council was to see that these forms of recognition—whether an award or a simple "thank you"—became consistently practiced throughout the division.

Rowe seemed a natural choice for the job. Except for a two-year hiatus, he had been at Micro Switch since 1977, first as an engineer, now as the director of materials, responsible for procurement under the vice president of operations. As a self-proclaimed "local boy" with "real, simple values," Rowe seemed to have a strong affinity for Micro Switch's employees, as well as a desire for them to

share his own enthusiasm. In particular, he wanted to prove to the work force that the division—under Alvarez—was now responsive to input from all levels of the company. "We're trying to institutionalize that we care, we show it, we go out and talk to people," he explained. "I'm really convinced that all of our employees should feel like I do: greatly empowered, very focused, basically happy, challenged, recognized in some form, and enjoying the work they have." He added: "People go out and self-actualize on bowling. Why can't we self-actualize more at work?"

According to Rowe, when Honeywell first announced that Alvarez would be taking over, many at Micro Switch—from factory workers to senior managers—were uneasy. "Everyone perceived that the guy who rose to the top was the guy who carried the biggest two-by-four, and the one who could really belt people around psychologically," Rowe recalled. Instead, Rowe said, Alvarez moved

EXHIBIT 5   The Eagle Ridge Session Agendas

Visioning for the 90s
Management Off-Site Meeting (November 1–3, 1989)

Objectives

1. Understand the Micro Switch vision.

   • "Growth through quality solutions to customer needs."
   • Where we need to be (i.e., 1992).
   • Define quality.

2. Gain an understanding of where we currently are.

   • Malcolm Baldrige National Quality Award report card.
   • Celebrate successes.
   • Identify improvement opportunities.

3. Direct and enhance the existing strategic planning process so as to ensure the development and implementation of a quality roadmap for reaching the vision.

   • Integration of quality into ongoing strategic management and planning process.
   • Define "World Class" more clearly using Malcolm Baldrige categories as a guide; identify where we need to be in general terms.
   • Identify requirements for the 1990 strategic planning process.
   • Generate ownership for Malcolm Baldrige categories, world-class definitions.
   • Leave with a roll-down plan for getting broader understanding and buy-in at the next level down.

4. Begin to mold directors and vice presidents into a team of change agents who understand and drive change through ownership and commitment to the vision and strategic plans.

Leading the 90s: How Do We Do It?
Management Off-Site Meeting (March 14–16, 1990)

Objectives

1. Develop a clear understanding of many of the changes needed within Micro Switch (what we are moving from and what we are moving to).
2. Gain insight into how we make the change happen. Develop and enhance change management skills. Leave with answers around the issues—"how do we do it, how do we move the organization, how do we create paradigm shifts?"
3. Learn how to identify, map, and manage processes. Develop an understanding of why it's important to manage processes instead of tasks (identify the "what's in it for me").
4. Reinforce the linkage between strategic planning, Malcolm Baldrige, APEX, Barrier Removals, and business issues (e.g., time-to-market, union avoidance, resource allocation).

cautiously, especially at first, in order to gain workers' trust and cooperation. "He took the opposite tack, which is to say we're good, we need to build on that, we need to create something, we need to regenerate, we need to rejuvenate the business," he recalled. "We need to put capital back into the facilities. The cow's been milked until she's about dead."

Many of these ideas weren't new to Rowe. He had always been intrigued by questions of organizational change and had tried to run his own piece of the organization in a more "enlightened" fashion than many other managers at Micro Switch, listening to worker concerns and delegating responsibility whenever possible. But instead of garnering praise for his efforts, Rowe had gained the reputation of being a renegade, not a team player. "Challenging anything we did was bad," he explained. "I was the 'bad cowboy.'"

Rowe claimed that his behavior didn't shift substantially after Alvarez's arrival. But now, the same actions that had been frowned on before were being held up as an example of the right way to operate. "Now I am a 'good cowboy' because I'm a change agent," he marveled. "I now have a desirable title as opposed to being someone who would rock the boat. Ray's tried to reach out and find the change makers who were still alive and well."

As newly appointed head of the recognition council, Rowe had been interviewing 300 randomly selected Micro Switch employees to elicit their ideas about rewards and recognition. The consensus on how to make people feel more appreciated turned out to be more simple than he expected: most important was to just say thank you. But Rowe uncovered other issues in the course of talking with coworkers, which he found more troubling and less easily solved. Among these was the issue of empowerment itself. "I think people absolutely have bought hook, line, and sinker that we have to change to survive," he mused. "Where we're getting hung up in the process right now is our people have said: 'OK, we buy it.' 'Boy, we're in trouble.' 'You guys in management, you tell us what to do now.' And our response back has been, 'Wait a minute, we want to empower you. And we want you to tell us what we should do.'" He added: "You essentially are empowered to do anything you want to do, but what hangs people up is you have to have the courage to use this power."

Not only were employees confused about how to suddenly take power into their own hands, Rowe said, the multiple changes taking place at Micro Switch had left many people at all levels of the company grasping for something to hang onto—something familiar or some point of safety. "When you're confronted with change and the unknown, for most people, it's very scary and they need an anchor," Rowe explained. "So I'm asking my people, 'What's the anchor for our factory? What's the anchor for our salaried people?' We would like to believe that management is the anchor for our employees."

Rowe also was concerned about how to keep Alvarez, the rest of the change agents, and himself from getting worn-down by the process. Even the apparently indefatigable Alvarez, he said, occasionally claimed he was tired. And with a possible five to eight additional years necessary to institute a major change at Micro Switch, there could be plenty of opportunity to become fatigued and frustrated. "There's a danger for change agents that you get so far ahead in understanding where the company needs to go, and then you look back and say, 'Where the hell is everybody?' '' Rowe noted. "That's scary. On a personal basis you're at risk because you're out there sticking your neck way out and you look back and no one's there. You get tired when you're too far out in front."

In this sense, change agents needed anchors just as much as anyone else involved in the process, Rowe insisted. But figuring out who or what should be the anchor for the change leaders was not so obvious, especially for Alvarez. "I was talking with one of my superintendents about anchors, and he said, 'What's your anchor?' '' Rowe recalled. "I said that I didn't know. For some people it probably is their peers or their superiors. And I suppose in one way, Ray may be more of an anchor than I think. I like to think I'm very independent. I'm still doing the same thing I've always done, only this time someone says, 'Gee, it's OK.' ''

Although Rowe might have been operating the same way he always did, the positive reinforcement he was feeling, and the excitement of working with others in the organization toward a common goal, was clearly a new and motivating sensation. "I wasn't ostracized before, but I felt I wasn't progressing at the rate I should," he remarked. "The real difference is it wasn't as much fun. This is like a playground! Right now, for someone like me, this environment we've created is like I've died and gone to heaven. I don't ever want this to end."

* * *

Four months later, it had become more apparent than ever that the business slump was not going away, and that Micro Switch's management team had to face the fact that Honeywell probably wouldn't provide funding for any of the more ambitious revitalization programs waiting in the wings. In fact, even some of the basic programs already in place were undergoing careful scrutiny. "I can see how far we've come in three years," Rowe insisted. "But the downside is that very few companies which have attempted to change succeed in the long run, principally because the owners can't endure the 7-to-10-year total transition period. In a lot of companies, the business doesn't quite measure up to standards, and someone who is holding the checkbook gets impatient."

The slump's timing was particularly hard for Micro Switch, Rowe contended, coinciding as it did with a natural slowdown in the change process itself. The easy changes already had been made. Now the company had to tackle deeply ingrained behaviors and processes which were holding the division back from reaching its goals. And while the first Eagle Ridge session had left most of the participants almost euphoric, the second session had felt more like plain work, and that sense had lingered. "We're at this lull where a lot of the excitement has worn off, and now we're into hard work," Rowe acknowledged. "Change takes so goddamn long. You get real frustrated by it and run the risk of losing people's attention."

Looking back over the change process of the past almost three years, Rowe's frustration seemed to grow. Eagle Ridge had been the first real opportunity for the directors to share training in change management, and it had been "an excellent solidifier," he said. "One of the big things Eagle Ridge did for us as a group was to create some degree of camaraderie, and also more of an element of trust," he reflected. "The degree of cooperation between functions here at the director level is the best that I've seen in years.''

But in retrospect, Rowe also felt that he could have benefitted from such training much earlier. "When I came into this job, I was given the task of transforming my part of the organization from its present state as an archetypical procurement organization into some undefined world-class operation," he explained, "but I wasn't given any real training. At Eagle Ridge, for the first time I felt like there was some laid-out method to the madness.'' He added: "As one of the so-called disciples, I've felt a little bit alone. I haven't felt as warm and comfortable and that I was doing the right thing as I should."

Rowe confronted Alvarez with these thoughts during a break at the second Eagle Ridge, but the general manager had defended his choice to hold off on the training. "Ray said, 'Some of you guys may be ready to go, but the rest of the organization is not. I can't let you get ahead of everybody else,' '' Rowe recounted. "So we could feel a little bit of the hand of control saying some of us may need to slow down." Despite Alvarez's cautioning, however, Rowe remained convinced that he and the other directors would have profited from earlier guidance and instruction. "I think there were a fair number of people who were confused," he explained. "Some people probably thought this is some kind of dictatorial commandment, and Ray's doing all this stuff, and they don't necessarily buy in. I think we could have got the buy-in a little bit sooner."

One of the key messages that stuck with Rowe after Eagle Ridge was that behaviors reflect beliefs: If you want to change someone's behavior, you must first change their underlying beliefs. But in addition to changing people's beliefs and rewarding the behaviors it wanted, something Micro Switch had done fairly successfully, Rowe maintained that it was also time for the division to get tougher about discouraging the behaviors it didn't want. "We haven't stressed enough of the attitude we're looking for in people,'' Rowe declared. "For a long time, we've said that, as long as people do an adequate job, that's OK. But if you think about anything else we do in life, we don't let people who have bad attitudes play on our teams, we get rid of them—we tell them that they can't play, or we trade them, or we let them go. Who says we have to employ people who don't want to be a part of our team?''

Reassigning or firing a large number of workers wouldn't be an easy move to make, Rowe admitted, particularly in Freeport, where Micro Switch was the main game in town. "It's real hard to look at people and to say, 'We didn't make you a manager for life,' '' he confessed. But according to Rowe, the time might have come for Micro Switch to make these hard choices in the interest of survival. "We're running out of time," he asserted. "My big concern is that in every case I've seen, it takes 7 to 10 years to make the change. I don't know that we've got 7 to 10 years.''

Deb Massof

A few days had passed since the second Eagle Ridge session and, like Rowe, Deb Massof was still struggling to digest all of the change-related topics presented there. "What's intriguing about Micro Switch right now is that there are so many changes going on at one time," she declared. "I think people do want to change. They do want to do good. But they're real frustrated at not knowing what to change.''

When Deb Massof joined Alvarez's management team early in 1988, she was immediately pegged as an outsider. For starters, at 32 years old, she was considerably younger than most of the managers. After recommending that Micro Switch focus more on its aerospace, ordnance, and marine (AOM) business by making it a separate unit, Massof was named the new unit's director of marketing, heading a staff whose members were typically between 40 and 60 years old, with 20 to 40 years of seniority. She was also a senior manager in a company unaccustomed to seeing women in professional positions. This, after all, was a division where—until Alvarez intervened—the only woman staff member had never been invited to a general manager's meeting and did not receive the same parking privileges the men enjoyed.

Finally, Massof—who had already amassed 12 years of experience at Honeywell—carried the stigma of coming from "Corporate." Since Honeywell bought Micro Switch in 1950, the relationship between the two organizations had evolved into an uneasy alliance. By 1987, senior management at Honeywell had become concerned by Micro Switch's apparent drive to stay independent. Micro Switch managers, for their part, believed Honeywell was milking Micro Switch dry without giving anything in return. Massof was well aware of these tensions. "It felt like those of us from Honeywell were suspect," she recalled. "For years and years they would ship the profits up the river . . . to us!"

Massof had her own misgivings about coming to Micro Switch. It wasn't just the move from Minneapolis, a thriving cosmopolitan center, to Freeport, a town of about 27,000 surrounded by farmland. It was also leaving behind the fast-paced environment of Honeywell for a division which appeared resistant to change. "I

used to think this place was stuck in a time warp," confessed Massof, who first visited Micro Switch a decade earlier. "Not many things have changed since 1980. That was probably the scariest thing for me. It's such a deep culture."

As Massof dug into her new job, some of her forebodings proved right on target. Her forthright and nonhierarchical style— which was among the traits that had appealed to Alvarez—came as a shock to managers accustomed to adhering to a rigid reporting structure. It took months, for example, before she could approach a product administrator two levels down in the organization without a product manager rushing to intervene, and without their assuming she had come to complain.

Moreover, Massof found herself responsible for marketing product lines which had basically lain dormant for more than a decade. For example, although she was told that Micro Switch was still a leader in military lighted push buttons—a product the company invented in the mid-1950s—Massof discovered that lead actually had dwindled away to an insignificant share. "In my particular business unit, the highest priority is making up for 15 years of no investment and no new products," she declared. "We're talking major, major change."

Massof's goals during her first 18 months with the AOM unit in many ways paralleled what Alvarez was trying to accomplish with the division overall: to make people aware of the need for change; to compensate for years of neglect; and to start drawing people into both the revitalization process and daily operations in ways they had never been involved before.

According to Massof, this was easier said than done. In her area, there was no time at first to think about "fine tuning" the change process. Instead, she was faced with getting much greater involvement in using management tools like market research and strategic planning in order to get the business moving again. "We were working very hard on just understanding this market we were in," she explained. "We thought we understood our customers, but I was shocked at how much we didn't know about the people we got all this money from."

Even in the process of implementing these steps, Massof was introducing her staff and employees to what for them was a radical new way of doing things. After just a few months on the job, for example, Massof called a general meeting to begin brainstorming for the unit's strategic plan, which Massof was determined to turn into a vital "living document"—a plan with daily significance for the entire unit. Because strategic planning at Micro Switch formerly had been the sole province of top management, employees at lower levels had never had a say in such issues before. She recalled the strategic planning kickoff meeting: "I got so many blank stares, as though to say, 'What on earth are you asking us to do?' All I heard was griping for weeks, and I thought, 'This is the biggest mistake I've ever made.'"

Massof didn't back down, however. She pressed her subordinates to continue meeting a couple of times a week, and, as the divisionwide strategic review process neared, the meetings increased to almost daily. The hardest part, Massof recounted, was to encourage independent thinking from employees who had never been expected to contribute before. Now, looking back on the process from a year's distance, Massof deemed it one of her group's greatest successes. When the time came for AOM to present its plan to the division, it was not Massof or her boss who introduced the strategy, but the cross-

functional business teams which had invested so much time, energy—and complaints—in crafting it. "To get them together in a room to do strategic management was real weird for them," she laughed. "But I think they're feeling better about it now, and better about themselves."

Although the strategic plan was a success, it didn't mean the AOM unit was looking forward to it the second time around. Massof had already heard complaints about the planning for 1991, which was set to begin. Partly because of the strain of trying to motivate her co-workers and subordinates, Massof was particularly eager to draw inspiration from the Eagle Ridge sessions, even though these signaled a more intense focus on change at Micro Switch. "I feel like I need to be smarter," she admitted. "Then I figure out that it's not related to my inexperience at all, it's just the situation. There are a lot of people who have a lot more experience than I do who are feeling the same way." She added, "The biggest thing that's hit me is that I can't do a lot of things at once. We have to show little successes. Then when you look back over 12 months you say, 'Well, we've come a long way.'"

*   *   *

Four months later, Massof seemed more at ease with the unsettling sensation of being in the midst of change. Moreover, now, in the middle of July 1990, she finally could point to a few examples of successful organizational change. Her group had recently completed its second strategic planning process, and this year—despite her initial forebodings—the participants had taken up the plan without complaining and had brought a new level of skill and detail to the task. "We spent very little time bemoaning the time it would take—we actually had buy-in!'' she exclaimed. ''We established a benchmark on change by doing something right in 12 months.'' She added: ''These people two years ago would not have had the confidence to get up in front of the general manager, and talk about their business, and tell the general manager what he should do.''

Massof also felt that the seeds of teamwork planted at Eagle Ridge were beginning to take root. Just the day before, for example, she had met Rick Rowe for lunch to discuss a number of issues, ranging from getting Rowe's procurement perspective on a major contract for her unit that Massof was renewing, to discussing how their Building Block Councils should complement each other. ''This helps the team-building process overall because we're setting an example,'' Massof explained. ''When people see us, they're going to realize that being from different areas of the organization doesn't make us enemies, and that we can work on problems together.''

Massof was still confronting many of the same obstacles which had discouraged her in March—in particular, the sheer number of changes waiting to be implemented. ''My major frustration is that there are too many things that you know *need* to be changed,'' she stated. But at the same time, Massof appeared less troubled by the sense of always having too much to do. ''We're all trying to be Super People— we're all trying to do everything at the same time, so we're spread a little thin,'' she mused. ''It's a natural part of the process, but as part of that process, you can also step back and say we need to focus.''

Specifically, Massof intended to focus more on her position as head of the Building Block Council on Customer Satisfac-

tion, a role which had taken a back seat to the strenuous strategic planning process of the previous few months, and which would probably continue to take a back seat to the overriding concern of keeping the business on track under very difficult market conditions. ''We're all doing this on the side of our desks,'' she sighed. ''The councils consist mostly of directors and managers, and just getting the three directors of marketing in one room at a time is an incredible job.''

As chair of the customer satisfaction council, Massof was charged with recommending and helping to implement the policies and systems Micro Switch needed to satisfy its mission of becoming a truly customer-driven organization. Among the priority items Massof wanted the council to consider were setting up a toll-free telephone number for customer inquires and creating a standard complaint system to replace the company's somewhat haphazard case-by-case approach.

According to Massof, Alvarez was ''very, very clear about his expectations'' for the division, yet she felt she had a great deal of autonomy. ''It's not dictatorial,'' she asserted. ''It's not like Ray's standing up there saying, '·'Thou shalt do this.' He's depending on a lot of different people to come up with the right solutions. And getting people together is not an easy thing to do when you're trying to run your business, too.'' She added: ''I don't feel like he's controlling us. In fact, I feel I have so much leeway that I always feel guilty that we're not doing enough.''

Ellis Stewart

The second Eagle Ridge session had ended just a few days before, but Ellis Stewart was already sifting through the materials he had brought back with him, trying to figure out how to incorporate the best of the new concepts into one of the many internal business manuals he had designed. Alvarez had named the 44-year-old Stewart to head the Building Block Council on Training just a few months before, but for Stewart, absorbing and repackaging change management techniques was a labor of love—one he had been doing on his own for years. "I do it because it's fun to do and it helps the cause," he claimed, and then gestured at a shelf piled high with management books. "There's no excuse for a business manager today not to know what is going on and not to have some ideas."

Stewart had logged almost 20 years at Micro Switch when Alvarez took over, and he had risen to the position of director of fabricating operations, responsible for producing precision engineered parts for Micro Switch and other Honeywell divisions. Stewart's roots went deep and revealed a loyalty which the last decade of management practices had not shaken. "When I came here, the place literally could do no wrong," he asserted. "In many markets we were the only game in town, so we named our price and got it. From the standpoint of a middle manager, this place has been a fantastic place to work."

Stewart grudgingly admitted that Micro Switch's dedication to delivering profits to Honeywell had gone too far—causing the company to skimp on internal investment and to resort to frequent layoffs. But he also insisted that many managers at the company had never lost sight of the quest for excellence. "Ray has said many times that the vision kind of got middle-aged," he said. "Some of us, especially people of my vintage, kind of resent that because we don't think we were ever caught up in that. Guys like Rick Rowe and me were off on

our own, having a chance to change things and influence things."

In fact, Stewart and Rowe recently had been the first employees to receive plaques—dubbed Eagle Visionary Commendations—honoring them for their contributions to the change process (see Exhibit 6). "If I got that award for any reason at all, I got it because of my guts—my willingness to experiment with my part of the organization and take some risks," Stewart declared. "But this stuff wasn't always appreciated. Some folks have labeled Rick a maverick; and when I was doing creative stuff back in 1982, I actually had my career threatened because people resented it."

Despite having won the award, Stewart still felt he had plenty of new things to learn, he hastened to add. The Eagle Ridge sessions, on top of the intensive strategic planning process which Alvarez had instituted, had begun to drive home a concept of cooperation and teamwork that was foreign to many of Micro Switch's managers. "We've got big egos, and teamwork becomes the biggest challenge," Stewart conceded. "We have some folks who think that if they don't control everything that they need, then they can't succeed. The ego thing tends to cloud objectivity—mine and everybody else's." He added: "It hasn't been until the last 18 months that we have tended to look around to see who's got something that's really good that we can copy. Up until then, it was, 'Well, Rick did something, but now I'll go do my own thing.' "

In addition to teamwork, Stewart also saw a number of other issues needing attention. "What is it going to take to get the rest of our management team to articulate the visions for their own areas as well as Ray can do it for the division, and as

EXHIBIT 6

The Eagle Visionary Commendation

Presented To

A visionary possesses a characteristic rare in today's fast-paced business environment: the ability to see beyond the urgency of today's demands to what *can* be reality tomorrow. This is not the ability to simply imagine what tomorrow might be like -- it is the ability to see that tomorrow so tangibly that it can be touched, understood and believed.

Some visionaries are traditionalists and some are mavericks. But all can articulate a vision in such a way that others may catch its essence. And all visionaries are leaders in that they help us create the blueprint to build those visions into towering realities. And then they challenge us all to make it happen.

And while they may be dreamers, visionaries are also doers: they see not only the future, but the path -- and its milestones -- that can take us there.

We salute and encourage this quality in the Honeywell MICRO SWITCH management team. It is a quality that will help us maintain a leadership position in our global marketplace and give us an unmatched competitive edge.

This commendation recognizes the visionary contributions made in ensuring our company's world-class citizenship in the business community of the 1990's.

Ramon A. Alvarez, Vice President and General Manager

MICRO SWITCH
a Honeywell Division

well as I and a number of other folks can do it for our parts of the division?'' he asked. ''That's a tall order. We have to learn a lot of things, we have to change the way we act a little, and we have to be a little less stuffy—get excited from time to time.''

Stewart seemed deeply committed to the changes taking place in the last two-and-a-half years. ''We have a general manager who has boundless energy and who sets the example,'' he declared. ''Not that he doesn't sometimes make us feel bad if he blows up at us, because that can happen. He's a very intense person. But his creative energy has changed the work environment.'' He added: ''We tried to remind our folks, we're optional. We've got to be the best there is in this kind of business, or eventually we won't be around—that's the law of nature.''

* * *

Four months later, Stewart's nervous energy seemed somewhat tempered. Like Rowe and Massof, Stewart worried that the business slump had hit at a particularly inopportune time—knocking the wind out of the change effort just when it needed a boost. ''We have lots of projects underway, lots of new product development work, tons of energy being expended, long workdays, people working on weekends and taking their work home, but there's just no growth,'' he lamented. ''What we need is some growth to take advantage of all the work we've done.''

Even Alvarez, whose energy and optimism had often sustained Micro Switch in the past, was showing signs of strain, Stewart said. ''Ray and a number of us are concerned that the organization is doing a lot of things, but doesn't appear to be changing rapidly enough to take advantage of the investments that we've made,''

he explained. ''We are not on this upward rocket that we'd expected to be on by now, and that is weighing extremely heavily.''

This increased level of stress might have contributed to the occasional friction some of the directors were experiencing, particularly as they wrestled with issues of autonomy and empowerment. In the past few months, for example, after a preliminary presentation to Alvarez and his executive staff, Stewart—in his role as head of the Building Block Council on Training—had overseen the planning, organization, and pilot run of a new employee training program known as APEX College. But instead of winning kudos for his fast work, Stewart and his associates had gotten their wrists slapped for acting without authorization. ''It was totally bewildering,'' he recalled. ''We said, 'Listen, damn it, we accepted the assignment, we went and did it, we're doing it on the corner of our desks, it's not anywhere *close* to the normal routine for a job like ours, so what the hell are you telling us now?' '' He added: ''There's an aura here that, if you don't move quickly, that's a problem, but in this case we got caught moving too quickly.''

Nevertheless, although Stewart was angry at the time, he said that, in retrospect, he saw the wisdom of the reprimand. ''Ray is tussling with the business of control versus empowerment,'' he explained. ''He's got to control the business, he's got his neck on the line for the success of this thing, he likes to have his mark on things, he wants to have his staff involved setting the tone and providing the leadership, and we went off and said, 'We don't need you guys.' We moved so quickly, we lost them.''

The issue of control versus empowerment was not the only dichotomy Micro Switch was struggling with, Stewart said.

The company also had a schism between those who were committed to change and those who were not. On the one hand were the change leaders like Rowe, Massof, and Stewart, himself, who were in danger of taking on more change than they could handle. And on the other hand was a group straddling all levels of the organization which still appeared unconvinced of the need for change.

Both of these groups needed attention, Stewart maintained. Those who had thrown themselves wholeheartedly behind change were in danger of burning out, or of becoming paralyzed by the sheer magnitude of the tasks they had taken on, he warned. "A friend of mine used to talk about the stool of life," Stewart mused. "There are four legs on that stool—your work, your hobbies, your family, and your religion—and as long as you keep those four legs the same length, it's a stable situation. But if you get one a lot shorter or longer than the others, it's unstable and the stool will fall over." He added: "I keep cautioning people in our career development workshops about that. At some point in time you have to live with a lopsided stool, but you can't live with it for long."

But even more threatening for the organization were the people who still weren't behind the change, Stewart warned. And like Rowe, he had begun to believe that the time for patience was past. "You have to provide the vision and the mission, but you also have to recognize that some folks won't see things that way and will hope to maintain the status quo," he stated. "If we choose to have a culture that's participative, and we have folks for whom that just isn't in their guts, then we have to reassign, reposition, or fire them. Our heritage here has been to be very patient, very tolerant—to coach, counsel, and hope for the best. We have to be more tough-minded now without being cruel and ruthless."

Providing more and better training was the first step in resolving many of these issues, Stewart insisted. "The key to this thing is a much more rapid introduction of empowerment techniques and training so we can get the entire work force to have an entrepreneurial spirit," he declared.

But in almost the same breath, Stewart admitted that there were times when he grew discouraged and brooded about some questions that simply couldn't be answered. "I think this is the right process, but I'm not so sure whether the timing was right," he reflected. "Is this the year—is this the decade—that we should have done this with Micro Switch? Could the business have continued to thrive and grow under the old way of working, and perhaps even done better during this same period of time? I don't know. I'm always going to wonder about that."

READING

CONVERTING MIDDLE POWERLESSNESS TO MIDDLE POWER: A SYSTEMS APPROACH

Barry Oshry
Management Consultant

Witches and Demons

We are in the Dark Ages of organizational understanding. In the years ahead we will be mocked for the primitiveness of our beliefs just as we now look condescendingly upon those who in great earnestness hung witches. In those dark days, when things went badly, people had their witches to blame; when things go badly for us in our organizations, we have our demons. They had their evidence, we have our evidence. They hung or burned their witches, we rotate our demons or fire them or humiliate them or hang them out to slowly twist in the wind. Looking back on the witch burners from our "modern day" perspective, we see how bizarre their beliefs were. When future "moderns" look back at us, what will they see?

Let me say something about our 20th century organizational demons. When things go wrong in our organizations, we see demons. We point the finger at particular people—they are the ones we blame, and they are the ones we "fix" or replace or fire. Yet I maintain that many of these demons are as innocent as the witches of yesteryear. You say, "Not so"—all the evidence of your senses tells you that they are in fact the culprits. And

From *National Productivity Review*.

I say, "Welcome to 20th century witchcraft."

Proust suggests that "the voyage of discovery rests not in seeking new lands but in seeing with new eyes." Which is precisely what we need—a new set of lenses for looking at organizational behavior. With the right lenses, our demons will disappear.

Like you, I am a primitive person living in the Dark Ages of organization behavior. My lenses are as primitive as yours. But over the past 30 years I have had the privilege of observing many hundreds of organizations. Some of these organizations are like the ones you work in and are familiar with, others are simulations we have created for purposes of education and research. I have seen things that give me a glimmer into what is missing—the lens we don't have.

What strikes me most about organizations is their regularity—the same scenarios keep happening again and again in the widest variety of settings—manufacturing, high technology, religious institutions, schools, community groups, government agencies, universities—the same patterns keep showing up. But rarely do people feel that they are living out a pattern; each event seems very specific to their unique organization, circumstances, and people. It matters little that all over the world many thousands of people in all varieties of organizations are having the very same experience.

The lens we are missing is a systemic one. We don't see systems, we just see people. We don't see system spaces, we see only the effects these spaces have on us. So when things go wrong, we blame what we see—the people, our demons.

The Middle Space

In this paper we direct our attention to the Middle Space. A Middle Space is a space that pulls us between others (see Figure 1). Whoever enters a Middle Space is caught between the conflicting agendas, perspectives, priorities, needs, and demands of two or more individuals or groups. Some middle spaces exist between contending vertical pressures (e.g., supervisors between their managers and their work groups); others exist between lateral pressures (e.g., a liaison between customers and producers); and many middle spaces have multiple contending forces vertically and laterally. Supervisors in plants and offices exist in middle spaces, as do department chairpersons and deans in universities, middle managers, heads of medical departments, union stewards, and people occupying many hundreds of other positions in the widest spectrum of organizations and institutions. (In our analyses we will for the most part limit our discussion to the relatively simple Middle Space between Above and Below.)

All of these are middle spaces. Some spaces are more middle than others—the greater the differences between Above and Below, in perspective, priorities, and needs, the more powerful the middleness of the space.

Put people into a Middle Space and there is a story that develops with great

FIGURE 1   The Middle Space—A Space That Pulls Us between Others

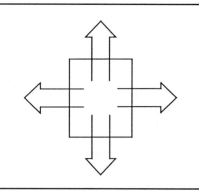

regularity. The story varies from situation to situation, but the basic pattern is the same. It is a story of gradual disempowerment in which reasonably healthy, confident, and competent people become transformed into anxious, tense, ineffective, and self-doubting wrecks. And when this happens we see these persons as our demons—it's too bad we're stuck with such weak and ineffective middles; fire them or fix them or rotate them or let them swing slowly in the wind.

The question is: If we look at these many different middle stories through a systematic lens, what new understanding and what new strategies for empowerment open up for us?

The Middle Story

"Middles live in a tearing world.

It is a world in which people are pulling you in different directions.

Tops have their priorities and they expect your support.

Bottoms have their priorities—which are generally different from Tops'—and *they* expect your support.

FIGURE 2   The Middle Story: From Healthy to Torn

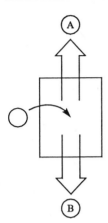 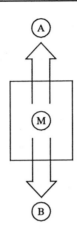 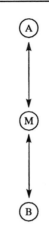 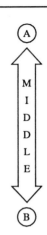

1. A perfectly healthy individual about to enter a middle space between above (A) and below (B).

2. **The individual in the middle space.**

3. Life becomes hectic.

4. **In time, a perfectly healthy individual becomes torn—confused, weak, powerless, disvalued, self-doubting.**

Tops want you to get production out of Bottoms, but you can't do that without the cooperation of Bottoms.

Bottoms want you to deliver on their needs and wants, but you can't do that without the cooperation of Tops.

When Tops and Bottoms are in conflict, one or the other or both try to draw you in on their side.

> You please one,
> you displease the other;
> you try to please both,
> you end up pleasing neither."[1]

Life in the Middle Space is hectic (see Figure 2). You are always on the go. So much to do—for everyone—so little time. You spend your time working in other people's spaces and on other people's

agendas. You feel squeezed. Tops are distant and remote; they're on another, less tangible wave length, talking about strategy and planning and organization. Meanwhile, Bottoms are looking to you for concrete direction and support; but you don't have the direction and support to give to them. You see the attitudes of Bottoms deteriorating and can't do anything about it. You feel useless, like a conduit simply carrying information back and forth. You spend your time going back and forth between Top and Bottom, explaining one to the other, justifying one to the other. There are lots of opportunities to let people down, and few opportunities to succeed. Tops don't seem to move your world ahead; they just give you more work and more uncertainty. You feel like a ping pong ball and Tops and Bottoms are the paddles. You are confused. (In the Middle Space, if you're not

---

[1] B. Oshry, *The Possibilities of Organization*, pp. 60–61, 1985.

confused, it means you're not paying attention. You talk to Tops and they make sense; you talk to Bottoms and they make sense, too. It's hard to figure out what *you* believe.) Your actions are weak, compromises, never quite strong enough to satisfy Tops or Bottoms. Sometimes you feel important yet insignificant—as a telephone wire is important; but the real action is not with you, it's on either end of the line. You take a lot of flak from Bottoms, and never feel you can give it back (it wouldn't be managerial). For some reason you feel like it's your responsibility to keep this system from flying apart. Yet, much of the time you feel invisible—when Tops and Bottoms are together they talk as if you're not even there. You feel inadequate, never doing quite enough for Tops or Bottoms, never quite measuring up to the job. In time, you begin to doubt yourself—maybe there *is* something wrong with you, maybe you're not smart or strong enough, maybe you're not as competent as you thought. And others in the organization mirror this impression. They see you as a nice person, trying hard, acting responsibly, maybe even well-intentioned. It's just too bad you're so weak and ineffective. Well, maybe with a little more training or meditation or aerobic exercise or therapy or a better diet. . . .

Primitive, primitive! There are no demons here. This is not a personal story; it's a space story. The solution lies not in fixing people but in seeing and mastering the Middle Space.

A Systemic Look at How We Disempower Ourselves in Middle Positions

Our methods of preparing people for middle positions are primitive. We pro-

mote them on the basis of dimensions that may be totally irrelevant to their ability to master middleness. We train them on the technical aspects of the job. At best, we offer them leadership or supervisory training—which is Top's way of telling Middle how to handle Top's agenda, but which leaves Middle totally unprepared for the fact that Bottom has its own agenda for Middle in relation to Top.

No dean, no supervisor, no department chair, no section head should enter such a position without first understanding the dynamics of middle positions and learning how to master the Middle Space.

There is a process that happens to us with great regularity when we enter the Middle Space, and this process lies at the heart of our disempowerment as Middles. (See Figure 3) Simply put, the process is this: We slide into the middle of *other people's* issues and conflicts and make these issues and conflicts *our own*. Once we slide into the middle, we are torn.

Objectively, even in middle positions, we are not torn until we put ourselves into the position to be torn. Objectively, Above has its agenda for Below, and Below has its agenda for Above. In that nano-second before sliding in, Middle could be relaxedly observing, "Isn't it interesting the conflicts *they* are having *with one another?* What's it got to do with *me?*"

That moment never happens or, if it does, it is too brief. As Middles, we slide into the Middle and become torn between Above and Below. In that torn condition we feel that it is our responsibility, *and our responsibility alone*, to resolve *their* issues and conflicts. Our self-esteem now rests on *their* evaluations of how well we satisfy *them*.

This "sliding in" process is not a conscious choice we make. It is more like a

FIGURE 3   We Slide into the Middle of Other People's Issues and Processes and Make Them Our Own

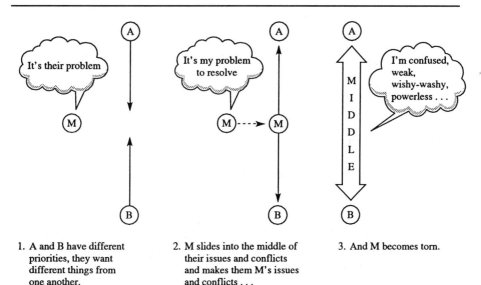

1. A and B have different priorities, they want different things from one another.

2. M slides into the middle of their issues and conflicts and makes them M's issues and conflicts . . .

3. And M becomes torn.

reflex. We don't *do* it, it *happens* to us. We see a conflict *between others*, and we feel the full weight of that conflict resting on *our* shoulders.

> Charlie complains to me, his supervisor, that the shower is not working. In a flash, I'm feeling that it's my fault that the shower is not working and that it's my responsibility to get it working. When I don't get it working fast enough, because I can't get the approval from upstairs or because maintenance has this huge backlog, Charlie gets on my case, and I'm feeling weak and foolish and ineffective.

> Louise has been called in to manage a meeting between Above and Below. This is an important meeting; Above and Below have a number of issues between them. Louise is very nervous; she feels that *her* success or failure rests on how well this meeting turns out.

If Charlie's supervisor or Louise had their systemic lenses on, they might see something else—a flashing sign: "Middleness—Beware of Sliding into the Middle!" And they might pause to consider if there might not be some more powerful way to handle this situation.

Coaching for Middleness: Two Strategies and Five Tactics for Empowering Yourself in the Middle

In the absence of a systemic lens, we see only specific events, specific circumstances, specific people—our demons— and we react. With a systemic lens, we see *middleness*, and that seeing opens up for us new strategies and tactics for mastering the Middle Space.

Strategy I: **Don't slide into the middle of *their* issues and conflicts and make them your own.** That is, at all times, be clear that this is not **your** problem. *They* are having an issue with one another. Do what you can to empower *them* to resolve *their* issues. Resist all efforts on their part to pull you into the Middle; the pressures can be quite strong. Understand that Above and Below don't mind at all having you feel responsible for resolving their problems.

Strategy II: **Do not lose *your* mind.** The Middle Space is an easy place to lose *your* mind—your view, your thoughts, your perspective on what needs to happen. When we are torn, our attention is on Above and Below—what they think, what they want, what will satisfy them. In that Middle Space, however, we are in a unique position to formulate our own vision of Below that confuses us and causes us great stress. That conflicting information, however, also can be the source of our unique strength. We need to seek out that information—rather than run from it. We need to allow it in and use it to formulate our unique Middle perspective.

With these two general strategies in mind, we can explore specific tactics by which we empower ourselves and others from the Middle position.

Tactic 1: **Be Top When You Can, and Take the Responsibility of Being Top.** Sometimes we beg for trouble, and then complain when we get it. In certain situations we make ourselves Middle when we could be Top. Two Middles walk away from a meeting with Tops. One Middle says to the other, "Say, we didn't ask them if we could do (such and such). Let's go back and ask." The second Middle says, "We didn't ask, and they didn't tell us. So why don't we decide what needs to happen. If they don't like it,

FIGURE 4 Be Top When You Can

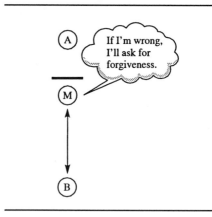

they'll tell us. " The first Middle is uncomfortable with this; he wants to go back, to be in the middle, to find out what **they** want, to ask permission. The second Middle is uncomfortable with going back; she wants to go ahead, she wants to be Top, to figure out what **she** thinks needs to happen, to do it, and, if it turns out poorly, to ask forgiveness (see Figure 4).

Tactic 2: **Be Bottom When You Should.** Middles sometimes describe themselves as "sewer pipes"—"any garbage that Tops send us we simply pass along to Bottoms . . . without question." Middle passes the garbage along to Bottom; Bottom complains about the garbage; Middle justifies the garbage, explaining that it's really good stuff; Bottom still sees it as garbage and continues to complain; Middle passes these complaints along to Tops; Tops explain to Middle how the garbage really is good stuff and chastise Middle for not doing a good enough job convincing Bottoms; and on it goes. Middles, if they haven't lost *their* minds, are often in a better position than Tops to recognize garbage as garbage. Don't just be a

FIGURE 5 Be Bottom When You Should

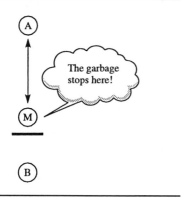

FIGURE 6 Coach

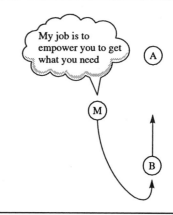

mindless funnel. Be Bottom. Work it out with Tops. The buck stops at the Top; the garbage stops in the Middle (see Figure 5).

Tactic 3: **Be coach.** When others bring their complaints to Middles, Middles assume that it's *their* job to handle these complaints—which is precisely what it means to slide into the middle. Middles feel ashamed if they *still* haven't fixed some lingering complaint; they feel embarrassed to admit that all their efforts to date have failed; they feel guilty about not having got around to it; they feel weak and inadequate for not being a more powerful, more effective, more competent Middle. Why all the shame, guilt, and self-doubt, Middle? *It is not your problem.* They're the ones with the complaints. This doesn't mean that you are to be callous, unsympathetic, unfeeling; nor does it mean that you have no important role to play. People have problems. Let them know that you understand their situation, that you empathize with their condition, *and* that you are not going to solve their problem for them. That's not your job. Your job is to empower others to solve

their own problems. Offer to be their coach—to work with them, to empower them so that *they* can do what *they* need to do to solve *their* problems. (See Figure 6)

Tactic 4: **Facilitate.** In the Middle we often find ourselves running back and forth between people, carrying messages from one to the other, explaining one to the other. We learn from the Customer what the Customer's needs are; we carry this information to the Producers; the Producers have questions, which we then bring back to the Customer; and then we carry the Customer's answers—along with a modified set of requirements—back to the Producers; and on and on it goes, sliding in the Middle. When we are in the middle of such a process, we are harried but with a sense of the importance of our role—we are needed by both sides. When we are caught up in this process, it may never occur to us to ask: Why am *I* doing all this running? Why not step out of the middle, bring together those people who need to be together, and do whatever it takes to make their interac-

FIGURE 7 Facilitate

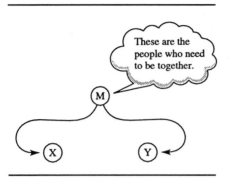

tion with one another as productive as possible?

New options open up for us when we see situations systemically. Our interactions in organizations are not simply people interacting with people—not isolated events in unique circumstances. People always interact with one another in systemic spaces. When we are blind to the effects of these system forces, we invite the space to disempower us. When we see systemically, we understand the space, we know what it can do to us, and we know what challenges we face in mastering the space (see Figure 7).

Tactic 5: **Integrate with One Another.** There is another factor that relates to the power and contribution of Middles, and that has to do with the nature of Middles' relationships with one another. Middles strengthen themselves and enhance their contributions to their organizations by developing strong peer group relationships—among supervisors, among deans, among sections heads, among plant managers, among department heads. Yet such relationships rarely develop. For most people the term *middle group* is an oxymoron—if it's a group then it can't be Middles, and if there are Middles then it can't be a group. Middles, left to their own

devices, do not become teams, they do not develop powerful and supportive relationships with one another. They generally resist all efforts at team development. This alienation from one another is a major contributor to their ineffectiveness in systems. So where does this dysfunctional alienation come from? Middles have their explanations: I have little in common with the others. . . . There are a number of them I don't particularly like. . . . There's no potential power in this group. . . . We bore one another. . . . I'm not particularly interested in their areas. . . . They are my competitors so why collaborate? . . . This one talks too much, that one's too emotional. . . . It's demons all over again.

Through the systemic lens, we see a different story. Here in our Dark Ages we are oblivious to the impact different system spaces have on us. As Tops we regularly fall into territorial struggles with one another; as Bottoms we regularly experience great pressures to conform to whatever the group opinion is; as Middles we regularly become isolated and alienated from one another.[2]

The Middle Space is a diffusing space; it pulls us apart from one another and toward other individuals and groups we service or manage (see Figure 8). We disperse. We spend our time away from one another. In that configuration our specialness becomes highlighted—our uniqueness, our separateness from one another, our differences. In the Top group we become territorial—a collection of "MINE"'s; in the Bottom group

---

[2] For further information on the predictable relationship problems that develop among Tops, among Bottoms, and among Middles, see Barry Oshry, "Them: A Conceptual Framework," *Journal of Organization Development* 6, no. 4 (1988), pp. 18–25.

FIGURE 8   The Vicious Cycle of Middle Alienation

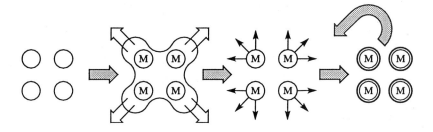

1. Four individuals who under other circumstances might get along perfectly well with one another . . .

2. Enter a middle space.

3. The space pulls them apart from one another and toward the groups they service or manage.

4. In their separateness they harden into an "I-ness" mentality which reinforces their staying apart.

we become a "WE"; and in the Middlegroup we become a collection of "I"'s. Whatever real differences exist among us become magnified. Each of us feels unique, special, different. We feel we have little in common with one another, we feel competitive with one another, we are critical of one another, we deal at the surface with one another, we are wary of one another, and we see little potential power in us as a collectivity.

There is a vicious cycle that happens to us in the Middle Space. The space pulls us apart from one another; that apartness heightens our separateness, our alienation from one another; and our alienation reinforces our staying apart—why would we want to spend time together when we have so little in common, we don't like one another, there is no potential for power in the collective, we are competitors, and so forth. So we stay apart, which reinforces the alienation, and on and on it goes. All of which is unfortunate because that Middle Space is a poten-

tially powerful space. There are productive relationships to be had and powerful contributions to be made.

Middle peer groups are, potentially, the integrating mechanisms for their systems. They are in the best position to tie these systems together, to provide strong and informed leadership to their Bottoms or to the groups they service, and to create consistency, evenness, and fairness throughout the system.

Middles integrate the system by integrating with one another. Each Middle moves out, manages, or services his or her part of the system and collects intelligence about what is happening there; Middles come together and share their intelligence; they move back out, and then come together—moving back and forth between diffusing and integrating. Goodbye demons. Goodbye, uninformed, weak, fractionated, surpriseable, uncoordinated Middles. Through this process, the Middle Space becomes the most solidly informed part of the system. Individual Middles are more knowledgeable about the total system, they are

FIGURE 9 Middles Integrate the System by Integrating with One Another

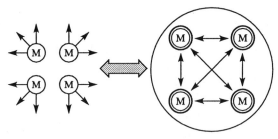

1. Middles move back and forth between servicing, managing, and collecting intelligence about their pieces of the system and . . .

2. Coming together integrating, sharing their intelligence.

able to provide more consistent information to others, they are better able to provide guidance and direction, there is less unproductive duplication among units, there is more evenness of treatment.

Middles who integrate are a potent force in their systems (see Figure 9). They develop a powerful support network for themselves; they provide informed leadership for others; and they lighten the burden of their Tops, making it possible for Tops to do the top work they should be doing. This is the possibility of middle integration. When Middles are in the grips of the Middle Space, however, they do not see integration as a possibility for *them*—"Maybe it's a good idea for some people in some circumstances but not in *our* organization, given the situation *we're* facing, and certainly not with this particular cast of characters; we have no reason to integrate, our responsibilities are diverse, we have so little in common, we don't get along, we are too competitive . . ." and so forth.

In the absence of a systemic lens, Middles feel that they do not integrate *because of* how they feel about one another. When viewed systemically, the truth is seen to be just the other way around: Middles feel the way they do as a consequence of not integrating; were they to integrate, they would feel quite differently toward one another.

Group empowerment supports individual empowerment. Without integration Middles face the tearing pressures of the Middle Space alone. With integration they create an informational and emotional base that strengthens each individual Middle.

You Don't Know What You Don't Know until You Know It

When Middles don't integrate, there is no basis for comprehending the possibilities of empowered middleness. Middles may think that the range of possibility is from *A* to *E,* and since they're at *D*, that's not so bad. Only when they integrate successfully do Middles realize that the range of possibility was from *A* to *Z*, and *D* wasn't so hot after all (see Figure 10).

Middle integration creates a whole new level of possibility for Middles. From

FIGURE 10   The Range of Middle Possibilities

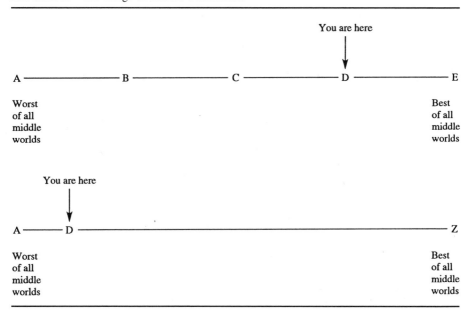

facing system pressures alone and unsupported, they become part of a powerful and supportive group. From being uninformed and surpriseable, they become part of the most well-informed part of the system. From being ping pong balls batted back and forth in other people's games, they become central players in creating and managing their own games.

So, for example, we find a middle group in a highly sensitive chemicals plant who have been integrating for over seven years. According to the plant manager, these Middles run the day-to-day business of the plant and do it better than he ever did. These Middles like, respect, and support one another—they have their own summer and winter uniforms, they are respected by Above and Below as a strong and informed leadership team, they do their own hiring into the group, they are rewarded (50 percent) for how well they individually manage their units and (50

percent) for how well they collectively integrate the system as a whole. Their plant manager is liberated by this process—rather than being mired in the details of day-to-day operations, he spends his time on "top business"— exploration of where the industry is heading and how to prepare for the future, community relations, interaction with headquarters, integration with his peers, and so forth. Not the way it usually goes with Middles.

In another setting, we find a Middle in a software company who had been having difficulty selling top management on a project idea. The Middle brought the project to the middle group, which had been integrating for several months. Without the knowledge or permission of senior management, the middle group took on the project. All the necessary expertise was in that group—marketing, sales, production, finance, and human resources.

They did their research meticulously, they put together a package top management could not and did not refuse. Great pride, great teamwork, great effectiveness, and significant contribution to profitability. Not the way it usually goes with Middles.

What *Are* Middles Good for?

Do we really need Middles? I am asked that question regularly. The truth is: We do not need weak, uninformed, torn, confused, wishy-washy, and fractionated Middles. That is, however, not the only available middle option. Middles do have a unique perspective in organizations and special contributions to make. These can be developed only as Middles learn to see their condition systemically and learn to master the Middle Space. That mastery does not come easily. To be "a Middle who stays out of the Middle" makes special demands on Middles. Middles may complain about their current "no-win" situation; yet, when they discover what it takes to empower themselves, they may decide they want no part of it.

There is great need for empowered Middles—Middles who act responsibly toward others, who are committed to their success, and who can deliver the infor-

mation, direction, and support that others need. The challenge for Middles is to do this while maintaining their own independence of thought and action. And that requires a different kind of fortitude, one that keeps Middles from being torn apart individually and collectively—preserving their boundaries, rather than allowing them to be overridden: shaping situations, rather than being shaped by them; standing up to both Above and Below; sometimes saying "no" or "not now" or "not this way," rather than dancing to every tune others play for them.

Middles who stay out of the middle, who empower themselves and others, who are Top when they can be, who are Bottom when they should be, who coach and who facilitate, and, above all else, who integrate with one another—these are a different order of Middles. They value themselves and they bring value to their systems.

What happened to the demons? What happened to those weak, confused, wishy-washy, fractionated, powerless Middles? They weren't sent off for therapy, they weren't replaced or fixed or fired. When Middles see and master the Middle Space, the demons—like the witches of yesteryear—simply disappear.

CASE

AT&T: THE DALLAS WORKS (A)

It was December 1988, and Sandy Ward felt a pulse of excitement as she prepared for the first meeting of the Quick JIT team. The last three months had been the most chaotic, yet exhilarating, period she had experienced since joining AT&T 10 years earlier. In September, a new vice president of manufacturing, Ken Weatherford, had been appointed to revitalize the Dallas Works—the AT&T plant in Mesquite, Texas, just outside of Dallas, where Ward had worked for the last four years. As part of that revitalization, Weatherford had cooked up the idea of the Quick JIT team—to spearhead the factory rearrangement and to solve problems in general—and had asked Ward to organize it.

Ward had held several different jobs at the Works—including customer service and shipping manager, human resources manager, and materials manager—and most recently had been trying to implement Just-in-Time (JIT) production initiatives at the plant. But whereas Ward had often found her efforts blocked by the inertia of a disinterested and lethargic management, with Weatherford's arrival Ward's proposals had received aggressive support from the top. In fact, Weatherford appeared willing to make whatever changes were necessary to transform the

plant into a world-class organization. Shortly after his arrival, he gave the 41-year-old Ward the title of JIT Implementation Manager, responsible for coordinating all production improvements, other than the actual physical makeover of the plant.

In her new position, Ward would be overseeing a broad range of action teams, working on everything from improving quality to facilitating materials flow. But the team that intrigued Ward the most was the group that was about to convene in her office for the first time. The Quick JIT team, in a sense, had been an afterthought—a final piece in a complex and integrated plan for recasting the Works. Yet, the expectations for the team were extremely high: In essence, Weatherford and Ward were counting on the team to be the catalyst that would break down barriers at the plant and make things happen. As Ward waited for the members to arrive, she wondered what she could say to prepare the team for the tasks that lay ahead.

* * *

Since the breakup of AT&T in January 1984, the Works—like other AT&T operations—had been struggling to reposition itself. The changeover from sheltered monopoly to open market competitor had not been an easy one. The factory, which had opened in 1969 as a producer of electronic switching systems, suddenly found itself faced with an array of competitive challenges. In part to meet these new challenges, the

This case was prepared by Research Associates Susan Rosegrant and Phillip Holland (under the direction of Professor Todd D. Jick).

Works had completely changed its product line in 1983 and 1984. Its new mission: "To become the world's leading supplier of power products by meeting customer needs with the highest quality levels."

After the reorganization, the Works had two major product lines: Electronic Power Supplies represented about two thirds of the plant's dollar output, while Energy Systems contributed the rest. Within the Electronic Power Supplies product line were three product groups: Board Mounted Power, Off-Line Switchers, and DC/DC Converters and Mature Products. All were used in most AT&T products. The Energy Systems line included DC reserve equipment (rectifiers, controllers, and distribution equipment) and Protected AC Power Supply equipment, providing power primarily for Regional Bell Operating Companies and AT&T's Network Operations Division.

The Works's major customers were internal AT&T customers—such as Network Systems (Oklahoma City Works, Columbus Works, and Merrimack Valley), and Information Systems (Denver Works)—and the Regional Bell Operating Companies. A small percentage of the output went to original equipment manufacturers, such as IBM, Hewlett-Packard, NAC, Tellabs, and Teradyne.

The 1984 product overhaul and revitalization had, in fact, achieved some of its goals, introducing state of the art power technology, flexible production methods based on JIT theories, and automation. One manager in 1988 described the plant as "reasonably acceptable," and insisted that the Works had been making steady—if slow—improvement. But this assessment was kinder than most. Other managers characterized the plant as another "Ma Bell," an "old Western Elec-

tric" factory that had not adapted to the needs of the current competitive marketplace. And, in fact, the Works continued to struggle. In September 1988, AT&T turned to Ken Weatherford to lead the revitalization of this troubled factory.

The task Weatherford faced was a daunting one. For starters, morale at the plant had been driven low by continual rounds of layoffs. Employment had fallen from a high of 3,500 in 1985 to 2,000 in 1988, consisting of roughly 1,400 production and direct workers and 600 salaried employees. Of these 600, about two thirds reported to manufacturing and the remainder to other organizations, including purchasing, systems control, material management, quality assurance, accounting, and personnel. The habitual layoffs had recently led to rumors that the plant would close and that production would be moved to AT&T's Matamoros plant in Mexico.

In addition, although the 1984 reorganization had improved the plant's technological capabilities, the plant was still not competitive in cost, cycle time, or access to customers. Quality control was a particular stumbling block: The plant would shut down one day a week because of materials problems, and it typically wrote off millions in scrap each year.

Problems such as these had damaged worker/management relations. Management characterized the operators, for example, as people who just "wanted to do one thing"; to come in and do their jobs, but not to grow or change. Workers, on the other hand, countered that management expected them to "check their brains at the door." One disgruntled manager, who described the plant as being in "disarray," complained that the management team was indecisive, not visible to people on the floor, and couldn't solve the plant's problems.

Workers' relationship with the union was almost equally unsettled. Although, in April 1987, the Communication Workers of America (CWA) members had elected new local leadership, workers typically distrusted both management and the union. As CWA local president David Amesquita put it: "At the time, the feeling was that if you were not screwed by the company, then you would be screwed by the union, or both. People didn't trust either one." In fact, in March 1988, just before Amesquita was elected, the local union went into a state of receivership.

Managing this array of quality, production, and personnel issues would have been a full plate in itself. But Weatherford, who had just completed a similar challenge as manufacturing director of AT&T's plant in Shreveport, Louisiana, had also been given the resources and the mandate to fundamentally restructure the entire Dallas Works operation. Indeed, most managers believed that the Works needed nothing less than a complete transformation to allow it first to survive, and then to become a competitive, world-class producer.

Weatherford moved fast and insisted that things change. First, he assembled a list of programs designed to snap the plant out of what he termed its "marginal" performance. His plan included the following actions:

- Reorganize into four "Focused Factories"—one for Energy Systems, and one each for the three Electronic Power Supplies groups—without shutting down production. The Focused Factories would be independent, stand-alone areas, occupying contiguous space on the shop floor, and would be managed by separate hierarchies. Process engineers, master schedulers, and production planners would all report for day-to-day direction to the Focused Factory managers.

- Lay out the four factories to accommodate Just-in-Time production techniques and total quality control principles. The work stations would use carefully sized Kanbans—carriers in which the product was moved from station to station—to eliminate excess inventory and to accommodate JIT flow.

- Reduce storeroom inventory and materials kept in the center of the shop floor and move them to a new stock shop—without ever closing the storeroom down.

- Cut the work force by an additional 500 people in response to economic conditions, productivity improvements, and a pruning of the management force. At the same time, form a "Flexible Work Pool" of surplus people to help with the factory rearrangements and other odd jobs. The pool would help lessen the number of additional layoffs.

- Move engineers' offices to the shop floor to encourage cooperation and communication and to boost productivity.

But even as Weatherford formulated these plans, a new level of complexity was added. AT&T corporate decided to establish Power Systems as a self-contained, strategic business unit. Not only would the Works have to learn to operate as a discrete business—encompassing research and development, manufacturing, and marketing operations at one site—but the facility would need to prepare for the transfer to Dallas of other members of the Power Systems Business Unit, such as AT&T Bell Laboratories research and development, from New Jersey and other locations. This decision required a second "crash" renovation project, since the transfers would require the Works to make available 150,000 square feet of additional lab and office space.

Weatherford's experience at AT&T's Shreveport facility had left him well aware of the potential pitfalls of implementing change, and, increasingly, the Dallas Works job was stacking up to be a major change. The transformation contemplated would not only require moving and realigning virtually every piece of equipment in the plant without stopping production, it would alter and redefine every job at the Works—from operator, to first line supervisor, to manager. Moreover, the immediate changes contemplated would be but the first step in setting the Works on a path toward continuous improvement.

As he prepared to get started, Weatherford huddled with Sandy Ward and other top managers to come up with structures and mechanisms to support the massive physical, organizational, and cultural changes that would soon be underway. The team-based program they devised— an effort to use cross-functional and multilevel groups to solve problems and to drive through the smorgasbord of contemplated changes—included the following initiatives:

• Designate a team of managers at the top to monitor the various change efforts and to oversee routine plant operations. This would provide a model for the teamwork and delegation they hoped to establish at all levels of the plant and would leave Weatherford free to concentrate on broader strategic issues.

• Appoint action teams to drive specific improvement efforts such as materials flow, quality improvement, and vendor partnerships.

• Create a permanent team structure—Vision Improvement People (VIP) teams—to tackle specific issues and to give employees experience with quality control, problem-solving methods, and interpersonal skills. The VIP teams would replace the union sanctioned and widely popular Quality of Work Life (QWL) teams that had been instituted earlier that decade. While the QWL teams had worked on problems unrelated, at least directly, to the plant's performance, the VIP teams would be operationally and process focused; a team might target improving the efficiency of a particular manufacturing line, for example, or tackle some other issue related to the factory's performance. Some teams would be ongoing, while others would be "task" teams, set up to solve a particular problem and then to disband.

• Form a Communications Committee—made up of a slice of nonsupervisory employees and union representatives from throughout the Works—to help replace rumors with solid information and to better link senior management and all employees. Other communications efforts would include sharing business and results-related information at "town meetings," rather than just functional information, as had been the practice.

• Provide supervisory training for middle managers, as well as human effectiveness, quality improvement, and problem-solving training for the entire work force.

• Consult union leaders and involve them in the process of making changes and of formulating new employee policies, such as an absenteeism policy, a "poor performers" program, more flexible work rules, and others.

• Revise the dress code so managers and engineers would no longer have to wear ties. This change would help break down the symbolic barriers that had long existed between operators and salaried employees.

• Increase the number of "celebrations" and other social events.

But even with these tools in hand, Weatherford wasn't satisfied. Although the Dallas Works had gone through a series of changes in the last four years, residue from the old "Ma Bell" attitude was blocking the plant from embracing continuous, ongoing change. Weatherford wanted to find a way to stir up the plant, to break through the inertia, and to prove to workers and managers alike that the old way of operating was dead. It was important to "get people's attention," he asserted, even though he was in a great hurry and had "no time to win people over." When he reviewed the plans for the plant's physical transformation with a team of engineers, they concluded it would take two years to accomplish. Weatherford insisted it be done in nine months.

As he searched for a way to quickly draw the whole plant into the process, Weatherford had an inspiration: He would pull a handful of production people and a few supervisors off their regular jobs and send them out into the factory as agents of change. What would be really special about this team, though, is that they would not be bound by the usual rules and red tape that made it so difficult and time-consuming to get things done.

Weatherford passed the idea of the team on to Ward, who called it Quick JIT. Before choosing the members, Ward turned for suggestions to local CWA president Davis Amesquita, who put together a list on the basis of what he called "communication skills" and the "ability to get along with others," though he knew none of the candidates well. After interviewing everyone on the list, Ward selected her team, looking for, as she described it, "people who were willing to use their heads." None of the nine team members— six hourly employees and three supervisors—had known each other prior to this new assignment.

*   *   *

Ward waited patiently for the first team members to arrive in her office. Probably her greatest strength, she reflected, was in getting things started. "Give me nothing and let me make something happen," she thought to herself with a smile. She was eager to get the change process underway.

But as the group began to assemble, her enthusiasm became tinged with doubt. She had never launched anything so open-ended before. Moreover, she began to wonder how much this team would be able to accomplish. The plant environment was already so unsettled that no one seemed to feel secure about what they were doing today, let alone what their jobs would be like tomorrow. "People are looking for reasons for things not to work," she mused. "We have to turn people into believers."

When the group was complete, the participants hurried through a round of perfunctory introductions. None of the members stood out in any distinctive way, Ward thought to herself; and, in fact, a couple of them had a reputation for being rabble-rousers. At the monent, the main mood in the room appeared to be a kind of wary expectation. After all, the team had no job description. Nor had they been told specifically what their job would be, other than helping with the plant's rearrangement, building hand fixtures for production, and doing anything else that was needed. Since the management team was "making it up as they went along," Ward herself didn't know precisely what the Quick JIT team would do.

Quickly, Ward ran through the few firm details she had. The Quick JIT members were not being made part of management, she announced, but they were expected to challenge management, if necessary, to get things done. They would receive no pay raise for the assignment, other than overtime pay for any extra hours they might spend. To help with some tasks, they would be assigned the Flexible Work Pool of extra skilled tradespeople that Weatherford had assembled. Finally, the team would stay together for about one year. "Your job," Ward concluded, "is to find out what problems are out there and fix them."

Ward had tried to communicate some of her own enthusiasm. More than anything else, she wanted the Quick JIT team to understand that it was not business as usual. But as she called for questions, Ward was met with an uneasy silence. Looking around the room, she saw nine people who were "trying to figure out what they had gotten themselves into."

CASE

AT&T: THE DALLAS WORKS (B)

Who the hell are you to come in here and question how we do our jobs?

Employee, at Dallas Works to Quick JIT team member

Looking back, the Quick JIT team members guessed that they had been selected because they represented a cross section of the plant, and because "they were not kiss-asses."

This case was prepared by Research Associates Susan Rosegrant and Phillip Holland (under the direction of Professor Todd D. Jick).

Copyright © 1991 by the President and Fellows of Harvard College. Harvard Business School case 9-492-024.

By November 1988, when the team first met, the reorganization of the factory had already begun and, by January, a major transformation was underway. In line with Weatherford's mandate, workers were shifting product lines to create the four Focused Factory areas; downsizing and relocating the job shop; moving the process platform, mailroom, model shop, and incoming inspection department in a matter of weeks; and shifting the central storeroom, which had been in the middle of the floor, to a high bay area—all without closing down.

The Quick JIT team descended on the factory against this backdrop of change and confusion. Although the team had not been charged with the redesign of the plant itself, Sandy Ward encouraged members to "go out and get ideas from people" wherever they could make a difference. There was painting, cleaning, and yardwork to do. Manufacturing lines needed to be rearranged, and inventory had to be reorganized—all without disrupting production, which Weatherford had declared could not stop. As the weeks went by, whether actually knocking down walls and rearranging equipment themselves, or coordinating this work by the Flexible Work Pool people, the Quick JIT members were everywhere.

One by one they ventured into the different production areas and began questioning the status quo. They asked why a certain operation was being done as it was. They asked why a certain piece of equipment was there. They wanted to know if any new tool or fixture might help the operators do their jobs. And if they didn't like the answer they got, they asked again. No one and nothing escaped their inquisition. Operators, supervisors, engineers, materials handlers—all were challenged.

As they set about their tasks, the group worked with a sense of urgency. They were motivated by fear that the plant would close or that there would be more layoffs; after all, Weatherford had already announced his intentions to let 500 people go. In addition, they believed that the Works had a deadline to become profitable—or else. Weatherford, they thought, had made clear the need to turn the place around.

Power and Resistance

Not everyone in the plant, however, felt this urgency. Moreover, not everyone welcomed the appearance of the Quick JIT team. "We infringed on [the workers'] particular domain," explained David Amesquita, CWA local president, who took some of the brunt of this animosity, as people stopped him in the hall to "cuss him out." His response: "We just have to change, so roll with it." To the Quick JIT team, it soon became apparent that winning acceptance would be a prerequisite to getting anything accomplished. "We caught a lot of hell," one Quick JIT team member recalled, "mainly from people we used to work beside."

Resistance to the Quick JIT team arose from a variety of sources. Many operators feared and opposed JIT, itself, because they believed it would cost them their jobs. The Quick JIT team became a convenient target for this opposition, hurled in such sayings as, "Quick JIT ain't worth it," or the more offensive, "Quick-shitters."

Others whom the team approached, while less hostile, were similarly unimpressed. Indeed, some of the *best* reactions were mocking. If a team member asked a particular operator what could be done to improve his or her job, for example, the operator would reel off a long list of requests, with a clear assumption that the question was not to be taken seriously, and that nothing would be accomplished.

The whole idea behind Quick JIT was to get things done quickly, and without red tape. But sometimes even their successes got them into trouble because they moved *too* quickly. For example, a supervisor might call the team in, point out a piece of equipment that hadn't been used for years, and ask them to take it away, which the team gladly did. Later, when engineers came looking for the equipment, or noticed it missing, they would find out what had happened—and go after the team. "They hated this," the team said, recalling some bouts with engineers. To avoid further misunderstandings, the team came up with a sign-off sheet—that included the supervisor, the engineer, and others—to be completed before anything was removed.

Yet, this compromise did not mean the team went any easier on the engineers or anyone else when it came to moving or removing a piece of equipment that appeared idle. "If the engineers really didn't want it moved," one team member said, "we challenged them. Do you really need it?" As a result, "We got them to use things they hadn't used, or to store things they rarely used." In fact, "Use it or lose it," became a classic Quick JIT phrase.

Not all the engineers acquiesced graciously to the team's demands; but if it came to a struggle, the team could wield their ultimate weapon. "If you don't want us to do this," they would tell an uncooperative engineer, or operator, or supervisor, "take it up with Brother Ken (Weatherford)." In fact, "Take it up with Brother Ken," became one of the team's biggest barrier breakers. It was not as if Weatherford had suggested to them that they drop his name should they need to; one day they just started doing it.

As momentum built, the "Quick Jitters" found they were routinely working 10-hour days, seven days a week. The team typically met informally or in passing every morning to check what each member planned to do, to see what else had come up, and to see if anyone on the team was out that day, and so had to have his or her work covered. While they used tradespeople and the Flexible Work Group as much as possible, if they were not available, the team often took it upon itself to get the job done—to the frequent annoyance of the union. One team member, for example, lifted herself in the power hoist so she could paint the ceiling to prepare for the next day's visitors. "We did not ask for permission," a member of the group said, summarizing how they approached the job. "We organized ourselves."

Quick Successes

During this early period, the Quick JIT team learned that cleaning up and changing operations was not just a matter of fighting but also of winning respect, helping people accomplish improvements they had pondered for years, and pushing to make their working lives easier. In fact, one team member said, it was the hell-raisers—the "Bell Heads," those who still had the old "Ma Bell mentality"—that they often approached first. "We asked them how we could help make their jobs better for them."

For example, if an operator claimed that a certain fixture would simplify a task, a team member would immediately go off and design that fixture, then take the design to the job shop to get it made. One particular team member designed or had designed over 200 items that year. "We picked the easiest things first," they said, like moving inventory to another spot, in order to achieve some early successes.

Often, when the formerly dubious operators saw how quickly the Quick JIT team could get something done for them—be it a rearrangement or the supply of a fixture—they "mellowed." Other departments started to call the team into their areas, daring the team, in a part friendly, part defiant challenge, to find something wrong with their operation.

Gradually, the plant began to unite behind the Quick JIT team. Part of the success came from the team's getting to know all the people they worked with so well. People were no longer "names in a crowd," because working that closely with someone, painting, cleaning up, rearranging, "you got to know their personalities." Whereas before team members had used Ken Weatherford's name to win cooperation, they now discovered that the Quick JIT name could stand on its own. In this indirect way, the team came to realize the power they actually had and began to use it. "It was really fun to watch people who had never really been expected to think," Sandy Ward recalled, "and to find them very capable of thinking and of making things happen." She added: "I didn't know the team was going to be this important."

By now, new ideas and requests were coming in so fast that the team had to keep a pad handy to be able to jot them all down. "We got involved with anything," the team concluded. "We attacked all kinds of problems, not just fixtures and rearrangements. Anything that people had anything to do with, we tried to help with."

As the Quick JIT effort came into its own, the factory rearrangement also went into high gear. In March, the ambitious transfer of the Power Systems product marketing and management and Bell Labs research and development units into the Dallas Works began. The cafeteria got a facelift; a new break area was built overlooking the plant; and engineering and maintenance offices were relocated to the factory floor, close to their operating counterparts. By August, with the help of the Quick JIT team, all the physical features of the factory rearrangement were in place.

For the next few months, the Quick JIT team continued to drive improvements and alterations at the newly revitalized operation. On all sides were striking visual examples of what the team had helped to accomplish. Even more important, there was a growing sense at the Works that change was possible—and that things could and should improve. "If there was a key to our being able to change so quickly and effectively, it was the Quick JIT team," declared Walt Boyko, who had accompanied Weatherford from Shreveport as his next-in-charge. "They did more than spearhead the rearrangement; they got the involvement of 1,000 people. If all we had needed was to get the work done, we could have hired carpenters and painters."

The Dallas Works was still changing. But with the physical transformation complete, Weatherford officially disbanded the Quick JIT team in November 1989. The team—never intended as a permanent organization—did not break up all at once. One at a time, the members took other positions with the hope that the organization could slowly pick up where they left off. They said:

> Ken used us as examples of what could be done. The whole concept was to work ourselves out of a job. We were examples. Then we would back off and let them do it themselves. People had to realize they could make things happen.

Overall, both the Quick JIT team and management felt that the change process so far had been an enormous success. In the team's view:

> Things have really changed. People today will pick up papers. Even supervisors push a broom. They all cleaned it up, and now they can show their families what they've done. It's like when you clean the garage; you don't want

anyone to mess it up. Even though we're no longer a team, people still look for changes because they believe they can. There's always more to do; the engineers are down there, and the people hadn't been allowed to solve problems before. They had ideas; some of them are very smart. But no one had listened before.

When it was over, Weatherford threw a party for everyone at the plant. Ward and others took the Quick JIT team out to dinner, but other than that, they were not singled out for a reward. This fact did not bother them. In fact, they seemed to dislike how much attention and credit they did get. As one member put it:

> Everyone should get the credit. During this whole transition, production never stopped. We moved entire areas around, painted, and so forth, but all the while quality and everything else actually went up! The people who were trying to

do their jobs with all the commotion, with all the building going on and the paint dripping and smelling, they deserve even more credit.

Part of the Works's success was clear from the changes in morale and attitudes at the end of the Quick JIT process. In addition, the plant—now the largest manufacturer of power equipment under one roof in the world—could boast of significant improvements in measured business performance. Between 1988 and 1990, the following changes took place:

- Productivity   +93%
- Inventory turns   +145%
- Inventory   −47%
- Vendor base   −25%
- Floor space   −30%
- Cost of quality   −6%

In addition, management summarized overall business unit integration results as follows:

Organizational	Operational
• Focused business unit teams • Colocation • Integrated engineering (RD&E) • End-to-end project management • Two less management levels • Forty percent reduction in expense personnel	• Best ever and industry leading quality • Cost of quality reduced by half • Reduced intervals—both PRP and manufacturing • Award winning service • Increased profit paid back project expense within first year

By any measure, then, what Weatherford had accomplished—with the help of the Quick JIT team—appeared to be a stunning success story. In slightly more than a year, they had rearranged the plant; reorganized production; improved management's relationship with the union;

largely integrated engineers and researchers from other sites; formed new problem-solving teams and communications committees; expanded education programs; and implemented new quality methods—all while improving the plant's performance in quality, cycle time,

EXHIBIT 1 Dallas Works Revitalization Timeline

1988

September: Ken Weatherford appointed new vice president of manufacturing.

October: Weatherford launches aggressive revitalization, including JIT and total quality control principles, and Focused Factories reorganization.

November: Relocation of job shop, process platform, mailroom, model shop, and incoming inspection department begins. AT&T designates Power Systems as a strategic business unit.

December: Sandy Ward holds first meeting with Quick JIT team.

1989

January: Major Focused Factory rearrangement begins. Central storeroom moved from center of floor without closing.

March: Transfer of Power Systems Bell Labs and product marketing units from New Jersey to Dallas requiring 150,000 square feet of additional lab and office space. Construction begins on two-story complex to accommodate new units.

April: Cafeteria and new break area built. Engineering and maintenance relocated close to operating counterparts. VIP team concept launched.

August: Construction completed, and all physical features of factory rearrangement implemented.

November: Quick JIT disbanded.

1990

January: Weatherford leaves. Boyko readies for transfer of New River Valley, Virginia, product line.

delivery, inventory management, and use of space. In short, they had completely overhauled the plant—physically, organizationally, and philosophically.

Looking to the Future

In January 1990, Ken Weatherford left the Dallas Works, and Walt Boyko was put in charge of operations. The plant that Boyko took over was a very different place than the factory that Weatherford had confronted back in the fall of 1988 (see Exhibit 1). Nevertheless, Boyko and his managers saw the accomplishments as only a beginning. Moreover, they understood the difficulty of the challenges that still lay ahead. At least four major issues promised to have

an immediate impact on the plant's progress and performance:

1. Completing the Integration. The Works was transforming itself from a factory to an end-to-end business. Product management, Bell Labs, and marketing people had all moved, or were moving to Dallas as part of this transformation. This meant the need to reorganize and to change from a traditional functional business to a more integrated organization. Engineers already sat on the shop floor with schedulers and planners, reporting to the Focused Factory managers. But much more could be done.

There were other challenges as well. Manufacturing people had already expressed their resentment at having to be at work at 7 A.M., while employees from Bell Labs—who had been granted flexible work hours—could start work later. In addition, there were questions about how to balance the compensation, benefits, perquisites, and educational opportunities of the new Bell Labs people with employees who had spent their careers at Dallas, particularly the engineers.

2. Physical Rearrangement. The Dallas Works's Focused Factory reorganization had been highly successful—so successful, in fact, that AT&T had decided to transfer in a fifth product line. In April 1990, the Works would begin rearranging again, this time to accept the Transformers and Inductors (T&I) business from the recently closed New River Valley, Virginia, plant. The line, with some juggling, would be wedged into the space in the center of the floor formerly occupied by excess inventory. The reorganization was to be completed by the end of the year.

Although the new line was a boon, guaranteeing increased production and new jobs at the factory, Boyko foresaw trouble in getting the plant geared up for another major renovation. After all, the previous major overhaul had just ended a few months before. Integrating the new line would mean a return to overtime and weekend work, as well as the daily disruption of trying to produce product in the middle of a construction project.

3. The "Culture Shock" of New Hires. The New River Valley plant had used 500 people to produce its T&I product line, and the initial expectation was that it would take the same in Dallas. This influx would mean about a 50 percent increase in the number of production workers at Dallas, over the roughly 1,000 it had in early 1990.

Most of these new workers would be hired locally, since few AT&T employees had chosen to transfer from Virginia. Legally, the Works was obligated to fill any new openings by hiring back those laid off in the previous three years. Not all of the 500 hires and rehires, however, would go to work in T&I; they would be spread out among the factories, and some people who already worked in other areas would shift to the new line. Mike Cassidy, manager of the existing Focused Factories, described one difficulty with adding so many people, whether new or rehired:

> None of these people, not even our rehires, have been through what we've been through in the past two years. Either they're from the "old style" or they're completely new and don't know what we're about. In the old days, to get even a bin turned around, you had to get the supervisor to write a request, an engineer to draw what it would look like—it all took three months. For the most part we threw this out with Quick JIT. To add all these people now might be a huge culture shock.

4. Matching Growth to Productivity Improvements. The Works faced the difficult task of growing the business as fast as it was improving productivity, so as to avoid future layoffs. With further integration of design and manufacturing, and with new VIP teams, quality measurements, and agreed-upon customer requirements, the potential to improve was enormous. But to improve without adding business would raise the fear— not only in perception, but in fact—that more layoffs were inevitable.

As Boyko considered these highly visible issues, he realized that there was another underlying—but critical—concern to address: how to get the entire factory empowered and involved in the pursuit of change.

Some people, like top managers and members of the Quick JIT team, still believed that the plant's future was at stake. They felt the need to keep going as strongly as they had felt the need to change in 1988. Although the Works had received an effective and much-needed facelift, there were more serious problems lurking under the surface. Moreover, Boyko needed to instill the philosophy, not of changing to survive, but of continuous improvement.

But many other people did not feel this urgency. The place looked clean and orderly, and it seemed to function smoothly. Performance measures were up. New people and new products were coming into the business, not going out. Without proper justification it would be easy for the managers to become known as the management team that cried, "Wolf!" and never stopped. "The first change was hell," asserted union leader Amesquita. "Now change is not the problem, but the vision is: Where do we go from here?"

Perhaps even more important, Boyko had to face whether the right structures were in place to allow employees to feel empowered and to create change. The Quick JIT team was disbanded. The 35 VIP teams were still active, but there was a need to get more people involved in the quest for continuous improvement. Part of that need might be met by a new team-based program adopted by Boyko's boss, Power Systems vice president Andrew Guarriello, and Guarriello's Quality Council. The program,

based on a Quality Improvement (QI) Story methodology developed by Florida Power and Light, would leave much of the responsibility for forming teams and selecting tasks to employees, as with the VIP effort. All Power Systems employees were to attend two days of intensive training in a seven-step problem-solving methodology. In addition, Boyko and his team established four Power Systems' imperatives: customer satisfaction, employee satisfaction, stakeholder satisfaction, and quality in daily work. These imperatives would give direction to the employees, who after their training would group into individual QI teams to identify and solve problems.

But Quick JIT would still be a hard act to follow. The Quick JIT team had set a precedent for how fast problems could be solved and what could be done by anyone who wanted to get involved. Some obstacles had been settled on the spot. In this respect, Quick JIT had been as much an agent of emotional change as it had been of physical change.

Of course, the team had always been seen as temporary. "If people indefinately relied on them to make things happen, then we had not done our job," Ward declared. "We had to force the initiatives and the ownership on the rest of the organization." Nevertheless, some people were convinced that the Quick JIT team had been shut down too soon. The debate was by no means dead about reviving the team, or some form of it, that was now credited with having accomplished so much.

Members of the Quick JIT team, for example, felt that with the team gone, things couldn't get done as quickly. Now people had to "go up the chain," and get their supervisors and others to approve changes in a way that involved more paperwork and procedures. Even many supervisors began to lament the team's dissolution. ''We had the biggest stick,'' the team said, adding:

> Many people think we should have continued this. It was a way to get around, for example, bad supervisors. We could take risks. We could make noise and take things right to the top, if we had to, though we almost never had to. The tie guys [supervisors] were rated, they were sensitive to their performance review, so they had something to lose.

Even Sandy Ward—who had strongly voiced her belief in the necessity of transferring the Quick JIT experience to the rest of the factory—voiced some doubts over the team's disbanding. ''I thought it was a little soon to expect that the ball was going to be received,'' she mused. ''We were throwing it, but we didn't know if anybody was going to catch it.''

CASE

NIGEL ANDREWS AND GENERAL ELECTRIC PLASTICS (A)

A slight frown crossed Nigel Andrews's brow as he hung up the phone. Andrews, recently installed general manager of the Silicones business of General Electric Plastics (GEP), had just finished speaking to the chair of his division's Workout steering committee, who seemed quite agitated. Could they get together later in the day for a brief meeting, the man had inquired? When Andrews agreed, they had arranged to meet at five o'clock. Everything appeared to be going well with Workout, Andrews brooded; the first session had been a great success, and the most recently concluded session had, by all accounts, been fruitful as well. He had been expecting the chair to call and set up a time for a debrief of this second meeting. Instead, this request for a rushed few

This case was prepared by Professor Todd D. Jick.

Copyright © 1991 by the President and Fellows of Harvard College. Harvard Business School case 9-492-020.

minutes later in the day—had something gone wrong?

Workout at GE

In January 1989, GE chairman Jack Welch, with the support of his two vice chairmen, launched a major organizational transformation called Workout. Its purpose was nothing short of radical cultural change, empowering the organization to eliminate unnecessary work, tasks, and activities left over from the company's significant downsizing and structural realignment of the 1980s. The goal was to move this 300,000-person, $50 billion organization away from centralized controls, multilevel approvals, and bureaucracy toward an operation characterized by ''speed, simplicity, and self-confidence.''

Silicones was to become the first GEP division to develop a Workout program. Three months after Welch's announcement, Andrews and his staff met with a Workout consultant to begin designing

EXHIBIT 1 Key Roles and Responsibilities for Workout at GE Silicones

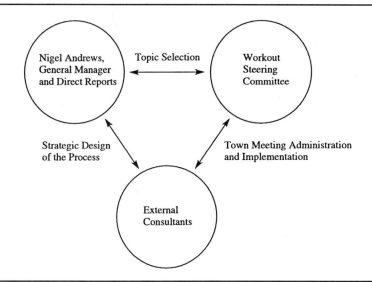

how to establish and introduce the new goals, and how the process might be implemented in "town meeting" style workshops. These two-day problem-solving sessions, made up of 50 to 75 participants, were to be used to identify bureaucratic encumbrances and devise action steps to change the way the division was operating. Another purpose was to reduce boundaries across functions.

At that initial meeting, Andrews and his staff made two decisions. First, a series of employee focus groups would help identify Workout issue opportunities. Second, a steering committee of employees, supervisors, and managers would work with Andrews's staff and the outside consultants as the "implementor" of the Workout process, and as a partner in its development (see Exhibit 1).

The Workout Steering Committee

In May, the Silicones human resource department selected steering committee candidates, inviting people from across all functions and levels with a broad range of experience. In all, 18 people agreed to participate. At its first meeting, the committee discussed the Workout concept, how the group would interact effectively, and began planning a first Town Meeting workshop for June. This workshop was to be organized around themes that had emerged from the focus group findings. After studying the data, Andrews's staff chose two major themes, and the steering committee added one more: The three issues were reports, approvals, and meeting management.

Despite some healthy skepticism and busy schedules, the members of the steering committee met frequently. There were no manuals to guide them—this was on-the-job training. First, the group planned the actual session: It split the three major themes into specific topics, chose 60 people to invite, and broke them into eight groups to attack the topic areas. Along with such procedural decisions, the group also dealt with invitations, hotel logistics, the workshop agenda, and other administrative matters. Its final task was to schedule the first five workshops, one a month from June to October, and to lock in the calendars of Andrews and his staff.

Workout I, June 6–7, 1989

When Workout I convened, the eight groups set out to reduce or eliminate wasteful, time-consuming, and unnecessary reports and approval steps at GE. The turning point came during the first evening's plenary at which all the teams presented their initial recommendations. After viewing the flip charts around the room and listening to the discussion, one participant demanded: "Why are we being so cautious? These aren't bold and groundbreaking suggestions. And why are we asking 'them' to do so much? Why can't we do more ourselves?" The evening concluded with a bonfire into which participants threw all the written reports they had brought along and now thought unnecessary.

During the second day, the teams refined and expanded their recommendations and devised action plans that were bolder and more within their own control. The groups made presentations to Andrews and the manager of finance for cutting back approval steps, eliminating reports, and streamlining certain business processes.

One recommendation, in particular, seemed to unite all the participants: to make Wednesdays "meeting-free" in order to cut down the volume of meetings and increase the time devoted to "work." The presenting group asked Andrews to decide whether Wednesday or Friday should be the meeting-free day. Because

customers often visited on Fridays, Andrews chose Wednesdays, starting the Wednesday after Labor Day, so people could plan accordingly. This proposal was greeted with thunderous applause, the loudest of the session.

Everyone declared Workout I a "victory," including the participants, the steering committee, the consultants, and Andrews. People left wearing buttons inscribed, "Ask Me about Workout!"

Workout II, July 18–19, 1989

Workout II followed the model of the first session. Based again on focus group findings, the steering committee chose two new themes, and Andrews's staff chose one. The steering committee then divided these issues into topics, selected new participants and teams, and set the agenda. Things were going smoothly.

Steering committee members opened the second meeting by endorsing the effort and sharing their perspectives on how Workout was faring. Over the next two days, they served as team facilitators, answering numerous questions about Workout I decisions, in particular "meeting-free Wednesdays." Toward the end of the session, as participants finalized their recommendations, the steering committee members informally began to map out the subsequent workshops. What would be the issues and who should attend? Who beyond Andrews should be sitting in to hear the recommendations? How would the union be included? But as these issues were debated, one question quickly overshadowed all others: the date for Workout IV.

Workout IV was scheduled for the Tuesday and Wednesday following Labor Day. But, given the decision to forbid meetings on Wednesdays (after Labor

Day), the committee realized that this session would violate the new policy. In late May, when the schedule originally had been set, these two days had been the only back-to-back dates Andrews had available in September. Further, GE vice chairman Larry Bossidy had called Andrews June 3 to arrange a time to observe a Workout session and had selected Wednesday, September 6. His date was now locked in and could take as long as three months to reschedule.

Bossidy wasn't just interested in Workout, Andrews knew. The vice chairman—often characterized as a terse, fast-moving, bottom-line[8] oriented decision maker—was visiting all 9 of the 13 GE divisions reporting directly to him to evaluate both Workout and business results.

Moreover, Silicones was likely to undergo particular scrutiny. The business had struggled in recent years, and, in 1988, had been rumored to be on the block. Andrews, in his first line management position, had replaced his fired predecessor just six months ago with the charge of revitalizing the business. He was anxious now to show Bossidy both the early indications of success with Workout and his progress at Silicones overall.

The Five O'Clock Meeting

The chair of the steering committee entered Andrews's office, wearing a distracted look. He came right to the point. The committee had informally caucused, he explained, at the conclusion of Workout II. The issue they now faced was one of principle, they agreed, and Andrews needed to be apprised of it immediately. He continued:

> We have to reschedule the September session. It lands on a Wednesday, and you know that's our meeting-free day. We just can't have a Workout on that day or it will kill Workout. And our own credibility is really on the line here. We have been telling everybody about this "win" and now we are going to violate it. You have to call Bossidy and tell him to come some other time. He can look us over whenever he wants but not on a Wednesday[1]

READING

GE KEEPS THOSE IDEAS COMING

Thomas A. Stewart

Calling General Electric just a company is like calling California just a state. GE has 298,000 employees, more people than live in Tampa, St. Paul, or Newark, New

Jersey. Last year they were paid $13 billion, a sum greater than the personal income of all the residents of Alaska, Montana, North Dakota, South Dakota, Vermont, or Wyoming. GE grossed $58.4 billion; its sales *growth*—$3.8 billion—exceeded the *total* sales of all but 126

Fortune 500 industrial companies.

Few corporations are bigger; none is as complex. GE makes 65-cent light bulbs, 400,000-pound locomotives, and billion-dollar power plants. It manages more credit cards than American Express and owns more commercial aircraft than American Airlines. Of the seven billion pounds of hamburger Americans tote home each year, 36 percent keeps fresh in GE refrigerators; and after dinner, one out of five couch potatoes tunes in GE's network, NBC.

This is the outfit that chairman John F. Welch, Jr., 55, wants to run like a small business. In the 90s, Welch believes, a corporate Gulliver is doomed without the Lilliputian virtues he calls "speed, simplicity, and self-confidence." To get them, the scrappy CEO has mounted a radical assault on the canons of modern management—which GE largely wrote.

"We've got to take out the boss element," Welch says. By his lights, 21st-century managers will forgo their old powers—to plan, organize, implement, and measure—for new duties: counseling groups, providing resources for them, helping them think for themselves. "We're going to win on our ideas," he says, "not by whips and chains."

A brave notion, even radical, verging on the touchy-feely. But at GE? Don't get us wrong. Welch is not about to sacrifice profit on the altar of lofty sentiments. As Stephen Joyce, a vice president at GE Capital, puts it, "Hey, this *is* GE." But Welch maintains there is no contradiction between his hard-nosed reputation for demanding superior performance and soft concepts like employee involvement. Explaining the point of the exercise, he says, "The only ideas that count are the *A* ideas. There is no second place. That means we have to get everybody in the

organization involved. If you do that right, the best ideas will rise to the top."

To get those ideas percolating, GE is dismantling executive power and handing pieces of it over to "process champions," who might be veeps in TV programming or janitors on a cleaning crew. Says Harvard business school professor Len Schlesinger, one of about two dozen academics and consultants GE has hired to coach employees through the change: "This is one of the biggest planned efforts to alter people's behavior since the Cultural Revolution."

Welch and his lieutenants have selected three weapons: management techniques called Work-Out, Best Practices, and Process Mapping. The first jimmies the locks that keep employees out of the decision-making process; the second seeks to smash the "not invented here" syndrome and to spread good ideas quickly from one part of GE to another; the third is the tool the others most depend on. All foster lots of employee involvement. Combined, they are designed to sustain the rapid growth in productivity that, Welch says, is the key to *any* corporation's survival in the competitive environment of the 90s.

That strategy has risks. No big old U.S. company has ever proved that "soft techniques" can deliver the goods over the long haul. But Welch is willing to bet his sterling reputation on the new initiatives. Rather than try them in pilot programs, he has, in effect, hurled them at the entire organization and yelled, "Catch!" With the game well under way, Fortune has become the first outsider allowed to range widely through the company to see how it is being played.

When the revolution hits GE, it's time to sit up and take notice. Concepts such as strategic planning, decentralization, and market research—indeed, the very notion that management is a discipline that can be taught and applied across a wide spectrum of business—were all either invented at GE, or first used systematically there. Those ideas formed the core curriculum at Crotonville, GE's Management Development Institute in Ossining, New York (see box). What's happening at GE now, says Schlesinger, "is an explicit rejection of many of the old principles."

Work-Out was conceived on a helicopter in September 1988. Welch was flying from Crotonville with its director, James Baughman, to headquarters in Fairfield,

---

The Harvard of Corporate America

It looks like a small, elite college: an ivy-covered classroom building, a wooded, rolling campus. But don't be fooled—this place is 100 percent business. It's Crotonville, home of General Electric's Management Development Institute, the Harvard of corporate America. "I've almost never missed a class," says CEO Jack Welch (PhD in chemical engineering, University of Illinois '60). His monthly visits to Crotonville are "a great way to take the pulse of the organization" in Q&A sessions with GE managers. The informal academic settings lets him hear from people he wouldn't encounter in the ordinary course of business.

The students, 120 a week, get an education that alumni and professors say can hold its own against the best university business schools. Says former vice chairman Lawrence Bossidy (BA, Colgate '57): "You get a better exposure to quantification at a place like the University of Chicago, but Crotonville might have a better management program. It's just so relevant." Crotonville's 160-page catalogue offers entry-level studies in manufacturing and sales, seminars in personnel relations and marketing strategy, a course for engineers and English majors called Eyawtkaf (Everything You Always Wanted to Know About Finance), and advanced management training. Tuition ranges from $800 for a half-week conference for all new professional hires to $14,000 for the four-week Executive Development Course, GE's most advanced offering. A student's home business pays the tab.

One of Crotonville's strengths is its faculty, headed by James Baughman, who gave up a professorship at Harvard Business School in 1980 to take the post. With no tenured professors, Baughman can cherry-pick, with the world as his orchard. In any given week you might find scholars from Harvard (John Kotter), Wharton (Ian MacMillan), Insead (André Laurent), and elsewhere.

Crotonville has long influenced business school curriculums. Noel Tichy, a professor at the University of Michigan and former head of management education at Crotonville, says the Blue Books—GE's bible of scientific management —"became the template for B-school curriculums in the 60s, helping those places become more than trade schools." The place is setting standards again. "Crotonville pioneered action learning and team learning, which are the innovations in business schools now," says Harvard's Len Schlesinger. Next spring, for instance, Tichy will offer students at Michigan a chance to spend seven weeks working intensively on real issues confronting GM, Kmart, and others, just the sort of thing Crotonville does using situations at GE. "If we pull it off," says Tichy, "every business school in the country will have to get into it."

Connecticut. They had just left the Pit, the classroom where GE executives are encouraged to put aside decorum and engage Welch in the rough-and-tumble debate he relishes. Pumped up, Welch told Baughman, "We've got to find a way to take this thing and transfer it out into the businesses."

GE was a different company from the one Welch had taken over in 1981. By 1989 he had squeezed 350 product lines and business units into 13 big businesses, each first or second in its industry. He had shed $9 billion of assets and spent $18 billion on acquisitions. He collapsed GE's management structure, a wedding cake that had towered up to nine layers high, and scraped off its ornate frosting of corporate staff; 29 pay levels became five broad bands. Victims dubbed Welch "Neutron Jack" after the neutron bomb, a Pentagon idea for a weapon that would kill people but leave buildings standing. That was a misnomer: Welch eliminated 100,000 jobs and flattened buildings, too. Those tough actions beefed up GE's total stock market value from $12 billion in 1980 (11th among U.S. corporations) to $65 billion today (second only to Exxon).

"The hardware was basically in place by mid-1988," Welch says. "We liked our businesses." But colleagues remember his frustration. Every time he visited the Pit, he told people, "I hope you're as brave when you're back home as you are here." They weren't. Former vice chairman Lawrence Bossidy (now CEO of Allied-Signal) recalls, "People were telling us, 'You say you want openness and candor, but that's not happening at our place.' " Further structural change wasn't the answer. Welch was asking for something much harder: cultural change.

Within a week of the helicopter conversation, Baughman had a plan. In January 1989, Welch announced it to 500 top operating managers at their annual confab in Boca Raton, Florida. They heard that Fairfield had a new program, that corporate was hiring top-flight consultants and B-school professors to facilitate it, and that it wasn't optional. It was called Work-Out.

Work-Out is, essentially, a place. It's a forum where three things can happen: Participants can get a mental workout; they can take unnecessary work out of their jobs; they can work out problems together. Work-Outs started in March 1989. Like kernels of corn in a hot pan, they began popping one at a time—in GE Plastics' Silicones unit in Waterford, New York; at NBC; in the lighting business— then in a great, noisy rush. No one keeps count, but Baughman guesses that 40,000 employees—better than one in eight—will take part in at least one Work-Out in 1991.

Initially, all followed the same format, which Welch likens to a New England town meeting. A group of 40 to 100 people, picked by management from all ranks and several functions, goes to a conference center or hotel. It's a gaffé to wear a tie. The three-day sessions begin with a talk by the boss, who roughs out an agenda—typically, to eliminate unnecessary meetings, forms, approvals, and other scutwork. Then the boss leaves. Aided by the outside facilitator, the group breaks into five or six teams, each to tackle part of the agenda. For a day and a half they go at it, listing complaints, debating solutions, and preparing presentations for the final day.

It's the third day that gives Work-Out its special power. The boss, ignorant of what has been going on, comes back and takes a place at the front of the room. Often senior executives come to watch.

One by one, team spokesmen rise to make their proposals. By the rules of the game, the boss can make only three responses: He can agree on the spot; he can say no; or he can ask for more information—in which case he must charter a team to get it by an agreed-upon date.

"I was wringing wet within half an hour," says Armand Lauzon, the burly, blunt-spoken head of plant services at the GE Aircraft Engines factory in Lynn, Massachusetts. His employees had set up the room so Lauzon had his back to his boss. "They had 108 proposals, I had about a minute to say yes or no to each one, and I couldn't make eye contact with my boss without turning around, which would show everyone in the room that I was chickenshit." Ideas ranged from designing a plant-services insignia as a morale booster to building a new tinsmith shop, and Lauzon said yes to all but eight.

Electrician Vic Slepoy makes no apology for the ordeal Lauzon suffered: "When you've been told to shut up for 20 years, and someone tells you to speak up—you're going to let them have it." Lauzon is not complaining. Work-Out proposals will save plant services more than $200,000 in 1991. The biggest hit: a yes to letting Lynn's tin knockers bid against an outside vendor to build new protective shields for grinding machines, based on a design an hourly worker sketched on a brown paper bag. They brought in the job for $16,000 versus the vendor's quoted $96,000.

That was an ideal Work-Out result: It not only saved GE money but it also brought work to a labor force that had plenty of reasons to mistrust the company. Lynn employs 8,000 people, down from 14,000 in 1986. The angry local of the International Union of Electronic Workers had voted down the previous

two national contracts. Welch, who grew up in nearby Salem, asked a gathering of union members last year, "Why do you guys poke your finger in my eye every three years?" Simple, explains Slepoy, his Massachusetts accent a lot like Welch's: "We had the feeling they were trying to phase us out. Now at least we have an avenue to make a pitch for our jobs."

They're more courtly in Louisville, Kentucky, where GE makes appliances, but no less theatrical. At a Work-Out held at the Ramada Inn in nearby Bardstown, one team's job was to find ways to improve the environment in Building One, which makes clothes washers and dryers. The place got so steamy in summer you'd think the machines on the assembly line were already hooked up and running. The fixes were simple: Open some vents that had been shut years ago for no remembered reason, and buy a few fans and blowers. To make their point, the team led boss Jeff Svoboda out to the parking lot. The temperature was in the 90s and team members took their sweet time setting up an easel and flip charts while Svoboda stood in the sun. They got one of the quicker okays in the annals of Work-Out.

Artificial? You bet. Steve Kerr, a USC business professor and Work-Out facilitator, says Work-Outs start as "unnatural acts in unnatural places." The stagecraft gives workers a safe way to taste empowerment. The same goes for the boss: Even if *his* boss is in the room, he is forced to make his own decisions. His boss can't overrule him later without jeopardizing the whole process. Kerr says Welch has made it plain that it's a "a career-limiting move" to obstruct the efforts of a Work-Out team.

By using early Work-Outs to go after

irksome minor issues like excess paperwork—"low-hanging fruit" in company parlance—GE gets quick victories on the board. The easy pickings often have big benefits. At NBC, Michael Sherlock's operations and technical services department used Work-Outs to scotch forms that totaled more than two million pieces of paper a year.

These first sessions are really about building trust. Says Welch: "You have to go through the administrivia part of it. If you jump right into complicated issues, no one speaks up, because those ideas are more dangerous." That's because they cross functional boundaries, where people feel their turf is being encroached upon. To make that step, the Work-Out process changes. Later Work-Outs are still "unnatural acts," but now they're "in natural places," in Kerr's words—meaning that teams are made up of people who work together day to day or who are involved in different steps of the same process, like packers and shippers or purchasing agents and parts managers. Often they are commissioned at town meetings to gather data on a knotty problem.

Technician Al Thomas led one such team at GE Plastics' Burkville, Alabama, plant, which makes Lexan, a polycarbonate used in auto bumpers and milk bottles. Its mission: to increase the "first-pass yield"—the percentage of resin that ends up as salable pellets without having to be melted and run again through the factory's extruders. "There were no home runs," Thomas says, but the team hit 26 singles. They installed a computer terminal on the extrusion floor to give workers early warning of problems upstream where resins are made. They realigned pipes that pour pellets into cartons to reduce spillage. They vetted the procedures manual;

a Post-it note on one page reads, "This procedure is totally unnecessary and useless." Hourly workers, not engineers, are writing a new version. The team met daily for three months and spent about $10,000. When they were done, 37 percent of the waste was gone. And, says Thomas, it was fun: "We learned a lot without bosses looking over our shoulders."

Now Work-Outs are enrolling customers and suppliers as well as colleagues. A team in the locomotive paintshop in Erie, Pennsylvania, found that a major cause of delays and rework was inconsistency in the paint, because GE was buying it from two suppliers. Team members persuaded their boss, Ralph Schumacher, to use just one, Glyptal Corporation, and asked its chemist to join up. Together they wrote standards for color and consistency, eliminated the need for dual inspections, and hooked up a direct phone line between the two shops. A paint job now takes 10 shifts, down from 11 or 12 before. GE's Monogram Retailer Credit Services, which manages Montgomery Ward's charge card business, teamed with Ward to tie its cash registers directly to GE's mainframes, cutting the time for opening a new customer account from 30 minutes to 90 seconds.

As Work-Out began to spread through GE, headquarters was laying in ammo for another assault on business-as-usual. Again the impetus was Welch's pursuit of ideas to increase productivity. It was Welch himself who first voiced what later seemed obvious. Other companies get higher productivity growth than GE. Why not kick their tires?

The assignment went to the business development staff in Fairfield, which scrutinizes acquisition candidates and, thus, has wide knowledge of other companies. In the summer of 1988, the group,

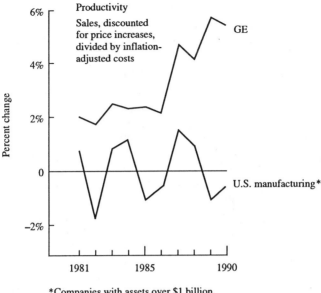

*Companies with assets over $1 billion.

then headed by Michael Fraizer, began scouring the business press and canvassing GE executives, looking for companies worth emulating. From an initial list of about 200, they found two dozen that had achieved faster productivity growth than GE and sustained it for at least 10 years. Also screened out: Direct competitors and companies that would not be credible to GE people. (Folks who make turbines have a hard time believing that a hot little cookiemaker can teach them much.) Half of the survivors agreed to the proposition GE made: Let us send some people to your shop to learn about your best management ideas; in return, we'll share the study with you and let you ask about our methods. Participants included electronic-components maker AMP, Chaparral Steel, Ford, Hewlett-Packard, Xerox, and three Japanese companies.

The project, which GE called Best Practices, took more than a year. There's a crucial difference between Best Prac-

tices and the benchmarking lots of companies do. Benchmarkers usually study nonpareils in particular functions—"What can our shipping department learn from L.L. Bean's?" GE was looking less for nuts and bolts than for attitudes and management practices. Basically, says Baughman, GE's question was, "What's the secret of your success?"

Surprise: The answers were remarkably similar. Almost every company emphasized managing processes, not functions; that is, they focused less on the performance of individual departments than on how they work together as products move from one to another. They also outhustled their competitors in introducing new products and treated their suppliers as partners. And they managed inventory so well that they tied up less working capital per dollar of sales than GE.

The implications of the Best Practices study were earthshaking. GE realized it was managing and measuring the wrong things. The company was setting goals and keeping score; instead, says business development manager George Zippel, "we should have focused more on *how* things got done than on *what* got done."

Best Practices provided an empirical basis for changing what GE manages. The corporate audit staff—GE's fearsome cadre of traveling checkers—altered its methods. Auditors, youngsters picked for their high potential, used to come from finance backgrounds; now half are operations or information systems experts. Says audit staff head Teresa LeGrand: "When I started 10 years ago, the first thing I did was count the $5,000 in the petty cash box. Today we look at the $5 million in inventory on the floor, searching for process improvements that will bring it down."

Crotonville turned the Best Practices findings into a course, which it gives to a dozen people a month from each of GE's 10 manufacturing businesses. The service businesses, which need to pay special attention to issues like managing information technology, have their own course, based on research at nonmanufacturing companies like American Express.

The class teaches three essential lessons. The first is that other companies have much to teach GE—something easy to forget in a century-old giant that hasn't had a down quarter in a decade. Second is the value of continuously improving processes, even in small ways, rather than taking big jumps. To develop a new product, for example, GE learned to make a multigenerational plan—aiming to introduce a first version that uses only tried-and-true technologies, then gradually introducing new ones as they are perfected. That gets the product to market faster and eliminates costly mishaps when

an unproven technology turns out to be full of bugs. GE also learned that rotating executives quickly through new jobs, long a proud practice at the company, created problems in new-product introductions, which go more smoothly when managers have long tenure.

The third lesson is that processes need owners—people whose responsibility and authority reach through the walls between departments. That's how Best Practices folds back into Work-Out and explains why, more and more, the people who go to Crotonville for the course are not senior management but Work-Out teams that are wrestling with, say, a supplier-relations issue.

Many ties established in the Best Practices study are still strong. GE and AMP visit one another several times a year, for example. Recently GE has been studying how AMP purchases, while AMP executives have been boning up on GE's executive development programs. And GE businesses have begun to copy the technique on their own—making a best practice of Best Practices. For example, NBC visited the United Nations, Citicorp, and others to learn how they cope with the frustrations of moving supplies and equipment in congested Manhattan.

"Demand for change creates demand for tools," says Baughman. GE meets it with Process Mapping, an old technique that the company has put on the dais along with Work-Out and Best Practices. A process map is a flow chart showing every step, no matter how small, that goes into making or doing something. Elaborate process maps use diamonds, circles, and squares to distinguish work that adds value from work that doesn't, like inspection. These are furbelows, not really necessary. What's essential is that every step be mapped, from the order clerk picking up the phone to the deliveryman getting a signed receipt.

Process mapping sounds simple, but it is not. To do it right, managers, employees, suppliers, and customers must work on the map together to make sure that what the company thinks happens really does. When a team from GE's Evendale, Ohio, plant mapped the process of making turbine shafts for jet engines, the job took more than a month, and the map went all around a conference room.

When a process is mapped, GE has—often for the first time—the ability to manage an operation in a coherent way from start to finish. Before, says John Chesson, general manager of component manufacturing at Evendale, "we strove for worker efficiency and machine efficiency. Now what drives us is the efficiency of total asset management." For example, in pursuit of 100 percent machine utilization, all rotating parts used to go to a central steam-cleaning facility between operations; now the shaftmakers have their own cleaning booths because the process map revealed that the time saved more than paid for the additional equipment. The map also helped the shaft team pinpoint sources of imperfect parts and rearrange equipment to achieve a more continuous flow through the factory. The result was a 50 percent time saving in 1991, a $4 million drop in inventory, and a good shot at getting seven inventory turns a year versus 2.6 before.

Nowhere have GE's new management techniques come together more impressively than in the appliance business. A year ago senior vice president Gary Rogers toured the Montreal plant of GE Appliances' Canadian subsidiary, Camco, to see how it had adapted the ideas of a small New Zealand appliance maker, Fisher & Paykel. Camco's manufacturing head, Serge Huot, had found a way to transfer Fisher & Paykel's job-shop techniques to the high-volume Canadian factory, dramatically speeding operations. The change hadn't been trouble free—Camco had problems making all models available at all times—but the normally taciturn Rogers was excited.

What happened next shows how GE's new management techniques work. Rogers called a town-meeting Work-Out to introduce the ideas and the vision—which amounts to a build-to-order manufacturing style. For example, building a dishwasher takes just hours, but it takes about 16 weeks for a change in the pattern of consumer demand to affect the product mix at the end of the assembly line in Louisville. The goal: reduce that cycle by 90 percent while actually increasing availability—the odds that a given model is on hand when a customer orders it. Finance manager David Cote assembled a cross-functional team to install Camco's system, now called Quick Response. Work-Out teams began sticking process maps on the walls—more than 500 in all. One result among many: Workers in the distribution center now get production schedules in a new way that allows them to tell truckers well in advance when their loads will be ready—a simple change that will save almost a day's time and will cut $3 million in inventory.

More than 200 Louisville managers and employees toured the Montreal operation. Others took a GE jet to Crotonville to take the Best Practices course, including a group with two shop stewards from the refrigerator plant. The trip was meant to show union and management leaders the potential payoff from process-oriented, nonhierarchical cooperation and to help soften a relationship that had become a rigid that's not-my-job-description face-off.

Another purpose was to study companies, one of them a textile manufacturer, that had mastered high-volume build-to-order manufacturing.

Two insights underlie Quick Response. First, no forecast, however accurate in the aggregate, can tell you precisely how many brown side-by-side refrigerators should be built with the freezer on the left. Conclusion: Forget about trying to pinpoint forecasting—if you can make to order, who needs it?—and drop that part of the cycle from six weeks to one. Second, although just 20 percent to 30 percent of the parts in any appliance are unique to that model, less than 5 percent are also complex and costly. If those come just-in-time from suppliers, you can carry buffer stock and still cut inventory costs. Manufacturing can be much more flexible if a company can design models to share more components, stock parts on the line rather than in storerooms, and speed up changeovers. A worker team in GE's factory in Decatur, Alabama, cut changeover time on a punch press from four hours to 15 minutes.

Since implementing Quick Response in January, GE Appliances has cut its 16-week cycle by more than half while increasing product availability 6 percent. Inventory costs have plunged more than 20 percent—a major reason the group has weathered the recession with steady profits despite a 5 percent decrease in volume. The program has cost less than $3 million, Rogers says, and has already returned a hundred times that.

That's not counting the benefits to other GE businesses. Quick Response, the result of a Best Practice from an outside company, has made Appliance Park the hottest destination on GE's internal Best Practices circuit. Two years ago the business's combination of low margins, tough unions, and brutal competition made Louisville the last place an ambitious GE manager wanted to be—"an isolation ward," says one. Now groups from every other GE business have taken up residence there to learn how to adapt the process to their needs.

The revolution at General Electric is still fragile, and middle management is one of the weaker points. David Genever-Watling, senior vice president of industrial and power systems, says, "You need unselfish, open-minded executives to run the process," and they are still a rare breed at GE or anywhere else. Many managers may have the courage of Welch's convictions: It's hard to know whether they fully understand their changed role or are simply responding to the fact that support for Work-Out has become one of the criteria in their annual review.

The same goes for workers. In Schenectady, New York, union business agent Lou Valenti says, "I'm behind the process 200 percent," and was reelected without opposition last year; at Lynn, workers who went through Work-Out were told by colleagues that it's a ploy to win votes for the new contract—but in July the Lynn local approved a three-year national pact for the first time since 1982. At NBC, excited network and affiliated station executives have decided to hold a Work-Out at the 1992 affiliates meeting—usually a gathering more memorable for sizzle than for steak. But Steve O'Donnell, head writer for the David Letterman show, says, "I've seen more boneheaded cost cutting than innovative management."

Change is catching on fast, however. So many Work-Outs are happening at GE that outside facilitators like Schlesinger and Kerr are training GE employees to take their place. Some are hourly workers. It's a tough job: Sessions can get frighteningly heated, and facilitators need to know when to step in, when to keep out, and how to get help from engineers and other experts if teams need it. Bob Huff, a machinist at Evendale, finds the job draws on his experience leading church groups and riding Brahman bulls in rodeos, as well as his study of consultant Marvin Weisbord's six-point model of organizational development.

Occasionally now, Work-Out teams form themselves, springing up in response to a problem or opportunity, rather than to a formal charter. Gary Rogers says he and his managers sometimes don't hear about a Work-Out till someone shows up to present its findings or ask for technical help.

And Welch can point to results where they will always matter most at GE, in the numbers. Productivity—which GE measures by dividing real revenues (with price increases factored out) by real costs (after discounting for inflation)—will rise 5 percent in 1991, according to Welch, "with almost no layoffs and, due to the recession, no increase in volume." GE expects to get five dollars in sales for every dollar of working capital invested—16.3 percent more than in 1988, the year before Work-Out and Best Practices began.

Welch admits that it will take a decade before GE's new culture becomes as hard to change as the one it is supplanting. By then, he says, GE's hierarchies could actually wither away: "Even in a horizontal structure you'll still have product managers, still need accountability," he says, "but the lines will blur. The functions will go away, if you will. There will be core technologies at the center of each business. Aircraft engines will always need real experts in combustion. They'll reside in the core. But teams will move together from left to right, from product idea to product delivery, reaching into the core as they need to in order to get the job done."

Ten years from now Welch will be 65. It is conceivable that he will have run GE for 20 years, longer than anyone since Charles Coffin, who retired in 1922 after 33 years at the helm. Looking ahead, he hopes to leave behind "a company that's able to change at least as fast as the world is changing, and people whose real income is secure because they're winning and whose psychic income is rising because every person is participating."

And managers? "They will be people who are comfortable facilitating, greasing, finding ways to make it all seamless, not controllers and directors. Work-Out is the fundamental underpinning of the training of the next generation of managers." In some evolved form, Work-Outs will be natural acts in natural places: No longer a means to change GE's culture, they will *be* the culture. Unrealistic? Perhaps. But, says Rodger Bricknell, who leads the effort in power systems, based in GE's ancient Schenectady works, there comes a point where employee involvement is impossible to turn off. As he says, "If you teach a bear to dance, you'd better be prepared to keep dancing till the bear wants to stop."

Investor's Snapshot
General Electric

Sales	
(latest four quarters)	$59.6 billion
Change from year earlier	up 6.2%
Net profit	$4.4 billion
Change	up 5.8%
Return on common stockholder's equity	19.7%
Five-year average	18.2%
Stock price range (last 12 months)	$50–$77.625
Recent share price	$71.75
Price earnings multiple	14
Total return to investors (12 months to 7/17)	−0.5%

READING

THE LEADER'S NEW WORK: BUILDING LEARNING ORGANIZATIONS

Peter M. Senge
MIT Sloan School of Management

Human beings are designed for learning. No one has to teach an infant to walk, or talk, or master the spatial relationships needed to stack eight building blocks that don't topple. Children come fully equipped with an insatiable drive to explore and experiment. Unfortunately, the primary institutions of our society are oriented predominantly toward controlling, rather than learning; rewarding individuals for performing for others, rather than for cultivating their natural curiosity and impulse to learn. The young child entering school discovers quickly that the name of the game is getting the right answer and avoiding mistakes—a mandate no less compelling to the aspiring manager.

"Our prevailing system of management has destroyed our people," writes W. Edwards Deming, leader in the quality movement.[1] "People are born with intrinsic motivation, self-esteem, dignity, curiosity to learn, joy in learning. The forces of destruction begin with toddlers—a prize for the best Halloween costume, grades in school, gold stars, and on up through the university. On the job, people, teams, divisions are ranked—reward for the one at the top, punishment at the bottom. MBO, quotas, incentive pay, business plans, put together separately, division by division, cause further loss, unknown and unknowable."

Ironically, by focusing on performing for someone else's approval, corporations create the very conditions that predestine them to mediocre performance. Over the long run, superior performance depends on superior learning. A Shell study showed that, according to former planning director Arie de Geus, "a full one third of the Fortune 500 industrials listed in 1970 had vanished by 1983."[2] Today, the average lifetime of the largest industrial enterprises is probably less than *half* the average lifetime of a person in an industrial society. On the other hand, de Geus and his colleagues at Shell also found a small number of companies that survived for 75 years or longer. Interestingly, the key to their survival was the ability to run "experiments in the margin," to continually explore new business and organizational opportunities that create potential new sources of growth.

If anything, the need for understanding how organizations learn and accelerating that learning is greater today than ever before. The old days when a Henry Ford, Alfred Sloan, or Tom Watson *learned for the organization* are gone. In an increasingly dynamic, interdependent, and unpredictable world, it is simply no longer possible for anyone to "figure it all out at the top." The old model, "the top thinks and the local acts," must now give way to

From *Sloan Management Review*, Fall 1990.

integrating thinking and acting at all levels. While the challenge is great, so is the potential payoff. "The person who figures out how to harness the collective genius of the people in his or her organization," according to former Citibank CEO Walter Wriston, "is going to blow the competition away."

Adaptive Learning and Generative Learning

The prevailing view of learning organizations emphasizes increased adaptability. Given the accelerating pace of change, or so the standard view goes, "the most successful corporation of the 1990s," according to *Fortune* magazine, "will be something called a learning organization, a consummately adaptive enterprise."[3] As the Shell study shows, examples of traditional authoritarian bureaucracies that responded too slowly to survive in changing business environments are legion.

But increasing adaptiveness is only the first stage in moving toward learning organizations. The impulse to learn in children goes deeper than desires to respond and adapt more effectively to environmental change. The impulse to learn, at its heart, is an impulse to be generative, to expand our capability. This is why leading corporations are focusing on *generative* learning, which is about creating, as well as *adaptive* learning, which is about coping.[4]

The total quality movement in Japan illustrates the evolution from adaptive to generative learning. With its emphasis on continuous experimentation and feedback, the total quality movement has been the first wave in building learning organizations. But Japanese firms' view of serving the customer has evolved. In the early years of total quality, the focus was on "fitness to standard," making a product reliably so that it would do what its designers intended it to do and what the firm told its customers it would do. Then came a focus on "fitness to need," understanding better what the customer wanted and then providing products that reliably met those needs. Today, leading-edge firms seek to understand and meet the "latent need" of the customer—what customers might truly value but have never experienced or would never think to ask for. As one Detroit executive commented recently, "You could never produce the Mazda Miata solely from market research. It required a leap of imagination to see what the customer *might* want."[5]

Generative learning, unlike adaptive learning, requires new ways of looking at the world, whether in understanding customers or in understanding how to better manage a business. For years, U.S. manufacturers sought competitive advantage in aggressive controls on inventories, incentives against overproduction, and rigid adherence to production forecasts. Despite these incentives, their performance was eventually eclipsed by Japanese firms who saw the challenges of manufacturing differently. They realized that eliminating delays in the production process was the key to reducing instability and improving cost, productivity, and service. They worked to build networks of relationships with trusted suppliers and to redesign physical production processes so as to reduce delays in materials procurement, production set up, and in-process inventory—a much higher-leverage approach to improving both cost and customer loyalty.

As Boston Consulting Group's George Stalk has observed, the Japanese saw the significance of delays because they saw the process of order entry, production scheduling, materials procurement, production, and distribution *as an integrated system.* "What distorts the system so badly is time," observed Stalk—the multiple delays between events and responses. "These distortions reverberate throughout the system, producing disruptions, waste, and inefficiency."[6] Generative learning requires seeing the systems that control events. When we fail to grasp the systemic source of problems, we are left to "push on" symptoms, rather than eliminate underlying causes. The best we can ever do is adaptive learning.

The Leader's New Work

"I talk with people all over the country about learning organizations, and the response is always very positive," says William O'Brien, CEO of the Hanover Insurance companies. "If this type of organization is so widely preferred, why don't people create such organizations? I think the answer is leadership. People have no real comprehension of the type of commitment it requires to build such an organization."[7]

Our traditional view of leaders—as special people who set the direction, make the key decisions, and energize the troops—is deeply rooted in an individualistic and nonsystemic worldview. Especially in the West, leaders are *heroes*—great men (and occasionally women) who rise to the fore in times of crisis. So long as such myths prevail, they reinforce a focus on short-term events and charismatic heroes rather than on systemic forces and collective learning.

Leadership in learning organizations centers on subtler and ultimately more important work. In a learning organization, leaders' roles differ dramatically from that of the charismatic decision maker. Leaders are designers, teachers,

and stewards. These roles require new skills: the ability to build shared vision, to bring to the surface and challenge prevailing mental models, and to foster more systemic patterns of thinking. In short, leaders in learning organizations are responsible for *building organizations* where people are continually expanding their capabilities to shape their future—that is, leaders are responsible for learning.

Creative Tension: The Integrating Principle

Leadership in a learning organization starts with the principle of creative tension.[8] Creative tension comes from seeing clearly where we want to be, our "vision," and telling the truth about where we are, our "current reality." The gap between the two generates a natural tension (see Figure 1).

Creative tension can be resolved in two basic ways: by raising current reality toward the vision, or by lowering the vision toward current reality. Individuals, groups, and organizations who learn how to work with creative tension learn how to use the energy it generates to move reality more reliably toward their visions.

The principle of creative tension has long been recognized by leaders. Martin Luther King, Jr., once said, "Just as Socrates felt that it was necessary to create a tension in the mind, so that individuals could rise from the bondage of myths and half truths . . . so must we . . . create the kind of tension in society that will help men rise from the dark depths of prejudice and racism."[9]

Without vision there is no creative tension. Creative tension cannot be generated from current reality alone. All the analysis in the world will never generate a vision.

FIGURE 1   The Principle of Creative
Tension

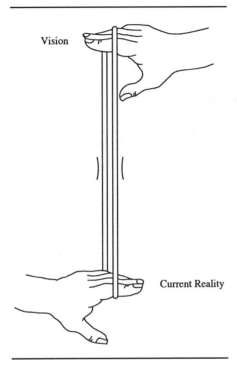

Vision

Current Reality

Many who are otherwise qualified to lead fail to do so because they try to substitute analysis for vision. They believe that, if only people understood current reality, they would surely feel the motivation to change. They are then disappointed to discover that people "resist" the personal and organizational changes that must be made to alter reality. What they never grasp is that the natural energy for changing reality comes from holding a picture of what might be that is more important to the people than what is.

But creative tension cannot be generated from vision alone; it demands an accurate picture of current reality as well. Just as King had a dream, so, too, did he continually strive to "dramatize the shameful conditions" of racism and prej-

udice so they could no longer be ignored. Vision without an understanding of current reality will more likely foster cynicism than creativity. The principle of creative tension teaches that *an accurate picture of current reality is just as important as a compelling picture of a desired future*.

Leading through creative tension is different than solving problems. In problem solving, the energy for change comes from attempting to get away from an aspect of current reality that is undesirable. With creative tension, the energy for change comes from the vision, from what we want to create, juxtaposed with current reality. While the distinction may seem small, the consequences are not. Many people and organizations find themselves motivated to change only when their problems are bad enough to cause them to change. This works for a while, but the change process runs out of steam as soon as the problems driving the change become less pressing. With problem solving, the motivation for change is extrinsic. With creative tension, the motivation is intrinsic. This distinction mirrors the distinction between adaptive and generative learning.

New Roles

The traditional authoritarian image of the leader as "the boss calling the shots" has been recognized as oversimplified and inadequate for some time. According to Edgar Schein, "Leadership is intertwined with culture formation." Building an organization's culture and shaping its evolution is the "unique and essential function" of leadership.[10] In a learning organization, the critical roles of leadership—designer, teacher, and steward—have antecedents in the ways leaders have contributed to building organizations in the past. But each role takes on new meaning in the learning organization and, as will be seen in the following sections, demands new skills and tools.

Leader as Designer. Imagine that your organization is an ocean liner and that you are "the leader." What is your role?

I have asked this question of groups of managers many times. The most common answer, not surprisingly, is "the captain." Others say, "The navigator, setting the direction." Still others say, "The helmsman, actually controlling the direction," or, "The engineer down there stoking the fire, providing energy," or, "The social director, making sure everybody's enrolled, involved, and communicating." While these are legitimate leadership roles, there is another which, in many ways, eclipses them all in importance. Yet rarely does anyone mention it.

The neglected leadership role is the *designer* of the ship. No one has a more sweeping influence than the designer. What good does it do for the captain to say, "Turn starboard 30 degrees," when the designer has built a rudder that will only turn to port, or which takes six hours to turn to starboard? It's fruitless to be the leader in an organization that is poorly designed.

The functions of design, or what some have called "social architecture," are rarely visible; they take place behind the scenes. The consequences that appear today are the result of work done long in the past, and work today will show its benefits far in the future. Those who aspire to lead out of a desire to control, or gain fame, or simply to be at the center of the action, will find little

to attract them to the quiet design work of leadership.

But what, specifically, is involved in organizational design? "Organization design is widely misconstrued as moving around boxes and lines," says Hanover's O'Brien. "The first task of organization design concerns designing the governing ideas of purpose, vision, and core values by which people will live." Few acts of leadership have a more enduring impact on an organization than building a foundation of purpose and core values.

In 1982, Johnson & Johnson found itself facing a corporate nightmare when bottles of its best-selling Tylenol were tampered with, resulting in several deaths. The corporation's immediate response was to pull all Tylenol off the shelves of retail outlets. Thirty-one million capsules were destroyed, even though they were tested and found safe. Although the immediate cost was significant, no other action was possible given the firm's credo. Authored almost 40 years earlier by president Robert Wood Johnson, Johnson & Johnson's credo states that permanent success is possible only when modern industry realizes that:

- Service to its customers comes first,
- Service to its employees and management comes second,
- Service to the community comes third,
- Service to its stockholders, last.

Such statements might seem like motherhood and apple pie to those who have not seen the way a clear sense of purpose and values can affect key business decisions. Johnson & Johnson's crisis management in this case was based on that credo. It was simple, it was right, and it worked.

If governing ideas constitute the first design task of leadership, the second design task involves the policies, strategies, and structures that translate guiding ideas into business decisions. Leadership theorist Philip Selznick calls policy and structure the "institutional embodiment of purpose."[11] "Policy making (the rules that guide decisions) ought to be separated from decision making," says Jay Forrester.[12] "Otherwise, short-term pressures will usurp time from policy creation."

Traditionally, writers like Selznick and Forrester have tended to see policy making and implementation as the work of a small number of senior managers. But that view is changing. Both the dynamic business environment and the mandate of the learning organization to engage people at all levels now make it clear that this second design task is more subtle. Henry Mintzberg has argued that strategy is less a rational plan arrived at in the abstract and implemented throughout the organization than an "emergent phenomenon." Successful organizations "craft strategy," according to Mintzberg, as they continually learn about shifting business conditions and balance what is desired and what is possible.[13] The key is not getting the right strategy but fostering strategic thinking. "The choice of individual action is only part of . . . the policymaker's need," according to Mason and Mitroff.[14] "More important is the need to achieve insight into the nature of the complexity and to formulate concepts and world views for coping with it."

Behind appropriate policies, strategies, and structures are effective learning processes; their creation is the third key design responsibility in learning organizations. This does not absolve senior managers of their strategic responsibilities. Actually, it deepens and extends those responsibilities. Now, they are not only responsible for ensuring that an organization have well-developed strategies and policies, but also for ensuring that processes exist whereby these are continually improved.

In the early 1970s, Shell was the weakest of the big seven oil companies. Today, Shell and Exxon are arguably the strongest, both in size and financial health. Shell's ascendance began with frustration. Around 1971, members of Shell's "Group Planning" in London began to foresee dramatic change and unpredictability in world oil markets. However, it proved impossible to persuade managers that the stable world of steady growth in oil demand and supply they had known for twenty years was about to change. Despite brilliant analysis and artful presentation, Shell's planners realized, in the words of Pierre Wack, that they "had failed to change behavior in much of the Shell organization."[15] Progress would probably have ended there, had the frustration not given way to a radically new view of corporate planning.

As they pondered this failure, the planners' view of their basic task shifted: "We no longer saw our task as producing a documented view of the future business environment five or ten years ahead. Our real target was the microcosm (the 'mental model') of our decision makers." Only when the planners reconceptualized their basic task as fostering learning rather than devising plans did their insights begin to have an impact. The initial tool used was "scenario analysis," through which planners encouraged operating managers to think through how they would manage in the future under different possible scenarios. It mattered not that the managers believed the planners' scenarios absolutely, only that they became engaged in ferreting out the implications. In this way, Shell's planners conditioned managers to be mentally prepared for a shift from low prices to high prices and from stability to instability. The results were significant. When OPEC became a reality, Shell quickly responded by increasing local operating company control (to enhance maneuverability in the new political environment), building buffer stocks, and accelerating development of non-OPEC sources—actions that its competitors took much more slowly or not at all.

Somewhat inadvertently, Shell planners had discovered the leverage of designing institutional learning processes, whereby, in the words of former planning director de Geus, "Management teams change their shared mental models of their company, their markets, and their competitors."[16] Since then, "planning as learning" has become a byword at Shell, and Group Planning has continually sought out new learning tools that can be integrated into the planning process. Some of these are described below.

Leader as Teacher. "The first responsibility of a leader," writes retired Herman Miller CEO Max de Pree, "is to define reality."[17] Much of the leverage leaders can actually exert lies in helping people achieve more accurate, more insightful, and more *empowering* views of reality.

Leader as teacher does *not* mean leader as authoritarian expert whose job it is to teach people the "correct" view of reality. Rather, it is about helping everyone in the organization, oneself included, to gain more insightful views of current reality. This is in line with a popular emerging view of leaders as coaches, guides, or facilitators.[18] In learning organizations, this teaching role is developed further by virtue of explicit attention to people's mental models and by the influence of the systems perspective.

The role of leader as teacher starts with bringing to the surface people's mental models of important issues. No one carries an organization, a market, or a state of technology in his or her head. What we carry in our heads are assumptions. These mental pictures of how the world works have a significant influence on how we perceive problems and opportunities, identify courses of action, and make choices.

One reason that mental models are so deeply entrenched is that they are largely tacit. Ian Mitroff, in his study of General Motors, argues that an assumption that prevailed for years was that, in the United States, "Cars are status symbols. Styling is therefore more important than quality."[19] The Detroit automakers didn't say, "We have a *mental model* that all people care about is styling." Few actual managers would even say publicly that all people care about is styling. So long as the view remained unexpressed, there was little possibility of challenging its validity or forming more accurate assumptions.

But working with mental models goes beyond revealing hidden assumptions. "Reality," as perceived by most people in most organizations, means pressures that must be borne, crises that must be reacted to, and limitations that must be accepted. Leaders as teachers help people *restructure their views of reality* to see beyond the superficial conditions and events into the underlying causes of problems—and therefore to see new possibilities for shaping the future.

Specifically, leaders can influence people to view reality at three distinct levels: events, patterns of behavior, and systemic structure.

Systemic Structure
(Generative)

↓

Patterns of Behavior
(Responsive)

↓

Events
(Reactive)

The key question becomes *where do leaders predominantly focus their own and their organization's attention?*

Contemporary society focuses predominantly on events. The media reinforces this perspective, with almost exclusive attention to short-term, dramatic events. This focus leads naturally to explaining what happens in terms of those events: "The Dow Jones average went up sixteen points because high fourth-quarter profits were announced yesterday."

Pattern-of-behavior explanations are rarer, in contemporary culture, than event explanations, but they do occur. "Trend analysis" is an example of seeing patterns of behavior. A good editorial that interprets a set of current events in the context of long-term historical changes is another example. Systemic, structural explanations go even further by addressing the question, "What causes the patterns of behavior?"

In some sense, all three levels of explanation are equally true. But their usefulness is quite different. Event explanations—who did what to whom—doom their holders to a reactive stance toward change. Pattern-of-behavior explanations focus on identifying long-term trends and assessing their implications. They at least suggest how, over time, we can respond to shifting conditions. Structural explanations are the most powerful. Only they address the underlying causes of behavior at a level such that patterns of behavior can be changed.

By and large, leaders of our current institutions focus their attention on events and patterns of behavior, and, under their influence, their organizations do likewise. That is why contemporary organizations are predominantly reactive, or at best responsive—rarely generative. On the other hand, leaders in learning organizations pay attention to all three levels, but focus especially on systemic structure; largely by example, they teach people throughout the organization to do likewise.

Leader as Steward. This is the subtlest role of leadership. Unlike the roles of designer and teacher, it is almost solely a matter of attitude. It is an attitude critical to learning organizations.

While stewardship has long been recognized as an aspect of leadership, its source is still not widely understood. I believe Robert Greenleaf came closest to explaining real stewardship, in his seminal book *Servant Leadership*.[20] There, Greenleaf argues that "The servant leader *is* servant first. . . . It begins with the natural feeling that one wants to serve, to serve *first*. This conscious choice brings one to aspire to lead. That person is sharply different from one who is leader first, perhaps because of the need to assuage an unusual power drive or to acquire material possessions."

Leaders' sense of stewardship operates on two levels: stewardship for the people they lead and stewardship for the larger purpose or mission that underlies the enterprise. The first type arises from a keen appreciation of the impact one's leadership can have on others. People can suffer economically, emotionally, and spiritually under inept leadership. If anything, people in a learning organization are more vulnerable because of their commitment and sense of shared ownership. Appreciating this naturally instills a sense of responsibility in leaders. The second type of stewardship arises from a leader's sense of personal purpose and commitment to the organization's larger mission. People's natural impulse to learn is unleashed when they are engaged in an endeavor they consider worthy of their fullest commitment. Or, as Lawrence Miller puts it, "Achieving return on equity does not, as a goal, mobilize the most noble forces of our soul."[21]

Leaders engaged in building learning organizations naturally feel part of a larger purpose that goes beyond their organization. They are part of changing the way businesses operate, not from a vague philanthropic urge, but from a conviction that their efforts will produce more productive organizations, capable of achieving higher levels of organizational success and personal satisfaction than more traditional organizations. Their sense of stewardship was succinctly captured by George Bernard Shaw when he said:

> This is the true joy in life, the being used for a purpose you consider a mighty one, being a force of nature rather than a feverish, selfish clod of ailments and grievances complaining that the world will not devote itself to making you happy.

New Skills

New leadership roles require new leadership skills. These skills can only be developed, in my judgment, through a lifelong commitment. It is not enough for one or two individuals to develop these skills. They must be distributed widely throughout the organization. This is one reason that understanding the *disciplines* of a learning organization is so important. These disciplines embody the principles and practices that can widely foster leadership development.

Three critical areas of skills (disciplines) are building shared vision, surfacing and challenging mental models, and engaging in systems thinking.[22]

Building Shared Vision. How do individual visions come together to create shared visions? A useful metaphor is the hologram, the three-dimensional image created by interacting light sources.

If you cut a photograph in half, each half shows only part of the whole image. But if you divide a hologram, each part, no matter how small, shows the whole image intact. Likewise, when a group of people come to share a vision for an organization, each person sees an individual picture of the organization at its best. Each shares responsibility for the whole, not just for one piece. But the component pieces of the hologram are not identical. Each represents the whole image from a different point of view. It's something like poking holes in a window shade; each hole offers a unique angle for viewing the whole image. So, too, is each individual's vision unique.

When you add up the pieces of a hologram, something interesting happens. The image becomes more intense, more lifelike. When more people come to share a vision, the vision becomes more real in the sense of a mental reality that people can truly imagine achieving. They now have partners, co-creators; the vision no longer rests on their shoulders alone. Early on, when they are nurturing an individual vision, people may say it is "my vision." But, as the shared vision develops, it becomes both "my vision" and "our vision."

The skills involved in building shared vision include the following:

- **Encouraging Personal Vision.** Shared visions emerge from personal visions. It is not that people only care about their own self-interest—in fact, people's values usually include dimensions that concern family, organization, community, and even the world. Rather, it is that people's capacity for caring is *personal*.

- **Communicating and Asking for Support.** Leaders must be willing to continually share their own vision, rather than being the official representative of the corporate vision. They also must be prepared to ask: "Is this vision worthy of your commitment?" This can be difficult for a person used to setting goals and presuming compliance.

- **Visioning as an Ongoing Process.** Building shared vision is a never-ending process. At any one point there will be a particular image of the future that is predominant, but that image will evolve. Today, too many managers want to dispense with the "vision business" by going off and writing the Official Vision Statement. Such statements almost

always lack the vitality, freshness, and excitement of a genuine vision that comes from people asking, "What do we really want to achieve?"

- **Blending Extrinsic and Intrinsic Visions.** Many energizing visions are extrinsic—that is, they focus on achieving something relative to an outsider, such as a competitor. But a goal that is limited to defeating an opponent can, once the vision is achieved, easily become a defensive posture. In contrast, intrinsic goals like creating a new type of product, taking an established product to a new level, or setting a new standard for customer satisfaction can call forth a new level of creativity and innovation. Intrinsic and extrinsic visions need to coexist; a vision solely predicated on defeating an adversary will eventually weaken an organization.

- **Distinguishing Positive from Negative Visions.** Many organizations only truly pull together when their survival is threatened. Similarly, most social movements aim at eliminating what people don't want: for example, anti-drugs, anti-smoking, or anti-nuclear arms movements. Negative visions carry a subtle message of powerlessness: people will only pull together when there is sufficient threat. Negative visions also tend to be short term. Two fundamental sources of energy can motivate organizations: fear and aspiration. Fear, the energy source behind negative visions, can produce extraordinary changes in short periods, but aspiration endures as a continuing source of learning and growth.

Surfacing and Testing Mental Models. Many of the best ideas in organizations never get put into practice. One reason is that new insights and initiatives often conflict with established mental models. The leadership task of challenging assumptions without invoking defensiveness requires reflection and inquiry skills possessed by few leaders in traditional controlling organizations.[23]

• **Seeing Leaps of Abstraction.** Our minds literally move at lightning speed. Ironically, this often slows our learning, because we leap to generalizations so quickly that we never think to test them. We then confuse our generalizations with the observable date upon which they are based, treating the generalizations *as if they were data*. The frustrated sales rep reports to the home office that "customers don't really care about quality, price is what matters," when what actually happened was that three consecutive large customers refused to place an order unless a larger discount was offered. The sales rep treats her generalization, "customers care only about price," as if it were absolute fact rather than an assumption (very likely an assumption reflecting her own views of customers and the market). This thwarts future learning because she starts to focus on how to offer attractive discounts rather than probing behind the customers' statements. For example, the customers may have been so disgruntled with the firm's delivery or customer service that they are unwilling to purchase again without larger discounts.

• **Balancing Inquiry and Advocacy.** Most managers are skilled at articulating their views and presenting them persuasively. While important, advocacy skills can become counterproductive as managers rise in responsibility and confront increasingly complex issues that require collaborative learning among different, equally knowledgeable people. Leaders in learning organizations need to have both inquiry *and* advocacy skills.[24]

• Specifically, when advocating a view, they need to be able to:
—explain the reasoning and data that led to their view;
—encourage others to test their view (e.g., Do you see gaps in my reasoning? Do you disagree with the data upon which my view is based?); and
—encourage others to provide different views (e.g., Do you have either different data, different conclusions, or both?).

• When inquiring into another's views, they need to:
—actively seek to understand the other's view, rather than simply restating their own view and how it differs from the other's view; and
—make their attributions about the other and the other's view explicit (e.g., Based on your statement that . . . ; I am assuming that you believe . . . ; Am I representing your views fairly?).

• If they reach an impasse (others no longer appear open to inquiry), they need to:
—ask what data or logic might unfreeze the impasse, or if an experiment (or some other inquiry) might be designed to provide new information.

• **Distinguishing Espoused Theory from Theory in Use.** We all like to think that we hold certain views, but often our actions reveal deeper views. For example, I may proclaim that people are trustworthy, but never lend friends money and jealously guard my possessions. Obviously, my deeper mental model (my theory in use) differs from my espoused theory. Recognizing gaps between espoused views and theories in use (which often requires the help of others) can be pivotal to deeper learning.

• **Recognizing and Defusing Defensive Routines.** As one CEO in our research program puts it, "Nobody ever talks about an issue at the 8:00 business meeting exactly the same way they talk about it at home that evening or over drinks at the end of the day." The reason is what Chris Argyris calls "defensive routines," entrenched habits used to protect ourselves from the embarrassment and threat that come with exposing our thinking. For most of us, such defenses began to build early in life in response to pressures to have the right answers in school or at home. Organizations add new levels of performance anxiety and thereby amplify and exacerbate this defensiveness. Ironically, this makes it even more difficult to expose hidden mental models, and thereby lessens learning.

The first challenge is to recognize defensive routines, then to inquire into their operation. Those who are best at revealing and defusing defensive routines operate with a high degree of self-disclosure regarding their own defensiveness (e.g., I notice that I am feeling uneasy about how this conversation is going. Perhaps I don't understand it or it is threatening to me in ways I don't yet see. Can you help me see this better?)

Systems Thinking. We all know that leaders should help people see the big picture. But the actual skills whereby leaders are supposed to achieve this are not well understood. In my experience, successful leaders often are "systems thinkers" to a considerable extent. They focus less on day-to-day events and more on underlying trends and forces of change. But they do this almost completely intuitively. The consequence is that they are often unable to explain their intuitions to others and feel frustrated that others cannot see the world the way they do.

One of the most significant developments in management science today is the gradual coalescence of managerial systems thinking as a field of study and practice. This field suggests some key skills for future leaders:

• **Seeing Interrelationships, Not Things, and Processes, Not Snapshots.** Most of us have been conditioned throughout our lives to focus on things and to see the world in static images. This leads us to linear explanations of systemic phenomenon. For instance, in an arms race each party is convinced that the other is *the cause* of problems. They react to each new move as an isolated event, not as part of a process. So long as they fail to see the interrelationships of these actions, they are trapped.

• **Moving beyond Blame.** We tend to blame each other or outside circumstances for our problems. But it is poorly designed systems, not incompetent or unmotivated individuals, that cause most organizational problems. Systems thinking shows us that there is no outside—that you and the cause of your problems are part of a single system.

• **Distinguishing Detail Complexity from Dynamic Complexity.** Some types of complexity are more important strategically than others. Detail complexity arises when there are many variables. Dynamic complexity arises when cause and effect are distant in time and space, and when the consequences over time of interventions are subtle and not obvious to many participants in the system. The leverage in most management situations lies in understanding dynamic complexity, not detail complexity.

• **Focusing on Areas of High Leverage.** Some have called systems thinking the "new dismal science" because it teaches that most obvious solutions don't work—at best, they improve matters in the short run, only to make things worse in the long run. But there is another side to the story. Systems thinking also shows that small, well-focused actions can produce significant, enduring improvements, if they are in the right place. Systems thinkers refer to this idea as the principle of "leverage." Tackling a difficult problem is often a matter of seeing where the high leverage lies, where a change—with a minimum of effort—would lead to lasting, significant improvement.

• **Avoiding Symptomatic Solutions.** The pressures to intervene

in management systems that are going awry can be overwhelming. Unfortunately, given the linear thinking that predominates in most organizations, interventions usually focus on symptomatic fixes, not underlying causes. This results in only temporary relief, and it tends to create still more pressures later on for further, low-leverage intervention. If leaders acquiesce to these pressures, they can be sucked into an endless spiral of increasing intervention. Sometimes the most difficult leadership acts are to refrain from intervening through popular quick fixes and to keep the pressure on everyone to identify more enduring solutions.

While leaders who can articulate systemic explanations are rare, those who *can* will leave their stamp on an organization. One person who had this gift was Bill Gore, the founder and long-time CEO of W. L. Gore and Associates (makers of Gore-Tex and other synthetic fiber products). Bill Gore was adept at telling stories that showed how the organization's core values of freedom and individual responsibility required particular operating policies. He was proud of his egalitarian organization, in which there were (and still are) no "employees," only "associates," all of whom own shares in the company and participate in its management. At one talk, he explained the company's policy of controlled growth: "Our limitation is not financial resources. Our limitation is the rate at which we can bring in new associates. Our experience has been that if we try to bring in more than a 25 percent per year increase, we begin to bog down. Twenty-five percent per year growth is a real limitation; you can do much better than that with an authoritarian organization." As Gore tells the story, one of the associates, Esther Baum, went home after this talk and reported the limitation to her husband. As it happened, he was an astronomer and mathematician at Lowell Observatory. He said, "That's a very interesting figure." He took out a pencil and paper and calculated and said, "Do you realize that in only 57 and a half years, everyone in the world will be working for Gore?"

Through this story, Gore explains the systemic rationale behind a key policy, limited growth rate—a policy that undoubtedly caused a lot of stress in the organization. He suggests that, at larger rates of growth, the adverse effects of attempting to integrate too many new people too rapidly would begin to dominate. (This is the "limits to growth" systems archetype explained below.) The story also reaffirms the organization's commitment to creating a unique environment for its associates and illustrates the types of sacrifices that the firm is prepared to make in order to remain true to its vision. The last part of the story shows that, despite the self-imposed limit, the company is still very much a growth company.

The consequences of leaders who lack systems thinking skills can be devastating. Many charismatic leaders manage almost exclusively at the level of events. They deal in visions and in crises, and little in between. Under their leadership, an organization hurtles from crisis to crisis. Eventually, the worldview of people in the organization becomes dominated by events and reactiveness. Many, especially those who are deeply committed, become burned out. Eventually, cynicism comes to pervade the organization. People have no control over their time, let alone their destiny.

Similar problems arise with the "visionary strategist," the leader with vision who sees both patterns of change and events. This leader is better prepared to manage change. He or she can explain strategies in terms of emerging trends, and thereby foster a climate that is less reactive. But such leaders still impart a responsive orientation rather than a generative one.

Many talented leaders have rich, highly systemic intuitions but cannot explain those intuitions to others. Ironically, they often end up being authoritarian leaders, even if they don't want to, because only they see the decisions that need to be made. They are unable to conceptualize their strategic insights so that these can become public knowledge, open to challenge and further improvement.

New Tools

Developing the skills described above requires new tools—tools that will enhance leaders' conceptual abilities and foster communication and collaborative inquiry. What follows is a sampling of tools starting to find use in learning organizations.

Systems Archetypes. One of the insights of the budding, managerial systems-thinking field is that certain types of systemic structures recur again and again. Countless systems grow for a period, then encounter problems and cease to grow (or even collapse) well before they have reached intrinsic limits to growth. Many other systems get locked in runaway vicious spirals where every actor has to run faster and faster to stay in the same place. Still others lure individual actors into doing what seems right locally, yet which eventually causes suffering for all.[25]

Some of the system archetypes that have the broadest relevance include:

• **Balancing Process with Delay.** In this archetype, decision makers fail to appreciate the time delays involved as they move toward a goal. As a result, they overshoot the goal and may even produce recurring cycles. Classic example: Real estate developers who keep starting new projects until the market has gone soft, by which time an eventual glut is guaranteed by the properties still under construction.

• **Limits to Growth.** A reinforcing cycle of growth grinds to a halt, and may even reverse itself, as limits are approached. The limits can be resource constraints, or external or internal responses to growth. Classic examples: Product life cycles that peak prematurely due to poor quality or service, the growth and decline of communication in a management team, and the spread of a new movement.

• **Shifting the Burden.** A short-term "solution" is used to correct a problem, with seemingly happy immediate results. As this correction is used more and more, fundamental long-term corrective measures are used less. Over time, the mechanisms of the fundamental solution may atrophy or become disabled, leading to even greater reliance on the symptomatic solution. Classic example: Using corporate human resource staff to solve local personnel problems, thereby keeping managers from developing their own interpersonal skills.

• **Eroding Goals.** When all else fails, lower your standards. This is like "shifting the burden," except that the short-term solution involves letting a fundamental goal, such as quality standards or employee morale standards, atrophy. Classic example: A company that responds to delivery problems by continually upping its quoted delivery times.

• **Escalation.** Two people or two organizations, who each see their welfare as depending on a relative advantage over the other, continually react to the other's advances. Whenever one side gets ahead, the other is threatened, leading it to act more aggressively to reestablish its advantage, which threatens the first, and so on. Classic examples: Arms race, gang warfare, price wars.

• **Tragedy of the Commons.**[26] Individuals keep intensifying their use of a commonly available but limited resource until all individuals start to experience severely diminishing returns. Classic examples: Sheepherders who keep increasing their flocks until they overgraze the common pasture; divisions in a firm that share a common sales force and compete for the use of sales reps by upping their sales targets, until the sales force burns out from overextension.

• **Growth and Underinvestment.** Rapid growth approaches a limit that could be eliminated or pushed into the future, but only by aggressive investment in physical and human capacity. Eroding goals or standards cause investment that is too weak, or too slow, and customers

FIGURE 2   "Shifting the Burden" Archetype Template

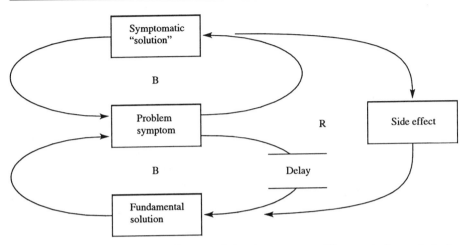

In the "shifting the burden" template, two balancing processes (B) compete for control of a problem symptom. Both solutions affect the symptom, but only the fundamental solution treats the cause. The symptomatic "solution" creates the additional side effect (R) of deferring the fundamental solution, making it harder and harder to achieve.

get increasingly unhappy, slowing demand growth and thereby making the needed investment (apparently) unnecessary or impossible. Classic example: Countless once-successful growth firms that allowed product or service quality to erode, and were unable to generate enough revenues to invest in remedies.

The Archetype template is a specific tool that is helping managers identify archetypes operating in their own strategic areas (see Figure 2).[27] The template shows the basic structural form of the archetype but lets managers fill in the variables of their own situation. For example, the shifting the burden template involves two balancing processes ("B") that compete for control of a problem symptom. The upper, symptomatic solution provides a short-term fix that will make the problem

symptom go away for a while. The lower, fundamental solution provides a more enduring solution. The side effect feedback ("R") around the outside of the diagram identifies unintended exacerbating effects of the symptomatic solution, which, over time, make it more and more difficult to invoke the fundamental solution.

Several years ago, a team of managers from a leading consumer goods producer used the shifting the burden archetype in a revealing way. The problem they focused on was financial stress, which could be dealt with in two different ways: by running marketing promotions (the symptomatic solution) or by product innovation (the fundamental solution). Marketing promotions were fast. The company was expert in their design and implementation. The results were highly predictable. Product innovation was slow and much less predictable, and the company had a history over the past 10 years of product-innovation mismanagement. Yet only through innovation could they retain a leadership position in their industry, which had slid over the past 10 to 20 years. What the managers saw clearly was that the more skillful they became at promotions, the more they shifted the burden away from product innovation. But what really struck home was when one member identified the unintended side effect: the last three CEOs had all come from the advertising function, which had become the politically dominant function in the corporation, thereby institutionalizing the symptomatic solution. Unless the political values shifted back toward product and process innovation, the managers realized, the firm's decline would accelerate—which is just the shift that has happened over the past several years.

Charting Strategic Dilemmas. Management teams typically come unglued when confronted with core dilemmas. A classic example was the way U.S. manufacturers faced the low-cost/high-quality choice. For years, most assumed that it was necessary to chose between the two. Not surprisingly, given the short-term pressures perceived by most managements, the prevailing choice was low cost. Firms that chose high quality usually perceived themselves as aiming exclusively for a high-quality/high-price market niche. The consequences of this perceived either-or choice have been disastrous, even fatal, as U.S. manufacturers have encountered increasing international competition from firms that have chosen to consistently improve quality *and* cost.

In a recent book, Charles Hampden-Turner presented a variety of tools for helping management teams confront strategic dilemmas creatively.[28] He summarizes the process in seven steps:

- **Eliciting the Dilemmas.** Identifying the opposed values that form the "horns" of the dilemma, for example, cost as opposed to quality, or local initiative as opposed to central coordination and control. Hampden-Turner suggests that humor can be a distinct asset in this process since "the admission that dilemmas even exist tends to be difficult for some companies."

- **Mapping.** Locating the opposing values at two axes and helping managers identify where they see themselves, or their organizations, along the axes.

- **Processing.** Getting rid of nouns to describe the axes of the dilemma. Present participles formed by adding "ing" convert rigid nouns into processes that imply movement. For example, central control versus local control becomes "strengthening national office" and "growing local initiatives." This loosens the bond of implied opposition between the two values. For example, it becomes possible to think of "strengthening national services from which local branches can benefit."

- **Framing/Contextualizing.** Further softening the adversarial structure among different values by letting "each side in turn be the frame or context for the other." This shifting of the "figure-ground" relationship undermines any implicit attempts to hold one value as intrinsically superior to the other, and thereby to become mentally closed to creative strategies for continuous improvement of both.

• **Sequencing.** Breaking the hold of static thinking. Very often, values like low cost and high quality appear to be in opposition because we think in terms of a point in time, not in terms of an ongoing process. For example, a strategy of investing in new process technology and developing a new production-floor culture of worker responsibility may take time and money in the near term yet reap significant long-term financial rewards.

• **Waving/Cycling.** Sometimes the strategic path toward improving both values involves cycles where both values will get "worse" for a time. Yet, at a deeper level, learning is occurring that will cause the next cycle to be at a higher plateau for both values.

• **Synergizing.** Achieving synergy where significant improvement is occurring along all axes of all relevant dilemmas. (This is the ultimate goal, of course.) Synergy, as Hampden-Turner points out, is a uniquely systemic notion, coming from the Greek *syn-ergo* or "work together."

"The Left-Hand Column": Surfacing Mental Models. The idea that mental models can dominate business decisions and that these models are often tacit and even contradictory to what people espouse can be very threatening to managers who pride themselves on rationality and judicious decision making. It is important to have tools to help managers discover for themselves how their mental models operate to undermine their own intentions.

One tool that has worked consistently to help managers see their own mental models in action is the "left-hand column" exercise developed by Chris Argyris and his colleagues. This tool is especially helpful in showing how we leap from data to generalization without testing the validity of our generalizations.

When working with managers, I start this exercise by selecting a specific situation in which I am interacting with other people in a way that is not working, that is not producing the learning that is needed. I write out a sample of the exchange, with the script on the right-hand side of the page. On the left-hand side, I write what I am thinking but not saying at each stage in the exchange (see boxed sidebar).

The left-hand column exercise not only brings hidden assumptions to the surface, it shows how they influence behavior. In the example, I make two key assumptions about Bill: he lacks confidence and he lacks initiative. Neither may be literally true, but both are evident in my internal dialogue, and both influence the way I handle the situation. Believing that he lacks confidence, I skirt the fact that I've heard the presentation was a bomb. I'm afraid that, if I say it directly, he will lose what little confidence he has, or he will see me as unsupportive. So I bring up the subject of the presentation obliquely. When I ask Bill what we should do next, he gives no specific course of action. Believing he lacks initiative, I take this as evidence of his laziness; he is content to do nothing when action is definitely required. I conclude that I will have to manufacture some form of pressure to motivate him, or else I will simply have to take matters into my own hands.

The Left-Hand Column: An Exercise

Imagine my exchange with a colleague, Bill, after he made a big presentation to our boss on a project we are doing together. I had to miss the presentation, but I've heard that it was poorly received.

Me: How did the presentation go?

Bill: Well, I don't know. It's really too early to say. Besides, we're breaking new ground here.

Me: Well, what do you think we should do? I believe that the issues you were raising are important.

Bill: I'm not so sure. Let's just wait and see what happens.

Me: You may be right, but I think we may need to do more than just wait.

Now, here is what the exchange looks like with my "left-hand column":

What I'm Thinking

Everyone says the presentation was a bomb. Does he really not know how bad it was? Or is he not willing to face up to it?

He really is afraid to see the truth. If he only had more confidence, he could probably learn from a situation like this.

I can't believe he doesn't realize how disastrous that presentation was to our moving ahead.

I've got to find some way to light a fire under the guy.

What Is Said

Me: How did the presentation go?

Bill: Well, I don't know. It's too early to say. Besides, we're breaking new ground here.

Me: Well, what do you think we should do? I believe that the issues you were raising are important.

Bill: I'm not so sure. Let's just wait and see what happens.

Me: You may be right, but I think we may need to do more than just wait.

The exercise reveals the elaborate webs of assumptions we weave, within which we become our own victims. Rather than dealing directly with my assumptions about Bill and the situation, we talk around the subject. The reasons for my avoidance are self-evident: I assume that, if I raised my doubts, I would provoke a defensive reaction that would only make matters worse. But the price of avoiding the issue is high. Instead of determining how to move forward to resolve our problems, we end our exchange with no clear course of action. My assumptions about Bill's limitations have been reinforced. I resort to a manipulative strategy to move things forward.

The exercise not only reveals the need for skills in surfacing assumptions, but that we are the ones most in need of help. There is no one right way to handle difficult situations like my exchange with Bill, but any productive strategy revolves around a high level of self-disclosure and willingness to have my views challenged. I need to recognize my own leaps of abstraction regarding Bill, share the events and reasoning that are leading to my concern over the project, and be open to Bill's views on both. The skills to carry on such conversations without invoking defensiveness take time to develop. But if both parties in a learning impasse start by doing their own left-hand column exercise and sharing them with each other, it is remarkable how quickly everyone recognizes their contribution to the impasse and progress starts to be made.

Learning Laboratories: Practice Fields for Management Teams. One of the most promising new tools is the learning laboratory or "microworld": constructed microcosms of real-life settings in which management teams can learn how to learn together.

The rationale behind learning laboratories can best be explained by analogy. Although most management teams have great difficulty learning (enhancing their collective intelligence and capacity to create), in other domains team learning is the norm, rather than the exception—team sports and the performing arts, for example. Great basketball teams do not start off great. They learn. But the process by which these teams learn is, by and large, absent from modern organizations. The process is a continual movement between practice and performance.

The vision guiding current research in management learning laboratories is to design and construct effective practice fields for management teams. Much remains to be done, but the broad outlines are emerging.

First, since team learning in organizations is an individual-to-individual and individual-to-system phenomenon, learning laboratories must combine meaning-ful business issues with meaningful interpersonal dynamics. Either alone is incomplete.

Second, the factors that thwart learning about complex business issues must be eliminated in the learning lab. Chief among these is the inability to experience the long-term, systemic consequences of key strategic decisions. We all learn best from experience, but we are unable to experience the consequences of many important organizational decisions. Learning laboratories remove this constraint through system dynamics simulation games that compress time and space.

Third, new learning skills must be developed. One constraint of learning is the inability of managers to reflect insightfully on their assumptions, and to inquire effectively into each other's assumptions. Both skills can be enhanced in a learning laboratory, where people can practice surfacing assumptions in a low-risk setting. A note of caution: It is far easier to design an entertaining learning laboratory than it is to have an impact on real management practices and firm traditions outside the learning lab. Research on management simulations has shown that they often have greater entertainment value than educational value. One of the reasons appears to be that many simulations do not offer deep insights into systemic structures causing business problems. Another reason is that they do not foster new learning skills. Also, there is no connection between experiments. These are significant problems that research on learning laboratory design is now addressing.

Developing Leaders and Learning Organizations

In a recently published retrospective on organization development in the 1980s,

Learning at Hanover Insurance

Hanover Insurance has gone from the bottom of the property and liability industry to a position among the top 25 percent of U.S. insurance companies over the past 20 years, largely through the efforts of CEO William O'Brien and his predecessor, Jack Adam. The following comments are excerpted from a series of interviews Senge conducted with O'Brien as background for his book.

Senge: Why do you think there is so much change occurring in management and organizations today? Is it primarily because of increased competitive pressures?

O'Brien: That's a factor, but not the most significant factor. The ferment in management will continue until we find models that are more congruent with human nature.

One of the great insights of modern psychology is the hierarchy of human needs. As Maslow expressed this idea, the most basic needs are food and shelter. Then comes belonging. Once these three basic needs are satisfied, people begin to aspire toward self-respect and esteem, and toward self-actualization—the fourth and fifth-order needs.

Our traditional hierarchical organizations are designed to provide for the first three levels, but not the fourth and fifth. These first three levels are now widely available to members of industrial society, but our organizations do not offer people sufficient opportunities for growth.

Senge: How would you assess Hanover's progress to date?

O'Brien: We have been on a long journey away from a traditional hierarchical culture. The journey began with everyone understanding some guiding ideas about purpose, vision, and values as a basis for participative management. This is a better way to begin building a participative culture than by simply "letting people in on decision making." Before there can be meaningful participation, people must share certain values and pictures about where we are trying to go. We discovered that people have a real need to feel that they're part of an enobling mission. But developing shared visions and values is not the end, only the beginning.

Next we had to get beyond mechanical, linear thinking. The essence of our jobs as managers is to deal with "divergent" problems—problems that have no simple answer. "Convergent" problems—problems that have a "right" answer—should be solved locally. Yet we are deeply conditioned to see the world in terms of convergent problems. Most managers try to force-fit simplistic solutions and undermine the potential for learning when divergent problems arise. Since everyone handles the linear issues fairly well, companies that learn how to handle divergent issues will have a great advantage.

The next basic stage in our progression was coming to understand inquiry and advocacy. We learned that real openness is rooted in people's ability to continually inquire into their own thinking. This requires exposing yourself to being wrong—not something that most managers are rewarded for. But learning is very difficult if you cannot look for errors or incompleteness in your own ideas.

What all this builds to is the capability throughout an organization to manage mental models. In a locally controlled organization, you have the fundamental challenge of learning how to help people make good decisions without coercing them into making *particular* decisions. By managing mental models, we create "self-concluding" decisions—decisions that people come to themselves—which will

---

Learning at Hanover Insurance *(concluded)*

result in deeper conviction, better implementation, and the ability to make better adjustments when the situation changes.

Senge: What concrete steps can top managers take to begin moving toward learning organizations?

O'Brien: Look at the signals you send through the organization. For example, one critical signal is how you spend your time. It's hard to build a learning organization if people are unable to take the time to think through important matters. I rarely set up an appointment for less than one hour. If the subject is not worth an hour, it shouldn't be on my calendar.

Senge: Why is this so hard for so many managers?

O'Brien: It comes back to what you believe about the nature of your work. The authoritarian manager has a "chain gang" mental model: "The speed of the boss is the speed of the gang. I've got to keep things moving fast, because I've got to keep people working." In a learning organization, the manager shoulders an almost sacred responsibility: to create conditions that enable people to have happy and productive lives. If you understand the effects the ideas we are discussing can have on the lives of people in your organization, you will take the time.

Marshall Sashkin and W. Warner Burke observe the return of an emphasis on developing leaders who can develop organizations.[29] They also note Schein's critique that most top executives are not qualified for the task of developing culture.[30] Learning organizations represent a potentially significant evolution of organizational culture. So it should come as no surprise that such organizations will remain a distant vision until the leadership capabilities they demand are developed. "The 1990s may be the period," suggest Sashkin and Burke, "during which organization development and (a new sort of) management development are reconnected."

I believe that this new sort of management development will focus on the roles, skills, and tools for leadership in learning organizations. Undoubtedly, the ideas offered above are only a rough approximation of this new territory. The sooner we begin seriously exploring the territory,

the sooner the initial map can be improved—and the sooner we will realize an age-old vision of leadership:

> The wicked leader is he who the people despise.
> The good leader is he who the people revere.
> The great leader is he who the people say, "We did it ourselves."

> Lao Tsu

References

1. P. Senge, *The Fifth Discipline: The Art and Practice of the Learning Organization* (New York: Doubleday/Currency, 1990).

2. A. P. de Geus, "Planning as Learning," *Harvard Business Review*, March–April 1988, pp. 70–74.

3. B. Domain, *Fortune*, 3 July 1989, pp. 48–62.

4. The distinction between adaptive and generative learning has its roots in the distinction between what Argyris and Schon

have called their "single-loop" learning, in which individuals or groups adjust their behavior relative to fixed goals, norms, and assumptions, and "double-loop" learning, in which goals, norms, and assumptions, as well as behavior, are open to change (e.g., see C. Argyris and D. Schon, *Organizational Learning: A Theory-in-Action Perspective* (Reading, Massachusetts: Addison-Wesley, 1978).

5. All unattributed quotes are from personal communications with the author.

6. G. Stalk, Jr., "Time: The Next Source of Competitive Advantage," *Harvard Business Review*, July–August 1988, pp. 41–51.

7. Senge (1990).

8. The principle of creative tension comes from Robert Fritz's work on creativity. See R. Fritz, *The Path of Least Resistance* (New York: Ballantine, 1989) and *Creating* (New York: Ballantine, 1990).

9. M. L. King, Jr., "Letter from Birmingham Jail," *American Visions*, January–February 1986, pp. 52–59.

10. E. Schein, *Organizational Culture and Leadership* (San Francisco: Jossey-Bass, 1985).

    Similar views have been expressed by many leadership theorists. For example, see: P. Selznick, *Leadership in Administration* (New York: Harper & Row, 1957); W. Bennis and B. Nanus, *Leaders* (New York: Harper & Row, 1985); and N. M. Tichy and M. A. Devanna, *The Transformational Leader* (New York: John Wiley & Sons, 1986).

11. Selznick (1957).

12. J. W. Forrester, "A New Corporate Design," *Sloan Management Review* (formerly *Industrial Management Review*), Fall 1965, pp. 5–17.

13. See, for example, H. Mintzberg, "Crafting Strategy," *Harvard Business Review*, July–August 1987, pp. 66–75.

14. R. Mason and I. Mitroff, *Challenging Strategic Planning Assumptions* (New York: John Wiley & Sons, 1981), p. 16.

15. P. Wack, "Scenarios: Unchartered Wa-

ters Ahead," *Harvard Business Review*, September–October 1985, pp. 73–89.

16. de Geus (1988).

17. M. de Pree, *Leadership Is an Art* (New York: Doubleday, 1989), p. 9.

18. For example, see T. Peters and N. Austin, *A Passion for Excellence* (New York: Random House, 1985) and J. M. Kouzes and B. Z. Posner, *The Leadership Challenge* (San Francisco: Jossey-Bass, 1987).

19. I. Mitroff, *Break-Away Thinking* (New York: John Wiley & Sons, 1988), pp. 66–67.

20. R. K. Greenleaf, *Servant Leadership: A Journey into the Nature of Legitimate Power and Greatness* (New York: Paulist Press, 1977).

21. L. Miller, *American Spirit: Visions of a New Corporate Culture* (New York: William Morrow, 1984), p. 15.

22. These points are condensed from the practices of the five disciplines examined in Senge (1990).

23. The ideas below are based to a considerable extent on the work of Chris Argyris, Donald Schon, and their Action Science colleagues: C. Argyris and D. Schon, *Organizational Learning: A Theory-in-Action Perspective* (Reading, Mass.: Addison-Wesley, 1978); C. Argyris, R. Putnam, and D. Smith, *Action Science* (San Francisco: Jossey-Bass, 1985); C. Argyris, *Strategy, Change, and Defensive Routines* (Boston: Pitman, 1985); and C. Argyris, *Overcoming Organizational Defenses* (Englewood Cliffs, New Jersey: Prentice Hall, 1990).

24. I am indebted to Diana Smith for the summary points below.

25. The system archetypes are one of several systems diagraming and communication tools. See D. H. Kim, "Toward Learning Organizations: Integrating Total Quality Control and Systems Thinking" (Cambridge, Mass.: MIT Sloan School of Management, Working Paper no. 3037-89-BPS, June 1989).

26. This archetype is closely associated with the work of ecologist Garrett Hardin,

who coined its label: G. Hardin, "The Tragedy of the Commons," *Science*, 13 December 1968.

27. These templates were originally developed by Jennifer Kemeny, Charles Kiefer, and Michael Goodman of Innovation Associates, Inc., Framingham, Massachusetts.

28. C. Hampden-Turner, *Charting the Corporate Mind* (New York: Free Press, 1990).

29. M. Sashkin and W. W. Burke, "Organization Development in the 1980s " and "An End-of the Eighties Retrospective," in *Advances in Organization Development*, ed. F. Masarik (Norwood, N.J.: Ablex, 1990).

30. E. Schein (1985).

READING

CUSTOMERS DRIVE A TECHNOLOGY-DRIVEN COMPANY: AN INTERVIEW WITH GEORGE FISHER

Bernard Avishai
William Taylor

On January 1, 1988, George M.C. Fisher became president and CEO of Motorola, Inc.—a company that has been "competing beyond technology" since it was founded more than 60 years ago. The first four decades of Motorola's history revolved around consumer electronics. It introduced the world's first car radio in 1930 and went on to develop an array of consumer products, including home audio equipment and television sets. In the early 1970s, however, under the leadership of CEO Robert Galvin, Motorola set out to reinvent itself. It abandoned the consumer market in favor of high-technology industrial electronics—and experienced one of the most successful transformations in U.S. business history.

Today Motorola is a world leader in a range of technology-intensive products and systems. It generates revenues of more than $8 billion per year through the sale of two-way private radio equipment, cellular telephones, pagers, microprocessors and other semiconductor devices, integrated networking systems, microcomputers, and automotive and industrial electronics. Motorola has also become a symbol of how the most effective U.S. companies can hold their own—and even make advances against—formidable Japanese rivals.

Like the company he heads, George Fisher has built his career around technology. He became Motorola's CEO 12 years after joining the company from AT&T Bell Laboratories, where he had spent more than a decade as an engineer and technical manager. He holds a master's degree in engineering and a doctorate in applied mathematics from Brown University. He also holds patents in optical wave-guide technology and digital

From *Harvard Business Review*, November-December 1989.

communications. The interview was conducted in Boston and at Motorola's Schaumburg, Illinois, headquarters by Harvard Business Review *associate editors Bernard Avishai and William Taylor.*

HBR: *In an increasingly technological world, no one can win on technology alone. How has Motorola responded to this paradox?*

George Fisher: Here's the question we're wrestling with—How do we get the people inside Motorola who know the customer best to have greater power? Our answer is to develop a management system that essentially flips the organization—a system that empowers the sales force.

Members of our sales force are surrogates for customers. They should be able to reach back into Motorola and pull out technologists and other people they need to solve problems and anticipate customer needs. We want to put the salesperson at the top of the organization. The rest of us then serve the salesperson. If we could get that mentality ingrained throughout Motorola, in a nonthreatening way, I think we would move a long way toward where we need to be.

But what an absolute threat to the technologists! I grew up in that world; I am a technologist. Many of us share a certain arrogance—we know all there is to know about technology, and technology is the only thing that matters. It's also a threat to the existing power structure inside technology companies. Sales just doesn't have the same stature as the technical side. It's an issue of heritage, I suppose. When most of these companies began, they were driven by brilliant technologists, so the organizations grew up revering the engineer and the scientist— we do at Motorola, and we always will.

But we don't have to turn our backs on our heritage to recognize the role of sales as a surrogate for customers. Most organizations, Motorola included, don't do that today. In fact, there's an adversarial relationship between sales and the technologists.

We don't know precisely how we're going to make this change. We've been having these discussions for a couple of years, and our thinking is still evolving. We also risk taking it to extremes; we don't want salespeople making complex technology decisions. But perhaps we have to err in the extreme direction for a while.

Would rotating people between technology and sales encourage this organizational shift?

We haven't done much of that, and I think it would be a mistake. Serious salespeople can't go in and out of technologist jobs, even it they have an engineering degree. In fact, many of our salespeople are engineers. But the half-life of an electrical engineering education today is about five years. If you're in sales for any length of time, you'd need serious study before you could go back to the lab. Likewise, serious technologists, who want to pursue technology as a career, would feel there's no benefit to being in sales. They are going to lose momentum. People get on a track early in their careers. It's just not effective to cross those tracks.

What steps are you taking to emphasize the customer's needs in a company that "reveres" technology?

First, we've established a massive program of increasing customer visits at all levels of the organization. We want everyone in Motorola, from top to bottom, to get out and see customers—to talk with them directly and understand their business better.

We did a survey on customer visits acouple of years ago—who's been visiting whom, how good or bad we are at it. It turned out our people were making thousands and thousands of visits every year—not enough, by any means, but people were getting out. But not enough of our top-level people were making these visits. So Bob Galvin, our chairman, pushed people at the top of the company to get more involved with customers. He personally went out and made 10 or 12 customer visits, and he wrote extensive trip reports on each one.

Those visits and reports produced two simple but powerful observations. Customers think we're pretty good; they like us. But they also think we could do one hell of a lot more business with them if we listened better and broadened the portfolio of products and systems we offered them. They *wanted* us to do that; they wanted to do more business with us.

After Bob's reports, we had long discussions in the policy committee, the company's top operating executives. We issued an edict: All members of the policy committee would make at least two visits per quarter to customers. We also insisted that everyone write trip reports and brief the policy committee: George Fisher visited three customers, here's who they were, here's what they said, and so on.

Are customer visits an effective solution to the technology-sales split?

We're still not doing a good enough job. In too many companies, and too much so in this company, the technologists who develop systems and the people who interact with customers are two separate groups. At our last policy commit-

tee meeting, we had an updated report on customer visits. That report showed that our technologists are still not visiting as many customers as we would like. I don't think it's a lack of desire on their part. People who don't give speeches aren't comfortable giving speeches. People who don't visit customers aren't comfortable visiting customers. So we've been trying to figure out how to promote more effective interaction between our technologists and our customers. How do we create an environment where technologists become comfortable doing that?

Let's say you succeed. Isn't there a danger of becoming too customer focused? Doesn't that work against pioneering new markets or introducing bold new products?

You're right; customers will always pull you in directions of interest to them. As a technology leader, sometimes we have to show people what we can do. The portable telephone is a good example. Motorola jumped way out in front on the car phone—so far out in front that there were pictures in magazines two or three years before the systems were actually available. We didn't have thousands of people saying, "We want portable telephones that look a certain way and have particular kinds of features." We presented it to the world. Unfortunately, the regulatory bureaucracy slowed us down once we introduced the product. Other people were able to catch up while we were forced to sit on our hands.

What's the other side of the coin—technologists who confuse the capability to produce a product with a customer need?

Many technologists have this problem. They look at a technology, get very excited, and say it's not a question of "whether," it's a question of "when." But "when" turns out to be a big question.

In the early 1970s, when I was still at AT&T Bell Labs, we had a grand vision of picture-phones. If you believed what we were saying then, by today everyone should have had a two-way video telephone sitting on his or her desk. Some of the technologists at Bell Labs really got caught up with it. They thought, "This is where the world is going!" Well, the world *is* going that way, no doubt about it. But we were much too early, even technically. The picture-phone needed a high-performance switching and transmission system that just didn't exist.

It didn't take long for me to realize I wasn't a marketing person. Invariably, the things I liked—and they were really great—were things the customers didn't like at the time. And yet 5 or 10 years later, we'd be selling tons of them. So I had to learn to discipline myself. Right now, for example, I could pull together the immense technology forces of Motorola and design the greatest device for ISDN digital communication you've ever seen. I could put 1.5 megabits per second under your desk, the cat's meow, everything you could ever want. You'd sit there, stare at it, and say, "What do I do now?" And the fact is, for many people there's not much you *can* do with it.

So how do you balance the two? How do you avoid both problems?

We are driving Motorola in one very clear direction: answer every question in the context of the customer. Everybody in this organization has to understand the customer much better. In fact, we've virtually outlawed use of the word "customer" except to refer to the ultimate

paying customer. For a while, people at Motorola thought they had "internal customers." They don't. There is only one customer—the person who pays the bills. That's the person we're serving.

We marry our technology development with a deep understanding of our customers' business needs. Notice I didn't say their communications needs. When we understand our customers' business needs, as well as what they believe to be their communications needs, we can develop products and systems they can't even imagine—but that are immensely valuable to them.

For example?

Take the radio data communications system we developed with IBM. We have an ongoing dialogue with IBM; I'm not even sure who came to whom on this project. One of the business problems IBM had talked with us about for a long time involved customer service. How could they keep track of maintenance records on computers and the availability of spare parts across the country? How could they reduce the need for their service people to borrow customers' telephone lines while they are on their premises? How could their service people make calls from near a computer where there's no telephone available? How could they better dispatch their field engineers?

IBM didn't identify radio communication solutions per se; they defined their problems. Talking through that situation led us to do something we had never done before. Together we saw how we could put up a nationwide, interconnected radio system with a portable, communicating computer in a very small package. It didn't exist, but we knew it was possible. So we worked together. IBM provided much of the software and the interface to their host computers. We put up the radio data network.

Micro TAC, our new personal telephone, is the other side of the balancing act. Micro TAC works to all our greatest strengths as a technology corporation. We are such a major force in the radio communications business that we virtually define the standard. The basics of the business are not all that complex, although the technical details are quite demanding. In portable equipment, which is the part of the company I grew up with, there are four critical forces: size, weight, current drain (a driving function of the size and weight of the battery), and cost. So in our formal technology planning, quite independent of market studies and planning for particular products, we develop 5-year and 10-year technology road maps of those four forces. Our ability to introduce a portable telephone that's the size of a wallet and weighs less than 11 ounces—that was driven by the technologists in our cellular and semiconductor groups and the people in corporate research.

Most of us who have been brought up in the portable equipment business—serving the needs of people and machines on the move—have developed pretty refined instincts as to what the next steps have to be technologically. When we go to customers with a new product, we don't expect many surprises. In part, that's because of the close interaction we've had with them over the years. But even more importantly, it's because of the instincts we've developed. This is a business we know very, very well.

Now, did our business leaders in the cellular group talk to customers? Absolutely. This was not done in a vacuum. We had focus groups and market studies, the

routine marketing things. But market research wasn't the primary force behind Micro TAC.

What's the CEO's role in striking this balance? Does a CEO today have to be a technologist to be effective?

I don't see how anybody could deal with the subjects I deal with on a daily basis—RISC processors, DRAM technology, cellular systems, paging—without a deep immersion in the technologies. It almost has to be second nature. Once it is second nature, of course, you wind up spending very little time on the technology itself.

Now, I don't want my friends from finance or legal to get too upset. Those functions are increasingly important to running a large corporation; I sometimes consider myself a finance wizard. But I contend it's easier for me to learn what I need to know about finance or law than it is for a lawyer to learn about RISC architecture or DRAMs. You have to understand where I come from. I'm a product of Bell Labs and Motorola. Top management in this company has always been technically aware and involved. Bob Galvin selected two key people who have driven this company for the last several decades—Bill Weisz, vice chairman and my predecessor as CEO, and John Mitchell, our vice chairman and former president. Both are engineers who've been deeply involved in communications and semiconductor technologies. Of course, some people raise the counterargument: "Aren't you micromanaging? Do you really need to be that involved in the details?" That's a long discussion.

Aren't you micromanaging? How do you answer the counterargument?

First of all, the "details" are awfully

important in our business. I go very deep sometimes, because in going very deep you learn a lot about the organization and the business. RISC architecture is the most recent example. Many of us in senior management got very involved in that technology, down into the statistics of the different machine language instructions used in a computer. What is the probability distribution of the various instructions a computer might be called on to perform? Lots of people, including my wife, asked why I was doing it. I was doing it because it lets me make linkages to my past, and a massive personal background in machine-level programming before there were sophisticated compilers and other tools. Those linkages give me a lot of leverage in understanding current technology.

Take our alliance with Toshiba. We exchanged some of our semiconductor technology for their help in gaining market share in Japan. That's a case where a technology background was critical to making a sound *business* decision. You can't understand whether an agreement is a technology giveaway if you don't really understand the technology: where it's been, where it's going, what kinds of investments are required to stay current, the different life cycles of microprocessors and memories, the nature of the software. Only by understanding the technology itself can you answer the most critical question: Are you giving away a core competence—a technological advantage that is key to the long-term prosperity of your corporation—or are you transferring discrete and replicable technology in return for comparable strategic benefits?

Motorola has been successful at encouraging different sectors of the company to collaborate on new products and systems. You've been able to tap the synergies that so many companies find elusive. What's your approach?

I'm not sure "synergy" is the right word, but I'll accept it. Motorola today is really built on a silicon foundation; our core strength is in semiconductors. The different groups and sectors in the company—two-way radio communication, pagers, computers, automotive components—utilize our semiconductor technology as one of their building blocks. So synergy in that respect is almost innate; it's what this company is designed to do. That doesn't mean we always manage to maximize technical cooperation.

There is one type of program that's almost universally successful in tapping synergy—a program driven by the needs of a big, strong customer like Federal Express, IBM, Apple, Ford, or General Motors. Or a program driven by a leading-edge customer, like the work we do with Steve Jobs and NeXT. When the customers drives it, synergy almost always follows.

The IBM project I discussed earlier is a good example. Our communications sector had a very strong interest in satisfying IBM. But it didn't have all the technical resources to put in the system. It had to turn for modems to our UDS operation in Huntsville, Alabama. It had to use the semiconductor sector for custom chips. It had to turn to the cellular people for network control processors. Without that kind of cooperation, the communications sector never could have pulled the project off.

Sometimes top management has to take the lead to make it work. A few years ago, the National Security Agency, with which we work closely, asked us and several other companies to bid on a secure telephone system that would encrypt wire-line voice and data communications. NSA wanted the phone to be used by all defense contractors; it also wanted a product with commercial potential to drive the price down.

Our government electronics group has world-class encryption technology. But it wasn't in the telephone business, and it doesn't make too many commercial products. So Bill Weisz pulled together the policy committee for a presentation on the NSA opportunity and the required cooperation between sectors: government electronics, communications, semiconductors, modems, even automotive components, which does lots of cost-sensitive volume manufacturing. We formed a team. That team talked to the people from NSA. It went through the company to figure our how we could use all of Motorola's strengths and where different technologies were headed. Members of that team just about lived together. We also formed an overseer group to make sure the team members were not inhibited by the normal corporate structure. It worked out extremely well. I suspect that will be a $500 million business, government and commercial, in not too many years.

Let's talk about Japan. How does U.S. industry stack up against Japan in its ability to compete on science and engineering?

First, let me say that we are lucky to have Japan. Japanese companies are very demanding and bring out the best in us—both as customers and competitors.

You have to distinguish between science and engineering. The United States has an inherent advantage over Japan in science. Our higher education system and our graduate-level science education system are second to none in the world. At the other extreme, of course, elementary and secondary education is in very bad shape comparatively. But high-level scientific education in this country is still superb.

In engineering, at least as it applies to consumer electronics, the advantage goes to Japan: the disciplined processes, the collegiality at all levels, the willingness to subjugate the interests of the individual to the good of the company. Those things are very real in Japan. I also see a greater willingness among Japan's young engineers to stay engineers and follow their products into the factory. Too many engineers in the United States think they have to be managers by the time they're 28 or they're washed up. The discipline of the Japanese culture favors them on technology execution.

Now let's add up the pluses and minuses. In a technology business, it only takes one great person to do something really important. There may be thousands of people in the supporting cast, but one real driving force with a creative mind can build a company. That's a tremendous source of strength for us relative to what I see in Japan. It's also a real challenge for big companies, by the way— to get out of the way of their most creative people and let them contribute.

Moreover, Japan's systemic discipline often makes them much less flexible. We are developing a distinctive competence in the United States based on the way we are. We are more receptive to change than the Japanese. And that's becoming an increasingly important factor for competitive success: to be able to change designs quickly, to be able to customize products for specific markets. The imperatives of business success are moving in directions that favor the strengths of the United States.

But haven't the Japanese led the world in cycle-time reduction, in the rapid introduction of new products, and in the rapid improvement and extension of existing products?

You're talking about incremental features; I'm talking about more fundamental changes in product. Changes at the feature level are almost a function of marketing. Don't get me wrong. The Japanese are superb at taking technology and turning over new features every few months. It's really incredible. That's one of the reasons we as a country weren't very good in consumer electronics. We never learned that very well, although we were pretty innovative.

But try to get behind the features you see on a VCR and change something inside the equipment. Put a RISC processor in there instead of the microprocessor they've got, or change the software quickly to suit a particular customer's needs. The Japanese find that very disruptive and, hence, difficult to do. They don't like to interrupt the status quo in their factories. I'm not even talking about great breakthrough ideas. There's a level of innovation between major breakthroughs and incremental features where the Japanese are very slow. They often find it very difficult to cope with change at the chip level—which ultimately drives product features, performance, and everything else.

How does Motorola leverage these U.S. strengths to compete against the Japanese?

Take our factory in Boynton Beach, Florida, where we build pagers. People who write about that plant usually empha-

size the assembly techniques and the robotics that we've "borrowed" from leading competitors, many of them Japanese. Actually, our factory, which was originally code-named Bandit, reflects a model of production that the United States is uniquely qualified to perfect. We're talking about lot-size-of-one manufacturing with cycle times on the order of two hours. That process used to take us two weeks.

Pagers are not commodity products. They have different frequencies, special labels, many customized features. With our system, you place an order from the field and 17 minutes later a bar-code reader will be scanning a blank circuit board in Florida. That bar code contains all the information the factory needs to make the pager. As the board goes down the line, each robot reads the bar code and executes the instructions. The pager right behind it could well be for a different customer with very different specifications.

Think of how you can link that manufacturing capability with a marketing strategy that drives mass producers like the Japanese crazy! You go to every customer and say, What do you want? Whatever it is, we can do it. If you drive that capability as a distinctive competence, while your competitor is building a million of the same gadgets at a very low cost, I'll bet the company that does something different for every customer is going to win. Companies in the United States are more likely to make that change than the Japanese.

Still, the Japanese are dominant in robotics. They're masters of factory automation.

But name one Japanese factory—just one—that integrates on-line customer information with robots and automatic pick-and-place machines. Sure, the Japanese are out in front of the world today in robotics. But that's pretty standard stuff, quite honestly. Anything you can do with robots everyone else can do. That's why I almost don't like people going through our factories like the Bandit plant. The casual observer oohs and aahs over a robot doing precise soldering or machine vision. But the real excitement is serving customers better with that capability. The manufacturing systems of the future will have brains that go right from the customer to the production line. Those systems are walking right into our strengths.

This is a critical point. What are the core competencies of the United States? Two of them are our computing capability and our strength in systems and software design. We are way out in front of the Japanese in those areas.

Even if U.S. companies have advantages on paper, haven't the Japanese shown time and again that they are masters at execution—the relentless attention to quality and the science of the production process?

We learn from a lot of very good companies—IBM, NTT, Xerox—who have done really brilliant things with their operations. We've borrowed from them, and their lessons are available for anyone to borrow. An increasing number of U.S. companies are learning from others and dramatically improving their operations.

There's another critical factor that will drive improvement—the supplier chain. Large companies like Hewlett-Packard, Xerox, and Motorola are creating ambient pressures that will force their very large supplier base to improve their operations, if they aren't already. Motorola, for example, now requires that all of our

suppliers apply for the Malcolm Baldrige National Quality Award or give us their time schedule as to when they will apply. If they expect to continue as a supplier to us, they have to commit to applying for the Baldrige award. This creates one more demanding review process our suppliers must go through. It forces companies to think through why they're not doing the things they need to do in order to improve quality and efficiency.

So demands on the supplier chain are going to accelerate the process of improvement in this country, just as they have in Japan. So far, the Japanese have done a more credible job in this area than we have.

So you'd argue that the United States is best suited to build the real factory of the future?

I don't know what the factory of the future is. I don't like the word "factory." It has all kinds of connotations, namely, less-skilled workers in a very structured environment. Successful companies are going to integrate the entire production and delivery chain—not necessarily around a factory but around a customer need. I'm talking about high-technology industries now; steel or textiles may be different. But to the extent that operations are all integrated for the sake of hitting demanding quality targets, or meeting a specialized customer need, or shortening cycle time so you're competitively responsive—that's where the real advantage is.

The bundling of services with production is also a natural. It's already happening. But is it happening in the factory? I'm not sure. It's happening with teams that include a company like Motorola, our suppliers, and the customer itself. We have to change the conventional ways we think about who really develops products and who bundles services. There's a team that satisfies a customer need. That team may even include the customer.

Another set of important linkages—as important as any taking place within companies—are between information systems of different companies. The electronic data interchange (EDI) systems that are being established between customers and suppliers are becoming two-way interfaces. The standards being established for them are also two-way.

What makes intercompany linkages so important?

Because my customers are also my suppliers. Take a company like Hewlett-Packard, which is a very big supplier to us—and a very big customer of ours. We have the need to link information systems. Well, you could dream a little and think about the ultimate ramifications of that, how with linked information systems we could drive each other's manufacturing processes.

In fact, it's already happening. Demand from HP factories can drive the forecasted materials planning systems in some of our semiconductor factories. Their forecast goes up, and that starts to load our material purchases and fab schedules. You have to have a very trusting relationship with a customer to do that. We will be doing that more and more, by the way. So marrying factory control systems with product design and development systems is very important. But to my way of thinking, the loop between suppliers and customers—in many cases, the same entities—is even more important.

What is Motorola doing today to be competitive 20 years from now?

Every organization is a victim of its own success. That's why we created a New Enterprises group as a stand-alone entity within Motorola. There's a strong belief in this company that the areas in which we're the leader today won't be the areas that make us healthy 20 or 30 years from now. We have example after example of that, starting with car radios. We were a world leader in car radios; it's what built this company. But we're no longer in that business. We were once a world leader in televisions. We're no longer in that business, either. If you were at Motorola when consumer electronics was king, people would tell you, "That little two-way radio business makes no sense, why are you interested in it?" When Dan Noble, one of the real geniuses of this corporation, wanted to move us into semiconductors, people said, "Why are you fooling around with that? That's a flaky technology; it will never prove out."

We wanted a vehicle to help create the semiconductor business of the future, the two-way radio businesses of the future—ventures that would never make the cut in our current businesses. New Enterprises is a way, fairly small at this point, to give people with bold ideas an opportunity to explore them outside the formal corporate structure. Plenty of very smart people are perfectly suited to the stability and time horizons of a giant corporation. Others aren't so comfortable. We want to make a home for both.

How does New Enterprises work?

First, these are very high-risk projects. I'm not talking about risks, I'm talking about *very high* risks. There also has to be a potential for building a really big business; otherwise it's just not worth our while. We now have six or seven companies under New Enterprises, in areas like factory automation, health care, and semiconductor equipment. We hope that within 10 years these businesses will generate between 5 to 10 percent of our total revenues—which means well over $1 billion. We will consider New Enterprises very successful if we get to that point.

New Enterprises reports directly to Bob Galvin and me. This way there are fewer of the quarter-to-quarter or year-to-year financial pressures and a much longer time horizon for building real businesses. Managers in these businesses don't participate in Motorola's standard compensation and benefit programs. They get equity; they can get rich if their company succeeds. Their salaries relate more to the industry they're in than to Motorola's structure. If they're in a computer operation, they may get higher salaries than they would in some parts of Motorola. If they're in medical electronics, like our Emtek health care unit, they're paid more on a scale with instrument companies and doctors and nurses. That's another important part of New Enterprises. It creates a different mix of talents. Emtek, for instance, is made up of engineers, scientists, nurses, doctors, and other medical professionals—a pool of people we wouldn't ordinarily get in the company.

You sound very optimistic.

We have to differentiate between companies and countries. The fact that Motorola and a group of companies like us turn out to be successful doesn't necessarily mean that the United States will maintain technological dominance or parity. Here's the basic question: Does being a successful global company headquartered in a particular country mean that country will also be successful as an economic entity? Increasingly, the answer is no. I'm not talking about national security now; I'm talking about competitiveness.

Companies have very direct measurement systems of success and failure. Good companies do what it takes to survive—and they know every year whether or not they're succeeding. It's much more difficult to measure success for a country. Moreover, countries can't act as quickly or decisively as companies can. I don't want to argue that companies will prosper on a global basis independent of how their home countries prosper. But the separation will grow. In Motorola's case, I hope the separation never gets so serious that it weakens the link between this company and the United States. I hope we never see the day when we operate independent of the fact that we are a U.S. company. There's still an innate strength in our believing we are a representative of the United States.

READING

MOTOROLA U: WHEN TRAINING BECOMES AN EDUCATION

William Wiggenhorn

William Wiggenhorn is Motorola's corporate vice president for training and education and the president of Motorola University.

At Motorola we require three things of our manufacturing employees. They must have communication and computation skills at the seventh grade level, soon going up to eighth and ninth. They must be able to do basic problem solving—not only as individuals but also as members of a team. And they must accept our definition of work and the work-week: the time it takes to ship perfect product to the customer who's ordered it. That can mean a work-week of 50 or even 60 hours, but we need people willing to work against quality and output instead of a time clock.

These requirements are relatively new. Ten years ago, we hired people to perform set tasks and didn't ask them to do a lot of thinking. If a machine went down, workers raised their hands, and a trouble-shooter came to fix it. Ten years ago, we saw quality control as a screening process, catching defects before they got out the door. Ten years ago, most workers and some managers learned their jobs by observation, experience, and trial and error. When we did train people, we simply taught them new techniques on top of the basic math and communication skills we supposed they brought with them from school or college.

Then all the rules of manufacturing and competition changed; and, in our drive to change with them, we found we had to rewrite the rules of corporate training and education. We learned that line workers had to actually understand their work and their equipment, that senior management had to exemplify and reinforce new methods and skills if they were going to stick, that change had to be continuous and participative, and that education—not just instruction—was the only way to make all this occur.

Finally, just as we began to capitalize on the change we thought we were achieving, we discovered to our utter astonishment that much of our work force was illiterate. They couldn't read. They couldn't do simple arithmetic like percentages and fractions. At one plant, a supplier changed its packaging, and we found in the nick of time that our people were working by the color of the package, not by what it said. In Illinois, we found a foreign-born employee who didn't know the difference between the present tense and the past. He was never sure if we were talking about what *was* happening or what *had* happened.

These discoveries led us into areas of education we had never meant to enter

From *Harvard Business Review*, July–August 1990.

and into budgetary realms we would have found unthinkable 10 years earlier. From the kind of skill instruction we envisioned at the onset, we moved out in both directions: down, toward grade school basics as fundamental as the three Rs; up, toward new concepts of work, quality, community, learning, and leadership. From a contemplated total budget of $35 million over a five-year period, a sum many thought excessive, we came to spend $60 million annually—plus another $60 million in lost work time—and everyone thought it was money well invested.

Today we expect workers to know their equipment and begin any troubleshooting process themselves. If they do need an expert, they must be able to describe the malfunction in detail. In other words, they have to be able to analyze problems and then communicate them.

Today we see quality as a process that prevents defects from occurring, a common corporate language that pervades the company and applies to security guards and secretaries as well as manufacturing staff. (For more about this, see the boxed insert, "The Language of Quality.")

Today Motorola has one of the most comprehensive and effective corporate training and education programs in the world and, in a recent leap of ambition, our own corporate university.

Why in the world, you ask, should any corporation have its own university? My answer is the story of how we came to have ours. In part, it is a kind of odyssey, a 10-year expedition full of well-meaning mistakes, heroic misapprehensions, and shocking discoveries. In part, it is a slowly unfolding definition of education and change that shows why successful companies in today's business climate must not only train workers but build educational systems.

An MBA in Four Weeks

In 1979, Bob Galvin, then Motorola's CEO and now chairman of the executive committee, asked the human resources department to put together a five-year training plan. He believed that all employees needed upgrading in their skills if the company was going to survive.

Galvin had made two earlier attempts at companywide education. The first focused on new tools, new technology, and teamwork, but it didn't produce the results he wanted. Plant managers brought in new equipment but wouldn't change the support systems and their own work patterns.

So he set up the Motorola Executive Institute, an intensive, one-time course for 400 executives that tried to give them an MBA in four weeks. The participants learned a great deal, but again, the ultimate results were disappointing.

Galvin, who understood that change had to force its way through a company from the top down, had been driving home the point that those who lead often lose their power—or their right to lead—because they're unwilling to change. He now realized that the top probably wasn't going to lead the attack until all employees wanted change to take place. Motorola had to educate everyone and make people see the need for change.

To carry out this training program, we set up an education service department— MTEC, the Motorola Training and Education Center—with its own board of directors consisting of Galvin himself, two of his top executives, and senior managers from each of Motorola's operating units. MTEC had two principal

The Language of Quality

The mathematics of quality are difficult. Even the vocabulary—bell curves, probability functions, standard deviations expressed in multiples of the Greek letter Σ—can be formidable. At Motorola, we have nevertheless tried to teach at least a basic version of this math to every employee and to extend the concepts and terminology of industrial quality into every corner of the business—training, public relations, finance, security, even cooking. In 1983, we thought three days of training on quality would be enough. Today we have 28 days of material—quality tools, quality strategy, quality techniques, quality feedback mechanisms—and over the course of several years, we expect our engineers and manufacturing middle managers to have all 28.

The corporate goal is to achieve a quality standard by 1992 equivalent to what the statisticians and industrial engineers call Six Sigma, which means six standard deviations from a statistical performance average. In plain English, Six Sigma translates into 3.4 defects per million opportunities, or production that is 99.99966 percent defect free. (By contrast, and according to formulas not worth explaining here, 5Σ is 233 defects per million, and 4Σ is 6,210. Airlines achieve 6.5Σ in safety—counting fatalities as defects—but only 3.5 to 4Σ in baggage handling. Doctors and pharmacists achieve an accuracy of just under 5Σ in writing and filling prescriptions.)

Motorola has not yet reached Six Sigma in manufacturing or in any other function. But we have achieved our initial goal of creating a common vocabulary that lets every person in the company speak the same quality language. Everyone pursues his or her own job version of Six Sigma,

and everyone shares a sense of what it means, objectively and subjectively, to take part in the process of getting from where we are to where we want to be. The idea of 3.4 defects per million opportunities may sound ridiculous for a course instructor or a chef, but there is always some way to apply the standard and strive for the goal. In effect, the Six Sigma process means changing the way people do things so that nothing can go wrong.

Applied to the chef, the process of reaching Six Sigma by 1992 means he can burn five muffins this year, two muffins next year, and eventually none at all. Of course, Six Sigma applied to muffins is in one sense a fiction; and, if we presented it to the chef as an ultimatum, it would also be insulting. The real point is that importing that quality language from manufacturing to the rest of the company stimulates a kind of discussion we might not otherwise have had. It also tells people they're important, since the time-cycle and quality standards so vital to manufacturing and product design now also apply to the chef, the security guard, and the clerical support people.

What we actually said to the chef was that he made a consistently Six Sigma chocolate chip cookie—in my opinion it ranks with the best in the world—and we wanted him to do the same with muffins. We asked him what changes we needed to make so he could accomplish that. He said, "The reason I can't make better muffins is that you don't trust me with the key to the freezer. I have to make the batter the night before, because when I get here in the morning the makings are still locked up. When batter sits for 12 hours, it's never as good as batter you make fresh and pop directly in the oven." He was right, of course. The

---

The Language of Quality *(concluded)*

language of quality can also be used to talk about trust.

Security guards are another good example. Every morning they have to get 12,000 employees and about 400 visitors through the gates in half an hour. What's their assignment—to keep people out, bring peo-ple in, protect property? As we now define it, their job is to make sure the right people get in quickly and, if there are problems, to handle them politely and professionally. Quality is measured accordingly—a "cus-tomer" complaint is a defect, and a cus-tomer is anyone who comes to the gate.

---

goals: to expand the participative man-agement process and to help improve product quality tenfold in five years.

Our charter was not so much to educate people as to be an agent of change, with an emphasis on retraining workers and rede-fining jobs. Our first order of business was to analyze the jobs that existed then, in 1980, and try to anticipate what they'd look like in the future. The first thing we learned was not to look too far ahead. If we made a two-year projection and trained people for that, then change didn't arrive quickly enough for people to make the shift. We had to anticipate, plan curricula, then train separately for each incremental change. We had thought progress would be made in leaps, but it took place one step at a time.

To meet the quality target, we devel-oped a five-part curriculum. First came statistical process control, which con-sisted of instruction in seven quality tools. Basic industrial problem solving was sec-ond. Third was a course on how to present conceptual material, a tricky assignment for an hourly worker presenting a techni-cal solution to an engineer. Fourth was a course on effective meetings that empha-sized the role of participant as well as that of chairperson. Finally we had a program on goal setting that taught people how to define objectives, how to describe them in writing, and how to measure progress.

So far so good. In the early 1980s, at a typical plant with 2,500 workers, MTEC was using 50,000 hours of employee time—a lot of time away from the job for what some people considered a pretty esoteric program. We thought it was worth the investment. Putting quality tools in the hands of every employee was the only way to overcome the old emphasis on shipment goals, even when meeting those goals meant shipping defective products.

Yet the skeptics were right. We were wasting everyone's time. We designed and taught courses, and people took them and went back to their jobs, and nothing changed. We had made a series of false assumptions.

Getting People to Want to Learn

Our first mistake was to assume that, once we described the courses, the people who needed them most would sign up to take them. They didn't. We also assumed that the courses would be popular, but enrollment was never in danger of swamp-ing our capacities.

The old approach had been to learn by watching others. When technology changed once in five years, on-the-job training made some sense, but people can't handle constant innovation by watching one another. Yet somehow the culture told them they didn't learn things any other way. Since people resisted formal classes, we developed self-help material so they could pick up a package and take it home. That failed, too. People just didn't see homework as real training, which left us in a bind: our employees didn't seem to believe the training was necessary; but, if it was necessary, then it had to take place in a formal classroom, not at home. So we dropped the learn-at-home program. Not because people couldn't learn that way but because we couldn't get people to *want* to learn that way.

Training, it appeared, was not something we could deliver like milk and expect people to consume spontaneously. It was not simply a matter of instructing or giving people a chance to instruct themselves. We had to motivate people to want to learn, and that meant overcoming complacency.

When Motorola hired people in the old days, we hired them for life. People grew up in their jobs, acquired competencies and titles, moved from work force to management. All employees became members of our Service Club at the end of 10 years, which meant we wouldn't terminate them except for poor performance or dishonesty. We never gave anyone an absolute right to lifelong employment, but we did provide an unmistakable opportunity to stay.

This was the employment model that built the corporation and made it successful, and we believed the loyalty it inspired gave us added value. We hadn't yet realized in the early 1980s that there was going to be a skill shortage, but we clearly needed to upgrade our training. A lot of our competitors, especially in the semiconductor business, hired people, used their skills, terminated them when their skills were out of date, then hired new people with new skills. But we had plants where 60 to 70 percent of the workers were Service Club members.

We didn't want to break a model that had worked for 50 years, but we had some people who thought that if they made that 10-year mark they could mentally retire, and that was an attitude we had to fix. In the end, we had to let people know that "poor performance" included an unwillingness to change. We had to abandon paternalism for shared responsibility.

A second major misconception was that senior managers needed only a briefing to understand the new quality systems. Conceptually, in fact, they grasped them very quickly and believed in their importance. But their behavior patterns didn't change, and that made life very difficult for middle managers.

Operations review is a good example. If a production team had mastered the new techniques and was eager to apply them, and if senior management paid lip service to quality but still placed its highest priority on shipping goals, middle managers got caught in the squeeze. Workers expected them to emphasize quality even if that made some deliveries late. Top management expected them to improve quality but not at the expense of schedule.

Workers began to wonder why they'd taken the training. They'd learned how to keep a Pareto chart and make an Ishikawa diagram, but no one ever appeared on the floor and asked to see one. On the contrary, some of their immediate managers wanted product shipped even if it wasn't perfect. Top managers, on the other hand, began to wonder why it was that people took the courses so carefully designed for them and then went back to their jobs and did nothing different. Shipping goals were being met, but quality was not improving.

At about this point in our frustration, we asked two universities to evaluate our return on investment. They identified three groups:

- In those few plants where the work force absorbed the whole curriculum of quality tools and process skills and where senior managers reinforced the training by means of new questions appropriate to the new methods, we were getting a $33 return for every dollar spent, including the cost of wages paid while people sat in class.

- Plants that made use of either the quality tools or the process skills but not both, and then reinforced what they taught, broke even.

- Finally, plants that taught all or part of the curriculum but failed to reinforce with follow-up meetings and a new, genuine emphasis on quality had a negative return on investment.

We were learning our first lesson all over again, that change is not just driven from the top—change must *begin* at the top. We had also begun to understand that one secret of manufacturing success was a language common to every employee, in this case a common language of quality. But if quality was to be the new language, every top manager had better learn to speak it like a native. Since Bob Galvin believed quality training was useless unless top managers gave quality even more attention than they gave quarterly results, he dramatized the point at operations review meetings. He insisted that quality reports come first, not last, on the agenda, and then he left before the financial results were discussed.

Thin Ice

By 1984, we were admittedly a little disappointed by what we had achieved so far, but we believed we could address the problem with a new, double-edged initiative. First, by hiring and training more carefully, we would bring our manufacturing talent up to the standard in product design, and second, having now learned our lesson about top executive involvement, we would offer the training to upper management as well as line workers.

There was no question that manufacturing was a second-class citizen. Our recruiting strategy had always been to find the best engineers, and the best engineers went into product design. We had never deliberately looked for the best manufacturing or materials-management people. We now consciously upgraded the status, rewards, and recruiting for Motorola manufacturing.

We also put together a two-week program of courses that tried to project what our kind of manufacturing would look like in 10 years and to think about the changes we would have to make to stay competitive. We wanted all the decision makers in manufacturing to take part.

We began, as so often before and since, by repeating a past mistake. We assumed the proper people at the top would sign up without prompting. What we found was that many simply delegated the program to subordinates. Our advisory board—Galvin and 11 senior managers—soon saw what was happening and changed the policy. From then on, the board "invited" people to take the training, and board members began by inviting themselves, then everyone else at the top.

The curriculum centered on manufacturing technologies—computer-aided design, new quality measurements, computer-integrated manufacturing, just-in-time—as well as on what we called "unity of purpose," our name for the empowered work force. We also began to focus on time. We used to take three to seven years to design a new product; now we were shooting for 18 months. Finally, we started talking about a contract book where marketing, product design, and manufacturing would meet, argue, and reach genuine agreement about the needs of the market, the right new product, and the schedules and responsibilities of each group in producing it.

Historically, such agreements had often been made but never kept. The three departments would meet and agree, product design would go home and invent something quite different but wonderfully state-of-the-art, manufacturing would do a complete redesign to permit actual production in the real world, and finally marketing would find itself with a product bearing little resemblance to what it had asked for and been promised.

We wanted to use the training to send a message to the company about achieving quality through the integration of efforts across functions, a message not just about quality of product but about quality of people, quality of service, quality of the total organization.

In 1985, we also started an annual training and education event for senior management. Each year, the CEO picks a topic of critical concern and brings his top executives together to thrash it out with the help of some carefully chosen experts.

That first year the topic was competition, especially Asian competition. There were Asian companies—whole Asian countries—going after every market segment we were in. Conversely, there were huge world markets we were ignoring:

India, mainland China, Eastern Europe. The goal was to scare the wits out of all the participants and wake them up to the perils and opportunities of our position. We had people calling themselves worldwide product or marketing managers who didn't even have a passport.

From 1985 to 1987, our top 200 people spent 17 days each in the classroom. Ten days on manufacturing, five days on global competition, and two more days on cycle-time management. We then drove that training down through the organization via the major components of the curriculum. What was 10 days for a vice president might have been eight hours for a production worker, but eventually they were all speaking the same language. Or so we believed.

In 1985, we decided after considerable fact finding and lengthy deliberation to open our new cellular manufacturing facility in the United States, rather than take it offshore. Top management had just gone through its workshop on foreign competition, and there was a general feeling that, with our manufacturing expertise, we should be able to compete with anyone in the world. We acknowledged the fact that it wasn't only low-cost labor we'd been going offshore to get but brains—first-rate manufacturing know-how. In our naive self-satisfaction over the success of our training programs, we figured we now had across-the-board know-how in Illinois.

Our work force in Arlington Heights, outside Chicago, knew radio technology, and, given the similarities, we believed these workers could make the bridge to cellular. In addition, they had improved quality tenfold in the first five years of training and were well on their way to doing it again. Nevertheless, we were making what was fundamentally an emotional commitment, not a hard-nosed business decision. However much quality had improved, it had probably not improved enough to compete in new technologies when our labor was going to cost us more than it cost our Asian competitors. However thoroughly the Arlington Heights workers understood radios, we were about to empower them to do much more than they had done in the past—not just one or two assembly functions but quality control, flexible manufacturing, and mentoring for the several thousand new-hires we'd eventually have to add.

Maybe we sensed the thin ice we were on. In any case, we did a quick math assessment to see exactly where we stood with regard to further training. The scores were a shock. Only 40 percent passed a test containing some questions as simple as "Ten is what percent of 100?"

The Work Force That Couldn't Read

Let me dwell for moment on the full drama of those results. The Arlington Heights work force was going to lead the company into global competition in a new technology, and 60 percent seemed to have trouble with simple arithmetic. We needed a work force capable of operating and maintaining sophisticated new equipment and facilities to a zero-defect standard, and most of them could not calculate decimals, fractions, and percents.

It took us several months and a number of math classes to discover that the real cause of much of this poor math performance was an inability to read or, in the case of many immigrants, to comprehend English as a second language. Those who'd missed the simple percentage question had been unable to read the words. In a sense, this was good news: it meant their math might not be as bad as we'd feared. But the news was bad enough even with

the silver lining. For years, we'd been moving computers into the work line to let everyone interface with a keyboard and a screen; since 1980, the number of computer terminals at Motorola had gone from 5,000 to 55,000. At the new plant, workers would need to feed data into these terminals and extract information from them. Now we had reason to wonder if they'd be able to use their computers effectively.

And yet these people were superior employees who had improved quality tenfold and more. How had they done that if they couldn't read? It was a mystery—and a great problem.

The mystery was easily solved. In the early 1980s, we had had several layers of middle managers who acted as translators. They took the directions on the screens and put them into spoken English or, in many cases, Polish or Spanish, and the workers—dedicated, motivated people— carried them out.

The problem, however, remained. In fact, it grew rapidly more serious as we began to set up the new plant. We had begun to remove layers of middle management in the mid-1980s, and in setting up the new factory we wanted to leave no more than two or three levels between the plant manager and the greenest entry-level hire. For that to work, we had to have people with basic skills who were quick to learn—and quick to teach. After all, we couldn't staff the whole plant with our current employees, even if they all had the necessary skills. We had to have a cadre of 400 to 500 people who could serve as teachers and role models for others as we brought them in.

In the old days, our selection criteria had been simply, "Are you willing to work? Do you have a good record of showing up for work? Are you motivated to work?'' We didn't ask people if they could read. We didn't ask them to do arithmetic. We didn't ask them to demonstrate an ability to solve problems or work on a team or do anything except show up and be productive for so many hours a week.

The obvious, drastic answer would have been to fire that old work force and hire people who could meet our standards, but that was not an acceptable approach for our company and probably not a realistic one given the educational level of the available labor pool. We quickly implemented a standard for new-hires based on seventh grade math and reading skills, but, as we recruited people from the outside, we found remarkably few who met that seventh grade standard.

We look for many things in our applicants, beyond literacy. For example, they must also be punctual and responsible. But at some installations, the requirements are even higher. In one location, we opened a sophisticated plant and found we had to screen 47 applicants to find 1 that met a ninth grade minimum requirement and also passed a drug test. This was admittedly an extreme situation, and the results were also skewed by the drug test. Still, at 1 applicant in 47, a company soon runs out of potential-hires, especially if anyone else is competing for the labor supply.

We quickly saw that a higher set of standards for new-hires was not the whole answer to our Illinois problem, particularly since we weren't willing to lay off dedicated people who'd been with us for years. And Arlington Heights was no isolated pocket. Documenting installations one by one, we concluded that about half of our 25,000 manufacturing and support people in the United States failed to meet the seventh grade yardstick in English and math.

At a plant in Florida, we offered English as a second language, thinking maybe 60 people would sign up, and we got 600—one out of three employees. By signing up, they were telling us they couldn't read the memos we sent them, the work order changes, the labels on boxes.

Joining Forces with the Schools

When we started MTEC in 1980, it was on the assumption that our people had the basic skills for the jobs they were doing. For five years, we saw ourselves as an agent of change, a school for the language of quality, a counselor and goal to senior management, a vocational instructor in the new skills and measurement systems that would enable our employees to lead the electronic industry in sophistication and quality control.

Our charter as an educational program was to provide continuous training to every employee. Then suddenly, to meet our business needs, we found we had to add remedial elementary education. We had never wanted to be in the grade school business, and it threw our investment strategy into chaos. An annual budget projected at $35 million to $40 million for the early 1980s had grown to $50 million a year by 1988, and we were going to need $35 million more over a three- to five-year period to correct the literacy problem.

Yet budget was only one of our problems. Morale was an even thornier issue. Remedial education made many people uncomfortable, and some were literally afraid of school, an environment in which they had failed as children. We didn't want to embarrass them; these weren't marginal workers, remember, but valuable, experienced employees. Yet they were also people with serious math and literacy problems, and we had to educate them.

We took the position that remedial math and language instruction was simply another form of skills training. We videotaped older employees within a few years of retirement and had them say to others their own age and younger, "Look, we're not going to get out of here without learning new skills. We need to go to class. Back in 1955, we had another moment of truth when we had to move from tubes to transistors. We did it then; we can do it now."

We also had Bob Galvin respond personally to letters. If a man wrote to ask if he really had to go back to school at 58 and study math, Bob would write back, "Yes, you do. But everyone does. You do your job well, but without more math you won't survive in the work environment another seven years."

We adopted a policy that said everyone had a right to retraining when technology changed. But, if people refused the retraining, then we said we'd dismiss them. In fact, we had refusals from 18 employees with long service, and we dismissed all but one. That sent another strong message.

There was also a flip side to the policy. It said that, if people took retraining and failed, then it was our job to figure out a way of helping them succeed. After all, nearly one fifth of the U.S. population has some kind of learning disability. If some of our employees couldn't learn to read and compute in conventional classrooms, we tried to help them learn some other way. If they couldn't learn at all but had met our hiring standards 20 or 30 years ago and worked hard ever since, we found jobs for them at Motorola, anyway.

Uncovering widespread math and reading problems was a great shock to the system, but it had the beneficial effect of pushing us into three watershed

decisions that shaped the whole future of MTEC and Motorola. First, we realized that remedial elementary education was not something we could do well ourselves, so we turned for help to community colleges and other local institutions. Second, we decided to take a harder look at certain other skills. We had always assumed, for example, that high school and junior college graduates came to us equipped with technical and business skills like accounting, computer operation, statistics, and basic electronics. When we discovered they did not—by this time nothing surprised us—we decided to go back to the community colleges that were already helping us with remedial math and English. We told them what we needed, and they had courses with the corresponding titles, so we sent them our people.

Our next surprise was that the courses weren't quite what the titles implied. The community colleges had fallen behind. Their theories, labs, and techniques were simply not up to modern industrial standards. They hadn't known where we were going, and we hadn't bothered to tell them.

This discovery forced our third major decision—to begin building the educational partnerships and dialogues that eventually led us to Motorola University.

We've deliberately tried to treat our educational suppliers the same way we treat our component and chemical suppliers. To begin with, that means acknowledging that in a certain sense we buy what they produce. To make that work, they have to know what we need, and we have to know what not to duplicate. We exchange faculty, jointly develop curriculum, share lab equipment, and tend our mutual feedback mechanisms. In half our plants, as an experiment, we have vocational training experts—community college staff members whom we pay full-time—to act as the ongoing bridge between the changes going on in our business and the changes necessary in the college curriculum. We're also developing dialogues with engineering schools, as well as elementary and secondary schools, about what we need and how it differs from what they provide.

Dialogue means not a single meeting, or two or three, but regular meetings every few weeks. We get presidents, deans, superintendents, principals, professors, and teachers to sit down with our vice presidents for manufacturing and quality, our CFO, the managers of various plants and functions and talk about our needs and theirs.

Schools and colleges have no self-evident need to collaborate with us to the extent we'd like them to. Some educators and academics believe businesspeople are universally unprincipled, that the reason for our involvement in education is to serve ourselves at the expense, somehow, of the community at large.

Yet in the course of talking and interacting, we've found that the benefits to all parties have emerged quite clearly. Some of our strongest support comes from the people who teach remedial English and math. They know how widespread the problem is beyond Motorola and seem grateful that we're eager to attack illiteracy without assessing blame. The point is not that our concern with education is utterly altruistic but that better and more relevant education helps business, labor, and schools themselves.

This last point is important. Take the case of a community college. To begin with, we supply them with, say, a thousand students a year, and a thousand tu-

itions. We also donate equipment. More important than either of these benefits, perhaps, is the fact that we offer an insight into what the globally competitive marketplace demands of students and educators. Most colleges are very resource poor. But the dialogue means that they can come into our plants, talk to us, study state-of-the-art manufacturing, and they can use our facilities to pursue their own staff development. We provide summer internships for their teachers and set aside a certain number of in-house training slots each year for community college faculty. We encourage them to use our labs and equipment to teach not only Motorolans but all their students. We believe—and I think they believe—that the mutual benefits are huge.

We've assigned one of our senior people to be the director of institutional relationships. His job is to understand and try to improve the supply lines that run from elementary schools, high schools, and colleges to Motorola. He's there to diagnose their needs, communicate ours, and fund projects that bridge the gap. Motorola has set up an account—in addition to the $60 million education budget—that we can use to invest in schools that are willing to undertake change and to work with us to address the needs of the populations that supply our work force.

For example, two of our scientists came up with an electronics kit that costs only $10 to produce. Then we discovered that the average high school physics teacher has only $2 per student to spend. So we decided to use the account to donate the kits to schools we draw students from and to teach the teachers how to use them.

We also sponsor a planning institute for superintendents from 52 school districts in

18 states on how to build strategic education plans and work with their business constituencies, of which we are one element. We're also trying to build a volunteer corps of Motorola employees who want to work with schools and teach, plan, or translate particular classes into industry-specific programs.

Open-Ended Education

In 1980, we thought we could provide *x* amount of training, get everybody up to speed, then back off. Now we know it's open-ended. Whenever we reach a certain level of expertise or performance, there's always another one to go for. Now we know it's a continuous investment from both sides—from the individuals who attend classes and apply new skills and from the corporation that designs new training programs and makes the time available to take them. In fact, we now know there is no real distinction between corporate education and every other kind. Education is a strenuous, universal, unending human activity that neither business nor society can live without. That insight was another that led us to Motorola University.

When Bob Galvin first suggested a university in 1979, the company wasn't ready. Galvin started interviewing presidents of real universities for advice and leads, but, in the meantime, I interviewed 22 senior Motorola executives to get their reactions. They were afraid a university, so called, would drain resources from the business, rather that add value. For my own part, I was afraid the name "university" was too pretentious. This wasn't to be a seat of free and open inquiry. This was to be training and education for work force and managers.

Instead, we set up MTEC as a service

division, with its own board of directors. That made us the only corporation in the United States with a training advisory board that included the CEO and other senior officers. But it didn't make us a university.

Then in 1989, CEO George Fisher made the suggestion. He believed the word university would give us greater autonomy. He also thought it would create an expectation we'd have to grow into.

A great deal had changed in those nine years. First of all, most of our senior clientele—the 22 executives and their fellow skeptics—had stopped seeing education as a cost and had begun to accept it as an indispensable investment. They'd seen returns. Most other people in the company had seen more than that. They'd seen themselves picking up marketable skills; they'd felt themselves growing in self-esteem and self-confidence.

Another difference was that by 1989 we were working closely with the schools, and, when public educators heard the word university, their response was positive, even enthusiastic. They took it to mean that we were serious about education, not just enthralled with our own bottom line.

But what *was* a university? And more to the point, what was a Motorola University? What kind of model should we work from? There were several that might apply, it seemed to me.

One came from the charter of the City University of New York, which says that one of the university's central missions is to meet the needs of the city's residents. What we had was a training department that focused on the needs of the organization. Becoming a university would mean a shift toward meeting the needs of individuals, the "residents" of the corporation.

Another possible model was the open university of the United Kingdom, which, instead of bringing people to the education, takes the education to the people and puts it in a context they can understand.

A third possibility was the model described by Cardinal Newman in *The Idea of a University*, which, after 150 years, is still the cornerstone of liberal education. Newman's ideal university had no place for vocational training, so in that sense he and we part ways. But in another sense, we're in complete agreement. Newman wanted his university to mold the kind of individual who can "fill any post with credit" and "master any subject with facility"—an excellent description of what we wanted Motorola University to do.

Our evolving vision of the university contains elements of all three models. We try to make our education relevant to the corporation, to the job, and to the individual. We also try to bridge the gap between our company and the institutions that supply us with people. We don't intend to grant degrees, but we do intend to design courses that accrediting boards will certify and that the universities that give degrees will count. (See the boxed insert "Curriculum Development at Motorola U.")

We are entering a new era of partnership with established universities. We give them feedback on the courses they teach and even on their faculties. Most companies have just blindly reimbursed tuition costs, but we think we have a legitimate interest in the schools that prepare our future employees and in the colleges that provide continuing adult education at our expense.

For example, Motorola and Northwestern jointly designed a quality course for the second year of Northwestern's MBA program. Northwestern also offers courses taught half-term by one of its professors and half-term by one of our experts—first half, theory; second half, application. We work closely with the Illinois Institute of Technology as well, and with Arizona State University. For the first time, we actually evaluate university services, not just assume they must be good.

We avoid collegiate trappings—no professors or basketball teams—but we do make academic appointments of a kind: we name people to staff positions, and for two or three years they leave their jobs and devote themselves to educational activities. (See the boxed insert "Finding and Training Faculty.") We also have a Motorola University Press that prints more than a million pages a month and plans to publish a series of books on design and quality written by one of our employees.

As for Newman's grander concept of the university, our commitment is not to buildings or a bureaucracy but to creating an environment for learning, a continuing openness to new ideas. We do teach vocational subjects, but we also teach supervocational subjects—functional skills raised to a higher level. We not only teach people how to respond quickly to new technologies we try to commit them to the goal of anticipating new technologies. We not only teach people how to lead a department to better performance and higher quality, we try to dedicate them to the idea of continuing, innovative leadership in the workplace and the marketplace. We not only teach skills, we try to breathe the very spirit of creativity and flexibility into manufacturing and management.

Curriculum Development at Motorola U

Motorola never farms out curriculum design—the road map that shows what we need to learn. But we may contract with an individual, a group, or a college to design a particular course, which we then turn over to our deans of delivery—one for the United States, one for the rest of the world—for distribution. Those deans search out instructors through the colleges or just hire free agents, whom we train. Sometimes, too, courses are packaged as software, as videos, or go out via satellite.

For each functional area we have a course-design team of instructional system designers whom we think of as product engineers in terms of title, pay, status, and job security. Their expertise is knowing how to extract the skill requirements from a job analysis and package them into training for adults.

Of 1,200 people involved in training and education at Motorola—including 110 full-time and 300 part-time staff at Motorola University—23 are product design engineers. They're like department chairs, and the senior product manager is like a dean. The faculty are the actual course writers, audiovisual specialists, and instructors.

We divide each functional curriculum—engineering, manufacturing, sales and marketing—into three parts: relational skills, technical skills, and business skills. M.U. itself is responsible for teaching relational skills—customer satisfaction, effective meetings, effective manufacturing supervision, negotiation, effective presentations. Since 1985, however, we have developed the curriculum for technical and business skills—basic math, electronics, accounting, computer operation, statistical process control—in cooperation with community colleges and technical schools.

As a result of what we've learned over the last decade, the Motorola curriculum has two more critically important elements. The first is culture. Culture in a corporation is partly a question of history and of common language—a form of tribal storytelling. At Motorola, for example, we believe in taking risks. Our history shows it was one of the things that made us great. Telling those stories creates a tradition of risk, invests it with value, and encourages young people to go out and do the same.

But culture is not only inherited, it's also created. Teamwork is an example. Our history is one of individual contributors, not teams. So training has to emphasize team building and downplay the Lone Ranger culture we valued in the 1950s and 1960s.

The second extra element is remedial reading and math, which today means algebra. In most of our factories, we want analyses and experiments requiring algebra done right on the line. As for reading, we've found that the engineering group writes work order changes, product specifications, and product manuals at a 14th to 17th grade level—to be read by people who read at the 4th to 6th grade level. We're trying to lower the former and raise the latter. When we talk about a literate work force by 1992, we mean seventh grade. But our goal remains ninth grade by 1995.

Finding and Training Faculty

I own a videotape of an all-day engineering class whose instructor, in closing the session, thanks the students for their active participation. In fact, except to breathe, not one of them has made a sound. In eight hours of teaching, the instructor never asks a question. He never makes eye contact. He is on top of his subject technically, but the class is boring beyond belief.

The teachers at Motorola University aren't there to implant data. They're there to transfer information and get it applied quickly. We design curricula and train teachers with that end in mind.

Training and certification of all teachers is in four phases of 40 hours each. The first phase is procedural: how to use flip charts, foils, chalkboards; how to manage a classroom; how to ask questions; how to observe, listen, and reinforce.

The second phase deals with the particular kinds of behavior we want to see teachers and students exhibit. We believe in participative management, so instructors must be models of openness and respect for other opinions. We also emphasize teamwork, so teachers must encourage mutual support and try to curb the competitive, who's-best model most people learned in school.

The third 40 hours deals with subject matter. We walk teachers through the course and then we walk them through the research that underlies it. We don't want them to teach *their* version of, say, Effective Meetings; we want them to teach *ours*. Not everyone can deliver on those terms. For example, few academics can do it our way. They're used to interpreting material independently, so after the first page, it tends to take on their own particular slant. It may make a fascinating course, but we can't have 3,000 people learning 35 different versions of Effective Meetings.

Finally, we assign teachers to master instructors who use them as coteachers and then have them teach on their own with feedback before turning them loose.

We have found three groups of people who make especially good teachers. The first is recently retired Motorola employees. We start talking to them six months out and try to get them through certification before retirement. Those who make it are superb. They believe in what they're teaching, they know how to apply it, and they can tell the stories from the past and relate them to the future.

We have one powerful, middle-management course on managing change—specifically, the change that must take place if Motorola is to prosper over the next decade—that is taught by insiders only. Bill Weisz, a former CEO and now a vice chairman of the board, devotes the last seven hours to the topic "I built this bureaucracy, and, if I was 25 years old, here's how I'd blow it up and build what we need for the next 10 years."

The second group consists of married women with college degrees whose children have left home. Lack of experience makes it hard for them to find jobs, so we've worked out programs with community colleges to screen them and reorient them to the business world. In courses like Effective Meetings, Interpersonal Skills, and Basic Sales Skills, they're our best performers by far. Most students think they're old business hands, but their actual experience—community politics, selling ideas to children, managing teenagers—is just as rich and certainly just as useful.

The third group represents a kind of talent sharing. Like most other companies, Motorola has a rule against rehiring people who've taken early retirement. Now we trade early retirement talent with other companies. AT&T gives us a list of 100 potential instructors who've just left, and

Finding and Training Faculty *(concluded)*

we give them our list. It's been a success. People like translating their experience from AT&T or IBM and making it relevant and effective in our different world. Eventually, we hope to change the rules so people who pass our certification will always have an alternative to early retirement.

Electrifying the Now and Future Employee

The word *university* is undeniably ambitious, but Motorola management has always tried to use words in ways that force people to rethink their assumptions. The term *university* will arouse curiosity and, I hope , raise the expectations of our work force and our training and education staff. We could have called it an "educational resource facility," but who would that have electrified?

As a first step, we have decided that Motorola University will be a global institution. We are already working on a formal relationship with the Asia Pacific International University, based in Macao. Motorola University is presently open to the employees of our suppliers, of our principal customers, and even of our educational partners, but we envision a time when the university will accept students from outside our immediate community of companies and institutions, people who will not necessarily work for Motorola or any of our suppliers or customers at any time in their lives.

At the same time, one of our goals is to have the best graduates of the best institutions want to work for us. To achieve that, we must attract young people into our classrooms so they'll know how good we are, and, just as important, so they'll know they have to take certain steps in their own development in order to work for us or someone like us as adults.

One of the things we have on the drawing board is a math-and-science summer institute for fifth, sixth, and seventh graders. Another is a simulation using an aircraft from the movie *Top Gun*. We'll stop the plane in mid-takeoff from a carrier and dissect it, showing the geometric and algebraic principles used in its design, then relate that back to the computer to show the same principles used in the design of other things. The goal is not to teach kids design but to show them that algebra is worth suffering through.

The point of a program like that is not to get kids to work for Motorola. We'd like the really inspired ones to want to work for us when that time comes. But if not, well, at least they'll be able to work for someone.

access control, database security, intrusion detection and prevention, malicious software, denial of service, firewalls, software security, physical security, human factors, auditing, legal and ethical aspects, and trusted systems. **Received the 2008 Text and Academic Authors Association (TAA) award for the best Computer Science and Engineering Textbook of the year.** ISBN 0-13-600424-5

NETWORK SECURITY ESSENTIALS, THIRD EDITION

A tutorial and survey on network security technology. The book covers important network security tools and applications, including S/MIME, IP Security, Kerberos, SSL/TLS, SET, and X509v3. In addition, methods for countering hackers and viruses are explored. ISBN 0-13-238033-1

WIRELESS COMMUNICATIONS AND NETWORKS, SECOND EDITION

A comprehensive, state-of-the art survey. Covers fundamental wireless communications topics, including antennas and propagation, signal encoding techniques, spread spectrum, and error correction techniques. Examines satellite, cellular, wireless local loop networks and wireless LANs, including Bluetooth and 802.11. Covers Mobile IP and WAP. ISBN 0-13-191835-4

COMPUTER NETWORKS WITH INTERNET PROTOCOLS AND TECHNOLOGY

An up-to-date survey of developments in the area of Internet-based protocols and algorithms. Using a top-down approach, this book covers applications, transport layer, Internet QoS, Internet routing, data link layer and computer networks, security, and network management. ISBN 0-13141098-9

HIGH-SPEED NETWORKS AND INTERNETS, SECOND EDITION

A state-of-the art survey of high-speed networks. Topics covered include TCP congestion control, ATM traffic management, Internet traffic management, differentiated and integrated services, Internet routing protocols and multicast routing protocols, resource reservation and RSVP, and lossless and lossy compression. Examines important topic of self-similar data traffic. ISBN 0-13-03221-0

COMPUTER ORGANIZATION AND ARCHITECTURE
DESIGNING FOR PERFORMANCE
EIGHTH EDITION

William Stallings

Prentice Hall
Upper Saddle River, NJ 07458

Library of Congress Cataloging-in-Publication Data On File

Vice President and Editorial Director: *Marcia J. Horton*
Editor-in-Chief: *Michael Hirsch*
Executive Editor: *Tracy Dunkelberger*
Associate Editor: *Melinda Haggerty*
Marketing Manager: *Erin Davis*
Senior Managing Editor: *Scott Disanno*
Production Editor: *Rose Kernan*
Operations Specialist: *Lisa McDowell*
Art Director: *Kenny Beck*
Cover Design: *Kristine Carney*
Director, Image Resource Center: *Melinda Patelli*
Manager, Rights and Permissions: *Zina Arabia*
Manager, Visual Research: *Beth Brenzel*
Manager, Cover Visual Research & Permissions: *Karen Sanatar*
Composition: *Rakesh Poddar, Aptara®, Inc.*
Cover Image: *Picturegarden / Image Bank / Getty Images, Inc.*

Pearson Education LTD. London
Pearson Education Singapore, Pte. Ltd
Pearson Education, Canada, Ltd
Pearson Education–Japan
Pearson Education Australia PTY, Limited

Pearson Education North Asia Ltd
Pearson Educación de Mexico, S.A. de C.V.
Pearson Education Malaysia, Pte. Ltd
Pearson Education, Upper Saddle River, New Jersey

Prentice Hall
is an imprint of

www.pearsonhighered.com

10 9 8 7 6 5 4 3 2
ISBN-13: 978-0-13-607373-4
ISBN-10:   0-13-607373-5

To Tricia (ATS),
my loving wife the kindest
and gentlest person

WEB SITE FOR COMPUTER ORGANIZATION AND ARCHITECTURE, EIGHTH EDITION

The Web site at WilliamStallings.com/COA/COA8e.html provides support for instructors and students using the book. It includes the following elements.

Course Support Materials

- A set of **PowerPoint** slides for use as lecture aids.
- Copies of **figures** from the book in PDF format.
- Copies of **tables** from the book in PDF format.
- **Computer Science Student Resource Site:** contains a number of links and documents that students may find useful in their ongoing computer science education. The site includes a review of basic, relevant mathematics; advice on research, writing, and doing homework problems; links to computer science research resources, such as report repositories and bibliographies; and other useful links.
- An **errata sheet** for the book, updated at most monthly.

Supplemental Documents

- A set of supplemental homework problems with solutions. Students can enhance their understanding of the material by working out the solutions to these problems and then checking their answers.
- Three online chapters: number systems, digital logic, and IA-64 architecture
- Nine online appendices that expand on the treatment in the book. Topics include recursion, and various topics related to memory.
- All of the Intel x86 and ARM architecture material from the book reproduced in two PDF documents for easy reference.
- Other useful documents

COA Courses

The Web site includes links to Web sites for courses taught using the book. These sites can provide useful ideas about scheduling and topic ordering, as well as a number of useful handouts and other materials.

Useful Web Sites

The Web site includes links to relevant Web sites. The links cover a broad spectrum of topics and will enable students to explore timely issues in greater depth.

Internet Mailing List

An Internet mailing list is maintained so that instructors using this book can exchange information, suggestions, and questions with each other and the author. Subscription information is provided at the book's Web site.

Simulation Tools for COA Projects

The Web site includes a number of interactive simulation tools, which are keyed to the topics of the book. The Web site also includes links to the SimpleScalar and SMPCache web sites. These are two software packages that serve as frameworks for project implementation. Each site includes downloadable software and background information.

CONTENTS

ABOUT THE AUTHOR

William Stallings has made a unique contribution to understanding the broad sweep of technical developments in computer security, computer networking and computer architecture. He has authored 17 titles, and counting revised editions, a total of 42 books on various aspects of these subjects. His writings have appeared in numerous ACM and IEEE publications, including the *Proceedings of the IEEE* and *ACM Computing Reviews*.

He has 10 times received the award for the best Computer Science textbook of the year from the Text and Academic Authors Association.

In over 30 years in the field, he has been a technical contributor, technical manager, and an executive with several high-technology firms. He has designed and implemented both TCP/IP-based and OSI-based protocol suites on a variety of computers and operating systems, ranging from microcomputers to mainframes. As a consultant, he has advised government agencies, computer and software vendors, and major users on the design, selection, and use of networking software and products.

He created and maintains the **Computer Science Student Resource Site** at WilliamStallings.com/StudentSupport.html. This site provides documents and links on a variety of subjects of general interest to computer science students (and professionals). He is a member of the editorial board of Cryptologia, a scholarly journal devoted to all aspects of cryptology.

Dr. Stallings holds a PhD from M.I.T. in Computer Science and a B.S. from Notre Dame in electrical engineering.

PREFACE

OBJECTIVES

This book is about the structure and function of computers. Its purpose is to present, as clearly and completely as possible, the nature and characteristics of modern-day computer systems.

This task is challenging for several reasons. First, there is a tremendous variety of products that can rightly claim the name of computer, from single-chip microprocessors costing a few dollars to supercomputers costing tens of millions of dollars. Variety is exhibited not only in cost, but also in size, performance, and application. Second, the rapid pace of change that has always characterized computer technology continues with no letup. These changes cover all aspects of computer technology, from the underlying integrated circuit technology used to construct computer components, to the increasing use of parallel organization concepts in combining those components.

In spite of the variety and pace of change in the computer field, certain fundamental concepts apply consistently throughout. The application of these concepts depends on the current state of the technology and the price/performance objectives of the designer. The intent of this book is to provide a thorough discussion of the fundamentals of computer organization and architecture and to relate these to contemporary design issues.

The subtitle suggests the theme and the approach taken in this book. It has always been important to design computer systems to achieve high performance, but never has this requirement been stronger or more difficult to satisfy than today. All of the basic performance characteristics of computer systems, including processor speed, memory speed, memory capacity, and interconnection data rates, are increasing rapidly. Moreover, they are increasing at different rates. This makes it difficult to design a balanced system that maximizes the performance and utilization of all elements. Thus, computer design increasingly becomes a game of changing the structure or function in one area to compensate for a performance mismatch in another area. We will see this game played out in numerous design decisions throughout the book.

A computer system, like any system, consists of an interrelated set of components. The system is best characterized in terms of structure—the way in which components are interconnected, and function—the operation of the individual components. Furthermore, a computer's organization is hierarchical. Each major component can be further described by decomposing it into its major subcomponents and describing their structure and function. For clarity and ease of understanding, this hierarchical organization is described in this book from the top down:

- **Computer system:** Major components are processor, memory, I/O.
- **Processor:** Major components are control unit, registers, ALU, and instruction execution unit.
- **Control Unit:** Provides control signals for the operation and coordination of all processor components. Traditionally, a microprogramming implementation has been used, in which major components are control memory, microinstruction sequencing logic, and registers. More recently, microprogramming has been less prominent but remains an important implementation technique.

The objective is to present the material in a fashion that keeps new material in a clear context. This should minimize the chance that the reader will get lost and should provide better motivation than a bottom-up approach.

Throughout the discussion, aspects of the system are viewed from the points of view of both architecture (those attributes of a system visible to a machine language programmer) and organization (the operational units and their interconnections that realize the architecture).

EXAMPLE SYSTEMS

This text is intended to acquaint the reader with the design principles and implementation issues of contemporary operating systems. Accordingly, a purely conceptual or theoretical treatment would be inadequate. To illustrate the concepts and to tie them to real-world design choices that must be made, two processor families have been chosen as running examples:

- **Intel x86 architecture:** The x86 architecture is the most widely used for non-embedded computer systems. The x86 is essentially a complex instruction set computer (CISC) with some RISC features. Recent members of the x86 family make use of superscalar and multicore design principles. The evolution of features in the x86 architecture provides a unique case study of the evolution of most of the design principles in computer architecture.
- **ARM:** The ARM embedded architecture is arguably the most widely used embedded processor, used in cell phones, iPods, remote sensor equipment, and many other devices. The ARM is essentially a reduced instruction set computer (RISC). Recent members of the ARM family make use of superscalar and multicore design principles.

Many, but by no means all, of the examples are drawn from these two computer families: the Intel x86, and the ARM embedded processor family. Numerous other systems, both contemporary and historical, provide examples of important computer architecture design features.

PLAN OF THE TEXT

The book is organized into five parts (see Chapter 0 for an overview)

- Overview
- The computer system
- The central processing unit
- The control unit
- Parallel organization, including multicore

The book includes a number of pedagogic features, including the use of interactive simulations and numerous figures and tables to clarify the discussion. Each chapter includes a list of key words, review questions, homework problems, suggestions for further reading, and recommended Web sites. The book also includes an extensive glossary, a list of frequently used acronyms, and a bibliography.

INTENDED AUDIENCE

The book is intended for both an academic and a professional audience. As a textbook, it is intended as a one- or two-semester undergraduate course for computer science, computer engineering, and electrical engineering majors. It covers all the topics in *CS 220 Computer Architecture,* which is one of the core subject areas in the *IEEE/ACM Computer Curricula 2001.*

For the professional interested in this field, the book serves as a basic reference volume and is suitable for self-study.

INSTRUCTIONAL SUPPORT MATERIALS

To support instructors, the following materials are provided:
- **Solutions manual:** Solutions to end-of-chapter Review Questions and Problems
- **Projects manual:** Suggested project assignments for all of the project categories listed below
- **PowerPoint slides:** A set of slides covering all chapters, suitable for use in lecturing
- **PDF files:** Reproductions of all figures and tables from the book
- **Test bank:** Includes true/false, multiple choice, and fill-in-the-blanks questions and answers

All of these support materials are available at the Instructor Resource Center (IRC) for this textbook. To gain access to the IRC, please contact your local Prentice Hall sales representative via prenhall.com/replocator or call Prentice Hall Faculty Services at 1-800-526-0485. You can also locate the IRC through **http://www.pearsonhighered.com/stallings**.

INTERNET SERVICES FOR INSTRUCTORS AND STUDENTS

There is a Web site for this book that provides support for students and instructors. The site includes links to other relevant sites and a set of useful documents. See the section, "Web Site for Computer Organization and Architecture," preceding this Preface, for more information. The Web page is at **williamstallings.com/COA/COA8e.html**.

New to this edition is a set of homework problems with solutions publicly available at this Web site. Students can enhance their understanding of the material by working out the solutions to these problems and then checking their answers.

An Internet mailing list has been set up so that instructors using this book can exchange information, suggestions, and questions with each other and with the author. As soon as typos or other errors are discovered, an errata list for this book will be available at **WilliamStallings.com**. Finally, I maintain the Computer Science Student Resource Site at **WilliamStallings.com/StudentSupport.html**.

PROJECTS AND OTHER STUDENT EXERCISES

For many instructors, an important component of a computer organization and architecture course is a project or set of projects by which the student gets hands-on experience to reinforce concepts from the text. This book provides an unparalleled degree of support for including a projects component in the course. The instructor's support materials available through Prentice Hall not only includes guidance on how to assign and structure the projects but also includes a set of user's manuals for various project types plus specific assignments, all written especially for this book. Instructors can assign work in the following areas:
- **Interactive simulation assignments:** Described subsequently.
- **Research projects:** A series of research assignments that instruct the student to research a particular topic on the Internet and write a report.

- **Simulation projects:** The IRC provides support for the use of the two simulation packages: SimpleScalar can be used to explore computer organization and architecture design issues. SMPCache provides a powerful educational tool for examining cache design issues for symmetric multiprocessors.
- **Assembly language projects:** A simplified assembly language, CodeBlue, is used and assignments based on the popular Core Wars concept are provided.
- **Reading/report assignments:** A list of papers in the literature, one or more for each chapter, that can be assigned for the student to read and then write a short report.
- **Writing assignments:** A list of writing assignments to facilitate learning the material.
- **Test bank:** Includes T/F, multiple choice, and fill-in-the-blanks questions and answers.

This diverse set of projects and other student exercises enables the instructor to use the book as one component in a rich and varied learning experience and to tailor a course plan to meet the specific needs of the instructor and students. See Appendix A in this book for details.

INTERACTIVE SIMULATIONS

New to this edition is the incorporation of interactive simulations. These simulations provide a powerful tool for understanding the complex design features of a modern computer system. A total of 20 interactive simulations are used to illustrate key functions and algorithms in computer organization and architecture design. At the relevant point in the book, an icon indicates that a relevant interactive simulation is available online for student use. Because the animations enable the user to set initial conditions, they can serve as the basis for student assignments. The instructor's supplement includes a set of assignments, one for each of the animations. Each assignment includes a several specific problems that can be assigned to students.

WHAT'S NEW IN THE EIGHTH EDITION

In the four years since the seventh edition of this book was published, the field has seen continued innovations and improvements. In this new edition, I try to capture these changes while maintaining a broad and comprehensive coverage of the entire field. To begin this process of revision, the seventh edition of this book was extensively reviewed by a number of professors who teach the subject and by professionals working in the field. The result is that, in many places, the narrative has been clarified and tightened, and illustrations have been improved. Also, a number of new "field-tested" homework problems have been added.

Beyond these refinements to improve pedagogy and user friendliness, there have been substantive changes throughout the book. Roughly the same chapter organization has been retained, but much of the material has been revised and new material has been added. The most noteworthy changes are as follows:

- **Interactive simulation:** Simulation provides a powerful tool for understanding the complex mechanisms of a modern processor. The eighth edition incorporates 20 separate interactive, Web-based simulation tools covering such areas as cache memory, main memory, I/O, branch prediction, instruction pipelining, and vector processing. At appropriate places in the book, the simulators are highlighted so that the student can invoke the simulation at the proper point in studying the book.

- **Embedded processors:** The eighth edition now includes coverage of embedded processors and the unique design issues they present. The ARM architecture is used as a case study.
- **Multicore processors:** The eighth edition now includes coverage of what has become the most prevalent new development in computer architecture: the use of multiple processors on a single chip. Chapter 18 is devoted to this topic.
- **Cache memory:** Chapter 4, which is devoted to cache memory, has been extensively revised, updated, and expanded to provide broader technical coverage and improved pedagogy through the use of numerous figures, as well as interactive simulation tools.
- **Performance assessment:** Chapter 2 includes a significantly expanded discussion of performance assessment, including a new discussion of benchmarks and an analysis of Amdahl's law.
- **Assembly language:** A new appendix has been added that covers assembly language and assemblers.
- **Programmable logic devices:** The discussion of PLDs in Chapter 20 on digital logic has been expanded to include an introduction to field-programmable gate arrays (FPGAs).
- **DDR SDRAM:** DDR has become the dominant main memory technology in desktops and servers, particularly DDR2 and DDR3. DDR technology is covered in Chapter 5, with additional details in Appendix K.
- **Linear tape open (LTO):** LTO has become the best selling "super tape" format and is widely used with small and large computer systems, especially for backup, LTO is covered in Chapter 6, with additional details in Appendix J.

With each new edition it is a struggle to maintain a reasonable page count while adding new material. In part this objective is realized by eliminating obsolete material and tightening the narrative. For this edition, chapters and appendices that are of less general interest have been moved online, as individual PDF files. This has allowed an expansion of material without the corresponding increase in size and price.

ACKNOWLEDGEMENTS

This new edition has benefited from review by a number of people, who gave generously of their time and expertise. The following people reviewed all or a large part of the manuscript: Azad Azadmanesh (*University of Nebraska–Omaha*); Henry Casanova (*University of Hawaii*); Marge Coahran (*Grinnell College*); Andree Jacobsen (*University of New Mexico*); Kurtis Kredo (*University of California—Davis*); Jiang Li (*Austin Peay State University*); Rachid Manseur (*SUNY, Oswego*); John Masiyowski (*George Mason University*); Fuad Muztaba (*Winston-Salem State University*); Bill Sverdlik (*Eastern Michigan University*); and Xiaobo Zhou (*University of Colorado Colorado Springs*).

Thanks also to the people who provided detailed technical reviews of a single chapter: Tim Mensch, Balbir Singh, Michael Spratte (Hewlett-Packard), François-Xavier Peretmere, John Levine, Jeff Kenton, Glen Herrmannsfeldt, Robert Thorpe, Grzegorz Mazur (Institute of Computer Science, Warsaw University of Technology), Ian Ameline, Terje Mathisen, Edward Brekelbaum (Varilog Research Inc), Paul DeMone, and Mikael Tillenius. I would also like to thank Jon Marsh of ARM Limited for the review of the material on ARM.

Professor Cindy Norris of Appalachian State University, Professor Bin Mu of the University of New Brunswick, and Professor Kenrick Mock of the University of Alaska kindly supplied homework problems.

Aswin Sreedhar of the University of Massachusetts developed the interactive simulation assignments and also wrote the test bank.

Professor Miguel Angel Vega Rodriguez, Professor Dr. Juan Manuel Sánchez Pérez, and Prof. Dr. Juan Antonio Gómez Pulido, all of University of Extremadura, Spain prepared the SMPCache problems in the instructors manual and authored the SMPCache User's Guide.

Todd Bezenek of the University of Wisconsin and James Stine of Lehigh University prepared the SimpleScalar problems in the instructor's manual, and Todd also authored the SimpleScalar User's Guide.

Thanks also to Adrian Pullin at Liverpool Hope University College, who developed the PowerPoint slides for the book.

Finally, I would like to thank the many people responsible for the publication of the book, all of whom did their usual excellent job. This includes my editor Tracy Dunkelberger, her assistant Melinda Haggerty, and production manager Rose Kernan. Also, Jake Warde of Warde Publishers managed the reviews; and Patricia M. Daly did the copy editing.

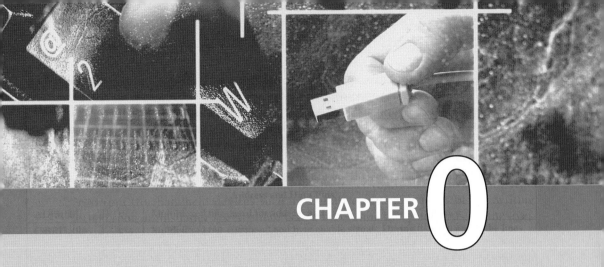

CHAPTER 0

READER'S GUIDE

This book, with its accompanying Web site, covers a lot of material. In this chapter, we give the reader an overview.

0.1 OUTLINE OF THE BOOK

The book is organized into five parts:

Part One: Provides an overview of computer organization and architecture and looks at how computer design has evolved.

Part Two: Examines the major components of a computer and their interconnections, both with each other and the outside world. This part also includes a detailed discussion of internal and external memory and of input–output (I/O). Finally, the relationship between a computer's architecture and the operating system running on that architecture is examined.

Part Three: Examines the internal architecture and organization of the processor. This part begins with an extended discussion of computer arithmetic. Then it looks at the instruction set architecture. The remainder of the part deals with the structure and function of the processor, including a discussion of reduced instruction set computer (RISC) and superscalar approaches.

Part Four: Discusses the internal structure of the processor's control unit and the use of microprogramming.

Part Five: Deals with parallel organization, including symmetric multiprocessing, clusters, and multicore architecture.

A number of online chapters and appendices at this book's Web site cover additional topics relevant to the book.

A more detailed, chapter-by-chapter summary of each part appears at the beginning of that part.

This text is intended to acquaint you with the design principles and implementation issues of contemporary computer organization and architecture. Accordingly, a purely conceptual or theoretical treatment would be inadequate. This book uses examples from a number of different machines to clarify and reinforce the concepts being presented. Many, but by no means all, of the examples are drawn from two computer families: the Intel x86 family and the ARM (Advanced RISC Machine) family. These two systems together encompass most of the current computer design trends. The Intel x86 architecture is essentially a complex instruction set computer (CISC) with some RISC features, while the ARM is essentially a RISC. Both systems make use of superscalar design principles and both support multiple processor and multicore configurations.

0.2 A ROADMAP FOR READERS AND INSTRUCTORS

This book follows a top-down approach to the presentation of the material. As we discuss in more detail in Section 1.2, a computer system can be viewed as a hierarchical structure. At a top level, we are concerned with the major components of the computers: processor, I/O, memory, peripheral devices. Part Two examines these components and looks in some detail at each component except the processor. This approach allows us to see the external functional requirements that drive the processor design, setting the stage for Part Three. In Part Three, we examine the processor in great detail. Because we have the context provided by Part Two, we are able, in Part Three, to see the design decisions that must be made so that the processor supports the overall function of the computer system. Next, in Part Four, we look at the control unit, which is at the heart of the processor. Again, the design of the control unit can best be explained in the context of the function it performs within the context of the processor. Finally, Part Five examines systems with multiple processors, including clusters, multiprocessor computers, and multi-core computers.

0.3 WHY STUDY COMPUTER ORGANIZATION AND ARCHITECTURE?

The *IEEE/ACM Computer Curricula 2001,* prepared by the Joint Task Force on Computing Curricula of the IEEE (Institute of Electrical and Electronics Engineers) Computer Society and ACM (Association for Computing Machinery), lists computer architecture as one of the core subjects that should be in the curriculum of all students in computer science and computer engineering. The report says the following:

> The computer lies at the heart of computing. Without it most of the computing disciplines today would be a branch of theoretical mathematics. To be a professional in any field of computing today, one should not regard the computer as just a black box that executes programs by magic. All students of computing should acquire some understanding and appreciation of a computer system's functional components, their characteristics, their performance, and their interactions. There are practical implications as well. Students need to understand computer architecture in order to structure a program so that it runs more efficiently on a real machine. In selecting a system to use, they should be able to understand the tradeoff among various components, such as CPU clock speed vs. memory size.

A more recent publication of the task force, *Computer Engineering 2004 Curriculum Guidelines,* emphasized the importance of Computer Architecture and Organization as follows:

> Computer architecture is a key component of computer engineering and the practicing computer engineer should have a practical understanding of this topic. It is concerned with all aspects of the design and organization of the central processing unit and the integration of the CPU into the computer system itself. Architecture extends upward into computer software because a processor's

architecture must cooperate with the operating system and system software. It is difficult to design an operating system well without knowledge of the underlying architecture. Moreover, the computer designer must have an understanding of software in order to implement the optimum architecture.

The computer architecture curriculum has to achieve multiple objectives. It must provide an overview of computer architecture and teach students the operation of a typical computing machine. It must cover basic principles, while acknowledging the complexity of existing commercial systems. Ideally, it should reinforce topics that are common to other areas of computer engineering; for example, teaching register indirect addressing reinforces the concept of pointers in C. Finally, students must understand how various peripheral devices interact with, and how they are interfaced to a CPU.

[CLEM00] gives the following examples as reasons for studying computer architecture:

1. Suppose a graduate enters the industry and is asked to select the most cost-effective computer for use throughout a large organization. An understanding of the implications of spending more for various alternatives, such as a larger cache or a higher processor clock rate, is essential to making the decision.

2. Many processors are not used in PCs or servers but in embedded systems. A designer may program a processor in C that is embedded in some real-time or larger system, such as an intelligent automobile electronics controller. Debugging the system may require the use of a logic analyzer that displays the relationship between interrupt requests from engine sensors and machine-level code.

3. Concepts used in computer architecture find application in other courses. In particular, the way in which the computer provides architectural support for programming languages and operating system facilities reinforces concepts from those areas.

As can be seen by perusing the table of contents of this book, computer organization and architecture encompasses a broad range of design issues and concepts. A good overall understanding of these concepts will be useful both in other areas of study and in future work after graduation.

0.4 INTERNET AND WEB RESOURCES

There are a number of resources available on the Internet and the Web that support this book and help readers keep up with developments in this field.

Web Sites for This Book

There is a Web page for this book at **WilliamStallings.com/COA/COA8e.html**. See the layout at the beginning of this book for a detailed description of that site.

An errata list for this book will be maintained at the Web site and updated as needed. Please e-mail any errors that you spot to me. Errata sheets for my other books are at **WilliamStallings.com**.

I also maintain the Computer Science Student Resource Site, at **WilliamStallings .com/StudentSupport.html**. The purpose of this site is to provide documents, information, and links for computer science students and professionals. Links and documents are organized into six categories:

- **Math:** Includes a basic math refresher, a queuing analysis primer, a number system primer, and links to numerous math sites.
- **How-to:** Advice and guidance for solving homework problems, writing technical reports, and preparing technical presentations.
- **Research resources:** Links to important collections of papers, technical reports, and bibliographies.
- **Miscellaneous:** A variety of other useful documents and links.
- **Computer science careers:** Useful links and documents for those considering a career in computer science.
- **Humor and other diversions:** You have to take your mind off your work once in a while.

Other Web Sites

There are numerous Web sites that provide information related to the topics of this book. In subsequent chapters, lists of specific Web sites can be found in the *Recommended Reading and Web Sites* section. Because the addresses for Web sites tend to change frequently, the book does not provide URLs. For all of the Web sites listed in the book, the appropriate link can be found at this book's Web site. Other links not mentioned in this book will be added to the Web site over time.

The following are Web sites of general interest related to computer organization and architecture:

- **WWW Computer Architecture Home Page:** A comprehensive index to information relevant to computer architecture researchers, including architecture groups and projects, technical organizations, literature, employment, and commercial information
- **CPU Info Center:** Information on specific processors, including technical papers, product information, and latest announcements
- **Processor Emporium:** Interesting and useful collection of information
- **ACM Special Interest Group on Computer Architecture:** Information on SIGARCH activities and publications
- **IEEE Technical Committee on Computer Architecture:** Copies of TCAA newsletter

USENET Newsgroups

A number of USENET newsgroups are devoted to some aspect of computer organization and architecture. As with virtually all USENET groups, there is a high noise-to-signal ratio, but it is worth experimenting to see if any meet your needs. The most relevant are as follows:

- **comp.arch:** A general newsgroup for discussion of computer architecture. Often quite good.
- **comp.arch.arithmetic:** Discusses computer arithmetic algorithms and standards.
- **comp.arch.storage:** Discussion ranges from products to technology to practical usage issues.
- **comp.parallel:** Discusses parallel computers and applications.

PART ONE

Overview

The purpose of Part One is to provide a background and context for the remainder of this book. The fundamental concepts of computer organization and architecture are presented.

ROAD MAP FOR PART ONE

Chapter 1 Introduction

Chapter 1 introduces the concept of the computer as a hierarchical system. A computer can be viewed as a structure of components and its function described in terms of the collective function of its cooperating components. Each component, in turn, can be described in terms of its internal structure and function. The major levels of this hierarchical view are introduced. The remainder of the book is organized, top down, using these levels.

Chapter 2 Computer Evolution and Performance

Chapter 2 serves two purposes. First, a discussion of the history of computer technology is an easy and interesting way of being introduced to the basic concepts of computer organization and architecture. The chapter also addresses the technology trends that have made performance the focus of computer system design and previews the various techniques and strategies that are used to achieve balanced, efficient performance.

CHAPTER 1

INTRODUCTION

This book is about the structure and function of computers. Its purpose is to present, as clearly and completely as possible, the nature and characteristics of modern-day computers. This task is a challenging one for two reasons.

First, there is a tremendous variety of products, from single-chip microcomputers costing a few dollars to supercomputers costing tens of millions of dollars, that can rightly claim the name *computer*. Variety is exhibited not only in cost, but also in size, performance, and application. Second, the rapid pace of change that has always characterized computer technology continues with no letup. These changes cover all aspects of computer technology, from the underlying integrated circuit technology used to construct computer components to the increasing use of parallel organization concepts in combining those components.

In spite of the variety and pace of change in the computer field, certain fundamental concepts apply consistently throughout. To be sure, the application of these concepts depends on the current state of technology and the price/performance objectives of the designer. The intent of this book is to provide a thorough discussion of the fundamentals of computer organization and architecture and to relate these to contemporary computer design issues. This chapter introduces the descriptive approach to be taken.

1.1   ORGANIZATION AND ARCHITECTURE

In describing computers, a distinction is often made between *computer architecture* and *computer organization*. Although it is difficult to give precise definitions for these terms, a consensus exists about the general areas covered by each (e.g., see [VRAN80], [SIEW82], and [BELL78a]); an interesting alternative view is presented in [REDD76].

Computer architecture refers to those attributes of a system visible to a programmer or, put another way, those attributes that have a direct impact on the logical execution of a program. **Computer organization** refers to the operational units and their interconnections that realize the architectural specifications. Examples of architectural attributes include the instruction set, the number of bits used to represent various data types (e.g., numbers, characters), I/O mechanisms, and techniques for addressing memory. Organizational attributes include those hardware details transparent to the programmer, such as control signals; interfaces between the computer and peripherals; and the memory technology used.

For example, it is an architectural design issue whether a computer will have a multiply instruction. It is an organizational issue whether that instruction will be implemented by a special multiply unit or by a mechanism that makes repeated use of the add unit of the system. The organizational decision may be based on the anticipated frequency of use of the multiply instruction, the relative speed of the two approaches, and the cost and physical size of a special multiply unit.

Historically, and still today, the distinction between architecture and organization has been an important one. Many computer manufacturers offer a family of computer models, all with the same architecture but with differences in organization. Consequently, the different models in the family have different price and performance characteristics. Furthermore, a particular architecture may span many years and encompass a number of different computer models, its organization changing with changing technology. A prominent example of both these phenomena is the

IBM System/370 architecture. This architecture was first introduced in 1970 and included a number of models. The customer with modest requirements could buy a cheaper, slower model and, if demand increased, later upgrade to a more expensive, faster model without having to abandon software that had already been developed. Over the years, IBM has introduced many new models with improved technology to replace older models, offering the customer greater speed, lower cost, or both. These newer models retained the same architecture so that the customer's software investment was protected. Remarkably, the System/370 architecture, with a few enhancements, has survived to this day as the architecture of IBM's mainframe product line.

In a class of computers called microcomputers, the relationship between architecture and organization is very close. Changes in technology not only influence organization but also result in the introduction of more powerful and more complex architectures. Generally, there is less of a requirement for generation-to-generation compatibility for these smaller machines. Thus, there is more interplay between organizational and architectural design decisions. An intriguing example of this is the reduced instruction set computer (RISC), which we examine in Chapter 13.

This book examines both computer organization and computer architecture. The emphasis is perhaps more on the side of organization. However, because a computer organization must be designed to implement a particular architectural specification, a thorough treatment of organization requires a detailed examination of architecture as well.

1.2   STRUCTURE AND FUNCTION

A computer is a complex system; contemporary computers contain millions of elementary electronic components. How, then, can one clearly describe them? The key is to recognize the hierarchical nature of most complex systems, including the computer [SIMO96]. A hierarchical system is a set of interrelated subsystems, each of the latter, in turn, hierarchical in structure until we reach some lowest level of elementary subsystem.

The hierarchical nature of complex systems is essential to both their design and their description. The designer need only deal with a particular level of the system at a time. At each level, the system consists of a set of components and their interrelationships. The behavior at each level depends only on a simplified, abstracted characterization of the system at the next lower level. At each level, the designer is concerned with structure and function:

- **Structure:** The way in which the components are interrelated
- **Function:** The operation of each individual component as part of the structure

In terms of description, we have two choices: starting at the bottom and building up to a complete description, or beginning with a top view and decomposing the system into its subparts. Evidence from a number of fields suggests that the top-down approach is the clearest and most effective [WEIN75].

The approach taken in this book follows from this viewpoint. The computer system will be described from the top down. We begin with the major components of a computer, describing their structure and function, and proceed to successively lower layers of the hierarchy. The remainder of this section provides a very brief overview of this plan of attack.

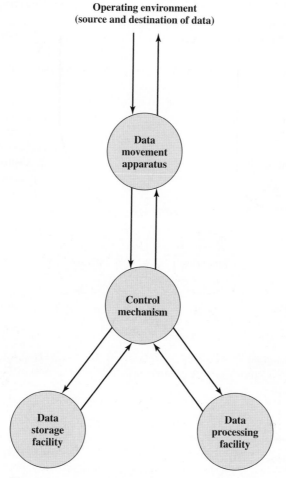

Figure 1.1 A Functional View of the Computer

Function

Both the structure and functioning of a computer are, in essence, simple. Figure 1.1 depicts the basic functions that a computer can perform. In general terms, there are only four:

- Data processing
- Data storage
- Data movement
- Control

The computer, of course, must be able to **process data**. The data may take a wide variety of forms, and the range of processing requirements is broad. However, we shall see that there are only a few fundamental methods or types of data processing.

It is also essential that a computer **store data**. Even if the computer is processing data on the fly (i.e., data come in and get processed, and the results go out immediately), the computer must temporarily store at least those pieces of data that are being

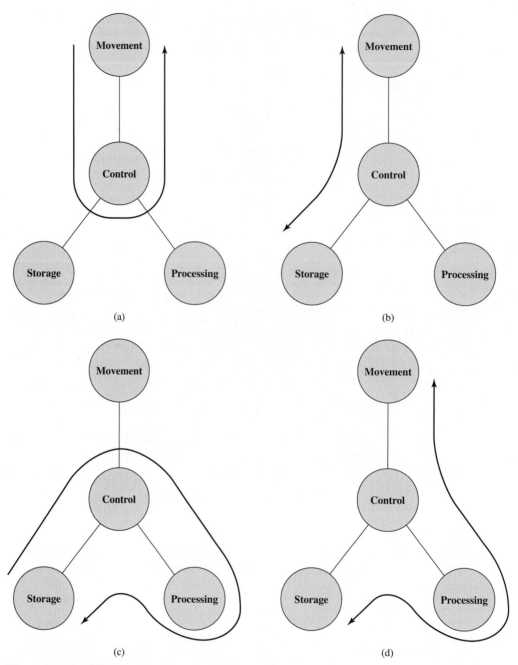

Figure 1.2   Possible Computer Operations

worked on at any given moment. Thus, there is at least a short-term data storage function. Equally important, the computer performs a long-term data storage function.
Files of data are stored on the computer for subsequent retrieval and update.

The computer must be able to **move data** between itself and the outside world.
The computer's operating environment consists of devices that serve as either

sources or destinations of data. When data are received from or delivered to a device that is directly connected to the computer, the process is known as *input–output* (I/O), and the device is referred to as a *peripheral*. When data are moved over longer distances, to or from a remote device, the process is known as *data communications*.

Finally, there must be **control** of these three functions. Ultimately, this control is exercised by the individual(s) who provides the computer with instructions. Within the computer, a control unit manages the computer's resources and orchestrates the performance of its functional parts in response to those instructions.

At this general level of discussion, the number of possible operations that can be performed is few. Figure 1.2 depicts the four possible types of operations. The computer can function as a data movement device (Figure 1.2a), simply transferring data from one peripheral or communications line to another. It can also function as a data storage device (Figure 1.2b), with data transferred from the external environment to computer storage (read) and vice versa (write). The final two diagrams show operations involving data processing, on data either in storage (Figure 1.2c) or en route between storage and the external environment (Figure 1.2d).

The preceding discussion may seem absurdly generalized. It is certainly possible, even at a top level of computer structure, to differentiate a variety of functions, but, to quote [SIEW82],

> There is remarkably little shaping of computer structure to fit the function to be performed. At the root of this lies the general-purpose nature of computers, in which all the functional specialization occurs at the time of programming and not at the time of design.

Structure

Figure 1.3 is the simplest possible depiction of a computer. The computer interacts in some fashion with its external environment. In general, all of its linkages to the external environment can be classified as peripheral devices or communication lines. We will have something to say about both types of linkages.

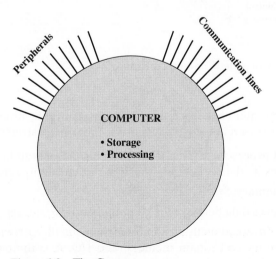

Figure 1.3 The Computer

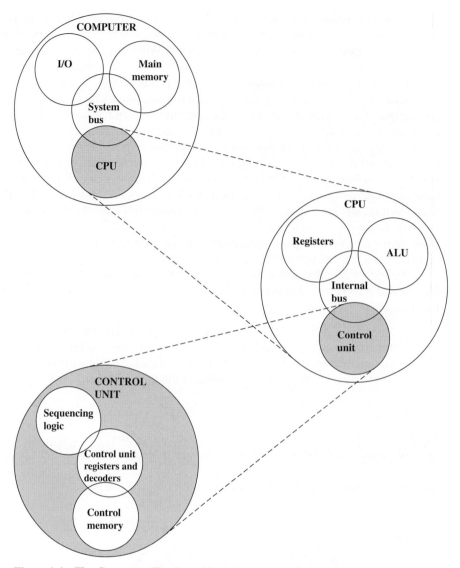

Figure 1.4 The Computer: Top-Level Structure

But of greater concern in this book is the internal structure of the computer itself, which is shown in Figure 1.4. There are four main structural components:

- **Central processing unit (CPU):** Controls the operation of the computer and performs its data processing functions; often simply referred to as **processor**.
- **Main memory:** Stores data.
- **I/O:** Moves data between the computer and its external environment.
- **System interconnection:** Some mechanism that provides for communication among CPU, main memory, and I/O. A common example of system

interconnection is by means of a **system bus**, consisting of a number of conducting wires to which all the other components attach.

There may be one or more of each of the aforementioned components. Traditionally, there has been just a single processor. In recent years, there has been increasing use of multiple processors in a single computer. Some design issues relating to multiple processors crop up and are discussed as the text proceeds; Part Five focuses on such computers.

Each of these components will be examined in some detail in Part Two. However, for our purposes, the most interesting and in some ways the most complex component is the CPU. Its major structural components are as follows:

- **Control unit:** Controls the operation of the CPU and hence the computer
- **Arithmetic and logic unit (ALU):** Performs the computer's data processing functions
- **Registers:** Provides storage internal to the CPU
- **CPU interconnection:** Some mechanism that provides for communication among the control unit, ALU, and registers

Each of these components will be examined in some detail in Part Three, where we will see that complexity is added by the use of parallel and pipelined organizational techniques. Finally, there are several approaches to the implementation of the control unit; one common approach is a *microprogrammed* implementation. In essence, a microprogrammed control unit operates by executing microinstructions that define the functionality of the control unit. With this approach, the structure of the control unit can be depicted, as in Figure 1.4. This structure will be examined in Part Four.

1.3 KEY TERMS AND REVIEW QUESTIONS

Key Terms

arithmetic and logic unit (ALU)	computer organization	processor
central processing unit (CPU)	control unit	registers
computer architecture	input–output (I/O)	system bus
	main memory	

Review Questions

1.1. What, in general terms, is the distinction between computer organization and computer architecture?

1.2. What, in general terms, is the distinction between computer structure and computer function?

1.3. What are the four main functions of a computer?

1.4. List and briefly define the main structural components of a computer.

1.5. List and briefly define the main structural components of a processor.

CHAPTER **2**

COMPUTER EVOLUTION AND PERFORMANCE

KEY POINTS

◆ The evolution of computers has been characterized by increasing processor speed, decreasing component size, increasing memory size, and increasing I/O capacity and speed.

◆ One factor responsible for the great increase in processor speed is the shrinking size of microprocessor components; this reduces the distance between components and hence increases speed. However, the true gains in speed in recent years have come from the organization of the processor, including heavy use of pipelining and parallel execution techniques and the use of speculative execution techniques (tentative execution of future instructions that might be needed). All of these techniques are designed to keep the processor busy as much of the time as possible.

◆ A critical issue in computer system design is balancing the performance of the various elements so that gains in performance in one area are not handicapped by a lag in other areas. In particular, processor speed has increased more rapidly than memory access time. A variety of techniques is used to compensate for this mismatch, including caches, wider data paths from memory to processor, and more intelligent memory chips.

We begin our study of computers with a brief history. This history is itself interesting and also serves the purpose of providing an overview of computer structure and function. Next, we address the issue of performance. A consideration of the need for balanced utilization of computer resources provides a context that is useful throughout the book. Finally, we look briefly at the evolution of the two systems that serve as key examples throughout the book: the Intel x86 and ARM processor families.

2.1 A BRIEF HISTORY OF COMPUTERS

The First Generation: Vacuum Tubes

ENIAC The ENIAC (Electronic Numerical Integrator And Computer), designed and constructed at the University of Pennsylvania, was the world's first general-purpose electronic digital computer. The project was a response to U.S. needs during World War II. The Army's Ballistics Research Laboratory (BRL), an agency responsible for developing range and trajectory tables for new weapons, was having difficulty supplying these tables accurately and within a reasonable time frame. Without these firing tables, the new weapons and artillery were useless to gunners. The BRL employed more than 200 people who, using desktop calculators, solved the necessary ballistics equations. Preparation of the tables for a single weapon would take one person many hours, even days.

John Mauchly, a professor of electrical engineering at the University of Pennsylvania, and John Eckert, one of his graduate students, proposed to build a general-purpose computer using vacuum tubes for the BRL's application. In 1943, the Army accepted this proposal, and work began on the ENIAC. The resulting machine was enormous, weighing 30 tons, occupying 1500 square feet of floor space, and containing more than 18,000 vacuum tubes. When operating, it consumed 140 kilowatts of power. It was also substantially faster than any electromechanical computer, capable of 5000 additions per second.

The ENIAC was a decimal rather than a binary machine. That is, numbers were represented in decimal form, and arithmetic was performed in the decimal system. Its memory consisted of 20 "accumulators," each capable of holding a 10-digit decimal number. A ring of 10 vacuum tubes represented each digit. At any time, only one vacuum tube was in the ON state, representing one of the 10 digits. The major drawback of the ENIAC was that it had to be programmed manually by setting switches and plugging and unplugging cables.

The ENIAC was completed in 1946, too late to be used in the war effort. Instead, its first task was to perform a series of complex calculations that were used to help determine the feasibility of the hydrogen bomb. The use of the ENIAC for a purpose other than that for which it was built demonstrated its general-purpose nature. The ENIAC continued to operate under BRL management until 1955, when it was disassembled.

THE VON NEUMANN MACHINE The task of entering and altering programs for the ENIAC was extremely tedious. The programming process could be facilitated if the program could be represented in a form suitable for storing in memory alongside the data. Then, a computer could get its instructions by reading them from memory, and a program could be set or altered by setting the values of a portion of memory.

This idea, known as the *stored-program concept,* is usually attributed to the ENIAC designers, most notably the mathematician John von Neumann, who was a consultant on the ENIAC project. Alan Turing developed the idea at about the same time. The first publication of the idea was in a 1945 proposal by von Neumann for a new computer, the EDVAC (Electronic Discrete Variable Computer).

In 1946, von Neumann and his colleagues began the design of a new stored-program computer, referred to as the IAS computer, at the Princeton Institute for Advanced Studies. The IAS computer, although not completed until 1952, is the prototype of all subsequent general-purpose computers.

Figure 2.1 shows the general structure of the IAS computer (compare to middle portion of Figure 1.4). It consists of

- A main memory, which stores both data and instructions[1]
- An arithmetic and logic unit (ALU) capable of operating on binary data

---

[1]In this book, unless otherwise noted, the term *instruction* refers to a machine instruction that is directly interpreted and executed by the processor, in contrast to an instruction in a high-level language, such as Ada or C++, which must first be compiled into a series of machine instructions before being executed.

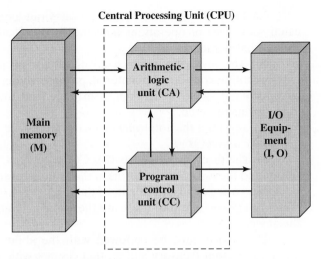

Figure 2.1   Structure of the IAS Computer

- A control unit, which interprets the instructions in memory and causes them to be executed
- Input and output (I/O) equipment operated by the control unit

This structure was outlined in von Neumann's earlier proposal, which is worth quoting at this point [VONN45]:

> 2.2 **First:** Because the device is primarily a computer, it will have to perform the elementary operations of arithmetic most frequently. These are addition, subtraction, multiplication and division. It is therefore reasonable that it should contain specialized organs for just these operations.
>
> It must be observed, however, that while this principle as such is probably sound, the specific way in which it is realized requires close scrutiny. At any rate a *central arithmetical* part of the device will probably have to exist and this constitutes *the first specific part: CA.*
>
> 2.3 **Second:** The logical control of the device, that is, the proper sequencing of its operations, can be most efficiently carried out by a central control organ. If the device is to be *elastic,* that is, as nearly as possible *all purpose,* then a distinction must be made between the specific instructions given for and defining a particular problem, and the general control organs which see to it that these instructions—no matter what they are—are carried out. The former must be stored in some way; the latter are represented by definite operating parts of the device. By the *central control* we mean this latter function only, and the organs which perform it form *the second specific part: CC.*

2.4 **Third:** Any device which is to carry out long and complicated sequences of operations (specifically of calculations) must
have a considerable memory . . .

(b) The instructions which govern a complicated problem
may constitute considerable material, particularly so, if the code is
circumstantial (which it is in most arrangements). This material
must be remembered.

At any rate, the total *memory* constitutes *the third specific
part of the device: M.*

2.6 The three specific parts CA, CC (together C), and M correspond to the *associative* neurons in the human nervous system. It
remains to discuss the equivalents of the *sensory* or *afferent* and the
motor or *efferent* neurons. These are the *input* and *output* organs of
the device.

The device must be endowed with the ability to maintain
input and output (sensory and motor) contact with some specific
medium of this type. The medium will be called the *outside recording medium of the device: R.*

2.7 **Fourth:** The device must have organs to transfer . . . information from R into its specific parts C and M. These organs form
its *input,* the *fourth specific part: I.* It will be seen that it is best to
make all transfers from R (by I) into M and never directly from C.

2.8 **Fifth:** The device must have organs to transfer . . . from its
specific parts C and M into R. These organs form its *output, the fifth
specific part: O.* It will be seen that it is again best to make all transfers from M (by O) into R, and never directly from C.

With rare exceptions, all of today's computers have this same general structure
and function and are thus referred to as von Neumann machines. Thus, it is worthwhile at this point to describe briefly the operation of the IAS computer [BURK46].
Following [HAYE98], the terminology and notation of von Neumann are changed
in the following to conform more closely to modern usage; the examples and illustrations accompanying this discussion are based on that latter text.

The memory of the IAS consists of 1000 storage locations, called *words,* of
40 binary digits (bits) each.[2] Both data and instructions are stored there. Numbers
are represented in binary form, and each instruction is a binary code. Figure 2.2
illustrates these formats. Each number is represented by a sign bit and a 39-bit value.
A word may also contain two 20-bit instructions, with each instruction consisting of
an 8-bit operation code (opcode) specifying the operation to be performed and a
12-bit address designating one of the words in memory (numbered from 0 to 999).

The control unit operates the IAS by fetching instructions from memory and
executing them one at a time. To explain this, a more detailed structure diagram is

---

[2]There is no universal definition of the term *word.* In general, a word is an ordered set of bytes or bits that
is the normal unit in which information may be stored, transmitted, or operated on within a given computer. Typically, if a processor has a fixed-length instruction set, then the instruction length equals the
word length.

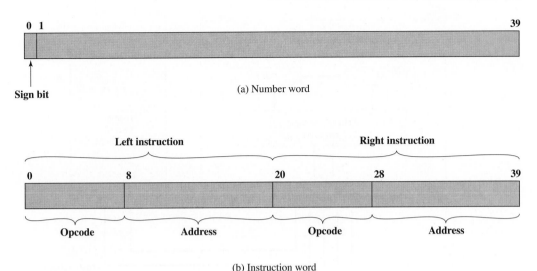

Figure 2.2   IAS Memory Formats

needed, as indicated in Figure 2.3. This figure reveals that both the control unit and the ALU contain storage locations, called *registers*, defined as follows:

- **Memory buffer register (MBR):** Contains a word to be stored in memory or sent to the I/O unit, or is used to receive a word from memory or from the I/O unit.
- **Memory address register (MAR):** Specifies the address in memory of the word to be written from or read into the MBR.
- **Instruction register (IR):** Contains the 8-bit opcode instruction being executed.
- **Instruction buffer register (IBR):** Employed to hold temporarily the right-hand instruction from a word in memory.
- **Program counter (PC):** Contains the address of the next instruction-pair to be fetched from memory.
- **Accumulator (AC) and multiplier quotient (MQ):** Employed to hold temporarily operands and results of ALU operations. For example, the result of multiplying two 40-bit numbers is an 80-bit number; the most significant 40 bits are stored in the AC and the least significant in the MQ.

The IAS operates by repetitively performing an *instruction cycle*, as shown in Figure 2.4. Each instruction cycle consists of two subcycles. During the *fetch cycle*, the opcode of the next instruction is loaded into the IR and the address portion is loaded into the MAR. This instruction may be taken from the IBR, or it can be obtained from memory by loading a word into the MBR, and then down to the IBR, IR, and MAR.

Why the indirection? These operations are controlled by electronic circuitry and result in the use of data paths. To simplify the electronics, there is only one

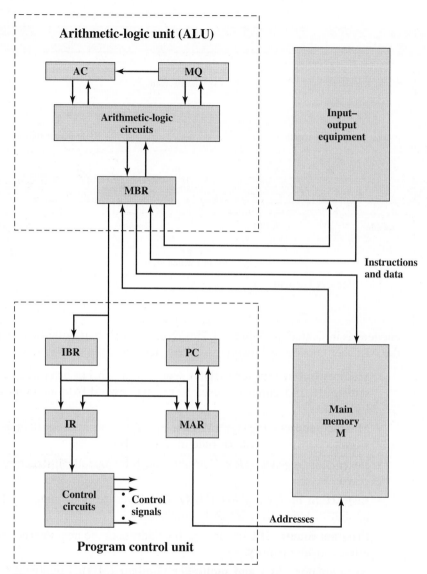

Figure 2.3 Expanded Structure of IAS Computer

register that is used to specify the address in memory for a read or write and only one register used for the source or destination.

Once the opcode is in the IR, the *execute cycle* is performed. Control circuitry interprets the opcode and executes the instruction by sending out the appropriate control signals to cause data to be moved or an operation to be performed by the ALU.

The IAS computer had a total of 21 instructions, which are listed in Table 2.1. These can be grouped as follows:

- **Data transfer:** Move data between memory and ALU registers or between two ALU registers.

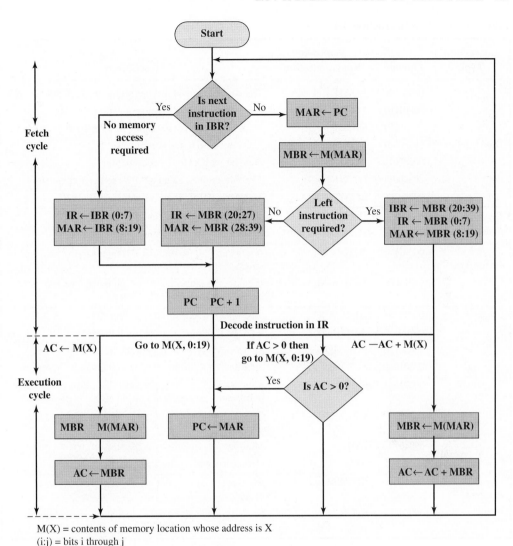

M(X) = contents of memory location whose address is X
(i:j) = bits i through j

Figure 2.4   Partial Flowchart of IAS Operation

- **Unconditional branch:** Normally, the control unit executes instructions in sequence from memory. This sequence can be changed by a branch instruction, which facilitates repetitive operations.
- **Conditional branch:** The branch can be made dependent on a condition, thus allowing decision points.
- **Arithmetic:** Operations performed by the ALU.
- **Address modify:** Permits addresses to be computed in the ALU and then inserted into instructions stored in memory. This allows a program considerable addressing flexibility.

Table 2.1 The IAS Instruction Set

Instruction Type	Opcode	Symbolic Representation	Description
Data transfer	00001010	LOAD MQ	Transfer contents of register MQ to the accumulator AC
	00001001	LOAD MQ,M(X)	Transfer contents of memory location X to MQ
	00100001	STOR M(X)	Transfer contents of accumulator to memory location X
	00000001	LOAD M(X)	Transfer M(X) to the accumulator
	00000010	LOAD −M(X)	Transfer −M(X) to the accumulator
	00000011	LOAD |M(X)|	Transfer absolute value of M(X) to the accumulator
	00000100	LOAD −|M(X)|	Transfer −|M(X)| to the accumulator
Unconditional branch	00001101	JUMP M(X,0:19)	Take next instruction from left half of M(X)
	00001110	JUMP M(X,20:39)	Take next instruction from right half of M(X)
Conditional branch	00001111	JUMP+ M(X,0:19)	If number in the accumulator is nonnegative, take next instruction from left half of M(X)
	00010000	JUMP+ M(X,20:39)	If number in the accumulator is nonnegative, take next instruction from right half of M(X)
Arithmetic	00000101	ADD M(X)	Add M(X) to AC; put the result in AC
	00000111	ADD |M(X)|	Add |M(X)| to AC; put the result in AC
	00000110	SUB M(X)	Subtract M(X) from AC; put the result in AC
	00001000	SUB |M(X)|	Subtract |M(X)| from AC; put the remainder in AC
	00001011	MUL M(X)	Multiply M(X) by MQ; put most significant bits of result in AC, put least significant bits in MQ
	00001100	DIV M(X)	Divide AC by M(X); put the quotient in MQ and the remainder in AC
	00010100	LSH	Multiply accumulator by 2; i.e., shift left one bit position
	00010101	RSH	Divide accumulator by 2; i.e., shift right one position
Address modify	00010010	STOR M(X,8:19)	Replace left address field at M(X) by 12 rightmost bits of AC
	00010011	STOR M(X,28:39)	Replace right address field at M(X) by 12 rightmost bits of AC

Table 2.1 presents instructions in a symbolic, easy-to-read form. Actually, each instruction must conform to the format of Figure 2.2b. The opcode portion (first 8 bits) specifies which of the 21 instructions is to be executed. The address portion (remaining 12 bits) specifies which of the 1000 memory locations is to be involved in the execution of the instruction.

Figure 2.4 shows several examples of instruction execution by the control unit. Note that each operation requires several steps. Some of these are quite elaborate. The multiplication operation requires 39 suboperations, one for each bit position except that of the sign bit.

COMMERCIAL COMPUTERS The 1950s saw the birth of the computer industry with two companies, Sperry and IBM, dominating the marketplace.

In 1947, Eckert and Mauchly formed the Eckert-Mauchly Computer Corporation to manufacture computers commercially. Their first successful machine was the UNIVAC I (Universal Automatic Computer), which was commissioned by the Bureau of the Census for the 1950 calculations. The Eckert-Mauchly Computer Corporation became part of the UNIVAC division of Sperry-Rand Corporation, which went on to build a series of successor machines.

The UNIVAC I was the first successful commercial computer. It was intended for both scientific and commercial applications. The first paper describing the system listed matrix algebraic computations, statistical problems, premium billings for a life insurance company, and logistical problems as a sample of the tasks it could perform.

The UNIVAC II, which had greater memory capacity and higher performance than the UNIVAC I, was delivered in the late 1950s and illustrates several trends that have remained characteristic of the computer industry. First, advances in technology allow companies to continue to build larger, more powerful computers. Second, each company tries to make its new machines *backward compatible*[3] with the older machines. This means that the programs written for the older machines can be executed on the new machine. This strategy is adopted in the hopes of retaining the customer base; that is, when a customer decides to buy a newer machine, he or she is likely to get it from the same company to avoid losing the investment in programs.

The UNIVAC division also began development of the 1100 series of computers, which was to be its major source of revenue. This series illustrates a distinction that existed at one time. The first model, the UNIVAC 1103, and its successors for many years were primarily intended for scientific applications, involving long and complex calculations. Other companies concentrated on business applications, which involved processing large amounts of text data. This split has largely disappeared, but it was evident for a number of years.

IBM, then the major manufacturer of punched-card processing equipment, delivered its first electronic stored-program computer, the 701, in 1953. The 701 was intended primarily for scientific applications [BASH81]. In 1955, IBM introduced the companion 702 product, which had a number of hardware features that suited it to business applications. These were the first of a long series of 700/7000 computers that established IBM as the overwhelmingly dominant computer manufacturer.

The Second Generation: Transistors

The first major change in the electronic computer came with the replacement of the vacuum tube by the transistor. The transistor is smaller, cheaper, and dissipates less heat than a vacuum tube but can be used in the same way as a vacuum tube to construct computers. Unlike the vacuum tube, which requires wires, metal plates, a glass capsule, and a vacuum, the transistor is a *solid-state device,* made from silicon.

The transistor was invented at Bell Labs in 1947 and by the 1950s had launched an electronic revolution. It was not until the late 1950s, however, that fully transistorized computers were commercially available. IBM again was not the first

---

[3]Also called *downward compatible*. The same concept, from the point of view of the older system, is referred to as *upward compatible,* or forward compatible.

Table 2.2 Computer Generations

Generation	Approximate Dates	Technology	Typical Speed (operations per second)
1	1946–1957	Vacuum tube	40,000
2	1958–1964	Transistor	200,000
3	1965–1971	Small and medium scale integration	1,000,000
4	1972–1977	Large scale integration	10,000,000
5	1978–1991	Very large scale integration	100,000,000
6	1991–	Ultra large scale integration	1,000,000,000

company to deliver the new technology. NCR and, more successfully, RCA were the front-runners with some small transistor machines. IBM followed shortly with the 7000 series.

The use of the transistor defines the *second generation* of computers. It has become widely accepted to classify computers into generations based on the fundamental hardware technology employed (Table 2.2). Each new generation is characterized by greater processing performance, larger memory capacity, and smaller size than the previous one.

But there are other changes as well. The second generation saw the introduction of more complex arithmetic and logic units and control units, the use of high-level programming languages, and the provision of *system software* with the computer.

The second generation is noteworthy also for the appearance of the Digital Equipment Corporation (DEC). DEC was founded in 1957 and, in that year, delivered its first computer, the PDP-1. This computer and this company began the minicomputer phenomenon that would become so prominent in the third generation.

THE IBM 7094 From the introduction of the 700 series in 1952 to the introduction of the last member of the 7000 series in 1964, this IBM product line underwent an evolution that is typical of computer products. Successive members of the product line show increased performance, increased capacity, and/or lower cost.

Table 2.3 illustrates this trend. The size of main memory, in multiples of 2^{10} 36-bit words, grew from 2K (1K = 2^{10}) to 32K words,[4] while the time to access one word of memory, the *memory cycle time,* fell from 30 μs to 1.4 μs. The number of opcodes grew from a modest 24 to 185.

The final column indicates the relative execution speed of the central processing unit (CPU). Speed improvements are achieved by improved electronics (e.g., a transistor implementation is faster than a vacuum tube implementation) and more complex circuitry. For example, the IBM 7094 includes an Instruction Backup Register, used to buffer the next instruction. The control unit fetches two adjacent words

---

[4]A discussion of the uses of numerical prefixes, such as kilo and giga, is contained in a supporting document at the Computer Science Student Resource Site at WilliamStallings.com/StudentSupport.html.

Table 2.3   Example members of the IBM 700/7000 Series

Model Number	First Delivery	CPU Technology	Memory Technology	Cycle Time (μs)	Memory Size (K)	Number of Opcodes	Number of Index Registers	Hardwired Floating-Point	I/O Overlap (Channels)	Instruction Fetch Overlap	Speed (relative to 701)
701	1952	Vacuum tubes	Electrostatic tubes	30	2-4	24	0	no	no	no	1
704	1955	Vacuum tubes	Core	12	4-32	80	3	yes	no	no	2.5
709	1958	Vacuum tubes	Core	12	32	140	3	yes	yes	no	4
7090	1960	Transistor	Core	2.18	32	169	3	yes	yes	no	25
7094 I	1962	Transistor	Core	2	32	185	7	yes (double precision)	yes	yes	30
7094 II	1964	Transistor	Core	1.4	32	185	7	yes (double precision)	yes	yes	50

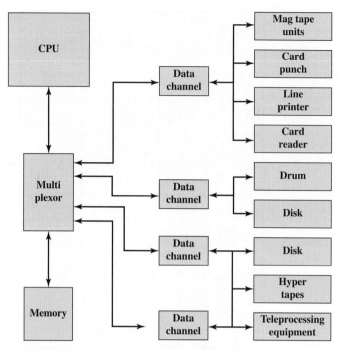

Figure 2.5   An IBM 7094 Configuration

from memory for an instruction fetch. Except for the occurrence of a branching in-struction, which is typically infrequent, this means that the control unit has to access memory for an instruction on only half the instruction cycles. This prefetching sig-nificantly reduces the average instruction cycle time.

The remainder of the columns of Table 2.3 will become clear as the text proceeds.

Figure 2.5 shows a large (many peripherals) configuration for an IBM 7094, which is representative of second-generation computers [BELL71]. Several differ-ences from the IAS computer are worth noting. The most important of these is the use of *data channels*. A data channel is an independent I/O module with its own processor and its own instruction set. In a computer system with such devices, the CPU does not execute detailed I/O instructions. Such instructions are stored in a main memory to be executed by a special-purpose processor in the data channel it-self. The CPU initiates an I/O transfer by sending a control signal to the data channel, instructing it to execute a sequence of instructions in memory. The data channel per-forms its task independently of the CPU and signals the CPU when the operation is complete. This arrangement relieves the CPU of a considerable processing burden.

Another new feature is the *multiplexor,* which is the central termination point for data channels, the CPU, and memory. The multiplexor schedules access to the memory from the CPU and data channels, allowing these devices to act independently.

The Third Generation: Integrated Circuits

A single, self-contained transistor is called a *discrete component*. Throughout the 1950s and early 1960s, electronic equipment was composed largely of discrete components—transistors, resistors, capacitors, and so on. Discrete components were manufactured separately, packaged in their own containers, and soldered or wired together onto masonite-like circuit boards, which were then installed in computers, oscilloscopes, and other electronic equipment. Whenever an electronic device called for a transistor, a little tube of metal containing a pinhead-sized piece of silicon had to be soldered to a circuit board. The entire manufacturing process, from transistor to circuit board, was expensive and cumbersome.

These facts of life were beginning to create problems in the computer industry. Early second-generation computers contained about 10,000 transistors. This figure grew to the hundreds of thousands, making the manufacture of newer, more powerful machines increasingly difficult.

In 1958 came the achievement that revolutionized electronics and started the era of microelectronics: the invention of the integrated circuit. It is the integrated circuit that defines the third generation of computers. In this section we provide a brief introduction to the technology of integrated circuits. Then we look at perhaps the two most important members of the third generation, both of which were introduced at the beginning of that era: the IBM System/360 and the DEC PDP-8.

MICROELECTRONICS Microelectronics means, literally, "small electronics." Since the beginnings of digital electronics and the computer industry, there has been a persistent and consistent trend toward the reduction in size of digital electronic circuits. Before examining the implications and benefits of this trend, we need to say something about the nature of digital electronics. A more detailed discussion is found in Chapter 20.

The basic elements of a digital computer, as we know, must perform storage, movement, processing, and control functions. Only two fundamental types of components are required (Figure 2.6): gates and memory cells. A gate is a device that implements a simple Boolean or logical function, such as IF *A* AND *B* ARE TRUE THEN *C* IS TRUE (AND gate). Such devices are called gates because they control data flow in much the same way that canal gates do. The memory cell is a device that can store one bit of data; that is, the device can be in one of two stable states at any time. By interconnecting large numbers of these fundamental devices, we can construct a computer. We can relate this to our four basic functions as follows:

- **Data storage:** Provided by memory cells.
- **Data processing:** Provided by gates.

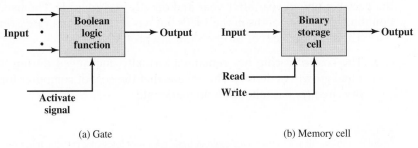

(a) Gate   (b) Memory cell

Figure 2.6 Fundamental Computer Elements

- **Data movement:** The paths among components are used to move data from memory to memory and from memory through gates to memory.
- **Control:** The paths among components can carry control signals. For example, a gate will have one or two data inputs plus a control signal input that activates the gate. When the control signal is ON, the gate performs its function on the data inputs and produces a data output. Similarly, the memory cell will store the bit that is on its input lead when the WRITE control signal is ON and will place the bit that is in the cell on its output lead when the READ control signal is ON.

Thus, a computer consists of gates, memory cells, and interconnections among these elements. The gates and memory cells are, in turn, constructed of simple digital electronic components.

The integrated circuit exploits the fact that such components as transistors, resistors, and conductors can be fabricated from a semiconductor such as silicon. It is merely an extension of the solid-state art to fabricate an entire circuit in a tiny piece of silicon rather than assemble discrete components made from separate pieces of silicon into the same circuit. Many transistors can be produced at the same time on a single wafer of silicon. Equally important, these transistors can be connected with a process of metallization to form circuits.

Figure 2.7 depicts the key concepts in an integrated circuit. A thin *wafer* of silicon is divided into a matrix of small areas, each a few millimeters square. The identical circuit pattern is fabricated in each area, and the wafer is broken up into *chips*. Each chip consists of many gates and/or memory cells plus a number of input and output attachment points. This chip is then packaged in housing that protects it and provides pins for attachment to devices beyond the chip. A number of these packages can then be interconnected on a printed circuit board to produce larger and more complex circuits.

Initially, only a few gates or memory cells could be reliably manufactured and packaged together. These early integrated circuits are referred to as *small-scale integration* (SSI). As time went on, it became possible to pack more and more components on the same chip. This growth in density is illustrated in Figure 2.8; it is one of the most remarkable technological trends ever recorded.[5] This figure reflects the famous Moore's law, which was propounded by Gordon Moore, cofounder of Intel, in 1965 [MOOR65]. Moore observed that the number of transistors that could be put on a single chip was doubling every year and correctly predicted that this pace would continue into the near future. To the surprise of many, including Moore, the pace continued year after year and decade after decade. The pace slowed to a doubling every 18 months in the 1970s but has sustained that rate ever since.

The consequences of Moore's law are profound:

1. The cost of a chip has remained virtually unchanged during this period of rapid growth in density. This means that the cost of computer logic and memory circuitry has fallen at a dramatic rate.

---

[5]Note that the vertical axis uses a log scale. A basic review of log scales is in the math refresher document at the Computer Science Student Support Site at WilliamStallings.com/StudentSupport.html.

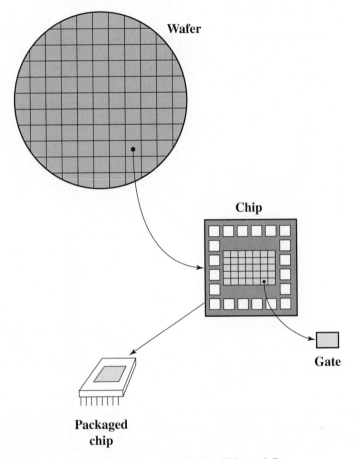

Figure 2.7   Relationship among Wafer, Chip, and Gate

2. Because logic and memory elements are placed closer together on more densely packed chips, the electrical path length is shortened, increasing operating speed.

3. The computer becomes smaller, making it more convenient to place in a variety of environments.

4. There is a reduction in power and cooling requirements.

5. The interconnections on the integrated circuit are much more reliable than solder connections. With more circuitry on each chip, there are fewer interchip connections.

IBM SYSTEM/360 By 1964, IBM had a firm grip on the computer market with its 7000 series of machines. In that year, IBM announced the System/360, a new family of computer products. Although the announcement itself was no surprise, it contained some unpleasant news for current IBM customers: the 360 product line was incompatible with older IBM machines. Thus, the transition to the 360 would be difficult for the current customer base. This was a bold step by IBM, but one IBM felt

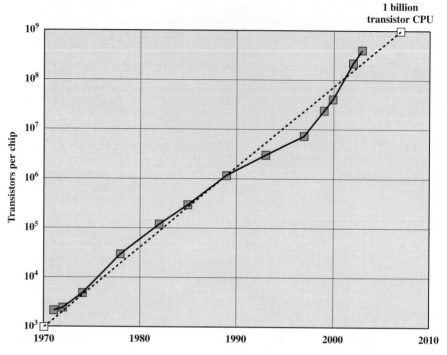

Figure 2.8   Growth in CPU Transistor Count [BOHR03]

was necessary to break out of some of the constraints of the 7000 architecture and to produce a system capable of evolving with the new integrated circuit technology [PADE81, GIFF87]. The strategy paid off both financially and technically. The 360 was the success of the decade and cemented IBM as the overwhelmingly dominant computer vendor, with a market share above 70%. And, with some modifications and extensions, the architecture of the 360 remains to this day the architecture of IBM's mainframe[6] computers. Examples using this architecture can be found throughout this text.

The System/360 was the industry's first planned family of computers. The family covered a wide range of performance and cost. Table 2.4 indicates some of the key characteristics of the various models in 1965 (each member of the family is distinguished by a model number). The models were compatible in the sense that a program written for one model should be capable of being executed by another model in the series, with only a difference in the time it takes to execute.

The concept of a family of compatible computers was both novel and extremely successful. A customer with modest requirements and a budget to match could start with the relatively inexpensive Model 30. Later, if the customer's needs grew, it was possible to upgrade to a faster machine with more memory without

---

[6]The term *mainframe* is used for the larger, most powerful computers other than supercomputers. Typical characteristics of a mainframe are that it supports a large database, has elaborate I/O hardware, and is used in a central data processing facility.

Table 2.4 Key Characteristics of the System/360 Family

Characteristic	Model 30	Model 40	Model 50	Model 65	Model 75
Maximum memory size (bytes)	64K	256K	256K	512K	512K
Data rate from memory (Mbytes/sec)	0.5	0.8	2.0	8.0	16.0
Processor cycle time μs)	1.0	0.625	0.5	0.25	0.2
Relative speed	1	3.5	10	21	50
Maximum number of data channels	3	3	4	6	6
Maximum data rate on one channel (Kbytes/s)	250	400	800	1250	1250

sacrificing the investment in already-developed software. The characteristics of a family are as follows:

- **Similar or identical instruction set:** In many cases, the exact same set of machine instructions is supported on all members of the family. Thus, a program that executes on one machine will also execute on any other. In some cases, the lower end of the family has an instruction set that is a subset of that of the top end of the family. This means that programs can move up but not down.
- **Similar or identical operating system:** The same basic operating system is available for all family members. In some cases, additional features are added to the higher-end members.
- **Increasing speed:** The rate of instruction execution increases in going from lower to higher family members.
- **Increasing number of I/O ports:** The number of I/O ports increases in going from lower to higher family members.
- **Increasing memory size:** The size of main memory increases in going from lower to higher family members.
- **Increasing cost:** At a given point in time, the cost of a system increases in going from lower to higher family members.

How could such a family concept be implemented? Differences were achieved based on three factors: basic speed, size, and degree of simultaneity [STEV64]. For example, greater speed in the execution of a given instruction could be gained by the use of more complex circuitry in the ALU, allowing suboperations to be carried out in parallel. Another way of increasing speed was to increase the width of the data path between main memory and the CPU. On the Model 30, only 1 byte (8 bits) could be fetched from main memory at a time, whereas 8 bytes could be fetched at a time on the Model 75.

The System/360 not only dictated the future course of IBM but also had a profound impact on the entire industry. Many of its features have become standard on other large computers.

DEC PDP-8 In the same year that IBM shipped its first System/360, another momentous first shipment occurred: PDP-8 from Digital Equipment Corporation

(DEC). At a time when the average computer required an air-conditioned room, the PDP-8 (dubbed a minicomputer by the industry, after the miniskirt of the day) was small enough that it could be placed on top of a lab bench or be built into other equipment. It could not do everything the mainframe could, but at $16,000, it was cheap enough for each lab technician to have one. In contrast, the System/360 series of mainframe computers introduced just a few months before cost hundreds of thousands of dollars.

The low cost and small size of the PDP-8 enabled another manufacturer to purchase a PDP-8 and integrate it into a total system for resale. These other manufacturers came to be known as original equipment manufacturers (OEMs), and the OEM market became and remains a major segment of the computer marketplace.

The PDP-8 was an immediate hit and made DEC's fortune. This machine and other members of the PDP-8 family that followed it (see Table 2.5) achieved a production status formerly reserved for IBM computers, with about 50,000 machines sold over the next dozen years. As DEC's official history puts it, the PDP-8 "established the concept of minicomputers, leading the way to a multibillion dollar industry." It also established DEC as the number one minicomputer vendor, and, by the time the PDP-8 had reached the end of its useful life, DEC was the number two computer manufacturer, behind IBM.

In contrast to the central-switched architecture (Figure 2.5) used by IBM on its 700/7000 and 360 systems, later models of the PDP-8 used a structure that is now virtually universal for microcomputers: the bus structure. This is illustrated in Figure 2.9. The PDP-8 bus, called the Omnibus, consists of 96 separate signal paths, used to carry control, address, and data signals. Because all system components share a common set of signal paths, their use must be controlled by the CPU. This architecture is highly flexible, allowing modules to be plugged into the bus to create various configurations.

Later Generations

Beyond the third generation there is less general agreement on defining generations of computers. Table 2.2 suggests that there have been a number of later generations, based on advances in integrated circuit technology. With the introduction of large-scale integration (LSI), more than 1000 components can be placed on a single integrated circuit chip. Very-large-scale integration (VLSI) achieved more than 10,000 components per chip, while current ultra-large-scale integration (ULSI) chips can contain more than one million components.

With the rapid pace of technology, the high rate of introduction of new products, and the importance of software and communications as well as hardware, the classification by generation becomes less clear and less meaningful. It could be said that the commercial application of new developments resulted in a major change in the early 1970s and that the results of these changes are still being worked out. In this section, we mention two of the most important of these results.

SEMICONDUCTOR MEMORY The first application of integrated circuit technology to computers was construction of the processor (the control unit and the arithmetic and logic unit) out of integrated circuit chips. But it was also found that this same technology could be used to construct memories.

Table 2.5 Evolution of the PDP-8 [VOEL88]

Model	First Shipped	Cost of Processor + 4K 12-bit Words of Memory ($1000s)	Data Rate from Memory (words/μsec)	Volume (cubic feet)	Innovations and Improvements
PDP-8	4/65	16.2	1.26	8.0	Automatic wire-wrapping production
PDP-8/5	9/66	8.79	0.08	3.2	Serial instruction implementation
PDP-8/1	4/68	11.6	1.34	8.0	Medium scale integrated circuits
PDP-8/L	11/68	7.0	1.26	2.0	Smaller cabinet
PDP-8/E	3/71	4.99	1.52	2.2	Omnibus
PDP-8/M	6/72	3.69	1.52	1.8	Half-size cabinet with fewer slots than 8/E
PDP-8/A	1/75	2.6	1.34	1.2	Semiconductor memory; floating-point processor

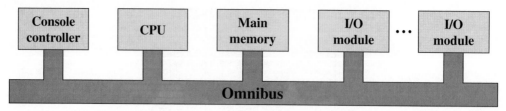

Figure 2.9   PDP-8 Bus Structure

In the 1950s and 1960s, most computer memory was constructed from tiny rings of ferromagnetic material, each about a sixteenth of an inch in diameter. These rings were strung up on grids of fine wires suspended on small screens inside the computer. Magnetized one way, a ring (called a *core*) represented a one; magnetized the other way, it stood for a zero. Magnetic-core memory was rather fast; it took as little as a millionth of a second to read a bit stored in memory. But it was expensive, bulky, and used destructive readout: The simple act of reading a core erased the data stored in it. It was therefore necessary to install circuits to restore the data as soon as it had been extracted.

Then, in 1970, Fairchild produced the first relatively capacious semiconductor memory. This chip, about the size of a single core, could hold 256 bits of memory. It was nondestructive and much faster than core. It took only 70 billionths of a second to read a bit. However, the cost per bit was higher than for that of core.

In 1974, a seminal event occurred: The price per bit of semiconductor memory dropped below the price per bit of core memory. Following this, there has been a continuing and rapid decline in memory cost accompanied by a corresponding increase in physical memory density. This has led the way to smaller, faster machines with memory sizes of larger and more expensive machines from just a few years earlier. Developments in memory technology, together with developments in processor technology to be discussed next, changed the nature of computers in less than a decade. Although bulky, expensive computers remain a part of the landscape, the computer has also been brought out to the "end user," with office machines and personal computers.

Since 1970, semiconductor memory has been through 13 generations: 1K, 4K, 16K, 64K, 256K, 1M, 4M, 16M, 64M, 256M, 1G, 4G, and, as of this writing, 16 Gbits on a single chip ($1K = 2^{10}$, $1M = 2^{20}$, $1G = 2^{30}$). Each generation has provided four times the storage density of the previous generation, accompanied by declining cost per bit and declining access time.

MICROPROCESSORS Just as the density of elements on memory chips has continued to rise, so has the density of elements on processor chips. As time went on, more and more elements were placed on each chip, so that fewer and fewer chips were needed to construct a single computer processor.

A breakthrough was achieved in 1971, when Intel developed its 4004. The 4004 was the first chip to contain *all* of the components of a CPU on a single chip: The microprocessor was born.

The 4004 can add two 4-bit numbers and can multiply only by repeated addition. By today's standards, the 4004 is hopelessly primitive, but it marked the beginning of a continuing evolution of microprocessor capability and power.

This evolution can be seen most easily in the number of bits that the processor deals with at a time. There is no clear-cut measure of this, but perhaps the best measure is the data bus width: the number of bits of data that can be brought into or sent out of the processor at a time. Another measure is the number of bits in the accumulator or in the set of general-purpose registers. Often, these measures coincide, but not always. For example, a number of microprocessors were developed that operate on 16-bit numbers in registers but can only read and write 8 bits at a time.

The next major step in the evolution of the microprocessor was the introduction in 1972 of the Intel 8008. This was the first 8-bit microprocessor and was almost twice as complex as the 4004.

Neither of these steps was to have the impact of the next major event: the introduction in 1974 of the Intel 8080. This was the first general-purpose microprocessor. Whereas the 4004 and the 8008 had been designed for specific applications, the 8080 was designed to be the CPU of a general-purpose microcomputer. Like the 8008, the 8080 is an 8-bit microprocessor. The 8080, however, is faster, has a richer instruction set, and has a large addressing capability.

About the same time, 16-bit microprocessors began to be developed. However, it was not until the end of the 1970s that powerful, general-purpose 16-bit microprocessors appeared. One of these was the 8086. The next step in this trend occurred in 1981, when both Bell Labs and Hewlett-Packard developed 32-bit, single-chip microprocessors. Intel introduced its own 32-bit microprocessor, the 80386, in 1985 (Table 2.6).

Table 2.6   Evolution of Intel Microprocessors

(a) 1970s Processors

	4004	8008	8080	8086	8088
Introduced	1971	1972	1974	1978	1979
Clock speeds	108 kHz	108 kHz	2 MHz	5 MHz, 8 MHz, 10 MHz	5 MHz, 8 MHz
Bus width	4 bits	8 bits	8 bits	16 bits	8 bits
Number of transistors	2,300	3,500	6,000	29,000	29,000
Feature size (μm)	10		6	3	6
Addressable memory	640 Bytes	16 KB	64 KB	1 MB	1 MB

(b) 1980s Processors

	80286	386TM DX	386TM SX	486TM DX CPU
Introduced	1982	1985	1988	1989
Clock speeds	6 MHz–12.5 MHz	16 MHz–33 MHz	16 MHz–33 MHz	25 MHz–50 MHz
Bus width	16 bits	32 bits	16 bits	32 bits
Number of transistors	134,000	275,000	275,000	1.2 million
Feature size (μm)	1.5	1	1	0.8–1
Addressable memory	16 MB	4 GB	16 MB	4 GB
Virtual memory	1 GB	64 TB	64 TB	64 TB
Cache	—	—	—	8 kB

Table 2.6 Continued

(c) 1990s Processors

	486TM SX	Pentium	Pentium Pro	Pentium II
Introduced	1991	1993	1995	1997
Clock speeds	16 MHz–33 MHz	60 MHz–166 MHz,	150 MHz–200 MHz	200 MHz–300 MHz
Bus width	32 bits	32 bits	64 bits	64 bits
Number of transistors	1.185 million	3.1 million	5.5 million	7.5 million
Feature size (μm)	1	0.8	0.6	0.35
Addressable memory	4 GB	4 GB	64 GB	64 GB
Virtual memory	64 TB	64 TB	64 TB	64 TB
Cache	8 kB	8 kB	512 kB L1 and 1 MB L2	512 kB L2

(d) Recent Processors

	Pentium III	Pentium 4	Core 2 Duo	Core 2 Quad
Introduced	1999	2000	2006	2008
Clock speeds	450–660 MHz	1.3–1.8 GHz	1.06–1.2 GHz	3 GHz
Bus sidth	64 bits	64 bits	64 bits	64 bits
Number of transistors	9.5 million	42 million	167 million	820 million
Feature size (nm)	250	180	65	45
Addressable memory	64 GB	64 GB	64 GB	64 GB
Virtual memory	64 TB	64 TB	64 TB	64 TB
Cache	512 kB L2	256 kB L2	2 MB L2	6 MB L2

2.2 DESIGNING FOR PERFORMANCE

Year by year, the cost of computer systems continues to drop dramatically, while the performance and capacity of those systems continue to rise equally dramatically. At a local warehouse club, you can pick up a personal computer for less than $1000 that packs the wallop of an IBM mainframe from 10 years ago. Thus, we have virtually "free" computer power. And this continuing technological revolution has enabled the development of applications of astounding complexity and power. For example, desktop applications that require the great power of today's microprocessor-based systems include

- Image processing
- Speech recognition
- Videoconferencing
- Multimedia authoring
- Voice and video annotation of files
- Simulation modeling

Workstation systems now support highly sophisticated engineering and scientific applications, as well as simulation systems, and have the ability to support image and video applications. In addition, businesses are relying on increasingly powerful servers to handle transaction and database processing and to support massive client/server networks that have replaced the huge mainframe computer centers of yesteryear.

What is fascinating about all this from the perspective of computer organization and architecture is that, on the one hand, the basic building blocks for today's computer miracles are virtually the same as those of the IAS computer from over 50 years ago, while on the other hand, the techniques for squeezing the last iota of performance out of the materials at hand have become increasingly sophisticated.

This observation serves as a guiding principle for the presentation in this book. As we progress through the various elements and components of a computer, two objectives are pursued. First, the book explains the fundamental functionality in each area under consideration, and second, the book explores those techniques required to achieve maximum performance. In the remainder of this section, we highlight some of the driving factors behind the need to design for performance.

Microprocessor Speed

What gives Intel x86 processors or IBM mainframe computers such mind-boggling power is the relentless pursuit of speed by processor chip manufacturers. The evolution of these machines continues to bear out Moore's law, mentioned previously. So long as this law holds, chipmakers can unleash a new generation of chips every three years—with four times as many transistors. In memory chips, this has quadrupled the capacity of dynamic random-access memory (DRAM), still the basic technology for computer main memory, every three years. In microprocessors, the addition of new circuits, and the speed boost that comes from reducing the distances between them, has improved performance four- or fivefold every three years or so since Intel launched its x86 family in 1978.

But the raw speed of the microprocessor will not achieve its potential unless it is fed a constant stream of work to do in the form of computer instructions. Anything that gets in the way of that smooth flow undermines the power of the processor. Accordingly, while the chipmakers have been busy learning how to fabricate chips of greater and greater density, the processor designers must come up with ever more elaborate techniques for feeding the monster. Among the techniques built into contemporary processors are the following:

- **Branch prediction:** The processor looks ahead in the instruction code fetched from memory and predicts which branches, or groups of instructions, are likely to be processed next. If the processor guesses right most of the time, it can prefetch the correct instructions and buffer them so that the processor is kept busy. The more sophisticated examples of this strategy predict not just the next branch but multiple branches ahead. Thus, branch prediction increases the amount of work available for the processor to execute.

- **Data flow analysis:** The processor analyzes which instructions are dependent on each other's results, or data, to create an optimized schedule of instructions.

In fact, instructions are scheduled to be executed when ready, independent of the original program order. This prevents unnecessary delay.

- **Speculative execution:** Using branch prediction and data flow analysis, some processors speculatively execute instructions ahead of their actual appearance in the program execution, holding the results in temporary locations. This enables the processor to keep its execution engines as busy as possible by executing instructions that are likely to be needed.

These and other sophisticated techniques are made necessary by the sheer power of the processor. They make it possible to exploit the raw speed of the processor.

Performance Balance

While processor power has raced ahead at breakneck speed, other critical components of the computer have not kept up. The result is a need to look for performance balance: an adjusting of the organization and architecture to compensate for the mismatch among the capabilities of the various components.

Nowhere is the problem created by such mismatches more critical than in the interface between processor and main memory. Consider the history depicted in Figure 2.10. While processor speed has grown rapidly, the speed with which data can be transferred between main memory and the processor has lagged badly. The interface between processor and main memory is the most crucial pathway in the entire computer because it is responsible for carrying a constant flow of program instructions and data between memory chips and the processor. If memory or the pathway fails to keep pace with the processor's insistent demands, the processor stalls in a wait state, and valuable processing time is lost.

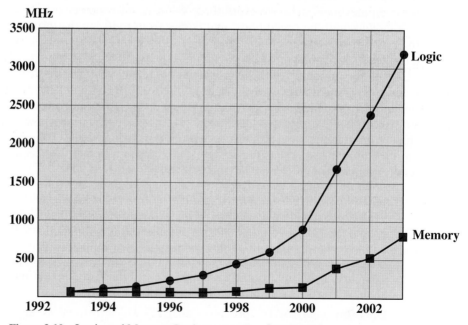

Figure 2.10   Logic and Memory Performance Gap [BORK03]

There are a number of ways that a system architect can attack this problem, all of which are reflected in contemporary computer designs. Consider the following examples:

- Increase the number of bits that are retrieved at one time by making DRAMs "wider" rather than "deeper" and by using wide bus data paths.
- Change the DRAM interface to make it more efficient by including a cache[7] or other buffering scheme on the DRAM chip.
- Reduce the frequency of memory access by incorporating increasingly complex and efficient cache structures between the processor and main memory. This includes the incorporation of one or more caches on the processor chip as well as on an off-chip cache close to the processor chip.
- Increase the interconnect bandwidth between processors and memory by using higher-speed buses and by using a hierarchy of buses to buffer and structure data flow.

Another area of design focus is the handling of I/O devices. As computers become faster and more capable, more sophisticated applications are developed that support the use of peripherals with intensive I/O demands. Figure 2.11 gives some

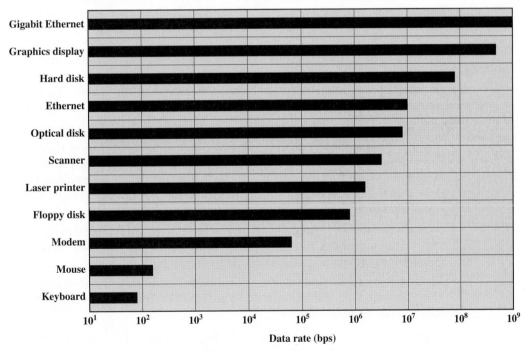

Figure 2.11 Typical I/O Device Data Rates

---

[7]A cache is a relatively small fast memory interposed between a larger, slower memory and the logic that accesses the larger memory. The cache holds recently accessed data, and is designed to speed up subsequent access to the same data. Caches are discussed in Chapter 4.

examples of typical peripheral devices in use on personal computers and workstations. These devices create tremendous data throughput demands. While the current generation of processors can handle the data pumped out by these devices, there remains the problem of getting that data moved between processor and peripheral. Strategies here include caching and buffering schemes plus the use of higher-speed interconnection buses and more elaborate structures of buses. In addition, the use of multiple-processor configurations can aid in satisfying I/O demands.

The key in all this is balance. Designers constantly strive to balance the throughput and processing demands of the processor components, main memory, I/O devices, and the interconnection structures. This design must constantly be rethought to cope with two constantly evolving factors:

- The rate at which performance is changing in the various technology areas (processor, buses, memory, peripherals) differs greatly from one type of element to another.

- New applications and new peripheral devices constantly change the nature of the demand on the system in terms of typical instruction profile and the data access patterns.

Thus, computer design is a constantly evolving art form. This book attempts to present the fundamentals on which this art form is based and to present a survey of the current state of that art.

Improvements in Chip Organization and Architecture

As designers wrestle with the challenge of balancing processor performance with that of main memory and other computer components, the need to increase processor speed remains. There are three approaches to achieving increased processor speed:

- Increase the hardware speed of the processor. This increase is fundamentally due to shrinking the size of the logic gates on the processor chip, so that more gates can be packed together more tightly and to increasing the clock rate. With gates closer together, the propagation time for signals is significantly reduced, enabling a speeding up of the processor. An increase in clock rate means that individual operations are executed more rapidly.

- Increase the size and speed of caches that are interposed between the processor and main memory. In particular, by dedicating a portion of the processor chip itself to the cache, cache access times drop significantly.

- Make changes to the processor organization and architecture that increase the effective speed of instruction execution. Typically, this involves using parallelism in one form or another.

Traditionally, the dominant factor in performance gains has been in increases in clock speed due and logic density. Figure 2.12 illustrates this trend for Intel processor chips. However, as clock speed and logic density increase, a number of obstacles become more significant [INTE04b]:

- **Power:** As the density of logic and the clock speed on a chip increase, so does the power density (Watts/cm^2). The difficulty of dissipating the heat generated

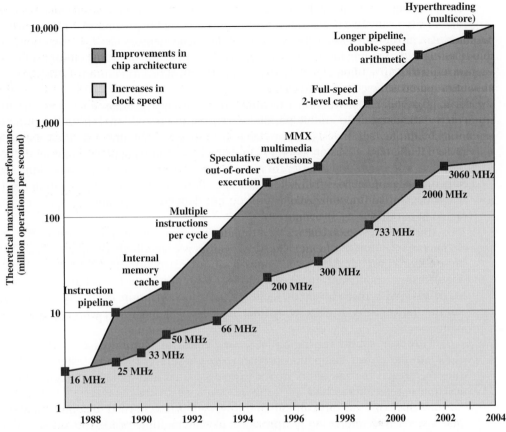

Figure 2.12   Intel Microprocessor Performance [GIBB04]

on high-density, high-speed chips is becoming a serious design issue ([GIBB04], [BORK03]).

- **RC delay:** The speed at which electrons can flow on a chip between transistors is limited by the resistance and capacitance of the metal wires connecting them; specifically, delay increases as the RC product increases. As components on the chip decrease in size, the wire interconnects become thinner, increasing resistance. Also, the wires are closer together, increasing capacitance.

- **Memory latency:** Memory speeds lag processor speeds, as previously discussed.

Thus, there will be more emphasis on organization and architectural approaches to improving performance. Figure 2.12 highlights the major changes that have been made over the years to increase the parallelism and therefore the computational efficiency of processors. These techniques are discussed in later chapters of the book.

Beginning in the late 1980s, and continuing for about 15 years, two main strategies have been used to increase performance beyond what can be achieved simply by increasing clock speed. First, there has been an increase in cache capacity. There are now typically two or three levels of cache between the processor and main memory. As chip density has increased, more of the cache memory has been incorporated on the chip, enabling faster cache access. For example, the original Pentium chip devoted about 10% of on-chip area to a cache. The most recent Pentium 4 chip devotes about half of the chip area to caches.

Second, the instruction execution logic within a processor has become increasingly complex to enable parallel execution of instructions within the processor. Two noteworthy design approaches have been pipelining and superscalar. A pipeline works much as an assembly line in a manufacturing plant enabling different stages of execution of different instructions to occur at the same time along the pipeline. A superscalar approach in essence allows multiple pipelines within a single processor so that instructions that do not depend on one another can be executed in parallel.

Both of these approaches are reaching a point of diminishing returns. The internal organization of contemporary processors is exceedingly complex and is able to squeeze a great deal of parallelism out of the instruction stream. It seems likely that further significant increases in this direction will be relatively modest [GIBB04]. With three levels of cache on the processor chip, each level providing substantial capacity, it also seems that the benefits from the cache are reaching a limit.

However, simply relying on increasing clock rate for increased performance runs into the power dissipation problem already referred to. The faster the clock rate, the greater the amount of power to be dissipated, and some fundamental physical limits are being reached.

With all of these difficulties in mind, designers have turned to a fundamentally new approach to improving performance: placing multiple processors on the same chip, with a large shared cache. The use of multiple processors on the same chip, also referred to as multiple cores, or **multicore**, provides the potential to increase performance without increasing the clock rate. Studies indicate that, within a processor, the increase in performance is roughly proportional to the square root of the increase in complexity [BORK03]. But if the software can support the effective use of multiple processors, then doubling the number of processors almost doubles performance. Thus, the strategy is to use two simpler processors on the chip rather than one more complex processor.

In addition, with two processors, larger caches are justified. This is important because the power consumption of memory logic on a chip is much less than that of processing logic. In coming years, we can expect that most new processor chips will have multiple processors.

2.3 THE EVOLUTION OF THE INTEL x86 ARCHITECTURE

Throughout this book, we rely on many concrete examples of computer design and implementation to illustrate concepts and to illuminate trade-offs. Most of the time, the book relies on examples from two computer families: the Intel x86 and the ARM architecture. The current x86 offerings represent the results of decades of design effort on complex instruction set computers (CISCs). The x86 incorporates the sophisticated design principles once found only on mainframes and supercomputers and serves as an excellent example of CISC design. An alternative approach to processor design in the reduced instruction set computer (RISC). The ARM architecture is used in a wide variety of embedded systems and is one of the most powerful and best-designed RISC-based systems on the market.

In this section and the next, we provide a brief overview of these two systems.

In terms of market share, Intel has ranked as the number one maker of microprocessors for non-embedded systems for decades, a position it seems unlikely to yield. The evolution of its flagship microprocessor product serves as a good indicator of the evolution of computer technology in general.

Table 2.6 shows that evolution. Interestingly, as microprocessors have grown faster and much more complex, Intel has actually picked up the pace. Intel used to develop microprocessors one after another, every four years. But Intel hopes to keep rivals at bay by trimming a year or two off this development time, and has done so with the most recent x86 generations.

It is worthwhile to list some of the highlights of the evolution of the Intel product line:

- **8080:** The world's first general-purpose microprocessor. This was an 8-bit machine, with an 8-bit data path to memory. The 8080 was used in the first personal computer, the Altair.
- **8086:** A far more powerful, 16-bit machine. In addition to a wider data path and larger registers, the 8086 sported an instruction cache, or queue, that prefetches a few instructions before they are executed. A variant of this processor, the 8088, was used in IBM's first personal computer, securing the success of Intel. The 8086 is the first appearance of the x86 architecture.
- **80286:** This extension of the 8086 enabled addressing a 16-MByte memory instead of just 1 MByte.
- **80386:** Intel's first 32-bit machine, and a major overhaul of the product. With a 32-bit architecture, the 80386 rivaled the complexity and power of minicomputers and mainframes introduced just a few years earlier. This was the first Intel processor to support multitasking, meaning it could run multiple programs at the same time.
- **80486:** The 80486 introduced the use of much more sophisticated and powerful cache technology and sophisticated instruction pipelining. The 80486 also offered a built-in math coprocessor, offloading complex math operations from the main CPU.
- **Pentium:** With the Pentium, Intel introduced the use of superscalar techniques, which allow multiple instructions to execute in parallel.
- **Pentium Pro:** The Pentium Pro continued the move into superscalar organization begun with the Pentium, with aggressive use of register renaming, branch prediction, data flow analysis, and speculative execution.
- **Pentium II:** The Pentium II incorporated Intel MMX technology, which is designed specifically to process video, audio, and graphics data efficiently.

- **Pentium III:** The Pentium III incorporates additional floating-point instructions to support 3D graphics software.
- **Pentium 4:** The Pentium 4 includes additional floating-point and other enhancements for multimedia.[8]
- **Core:** This is the first Intel x86 microprocessor with a dual core, referring to the implementation of two processors on a single chip.
- **Core 2:** The Core 2 extends the architecture to 64 bits. The Core 2 Quad provides four processors on a single chip.

Over 30 years after its introduction in 1978, the x86 architecture continues to dominate the processor market outside of embedded systems. Although the organization and technology of the x86 machines has changed dramatically over the decades, the instruction set architecture has evolved to remain backward compatible with earlier versions. Thus, any program written on an older version of the x86 architecture can execute on newer versions. All changes to the instruction set architecture have involved additions to the instruction set, with no subtractions. The rate of change has been the addition of roughly one instruction per month added to the architecture over the 30 years [ANTH08], so that there are now over 500 instructions in the instruction set.

The x86 provides an excellent illustration of the advances in computer hardware over the past 30 years. The 1978 8086 was introduced with a clock speed of 5 MHz and had 29,000 transistors. A quad-core Intel Core 2 introduced in 2008 operates at 3 GHz, a speedup of a factor of 600, and has 820 million transistors, about 28,000 times as many as the 8086. Yet the Core 2 is in only a slightly larger package than the 8086 and has a comparable cost.

2.4   EMBEDDED SYSTEMS AND THE ARM

The ARM architecture refers to a processor architecture that has evolved from RISC design principles and is used in embedded systems. Chapter 13 examines RISC design principles in detail. In this section, we give a brief overview of the concept of embedded systems, and then look at the evolution of the ARM.

Embedded Systems

The term *embedded system* refers to the use of electronics and software within a product, as opposed to a general-purpose computer, such as a laptop or desktop system. The following is a good general definition:[9]

> **Embedded system.** A combination of computer hardware and software, and perhaps additional mechanical or other parts, designed to perform a dedicated function. In many cases, embedded systems are part of a larger system or product, as in the case of an antilock braking system in a car.

---

[8]With the Pentium 4, Intel switched from Roman numerals to Arabic numerals for model numbers.
[9]Michael Barr, *Embedded Systems Glossary*. Netrino Technical Library. http://www.netrino.com/Publications/Glossary/index.php

Table 2.7   Examples of Embedded Systems and Their Markets [NOER05]

Market	Embedded Device
Automotive	Ignition system Engine control Brake system
Consumer electronics	Digital and analog televisions Set-top boxes (DVDs, VCRs, Cable boxes) Personal digital assistants (PDAs) Kitchen appliances (refrigerators, toasters, microwave ovens) Automobiles Toys/games Telephones/cell phones/pagers Cameras Global positioning systems
Industrial control	Robotics and controls systems for manufacturing Sensors
Medical	Infusion pumps Dialysis machines Prosthetic devices Cardiac monitors
Office automation	Fax machine Photocopier Printers Monitors Scanners

Embedded systems far outnumber general-purpose computer systems, encompassing a broad range of applications (Table 2.7). These systems have widely varying requirements and constraints, such as the following [GRIM05]:

- Small to large systems, implying very different cost constraints, thus different needs for optimization and reuse
- Relaxed to very strict requirements and combinations of different quality requirements, for example, with respect to safety, reliability, real-time, flexibility, and legislation
- Short to long life times
- Different environmental conditions in terms of, for example, radiation, vibrations, and humidity
- Different application characteristics resulting in static versus dynamic loads, slow to fast speed, compute versus interface intensive tasks, and/or combinations thereof
- Different models of computation ranging from discrete-event systems to those involving continuous time dynamics (usually referred to as hybrid systems)

Often, embedded systems are tightly coupled to their environment. This can give rise to real-time constraints imposed by the need to interact with the environment. Constraints, such as required speeds of motion, required precision of measurement, and required time durations, dictate the timing of software operations.

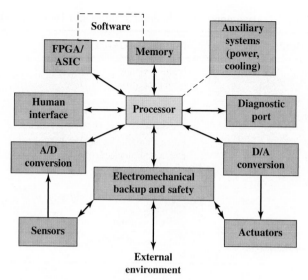

Figure 2.13 Possible Organization of an Embedded System

If multiple activities must be managed simultaneously, this imposes more complex real-time constraints.

Figure 2.13, based on [KOOP96], shows in general terms an embedded system organization. In addition to the processor and memory, there are a number of elements that differ from the typical desktop or laptop computer:

- There may be a variety of interfaces that enable the system to measure, manipulate, and otherwise interact with the external environment.
- The human interface may be as simple as a flashing light or as complicated as real-time robotic vision.
- The diagnostic port may be used for diagnosing the system that is being controlled—not just for diagnosing the computer.
- Special-purpose field programmable (FPGA), application specific (ASIC), or even nondigital hardware may be used to increase performance or safety.
- Software often has a fixed function and is specific to the application.

ARM Evolution

ARM is a family of RISC-based microprocessors and microcontrollers designed by ARM Inc., Cambridge, England. The company doesn't make processors but instead designs microprocessor and multicore architectures and licenses them to manufacturers. ARM chips are high-speed processors that are known for their small die size and low power requirements. They are widely used in PDAs and other handheld devices, including games and phones as well as a large variety of consumer products. ARM chips are the processors in Apple's popular iPod and iPhone devices. ARM is probably the most widely used embedded processor architecture and indeed the most widely used processor architecture of any kind in the world.

The origins of ARM technology can be traced back to the British-based Acorn Computers company. In the early 1980s, Acorn was awarded a contract by the

Table 2.8   ARM Evolution

Family	Notable Features	Cache	Typical MIPS @ MHz
ARM1	32-bit RISC	None	
ARM2	Multiply and swap instructions; Integrated memory management unit, graphics and I/O processor	None	7 MIPS @ 12 MHz
ARM3	First use of processor cache	4 KB unified	12 MIPS @ 25 MHz
ARM6	First to support 32-bit addresses; floating-point unit	4 KB unified	28 MIPS @ 33 MHz
ARM7	Integrated SoC	8 KB unified	60 MIPS @ 60 MHz
ARM8	5-stage pipeline; static branch prediction	8 KB unified	84 MIPS @ 72 MHz
ARM9		16 KB/16 KB	300 MIPS @ 300 MHz
ARM9E	Enhanced DSP instructions	16 KB/16 KB	220 MIPS @ 200 MHz
ARM10E	6-stage pipeline	32 KB/32 KB	
ARM11	9-stage pipeline	Variable	740 MIPS @ 665 MHz
Cortex	13-stage superscalar pipeline	Variable	2000 MIPS @ 1 GHz
XScale	Applications processor; 7-stage pipeline	32 KB/32 KB L1 512 KB L2	1000 MIPS @ 1.25 GHz

DSP = digital signal processor
SoC = system on a chip

British Broadcasting Corporation (BBC) to develop a new microcomputer architecture for the BBC Computer Literacy Project. The success of this contract enabled Acorn to go on to develop the first commercial RISC processor, the Acorn RISC Machine (ARM). The first version, ARM1, became operational in 1985 and was used for internal research and development as well as being used as a coprocessor in the BBC machine. Also in 1985, Acorn released the ARM2, which had greater functionality and speed within the same physical space. Further improvements were achieved with the release in 1989 of the ARM3.

Throughout this period, Acorn used the company VLSI Technology to do the actual fabrication of the processor chips. VLSI was licensed to market the chip on its own and had some success in getting other companies to use the ARM in their products, particularly as an embedded processor.

The ARM design matched a growing commercial need for a high-performance, low-power-consumption, small-size and low-cost processor for embedded applications. But further development was beyond the scope of Acorns capabilities. Accordingly, a new company was organized, with Acorn, VLSI, and Apple Computer as founding partners, known as ARM Ltd. The Acorn RISC Machine became the Advanced RISC Machine.[10] The new company's first offering, an improvement on the ARM3, was designated ARM6. Subsequently, the company has introduced a number of new families, with increasing functionality and performance. Table 2.8

---

[10]The company dropped the designation *Advanced RISC Machine* in the late 1990s. It is now simply known as the ARM architecture.

shows some characteristics of the various ARM architecture families. The numbers in this table are only approximate guides; actual values vary widely for different implementations.

According to the ARM Web site arm.com, ARM processors are designed to meet the needs of three system categories:

- **Embedded real-time systems:** Systems for storage, automotive body and power-train, industrial, and networking applications
- **Application platforms:** Devices running open operating systems including Linux, Palm OS, Symbian OS, and Windows CE in wireless, consumer entertainment and digital imaging applications
- **Secure applications:** Smart cards, SIM cards, and payment terminals

2.5 PERFORMANCE ASSESSMENT

In evaluating processor hardware and setting requirements for new systems, performance is one of the key parameters to consider, along with cost, size, security, reliability, and, in some cases power consumption.

It is difficult to make meaningful performance comparisons among different processors, even among processors in the same family. Raw speed is far less important than how a processor performs when executing a given application. Unfortunately, application performance depends not just on the raw speed of the processor, but on the instruction set, choice of implementation language, efficiency of the compiler, and skill of the programming done to implement the application.

We begin this section with a look at some traditional measures of processor speed. Then we examine the most common approach to assessing processor and computer system performance. We follow this with a discussion of how to average results from multiple tests. Finally, we look at the insights produced by considering Amdahl's law.

Clock Speed and Instructions per Second

THE SYSTEM CLOCK Operations performed by a processor, such as fetching an instruction, decoding the instruction, performing an arithmetic operation, and so on, are governed by a system clock. Typically, all operations begin with the pulse of the clock. Thus, at the most fundamental level, the speed of a processor is dictated by the pulse frequency produced by the clock, measured in cycles per second, or Hertz (Hz).

Typically, clock signals are generated by a quartz crystal, which generates a constant signal wave while power is applied. This wave is converted into a digital voltage pulse stream that is provided in a constant flow to the processor circuitry (Figure 2.14). For example, a 1-GHz processor receives 1 billion pulses per second. The rate of pulses is known as the **clock rate**, or **clock speed**. One increment, or pulse, of the clock is referred to as a **clock cycle**, or a **clock tick**. The time between pulses is the **cycle time**.

The clock rate is not arbitrary, but must be appropriate for the physical layout of the processor. Actions in the processor require signals to be sent from one processor element to another. When a signal is placed on a line inside the processor,

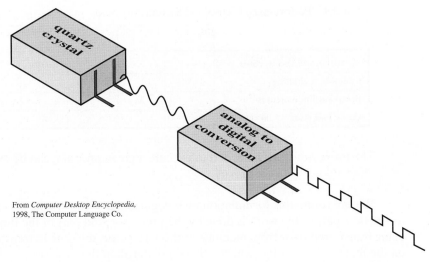

From *Computer Desktop Encyclopedia*,
1998, The Computer Language Co.

Figure 2.14   System Clock

it takes some finite amount of time for the voltage levels to settle down so that an accurate value (1 or 0) is available. Furthermore, depending on the physical layout of the processor circuits, some signals may change more rapidly than others. Thus, operations must be synchronized and paced so that the proper electrical signal (voltage) values are available for each operation.

The execution of an instruction involves a number of discrete steps, such as fetching the instruction from memory, decoding the various portions of the instruction, loading and storing data, and performing arithmetic and logical operations. Thus, most instructions on most processors require multiple clock cycles to complete. Some instructions may take only a few cycles, while others require dozens. In addition, when pipelining is used, multiple instructions are being executed simultaneously. Thus, a straight comparison of clock speeds on different processors does not tell the whole story about performance.

INSTRUCTION EXECUTION RATE A processor is driven by a clock with a constant frequency f or, equivalently, a constant cycle time τ, where $\tau = 1/f$. Define the instruction count, I_c, for a program as the number of machine instructions executed for that program until it runs to completion or for some defined time interval. Note that this is the number of instruction executions, not the number of instructions in the object code of the program. An important parameter is the average cycles per instruction CPI for a program. If all instructions required the same number of clock cycles, then CPI would be a constant value for a processor. However, on any give processor, the number of clock cycles required varies for different types of instructions, such as load, store, branch, and so on. Let CPI_i be the number of cycles required for instruction type i. and I_i be the number of executed instructions of type i for a given program. Then we can calculate an overall CPI as follows:

$$CPI = \frac{\sum_{i=1}^{n}(CPI_i \times I_i)}{I_c} \tag{2.1}$$

Table 2.9   Performance Factors and System Attributes

	I_c	p	m	k	τ
Instruction set architecture	X	X			
Compiler technology	X	X	X		
Processor implementation		X			X
Cache and memory hierarchy				X	X

The processor time T needed to execute a given program can be expressed as

$$T = I_c \times CPI \times \tau$$

We can refine this formulation by recognizing that during the execution of an instruction, part of the work is done by the processor, and part of the time a word is being transferred to or from memory. In this latter case, the time to transfer depends on the memory cycle time, which may be greater than the processor cycle time. We can rewrite the preceding equation as

$$T = I_c \times [p + (m \times k)] \times \tau$$

where p is the number of processor cycles needed to decode and execute the instruction, m is the number of memory references needed, and k is the ratio between memory cycle time and processor cycle time. The five performance factors in the preceding equation (I_c, p, m, k, τ) are influenced by four system attributes: the design of the instruction set (known as *instruction set architecture*), compiler technology (how effective the compiler is in producing an efficient machine language program from a high-level language program), processor implementation, and cache and memory hierarchy. Table 2.9, based on [HWAN93], is a matrix in which one dimension shows the five performance factors and the other dimension shows the four system attributes. An X in a cell indicates a system attribute that affects a performance factor.

A common measure of performance for a processor is the rate at which instructions are executed, expressed as millions of instructions per second (MIPS), referred to as the **MIPS rate**. We can express the MIPS rate in terms of the clock rate and CPI as follows:

$$\text{MIPS rate} = \frac{I_c}{T \times 10^6} = \frac{f}{CPI \times 10^6} \tag{2.2}$$

For example, consider the execution of a program which results in the execution of 2 million instructions on a 400-MHz processor. The program consists of four major types of instructions. The instruction mix and the CPI for each instruction type are given below based on the result of a program trace experiment:

Instruction Type	CPI	Instruction Mix
Arithmetic and logic	1	60%
Load/store with cache hit	2	18%
Branch	4	12%
Memory reference with cache miss	8	10%

The average CPI when the program is executed on a uniprocessor with the above trace results is $CPI = 0.6 + (2 \times 0.18) + (4 \times 0.12) + (8 \times 0.1) = 2.24$. The corresponding MIPS rate is $(400 \times 10^6)/(2.24 \times 10^6) \approx 178$.

Another common performance measure deals only with floating-point instructions. These are common in many scientific and game applications. Floating-point performance is expressed as millions of floating-point operations per second (MFLOPS), defined as follows:

$$\text{MFLOPS rate} = \frac{\textit{Number of executed floating-point operations in a program}}{\textit{Execution time} \times 10^6}$$

Benchmarks

Measures such as MIPS and MFLOPS have proven inadequate to evaluating the performance of processors. Because of differences in instruction sets, the instruction execution rate is not a valid means of comparing the performance of different architectures. For example, consider this high-level language statement:

```
A = B + C    /* assume all quantities in main memory */
```

With a traditional instruction set architecture, referred to as a complex instruction set computer (CISC), this instruction can be compiled into one processor instruction:

```
add    mem(B), mem(C), mem (A)
```

On a typical RISC machine, the compilation would look something like this:

```
load   mem(B), reg(1);
load   mem(C), reg(2);
add    reg(1), reg(2), reg(3);
store  reg(3), mem (A)
```

Because of the nature of the RISC architecture (discussed in Chapter 13), both machines may execute the original high-level language instruction in about the same time. If this example is representative of the two machines, then if the CISC machine is rated at 1 MIPS, the RISC machine would be rated at 4 MIPS. But both do the same amount of high-level language work in the same amount of time.

Further, the performance of a given processor on a given program may not be useful in determining how that processor will perform on a very different type of application. Accordingly, beginning in the late 1980s and early 1990s, industry and academic interest shifted to measuring the performance of systems using a set of benchmark programs. The same set of programs can be run on different machines and the execution times compared.

[WEIC90] lists the following as desirable characteristics of a benchmark program:

1. It is written in a high-level language, making it portable across different machines.

2. It is representative of a particular kind of programming style, such as systems programming, numerical programming, or commercial programming.

3. It can be measured easily.
4. It has wide distribution.

SPEC BENCHMARKS The common need in industry and academic and research communities for generally accepted computer performance measurements has led to the development of standardized benchmark suites. A benchmark suite is a collection of programs, defined in a high-level language, that together attempt to provide a representative test of a computer in a particular application or system programming area. The best known such collection of benchmark suites is defined and maintained by the System Performance Evaluation Corporation (SPEC), an industry consortium. SPEC performance measurements are widely used for comparison and research purposes.

The best known of the SPEC benchmark suites is SPEC CPU2006. This is the industry standard suite for processor-intensive applications. That is, SPEC CPU2006 is appropriate for measuring performance for applications that spend most of their time doing computation rather than I/O. The CPU2006 suite is based on existing applications that have already been ported to a wide variety of platforms by SPEC industry members. It consists of 17 floating-point programs written in C, C++, and Fortran; and 12 integer programs written in C and C++. The suite contains over 3 million lines of code. This is the fifth generation of processor-intensive suites from SPEC, replacing SPEC CPU2000, SPEC CPU95, SPEC CPU92, and SPEC CPU89 [HENN07].

Other SPEC suites include the following:

- **SPECjvm98:** Intended to evaluate performance of the combined hardware and software aspects of the Java Virtual Machine (JVM) client platform
- **SPECjbb2000 (Java Business Benchmark):** A benchmark for evaluating server-side Java-based electronic commerce applications
- **SPECweb99:** Evaluates the performance of World Wide Web (WWW) servers
- **SPECmail2001:** Designed to measure a system's performance acting as a mail server

AVERAGING RESULTS To obtain a reliable comparison of the performance of various computers, it is preferable to run a number of different benchmark programs on each machine and then average the results. For example, if m different benchmark program, then a simple **arithmetic mean** can be calculated as follows:

$$R_A = \frac{1}{m} \sum_{i=1}^{m} R_i \tag{2.3}$$

where R_i is the high-level language instruction execution rate for the ith benchmark program.

An alternative is to take the **harmonic mean**:

$$R_H = \frac{m}{\sum_{i=1}^{m} \frac{1}{R_i}} \tag{2.4}$$

Ultimately, the user is concerned with the execution time of a system, not its execution rate. If we take arithmetic mean of the instruction rates of various benchmark programs, we get a result that is proportional to the sum of the inverses of execution times. But this is not inversely proportional to the sum of execution times. In other words, the arithmetic mean of the instruction rate does not cleanly relate to execution time. On the other hand, the harmonic mean instruction rate is the inverse of the average execution time.

SPEC benchmarks do not concern themselves with instruction execution rates. Rather, two fundamental metrics are of interest: a speed metric and a rate metric. The **speed metric** measures the ability of a computer to complete a single task. SPEC defines a base runtime for each benchmark program using a reference machine. Results for a system under test are reported as the **ratio** of the reference run time to the system run time. The ratio is calculated as follows:

$$r_i = \frac{Tref_i}{Tsut_i} \tag{2.5}$$

where $Tref_i$ is the execution time of benchmark program i on the reference system and $Tsut_i$ is the execution time of benchmark program i on the system under test.

As an example of the calculation and reporting, consider the Sun Blade 6250, which consists of two chips with four cores, or processors, per chip. One of the SPEC CPU2006 integer benchmark is 464.h264ref. This is a reference implementation of H.264/AVC (Advanced Video Coding), the latest state-of-the-art video compression standard. The Sun system executes this program in 934 seconds. The reference implementation requires 22,135 seconds. The ratio is calculated as: 22136/934 = 23.7.

Because the time for the system under test is in the denominator, the larger the ratio, the higher the speed. An overall performance measure for the system under test is calculated by averaging the values for the ratios for all 12 integer benchmarks. SPEC specifies the use of a **geometric mean**, defined as follows:

$$r_G = \left(\prod_{i=1}^{n} r_i \right)^{1/n} \tag{2.6}$$

where r_i is the ratio for the ith benchmark program. For the Sun Blade 6250, the SPEC integer speed ratios were reported as follows:

Benchmark	Ratio	Benchmark	Ratio
400.perlbench	17.5	458.sjeng	17.0
401.bzip2	14.0	462.libquantum	31.3
403.gcc	13.7	464.h264ref	23.7
429.mcf	17.6	471.omnetpp	9.23
445.gobmk	14.7	473.astar	10.9
456.hmmer	18.6	483.xalancbmk	14.7

The speed metric is calculated by taking the twelfth root of the product of the ratios:

$$(17.5 \times 14 \times 13.7 \times 17.6 \times 14.7 \times 18.6 \times 17 \times 31.3 \times 23.7 \times 9.23 \times 10.9 \times 14.7)^{1/12} = 18.5$$

The **rate metric** measures the throughput or rate of a machine carrying out a number of tasks. For the rate metrics, multiple copies of the benchmarks are run simultaneously. Typically, the number of copies is the same as the number of processors on the machine. Again, a ratio is used to report results, although the calculation is more complex. The ratio is calculated as follows:

$$r_i = \frac{N \times Tref_i}{Tsut_i} \tag{2.7}$$

where $Tref_i$ is the reference execution time for benchmark i, N is the number of copies of the program that are run simultaneously, and $Tsut_i$ is the elapsed time from the start of the execution of the program on all N processors of the system under test until the completion of all the copies of the program. Again, a geometric mean is calculated to determine the overall performance measure.

SPEC chose to use a geometric mean because it is the most appropriate for normalized numbers, such as ratios. [FLEM86] demonstrates that the geometric mean has the property of performance relationships consistently maintained regardless of the computer that is used as the basis for normalization.

Amdahl's Law

When considering system performance, computer system designers look for ways to improve performance by improvement in technology or change in design. Examples include the use of parallel processors, the use of a memory cache hierarchy, and speedup in memory access time and I/O transfer rate due to technology improvements. In all of these cases, it is important to note that a speedup in one aspect of the technology or design does not result in a corresponding improvement in performance. This limitation is succinctly expressed by Amdahl's law.

Amdahl's law was first proposed by Gene Amdahl in [AMDA67] and deals with the potential speedup of a program using multiple processors compared to a single processor. Consider a program running on a single processor such that a fraction $(1 - f)$ of the execution time involves code that is inherently serial and a fraction f that involves code that is infinitely parallelizable with no scheduling overhead. Let T be the total execution time of the program using a single processor. Then the speedup using a parallel processor with N processors that fully exploits the parallel portion of the program is as follows:

$$\text{Speedup} = \frac{\text{time to execute program on a single processor}}{\text{time to execute program on N parallel processors}}$$

$$= \frac{T(1 - f) + Tf}{T(1 - f) + \dfrac{Tf}{N}} = \frac{1}{(1 - f) + \dfrac{f}{N}}$$

Two important conclusions can be drawn:

1. When f is small, the use of parallel processors has little effect.
2. As N approaches infinity, speedup is bound by $1/(1 - f)$, so that there are diminishing returns for using more processors.

These conclusions are too pessimistic, an assertion first put forward in [GUST88]. For example, a server can maintain multiple threads or multiple tasks to handle multiple clients and execute the threads or tasks in parallel up to the limit of the number of processors. Many database applications involve computations on massive amounts of data that can be split up into multiple parallel tasks. Nevertheless,

Amdahl's law illustrates the problems facing industry in the development of multi-core machines with an ever-growing number of cores: The software that runs on such machines must be adapted to a highly parallel execution environment to exploit the power of parallel processing.

Amdahl's law can be generalized to evaluate any design or technical improvement in a computer system. Consider any enhancement to a feature of a system that results in a speedup. The speedup can be expressed as

$$\text{Speedup} = \frac{\text{Performance after enhancement}}{\text{Performance before enhancement}} = \frac{\text{Execution time before enhancement}}{\text{Execution time after enhancement}} \quad (2.8)$$

Suppose that a feature of the system is used during execution a fraction of the time f, before enhancement, and that the speedup of that feature after enhancement is SU_f. Then the overall speedup of the system is

$$\text{Speedup} = \frac{1}{(1 - f) + \dfrac{f}{SU_f}}$$

For example, suppose that a task makes extensive use of floating-point operations, with 40% of the time is consumed by floating-point operations. With a new hardware design, the floating-point module is speeded up by a factor of K. Then the overall speedup is:

$$\text{Speedup} = \frac{1}{0.6 + \dfrac{0.4}{K}}$$

Thus, independent of K, the maximum speedup is 1.67.

2.6 RECOMMENDED READING AND WEB SITES

A description of the IBM 7000 series can be found in [BELL71]. There is good coverage of the IBM 360 in [SIEW82] and of the PDP-8 and other DEC machines in [BELL78a]. These three books also contain numerous detailed examples of other computers spanning the history of computers through the early 1980s. A more recent book that includes an excellent set of case studies of historical machines is [BLAA97]. A good history of the microprocessor is [BETK97].

[OLUK96], [HAMM97], and [SAKA02] discuss the motivation for multiple processors on a single chip.

[BREY09] provides a good survey of the Intel microprocessor line. The Intel documentation itself is also good [INTE08].

The most thorough documentation available for the ARM architecture is [SEAL00].[11] [FURB00] is another excellent source of information. [SMIT08] is an interesting comparison of the ARM and x86 approaches to embedding processors in mobile wireless devices.

For interesting discussions of Moore's law and its consequences, see [HUTC96], [SCHA97], and [BOHR98].

[HENN06] provides a detailed description of each of the benchmarks in CPU2006. [SMIT88] discusses the relative merits of arithmetic, harmonic, and geometric means.

---

[11]Known in the ARM community as the "ARM ARM."

BELL71   Bell, C., and Newell, A. *Computer Structures: Readings and Examples.* New York: McGraw-Hill, 1971.

BELL78A   Bell, C.; Mudge, J.; and McNamara, J. *Computer Engineering: A DEC View of Hardware Systems Design.* Bedford, MA: Digital Press, 1978.

BETK97   Betker, M.; Fernando, J.; and Whalen, S. "The History of the Microprocessor." *Bell Labs Technical Journal,* Autumn 1997.

BLAA97   Blaauw, G., and Brooks, F. *Computer Architecture: Concepts and Evolution.* Reading, MA: Addison-Wesley, 1997.

BOHR98   Bohr, M. "Silicon Trends and Limits for Advanced Microprocessors." *Communications of the ACM,* March 1998.

BREY09   Brey, B. *The Intel Microprocessors: 8086/8066, 80186/80188, 80286, 80386, 80486, Pentium, Pentium Pro Processor, Pentium II, Pentium III, Pentium 4 and Core2 with 64-bit Extensions.* Upper Saddle River, NJ: Prentice Hall, 2009.

FURB00   Furber, S. *ARM System-On-Chip Architecture.* Reading, MA: Addison-Wesley, 2000.

HAMM97   Hammond, L.; Nayfay, B.; and Olukotun, K. "A Single-Chip Multiprocessor." *Computer,* September 1997.

HENN06   Henning, J. "SPEC CPU2006 Benchmark Descriptions." *Computer Architecture News,* September 2006.

HUTC96   Hutcheson, G., and Hutcheson, J. "Technology and Economics in the Semiconductor Industry." *Scientific American,* January 1996.

INTE08   Intel Corp. Intel ® 64 and *IA-32 Intel Architectures Software Developer's Manual (3 volumes).* Denver, CO, 2008. intel.com/products/processor/manuals

OLUK96   Olukotun, K., et al. "The Case for a Single-Chip Multiprocessor." *Proceedings, Seventh International Conference on Architectural Support for Programming Languages and Operating Systems,* 1996.

SAKA02   Sakai, S. "CMP on SoC: Architect's View." *Proceedings. 15th International Symposium on System Synthesis,* 2002.

SCHA97   Schaller, R. "Moore's Law: Past, Present, and Future." *IEEE Spectrum,* June 1997.

SEAL00   Seal, D., ed. *ARM Architecture Reference Manual.* Reading, MA: Addison-Wesley, 2000.

SIEW82   Siewiorek, D.; Bell, C.; and Newell, A. *Computer Structures: Principles and Examples.* New York: McGraw-Hill, 1982.

SMIT88   Smith, J. "Characterizing Computer Performance with a Single Number." *Communications of the ACM,* October 1988.

SMIT08   Smith, B. "ARM and Intel Battle over the Mobile Chip's Future." *Computer,* May 2008.

Recommended Web sites:

- **Intel Developer's Page:** Intel's Web page for developers; provides a starting point for accessing Pentium information. Also includes the Intel Technology Journal.
- **ARM:** Home page of ARM Limited, developer of the ARM architecture. Includes technical documentation.

- **Standard Performance Evaluation Corporation:** SPEC is a widely recognized organization in the computer industry for its development of standardized benchmarks used to measure and compare performance of different computer systems.
- **Top500 Supercomputer Site:** Provides brief description of architecture and organization of current supercomputer products, plus comparisons.
- **Charles Babbage Institute:** Provides links to a number of Web sites dealing with the history of computers.

2.7 KEY TERMS, REVIEW QUESTIONS, AND PROBLEMS

Key Terms

accumulator (AC)	instruction cycle	opcode
Amdahl's law	instruction register (IR)	original equipment manufac-
arithmetic and logic unit (ALU)	instruction set	turer (OEM)
benchmark	integrated circuit (IC)	program control unit
chip	main memory	program counter (PC)
data channel	memory address register	SPEC
embedded system	(MAR)	stored program computer
execute cycle	memory buffer register (MBR)	upward compatible
fetch cycle	microprocessor	von Neumann machine
input-output (I/O)	multicore	wafer
instruction buffer register (IBR)	multiplexor	word

Review Questions

2.1. What is a stored program computer?

2.2. What are the four main components of any general-purpose computer?

2.3. At the integrated circuit level, what are the three principal constituents of a computer system?

2.4. Explain Moore's law.

2.5. List and explain the key characteristics of a computer family.

2.6. What is the key distinguishing feature of a microprocessor?

Problems

2.1. Let $\mathbf{A}$ = A(1), A(2), . . . , A(1000) and $\mathbf{B}$ = B(1), B(2), . . . , B(1000) be two vectors (one-dimensional arrays) comprising 1000 numbers each that are to be added to form an array C such that C(I) = A(I) + B(I) for I = 1, 2, . . . , 1000. Using the IAS instruction set, write a program for this problem. Ignore the fact that the IAS was designed to have only 1000 words of storage.

2.2. a. On the IAS, what would the machine code instruction look like to load the contents of memory address 2?

b. How many trips to memory does the CPU need to make to complete this instruction during the instruction cycle?

2.3. On the IAS, describe in English the process that the CPU must undertake to read a value from memory and to write a value to memory in terms of what is put into the MAR, MBR, address bus, data bus, and control bus.

2.4. Given the memory contents of the IAS computer shown below,

Address	Contents
08A	010FA210FB
08B	010FA0F08D
08C	020FA210FB

show the assembly language code for the program, starting at address 08A. Explain what this program does.

2.5. In Figure 2.3, indicate the width, in bits, of each data path (e.g., between AC and ALU).

2.6. In the IBM 360 Models 65 and 75, addresses are staggered in two separate main memory units (e.g., all even-numbered words in one unit and all odd-numbered words in another). What might be the purpose of this technique?

2.7. With reference to Table 2.4, we see that the relative performance of the IBM 360 Model 75 is 50 times that of the 360 Model 30, yet the instruction cycle time is only 5 times as fast. How do you account for this discrepancy?

2.8. While browsing at Billy Bob's computer store, you overhear a customer asking Billy Bob what is the fastest computer in the store that he can buy. Billy Bob replies, "You're looking at our Macintoshes. The fastest Mac we have runs at a clock speed of 1.2 gigahertz. If you really want the fastest machine, you should buy our 2.4-gigahertz Intel Pentium IV instead." Is Billy Bob correct? What would you say to help this customer?

2.9. The ENIAC was a decimal machine, where a register was represented by a ring of 10 vacuum tubes. At any time, only one vacuum tube was in the ON state, representing one of the 10 digits. Assuming that ENIAC had the capability to have multiple vacuum tubes in the ON and OFF state simultaneously, why is this representation "wasteful" and what range of integer values could we represent using the 10 vacuum tubes?

2.10. A benchmark program is run on a 40 MHz processor. The executed program consists of 100,000 instruction executions, with the following instruction mix and clock cycle count:

Instruction Type	Instruction Count	Cycles per Instruction
Integer arithmetic	45000	1
Data transfer	32000	2
Floating point	15000	2
Control transfer	8000	2

Determine the effective CPI, MIPS rate, and execution time for this program.

2.11. Consider two different machines, with two different instruction sets, both of which have a clock rate of 200 MHz. The following measurements are recorded on the two machines running a given set of benchmark programs:

Instruction Type	Instruction Count (millions)	Cycles per Instruction
Machine A		
Arithmetic and logic	8	1
Load and store	4	3
Branch	2	4
Others	4	3
Machine A		
Arithmetic and logic	10	1
Load and store	8	2
Branch	2	4
Others	4	3

a. Determine the effective CPI, MIPS rate, and execution time for each machine.
b. Comment on the results.

2.12. Early examples of CISC and RISC design are the VAX 11/780 and the IBM RS/6000, respectively. Using a typical benchmark program, the following machine characteristics result:

Processor	Clock Frequency	Performance	CPU Time
VAX 11/780	5 MHz	1 MIPS	12 x seconds
IBM RS/6000	25 MHz	18 MIPS	x seconds

The final column shows that the VAX required 12 times longer than the IBM measured in CPU time.

a. What is the relative size of the instruction count of the machine code for this benchmark program running on the two machines?
b. What are the *CPI* values for the two machines?

2.13. Four benchmark programs are executed on three computers with the following results:

	Computer A	Computer B	Computer C
Program 1	1	10	20
Program 2	1000	100	20
Program 3	500	1000	50
Program 4	100	800	100

The table shows the execution time in seconds, with 100,000,000 instructions executed in each of the four programs. Calculate the MIPS values for each computer for each program. Then calculate the arithmetic and harmonic means assuming equal weights for the four programs, and rank the computers based on arithmetic mean and harmonic mean.

2.14. The following table, based on data reported in the literature [HEAT84], shows the execution times, in seconds, for five different benchmark programs on three machines.

Benchmark	Processor		
	R	M	Z
E	417	244	134
F	83	70	70
H	66	153	135
I	39,449	35,527	66,000
K	772	368	369

a. Compute the speed metric for each processor for each benchmark, normalized to machine R. That is, the ratio values for R are all 1.0. Other ratios are calculated using Equation (2.5) with R treated as the reference system. Then compute the arithmetic mean value for each system using Equation (2.3). This is the approach taken in [HEAT84].
b. Repeat part (a) using M as the reference machine. This calculation was not tried in [HEAT84].
c. Which machine is the slowest based on each of the preceding two calculations?
d. Repeat the calculations of parts (a) and (b) using the geometric mean, defined in Equation (2.6). Which machine is the slowest based on the two calculations?

2.15. To clarify the results of the preceding problem, we look at a simpler example.

Benchmark	Processor		
	X	Y	Z
1	20	10	40
2	40	80	20

    a. Compute the arithmetic mean value for each system using X as the reference machine and then using Y as the reference machine. Argue that intuitively the three machines have roughly equivalent performance and that the arithmetic mean gives misleading results.

    b. Compute the geometric mean value for each system using X as the reference machine and then using Y as the reference machine. Argue that the results are more realistic than with the arithmetic mean.

2.16. Consider the example in Section 2.5 for the calculation of average CPI and MIPS rate, which yielded the result of CPI $= 2.24$ and MIPS rate $= 178$. Now assume that the program can be executed in eight parallel tasks or threads with roughly equal number of instructions executed in each task. Execution is on an 8-core system with each core (processor) having the same performance as the single processor originally used. Coordination and synchronization between the parts adds an extra 25,000 instruction executions to each task. Assume the same instruction mix as in the example for each task, but increase the CPI for memory reference with cache miss to 12 cycles due to contention for memory.

    a. Determine the average CPI.

    b. Determine the corresponding MIPS rate.

    c. Calculate the speedup factor.

    d. Compare the actual speedup factor with the theoretical speedup factor determined by Amdhal's law.

2.17. A processor accesses main memory with an average access time of T_2. A smaller cache memory is interposed between the processor and main memory. The cache has a significantly faster access time of $T_1 < T_2$. The cache holds, at any time, copies of some main memory words and is designed so that the words more likely to be accessed in the near future are in the cache. Assume that the probability that the next word accessed by the processor is in the cache is H, known as the hit ratio.

    a. For any single memory access, what is the theoretical speedup of accessing the word in the cache rather than in main memory?

    b. Let T be the average access time. Express T as a function of T_1, T_2, and H. What is the overall speedup as a function of H?

    c. In practice, a system may be designed so that the processor must first access the cache to determine if the word is in the cache and, if it is not, then access main memory, so that on a miss (opposite of a hit), memory access time is $T_1 + T_2$. Express T as a function of T_1, T_2, and H. Now calculate the speedup and compare to the result produced in part (b).

PART TWO

The Computer System

P.1 ISSUES FOR PART TWO

A computer system consists of a processor, memory, I/O, and the interconnections among these major components. With the exception of the processor, which is sufficiently complex to devote Part Three to its study, Part Two examines each of these components in detail.

ROAD MAP FOR PART TWO

Chapter 3 A Top-Level View of Computer Function and Interconnection

At a top level, a computer consists of a processor, memory, and I/O components. The functional behavior of the system consists of the exchange of data and control signals among these components. To support this exchange, these components must be interconnected. Chapter 3 begins with a brief examination of the computer's components and their input–output requirements. The chapter then looks at key issues that affect interconnection design, especially the need to support interrupts. The bulk of the chapter is devoted to a study of the most common approach to interconnection: the use of a structure of buses.

Chapter 4 Cache Memory

Computer memory exhibits a wide range of type, technology, organization, performance, and cost. The typical computer system is equipped with a hierarchy of memory subsystems, some internal (directly accessible by the processor) and some external (accessible by the processor via an I/O module). Chapter 4 begins with an overview of this hierarchy. Next, the chapter deals in detail with the design of cache memory, including separate code and data caches and two-level caches.

Chapter 5 Internal Memory

The design of a main memory system is a never-ending battle among three competing design requirements: large storage capacity, rapid access time, and low cost. As memory technology evolves, each of these three characteristics is changing, so that the design decisions in organizing main memory must be revisited anew with each new implementation. Chapter 5 focuses on design issues related to internal memory. First, the nature and organization of semiconductor main memory is examined. Then, recent advanced DRAM memory organizations are explored.

Chapter 6 External Memory

For truly large storage capacity and for more permanent storage than is available with main memory, an external memory organization is needed. The most widely used type of external memory is magnetic disk, and much of Chapter 6 concentrates on this topic. First, we look at magnetic disk technology and design considerations. Then, we look at the use of RAID organization to improve disk memory performance. Chapter 6 also examines optical and tape storage.

Chapter 7 Input/Output

I/O modules are interconnected with the processor and main memory, and each controls one or more external devices. Chapter 7 is devoted to the various aspects of I/O organization. This is a complex area, and less well understood than other areas of computer system design in terms of meeting performance demands. Chapter 7 examines the mechanisms by which an I/O module interacts with the rest of the computer system, using the techniques of programmed I/O, interrupt I/O, and direct memory access (DMA). The interface between an I/O module and external devices is also described.

Chapter 8 Operating System Support

A detailed examination of operating systems (OSs) is beyond the scope of this book. However, it is important to understand the basic functions of an operating system and how the OS exploits hardware to provide the desired performance. Chapter 8 describes the basic principles of operating systems and discusses the specific design features in the computer hardware intended to provide support for the operating system. The chapter begins with a brief history, which serves to identify the major types of operating systems and to motivate their use. Next, multiprogramming is explained by examining the long-term and short-term scheduling functions. Finally, an examination of memory management includes a discussion of segmentation, paging, and virtual memory.

CHAPTER 3

A TOP-LEVEL VIEW OF COMPUTER FUNCTION AND INTERCONNECTION

65

KEY POINTS

- An instruction cycle consists of an instruction fetch, followed by zero or more operand fetches, followed by zero or more operand stores, followed by an interrupt check (if interrupts are enabled).

- The major computer system components (processor, main memory, I/O modules) need to be interconnected in order to exchange data and control signals. The most popular means of interconnection is the use of a shared system bus consisting of multiple lines. In contemporary systems, there typically is a hierarchy of buses to improve performance.

- Key design elements for buses include arbitration (whether permission to send signals on bus lines is controlled centrally or in a distributed fashion); timing (whether signals on the bus are synchronized to a central clock or are sent asynchronously based on the most recent transmission); and width (number of address lines and number of data lines).

At a top level, a computer consists of CPU (central processing unit), memory, and I/O components, with one or more modules of each type. These components are interconnected in some fashion to achieve the basic function of the computer, which is to execute programs. Thus, at a top level, we can describe a computer system by (1) describing the external behavior of each component—that is, the data and control signals that it exchanges with other components; and (2) describing the interconnection structure and the controls required to manage the use of the interconnection structure.

This top-level view of structure and function is important because of its explanatory power in understanding the nature of a computer. Equally important is its use to understand the increasingly complex issues of performance evaluation. A grasp of the top-level structure and function offers insight into system bottlenecks, alternate pathways, the magnitude of system failures if a component fails, and the ease of adding performance enhancements. In many cases, requirements for greater system power and fail-safe capabilities are being met by changing the design rather than merely increasing the speed and reliability of individual components.

This chapter focuses on the basic structures used for computer component interconnection. As background, the chapter begins with a brief examination of the basic components and their interface requirements. Then a functional overview is provided. We are then prepared to examine the use of buses to interconnect system components.

3.1 COMPUTER COMPONENTS

As discussed in Chapter 2, virtually all contemporary computer designs are based on concepts developed by John von Neumann at the Institute for Advanced Studies, Princeton. Such a design is referred to as the *von Neumann architecture* and is based on three key concepts:

- Data and instructions are stored in a single read–write memory.
- The contents of this memory are addressable by location, without regard to the type of data contained there.
- Execution occurs in a sequential fashion (unless explicitly modified) from one instruction to the next.

The reasoning behind these concepts was discussed in Chapter 2 but is worth summarizing here. There is a small set of basic logic components that can be combined in various ways to store binary data and to perform arithmetic and logical operations on that data. If there is a particular computation to be performed, a configuration of logic components designed specifically for that computation could be constructed. We can think of the process of connecting the various components in the desired configuration as a form of programming. The resulting "program" is in the form of hardware and is termed a *hardwired program.*

Now consider this alternative. Suppose we construct a general-purpose configuration of arithmetic and logic functions. This set of hardware will perform various functions on data depending on control signals applied to the hardware. In the original case of customized hardware, the system accepts data and produces results (Figure 3.1a). With general-purpose hardware, the system accepts data and control signals and produces results. Thus, instead of rewiring the hardware for each new program, the programmer merely needs to supply a new set of control signals.

How shall control signals be supplied? The answer is simple but subtle. The entire program is actually a sequence of steps. At each step, some arithmetic or logical

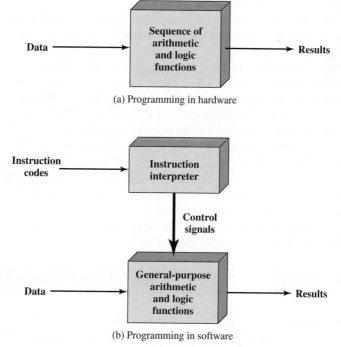

(a) Programming in hardware

(b) Programming in software

Figure 3.1   Hardware and Software Approaches

operation is performed on some data. For each step, a new set of control signals is needed. Let us provide a unique code for each possible set of control signals, and let us add to the general-purpose hardware a segment that can accept a code and generate control signals (Figure 3.1b).

Programming is now much easier. Instead of rewiring the hardware for each new program, all we need to do is provide a new sequence of codes. Each code is, in effect, an instruction, and part of the hardware interprets each instruction and generates control signals. To distinguish this new method of programming, a sequence of codes or instructions is called *software*.

Figure 3.1b indicates two major components of the system: an instruction interpreter and a module of general-purpose arithmetic and logic functions. These two constitute the CPU. Several other components are needed to yield a functioning computer. Data and instructions must be put into the system. For this we need some sort of input module. This module contains basic components for accepting data and instructions in some form and converting them into an internal form of signals usable by the system. A means of reporting results is needed, and this is in the form of an output module. Taken together, these are referred to as *I/O components*.

One more component is needed. An input device will bring instructions and data in sequentially. But a program is not invariably executed sequentially; it may jump around (e.g., the IAS jump instruction). Similarly, operations on data may require access to more than just one element at a time in a predetermined sequence. Thus, there must be a place to store temporarily both instructions and data. That module is called *memory,* or *main memory* to distinguish it from external storage or peripheral devices. Von Neumann pointed out that the same memory could be used to store both instructions and data.

Figure 3.2 illustrates these top-level components and suggests the interactions among them. The CPU exchanges data with memory. For this purpose, it typically makes use of two internal (to the CPU) registers: a memory address register (MAR), which specifies the address in memory for the next read or write, and a memory buffer register (MBR), which contains the data to be written into memory or receives the data read from memory. Similarly, an I/O address register (I/OAR) specifies a particular I/O device. An I/O buffer (I/OBR) register is used for the exchange of data between an I/O module and the CPU.

A memory module consists of a set of locations, defined by sequentially numbered addresses. Each location contains a binary number that can be interpreted as either an instruction or data. An I/O module transfers data from external devices to CPU and memory, and vice versa. It contains internal buffers for temporarily holding these data until they can be sent on.

Having looked briefly at these major components, we now turn to an overview of how these components function together to execute programs.

3.2 COMPUTER FUNCTION

The basic function performed by a computer is execution of a program, which consists of a set of instructions stored in memory. The processor does the actual work by executing instructions specified in the program. This section provides an overview of

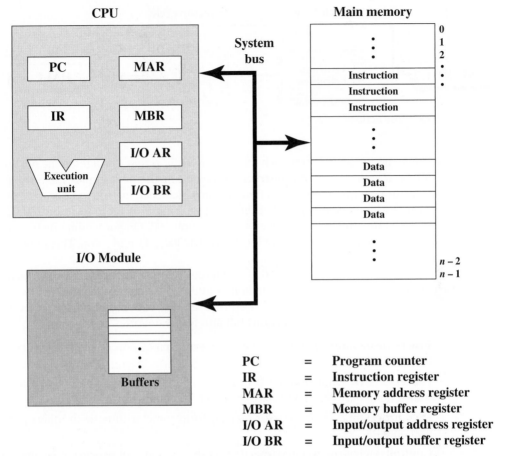

PC	=	Program counter
IR	=	Instruction register
MAR	=	Memory address register
MBR	=	Memory buffer register
I/O AR	=	Input/output address register
I/O BR	=	Input/output buffer register

Figure 3.2 Computer Components:Top-Level View

the key elements of program execution. In its simplest form, instruction processing consists of two steps: The processor reads (*fetches*) instructions from memory one at a time and executes each instruction. Program execution consists of repeating the process of instruction fetch and instruction execution. The instruction execution may involve several operations and depends on the nature of the instruction (see, for example, the lower portion of Figure 2.4).

The processing required for a single instruction is called an *instruction cycle*. Using the simplified two-step description given previously, the instruction cycle is depicted in Figure 3.3. The two steps are referred to as the *fetch cycle* and the *execute cycle*. Program execution halts only if the machine is turned off, some sort of unrecoverable error occurs, or a program instruction that halts the computer is encountered.

Instruction Fetch and Execute

At the beginning of each instruction cycle, the processor fetches an instruction from memory. In a typical processor, a register called the program counter (PC) holds the address of the instruction to be fetched next. Unless told otherwise, the processor

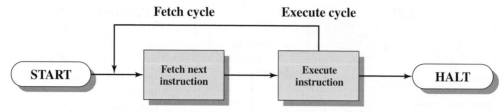

Figure 3.3 Basic Instruction Cycle

always increments the PC after each instruction fetch so that it will fetch the next instruction in sequence (i.e., the instruction located at the next higher memory address). So, for example, consider a computer in which each instruction occupies one 16-bit word of memory. Assume that the program counter is set to location 300. The processor will next fetch the instruction at location 300. On succeeding instruction cycles, it will fetch instructions from locations 301, 302, 303, and so on. This sequence may be altered, as explained presently.

The fetched instruction is loaded into a register in the processor known as the instruction register (IR). The instruction contains bits that specify the action the processor is to take. The processor interprets the instruction and performs the required action. In general, these actions fall into four categories:

- **Processor-memory:** Data may be transferred from processor to memory or from memory to processor.
- **Processor-I/O:** Data may be transferred to or from a peripheral device by transferring between the processor and an I/O module.
- **Data processing:** The processor may perform some arithmetic or logic operation on data.
- **Control:** An instruction may specify that the sequence of execution be altered. For example, the processor may fetch an instruction from location 149, which specifies that the next instruction be from location 182. The processor will remember this fact by setting the program counter to 182. Thus, on the next fetch cycle, the instruction will be fetched from location 182 rather than 150.

An instruction's execution may involve a combination of these actions.

Consider a simple example using a hypothetical machine that includes the characteristics listed in Figure 3.4. The processor contains a single data register, called an accumulator (AC). Both instructions and data are 16 bits long. Thus, it is convenient to organize memory using 16-bit words. The instruction format provides 4 bits for the opcode, so that there can be as many as $2^4 = 16$ different opcodes, and up to $2^{12} = 4096$ (4K) words of memory can be directly addressed.

Figure 3.5 illustrates a partial program execution, showing the relevant portions of memory and processor registers.[1] The program fragment shown adds the contents of the memory word at address 940 to the contents of the memory word at

---

[1]Hexadecimal notation is used, in which each digit represents 4 bits. This is the most convenient notation for representing the contents of memory and registers when the word length is a multiple of 4. See Chapter 19 for a basic refresher on number systems (decimal, binary, hexadecimal).

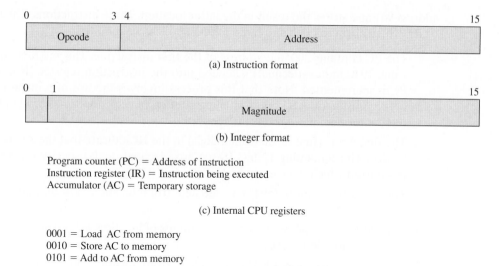

(a) Instruction format

(b) Integer format

Program counter (PC) = Address of instruction
Instruction register (IR) = Instruction being executed
Accumulator (AC) = Temporary storage

(c) Internal CPU registers

0001 = Load AC from memory
0010 = Store AC to memory
0101 = Add to AC from memory

(d) Partial list of opcodes

Figure 3.4 Characteristics of a Hypothetical Machine

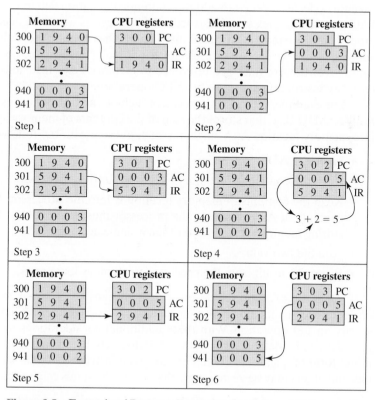

Figure 3.5 Example of Program Execution (contents of memory and registers in hexadecimal)

address 941 and stores the result in the latter location. Three instructions, which can be described as three fetch and three execute cycles, are required:

1. The PC contains 300, the address of the first instruction. This instruction (the value 1940 in hexadecimal) is loaded into the instruction register IR and the PC is incremented. Note that this process involves the use of a memory address register (MAR) and a memory buffer register (MBR). For simplicity, these intermediate registers are ignored.

2. The first 4 bits (first hexadecimal digit) in the IR indicate that the AC is to be loaded. The remaining 12 bits (three hexadecimal digits) specify the address (940) from which data are to be loaded.

3. The next instruction (5941) is fetched from location 301 and the PC is incremented.

4. The old contents of the AC and the contents of location 941 are added and the result is stored in the AC.

5. The next instruction (2941) is fetched from location 302 and the PC is incremented.

6. The contents of the AC are stored in location 941.

In this example, three instruction cycles, each consisting of a fetch cycle and an execute cycle, are needed to add the contents of location 940 to the contents of 941. With a more complex set of instructions, fewer cycles would be needed. Some older processors, for example, included instructions that contain more than one memory address. Thus the execution cycle for a particular instruction on such processors could involve more than one reference to memory. Also, instead of memory references, an instruction may specify an I/O operation.

For example, the PDP-11 processor includes an instruction, expressed symbolically as ADD B,A, that stores the sum of the contents of memory locations B and A into memory location A. A single instruction cycle with the following steps occurs:

- Fetch the ADD instruction.
- Read the contents of memory location A into the processor.
- Read the contents of memory location B into the processor. In order that the contents of A are not lost, the processor must have at least two registers for storing memory values, rather than a single accumulator.
- Add the two values.
- Write the result from the processor to memory location A.

Thus, the execution cycle for a particular instruction may involve more than one reference to memory. Also, instead of memory references, an instruction may specify an I/O operation. With these additional considerations in mind, Figure 3.6 provides a more detailed look at the basic instruction cycle of Figure 3.3. The figure is in the form of a state diagram. For any given instruction cycle, some states may be null and others may be visited more than once. The states can be described as follows:

- **Instruction address calculation (iac):** Determine the address of the next instruction to be executed. Usually, this involves adding a fixed number to the

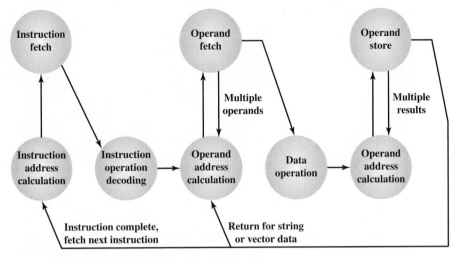

Figure 3.6   Instruction Cycle State Diagram

address of the previous instruction. For example, if each instruction is 16 bits long and memory is organized into 16-bit words, then add 1 to the previous address. If, instead, memory is organized as individually addressable 8-bit bytes, then add 2 to the previous address.

- **Instruction fetch (if):** Read instruction from its memory location into the processor.
- **Instruction operation decoding (iod):** Analyze instruction to determine type of operation to be performed and operand(s) to be used.
- **Operand address calculation (oac):** If the operation involves reference to an operand in memory or available via I/O, then determine the address of the operand.
- **Operand fetch (of):** Fetch the operand from memory or read it in from I/O.
- **Data operation (do):** Perform the operation indicated in the instruction.
- **Operand store (os):** Write the result into memory or out to I/O.

States in the upper part of Figure 3.6 involve an exchange between the processor and either memory or an I/O module. States in the lower part of the diagram involve only internal processor operations. The oac state appears twice, because an instruction may involve a read, a write, or both. However, the action performed during that state is fundamentally the same in both cases, and so only a single state identifier is needed.

Also note that the diagram allows for multiple operands and multiple results, because some instructions on some machines require this. For example, the PDP-11 instruction ADD A,B results in the following sequence of states: iac, if, iod, oac, of, oac, of, do, oac, os.

Finally, on some machines, a single instruction can specify an operation to be performed on a vector (one-dimensional array) of numbers or a string (one-dimensional array) of characters. As Figure 3.6 indicates, this would involve repetitive operand fetch and/or store operations.

Table 3.1 Classes of Interrupts

Program	Generated by some condition that occurs as a result of an instruction execution, such as arithmetic overflow, division by zero, attempt to execute an illegal machine instruction, or reference outside a user's allowed memory space.
Timer	Generated by a timer within the processor. This allows the operating system to perform certain functions on a regular basis.
I/O	Generated by an I/O controller, to signal normal completion of an operation or to signal a variety of error conditions.
Hardware failure	Generated by a failure such as power failure or memory parity error.

Interrupts

Virtually all computers provide a mechanism by which other modules (I/O, memory) may interrupt the normal processing of the processor. Table 3.1 lists the most common classes of interrupts. The specific nature of these interrupts is examined later in this book, especially in Chapters 7 and 12. However, we need to introduce the concept now to understand more clearly the nature of the instruction cycle and the implications of interrupts on the interconnection structure. The reader need not be concerned at this stage about the details of the generation and processing of interrupts, but only focus on the communication between modules that results from interrupts.

Interrupts are provided primarily as a way to improve processing efficiency. For example, most external devices are much slower than the processor. Suppose that the processor is transferring data to a printer using the instruction cycle scheme of Figure 3.3. After each write operation, the processor must pause and remain idle until the printer catches up. The length of this pause may be on the order of many hundreds or even thousands of instruction cycles that do not involve memory. Clearly, this is a very wasteful use of the processor.

Figure 3.7a illustrates this state of affairs. The user program performs a series of WRITE calls interleaved with processing. Code segments 1, 2, and 3 refer to sequences of instructions that do not involve I/O. The WRITE calls are to an I/O program that is a system utility and that will perform the actual I/O operation. The I/O program consists of three sections:

- A sequence of instructions, labeled 4 in the figure, to prepare for the actual I/O operation. This may include copying the data to be output into a special buffer and preparing the parameters for a device command.
- The actual I/O command. Without the use of interrupts, once this command is issued, the program must wait for the I/O device to perform the requested function (or periodically poll the device). The program might wait by simply repeatedly performing a test operation to determine if the I/O operation is done.
- A sequence of instructions, labeled 5 in the figure, to complete the operation. This may include setting a flag indicating the success or failure of the operation.

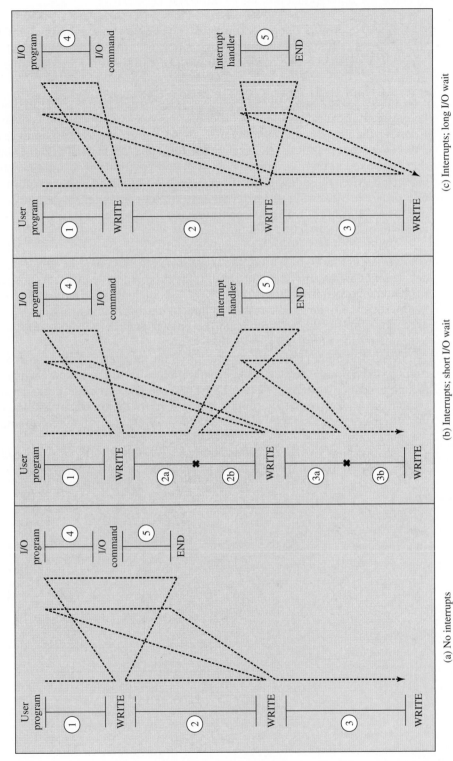

(a) No interrupts

(b) Interrupts; short I/O wait

(c) Interrupts; long I/O wait

Figure 3.7 Program Flow of Control without and with Interrupts

75

Because the I/O operation may take a relatively long time to complete, the I/O program is hung up waiting for the operation to complete; hence, the user program is stopped at the point of the WRITE call for some considerable period of time.

INTERRUPTS AND THE INSTRUCTION CYCLE With interrupts, the processor can be engaged in executing other instructions while an I/O operation is in progress. Consider the flow of control in Figure 3.7b. As before, the user program reaches a point at which it makes a system call in the form of a WRITE call. The I/O program that is invoked in this case consists only of the preparation code and the actual I/O command. After these few instructions have been executed, control returns to the user program. Meanwhile, the external device is busy accepting data from computer memory and printing it. This I/O operation is conducted concurrently with the execution of instructions in the user program.

When the external device becomes ready to be serviced—that is, when it is ready to accept more data from the processor,—the I/O module for that external device sends an *interrupt request* signal to the processor. The processor responds by suspending operation of the current program, branching off to a program to service that particular I/O device, known as an interrupt handler, and resuming the original execution after the device is serviced. The points at which such interrupts occur are indicated by an asterisk in Figure 3.7b.

From the point of view of the user program, an interrupt is just that: an interruption of the normal sequence of execution. When the interrupt processing is completed, execution resumes (Figure 3.8). Thus, the user program does not have to contain any special code to accommodate interrupts; the processor and the operating system are responsible for suspending the user program and then resuming it at the same point.

To accommodate interrupts, an *interrupt cycle* is added to the instruction cycle, as shown in Figure 3.9. In the interrupt cycle, the processor checks to see if any

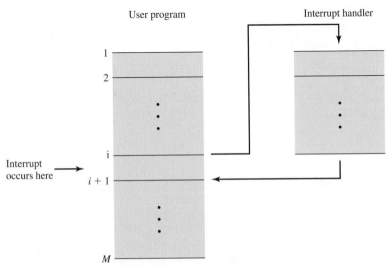

Figure 3.8 Transfer of Control via Interrupts

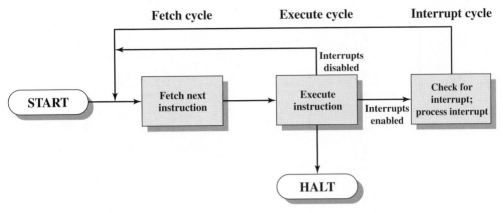

Figure 3.9   Instruction Cycle with Interrupts

interrupts have occurred, indicated by the presence of an interrupt signal. If no interrupts are pending, the processor proceeds to the fetch cycle and fetches the next instruction of the current program. If an interrupt is pending, the processor does the following:

- It suspends execution of the current program being executed and saves its context. This means saving the address of the next instruction to be executed (current contents of the program counter) and any other data relevant to the processor's current activity.

- It sets the program counter to the starting address of an *interrupt handler* routine.

The processor now proceeds to the fetch cycle and fetches the first instruction in the interrupt handler program, which will service the interrupt. The interrupt handler program is generally part of the operating system. Typically, this program determines the nature of the interrupt and performs whatever actions are needed. In the example we have been using, the handler determines which I/O module generated the interrupt and may branch to a program that will write more data out to that I/O module. When the interrupt handler routine is completed, the processor can resume execution of the user program at the point of interruption.

It is clear that there is some overhead involved in this process. Extra instructions must be executed (in the interrupt handler) to determine the nature of the interrupt and to decide on the appropriate action. Nevertheless, because of the relatively large amount of time that would be wasted by simply waiting on an I/O operation, the processor can be employed much more efficiently with the use of interrupts.

To appreciate the gain in efficiency, consider Figure 3.10, which is a timing diagram based on the flow of control in Figures 3.7a and 3.7b. Figures 3.7b and 3.10 assume that the time required for the I/O operation is relatively short: less than the time to complete the execution of instructions between write operations in the user program. The more typical case, especially for a slow device such as a printer, is that the I/O operation will take much more time than executing a sequence of user instructions. Figure 3.7c indicates this state of affairs. In this case, the user program reaches the second WRITE call before the I/O operation spawned by the first call is

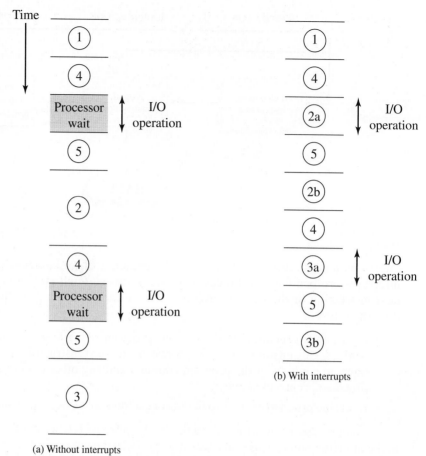

Figure 3.10 Program Timing: Short I/O Wait

complete. The result is that the user program is hung up at that point. When the preceding I/O operation is completed, this new WRITE call may be processed, and a new I/O operation may be started. Figure 3.11 shows the timing for this situation with and without the use of interrupts. We can see that there is still a gain in efficiency because part of the time during which the I/O operation is underway overlaps with the execution of user instructions.

Figure 3.12 shows a revised instruction cycle state diagram that includes interrupt cycle processing.

MULTIPLE INTERRUPTS The discussion so far has focused only on the occurrence of a single interrupt. Suppose, however, that multiple interrupts can occur. For example, a program may be receiving data from a communications line and printing results. The printer will generate an interrupt every time that it completes a print operation. The communication line controller will generate an interrupt every time a unit of data arrives. The unit could either be a single character or a block, depending on the nature of the communications discipline.

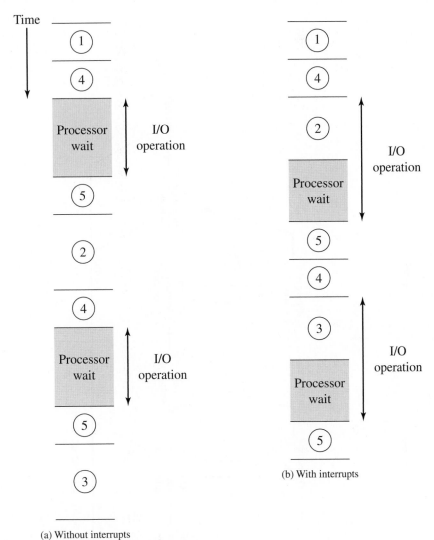

(a) Without interrupts

(b) With interrupts

Figure 3.11   Program Timing: Long I/O Wait

In any case, it is possible for a communications interrupt to occur while a printer interrupt is being processed.

Two approaches can be taken to dealing with multiple interrupts. The first is to disable interrupts while an interrupt is being processed. A *disabled interrupt* simply means that the processor can and will ignore that interrupt request signal. If an interrupt occurs during this time, it generally remains pending and will be checked by the processor after the processor has enabled interrupts. Thus, when a user program is executing and an interrupt occurs, interrupts are disabled immediately. After the interrupt handler routine completes, interrupts are enabled before resuming the user program, and the processor checks to see if additional interrupts have occurred. This approach is nice and simple, as interrupts are handled in strict sequential order (Figure 3.13a).

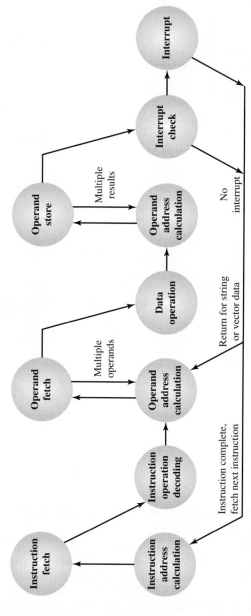

Figure 3.12 Instruction Cycle State Diagram, with Interrupts

80

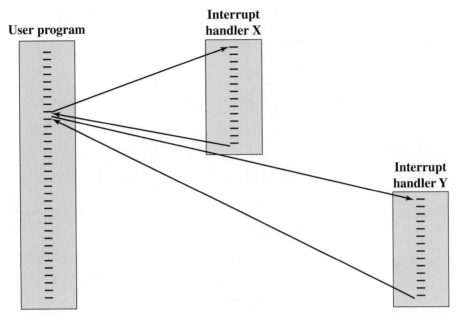

(a) Sequential interrupt processing

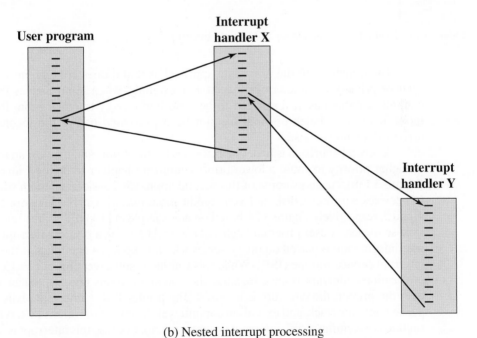

(b) Nested interrupt processing

Figure 3.13   Transfer of Control with Multiple Interrupts

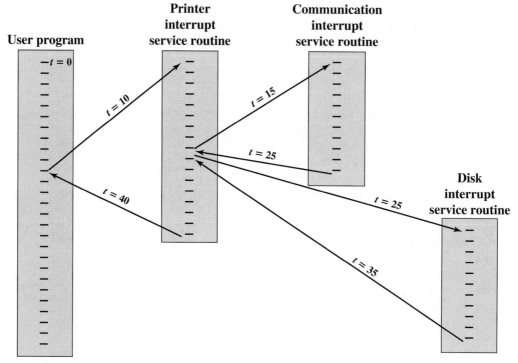

Figure 3.14   Example Time Sequence of Multiple Interrupts

The drawback to the preceding approach is that it does not take into account relative priority or time-critical needs. For example, when input arrives from the communications line, it may need to be absorbed rapidly to make room for more input. If the first batch of input has not been processed before the second batch arrives, data may be lost.

A second approach is to define priorities for interrupts and to allow an interrupt of higher priority to cause a lower-priority interrupt handler to be itself interrupted (Figure 3.13b). As an example of this second approach, consider a system with three I/O devices: a printer, a disk, and a communications line, with increasing priorities of 2, 4, and 5, respectively. Figure 3.14, based on an example in [TANE97], illustrates a possible sequence. A user program begins at $t = 0$. At $t = 10$, a printer interrupt occurs; user information is placed on the system stack and execution continues at the printer interrupt service routine (ISR). While this routine is still executing, at $t = 15$, a communications interrupt occurs. Because the communications line has higher priority than the printer, the interrupt is honored. The printer ISR is interrupted, its state is pushed onto the stack, and execution continues at the communications ISR. While this routine is executing, a disk interrupt occurs ($t = 20$). Because this interrupt is of lower priority, it is simply held, and the communications ISR runs to completion.

When the communications ISR is complete ($t = 25$), the previous processor state is restored, which is the execution of the printer ISR. However, before even a single instruction in that routine can be executed, the processor honors the higher-priority disk interrupt and control transfers to the disk ISR. Only when that routine is complete ($t = 35$) is the printer ISR resumed. When that routine completes ($t = 40$), control finally returns to the user program.

I/O Function

Thus far, we have discussed the operation of the computer as controlled by the processor, and we have looked primarily at the interaction of processor and memory. The discussion has only alluded to the role of the I/O component. This role is discussed in detail in Chapter 7, but a brief summary is in order here.

An I/O module (e.g., a disk controller) can exchange data directly with the processor. Just as the processor can initiate a read or write with memory, designating the address of a specific location, the processor can also read data from or write data to an I/O module. In this latter case, the processor identifies a specific device that is controlled by a particular I/O module. Thus, an instruction sequence similar in form to that of Figure 3.5 could occur, with I/O instructions rather than memory-referencing instructions.

In some cases, it is desirable to allow I/O exchanges to occur directly with memory. In such a case, the processor grants to an I/O module the authority to read from or write to memory, so that the I/O-memory transfer can occur without tying up the processor. During such a transfer, the I/O module issues read or write commands to memory, relieving the processor of responsibility for the exchange. This operation is known as direct memory access (DMA) and is examined Chapter 7.

3.3 INTERCONNECTION STRUCTURES

A computer consists of a set of components or modules of three basic types (processor, memory, I/O) that communicate with each other. In effect, a computer is a network of basic modules. Thus, there must be paths for connecting the modules.

The collection of paths connecting the various modules is called the *interconnection structure*. The design of this structure will depend on the exchanges that must be made among modules.

Figure 3.15 suggests the types of exchanges that are needed by indicating the major forms of input and output for each module type:[2]

- **Memory:** Typically, a memory module will consist of N words of equal length. Each word is assigned a unique numerical address $(0, 1, \ldots, N-1)$. A word of data can be read from or written into the memory. The nature of the operation is indicated by read and write control signals. The location for the operation is specified by an address.
- **I/O module:** From an internal (to the computer system) point of view, I/O is functionally similar to memory. There are two operations, read and write. Further, an I/O module may control more than one external device. We can refer to each of the interfaces to an external device as a *port* and give each a unique address (e.g., $0, 1, \ldots, M-1$). In addition, there are external data paths for the

---

[2]The wide arrows represent multiple signal lines carrying multiple bits of information in parallel. Each narrow arrows represents a single signal line.

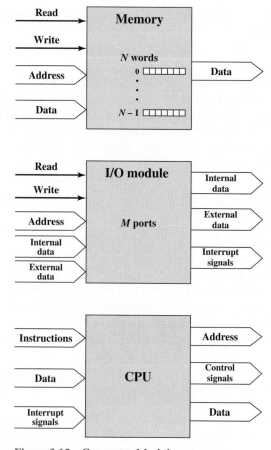

Figure 3.15   Computer Modules

input and output of data with an external device. Finally, an I/O module may be able to send interrupt signals to the processor.

- **Processor:** The processor reads in instructions and data, writes out data after processing, and uses control signals to control the overall operation of the system. It also receives interrupt signals.

The preceding list defines the data to be exchanged. The interconnection structure must support the following types of transfers:

- **Memory to processor:** The processor reads an instruction or a unit of data from memory.
- **Processor to memory:** The processor writes a unit of data to memory.
- **I/O to processor:** The processor reads data from an I/O device via an I/O module.
- **Processor to I/O:** The processor sends data to the I/O device.
- **I/O to or from memory:** For these two cases, an I/O module is allowed to exchange data directly with memory, without going through the processor, using direct memory access (DMA).

Over the years, a number of interconnection structures have been tried. By far the most common is the bus and various multiple-bus structures. The remainder of this chapter is devoted to an assessment of bus structures.

3.4   BUS INTERCONNECTION

A bus is a communication pathway connecting two or more devices. A key characteristic of a bus is that it is a shared transmission medium. Multiple devices connect to the bus, and a signal transmitted by any one device is available for reception by all other devices attached to the bus. If two devices transmit during the same time period, their signals will overlap and become garbled. Thus, only one device at a time can successfully transmit.

Typically, a bus consists of multiple communication pathways, or lines. Each line is capable of transmitting signals representing binary 1 and binary 0. Over time, a sequence of binary digits can be transmitted across a single line. Taken together, several lines of a bus can be used to transmit binary digits simultaneously (in parallel). For example, an 8-bit unit of data can be transmitted over eight bus lines.

Computer systems contain a number of different buses that provide pathways between components at various levels of the computer system hierarchy. A bus that connects major computer components (processor, memory, I/O) is called a *system bus*. The most common computer interconnection structures are based on the use of one or more system buses.

Bus Structure

A system bus consists, typically, of from about 50 to hundreds of separate lines. Each line is assigned a particular meaning or function. Although there are many different bus designs, on any bus the lines can be classified into three functional groups (Figure 3.16): data, address, and control lines. In addition, there may be power distribution lines that supply power to the attached modules.

The **data lines** provide a path for moving data among system modules. These lines, collectively, are called the *data bus*. The data bus may consist of 32, 64, 128, or even more separate lines, the number of lines being referred to as the *width* of the data bus. Because each line can carry only 1 bit at a time, the number of lines determines how many bits can be transferred at a time. The width of the data bus is a key

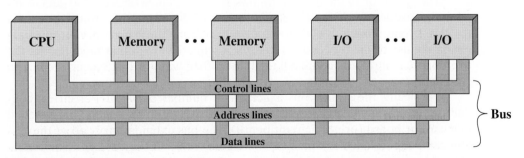

Figure 3.16 Bus Interconnection Scheme

factor in determining overall system performance. For example, if the data bus is 32 bits wide and each instruction is 64 bits long, then the processor must access the memory module twice during each instruction cycle.

The **address lines** are used to designate the source or destination of the data on the data bus. For example, if the processor wishes to read a word (8, 16, or 32 bits) of data from memory, it puts the address of the desired word on the address lines. Clearly, the width of the address bus determines the maximum possible memory capacity of the system. Furthermore, the address lines are generally also used to address I/O ports. Typically, the higher-order bits are used to select a particular module on the bus, and the lower-order bits select a memory location or I/O port within the module. For example, on an 8-bit address bus, address 01111111 and below might reference locations in a memory module (module 0) with 128 words of memory, and address 10000000 and above refer to devices attached to an I/O module (module 1).

The **control lines** are used to control the access to and the use of the data and address lines. Because the data and address lines are shared by all components, there must be a means of controlling their use. Control signals transmit both command and timing information among system modules. Timing signals indicate the validity of data and address information. Command signals specify operations to be performed. Typical control lines include

- **Memory write:** Causes data on the bus to be written into the addressed location
- **Memory read:** Causes data from the addressed location to be placed on the bus
- **I/O write:** Causes data on the bus to be output to the addressed I/O port
- **I/O read:** Causes data from the addressed I/O port to be placed on the bus
- **Transfer ACK:** Indicates that data have been accepted from or placed on the bus
- **Bus request:** Indicates that a module needs to gain control of the bus
- **Bus grant:** Indicates that a requesting module has been granted control of the bus
- **Interrupt request:** Indicates that an interrupt is pending
- **Interrupt ACK:** Acknowledges that the pending interrupt has been recognized
- **Clock:** Is used to synchronize operations
- **Reset:** Initializes all modules

The operation of the bus is as follows. If one module wishes to send data to another, it must do two things: (1) obtain the use of the bus, and (2) transfer data via the bus. If one module wishes to request data from another module, it must (1) obtain the use of the bus, and (2) transfer a request to the other module over the appropriate control and address lines. It must then wait for that second module to send the data.

Physically, the system bus is actually a number of parallel electrical conductors. In the classic bus arrangement, these conductors are metal lines etched in a card or board (printed circuit board). The bus extends across all of the system components, each of which taps into some or all of the bus lines. The classic physical arrangement is depicted in Figure 3.17. In this example, the bus consists

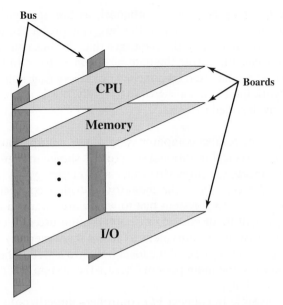

Figure 3.17 Typical Physical Realization of a Bus Architecture

of two vertical columns of conductors. At regular intervals along the columns, there are attachment points in the form of slots that extend out horizontally to support a printed circuit board. Each of the major system components occupies one or more boards and plugs into the bus at these slots. The entire arrangement is housed in a chassis. This scheme can still be used for some of the buses associated with a computer system. However, modern systems tend to have all of the major components on the same board with more elements on the same chip as the processor. Thus, an on-chip bus may connect the processor and cache memory, whereas an on-board bus may connect the processor to main memory and other components.

This arrangement is most convenient. A small computer system may be acquired and then expanded later (more memory, more I/O) by adding more boards. If a component on a board fails, that board can easily be removed and replaced.

Multiple-Bus Hierarchies

If a great number of devices are connected to the bus, performance will suffer. There are two main causes:

1. In general, the more devices attached to the bus, the greater the bus length and hence the greater the propagation delay. This delay determines the time it takes for devices to coordinate the use of the bus. When control of the bus passes from one device to another frequently, these propagation delays can noticeably affect performance.

2. The bus may become a bottleneck as the aggregate data transfer demand approaches the capacity of the bus. This problem can be countered to some extent by increasing the data rate that the bus can carry and by using wider buses (e.g., increasing the data bus from 32 to 64 bits). However, because the data rates generated by attached devices (e.g., graphics and video controllers, network interfaces) are growing rapidly, this is a race that a single bus is ultimately destined to lose.

Accordingly, most computer systems use multiple buses, generally laid out in a hierarchy. A typical traditional structure is shown in Figure 3.18a. There is a local bus that connects the processor to a cache memory and that may support one or more local devices. The cache memory controller connects the cache not only to this local bus, but to a system bus to which are attached all of the main memory modules. As will be discussed in Chapter 4, the use of a cache structure insulates the processor from a requirement to access main memory frequently. Hence, main memory can be moved off of the local bus onto a system bus. In this way, I/O transfers to and from the main memory across the system bus do not interfere with the processor's activity.

It is possible to connect I/O controllers directly onto the system bus. A more efficient solution is to make use of one or more expansion buses for this purpose. An expansion bus interface buffers data transfers between the system bus and the I/O controllers on the expansion bus. This arrangement allows the system to support a wide variety of I/O devices and at the same time insulate memory-to-processor traffic from I/O traffic.

Figure 3.18a shows some typical examples of I/O devices that might be attached to the expansion bus. Network connections include local area networks (LANs) such as a 10-Mbps Ethernet and connections to wide area networks (WANs) such as a packet-switching network. SCSI (small computer system interface) is itself a type of bus used to support local disk drives and other peripherals. A serial port could be used to support a printer or scanner.

This traditional bus architecture is reasonably efficient but begins to break down as higher and higher performance is seen in the I/O devices. In response to these growing demands, a common approach taken by industry is to build a high-speed bus that is closely integrated with the rest of the system, requiring only a bridge between the processor's bus and the high-speed bus. This arrangement is sometimes known as a mezzanine architecture.

Figure 3.18b shows a typical realization of this approach. Again, there is a local bus that connects the processor to a cache controller, which is in turn connected to a system bus that supports main memory. The cache controller is integrated into a bridge, or buffering device, that connects to the high-speed bus. This bus supports connections to high-speed LANs, such as Fast Ethernet at 100 Mbps, video and graphics workstation controllers, as well as interface controllers to local peripheral buses, including SCSI and FireWire. The latter is a high-speed bus arrangement specifically designed to support high-capacity I/O devices. Lower-speed devices are still supported off an expansion bus, with an interface buffering traffic between the expansion bus and the high-speed bus.

The advantage of this arrangement is that the high-speed bus brings high-demand devices into closer integration with the processor and at the same time is

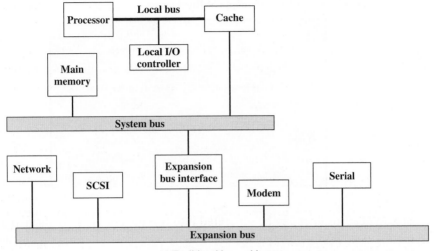

(a) Traditional bus architecture

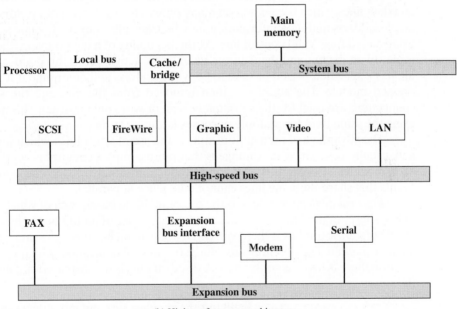

(b) High-performance architecture

Figure 3.18 Example Bus Configurations

independent of the processor. Thus, differences in processor and high-speed bus speeds and signal line definitions are tolerated. Changes in processor architecture do not affect the high-speed bus, and vice versa.

Elements of Bus Design

Although a variety of different bus implementations exist, there are a few basic parameters or design elements that serve to classify and differentiate buses. Table 3.2 lists key elements.

Table 3.2 Elements of Bus Design

Type	Bus Width
Dedicated	Address
Multiplexed	Data
Method of Arbitration	**Data Transfer Type**
Centralized	Read
Distributed	Write
Timing	Read-modify-write
Synchronous	Read-after-write
Asynchronous	Block

BUS TYPES Bus lines can be separated into two generic types: dedicated and multiplexed. A dedicated bus line is permanently assigned either to one function or to a physical subset of computer components.

An example of functional dedication is the use of separate dedicated address and data lines, which is common on many buses. However, it is not essential. For example, address and data information may be transmitted over the same set of lines using an Address Valid control line. At the beginning of a data transfer, the address is placed on the bus and the Address Valid line is activated. At this point, each module has a specified period of time to copy the address and determine if it is the addressed module. The address is then removed from the bus, and the same bus connections are used for the subsequent read or write data transfer. This method of using the same lines for multiple purposes is known as *time multiplexing.*

The advantage of time multiplexing is the use of fewer lines, which saves space and, usually, cost. The disadvantage is that more complex circuitry is needed within each module. Also, there is a potential reduction in performance because certain events that share the same lines cannot take place in parallel.

Physical dedication refers to the use of multiple buses, each of which connects only a subset of modules. A typical example is the use of an I/O bus to interconnect all I/O modules; this bus is then connected to the main bus through some type of I/O adapter module. The potential advantage of physical dedication is high throughput, because there is less bus contention. A disadvantage is the increased size and cost of the system.

METHOD OF ARBITRATION In all but the simplest systems, more than one module may need control of the bus. For example, an I/O module may need to read or write directly to memory, without sending the data to the processor. Because only one unit at a time can successfully transmit over the bus, some method of arbitration is needed. The various methods can be roughly classified as being either centralized or distributed. In a centralized scheme, a single hardware device, referred to as a *bus controller* or *arbiter,* is responsible for allocating time on the bus. The device may be a separate module or part of the processor. In a distributed scheme, there is no central controller. Rather, each module contains access control logic and the modules act together to share the bus. With both methods of arbitration, the purpose is to designate one device, either the processor or an I/O module, as master. The master may then initiate a data transfer (e.g., read or write) with some other device, which acts as slave for this particular exchange.

TIMING Timing refers to the way in which events are coordinated on the bus. Buses use either synchronous timing or asynchronous timing.

With **synchronous timing**, the occurrence of events on the bus is determined by a clock. The bus includes a clock line upon which a clock transmits a regular sequence of alternating 1s and 0s of equal duration. A single 1–0 transmission is referred to as a *clock cycle* or *bus cycle* and defines a time slot. All other devices on the bus can read the clock line, and all events start at the beginning of a clock cycle. Figure 3.19 shows a typical, but simplified, timing diagram for synchronous read and write operations (see Appendix 3A for a description of timing diagrams). Other bus signals may change at the leading edge of the clock signal (with a slight reaction delay). Most events occupy a single clock cycle. In this simple example, the processor places a memory address on the address lines during the first

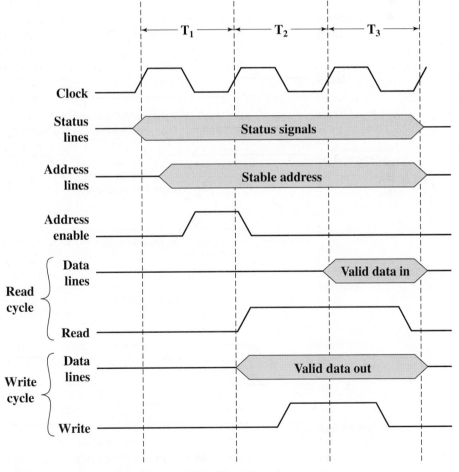

Figure 3.19   Timing of Synchronous Bus Operations

clock cycle and may assert various status lines. Once the address lines have stabilized, the processor issues an address enable signal. For a read operation, the processor issues a read command at the start of the second cycle. A memory module recognizes the address and, after a delay of one cycle, places the data on the data lines. The processor reads the data from the data lines and drops the read signal. For a write operation, the processor puts the data on the data lines at the start of the second cycle, and issues a write command after the data lines have stabilized. The memory module copies the information from the data lines during the third clock cycle.

With **asynchronous timing**, the occurrence of one event on a bus follows and depends on the occurrence of a previous event. In the simple read example of Figure 3.20a, the processor places address and status signals on the bus. After

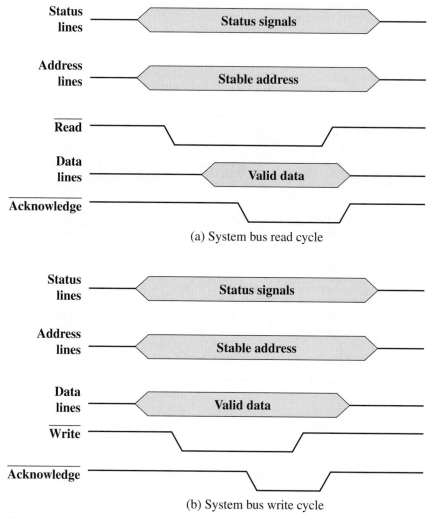

(a) System bus read cycle

(b) System bus write cycle

Figure 3.20 Timing of Asynchronous Bus Operations

pausing for these signals to stabilize, it issues a read command, indicating the presence of valid address and control signals. The appropriate memory decodes the address and responds by placing the data on the data line. Once the data lines have stabilized, the memory module asserts the acknowledged line to signal the processor that the data are available. Once the master has read the data from the data lines, it deasserts the read signal. This causes the memory module to drop the data and acknowledge lines. Finally, once the acknowledge line is dropped, the master removes the address information.

Figure 3.20b shows a simple asynchronous write operation. In this case, the master places the data on the data line at the same time that is puts signals on the status and address lines. The memory module responds to the write command by copying the data from the data lines and then asserting the acknowledge line. The master then drops the write signal and the memory module drops the acknowledge signal.

Synchronous timing is simpler to implement and test. However, it is less flexible than asynchronous timing. Because all devices on a synchronous bus are tied to a fixed clock rate, the system cannot take advantage of advances in device performance. With asynchronous timing, a mixture of slow and fast devices, using older and newer technology, can share a bus.

BUS WIDTH We have already addressed the concept of bus width. The width of the data bus has an impact on system performance: The wider the data bus, the greater the number of bits transferred at one time. The width of the address bus has an impact on system capacity: the wider the address bus, the greater the range of locations that can be referenced.

DATA TRANSFER TYPE Finally, a bus supports various data transfer types, as illustrated in Figure 3.21. All buses support both write (master to slave) and read (slave to master) transfers. In the case of a multiplexed address/data bus, the bus is first used for specifying the address and then for transferring the data. For a read operation, there is typically a wait while the data are being fetched from the slave to be put on the bus. For either a read or a write, there may also be a delay if it is necessary to go through arbitration to gain control of the bus for the remainder of the operation (i.e., seize the bus to request a read or write, then seize the bus again to perform a read or write).

In the case of dedicated address and data buses, the address is put on the address bus and remains there while the data are put on the data bus. For a write operation, the master puts the data onto the data bus as soon as the address has stabilized and the slave has had the opportunity to recognize its address. For a read operation, the slave puts the data onto the data bus as soon as it has recognized its address and has fetched the data.

There are also several combination operations that some buses allow. A read–modify–write operation is simply a read followed immediately by a write to the same address. The address is only broadcast once at the beginning of the operation. The whole operation is typically indivisible to prevent any access to the data element by other potential bus masters. The principal purpose of this

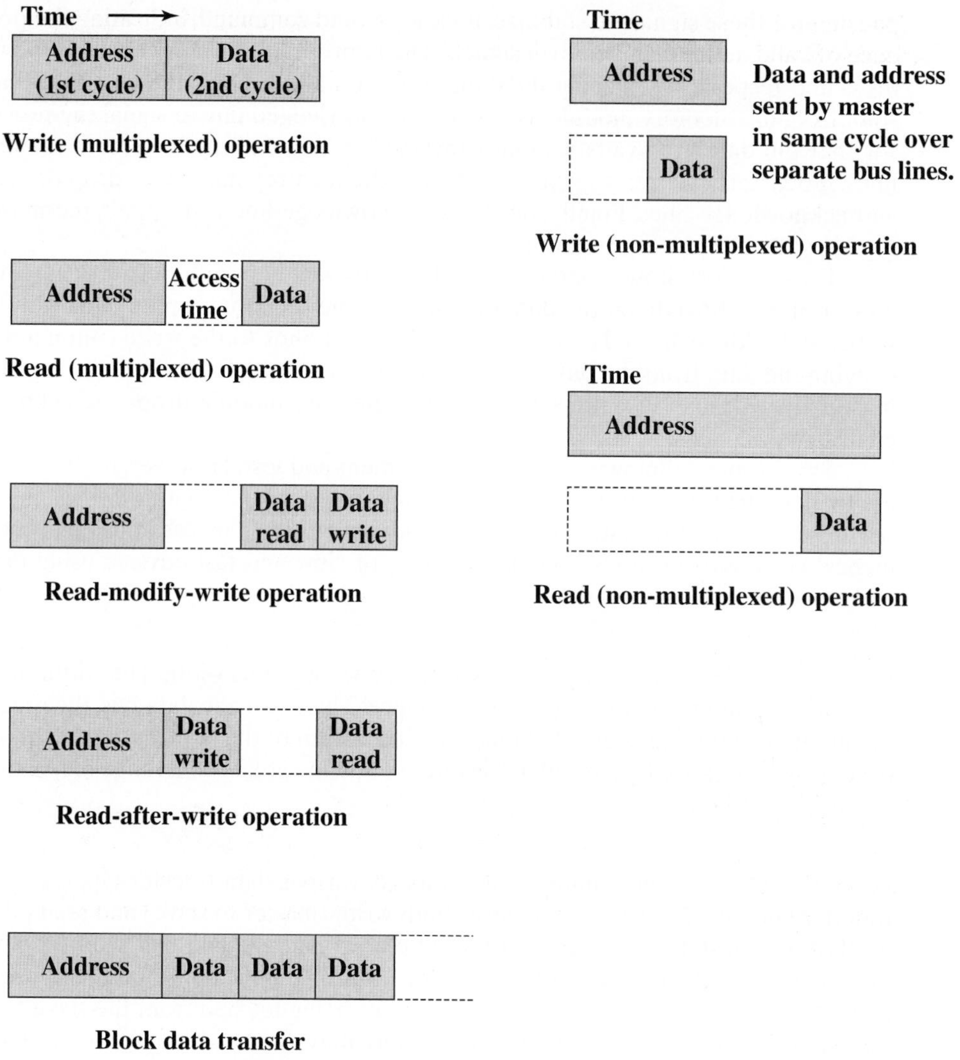

Time ⟶

Address (1st cycle)	Data (2nd cycle)

Write (multiplexed) operation

Time

Address	

Data and address
sent by master
in same cycle over
separate bus lines.

	Data

Write (non-multiplexed) operation

Address	Access time	Data

Read (multiplexed) operation

Time

Address

	Data

Read (non-multiplexed) operation

Address		Data read	Data write

Read-modify-write operation

Address	Data write		Data read

Read-after-write operation

Address	Data	Data	Data	

Block data transfer

Figure 3.21   Bus Data Transfer Types

capability is to protect shared memory resources in a multiprogramming system (see Chapter 8).

Read-after-write is an indivisible operation consisting of a write followed immediately by a read from the same address. The read operation may be performed for checking purposes.

Some bus systems also support a block data transfer. In this case, one address cycle is followed by *n* data cycles. The first data item is transferred to or from the specified address; the remaining data items are transferred to or from subsequent addresses.

3.5   PCI

The peripheral component interconnect (PCI) is a popular high-bandwidth, processor-independent bus that can function as a mezzanine or peripheral bus. Compared with other common bus specifications, PCI delivers better system performance for high-speed I/O subsystems (e.g., graphic display adapters, network interface controllers, disk controllers, and so on). The current standard allows the use of up to 64 data lines at 66 MHz, for a raw transfer rate of 528 MByte/s, or 4.224 Gbps. But it is not just a high speed that makes PCI attractive. PCI is specifically designed to meet economically the I/O requirements of modern systems; it requires very few chips to implement and supports other buses attached to the PCI bus.

Intel began work on PCI in 1990 for its Pentium-based systems. Intel soon released all the patents to the public domain and promoted the creation of an industry association, the PCI Special Interest Group (SIG), to develop further and maintain the compatibility of the PCI specifications. The result is that PCI has been widely adopted and is finding increasing use in personal computer, workstation, and server systems. Because the specification is in the public domain and is supported by a broad cross section of the microprocessor and peripheral industry, PCI products built by different vendors are compatible.

PCI is designed to support a variety of microprocessor-based configurations, including both single- and multiple-processor systems. Accordingly, it provides a general-purpose set of functions. It makes use of synchronous timing and a centralized arbitration scheme.

Figure 3.22a shows a typical use of PCI in a single-processor system. A combined DRAM controller and bridge to the PCI bus provides tight coupling with the processor and the ability to deliver data at high speeds. The bridge acts as a data buffer so that the speed of the PCI bus may differ from that of the processor's I/O capability. In a multiprocessor system (Figure 3.22b), one or more PCI configurations may be connected by bridges to the processor's system bus. The system bus supports only the processor/cache units, main memory, and the PCI bridges. Again, the use of bridges keeps the PCI independent of the processor speed yet provides the ability to receive and deliver data rapidly.

Bus Structure

PCI may be configured as a 32- or 64-bit bus. Table 3.3 defines the 49 mandatory signal lines for PCI. These are divided into the following functional groups:

- **System pins:** Include the clock and reset pins.
- **Address and data pins:** Include 32 lines that are time multiplexed for addresses and data. The other lines in this group are used to interpret and validate the signal lines that carry the addresses and data.
- **Interface control pins:** Control the timing of transactions and provide coordination among initiators and targets.

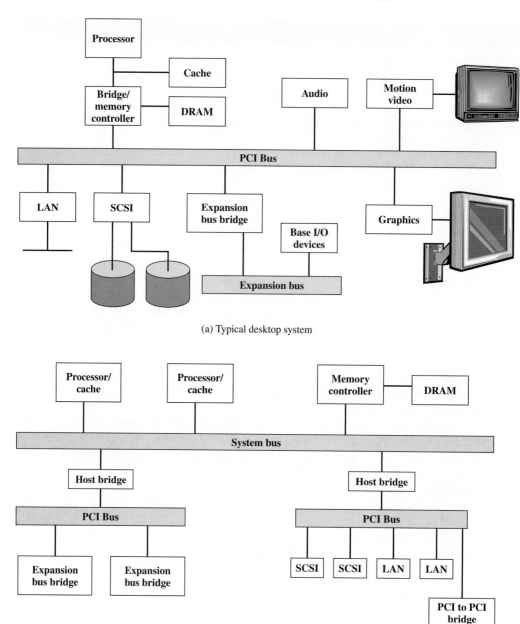

(a) Typical desktop system

(b) Typical server system

Figure 3.22 Example PCI Configurations

- **Arbitration pins:** Unlike the other PCI signal lines, these are not shared lines. Rather, each PCI master has its own pair of arbitration lines that connect it directly to the PCI bus arbiter.
- **Error reporting pins:** Used to report parity and other errors.

Table 3.3 Mandatory PCI Signal Lines

Designation	Type	Description
System Pins		
CLK	in	Provides timing for all transactions and is sampled by all inputs on the rising edge. Clock rates up to 33 MHz are supported.
RST#	in	Forces all PCI-specific registers, sequencers, and signals to an initialized state.
Address and Data Pins		
AD[31::0]	t/s	Multiplexed lines used for address and data
C/BE[3::0]#	t/s	Multiplexed bus command and byte enable signals. During the data phase, the lines indicate which of the four byte lanes carry meaningful data.
PAR	t/s	Provides even parity across AD and C/BE lines one clock cycle later. The master drives PAR for address and write data phases; the target drive PAR for read data phases.
Interface Control Pins		
FRAME#	s/t/s	Driven by current master to indicate the start and duration of a transaction. It is asserted at the start and deasserted when the initiator is ready to begin the final data phase.
IRDY#	s/t/s	Initiator Ready. Driven by current bus master (initiator of transaction). During a read, indicates that the master is prepared to accept data; during a write, indicates that valid data are present on AD.
TRDY#	s/t/s	Target Ready. Driven by the target (selected device). During a read, indicates that valid data are present on AD; during a write, indicates that target is ready to accept data.
STOP#	s/t/s	Indicates that current target wishes the initiator to stop the current transaction.
IDSEL	in	Initialization Device Select. Used as a chip select during configuration read and write transactions.
DEVSEL#	in	Device Select. Asserted by target when it has recognized its address. Indicates to current initiator whether any device has been selected.
Arbitration Pins		
REQ#	t/s	Indicates to the arbiter that this device requires use of the bus. This is a device-specific point-to-point line.
GNT#	t/s	Indicates to the device that the arbiter has granted bus access. This is a device-specific point-to-point line.
Error Reporting Pins		
PERR#	s/t/s	Parity Error. Indicates a data parity error is detected by a target during a write data phase or by an initiator during a read data phase.
SERR#	o/d	System Error. May be pulsed by any device to report address parity errors and critical errors other than parity.

In addition, the PCI specification defines 51 optional signal lines (Table 3.4), divided into the following functional groups:

- **Interrupt pins:** These are provided for PCI devices that must generate requests for service. As with the arbitration pins, these are not shared lines. Rather, each PCI device has its own interrupt line or lines to an interrupt controller.

Table 3.4   Optional PCI Signal Lines

Designation	Type	Description
Interrupt Pins		
INTA#	o/d	Used to request an interrupt.
INTB#	o/d	Used to request an interrupt; only has meaning on a multifunction device.
INTC#	o/d	Used to request an interrupt; only has meaning on a multifunction device.
INTD#	o/d	Used to request an interrupt; only has meaning on a multifunction device.
Cache Support Pins		
SBO#	in/out	Snoop Backoff. Indicates a hit to a modified line.
SDONE	in/out	Snoop Done. Indicates the status of the snoop for the current access. Asserted when snoop has been completed.
64-Bit Bus Extension Pins		
AD[63::32]	t/s	Multiplexed lines used for address and data to extend bus to 64 bits.
C/BE[7::4]#	t/s	Multiplexed bus command and byte enable signals. During the address phase, the lines provide additional bus commands. During the data phase, the lines indicate which of the four extended byte lanes carry meaningful data.
REQ64#	s/t/s	Used to request 64-bit transfer.
ACK64#	s/t/s	Indicates target is willing to perform 64-bit transfer.
PAR64	t/s	Provides even parity across extended AD and C/BE lines one clock cycle later.
JTAG/Boundary Scan Pins		
TCK	in	Test clock. Used to clock state information and test data into and out of the device during boundary scan.
TDI	in	Test input. Used to serially shift test data and instructions into the device.
TDO	out	Test output. Used to serially shift test data and instructions out of the device.
TMS	in	Test mode Select. Used to control state of test access port controller.
TRST#	in	Test reset. Used to initialize test access port controller.

in   Input-only signal
out   Output-only signal
t/s   Bidirectional, tri-state, I/O signal
s/t/s   Sustained tri-state signal driven by only one owner at a time
o/d   Open drain: allows multiple devices to share as a wire-OR
Signal's active state occurs at low voltage

- **Cache support pins:** These pins are needed to support a memory on PCI that can be cached in the processor or another device. These pins support snoopy cache protocols (see Chapter 18 for a discussion of such protocols).

- **64-bit bus extension pins:** Include 32 lines that are time multiplexed for addresses and data and that are combined with the mandatory address/data lines to form a 64-bit address/data bus. Other lines in this group are used to interpret and validate the signal lines that carry the addresses and data. Finally, there are two lines that enable two PCI devices to agree to the use of the 64-bit capability.

- **JTAG/boundary scan pins:** These signal lines support testing procedures defined in IEEE Standard 1149.1.

PCI Commands

Bus activity occurs in the form of transactions between an initiator, or master, and a target. When a bus master acquires control of the bus, it determines the type of transaction that will occur next. During the address phase of the transaction, the C/BE lines are used to signal the transaction type. The commands are as follows:

- Interrupt Acknowledge
- Special Cycle
- I/O Read
- I/O Write
- Memory Read
- Memory Read Line
- Memory Read Multiple
- Memory Write
- Memory Write and Invalidate
- Configuration Read
- Configuration Write
- Dual address Cycle

Interrupt Acknowledge is a read command intended for the device that functions as an interrupt controller on the PCI bus. The address lines are not used during the address phase, and the byte enable lines indicate the size of the interrupt identifier to be returned.

The Special Cycle command is used by the initiator to broadcast a message to one or more targets.

The I/O Read and Write commands are used to transfer data between the initiator and an I/O controller. Each I/O device has its own address space, and the address lines are used to indicate a particular device and to specify the data to be transferred to or from that device. The concept of I/O addresses is explored in Chapter 7.

The memory read and write commands are used to specify the transfer of a burst of data, occupying one or more clock cycles. The interpretation of these commands depends on whether or not the memory controller on the PCI bus supports the PCI protocol for transfers between memory and cache. If so, the transfer of data to and from the memory is typically in terms of cache lines, or blocks.[3] The three memory read commands have the uses outlined in Table 3.5. The Memory Write command is used to transfer data in one or more data cycles to memory. The Memory Write and Invalidate command transfers data in one or more cycles to memory. In addition, it guarantees that at least one cache line is written. This command supports the cache function of writing back a line to memory.

The two configuration commands enable a master to read and update configuration parameters in a device connected to the PCI. Each PCI device may include

---

[3]The fundamental principles of cache memory are described in Chapter 4; bus-based cache protocols are described in Chapter 17.

Table 3.5 Interpretation of PCI Read Commands

Read Command Type	For Cachable Memory	For Noncachable Memory
Memory Read	Bursting one-half or less of a cache line	Bursting 2 data transfer cycles or less
Memory Read Line	Bursting more than one-half a cache line to three cache lines	Bursting 3 to 12 data transfers
Memory Read Multiple	Bursting more than three cache lines	Bursting more than 12 data transfers

up to 256 internal registers that are used during system initialization to configure that device.

The Dual Address Cycle command is used by an initiator to indicate that it is using 64-bit addressing.

Data Transfers

Every data transfer on the PCI bus is a single transaction consisting of one address phase and one or more data phases. In this discussion, we illustrate a typical read operation; a write operation proceeds similarly.

Figure 3.23 shows the timing of the read transaction. All events are synchronized to the falling transitions of the clock, which occur in the middle of each clock cycle. Bus devices sample the bus lines on the rising edge at the beginning of a bus cycle. The following are the significant events, labeled on the diagram:

a. Once a bus master has gained control of the bus, it may begin the transaction by asserting FRAME. This line remains asserted until the initiator is ready to complete the last data phase. The initiator also puts the start address on the address bus, and the read command on the C/BE lines.

b. At the start of clock 2, the target device will recognize its address on the AD lines.

c. The initiator ceases driving the AD bus. A turnaround cycle (indicated by the two circular arrows) is required on all signal lines that may be driven by more than one device, so that the dropping of the address signal will prepare the bus for use by the target device. The initiator changes the information on the C/BE lines to designate which AD lines are to be used for transfer for the currently addressed data (from 1 to 4 bytes). The initiator also asserts IRDY to indicate that it is ready for the first data item.

d. The selected target asserts DEVSEL to indicate that it has recognized its address and will respond. It places the requested data on the AD lines and asserts TRDY to indicate that valid data are present on the bus.

e. The initiator reads the data at the beginning of clock 4 and changes the byte enable lines as needed in preparation for the next read.

f. In this example, the target needs some time to prepare the second block of data for transmission. Therefore, it deasserts TRDY to signal the initiator that there will not be new data during the coming cycle. Accordingly, the initiator does not read the data lines at the beginning of the fifth clock cycle and does not change byte enable during that cycle. The block of data is read at beginning of clock 6.

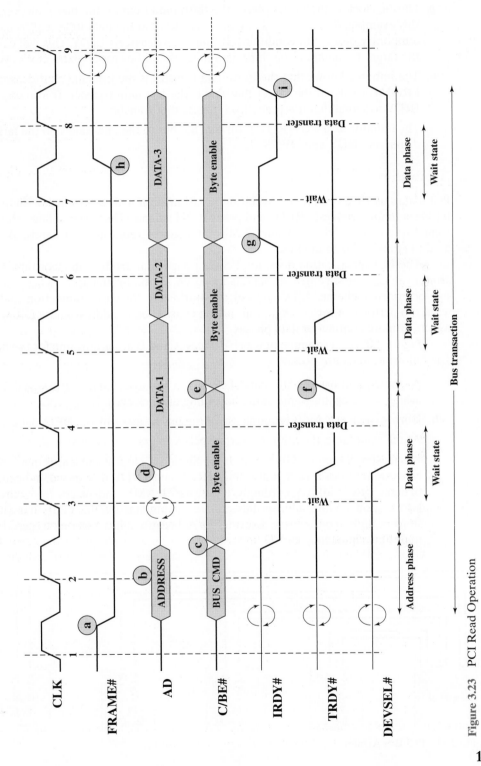

Figure 3.23 PCI Read Operation

101

g. During clock 6, the target places the third data item on the bus. However, in this example, the initiator is not yet ready to read the data item (e.g., it has a temporary buffer full condition). It therefore deasserts IRDY. This will cause the target to maintain the third data item on the bus for an extra clock cycle.

h. The initiator knows that the third data transfer is the last, and so it deasserts FRAME to signal the target that this is the last data transfer. It also asserts IRDY to signal that it is ready to complete that transfer.

i. The initiator deasserts IRDY, returning the bus to the idle state, and the target deasserts TRDY and DEVSEL.

Arbitration

PCI makes use of a centralized, synchronous arbitration scheme in which each master has a unique request (REQ) and grant (GNT) signal. These signal lines are attached to a central arbiter (Figure 3.24) and a simple request–grant handshake is used to grant access to the bus.

The PCI specification does not dictate a particular arbitration algorithm. The arbiter can use a first-come-first-served approach, a round-robin approach, or some sort of priority scheme. A PCI master must arbitrate for each transaction that it wishes to perform, where a single transaction consists of an address phase followed by one or more contiguous data phases.

Figure 3.25 is an example in which devices A and B are arbitrating for the bus. The following sequence occurs:

a. At some point prior to the start of clock 1, A has asserted its REQ signal. The arbiter samples this signal at the beginning of clock cycle 1.

b. During clock cycle 1, B requests use of the bus by asserting its REQ signal.

c. At the same time, the arbiter asserts GNT-A to grant bus access to A.

d. Bus master A samples GNT-A at the beginning of clock 2 and learns that it has been granted bus access. It also finds IRDY and TRDY deasserted, indicating that the bus is idle. Accordingly, it asserts FRAME and places the address information on the address bus and the command on the C/BE bus (not shown). It also continues to assert REQ-A, because it has a second transaction to perform after this one.

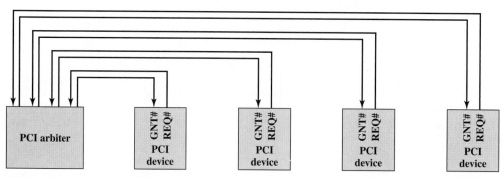

Figure 3.24   PCI Bus Arbiter

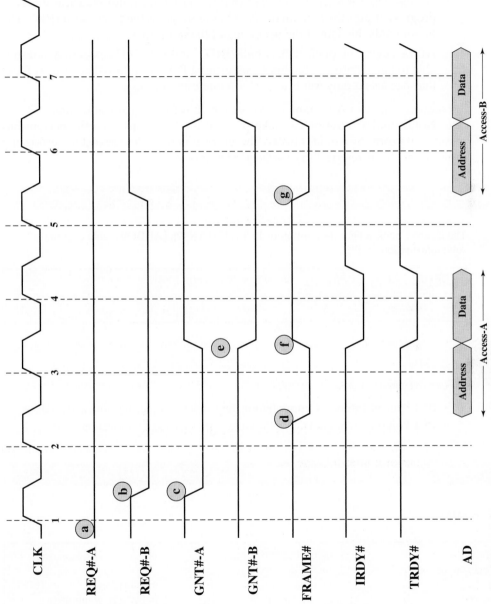

Figure 3.25   PCI Bus Arbitration between Two Masters

103

    e. The bus arbiter samples all REQ lines at the beginning of clock 3 and makes an arbitration decision to grant the bus to B for the next transaction. It then asserts GNT-B and deasserts GNT-A. B will not be able to use the bus until it returns to an idle state.

    f. A deasserts FRAME to indicate that the last (and only) data transfer is in progress. It puts the data on the data bus and signals the target with IRDY. The target reads the data at the beginning of the next clock cycle.

    g. At the beginning of clock 5, B finds IRDY and FRAME deasserted and so is able to take control of the bus by asserting FRAME. It also deasserts its REQ line, because it only wants to perform one transaction.

Subsequently, master A is granted access to the bus for its next transaction.

Notice that arbitration can take place at the same time that the current bus master is performing a data transfer. Therefore, no bus cycles are lost in performing arbitration. This is referred to as *hidden arbitration.*

3.6 RECOMMENDED READING AND WEB SITES

The clearest book-length description of PCI is [SHAN99]. [ABBO04] also contains a lot of solid information on PCI.

ABBO04   Abbot, D. *PCI Bus Demystified.* New York: Elsevier, 2004.
SHAN99   Shanley, T., and Anderson, D. *PCI Systems Architecture.* Richardson, TX: Mindshare Press, 1999.

 Recommended Web sites:

- **PCI Special Interest Group:** Information about PCI specifications and products
- **PCI Pointers:** Links to PCI vendors and other sources of information

3.7 KEY TERMS, REVIEW QUESTIONS, AND PROBLEMS

Key Terms

address bus	distributed arbitration	memory address register
asynchronous timing	instruction cycle	(MAR)
bus	instruction execute	memory buffer register (MBR)
bus arbitration	instruction fetch	peripheral component
bus width	interrupt	interconnect (PCI)
centralized arbitration	interrupt handler	synchronous timing
data bus	interrupt service routine	system bus
disabled interrupt		

Review Questions

3.1 What general categories of functions are specified by computer instructions?

3.2 List and briefly define the possible states that define an instruction execution.

3.3 List and briefly define two approaches to dealing with multiple interrupts.

3.4 What types of transfers must a computer's interconnection structure (e.g., bus) support?

3.5 What is the benefit of using a multiple-bus architecture compared to a single-bus architecture?

3.6 List and briefly define the functional groups of signal lines for PCI.

Problems

3.1 The hypothetical machine of Figure 3.4 also has two I/O instructions:

$$0011 = \text{Load AC from I/O}$$
$$0011 = \text{Store AC to I/O}$$

In these cases, the 12-bit address identifies a particular I/O device. Show the program execution (using the format of Figure 3.5) for the following program:
1. Load AC from device 5.
2. Add contents of memory location 940.
3. Store AC to device 6.

Assume that the next value retrieved from device 5 is 3 and that location 940 contains a value of 2.

3.2 The program execution of Figure 3.5 is described in the text using six steps. Expand this description to show the use of the MAR and MBR.

3.3 Consider a hypothetical 32-bit microprocessor having 32-bit instructions composed of two fields: the first byte contains the opcode and the remainder the immediate operand or an operand address.
   a. What is the maximum directly addressable memory capacity (in bytes)?
   b. Discuss the impact on the system speed if the microprocessor bus has
      1. a 32-bit local address bus and a 16-bit local data bus, or
      2. a 16-bit local address bus and a 16-bit local data bus.
   c. How many bits are needed for the program counter and the instruction register?

3.4 Consider a hypothetical microprocessor generating a 16-bit address (for example, assume that the program counter and the address registers are 16 bits wide) and having a 16-bit data bus.
   a. What is the maximum memory address space that the processor can access directly if it is connected to a "16-bit memory"?
   b. What is the maximum memory address space that the processor can access directly if it is connected to an "8-bit memory"?
   c. What architectural features will allow this microprocessor to access a separate "I/O space"?
   d. If an input and an output instruction can specify an 8-bit I/O port number, how many 8-bit I/O ports can the microprocessor support? How many 16-bit I/O ports? Explain.

3.5 Consider a 32-bit microprocessor, with a 16-bit external data bus, driven by an 8-MHz input clock. Assume that this microprocessor has a bus cycle whose minimum duration equals four input clock cycles. What is the maximum data transfer rate across the bus that this microprocessor can sustain, in bytes/s? To increase its performance, would it be better to make its external data bus 32 bits or to double the external clock frequency supplied to the microprocessor? State any other assumptions you make, and explain. *Hint:* Determine the number of bytes that can be transferred per bus cycle.

3.6   Consider a computer system that contains an I/O module controlling a simple keyboard/printer teletype. The following registers are contained in the processor and connected directly to the system bus:

INPR: Input Register, 8 bits
OUTR: Output Register, 8 bits
FGI: Input Flag, 1 bit
FGO: Output Flag, 1 bit
IEN: Interrupt Enable, 1 bit

Keystroke input from the teletype and printer output to the teletype are controlled by the I/O module. The teletype is able to encode an alphanumeric symbol to an 8-bit word and decode an 8-bit word into an alphanumeric symbol.

   a. Describe how the processor, using the first four registers listed in this problem, can achieve I/O with the teletype.
   b. Describe how the function can be performed more efficiently by also employing IEN.

3.7   Consider two microprocessors having 8- and 16-bit-wide external data buses, respectively. The two processors are identical otherwise and their bus cycles take just as long.

   a. Suppose all instructions and operands are two bytes long. By what factor do the maximum data transfer rates differ?
   b. Repeat assuming that half of the operands and instructions are one byte long.

3.8   Figure 3.26 indicates a distributed arbitration scheme that can be used with an obsolete bus scheme known as Multibus I. Agents are daisy-chained physically in priority order. The left-most agent in the diagram receives a constant *bus priority in* (BPRN) signal indicating that no higher-priority agent desires the bus. If the agent does not require the bus, it asserts its *bus priority out* (BPRO) line. At the beginning of a clock cycle, any agent can request control of the bus by lowering its BPRO line. This lowers the BPRN line of the next agent in the chain, which is in turn required to lower its BPRO line. Thus, the signal is propagated the length of the chain. At the end of this chain reaction, there should be only one agent whose BPRN is asserted and whose BPRO is not. This agent has priority. If, at the beginning of a bus cycle, the bus is not busy (BUSY inactive), the agent that has priority may seize control of the bus by asserting the BUSY line.

It takes a certain amount of time for the BPR signal to propagate from the highest-priority agent to the lowest. Must this time be less than the clock cycle? Explain.

3.9   The VAX SBI bus uses a distributed, synchronous arbitration scheme. Each SBI device (i.e., processor, memory, I/O module) has a unique priority and is assigned a

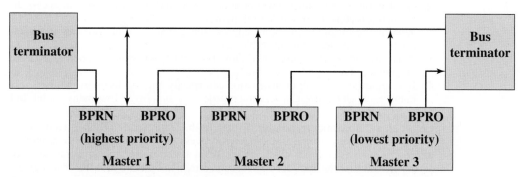

Figure 3.26   Multibus I Distributed Arbitration

unique transfer request (TR) line. The SBI has 16 such lines (TR0, TR1, . . ., TR15), with TR0 having the highest priority. When a device wants to use the bus, it places a reservation for a future time slot by asserting its TR line during the current time slot. At the end of the current time slot, each device with a pending reservation examines the TR lines; the highest-priority device with a reservation uses the next time slot.

A maximum of 17 devices can be attached to the bus. The device with priority 16 has no TR line. Why not?

3.10 On the VAX SBI, the lowest-priority device usually has the lowest average wait time. For this reason, the processor is usually given the lowest priority on the SBI. Why does the priority 16 device usually have the lowest average wait time? Under what circumstances would this not be true?

3.11 For a synchronous read operation (Figure 3.19), the memory module must place the data on the bus sufficiently ahead of the falling edge of the Read signal to allow for signal settling. Assume a microprocessor bus is clocked at 10 MHz and that the Read signal begins to fall in the middle of the second half of T_3.
   a. Determine the length of the memory read instruction cycle.
   b. When, at the latest, should memory data be placed on the bus? Allow 20 ns for the settling of data lines.

3.12 Consider a microprocessor that has a memory read timing as shown in Figure 3.19. After some analysis, a designer determines that the memory falls short of providing read data on time by about 180 ns.
   a. How many wait states (clock cycles) need to be inserted for proper system operation if the bus clocking rate is 8 MHz?
   b. To enforce the wait states, a Ready status line is employed. Once the processor has issued a Read command, it must wait until the Ready line is asserted before attempting to read data. At what time interval must we keep the Ready line low in order to force the processor to insert the required number of wait states?

3.13 A microprocessor has a memory write timing as shown in Figure 3.19. Its manufacturer specifies that the width of the Write signal can be determined by $T - 50$, where T is the clock period in ns.
   a. What width should we expect for the Write signal if bus clocking rate is 5 MHz?
   b. The data sheet for the microprocessor specifies that the data remain valid for 20 ns after the falling edge of the Write signal. What is the total duration of valid data presentation to memory?
   c. How many wait states should we insert if memory requires valid data presentation for at least 190 ns?

3.14 A microprocessor has an increment memory direct instruction, which adds 1 to the value in a memory location. The instruction has five stages: fetch opcode (four bus clock cycles), fetch operand address (three cycles), fetch operand (three cycles), add 1 to operand (three cycles), and store operand (three cycles).
   a. By what amount (in percent) will the duration of the instruction increase if we have to insert two bus wait states in each memory read and memory write operation?
   b. Repeat assuming that the increment operation takes 13 cycles instead of 3 cycles.

3.15 The Intel 8088 microprocessor has a read bus timing similar to that of Figure 3.19, but requires four processor clock cycles. The valid data is on the bus for an amount of time that extends into the fourth processor clock cycle. Assume a processor clock rate of 8 MHz.
   a. What is the maximum data transfer rate?
   b. Repeat but assume the need to insert one wait state per byte transferred.

3.16 The Intel 8086 is a 16-bit processor similar in many ways to the 8-bit 8088. The 8086 uses a 16-bit bus that can transfer 2 bytes at a time, provided that the lower-order byte has an even address. However, the 8086 allows both even- and odd-aligned word operands. If an odd-aligned word is referenced, two memory cycles, each consisting of four bus cycles, are required to transfer the word. Consider an instruction on the 8086 that involves two 16-bit operands. How long does it take to fetch the operands? Give the range of possible answers. Assume a clocking rate of 4 MHz and no wait states.

3.17 Consider a 32-bit microprocessor whose bus cycle is the same duration as that of a 16-bit microprocessor. Assume that, on average, 20% of the operands and instructions are 32 bits long, 40% are 16 bits long, and 40% are only 8 bits long. Calculate the improvement achieved when fetching instructions and operands with the 32-bit microprocessor.

3.18 The microprocessor of Problem 3.14 initiates the fetch operand stage of the increment memory direct instruction at the same time that a keyboard actives an interrupt request line. After how long does the processor enter the interrupt processing cycle? Assume a bus clocking rate of 10 MHz.

3.19 Draw and explain a timing diagram for a PCI write operation (similar to Figure 3.23).

APPENDIX 3A   TIMING DIAGRAMS

In this chapter, timing diagrams are used to illustrate sequences of events and dependencies among events. For the reader unfamiliar with timing diagrams, this appendix provides a brief explanation.

Communication among devices connected to a bus takes place along a set of lines capable of carrying signals. Two different signal levels (voltage levels), representing binary 0 and binary 1, may be transmitted. A timing diagram shows the signal level on a line as a function of time (Figure 3.27a). By convention, the binary 1 signal level is depicted as a higher level than that of binary 0. Usually, binary 0 is the default value. That is, if no data or other signal is being transmitted, then the level on a line is that which represents binary 0. A signal transition from 0 to 1 is frequently referred to as the signal's *leading edge;* a transition from 1 to 0 is referred to as a *trailing edge.* Such transitions are not instantaneous, but this transition time is usually small compared with the duration of a signal level. For clarity, the transition is usually depicted as an angled line that exaggerates the relative amount of time that the transition takes. Occasionally, you will see diagrams that use vertical lines, which incorrectly suggests that the transition is instantaneous. On a timing diagram, it may happen that a variable or at least irrelevant amount of time elapses between events of interest. This is depicted by a gap in the time line.

Signals are sometimes represented in groups (Figure 3.27b). For example, if data are transferred a byte at a time, then eight lines are required. Generally, it is not important to know the exact value being transferred on such a group, but rather whether signals are present or not.

A signal transition on one line may trigger an attached device to make signal changes on other lines. For example, if a memory module detects a read control signal (0 or 1 transition), it will place data signals on the data lines. Such cause-and-effect relationships produce sequences of events. Arrows are used on timing diagrams to show these dependencies (Figure 3.27c).

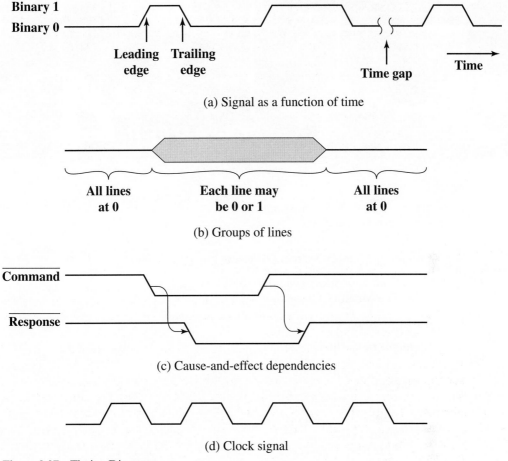

Figure 3.27   Timing Diagrams

In Figure 3.27c, the overbar over the signal name indicates that the signal is active low as shown. For example, $\overline{\text{Command}}$ is active, or asserted, at 0 volts. This means that $\overline{\text{Command}} = 0$ is interpreted as logical 1, or true.

A clock line is often part of a system bus. An electronic clock is connected to the clock line and provides a repetitive, regular sequence of transitions (Figure 3.27d). Other events may be synchronized to the clock signal.

CHAPTER 4

CACHE MEMORY

KEY POINTS

◆ Computer memory is organized into a hierarchy. At the highest level (closest to the processor) are the processor registers. Next comes one or more levels of cache, When multiple levels are used, they are denoted L1, L2, and so on. Next comes main memory, which is usually made out of dynamic random-access memory (DRAM). All of these are considered internal to the computer system. The hierarchy continues with external memory, with the next level typically being a fixed hard disk, and one or more levels below that consisting of removable media such as optical disks and tape.

◆ As one goes down the memory hierarchy, one finds decreasing cost/bit, increasing capacity, and slower access time. It would be nice to use only the fastest memory, but because that is the most expensive memory, we trade off access time for cost by using more of the slower memory. The design challenge is to organize the data and programs in memory so that the accessed memory words are usually in the faster memory.

◆ In general, it is likely that most future accesses to main memory by the processor will be to locations recently accessed. So the cache automatically retains a copy of some of the recently used words from the DRAM. If the cache is designed properly, then most of the time the processor will request memory words that are already in the cache.

Although seemingly simple in concept, computer memory exhibits perhaps the widest range of type, technology, organization, performance, and cost of any feature of a computer system. No one technology is optimal in satisfying the memory requirements for a computer system. As a consequence, the typical computer system is equipped with a hierarchy of memory subsystems, some internal to the system (directly accessible by the processor) and some external (accessible by the processor via an I/O module).

This chapter and the next focus on internal memory elements, while Chapter 6 is devoted to external memory. To begin, the first section examines key characteristics of computer memories. The remainder of the chapter examines an essential element of all modern computer systems: cache memory.

4.1 COMPUTER MEMORY SYSTEM OVERVIEW

Characteristics of Memory Systems

The complex subject of computer memory is made more manageable if we classify memory systems according to their key characteristics. The most important of these are listed in Table 4.1.

The term **location** in Table 4.1 refers to whether memory is internal and external to the computer. Internal memory is often equated with main memory. But there are other forms of internal memory. The processor requires its own local memory, in

Table 4.1 Key Characteristics of Computer Memory Systems

Location	Performance
Internal (e.g. processor registers, main memory, cache)	Access time
	Cycle time
External (e.g. optical disks, magnetic disks, tapes)	Transfer rate
Capacity	**Physical Type**
	Semiconductor
Number of words	Magnetic
Number of bytes	Optical
Unit of Transfer	Magneto-optical
Word	**Physical Characteristics**
Block	Volatile/nonvolatile
Access Method	Erasable/nonerasable
Sequential	**Organization**
Direct	Memory modules
Random	
Associative	

the form of registers (e.g., see Figure 2.3). Further, as we shall see, the control unit portion of the processor may also require its own internal memory. We will defer discussion of these latter two types of internal memory to later chapters. Cache is another form of internal memory. External memory consists of peripheral storage devices, such as disk and tape, that are accessible to the processor via I/O controllers.

An obvious characteristic of memory is its **capacity**. For internal memory, this is typically expressed in terms of bytes (1 byte = 8 bits) or words. Common word lengths are 8, 16, and 32 bits. External memory capacity is typically expressed in terms of bytes.

A related concept is the **unit of transfer**. For internal memory, the unit of transfer is equal to the number of electrical lines into and out of the memory module. This may be equal to the word length, but is often larger, such as 64, 128, or 256 bits. To clarify this point, consider three related concepts for internal memory:

- **Word:** The "natural" unit of organization of memory. The size of the word is typically equal to the number of bits used to represent an integer and to the instruction length. Unfortunately, there are many exceptions. For example, the CRAY C90 (an older model CRAY supercomputer) has a 64-bit word length but uses a 46-bit integer representation. The Intel x86 architecture has a wide variety of instruction lengths, expressed as multiples of bytes, and a word size of 32 bits.

- **Addressable units:** In some systems, the addressable unit is the word. However, many systems allow addressing at the byte level. In any case, the relationship between the length in bits A of an address and the number N of addressable units is $2^A = N$.

- **Unit of transfer:** For main memory, this is the number of bits read out of or written into memory at a time. The unit of transfer need not equal a word or an addressable unit. For external memory, data are often transferred in much larger units than a word, and these are referred to as blocks.

Another distinction among memory types is the **method of accessing** units of data. These include the following:

- **Sequential access:** Memory is organized into units of data, called records. Access must be made in a specific linear sequence. Stored addressing information is used to separate records and assist in the retrieval process. A shared read–write mechanism is used, and this must be moved from its current location to the desired location, passing and rejecting each intermediate record. Thus, the time to access an arbitrary record is highly variable. Tape units, discussed in Chapter 6, are sequential access.

- **Direct access:** As with sequential access, direct access involves a shared read–write mechanism. However, individual blocks or records have a unique address based on physical location. Access is accomplished by direct access to reach a general vicinity plus sequential searching, counting, or waiting to reach the final location. Again, access time is variable. Disk units, discussed in Chapter 6, are direct access.

- **Random access:** Each addressable location in memory has a unique, physically wired-in addressing mechanism. The time to access a given location is independent of the sequence of prior accesses and is constant. Thus, any location can be selected at random and directly addressed and accessed. Main memory and some cache systems are random access.

- **Associative:** This is a random access type of memory that enables one to make a comparison of desired bit locations within a word for a specified match, and to do this for all words simultaneously. Thus, a word is retrieved based on a portion of its contents rather than its address. As with ordinary random-access memory, each location has its own addressing mechanism, and retrieval time is constant independent of location or prior access patterns. Cache memories may employ associative access.

From a user's point of view, the two most important characteristics of memory are capacity and **performance**. Three performance parameters are used:

- **Access time (latency):** For random-access memory, this is the time it takes to perform a read or write operation, that is, the time from the instant that an address is presented to the memory to the instant that data have been stored or made available for use. For non-random-access memory, access time is the time it takes to position the read–write mechanism at the desired location.

- **Memory cycle time:** This concept is primarily applied to random-access memory and consists of the access time plus any additional time required before a second access can commence. This additional time may be required for transients to die out on signal lines or to regenerate data if they are read destructively. Note that memory cycle time is concerned with the system bus, not the processor.

- **Transfer rate:** This is the rate at which data can be transferred into or out of a memory unit. For random-access memory, it is equal to 1/(cycle time).

For non-random-access memory, the following relationship holds:

$$T_N = T_A + \frac{n}{R}$$ (4.1)

where

T_N = Average time to read or write N bits

T_A = Average access time

n = Number of bits

R = Transfer rate, in bits per second (bps)

A variety of **physical types** of memory have been employed. The most common today are semiconductor memory, magnetic surface memory, used for disk and tape, and optical and magneto-optical.

Several **physical characteristics** of data storage are important. In a volatile memory, information decays naturally or is lost when electrical power is switched off. In a nonvolatile memory, information once recorded remains without deterioration until deliberately changed; no electrical power is needed to retain information. Magnetic-surface memories are nonvolatile. Semiconductor memory may be either volatile or nonvolatile. Nonerasable memory cannot be altered, except by destroying the storage unit. Semiconductor memory of this type is known as *read-only memory* (ROM). Of necessity, a practical nonerasable memory must also be nonvolatile.

For random-access memory, the **organization** is a key design issue. By *organization* is meant the physical arrangement of bits to form words. The obvious arrangement is not always used, as is explained in Chapter 5.

The Memory Hierarchy

The design constraints on a computer's memory can be summed up by three questions: How much? How fast? How expensive?

The question of how much is somewhat open ended. If the capacity is there, applications will likely be developed to use it. The question of how fast is, in a sense, easier to answer. To achieve greatest performance, the memory must be able to keep up with the processor. That is, as the processor is executing instructions, we would not want it to have to pause waiting for instructions or operands. The final question must also be considered. For a practical system, the cost of memory must be reasonable in relationship to other components.

As might be expected, there is a trade-off among the three key characteristics of memory: namely, capacity, access time, and cost. A variety of technologies are used to implement memory systems, and across this spectrum of technologies, the following relationships hold:

- Faster access time, greater cost per bit
- Greater capacity, smaller cost per bit
- Greater capacity, slower access time

The dilemma facing the designer is clear. The designer would like to use memory technologies that provide for large-capacity memory, both because the capacity is needed and because the cost per bit is low. However, to meet performance requirements, the designer needs to use expensive, relatively lower-capacity memories with short access times.

The way out of this dilemma is not to rely on a single memory component or technology, but to employ a **memory hierarchy**. A typical hierarchy is illustrated in Figure 4.1. As one goes down the hierarchy, the following occur:

a. Decreasing cost per bit

b. Increasing capacity

c. Increasing access time

d. Decreasing frequency of access of the memory by the processor

Thus, smaller, more expensive, faster memories are supplemented by larger, cheaper, slower memories. The key to the success of this organization is item (d): decreasing frequency of access. We examine this concept in greater detail when we discuss the cache, later in this chapter, and virtual memory in Chapter 8. A brief explanation is provided at this point.

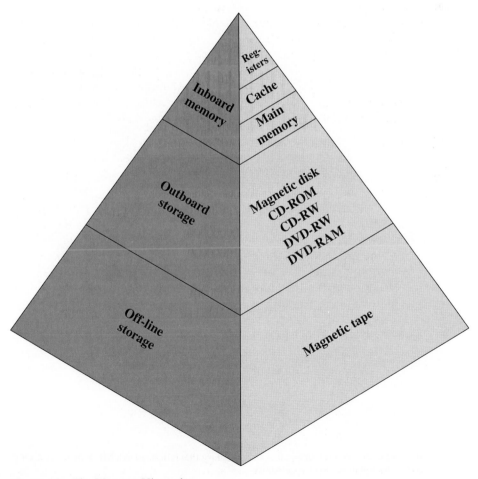

Figure 4.1   The Memory Hierarchy

Example 4.1   Suppose that the processor has access to two levels of memory. Level 1 contains 1000 words and has an access time of 0.01 μs; level 2 contains 100,000 words and has an access time of 0.1 μs. Assume that if a word to be accessed is in level 1, then the processor accesses it directly. If it is in level 2, then the word is first transferred to level 1 and then accessed by the processor. For simplicity, we ignore the time required for the processor to determine whether the word is in level 1 or level 2. Figure 4.2 shows the general shape of the curve that covers this situation. The figure shows the average access time to a two-level memory as a function of the hit ratio H, where H is defined as the fraction of all memory accesses that are found in the faster memory (e.g., the cache), T_1 is the access time to level 1, and T_2 is the access time to level 2.[1] As can be seen, for high percentages of level 1 access, the average total access time is much closer to that of level 1 than that of level 2.

In our example, suppose 95% of the memory accesses are found in the cache. Then the average time to access a word can be expressed as

$$(0.95)(0.01 \ \mu s) + (0.05)(0.01 \ \mu s + 0.1 \ \mu s) = 0.0095 + 0.0055 = 0.015 \ \mu s$$

The average access time is much closer to 0.01 μs than to 0.1 μs, as desired.

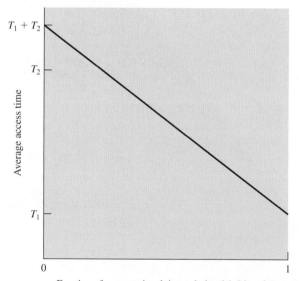

Figure 4.2   Performance of accesses involving only level 1 (hit ratio)

---

[1]If the accessed word is found in the faster memory, that is defined as a **hit**. A **miss** occurs if the accessed word is not found in the faster memory.

The use of two levels of memory to reduce average access time works in principle, but only if conditions (a) through (d) apply. By employing a variety of technologies, a spectrum of memory systems exists that satisfies conditions (a) through (c). Fortunately, condition (d) is also generally valid.

The basis for the validity of condition (d) is a principle known as **locality of reference** [DENN68]. During the course of execution of a program, memory references by the processor, for both instructions and data, tend to cluster. Programs typically contain a number of iterative loops and subroutines. Once a loop or subroutine is entered, there are repeated references to a small set of instructions. Similarly, operations on tables and arrays involve access to a clustered set of data words. Over a long period of time, the clusters in use change, but over a short period of time, the processor is primarily working with fixed clusters of memory references.

Accordingly, it is possible to organize data across the hierarchy such that the percentage of accesses to each successively lower level is substantially less than that of the level above. Consider the two-level example already presented. Let level 2 memory contain all program instructions and data. The current clusters can be temporarily placed in level 1. From time to time, one of the clusters in level 1 will have to be swapped back to level 2 to make room for a new cluster coming in to level 1. On average, however, most references will be to instructions and data contained in level 1.

This principle can be applied across more than two levels of memory, as suggested by the hierarchy shown in Figure 4.1. The fastest, smallest, and most expensive type of memory consists of the registers internal to the processor. Typically, a processor will contain a few dozen such registers, although some machines contain hundreds of registers. Skipping down two levels, main memory is the principal internal memory system of the computer. Each location in main memory has a unique address. Main memory is usually extended with a higher-speed, smaller cache. The cache is not usually visible to the programmer or, indeed, to the processor. It is a device for staging the movement of data between main memory and processor registers to improve performance.

The three forms of memory just described are, typically, volatile and employ semiconductor technology. The use of three levels exploits the fact that semiconductor memory comes in a variety of types, which differ in speed and cost. Data are stored more permanently on external mass storage devices, of which the most common are hard disk and removable media, such as removable magnetic disk, tape, and optical storage. External, nonvolatile memory is also referred to as **secondary memory** or **auxiliary memory**. These are used to store program and data files and are usually visible to the programmer only in terms of files and records, as opposed to individual bytes or words. Disk is also used to provide an extension to main memory known as virtual memory, which is discussed in Chapter 8.

Other forms of memory may be included in the hierarchy. For example, large IBM mainframes include a form of internal memory known as expanded storage. This uses a semiconductor technology that is slower and less expensive than that of main memory. Strictly speaking, this memory does not fit into the hierarchy but is a side branch: Data can be moved between main memory and expanded storage but not between expanded storage and external memory. Other forms of secondary memory include optical and magneto-optical disks. Finally, additional levels can be effectively added to the hierarchy in software. A portion of main memory can be used as a buffer to hold data temporarily that is to be read out to disk. Such a technique, sometimes referred to as a disk cache,[2] improves performance in two ways:

- Disk writes are clustered. Instead of many small transfers of data, we have a few large transfers of data. This improves disk performance and minimizes processor involvement.
- Some data destined for write-out may be referenced by a program before the next dump to disk. In that case, the data are retrieved rapidly from the software cache rather than slowly from the disk.

Appendix 4A examines the performance implications of multilevel memory structures.

4.2 CACHE MEMORY PRINCIPLES

Cache memory is intended to give memory speed approaching that of the fastest memories available, and at the same time provide a large memory size at the price of less expensive types of semiconductor memories. The concept is illustrated in Figure 4.3a. There is a relatively large and slow main memory together with a smaller, faster cache memory. The cache contains a copy of portions of main memory. When the processor attempts to read a word of memory, a check is made to

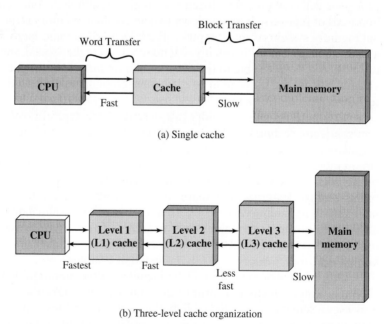

(a) Single cache

(b) Three-level cache organization

Figure 4.3   Cache and Main Memory

---

[2]Disk cache is generally a purely software technique and is not examined in this book. See [STAL09] for a discussion.

determine if the word is in the cache. If so, the word is delivered to the processor. If not, a block of main memory, consisting of some fixed number of words, is read into the cache and then the word is delivered to the processor. Because of the phenomenon of locality of reference, when a block of data is fetched into the cache to satisfy a single memory reference, it is likely that there will be future references to that same memory location or to other words in the block.

Figure 4.3b depicts the use of multiple levels of cache. The L2 cache is slower and typically larger than the L1 cache, and the L3 cache is slower and typically larger than the L2 cache.

Figure 4.4 depicts the structure of a cache/main-memory system. Main memory consists of up to 2^n addressable words, with each word having a unique n-bit address. For mapping purposes, this memory is considered to consist of a number of fixed-length blocks of K words each. That is, there are $M = 2^n/K$ blocks in main memory. The cache consists of m blocks, called **lines**.[3] Each line contains K words, plus a tag of a few bits. Each line also includes control bits (not shown), such as a bit to indicate

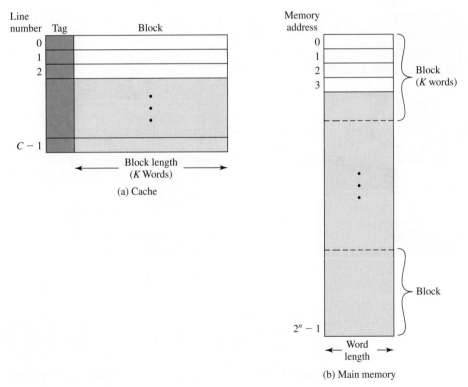

Figure 4.4   Cache/Main Memory Structure

---

[3]In referring to the basic unit of the cache, the term *line* is used, rather than the term *block*, for two reasons: (1) to avoid confusion with a main memory block, which contains the same number of data words as a cache line; and (2) because a cache line includes not only K words of data, just as a main memory block, but also include tag and control bits.

whether the line has been modified since being loaded into the cache. The length of a line, not including tag and control bits, is the **line size**. The line size may be as small as 32 bits, with each "word" being a single byte; in this case the line size is 4 bytes. The number of lines is considerably less than the number of main memory blocks ($m \ll M$). At any time, some subset of the blocks of memory resides in lines in the cache. If a word in a block of memory is read, that block is transferred to one of the lines of the cache. Because there are more blocks than lines, an individual line cannot be uniquely and permanently dedicated to a particular block. Thus, each line includes a **tag** that identifies which particular block is currently being stored. The tag is usually a portion of the main memory address, as described later in this section.

Figure 4.5 illustrates the read operation. The processor generates the read address (RA) of a word to be read. If the word is contained in the cache, it is delivered

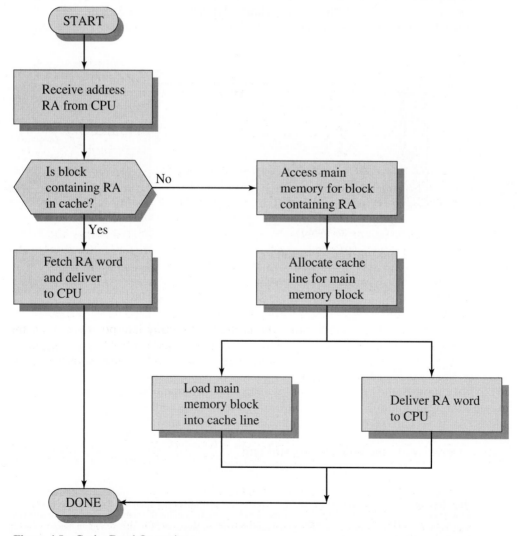

Figure 4.5 Cache Read Operation

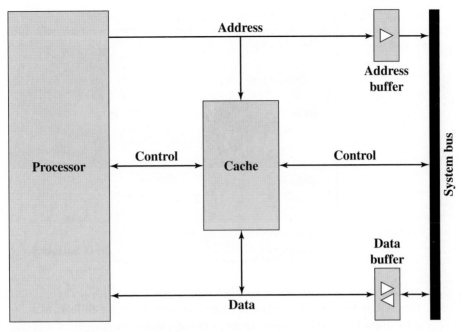

Figure 4.6 Typical Cache Organization

to the processor. Otherwise, the block containing that word is loaded into the cache, and the word is delivered to the processor. Figure 4.5 shows these last two operations occurring in parallel and reflects the organization shown in Figure 4.6, which is typical of contemporary cache organizations. In this organization, the cache connects to the processor via data, control, and address lines. The data and address lines also attach to data and address buffers, which attach to a system bus from which main memory is reached. When a cache hit occurs, the data and address buffers are disabled and communication is only between processor and cache, with no system bus traffic. When a cache miss occurs, the desired address is loaded onto the system bus and the data are returned through the data buffer to both the cache and the processor. In other organizations, the cache is physically interposed between the processor and the main memory for all data, address, and control lines. In this latter case, for a cache miss, the desired word is first read into the cache and then transferred from cache to processor.

A discussion of the performance parameters related to cache use is contained in Appendix 4A.

4.3 ELEMENTS OF CACHE DESIGN

This section provides an overview of cache design parameters and reports some typical results. We occasionally refer to the use of caches in high-performance computing (HPC). HPC deals with supercomputers and supercomputer software, especially for scientific applications that involve large amounts of data, vector and matrix

Table 4.2   Elements of Cache Design

Cache Addresses	Write Policy
Logical	Write through
Physical	Write back
Cache Size	Write once
Mapping Function	**Line Size**
Direct	**Number of caches**
Associative	Single or two level
Set Associative	Unified or split
Replacement Algorithm	
Least recently used (LRU)	
First in first out (FIFO)	
Least frequently used (LFU)	
Random	

computation, and the use of parallel algorithms. Cache design for HPC is quite different than for other hardware platforms and applications. Indeed, many researchers have found that HPC applications perform poorly on computer architectures that employ caches [BAIL93]. Other researchers have since shown that a cache hierarchy can be useful in improving performance if the application software is tuned to exploit the cache [WANG99, PRES01].[4]

Although there are a large number of cache implementations, there are a few basic design elements that serve to classify and differentiate cache architectures. Table 4.2 lists key elements.

Cache Addresses

Almost all nonembedded processors, and many embedded processors, support virtual memory, a concept discussed in Chapter 8. In essence, virtual memory is a facility that allows programs to address memory from a logical point of view, without regard to the amount of main memory physically available. When virtual memory is used, the address fields of machine instructions contain virtual addresses. For reads to and writes from main memory, a hardware memory management unit (MMU) translates each virtual address into a physical address in main memory.

When virtual addresses are used, the system designer may choose to place the cache between the processor and the MMU or between the MMU and main memory (Figure 4.7). A **logical cache**, also known as a **virtual cache**, stores data using **virtual addresses**. The processor accesses the cache directly, without going through the MMU. A physical cache stores data using main memory **physical addresses**.

One obvious advantage of the logical cache is that cache access speed is faster than for a physical cache, because the cache can respond before the MMU performs

[4]For a general discussion of HPC, see [DOWD98].

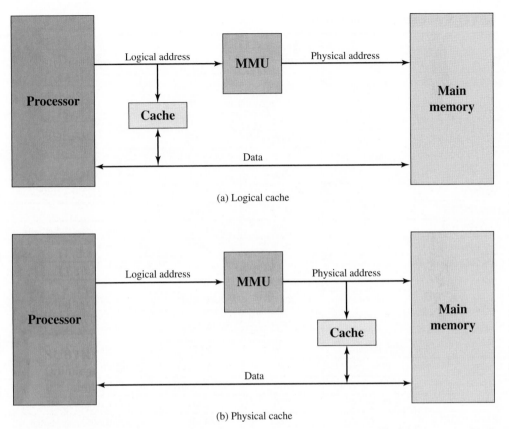

(a) Logical cache

(b) Physical cache

Figure 4.7   Logical and Physical Caches

an address translation. The disadvantage has to do with the fact that most virtual memory systems supply each application with the same virtual memory address space. That is, each application sees a virtual memory that starts at address 0. Thus, the same virtual address in two different applications refers to two different physical addresses. The cache memory must therefore be completely flushed with each application context switch, or extra bits must be added to each line of the cache to identify which virtual address space this address refers to.

The subject of logical versus physical cache is a complex one, and beyond the scope of this book. For a more in-depth discussion, see [CEKL97] and [JACO08].

Cache Size

The first item in Table 4.2, cache size, has already been discussed. We would like the size of the cache to be small enough so that the overall average cost per bit is close to that of main memory alone and large enough so that the overall average access time is close to that of the cache alone. There are several other motivations for minimizing cache size. The larger the cache, the larger the number of gates involved in addressing the cache. The result is that large caches tend to be slightly slower than small ones—even when built with the same integrated circuit technology and put in the

Table 4.3 Cache Sizes of Some Processors

Processor	Type	Year of Introduction	L1 Cache[a]	L2 Cache	L3 Cache
IBM 360/85	Mainframe	1968	16 to 32 kB	—	—
PDP-11/70	Minicomputer	1975	1 kB	—	—
VAX 11/780	Minicomputer	1978	16 kB	—	—
IBM 3033	Mainframe	1978	64 kB	—	—
IBM 3090	Mainframe	1985	128 to 256 kB	—	—
Intel 80486	PC	1989	8 kB	—	—
Pentium	PC	1993	8 kB/8 kB	256 to 512 KB	—
PowerPC 601	PC	1993	32 kB	—	—
PowerPC 620	PC	1996	32 kB/32 kB	—	—
PowerPC G4	PC/server	1999	32 kB/32 kB	256 KB to 1 MB	2 MB
IBM S/390 G4	Mainframe	1997	32 kB	256 KB	2 MB
IBM S/390 G6	Mainframe	1999	256 kB	8 MB	—
Pentium 4	PC/server	2000	8 kB/8 kB	256 KB	—
IBM SP	High-end server/ supercomputer	2000	64 kB/32 kB	8 MB	—
CRAY MTA[b]	Supercomputer	2000	8 kB	2 MB	—
Itanium	PC/server	2001	16 kB/16 kB	96 KB	4 MB
SGI Origin 2001	High-end server	2001	32 kB/32 kB	4 MB	—
Itanium 2	PC/server	2002	32 kB	256 KB	6 MB
IBM POWER5	High-end server	2003	64 kB	1.9 MB	36 MB
CRAY XD-1	Supercomputer	2004	64 kB/64 kB	1 MB	—
IBM POWER6	PC/server	2007	64 kB/64 kB	4 MB	32 MB
IBM z10	Mainframe	2008	64 kB/128 kB	3 MB	24–48 MB

[a] Two values separated by a slash refer to instruction and data caches.
[b] Both caches are instruction only; no data caches.

same place on chip and circuit board. The available chip and board area also limits cache size. Because the performance of the cache is very sensitive to the nature of the workload, it is impossible to arrive at a single "optimum" cache size. Table 4.3 lists the cache sizes of some current and past processors.

Mapping Function

Because there are fewer cache lines than main memory blocks, an algorithm is needed for mapping main memory blocks into cache lines. Further, a means is needed for determining which main memory block currently occupies a cache line. The choice of the mapping function dictates how the cache is organized. Three techniques can be used: direct, associative, and set associative. We examine each of these in turn. In each case, we look at the general structure and then a specific example.

Example 4.2 For all three cases, the example includes the following elements:

- The cache can hold 64 KBytes.
- Data are transferred between main memory and the cache in blocks of 4 bytes each. This means that the cache is organized as $16K = 2^{14}$ lines of 4 bytes each.
- The main memory consists of 16 Mbytes, with each byte directly addressable by a 24-bit address ($2^{24} = 16M$). Thus, for mapping purposes, we can consider main memory to consist of 4M blocks of 4 bytes each.

DIRECT MAPPING The simplest technique, known as direct mapping, maps each block of main memory into only one possible cache line. The mapping is expressed as

$$i = j \bmod m$$

where

i = cache line number

j = main memory block number

m = number of lines in the cache

Figure 4.8a shows the mapping for the first m blocks of main memory. Each block of main memory maps into one unique line of the cache. The next m blocks of main memory map into the cache in the same fashion; that is, block B_m of main memory maps into line L_0 of cache, block B_{m+1} maps into line L_1, and so on.

The mapping function is easily implemented using the main memory address. Figure 4.9 illustrates the general mechanism. For purposes of cache access, each main memory address can be viewed as consisting of three fields. The least significant w bits identify a unique word or byte within a block of main memory; in most contemporary machines, the address is at the byte level. The remaining s bits specify one of the 2^s blocks of main memory. The cache logic interprets these s bits as a tag of $s - r$ bits (most significant portion) and a line field of r bits. This latter field identifies one of the $m = 2^r$ lines of the cache. To summarize,

- Address length = $(s + w)$ bits
- Number of addressable units = 2^{s+w} words or bytes
- Block size = line size = 2^w words or bytes
- Number of blocks in main memory = $\dfrac{2^{s+w}}{2^w} = 2^s$
- Number of lines in cache = $m = 2^r$
- Size of cache = 2^{r+w} words or bytes
- Size of tag = $(s - r)$ bits

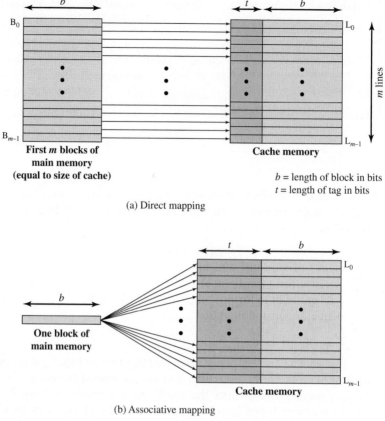

$b = $ length of block in bits
$t = $ length of tag in bits

(a) Direct mapping

(b) Associative mapping

Figure 4.8 Mapping from Main Memory to Cache: Direct and Associative

The effect of this mapping is that blocks of main memory are assigned to lines of the cache as follows:

Cache line	Main memory blocks assigned
0	$0, m, 2m, \ldots, 2^s - m$
1	$1, m + 1, 2m + 1, \ldots, 2^s - m + 1$
$\vdots$	$\vdots$
$m - 1$	$m - 1, 2m - 1, 3m - 1, \ldots, 2^s - 1$

Thus, the use of a portion of the address as a line number provides a unique mapping of each block of main memory into the cache. When a block is actually read into its assigned line, it is necessary to tag the data to distinguish it from other blocks that can fit into that line. The most significant $s - r$ bits serve this purpose.

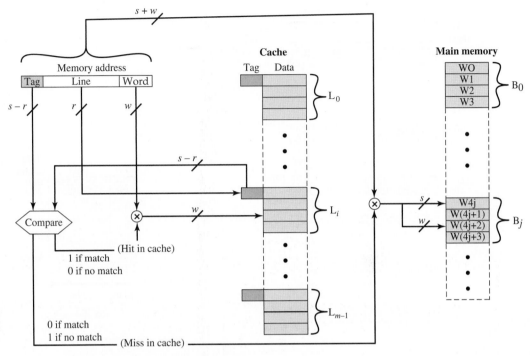

Figure 4.9   Direct-Mapping Cache Organization

Example 4.2a   Figure 4.10 shows our example system using direct mapping.[5] In the example, $m = 16K = 2^{14}$ and $i = j$ modulo 2^{14}. The mapping becomes

Cache Line	Starting Memory Address of Block
0	000000, 010000, ..., FF0000
1	000004, 010004, ..., FF0004
⋮	⋮
$2^{14} - 1$	00FFFC, 01FFFC, ..., FFFFFC

Note that no two blocks that map into the same line number have the same tag number. Thus, blocks with starting addresses 000000, 010000, ..., FF0000 have tag numbers 00, 01, ..., FF, respectively.

Referring back to Figure 4.5, a read operation works as follows. The cache system is presented with a 24-bit address. The 14-bit line number is used as an index into the cache to access a particular line. If the 8-bit tag number matches the tag number currently stored in that line, then the 2-bit word number is used to select one of the 4 bytes in that line. Otherwise, the 22-bit tag-plus-line field is used to fetch a block from main memory. The actual address that is used for the fetch is the 22-bit tag-plus-line concatenated with two 0 bits, so that 4 bytes are fetched starting on a block boundary.

---

[5]In this and subsequent figures, memory values are represented in hexadecimal notation. See Chapter 19 for a basic refresher on number systems (decimal, binary, hexadecimal).

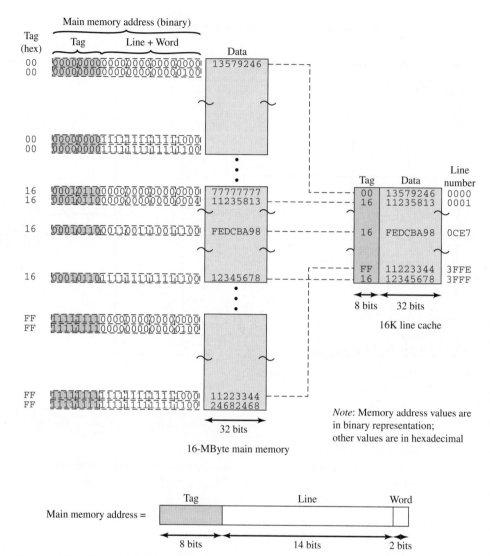

Figure 4.10 Direct Mapping Example

The direct mapping technique is simple and inexpensive to implement. Its main disadvantage is that there is a fixed cache location for any given block. Thus, if a program happens to reference words repeatedly from two different blocks that map into the same line, then the blocks will be continually swapped in the cache, and the hit ratio will be low (a phenomenon known as *thrashing*).

Selective Victim Cache Simulator

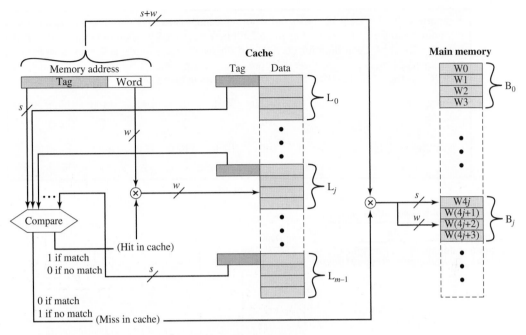

Figure 4.11 Fully Associative Cache Organization

One approach to lower the miss penalty is to remember what was discarded in case it is needed again. Since the discarded data has already been fetched, it can be used again at a small cost. Such recycling is possible using a victim cache. Victim cache was originally proposed as an approach to reduce the conflict misses of direct mapped caches without affecting its fast access time. Victim cache is a fully associative cache, whose size is typically 4 to 16 cache lines, residing between a direct mapped L1 cache and the next level of memory. This concept is explored in Appendix D.

ASSOCIATIVE MAPPING Associative mapping overcomes the disadvantage of direct mapping by permitting each main memory block to be loaded into any line of the cache (Figure 4.8b). In this case, the cache control logic interprets a memory address simply as a Tag and a Word field. The Tag field uniquely identifies a block of main memory. To determine whether a block is in the cache, the cache control logic must simultaneously examine every line's tag for a match. Figure 4.11 illustrates the logic. Note that no field in the address corresponds to the line number, so that the number of lines in the cache is not determined by the address format. To summarize,

- Address length = $(s + w)$ bits
- Number of addressable units = 2^{s+w} words or bytes
- Block size = line size = 2^w words or bytes
- Number of blocks in main memory = $\dfrac{2^{s+w}}{2^w} = 2^s$
- Number of lines in cache = undetermined
- Size of tag = s bits

Example 4.2b Figure 4.12 shows our example using associative mapping. A main memory address consists of a 22-bit tag and a 2-bit byte number. The 22-bit tag must be stored with the 32-bit block of data for each line in the cache. Note that it is the leftmost (most significant) 22 bits of the address that form the tag. Thus, the 24-bit hexadecimal address 16339C has the 22-bit tag 058CE7. This is easily seen in binary notation:

memory address	0001	0110	0011	0011	1001	1100	(binary)
	1	6	3	3	9	C	(hex)
tag (leftmost 22 bits)	00	0101	1000	1100	1110	0111	(binary)
	0	5	8	C	E	7	(hex)

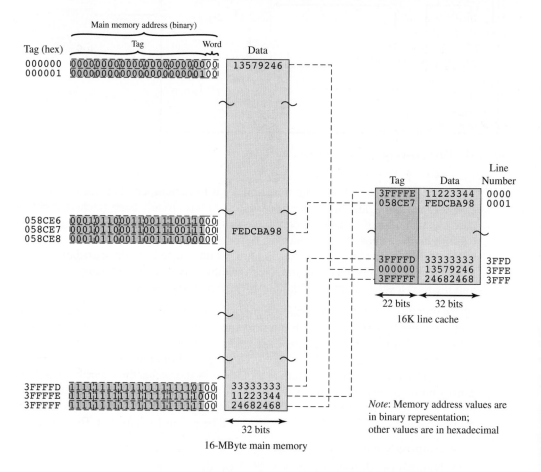

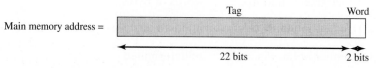

Figure 4.12   Associative Mapping Example

With associative mapping, there is flexibility as to which block to replace when a new block is read into the cache. Replacement algorithms, discussed later in this section, are designed to maximize the hit ratio. The principal disadvantage of associative mapping is the complex circuitry required to examine the tags of all cache lines in parallel.

Cache Time Analysis Simulator

SET-ASSOCIATIVE MAPPING Set-associative mapping is a compromise that exhibits the strengths of both the direct and associative approaches while reducing their disadvantages.

In this case, the cache consists of a number sets, each of which consists of a number of lines. The relationships are

$$m = v \times k$$
$$i = j \bmod v$$

where

i = cache set number
j = main memory block number
m = number of lines in the cache
v = number of sets
k = number of lines in each set

This is referred to as k-way set-associative mapping. With set-associative mapping, block B_j can be mapped into any of the lines of set j. Figure 4.13a illustrates this mapping for the first v blocks of main memory. As with associative mapping, each word maps into multiple cache lines. For set-associative mapping, each word maps into all the cache lines in a specific set, so that main memory block B_0 maps into set 0, and so on. Thus, the set-associative cache can be physically implemented as v associative caches. It is also possible to implement the set-associative cache as k direct mapping caches, as shown in Figure 4.13b. Each direct-mapped cache is referred to as a *way,* consisting of v lines. The first v lines of main memory are direct mapped into the v lines of each way; the next group of v lines of main memory are similarly mapped, and so on. The direct-mapped implementation is typically used for small degrees of associativity (small values of k) while the associative-mapped implementation is typically used for higher degrees of associativity [JACO08].

For set-associative mapping, the cache control logic interprets a memory address as three fields: Tag, Set, and Word. The d set bits specify one of $v = 2^d$ sets. The s bits of the Tag and Set fields specify one of the 2^s blocks of main memory. Figure 4.14 illustrates the cache control logic. With fully associative mapping, the tag in a memory address is quite large and must be compared to the tag of every line in the cache. With k-way set-associative mapping, the tag in a memory

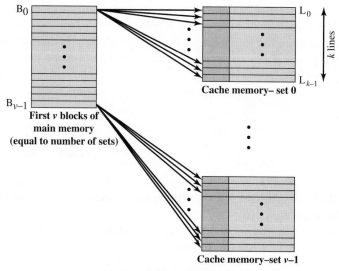

(a) v Associative–mapped caches

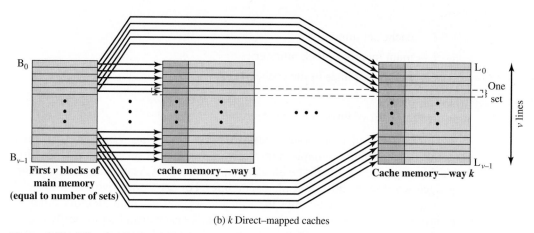

(b) k Direct–mapped caches

Figure 4.13   Mapping from Main Memory to Cache: k-way Set Associative

address is much smaller and is only compared to the k tags within a single set. To summarize,

- Address length $= (s + w)$ bits
- Number of addressable units $= 2^{s+w}$ words or bytes
- Block size $=$ line size $= 2^w$ words or bytes
- Number of blocks in main memory $= \dfrac{2^{s+w}}{2^w} = 2^s$
- Number of lines in set $= k$
- Number of sets $= v = 2^d$

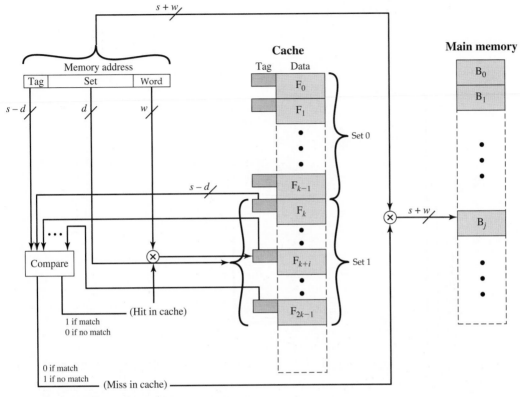

Figure 4.14 *K*-Way Set Associative Cache Organization

- Number of lines in cache $= m = kv = k \times 2^d$
- Size of cache $= k \times 2^{d+w}$ words or bytes
- Size of tag $= (s - d)$ bits

Example 4.2c Figure 4.15 shows our example using set-associative mapping with two lines in each set, referred to as two-way set-associative. The 13-bit set number identifies a unique set of two lines within the cache. It also gives the number of the block in main memory, modulo 2^{13}. This determines the mapping of blocks into lines. Thus, blocks 000000, 008000, ..., FF8000 of main memory map into cache set 0. Any of those blocks can be loaded into either of the two lines in the set. Note that no two blocks that map into the same cache set have the same tag number. For a read operation, the 13-bit set number is used to determine which set of two lines is to be examined. Both lines in the set are examined for a match with the tag number of the address to be accessed.

In the extreme case of $v = m, k = 1$, the set-associative technique reduces to direct mapping, and for $v = 1, k = m$, it reduces to associative mapping. The use of two lines per set ($v = m/2, k = 2$) is the most common set-associative organization.

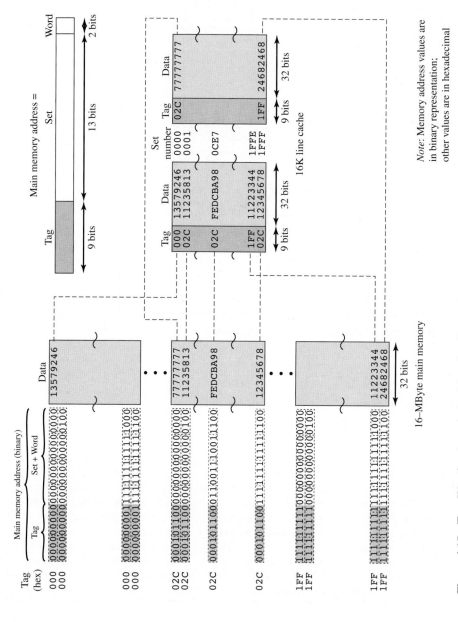

Figure 4.15 Two-Way Set Associative Mapping Example

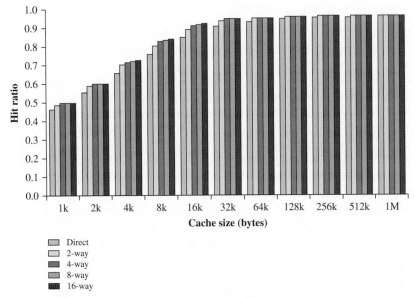

Figure 4.16 Varying Associativity over Cache Size

It significantly improves the hit ratio over direct mapping. Four-way set associative ($v = m/4$, $k = 4$) makes a modest additional improvement for a relatively small additional cost [MAYB84, HILL89]. Further increases in the number of lines per set have little effect.

Figure 4.16 shows the results of one simulation study of set-associative cache performance as a function of cache size [GENU04]. The difference in performance between direct and two-way set associative is significant up to at least a cache size of 64 kB. Note also that the difference between two-way and four-way at 4 kB is much less than the difference in going from for 4 kB to 8 kB in cache size. The complexity of the cache increases in proportion to the associativity, and in this case would not be justifiable against increasing cache size to 8 or even 16 Kbytes. A final point to note is that beyond about 32 kB, increase in cache size brings no significant increase in performance.

The results of Figure 4.16 are based on simulating the execution of a GCC compiler. Different applications may yield different results. For example, [CANT01] reports on the results for cache performance using many of the CPU2000 SPEC benchmarks. The results of [CANT01] in comparing hit ratio to cache size follow the same pattern as Figure 4.16, but the specific values are somewhat different.

Cache Simulator
Multitask Cache Simulator

Replacement Algorithms

Once the cache has been filled, when a new block is brought into the cache, one of the existing blocks must be replaced. For direct mapping, there is only one possible line for any particular block, and no choice is possible. For the associative and set-associative techniques, a replacement algorithm is needed. To achieve high speed, such an algorithm must be implemented in hardware. A number of algorithms have been tried. We mention four of the most common. Probably the most effective is least recently used (LRU): Replace that block in the set that has been in the cache longest with no reference to it. For two-way set associative, this is easily implemented. Each line includes a USE bit. When a line is referenced, its USE bit is set to 1 and the USE bit of the other line in that set is set to 0. When a block is to be read into the set, the line whose USE bit is 0 is used. Because we are assuming that more recently used memory locations are more likely to be referenced, LRU should give the best hit ratio. LRU is also relatively easy to implement for a fully associative cache. The cache mechanism maintains a separate list of indexes to all the lines in the cache. When a line is referenced, it moves to the front of the list. For replacement, the line at the back of the list is used. Because of its simplicity of implementation, LRU is the most popular replacement algorithm.

Another possibility is first-in-first-out (FIFO): Replace that block in the set that has been in the cache longest. FIFO is easily implemented as a round-robin or circular buffer technique. Still another possibility is least frequently used (LFU): Replace that block in the set that has experienced the fewest references. LFU could be implemented by associating a counter with each line. A technique not based on usage (i.e., not LRU, LFU, FIFO, or some variant) is to pick a line at random from among the candidate lines. Simulation studies have shown that random replacement provides only slightly inferior performance to an algorithm based on usage [SMIT82].

Write Policy

When a block that is resident in the cache is to be replaced, there are two cases to consider. If the old block in the cache has not been altered, then it may be overwritten with a new block without first writing out the old block. If at least one write operation has been performed on a word in that line of the cache, then main memory must be updated by writing the line of cache out to the block of memory before bringing in the new block. A variety of write policies, with performance and economic trade-offs, is possible. There are two problems to contend with. First, more than one device may have access to main memory. For example, an I/O module may be able to read-write directly to memory. If a word has been altered only in the cache, then the corresponding memory word is invalid. Further, if the I/O device has altered main memory, then the cache word is invalid. A more complex problem occurs when multiple processors are attached to the same bus and each processor has its own local cache. Then, if a word is altered in one cache, it could conceivably invalidate a word in other caches.

The simplest technique is called **write through**. Using this technique, all write operations are made to main memory as well as to the cache, ensuring that main memory is always valid. Any other processor–cache module can monitor traffic to main memory to maintain consistency within its own cache. The main disadvantage of this technique is that it generates substantial memory traffic and may create a bottleneck. An alternative technique, known as **write back**, minimizes memory writes. With write back, updates are made only in the cache. When an update occurs, a **dirty bit**, or **use bit**, associated with the line is set. Then, when a block is replaced, it is written back to main memory if and only if the dirty bit is set. The problem with write back is that portions of main memory are invalid, and hence accesses by I/O modules can be allowed only through the cache. This makes for complex circuitry and a potential bottleneck. Experience has shown that the percentage of memory references that are writes is on the order of 15% [SMIT82]. However, for HPC applications, this number may approach 33% (vector-vector multiplication) and can go as high as 50% (matrix transposition).

Example 4.3 Consider a cache with a line size of 32 bytes and a main memory that requires 30 ns to transfer a 4-byte word. For any line that is written at least once before being swapped out of the cache, what is the average number of times that the line must be written before being swapped out for a write-back cache to be more efficient that a write-through cache?

For the write-back case, each dirty line is written back once, at swap-out time, taking $8 \times 30 = 240$ ns. For the write-through case, each update of the line requires that one word be written out to main memory, taking 30 ns. Therefore, if the average line that gets written at least once gets written more than 8 times before swap out, then write back is more efficient.

In a bus organization in which more than one device (typically a processor) has a cache and main memory is shared, a new problem is introduced. If data in one cache are altered, this invalidates not only the corresponding word in main memory, but also that same word in other caches (if any other cache happens to have that same word). Even if a write-through policy is used, the other caches may contain invalid data. A system that prevents this problem is said to maintain cache coherency. Possible approaches to cache coherency include the following:

- **Bus watching with write through:** Each cache controller monitors the address lines to detect write operations to memory by other bus masters. If another master writes to a location in shared memory that also resides in the cache memory, the cache controller invalidates that cache entry. This strategy depends on the use of a write-through policy by all cache controllers.

- **Hardware transparency:** Additional hardware is used to ensure that all updates to main memory via cache are reflected in all caches. Thus, if one processor modifies a word in its cache, this update is written to main memory. In addition, any matching words in other caches are similarly updated.

- **Noncacheable memory:** Only a portion of main memory is shared by more than one processor, and this is designated as noncacheable. In such a system, all accesses to shared memory are cache misses, because the shared memory is never copied into the cache. The noncacheable memory can be identified using chip-select logic or high-address bits.

Cache coherency is an active field of research. This topic is explored further in Part Five.

Line Size

Another design element is the line size. When a block of data is retrieved and placed in the cache, not only the desired word but also some number of adjacent words are retrieved. As the block size increases from very small to larger sizes, the hit ratio will at first increase because of the principle of locality, which states that data in the vicinity of a referenced word are likely to be referenced in the near future. As the block size increases, more useful data are brought into the cache. The hit ratio will begin to decrease, however, as the block becomes even bigger and the probability of using the newly fetched information becomes less than the probability of reusing the information that has to be replaced. Two specific effects come into play:

- Larger blocks reduce the number of blocks that fit into a cache. Because each block fetch overwrites older cache contents, a small number of blocks results in data being overwritten shortly after they are fetched.
- As a block becomes larger, each additional word is farther from the requested word and therefore less likely to be needed in the near future.

The relationship between block size and hit ratio is complex, depending on the locality characteristics of a particular program, and no definitive optimum value has been found. A size of from 8 to 64 bytes seems reasonably close to optimum [SMIT87, PRZY88, PRZY90, HAND98]. For HPC systems, 64- and 128-byte cache line sizes are most frequently used.

Number of Caches

When caches were originally introduced, the typical system had a single cache. More recently, the use of multiple caches has become the norm. Two aspects of this design issue concern the number of levels of caches and the use of unified versus split caches.

MULTILEVEL CACHES As logic density has increased, it has become possible to have a cache on the same chip as the processor: the on-chip cache. Compared with a cache reachable via an external bus, the on-chip cache reduces the processor's external bus activity and therefore speeds up execution times and increases overall system performance. When the requested instruction or data is found in the on-chip cache, the bus access is eliminated. Because of the short data paths internal to the processor, compared with bus lengths, on-chip cache accesses will complete appreciably faster than would even zero-wait state bus cycles. Furthermore, during this period the bus is free to support other transfers.

The inclusion of an on-chip cache leaves open the question of whether an off-chip, or external, cache is still desirable. Typically, the answer is yes, and most contemporary designs include both on-chip and external caches. The simplest such organization is known as a two-level cache, with the internal cache designated as level 1 (L1) and the external cache designated as level 2 (L2). The reason for including an L2 cache is the following: If there is no L2 cache and the processor makes an access request for a memory location not in the L1 cache, then the processor must access

DRAM or ROM memory across the bus. Due to the typically slow bus speed and slow memory access time, this results in poor performance. On the other hand, if an L2 SRAM (static RAM) cache is used, then frequently the missing information can be quickly retrieved. If the SRAM is fast enough to match the bus speed, then the data can be accessed using a zero-wait state transaction, the fastest type of bus transfer.

Two features of contemporary cache design for multilevel caches are noteworthy. First, for an off-chip L2 cache, many designs do not use the system bus as the path for transfer between the L2 cache and the processor, but use a separate data path, so as to reduce the burden on the system bus. Second, with the continued shrinkage of processor components, a number of processors now incorporate the L2 cache on the processor chip, improving performance.

The potential savings due to the use of an L2 cache depends on the hit rates in both the L1 and L2 caches. Several studies have shown that, in general, the use of a second-level cache does improve performance (e.g., see [AZIM92], [NOVI93], [HAND98]). However, the use of multilevel caches does complicate all of the design issues related to caches, including size, replacement algorithm, and write policy; see [HAND98] and [PEIR99] for discussions.

Figure 4.17 shows the results of one simulation study of two-level cache performance as a function of cache size [GENU04]. The figure assumes that both caches have the same line size and shows the total hit ratio. That is, a hit is counted if the desired data appears in either the L1 or the L2 cache. The figure shows the impact of L2 on total hits with respect to L1 size. L2 has little effect on the total number of cache hits until it is at least double the L1 cache size. Note that the steepest part of the slope for an L1 cache of 8 Kbytes is for an L2 cache of 16 Kbytes. Again for an L1 cache of 16 Kbytes, the steepest part of the curve is for an L2 cache size of 32 Kbytes. Prior to that point, the L2 cache has little, if any, impact on total cache

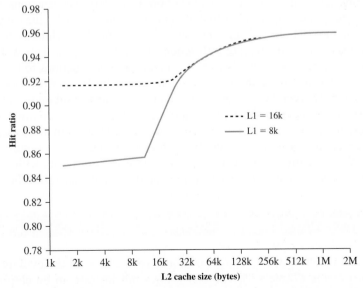

Figure 4.17 Total Hit Ratio (L1 and L2) for 8-Kbyte and 16-Kbyte L1

performance. The need for the L2 cache to be larger than the L1 cache to affect performance makes sense. If the L2 cache has the same line size and capacity as the L1 cache, its contents will more or less mirror those of the L1 cache.

With the increasing availability of on-chip area available for cache, most contemporary microprocessors have moved the L2 cache onto the processor chip and added an L3 cache. Originally, the L3 cache was accessible over the external bus. More recently, most microprocessors have incorporated an on-chip L3 cache. In either case, there appears to be a performance advantage to adding the third level (e.g., see [GHAI98]).

UNIFIED VERSUS SPLIT CACHES When the on-chip cache first made an appearance, many of the designs consisted of a single cache used to store references to both data and instructions. More recently, it has become common to split the cache into two: one dedicated to instructions and one dedicated to data. These two caches both exist at the same level, typically as two L1 caches. When the processor attempts to fetch an instruction from main memory, it first consults the instruction L1 cache, and when the processor attempts to fetch data from main memory, it first consults the data L1 cache.

There are two potential advantages of a unified cache:

- For a given cache size, a unified cache has a higher hit rate than split caches because it balances the load between instruction and data fetches automatically. That is, if an execution pattern involves many more instruction fetches than data fetches, then the cache will tend to fill up with instructions, and if an execution pattern involves relatively more data fetches, the opposite will occur.
- Only one cache needs to be designed and implemented.

Despite these advantages, the trend is toward split caches, particularly for superscalar machines such as the Pentium and PowerPC, which emphasize parallel instruction execution and the prefetching of predicted future instructions. The key advantage of the split cache design is that it eliminates contention for the cache between the instruction fetch/decode unit and the execution unit. This is important in any design that relies on the pipelining of instructions. Typically, the processor will fetch instructions ahead of time and fill a buffer, or pipeline, with instructions to be executed. Suppose now that we have a unified instruction/data cache. When the execution unit performs a memory access to load and store data, the request is submitted to the unified cache. If, at the same time, the instruction prefetcher issues a read request to the cache for an instruction, that request will be temporarily blocked so that the cache can service the execution unit first, enabling it to complete the currently executing instruction. This cache contention can degrade performance by interfering with efficient use of the instruction pipeline. The split cache structure overcomes this difficulty.

4.4   PENTIUM 4 CACHE ORGANIZATION

The evolution of cache organization is seen clearly in the evolution of Intel microprocessors (Table 4.4). The 80386 does not include an on-chip cache. The 80486 includes a single on-chip cache of 8 KBytes, using a line size of 16 bytes and a four-way

Table 4.4   Intel Cache Evolution

Problem	Solution	Processor on which Feature First Appears
External memory slower than the system bus.	Add external cache using faster memory technology.	386
Increased processor speed results in external bus becoming a bottleneck for cache access.	Move external cache on-chip, operating at the same speed as the processor.	486
Internal cache is rather small, due to limited space on chip	Add external L2 cache using faster technology than main memory	486
Contention occurs when both the Instruction Prefetcher and the Execution Unit simultaneously require access to the cache. In that case, the Prefetcher is stalled while the Execution Unit's data access takes place.	Create separate data and instruction caches.	Pentium
Increased processor speed results in external bus becoming a bottleneck for L2 cache access.	Create separate back-side bus that runs at higher speed than the main (front-side) external bus. The BSB is dedicated to the L2 cache.	Pentium Pro
	Move L2 cache on to the processor chip.	Pentium II
Some applications deal with massive databases and must have rapid access to large amounts of data. The on-chip caches are too small.	Add external L3 cache.	Pentium III
	Move L3 cache on-chip.	Pentium 4

set-associative organization. All of the Pentium processors include two on-chip L1 caches, one for data and one for instructions. For the Pentium 4, the L1 data cache is 16 KBytes, using a line size of 64 bytes and a four-way set-associative organization. The Pentium 4 instruction cache is described subsequently. The Pentium II also includes an L2 cache that feeds both of the L1 caches. The L2 cache is eight-way set associative with a size of 512 KB and a line size of 128 bytes. An L3 cache was added for the Pentium III and became on-chip with high-end versions of the Pentium 4.

Figure 4.18 provides a simplified view of the Pentium 4 organization, highlighting the placement of the three caches. The processor core consists of four major components:

- **Fetch/decode unit:** Fetches program instructions in order from the L2 cache, decodes these into a series of micro-operations, and stores the results in the L1 instruction cache.
- **Out-of-order execution logic:** Schedules execution of the micro-operations subject to data dependencies and resource availability; thus, micro-operations may be scheduled for execution in a different order than they were fetched from the instruction stream. As time permits, this unit schedules speculative execution of micro-operations that may be required in the future.

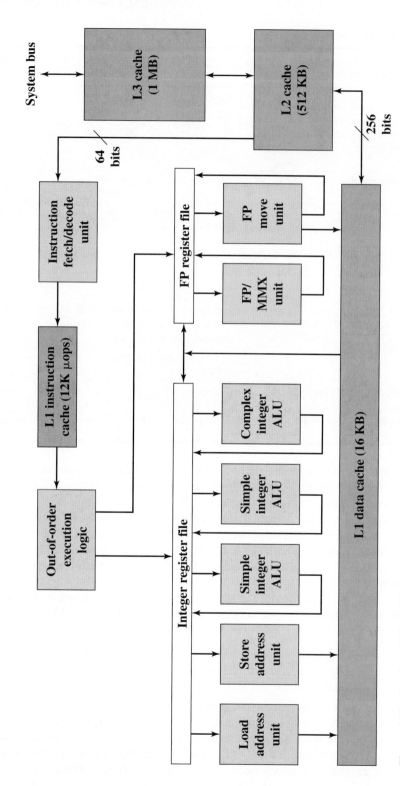

Figure 4.18 Pentium 4 Block Diagram

Table 4.5   Pentium 4 Cache Operating Modes

Control Bits		Operating Mode		
CD	NW	Cache Fills	Write Throughs	Invalidates
0	0	Enabled	Enabled	Enabled
1	0	Disabled	Enabled	Enabled
1	1	Disabled	Disabled	Disabled

Note: CD = 0; NW = 1 is an invalid combination.

- **Execution units:** These units executes micro-operations, fetching the required data from the L1 data cache and temporarily storing results in registers.
- **Memory subsystem:** This unit includes the L2 and L3 caches and the system bus, which is used to access main memory when the L1 and L2 caches have a cache miss and to access the system I/O resources.

Unlike the organization used in all previous Pentium models, and in most other processors, the Pentium 4 instruction cache sits between the instruction decode logic and the execution core. The reasoning behind this design decision is as follows: As discussed more fully in Chapter 14, the Pentium process decodes, or translates, Pentium machine instructions into simple RISC-like instructions called micro-operations. The use of simple, fixed-length micro-operations enables the use of superscalar pipelining and scheduling techniques that enhance performance. However, the Pentium machine instructions are cumbersome to decode; they have a variable number of bytes and many different options. It turns out that performance is enhanced if this decoding is done independently of the scheduling and pipelining logic. We return to this topic in Chapter 14.

The data cache employs a write-back policy: Data are written to main memory only when they are removed from the cache and there has been an update. The Pentium 4 processor can be dynamically configured to support write-through caching.

The L1 data cache is controlled by two bits in one of the control registers, labeled the CD (cache disable) and NW (not write-through) bits (Table 4.5). There are also two Pentium 4 instructions that can be used to control the data cache: INVD invalidates (flushes) the internal cache memory and signals the external cache (if any) to invalidate. WBINVD writes back and invalidates internal cache and then writes back and invalidates external cache.

Both the L2 and L3 caches are eight-way setassociative with a line size of 128 bytes.

4.5   ARM CACHE ORGANIZATION

The ARM cache organization has evolved with the overall architecture of the ARM family, reflecting the relentless pursuit of performance that is the driving force for all microprocessor designers.

Table 4.6 ARM Cache Features

Core	Cache Type	Cache Size (kB)	Cache Line Size (words)	Associativity	Location	Write Buffer Size (words)
ARM720T	Unified	8	4	4-way	Logical	8
ARM920T	Split	16/16 D/I	8	64-way	Logical	16
ARM926EJ-S	Split	4-128/4-128 D/I	8	4-way	Logical	16
ARM1022E	Split	16/16 D/I	8	64-way	Logical	16
ARM1026EJ-S	Split	4-128/4-128 D/I	8	4-way	Logical	8
Intel StrongARM	Split	16/16 D/I	4	32-way	Logical	32
Intel Xscale	Split	32/32 D/I	8	32-way	Logical	32
ARM1136-JF-S	Split	4-64/4-64 D/I	8	4-way	Physical	32

Table 4.6 shows this evolution. The ARM7 models used a unified L1 cache, while all subsequent models use a split instruction/data cache. All of the ARM designs use a set-associative cache, with the degree of associativity and the line size varying. ARM cached cores with an MMU use a logical cache for processor families ARM7 through ARM10, including the Intel StongARM and Intel Xscale processors. The ARM11 family uses a physical cache. The distinction between logical and physical cache is discussed earlier in this chapter (Figure 4.7).

An interesting feature of the ARM architecture is the use of a small first-in-first out (FIFO) write buffer to enhance memory write performance. The write buffer is interposed between the cache and main memory and consists of a set of addresses and a set of data words. The write buffer is small compared to the cache, and may hold up to four independent addresses. Typically, the write buffer is enabled for all of main memory, although it may be selectively disabled at the page level. Figure 4.19, taken from [SLOS04], shows the relationship among the write buffer, cache, and main memory.

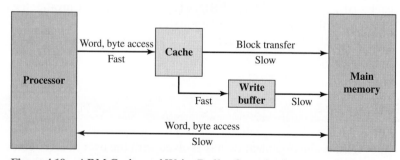

Figure 4.19 ARM Cache and Write Buffer Organization

The write buffer operates as follows: When the processor performs a write to a bufferable area, the data are placed in the write buffer at processor clock speed and the processor continues execution. A write occurs when data in the cache are written back to main memory. Thus, the data to be written are transferred from the cache to the write buffer. The write buffer then performs the external write in parallel. If, however, the write buffer is full (either because there are already the maximum number of words of data in the buffer or because there is no slot for the new address) then the processor is stalled until there is sufficient space in the buffer. As non-write operations proceed, the write buffer continues to write to main memory until the buffer is completely empty.

Data written to the write buffer are not available for reading back into the cache until the data have transferred from the write buffer to main memory. This is the principal reason that the write buffer is quite small. Even so, unless there is a high proportion of writes in an executing program, the write buffer improves performance.

4.6 RECOMMENDED READING

[JACO08] is an excellent, up-to-date treatment of cache design. Another thorough treatment is [HAND98]. A classic paper that is still well worth reading is [SMIT82]; it surveys the various elements of cache design and presents the results of an extensive set of analyses. Another interesting classic is [WILK65], which is probably the first paper to introduce the concept of the cache. [GOOD83] also provides a useful analysis of cache behavior. Another worthwhile analysis is [BELL74]. [AGAR89] presents a detailed examination of a variety of cache design issues related to multiprogramming and multiprocessing. [HIGB90] provides a set of simple formulas that can be used to estimate cache performance as a function of various cache parameters.

AGAR89   Agarwal, A. *Analysis of Cache Performance for Operating Systems and Multi-programming.* Boston: Kluwer Academic Publishers, 1989.

BELL74   Bell, J.; Casasent, D.; and Bell, C. "An Investigation into Alternative Cache Organizations." *IEEE Transactions on Computers*, April 1974. **http://research .microsoft.com/users/GBell/gbvita.htm**.

GOOD83   Goodman, J. "Using Cache Memory to Reduce Processor-Memory Bandwidth." *Proceedings, 10th Annual International Symposium on Computer Architecture*, 1983. Reprinted in [HILL00].

HAND98   Handy, J. *The Cache Memory Book.* San Diego: Academic Press, 1993.

HIGB90   Higbie, L. "Quick and Easy Cache Performance Analysis." *Computer Architecture News*, June 1990.

JACO08   Jacob, B.; Ng, S.; and Wang, D. *Memory Systems: Cache, DRAM, Disk.* Boston: Morgan Kaufmann, 2008.

SMIT82   Smith, A. "Cache Memories." *ACM Computing Surveys*, September 1992.

WILK65   Wilkes, M. "Slave Memories and Dynamic Storage Allocation," *IEEE Transactions on Electronic Computers*, April 1965. Reprinted in [HILL00].

4.7   KEY TERMS, REVIEW QUESTIONS, AND PROBLEMS

Key Terms

access time	hit ratio	sequential access
associative mapping	instruction cache	set-associative mapping
cache hit	L1 cache	spatial locality
cache line	L2 cache	split cache
cache memory	L3 cache	tag
cache miss	locality	temporal locality
cache set	logical cache	unified cache
data cache	memory hierarchy	virtual cache
direct access	multilevel cache	write back
direct mapping	physical cache	write once
high-performance computing	random access	write through
(HPC)	replacement algorithm	

Review Questions

4.1   What are the differences among sequential access, direct access, and random access?

4.2   What is the general relationship among access time, memory cost, and capacity?

4.3   How does the principle of locality relate to the use of multiple memory levels?

4.4   What are the differences among direct mapping, associative mapping, and set-associative mapping?

4.5   For a direct-mapped cache, a main memory address is viewed as consisting of three fields. List and define the three fields.

4.6   For an associative cache, a main memory address is viewed as consisting of two fields. List and define the two fields.

4.7   For a set-associative cache, a main memory address is viewed as consisting of three fields. List and define the three fields.

4.8   What is the distinction between spatial locality and temporal locality?

4.9   In general, what are the strategies for exploiting spatial locality and temporal locality?

Problems

4.1   A set-associative cache consists of 64 lines, or slots, divided into four-line sets. Main memory contains 4K blocks of 128 words each. Show the format of main memory addresses.

4.2   A two-way set-associative cache has lines of 16 bytes and a total size of 8 kbytes. The 64-Mbyte main memory is byte addressable. Show the format of main memory addresses.

4.3   For the hexadecimal main memory addresses 111111, 666666, BBBBBB, show the following information, in hexadecimal format:
   a.   Tag, Line, and Word values for a direct-mapped cache, using the format of Figure 4.10
   b.   Tag and Word values for an associative cache, using the format of Figure 4.12
   c.   Tag, Set, and Word values for a two-way set-associative cache, using the format of Figure 4.15

4.4 List the following values:
  a. For the direct cache example of Figure 4.10: address length, number of addressable units, block size, number of blocks in main memory, number of lines in cache, size of tag
  b. For the associative cache example of Figure 4.12: address length, number of addressable units, block size, number of blocks in main memory, number of lines in cache, size of tag
  c. For the two-way set-associative cache example of Figure 4.15: address length, number of addressable units, block size, number of blocks in main memory, number of lines in set, number of sets, number of lines in cache, size of tag

4.5 Consider a 32-bit microprocessor that has an on-chip 16-KByte four-way set-associative cache. Assume that the cache has a line size of four 32-bit words. Draw a block diagram of this cache showing its organization and how the different address fields are used to determine a cache hit/miss. Where in the cache is the word from memory location ABCDE8F8 mapped?

4.6 Given the following specifications for an external cache memory: four-way set associative; line size of two 16-bit words; able to accommodate a total of 4K 32-bit words from main memory; used with a 16-bit processor that issues 24-bit addresses. Design the cache structure with all pertinent information and show how it interprets the processor's addresses.

4.7 The Intel 80486 has an on-chip, unified cache. It contains 8 KBytes and has a four-way set-associative organization and a block length of four 32-bit words. The cache is organized into 128 sets. There is a single "line valid bit" and three bits, B0, B1, and B2 (the "LRU" bits), per line. On a cache miss, the 80486 reads a 16-byte line from main memory in a bus memory read burst. Draw a simplified diagram of the cache and show how the different fields of the address are interpreted.

4.8 Consider a machine with a byte addressable main memory of 2^{16} bytes and block size of 8 bytes. Assume that a direct mapped cache consisting of 32 lines is used with this machine.
  a. How is a 16-bit memory address divided into tag, line number, and byte number?
  b. Into what line would bytes with each of the following addresses be stored?

  0001 0001 0001 1011
  1100 0011 0011 0100
  1101 0000 0001 1101
  1010 1010 1010 1010

  c. Suppose the byte with address 0001 1010 0001 1010 is stored in the cache. What are the addresses of the other bytes stored along with it?
  d. How many total bytes of memory can be stored in the cache?
  e. Why is the tag also stored in the cache?

4.9 For its on-chip cache, the Intel 80486 uses a replacement algorithm referred to as **pseudo least recently used**. Associated with each of the 128 sets of four lines (labeled L0, L1, L2, L3) are three bits B0, B1, and B2. The replacement algorithm works as follows: When a line must be replaced, the cache will first determine whether the most recent use was from L0 and L1 or L2 and L3. Then the cache will determine which of the pair of blocks was least recently used and mark it for replacement. Figure 4.20 illustrates the logic.
  a. Specify how the bits B0, B1, and B2 are set and then describe in words how they are used in the replacement algorithm depicted in Figure 4.20.
  b. Show that the 80486 algorithm approximates a true LRU algorithm. *Hint:* Consider the case in which the most recent order of usage is L0, L2, L3, L1.
  c. Demonstrate that a true LRU algorithm would require 6 bits per set.

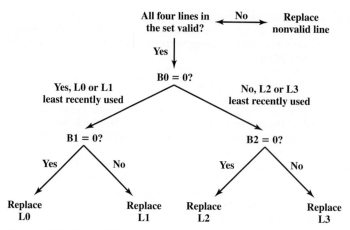

Figure 4.20   Intel 80486 On-Chip Cache Replacement Strategy

4.10   A set-associative cache has a block size of four 16-bit words and a set size of 2. The cache can accommodate a total of 4096 words. The main memory size that is cacheable is 64K × 32 bits. Design the cache structure and show how the processor's addresses are interpreted.

4.11   Consider a memory system that uses a 32-bit address to address at the byte level, plus a cache that uses a 64-byte line size.
   a.   Assume a direct mapped cache with a tag field in the address of 20 bits. Show the address format and determine the following parameters: number of addressable units, number of blocks in main memory, number of lines in cache, size of tag.
   b.   Assume an associative cache. Show the address format and determine the following parameters: number of addressable units, number of blocks in main memory, number of lines in cache, size of tag.
   c.   Assume a four-way set-associative cache with a tag field in the address of 9 bits. Show the address format and determine the following parameters: number of addressable units, number of blocks in main memory, number of lines in set, number of sets in cache, number of lines in cache, size of tag.

4.12   Consider a computer with the following characteristics: total of 1Mbyte of main memory; word size of 1 byte; block size of 16 bytes; and cache size of 64 Kbytes.
   a.   For the main memory addresses of F0010, 01234, and CABBE, give the corresponding tag, cache line address, and word offsets for a direct-mapped cache.
   b.   Give any two main memory addresses with different tags that map to the same cache slot for a direct-mapped cache.
   c.   For the main memory addresses of F0010 and CABBE, give the corresponding tag and offset values for a fully-associative cache.
   d.   For the main memory addresses of F0010 and CABBE, give the corresponding tag, cache set, and offset values for a two-way set-associative cache.

4.13   Describe a simple technique for implementing an LRU replacement algorithm in a four-way set-associative cache.

4.14   Consider again Example 4.3. How does the answer change if the main memory uses a block transfer capability that has a first-word access time of 30 ns and an access time of 5 ns for each word thereafter?

4.15   Consider the following code:

```
for (i = 0; i < 20; i++)
    for (j = 0; j < 10; j++)
        a[i] = a[i]* j
```

   a. Give one example of the spatial locality in the code.
   b. Give one example of the temporal locality in the code.

4.16   Generalize Equations (4.2) and (4.3), in Appendix 4A, to N-level memory hierarchies.

4.17   A computer system contains a main memory of 32K 16-bit words. It also has a 4K-word cache divided into four-line sets with 64 words per line. Assume that the cache is initially empty. The processor fetches words from locations 0, 1, 2, . . ., 4351 in that order. It then repeats this fetch sequence nine more times. The cache is 10 times faster than main memory. Estimate the improvement resulting from the use of the cache. Assume an LRU policy for block replacement.

4.18   Consider a cache of 4 lines of 16 bytes each. Main memory is divided into blocks of 16 bytes each. That is, block 0 has bytes with addresses 0 through 15, and so on. Now consider a program that accesses memory in the following sequence of addresses:

Once: 63 through 70

Loop ten times: 15 through 32; 80 through 95

   a. Suppose the cache is organized as direct mapped. Memory blocks 0, 4, and so on are assigned to line 1; blocks 1, 5, and so on to line 2; and so on. Compute the hit ratio.
   b. Suppose the cache is organized as two-way set associative, with two sets of two lines each. Even-numbered blocks are assigned to set 0 and odd-numbered blocks are assigned to set 1. Compute the hit ratio for the two-way set-associative cache using the least recently used replacement scheme.

4.19.   Consider a memory system with the following parameters:

$$T_c = 100 \text{ ns} \qquad C_c = 10^{-4} \text{ \$/bit}$$
$$T_m = 1200 \text{ ns} \qquad C_m = 10^{-5} \text{ \$/bit}$$

   a. What is the cost of 1 Mbyte of main memory?
   b. What is the cost of 1 Mbyte of main memory using cache memory technology?
   c. If the effective access time is 10% greater than the cache access time, what is the hit ratio H?

4.20   a. Consider an L1 cache with an access time of 1 ns and a hit ratio of $H = 0.95$. Suppose that we can change the cache design (size of cache, cache organization) such that we increase H to 0.97, but increase access time to 1.5 ns. What conditions must be met for this change to result in improved performance?
   b. Explain why this result makes intuitive sense.

4.21   Consider a single-level cache with an access time of 2.5 ns, a line size of 64 bytes, and a hit ratio of $H = 0.95$. Main memory uses a block transfer capability that has a first-word (4 bytes) access time of 50 ns and an access time of 5 ns for each word thereafter.
   a. What is the access time when there is a cache miss? Assume that the cache waits until the line has been fetched from main memory and then re-executes for a hit.
   b. Suppose that increasing the line size to 128 bytes increases the H to 0.97. Does this reduce the average memory access time?

4.22   A computer has a cache, main memory, and a disk used for virtual memory. If a referenced word is in the cache, 20 ns are required to access it. If it is in main memory but not in the cache, 60 ns are needed to load it into the cache, and then the reference is started again. If the word is not in main memory, 12 ms are required to fetch the word from disk, followed by 60 ns to copy it to the cache, and then the reference is started again. The cache hit ratio is 0.9 and the main memory hit ratio is 0.6. What is the average time in nanoseconds required to access a referenced word on this system?

4.23   Consider a cache with a line size of 64 bytes. Assume that on average 30% of the lines in the cache are dirty. A word consists of 8 bytes.
  a.   Assume there is a 3% miss rate (0.97 hit ratio). Compute the amount of main memory traffic, in terms of bytes per instruction for both write-through and write-back policies. Memory is read into cache one line at a time. However, for write back, a single word can be written from cache to main memory.
  b.   Repeat part a for a 5% rate.
  c.   Repeat part a for a 7% rate.
  d.   What conclusion can you draw from these results?

4.24   On the Motorola 68020 microprocessor, a cache access takes two clock cycles. Data access from main memory over the bus to the processor takes three clock cycles in the case of no wait state insertion; the data are delivered to the processor in parallel with delivery to the cache.
  a.   Calculate the effective length of a memory cycle given a hit ratio of 0.9 and a clocking rate of 16.67 MHz.
  b.   Repeat the calculations assuming insertion of two wait states of one cycle each per memory cycle. What conclusion can you draw from the results?

4.25   Assume a processor having a memory cycle time of 300 ns and an instruction processing rate of 1 MIPS. On average, each instruction requires one bus memory cycle for instruction fetch and one for the operand it involves.
  a.   Calculate the utilization of the bus by the processor.
  b.   Suppose the processor is equipped with an instruction cache and the associated hit ratio is 0.5. Determine the impact on bus utilization.

4.26   The performance of a single-level cache system for a read operation can be characterized by the following equation:

$$T_a = T_c + (1 - H)T_m$$

where T_a is the average access time, T_c is the cache access time, T_m is the memory access time (memory to processor register), and H is the hit ratio. For simplicity, we assume that the word in question is loaded into the cache in parallel with the load to processor register. This is the same form as Equation (4.2).
  a.   Define T_b = time to transfer a line between cache and main memory, and W = fraction of write references. Revise the preceding equation to account for writes as well as reads, using a write-through policy.
  b.   Define W_b as the probability that a line in the cache has been altered. Provide an equation for T_a for the write-back policy.

4.27   For a system with two levels of cache, define T_{c1} = first-level cache access time; T_{c2} = second-level cache access time; T_m = memory access time; H_1 = first-level cache hit ratio; H_2 = combined first/second level cache hit ratio. Provide an equation for T_a for a read operation.

4.28   Assume the following performance characteristics on a cache read miss: one clock cycle to send an address to main memory and four clock cycles to access a 32-bit word from main memory and transfer it to the processor and cache.
  a.   If the cache line size is one word, what is the miss penalty (i.e., additional time required for a read in the event of a read miss)?
  b.   What is the miss penalty if the cache line size is four words and a multiple, non-burst transfer is executed?
  c.   What is the miss penalty if the cache line size is four words and a transfer is executed, with one clock cycle per word transfer?

4.29   For the cache design of the preceding problem, suppose that increasing the line size from one word to four words results in a decrease of the read miss rate from 3.2% to 1.1%. For both the nonburst transfer and the burst transfer case, what is the average miss penalty, averaged over all reads, for the two different line sizes?

APPENDIX 4A PERFORMANCE CHARACTERISTICS OF TWO-LEVEL MEMORIES

In this chapter, reference is made to a cache that acts as a buffer between main memory and processor, creating a two-level internal memory. This two-level architecture exploits a property known as locality to provide improved performance over a comparable one-level memory.

The main memory cache mechanism is part of the computer architecture, implemented in hardware and typically invisible to the operating system. There are two other instances of a two-level memory approach that also exploit locality and that are, at least partially, implemented in the operating system: virtual memory and the disk cache (Table 4.7). Virtual memory is explored in Chapter 8; disk cache is beyond the scope of this book but is examined in [STAL09]. In this appendix, we look at some of the performance characteristics of two-level memories that are common to all three approaches.

Locality

The basis for the performance advantage of a two-level memory is a principle known as **locality of reference** [DENN68]. This principle states that memory references tend to cluster. Over a long period of time, the clusters in use change, but over a short period of time, the processor is primarily working with fixed clusters of memory references.

Intuitively, the principle of locality makes sense. Consider the following line of reasoning:

1. Except for branch and call instructions, which constitute only a small fraction of all program instructions, program execution is sequential. Hence, in most cases, the next instruction to be fetched immediately follows the last instruction fetched.

2. It is rare to have a long uninterrupted sequence of procedure calls followed by the corresponding sequence of returns. Rather, a program remains confined to a

Table 4.7 Characteristics of Two-Level Memories

	Main Memory Cache	Virtual Memory (paging)	Disk Cache
Typical access time ratios	5 : 1 (main memory vs. cache)	10^6 : 1 (main memory vs. disk)	10^6 : 1 (main memory vs. disk)
Memory management system	Implemented by special hardware	Combination of hardware and system software	System software
Typical block or page size	4 to 128 bytes (cache block)	64 to 4096 bytes (virtual memory page)	64 to 4096 bytes (disk block or pages)
Access of processor to second level	Direct access	Indirect access	Indirect access

Table 4.8   Relative Dynamic Frequency of High-Level Language Operations

Study	[HUCK83]	[KNUT71]	[PATT82a]		[TANE78]
Language	Pascal	FORTRAN	Pascal	C	SAL
Workload	Scientific	Student	System	System	System
Assign	74	67	45	38	42
Loop	4	3	5	3	4
Call	1	3	15	12	12
IF	20	11	29	43	36
GOTO	2	9	–	3	–
Other	–	7	6	1	6

rather narrow window of procedure-invocation depth. Thus, over a short period of time references to instructions tend to be localized to a few procedures.

3. Most iterative constructs consist of a relatively small number of instructions repeated many times. For the duration of the iteration, computation is therefore confined to a small contiguous portion of a program.

4. In many programs, much of the computation involves processing data structures, such as arrays or sequences of records. In many cases, successive references to these data structures will be to closely located data items.

This line of reasoning has been confirmed in many studies. With reference to point 1, a variety of studies have analyzed the behavior of high-level language programs. Table 4.8 includes key results, measuring the appearance of various statement types during execution, from the following studies. The earliest study of programming language behavior, performed by Knuth [KNUT71], examined a collection of FORTRAN programs used as student exercises. Tanenbaum [TANE78] published measurements collected from over 300 procedures used in operating-system programs and written in a language that supports structured programming (SAL). Patterson and Sequein [PATT82a] analyzed a set of measurements taken from compilers and programs for typesetting, computer-aided design (CAD), sorting, and file comparison. The programming languages C and Pascal were studied. Huck [HUCK83] analyzed four programs intended to represent a mix of general-purpose scientific computing, including fast Fourier transform and the integration of systems of differential equations. There is good agreement in the results of this mixture of languages and applications that branching and call instructions represent only a fraction of statements executed during the lifetime of a program. Thus, these studies confirm assertion 1.

With respect to assertion 2, studies reported in [PATT85a] provide confirmation. This is illustrated in Figure 4.21, which shows call-return behavior. Each call is represented by the line moving down and to the right, and each return by the line moving up and to the right. In the figure, a *window* with depth equal to 5 is defined. Only a sequence of calls and returns with a net movement of 6 in either direction causes the window to move. As can be seen, the executing program can remain within a stationary window for long periods of time. A study by the same analysts of C and Pascal programs showed that a window of depth 8 will need to shift only on less than 1% of the calls or returns [TAMI83].

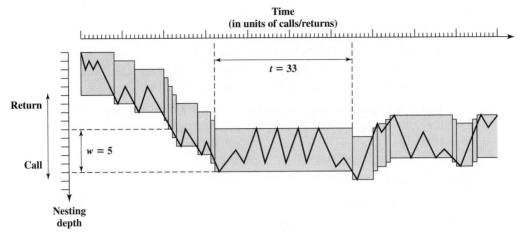

Figure 4.21 Example Call-Return Behavior of a Program

A distinction is made in the literature between spatial locality and temporal locality. **Spatial locality** refers to the tendency of execution to involve a number of memory locations that are clustered. This reflects the tendency of a processor to access instructions sequentially. Spatial location also reflects the tendency of a program to access data locations sequentially, such as when processing a table of data. **Temporal locality** refers to the tendency for a processor to access memory locations that have been used recently. For example, when an iteration loop is executed, the processor executes the same set of instructions repeatedly.

Traditionally, temporal locality is exploited by keeping recently used instruction and data values in cache memory and by exploiting a cache hierarchy. Spatial locality is generally exploited by using larger cache blocks and by incorporating prefetching mechanisms (fetching items of anticipated use) into the cache control logic. Recently, there has been considerable research on refining these techniques to achieve greater performance, but the basic strategies remain the same.

Operation of Two–Level Memory

The locality property can be exploited in the formation of a two-level memory. The upper-level memory (M1) is smaller, faster, and more expensive (per bit) than the lower-level memory (M2). M1 is used as a temporary store for part of the contents of the larger M2. When a memory reference is made, an attempt is made to access the item in M1. If this succeeds, then a quick access is made. If not, then a block of memory locations is copied from M2 to M1 and the access then takes place via M1. Because of locality, once a block is brought into M1, there should be a number of accesses to locations in that block, resulting in fast overall service.

To express the average time to access an item, we must consider not only the speeds of the two levels of memory, but also the probability that a given reference can be found in M1. We have

$$T_s = H \times T_1 + (1 - H) \times (T_1 + T_2)$$
$$= T_1 + (1 - H) \times T_2 \tag{4.2}$$

where

T_s = average (system) access time
T_1 = access time of M1 (e.g., cache, disk cache)
T_2 = access time of M2 (e.g., main memory, disk)
H = hit ratio (fraction of time reference is found in M1)

Figure 4.2 shows average access time as a function of hit ratio. As can be seen, for a high percentage of hits, the average total access time is much closer to that of M1 than M2.

Performance

Let us look at some of the parameters relevant to an assessment of a two-level memory mechanism. First consider cost. We have

$$C_s = \frac{C_1 S_1 + C_2 S_2}{S_1 + S_2} \qquad \textbf{(4.3)}$$

where

C_s = average cost per bit for the combined two-level memory
C_1 = average cost per bit of upper-level memory M1
C_2 = average cost per bit of lower-level memory M2
S_1 = size of M1
S_2 = size of M2

We would like $C_s \approx C_2$. Given that $C_1 \gg C_2$, this requires $S_1 \ll S_2$. Figure 4.22 shows the relationship.

Next, consider access time. For a two-level memory to provide a significant performance improvement, we need to have T_s approximately equal to T_1 ($T_s \approx T_1$). Given that T_1 is much less than T_2 ($T_1 \ll T_2$), a hit ratio of close to 1 is needed.

So we would like M1 to be small to hold down cost, and large to improve the hit ratio and therefore the performance. Is there a size of M1 that satisfies both requirements to a reasonable extent? We can answer this question with a series of subquestions:

• What value of hit ratio is needed so that $T_s \approx T_1$?
• What size of M1 will assure the needed hit ratio?
• Does this size satisfy the cost requirement?

To get at this, consider the quantity T_1/T_s, which is referred to as the *access efficiency*. It is a measure of how close average access time (T_s) is to M1 access time (T_1). From Equation (4.2),

$$\frac{T_1}{T_s} = \frac{1}{1 + (1 - H)\dfrac{T_2}{T_1}} \qquad \textbf{(4.4)}$$

Figure 4.23 plots T_1/T_s as a function of the hit ratio H, with the quantity T_2/T_1 as a parameter. Typically, on-chip cache access time is about 25 to 50 times faster than main

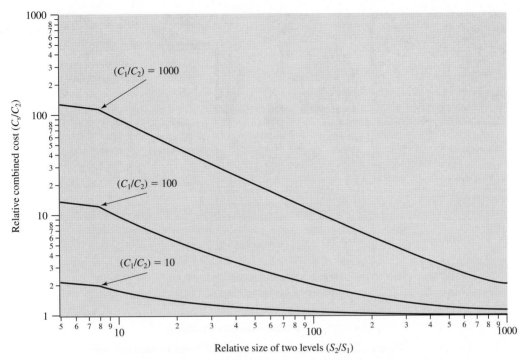

Figure 4.22   Relationship of Average Memory Cost to Relative Memory Size for a Two-Level Memory

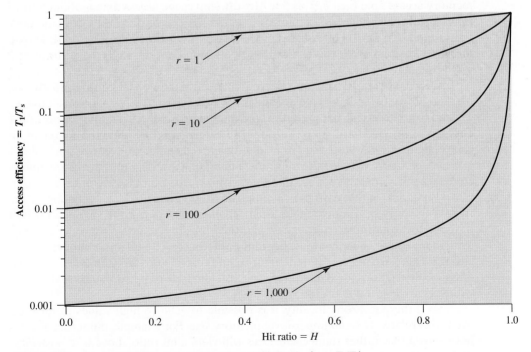

Figure 4.23   Access Efficiency as a Function of Hit Ratio ($r = T_2/T_1$)

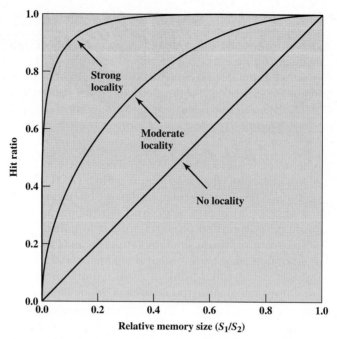

Figure 4.24   Hit Ratio as a Function of Relative Memory Size

memory access time (i.e., T_2/T_1 is 5 to 10), off-chip cache access time is about 5 to 15 times faster than main memory access time (i.e., T_2/T_1 is 5 to 15), and main memory access time is about 1000 times faster than disk access time ($T_2/T_1 = 1000$). Thus, a hit ratio in the range of near 0.9 would seem to be needed to satisfy the performance requirement.

We can now phrase the question about relative memory size more exactly. Is a hit ratio of, say, 0.8 or better reasonable for $S_1 \ll S_2$? This will depend on a number of factors, including the nature of the software being executed and the details of the design of the two-level memory. The main determinant is, of course, the degree of locality. Figure 4.24 suggests the effect that locality has on the hit ratio. Clearly, if M1 is the same size as M2, then the hit ratio will be 1.0: All of the items in M2 are always stored also in M1. Now suppose that there is no locality; that is, references are completely random. In that case the hit ratio should be a strictly linear function of the relative memory size. For example, if M1 is half the size of M2, then at any time half of the items from M2 are also in M1 and the hit ratio will be 0.5. In practice, however, there is some degree of locality in the references. The effects of moderate and strong locality are indicated in the figure. Note that Figure 4.24 is not derived from any specific data or model; the figure suggests the type of performance that is seen with various degrees of locality.

So if there is strong locality, it is possible to achieve high values of hit ratio even with relatively small upper-level memory size. For example, numerous studies have shown that rather small cache sizes will yield a hit ratio above 0.75 *regardless of the size of main memory* (e.g., [AGAR89], [PRZY88], [STRE83], and [SMIT82]).

A cache in the range of 1K to 128K words is generally adequate, whereas main memory is now typically in the gigabyte range. When we consider virtual memory and disk cache, we will cite other studies that confirm the same phenomenon, namely that a relatively small M1 yields a high value of hit ratio because of locality.

This brings us to the last question listed earlier: Does the relative size of the two memories satisfy the cost requirement? The answer is clearly yes. If we need only a relatively small upper-level memory to achieve good performance, then the average cost per bit of the two levels of memory will approach that of the cheaper lower-level memory.

Please note that with L2 cache, or even L2 and L3 caches, involved, analysis is much more complex. See [PEIR99] and [HAND98] for discussions.

CHAPTER 5

INTERNAL MEMORY

158

KEY POINTS

◆ The two basic forms of semiconductor random access memory are dynamic RAM (DRAM) and static RAM (SRAM). SRAM is faster, more expensive, and less dense than DRAM, and is used for cache memory. DRAM is used for main memory.

◆ Error correction techniques are commonly used in memory systems. These involve adding redundant bits that are a function of the data bits to form an error-correcting code. If a bit error occurs, the code will detect and, usually, correct the error.

◆ To compensate for the relatively slow speed of DRAM, a number of advanced DRAM organizations have been introduced. The two most common are synchronous DRAM and RamBus DRAM. Both of these involve using the system clock to provide for the transfer of blocks of data.

We begin this chapter with a survey of semiconductor main memory subsystems, including ROM, DRAM, and SRAM memories. Then we look at error control techniques used to enhance memory reliability. Following this, we look at more advanced DRAM architectures.

5.1 SEMICONDUCTOR MAIN MEMORY

In earlier computers, the most common form of random-access storage for computer main memory employed an array of doughnut-shaped ferromagnetic loops referred to as *cores*. Hence, main memory was often referred to as *core,* a term that persists to this day. The advent of, and advantages of, microelectronics has long since vanquished the magnetic core memory. Today, the use of semiconductor chips for main memory is almost universal. Key aspects of this technology are explored in this section.

Organization

The basic element of a semiconductor memory is the memory cell. Although a variety of electronic technologies are used, all semiconductor memory cells share certain properties:

- They exhibit two stable (or semistable) states, which can be used to represent binary 1 and 0.
- They are capable of being written into (at least once), to set the state.
- They are capable of being read to sense the state.

Figure 5.1 depicts the operation of a memory cell. Most commonly, the cell has three functional terminals capable of carrying an electrical signal. The select

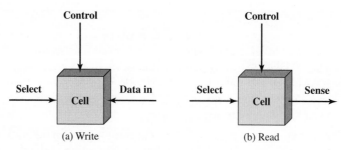

Figure 5.1 Memory Cell Operation

terminal, as the name suggests, selects a memory cell for a read or write operation. The control terminal indicates read or write. For writing, the other terminal provides an electrical signal that sets the state of the cell to 1 or 0. For reading, that terminal is used for output of the cell's state. The details of the internal organization, functioning, and timing of the memory cell depend on the specific integrated circuit technology used and are beyond the scope of this book, except for a brief summary. For our purposes, we will take it as given that individual cells can be selected for reading and writing operations.

DRAM and SRAM

All of the memory types that we will explore in this chapter are random access. That is, individual words of memory are directly accessed through wired-in addressing logic.

Table 5.1 lists the major types of semiconductor memory. The most common is referred to as *random-access memory* (RAM). This is, of course, a misuse of the term, because all of the types listed in the table are random access. One distinguishing characteristic of RAM is that it is possible both to read data from the memory and to write new data into the memory easily and rapidly. Both the reading and writing are accomplished through the use of electrical signals.

Table 5.1 Semiconductor Memory Types

Memory Type	Category	Erasure	Write Mechanism	Volatility
Random-access memory (RAM)	Read-write memory	Electrically, byte-level	Electrically	Volatile
Read-only memory (ROM)	Read-only memory	Not possible	Masks	Nonvolatile
Programmable ROM (PROM)				
Erasable PROM (EPROM)	Read-mostly memory	UV light, chip-level	Electrically	
Electrically Erasable PROM (EEPROM)		Electrically, byte-level		
Flash memory		Electrically, block-level		

The other distinguishing characteristic of RAM is that it is volatile. A RAM must be provided with a constant power supply. If the power is interrupted, then the data are lost. Thus, RAM can be used only as temporary storage. The two traditional forms of RAM used in computers are DRAM and SRAM.

DYNAMIC RAM RAM technology is divided into two technologies: dynamic and static. A dynamic RAM (DRAM) is made with cells that store data as charge on capacitors. The presence or absence of charge in a capacitor is interpreted as a binary 1 or 0. Because capacitors have a natural tendency to discharge, dynamic RAMs require periodic charge refreshing to maintain data storage. The term *dynamic* refers to this tendency of the stored charge to leak away, even with power continuously applied.

Figure 5.2a is a typical DRAM structure for an individual cell that stores 1 bit. The address line is activated when the bit value from this cell is to be read or written. The transistor acts as a switch that is closed (allowing current to flow) if a voltage is applied to the address line and open (no current flows) if no voltage is present on the address line.

For the write operation, a voltage signal is applied to the bit line; a high voltage represents 1, and a low voltage represents 0. A signal is then applied to the address line, allowing a charge to be transferred to the capacitor.

For the read operation, when the address line is selected, the transistor turns on and the charge stored on the capacitor is fed out onto a bit line and to a sense amplifier. The sense amplifier compares the capacitor voltage to a reference value and determines if the cell contains a logic 1 or a logic 0. The readout from the cell discharges the capacitor, which must be restored to complete the operation.

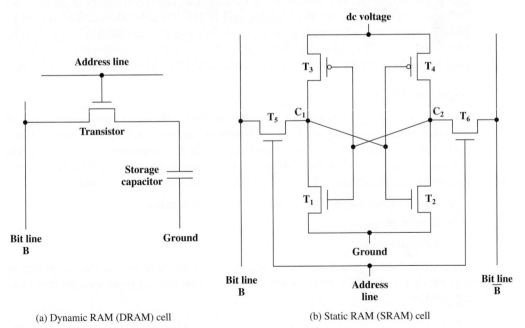

(a) Dynamic RAM (DRAM) cell   (b) Static RAM (SRAM) cell

Figure 5.2 Typical Memory Cell Structures

Although the DRAM cell is used to store a single bit (0 or 1), it is essentially an analog device. The capacitor can store any charge value within a range; a threshold value determines whether the charge is interpreted as 1 or 0.

STATIC RAM In contrast, a static RAM (SRAM) is a digital device that uses the same logic elements used in the processor. In a SRAM, binary values are stored using traditional flip-flop logic-gate configurations (see Chapter 20 for a description of flip-flops). A static RAM will hold its data as long as power is supplied to it.

Figure 5.2b is a typical SRAM structure for an individual cell. Four transistors (T_1, T_2, T_3, T_4) are cross connected in an arrangement that produces a stable logic state. In logic state 1, point C_1 is high and point C_2 is low; in this state, T_1 and T_4 are off and T_2 and T_3 are on.[1] In logic state 0, point C_1 is low and point C_2 is high; in this state, T_1 and T_4 are on and T_2 and T_3 are off. Both states are stable as long as the direct current (dc) voltage is applied. Unlike the DRAM, no refresh is needed to retain data.

As in the DRAM, the SRAM address line is used to open or close a switch. The address line controls two transistors $(T_5$ and $T_6)$. When a signal is applied to this line, the two transistors are switched on, allowing a read or write operation. For a write operation, the desired bit value is applied to line B, while its complement is applied to line $\overline{B}$. This forces the four transistors (T_1, T_2, T_3, T_4) into the proper state. For a read operation, the bit value is read from line B.

SRAM VERSUS DRAM Both static and dynamic RAMs are volatile; that is, power must be continuously supplied to the memory to preserve the bit values. A dynamic memory cell is simpler and smaller than a static memory cell. Thus, a DRAM is more dense (smaller cells = more cells per unit area) and less expensive than a corresponding SRAM. On the other hand, a DRAM requires the supporting refresh circuitry. For larger memories, the fixed cost of the refresh circuitry is more than compensated for by the smaller variable cost of DRAM cells. Thus, DRAMs tend to be favored for large memory requirements. A final point is that SRAMs are generally somewhat faster than DRAMs. Because of these relative characteristics, SRAM is used for cache memory (both on and off chip), and DRAM is used for main memory.

Types of ROM

As the name suggests, a **read-only memory** (ROM) contains a permanent pattern of data that cannot be changed. A ROM is nonvolatile; that is, no power source is required to maintain the bit values in memory. While it is possible to read a ROM, it is not possible to write new data into it. An important application of ROMs is microprogramming, discussed in Part Four. Other potential applications include

- Library subroutines for frequently wanted functions
- System programs
- Function tables

For a modest-sized requirement, the advantage of ROM is that the data or program is permanently in main memory and need never be loaded from a secondary storage device.

---

[1]The circles at the head of T_3 and T_4 indicate signal negation.

A ROM is created like any other integrated circuit chip, with the data actually wired into the chip as part of the fabrication process. This presents two problems:

- The data insertion step includes a relatively large fixed cost, whether one or thousands of copies of a particular ROM are fabricated.
- There is no room for error. If one bit is wrong, the whole batch of ROMs must be thrown out.

When only a small number of ROMs with a particular memory content is needed, a less expensive alternative is the **programmable ROM** (PROM). Like the ROM, the PROM is nonvolatile and may be written into only once. For the PROM, the writing process is performed electrically and may be performed by a supplier or customer at a time later than the original chip fabrication. Special equipment is required for the writing or "programming" process. PROMs provide flexibility and convenience. The ROM remains attractive for high-volume production runs.

Another variation on read-only memory is the read-mostly memory, which is useful for applications in which read operations are far more frequent than write operations but for which nonvolatile storage is required. There are three common forms of read-mostly memory: EPROM, EEPROM, and flash memory.

The optically **erasable programmable read-only memory** (EPROM) is read and written electrically, as with PROM. However, before a write operation, all the storage cells must be erased to the same initial state by exposure of the packaged chip to ultraviolet radiation. Erasure is performed by shining an intense ultraviolet light through a window that is designed into the memory chip. This erasure process can be performed repeatedly; each erasure can take as much as 20 minutes to perform. Thus, the EPROM can be altered multiple times and, like the ROM and PROM, holds its data virtually indefinitely. For comparable amounts of storage, the EPROM is more expensive than PROM, but it has the advantage of the multiple update capability.

A more attractive form of read-mostly memory is **electrically erasable programmable read-only memory** (EEPROM). This is a read-mostly memory that can be written into at any time without erasing prior contents; only the byte or bytes addressed are updated. The write operation takes considerably longer than the read operation, on the order of several hundred microseconds per byte. The EEPROM combines the advantage of nonvolatility with the flexibility of being updatable in place, using ordinary bus control, address, and data lines. EEPROM is more expensive than EPROM and also is less dense, supporting fewer bits per chip.

Another form of semiconductor memory is **flash memory** (so named because of the speed with which it can be reprogrammed). First introduced in the mid-1980s, flash memory is intermediate between EPROM and EEPROM in both cost and functionality. Like EEPROM, flash memory uses an electrical erasing technology. An entire flash memory can be erased in one or a few seconds, which is much faster than EPROM. In addition, it is possible to erase just blocks of memory rather than an entire chip. Flash memory gets its name because the microchip is organized so that a section of memory cells are erased in a single action or "flash." However, flash memory does not provide byte-level erasure. Like EPROM, flash memory uses only one transistor per bit, and so achieves the high density (compared with EEPROM) of EPROM.

Chip Logic

As with other integrated circuit products, semiconductor memory comes in packaged chips (Figure 2.7). Each chip contains an array of memory cells.

In the memory hierarchy as a whole, we saw that there are trade-offs among speed, capacity, and cost. These trade-offs also exist when we consider the organization of memory cells and functional logic on a chip. For semiconductor memories, one of the key design issues is the number of bits of data that may be read/written at a time. At one extreme is an organization in which the physical arrangement of cells in the array is the same as the logical arrangement (as perceived by the processor) of words in memory. The array is organized into W words of B bits each. For example, a 16-Mbit chip could be organized as 1M 16-bit words. At the other extreme is the so-called 1-bit-per-chip organization, in which data are read/written 1 bit at a time. We will illustrate memory chip organization with a DRAM; ROM organization is similar, though simpler.

Figure 5.3 shows a typical organization of a 16-Mbit DRAM. In this case, 4 bits are read or written at a time. Logically, the memory array is organized as four square arrays of 2048 by 2048 elements. Various physical arrangements are possible. In any case, the elements of the array are connected by both horizontal (row) and vertical (column) lines. Each horizontal line connects to the Select terminal of each cell in its row; each vertical line connects to the Data-In/Sense terminal of each cell in its column.

Address lines supply the address of the word to be selected. A total of $\log_2 W$ lines are needed. In our example, 11 address lines are needed to select one of 2048 rows. These 11 lines are fed into a row decoder, which has 11 lines of input and 2048 lines for output. The logic of the decoder activates a single one of the 2048 outputs depending on the bit pattern on the 11 input lines ($2^{11} = 2048$).

An additional 11 address lines select one of 2048 columns of 4 bits per column. Four data lines are used for the input and output of 4 bits to and from a data buffer. On input (write), the bit driver of each bit line is activated for a 1 or 0 according to the value of the corresponding data line. On output (read), the value of each bit line is passed through a sense amplifier and presented to the data lines. The row line selects which row of cells is used for reading or writing.

Because only 4 bits are read/written to this DRAM, there must be multiple DRAMs connected to the memory controller to read/write a word of data to the bus.

Note that there are only 11 address lines (A0–A10), half the number you would expect for a 2048 × 2048 array. This is done to save on the number of pins. The 22 required address lines are passed through select logic external to the chip and multiplexed onto the 11 address lines. First, 11 address signals are passed to the chip to define the row address of the array, and then the other 11 address signals are presented for the column address. These signals are accompanied by row address select ($\overline{RAS}$) and column address select ($\overline{CAS}$) signals to provide timing to the chip.

The write enable ($\overline{WE}$) and output enable ($\overline{OE}$) pins determine whether a write or read operation is performed. Two other pins, not shown in Figure 5.3, are ground (Vss) and a voltage source (Vcc).

As an aside, multiplexed addressing plus the use of square arrays result in a quadrupling of memory size with each new generation of memory chips. One more pin devoted to addressing doubles the number of rows and columns, and so the size of the chip memory grows by a factor of 4.

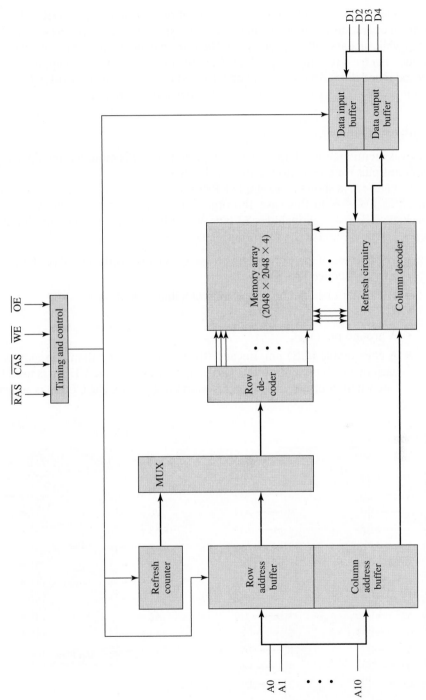

Figure 5.3 Typical 16 Megabit DRAM (4M × 4)

165

Figure 5.3 also indicates the inclusion of refresh circuitry. All DRAMs require a refresh operation. A simple technique for refreshing is, in effect, to disable the DRAM chip while all data cells are refreshed. The refresh counter steps through all of the row values. For each row, the output lines from the refresh counter are supplied to the row decoder and the RAS line is activated. The data are read out and written back into the same location. This causes each cell in the row to be refreshed.

Chip Packaging

As was mentioned in Chapter 2, an integrated circuit is mounted on a package that contains pins for connection to the outside world.

Figure 5.4a shows an example EPROM package, which is an 8-Mbit chip organized as 1M × 8. In this case, the organization is treated as a one-word-per-chip package. The package includes 32 pins, which is one of the standard chip package sizes. The pins support the following signal lines:

- The address of the word being accessed. For 1M words, a total of 20 (2^{20} = 1M) pins are needed (A0–A19).
- The data to be read out, consisting of 8 lines (D0–D7).
- The power supply to the chip (V_{cc}).
- A ground pin (V_{ss}).
- A chip enable (CE) pin. Because there may be more than one memory chip, each of which is connected to the same address bus, the CE pin is used to indicate whether or not the address is valid for this chip. The CE pin is activated by

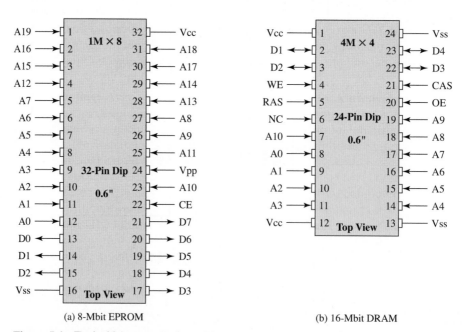

(a) 8-Mbit EPROM   (b) 16-Mbit DRAM

Figure 5.4 Typical Memory Package Pins and Signals

logic connected to the higher-order bits of the address bus (i.e., address bits above A19). The use of this signal is illustrated presently.

- A program voltage (V_{pp}) that is supplied during programming (write operations).

A typical DRAM pin configuration is shown in Figure 5.4b, for a 16-Mbit chip organized as 4M × 4. There are several differences from a ROM chip. Because a RAM can be updated, the data pins are input/output. The write enable (WE) and output enable (OE) pins indicate whether this is a write or read operation. Because the DRAM is accessed by row and column, and the address is multiplexed, only 11 address pins are needed to specify the 4M row/column combinations ($2^{11} \times 2^{11} = 2^{22} = 4M$). The functions of the row address select (RAS) and column address select (CAS) pins were discussed previously. Finally, the no connect (NC) pin is provided so that there are an even number of pins.

Module Organization

If a RAM chip contains only 1 bit per word, then clearly we will need at least a number of chips equal to the number of bits per word. As an example, Figure 5.5 shows

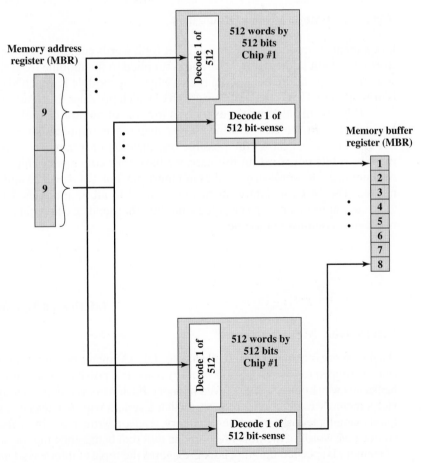

Figure 5.5   256-KByte Memory Organization

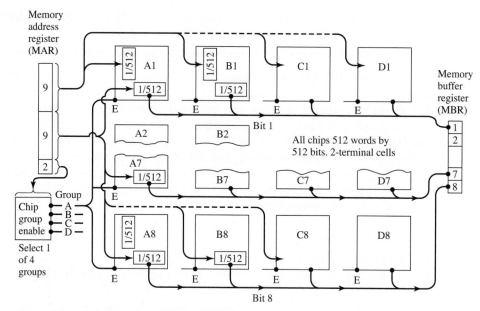

Figure 5.6 1-Mbyte Memory Organization

how a memory module consisting of 256K 8-bit words could be organized. For 256K words, an 18-bit address is needed and is supplied to the module from some external source (e.g., the address lines of a bus to which the module is attached). The address is presented to 8 256K × 1-bit chips, each of which provides the input/output of 1 bit.

This organization works as long as the size of memory equals the number of bits per chip. In the case in which larger memory is required, an array of chips is needed. Figure 5.6 shows the possible organization of a memory consisting of 1M word by 8 bits per word. In this case, we have four columns of chips, each column containing 256K words arranged as in Figure 5.5. For 1M word, 20 address lines are needed. The 18 least significant bits are routed to all 32 modules. The high-order 2 bits are input to a group select logic module that sends a chip enable signal to one of the four columns of modules.

Interleaved Memory Simulator

Interleaved Memory

Main memory is composed of a collection of DRAM memory chips. A number of chips can be grouped together to form a *memory bank*. It is possible to organize the memory banks in a way known as interleaved memory. Each bank is independently able to service a memory read or write request, so that a system with K banks can service K requests simultaneously, increasing memory read or write rates by a factor of K. If consecutive words of memory are stored in different banks, then the transfer of a block of memory is speeded up. Appendix E explores the topic of interleaved memory.

5.2 ERROR CORRECTION

A semiconductor memory system is subject to errors. These can be categorized as hard failures and soft errors. A **hard failure** is a permanent physical defect so that the memory cell or cells affected cannot reliably store data but become stuck at 0 or 1 or switch erratically between 0 and 1. Hard errors can be caused by harsh environmental abuse, manufacturing defects, and wear. A **soft error** is a random, nondestructive event that alters the contents of one or more memory cells without damaging the memory. Soft errors can be caused by power supply problems or alpha particles. These particles result from radioactive decay and are distressingly common because radioactive nuclei are found in small quantities in nearly all materials. Both hard and soft errors are clearly undesirable, and most modern main memory systems include logic for both detecting and correcting errors.

Figure 5.7 illustrates in general terms how the process is carried out. When data are to be read into memory, a calculation, depicted as a function f, is performed on the data to produce a code. Both the code and the data are stored. Thus, if an M-bit word of data is to be stored and the code is of length K bits, then the actual size of the stored word is $M + K$ bits.

When the previously stored word is read out, the code is used to detect and possibly correct errors. A new set of K code bits is generated from the M data bits and compared with the fetched code bits. The comparison yields one of three results:

- No errors are detected. The fetched data bits are sent out.
- An error is detected, and it is possible to correct the error. The data bits plus error correction bits are fed into a corrector, which produces a corrected set of M bits to be sent out.
- An error is detected, but it is not possible to correct it. This condition is reported.

Codes that operate in this fashion are referred to as *error-correcting codes.* A code is characterized by the number of bit errors in a word that it can correct and detect.

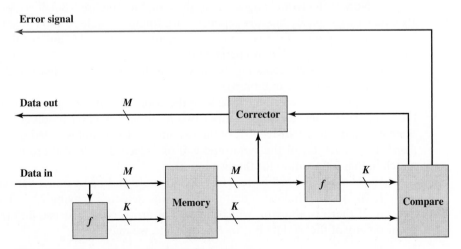

Figure 5.7 Error-Correcting Code Function

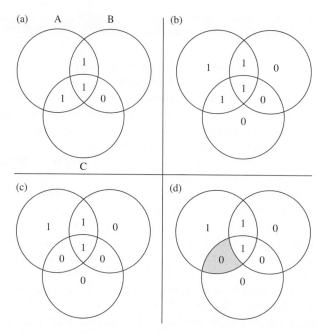

Figure 5.8   Hamming Error-Correcting Code

The simplest of the error-correcting codes is the *Hamming code* devised by Richard Hamming at Bell Laboratories. Figure 5.8 uses Venn diagrams to illustrate the use of this code on 4-bit words ($M = 4$). With three intersecting circles, there are seven compartments. We assign the 4 data bits to the inner compartments (Figure 5.8a). The remaining compartments are filled with what are called *parity bits*. Each parity bit is chosen so that the total number of 1s in its circle is even (Figure 5.8b). Thus, because circle A includes three data 1s, the parity bit in that circle is set to 1. Now, if an error changes one of the data bits (Figure 5.8c), it is easily found. By checking the parity bits, discrepancies are found in circle A and circle C but not in circle B. Only one of the seven compartments is in A and C but not B. The error can therefore be corrected by changing that bit.

To clarify the concepts involved, we will develop a code that can detect and correct single-bit errors in 8-bit words.

To start, let us determine how long the code must be. Referring to Figure 5.7, the comparison logic receives as input two K-bit values. A bit-by-bit comparison is done by taking the exclusive-OR of the two inputs. The result is called the *syndrome word*. Thus, each bit of the syndrome is 0 or 1 according to if there is or is not a match in that bit position for the two inputs.

The syndrome word is therefore K bits wide and has a range between 0 and $2^K - 1$. The value 0 indicates that no error was detected, leaving $2^K - 1$ values to indicate, if there is an error, which bit was in error. Now, because an error could occur on any of the M data bits or K check bits, we must have

$$2^K - 1 \geq M + K$$

Table 5.2   Increase in Word Length with Error Correction

Data Bits	Single-Error Correction			Single-Error Correction/ Double-Error Detection	
	Check Bits	% Increase		Check Bits	% Increase
8	4	50		5	62.5
16	5	31.25		6	37.5
32	6	18.75		7	21.875
64	7	10.94		8	12.5
128	8	6.25		9	7.03
256	9	3.52		10	3.91

This inequality gives the number of bits needed to correct a single bit error in a word containing M data bits. For example, for a word of 8 data bits ($M = 8$), we have

- $K = 3: 2^3 - 1 < 8 + 3$
- $K = 4: 2^4 - 1 > 8 + 4$

Thus, eight data bits require four check bits. The first three columns of Table 5.2 lists the number of check bits required for various data word lengths.

For convenience, we would like to generate a 4-bit syndrome for an 8-bit data word with the following characteristics:

- If the syndrome contains all 0s, no error has been detected.
- If the syndrome contains one and only one bit set to 1, then an error has occurred in one of the 4 check bits. No correction is needed.
- If the syndrome contains more than one bit set to 1, then the numerical value of the syndrome indicates the position of the data bit in error. This data bit is inverted for correction.

To achieve these characteristics, the data and check bits are arranged into a 12-bit word as depicted in Figure 5.9. The bit positions are numbered from 1 to 12. Those bit positions whose position numbers are powers of 2 are designated as check bits. The check bits are calculated as follows, where the symbol $\oplus$ designates the exclusive-OR operation:

$$C1 = D1 \oplus D2 \oplus \quad\quad D4 \oplus D5 \oplus \quad\quad D7$$
$$C2 = D1 \oplus \quad\quad D3 \oplus D4 \oplus \quad\quad D6 \oplus D7$$
$$C4 = \quad\quad D2 \oplus D3 \oplus D4 \oplus \quad\quad\quad\quad D8$$
$$C8 = \quad\quad\quad\quad\quad\quad\quad\quad D5 \oplus D6 \oplus D7 \oplus D8$$

Bit position	12	11	10	9	8	7	6	5	4	3	2	1
Position number	1100	1011	1010	1001	1000	0111	0110	0101	0100	0011	0010	0001
Data bit	D8	D7	D6	D5		D4	D3	D2		D1		
Check bit					C8				C4		C2	C1

Figure 5.9   Layout of Data Bits and Check Bits

Each check bit operates on every data bit whose position number contains a 1 in the same bit position as the position number of that check bit. Thus, data bit positions 3, 5, 7, 9, and 11 (D1, D2, D4, D5, D7) all contain a 1 in the least significant bit of their position number as does C1; bit positions 3, 6, 7, 10, and 11 all contain a 1 in the second bit position, as does C2; and so on. Looked at another way, bit position n is checked by those bits C_i such that $\Sigma_i = n$. For example, position 7 is checked by bits in position 4, 2, and 1; and $7 = 4 + 2 + 1$.

Let us verify that this scheme works with an example. Assume that the 8-bit input word is 00111001, with data bit D1 in the rightmost position. The calculations are as follows:

$$C1 = 1 \oplus 0 \oplus 1 \oplus 1 \oplus 0 = 1$$
$$C2 = 1 \oplus 0 \oplus 1 \oplus 1 \oplus 0 = 1$$
$$C4 = 0 \oplus 0 \oplus 1 \oplus 0 = 1$$
$$C8 = 1 \oplus 1 \oplus 0 \oplus 0 = 0$$

Suppose now that data bit 3 sustains an error and is changed from 0 to 1. When the check bits are recalculated, we have

$$C1 = 1 \oplus 0 \oplus 1 \oplus 1 \oplus 0 = 1$$
$$C2 = 1 \oplus 1 \oplus 1 \oplus 1 \oplus 0 = 0$$
$$C4 = 0 \oplus 1 \oplus 1 \oplus 0 = 0$$
$$C8 = 1 \oplus 1 \oplus 0 \oplus 0 = 0$$

When the new check bits are compared with the old check bits, the syndrome word is formed:

	C8	C4	C2	C1
	0	1	1	1
$\oplus$	0	0	0	1
	0	1	1	0

The result is 0110, indicating that bit position 6, which contains data bit 3, is in error.

Figure 5.10 illustrates the preceding calculation. The data and check bits are positioned properly in the 12-bit word. Four of the data bits have a value 1 (shaded in the

Bit position	12	11	10	9	8	7	6	5	4	3	2	1
Position number	1100	1011	1010	1001	1000	0111	0110	0101	0100	0011	0010	0001
Data bit	D8	D7	D6	D5		D4	D3	D2		D1		
Check bit					C8				C4		C2	C1
Word stored as	0	0	1	1	0	1	0	0	1	1	1	1
Word fetched as	0	0	1	1	0	1	1	0	1	1	1	1
Position number	1100	1011	1010	1001	1000	0111	0110	0101	0100	0011	0010	0001
Check bit					0				0		0	1

Figure 5.10   Check Bit Calculation

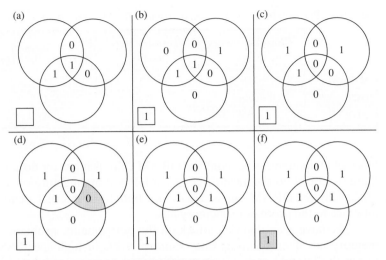

Figure 5.11   Hamming SEC-DEC Code

table), and their bit position values are XORed to produce the Hamming code 0111, which forms the four check digits. The entire block that is stored is 001101001111. Suppose now that data bit 3, in bit position 6, sustains an error and is changed from 0 to 1. The resulting block is 001101101111, with a Hamming code of 0111. An XOR of the Hamming code and all of the bit position values for nonzero data bits results in 0110. The nonzero result detects an error and indicates that the error is in bit position 6.

The code just described is known as a *single-error-correcting* (SEC) code. More commonly, semiconductor memory is equipped with a single-error-correcting, double-error-detecting (SEC-DED) code. As Table 5.2 shows, such codes require one additional bit compared with SEC codes.

Figure 5.11 illustrates how such a code works, again with a 4-bit data word. The sequence shows that if two errors occur (Figure 5.11c), the checking procedure goes astray (d) and worsens the problem by creating a third error (e). To overcome the problem, an eighth bit is added that is set so that the total number of 1s in the diagram is even. The extra parity bit catches the error (f).

An error-correcting code enhances the reliability of the memory at the cost of added complexity. With a 1-bit-per-chip organization, an SEC-DED code is generally considered adequate. For example, the IBM 30xx implementations used an 8-bit SEC-DED code for each 64 bits of data in main memory. Thus, the size of main memory is actually about 12% larger than is apparent to the user. The VAX computers used a 7-bit SEC-DED for each 32 bits of memory, for a 22% overhead. A number of contemporary DRAMs use 9 check bits for each 128 bits of data, for a 7% overhead [SHAR97].

5.3   ADVANCED DRAM ORGANIZATION

As discussed in Chapter 2, one of the most critical system bottlenecks when using high-performance processors is the interface to main internal memory. This interface is the most important pathway in the entire computer system. The basic building

Table 5.3 Performance Comparison of Some DRAM Alternatives

	Clock Frequency (MHz)	Transfer Rate (GB/s)	Access Time (ns)	Pin Count
SDRAM	166	1.3	18	168
DDR	200	3.2	12.5	184
RDRAM	600	4.8	12	162

block of main memory remains the DRAM chip, as it has for decades; until recently, there had been no significant changes in DRAM architecture since the early 1970s. The traditional DRAM chip is constrained both by its internal architecture and by its interface to the processor's memory bus.

We have seen that one attack on the performance problem of DRAM main memory has been to insert one or more levels of high-speed SRAM cache between the DRAM main memory and the processor. But SRAM is much costlier than DRAM, and expanding cache size beyond a certain point yields diminishing returns.

In recent years, a number of enhancements to the basic DRAM architecture have been explored, and some of these are now on the market. The schemes that currently dominate the market are SDRAM, DDR-DRAM, and RDRAM. Table 5.3 provides a performance comparison. CDRAM has also received considerable attention. We examine each of these approaches in this section.

Synchronous DRAM

One of the most widely used forms of DRAM is the synchronous DRAM (SDRAM) [VOGL94]. Unlike the traditional DRAM, which is asynchronous, the SDRAM exchanges data with the processor synchronized to an external clock signal and running at the full speed of the processor/memory bus without imposing wait states.

In a typical DRAM, the processor presents addresses and control levels to the memory, indicating that a set of data at a particular location in memory should be either read from or written into the DRAM. After a delay, the access time, the DRAM either writes or reads the data. During the access-time delay, the DRAM performs various internal functions, such as activating the high capacitance of the row and column lines, sensing the data, and routing the data out through the output buffers. The processor must simply wait through this delay, slowing system performance.

With synchronous access, the DRAM moves data in and out under control of the system clock. The processor or other master issues the instruction and address information, which is latched by the DRAM. The DRAM then responds after a set number of clock cycles. Meanwhile, the master can safely do other tasks while the SDRAM is processing the request.

Figure 5.12 shows the internal logic of IBM's 64-Mb SDRAM [IBM01], which is typical of SDRAM organization, and Table 5.4 defines the various pin assignments.

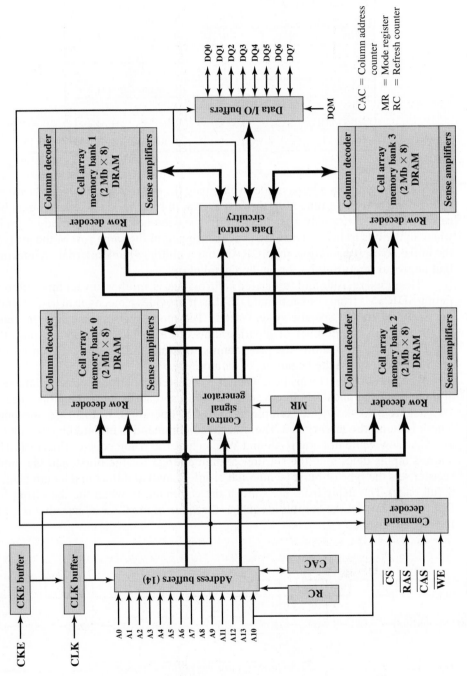

Figure 5.12 Synchronous Dynamic RAM (SDRAM)

175

Table 5.4   SDRAM Pin Assignments

A0 to A13	Address inputs
CLK	Clock input
CKE	Clock enable
$\overline{CS}$	Chip select
$\overline{RAS}$	Row address strobe
$\overline{CAS}$	Column address strobe
$\overline{WE}$	Write enable
DQ0 to DQ7	Data input/output
DQM	Data mask

The SDRAM employs a burst mode to eliminate the address setup time and row and column line precharge time after the first access. In burst mode, a series of data bits can be clocked out rapidly after the first bit has been accessed. This mode is useful when all the bits to be accessed are in sequence and in the same row of the array as the initial access. In addition, the SDRAM has a multiple-bank internal architecture that improves opportunities for on-chip parallelism.

The mode register and associated control logic is another key feature differentiating SDRAMs from conventional DRAMs. It provides a mechanism to customize the SDRAM to suit specific system needs. The mode register specifies the burst length, which is the number of separate units of data synchronously fed onto the bus. The register also allows the programmer to adjust the latency between receipt of a read request and the beginning of data transfer.

The SDRAM performs best when it is transferring large blocks of data serially, such as for applications like word processing, spreadsheets, and multimedia.

Figure 5.13 shows an example of SDRAM operation. In this case, the burst length is 4 and the latency is 2. The burst read command is initiated by having $\overline{CS}$ and $\overline{CAS}$ low while holding $\overline{RAS}$ and $\overline{WE}$ high at the rising edge of the clock. The address inputs determine the starting column address for the burst, and the mode register sets the type of burst (sequential or interleave) and the burst length (1, 2, 4, 8, full page). The delay from the start of the command to when the data from the first cell appears on the outputs is equal to the value of the $\overline{CAS}$ latency that is set in the mode register.

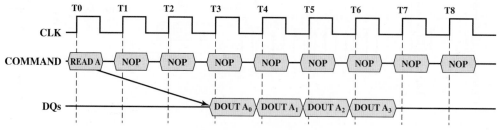

Figure 5.13   SDRAM Read Timing (burst length = 4, $\overline{CAS}$ latency = 2)

There is now an enhanced version of SDRAM, known as double data rate SDRAM (DDR-SDRAM) that overcomes the once-per-cycle limitation. DDR-SDRAM can send data to the processor twice per clock cycle.

Rambus DRAM

RDRAM, developed by Rambus [FARM92, CRIS97], has been adopted by Intel for its Pentium and Itanium processors. It has become the main competitor to SDRAM. RDRAM chips are vertical packages, with all pins on one side. The chip exchanges data with the processor over 28 wires no more than 12 centimeters long. The bus can address up to 320 RDRAM chips and is rated at 1.6 GBps.

The special RDRAM bus delivers address and control information using an asynchronous block-oriented protocol. After an initial 480 ns access time, this produces the 1.6 GBps data rate. What makes this speed possible is the bus itself, which defines impedances, clocking, and signals very precisely. Rather than being controlled by the explicit RAS, CAS, R/W, and CE signals used in conventional DRAMs, an RDRAM gets a memory request over the high-speed bus. This request contains the desired address, the type of operation, and the number of bytes in the operation.

Figure 5.14 illustrates the RDRAM layout. The configuration consists of a controller and a number of RDRAM modules connected via a common bus. The controller is at one end of the configuration, and the far end of the bus is a parallel termination of the bus lines. The bus includes 18 data lines (16 actual data, two parity) cycling at twice the clock rate; that is, 1 bit is sent at the leading and following edge of each clock signal. This results in a signal rate on each data line of 800 Mbps. There is a separate set of 8 lines (RC) used for address and control signals. There is also a clock signal that starts at the far end from the controller propagates to the controller end and then loops back. A RDRAM module sends data to the controller synchronously to the clock to master, and the controller sends data to an RDRAM synchronously with the clock signal in the opposite direction. The remaining bus lines include a reference voltage, ground, and power source.

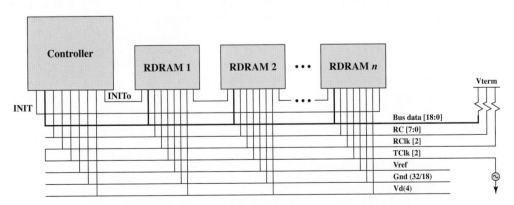

Figure 5.14   RDRAM Structure

DDR SDRAM

SDRAM is limited by the fact that it can only send data to the processor once per bus clock cycle. A new version of SDRAM, referred to as double-data-rate SDRAM can send data twice per clock cycle, once on the rising edge of the clock pulse and once on the falling edge.

DDR DRAM was developed by the JEDEC Solid State Technology Association, the Electronic Industries Alliance's semiconductor-engineering-standardization body. Numerous companies make DDR chips, which are widely used in desktop computers and servers.

Figure 5.15 shows the basic timing for a DDR read. The data transfer is synchronized to both the rising and falling edge of the clock. It is also synchronized to a bidirectional data strobe (DQS) signal that is provided by the memory controller during a read and by the DRAM during a write. In typical implementations the DQS is ignored during the read. An explanation of the use of DQS on writes is beyond our scope; see [JACO08] for details.

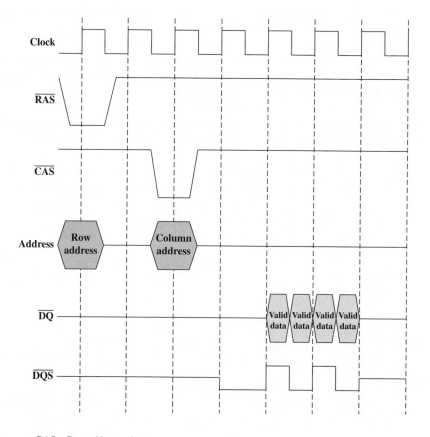

RAS = Row address select
CAS = Column address select
DQ = Data (in or out)
DQS = DQ select

Figure 5.15   DDR SDRAM Road Timing

There have been two generations of improvement to the DDR technology. DDR2 increases the data transfer rate by increasing the operational frequency of the RAM chip and by increasing the prefetch buffer from 2 bits to 4 bits per chip. The prefetch buffer is a memory cache located on the RAM chip. The buffer enables the RAM chip to preposition bits to be placed on the data base as rapidly as possible. DDR3, introduced in 2007, increases the prefetch buffer size to 8 bits.

Theoretically, a DDR module can transfer data at a clock rate in the range of 200 to 600 MHz; a DDR2 module transfers at a clock rate of 400 to 1066 MHz; and a DDR3 module transfers at a clock rate of 800 to 1600 MHz. In practice, somewhat smaller rates are achieved.

Appendix K provides more detail on DDR technology.

Cache DRAM

Cache DRAM (CDRAM), developed by Mitsubishi [HIDA90, ZHAN01], integrates a small SRAM cache (16 Kb) onto a generic DRAM chip.

The SRAM on the CDRAM can be used in two ways. First, it can be used as a true cache, consisting of a number of 64-bit lines. The cache mode of the CDRAM is effective for ordinary random access to memory.

The SRAM on the CDRAM can also be used as a buffer to support the serial access of a block of data. For example, to refresh a bit-mapped screen, the CDRAM can prefetch the data from the DRAM into the SRAM buffer. Subsequent accesses to the chip result in accesses solely to the SRAM.

5.4 RECOMMENDED READING AND WEB SITES

[PRIN97] provides a comprehensive treatment of semiconductor memory technologies, including SRAM, DRAM, and flash memories. [SHAR97] covers the same material, with more emphasis on testing and reliability issues. [SHAR03] and [PRIN02] focus on advanced DRAM and SRAM architectures. For an in-depth look at DRAM, see [JACO08] and [KEET01]. [CUPP01] provides an interesting performance comparison of various DRAM schemes. [BEZ03] is a comprehensive introduction to flash memory technology.

A good explanation of error-correcting codes is contained in [MCEL85]. For a deeper study, worthwhile book-length treatments are [ADAM91] and [BLAH83]. A readable theoretical and mathematical treatment of error-correcting codes is [ASH90]. [SHAR97] contains a good survey of codes used in contemporary main memories.

ADAM91 Adamek, J. *Foundations of Coding.* New York: Wiley, 1991.

ASH90 Ash, R. *Information Theory.* New York: Dover, 1990.

BEZ03 Bez, R.; et al. Introduction to Flash Memory. *Proceedings of the IEEE,* April 2003.

BLAH83 Blahut, R. *Theory and Practice of Error Control Codes.* Reading, MA: Addison-Wesley, 1983.

CUPP01 Cuppu, V., et al. "High Performance DRAMS in Workstation Environments." *IEEE Transactions on Computers,* November 2001.

JACO08 Jacob, B.; Ng, S.; and Wang, D. *Memory Systems: Cache, DRAM, Disk.* Boston: Morgan Kaufmann, 2008.

KEET01 Keeth, B., and Baker, R. *DRAM Circuit Design: A Tutorial.* Piscataway, NJ: IEEE Press, 2001.

MCEL85   McEliece, R. "The Reliability of Computer Memories." *Scientific American*, January 1985.

PRIN97   Prince, B. *Semiconductor Memories.* New York: Wiley, 1997.

PRIN02   Prince, B. *Emerging Memories: Technologies and Trends.* Norwell, MA: Kluwer, 2002.

SHAR97   Sharma, A. *Semiconductor Memories: Technology, Testing, and Reliability.* New York: IEEE Press, 1997.

SHAR03   Sharma, A. *Advanced Semiconductor Memories: Architectures, Designs, and Applications.* New York: IEEE Press, 2003.

Recommended Web sites:

- **The RAM Guide:** Good overview of RAM technology plus a number of useful links
- **RDRAM:** Another useful site for RDRAM information

5.5   KEY TERMS, REVIEW QUESTIONS, AND PROBLEMS

Key Terms

cache DRAM (CDRAM)	hard failure	single-error-correcting,
dynamic RAM (DRAM)	nonvolatile memory	double-error-detecting
electrically erasable program-	programmable ROM	(SEC-DED) code
mable ROM (EEPROM)	(PROM)	soft error
erasable programmable ROM	RamBus DRAM (RDRAM)	static RAM (SRAM)
(EPROM)	read-mostly memory	synchronous DRAM
error correcting code (ECC)	read-only memory (ROM)	(SDRAM)
error correction	semiconductor memory	syndrome
flash memory	single-error-correcting (SEC)	volatile memory
Hamming code	code	

Review Questions

5.1   What are the key properties of semiconductor memory?

5.2   What are two senses in which the term *random-access memory* is used?

5.3   What is the difference between DRAM and SRAM in terms of application?

5.4   What is the difference between DRAM and SRAM in terms of characteristics such as speed, size, and cost?

5.5   Explain why one type of RAM is considered to be analog and the other digital.

5.6   What are some applications for ROM?

5.7   What are the differences among EPROM, EEPROM, and flash memory?

5.8   Explain the function of each pin in Figure 5.4b.

5.9 What is a parity bit?

5.10 How is the syndrome for the Hamming code interpreted?

5.11 How does SDRAM differ from ordinary DRAM?

Problems

5.1 Suggest reasons why RAMs traditionally have been organized as only 1 bit per chip whereas ROMs are usually organized with multiple bits per chip.

5.2 Consider a dynamic RAM that must be given a refresh cycle 64 times per ms. Each refresh operation requires 150 ns; a memory cycle requires 250 ns. What percentage of the memory's total operating time must be given to refreshes?

5.3 Figure 5.16 shows a simplified timing diagram for a DRAM read operation over a bus. The access time is considered to last from t_1 to t_2. Then there is a recharge time, lasting from t_2 to t_3, during which the DRAM chips will have to recharge before the processor can access them again.

  a. Assume that the access time is 60 ns and the recharge time is 40 ns. What is the memory cycle time? What is the maximum data rate this DRAM can sustain, assuming a 1-bit output?

  b. Constructing a 32-bit wide memory system using these chips yields what data transfer rate?

5.4 Figure 5.6 indicates how to construct a module of chips that can store 1 MByte based on a group of four 256-Kbyte chips. Let's say this module of chips is packaged as a single 1-Mbyte chip, where the word size is 1 byte. Give a high-level chip diagram of how to construct an 8-Mbyte computer memory using eight 1-Mbyte chips. Be sure to show the address lines in your diagram and what the address lines are used for.

5.5 On a typical Intel 8086-based system, connected via system bus to DRAM memory, for a read operation, $\overline{\text{RAS}}$ is activated by the trailing edge of the Address Enable signal (Figure 3.19). However, due to propagation and other delays, $\overline{\text{RAS}}$ does not go active until 50 ns after Address Enable returns to a low. Assume the latter occurs in the middle of the second half of state T_1 (somewhat earlier than in Figure 3.19). Data are read by the processor at the end of T_3. For timely presentation to the processor, however, data must be provided 60 ns earlier by memory. This interval accounts for

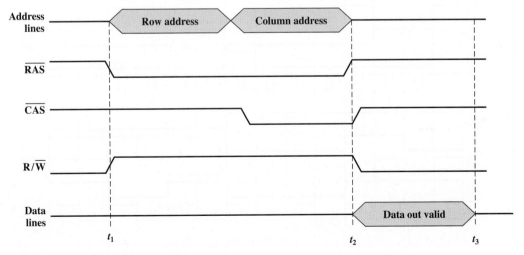

Figure 5.16 Simplified DRAM Read Timing

propagation delays along the data paths (from memory to processor) and processor data hold time requirements. Assume a clocking rate of 10 MHz.

a. How fast (access time) should the DRAMs be if no wait states are to be inserted?

b. How many wait states do we have to insert per memory read operation if the access time of the DRAMs is 150 ns?

5.6 The memory of a particular microcomputer is built from 64K × 1 DRAMs. According to the data sheet, the cell array of the DRAM is organized into 256 rows. Each row must be refreshed at least once every 4 ms. Suppose we refresh the memory on a strictly periodic basis.

a. What is the time period between successive refresh requests?

b. How long a refresh address counter do we need?

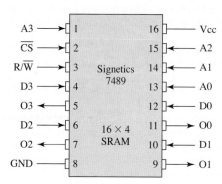

(a) Pin layout

Operating Mode	Inputs			Outputs
	$\overline{CS}$	$R/\overline{W}$	Dn	On
Write	L	L	L	L
	L	L	H	H
Read	L	H	X	Data
Inhibit writing	H	L	L	H
	H	L	H	L
Store - disable outputs	H	H	X	H

H = high voltage level
L = low voltage level
X = don't care

(b) Truth table

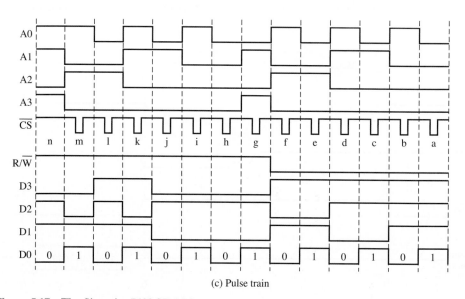

(c) Pulse train

Figure 5.17   The Signetics 7489 SRAM

5.7 Figure 5.17 shows one of the early SRAMs, the 16×4 Signetics 7489 chip, which stores 16 4-bit words.
  a. List the mode of operation of the chip for each $\overline{\text{CS}}$ input pulse shown in Figure 5.17c.
  b. List the memory contents of word locations 0 through 6 after pulse n.
  c. What is the state of the output data leads for the input pulses h through m?

5.8 Design a 16-bit memory of total capacity 8192 bits using SRAM chips of size 64×1 bit. Give the array configuration of the chips on the memory board showing all required input and output signals for assigning this memory to the lowest address space. The design should allow for both byte and 16-bit word accesses.

5.9 A common unit of measure for failure rates of electronic components is the **Failure unIT** (FIT), expressed as a rate of failures per billion device hours. Another well known but less used measure is **mean time between failures** (MTBF), which is the average time of operation of a particular component until it fails. Consider a 1 MB memory of a 16-bit microprocessor with $256\text{K} \times 1$ DRAMs. Calculate its MTBF assuming 2000 FITS for each DRAM.

5.10 For the Hamming code shown in Figure 5.10, show what happens when a check bit rather than a data bit is in error?

5.11 Suppose an 8-bit data word stored in memory is 11000010. Using the Hamming algorithm, determine what check bits would be stored in memory with the data word. Show how you got your answer.

5.12 For the 8-bit word 00111001, the check bits stored with it would be 0111. Suppose when the word is read from memory, the check bits are calculated to be 1101. What is the data word that was read from memory?

5.13 How many check bits are needed if the Hamming error correction code is used to detect single bit errors in a 1024-bit data word?

5.14 Develop an SEC code for a 16-bit data word. Generate the code for the data word 0101000000111001. Show that the code will correctly identify an error in data bit 5.

CHAPTER 6

EXTERNAL MEMORY

KEY POINTS

◆ Magnetic disks remain the most important component of external memory. Both removable and fixed, or hard, disks are used in systems ranging from personal computers to mainframes and supercomputers.

◆ To achieve greater performance and higher availability, servers and larger systems use RAID disk technology. RAID is a family of techniques for using multiple disks as a parallel array of data storage devices, with redundancy built in to compensate for disk failure.

◆ Optical storage technology has become increasingly important in all types of computer systems. While CD-ROM has been widely used for many years, more recent technologies, such as writable CD and DVD, are becoming increasingly important.

This chapter examines a range of external memory devices and systems. We begin with the most important device, the magnetic disk. Magnetic disks are the foundation of external memory on virtually all computer systems. The next section examines the use of disk arrays to achieve greater performance, looking specifically at the family of systems known as RAID (Redundant Array of Independent Disks). An increasingly important component of many computer systems is external optical memory, and this is examined in the third section. Finally, magnetic tape is described.

6.1 MAGNETIC DISK

A disk is a circular platter constructed of nonmagnetic material, called the substrate, coated with a magnetizable material. Traditionally, the substrate has been an aluminum or aluminum alloy material. More recently, glass substrates have been introduced. The glass substrate has a number of benefits, including the following:

- Improvement in the uniformity of the magnetic film surface to increase disk reliability
- A significant reduction in overall surface defects to help reduce read-write errors
- Ability to support lower fly heights (described subsequently)
- Better stiffness to reduce disk dynamics
- Greater ability to withstand shock and damage

Magnetic Read and Write Mechanisms

Data are recorded on and later retrieved from the disk via a conducting coil named the **head**; in many systems, there are two heads, a read head and a write head. During a read or write operation, the head is stationary while the platter rotates beneath it.

The write mechanism exploits the fact that electricity flowing through a coil produces a magnetic field. Electric pulses are sent to the write head, and the resulting

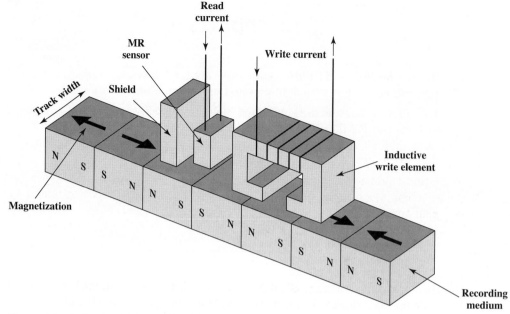

Figure 6.1   Inductive Write/Magnetoresistive Read Head

magnetic patterns are recorded on the surface below, with different patterns for positive and negative currents. The write head itself is made of easily magnetizable material and is in the shape of a rectangular doughnut with a gap along one side and a few turns of conducting wire along the opposite side (Figure 6.1). An electric current in the wire induces a magnetic field across the gap, which in turn magnetizes a small area of the recording medium. Reversing the direction of the current reverses the direction of the magnetization on the recording medium.

The traditional read mechanism exploits the fact that a magnetic field moving relative to a coil produces an electrical current in the coil. When the surface of the disk passes under the head, it generates a current of the same polarity as the one already recorded. The structure of the head for reading is in this case essentially the same as for writing and therefore the same head can be used for both. Such single heads are used in floppy disk systems and in older rigid disk systems.

Contemporary rigid disk systems use a different read mechanism, requiring a separate read head, positioned for convenience close to the write head. The read head consists of a partially shielded magnetoresistive (MR) sensor. The MR material has an electrical resistance that depends on the direction of the magnetization of the medium moving under it. By passing a current through the MR sensor, resistance changes are detected as voltage signals. The MR design allows higher-frequency operation, which equates to greater storage densities and operating speeds.

Data Organization and Formatting

The head is a relatively small device capable of reading from or writing to a portion of the platter rotating beneath it. This gives rise to the organization of data on the

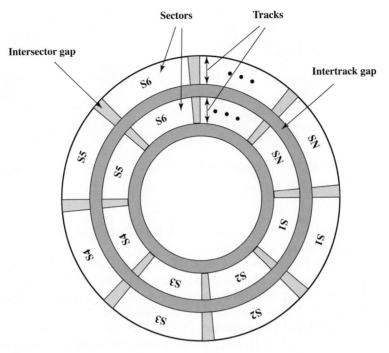

Figure 6.2   Disk Data Layout

platter in a concentric set of rings, called **tracks**. Each track is the same width as the head. There are thousands of tracks per surface.

Figure 6.2 depicts this data layout. Adjacent tracks are separated by **gaps**. This prevents, or at least minimizes, errors due to misalignment of the head or simply interference of magnetic fields.

Data are transferred to and from the disk in **sectors** (Figure 6.2). There are typically hundreds of sectors per track, and these may be of either fixed or variable length. In most contemporary systems, fixed-length sectors are used, with 512 bytes being the nearly universal sector size. To avoid imposing unreasonable precision requirements on the system, adjacent sectors are separated by intratrack (intersector) gaps.

A bit near the center of a rotating disk travels past a fixed point (such as a read–write head) slower than a bit on the outside. Therefore, some way must be found to compensate for the variation in speed so that the head can read all the bits at the same rate. This can be done by increasing the spacing between bits of information recorded in segments of the disk. The information can then be scanned at the same rate by rotating the disk at a fixed speed, known as the **constant angular velocity** (CAV). Figure 6.3a shows the layout of a disk using CAV. The disk is divided into a number of pie-shaped sectors and into a series of concentric tracks. The advantage of using CAV is that individual blocks of data can be directly addressed by track and sector. To move the head from its current location to a specific address, it only takes a short movement of the head to a specific track and a short wait for the proper sector to spin under the head. The disadvantage of CAV is that the amount of data that

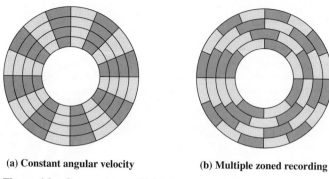

(a) Constant angular velocity   (b) Multiple zoned recording

Figure 6.3   Comparison of Disk Layout Methods

can be stored on the long outer tracks is the only same as what can be stored on the short inner tracks.

Because the **density**, in bits per linear inch, increases in moving from the outermost track to the innermost track, disk storage capacity in a straightforward CAV system is limited by the maximum recording density that can be achieved on the innermost track. To increase density, modern hard disk systems use a technique known as **multiple zone recording**, in which the surface is divided into a number of concentric zones (16 is typical). Within a zone, the number of bits per track is constant. Zones farther from the center contain more bits (more sectors) than zones closer to the center. This allows for greater overall storage capacity at the expense of somewhat more complex circuitry. As the disk head moves from one zone to another, the length (along the track) of individual bits changes, causing a change in the timing for reads and writes. Figure 6.3b suggests the nature of multiple zone recording; in this illustration, each zone is only a single track wide.

Some means is needed to locate sector positions within a track. Clearly, there must be some starting point on the track and a way of identifying the start and end of each sector. These requirements are handled by means of control data recorded on the disk. Thus, the disk is formatted with some extra data used only by the disk drive and not accessible to the user.

An example of disk formatting is shown in Figure 6.4. In this case, each track contains 30 fixed-length sectors of 600 bytes each. Each sector holds 512 bytes of data plus control information useful to the disk controller. The ID field is a unique identifier or address used to locate a particular sector. The SYNCH byte is a special bit pattern that delimits the beginning of the field. The track number identifies a track on a surface. The head number identifies a head, because this disk has multiple surfaces (explained presently). The ID and data fields each contain an error-detecting code.

Physical Characteristics

Table 6.1 lists the major characteristics that differentiate among the various types of magnetic disks. First, the head may either be fixed or movable with respect to the radial direction of the platter. In a **fixed-head disk**, there is one read-write head per

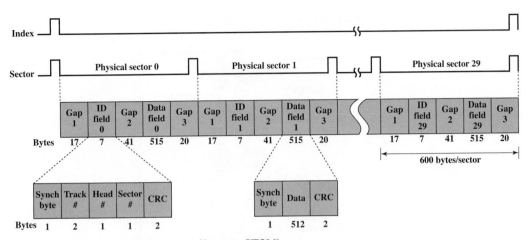

Figure 6.4   Winchester Disk Format (Seagate ST506)

track. All of the heads are mounted on a rigid arm that extends across all tracks; such systems are rare today. In a **movable-head disk**, there is only one read-write head. Again, the head is mounted on an arm. Because the head must be able to be positioned above any track, the arm can be extended or retracted for this purpose.

The disk itself is mounted in a disk drive, which consists of the arm, a spindle that rotates the disk, and the electronics needed for input and output of binary data. A **nonremovable disk** is permanently mounted in the disk drive; the hard disk in a personal computer is a nonremovable disk. A **removable disk** can be removed and replaced with another disk. The advantage of the latter type is that unlimited amounts of data are available with a limited number of disk systems. Furthermore, such a disk may be moved from one computer system to another. Floppy disks and ZIP cartridge disks are examples of removable disks.

For most disks, the magnetizable coating is applied to both sides of the platter, which is then referred to as **double sided**. Some less expensive disk systems use **single-sided** disks.

Table 6.1   Physical Characteristics of Disk Systems

Head Motion	**Platters**
Fixed head (one per track)	Single platter
Movable head (one per surface)	Multiple platter
Disk Portability	**Head Mechanism**
Nonremovable disk	Contact (floppy)
Removable disk	Fixed gap
	Aerodynamic gap (Winchester)
Sides	
Single sided	
Double sided	

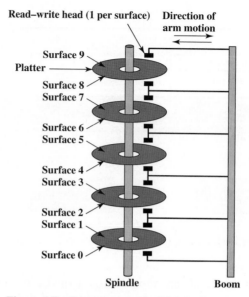

Figure 6.5   Components of a Disk Drive

Some disk drives accommodate **multiple platters** stacked vertically a fraction of an inch apart. Multiple arms are provided (Figure 6.5). Multiple–platter disks employ a movable head, with one read-write head per platter surface. All of the heads are mechanically fixed so that all are at the same distance from the center of the disk and move together. Thus, at any time, all of the heads are positioned over tracks that are of equal distance from the center of the disk. The set of all the tracks in the same relative position on the platter is referred to as a **cylinder**. For example, all of the shaded tracks in Figure 6.6 are part of one cylinder.

Finally, the head mechanism provides a classification of disks into three types. Traditionally, the read-write head has been positioned a fixed distance above the

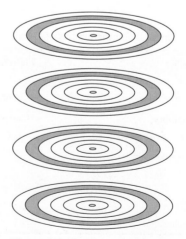

Figure 6.6   Tracks and Cylinders

platter, allowing an air gap. At the other extreme is a head mechanism that actually comes into physical contact with the medium during a read or write operation. This mechanism is used with the **floppy disk**, which is a small, flexible platter and the least expensive type of disk.

To understand the third type of disk, we need to comment on the relationship between data density and the size of the air gap. The head must generate or sense an electromagnetic field of sufficient magnitude to write and read properly. The narrower the head is, the closer it must be to the platter surface to function. A narrower head means narrower tracks and therefore greater data density, which is desirable. However, the closer the head is to the disk, the greater the risk of error from impurities or imperfections. To push the technology further, the Winchester disk was developed. Winchester heads are used in sealed drive assemblies that are almost free of contaminants. They are designed to operate closer to the disk's surface than conventional rigid disk heads, thus allowing greater data density. The head is actually an aerodynamic foil that rests lightly on the platter's surface when the disk is motionless. The air pressure generated by a spinning disk is enough to make the foil rise above the surface. The resulting noncontact system can be engineered to use narrower heads that operate closer to the platter's surface than conventional rigid disk heads.[1]

Table 6.2 gives disk parameters for typical contemporary high-performance disks.

Table 6.2   Typical Hard Disk Drive Parameters

Characteristics	Seagate Barracuda ES.2	Seagate Barracuda 7200.10	Seagate Barracuda 7200.9	Seagate	Hitachi Micro-drive
Application	High-capacity server	High-performance desktop	Entry-level desktop	Laptop	Handheld devices
Capacity	1 TB	750 GB	160 GB	120 GB	8 GB
Minimum track-to-track seek time	0.8 ms	0.3 ms	1.0 ms	–	1.0 ms
Average seek time	8.5 ms	3.6 ms	9.5 ms	12.5 ms	12 ms
Spindle speed	7200 rpm	7200 rpm	7200	5400 rpm	3600 rpm
Average rotational delay	4.16 ms	4.16 ms	4.17 ms	5.6 ms	8.33 ms
Maximum transfer rate	3 GB/s	300 MB/s	300 MB/s	150 MB/s	10 MB/s
Bytes per sector	512	512	512	512	512
Tracks per cylinder (number of platter surfaces)	8	8	2	8	2

---

[1]As a matter of historical interest, the term *Winchester* was originally used by IBM as a code name for the 3340 disk model prior to its announcement. The 3340 was a removable disk pack with the heads sealed within the pack. The term is now applied to any sealed-unit disk drive with aerodynamic head design. The Winchester disk is commonly found built in to personal computers and workstations, where it is referred to as a *hard disk*.

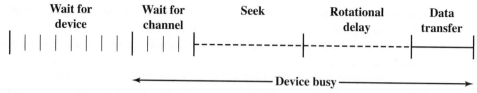

Figure 6.7 Timing of a Disk I/O Transfer

Disk Performance Parameters

The actual details of disk I/O operation depend on the computer system, the operating system, and the nature of the I/O channel and disk controller hardware. A general timing diagram of disk I/O transfer is shown in Figure 6.7.

When the disk drive is operating, the disk is rotating at constant speed. To read or write, the head must be positioned at the desired track and at the beginning of the desired sector on that track. Track selection involves moving the head in a movable-head system or electronically selecting one head on a fixed-head system. On a movable-head system, the time it takes to position the head at the track is known as **seek time**. In either case, once the track is selected, the disk controller waits until the appropriate sector rotates to line up with the head. The time it takes for the beginning of the sector to reach the head is known as **rotational delay**, or *rotational latency*. The sum of the seek time, if any, and the rotational delay equals the **access time**, which is the time it takes to get into position to read or write. Once the head is in position, the read or write operation is then performed as the sector moves under the head; this is the data transfer portion of the operation; the time required for the transfer is the **transfer time**.

In addition to the access time and transfer time, there are several queuing delays normally associated with a disk I/O operation. When a process issues an I/O request, it must first wait in a queue for the device to be available. At that time, the device is assigned to the process. If the device shares a single I/O channel or a set of I/O channels with other disk drives, then there may be an additional wait for the channel to be available. At that point, the seek is performed to begin disk access.

In some high-end systems for servers, a technique known as rotational positional sensing (RPS) is used. This works as follows: When the seek command has been issued, the channel is released to handle other I/O operations. When the seek is completed, the device determines when the data will rotate under the head. As that sector approaches the head, the device tries to reestablish the communication path back to the host. If either the control unit or the channel is busy with another I/O, then the reconnection attempt fails and the device must rotate one whole revolution before it can attempt to reconnect, which is called an RPS miss. This is an extra delay element that must be added to the timeline of Figure 6.7.

SEEK TIME Seek time is the time required to move the disk arm to the required track. It turns out that this is a difficult quantity to pin down. The seek time consists of two key components: the initial startup time, and the time taken to traverse the tracks that have to be crossed once the access arm is up to speed. Unfortunately, the traversal time is not a linear function of the number of tracks, but includes a settling time (time after positioning the head over the target track until track identification is confirmed).

Much improvement comes from smaller and lighter disk components. Some years ago, a typical disk was 14 inches (36 cm) in diameter, whereas the most common size today is 3.5 inches (8.9 cm), reducing the distance that the arm has to travel. A typical average seek time on contemporary hard disks is under 10 ms.

ROTATIONAL DELAY Disks, other than floppy disks, rotate at speeds ranging from 3600 rpm (for handheld devices such as digital cameras) up to, as of this writing, 20,000 rpm; at this latter speed, there is one revolution per 3 ms. Thus, on the average, the rotational delay will be 1.5 ms.

TRANSFER TIME The transfer time to or from the disk depends on the rotation speed of the disk in the following fashion:

$$T = \frac{b}{rN}$$

where

$\quad T$ = transfer time

$\quad b$ = number of bytes to be transferred

$\quad N$ = number of bytes on a track

$\quad r$ = rotation speed, in revolutions per second

Thus the total average access time can be expressed as

$$T_a = T_s + \frac{1}{2r} + \frac{b}{rN}$$

where T_s is the average seek time. Note that on a zoned drive, the number of bytes per track is variable, complicating the calculation.[2]

A TIMING COMPARISON With the foregoing parameters defined, let us look at two different I/O operations that illustrate the danger of relying on average values. Consider a disk with an advertised average seek time of 4 ms, rotation speed of 15,000 rpm, and 512-byte sectors with 500 sectors per track. Suppose that we wish to read a file consisting of 2500 sectors for a total of 1.28 Mbytes. We would like to estimate the total time for the transfer.

First, let us assume that the file is stored as compactly as possible on the disk. That is, the file occupies all of the sectors on 5 adjacent tracks (5 tracks × 500 sectors/track = 2500 sectors). This is known as *sequential organization*. Now, the time to read the first track is as follows:

Average seek	4 ms
Average rotational delay	2 ms
Read 500 sectors	4 ms
	10 ms

---

[2]Compare the two preceding equations to Equation (4.1).

Suppose that the remaining tracks can now be read with essentially no seek time. That is, the I/O operation can keep up with the flow from the disk. Then, at most, we need to deal with rotational delay for each succeeding track. Thus each successive track is read in $2 + 4 = 6$ ms. To read the entire file,

$$\text{Total time} = 10 + (4 \times 6) = 34 \text{ ms} = 0.034 \text{ seconds}$$

Now let us calculate the time required to read the same data using random access rather than sequential access; that is, accesses to the sectors are distributed randomly over the disk. For each sector, we have

Average seek	4	ms
Rotational delay	2	ms
Read 1 sectors	0.008 ms	
	6.008 ms	

$$\text{Total time} = 2500 \times 6.008 = 15020 \text{ ms} = 15.02 \text{ seconds}$$

It is clear that the order in which sectors are read from the disk has a tremendous effect on I/O performance. In the case of file access in which multiple sectors are read or written, we have some control over the way in which sectors of data are deployed. However, even in the case of a file access, in a multiprogramming environment, there will be I/O requests competing for the same disk. Thus, it is worthwhile to examine ways in which the performance of disk I/O can be improved over that achieved with purely random access to the disk. This leads to a consideration of disk scheduling algorithms, which is the province of the operating system and beyond the scope of this book (see [STAL09] for a discussion).

RAID Simulator

6.2 RAID

As discussed earlier, the rate in improvement in secondary storage performance has been considerably less than the rate for processors and main memory. This mismatch has made the disk storage system perhaps the main focus of concern in improving overall computer system performance.

As in other areas of computer performance, disk storage designers recognize that if one component can only be pushed so far, additional gains in performance are to be had by using multiple parallel components. In the case of disk storage, this leads to the development of arrays of disks that operate independently and in parallel. With multiple disks, separate I/O requests can be handled in parallel, as long as the data required reside on separate disks. Further, a single I/O request can be executed in parallel if the block of data to be accessed is distributed across multiple disks.

With the use of multiple disks, there is a wide variety of ways in which the data can be organized and in which redundancy can be added to improve reliability. This could make it difficult to develop database schemes that are usable on a number of platforms and operating systems. Fortunately, industry has agreed on a standardized scheme for multiple-disk database design, known as RAID (Redundant Array of Independent Disks). The RAID scheme consists of seven levels,[3] zero through six. These levels do not imply a hierarchical relationship but designate different design architectures that share three common characteristics:

1. RAID is a set of physical disk drives viewed by the operating system as a single logical drive.
2. Data are distributed across the physical drives of an array in a scheme known as striping, described subsequently.
3. Redundant disk capacity is used to store parity information, which guarantees data recoverability in case of a disk failure.

The details of the second and third characteristics differ for the different RAID levels. RAID 0 and RAID 1 do not support the third characteristic.

The term *RAID* was originally coined in a paper by a group of researchers at the University of California at Berkeley [PATT88].[4] The paper outlined various RAID configurations and applications and introduced the definitions of the RAID levels that are still used. The RAID strategy employs multiple disk drives and distributes data in such a way as to enable simultaneous access to data from multiple drives, thereby improving I/O performance and allowing easier incremental increases in capacity.

The unique contribution of the RAID proposal is to address effectively the need for redundancy. Although allowing multiple heads and actuators to operate simultaneously achieves higher I/O and transfer rates, the use of multiple devices increases the probability of failure. To compensate for this decreased reliability, RAID makes use of stored parity information that enables the recovery of data lost due to a disk failure.

We now examine each of the RAID levels. Table 6.3 provides a rough guide to the seven levels. In the table, I/O performance is shown both in terms of data transfer capacity, or ability to move data, and I/O request rate, or ability to satisfy I/O requests, since these RAID levels inherently perform differently relative to these two

---

[3]Additional levels have been defined by some researchers and some companies, but the seven levels described in this section are the ones universally agreed on.

[4]In that paper, the acronym RAID stood for Redundant Array of Inexpensive Disks. The term *inexpensive* was used to contrast the small relatively inexpensive disks in the RAID array to the alternative, a single large expensive disk (SLED). The SLED is essentially a thing of the past, with similar disk technology being used for both RAID and non-RAID configurations. Accordingly, the industry has adopted the term *independent* to emphasize that the RAID array creates significant performance and reliability gains.

Table 6.3 RAID Levels

Category	Level	Description	Disks Required	Data Availability	Large I/O Data Transfer Capacity	Small I/O Request Rate
Striping	0	Nonredundant	N	Lower than single disk	Very high	Very high for both read and write
Mirroring	1	Mirrored	$2N$	Higher than RAID 2, 3, 4, or 5; lower than RAID 6	Higher than single disk for read; similar to single disk for write	Up to twice that of a single disk for read; similar to single disk for write
Parallel access	2	Redundant via Hamming code	$N + m$	Much higher than single disk; comparable to RAID 3, 4, or 5	Highest of all listed alternatives	Approximately twice that of a single disk
	3	Bit-interleaved parity	$N + 1$	Much higher than single disk; comparable to RAID 2, 4, or 5	Highest of all listed alternatives	Approximately twice that of a single disk
	4	Block-interleaved parity	$N + 1$	Much higher than single disk; comparable to RAID 2, 3, or 5	Similar to RAID 0 for read; significantly lower than single disk for write	Similar to RAID 0 for read; significantly lower than single disk for write
Independent access	5	Block-interleaved distributed parity	$N + 1$	Much higher than single disk; comparable to RAID 2, 3, or 4	Similar to RAID 0 for read; lower than single disk for write	Similar to RAID 0 for read; generally lower than single disk for write
	6	Block-interleaved dual distributed parity	$N + 2$	Highest of all listed alternatives	Similar to RAID 0 for read; lower than RAID 5 for write	Similar to RAID 0 for read; significantly lower than RAID 5 for write

N = number of data disks; m proportional to log N

196

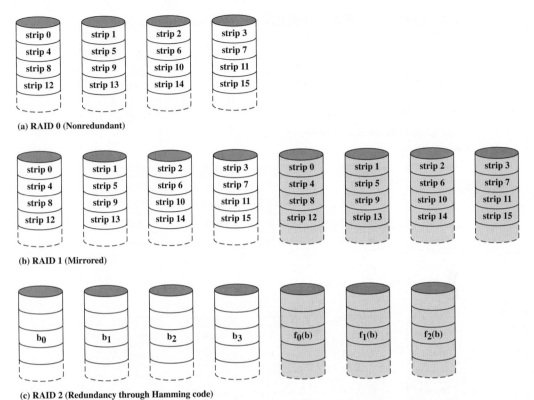

(a) RAID 0 (Nonredundant)

(b) RAID 1 (Mirrored)

(c) RAID 2 (Redundancy through Hamming code)

Figure 6.8   RAID Levels

metrics. Each RAID level's strong point is highlighted by darker shading. Figure 6.8 illustrates the use of the seven RAID schemes to support a data capacity requiring four disks with no redundancy. The figures highlight the layout of user data and redundant data and indicates the relative storage requirements of the various levels. We refer to these figures throughout the following discussion.

RAID Level 0

RAID level 0 is not a true member of the RAID family because it does not include redundancy to improve performance. However, there are a few applications, such as some on supercomputers in which performance and capacity are primary concerns and low cost is more important than improved reliability.

For RAID 0, the user and system data are distributed across all of the disks in the array. This has a notable advantage over the use of a single large disk: If two different I/O requests are pending for two different blocks of data, then there is a good chance that the requested blocks are on different disks. Thus, the two requests can be issued in parallel, reducing the I/O queuing time.

But RAID 0, as with all of the RAID levels, goes further than simply distributing the data across a disk array: The data are *striped* across the available disks. This is best understood by considering Figure 6.9. All of the user and system data are viewed

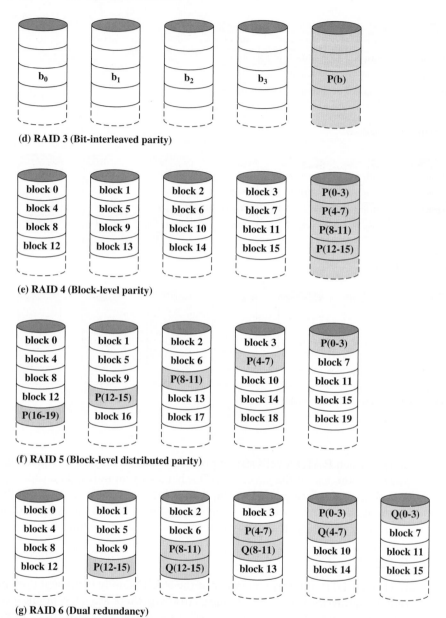

(d) RAID 3 (Bit-interleaved parity)

(e) RAID 4 (Block-level parity)

(f) RAID 5 (Block-level distributed parity)

(g) RAID 6 (Dual redundancy)

Figure 6.8 RAID Levels (*continued*)

as being stored on a logical disk. The logical disk is divided into strips; these strips may be physical blocks, sectors, or some other unit. The strips are mapped round robin to consecutive physical disks in the RAID array. A set of logically consecutive strips that maps exactly one strip to each array member is referred to as a **stripe**. In an n-disk array, the first n logical strips are physically stored as the first strip on each of the n disks, forming the first stripe; the second n strips are distributed as the second

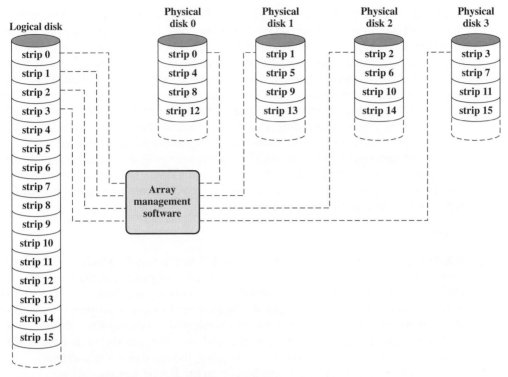

Figure 6.9 Data Mapping for a RAID Level 0 Array

strips on each disk; and so on. The advantage of this layout is that if a single I/O request consists of multiple logically contiguous strips, then up to *n* strips for that request can be handled in parallel, greatly reducing the I/O transfer time.

Figure 6.9 indicates the use of array management software to map between logical and physical disk space. This software may execute either in the disk subsystem or in a host computer.

RAID 0 FOR HIGH DATA TRANSFER CAPACITY The performance of any of the RAID levels depends critically on the request patterns of the host system and on the layout of the data. These issues can be most clearly addressed in RAID 0, where the impact of redundancy does not interfere with the analysis. First, let us consider the use of RAID 0 to achieve a high data transfer rate. For applications to experience a high transfer rate, two requirements must be met. First, a high transfer capacity must exist along the entire path between host memory and the individual disk drives. This includes internal controller buses, host system I/O buses, I/O adapters, and host memory buses.

The second requirement is that the application must make I/O requests that drive the disk array efficiently. This requirement is met if the typical request is for large amounts of logically contiguous data, compared to the size of a strip. In this case, a single I/O request involves the parallel transfer of data from multiple disks, increasing the effective transfer rate compared to a single-disk transfer.

RAID 0 FOR HIGH I/O REQUEST RATE In a transaction-oriented environment, the user is typically more concerned with response time than with transfer rate. For an individual I/O request for a small amount of data, the I/O time is dominated by the motion of the disk heads (seek time) and the movement of the disk (rotational latency).

In a transaction environment, there may be hundreds of I/O requests per second. A disk array can provide high I/O execution rates by balancing the I/O load across multiple disks. Effective load balancing is achieved only if there are typically multiple I/O requests outstanding. This, in turn, implies that there are multiple independent applications or a single transaction-oriented application that is capable of multiple asynchronous I/O requests. The performance will also be influenced by the strip size. If the strip size is relatively large, so that a single I/O request only involves a single disk access, then multiple waiting I/O requests can be handled in parallel, reducing the queuing time for each request.

RAID Level 1

RAID 1 differs from RAID levels 2 through 6 in the way in which redundancy is achieved. In these other RAID schemes, some form of parity calculation is used to introduce redundancy, whereas in RAID 1, redundancy is achieved by the simple expedient of duplicating all the data. As Figure 6.8b shows, data striping is used, as in RAID 0. But in this case, each logical strip is mapped to two separate physical disks so that every disk in the array has a mirror disk that contains the same data. RAID 1 can also be implemented without data striping, though this is less common.

There are a number of positive aspects to the RAID 1 organization:

1. A read request can be serviced by either of the two disks that contains the requested data, whichever one involves the minimum seek time plus rotational latency.

2. A write request requires that both corresponding strips be updated, but this can be done in parallel. Thus, the write performance is dictated by the slower of the two writes (i.e., the one that involves the larger seek time plus rotational latency). However, there is no "write penalty" with RAID 1. RAID levels 2 through 6 involve the use of parity bits. Therefore, when a single strip is updated, the array management software must first compute and update the parity bits as well as updating the actual strip in question.

3. Recovery from a failure is simple. When a drive fails, the data may still be accessed from the second drive.

The principal disadvantage of RAID 1 is the cost; it requires twice the disk space of the logical disk that it supports. Because of that, a RAID 1 configuration is likely to be limited to drives that store system software and data and other highly critical files. In these cases, RAID 1 provides real-time copy of all data so that in the event of a disk failure, all of the critical data are still immediately available.

In a transaction-oriented environment, RAID 1 can achieve high I/O request rates if the bulk of the requests are reads. In this situation, the performance of RAID 1 can approach double of that of RAID 0. However, if a substantial fraction of the I/O requests are write requests, then there may be no significant performance gain over RAID 0. RAID 1 may also provide improved performance over RAID 0 for data transfer intensive applications with a high percentage of reads. Improvement occurs if the application can split each read request so that both disk members participate.

RAID Level 2

RAID levels 2 and 3 make use of a parallel access technique. In a parallel access array, all member disks participate in the execution of every I/O request. Typically, the spindles of the individual drives are synchronized so that each disk head is in the same position on each disk at any given time.

As in the other RAID schemes, data striping is used. In the case of RAID 2 and 3, the strips are very small, often as small as a single byte or word. With RAID 2, an error-correcting code is calculated across corresponding bits on each data disk, and the bits of the code are stored in the corresponding bit positions on multiple parity disks. Typically, a Hamming code is used, which is able to correct single-bit errors and detect double-bit errors.

Although RAID 2 requires fewer disks than RAID 1, it is still rather costly. The number of redundant disks is proportional to the log of the number of data disks. On a single read, all disks are simultaneously accessed. The requested data and the associated error-correcting code are delivered to the array controller. If there is a single-bit error, the controller can recognize and correct the error instantly, so that the read access time is not slowed. On a single write, all data disks and parity disks must be accessed for the write operation.

RAID 2 would only be an effective choice in an environment in which many disk errors occur. Given the high reliability of individual disks and disk drives, RAID 2 is overkill and is not implemented.

RAID Level 3

RAID 3 is organized in a similar fashion to RAID 2. The difference is that RAID 3 requires only a single redundant disk, no matter how large the disk array. RAID 3 employs parallel access, with data distributed in small strips. Instead of an error-correcting code, a simple parity bit is computed for the set of individual bits in the same position on all of the data disks.

REDUNDANCY In the event of a drive failure, the parity drive is accessed and data is reconstructed from the remaining devices. Once the failed drive is replaced, the missing data can be restored on the new drive and operation resumed.

Data reconstruction is simple. Consider an array of five drives in which X0 through X3 contain data and X4 is the parity disk. The parity for the ith bit is calculated as follows:

$$X4(i) = X3(i) \oplus X2(i) \oplus X1(i) \oplus X0(i)$$

where $\oplus$ is exclusive-OR function.

Suppose that drive X1 has failed. If we add $X4(i) \oplus X1(i)$ to both sides of the preceding equation, we get

$$X1(i) = X4(i) \oplus X3(i) \oplus X2(i) \oplus X0(i)$$

Thus, the contents of each strip of data on X1 can be regenerated from the contents of the corresponding strips on the remaining disks in the array. This principle is true for RAID levels 3 through 6.

In the event of a disk failure, all of the data are still available in what is referred to as reduced mode. In this mode, for reads, the missing data are regenerated on the fly using the exclusive-OR calculation. When data are written to a reduced RAID 3 array, consistency of the parity must be maintained for later regeneration. Return to full operation requires that the failed disk be replaced and the entire contents of the failed disk be regenerated on the new disk.

PERFORMANCE Because data are striped in very small strips, RAID 3 can achieve very high data transfer rates. Any I/O request will involve the parallel transfer of data from all of the data disks. For large transfers, the performance improvement is especially noticeable. On the other hand, only one I/O request can be executed at a time. Thus, in a transaction-oriented environment, performance suffers.

RAID Level 4

RAID levels 4 through 6 make use of an independent access technique. In an independent access array, each member disk operates independently, so that separate I/O requests can be satisfied in parallel. Because of this, independent access arrays are more suitable for applications that require high I/O request rates and are relatively less suited for applications that require high data transfer rates.

As in the other RAID schemes, data striping is used. In the case of RAID 4 through 6, the strips are relatively large. With RAID 4, a bit-by-bit parity strip is calculated across corresponding strips on each data disk, and the parity bits are stored in the corresponding strip on the parity disk.

RAID 4 involves a write penalty when an I/O write request of small size is performed. Each time that a write occurs, the array management software must update not only the user data but also the corresponding parity bits. Consider an array of five drives in which X0 through X3 contain data and X4 is the parity disk. Suppose that a write is performed that only involves a strip on disk X1. Initially, for each bit i, we have the following relationship:

$$X4(i) = X3(i) \oplus X2(i) \oplus X1(i) \oplus X0(i) \tag{6.1}$$

After the update, with potentially altered bits indicated by a prime symbol:

$$
\begin{aligned}
X4'(i) &= X3(i) \oplus X2(i) \oplus X1'(i) \oplus X0(i) \\
&= X3(i) \oplus X2(i) \oplus X1'(i) \oplus X0(i) \oplus X1(i) \oplus X1(i) \\
&= X3(i) \oplus X2(i) \oplus X1(i) \oplus X0(i) \oplus X1(i) \oplus X1'(i) \\
&= X4(i) \oplus X1(i) \oplus X1'(i)
\end{aligned}
$$

The preceding set of equations is derived as follows. The first line shows that a change in X1 will also affect the parity disk X4. In the second line, we add the terms $\oplus X1(i) \oplus X1(i)]$. Because the exclusive-OR of any quantity with itself is 0, this does not affect the equation. However, it is a convenience that is used to create the third line, by reordering. Finally, Equation (6.1) is used to replace the first four terms by X4(i).

To calculate the new parity, the array management software must read the old user strip and the old parity strip. Then it can update these two strips with the new data and the newly calculated parity. Thus, each strip write involves two reads and two writes.

In the case of a larger size I/O write that involves strips on all disk drives, parity is easily computed by calculation using only the new data bits. Thus, the parity drive can be updated in parallel with the data drives and there are no extra reads or writes.

In any case, every write operation must involve the parity disk, which therefore can become a bottleneck.

RAID Level 5

RAID 5 is organized in a similar fashion to RAID 4. The difference is that RAID 5 distributes the parity strips across all disks. A typical allocation is a round-robin scheme, as illustrated in Figure 6.8f. For an n-disk array, the parity strip is on a different disk for the first n stripes, and the pattern then repeats.

The distribution of parity strips across all drives avoids the potential I/O bottleneck found in RAID 4.

RAID Level 6

RAID 6 was introduced in a subsequent paper by the Berkeley researchers [KATZ89]. In the RAID 6 scheme, two different parity calculations are carried out and stored in separate blocks on different disks. Thus, a RAID 6 array whose user data require N disks consists of $N + 2$ disks.

Figure 6.8g illustrates the scheme. P and Q are two different data check algorithms. One of the two is the exclusive-OR calculation used in RAID 4 and 5. But the other is an independent data check algorithm. This makes it possible to regenerate data even if two disks containing user data fail.

The advantage of RAID 6 is that it provides extremely high data availability. Three disks would have to fail within the MTTR (mean time to repair) interval to cause data to be lost. On the other hand, RAID 6 incurs a substantial write penalty, because each write affects two parity blocks. Performance benchmarks [EISC07] show a RAID 6 controller can suffer more than a 30% drop in overall write performance compared with a RAID 5 implementation. RAID 5 and RAID 6 read performance is comparable.

Table 6.4 is a comparative summary of the seven levels.

6.3 OPTICAL MEMORY

In 1983, one of the most successful consumer products of all time was introduced: the compact disk (CD) digital audio system. The CD is a nonerasable disk that can store more than 60 minutes of audio information on one side. The huge commercial success of the CD enabled the development of low-cost optical-disk storage technology that has revolutionized computer data storage. A variety of optical-disk systems have been introduced (Table 6.5). We briefly review each of these.

Table 6.4 RAID Comparison

Level	Advantages	Disadvantages	Applications
0	I/O performance is greatly improved by spreading the I/O load across many channels and drives No parity calculation overhead is involved Very simple design Easy to implement	The failure of just one drive will result in all data in an array being lost	Video production and editing Image Editing Pre-press applications Any application requiring high bandwidth
1	100% redundancy of data means no rebuild is necessary in case of a disk failure, just a copy to the replacement disk Under certain circumstances, RAID 1 can sustain multiple simultaneous drive failures Simplest RAID storage subsystem design	Highest disk overhead of all RAID types (100%)—inefficient	Accounting Payroll Financial Any application requiring very high availability
2	Extremely high data transfer rates possible The higher the data transfer rate required, the better the ratio of data disks to ECC disks Relatively simple controller design compared to RAID levels 3, 4 & 5	Very high ratio of ECC disks to data disks with smaller word sizes— inefficient Entry level cost very high—requires very high transfer rate requirement to justify	No commercial implementations exist/ not commercially viable
3	Very high read data transfer rate Very high write data transfer rate Disk failure has an insignificant impact on throughput Low ratio of ECC (parity) disks to data disks means high efficiency	Transaction rate equal to that of a single disk drive at best (if spindles are synchronized) Controller design is fairly complex	Video production and live streaming Image editing Video editing Prepress applications Any application requiring high throughput
4	Very high Read data transaction rate Low ratio of ECC (parity) disks to data disks means high efficiency	Quite complex controller design Worst write transaction rate and Write aggregate transfer rate Difficult and inefficient data rebuild in the event of disk failure	No commercial implementations exist/ not commercially viable

(Continued)

Table 6.4   Continued

Level	Advantages	Disadvantages	Applications
5	Highest Read data transaction rate Low ratio of ECC (parity) disks to data disks means high efficiency Good aggregate transfer rate	Most complex controller design Difficult to rebuild in the event of a disk failure (as compared to RAID level 1)	File and application servers Database servers Web, e-mail, and news servers Intranet servers Most versatile RAID level
6	Provides for an extremely high data fault tolerance and can sustain multiple simultaneous drive failures	More complex controller design Controller overhead to compute parity addresses is extremely high	Perfect solution for mission critical applications

Table 6.5   Optical Disk Products

CD

Compact Disk. A nonerasable disk that stores digitized audio information. The standard system uses 12-cm disks and can record more than 60 minutes of uninterrupted playing time.

CD-ROM

Compact Disk Read-Only Memory. A nonerasable disk used for storing computer data. The standard system uses 12-cm disks and can hold more than 650 Mbytes.

CD-R

CD Recordable. Similar to a CD-ROM. The user can write to the disk only once.

CD-RW

CD Rewritable. Similar to a CD-ROM. The user can erase and rewrite to the disk multiple times.

DVD

Digital Versatile Disk. A technology for producing digitized, compressed representation of video information, as well as large volumes of other digital data. Both 8 and 12 cm diameters are used, with a double-sided capacity of up to 17 Gbytes. The basic DVD is read-only (DVD-ROM).

DVD-R

DVD Recordable. Similar to a DVD-ROM. The user can write to the disk only once. Only one-sided disks can be used.

DVD-RW

DVD Rewritable. Similar to a DVD-ROM. The user can erase and rewrite to the disk multiple times. Only one-sided disks can be used.

Blu-Ray DVD

High definition video disk. Provides considerably greater data storage density than DVD, using a 405-nm (blue-violet) laser. A single layer on a single side can store 25 Gbytes.

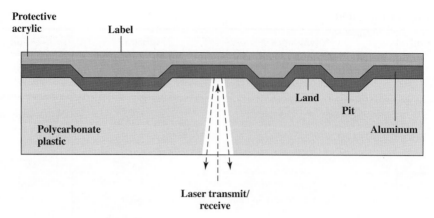

Figure 6.10   CD Operation

Compact Disk

CD-ROM Both the audio CD and the CD-ROM (compact disk read-only memory) share a similar technology. The main difference is that CD-ROM players are more rugged and have error correction devices to ensure that data are properly transferred from disk to computer. Both types of disk are made the same way. The disk is formed from a resin, such as polycarbonate. Digitally recorded information (either music or computer data) is imprinted as a series of microscopic pits on the surface of the poly-carbonate. This is done, first of all, with a finely focused, high-intensity laser to create a master disk. The master is used, in turn, to make a die to stamp out copies onto poly-carbonate. The pitted surface is then coated with a highly reflective surface, usually aluminum or gold. This shiny surface is protected against dust and scratches by a top coat of clear acrylic. Finally, a label can be silkscreened onto the acrylic.

Information is retrieved from a CD or CD-ROM by a low-powered laser housed in an optical-disk player, or drive unit. The laser shines through the clear polycarbonate while a motor spins the disk past it (Figure 6.10). The intensity of the reflected light of the laser changes as it encounters a pit. Specifically, if the laser beam falls on a pit, which has a somewhat rough surface, the light scatters and a low intensity is reflected back to the source. The areas between pits are called *lands*. A land is a smooth surface, which reflects back at higher intensity. The change between pits and lands is detected by a photosensor and converted into a digital signal. The sensor tests the surface at regular intervals. The beginning or end of a pit represents a 1; when no change in elevation occurs between intervals, a 0 is recorded.

Recall that on a magnetic disk, information is recorded in concentric tracks. With the simplest constant angular velocity (CAV) system, the number of bits per track is constant. An increase in density is achieved with multiple zoned recording, in which the surface is divided into a number of zones, with zones farther from the center containing more bits than zones closer to the center. Although this technique increases capacity, it is still not optimal.

To achieve greater capacity, CDs and CD-ROMs do not organize information on concentric tracks. Instead, the disk contains a single spiral track, beginning near

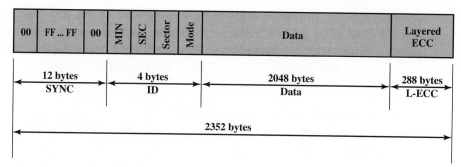

Figure 6.11   CD-ROM Block Format

the center and spiraling out to the outer edge of the disk. Sectors near the outside of the disk are the same length as those near the inside. Thus, information is packed evenly across the disk in segments of the same size and these are scanned at the same rate by rotating the disk at a variable speed. The pits are then read by the laser at a **constant linear velocity** (CLV). The disk rotates more slowly for accesses near the outer edge than for those near the center. Thus, the capacity of a track and the rotational delay both increase for positions nearer the outer edge of the disk. The data capacity for a CD-ROM is about 680 MB.

Data on the CD-ROM are organized as a sequence of blocks. A typical block format is shown in Figure 6.11. It consists of the following fields:

- **Sync:** The sync field identifies the beginning of a block. It consists of a byte of all 0s, 10 bytes of all 1s, and a byte of all 0s.
- **Header:** The header contains the block address and the mode byte. Mode 0 specifies a blank data field; mode 1 specifies the use of an error-correcting code and 2048 bytes of data; mode 2 specifies 2336 bytes of user data with no error-correcting code.
- **Data:** User data.
- **Auxiliary:** Additional user data in mode 2. In mode 1, this is a 288-byte error-correcting code.

With the use of CLV, random access becomes more difficult. Locating a specific address involves moving the head to the general area, adjusting the rotation speed and reading the address, and then making minor adjustments to find and access the specific sector.

CD-ROM is appropriate for the distribution of large amounts of data to a large number of users. Because of the expense of the initial writing process, it is not appropriate for individualized applications. Compared with traditional magnetic disks, the CD-ROM has two advantages:

- The optical disk together with the information stored on it can be mass replicated inexpensively—unlike a magnetic disk. The database on a magnetic disk has to be reproduced by copying one disk at a time using two disk drives.

- The optical disk is removable, allowing the disk itself to be used for archival storage. Most magnetic disks are nonremovable. The information on nonremovable magnetic disks must first be copied to another storage medium before the disk drive/disk can be used to store new information.

The disadvantages of CD-ROM are as follows:

- It is read-only and cannot be updated.
- It has an access time much longer than that of a magnetic disk drive, as much as half a second.

CD RECORDABLE To accommodate applications in which only one or a small number of copies of a set of data is needed, the write-once read-many CD, known as the CD recordable (CD-R), has been developed. For CD-R, a disk is prepared in such a way that it can be subsequently written once with a laser beam of modest intensity. Thus, with a somewhat more expensive disk controller than for CD-ROM, the customer can write once as well as read the disk.

The CD-R medium is similar to but not identical to that of a CD or CD-ROM. For CDs and CD-ROMs, information is recorded by the pitting of the surface of the medium, which changes reflectivity. For a CD-R, the medium includes a dye layer. The dye is used to change reflectivity and is activated by a high-intensity laser. The resulting disk can be read on a CD-R drive or a CD-ROM drive.

The CD-R optical disk is attractive for archival storage of documents and files. It provides a permanent record of large volumes of user data.

CD REWRITABLE The CD-RW optical disk can be repeatedly written and overwritten, as with a magnetic disk. Although a number of approaches have been tried, the only pure optical approach that has proved attractive is called **phase change**. The phase change disk uses a material that has two significantly different reflectivities in two different phase states. There is an amorphous state, in which the molecules exhibit a random orientation that reflects light poorly; and a crystalline state, which has a smooth surface that reflects light well. A beam of laser light can change the material from one phase to the other. The primary disadvantage of phase change optical disks is that the material eventually and permanently loses its desirable properties. Current materials can be used for between 500,000 and 1,000,000 erase cycles.

The CD-RW has the obvious advantage over CD-ROM and CD-R that it can be rewritten and thus used as a true secondary storage. As such, it competes with magnetic disk. A key advantage of the optical disk is that the engineering tolerances for optical disks are much less severe than for high-capacity magnetic disks. Thus, they exhibit higher reliability and longer life.

Digital Versatile Disk

With the capacious digital versatile disk (DVD), the electronics industry has at last found an acceptable replacement for the analog VHS video tape. The DVD has replaced the videotape used in video cassette recorders (VCRs) and, more important for this discussion, replace the CD-ROM in personal computers and servers. The DVD takes video into the digital age. It delivers movies with impressive picture quality, and it can be randomly accessed like audio CDs, which DVD machines can also play. Vast volumes of data can be crammed onto the disk, currently seven times as

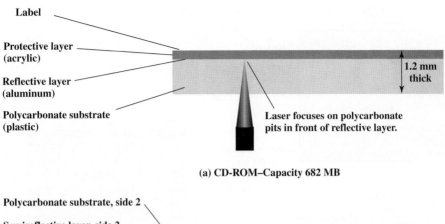

(a) CD-ROM–Capacity 682 MB

(b) DVD-ROM, double-sided, dual-layer–Capacity 17 GB

Figure 6.12   CD-ROM and DVD-ROM

much as a CD-ROM. With DVD's huge storage capacity and vivid quality, PC games have become more realistic and educational software incorporates more video. Following in the wake of these developments has been a new crest of traffic over the Internet and corporate intranets, as this material is incorporated into Web sites.

The DVD's greater capacity is due to three differences from CDs (Figure 6.12):

1. Bits are packed more closely on a DVD. The spacing between loops of a spiral on a CD is 1.6 μm and the minimum distance between pits along the spiral is 0.834 μm. The DVD uses a laser with shorter wavelength and achieves a loop spacing of 0.74 μm and a minimum distance between pits of 0.4 μm. The result of these two improvements is about a seven-fold increase in capacity, to about 4.7 GB.

2. The DVD employs a second layer of pits and lands on top of the first layer. A dual-layer DVD has a semireflective layer on top of the reflective layer, and by adjusting focus, the lasers in DVD drives can read each layer separately. This technique almost doubles the capacity of the disk, to about 8.5 GB. The lower reflectivity of the second layer limits its storage capacity so that a full doubling is not achieved.

3. The DVD-ROM can be two sided, whereas data are recorded on only one side of a CD. This brings total capacity up to 17 GB.

As with the CD, DVDs come in writeable as well as read-only versions (Table 6.5).

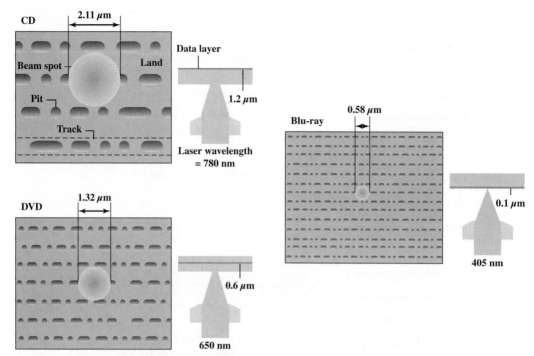

Figure 6.13 Optical Memory Characteristics

High–Definition Optical Disks

High-definition optical disks are designed to store high-definition videos and to provide significantly greater storage capacity compared to DVDs. The higher bit density is achieved by using a laser with a shorter wavelength, in the blue-violet range. The data pits, which constitute the digital 1s and 0s, are smaller on the high-definition optical disks compared to DVD because of the shorter laser wavelength.

Two competing disk formats and technologies initially competed for market acceptance: HD DVD and Blu-ray DVD. The Blu-ray scheme ultimately achieved market dominance. The HD DVD scheme can store 15 GB on a single layer on a single side. Blu-ray positions the data layer on the disk closer to the laser (shown on the right-hand side of each diagram in Figure 6.13). This enables a tighter focus and less distortion and thus smaller pits and tracks. Blu-ray can store 25 GB on a single layer. Three versions are available: read only (BD-ROM), recordable once (BD-R), and rerecordable (BD-RE).

6.4 MAGNETIC TAPE

Tape systems use the same reading and recording techniques as disk systems. The medium is flexible polyester (similar to that used in some clothing) tape coated with magnetizable material. The coating may consist of particles of pure metal in special binders or vapor-plated metal films. The tape and the tape drive are analogous to a home tape recorder system. Tape widths vary from 0.38 cm (0.15 inch) to 1.27 cm

(0.5 inch). Tapes used to be packaged as open reels that have to be threaded through a second spindle for use. Today, virtually all tapes are housed in cartridges.

Data on the tape are structured as a number of parallel tracks running lengthwise. Earlier tape systems typically used nine tracks. This made it possible to store data one byte at a time, with an additional parity bit as the ninth track. This was followed by tape systems using 18 or 36 tracks, corresponding to a digital word or double word. The recording of data in this form is referred to as **parallel recording**. Most modern systems instead use **serial recording**, in which data are laid out as a sequence of bits along each track, as is done with magnetic disks. As with the disk, data are read and written in contiguous blocks, called *physical records,* on a tape. Blocks on the tape are separated by gaps referred to as *interrecord* gaps. As with the disk, the tape is formatted to assist in locating physical records.

The typical recording technique used in serial tapes is referred to as **serpentine recording**. In this technique, when data are being recorded, the first set of bits is recorded along the whole length of the tape. When the end of the tape is reached, the heads are repositioned to record a new track, and the tape is again recorded on its whole length, this time in the opposite direction. That process continues, back and forth, until the tape is full (Figure 6.14a). To increase speed, the

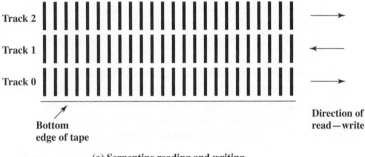

(a) Serpentine reading and writing

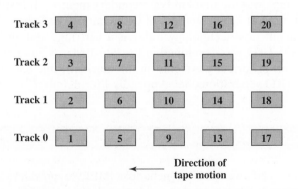

(b) Block layout for system that reads—writes four tracks simultaneously

Figure 6.14   Typical Magnetic Tape Features

Table 6.6 LTO Tape Drives

	LTO-1	**LTO-2**	**LTO-3**	**LTO-4**	**LTO-5**	**LTO-6**
Release date	2000	2003	2005	2007	TBA	TBA
Compressed capacity	200 GB	400 GB	800 GB	1600 GB	3.2 TB	6.4 TB
Compressed transfer rate (MB/s)	40	80	160	240	360	540
Linear density (bits/mm)	4880	7398	9638	13300		
Tape tracks	384	512	704	896		
Tape length	609 m	609 m	680 m	820 m		
Tape width (cm)	1.27	1.27	1.27	1.27		
Write elements	8	8	16	16		

read-write head is capable of reading and writing a number of adjacent tracks simultaneously (typically two to eight tracks). Data are still recorded serially along individual tracks, but blocks in sequence are stored on adjacent tracks, as suggested by Figure 6.14b.

A tape drive is a *sequential-access* device. If the tape head is positioned at record 1, then to read record N, it is necessary to read physical records 1 through $N - 1$, one at a time. If the head is currently positioned beyond the desired record, it is necessary to rewind the tape a certain distance and begin reading forward. Unlike the disk, the tape is in motion only during a read or write operation.

In contrast to the tape, the disk drive is referred to as a *direct-access* device. A disk drive need not read all the sectors on a disk sequentially to get to the desired one. It must only wait for the intervening sectors within one track and can make successive accesses to any track.

Magnetic tape was the first kind of secondary memory. It is still widely used as the lowest-cost, slowest-speed member of the memory hierarchy.

The dominant tape technology today is a cartridge system known as linear tape-open (LTO). LTO was developed in the late 1990s as an open-source alternative to the various proprietary systems on the market. Table 6.6 shows parameters for the various LTO generations. See Appendix J for details.

6.5 RECOMMENDED READING AND WEB SITES

[JACO08] provides solid coverage of magnetic disks. [MEE96a] provides a good survey of the underlying recording technology of disk and tape systems. [MEE96b] focuses on the data storage techniques for disk and tape systems. [COME00] is a short but instructive article on current trends in magnetic disk storage technology. [RADD08] and [ANDE03] provide a more recent discussion of magnetic disk storage technology.

An excellent survey of RAID technology, written by the inventors of the RAID concept, is [CHEN94]. A good overview paper is [FRIE96]. A good performance comparison of the RAID architectures is [CHEN96].

[MARC90] gives an excellent overview of the optical storage field. A good survey of the underlying recording and reading technology is [MANS97].

[ROSC03] provides a comprehensive overview of all types of external memory systems, with a modest amount of technical detail on each. [KHUR01] is another good survey.

[HAEU07] provides a detailed treatment of LTO.

ANDE03 Anderson, D. "You Don't Know Jack About Disks." *ACM Queue*, June 2003.

CHEN94 Chen, P.; Lee, E.; Gibson, G.; Katz, R.; and Patterson, D. "RAID: High-Performance, Reliable Secondary Storage." *ACM Computing Surveys*, June 1994.

CHEN96 Chen, S., and Towsley, D. "A Performance Evaluation of RAID Architectures." *IEEE Transactions on Computers*, October 1996.

COME00 Comerford, R. "Magnetic Storage: The Medium that Wouldn't Die." *IEEE Spectrum*, December 2000.

FRIE96 Friedman, M. "RAID Keeps Going and Going and . . ." *IEEE Spectrum*, April 1996.

HAUE08 Haeusser, B., et al. *IBM System Storage Tape Library Guide for Open Systems.* IBM Redbook SG24-5946-05, October 2007. ibm.com/redbooks

JACO08 Jacob, B.; Ng, S.; and Wang, D. *Memory Systems: Cache, DRAM, Disk.* Boston: Morgan Kaufmann, 2008.

KHUR01 Khurshudov, A. *The Essential Guide to Computer Data Storage.* Upper Saddle River, NJ: Prentice Hall, 2001.

MANS97 Mansuripur, M., and Sincerbox, G. "Principles and Techniques of Optical Data Storage." *Proceedings of the IEEE*, November 1997.

MARC90 Marchant, A. *Optical Recording.* Reading, MA: Addison-Wesley, 1990.

MEE96a Mee, C., and Daniel, E. eds. *Magnetic Recording Technology.* New York: McGraw-Hill, 1996.

MEE96b Mee, C., and Daniel, E. eds. *Magnetic Storage Handbook.* New York: McGraw-Hill, 1996.

RADD08 Radding, A. "Small Disks, Big Specs." *Storage Magazine*, September 2008

ROSC03 Rosch, W. *Winn L. Rosch Hardware Bible.* Indianapolis, IN: Que Publishing, 2003.

Recommended Web sites:

- **Optical Storage Technology Association:** Good source of information about optical storage technology and vendors, plus extensive list of relevant links
- **LTO Web site:** Provides information about LTO technology and licensed vendors

6.6 KEY TERMS, REVIEW QUESTIONS, AND PROBLEMS

Key Terms

access time	DVD-RW	pit
Blu-ray	fixed-head disk	platter
CD	floppy disk	RAID
CD-ROM	gap	removable disk
CD-R	head	rotational delay
CD-RW	land	sector
constant angular velocity	magnetic disk	seek time
(CAV)	magnetic tape	serpentine recording
constant linear velocity (CLV)	magnetoresistive	striped data
cylinder	movable-head disk	substrate
DVD	multiple zoned recording	track
DVD-ROM	nonremovable disk	transfer time
DVD-R	optical memory	

Review Questions

6.1 What are the advantages of using a glass substrate for a magnetic disk?

6.2 How are data written onto a magnetic disk?

6.3 How are data read from a magnetic disk?

6.4 Explain the difference between a simple CAV system and a multiple zoned recording system.

6.5 Define the terms *track, cylinder,* and *sector*.

6.6 What is the typical disk sector size?

6.7 Define the terms *seek time, rotational delay, access time,* and *transfer time*.

6.8 What common characteristics are shared by all RAID levels?

6.9 Briefly define the seven RAID levels.

6.10 Explain the term *striped data*.

6.11 How is redundancy achieved in a RAID system?

6.12 In the context of RAID, what is the distinction between parallel access and independent access?

6.13 What is the difference between CAV and CLV?

6.14 What differences between a CD and a DVD account for the larger capacity of the latter?

6.15 Explain serpentine recording.

Problems

6.1 Consider a disk with N tracks numbered from 0 to $(N - 1)$ and assume that requested sectors are distributed randomly and evenly over the disk. We want to calculate the average number of tracks traversed by a seek.

a. First, calculate the probability of a seek of length j when the head is currently positioned over track t. *Hint:* This is a matter of determining the total number of combinations, recognizing that all track positions for the destination of the seek are equally likely.

b. Next, calculate the probability of a seek of length K. *Hint:* this involves the summing over all possible combinations of movements of K tracks.

c. Calculate the average number of tracks traversed by a seek, using the formula for expected value

$$E[x] = \sum_{i=0}^{N-1} i \times \Pr[x = i]$$

Hint: Use the equalities: $\sum_{i=1}^{n} i = \dfrac{n(n+1)}{2}; \sum_{i=1}^{n} i^2 = \dfrac{n(n+1)(2n+1)}{6}$.

d. Show that for large values of N, the average number of tracks traversed by a seek approaches $N/3$.

6.2 Define the following for a disk system:

t_s = seek time; average time to position head over track

r = rotation speed of the disk, in revolutions per second

n = number of bits per sector

N = capacity of a track, in bits

t_A = time to access a sector

Develop a formula for t_A as a function of the other parameters.

6.3 Consider a magnetic disk drive with 8 surfaces, 512 tracks per surface, and 64 sectors per track. Sector size is 1 KB. The average seek time is 8 ms, the track-to-track access time is 1.5 ms, and the drive rotates at 3600 rpm. Successive tracks in a cylinder can be read without head movement.

a. What is the disk capacity?

b. What is the average access time? Assume this file is stored in successive sectors and tracks of successive cylinders, starting at sector 0, track 0, of cylinder i.

c. Estimate the time required to transfer a 5-MB file.

d. What is the burst transfer rate?

6.4 Consider a single-platter disk with the following parameters: rotation speed: 7200 rpm; number of tracks on one side of platter: 30,000; number of sectors per track: 600; seek time: one ms for every hundred tracks traversed. Let the disk receive a request to access a random sector on a random track and assume the disk head starts at track 0.

a. What is the average seek time?

b. What is the average rotational latency?

c. What is the transfer time for a sector?

d. What is the total average time to satisfy a request?

6.5 A distinction is made between physical records and logical records. A **logical record** is a collection of related data elements treated as a conceptual unit, independent of how or where the information is stored. A **physical record** is a contiguous area of storage space that is defined by the characteristics of the storage device and operating system. Assume a disk system in which each physical record contains thirty 120-byte logical records. Calculate how much disk space (in sectors, tracks, and surfaces) will be required to store 300,000 logical records if the disk is fixed-sector with 512 bytes/sector, with 96 sectors/track, 110 tracks per surface, and 8 usable surfaces. Ignore any file header record(s) and track indexes, and assume that records cannot span two sectors.

6.6 Consider a disk that rotates at 3600 rpm. The seek time to move the head between adjacent tracks is 2 ms. There are 32 sectors per track, which are stored in linear order from sector 0 through sector 31. The head sees the sectors in ascending order. Assume the read/write head is positioned at the start of sector 1 on track 8. There is a main memory buffer large enough to hold an entire track. Data is transferred between disk locations by reading from the source track into the main memory buffer and then writing the date from the buffer to the target track.

   a. How long will it take to transfer sector 1 on track 8 to sector 1 on track 9?

   b. How long will it take to transfer all the sectors of track 8 to the corresponding sectors of track 9?

6.7 It should be clear that disk striping can improve data transfer rate when the strip size is small compared to the I/O request size. It should also be clear that RAID 0 provides improved performance relative to a single large disk, because multiple I/O requests can be handled in parallel. However, in this latter case, is disk striping necessary? That is, does disk striping improve I/O request rate performance compared to a comparable disk array without striping?

6.8 Consider a 4-drive, 200GB-per-drive RAID array. What is the available data storage capacity for each of the RAID levels, 0, 1, 3, 4, 5, and 6?

6.9 For a compact disk, audio is converted to digital with 16-bit samples, and is treated a stream of 8-bit bytes for storage. One simple scheme for storing this data, called direct recording, would be to represent a 1 by a land and a 0 by a pit. Instead, each byte is expanded into a 14-bit binary number. It turns out that exactly 256 (2^8) of the total of 16,134 (2^{14}) 14-bit numbers have at least two 0s between every pair of 1s, and these are the numbers selected for the expansion from 8 to 14 bits. The optical system detects the presence of 1s by detecting a transition for pit to land or land to pit. It detects 0s by measuring the distances between intensity changes. This scheme requires that there are no 1s in succession; hence the use of the 8-to-14 code.

    The advantage of this scheme is as follows. For a given laser beam diameter, there is a minimum-pit size, regardless of how the bits are represented. With this scheme, this minimum-pit size stores 3 bits, because at least two 0s follow every 1. With direct recording, the same pit would be able to store only one bit. Considering both the number of bits stored per pit and the 8-to-14 bit expansion, which scheme stores the most bits and by what factor?

6.10 Design a backup strategy for a computer system. One option is to use plug-in external disks, which cost $150 for each 500 GB drive. Another option is to buy a tape drive for $2500, and 400 GB tapes for $50 apiece. (These were realistic prices in 2008.) A typical backup strategy is to have two sets of backup media onsite, with backups alternately written on them so in case the system fails while making a backup, the previous version is still intact. There's also a third set kept offsite, with the offsite set periodically swapped with an on-site set.

   a. Assume you have 1 TB (1000 GB) of data to back up. How much would a disk backup system cost?

   b. How much would a tape backup system cost for 1 TB?

   c. How large would each backup have to be in order for a tape strategy to be less expensive?

   d. What kind of backup strategy favors tapes?

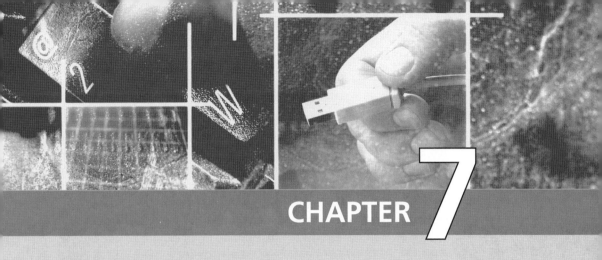

CHAPTER 7

INPUT/OUTPUT

217

KEY POINTS

◆ The computer system's I/O architecture is its interface to the outside world. This architecture provides a systematic means of controlling interaction with the outside world and provides the operating system with the information it needs to manage I/O activity effectively.

◆ The are three principal I/O techniques: **programmed I/O**, in which I/O occurs under the direct and continuous control of the program requesting the I/O operation; **interrupt-driven I/O**, in which a program issues an I/O command and then continues to execute, until it is interrupted by the I/O hardware to signal the end of the I/O operation; and **direct memory access (DMA)**, in which a specialized I/O processor takes over control of an I/O operation to move a large block of data.

◆ Two important examples of external I/O interfaces are **FireWire** and **Infiniband**.

I/O System Design Tool

In addition to the processor and a set of memory modules, the third key element of a computer system is a set of I/O modules. Each module interfaces to the system bus or central switch and controls one or more peripheral devices. An I/O module is not simply a set of mechanical connectors that wire a device into the system bus. Rather, the I/O module contains logic for performing a communication function between the peripheral and the bus.

The reader may wonder why one does not connect peripherals directly to the system bus. The reasons are as follows:

• There are a wide variety of peripherals with various methods of operation. It would be impractical to incorporate the necessary logic within the processor to control a range of devices.

• The data transfer rate of peripherals is often much slower than that of the memory or processor. Thus, it is impractical to use the high-speed system bus to communicate directly with a peripheral.

• On the other hand, the data transfer rate of some peripherals is faster than that of the memory or processor. Again, the mismatch would lead to inefficiencies if not managed properly.

• Peripherals often use different data formats and word lengths than the computer to which they are attached.

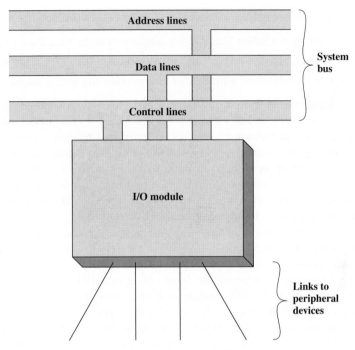

Figure 7.1   Generic Model of an I/O Module

Thus, an I/O module is required. This module has two major functions (Figure 7.1):

- Interface to the processor and memory via the system bus or central switch
- Interface to one or more peripheral devices by tailored data links

We begin this chapter with a brief discussion of external devices, followed by an overview of the structure and function of an I/O module. Then we look at the various ways in which the I/O function can be performed in cooperation with the processor and memory: the internal I/O interface. Finally, we examine the external I/O interface, between the I/O module and the outside world.

7.1 EXTERNAL DEVICES

I/O operations are accomplished through a wide assortment of external devices that provide a means of exchanging data between the external environment and the computer. An external device attaches to the computer by a link to an I/O module (Figure 7.1). The link is used to exchange control, status, and data between the I/O module and the external device. An external device connected to an I/O module is often referred to as a *peripheral device* or, simply, a *peripheral*.

We can broadly classify external devices into three categories:

- **Human readable:** Suitable for communicating with the computer user
- **Machine readable:** Suitable for communicating with equipment
- **Communication:** Suitable for communicating with remote devices

Examples of human-readable devices are video display terminals (VDTs) and printers. Examples of machine-readable devices are magnetic disk and tape systems, and sensors and actuators, such as are used in a robotics application. Note that we are viewing disk and tape systems as I/O devices in this chapter, whereas in Chapter 6 we viewed them as memory devices. From a functional point of view, these devices are part of the memory hierarchy, and their use is appropriately discussed in Chapter 6. From a structural point of view, these devices are controlled by I/O modules and are hence to be considered in this chapter.

Communication devices allow a computer to exchange data with a remote device, which may be a human-readable device, such as a terminal, a machine-readable device, or even another computer.

In very general terms, the nature of an external device is indicated in Figure 7.2. The interface to the I/O module is in the form of control, data, and status signals. *Control signals* determine the function that the device will perform, such as send data to the I/O module (INPUT or READ), accept data from the I/O module (OUTPUT or WRITE), report status, or perform some control function particular to the device (e.g., position a disk head). *Data* are in the form of a set of bits to be sent to or received from the I/O module. *Status signals* indicate the state of the device. Examples are READY/NOT-READY to show whether the device is ready for data transfer.

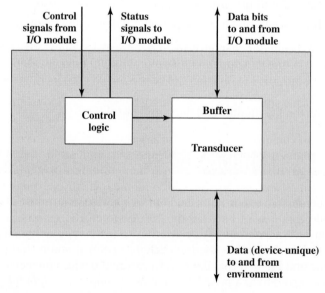

Figure 7.2 Block Diagram of an External Device

Control logic associated with the device controls the device's operation in response to direction from the I/O module. The *transducer* converts data from electrical to other forms of energy during output and from other forms to electrical during input. Typically, a buffer is associated with the transducer to temporarily hold data being transferred between the I/O module and the external environment; a buffer size of 8 to 16 bits is common.

The interface between the I/O module and the external device will be examined in Section 7.7. The interface between the external device and the environment is beyond the scope of this book, but several brief examples are given here.

Keyboard/Monitor

The most common means of computer/user interaction is a keyboard/monitor arrangement. The user provides input through the keyboard. This input is then transmitted to the computer and may also be displayed on the monitor. In addition, the monitor displays data provided by the computer.

The basic unit of exchange is the character. Associated with each character is a code, typically 7 or 8 bits in length. The most commonly used text code is the International Reference Alphabet (IRA).[1] Each character in this code is represented by a unique 7-bit binary code; thus, 128 different characters can be represented. Characters are of two types: printable and control. Printable characters are the alphabetic, numeric, and special characters that can be printed on paper or displayed on a screen. Some of the control characters have to do with controlling the printing or displaying of characters; an example is carriage return. Other control characters are concerned with communications procedures. See Appendix F for details.

For keyboard input, when the user depresses a key, this generates an electronic signal that is interpreted by the transducer in the keyboard and translated into the bit pattern of the corresponding IRA code. This bit pattern is then transmitted to the I/O module in the computer. At the computer, the text can be stored in the same IRA code. On output, IRA code characters are transmitted to an external device from the I/O module. The transducer at the device interprets this code and sends the required electronic signals to the output device either to display the indicated character or perform the requested control function.

Disk Drive

A disk drive contains electronics for exchanging data, control, and status signals with an I/O module plus the electronics for controlling the disk read/write mechanism. In a fixed-head disk, the transducer is capable of converting between the magnetic patterns on the moving disk surface and bits in the device's buffer (Figure 7.2). A moving-head disk must also be able to cause the disk arm to move radially in and out across the disk's surface.

---

[1]IRA is defined in ITU-T Recommendation T.50 and was formerly known as International Alphabet Number 5 (IA5). The U.S. national version of IRA is referred to as the American Standard Code for Information Interchange (ASCII).

7.2 I/O MODULES

Module Function

The major functions or requirements for an I/O module fall into the following categories:

- Control and timing
- Processor communication
- Device communication
- Data buffering
- Error detection

During any period of time, the processor may communicate with one or more external devices in unpredictable patterns, depending on the program's need for I/O. The internal resources, such as main memory and the system bus, must be shared among a number of activities, including data I/O. Thus, the I/O function includes a **control and timing** requirement, to coordinate the flow of traffic between internal resources and external devices. For example, the control of the transfer of data from an external device to the processor might involve the following sequence of steps:

1. The processor interrogates the I/O module to check the status of the attached device.
2. The I/O module returns the device status.
3. If the device is operational and ready to transmit, the processor requests the transfer of data, by means of a command to the I/O module.
4. The I/O module obtains a unit of data (e.g., 8 or 16 bits) from the external device.
5. The data are transferred from the I/O module to the processor.

If the system employs a bus, then each of the interactions between the processor and the I/O module involves one or more bus arbitrations.

The preceding simplified scenario also illustrates that the I/O module must communicate with the processor and with the external device. **Processor communication** involves the following:

- **Command decoding:** The I/O module accepts commands from the processor, typically sent as signals on the control bus. For example, an I/O module for a disk drive might accept the following commands: READ SECTOR, WRITE SECTOR, SEEK track number, and SCAN record ID. The latter two commands each include a parameter that is sent on the data bus.

- **Data:** Data are exchanged between the processor and the I/O module over the data bus.

- **Status reporting:** Because peripherals are so slow, it is important to know the status of the I/O module. For example, if an I/O module is asked to send data to the processor (read), it may not be ready to do so because it is still working on the previous I/O command. This fact can be reported with a status signal.

Common status signals are BUSY and READY. There may also be signals to report various error conditions.

- **Address recognition:** Just as each word of memory has an address, so does each I/O device. Thus, an I/O module must recognize one unique address for each peripheral it controls.

On the other side, the I/O module must be able to perform **device communication**. This communication involves commands, status information, and data (Figure 7.2).

An essential task of an I/O module is **data buffering**. The need for this function is apparent from Figure 2.11. Whereas the transfer rate into and out of main memory or the processor is quite high, the rate is orders of magnitude lower for many peripheral devices and covers a wide range. Data coming from main memory are sent to an I/O module in a rapid burst. The data are buffered in the I/O module and then sent to the peripheral device at its data rate. In the opposite direction, data are buffered so as not to tie up the memory in a slow transfer operation. Thus, the I/O module must be able to operate at both device and memory speeds. Similarly, if the I/O device operates at a rate higher than the memory access rate, then the I/O module performs the needed buffering operation.

Finally, an I/O module is often responsible for **error detection** and for subsequently reporting errors to the processor. One class of errors includes mechanical and electrical malfunctions reported by the device (e.g., paper jam, bad disk track). Another class consists of unintentional changes to the bit pattern as it is transmitted from device to I/O module. Some form of error-detecting code is often used to detect transmission errors. A simple example is the use of a parity bit on each character of data. For example, the IRA character code occupies 7 bits of a byte. The eighth bit is set so that the total number of 1s in the byte is even (even parity) or odd (odd parity). When a byte is received, the I/O module checks the parity to determine whether an error has occurred.

I/O Module Structure

I/O modules vary considerably in complexity and the number of external devices that they control. We will attempt only a very general description here. (One specific device, the Intel 82C55A, is described in Section 7.4.) Figure 7.3 provides a general block diagram of an I/O module. The module connects to the rest of the computer through a set of signal lines (e.g., system bus lines). Data transferred to and from the module are buffered in one or more data registers. There may also be one or more status registers that provide current status information. A status register may also function as a control register, to accept detailed control information from the processor. The logic within the module interacts with the processor via a set of control lines. The processor uses the control lines to issue commands to the I/O module. Some of the control lines may be used by the I/O module (e.g., for arbitration and status signals). The module must also be able to recognize and generate addresses associated with the devices it controls. Each I/O module has a unique address or, if it controls more than one external device, a unique set of addresses. Finally, the I/O module contains logic specific to the interface with each device that it controls.

An I/O module functions to allow the processor to view a wide range of devices in a simple-minded way. There is a spectrum of capabilities that may be provided. The

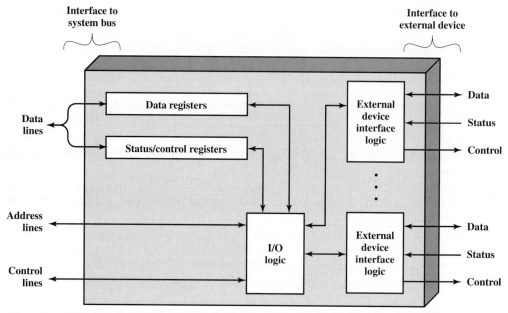

Figure 7.3 Block Diagram of an I/O Module

I/O module may hide the details of timing, formats, and the electromechanics of an external device so that the processor can function in terms of simple read and write commands, and possibly open and close file commands. In its simplest form, the I/O module may still leave much of the work of controlling a device (e.g., rewind a tape) visible to the processor.

An I/O module that takes on most of the detailed processing burden, presenting a high-level interface to the processor, is usually referred to as an *I/O channel* or *I/O processor.* An I/O module that is quite primitive and requires detailed control is usually referred to as an *I/O controller* or *device controller.* I/O controllers are commonly seen on microcomputers, whereas I/O channels are used on mainframes.

In what follows, we will use the generic term *I/O module* when no confusion results and will use more specific terms where necessary.

7.3 PROGRAMMED I/O

Three techniques are possible for I/O operations. With *programmed I/O,* data are exchanged between the processor and the I/O module. The processor executes a program that gives it direct control of the I/O operation, including sensing device status, sending a read or write command, and transferring the data. When the processor issues a command to the I/O module, it must wait until the I/O operation is complete. If the processor is faster than the I/O module, this is wasteful of processor time. With *interrupt-driven I/O,* the processor issues an I/O command, continues to execute other instructions, and is interrupted by the I/O module when the latter has completed its work. With both programmed and interrupt I/O, the processor is

Table 7.1   I/O Techniques

	No Interrupts	Use of Interrupts
I/O-to-memory transfer through processor	Programmed I/O	Interrupt-driven I/O
Direct I/O-to-memory transfer		Direct memory access (DMA)

responsible for extracting data from main memory for output and storing data in main memory for input. The alternative is known as *direct memory access* (DMA). In this mode, the I/O module and main memory exchange data directly, without processor involvement.

Table 7.1 indicates the relationship among these three techniques. In this section, we explore programmed I/O. Interrupt I/O and DMA are explored in the following two sections, respectively.

Overview of Programmed I/O

When the processor is executing a program and encounters an instruction relating to I/O, it executes that instruction by issuing a command to the appropriate I/O module. With programmed I/O, the I/O module will perform the requested action and then set the appropriate bits in the I/O status register (Figure 7.3). The I/O module takes no further action to alert the processor. In particular, it does not interrupt the processor. Thus, it is the responsibility of the processor periodically to check the status of the I/O module until it finds that the operation is complete.

To explain the programmed I/O technique, we view it first from the point of view of the I/O commands issued by the processor to the I/O module, and then from the point of view of the I/O instructions executed by the processor.

I/O Commands

To execute an I/O-related instruction, the processor issues an address, specifying the particular I/O module and external device, and an I/O command. There are four types of I/O commands that an I/O module may receive when it is addressed by a processor:

- **Control:** Used to activate a peripheral and tell it what to do. For example, a magnetic-tape unit may be instructed to rewind or to move forward one record. These commands are tailored to the particular type of peripheral device.
- **Test:** Used to test various status conditions associated with an I/O module and its peripherals. The processor will want to know that the peripheral of interest is powered on and available for use. It will also want to know if the most recent I/O operation is completed and if any errors occurred.
- **Read:** Causes the I/O module to obtain an item of data from the peripheral and place it in an internal buffer (depicted as a data register in Figure 7.3). The processor can then obtain the data item by requesting that the I/O module place it on the data bus.
- **Write:** Causes the I/O module to take an item of data (byte or word) from the data bus and subsequently transmit that data item to the peripheral.

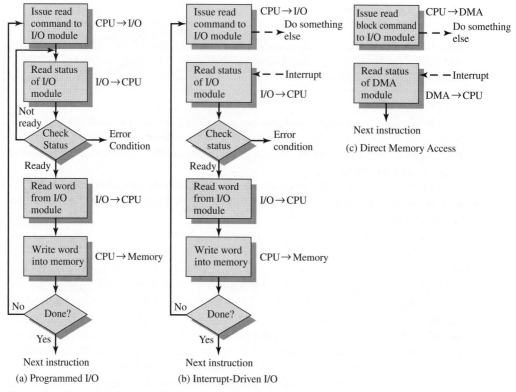

Figure 7.4 Three Techniques for Input of a Block of Data

Figure 7.4a gives an example of the use of programmed I/O to read in a block of data from a peripheral device (e.g., a record from tape) into memory. Data are read in one word (e.g., 16 bits) at a time. For each word that is read in, the processor must remain in a status-checking cycle until it determines that the word is available in the I/O module's data register. This flowchart highlights the main disadvantage of this technique: it is a time-consuming process that keeps the processor busy needlessly.

I/O Instructions

With programmed I/O, there is a close correspondence between the I/O-related instructions that the processor fetches from memory and the I/O commands that the processor issues to an I/O module to execute the instructions. That is, the instructions are easily mapped into I/O commands, and there is often a simple one-to-one relationship. The form of the instruction depends on the way in which external devices are addressed.

Typically, there will be many I/O devices connected through I/O modules to the system. Each device is given a unique identifier or address. When the processor issues an I/O command, the command contains the address of the desired device. Thus, each I/O module must interpret the address lines to determine if the command is for itself.

When the processor, main memory, and I/O share a common bus, two modes of addressing are possible: memory mapped and isolated. With **memory-mapped I/O**, there is a single address space for memory locations and I/O devices. The processor treats the status and data registers of I/O modules as memory locations and uses the same machine instructions to access both memory and I/O devices. So, for example, with 10 address lines, a combined total of $2^{10} = 1024$ memory locations and I/O addresses can be supported, in any combination.

With memory-mapped I/O, a single read line and a single write line are needed on the bus. Alternatively, the bus may be equipped with memory read and write plus input and output command lines. Now, the command line specifies whether the address refers to a memory location or an I/O device. The full range of addresses may be available for both. Again, with 10 address lines, the system may now support both 1024 memory locations and 1024 I/O addresses. Because the address space for I/O is isolated from that for memory, this is referred to as **isolated I/O**.

Figure 7.5 contrasts these two programmed I/O techniques. Figure 7.5a shows how the interface for a simple input device such as a terminal keyboard might appear to a programmer using memory-mapped I/O. Assume a 10-bit address, with a 512-bit memory (locations 0–511) and up to 512 I/O addresses (locations 512–1023). Two addresses are dedicated to keyboard input from a particular terminal. Address 516 refers to the data register and address 517 refers to the status register, which also functions as a control register for receiving processor commands. The program

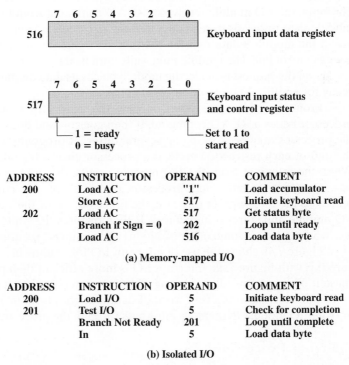

Figure 7.5   Memory-Mapped and Isolated I/O

shown will read 1 byte of data from the keyboard into an accumulator register in the processor. Note that the processor loops until the data byte is available.

With isolated I/O (Figure 7.5b), the I/O ports are accessible only by special I/O commands, which activate the I/O command lines on the bus.

For most types of processors, there is a relatively large set of different instructions for referencing memory. If isolated I/O is used, there are only a few I/O instructions. Thus, an advantage of memory-mapped I/O is that this large repertoire of instructions can be used, allowing more efficient programming. A disadvantage is that valuable memory address space is used up. Both memory-mapped and isolated I/O are in common use.

7.4   INTERRUPT-DRIVEN I/O

The problem with programmed I/O is that the processor has to wait a long time for the I/O module of concern to be ready for either reception or transmission of data. The processor, while waiting, must repeatedly interrogate the status of the I/O module. As a result, the level of the performance of the entire system is severely degraded.

An alternative is for the processor to issue an I/O command to a module and then go on to do some other useful work. The I/O module will then interrupt the processor to request service when it is ready to exchange data with the processor. The processor then executes the data transfer, as before, and then resumes its former processing.

Let us consider how this works, first from the point of view of the I/O module. For input, the I/O module receives a READ command from the processor. The I/O module then proceeds to read data in from an associated peripheral. Once the data are in the module's data register, the module signals an interrupt to the processor over a control line. The module then waits until its data are requested by the processor. When the request is made, the module places its data on the data bus and is then ready for another I/O operation.

From the processor's point of view, the action for input is as follows. The processor issues a READ command. It then goes off and does something else (e.g., the processor may be working on several different programs at the same time). At the end of each instruction cycle, the processor checks for interrupts (Figure 3.9). When the interrupt from the I/O module occurs, the processor saves the context (e.g., program counter and processor registers) of the current program and processes the interrupt. In this case, the processor reads the word of data from the I/O module and stores it in memory. It then restores the context of the program it was working on (or some other program) and resumes execution.

Figure 7.4b shows the use of interrupt I/O for reading in a block of data. Compare this with Figure 7.4a. Interrupt I/O is more efficient than programmed I/O because it eliminates needless waiting. However, interrupt I/O still consumes a lot of processor time, because every word of data that goes from memory to I/O module or from I/O module to memory must pass through the processor.

Interrupt Processing

Let us consider the role of the processor in interrupt-driven I/O in more detail. The occurrence of an interrupt triggers a number of events, both in the processor hardware

Hardware   **Software**

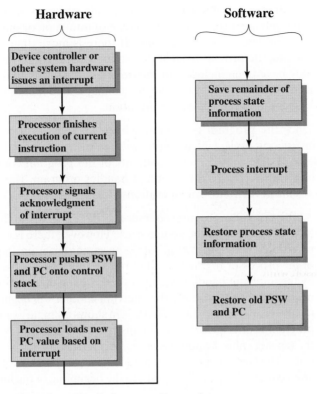

Figure 7.6 Simple Interrupt Processing

and in software. Figure 7.6 shows a typical sequence. When an I/O device completes an I/O operation, the following sequence of hardware events occurs:

1. The device issues an interrupt signal to the processor.

2. The processor finishes execution of the current instruction before responding to the interrupt, as indicated in Figure 3.9.

3. The processor tests for an interrupt, determines that there is one, and sends an acknowledgment signal to the device that issued the interrupt. The acknowledgment allows the device to remove its interrupt signal.

4. The processor now needs to prepare to transfer control to the interrupt routine. To begin, it needs to save information needed to resume the current program at the point of interrupt. The minimum information required is (a) the status of the processor, which is contained in a register called the program status word (PSW), and (b) the location of the next instruction to be executed, which is contained in the program counter. These can be pushed onto the system control stack.[2]

5. The processor now loads the program counter with the entry location of the interrupt-handling program that will respond to this interrupt. Depending on

---

[2]See Appendix 10A for a discussion of stack operation.

the computer architecture and operating system design, there may be a single program; one program for each type of interrupt; or one program for each device and each type of interrupt. If there is more than one interrupt-handling routine, the processor must determine which one to invoke. This information may have been included in the original interrupt signal, or the processor may have to issue a request to the device that issued the interrupt to get a response that contains the needed information.

Once the program counter has been loaded, the processor proceeds to the next instruction cycle, which begins with an instruction fetch. Because the instruction fetch is determined by the contents of the program counter, the result is that control is transferred to the interrupt-handler program. The execution of this program results in the following operations:

6. At this point, the program counter and PSW relating to the interrupted program have been saved on the system stack. However, there is other information that is considered part of the "state" of the executing program. In particular, the contents of the processor registers need to be saved, because these registers may be used by the interrupt handler. So, all of these values, plus any other state information, need to be saved. Typically, the interrupt handler will begin by saving the contents of all registers on the stack. Figure 7.7a shows a simple example. In this case, a user program is interrupted after the instruction at location N. The contents of all of the registers plus the address of the next instruction $(N + 1)$ are pushed onto the stack. The stack pointer is updated to point to the new top of stack, and the program counter is updated to point to the beginning of the interrupt service routine.

7. The interrupt handler next processes the interrupt. This includes an examination of status information relating to the I/O operation or other event that caused an interrupt. It may also involve sending additional commands or acknowledgments to the I/O device.

8. When interrupt processing is complete, the saved register values are retrieved from the stack and restored to the registers (e.g., see Figure 7.7b).

9. The final act is to restore the PSW and program counter values from the stack. As a result, the next instruction to be executed will be from the previously interrupted program.

Note that it is important to save all the state information about the interrupted program for later resumption. This is because the interrupt is not a routine called from the program. Rather, the interrupt can occur at any time and therefore at any point in the execution of a user program. Its occurrence is unpredictable. Indeed, as we will see in the next chapter, the two programs may not have anything in common and may belong to two different users.

Design Issues

Two design issues arise in implementing interrupt I/O. First, because there will almost invariably be multiple I/O modules, how does the processor determine which device issued the interrupt? And second, if multiple interrupts have occurred, how does the processor decide which one to process?

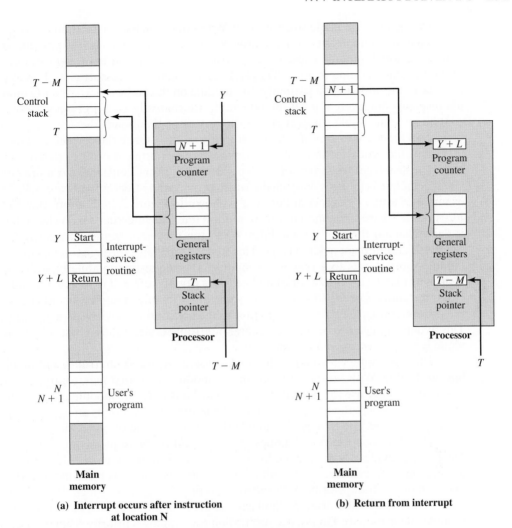

Figure 7.7 Changes in Memory and Registers for an Interrupt

Let us consider device identification first. Four general categories of techniques are in common use:

- Multiple interrupt lines
- Software poll
- Daisy chain (hardware poll, vectored)
- Bus arbitration (vectored)

The most straightforward approach to the problem is to provide **multiple interrupt lines** between the processor and the I/O modules. However, it is impractical to dedicate more than a few bus lines or processor pins to interrupt lines. Consequently, even if multiple lines are used, it is likely that each line will have multiple I/O modules attached to it. Thus, one of the other three techniques must be used on each line.

One alternative is the **software poll**. When the processor detects an interrupt, it branches to an interrupt-service routine whose job it is to poll each I/O module to determine which module caused the interrupt. The poll could be in the form of a separate command line (e.g., TESTI/O). In this case, the processor raises TESTI/O and places the address of a particular I/O module on the address lines. The I/O module responds positively if it set the interrupt. Alternatively, each I/O module could contain an addressable status register. The processor then reads the status register of each I/O module to identify the interrupting module. Once the correct module is identified, the processor branches to a device-service routine specific to that device.

The disadvantage of the software poll is that it is time consuming. A more efficient technique is to use a **daisy chain**, which provides, in effect, a hardware poll. An example of a daisy-chain configuration is shown in Figure 3.26. For interrupts, all I/O modules share a common interrupt request line. The interrupt acknowledge line is daisy chained through the modules. When the processor senses an interrupt, it sends out an interrupt acknowledge. This signal propagates through a series of I/O modules until it gets to a requesting module. The requesting module typically responds by placing a word on the data lines. This word is referred to as a *vector* and is either the address of the I/O module or some other unique identifier. In either case, the processor uses the vector as a pointer to the appropriate device-service routine. This avoids the need to execute a general interrupt-service routine first. This technique is called a *vectored interrupt*.

There is another technique that makes use of vectored interrupts, and that is **bus arbitration**. With bus arbitration, an I/O module must first gain control of the bus before it can raise the interrupt request line. Thus, only one module can raise the line at a time. When the processor detects the interrupt, it responds on the interrupt acknowledge line. The requesting module then places its vector on the data lines.

The aforementioned techniques serve to identify the requesting I/O module. They also provide a way of assigning priorities when more than one device is requesting interrupt service. With multiple lines, the processor just picks the interrupt line with the highest priority. With software polling, the order in which modules are polled determines their priority. Similarly, the order of modules on a daisy chain determines their priority. Finally, bus arbitration can employ a priority scheme, as discussed in Section 3.4.

We now turn to two examples of interrupt structures.

Intel 82C59A Interrupt Controller

The Intel 80386 provides a single Interrupt Request (INTR) and a single Interrupt Acknowledge (INTA) line. To allow the 80386 to handle a variety of devices and priority structures, it is usually configured with an external interrupt arbiter, the 82C59A. External devices are connected to the 82C59A, which in turn connects to the 80386.

Figure 7.8 shows the use of the 82C59A to connect multiple I/O modules for the 80386. A single 82C59A can handle up to eight modules. If control for more than eight modules is required, a cascade arrangement can be used to handle up to 64 modules.

The 82C59A's sole responsibility is the management of interrupts. It accepts interrupt requests from attached modules, determines which interrupt has the highest priority, and then signals the processor by raising the INTR line. The processor acknowledges via the INTA line. This prompts the 82C59A to place the appropriate

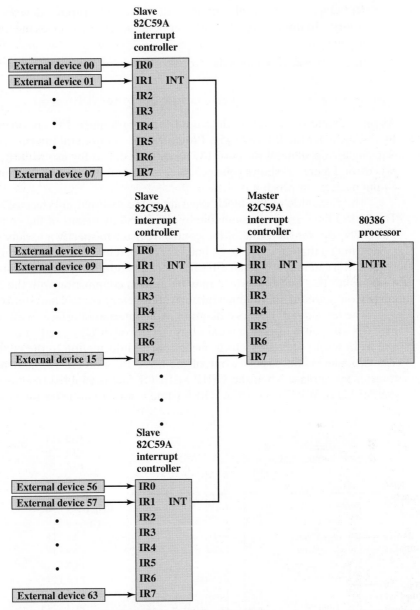

Figure 7.8 Use of the 82C59A Interrupt Controller

vector information on the data bus. The processor can then proceed to process the interrupt and to communicate directly with the I/O module to read or write data.

The 82C59A is programmable. The 80386 determines the priority scheme to be used by setting a control word in the 82C59A. The following interrupt modes are possible:

- **Fully nested:** The interrupt requests are ordered in priority from 0 (IR0) through 7 (IR7).

- **Rotating:** In some applications a number of interrupting devices are of equal priority. In this mode a device, after being serviced, receives the lowest priority in the group.
- **Special mask:** This allows the processor to inhibit interrupts from certain devices.

The Intel 82C55A Programmable Peripheral Interface

As an example of an I/O module used for programmed I/O and interrupt-driven I/O, we consider the Intel 82C55A Programmable Peripheral Interface. The 82C55A is a single-chip, general-purpose I/O module designed for use with the Intel 80386 processor. Figure 7.9 shows a general block diagram plus the pin assignment for the 40-pin package in which it is housed.

The right side of the block diagram is the external interface of the 82C55A. The 24 I/O lines are programmable by the 80386 by means of the control register. The 80386 can set the value of the control register to specify a variety of operating modes and configurations. The 24 lines are divided into three 8-bit groups (A, B, C). Each group can function as an 8-bit I/O port. In addition, group C is subdivided into 4-bit groups (C_A and C_B), which may be used in conjunction with the A and B I/O ports. Configured in this manner, group C lines carry control and status signals.

The left side of the block diagram is the internal interface to the 80386 bus. It includes an 8-bit bidirectional data bus (D0 through D7), used to transfer data to and from the I/O ports and to transfer control information to the control register. The two address lines specify one of the three I/O ports or the control register. A transfer takes place when the CHIP SELECT line is enabled together with either the READ or WRITE line. The RESET line is used to initialize the module.

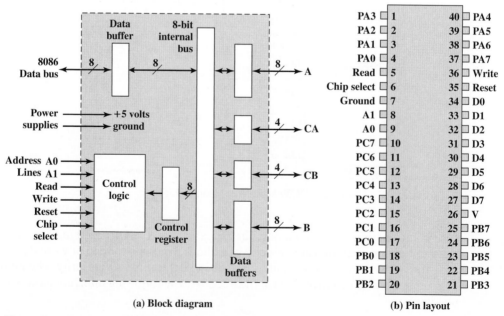

(a) Block diagram   (b) Pin layout

Figure 7.9   The Intel 82C55A Programmable Peripheral Interface

The control register is loaded by the processor to control the mode of operation and to define signals, if any. In Mode 0 operation, the three groups of eight external lines function as three 8-bit I/O ports. Each port can be designated as input or output. Otherwise, groups A and B function as I/O ports, and the lines of group C serve as control lines for A and B. The control signals serve two principal purposes: "handshaking" and interrupt request. Handshaking is a simple timing mechanism. One control line is used by the sender as a DATA READY line, to indicate when the data are present on the I/O data lines. Another line is used by the receiver as an ACKNOWLEDGE, indicating that the data have been read and the data lines may be cleared. Another line may be designated as an INTERRUPT REQUEST line and tied back to the system bus.

Because the 82C55A is programmable via the control register, it can be used to control a variety of simple peripheral devices. Figure 7.10 illustrates its use to

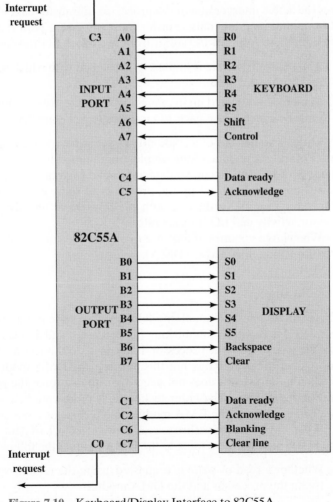

Figure 7.10   Keyboard/Display Interface to 82C55A

control a keyboard/display terminal. The keyboard provides 8 bits of input. Two of these bits, SHIFT and CONTROL, have special meaning to the keyboard-handling program executing in the processor. However, this interpretation is transparent to the 82C55A, which simply accepts the 8 bits of data and presents them on the system data bus. Two handshaking control lines are provided for use with the keyboard.

The display is also linked by an 8-bit data port. Again, two of the bits have special meanings that are transparent to the 82C55A. In addition to two handshaking lines, two lines provide additional control functions.

7.5   DIRECT MEMORY ACCESS

Drawbacks of Programmed and Interrupt-Driven I/O

Interrupt-driven I/O, though more efficient than simple programmed I/O, still requires the active intervention of the processor to transfer data between memory and an I/O module, and any data transfer must traverse a path through the processor. Thus, both these forms of I/O suffer from two inherent drawbacks:

1. The I/O transfer rate is limited by the speed with which the processor can test and service a device.
2. The processor is tied up in managing an I/O transfer; a number of instructions must be executed for each I/O transfer (e.g., Figure 7.5).

There is somewhat of a trade-off between these two drawbacks. Consider the transfer of a block of data. Using simple programmed I/O, the processor is dedicated to the task of I/O and can move data at a rather high rate, at the cost of doing nothing else. Interrupt I/O frees up the processor to some extent at the expense of the I/O transfer rate. Nevertheless, both methods have an adverse impact on both processor activity and I/O transfer rate.

When large volumes of data are to be moved, a more efficient technique is required: direct memory access (DMA).

DMA Function

DMA involves an additional module on the system bus. The DMA module (Figure 7.11) is capable of mimicking the processor and, indeed, of taking over control of the system from the processor. It needs to do this to transfer data to and from memory over the system bus. For this purpose, the DMA module must use the bus only when the processor does not need it, or it must force the processor to suspend operation temporarily. The latter technique is more common and is referred to as *cycle stealing,* because the DMA module in effect steals a bus cycle.

When the processor wishes to read or write a block of data, it issues a command to the DMA module, by sending to the DMA module the following information:

- Whether a read or write is requested, using the read or write control line between the processor and the DMA module

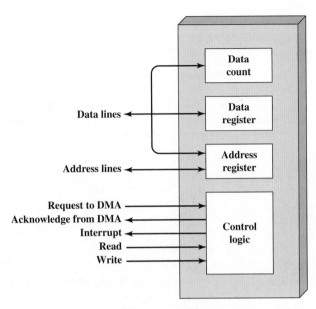

Figure 7.11   Typical DMA Block Diagram

- The address of the I/O device involved, communicated on the data lines
- The starting location in memory to read from or write to, communicated on the data lines and stored by the DMA module in its address register
- The number of words to be read or written, again communicated via the data lines and stored in the data count register

The processor then continues with other work. It has delegated this I/O operation to the DMA module. The DMA module transfers the entire block of data, one word at a time, directly to or from memory, without going through the processor. When the transfer is complete, the DMA module sends an interrupt signal to the processor. Thus, the processor is involved only at the beginning and end of the transfer (Figure 7.4c).

Figure 7.12 shows where in the instruction cycle the processor may be suspended. In each case, the processor is suspended just before it needs to use the bus. The DMA module then transfers one word and returns control to the processor. Note that this is not an interrupt; the processor does not save a context and do something else. Rather, the processor pauses for one bus cycle. The overall effect is to cause the processor to execute more slowly. Nevertheless, for a multiple-word I/O transfer, DMA is far more efficient than interrupt-driven or programmed I/O.

The DMA mechanism can be configured in a variety of ways. Some possibilities are shown in Figure 7.13. In the first example, all modules share the same system bus. The DMA module, acting as a surrogate processor, uses programmed I/O to exchange data between memory and an I/O module through the DMA

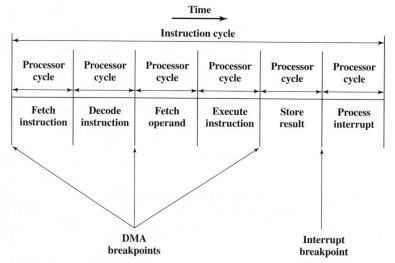

Figure 7.12 DMA and Interrupt Breakpoints during an Instruction Cycle

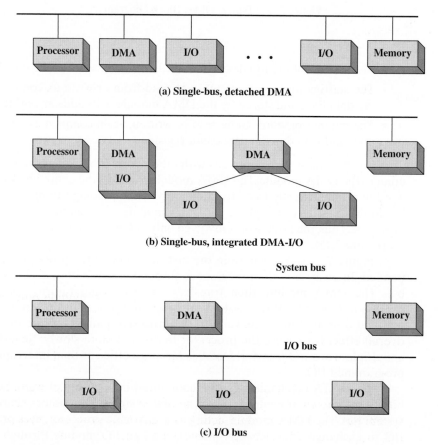

Figure 7.13 Alternative DMA Configurations

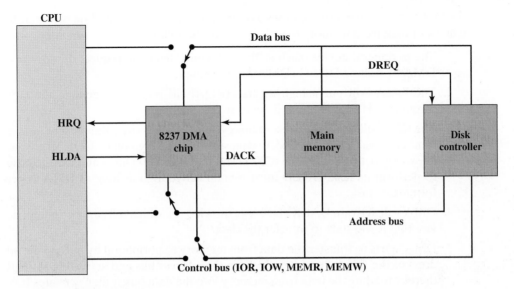

DACK = DMA acknowledge
DREQ = DMA request
HLDA = HOLD acknowledge
HRQ = HOLD request

Figure 7.14 8237 DMA Usage of System Bus

module. This configuration, while it may be inexpensive, is clearly inefficient. As with processor-controlled programmed I/O, each transfer of a word consumes two bus cycles.

The number of required bus cycles can be cut substantially by integrating the DMA and I/O functions. As Figure 7.13b indicates, this means that there is a path between the DMA module and one or more I/O modules that does not include the system bus. The DMA logic may actually be a part of an I/O module, or it may be a separate module that controls one or more I/O modules. This concept can be taken one step further by connecting I/O modules to the DMA module using an I/O bus (Figure 7.13c). This reduces the number of I/O interfaces in the DMA module to one and provides for an easily expandable configuration. In both of these cases (Figures 7.13b and c), the system bus that the DMA module shares with the processor and memory is used by the DMA module only to exchange data with memory. The exchange of data between the DMA and I/O modules takes place off the system bus.

Intel 8237A DMA Controller

The Intel 8237A DMA controller interfaces to the 80x86 family of processors and to DRAM memory to provide a DMA capability. Figure 7.14 indicates the location of the DMA module. When the DMA module needs to use the system buses (data, address, and control) to transfer data, it sends a signal called HOLD to the processor. The processor responds with the HLDA (hold acknowledge) signal, indicating that the DMA module can use the buses. For example, if the DMA module is to transfer a block of data from memory to disk, it will do the following:

1. The peripheral device (such as the disk controller) will request the service of DMA by pulling DREQ (DMA request) high.

2. The DMA will put a high on its HRQ (hold request), signaling the CPU through its HOLD pin that it needs to use the buses.

3. The CPU will finish the present bus cycle (not necessarily the present instruction) and respond to the DMA request by putting high on its HDLA (hold acknowledge), thus telling the 8237 DMA that it can go ahead and use the buses to perform its task. HOLD must remain active high as long as DMA is performing its task.

4. DMA will activate DACK (DMA acknowledge), which tells the peripheral device that it will start to transfer the data.

5. DMA starts to transfer the data from memory to peripheral by putting the address of the first byte of the block on the address bus and activating MEMR, thereby reading the byte from memory into the data bus; it then activates IOW to write it to the peripheral. Then DMA decrements the counter and increments the address pointer and repeats this process until the count reaches zero and the task is finished.

6. After the DMA has finished its job it will deactivate HRQ, signaling the CPU that it can regain control over its buses.

While the DMA is using the buses to transfer data, the processor is idle. Similarly, when the processor is using the bus, the DMA is idle. The 8237 DMA is known as a *fly-by* DMA controller. This means that the data being moved from one location to another does not pass through the DMA chip and is not stored in the DMA chip. Therefore, the DMA can only transfer data between an I/O port and a memory address, but not between two I/O ports or two memory locations. However, as explained subsequently, the DMA chip can perform a memory-to-memory transfer via a register.

The 8237 contains four DMA channels that can be programmed independently, and any one of the channels may be active at any moment. These channels are numbered 0, 1, 2, and 3.

The 8237 has a set of five control/command registers to program and control DMA operation over one of its channels (Table 7.2):

- **Command:** The processor loads this register to control the operation of the DMA. D0 enables a memory-to-memory transfer, in which channel 0 is used to transfer a byte into an 8237 temporary register and channel 1 is used to transfer the byte from the register to memory. When memory-to-memory is enabled, D1 can be used to disable increment/decrement on channel 0 so that a fixed value can be written into a block of memory. D2 enables or disables DMA.

- **Status:** The processor reads this register to determine DMA status. Bits D0–D3 are used to indicate if channels 0–3 have reached their TC (terminal count). Bits D4–D7 are used by the processor to determine if any channel has a DMA request pending.

Table 7.2 Intel 8237A Registers

Bit	Command	Status	Mode	Single Mask	All Mask
D0	Memory-to-memory E/D	Channel 0 has reached TC	Channel select	Select channel mask bit	Clear/set channel 0 mask bit
D1	Channel 0 address hold E/D	Channel 1 has reached TC			Clear/set channel 1 mask bit
D2	Controller E/D	Channel 2 has reached TC	Verify/write/ read transfer	Clear/set mask bit	Clear/set channel 2 mask bit
D3	Normal/compressed timing	Channel 3 has reached TC	Auto-initialization E/D		Clear/set channel 3 mask bit
D4	Fixed/rotating priority	Channel 0 request	Address increment/ decrement select	Not used	Not used
D5	Late/extended write selection	Channel 0 request			
D6	DREQ sense active high/low	Channel 0 request			
D7	DACK sense active high/low	Channel 0 request	Demand/single/block/ cascade mode select		

E/D = enable/disable
TC = terminal count

241

- **Mode:** The processor sets this register to determine the mode of operation of the DMA. Bits D0 and D1 are used to select a channel. The other bits select various operation modes for the selected channel. Bits D2 and D3 determine if the transfer is a from an I/O device to memory (write) or from memory to I/O (read), or a verify operation. If D4 is set, then the memory address register and the count register are reloaded with their original values at the end of a DMA data transfer. Bits D6 and D7 determine the way in which the 8237 is used. In single mode, a single byte of data is transferred. Block and demand modes are used for a block transfer, with the demand mode allowing for premature ending of the transfer. Cascade mode allows multiple 8237s to be cascaded to expand the number of channels to more than 4.

- **Single Mask:** The processor sets this register. Bits D0 and D1 select the channel. Bit D2 clears or sets the mask bit for that channel. It is through this register that the DREQ input of a specific channel can be masked (disabled) or unmasked (enabled). While the command register can be used to disable the whole DMA chip, the single mask register allows the programmer to disable or enable a specific channel.

- **All Mask:** This register is similar to the single mask register except that all four channels can be masked or unmasked with one write operation.

In addition, the 8237A has eight data registers: one memory address register and one count register for each channel. The processor sets these registers to indicate the location of size of main memory to be affected by the transfers.

7.6   I/O CHANNELS AND PROCESSORS

The Evolution of the I/O Function

As computer systems have evolved, there has been a pattern of increasing complexity and sophistication of individual components. Nowhere is this more evident than in the I/O function. We have already seen part of that evolution. The evolutionary steps can be summarized as follows:

1. The CPU directly controls a peripheral device. This is seen in simple microprocessor-controlled devices.

2. A controller or I/O module is added. The CPU uses programmed I/O without interrupts. With this step, the CPU becomes somewhat divorced from the specific details of external device interfaces.

3. The same configuration as in step 2 is used, but now interrupts are employed. The CPU need not spend time waiting for an I/O operation to be performed, thus increasing efficiency.

4. The I/O module is given direct access to memory via DMA. It can now move a block of data to or from memory without involving the CPU, except at the beginning and end of the transfer.

5. The I/O module is enhanced to become a processor in its own right, with a specialized instruction set tailored for I/O. The CPU directs the I/O processor to execute an I/O program in memory. The I/O processor fetches and executes these instructions without CPU intervention. This allows the CPU to specify a sequence of I/O activities and to be interrupted only when the entire sequence has been performed.

6. The I/O module has a local memory of its own and is, in fact, a computer in its own right. With this architecture, a large set of I/O devices can be controlled, with minimal CPU involvement. A common use for such an architecture has been to control communication with interactive terminals. The I/O processor takes care of most of the tasks involved in controlling the terminals.

As one proceeds along this evolutionary path, more and more of the I/O function is performed without CPU involvement. The CPU is increasingly relieved of I/O-related tasks, improving performance. With the last two steps (5–6), a major change occurs with the introduction of the concept of an I/O module capable of executing a program. For step 5, the I/O module is often referred to as an *I/O channel.* For step 6, the term *I/O processor* is often used. However, both terms are on occasion applied to both situations. In what follows, we will use the term *I/O channel.*

Characteristics of I/O Channels

The I/O channel represents an extension of the DMA concept. An I/O channel has the ability to execute I/O instructions, which gives it complete control over I/O operations. In a computer system with such devices, the CPU does not execute I/O instructions. Such instructions are stored in main memory to be executed by a special-purpose processor in the I/O channel itself. Thus, the CPU initiates an I/O transfer by instructing the I/O channel to execute a program in memory. The program will specify the device or devices, the area or areas of memory for storage, priority, and actions to be taken for certain error conditions. The I/O channel follows these instructions and controls the data transfer.

Two types of I/O channels are common, as illustrated in Figure 7.15. A *selector channel* controls multiple high-speed devices and, at any one time, is dedicated to the transfer of data with one of those devices. Thus, the I/O channel selects one device and effects the data transfer. Each device, or a small set of devices, is handled by a *controller,* or I/O module, that is much like the I/O modules we have been discussing. Thus, the I/O channel serves in place of the CPU in controlling these I/O controllers. A *multiplexor channel* can handle I/O with multiple devices at the same time. For low-speed devices, a *byte multiplexor* accepts or transmits characters as fast as possible to multiple devices. For example, the resultant character stream from three devices with different rates and individual streams $A_1A_2A_3A_4\ldots$, $B_1B_2B_3B_4\ldots$, and $C_1C_2C_3C_4\ldots$ might be $A_1B_1C_1A_2C_2A_3B_2C_3A_4$, and so on. For high-speed devices, a *block multiplexor* interleaves blocks of data from several devices.

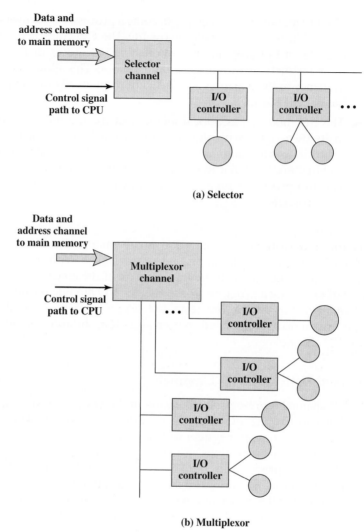

Figure 7.15   I/O Channel Architecture

7.7   THE EXTERNAL INTERFACE: FIREWIRE AND INFINIBAND

Types of Interfaces

The interface to a peripheral from an I/O module must be tailored to the nature and operation of the peripheral. One major characteristic of the interface is whether it is serial or parallel (Figure 7.16). In a **parallel interface**, there are multiple lines connecting the I/O module and the peripheral, and multiple bits are transferred simultaneously, just as all of the bits of a word are transferred simultaneously over the data bus. In a **serial interface**, there is only one line used to transmit data, and bits must be transmitted one at a time. A parallel interface has traditionally been used

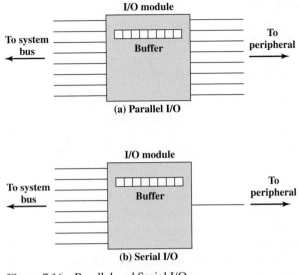

Figure 7.16   Parallel and Serial I/O

for higher-speed peripherals, such as tape and disk, while the serial interface has tra-ditionally been used for printers and terminals. With a new generation of high-speed serial interfaces, parallel interfaces are becoming much less common.

In either case, the I/O module must engage in a dialogue with the peripheral. In general terms, the dialogue for a write operation is as follows:

1. The I/O module sends a control signal requesting permission to send data.
2. The peripheral acknowledges the request.
3. The I/O module transfers data (one word or a block depending on the periph-eral).
4. The peripheral acknowledges receipt of the data.

A read operation proceeds similarly.

Key to the operation of an I/O module is an internal buffer that can store data being passed between the peripheral and the rest of the system. This buffer allows the I/O module to compensate for the differences in speed between the system bus and its external lines.

Point-to-Point and Multipoint Configurations

The connection between an I/O module in a computer system and external devices can be either point-to-point or multipoint. A point-to-point interface provides a dedicated line between the I/O module and the external device. On small systems (PCs, workstations), typical point-to-point links include those to the keyboard, printer, and external modem. A typical example of such an interface is the EIA-232 specification (see [STAL07] for a description).

Of increasing importance are multipoint external interfaces, used to sup-port external mass storage devices (disk and tape drives) and multimedia devices

(CD-ROMs, video, audio). These multipoint interfaces are in effect external buses, and they exhibit the same type of logic as the buses discussed in Chapter 3. In this section, we look at two key examples: FireWire and Infiniband.

FireWire Serial Bus

With processor speeds reaching gigahertz range and storage devices holding multiple gigabits, the I/O demands for personal computers, workstations, and servers are formidable. Yet the high-speed I/O channel technologies that have been developed for mainframe and supercomputer systems are too expensive and bulky for use on these smaller systems. Accordingly, there has been great interest in developing a high-speed alternative to Small Computer System Interface (SCSI) and other small-system I/O interfaces. The result is the IEEE standard 1394, for a High Performance Serial Bus, commonly known as FireWire.

FireWire has a number of advantages over older I/O interfaces. It is very high speed, low cost, and easy to implement. In fact, FireWire is finding favor not only for computer systems, but also in consumer electronics products, such as digital cameras, DVD players/recorders, and televisions. In these products, FireWire is used to transport video images, which are increasingly coming from digitized sources.

One of the strengths of the FireWire interface is that it uses serial transmission (bit at a time) rather than parallel. Parallel interfaces, such as SCSI, require more wires, which means wider, more expensive cables and wider, more expensive connectors with more pins to bend or break. A cable with more wires requires shielding to prevent electrical interference between the wires. Also, with a parallel interface, synchronization between wires becomes a requirement, a problem that gets worse with increased cable length.

In addition, computers are getting physically smaller even as they expand in computing power and I/O needs. Handheld and pocket-size computers have little room for connectors yet need high data rates to handle images and video.

The intent of FireWire is to provide a single I/O interface with a simple connector that can handle numerous devices through a single port, so that the mouse, laser printer, external disk drive, sound, and local area network hookups can be replaced with this single connector.

FIREWIRE CONFIGURATIONS FireWire uses a daisy-chain configuration, with up to 63 devices connected off a single port. Moreover, up to 1022 FireWire buses can be interconnected using bridges, enabling a system to support as many peripherals as required.

FireWire provides for what is known as hot plugging, which makes it possible to connect and disconnect peripherals without having to power the computer system down or reconfigure the system. Also, FireWire provides for automatic configuration; it is not necessary manually to set device IDs or to be concerned with the relative position of devices. Figure 7.17 shows a simple FireWire configuration. With FireWire, there are no terminations, and the system automatically performs a configuration function to assign addresses. Also note that a FireWire bus need not be a strict daisy chain. Rather, a tree-structured configuration is possible.

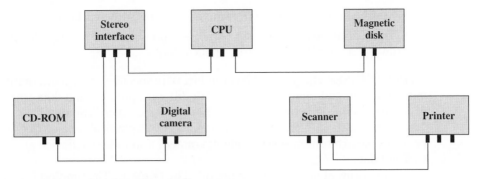

Figure 7.17   Simple FireWire Configuration

An important feature of the FireWire standard is that it specifies a set of three layers of protocols to standardize the way in which the host system interacts with the peripheral devices over the serial bus. Figure 7.18 illustrates this stack. The three layers of the stack are as follows:

- **Physical layer:** Defines the transmission media that are permissible under FireWire and the electrical and signaling characteristics of each

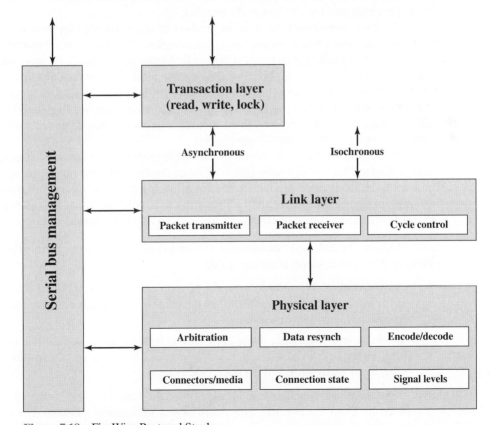

Figure 7.18   FireWire Protocol Stack

- **Link layer:** Describes the transmission of data in the packets
- **Transaction layer:** Defines a request–response protocol that hides the lower-layer details of FireWire from applications

PHYSICAL LAYER The physical layer of FireWire specifies several alternative transmission media and their connectors, with different physical and data transmission properties. Data rates from 25 to 3200 Mbps are defined. The physical layer converts binary data into electrical signals for various physical media. This layer also provides the arbitration service that guarantees that only one device at a time will transmit data.

Two forms of arbitration are provided by FireWire. The simplest form is based on the tree-structured arrangement of the nodes on a FireWire bus, mentioned earlier. A special case of this structure is a linear daisy chain. The physical layer contains logic that allows all the attached devices to configure themselves so that one node is designated as the root of the tree and other nodes are organized in a parent/child relationship forming the tree topology. Once this configuration is established, the root node acts as a central arbiter and processes requests for bus access in a first-come-first-served fashion. In the case of simultaneous requests, the node with the highest natural priority is granted access. The natural priority is determined by which competing node is closest to the root and, among those of equal distance from the root, which one has the lower ID number.

The aforementioned arbitration method is supplemented by two additional functions: fairness arbitration and urgent arbitration. With fairness arbitration, time on the bus is organized into *fairness intervals.* At the beginning of an interval, each node sets an arbitration_enable flag. During the interval, each node may compete for bus access. Once a node has gained access to the bus, it resets its arbitration_enable flag and may not again compete for fair access during this interval. This scheme makes the arbitration fairer, in that it prevents one or more busy high-priority devices from monopolizing the bus.

In addition to the fairness scheme, some devices may be configured as having *urgent* priority. Such nodes may gain control of the bus multiple times during a fairness interval. In essence, a counter is used at each high-priority node that enables the high-priority nodes to control 75% of the available bus time. For each packet that is transmitted as nonurgent, three packets may be transmitted as urgent.

LINK LAYER The link layer defines the transmission of data in the form of packets. Two types of transmission are supported:

- **Asynchronous:** A variable amount of data and several bytes of transaction layer information are transferred as a packet to an explicit address and an acknowledgment is returned.
- **Isochronous:** A variable amount of data is transferred in a sequence of fixed-size packets transmitted at regular intervals. This form of transmission uses simplified addressing and no acknowledgment.

Asynchronous transmission is used by data that have no fixed data rate requirements. Both the fair arbitration and urgent arbitration schemes may be used for asynchronous transmission. The default method is fair arbitration. Devices that

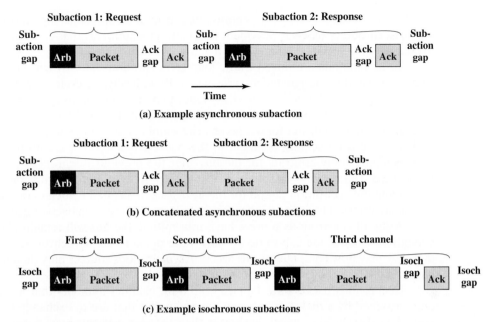

Figure 7.19 FireWire Subactions

desire a substantial fraction of the bus capacity or have severe latency requirements use the urgent arbitration method. For example, a high-speed real-time data collection node may use urgent arbitration when critical data buffers are more than half full.

Figure 7.19a depicts a typical asynchronous transaction. The process of delivering a single packet is called a subaction. The subaction consists of five time periods:

- **Arbitration sequence:** This is the exchange of signals required to give one device control of the bus.
- **Packet transmission:** Every packet includes a header containing the source and destination IDs. The header also contains packet type information, a CRC (cyclic redundancy check) checksum, and parameter information for the specific packet type. A packet may also include a data block consisting of user data and another CRC.
- **Acknowledgment gap:** This is the time delay for the destination to receive and decode a packet and generate an acknowledgment.
- **Acknowledgment:** The recipient of the packet returns an acknowledgment packet with a code indicating the action taken by the recipient.
- **Subaction gap:** This is an enforced idle period to ensure that other nodes on the bus do not begin arbitrating before the acknowledgment packet has been transmitted.

At the time that the acknowledgment is sent, the acknowledging node is in control of the bus. Therefore, if the exchange is a request/response interaction between two nodes, then the responding node can immediately transmit the response packet without going through an arbitration sequence (Figure 7.19b).

For devices that regularly generate or consume data, such as digital sound or video, isochronous access is provided. This method guarantees that data can be delivered within a specified latency with a guaranteed data rate.

To accommodate a mixed traffic load of isochronous and asynchronous data sources, one node is designated as *cycle master*. Periodically, the cycle master issues a cycle_start packet. This signals all other nodes that an isochronous cycle has begun. During this cycle, only isochronous packets may be sent (Figure 7.19c). Each isochronous data source arbitrates for bus access. The winning node immediately transmits a packet. There is no acknowledgment to this packet, and so other isochronous data sources immediately arbitrate for the bus after the previous isochronous packet is transmitted. The result is that there is a small gap between the transmission of one packet and the arbitration period for the next packet, dictated by delays on the bus. This delay, referred to as the isochronous gap, is smaller than a subaction gap.

After all isochronous sources have transmitted, the bus will remain idle long enough for a subaction gap to occur. This is the signal to the asynchronous sources that they may now compete for bus access. Asynchronous sources may then use the bus until the beginning of the next isochronous cycle.

Isochronous packets are labeled with 8-bit channel numbers that are previously assigned by a dialogue between the two nodes that are to exchange isochronous data. The header, which is shorter than that for asynchronous packets, also includes a data length field and a header CRC.

InfiniBand

InfiniBand is a recent I/O specification aimed at the high-end server market.[3] The first version of the specification was released in early 2001 and has attracted numerous vendors. The standard describes an architecture and specifications for data flow among processors and intelligent I/O devices. InfiniBand has become a popular interface for storage area networking and other large storage configurations. In essence, InfiniBand enables servers, remote storage, and other network devices to be attached in a central fabric of switches and links. The switch-based architecture can connect up to 64,000 servers, storage systems, and networking devices.

INFINIBAND ARCHITECTURE Although PCI is a reliable interconnect method and continues to provide increased speeds, up to 4 Gbps, it is a limited architecture compared to Infiniband. With InfiniBand, it is not necessary to have the basic I/O interface hardware inside the server chassis. With InfiniBand, remote storage, networking, and connections between servers are accomplished by attaching all devices to a central fabric of switches and links. Removing I/O from the server chassis allows greater server density and allows for a more flexible and scalable data center, as independent nodes may be added as needed.

Unlike PCI, which measures distances from a CPU motherboard in centimeters, InfiniBand's channel design enables I/O devices to be placed up to 17 meters away from the server using copper, up to 300 m using multimode optical fiber, and

---

[3]Infiniband is the result of the merger of two competing projects: Future I/O (backed by Cisco, HP, Compaq, and IBM) and Next Generation I/O (developed by Intel and backed by a number of other companies).

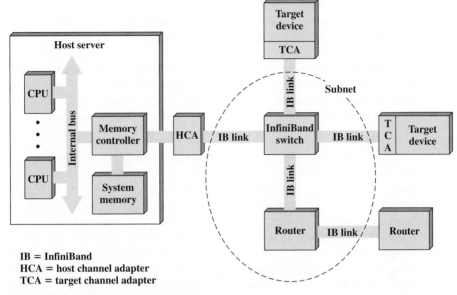

Figure 7.20   InfiniBand Switch Fabric

up to 10 km with single-mode optical fiber. Transmission rates has high as 30 Gbps can be achieved.

Figure 7.20 illustrates the InfiniBand architecture. The key elements are as follows:

- **Host channel adapter (HCA):** Instead of a number of PCI slots, a typical server needs a single interface to an HCA that links the server to an Infini-Band switch. The HCA attaches to the server at a memory controller, which has access to the system bus and controls traffic between the processor and memory and between the HCA and memory. The HCA uses direct-memory access (DMA) to read and write memory.

- **Target channel adapter (TCA):** A TCA is used to connect storage systems, routers, and other peripheral devices to an InfiniBand switch.

- **InfiniBand switch:** A switch provides point-to-point physical connections to a variety of devices and switches traffic from one link to another. Servers and devices communicate through their adapters, via the switch. The switch's intelligence manages the linkage without interrupting the servers' operation.

- **Links:** The link between a switch and a channel adapter, or between two switches.

- **Subnet:** A subnet consists of one or more interconnected switches plus the links that connect other devices to those switches. Figure 7.20 shows a subnet with a single switch, but more complex subnets are required when a large number of devices are to be interconnected. Subnets allow administrators to confine broadcast and multicast transmissions within the subnet.

- **Router:** Connects InfiniBand subnets, or connects an Infiniband switch to a network, such as a local area network, wide area network, or storage area network.

The channel adapters are intelligent devices that handle all I/O functions without the need to interrupt the server's processor. For example, there is a control protocol by which a switch discovers all TCAs and HCAs in the fabric and assigns logical addresses to each. This is done without processor involvement.

The Infiniband switch temporarily opens up channels between the processor and devices with which it is communicating. The devices do not have to share a channel's capacity, as is the case with a bus-based design such as PCI, which requires that devices arbitrate for access to the processor. Additional devices are added to the configuration by hooking up each device's TCA to the switch.

INFINIBAND OPERATION Each physical link between a switch and an attached interface (HCA or TCA) can be support up to 16 logical channels, called **virtual lanes**. One lane is reserved for fabric management and the other lanes for data transport. Data are sent in the form of a stream of packets, with each packet containing some portion of the total data to be transferred, plus addressing and control information. Thus, a set of communications protocols are used to manage the transfer of data. A virtual lane is temporarily dedicated to the transfer of data from one end node to another over the InfiniBand fabric. The InfiniBand switch maps traffic from an incoming lane to an outgoing lane to route the data between the desired end points.

Figure 7.21 indicates the logical structure used to support exchanges over InfiniBand. To account for the fact that some devices can send data faster than another destination device can receive it, a pair of queues at both ends of each link temporarily buffers excess outbound and inbound data. The queues can be located in the channel adapter or in the attached device's memory. A separate pair of

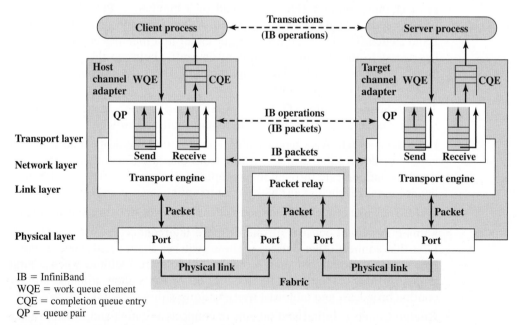

IB = InfiniBand
WQE = work queue element
CQE = completion queue entry
QP = queue pair

Figure 7.21 InfiniBand Communication Protocol Stack

Table 7.3   InfiniBand Links and Data Throughput Rates

Link	Signal rate (unidirectional)	Usable capacity (80% of signal rate)	Effective data throughput (send + receive)
1-wide	2.5 Gbps	2 Gbps (250 MBps)	(250 + 250) MBps
4-wide	10 Gbps	8 Gbps (1 GBps)	(1 + 1) GBps
12-wide	30 Gbps	24 Gbps (3 GBps)	(3 + 3) Gbps

queues is used for each virtual lane. The host uses these queues in the following fashion. The host places a transaction, called a work queue entry (WQE) into either the send or receive queue of the queue pair. The two most important WQEs are SEND and RECEIVE. For a SEND operation, the WQE specifies a block of data in the device's memory space for the hardware to send to the destination. A RECEIVE WQE specifies where the hardware is to place data received from another device when that consumer executes a SEND operation. The channel adapter processes each posted WQE in the proper prioritized order and generates a completion queue entry (CQE) to indicate the completion status.

Figure 7.21 also indicates that a layered protocol architecture is used, consisting of four layers:

- **Physical:** The physical-layer specification defines three link speeds (1X, 4X, and 12X) giving transmission rates of 2.5, 10, and 30 Gbps, respectively (Table 7.3). The physical layer also defines the physical media, including copper and optical fiber.

- **Link:** This layer defines the basic packet structure used to exchange data, including an addressing scheme that assigns a unique link address to every device in a subnet. This level includes the logic for setting up virtual lanes and for switching data through switches from source to destination within a subnet. The packet structure includes an error-detection code to provide reliability.

- **Network:** The network layer routes packets between different InfiniBand subnets.

- **Transport:** The transport layer provides reliability mechanism for end-to-end transfer of packets across one or more subnets.

7.8   RECOMMENDED READING AND WEB SITES

A good discussion of Intel I/O modules and architecture, including the 82C59A, 82C55A, and 8237A, can be found in [BREY09] and [MAZI03].

FireWire is covered in great detail in [ANDE98]. [WICK97] and [THOM00] provide concise overviews of FireWire.

InfiniBand is covered in great detail in [SHAN03] and [FUTR01]. [KAGA01] provides a concise overview.

ANDE98   Anderson, D. *FireWire System Architecture.* Reading, MA: Addison-Wesley, 1998.

BREY09   Brey, B. *The Intel Microprocessors: 8086/8066, 80186/80188, 80286, 80386, 80486, Pentium, Pentium Pro Processor, Pentium II, Pentium III, Pentium 4 and Core2 with 64-bit Extensions.* Upper Saddle River, NJ: Prentice Hall, 2009.

FUTR01   Futral, W. *InfiniBand Architecture: Development and Deployment.* Hillsboro, OR: Intel Press, 2001.

KAGA01   Kagan, M. "InfiniBand: Thinking Outside the Box Design." *Communications System Design,* September 2001. (www.csdmag.com)

MAZI03   Mazidi, M., and Mazidi, J. *The 80x86 IBM PC and Compatible Computers: Assembly Language, Design and Interfacing.* Upper Saddle River, NJ: Prentice Hall, 2003.

SHAN03   Shanley, T. *InfinBand Network Architecture.* Reading, MA: Addison-Wesley, 2003.

THOM00   Thompson, D. "IEEE 1394: Changing the Way We Do Multimedia Communications." *IEEE Multimedia,* April-June 2000.

WICK97   Wickelgren, I. "The Facts about FireWire." *IEEE Spectrum,* April 1997.

Recommended Web sites:

- **T10 Home Page:** T10 is a Technical Committee of the National Committee on Information Technology Standards and is responsible for lower-level interfaces. Its principal work is the Small Computer System Interface (SCSI).

- **1394 Trade Association:** Includes technical information and vendor pointers on FireWire.

- **Infiniband Trade Association:** Includes technical information and vendor pointers on Infiniband.

- **National Facility for I/O Characterization and Optimization:** A facility dedicated to education and research in the area of I/O design and performance. Useful tools and tutorials.

7.9 KEY TERMS, REVIEW QUESTIONS, AND PROBLEMS

Key Terms

cycle stealing	I/O channel	multiplexor channel
direct memory access (DMA)	I/O command	parallel I/O
FireWire	I/O module	peripheral device
InfiniBand	I/O processor	programmed I/O
interrupt	isolated I/O	selector channel
interrupt-driven I/O	memory-mapped I/O	serial I/O

Review Questions

7.1 List three broad classifications of external, or peripheral, devices.

7.2 What is the International Reference Alphabet?

7.3 What are the major functions of an I/O module?

7.4 List and briefly define three techniques for performing I/O.

7.5 What is the difference between memory-mapped I/O and isolated I/O?

7.6 When a device interrupt occurs, how does the processor determine which device issued the interrupt?

7.7 When a DMA module takes control of a bus, and while it retains control of the bus, what does the processor do?

Problems

7.1 On a typical microprocessor, a distinct I/O address is used to refer to the I/O data registers and a distinct address for the control and status registers in an I/O controller for a given device. Such registers are referred to as **ports**. In the Intel 8088, two I/O instruction formats are used. In one format, the 8-bit opcode specifies an I/O operation; this is followed by an 8-bit port address. Other I/O opcodes imply that the port address is in the 16-bit DX register. How many ports can the 8088 address in each I/O addressing mode? .

7.2 A similar instruction format is used in the Zilog Z8000 microprocessor family. In this case, there is a direct port addressing capability, in which a 16-bit port address is part of the instruction, and an indirect port addressing capability, in which the instruction references one of the 16-bit general purpose registers, which contains the port address. How many ports can the Z8000 address in each I/O addressing mode?

7.3 The Z8000 also includes a block I/O transfer capability that, unlike DMA, is under the direct control of the processor. The block transfer instructions specify a port address register (Rp), a count register (Rc), and a destination register (Rd). Rd contains the main memory address at which the first byte read from the input port is to be stored. Rc is any of the 16-bit general purpose registers. How large a data block can be transferred?

7.4 Consider a microprocessor that has a block I/O transfer instruction such as that found on the Z8000. Following its first execution, such an instruction takes five clock cycles to re-execute. However, if we employ a nonblocking I/O instruction, it takes a total of 20 clock cycles for fetching and execution. Calculate the increase in speed with the block I/O instruction when transferring blocks of 128 bytes.

7.5 A system is based on an 8-bit microprocessor and has two I/O devices. The I/O controllers for this system use separate control and status registers. Both devices handle data on a 1-byte-at-a-time basis. The first device has two status lines and three control lines. The second device has three status lines and four control lines.

    a. How many 8-bit I/O control module registers do we need for status reading and control of each device?

    b. What is the total number of needed control module registers given that the first device is an output-only device?

    c. How many distinct addresses are needed to control the two devices?

7.6 For programmed I/O, Figure 7.5 indicates that the processor is stuck in a wait loop doing status checking of an I/O device. To increase efficiency, the I/O software could be written so that the processor periodically checks the status of the device. If the device is not ready, the processor can jump to other tasks. After some timed interval, the processor comes back to check status again.

    a. Consider the above scheme for outputting data one character at a time to a printer that operates at 10 characters per second (cps). What will happen if its status is scanned every 200 ms?

b. Next consider a keyboard with a single character buffer. On average, characters are entered at a rate of 10 cps. However, the time interval between two consecutive key depressions can be as short as 60 ms. At what frequency should the keyboard be scanned by the I/O program?

7.7 A microprocessor scans the status of an output I/O device every 20 ms. This is accomplished by means of a timer alerting the processor every 20 ms. The interface of the device includes two ports: one for status and one for data output. How long does it take to scan and service the device given a clocking rate of 8 MHz? Assume for simplicity that all pertinent instruction cycles take 12 clock cycles.

7.8 In Section 7.3, one advantage and one disadvantage of memory-mapped I/O, compared with isolated I/O, were listed. List two more advantages and two more disadvantages.

7.9 A particular system is controlled by an operator through commands entered from a keyboard. The average number of commands entered in an 8-hour interval is 60.
  a. Suppose the processor scans the keyboard every 100 ms. How many times will the keyboard be checked in an 8-hour period?
  b. By what fraction would the number of processor visits to the keyboard be reduced if interrupt-driven I/O were used?

7.10 Consider a system employing interrupt-driven I/O for a particular device that transfers data at an average of 8 KB/s on a continuous basis.
  a. Assume that interrupt processing takes about 100 μs (i.e., the time to jump to the interrupt service routine (ISR), execute it, and return to the main program). Determine what fraction of processor time is consumed by this I/O device if it interrupts for every byte.
  b. Now assume that the device has two 16-byte buffers and interrupts the processor when one of the buffers is full. Naturally, interrupt processing takes longer, because the ISR must transfer 16 bytes. While executing the ISR, the processor takes about 8 μs for the transfer of each byte. Determine what fraction of processor time is consumed by this I/O device in this case.
  c. Now assume that the processor is equipped with a block transfer I/O instruction such as that found on the Z8000. This permits the associated ISR to transfer each byte of a block in only 2 μs. Determine what fraction of processor time is consumed by this I/O device in this case.

7.11 In virtually all systems that include DMA modules, DMA access to main memory is given higher priority than CPU access to main memory. Why?

7.12 A DMA module is transferring characters to memory using cycle stealing, from a device transmitting at 9600 bps. The processor is fetching instructions at the rate of 1 million instructions per second (1 MIPS). By how much will the processor be slowed down due to the DMA activity?

7.13 Consider a system in which bus cycles takes 500 ns. Transfer of bus control in either direction, from processor to I/O device or vice versa, takes 250 ns. One of the I/O devices has a data transfer rate of 50 KB/s and employs DMA. Data are transferred one byte at a time.
  a. Suppose we employ DMA in a burst mode. That is, the DMA interface gains bus mastership prior to the start of a block transfer and maintains control of the bus until the whole block is transferred. For how long would the device tie up the bus when transferring a block of 128 bytes?
  b. Repeat the calculation for cycle-stealing mode.

7.14 Examination of the timing diagram of the 8237A indicates that once a block transfer begins, it takes three bus clock cycles per DMA cycle. During the DMA cycle, the 8237A transfers one byte of information between memory and I/O device.
  a. Suppose we clock the 8237A at a rate of 5 MHz. How long does it take to transfer one byte?
  b. What would be the maximum attainable data transfer rate?
  c. Assume that the memory is not fast enough and we have to insert two wait states per DMA cycle. What will be the actual data transfer rate?

7.15 Assume that in the system of the preceding problem, a memory cycle takes 750 ns. To what value could we reduce the clocking rate of the bus without effect on the attainable data transfer rate?

7.16 A DMA controller serves four receive-only telecommunication links (one per DMA channel) having a speed of 64 Kbps each.
   a. Would you operate the controller in burst mode or in cycle-stealing mode?
   b. What priority scheme would you employ for service of the DMA channels?

7.17 A 32-bit computer has two selector channels and one multiplexor channel. Each selector channel supports two magnetic disk and two magnetic tape units. The multiplexor channel has two line printers, two card readers, and 10 VDT terminals connected to it. Assume the following transfer rates:

Disk drive	800 KBytes/s
Magnetic tape drive	200 KBytes/s
Line printer	6.6 KBytes/s
Card reader	1.2 KBytes/s
VDT	1 KBytes/s

Estimate the maximum aggregate I/O transfer rate in this system.

7.18 A computer consists of a processor and an I/O device D connected to main memory M via a shared bus with a data bus width of one word. The processor can execute a maximum of 10^6 instructions per second. An average instruction requires five machine cycles, three of which use the memory bus. A memory read or write operation uses one machine cycle. Suppose that the processor is continuously executing "background" programs that require 95% of its instruction execution rate but not any I/O instructions. Assume that one processor cycle equals one bus cycle. Now suppose the I/O device is to be used to transfer very large blocks of data between M and D.
   a. If programmed I/O is used and each one-word I/O transfer requires the processor to execute two instructions, estimate the maximum I/O data-transfer rate, in words per second, possible through D.
   b. Estimate the same rate if DMA is used.

7.19 A data source produces 7-bit IRA characters, to each of which is appended a parity bit. Derive an expression for the maximum effective data rate (rate of IRA data bits) over an R-bps line for the following:
   a. Asynchronous transmission, with a 1.5-unit stop bit
   b. Bit-synchronous transmission, with a frame consisting of 48 control bits and 128 information bits
   c. Same as (b), with a 1024-bit information field
   d. Character-synchronous, with 9 control characters per frame and 16 information characters
   e. Same as (d), with 128 information characters

7.20 The following problem is based on a suggested illustration of I/O mechanisms in [ECKE90] (Figure 7.22):
      Two women are on either side of a high fence. One of the women, named Apple-server, has a beautiful apple tree loaded with delicious apples growing on her side of the fence; she is happy to supply apples to the other woman whenever needed. The other woman, named Apple-eater, loves to eat apples but has none. In fact, she must eat her apples at a fixed rate (an apple a day keeps the doctor away). If she eats them faster than that rate, she will get sick. If she eats them slower, she will suffer malnutrition. Neither woman can talk, and so the problem is to get apples from Apple-server to Apple-eater at the correct rate.
   a. Assume that there is an alarm clock sitting on top of the fence and that the clock can have multiple alarm settings. How can the clock be used to solve the problem? Draw a timing diagram to illustrate the solution.
   b. Now assume that there is no alarm clock. Instead Apple-eater has a flag that she can wave whenever she needs an apple. Suggest a new solution. Would it be

Figure 7.22   An Apple Problem

helpful for Apple-server also to have a flag? If so, incorporate this into the solution. Discuss the drawbacks of this approach.

c. Now take away the flag and assume the existence of a long piece of string. Suggest a solution that is superior to that of (b) using the string.

7.21   Assume that one 16-bit and two 8-bit microprocessors are to be interfaced to a system bus. The following details are given:

1. All microprocessors have the hardware features necessary for any type of data transfer: programmed I/O, interrupt-driven I/O, and DMA.
2. All microprocessors have a 16-bit address bus.
3. Two memory boards, each of 64 KBytes capacity, are interfaced with the bus. The designer wishes to use a shared memory that is as large as possible.
4. The system bus supports a maximum of four interrupt lines and one DMA line.

Make any other assumptions necessary, and

a. Give the system bus specifications in terms of number and types of lines.
b. Describe a possible protocol for communicating on the bus (i.e., read-write, interrupt, and DMA sequences).
c. Explain how the aforementioned devices are interfaced to the system bus.

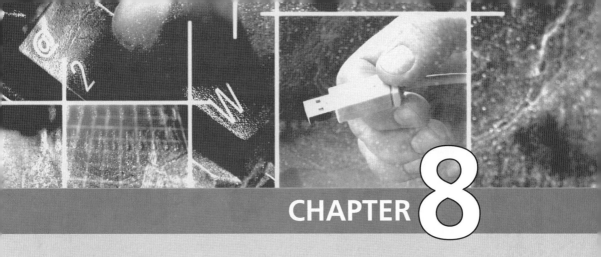

CHAPTER 8

OPERATING SYSTEM SUPPORT

259

KEY POINTS

◆ The operating system (OS) is the software that controls the execution of programs on a processor and that manages the processor's resources. A number of the functions performed by the OS, including process scheduling and memory management, can only be performed efficiently and rapidly if the processor hardware includes capabilities to support the OS. Virtually all processors include such capabilities to a greater or lesser extent, including virtual memory management hardware and process management hardware. The hardware includes special purpose registers and buffers, as well as circuitry to perform basic resource management tasks.

◆ One of the most important functions of the OS is the scheduling of processes, or tasks. The OS determines which process should run at any given time. Typically, the hardware will interrupt a running process from time to time to enable the OS to make a new scheduling decision so as to share processor time fairly among a number of processes.

◆ Another important OS function is memory management. Most contemporary operating systems include a virtual memory capability, which has two benefits: (1) A process can run in main memory without all of the instructions and data for that program being present in main memory at one time, and (2) the total memory space available to a program may far exceed the actual main memory on the system. Although memory management is performed in software, the OS relies on hardware support in the processor, including paging and segmentation hardware.

Although the focus of this text is computer hardware, there is one area of software that needs to be addressed: the computer's OS. The OS is a program that manages the computer's resources, provides services for programmers, and schedules the execution of other programs. Some understanding of operating systems is essential to appreciate the mechanisms by which the CPU controls the computer system. In particular, explanations of the effect of interrupts and of the management of the memory hierarchy are best explained in this context.

The chapter begins with an overview and brief history of operating systems. The bulk of the chapter looks at the two OS functions that are most relevant to the study of computer organization and architecture: scheduling and memory management.

8.1 OPERATING SYSTEM OVERVIEW

Operating System Objectives and Functions

An OS is a program that controls the execution of application programs and acts as an interface between the user of a computer and the computer hardware. It can be thought of as having two objectives:

- **Convenience:** An OS makes a computer more convenient to use.
- **Efficiency:** An OS allows the computer system resources to be used in an efficient manner.

Let us examine these two aspects of an OS in turn.

THE OPERATING SYSTEM AS A USER/COMPUTER INTERFACE The hardware and software used in providing applications to a user can be viewed in a layered or hierarchical fashion, as depicted in Figure 8.1. The user of those applications, the end user, generally is not concerned with the computer's architecture. Thus the end user views a computer system in terms of an application. That application can be expressed in a programming language and is developed by an application programmer. To develop an application program as a set of processor instructions that is completely responsible for controlling the computer hardware would be an overwhelmingly complex task. To ease this task, a set of systems programs is provided. Some of these programs are referred to as **utilities**. These implement frequently used functions that assist in program creation, the management of files, and the control of I/O devices. A programmer makes use of these facilities in developing an application, and the application, while it is running, invokes the utilities to perform certain functions. The most important system program is the OS. The OS masks the details of the hardware from the programmer and provides the programmer with a convenient interface for using the system. It acts as mediator, making it easier for the programmer and for application programs to access and use those facilities and services.

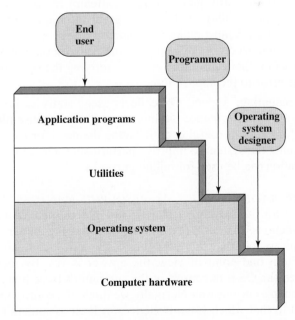

Figure 8.1 Layers and Views of a Computer System

Briefly, the OS typically provides services in the following areas:

- **Program creation:** The OS provides a variety of facilities and services, such as editors and debuggers, to assist the programmer in creating programs. Typically, these services are in the form of utility programs that are not actually part of the OS but are accessible through the OS.

- **Program execution:** A number of tasks need to be performed to execute a program. Instructions and data must be loaded into main memory, I/O devices and files must be initialized, and other resources must be prepared. The OS handles all of this for the user.

- **Access to I/O devices:** Each I/O device requires its own specific set of instructions or control signals for operation. The OS takes care of the details so that the programmer can think in terms of simple reads and writes.

- **Controlled access to files:** In the case of files, control must include an understanding of not only the nature of the I/O device (disk drive, tape drive) but also the file format on the storage medium. Again, the OS worries about the details. Further, in the case of a system with multiple simultaneous users, the OS can provide protection mechanisms to control access to the files.

- **System access:** In the case of a shared or public system, the OS controls access to the system as a whole and to specific system resources. The access function must provide protection of resources and data from unauthorized users and must resolve conflicts for resource contention.

- **Error detection and response:** A variety of errors can occur while a computer system is running. These include internal and external hardware errors, such as a memory error, or a device failure or malfunction; and various software errors, such as arithmetic overflow, attempt to access forbidden memory location, and inability of the OS to grant the request of an application. In each case, the OS must make the response that clears the error condition with the least impact on running applications. The response may range from ending the program that caused the error, to retrying the operation, to simply reporting the error to the application.

- **Accounting:** A good OS collects usage statistics for various resources and monitor performance parameters such as response time. On any system, this information is useful in anticipating the need for future enhancements and in tuning the system to improve performance. On a multiuser system, the information can be used for billing purposes.

THE OPERATING SYSTEM AS RESOURCE MANAGER A computer is a set of resources for the movement, storage, and processing of data and for the control of these functions. The OS is responsible for managing these resources.

Can we say that the OS controls the movement, storage, and processing of data? From one point of view, the answer is yes: By managing the computer's resources, the OS is in control of the computer's basic functions. But this control is exercised in a curious way. Normally, we think of a control mechanism as something external to that which is controlled, or at least as something that is a distinct and separate part of that which is controlled. (For example, a residential heating system is controlled by a thermostat, which is completely distinct from the heat-generation and heat-distribution apparatus.) This is not the case with the OS, which as a control mechanism is unusual in two respects:

- The OS functions in the same way as ordinary computer software; that is, it is a program executed by the processor.
- The OS frequently relinquishes control and must depend on the processor to allow it to regain control.

The OS is, in fact, nothing more than a computer program. Like other computer programs, it provides instructions for the processor. The key difference is in the intent of the program. The OS directs the processor in the use of the other system resources and in the timing of its execution of other programs. But in order for the processor to do any of these things, it must cease executing the OS program and execute other programs. Thus, the OS relinquishes control for the processor to do some "useful" work and then resumes control long enough to prepare the processor to do the next piece of work. The mechanisms involved in all this should become clear as the chapter proceeds.

Figure 8.2 suggests the main resources that are managed by the OS. A portion of the OS is in main memory. This includes the **kernel**, or **nucleus**, which contains the most frequently used functions in the OS and, at a given time, other portions of the OS currently in use. The remainder of main memory contains user programs and data. The allocation of this resource (main memory) is controlled jointly by the OS and memory-management hardware in the processor, as we shall see. The OS decides when an I/O

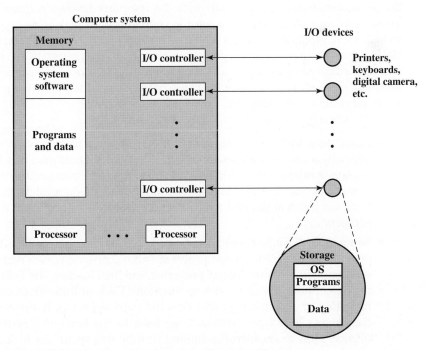

Figure 8.2   The Operating System as Resource Manager

device can be used by a program in execution, and controls access to and use of files. The processor itself is a resource, and the OS must determine how much processor time is to be devoted to the execution of a particular user program. In the case of a multiple-processor system, this decision must span all of the processors.

Types of Operating Systems

Certain key characteristics serve to differentiate various types of operating systems. The characteristics fall along two independent dimensions. The first dimension specifies whether the system is batch or interactive. In an **interactive** system, the user/programmer interacts directly with the computer, usually through a keyboard/display terminal, to request the execution of a job or to perform a transaction. Furthermore, the user may, depending on the nature of the application, communicate with the computer during the execution of the job. A **batch** system is the opposite of interactive. The user's program is batched together with programs from other users and submitted by a computer operator. After the program is completed, results are printed out for the user. Pure batch systems are rare today. However, it will be useful to the description of contemporary operating systems to examine batch systems briefly.

An independent dimension specifies whether the system employs **multiprogramming** or not. With multiprogramming, the attempt is made to keep the processor as busy as possible, by having it work on more than one program at a time. Several programs are loaded into memory, and the processor switches rapidly among them. The alternative is a **uniprogramming** system that works only one program at a time.

EARLY SYSTEMS With the earliest computers, from the late 1940s to the mid-1950s, the programmer interacted directly with the computer hardware; there was no OS. These processors were run from a console, consisting of display lights, toggle switches, some form of input device, and a printer. Programs in processor code were loaded via the input device (e.g., a card reader). If an error halted the program, the error condition was indicated by the lights. The programmer could proceed to examine registers and main memory to determine the cause of the error. If the program proceeded to a normal completion, the output appeared on the printer.

These early systems presented two main problems.:

- **Scheduling:** Most installations used a sign-up sheet to reserve processor time. Typically, a user could sign up for a block of time in multiples of a half hour or so. A user might sign up for an hour and finish in 45 minutes; this would result in wasted computer idle time. On the other hand, the user might run into problems, not finish in the allotted time, and be forced to stop before resolving the problem.

- **Setup time:** A single program, called a **job**, could involve loading the compiler plus the high-level language program (source program) into memory, saving the compiled program (object program), and then loading and linking together the object program and common functions. Each of these steps could involve mounting or dismounting tapes, or setting up card decks. If an error occurred, the hapless user typically had to go back to the beginning of the setup sequence. Thus a considerable amount of time was spent just in setting up the program to run.

This mode of operation could be termed serial processing, reflecting the fact that users have access to the computer in series. Over time, various system software tools were developed to attempt to make serial processing more efficient. These include libraries of common functions, linkers, loaders, debuggers, and I/O driver routines that were available as common software for all users.

SIMPLE BATCH SYSTEMS Early processors were very expensive, and therefore it was important to maximize processor utilization. The wasted time due to scheduling and setup time was unacceptable.

To improve utilization, simple batch operating systems were developed. With such a system, also called a **monitor,** the user no longer has direct access to the processor. Rather, the user submits the job on cards or tape to a computer operator, who *batches* the jobs together sequentially and places the entire batch on an input device, for use by the monitor.

To understand how this scheme works, let us look at it from two points of view: that of the monitor and that of the processor. From the point of view of the monitor, the monitor controls the sequence of events. For this to be so, much of the monitor must always be in main memory and available for execution (Figure 8.3). That portion is referred to as the **resident monitor.** The rest of the monitor consists of utilities and common functions that are loaded as subroutines to the user program at the beginning of any job that requires them. The monitor reads in jobs one at a time from the input device (typically a card reader or magnetic tape drive). As it is read in, the current job is placed in the user program area, and control is passed to this job. When the job is completed, it returns control to the monitor, which immediately reads in the next job. The results of each job are printed out for delivery to the user.

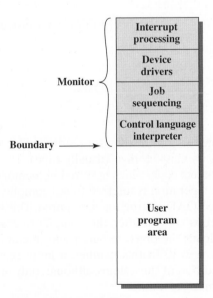

Figure 8.3   Memory Layout for a Resident Monitor

Now consider this sequence from the point of view of the processor. At a certain point in time, the processor is executing instructions from the portion of main memory containing the monitor. These instructions cause the next job to be read in to another portion of main memory. Once a job has been read in, the processor will encounter in the monitor a branch instruction that instructs the processor to continue execution at the start of the user program. The processor will then execute the instruction in the user's program until it encounters an ending or error condition. Either event causes the processor to fetch its next instruction from the monitor program. Thus the phrase "control is passed to a job" simply means that the processor is now fetching and executing instructions in a user program, and "control is returned to the monitor" means that the processor is now fetching and executing instructions from the monitor program.

It should be clear that the monitor handles the scheduling problem. A batch of jobs is queued up, and jobs are executed as rapidly as possible, with no intervening idle time.

How about the job setup time? The monitor handles this as well. With each job, instructions are included in a **job control language** (JCL). This is a special type of programming language used to provide instructions to the monitor. A simple example is that of a user submitting a program written in FORTRAN plus some data to be used by the program. Each FORTRAN instruction and each item of data is on a separate punched card or a separate record on tape. In addition to FORTRAN and data lines, the job includes job control instructions, which are denoted by the beginning "$". The overall format of the job looks like this:

$JOB

$FTN

    ⋮   } FORTRAN instructions

$LOAD

$RUN

    ⋮   } Data

$END

To execute this job, the monitor reads the $FTN line and loads the appropriate compiler from its mass storage (usually tape). The compiler translates the user's program into object code, which is stored in memory or mass storage. If it is stored in memory, the operation is referred to as "compile, load, and go." If it is stored on tape, then the $LOAD instruction is required. This instruction is read by the monitor, which regains control after the compile operation. The monitor invokes the loader, which loads the object program into memory in place of the compiler and transfers control to it. In this manner, a large segment of main memory can be shared among different subsystems, although only one such subsystem could be resident and executing at a time.

We see that the monitor, or batch OS, is simply a computer program. It relies on the ability of the processor to fetch instructions from various portions of main

Read one record from file	15 μs
Execute 100 instructions	1 μs
Write one record to file	15 μs
TOTAL	31 μs

Percent CPU utilization $= \dfrac{1}{31} = 0.032 = 3.2\%$

Figure 8.4 System Utilization Example

memory in order to seize and relinquish control alternately. Certain other hardware features are also desirable:

- **Memory protection:** While the user program is executing, it must not alter the memory area containing the monitor. If such an attempt is made, the processor hardware should detect an error and transfer control to the monitor. The monitor would then abort the job, print out an error message, and load the next job.
- **Timer:** A timer is used to prevent a single job from monopolizing the system. The timer is set at the beginning of each job. If the timer expires, an interrupt occurs, and control returns to the monitor.
- **Privileged instructions:** Certain instructions are designated privileged and can be executed only by the monitor. If the processor encounters such an instruction while executing a user program, an error interrupt occurs. Among the privileged instructions are I/O instructions, so that the monitor retains control of all I/O devices. This prevents, for example, a user program from accidentally reading job control instructions from the next job. If a user program wishes to perform I/O, it must request that the monitor perform the operation for it. If a privileged instruction is encountered by the processor while it is executing a user program, the processor hardware considers this an error and transfers control to the monitor.
- **Interrupts:** Early computer models did not have this capability. This feature gives the OS more flexibility in relinquishing control to and regaining control from user programs.

Processor time alternates between execution of user programs and execution of the monitor. There have been two sacrifices: Some main memory is now given over to the monitor and some processor time is consumed by the monitor. Both of these are forms of overhead. Even with this overhead, the simple batch system improves utilization of the computer.

MULTIPROGRAMMED BATCH SYSTEMS Even with the automatic job sequencing provided by a simple batch OS, the processor is often idle. The problem is that I/O devices are slow compared to the processor. Figure 8.4 details a representative calculation. The calculation concerns a program that processes a file of records and performs, on average, 100 processor instructions per record. In this example the computer spends over 96% of its time waiting for I/O devices to finish transferring data! Figure 8.5a illustrates this situation. The processor spends a certain amount of time executing, until it reaches an I/O instruction. It must then wait until that I/O instruction concludes before proceeding.

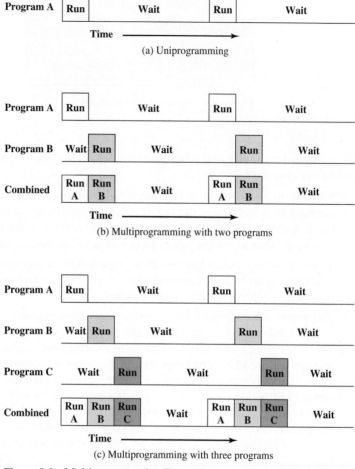

Figure 8.5   Multiprogramming Example

This inefficiency is not necessary. We know that there must be enough memory to hold the OS (resident monitor) and one user program. Suppose that there is room for the OS and two user programs. Now, when one job needs to wait for I/O, the processor can switch to the other job, which likely is not waiting for I/O (Figure 8.5b). Furthermore, we might expand memory to hold three, four, or more programs and switch among all of them (Figure 8.5c). This technique is known as **multiprogramming**, or **multitasking**.[1] It is the central theme of modern operating systems.

---

[1]The term *multitasking* is sometimes reserved to mean multiple tasks within the same program that may be handled concurrently by the OS, in contrast to *multiprogramming,* which would refer to multiple processes from multiple programs. However, it is more common to equate the terms *multitasking* and *multiprogramming,* as is done in most standards dictionaries (e.g., IEEE Std 100-1992, *The New IEEE Standard Dictionary of Electrical and Electronics Terms*).

Table 8.1   Sample Program Execution Attributes

	JOB1	JOB2	JOB3
Type of job	Heavy compute	Heavy I/O	Heavy I/O
Duration	5 min	15 min	10 min
Memory required	50 M	100 M	80 M
Need disk?	No	No	Yes
Need terminal?	No	Yes	No
Need printer?	No	No	Yes

Example 8.1   This example illustrates the benefit of multiprogramming. Consider a computer with 250 MBytes of available memory (not used by the OS), a disk, a terminal, and a printer. Three programs, JOB1, JOB2, and JOB3, are submitted for execution at the same time, with the attributes listed in Table 8.1. We assume minimal processor requirements for JOB2 and JOB3 and continuous disk and printer use by JOB3. For a simple batch environment, these jobs will be executed in sequence. Thus, JOB1 completes in 5 minutes. JOB2 must wait until the 5 minutes is over and then completes 15 minutes after that. JOB3 begins after 20 minutes and completes at 30 minutes from the time it was initially submitted. The average resource utilization, throughput, and response times are shown in the uniprogramming column of Table 8.2. Device-by-device utilization is illustrated in Figure 8.6a. It is evident that there is gross underutilization for all resources when averaged over the required 30-minute time period.

   Now suppose that the jobs are run concurrently under a multiprogramming OS. Because there is little resource contention between the jobs, all three can run in nearly minimum time while coexisting with the others in the computer (assuming that JOB2 and JOB3 are allotted enough processor time to keep their input and output operations active). JOB1 will still require 5 minutes to complete but at the end of that time, JOB2 will be one-third finished, and JOB3 will be half finished. All three jobs will have finished within 15 minutes. The improvement is evident when examining the multiprogramming column of Table 8.2, obtained from the histogram shown in Figure 8.6b.

As with a simple batch system, a multiprogramming batch system must rely on certain computer hardware features. The most notable additional feature that is useful for multiprogramming is the hardware that supports I/O interrupts and DMA.

Table 8.2   Effects of Multiprogramming on Resource Utilization

	Uniprogramming	Multiprogramming
Processor use	20%	40%
Memory use	33%	67%
Disk use	33%	67%
Printer use	33%	67%
Elapsed time	30 min	15 min
Throughput rate	6 jobs/hr	12 jobs/hr
Mean response time	18 min	10 min

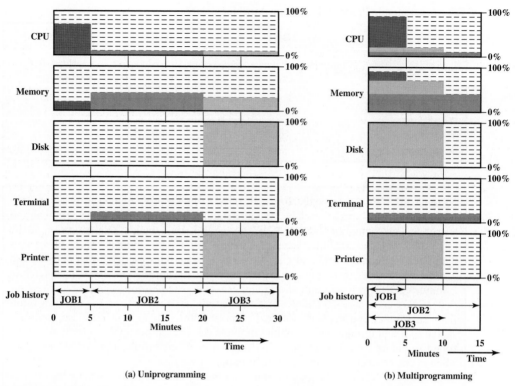

Figure 8.6 Utilization Histograms

With interrupt-driven I/O or DMA, the processor can issue an I/O command for one job and proceed with the execution of another job while the I/O is carried out by the device controller. When the I/O operation is complete, the processor is interrupted and control is passed to an interrupt-handling program in the OS. The OS will then pass control to another job.

Multiprogramming operating systems are fairly sophisticated compared to single-program, or **uniprogramming**, systems. To have several jobs ready to run, the jobs must be kept in main memory, requiring some form of **memory management**. In addition, if several jobs are ready to run, the processor must decide which one to run, which requires some algorithm for scheduling. These concepts are discussed later in this chapter.

TIME-SHARING SYSTEMS With the use of multiprogramming, batch processing can be quite efficient. However, for many jobs, it is desirable to provide a mode in which the user interacts directly with the computer. Indeed, for some jobs, such as transaction processing, an interactive mode is essential.

Today, the requirement for an interactive computing facility can be, and often is, met by the use of a dedicated microcomputer. That option was not available in the 1960s, when most computers were big and costly. Instead, time sharing was developed.

Just as multiprogramming allows the processor to handle multiple batch jobs at a time, multiprogramming can be used to handle multiple interactive jobs. In this latter case, the technique is referred to as time sharing, because the processor's time is shared among multiple users. In a time-sharing system, multiple users simultaneously

Table 8.3 Batch Multiprogramming versus Time Sharing

	Batch Multiprogramming	**Time Sharing**
Principal objective	Maximize processor use	Minimize response time
Source of directives to operating system	Job control language commands provided with the job	Commands entered at the terminal

access the system through terminals, with the OS interleaving the execution of each user program in a short burst or quantum of computation. Thus, if there are *n* users actively requesting service at one time, each user will only see on the average 1/*n* of the effective computer speed, not counting OS overhead. However, given the relatively slow human reaction time, the response time on a properly designed system should be comparable to that on a dedicated computer.

Both batch multiprogramming and time sharing use multiprogramming. The key differences are listed in Table 8.3.

8.2 SCHEDULING

The key to multiprogramming is scheduling. In fact, four types of scheduling are typically involved (Table 8.4). We will explore these presently. But first, we introduce the concept of **process**. This term was first used by the designers of the Multics OS in the 1960s. It is a somewhat more general term than *job*. Many definitions have been given for the term *process,* including

- A program in execution
- The "animated spirit" of a program
- That entity to which a processor is assigned

This concept should become clearer as we proceed.

Long–Term Scheduling

The long-term scheduler determines which programs are admitted to the system for processing. Thus, it controls the degree of multiprogramming (number of processes in memory). Once admitted, a job or user program becomes a process and is added to the queue for the short-term scheduler. In some systems, a newly created process

Table 8.4 Types of Scheduling

Long-term scheduling	The decision to add to the pool of processes to be executed
Medium-term scheduling	The decision to add to the number of processes that are partially or fully in main memory
Short-term scheduling	The decision as to which available process will be executed by the processor
I/O scheduling	The decision as to which process's pending I/O request shall be handled by an available I/O device

begins in a swapped-out condition, in which case it is added to a queue for the medium-term scheduler.

In a batch system, or for the batch portion of a general-purpose OS, newly submitted jobs are routed to disk and held in a batch queue. The long-term scheduler creates processes from the queue when it can. There are two decisions involved here. First, the scheduler must decide that the OS can take on one or more additional processes. Second, the scheduler must decide which job or jobs to accept and turn into processes. The criteria used may include priority, expected execution time, and I/O requirements.

For interactive programs in a time-sharing system, a process request is generated when a user attempts to connect to the system. Time-sharing users are not simply queued up and kept waiting until the system can accept them. Rather, the OS will accept all authorized comers until the system is saturated, using some predefined measure of saturation. At that point, a connection request is met with a message indicating that the system is full and the user should try again later.

Medium-Term Scheduling

Medium-term scheduling is part of the swapping function, described in Section 8.3. Typically, the swapping-in decision is based on the need to manage the degree of multiprogramming. On a system that does not use virtual memory, memory management is also an issue. Thus, the swapping-in decision will consider the memory requirements of the swapped-out processes.

Short-Term Scheduling

The long-term scheduler executes relatively infrequently and makes the coarse-grained decision of whether or not to take on a new process, and which one to take. The short-term scheduler, also known as the **dispatcher**, executes frequently and makes the fine-grained decision of which job to execute next.

PROCESS STATES To understand the operation of the short-term scheduler, we need to consider the concept of a **process state**. During the lifetime of a process, its status will change a number of times. Its status at any point in time is referred to as a *state*. The term *state* is used because it connotes that certain information exists that defines

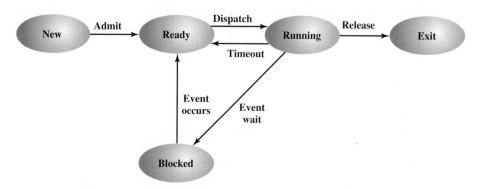

Figure 8.7 Five-State Process Model

the status at that point. At minimum, there are five defined states for a process (Figure 8.7):

- **New:** A program is admitted by the high-level scheduler but is not yet ready to execute. The OS will initialize the process, moving it to the ready state.
- **Ready:** The process is ready to execute and is awaiting access to the processor.
- **Running:** The process is being executed by the processor.
- **Waiting:** The process is suspended from execution waiting for some system resource, such as I/O.
- **Halted:** The process has terminated and will be destroyed by the OS.

For each process in the system, the OS must maintain information indicating the state of the process and other information necessary for process execution. For this purpose, each process is represented in the OS by a **process control block** (Figure 8.8), which typically contains

- **Identifier:** Each current process has a unique identifier.
- **State:** The current state of the process (new, ready, and so on).
- **Priority:** Relative priority level.
- **Program counter:** The address of the next instruction in the program to be executed.
- **Memory pointers:** The starting and ending locations of the process in memory.
- **Context data:** These are data that are present in registers in the processor while the process is executing, and they will be discussed in Part Three. For now, it is

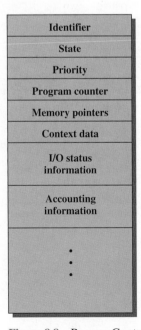

Figure 8.8 Process Control Block

enough to say that these data represent the "context" of the process. The context data plus the program counter are saved when the process leaves the running state. They are retrieved by the processor when it resumes execution of the process.

- **I/O status information:** Includes outstanding I/O requests, I/O devices (e.g., tape drives) assigned to this process, a list of files assigned to the process, and so on.
- **Accounting information:** May include the amount of processor time and clock time used, time limits, account numbers, and so on.

When the scheduler accepts a new job or user request for execution, it creates a blank process control block and places the associated process in the new state. After the system has properly filled in the process control block, the process is transferred to the ready state.

SCHEDULING TECHNIQUES To understand how the OS manages the scheduling of the various jobs in memory, let us begin by considering the simple example in Figure 8.9. The figure shows how main memory is partitioned at a given point in time. The kernel

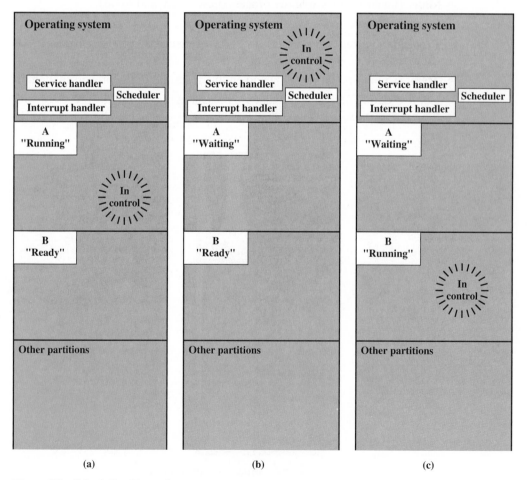

(a)   (b)   (c)

Figure 8.9   Scheduling Example

of the OS is, of course, always resident. In addition, there are a number of active processes, including A and B, each of which is allocated a portion of memory.

We begin at a point in time when process A is running. The processor is executing instructions from the program contained in A's memory partition. At some later point in time, the processor ceases to execute instructions in A and begins executing instructions in the OS area. This will happen for one of three reasons:

1. Process A issues a service call (e.g., an I/O request) to the OS. Execution of A is suspended until this call is satisfied by the OS.

2. Process A causes an *interrupt*. An interrupt is a hardware-generated signal to the processor. When this signal is detected, the processor ceases to execute A and transfers to the interrupt handler in the OS. A variety of events related to A will cause an interrupt. One example is an error, such as attempting to execute a privileged instruction. Another example is a timeout; to prevent any one process from monopolizing the processor, each process is only granted the processor for a short period at a time.

3. Some event unrelated to process A that requires attention causes an interrupt. An example is the completion of an I/O operation.

In any case, the result is the following. The processor saves the current context data and the program counter for A in A's process control block and then begins executing in the OS. The OS may perform some work, such as initiating an I/O operation. Then the short-term-scheduler portion of the OS decides which process should be executed next. In this example, B is chosen. The OS instructs the processor to restore B's context data and proceed with the execution of B where it left off.

This simple example highlights the basic functioning of the short-term scheduler. Figure 8.10 shows the major elements of the OS involved in the multiprogramming

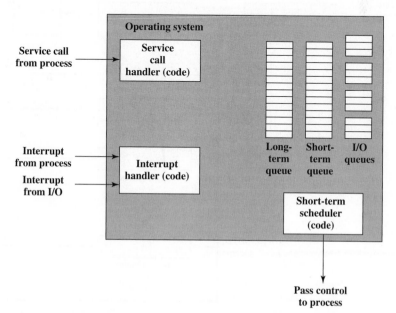

Figure 8.10 Key Elements of an Operating System for Multiprogramming

and scheduling of processes. The OS receives control of the processor at the interrupt handler if an interrupt occurs and at the service-call handler if a service call occurs. Once the interrupt or service call is handled, the short-term scheduler is invoked to select a process for execution.

To do its job, the OS maintains a number of queues. Each queue is simply a waiting list of processes waiting for some resource. The **long-term queue** is a list of jobs waiting to use the system. As conditions permit, the high-level scheduler will allocate memory and create a process for one of the waiting items. The **short-term queue** consists of all processes in the ready state. Any one of these processes could use the processor next. It is up to the short-term scheduler to pick one. Generally, this is done with a round-robin algorithm, giving each process some time in turn. Priority levels may also be used. Finally, there is an **I/O queue** for each I/O device. More than one process may request the use of the same I/O device. All processes waiting to use each device are lined up in that device's queue.

Figure 8.11 suggests how processes progress through the computer under the control of the OS. Each process request (batch job, user-defined interactive job) is placed in the long-term queue. As resources become available, a process request becomes a process and is then placed in the ready state and put in the short-term queue. The processor alternates between executing OS instructions and executing user processes. While the OS is in control, it decides which process in the short-term queue should be executed next. When the OS has finished its immediate tasks, it turns the processor over to the chosen process.

As was mentioned earlier, a process being executed may be suspended for a variety of reasons. If it is suspended because the process requests I/O, then it is

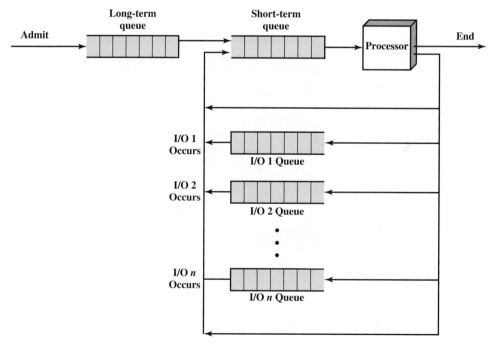

Figure 8.11   Queuing Diagram Representation of Processor Scheduling

placed in the appropriate I/O queue. If it is suspended because of a timeout or because the OS must attend to pressing business, then it is placed in the ready state and put into the short-term queue.

Finally, we mention that the OS also manages the I/O queues. When an I/O operation is completed, the OS removes the satisfied process from that I/O queue and places it in the short-term queue. It then selects another waiting process (if any) and signals for the I/O device to satisfy that process's request.

8.3 MEMORY MANAGEMENT

In a uniprogramming system, main memory is divided into two parts: one part for the OS (resident monitor) and one part for the program currently being executed. In a multiprogramming system, the "user" part of memory is subdivided to accommodate multiple processes. The task of subdivision is carried out dynamically by the OS and is known as **memory management**.

Effective memory management is vital in a multiprogramming system. If only a few processes are in memory, then for much of the time all of the processes will be waiting for I/O and the processor will be idle. Thus, memory needs to be allocated efficiently to pack as many processes into memory as possible.

Swapping

Referring back to Figure 8.11, we have discussed three types of queues: the long-term queue of requests for new processes, the short-term queue of processes ready to use the processor, and the various I/O queues of processes that are not ready to use the processor. Recall that the reason for this elaborate machinery is that I/O activities are much slower than computation and therefore the processor in a uniprogramming system is idle most of the time.

But the arrangement in Figure 8.11 does not entirely solve the problem. It is true that, in this case, memory holds multiple processes and that the processor can move to another process when one process is waiting. But the processor is so much faster than I/O that it will be common for *all* the processes in memory to be waiting on I/O. Thus, even with multiprogramming, a processor could be idle most of the time.

What to do? Main memory could be expanded, and so be able to accommodate more processes. But there are two flaws in this approach. First, main memory is expensive, even today. Second, the appetite of programs for memory has grown as fast as the cost of memory has dropped. So larger memory results in larger processes, not more processes.

Another solution is *swapping,* depicted in Figure 8.12. We have a long-term queue of process requests, typically stored on disk. These are brought in, one at a time, as space becomes available. As processes are completed, they are moved out of main memory. Now the situation will arise that none of the processes in memory are in the ready state (e.g., all are waiting on an I/O operation). Rather than remain idle, the processor *swaps* one of these processes back out to disk into an *intermediate queue.* This is a queue of existing processes that have been temporarily kicked out of memory. The OS then brings in another process from the intermediate queue, or it

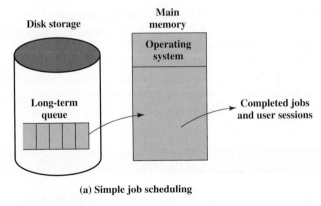

(a) Simple job scheduling

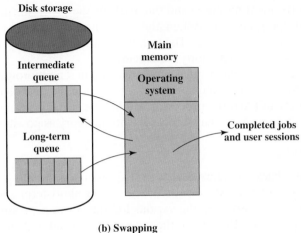

(b) Swapping

Figure 8.12 The Use of Swapping

honors a new process request from the long-term queue. Execution then continues with the newly arrived process.

Swapping, however, is an I/O operation, and therefore there is the potential for making the problem worse, not better. But because disk I/O is generally the fastest I/O on a system (e.g., compared with tape or printer I/O), swapping will usually enhance performance. A more sophisticated scheme, involving virtual memory, improves performance over simple swapping. This will be discussed shortly. But first, we must prepare the ground by explaining partitioning and paging.

Partitioning

The simplest scheme for partitioning available memory is to use *fixed-size partitions*, as shown in Figure 8.13. Note that, although the partitions are of fixed size, they need not be of equal size. When a process is brought into memory, it is placed in the smallest available partition that will hold it.

Even with the use of unequal fixed-size partitions, there will be wasted memory. In most cases, a process will not require exactly as much memory as provided by the

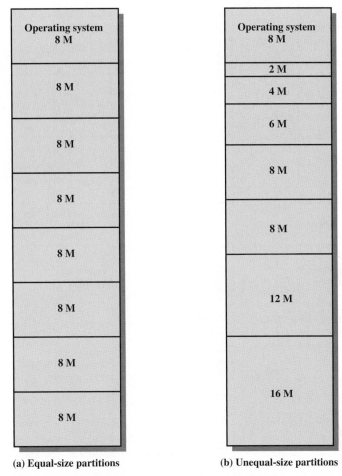

(a) Equal-size partitions   (b) Unequal-size partitions

Figure 8.13   Example of Fixed Partitioning of a 64-Mbyte Memory

partition. For example, a process that requires 3M bytes of memory would be placed in the 4M partition of Figure 8.13b, wasting 1M that could be used by another process.

A more efficient approach is to use *variable-size partitions*. When a process is brought into memory, it is allocated exactly as much memory as it requires and no more.

Example 8.2   An example, using 64 MBytes of main memory, is shown in Figure 8.14. Initially, main memory is empty, except for the OS (a). The first three processes are loaded in, starting where the OS ends and occupying just enough space for each process (b, c, d). This leaves a "hole" at the end of memory that is too small for a fourth process. At some point, none of the processes in memory is ready. The OS swaps out process 2 (e), which leaves sufficient room to load a new process, process 4 (f). Because process 4 is smaller than process 2, another small hole is created. Later, a point is reached at which none of the processes in main memory is ready, but process 2, in the Ready-Suspend state, is available. Because there is insufficient room in memory for process 2, the OS swaps process 1 out (g) and swaps process 2 back in (h).

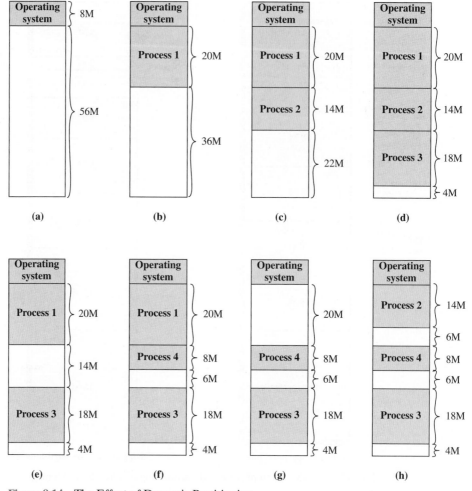

Figure 8.14 The Effect of Dynamic Partitioning

As this example shows, this method starts out well, but eventually it leads to a situation in which there are a lot of small holes in memory. As time goes on, memory becomes more and more fragmented, and memory utilization declines. One technique for overcoming this problem is **compaction**: From time to time, the OS shifts the processes in memory to place all the free memory together in one block. This is a time-consuming procedure, wasteful of processor time.

Before we consider ways of dealing with the shortcomings of partitioning, we must clear up one loose end. Consider Figure 8.14; it should be obvious that a process is not likely to be loaded into the same place in main memory each time it is swapped in. Furthermore, if compaction is used, a process may be shifted while in main memory. A process in memory consists of instructions plus data. The instructions will contain addresses for memory locations of two types:

- Addresses of data items
- Addresses of instructions, used for branching instructions

But these addresses are not fixed. They will change each time a process is swapped in. To solve this problem, a distinction is made between logical addresses and physical addresses. A **logical address** is expressed as a location relative to the beginning of the program. Instructions in the program contain only logical addresses. A **physical address** is an actual location in main memory. When the processor executes a process, it automatically converts from logical to physical address by adding the current starting location of the process, called its **base address**, to each logical address. This is another example of a processor hardware feature designed to meet an OS requirement. The exact nature of this hardware feature depends on the memory management strategy in use. We will see several examples later in this chapter.

Paging

Both unequal fixed-size and variable-size partitions are inefficient in the use of memory. Suppose, however, that memory is partitioned into equal fixed-size chunks that are relatively small, and that each process is also divided into small fixed-size chunks of some size. Then the chunks of a program, known as **pages**, could be assigned to available chunks of memory, known as **frames**, or page frames. At most, then, the wasted space in memory for that process is a fraction of the last page.

Figure 8.15 shows an example of the use of pages and frames. At a given point in time, some of the frames in memory are in use and some are free. The list of free

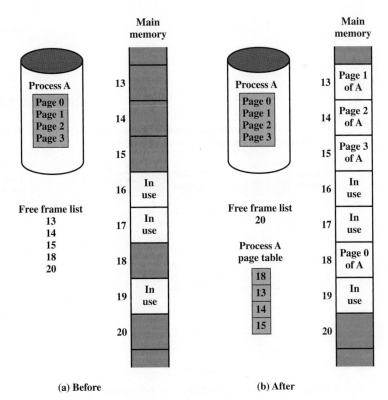

(a) Before   (b) After

Figure 8.15   Allocation of Free Frames

frames is maintained by the OS. Process A, stored on disk, consists of four pages. When it comes time to load this process, the OS finds four free frames and loads the four pages of the process A into the four frames.

Now suppose, as in this example, that there are not sufficient unused contiguous frames to hold the process. Does this prevent the OS from loading A? The answer is no, because we can once again use the concept of logical address. A simple base address will no longer suffice. Rather, the OS maintains a **page table** for each process. The page table shows the frame location for each page of the process. Within the program, each logical address consists of a page number and a relative address within the page. Recall that in the case of simple partitioning, a logical address is the location of a word relative to the beginning of the program; the processor translates that into a physical address. With paging, the logical-to-physical address translation is still done by processor hardware. The processor must know how to access the page table of the current process. Presented with a logical address (page number, relative address), the processor uses the page table to produce a physical address (frame number, relative address). An example is shown in Figure 8.16.

This approach solves the problems raised earlier. Main memory is divided into many small equal-size frames. Each process is divided into frame-size pages: smaller processes require fewer pages, larger processes require more. When a process is brought in, its pages are loaded into available frames, and a page table is set up.

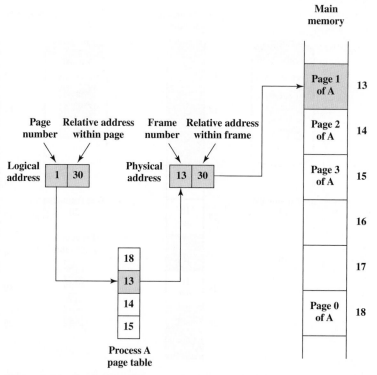

Figure 8.16 Logical and Physical Addresses

Virtual Memory

DEMAND PAGING With the use of paging, truly effective multiprogramming systems came into being. Furthermore, the simple tactic of breaking a process up into pages led to the development of another important concept: virtual memory.

To understand virtual memory, we must add a refinement to the paging scheme just discussed. That refinement is **demand paging**, which simply means that each page of a process is brought in only when it is needed, that is, on demand.

Consider a large process, consisting of a long program plus a number of arrays of data. Over any short period of time, execution may be confined to a small section of the program (e.g., a subroutine), and perhaps only one or two arrays of data are being used. This is the principle of locality, which we introduced in Appendix 4A. It would clearly be wasteful to load in dozens of pages for that process when only a few pages will be used before the program is suspended. We can make better use of memory by loading in just a few pages. Then, if the program branches to an instruction on a page not in main memory, or if the program references data on a page not in memory, a **page fault** is triggered. This tells the OS to bring in the desired page.

Thus, at any one time, only a few pages of any given process are in memory, and therefore more processes can be maintained in memory. Furthermore, time is saved because unused pages are not swapped in and out of memory. However, the OS must be clever about how it manages this scheme. When it brings one page in, it must throw another page out; this is known as **page replacement**. If it throws out a page just before it is about to be used, then it will just have to go get that page again almost immediately. Too much of this leads to a condition known as **thrashing**: the processor spends most of its time swapping pages rather than executing instructions. The avoidance of thrashing was a major research area in the 1970s and led to a variety of complex but effective algorithms. In essence, the OS tries to guess, based on recent history, which pages are least likely to be used in the near future.

Page Replacement Algorithm Simulators

A discussion of page replacement algorithms is beyond the scope of this chapter. A potentially effective technique is least recently used (LRU), the same algorithm discussed in Chapter 4 for cache replacement. In practice, LRU is difficult to implement for a virtual memory paging scheme. Several alternative approaches that seek to approximate the performance of LRU are in use; see Appendix F for details.

With demand paging, it is not necessary to load an entire process into main memory. This fact has a remarkable consequence: *It is possible for a process to be larger than all of main memory.* One of the most fundamental restrictions in programming has been lifted. Without demand paging, a programmer must be acutely aware of how much memory is available. If the program being written is too large, the programmer must devise ways to structure the program into pieces that can be loaded one at a time. With demand paging, that job is left to the OS and the hardware. As far as the programmer is concerned, he or she is dealing with a huge memory, the size associated with disk storage.

Because a process executes only in main memory, that memory is referred to as **real memory**. But a programmer or user perceives a much larger memory—that which is allocated on the disk. This latter is therefore referred to as **virtual memory**. Virtual memory allows for very effective multiprogramming and relieves the user of the unnecessarily tight constraints of main memory.

PAGE TABLE STRUCTURE The basic mechanism for reading a word from memory involves the translation of a virtual, or logical, address, consisting of page number and offset, into a physical address, consisting of frame number and offset, using a page table. Because the page table is of variable length, depending on the size of the process, we cannot expect to hold it in registers. Instead, it must be in main memory to be accessed. Figure 8.16 suggests a hardware implementation of this scheme. When a particular process is running, a register holds the starting address of the page table for that process. The page number of a virtual address is used to index that table and look up the corresponding frame number. This is combined with the offset portion of the virtual address to produce the desired real address.

In most systems, there is one page table per process. But each process can occupy huge amounts of virtual memory. For example, in the VAX architecture, each process can have up to $2^{31} = 2$ GBytes of virtual memory. Using $2^9 = 512$-byte pages, that means that as many as 2^{22} page table entries are required *per process*. Clearly, the amount of memory devoted to page tables alone could be unacceptably high. To overcome this problem, most virtual memory schemes store page tables in virtual memory rather than real memory. This means that page tables are subject to paging just as other pages are. When a process is running, at least a part of its page table must be in main memory, including the page table entry of the currently executing page. Some processors make use of a two-level scheme to organize large page tables. In this scheme, there is a page directory, in which each entry points to a page table. Thus, if the length of the page directory is X, and if the maximum length of a page table is Y, then a process can consist of up to $X \times Y$ pages. Typically, the maximum length of a page table is restricted to be equal to one page. We will see an example of this two-level approach when we consider the Pentium II later in this chapter.

An alternative approach to the use of one- or two-level page tables is the use of an inverted page table structure (Figure 8.17). Variations on this approach are used on the PowerPC, UltraSPARC, and the IA-64 architecture. An implementation of the Mach OS on the RT-PC also uses this technique.

In this approach, the page number portion of a virtual address is mapped into a hash value using a simple hashing function.[2] The hash value is a pointer to

---

[2] A hash function maps numbers in the range 0 through M into numbers in the range 0 through N, where $M > N$. The output of the hash function is used as an index into the hash table. Since more than one input maps into the same output, it is possible for an input item to map to a hash table entry that is already occupied. In that case, the new item must *overflow* into another hash table location. Typically, the new item is placed in the first succeeding empty space, and a pointer from the original location is provided to chain the entries together. See Appendix C for more information on hash functions.

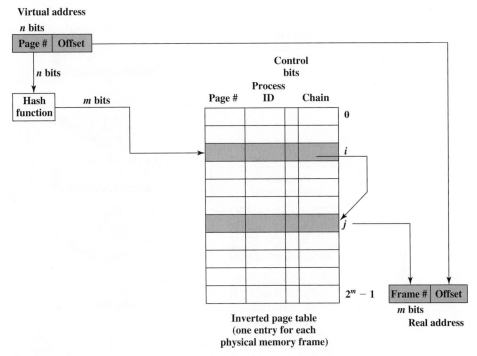

Figure 8.17   Inverted Page Table Structure

the inverted page table, which contains the page table entries. There is one entry in the inverted page table for each real memory page frame rather than one per virtual page. Thus a fixed proportion of real memory is required for the tables regardless of the number of processes or virtual pages supported. Because more than one virtual address may map into the same hash table entry, a chaining technique is used for managing the overflow. The hashing technique results in chains that are typically short—between one and two entries. The page table's structure is called *inverted* because it indexes page table entries by frame number rather than by virtual page number.

Translation Lookaside Buffer

In principle, then, every virtual memory reference can cause two physical memory accesses: one to fetch the appropriate page table entry, and one to fetch the desired data. Thus, a straightforward virtual memory scheme would have the effect of doubling the memory access time. To overcome this problem, most virtual memory schemes make use of a special cache for page table entries, usually called a translation lookaside buffer (TLB). This cache functions in the same way as a memory cache and contains those page table entries that have been most recently used. Figure 8.18 is a flowchart that shows the use of the TLB. By the principle of locality, most virtual memory references will be to locations in recently used pages. Therefore, most references will involve page table entries in the cache. Studies of the VAX TLB have shown that this scheme can significantly improve performance [CLAR85, SATY81].

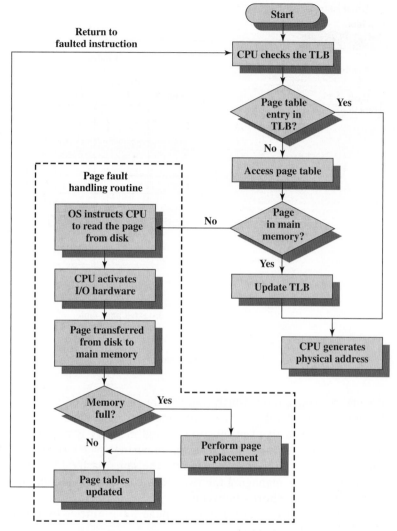

Figure 8.18 Operation of Paging and Translation Lookaside Buffer (TLB)

Note that the virtual memory mechanism must interact with the cache system (not the TLB cache, but the main memory cache). This is illustrated in Figure 8.19. A virtual address will generally be in the form of a page number, offset. First, the memory system consults the TLB to see if the matching page table entry is present. If it is, the real (physical) address is generated by combining the frame number with the offset. If not, the entry is accessed from a page table. Once the real address is generated, which is in the form of a tag and a remainder, the cache is consulted to see if the block containing that word is present (see Figure 4.5). If so, it is returned to the processor. If not, the word is retrieved from main memory.

The reader should be able to appreciate the complexity of the processor hardware involved in a single memory reference. The virtual address is translated into a

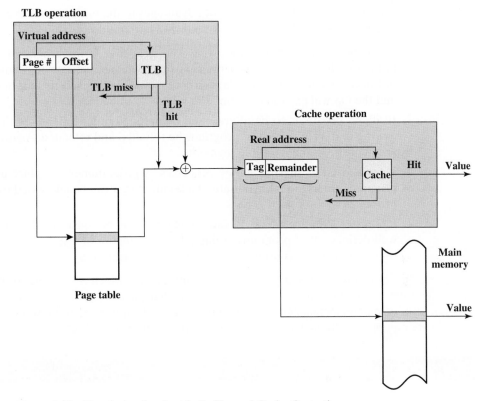

Figure 8.19   Translation Lookaside Buffer and Cache Operation

real address. This involves reference to a page table, which may be in the TLB, in main memory, or on disk. The referenced word may be in cache, in main memory, or on disk. In the latter case, the page containing the word must be loaded into main memory and its block loaded into the cache. In addition, the page table entry for that page must be updated.

Segmentation

There is another way in which addressable memory can be subdivided, known as *segmentation*. Whereas paging is invisible to the programmer and serves the purpose of providing the programmer with a larger address space, segmentation is usually visible to the programmer and is provided as a convenience for organizing programs and data and as a means for associating privilege and protection attributes with instructions and data.

Segmentation allows the programmer to view memory as consisting of multiple address spaces or segments. Segments are of variable, indeed dynamic, size. Typically, the programmer or the OS will assign programs and data to different segments. There may be a number of program segments for various types of programs as well as a number of data segments. Each segment may be assigned access and usage rights. Memory references consist of a (segment number, offset) form of address.

This organization has a number of advantages to the programmer over a non-segmented address space:

1. It simplifies the handling of growing data structures. If the programmer does not know ahead of time how large a particular data structure will become, it is not necessary to guess. The data structure can be assigned its own segment, and the OS will expand or shrink the segment as needed.

2. It allows programs to be altered and recompiled independently without requiring that an entire set of programs be relinked and reloaded. Again, this is accomplished using multiple segments.

3. It lends itself to sharing among processes. A programmer can place a utility program or a useful table of data in a segment that can be addressed by other processes.

4. It lends itself to protection. Because a segment can be constructed to contain a well-defined set of programs or data, the programmer or a system administrator can assign access privileges in a convenient fashion.

These advantages are not available with paging, which is invisible to the programmer. On the other hand, we have seen that paging provides for an efficient form of memory management. To combine the advantages of both, some systems are equipped with the hardware and OS software to provide both.

8.4   PENTIUM MEMORY MANAGEMENT

Since the introduction of the 32-bit architecture, microprocessors have evolved sophisticated memory management schemes that build on the lessons learned with medium- and large-scale systems. In many cases, the microprocessor versions are superior to their larger-system antecedents. Because the schemes were developed by the microprocessor hardware vendor and may be employed with a variety of operating systems, they tend to be quite general purpose. A representative example is the scheme used on the Pentium II. The Pentium II memory management hardware is essentially the same as that used in the Intel 80386 and 80486 processors, with some refinements.

Address Spaces

The Pentium II includes hardware for both segmentation and paging. Both mechanisms can be disabled, allowing the user to choose from four distinct views of memory:

- **Unsegmented unpaged memory:** In this case, the virtual address is the same as the physical address. This is useful, for example, in low-complexity, high-performance controller applications.

- **Unsegmented paged memory:** Here memory is viewed as a paged linear address space. Protection and management of memory is done via paging. This is favored by some operating systems (e.g., Berkeley UNIX).

- **Segmented unpaged memory:** Here memory is viewed as a collection of logical address spaces. The advantage of this view over a paged approach is that it affords protection down to the level of a single byte, if necessary. Furthermore, unlike paging, it guarantees that the translation table needed (the segment table) is on-chip when the segment is in memory. Hence, segmented unpaged memory results in predictable access times.

- **Segmented paged memory:** Segmentation is used to define logical memory partitions subject to access control, and paging is used to manage the allocation of memory within the partitions. Operating systems such as UNIX System V favor this view.

Segmentation

When segmentation is used, each virtual address (called a logical address in the Pentium II documentation) consists of a 16-bit segment reference and a 32-bit offset. Two bits of the segment reference deal with the protection mechanism, leaving 14 bits for specifying a particular segment. Thus, with unsegmented memory, the user's virtual memory is $2^{32} = 4$ GBytes. With segmented memory, the total virtual memory space as seen by a user is $2^{46} = 64$ terabytes (TBytes). The physical address space employs a 32-bit address for a maximum of 4 GBytes.

The amount of virtual memory can actually be larger than the 64 TBytes. This is because the processor's interpretation of a virtual address depends on which process is currently active. Virtual address space is divided into two parts. One-half of the virtual address space (8K segments $\times$ 4 GBytes) is global, shared by all processes; the remainder is local and is distinct for each process.

Associated with each segment are two forms of protection: privilege level and access attribute. There are four privilege levels, from most protected (level 0) to least protected (level 3). The privilege level associated with a data segment is its "classification"; the privilege level associated with a program segment is its "clearance." An executing program may only access data segments for which its clearance level is lower than (more privileged) or equal to (same privilege) the privilege level of the data segment.

The hardware does not dictate how these privilege levels are to be used; this depends on the OS design and implementation. It was intended that privilege level 1 would be used for most of the OS, and level 0 would be used for that small portion of the OS devoted to memory management, protection, and access control. This leaves two levels for applications. In many systems, applications will reside at level 3, with level 2 being unused. Specialized application subsystems that must be protected because they implement their own security mechanisms are good candidates for level 2. Some examples are database management systems, office automation systems, and software engineering environments.

In addition to regulating access to data segments, the privilege mechanism limits the use of certain instructions. Some instructions, such as those dealing with memory-management registers, can only be executed in level 0. I/O instructions can only be executed up to a certain level that is designated by the OS; typically, this will be level 1.

The access attribute of a data segment specifies whether read/write or read-only accesses are permitted. For program segments, the access attribute specifies read/execute or read-only access.

The address translation mechanism for segmentation involves mapping a virtual address into what is referred to as a linear address (Figure 8.20b). A virtual

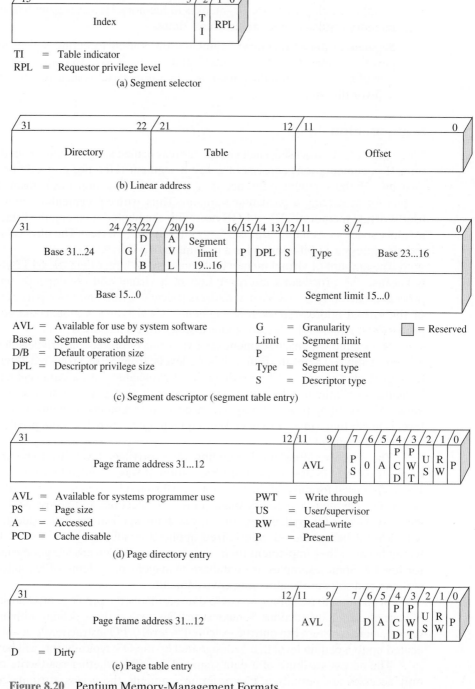

TI   = Table indicator
RPL = Requestor privilege level

(a) Segment selector

(b) Linear address

AVL = Available for use by system software
Base = Segment base address
D/B = Default operation size
DPL = Descriptor privilege size

G   = Granularity
Limit = Segment limit
P   = Segment present
Type = Segment type
S   = Descriptor type

☐ = Reserved

(c) Segment descriptor (segment table entry)

AVL = Available for systems programmer use
PS   = Page size
A   = Accessed
PCD = Cache disable

PWT = Write through
US   = User/supervisor
RW = Read–write
P   = Present

(d) Page directory entry

D   = Dirty

(e) Page table entry

Figure 8.20   Pentium Memory-Management Formats

address consists of the 32-bit offset and a 16-bit segment selector (Figure 8.20a). The segment selector consists of the following fields:

- **Table Indicator (TI):** Indicates whether the global segment table or a local segment table should be used for translation.
- **Segment Number:** The number of the segment. This serves as an index into the segment table.
- **Requested Privilege Level (RPL):** The privilege level requested for this access.

Each entry in a segment table consists of 64 bits, as shown in Figure 8.20c. The fields are defined in Table 8.5.

Paging

Segmentation is an optional feature and may be disabled. When segmentation is in use, addresses used in programs are virtual addresses and are converted into linear addresses, as just described. When segmentation is not in use, linear addresses are used in programs. In either case, the following step is to convert that linear address into a real 32-bit address.

To understand the structure of the linear address, you need to know that the Pentium II paging mechanism is actually a two-level table lookup operation. The first level is a page directory, which contains up to 1024 entries. This splits the 4-GByte linear memory space into 1024 page groups, each with its own page table, and each 4 MBytes in length. Each page table contains up to 1024 entries; each entry corresponds to a single 4-KByte page. Memory management has the option of using one page directory for all processes, one page directory for each process, or some combination of the two. The page directory for the current task is always in main memory. Page tables may be in virtual memory.

Figure 8.20 shows the formats of entries in page directories and page tables, and the fields are defined in Table 8.5. Note that access control mechanisms can be provided on a page or page group basis.

The Pentium II also makes use of a translation lookaside buffer. The buffer can hold 32 page table entries. Each time that the page directory is changed, the buffer is cleared.

Figure 8.21 illustrates the combination of segmentation and paging mechanisms. For clarity, the translation lookaside buffer and memory cache mechanisms are not shown.

Finally, the Pentium II includes a new extension not found on the 80386 or 80486, the provision for two page sizes. If the PSE (page size extension) bit in control register 4 is set to 1, then the paging unit permits the OS programmer to define a page as either 4 KByte or 4 MByte in size.

When 4-MByte pages are used, there is only one level of table lookup for pages. When the hardware accesses the page directory, the page directory entry (Figure 8.20d) has the PS bit set to 1. In this case, bits 9 through 21 are ignored and bits 22 through 31 define the base address for a 4-MByte page in memory. Thus, there is a single page table.

Table 8.5 Pentium II Memory Management Parameters

Segment Descriptor (Segment Table Entry)

Base

Defines the starting address of the segment within the 4-GByte linear address space.

D/B bit

In a code segment, this is the D bit and indicates whether operands and addressing modes are 16 or 32 bits.

Descriptor Privilege Level (DPL)

Specifies the privilege level of the segment referred to by this segment descriptor.

Granularity bit (G)

Indicates whether the Limit field is to be interpreted in units by one byte or 4 KBytes.

Limit

Defines the size of the segment. The processor interprets the limit field in one of two ways, depending on the granularity bit: in units of one byte, up to a segment size limit of 1 MByte, or in units of 4 KBytes, up to a segment size limit of 4 GBytes.

S bit

Determines whether a given segment is a system segment or a code or data segment.

Segment Present bit (P)

Used for nonpaged systems. It indicates whether the segment is present in main memory. For paged systems, this bit is always set to 1.

Type

Distinguishes between various kinds of segments and indicates the access attributes.

Page Directory Entry and Page Table Entry

Accessed bit (A)

This bit is set to 1 by the processor in both levels of page tables when a read or write operation to the corresponding page occurs.

Dirty bit (D)

This bit is set to 1 by the processor when a write operation to the corresponding page occurs.

Page Frame Address

Provides the physical address of the page in memory if the present bit is set. Since page frames are aligned on 4K boundaries, the bottom 12 bits are 0, and only the top 20 bits are included in the entry. In a page directory, the address is that of a page table.

Page Cache Disable bit (PCD)

Indicates whether data from page may be cached.

Page Size bit (PS)

Indicates whether page size is 4 KByte or 4 MByte.

Page Write Through bit (PWT)

Indicates whether write-through or write-back caching policy will be used for data in the corresponding page.

Present bit (P)

Indicates whether the page table or page is in main memory.

Read/Write bit (RW)

For user-level pages, indicates whether the page is read-only access or read/write access for user-level programs.

User/Supervisor bit (US)

Indicates whether the page is available only to the operating system (supervisor level) or is available to both operating system and applications (user level).

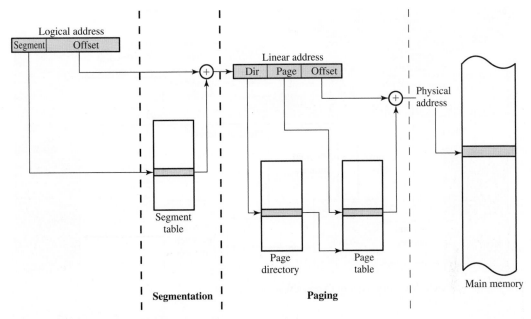

Figure 8.21 Pentium Memory Address Translation Mechanisms

The use of 4-MByte pages reduces the memory-management storage requirements for large main memories. With 4-KByte pages, a full 4-GByte main memory
requires about 4 MBytes of memory just for the page tables. With 4-MByte pages, a
single table, 4 KBytes in length, is sufficient for page memory management.

8.5 ARM MEMORY MANAGEMENT

ARM provides a versatile virtual memory system architecture that can be tailored
to the needs of the embedded system designer.

Memory System Organization

Figure 8.22 provides an overview of the memory management hardware in the
ARM for virtual memory. The virtual memory translation hardware uses one or two
levels of tables for translation from virtual to physical addresses, as explained subsequently. The translation lookaside buffer (TLB) is a cache of recent page table entries. If an entry is available in the TLB, then the TLB directly sends a physical
address to main memory for a read or write operation. As explained in Chapter 4,
data is exchanged between the processor and main memory via the cache. If a logical cache organization is used (Figure 4.7a), then the ARM supplies that address directly to the cache as well as supplying it to the TLB when a cache miss occurs. If a
physical cache organization is used (Figure 4.7b), then the TLB must supply the
physical address to the cache.

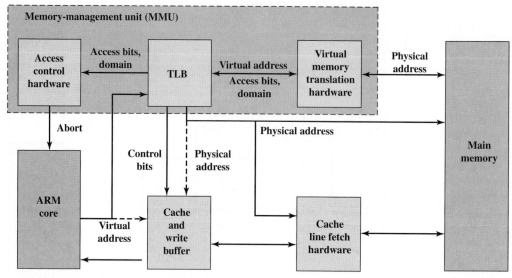

Figure 8.22   ARM Memory System Overview

Entries in the translation tables also include access control bits, which deter-mine whether a given process may access a given portion of memory. If access is de-nied, access control hardware supplies an abort signal to the ARM processor.

Virtual Memory Address Translation

The ARM supports memory access based on either sections or pages:

- **Supersections (optional):** Consist of 16-MB blocks of main memory
- **Sections:** Consist of 1-MB blocks of main memory
- **Large pages:** Consist of 64-KB blocks of main memory
- **Small pages:** Consist of 4-KB blocks of main memory

Sections and supersections are supported to allow mapping of a large re-gion of memory while using only a single entry in the TLB. Additional access con-trol mechanisms are extended within small pages to 1KB subpages, and within large pages to 16KB subpages. The translation table held in main memory has two levels:

- **First-level table:** Holds section and supersection translations, and pointers to second-level tables
- **Second-level tables:** Hold both large and small page translations

The memory-management unit (MMU) translates virtual addresses generated by the processor into physical addresses to access main memory, and also derives and checks the access permission. Translations occur as the result of a TLB miss, and start with a first-level fetch. A section-mapped access only requires a first-level fetch, whereas a page-mapped access also requires a second-level fetch.

Figure 8.23 shows the two-level address translation process for small pages. There is a single level 1 (L1) page table with 4K 32-bit entries. Each L1 entry points

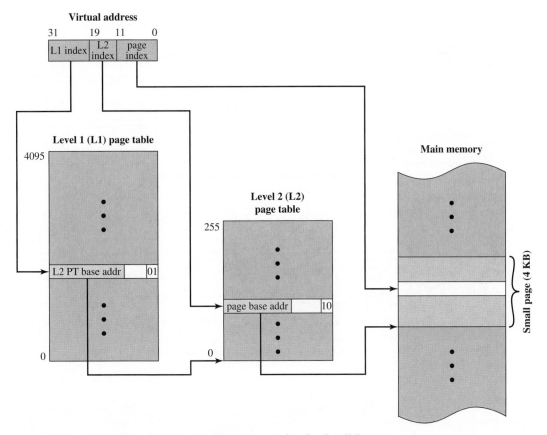

Figure 8.23 ARM Virtual Memory Address Translation for Small Pages

to a level 2 (L2) page table with 255 32-bit entries. Each of the L2 entry points to a 4-KB page in main memory. The 32-bit virtual address is interpreted as follows: The most significant 12 bits are an index into the L1 page table. The next 8 bits are an index into the relevant L2 page table. The least significant 12 bits index a byte in the relevant page in main memory.

A similar two-page lookup procedure is used for large pages. For sections and supersection, only the L1 page table lookup is required.

Memory-Management Formats

To get a better understanding of the ARM memory management scheme, we consider the key formats, as shown in Figure 8.24. The control bits shown in this figure are defined in Table 8.6.

For the L1 table, each entry is a descriptor of how its associated 1-MB virtual address range is mapped. Each entry has one of four alternative formats:

- **Bits [1:0] = 00:** The associated virtual addresses are unmapped, and attempts to access them generate a translation fault.
- **Bits [1:0] = 01:** The entry gives the physical address of an L2 page table, which specifies how the associated virtual address range is mapped.

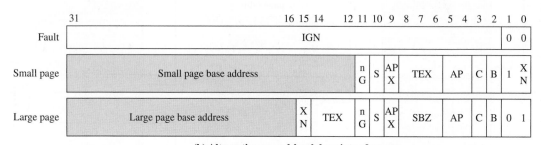

(a) Alternative first-level descriptor formats

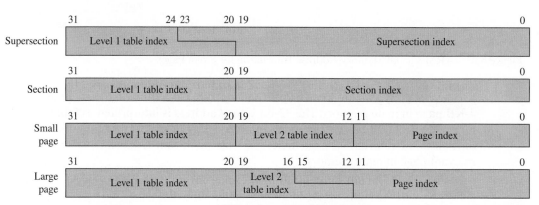

(b) Alternative second-level descriptor formats

(c) Virtual memory address formats

Figure 8.24 ARMv6 Memory-Management Formats

- **Bits [1:0] = 01 and bit 19 = 0:** The entry is a section descriptor for its associated virtual addresses.

- **Bits [1:0] = 01 and bit 19 = 1:** The entry is a supersection descriptor for its associated virtual addresses.

Entries with bits [1:0] = 11 are reserved.

For memory structured into pages, a two-level page table access is required. Bits [31:10] of the L1 page entry contain a pointer to a L1 page table. For small

Table 8.6   ARM Memory-Management Parameters

Access Permission (AP), Access Permission Extension (APX)
   These bits control access to the corresponding memory region. If an access is made to an area of memory without the required permissions, a Permission Fault is raised.

Bufferable (B) bit
   Determines, with the TEX bits, how the write buffer is used for cacheable memory.

Cacheable (C) bit
   Determines whether this memory region can be mapped through the cache.

Domain
   Collection of memory regions. Access control can be applied on the basis of domain.

not Global (nG)
   Determines whether the translation should be marked as global (0), or process specific (1).

Shared (S)
   Determines whether the translation is for not-shared (0), or shared (1) memory.

SBZ
   Should be zero.

Type Extension (TEX)
   These bits, together with the B and C bits, control accesses to the caches, how the write buffer is used, and if the memory region is shareable and therefore must be kept coherent.

Execute Never (XN)
   Determines whether the region is executable (0) or not executable (1).

---

pages, the L2 entry contains a 20-bit pointer to the base address of a 4-KB page in main memory.

   For large pages, the structure is more complex. As with virtual addresses for small pages, a virtual address for a large page structure includes a 12-bit index into the level one table and an 8-bit index into the L2 table. For the 64-KB large pages, the page index portion of the virtual address must be 16 bits. To accommodate all of these bits in a 32-bit format, there is a 4-bit overlap between the page index field and the L2 table index field. ARM accommodates this overlap by requiring that each page table entry in a L2 page table that supports large pages be replicated 16 times. In effect, the size of the L2 page table is reduced from 256 entries to 16 entries, if all of the entries refer to large pages. However, a given L2 page can service a mixture of large and small pages, hence the need for the replication for large page entries.

   For memory structured into sections or supersections, a one-level page table access is required. For sections, bits [31:20] of the L1 entry contain a 12-bit pointer to the base of the 1-MB section in main memory.

   For supersections, bits [31:24] of the L1 entry contain an 8-bit pointer to the base of the 16-MB section in main memory. As with large pages, a page table entry replication is required. In the case of supersections, the L1 table index portion of the virtual address overlaps by 4 bits with the supersection index portion of the virtual address Therefore, 16 identical L1 page table entries are required.

   The range of physical address space can be expanded by up to eight additional address bits (bits [23:20] and [8:5]). The number of additional bits is implementation dependent. These additional bits can be interpreted as extending the size of physical memory by as much as a factor of $2^8 = 256$. Thus, physical memory may in fact be as much as 256 times as large as the memory space available to each individual process.

Access Control

The AP access control bits in each table entry control access to a region of memory by a given process. A region of memory can be designated as no access, read only, or read-write. Further, the region can be designated as privileged access only, reserved for use by the OS and not by applications.

ARM also employs the concept of a domain, which is a collection of sections and/or pages that have particular access permissions. The ARM architecture supports 16 domains. The domain feature allows multiple processes to use the same translation tables while maintaining some protection from each other.

Each page table entry and TLB entry contains a field that specifies which domain the entry is in. A 2-bit field in the Domain Access Control Register controls access to each domain. Each field allows the access to an entire domain to be enabled and disabled very quickly, so that whole memory areas can be swapped in and out of virtual memory very efficiently. Two kinds of domain access are supported:

- **Clients:** Users of domains (execute programs and access data) that must observe the access permissions of the individual sections and/or pages that make up that domain
- **Managers:** Control the behavior of the domain (the current sections and pages in the domain, and the domain access), and bypass the access permissions for table entries in that domain

One program can be a client of some domains, and a manager of some other domains, and have no access to the remaining domains. This allows very flexible memory protection for programs that access different memory resources.

8.6   RECOMMENDED READING AND WEB SITES

[STAL09] covers the topics of this chapter in detail.

> **STAL09**   Stallings, W. *Operating Systems, Internals and Design Principles, Sixth Edition.* Upper Saddle River, NJ: Prentice Hall, 2009.

Recommended Web sites:

- **Operating System Resource Center:** A useful collection of documents and papers on a wide range of OS topics
- **ACM Special Interest Group on Operating Systems:** Information on SIGOPS publications and conferences
- **IEEE Technical Committee on Operating Systems and Applications:** Includes an online newsletter and links to other sites

Key Terms

batch system	multitasking	resident monitor
demand paging	nucleus	segmentation
interactive operating system	operating system (OS)	short-term scheduling
interrupt	paging	swapping
job control language (JCL)	page table	thrashing
kernel	partitioning	time-sharing system
logical address	physical address	translation lookaside buffer
long-term scheduling	privileged instruction	(TLB)
medium-term scheduling	process	utility
memory management	process control block	virtual memory
memory protection	process state	
multiprogramming	real memory	

Review Questions

8.1 What is an operating system?
8.2 List and briefly define the key services provided by an OS.
8.3 List and briefly define the major types of OS scheduling.
8.4 What is the difference between a process and a program?
8.5 What is the purpose of swapping?
8.6 If a process may be dynamically assigned to different locations in main memory, what is the implication for the addressing mechanism?
8.7 Is it necessary for all of the pages of a process to be in main memory while the process is executing?
8.8 Must the pages of a process in main memory be contiguous?
8.9 Is it necessary for the pages of a process in main memory to be in sequential order?
8.10 What is the purpose of a translation lookaside buffer?

Problems

8.1 Suppose that we have a multiprogrammed computer in which each job has identical characteristics. In one computation period, T, for a job, half the time is spent in I/O and the other half in processor activity. Each job runs for a total of N periods. Assume that a simple round-robin priority is used, and that I/O operations can overlap with processor operation. Define the following quantities:
  • Turnaround time = actual time to complete a job
  • Throughput = average number of jobs completed per time period T
  • Processor utilization = percentage of time that the processor is active (not waiting)
Compute these quantities for one, two, and four simultaneous jobs, assuming that the period T is distributed in each of the following ways:
  a. I/O first half, processor second half
  b. I/O first and fourth quarters, processor second and third quarters
8.2 An I/O-bound program is one that, if run alone, would spend more time waiting for I/O than using the processor. A processor-bound program is the opposite. Suppose a

short-term scheduling algorithm favors those programs that have used little processor time in the recent past. Explain why this algorithm favors I/O-bound programs and yet does not permanently deny processor time to processor-bound programs.

8.3 A program computes the row sums

$$C_i = \sum_{j=1}^{n} a_{ij}$$

of an array A that is 100 by 100. Assume that the computer uses demand paging with a page size of 1000 words, and that the amount of main memory allotted for data is five page frames. Is there any difference in the page fault rate if A were stored in virtual memory by rows or columns? Explain.

8.4 Consider a fixed partitioning scheme with equal-size partitions of 2^{16} bytes and a total main memory size of 2^{24} bytes. A process table is maintained that includes a pointer to a partition for each resident process. How many bits are required for the pointer?

8.5 Consider a dynamic partitioning scheme. Show that, on average, the memory contains half as many holes as segments.

8.6 Suppose the page table for the process currently executing on the processor looks like the following. All numbers are decimal, everything is numbered starting from zero, and all addresses are memory byte addresses. The page size is 1024 bytes.

Virtual page number	Valid bit	Reference bit	Modify bit	Page frame number
0	1	1	0	4
1	1	1	1	7
2	0	0	0	—
3	1	0	0	2
4	0	0	0	—
5	1	0	1	0

a. Describe exactly how, in general, a virtual address generated by the CPU is translated into a physical main memory address.
b. What physical address, if any, would each of the following virtual addresses correspond to? (Do not try to handle any page faults, if any.)
   (i) 1052
   (ii) 2221
   (iii) 5499

8.7 Give reasons that the page size in a virtual memory system should be neither very small nor very large.

8.8 A process references five pages, A, B, C, D, and E, in the following order:

A; B; C; D; A; B; E; A; B; C; D; E

Assume that the replacement algorithm is first-in-first-out and find the number of page transfers during this sequence of references starting with an empty main memory with three page frames. Repeat for four page frames.

8.9 The following sequence of virtual page numbers is encountered in the course of execution on a computer with virtual memory:

3 4 2 6 4 7 1 3 2 6 3 5 1 2 3

Assume that a least recently used page replacement policy is adopted. Plot a graph of page hit ratio (fraction of page references in which the page is in main memory) as a function of main-memory page capacity n for $1 \leq n \leq 8$. Assume that main memory is initially empty.

8.10 In the VAX computer, user page tables are located at virtual addresses in the system space. What is the advantage of having user page tables in virtual rather than main memory? What is the disadvantage?

8.11 Suppose the program statement

$$\textbf{for } (i = 1; i <= n; i++)$$
$$a[i] = b[i] + c[i];$$

is executed in a memory with page size of 1000 words. Let $n = 1000$. Using a machine that has a full range of register-to-register instructions and employs index registers, write a hypothetical program to implement the foregoing statement. Then show the sequence of page references during execution.

8.12 The IBM System/370 architecture uses a two-level memory structure and refers to the two levels as segments and pages, although the segmentation approach lacks many of the features described earlier in this chapter. For the basic 370 architecture, the page size may be either 2 Kbytes or 4 Kbytes, and the segment size is fixed at either 64 Kbytes or 1 MByte. For the 370/XA and 370/ESA architectures, the page size is 4 Kbytes and the segment size is 1 MByte. Which advantages of segmentation does this scheme lack? What is the benefit of segmentation for the 370?

8.13 Consider a computer system with both segmentation and paging. When a segment is in memory, some words are wasted on the last page. In addition, for a segment size s and a page size p, there are s/p page table entries. The smaller the page size, the less waste in the last page of the segment, but the larger the page table. What page size minimizes the total overhead?

8.14 A computer has a cache, main memory, and a disk used for virtual memory. If a referenced word is in the cache, 20 ns are required to access it. If it is in main memory but not in the cache, 60 ns are needed to load it into the cache, and then the reference is started again. If the word is not in main memory, 12 ms are required to fetch the word from disk, followed by 60 ns to copy it to the cache, and then the reference is started again. The cache hit ratio is 0.9 and the main-memory hit ratio is 0.6. What is the average time in ns required to access a referenced word on this system?

8.15 Assume a task is divided into four equal-sized segments and that the system builds an eight-entry page descriptor table for each segment. Thus, the system has a combination of segmentation and paging. Assume also that the page size is 2 KBytes.
  a. What is the maximum size of each segment?
  b. What is the maximum logical address space for the task?
  c. Assume that an element in physical location 00021ABC is accessed by this task. What is the format of the logical address that the task generates for it? What is the maximum physical address space for the system?

8.16 Assume a microprocessor capable of accessing up to 2^{32} bytes of physical main memory. It implements one segmented logical address space of maximum size 2^{31} bytes. Each instruction contains the whole two-part address. External memory management units (MMUs) are used, whose management scheme assigns contiguous blocks of physical memory of fixed size 2^{22} bytes to segments. The starting physical address of a segment is always divisible by 1024. Show the detailed interconnection of the external mapping mechanism that converts logical addresses to physical addresses using the appropriate number of MMUs, and show the detailed internal structure of an MMU (assuming that each MMU contains a 128-entry directly mapped segment descriptor cache) and how each MMU is selected.

8.17 Consider a paged logical address space (composed of 32 pages of 2 KBytes each) mapped into a 1-MByte physical memory space.
  a. What is the format of the processor's logical address?
  b. What is the length and width of the page table (disregarding the "access rights" bits)?
  c. What is the effect on the page table if the physical memory space is reduced by half?

8.18 In IBM's mainframe operating system, OS/390, one of the major modules in the kernel is the System Resource Manager (SRM). This module is responsible for the allocation of resources among address spaces (processes). The SRM gives OS/390 a degree of sophistication unique among operating systems. No other mainframe OS, and certainly no other type of OS, can match the functions performed by SRM. The concept of resource includes processor, real memory, and I/O channels. SRM accumulates statistics pertaining to utilization of processor, channel, and various key data structures. Its purpose is to provide optimum performance based on performance monitoring and analysis. The installation sets forth various performance objectives, and these serve as guidance to the SRM, which dynamically modifies installation and job performance characteristics based on system utilization. In turn, the SRM provides reports that enable the trained operator to refine the configuration and parameter settings to improve user service.

This problem concerns one example of SRM activity. Real memory is divided into equal-sized blocks called frames, of which there may be many thousands. Each frame can hold a block of virtual memory referred to as a page. SRM receives control approximately 20 times per second and inspects each and every page frame. If the page has not been referenced or changed, a counter is incremented by 1. Over time, SRM averages these numbers to determine the average number of seconds that a page frame in the system goes untouched. What might be the purpose of this and what action might SRM take?

8.19 For each of the ARM virtual address formats shown in Figure 8.24, show the physical address format.

8.20 Draw a figure similar to Figure 8.23 for ARM virtual memory translation when main memory is divided into sections.

PART THREE

The Central Processing Unit

Up to this point, we have viewed the processor essentially as a "black box" and have considered its interaction with I/O and memory. Part Three examines the internal structure and function of the processor. The processor consists of registers, the arithmetic and logic unit, the instruction execution unit, a control unit, and the interconnections among these components. Architectural issues, such as instruction set design and data types, are covered. The part also looks at organizational issues, such as pipelining.

ROAD MAP FOR PART THREE

Chapter 9 Computer Arithmetic

Chapter 9 examines the functionality of the arithmetic and logic unit (ALU) and focuses on the representation of numbers and techniques for implementing arithmetic operations. Processors typically support two types of arithmetic: integer, or fixed point, and floating point. For both cases, the chapter first examines the representation of numbers and then discusses arithmetic operations. The important IEEE 754 floating-point standard is examined in detail.

Chapter 10 Instruction Sets: Characteristics and Functions

From a programmer's point of view, the best way to understand the operation of a processor is to learn the machine instruction set that it executes. The complex topic of instruction set design occupies Chapters 10 and 11. Chapter 10 focuses on the functional aspects of instruction set design. The chapter examines the types of functions that are specified by computer instructions and then looks specifically at the types of operands (which specify the data to be operated on) and the types of operations (which specify the operations to be performed) commonly found in instruction sets. Then

303

the relationship of processor instructions to assembly language is briefly explained.

Chapter 11 Instruction Sets: Addressing Modes and Formats

Whereas Chapter 10 can be viewed as dealing with the semantics of instruction sets, Chapter 11 is more concerned with the syntax of instruction sets. Specifically, Chapter 11 looks at the way in which memory addresses are specified and at the overall format of computer instructions.

Chapter 12 Processor Structure and Function

Chapter 12 is devoted to a discussion of the internal structure and function of the processor. The chapter describes the use of registers as the CPU's internal memory and then pulls together all of the material covered so far to provide an overview of CPU structure and function. The overall organization (ALU, register file, control unit) is reviewed. Then the organization of the register file is discussed. The remainder of the chapter describes the functioning of the processor in executing machine instructions. The instruction cycle is examined to show the function and interrelationship of fetch, indirect, execute, and interrupt cycles. Finally, the use of pipelining to improve performance is explored in depth.

Chapter 13 Reduced Instruction Set Computers

The remainder of Part Three looks in more detail at the key trends in CPU design. Chapter 13 describes the approach associated with the concept of a reduced instruction set computer (RISC), which is one of the most significant innovations in computer organization and architecture in recent years. RISC architecture is a dramatic departure from the historical trend in processor architecture. An analysis of this approach brings into focus many of the important issues in computer organization and architecture. The chapter examines the motivation for the use of RISC design and then looks at the details of RISC instruction set design and RISC CPU architecture and compares RISC with the complex instruction set computer (CISC) approach.

Chapter 14 Instruction-Level Parallelism and Superscalar Processors

Chapter 14 examines an even more recent and equally important design innovation: the superscalar processor. Although superscalar technology can be used on any processor, it is especially well suited to a RISC architecture. The chapter also looks at the general issue of instruction-level parallelism.

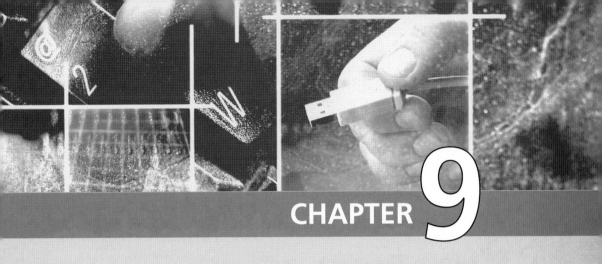

CHAPTER 9

COMPUTER ARITHMETIC

KEY POINTS

◆ The two principal concerns for computer arithmetic are the way in which numbers are represented (the binary format) and the algorithms used for the basic arithmetic operations (add, subtract, multiply, divide). These two considerations apply both to integer and floating-point arithmetic.

◆ Floating-point numbers are expressed as a number (significand) multiplied by a constant (base) raised to some integer power (exponent). Floating-point numbers can be used to represent very large and very small numbers.

◆ Most processors implement the IEEE 754 standard for floating-point representation and floating-point arithmetic. IEEE 754 defines both a 32-bit and a 64-bit format.

We begin our examination of the processor with an overview of the arithmetic and logic unit (ALU). The chapter then focuses on the most complex aspect of the ALU, computer arithmetic. The logic functions that are part of the ALU are described in Chapter 10, and implementations of simple logic and arithmetic functions in digital logic are described in Chapter 20.

Computer arithmetic is commonly performed on two very different types of numbers: integer and floating point. In both cases, the representation chosen is a crucial design issue and is treated first, followed by a discussion of arithmetic operations.

This chapter includes a number of examples, each of which is highlighted in a shaded box.

9.1   THE ARITHMETIC AND LOGIC UNIT

The ALU is that part of the computer that actually performs arithmetic and logical operations on data. All of the other elements of the computer system—control unit, registers, memory, I/O—are there mainly to bring data into the ALU for it to process and then to take the results back out. We have, in a sense, reached the core or essence of a computer when we consider the ALU.

An ALU and, indeed, all electronic components in the computer are based on the use of simple digital logic devices that can store binary digits and perform simple Boolean logic operations. For the interested reader, Chapter 20 explores digital logic implementation.

Figure 9.1 indicates, in general terms, how the ALU is interconnected with the rest of the processor. Data are presented to the ALU in registers, and the results of an operation are stored in registers. These registers are temporary storage locations within the processor that are connected by signal paths to the ALU (e.g., see Figure 2.3). The ALU may also set flags as the result of an operation. For example, an overflow flag is set to 1 if the result of a computation exceeds the length of the register into which it is to be stored. The flag values are also stored in registers

Figure 9.1   ALU Inputs and Outputs

within the processor. The control unit provides signals that control the operation of the ALU and the movement of the data into and out of the ALU.

9.2   INTEGER REPRESENTATION

In the binary number system,[1] arbitrary numbers can be represented with just the digits zero and one, the minus sign, and the period, or **radix point**.

$$-1101.0101_2 = -13.3125_{10}$$

For purposes of computer storage and processing, however, we do not have the benefit of minus signs and periods. Only binary digits (0 and 1) may be used to represent numbers. If we are limited to nonnegative integers, the representation is straightforward.

An 8-bit word can represent the numbers from 0 to 255, including

$$00000000 = \quad 0$$
$$00000001 = \quad 1$$
$$00101001 = \quad 41$$
$$10000000 = 128$$
$$11111111 = 255$$

In general, if an n-bit sequence of binary digits $a_{n-1}a_{n-2}\ldots a_1a_0$ is interpreted as an unsigned integer A, its value is

$$A = \sum_{i=0}^{n-1} 2^i a_i$$

---

[1]See Chapter 19 for a basic refresher on number systems (decimal, binary, hexadecimal).

Sign–Magnitude Representation

There are several alternative conventions used to represent negative as well as positive integers, all of which involve treating the most significant (leftmost) bit in the word as a sign bit. If the sign bit is 0, the number is positive; if the sign bit is 1, the number is negative.

The simplest form of representation that employs a sign bit is the sign-magnitude representation. In an n-bit word, the rightmost $n - 1$ bits hold the magnitude of the integer.

$$+ 18 \quad = 00010010$$
$$- 18 \quad = 10010010 \quad \text{(sign magnitude)}$$

The general case can be expressed as follows:

Sign Magnitude
$$A = \begin{cases} \sum_{i=0}^{n-2} 2^i a_i & \text{if } a_{n-1} = 0 \\ -\sum_{i=0}^{n-2} 2^i a_i & \text{if } a_{n-1} = 1 \end{cases} \tag{9.1}$$

There are several drawbacks to sign-magnitude representation. One is that addition and subtraction require a consideration of both the signs of the numbers and their relative magnitudes to carry out the required operation. This should become clear in the discussion in Section 9.3. Another drawback is that there are two representations of 0:

$$+0_{10} \quad = 00000000$$
$$-0_{10} \quad = 10000000 \quad \text{(sign magnitude)}$$

This is inconvenient because it is slightly more difficult to test for 0 (an operation performed frequently on computers) than if there were a single representation.

Because of these drawbacks, sign-magnitude representation is rarely used in implementing the integer portion of the ALU. Instead, the most common scheme is twos complement representation.[2]

Twos Complement Representation

Like sign magnitude, twos complement representation uses the most significant bit as a sign bit, making it easy to test whether an integer is positive or negative. It differs from the use of the sign-magnitude representation in the way that the other bits are interpreted. Table 9.1 highlights key characteristics of twos complement representation and arithmetic, which are elaborated in this section and the next.

Most treatments of twos complement representation focus on the rules for producing negative numbers, with no formal proof that the scheme "works." Instead,

---

[2]In the literature, the terms *two's complement* or *2's complement* are often used. Here we follow the practice used in standards documents and omit the apostrophe (e.g., IEEE Std 100-1992, *The New IEEE Standard Dictionary of Electrical and Electronics Terms*).

Table 9.1   Characteristics of Twos Complement Representation and Arithmetic

Range	-2^{n-1} through $2^{n-1} - 1$
Number of Representations of Zero	One
Negation	Take the Boolean complement of each bit of the corresponding positive number, then add 1 to the resulting bit pattern viewed as an unsigned integer.
Expansion of Bit Length	Add additional bit positions to the left and fill in with the value of the original sign bit.
Overflow Rule	If two numbers with the same sign (both positive or both negative) are added, then overflow occurs if and only if the result has the opposite sign.
Subtraction Rule	To subtract B from A, take the twos complement of B and add it to A.

our presentation of twos complement integers in this section and in Section 9.3 is based on [DATT93], which suggests that twos complement representation is best understood by defining it in terms of a weighted sum of bits, as we did previously for unsigned and sign-magnitude representations. The advantage of this treatment is that it does not leave any lingering doubt that the rules for arithmetic operations in twos complement notation may not work for some special cases.

Consider an n-bit integer, A, in twos complement representation. If A is positive, then the sign bit, a_{n-1}, is zero. The remaining bits represent the magnitude of the number in the same fashion as for sign magnitude:

$$A = \sum_{i=0}^{n-2} 2^i a_i \qquad \text{for } A \geq 0$$

The number zero is identified as positive and therefore has a 0 sign bit and a magnitude of all 0s. We can see that the range of positive integers that may be represented is from 0 (all of the magnitude bits are 0) through $2^{n-1} - 1$ (all of the magnitude bits are 1). Any larger number would require more bits.

Now, for a negative number A ($A < 0$), the sign bit, a_{n-1}, is one. The remaining $n - 1$ bits can take on any one of 2^{n-1} values. Therefore, the range of negative integers that can be represented is from -1 to -2^{n-1}. We would like to assign the bit values to negative integers in such a way that arithmetic can be handled in a straightforward fashion, similar to unsigned integer arithmetic. In unsigned integer representation, to compute the value of an integer from the bit representation, the weight of the most significant bit is $+2^{n-1}$. For a representation with a sign bit, it turns out that the desired arithmetic properties are achieved, as we will see in Section 9.3, if the weight of the most significant bit is -2^{n-1}. This is the convention used in twos complement representation, yielding the following expression for negative numbers:

$$\textbf{Twos Complement} \qquad A = -2^{n-1} a_{n-1} + \sum_{i=0}^{n-2} 2^i a_i \qquad \text{(9.2)}$$

Equation (9.2) defines the twos complement representation for both positive and negative numbers. For $a_{n-1} = 0$, the term $-2^{n-1} a_{n-1} = 0$ and the equation defines a

Table 9.2   Alternative Representations for 4-Bit Integers

Decimal Representation	Sign-Magnitude Representation	Twos Complement Representation	Biased Representation
+8	—	—	1111
+7	0111	0111	1110
+6	0110	0110	1101
+5	0101	0101	1100
+4	0100	0100	1011
+3	0011	0011	1010
+2	0010	0010	1001
+1	0001	0001	1000
+0	0000	0000	0111
−0	1000	—	—
−1	1001	1111	0110
−2	1010	1110	0101
−3	1011	1101	0100
−4	1100	1100	0011
−5	1101	1011	0010
−6	1110	1010	0001
−7	1111	1001	0000
−8	—	1000	—

nonnegative integer. When $a_{n-1} = 1$, the term 2^{n-1} is subtracted from the summation term, yielding a negative integer.

Table 9.2 compares the sign-magnitude and twos complement representations for 4-bit integers. Although twos complement is an awkward representation from the human point of view, we will see that it facilitates the most important arithmetic operations, addition and subtraction. For this reason, it is almost universally used as the processor representation for integers.

A useful illustration of the nature of twos complement representation is a value box, in which the value on the far right in the box is 1 (2^0) and each succeeding position to the left is double in value, until the leftmost position, which is negated. As you can see in Figure 9.2a, the most negative twos complement number that can be represented is -2^{n-1}; if any of the bits other than the sign bit is one, it adds a positive amount to the number. Also, it is clear that a negative number must have a 1 at its leftmost position and a positive number must have a 0 in that position. Thus, the largest positive number is a 0 followed by all 1s, which equals $2^{n-1} - 1$.

The rest of Figure 9.2 illustrates the use of the value box to convert from twos complement to decimal and from decimal to twos complement.

Converting between Different Bit Lengths

It is sometimes desirable to take an n-bit integer and store it in m bits, where $m > n$. In sign-magnitude notation, this is easily accomplished: simply move the sign bit to the new leftmost position and fill in with zeros.

−128	64	32	16	8	4	2	1

(a) An eight-position twos complement value box

−128	64	32	16	8	4	2	1
1	0	0	0	0	0	1	1

−128   +2   +1 = −125

(b) Convert binary 10000011 to decimal

−128	64	32	16	8	4	2	1
1	0	0	0	1	0	0	0

−120 = −128   +8

(c) Convert decimal −120 to binary

Figure 9.2 Use of a Value Box for Conversion between Twos Complement Binary and Decimal

+18	=		00010010	(sign magnitude, 8 bits)
+18	=		0000000000010010	(sign magnitude, 16 bits)
−18	=		10010010	(sign magnitude, 8 bits)
−18	=		1000000000010010	(sign magnitude, 16 bits)

This procedure will not work for twos complement negative integers. Using the same example,

+18	=		00010010	(twos complement, 8 bits)
+18	=		0000000000010010	(twos complement, 16 bits)
−18	=		11101110	(twos complement, 8 bits)
−32,658	=		1000000001101110	(twos complement, 16 bits)

The next to last line is easily seen using the value box of Figure 9.2. The last line can be verified using Equation (9.2) or a 16-bit value box.

Instead, the rule for twos complement integers is to move the sign bit to the new leftmost position and fill in with copies of the sign bit. For positive numbers, fill in with zeros, and for negative numbers, fill in with ones. This is called sign extension.

−18	=		11101110	(twos complement, 8 bits)
−18	=		1111111111101110	(twos complement, 16 bits)

To see why this rule works, let us again consider an n-bit sequence of binary digits $a_{n-1}a_{n-2} \dots a_1 a_0$ interpreted as a twos complement integer A, so that its value is

$$A = -2^{n-1}a_{n-1} + \sum_{i=0}^{n-2} 2^i a_i$$

If A is a positive number, the rule clearly works. Now, if A is negative and we want to construct an m-bit representation, with $m > n$. Then

$$A = -2^{m-1}a_{m-1} + \sum_{i=0}^{m-2} 2^i a_i$$

The two values must be equal:

$$-2^{m-1} + \sum_{i=0}^{m-2} 2^i a_i = -2^{n-1} + \sum_{i=0}^{n-2} 2^i a_i$$

$$-2^{m-1} + \sum_{i=n-1}^{m-2} 2^i a_i = -2^{n-1}$$

$$2^{n-1} + \sum_{i=n-1}^{m-2} 2^i a_i = 2^{m-1}$$

$$1 + \sum_{i=0}^{n-2} 2^i + \sum_{i=n-1}^{m-2} 2^i a_i = 1 + \sum_{i=0}^{m-2} 2^i$$

$$\sum_{i=n-1}^{m-2} 2^i a_i = \sum_{i=n-1}^{m-2} 2^i$$

$$\Rightarrow \quad a_{m-2} = \cdots = a_{n-2} = a_{n-1} = 1$$

In going from the first to the second equation, we require that the least significant $n - 1$ bits do not change between the two representations. Then we get to the next to last equation, which is only true if all of the bits in positions $n - 1$ through $m - 2$ are 1. Therefore, the sign-extension rule works. The reader may find the rule easier to grasp after studying the discussion on twos-complement negation at the beginning of Section 9.3.

Fixed-Point Representation

Finally, we mention that the representations discussed in this section are sometimes referred to as fixed point. This is because the radix point (binary point) is fixed and assumed to be to the right of the rightmost digit. The programmer can use the same representation for binary fractions by scaling the numbers so that the binary point is implicitly positioned at some other location.

9.3 INTEGER ARITHMETIC

This section examines common arithmetic functions on numbers in twos complement representation.

Negation

In sign-magnitude representation, the rule for forming the negation of an integer is simple: invert the sign bit. In twos complement notation, the negation of an integer can be formed with the following rules:

1. Take the Boolean complement of each bit of the integer (including the sign bit). That is, set each 1 to 0 and each 0 to 1.
2. Treating the result as an unsigned binary integer, add 1.

This two-step process is referred to as the **twos complement operation**, or the taking of the twos complement of an integer.

$$
\begin{array}{rcl}
+18 & = & 00010010 \ \text{(twos complement)} \\
\text{bitwise complement} & = & 11101101 \\
& + & \quad\quad\quad 1 \\
\hline
& & 11101110 = -18
\end{array}
$$

As expected, the negative of the negative of that number is itself:

$$
\begin{array}{rcl}
-18 & = & 11101110 \ \text{(twos complement)} \\
\text{bitwise complement} & = & 00010001 \\
& + & \quad\quad\quad 1 \\
\hline
& & 00010010 = +18
\end{array}
$$

We can demonstrate the validity of the operation just described using the definition of the twos complement representation in Equation (9.2). Again, interpret an n-bit sequence of binary digits $a_{n-1}a_{n-2}\ldots a_1 a_0$ as a twos complement integer A, so that its value is

$$
A = -2^{n-1}a_{n-1} + \sum_{i=0}^{n-2} 2^i a_i
$$

Now form the bitwise complement, $\overline{a_{n-1}}\,\overline{a_{n-2}}\ldots\overline{a_0}$, and, treating this is an unsigned integer, add 1. Finally, interpret the resulting n-bit sequence of binary digits as a twos complement integer B, so that its value is

$$
B = -2^{n-1}\overline{a_{n-1}} + 1 + \sum_{i=0}^{n-2} 2^i \overline{a_i}
$$

Now, we want $A = -B$, which means $A + B = 0$. This is easily shown to be true:

$$
A + B = -(a_{n-1} + \overline{a_{n-1}})2^{n-1} + 1 + \left(\sum_{i=0}^{n-2} 2^i (a_i + \overline{a_i}) \right)
$$

$$
= -2^{n-1} + 1 + \left(\sum_{i=0}^{n-2} 2^i \right)
$$

$$
= -2^{n-1} + 1 + (2^{n-1} - 1)
$$

$$
= -2^{n-1} + 2^{n-1} = 0
$$

The preceding derivation assumes that we can first treat the bitwise complement of A as an unsigned integer for the purpose of adding 1, and then treat the result as a twos complement integer. There are two special cases to consider. First, consider $A = 0$. In that case, for an 8-bit representation:

$$
\begin{array}{rcl}
0 & = & 00000000 \ (\text{twos complement}) \\
\text{bitwise complement} & = & 11111111 \\
+ & & 1 \\
\hline
& & 100000000 = 0
\end{array}
$$

There is *carry* out of the most significant bit position, which is ignored. The result is that the negation of 0 is 0, as it should be.

The second special case is more of a problem. If we take the negation of the bit pattern of 1 followed by $n - 1$ zeros, we get back the same number. For example, for 8-bit words,

$$
\begin{array}{rcl}
-128 & = & 10000000 \ (\text{twos complement}) \\
\text{bitwise complement} & = & 01111111 \\
+ & & 1 \\
\hline
& & 10000000 = -128
\end{array}
$$

Some such anomaly is unavoidable. The number of different bit patterns in an n-bit word is 2^n, which is an even number. We wish to represent positive and negative integers and 0. If an equal number of positive and negative integers are represented (sign magnitude), then there are two representations for 0. If there is only one representation of 0 (twos complement), then there must be an unequal number of negative and positive numbers represented. In the case of twos complement, for an n-bit length, there is a representation for -2^{n-1} but not for $+2^{n-1}$.

Addition and Subtraction

Addition in twos complement is illustrated in Figure 9.3. Addition proceeds as if the two numbers were unsigned integers. The first four examples illustrate successful operations. If the result of the operation is positive, we get a positive number in twos complement form, which is the same as in unsigned-integer form. If the result of the operation is negative, we get a negative number in twos complement form. Note that, in some instances, there is a carry bit beyond the end of the word (indicated by shading), which is ignored.

On any addition, the result may be larger than can be held in the word size being used. This condition is called **overflow**. When overflow occurs, the ALU must signal this fact so that no attempt is made to use the result. To detect overflow, the following rule is observed:

OVERFLOW RULE: If two numbers are added, and they are both positive or both negative, then overflow occurs if and only if the result has the opposite sign.

1001 = −7 +0101 = 5 1110 = −2 (a) (−7) + (+5)	1100 = −4 +0100 = 4 10000 = 0 (b) (−4) + (+4)
0011 = 3 +0100 = 4 0111 = 7 (c) (+3) + (+4)	1100 = −4 +1111 = −1 11011 = −5 (d) (−4) + (−1)
0101 = 5 +0100 = 4 1001 = Overflow (e) (+5) + (+4)	1001 = −7 +1010 = −6 10011 = Overflow (f) (−7) + (−6)

Figure 9.3 Addition of Numbers in Twos Complement Representation

Figures 9.3e and f show examples of overflow. Note that overflow can occur whether or not there is a carry.

Subtraction is easily handled with the following rule:

SUBTRACTION RULE: To subtract one number (subtrahend) from another (minuend), take the twos complement (negation) of the subtrahend and add it to the minuend.

Thus, subtraction is achieved using addition, as illustrated in Figure 9.4. The last two examples demonstrate that the overflow rule still applies.

0010 =   2
+1001 = −7
1011 = −5
 	
(a) M = 2 = 0010
    S = 7 = 0111
  −S =   1001
	0101 = 5
	+1110 = −2
	10011 = 3
	
	(b) M = 5 = 0101
	    S = 2 = 0010
	  −S = 1110

1011 = −5
+1110 = −2
11001 = −7
 	
(c) M = −5 = 1011
    S =   2 = 0010
  −S =   1110
	0101 = 5
	+0010 = 2
	0111 = 7
	
	(d) M = 5 = 0101
	    S = −2 = 1110
	  −S = 0010

0111 = 7
+0111 = 7
1110 = Overflow
 	
(e) M =   7 = 0111
    S = −7 = 1001
  −S =   0111
	1010 = −6
	+1100 = −4
	10110 = Overflow
	
	(f) M = −6 = 1010
	    S = 4 = 0100
	  −S = 1100

Figure 9.4 Subtraction of Numbers in Twos Complement Representation (M − S)

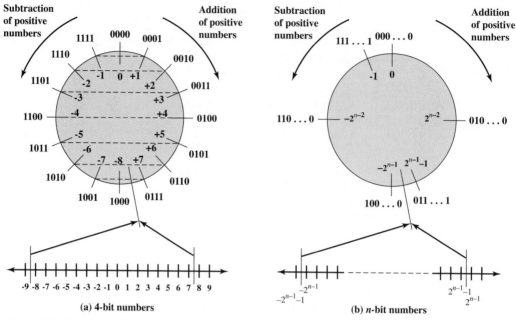

Figure 9.5 Geometric Depiction of Twos Complement Integers

Some insight into twos complement addition and subtraction can be gained by looking at a geometric depiction [BENH92], as shown in Figure 9.5. The circle in the upper half of each part of the figure is formed by selecting the appropriate segment of the number line and joining the endpoints. Note that when the numbers are laid out on a circle, the twos complement of any number is horizontally opposite that number (indicated by dashed horizontal lines). Starting at any number on the circle, we can add positive k (or subtract negative k) to that number by moving k positions clockwise, and we can subtract positive k (or add negative k) from that number by moving k positions counterclockwise. If an arithmetic operation results in traversal of the point where the endpoints are joined, an incorrect answer is given (overflow).

All of the examples of Figures 9.3 and 9.4 are easily traced in the circle of Figure 9.5.

Figure 9.6 suggests the data paths and hardware elements needed to accomplish addition and subtraction. The central element is a binary adder, which is presented two numbers for addition and produces a sum and an overflow indication. The binary adder treats the two numbers as unsigned integers. (A logic implementation of an adder is given in Chapter 20.) For addition, the two numbers are presented to the adder from two registers, designated in this case as A and B registers. The result may be stored in one of these registers or in a third. The overflow indication is stored in a 1-bit overflow flag (0 = no overflow; 1 = overflow). For subtraction, the subtrahend (B register) is passed through a twos complementer so that its twos complement is presented to the adder. Note that Figure 9.6 only shows the data paths. Control signals are needed to control whether or not the complementer is used, depending on whether the operation is addition or subtraction.

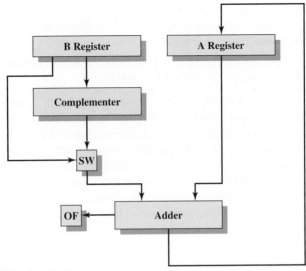

OF = Overflow bit
SW = Switch (select addition or subtraction)

Figure 9.6   Block Diagram of Hardware for Addition and Subtraction

Multiplication

Compared with addition and subtraction, multiplication is a complex operation, whether performed in hardware or software. A wide variety of algorithms have been used in various computers. The purpose of this subsection is to give the reader some feel for the type of approach typically taken. We begin with the simpler problem of multiplying two unsigned (nonnegative) integers, and then we look at one of the most common techniques for multiplication of numbers in twos complement representation.

UNSIGNED INTEGERS Figure 9.7 illustrates the multiplication of unsigned binary integers, as might be carried out using paper and pencil. Several important observations can be made:

1. Multiplication involves the generation of partial products, one for each digit in the multiplier. These partial products are then summed to produce the final product.
2. The partial products are easily defined. When the multiplier bit is 0, the partial product is 0. When the multiplier is 1, the partial product is the multiplicand.

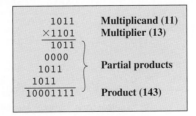

Figure 9.7   Multiplication of Unsigned Binary Integers

3. The total product is produced by summing the partial products. For this operation, each successive partial product is shifted one position to the left relative to the preceding partial product.

4. The multiplication of two n-bit binary integers results in a product of up to $2n$ bits in length (e.g., $11 \times 11 = 1001$).

Compared with the pencil-and-paper approach, there are several things we can do to make computerized multiplication more efficient. First, we can perform a running addition on the partial products rather than waiting until the end. This eliminates the need for storage of all the partial products; fewer registers are needed. Second, we can save some time on the generation of partial products. For each 1 on the multiplier, an add and a shift operation are required; but for each 0, only a shift is required.

Figure 9.8a shows a possible implementation employing these measures. The multiplier and multiplicand are loaded into two registers (Q and M). A third register,

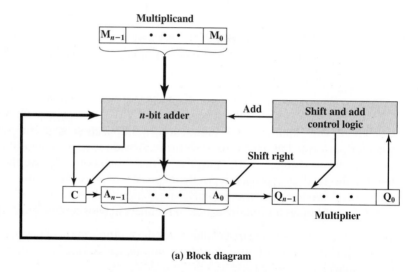

(a) Block diagram

C	A	Q	M		
0	0000	1101	1011	Initial values	
0	1011	1101	1011	Add	First
0	0101	1110	1011	Shift	cycle
0	0010	1111	1011	Shift	Second cycle
0	1101	1111	1011	Add	Third
0	0110	1111	1011	Shift	cycle
1	0001	1111	1011	Add	Fourth
0	1000	1111	1011	Shift	cycle

(b) Example from Figure 9.7 (product in A, Q)

Figure 9.8   Hardware Implementation of Unsigned Binary Multiplication

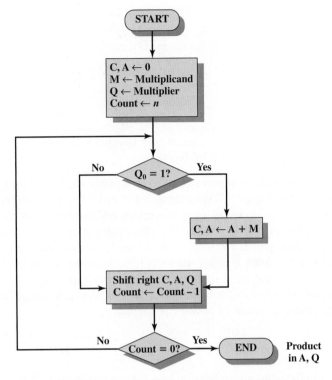

Figure 9.9 Flowchart for Unsigned Binary Multiplication

the A register, is also needed and is initially set to 0. There is also a 1-bit C register, initialized to 0, which holds a potential carry bit resulting from addition.

The operation of the multiplier is as follows. Control logic reads the bits of the multiplier one at a time. If Q_0 is 1, then the multiplicand is added to the A register and the result is stored in the A register, with the C bit used for overflow. Then all of the bits of the C, A, and Q registers are shifted to the right one bit, so that the C bit goes into A_{n-1}, A_0 goes into Q_{n-1}, and Q_0 is lost. If Q_0 is 0, then no addition is performed, just the shift. This process is repeated for each bit of the original multiplier. The resulting 2n-bit product is contained in the A and Q registers. A flowchart of the operation is shown in Figure 9.9, and an example is given in Figure 9.8b. Note that on the second cycle, when the multiplier bit is 0, there is no add operation.

TWOS COMPLEMENT MULTIPLICATION We have seen that addition and subtraction can be performed on numbers in twos complement notation by treating them as unsigned integers. Consider

$$
\begin{array}{r}
1001 \\
+0011 \\
\hline
1100
\end{array}
$$

If these numbers are considered to be unsigned integers, then we are adding 9 (1001) plus 3 (0011) to get 12 (1100). As twos complement integers, we are adding −7 (1001) to 3 (0011) to get −4 (1100).

```
        1011
      × 1101
    00001011    1011 × 1 × 2⁰
    00000000    1011 × 0 × 2¹
    00101100    1011 × 1 × 2²
    01011000    1011 × 1 × 2³
    10001111
```

Figure 9.10   Multiplication of Two
Unsigned 4-Bit Integers Yielding an
8-Bit Result

Unfortunately, this simple scheme will not work for multiplication. To see this, consider again Figure 9.7. We multiplied 11 (1011) by 13 (1101) to get 143 (10001111). If we interpret these as twos complement numbers, we have −5 (1011) times −3 (1101) equals −113 (10001111). This example demonstrates that straightforward multiplication will not work if both the multiplicand and multiplier are negative. In fact, it will not work if either the multiplicand or the multiplier is negative. To justify this statement, we need to go back to Figure 9.7 and explain what is being done in terms of operations with powers of 2. Recall that any unsigned binary number can be expressed as a sum of powers of 2. Thus,

$$1101 = 1 \times 2^3 + 1 \times 2^2 + 0 \times 2^1 + 1 \times 2^0$$
$$= 2^3 + 2^2 + 2^0$$

Further, the multiplication of a binary number by 2^n is accomplished by shifting that number to the left n bits. With this in mind, Figure 9.10 recasts Figure 9.7 to make the generation of partial products by multiplication explicit. The only difference in Figure 9.10 is that it recognizes that the partial products should be viewed as $2n$-bit numbers generated from the n-bit multiplicand.

Thus, as an unsigned integer, the 4-bit multiplicand 1011 is stored in an 8-bit word as 00001011. Each partial product (other than that for 2^0) consists of this number shifted to the left, with the unoccupied positions on the right filled with zeros (e.g., a shift to the left of two places yields 00101100).

Now we can demonstrate that straightforward multiplication will not work if the multiplicand is negative. The problem is that each contribution of the negative multiplicand as a partial product must be a negative number on a $2n$-bit field; the sign bits of the partial products must line up. This is demonstrated in Figure 9.11, which shows that multiplication of 1001 by 0011. If these are treated as unsigned integers, the multiplication of 9 × 3 = 27 proceeds simply. However, if 1001 is interpreted as

```
      1001  (9)                      1001  (−7)
    × 0011  (3)                    × 0011  (3)
    00001001  1001 × 2⁰            11111001  (−7) × 2⁰ = (−7)
    00010010  1001 × 2¹            11110010  (−7) × 2¹ = (−14)
    00011011  (27)                 11101011  (−21)
```

     (a) Unsigned integers   (b) Twos complement integers

Figure 9.11   Comparison of Multiplication of Unsigned and Twos
Complement Integers

the twos complement value -7, then each partial product must be a negative twos complement number of $2n$ (8) bits, as shown in Figure 9.11b. Note that this is accomplished by padding out each partial product to the left with binary 1s.

If the multiplier is negative, straightforward multiplication also will not work. The reason is that the bits of the multiplier no longer correspond to the shifts or multiplications that must take place. For example, the 4-bit decimal number -3 is written 1101 in twos complement. If we simply took partial products based on each bit position, we would have the following correspondence:

$$1101 \longleftrightarrow -(1 \times 2^3 + 1 \times 2^2 + 0 \times 2^1 + 1 \times 2^0) = -(2^3 + 2^2 + 2^0)$$

In fact, what is desired is $-(2^1 + 2^0)$. So this multiplier cannot be used directly in the manner we have been describing.

There are a number of ways out of this dilemma. One would be to convert both multiplier and multiplicand to positive numbers, perform the multiplication, and then take the twos complement of the result if and only if the sign of the two original numbers differed. Implementers have preferred to use techniques that do not require this final transformation step. One of the most common of these is Booth's algorithm. This algorithm also has the benefit of speeding up the multiplication process, relative to a more straightforward approach.

Booth's algorithm is depicted in Figure 9.12 and can be described as follows. As before, the multiplier and multiplicand are placed in the Q and M registers,

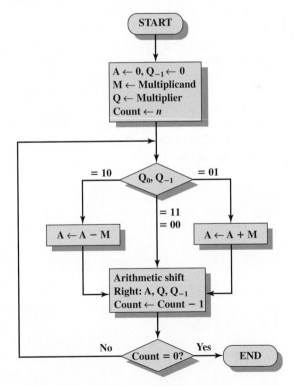

Figure 9.12 Booth's Algorithm for Twos Complement Multiplication

A	Q	Q_{-1}	M		
0000	0011	0	0111	Initial values	
1001	0011	0	0111	A ← A − M	First
1100	1001	1	0111	Shift	cycle
1110	0100	1	0111	Shift	Second cycle
0101	0100	1	0111	A ← A + M	Third
0010	1010	0	0111	Shift	cycle
0001	0101	0	0111	Shift	Fourth cycle

Figure 9.13 Example of Booth's Algorithm (7 × 3)

respectively. There is also a 1-bit register placed logically to the right of the least significant bit (Q_0) of the Q register and designated Q_{-1}; its use is explained shortly. The results of the multiplication will appear in the A and Q registers. A and Q_{-1} are initialized to 0. As before, control logic scans the bits of the multiplier one at a time. Now, as each bit is examined, the bit to its right is also examined. If the two bits are the same (1–1 or 0–0), then all of the bits of the A, Q, and Q_{-1} registers are shifted to the right 1 bit. If the two bits differ, then the multiplicand is added to or subtracted from the A register, depending on whether the two bits are 0–1 or 1–0. Following the addition or subtraction, the right shift occurs. In either case, the right shift is such that the leftmost bit of A, namely A_{n-1}, not only is shifted into A_{n-2}, but also remains in A_{n-1}. This is required to preserve the sign of the number in A and Q. It is known as an **arithmetic shift**, because it preserves the sign bit.

Figure 9.13 shows the sequence of events in Booth's algorithm for the multiplication of 7 by 3. More compactly, the same operation is depicted in Figure 9.14a. The rest of Figure 9.14 gives other examples of the algorithm. As can be seen, it works with any combination of positive and negative numbers. Note also the efficiency of the algorithm. Blocks of 1s or 0s are skipped over, with an average of only one addition or subtraction per block.

```
     0111                          0111
   × 0011    (0)                 × 1101    (0)
  11111001   1–0                11111001   1–0
  0000000    1–1                0000111    0–1
  000111     0–1                111001     1–0
  00010101   (21)               11101011   (−21)
```
(a) (7) × (3) = (21)   (b) (7) × (−3) = (−21)

```
     1001                          1001
   × 0011    (0)                 × 1101    (0)
  00000111   1–0                00000111   1–0
  0000000    1–1                1111001    0–1
  111001     0–1                000111     1–0
  11101011   (−21)              00010101   (21)
```
(c) (−7) × (3) = (−21)   (d) (−7) × (−3) = (21)

Figure 9.14 Examples Using Booth's Algorithm

Why does Booth's algorithm work? Consider first the case of a positive multiplier. In particular, consider a positive multiplier consisting of one block of 1s surrounded by 0s (for example, 00011110). As we know, multiplication can be achieved by adding appropriately shifted copies of the multiplicand:

$$M \times (00011110) = M \times (2^4 + 2^3 + 2^2 + 2^1)$$
$$= M \times (16 + 8 + 4 + 2)$$
$$= M \times 30$$

The number of such operations can be reduced to two if we observe that

$$2^n + 2^{n-1} + \cdots + 2^{n-K} = 2^{n+1} - 2^{n-K} \tag{9.3}$$

$$M \times (00011110) = M \times (2^5 - 2^1)$$
$$= M \times (32 - 2)$$
$$= M \times 30$$

So the product can be generated by one addition and one subtraction of the multiplicand. This scheme extends to any number of blocks of 1s in a multiplier, including the case in which a single 1 is treated as a block.

$$M \times (01111010) = M \times (2^6 + 2^5 + 2^4 + 2^3 + 2^1)$$
$$= M \times (2^7 - 2^3 + 2^2 - 2^1)$$

Booth's algorithm conforms to this scheme by performing a subtraction when the first 1 of the block is encountered (1–0) and an addition when the end of the block is encountered (0–1).

To show that the same scheme works for a negative multiplier, we need to observe the following. Let X be a negative number in twos complement notation:

$$\text{Representation of } X = \{1x_{n-2}x_{n-3} \ldots x_1 x_0\}$$

Then the value of X can be expressed as follows:

$$X = -2^{n-1} + (x_{n-2} \times 2^{n-2}) + (x_{n-3} \times 2^{n-3}) + \cdots + (x_1 \times 2^1) + (x_0 \times 2^0) \tag{9.4}$$

The reader can verify this by applying the algorithm to the numbers in Table 9.2.

The leftmost bit of X is 1, because X is negative. Assume that the leftmost 0 is in the kth position. Thus, X is of the form

$$\text{Representation of } X = \{111 \ldots 10x_{k-1}x_{k-2} \ldots x_1 x_0\} \tag{9.5}$$

Then the value of X is

$$X = -2^{n-1} + 2^{n-2} + \cdots + 2^{k+1} + (x_{k-1} \times 2^{k-1}) + \cdots + (x_0 \times 2^0) \tag{9.6}$$

From Equation (9.3), we can say that

$$2^{n-2} + 2^{n-3} + \cdots + 2^{k+1} = 2^{n-1} - 2^{k+1}$$

Rearranging

$$-2^{n-1} + 2^{n-2} + 2^{n-3} + \cdots + 2^{k+1} = -2^{k+1} \qquad \textbf{(9.7)}$$

Substituting Equation (9.7) into Equation (9.6), we have

$$X = -2^{k+1} + (x_{k-1} \times 2^{k-1}) + \cdots + (x_0 \times 2^0) \qquad \textbf{(9.8)}$$

At last we can return to Booth's algorithm. Remembering the representation of X [Equation (9.5)], it is clear that all of the bits from x_0 up to the leftmost 0 are handled properly because they produce all of the terms in Equation (9.8) but (-2^{k+1}) and thus are in the proper form. As the algorithm scans over the leftmost 0 and encounters the next 1 (2^{k+1}), a 1–0 transition occurs and a subtraction takes place (-2^{k+1}). This is the remaining term in Equation (9.8).

As an example, consider the multiplication of some multiplicand by (-6). In twos complement representation, using an 8-bit word, (-6) is represented as 11111010. By Equation (9.4), we know that

$$-6 = -2^7 + 2^6 + 2^5 + 2^4 + 2^3 + 2^1$$

which the reader can easily verify. Thus,

$$M \times (11111010) = M \times (-2^7 + 2^6 + 2^5 + 2^4 + 2^3 + 2^1)$$

Using Equation (9.7),

$$M \times (11111010) = M \times (-2^3 + 2^1)$$

which the reader can verify is still $M \times (-6)$. Finally, following our earlier line of reasoning,

$$M \times (11111010) = M \times (-2^3 + 2^2 - 2^1)$$

We can see that Booth's algorithm conforms to this scheme. It performs a subtraction when the first 1 is encountered (1–0), an addition when (01) is encountered, and finally another subtraction when the first 1 of the next block of 1s is encountered. Thus, Booth's algorithm performs fewer additions and subtractions than a more straightforward algorithm.

Division

Division is somewhat more complex than multiplication but is based on the same general principles. As before, the basis for the algorithm is the paper-and-pencil approach, and the operation involves repetitive shifting and addition or subtraction.

Figure 9.15 shows an example of the long division of unsigned binary integers. It is instructive to describe the process in detail. First, the bits of the dividend are examined from left to right, until the set of bits examined represents a number greater than or equal to the divisor; this is referred to as the divisor being able to divide the number. Until this event occurs, 0s are placed in the quotient from left to right. When the event occurs, a 1 is placed in the quotient and the divisor is subtracted from the partial dividend. The result is referred to as a *partial remainder*. From this point on,

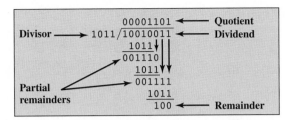

Figure 9.15 Example of Division of Unsigned Binary Integers

the division follows a cyclic pattern. At each cycle, additional bits from the dividend are appended to the partial remainder until the result is greater than or equal to the divisor. As before, the divisor is subtracted from this number to produce a new partial remainder. The process continues until all the bits of the dividend are exhausted.

Figure 9.16 shows a machine algorithm that corresponds to the long division process. The divisor is placed in the M register, the dividend in the Q register. At each

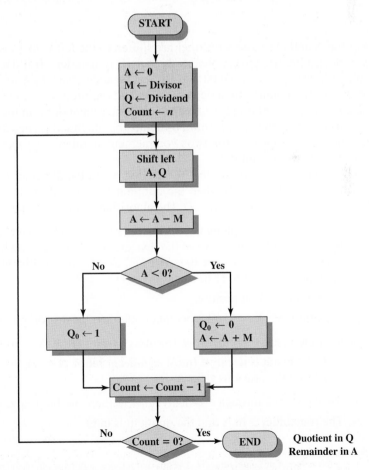

Figure 9.16 Flowchart for Unsigned Binary Division

A	Q	
0000	0111	Initial value
0000	1110	Shift
1101		Use twos complement of 0011 for subtraction
1101		Subtract
0000	1110	Restore, set $Q_0 = 0$
0001	1100	Shift
1101		
1110		Subtract
0001	1100	Restore, set $Q_0 = 0$
0011	1000	Shift
1101		
0000	1001	Subtract, set $Q_0 = 1$
0001	0010	Shift
1101		
1110		Subtract
0001	0010	Restore, set $Q_0 = 0$

Figure 9.17   Example of Restoring Twos Complement Division (7/3)

step, the A and Q registers together are shifted to the left 1 bit. M is subtracted from A to determine whether A divides the partial remainder.[3] If it does, then Q_0 gets a 1 bit. Otherwise, Q_0 gets a 0 bit and M must be added back to A to restore the previous value. The count is then decremented, and the process continues for n steps. At the end, the quotient is in the Q register and the remainder is in the A register.

This process can, with some difficulty, be extended to negative numbers. We give here one approach for twos complement numbers. An example of this approach is shown in Figure 9.17.

The algorithm assumes that the divisor V and the dividend D are positive and that $|V| < |D|$. If $|V| = |D|$, then the quotient $Q = 1$ and the remainder $R = 0$. If $|V| > |D|$, then $Q = 0$ and $R = D$. The algorithm can be summarized as follows:

1. Load the twos complement of the divisor into the M register; that is, the M register contains the negative of the divisor. Load the dividend into the A, Q registers. The dividend must be expressed as a $2n$-bit positive number. Thus, for example, the 4-bit 0111 becomes 00000111.

2. Shift A, Q left 1 bit position.

3. Perform $A \leftarrow A - M$. This operation subtracts the divisor from the contents of A.

4. a. If the result is nonnegative (most significant bit of A = 0), then set $Q_0 \leftarrow 1$.

   b. If the result is negative (most significant bit of A = 1), then set $Q_0 \leftarrow 0$ and restore the previous value of A.

5. Repeat steps 2 through 4 as many times as there are bit positions in Q.

6. The remainder is in A and the quotient is in Q.

---

[3]This is subtraction of unsigned integers. A result that requires a borrow out of the most significant bit is a negative result.

To deal with negative numbers, we recognize that the remainder is defined by
This is because the remainder is defined by

$$D = Q \times V + R$$

Consider the following examples of integer division with all possible combinations of signs of D and V:

$$
\begin{array}{llll}
D = 7 & V = 3 & \Rightarrow Q = 2 & R = 1 \\
D = 7 & V = -3 & \Rightarrow Q = -2 & R = 1 \\
D = -7 & V = 3 & \Rightarrow Q = -2 & R = -1 \\
D = -7 & V = -3 & \Rightarrow Q = 2 & R = -1
\end{array}
$$

The reader will note from Figure 9.17 that $(-7)/(3)$ and $(7)/(-3)$ produce different remainders. We see that the magnitudes of Q and R are unaffected by the input signs and that the signs of Q and R are easily derivable form the signs of D and V. Specifically, $\text{sign}(R) = \text{sign}(D)$ and $\text{sign}(Q) = \text{sign}(D) \times \text{sign}(V)$. Hence, one way to do twos complement division is to convert the operands into unsigned values and, at the end, to account for the signs by complementation where needed. This is the method of choice for the restoring division algorithm [PARH00].

9.4 FLOATING-POINT REPRESENTATION

Principles

With a fixed-point notation (e.g., twos complement) it is possible to represent a range of positive and negative integers centered on 0. By assuming a fixed binary or radix point, this format allows the representation of numbers with a fractional component as well.

This approach has limitations. Very large numbers cannot be represented, nor can very small fractions. Furthermore, the fractional part of the quotient in a division of two large numbers could be lost.

For decimal numbers, we get around this limitation by using scientific notation. Thus, 976,000,000,000,000 can be represented as 9.76×10^{14}, and 0.0000000000000976 can be represented as 9.76×10^{-14}. What we have done, in effect, is dynamically to slide the decimal point to a convenient location and use the exponent of 10 to keep track of that decimal point. This allows a range of very large and very small numbers to be represented with only a few digits.

This same approach can be taken with binary numbers. We can represent a number in the form

$$\pm S \times B^{\pm E}$$

This number can be stored in a binary word with three fields:

- Sign: plus or minus
- Significand S
- Exponent E

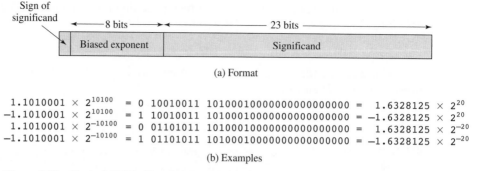

(a) Format

$$
\begin{array}{llllll}
1.1010001 \times 2^{10100} & = & 0 & 10010011 & 10100010000000000000000 & = & 1.6328125 \times 2^{20} \\
-1.1010001 \times 2^{10100} & = & 1 & 10010011 & 10100010000000000000000 & = & -1.6328125 \times 2^{20} \\
1.1010001 \times 2^{-10100} & = & 0 & 01101011 & 10100010000000000000000 & = & 1.6328125 \times 2^{-20} \\
-1.1010001 \times 2^{-10100} & = & 1 & 01101011 & 10100010000000000000000 & = & -1.6328125 \times 2^{-20}
\end{array}
$$

(b) Examples

Figure 9.18 Typical 32-Bit Floating-Point Format

The **base** B is implicit and need not be stored because it is the same for all numbers. Typically, it is assumed that the radix point is to the right of the leftmost, or most significant, bit of the significand. That is, there is one bit to the left of the radix point.

The principles used in representing binary floating-point numbers are best explained with an example. Figure 9.18a shows a typical 32-bit floating-point format. The leftmost bit stores the **sign** of the number (0 = positive, 1 = negative). The **exponent** value is stored in the next 8 bits. The representation used is known as a **biased representation**. A fixed value, called the bias, is subtracted from the field to get the true exponent value. Typically, the bias equals $(2^{k-1} - 1)$, where k is the number of bits in the binary exponent. In this case, the 8-bit field yields the numbers 0 through 255. With a bias of 127 ($2^7 - 1$), the true exponent values are in the range -127 to $+128$. In this example, the base is assumed to be 2.

Table 9.2 shows the biased representation for 4-bit integers. Note that when the bits of a biased representation are treated as unsigned integers, the relative magnitudes of the numbers do not change. For example, in both biased and unsigned representations, the largest number is 1111 and the smallest number is 0000. This is not true of sign-magnitude or twos complement representation. An advantage of biased representation is that nonnegative floating-point numbers can be treated as integers for comparison purposes.

The final portion of the word (23 bits in this case) is the **significand**.[4]

Any floating-point number can be expressed in many ways.

The following are equivalent, where the significand is expressed in binary form:

$$0.110 \times 2^5$$
$$110 \times 2^2$$
$$0.0110 \times 2^6$$

To simplify operations on floating-point numbers, it is typically required that they be normalized. A **normalized number** is one in which the most significant digit of

---

[4]The term *mantissa,* sometimes used instead of *significand,* is considered obsolete. *Mantissa* also means "the fractional part of a logarithm," so is best avoided in this context.

the significand is nonzero. For base 2 representation, a normalized number is therefore one in which the most significant bit of the significand is one. As was mentioned, the typical convention is that there is one bit to the left of the radix point. Thus, a normalized nonzero number is one in the form

$$\pm 1.bbb\dots b \times 2^{\pm E}$$

where b is either binary digit (0 or 1). Because the most significant bit is always one, it is unnecessary to store this bit; rather, it is implicit. Thus, the 23-bit field is used to store a 24-bit significand with a value in the half open interval $[1, 2)$. Given a number that is not normalized, the number may be normalized by shifting the radix point to the right of the leftmost 1 bit and adjusting the exponent accordingly.

Figure 9.18b gives some examples of numbers stored in this format. For each example, on the left is the binary number; in the center is the corresponding bit pattern; on the right is the decimal value. Note the following features:

- The sign is stored in the first bit of the word.
- The first bit of the true significand is always 1 and need not be stored in the significand field.
- The value 127 is added to the true exponent to be stored in the exponent field.
- The base is 2.

For comparison, Figure 9.19 indicates the range of numbers that can be represented in a 32-bit word. Using twos complement integer representation, all of the integers from -2^{31} to $2^{31} - 1$ can be represented, for a total of 2^{32} different numbers. With the example floating-point format of Figure 9.18, the following ranges of numbers are possible:

- Negative numbers between $-(2 - 2^{-23}) \times 2^{128}$ and -2^{-127}
- Positive numbers between 2^{-127} and $(2 - 2^{-23}) \times 2^{128}$

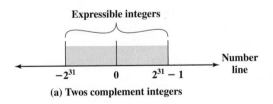

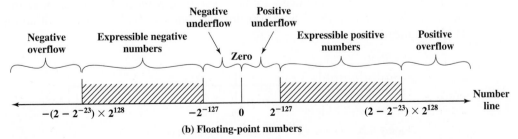

Figure 9.19 Expressible Numbers in Typical 32-Bit Formats

Five regions on the number line are not included in these ranges:

- Negative numbers less than $-(2 - 2^{-23}) \times 2^{128}$, called **negative overflow**
- Negative numbers greater than 2^{-127}, called **negative underflow**
- Zero
- Positive numbers less than 2^{-127}, called **positive underflow**
- Positive numbers greater than $(2 - 2^{-23}) \times 2^{128}$, called **positive overflow**

The representation as presented will not accommodate a value of 0. However, as we shall see, actual floating-point representations include a special bit pattern to designate zero. Overflow occurs when an arithmetic operation results in a magnitude greater than can be expressed with an exponent of 128 (e.g., $2^{120} \times 2^{100} = 2^{220}$). Underflow occurs when the fractional magnitude is too small (e.g., $2^{-120} \times 2^{-100} = 2^{-220}$). Underflow is a less serious problem because the result can generally be satisfactorily approximated by 0.

It is important to note that we are not representing more individual values with floating-point notation. The maximum number of different values that can be represented with 32 bits is still 2^{32}. What we have done is to spread those numbers out in two ranges, one positive and one negative. In practice, most floating-point numbers that one would wish to represent are represented only approximately. However, for moderate sized integers, the representation is exact.

Also, note that the numbers represented in floating-point notation are not spaced evenly along the number line, as are fixed-point numbers. The possible values get closer together near the origin and farther apart as you move away, as shown in Figure 9.20. This is one of the trade-offs of floating-point math: Many calculations produce results that are not exact and have to be rounded to the nearest value that the notation can represent.

In the type of format depicted in Figure 9.18, there is a trade-off between range and precision. The example shows 8 bits devoted to the exponent and 23 to the significand. If we increase the number of bits in the exponent, we expand the range of expressible numbers. But because only a fixed number of different values can be expressed, we have reduced the density of those numbers and therefore the precision. The only way to increase both range and precision is to use more bits. Thus, most computers offer, at least, single-precision numbers and double-precision numbers. For example, a single-precision format might be 32 bits, and a double-precision format 64 bits.

So there is a trade-off between the number of bits in the exponent and the number of bits in the significand. But it is even more complicated than that. The implied base of the exponent need not be 2. The IBM S/390 architecture, for example, uses a base of 16 [ANDE67b]. The format consists of a 7-bit exponent and a 24-bit significand.

Figure 9.20   Density of Floating-Point Numbers

In the IBM base-16 format,

$$0.11010001 \times 2^{10100} = 0.11010001 \times 16^{101}$$

and the exponent is stored to represent 5 rather than 20.

The advantage of using a larger exponent is that a greater range can be achieved for the same number of exponent bits. But remember, we have not increased the number of different values that can be represented. Thus, for a fixed format, a larger exponent base gives a greater range at the expense of less precision.

IEEE Standard for Binary Floating–Point Representation

The most important floating-point representation is defined in IEEE Standard 754, adopted in 1985. This standard was developed to facilitate the portability of programs from one processor to another and to encourage the development of sophisticated, numerically oriented programs. The standard has been widely adopted and is used on virtually all contemporary processors and arithmetic coprocessors.

The IEEE standard defines both a 32-bit single and a 64-bit double format (Figure 9.21), with 8-bit and 11-bit exponents, respectively. The implied base is 2. In addition, the standard defines two extended formats, single and double, whose exact format is implementation dependent. The extended formats include additional bits in the exponent (extended range) and in the significand (extended precision). The extended formats are to be used for intermediate calculations. With their greater precision, the extended formats lessen the chance of a final result that has been contaminated by excessive roundoff error; with their greater range, they also lessen the chance of an intermediate overflow aborting a computation whose final result would have been representable in a basic format. An additional motivation for the single extended format is that it affords some of the benefits of a double format without incurring the time penalty usually associated with higher precision. Table 9.3 summarizes the characteristics of the four formats.

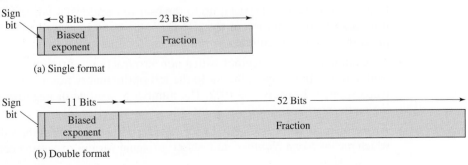

(a) Single format

(b) Double format

Figure 9.21   IEEE 754 Formats

Table 9.3   IEEE 754 Format Parameters

Parameter	Format			
	Single	Single Extended	Double	Double Extended
Word width (bits)	32	≥43	64	≥79
Exponent width (bits)	8	≥11	11	≥15
Exponent bias	127	unspecified	1023	unspecified
Maximum exponent	127	≥1023	1023	≥16383
Minimum exponent	−126	≤−1022	−1022	≤−16382
Number range (base 10)	$10^{-38}, 10^{+38}$	unspecified	$10^{-308}, 10^{+308}$	unspecified
Significand width (bits)*	23	≥31	52	≥63
Number of exponents	254	unspecified	2046	unspecified
Number of fractions	2^{23}	unspecified	2^{52}	unspecified
Number of values	1.98×2^{31}	unspecified	1.99×2^{63}	unspecified

*not including implied bit

Not all bit patterns in the IEEE formats are interpreted in the usual way; instead, some bit patterns are used to represent special values. Table 9.4 indicates the values assigned to various bit patterns. The extreme exponent values of all zeros (0) and all ones (255 in single format, 2047 in double format) define special values. The following classes of numbers are represented:

• For exponent values in the range of 1 through 254 for single format and 1 through 2046 for double format, normalized nonzero floating-point numbers are represented. The exponent is biased, so that the range of exponents is −126 through +127 for single format and −1022 through +1023 for double format. A normalized number requires a 1 bit to the left of the binary point; this bit is implied, giving an effective 24-bit or 53-bit significand (called *fraction* in the standard).

• An exponent of zero together with a fraction of zero represents positive or negative zero, depending on the sign bit. As was mentioned, it is useful to have an exact value of 0 represented.

• An exponent of all ones together with a fraction of zero represents positive or negative infinity, depending on the sign bit. It is also useful to have a representation of infinity. This leaves it up to the user to decide whether to treat overflow as an error condition or to carry the value ∞ and proceed with whatever program is being executed.

• An exponent of zero together with a nonzero fraction represents a denormalized number. In this case, the bit to the left of the binary point is zero and the true exponent is −126 or −1022. The number is positive or negative depending on the sign bit.

• An exponent of all ones together with a nonzero fraction is given the value NaN, which means *Not a Number,* and is used to signal various exception conditions.

The significance of denormalized numbers and NaNs is discussed in Section 9.5.

Table 9.4   Interpretation of IEEE 754 Floating-Point Numbers

	Single Precision (32 bits)				Double Precision (64 bits)			
	Sign	Biased exponent	Fraction	Value	Sign	Biased exponent	Fraction	Value
positive zero	0	0	0	0	0	0	0	0
negative zero	1	0	0	-0	1	0	0	-0
plus infinity	0	255 (all 1s)	0	∞	0	2047 (all 1s)	0	∞
minus infinity	1	255 (all 1s)	0	$-\infty$	1	2047 (all 1s)	0	$-\infty$
quiet NaN	0 or 1	255 (all 1s)	$\neq 0$	NaN	0 or 1	2047 (all 1s)	$\neq 0$	NaN
signaling NaN	0 or 1	255 (all 1s)	$\neq 0$	NaN	0 or 1	2047 (all 1s)	$\neq 0$	NaN
positive normalized nonzero	0	$0 < e < 255$	f	$2^{e-127}(1.f)$	0	$0 < e < 2047$	f	$2^{e-1023}(1.f)$
negative normalized nonzero	1	$0 < e < 255$	f	$-2^{e-127}(1.f)$	1	$0 < e < 2047$	f	$-2^{e-1023}(1.f)$
positive denormalized	0	0	$f \neq 0$	$2^{e-126}(0.f)$	0	0	$f \neq 0$	$2^{e-1022}(0.f)$
negative denormalized	1	0	$f \neq 0$	$-2^{e-126}(0.f)$	1	0	$f \neq 0$	$-2^{e-1022}(0.f)$

9.5 FLOATING-POINT ARITHMETIC

Table 9.5 summarizes the basic operations for floating-point arithmetic. For addition and subtraction, it is necessary to ensure that both operands have the same exponent value. This may require shifting the radix point on one of the operands to achieve alignment. Multiplication and division are more straightforward.

A floating-point operation may produce one of these conditions:

- **Exponent overflow:** A positive exponent exceeds the maximum possible exponent value. In some systems, this may be designated as $+\infty$ or $-\infty$.
- **Exponent underflow:** A negative exponent is less than the minimum possible exponent value (e.g., -200 is less than -127). This means that the number is too small to be represented, and it may be reported as 0.
- **Significand underflow:** In the process of aligning significands, digits may flow off the right end of the significand. As we shall discuss, some form of rounding is required.
- **Significand overflow:** The addition of two significands of the same sign may result in a carry out of the most significant bit. This can be fixed by realignment, as we shall explain.

Addition and Subtraction

In floating-point arithmetic, addition and subtraction are more complex than multiplication and division. This is because of the need for alignment. There are four basic phases of the algorithm for addition and subtraction:

1. Check for zeros.
2. Align the significands.
3. Add or subtract the significands.
4. Normalize the result.

Table 9.5 Floating-Point Numbers and Arithmetic Operations

Floating Point Numbers	Arithmetic Operations
$X = X_S \times B^{X_E}$ $Y = Y_S \times B^{Y_E}$	$\left. \begin{array}{l} X + Y = (X_S \times B^{X_E-Y_E} + Y_S) \times B^{Y_E} \\ X - Y = (X_S \times B^{X_E-Y_E} - Y_S) \times B^{Y_E} \end{array} \right\} X_E \leq Y_E$ $X \times Y = (X_S \times Y_S) \times B^{X_E+Y_E}$ $\dfrac{X}{Y} = \left(\dfrac{X_S}{Y_S}\right) \times B^{X_E-Y_E}$

Examples:

$X = 0.3 \times 10^2 = 30$
$Y = 0.2 \times 10^3 = 200$

$X + Y = (0.3 \times 10^{2-3} + 0.2) \times 10^3 = 0.23 \times 10^3 = 230$
$X - Y = (0.3 \times 10^{2-3} - 0.2) \times 10^3 = (-0.17) \times 10^3 = -170$
$X \times Y = (0.3 \times 0.2) \times 10^{2+3} = 0.06 \times 10^5 = 6000$
$X \div Y = (0.3 \div 0.2) \times 10^{2-3} = 1.5 \times 10^{-1} = 0.15$

A typical flowchart is shown in Figure 9.22. A step-by-step narrative highlights the main functions required for floating-point addition and subtraction. We assume a format similar to those of Figure 9.21. For the addition or subtraction operation, the two operands must be transferred to registers that will be used by the ALU. If the floating-point format includes an implicit significand bit, that bit must be made explicit for the operation.

Phase 1: Zero check. Because addition and subtraction are identical except for a sign change, the process begins by changing the sign of the subtrahend if it is a subtract operation. Next, if either operand is 0, the other is reported as the result.

Phase 2: Significand alignment. The next phase is to manipulate the numbers so that the two exponents are equal.

To see the need for aligning exponents, consider the following decimal addition:

$$(123 \times 10^0) + (456 \times 10^{-2})$$

Clearly, we cannot just add the significands. The digits must first be set into equivalent positions, that is, the 4 of the second number must be aligned with the 3 of the first. Under these conditions, the two exponents will be equal, which is the mathematical condition under which two numbers in this form can be added. Thus,

$$(123 \times 10^0) + (456 \times 10^{-2}) = (123 \times 10^0) + (4.56 \times 10^0) = 127.56 \times 10^0$$

Alignment may be achieved by shifting either the smaller number to the right (increasing its exponent) or shifting the larger number to the left. Because either operation may result in the loss of digits, it is the smaller number that is shifted; any digits that are lost are therefore of relatively small significance. The alignment is achieved by repeatedly shifting the magnitude portion of the significand right 1 digit and incrementing the exponent until the two exponents are equal. (Note that if the implied base is 16, a shift of 1 digit is a shift of 4 bits.) If this process results in a 0 value for the significand, then the other number is reported as the result. Thus, if two numbers have exponents that differ significantly, the lesser number is lost.

Phase 3: Addition. Next, the two significands are added together, taking into account their signs. Because the signs may differ, the result may be 0. There is also the possibility of significand overflow by 1 digit. If so, the significand of the result is shifted right and the exponent is incremented. An exponent overflow could occur as a result; this would be reported and the operation halted.

Phase 4: Normalization. The final phase normalizes the result. Normalization consists of shifting significand digits left until the most significant digit (bit, or 4 bits for base-16 exponent) is nonzero. Each shift causes a decrement of the exponent and thus could cause an exponent underflow. Finally, the result must be rounded off and then reported. We defer a discussion of rounding until after a discussion of multiplication and division.

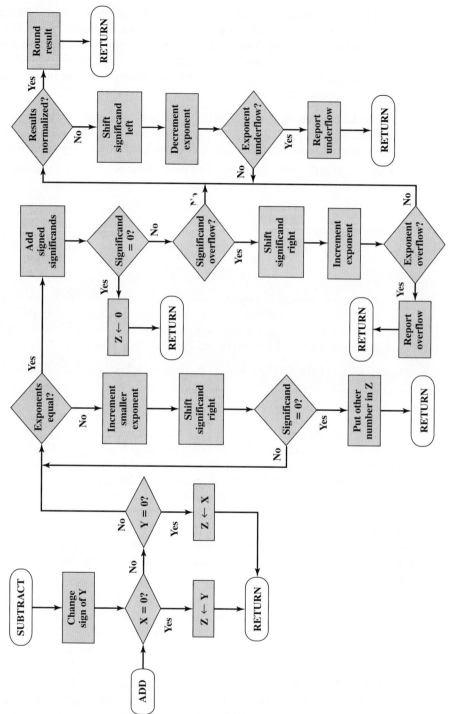

Figure 9.22 Floating-Point Addition and Subtraction $(Z \leftarrow Z \pm Y)$

336

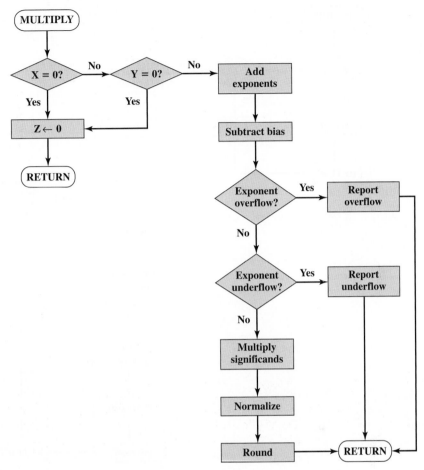

Figure 9.23 Floating-Point Multiplication $(Z \leftarrow X \times Y)$

Multiplication and Division

Floating-point multiplication and division are much simpler processes than addition and subtraction, as the following discussion indicates.

We first consider multiplication, illustrated in Figure 9.23. First, if either operand is 0, 0 is reported as the result. The next step is to add the exponents. If the exponents are stored in biased form, the exponent sum would have doubled the bias. Thus, the bias value must be subtracted from the sum. The result could be either an exponent overflow or underflow, which would be reported, ending the algorithm.

If the exponent of the product is within the proper range, the next step is to multiply the significands, taking into account their signs. The multiplication is performed in the same way as for integers. In this case, we are dealing with a sign–magnitude representation, but the details are similar to those for twos complement representation. The product will be double the length of the multiplier and multiplicand. The extra bits will be lost during rounding.

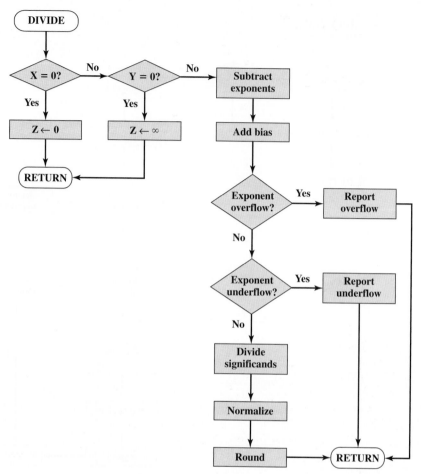

Figure 9.24 Floating-Point Division $(Z \leftarrow X/Y)$

After the product is calculated, the result is then normalized and rounded, as was done for addition and subtraction. Note that normalization could result in exponent underflow.

Finally, let us consider the flowchart for division depicted in Figure 9.24. Again, the first step is testing for 0. If the divisor is 0, an error report is issued, or the result is set to infinity, depending on the implementation. A dividend of 0 results in 0. Next, the divisor exponent is subtracted from the dividend exponent. This removes the bias, which must be added back in. Tests are then made for exponent underflow or overflow.

The next step is to divide the significands. This is followed with the usual normalization and rounding.

Precision Considerations

GUARD BITS We mentioned that, prior to a floating-point operation, the exponent and significand of each operand are loaded into ALU registers. In the case of the

```
x = 1.000.....00 × 2¹
-y = 0.111.....11 × 2¹
 z = 0.000.....01 × 2¹
   = 1.000.....00 × 2⁻²²
```

$$x = 1.000\ldots00 \times 2^1$$
$$-y = 0.111\ldots11 \times 2^1$$
$$z = 0.000\ldots01 \times 2^1$$
$$= 1.000\ldots00 \times 2^{-22}$$

$$x = .100000 \times 16^1$$
$$-y = .0FFFFF \times 16^1$$
$$z = .000001 \times 16^1$$
$$= .100000 \times 16^{-4}$$

(a) Binary example, without guard bits

(c) Hexadecimal example, without guard bits

$$x = 1.000\ldots00\ 0000 \times 2^1$$
$$-y = 0.111\ldots11\ 1000 \times 2^1$$
$$z = 0.000\ldots00\ 1000 \times 2^1$$
$$= 1.000\ldots00\ 0000 \times 2^{-23}$$

$$x = .100000\ 00 \times 16^1$$
$$-y = .0FFFFF\ F0 \times 16^1$$
$$z = .000000\ 10 \times 16^1$$
$$= .100000\ 00 \times 16^{-5}$$

(b) Binary example, with guard bits

(d) Hexadecimal example, with guard bits

Figure 9.25 The Use of Guard Bits

significand, the length of the register is almost always greater than the length of the significand plus an implied bit. The register contains additional bits, called guard bits, which are used to pad out the right end of the significand with 0s.

The reason for the use of guard bits is illustrated in Figure 9.25. Consider numbers in the IEEE format, which has a 24-bit significand, including an implied 1 bit to the left of the binary point. Two numbers that are very close in value are $x = 1.00\ldots00 \times 2^1$ and $y = 1.11\ldots11 \times 2^0$. If the smaller number is to be subtracted from the larger, it must be shifted right 1 bit to align the exponents. This is shown in Figure 9.25a. In the process, y loses 1 bit of significance; the result is 2^{-22}. The same operation is repeated in part (b) with the addition of guard bits. Now the least significant bit is not lost due to alignment, and the result is 2^{-23}, a difference of a factor of 2 from the previous answer. When the radix is 16, the loss of precision can be greater. As Figures 9.25c and d show, the difference can be a factor of 16.

ROUNDING Another detail that affects the precision of the result is the rounding policy. The result of any operation on the significands is generally stored in a longer register. When the result is put back into the floating-point format, the extra bits must be disposed of.

A number of techniques have been explored for performing rounding. In fact, the IEEE standard lists four alternative approaches:

- **Round to nearest:** The result is rounded to the nearest representable number.
- **Round toward $+\infty$:** The result is rounded up toward plus infinity.
- **Round toward $-\infty$:** The result is rounded down toward negative infinity.
- **Round toward 0:** The result is rounded toward zero.

Let us consider each of these policies in turn. **Round to nearest** is the default rounding mode listed in the standard and is defined as follows: The representable value nearest to the infinitely precise result shall be delivered.

If the extra bits, beyond the 23 bits that can be stored, are 10010, then the extra bits amount to more than one-half of the last representable bit position. In this case, the correct answer is to add binary 1 to the last representable bit, rounding up to the next representable number. Now consider that the extra bits are 01111. In this case, the extra bits amount to less than one-half of the last representable bit position. The correct answer is simply to drop the extra bits (truncate), which has the effect of rounding down to the next representable number.

The standard also addresses the special case of extra bits of the form 10000 . . . . Here the result is exactly halfway between the two possible representable values. One possible technique here would be to always truncate, as this would be the simplest operation. However, the difficulty with this simple approach is that it introduces a small but cumulative bias into a sequence of computations. What is required is an unbiased method of rounding. One possible approach would be to round up or down on the basis of a random number so that, on average, the result would be unbiased. The argument against this approach is that it does not produce predictable, deterministic results. The approach taken by the IEEE standard is to force the result to be even: If the result of a computation is exactly midway between two representable numbers, the value is rounded up if the last representable bit is currently 1 and not rounded up if it is currently 0.

The next two options, **rounding to plus** and **minus infinity**, are useful in implementing a technique known as interval arithmetic. Interval arithmetic provides an efficient method for monitoring and controlling errors in floating-point computations by producing two values for each result. The two values correspond to the lower and upper endpoints of an interval that contains the true result. The width of the interval, which is the difference between the upper and lower endpoints, indicates the accuracy of the result. If the endpoints of an interval are not representable, then the interval endpoints are rounded down and up, respectively. Although the width of the interval may vary according to implementation, many algorithms have been designed to produce narrow intervals. If the range between the upper and lower bounds is sufficiently narrow, then a sufficiently accurate result has been obtained. If not, at least we know this and can perform additional analysis.

The final technique specified in the standard is **round toward zero**. This is, in fact, simple truncation: The extra bits are ignored. This is certainly the simplest technique. However, the result is that the magnitude of the truncated value is always less than or equal to the more precise original value, introducing a consistent bias toward zero in the operation. This is a serious bias because it affects every operation for which there are nonzero extra bits.

IEEE Standard for Binary Floating-Point Arithmetic

IEEE 754 goes beyond the simple definition of a format to lay down specific practices and procedures so that floating-point arithmetic produces uniform, predictable results independent of the hardware platform. One aspect of this has already been discussed, namely rounding. This subsection looks at three other topics: infinity, NaNs, and denormalized numbers.

INFINITY Infinity arithmetic is treated as the limiting case of real arithmetic, with the infinity values given the following interpretation:

$$-\infty < \text{(every finite number)} < +\infty$$

With the exception of the special cases discussed subsequently, any arithmetic operation involving infinity yields the obvious result.

For example:

$$5 + (+\infty) = +\infty \qquad 5 \div (+\infty) \quad = +0$$
$$5 - (+\infty) = -\infty \qquad (+\infty) + (+\infty) = +\infty$$
$$5 + (-\infty) = -\infty \qquad (-\infty) + (-\infty) = -\infty$$
$$5 - (-\infty) = +\infty \qquad (-\infty) - (+\infty) = -\infty$$
$$5 \times (+\infty) = +\infty \qquad (+\infty) - (-\infty) = +\infty$$

QUIET AND SIGNALING NaNS A NaN is a symbolic entity encoded in floating-point format, of which there are two types: signaling and quiet. A signaling NaN signals an invalid operation exception whenever it appears as an operand. Signaling NaNs afford values for uninitialized variables and arithmetic-like enhancements that are not the subject of the standard. A quiet NaN propagates through almost every arithmetic operation without signaling an exception. Table 9.6 indicates operations that will produce a quiet NaN.

Note that both types of NaNs have the same general format (Table 9.4): an exponent of all ones and a nonzero fraction. The actual bit pattern of the nonzero fraction is implementation dependent; the fraction values can be used to distinguish quiet NaNs from signaling NaNs and to specify particular exception conditions.

Table 9.6   Operations that Produce a Quiet NaN

Operation	Quiet NaN Produced by
Any	Any operation on a signaling NaN
Add or subtract	Magnitude subtraction of infinities: $(+\infty) + (-\infty)$ $(-\infty) + (+\infty)$ $(+\infty) - (+\infty)$ $(-\infty) - (-\infty)$
Multiply	$0 \times \infty$
Division	$\dfrac{0}{0}$ or $\dfrac{\infty}{\infty}$
Remainder	x REM 0 or ∞ REM y
Square root	$\sqrt{x}$, where $x < 0$

(a) 32-Bit format without denormalized numbers

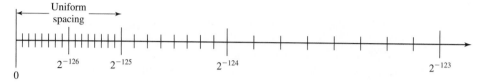

(b) 32-Bit format with denormalized numbers

Figure 9.26   The Effect of IEEE 754 Denormalized Numbers

DENORMALIZED NUMBERS Denormalized numbers are included in IEEE 754 to handle cases of exponent underflow. When the exponent of the result becomes too small (a negative exponent with too large a magnitude), the result is denormalized by right shifting the fraction and incrementing the exponent for each shift until the exponent is within a representable range.

Figure 9.26 illustrates the effect of including denormalized numbers. The representable numbers can be grouped into intervals of the form $[2^n, 2^{n+1}]$. Within each such interval, the exponent portion of the number remains constant while the fraction varies, producing a uniform spacing of representable numbers within the interval. As we get closer to zero, each successive interval is half the width of the preceding interval but contains the same number of representable numbers. Hence the density of representable numbers increases as we approach zero. However, if only normalized numbers are used, there is a gap between the smallest normalized number and 0. In the case of the 32-bit IEEE 754 format, there are 2^{23} representable numbers in each interval, and the smallest representable positive number is 2^{-126}. With the addition of denormalized numbers, an additional $2^{23} - 1$ numbers are uniformly added between 0 and 2^{-126}.

The use of denormalized numbers is referred to as *gradual underflow* [COON81]. Without denormalized numbers, the gap between the smallest representable nonzero number and zero is much wider than the gap between the smallest representable nonzero number and the next larger number. Gradual underflow fills in that gap and reduces the impact of exponent underflow to a level comparable with roundoff among the normalized numbers.

9.6   RECOMMENDED READING AND WEB SITES

[ERCE04] and [PARH00] are excellent treatments of computer arithmetic, covering all of the topics in this chapter in detail. [FLYN01] is a useful discussion that focuses on practical design and implementation issues. For the serious student of computer arithmetic, a very useful reference is the two-volume [SWAR90]. Volume I was originally published in 1980 and provides key papers (some very difficult to obtain otherwise) on computer arithmetic fundamentals. Volume II contains more recent papers, covering theoretical, design, and implementation aspects of computer arithmetic.

For floating-point arithmetic, [GOLD91] is well named: "What Every Computer Scientist Should Know About Floating-Point Arithmetic." Another excellent treatment of the topic is contained in [KNUT98], which also covers integer computer arithmetic. The following more in-depth treatments are also worthwhile: [OVER01, EVEN00a, OBER97a, OBER97b, SODE96]. [KUCK77] is a good discussion of rounding methods in floating-point arithmetic. [EVEN00b] examines rounding with respect to IEEE 754.

[SCHW99] describes the first IBM S/390 processor to integrate radix-16 and IEEE 754 floating-point arithmetic in the same floating-point unit.

ERCE04 Ercegovac, M., and Lang, T. *Digital Arithmetic*. San Francisco: Morgan Kaufmann, 2004.

EVEN00a Even, G., and Paul, W. "On the Design of IEEE Compliant Floating-Point Units." *IEEE Transactions on Computers,* May 2000.

EVEN00b Even, G., and Seidel, P. "A Comparison of Three Rounding Algorithms for IEEE Floating-Point Multiplication." *IEEE Transactions on Computers,* July 2000.

FLYN01 Flynn, M., and Oberman, S. *Advanced Computer Arithmetic Design*. New York: Wiley, 2001.

GOLD91 Goldberg, D. "What Every Computer Scientist Should Know About Floating-Point Arithmetic." *ACM Computing Surveys,* March 1991.

KNUT98 Knuth, D. *The Art of Computer Programming, Volume 2: Seminumerical Algorithms*. Reading, MA: Addison-Wesley, 1998.

KUCK77 Kuck, D.; Parker, D.; and Sameh, A. "An Analysis of Rounding Methods in Floating-Point Arithmetic." *IEEE Transactions on Computers*. July 1977.

OBER97a Oberman, S., and Flynn, M. "Design Issues in Division and Other Floating-Point Operations." *IEEE Transactions on Computers,* February 1997.

OBER97b Oberman, S., and Flynn, M. "Division Algorithms and Implementations." *IEEE Transactions on Computers,* August 1997.

OVER01 Overton, M. *Numerical Computing with IEEE Floating Point Arithmetic*. Philadelphia, PA: Society for Industrial and Applied Mathematics, 2001.

PARH00 Parhami, B. *Computer Arithmetic: Algorithms and Hardware Design*. Oxford: Oxford University Press, 2000.

SCHW99 Schwarz, E., and Krygowski, C. "The S/390 G5 Floating-Point Unit." *IBM Journal of Research and Development,* September/November 1999.

SODE96 Soderquist, P., and Leeser, M. "Area and Performance Tradeoffs in Floating-Point Divide and Square-Root Implementations." *ACM Computing Surveys,* September 1996.

SWAR90 Swartzlander, E., editor. *Computer Arithmetic, Volumes I and II*. Los Alamitos, CA: IEEE Computer Society Press, 1990.

Recommended Web site:

- **IEEE 754:** The IEEE 754 documents, related publications and papers, and a useful set of links related to computer arithmetic

9.7 KEY TERMS, REVIEW QUESTIONS, AND PROBLEMS

Key Terms

arithmetic and logic unit (ALU)	mantissa	quotient
arithmetic shift	minuend	radix point
base	multiplicand	remainder
biased representation	multiplier	rounding
denormalized number	negative overflow	sign bit
dividend	negative underflow	significand
divisor	normalized number	significand overflow
exponent	ones complement	significand underflow
exponent overflow	representation	sign-magnitude
exponent underflow	overflow	representation
fixed-point representation	partial product	subtrahend
floating-point representation	positive overflow	twos complement
guard bits	positive underflow	representation
	product	

Review Questions

9.1 Briefly explain the following representations: sign magnitude, twos complement, biased.

9.2 Explain how to determine if a number is negative in the following representations: sign magnitude, twos complement, biased.

9.3 What is the sign-extension rule for twos complement numbers?

9.4 How can you form the negation of an integer in twos complement representation?

9.5 In general terms, when does the twos complement operation on an n-bit integer produce the same integer?

9.6 What is the difference between the twos complement representation of a number and the twos complement of a number?

9.7 If we treat 2 twos complement numbers as unsigned integers for purposes of addition, the result is correct if interpreted as a twos complement number. This is not true for multiplication. Why?

9.8 What are the four essential elements of a number in floating-point notation?

9.9 What is the benefit of using biased representation for the exponent portion of a floating-point number?

9.10 What are the differences among positive overflow, exponent overflow, and significand overflow?

9.11 What are the basic elements of floating-point addition and subtraction?

9.12 Give a reason for the use of guard bits.

9.13 List four alternative methods of rounding the result of a floating-point operation.

Problems

9.1 Represent the following decimal numbers in both binary sign/magnitude and twos complement using 16 bits: +512; −29.

9.2 Represent the following twos complement values in decimal: 1101011; 0101101.

9.3 Another representation of binary integers that is sometimes encountered is **ones complement**. Positive integers are represented in the same way as sign magnitude. A negative integer is represented by taking the Boolean complement of each bit of the corresponding positive number.

    a. Provide a definition of ones complement numbers using a weighted sum of bits, similar to Equations (9.1) and (9.2).

    b. What is the range of numbers that can be represented in ones complement?

    c. Define an algorithm for performing addition in ones complement arithmetic.

    Note: Ones complement arithmetic disappeared from hardware in the 1960s, but still survives checksum calculations for the Internet Protocol (IP) and the Transmission Control Protocol (TCP).

9.4 Add columns to Table 9.1 for sign magnitude and ones complement.

9.5 Consider the following operation on a binary word. Start with the least significant bit. Copy all bits that are 0 until the first bit is reached and copy that bit, too. Then take the complement of each bit thereafter. What is the result?

9.6 In Section 9.3, the twos complement operation is defined as follows. To find the twos complement of X, take the Boolean complement of each bit of X, and then add 1.

    a. Show that the following is an equivalent definition. For an n-bit integer X, the twos complement of X is formed by treating X as an unsigned integer and calculating $(2_n - X)$.

    b. Demonstrate that Figure 9.5 can be used to support graphically the claim in part (a), by showing how a clockwise movement is used to achieve subtraction.

9.7 The r's complement of an n-digit number N in base r is defined as $r^n - N$ for $N \neq 0$ and 0 for $N = 0$. Find the tens complement of the decimal number 13250.

9.8 Calculate $(72530 - 13250)$ using tens complement arithmetic. Assume rules similar to those for twos complement arithmetic.

9.9 Consider the twos complement addition of two n-bit numbers:

$$z_{n-1}z_{n-2}\ldots z_0 = x_{n-1}x_{n-2}\ldots x_0 + y_{n-1}y_{n-2}\ldots y_0$$

Assume that bitwise addition is performed with a carry bit c_i generated by the addition of x_i, y_i, and c_{i-1}. Let v be a binary variable indicating overflow when $v = 1$. Fill in the values in the table.

Input	x_{n-1}	0	0	0	0	1	1	1	1
	y_{n-1}	0	0	1	1	0	0	1	1
	c_{n-2}	0	1	0	1	0	1	0	1
Output	z_{n-1}								
	v								

9.10 Assume numbers are represented in 8-bit twos complement representation. Show the calculation of the following:

    a. $6 + 13$ **b.** $-6 + 13$ **c.** $6 - 13$ **d.** $-6 - 13$

9.11 Find the following differences using twos complement arithmetic:

    a.   111000   **b.**   11001100   **c.**   111100001111   **d.**   11000011

        -110011 $- \;\; 101110$ -110011110011 -11101000

9.12 Is the following a valid alternative definition of overflow in twos complement arithmetic?

    If the exclusive-OR of the carry bits into and out of the leftmost column is 1, then there is an overflow condition. Otherwise, there is not.

9.13   Compare Figures 9.9 and 9.12. Why is the C bit not used in the latter?

9.14   Given $x = 0101$ and $y = 1010$ in twos complement notation (i.e., $x = 5, y = -6$), compute the product $p = x \times y$ with Booth's algorithm.

9.15   Use the Booth algorithm to multiply 23 (multiplicand) by 29 (multiplier), where each number is represented using 6 bits.

9.16   Prove that the multiplication of two n-digit numbers in base B gives a product of no more than $2n$ digits.

9.17   Verify the validity of the unsigned binary division algorithm of Figure 9.16 by showing the steps involved in calculating the division depicted in Figure 9.15. Use a presentation similar to that of Figure 9.17.

9.18   The twos complement integer division algorithm described in Section 9.3 is known as the restoring method because the value in the A register must be restored following unsuccessful subtraction. A slightly more complex approach, known as nonrestoring, avoids the unnecessary subtraction and addition. Propose an algorithm for this latter approach.

9.19   Under computer integer arithmetic, the quotient J/K of two integers J and K is less than or equal to the usual quotient. True or false?

9.20   Divide -145 by 13 in binary twos complement notation, using 12-bit words. Use the algorithm described in Section 9.3.

9.21   **a.** Consider a fixed-point representation using decimal digits, in which the implied radix point can be in any position (e.g., to the right of the least significant digit, to the right of the most significant digit, and so on). How many decimal digits are needed to represent the approximations of both Planck's constant (6.63×10^{-27}) and Avogadro's number (6.02×10^{23})? The implied radix point must be in the same position for both numbers.
   b. Now consider a decimal floating-point format with the exponent stored in a biased representation with a bias of 50. A normalized representation is assumed. How many decimal digits are needed to represent these constants in this floating-point format?

9.22   Assume that the exponent e is constrained to lie in the range $0 \le e \le X$, with a bias of q, that the base is b, and that the significand is p digits in length.
   a. What are the largest and smallest positive values that can be written?
   b. What are the largest and smallest positive values that can be written as normalized floating-point numbers?

9.23   Express the following numbers in IEEE 32-bit floating-point format:
   a. -5 **b.** -6 **c.** -1.5 **d.** 384   **e.** 1/16   **f.** $-1/32$

9.24   The following numbers use the IEEE 32-bit floating-point format. What is the equivalent decimal value?
   a. 1 10000011 11000000000000000000000
   b. 0 01111110 10100000000000000000000
   c. 0 10000000 00000000000000000000000

9.25   Consider a reduced 7-bit IEEE floating-point format, with 3 bits for the exponent and 3 bits for the significand. List all 127 values.

9.26   Express the following numbers in IBM's 32-bit floating-point format, which uses a 7-bit exponent with an implied base of 16 and an exponent bias of 64 (40 hexadecimal). A normalized floating-point number requires that the leftmost hexadecimal digit be nonzero; the implied radix point is to the left of that digit.

| a. 1.0 | c. 1/64 | e. -15.0 | g. 7.2×10^{75} |
| b. 0.5 | d. 0.0 | f. 5.4×10^{-79} | h. 65535 |

9.27   Let 5BCA0000 be a floating-point number in IBM format, expressed in hexadecimal. What is the decimal value of the number?

9.28   What would be the bias value for
  a. A base-2 exponent ($B = 2$) in a 6-bit field?
  b. A base-8 exponent ($B = 8$) in a 7-bit field?

9.29   Draw a number line similar to that in Figure 9.19b for the floating-point format of Figure 9.21b.

9.30   Consider a floating-point format with 8 bits for the biased exponent and 23 bits for the significand. Show the bit pattern for the following numbers in this format:
  a. -720 **b.** 0.645

9.31   The text mentions that a 32-bit format can represent a maximum of 2^{32} different numbers. How many different numbers can be represented in the IEEE 32-bit format? Explain.

9.32   Any floating-point representation used in a computer can represent only certain real numbers exactly; all others must be approximated. If A' is the stored value approximating the real value A, then the relative error, r, is expressed as

$$r = \frac{A - A'}{A}$$

Represent the decimal quantity $+0.4$ in the following floating-point format: base $= 2$; exponent: biased, 4 bits; significand, 7 bits. What is the relative error?

9.33   If $A = 1.427$, find the relative error if A is truncated to 1.42 and if it is rounded to 1.43.

9.34   When people speak about inaccuracy in floating-point arithmetic, they often ascribe errors to cancellation that occurs during the subtraction of nearly equal quantities. But when X and Y are approximately equal, the difference $X - Y$ is obtained exactly, with no error. What do these people really mean?

9.35   Numerical values A and B are stored in the computer as approximations A' and B'. Neglecting any further truncation or roundoff errors, show that the relative error of the product is approximately the sum of the relative errors in the factors.

9.36   One of the most serious errors in computer calculations occurs when two nearly equal numbers are subtracted. Consider $A = 0.22288$ and $B = 0.22211$. The computer truncates all values to four decimal digits. Thus $A' = 0.2228$ and $B' = 0.2221$.
  a. What are the relative errors for A' and B'?
  b. What is the relative error for $C' = A' - B'$?

9.37   To get some feel for the effects of denormalization and gradual underflow, consider a decimal system that provides 6 decimal digits for the significand and for which the smallest normalized number is 10^{-99}. A normalized number has one nonzero decimal digit to the left of the decimal point. Perform the following calculations and denormalize the results. Comment on the results.
  a. $(2.50000 \times 10^{-60}) \times (3.50000 \times 10^{-43})$
  b. $(2.50000 \times 10^{-60}) \times (3.50000 \times 10^{-60})$
  c. $(5.67834 \times 10^{-97}) - (5.67812 \times 10^{-97})$

9.38   Show how the following floating-point additions are performed (where significands are truncated to 4 decimal digits). Show the results in normalized form.
  a. $5.566 \times 10^2 + 7.777 \times 10^2$ **b.** $3.344 \times 10^1 + 8.877 \times 10^{-2}$

9.39   Show how the following floating-point subtractions are performed (where significands are truncated to 4 decimal digits). Show the results in normalized form.
  a. $7.744 \times 10^{-3} - 6.666 \times 10^{-3}$ **b.** $8.844 \times 10^{-3} - 2.233 \times 10^{-1}$

9.40   Show how the following floating-point calculations are performed (where significands are truncated to 4 decimal digits). Show the results in normalized form.
  a. $(2.255 \times 10^1) \times (1.234 \times 10^0)$ **b.** $(8.833 \times 10^2) \div (5.555 \times 10^4)$

CHAPTER 10

INSTRUCTION SETS: CHARACTERISTICS AND FUNCTIONS

KEY POINTS

♦   The essential elements of a computer instruction are the opcode, which specifies the operation to be performed; the source and destination operand references, which specify the input and output locations for the operation; and a next instruction reference, which is usually implicit.

♦   Opcodes specify operations in one of the following general categories: arithmetic and logic operations; movement of data between two registers, register and memory, or two memory locations; I/O; and control.

♦   Operand references specify a register or memory location of operand data. The type of data may be addresses, numbers, characters, or logical data.

♦   A common architectural feature in processors is the use of a stack, which may or may not be visible to the programmer. Stacks are used to manage procedure calls and returns and may be provided as an alternative form of addressing memory. The basic stack operations are PUSH, POP, and operations on the top one or two stack locations. Stacks typically are implemented to grow from higher addresses to lower addresses.

♦   Byte-addressable processors may be categorized as big endian, little endian, or bi-endian. A multibyte numerical value stored with the most significant byte in the lowest numerical address is stored in big-endian fashion. The little-endian style stores the most significant byte in the highest numerical address. A bi-endian processor can handle both styles.

Much of what is discussed in this book is not readily apparent to the user or programmer of a computer. If a programmer is using a high-level language, such as Pascal or Ada, very little of the architecture of the underlying machine is visible.

One boundary where the computer designer and the computer programmer can view the same machine is the machine instruction set. From the designer's point of view, the machine instruction set provides the functional requirements for the processor: implementing the processor is a task that in large part involves implementing the machine instruction set. The user who chooses to program in machine language (actually, in assembly language; see Appendix B) becomes aware of the register and memory structure, the types of data directly supported by the machine, and the functioning of the ALU.

A description of a computer's machine instruction set goes a long way toward explaining the computer's processor. Accordingly, we focus on machine instructions in this chapter and the next.

10.1 MACHINE INSTRUCTION CHARACTERISTICS

The operation of the processor is determined by the instructions it executes, referred to as *machine instructions* or *computer instructions*. The collection of different instructions that the processor can execute is referred to as the processor's *instruction set*.

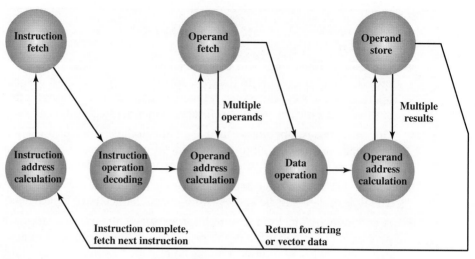

Figure 10.1   Instruction Cycle State Diagram

Elements of a Machine Instruction

Each instruction must contain the information required by the processor for execution. Figure 10.1, which repeats Figure 3.6, shows the steps involved in instruction execution and, by implication, defines the elements of a machine instruction. These elements are as follows:

- **Operation code:** Specifies the operation to be performed (e.g., ADD, I/O). The operation is specified by a binary code, known as the operation code, or **opcode**.
- **Source operand reference:** The operation may involve one or more source operands, that is, operands that are inputs for the operation.
- **Result operand reference:** The operation may produce a result.
- **Next instruction reference:** This tells the processor where to fetch the next instruction after the execution of this instruction is complete.

The address of the next instruction to be fetched could be either a real address or a virtual address, depending on the architecture. Generally, the distinction is transparent to the instruction set architecture. In most cases, the next instruction to be fetched immediately follows the current instruction. In those cases, there is no explicit reference to the next instruction. When an explicit reference is needed, then the main memory or virtual memory address must be supplied. The form in which that address is supplied is discussed in Chapter 11.

Source and result operands can be in one of four areas:

- **Main or virtual memory:** As with next instruction references, the main or virtual memory address must be supplied.
- **Processor register:** With rare exceptions, a processor contains one or more registers that may be referenced by machine instructions. If only one register exists,

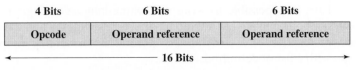

Figure 10.2 A Simple Instruction Format

reference to it may be implicit. If more than one register exists, then each register is assigned a unique name or number, and the instruction must contain the number of the desired register.

- **Immediate:** The value of the operand is contained in a field in the instruction being executed.
- **I/O device:** The instruction must specify the I/O module and device for the operation. If memory-mapped I/O is used, this is just another main or virtual memory address.

Instruction Representation

Within the computer, each instruction is represented by a sequence of bits. The instruction is divided into fields, corresponding to the constituent elements of the instruction. A simple example of an instruction format is shown in Figure 10.2. As another example, the IAS instruction format is shown in Figure 2.2. With most instruction sets, more than one format is used. During instruction execution, an instruction is read into an instruction register (IR) in the processor. The processor must be able to extract the data from the various instruction fields to perform the required operation.

It is difficult for both the programmer and the reader of textbooks to deal with binary representations of machine instructions. Thus, it has become common practice to use a *symbolic representation* of machine instructions. An example of this was used for the IAS instruction set, in Table 2.1.

Opcodes are represented by abbreviations, called *mnemonics,* that indicate the operation. Common examples include

ADD	Add
SUB	Subtract
MUL	Multiply
DIV	Divide
LOAD	Load data from memory
STOR	Store data to memory

Operands are also represented symbolically. For example, the instruction

ADD R, Y

may mean add the value contained in data location Y to the contents of register R. In this example, Y refers to the address of a location in memory, and R refers to a particular register. Note that the operation is performed on the contents of a location, not on its address.

Thus, it is possible to write a machine-language program in symbolic form. Each symbolic opcode has a fixed binary representation, and the programmer specifies the location of each symbolic operand. For example, the programmer might begin with a list of definitions:

$$X = 513$$
$$Y = 514$$

and so on. A simple program would accept this symbolic input, convert opcodes and operand references to binary form, and construct binary machine instructions.

Machine-language programmers are rare to the point of nonexistence. Most programs today are written in a high-level language or, failing that, assembly language, which is discussed in Appencix B. However, symbolic machine language remains a useful tool for describing machine instructions, and we will use it for that purpose.

Instruction Types

Consider a high-level language instruction that could be expressed in a language such as BASIC or FORTRAN. For example,

$$X = X + Y$$

This statement instructs the computer to add the value stored in Y to the value stored in X and put the result in X. How might this be accomplished with machine instructions? Let us assume that the variables X and Y correspond to locations 513 and 514. If we assume a simple set of machine instructions, this operation could be accomplished with three instructions:

1. Load a register with the contents of memory location 513.
2. Add the contents of memory location 514 to the register.
3. Store the contents of the register in memory location 513.

As can be seen, the single BASIC instruction may require three machine instructions. This is typical of the relationship between a high-level language and a machine language. A high-level language expresses operations in a concise algebraic form, using variables. A machine language expresses operations in a basic form involving the movement of data to or from registers.

With this simple example to guide us, let us consider the types of instructions that must be included in a practical computer. A computer should have a set of instructions that allows the user to formulate any data processing task. Another way to view it is to consider the capabilities of a high-level programming language. Any program written in a high-level language must be translated into machine language to be executed. Thus, the set of machine instructions must be sufficient to express any of the instructions from a high-level language. With this in mind we can categorize instruction types as follows:

- **Data processing:** Arithmetic and logic instructions
- **Data storage:** Movement of data into or out of register and or memory locations

- **Data movement:** I/O instructions
- **Control:** Test and branch instructions

Arithmetic instructions provide computational capabilities for processing numeric data. *Logic* (Boolean) instructions operate on the bits of a word as bits rather than as numbers; thus, they provide capabilities for processing any other type of data the user may wish to employ. These operations are performed primarily on data in processor registers. Therefore, there must be *memory* instructions for moving data between memory and the registers. *I/O* instructions are needed to transfer programs and data into memory and the results of computations back out to the user. *Test* instructions are used to test the value of a data word or the status of a computation. *Branch* instructions are then used to branch to a different set of instructions depending on the decision made.

We will examine the various types of instructions in greater detail later in this chapter.

Number of Addresses

One of the traditional ways of describing processor architecture is in terms of the number of addresses contained in each instruction. This dimension has become less significant with the increasing complexity of processor design. Nevertheless, it is useful at this point to draw and analyze this distinction.

What is the maximum number of addresses one might need in an instruction? Evidently, arithmetic and logic instructions will require the most operands. Virtually all arithmetic and logic operations are either unary (one source operand) or binary (two source operands). Thus, we would need a maximum of two addresses to reference source operands. The result of an operation must be stored, suggesting a third address, which defines a destination operand. Finally, after completion of an instruction, the next instruction must be fetched, and its address is needed.

This line of reasoning suggests that an instruction could plausibly be required to contain four address references: two source operands, one destination operand, and the address of the next instruction. In most architectures, most instructions have one, two, or three operand addresses, with the address of the next instruction being implicit (obtained from the program counter). Most architectures also have a few special-purpose instructions with more operands. For example, the load and store multiple instructions of the ARM architecture, described in Chapter 11, designate up to 17 register operands in a single instruction.

Figure 10.3 compares typical one-, two-, and three-address instructions that could be used to compute $Y = (A - B)/[C + (D \times E)]$. With three addresses, each instruction specifies two source operand locations and a destination operand location. Because we choose not to alter the value of any of the operand locations, a temporary location, T, is used to store some intermediate results. Note that there are four instructions and that the original expression had five operands.

Three-address instruction formats are not common because they require a relatively long instruction format to hold the three address references. With two-address instructions, and for binary operations, one address must do double duty as both an operand and a result. Thus, the instruction SUB Y, B carries out the calculation

Instruction		Comment
SUB	Y, A, B	Y ← A − B
MPY	T, D, E	T ← D × E
ADD	T, T, C	T ← T + C
DIV	Y, Y, T	Y ← Y ÷ T

(a) Three-address instructions

Instruction	Comment
LOAD D	AC ← D
MPY E	AC ← AC × E
ADD C	AC ← AC + C
STOR Y	Y ← AC
LOAD A	AC ← A
SUB B	AC ← AC − B
DIV Y	AC ← AC ÷ Y
STOR Y	Y ← AC

(c) One-address instructions

Instruction		Comment
MOVE Y, A		Y ← A
SUB	Y, B	Y ← Y − B
MOVE T, D		T ← D
MPY	T, E	T ← T × E
ADD	T, C	T ← T + C
DIV	Y, T	Y ← Y ÷ T

(b) Two-address instructions

Figure 10.3   Programs to Execute $Y = \dfrac{A - B}{C + (D \times E)}$

$Y - B$ and stores the result in Y. The two-address format reduces the space requirement but also introduces some awkwardness. To avoid altering the value of an operand, a MOVE instruction is used to move one of the values to a result or temporary location before performing the operation. Our sample program expands to six instructions.

Simpler yet is the one-address instruction. For this to work, a second address must be implicit. This was common in earlier machines, with the implied address being a processor register known as the **accumulator** (AC). The accumulator contains one of the operands and is used to store the result. In our example, eight instructions are needed to accomplish the task.

It is, in fact, possible to make do with zero addresses for some instructions. Zero-address instructions are applicable to a special memory organization, called a *stack*. A stack is a last-in-first-out set of locations. The stack is in a known location and, often, at least the top two elements are in processor registers. Thus, zero-address instructions would reference the top two stack elements. Stacks are described in Appendix 10A. Their use is explored further later in this chapter and in Chapter 11.

Table 10.1 summarizes the interpretations to be placed on instructions with zero, one, two, or three addresses. In each case in the table, it is assumed that the address of the next instruction is implicit, and that one operation with two source operands and one result operand is to be performed.

The number of addresses per instruction is a basic design decision. Fewer addresses per instruction result in instructions that are more primitive, requiring a less complex processor. It also results in instructions of shorter length. On the other hand, programs contain more total instructions, which in general results in longer execution

Table 10.1 Utilization of Instruction Addresses (Nonbranching Instructions)

Number of Addresses	Symbolic Representation	Interpretation
3	OP A, B, C	$A \leftarrow B \ OP \ C$
2	OP A, B	$A \leftarrow A \ OP \ B$
1	OP A	$AC \leftarrow AC \ OP \ A$
0	OP	$T \leftarrow (T - 1) \ OP \ T$

AC   = accumulator
T   = top of stack
(T − 1) = second element of stack
A, B, C = memory or register locations

times and longer, more complex programs. Also, there is an important threshold between one-address and multiple-address instructions. With one-address instructions,
the programmer generally has available only one general-purpose register, the accumulator. With multiple-address instructions, it is common to have multiple general-
purpose registers. This allows some operations to be performed solely on registers.
Because register references are faster than memory references, this speeds up execution. For reasons of flexibility and ability to use multiple registers, most contemporary machines employ a mixture of two- and three-address instructions.

The design trade-offs involved in choosing the number of addresses per instruction are complicated by other factors. There is the issue of whether an address
references a memory location or a register. Because there are fewer registers, fewer
bits are needed for a register reference. Also, as we shall see in the next chapter, a
machine may offer a variety of addressing modes, and the specification of mode
takes one or more bits. The result is that most processor designs involve a variety of
instruction formats.

Instruction Set Design

One of the most interesting, and most analyzed, aspects of computer design is instruction set design. The design of an instruction set is very complex because it affects so
many aspects of the computer system. The instruction set defines many of the functions
performed by the processor and thus has a significant effect on the implementation of
the processor. The instruction set is the programmer's means of controlling the processor. Thus, programmer requirements must be considered in designing the instruction set.

It may surprise you to know that some of the most fundamental issues relating
to the design of instruction sets remain in dispute. Indeed, in recent years, the level
of disagreement concerning these fundamentals has actually grown. The most important of these fundamental design issues include the following:

- **Operation repertoire:** How many and which operations to provide, and how
  complex operations should be
- **Data types:** The various types of data upon which operations are performed
- **Instruction format:** Instruction length (in bits), number of addresses, size of
  various fields, and so on

- **Registers:** Number of processor registers that can be referenced by instructions, and their use
- **Addressing:** The mode or modes by which the address of an operand is specified

These issues are highly interrelated and must be considered together in designing an instruction set. This book, of course, must consider them in some sequence, but an attempt is made to show the interrelationships.

Because of the importance of this topic, much of Part Three is devoted to instruction set design. Following this overview section, this chapter examines data types and operation repertoire. Chapter 11 examines addressing modes (which includes a consideration of registers) and instruction formats. Chapter 13 examines the reduced instruction set computer (RISC). RISC architecture calls into question many of the instruction set design decisions traditionally made in commercial computers.

10.2 TYPES OF OPERANDS

Machine instructions operate on data. The most important general categories of data are

- Addresses
- Numbers
- Characters
- Logical data

We shall see, in discussing addressing modes in Chapter 11, that addresses are, in fact, a form of data. In many cases, some calculation must be performed on the operand reference in an instruction to determine the main or virtual memory address. In this context, addresses can be considered to be unsigned integers.

Other common data types are numbers, characters, and logical data, and each of these is briefly examined in this section. Beyond that, some machines define specialized data types or data structures. For example, there may be machine operations that operate directly on a list or a string of characters.

Numbers

All machine languages include numeric data types. Even in nonnumeric data processing, there is a need for numbers to act as counters, field widths, and so forth. An important distinction between numbers used in ordinary mathematics and numbers stored in a computer is that the latter are limited. This is true in two senses. First, there is a limit to the magnitude of numbers representable on a machine and second, in the case of floating-point numbers, a limit to their precision. Thus, the programmer is faced with understanding the consequences of rounding, overflow, and underflow.

Three types of numerical data are common in computers:

- Binary integer or binary fixed point
- Binary floating point
- Decimal

We examined the first two in some detail in Chapter 9. It remains to say a few words about decimal numbers.

Although all internal computer operations are binary in nature, the human users of the system deal with decimal numbers. Thus, there is a necessity to convert from decimal to binary on input and from binary to decimal on output. For applications in which there is a great deal of I/O and comparatively little, comparatively simple computation, it is preferable to store and operate on the numbers in decimal form. The most common representation for this purpose is **packed decimal**.[1]

With packed decimal, each decimal digit is represented by a 4-bit code, in the obvious way, with two digits stored per byte. Thus, $0 = 0000$, $1 = 0001, \ldots, 8 = 1000$, and $9 = 1001$. Note that this is a rather inefficient code because only 10 of 16 possible 4-bit values are used. To form numbers, 4-bit codes are strung together, usually in multiples of 8 bits. Thus, the code for 246 is 0000 0010 0100 0110. This code is clearly less compact than a straight binary representation, but it avoids the conversion overhead. Negative numbers can be represented by including a 4-bit sign digit at either the left or right end of a string of packed decimal digits. Standard sign values are 1100 for positive $(+)$ and 1101 for negative $(-)$.

Many machines provide arithmetic instructions for performing operations directly on packed decimal numbers. The algorithms are quite similar to those described in Section 9.3 but must take into account the decimal carry operation.

Characters

A common form of data is text or character strings. While textual data are most convenient for human beings, they cannot, in character form, be easily stored or transmitted by data processing and communications systems. Such systems are designed for binary data. Thus, a number of codes have been devised by which characters are represented by a sequence of bits. Perhaps the earliest common example of this is the Morse code. Today, the most commonly used character code in the International Reference Alphabet (IRA), referred to in the United States as the American Standard Code for Information Interchange (ASCII; see Appendix F). Each character in this code is represented by a unique 7-bit pattern; thus, 128 different characters can be represented. This is a larger number than is necessary to represent printable characters, and some of the patterns represent *control* characters. Some of these control characters have to do with controlling the printing of characters on a page. Others are concerned with communications procedures. IRA-encoded characters are almost always stored and transmitted using 8 bits per character. The eighth bit may be set to 0 or used as a parity bit for error detection. In the latter case, the bit is set such that the total number of binary 1s in each octet is always odd (odd parity) or always even (even parity).

Note in Table F.1 (Appendix F) that for the IRA bit pattern 011XXXX, the digits 0 through 9 are represented by their binary equivalents, 0000 through 1001, in

---

[1]Textbooks often refer to this as binary coded decimal (BCD). Strictly speaking, BCD refers to the encoding of each decimal digit by a unique 4-bit sequence. Packed decimal refers to the storage of BCD-encoded digits using one byte for each two digits.

the rightmost 4 bits. This is the same code as packed decimal. This facilitates conversion between 7-bit IRA and 4-bit packed decimal representation.

Another code used to encode characters is the Extended Binary Coded Decimal Interchange Code (EBCDIC). EBCDIC is used on IBM mainframes. It is an 8-bit code. As with IRA, EBCDIC is compatible with packed decimal. In the case of EBCDIC, the codes 11110000 through 11111001 represent the digits 0 through 9.

Logical Data

Normally, each word or other addressable unit (byte, halfword, and so on) is treated as a single unit of data. It is sometimes useful, however, to consider an *n*-bit unit as consisting of *n* 1-bit items of data, each item having the value 0 or 1. When data are viewed this way, they are considered to be *logical* data.

There are two advantages to the bit-oriented view. First, we may sometimes wish to store an array of Boolean or binary data items, in which each item can take on only the values 1 (true) and 0 (false). With logical data, memory can be used most efficiently for this storage. Second, there are occasions when we wish to manipulate the bits of a data item. For example, if floating-point operations are implemented in software, we need to be able to shift significant bits in some operations. Another example: To convert from IRA to packed decimal, we need to extract the rightmost 4 bits of each byte.

Note that, in the preceding examples, the same data are treated sometimes as logical and other times as numerical or text. The "type" of a unit of data is determined by the operation being performed on it. While this is not normally the case in high-level languages, it is almost always the case with machine language.

10.3 INTEL x86 AND ARM DATA TYPES

x86 Data Types

The x86 can deal with data types of 8 (byte), 16 (word), 32 (doubleword), 64 (quadword), and 128 (double quadword) bits in length. To allow maximum flexibility in data structures and efficient memory utilization, words need not be aligned at even-numbered addresses; doublewords need not be aligned at addresses evenly divisible by 4; and quadwords need not be aligned at addresses evenly divisible by 8, and so on. However, when data are accessed across a 32-bit bus, data transfers take place in units of doublewords, beginning at addresses divisible by 4. The processor converts the request for misaligned values into a sequence of requests for the bus transfer. As with all of the Intel 80x86 machines, the x86 uses the little-endian style; that is, the least significant byte is stored in the lowest address (see Appendix 10B for a discussion of endianness).

The byte, word, doubleword, quadword, and double quadword are referred to as general data types. In addition, the x86 supports an impressive array of specific data types that are recognized and operated on by particular instructions. Table 10.2 summarizes these types.

Table 10.2   x86 Data Types

Data Type	Description
General	Byte, word (16 bits), doubleword (32 bits), quadword (64 bits), and double quadword (128 bits) locations with arbitrary binary contents.
Integer	A signed binary value contained in a byte, word, or doubleword, using twos complement representation.
Ordinal	An unsigned integer contained in a byte, word, or doubleword.
Unpacked binary coded decimal (BCD)	A representation of a BCD digit in the range 0 through 9, with one digit in each byte.
Packed BCD	Packed byte representation of two BCD digits; value in the range 0 to 99.
Near pointer	A 16-bit, 32-bit, or 64-bit effective address that represents the offset within a segment. Used for all pointers in a nonsegmented memory and for references within a segment in a segmented memory.
Far pointer	A logical address consisting of a 16-bit segment selector and an offset of 16, 32, or 64 bits. Far pointers are used for memory references in a segmented memory model where the identity of a segment being accessed must be specified explicitly.
Bit field	A contiguous sequence of bits in which the position of each bit is considered as an independent unit. A bit string can begin at any bit position of any byte and can contain up to 32 bits.
Bit string	A contiguous sequence of bits, containing from zero to $2^{32} - 1$ bits.
Byte string	A contiguous sequence of bytes, words, or doublewords, containing from zero to $2^{32} - 1$ bytes.
Floating point	See Figure 10.4.
Packed SIMD (single instruction, multiple data)	Packed 64-bit and 128-bit data types

Figure 10.4 illustrates the x86 numerical data types. The signed integers are in twos complement representation and may be 16, 32, or 64 bits long. The floating-point type actually refers to a set of types that are used by the floating-point unit and operated on by floating-point instructions. The three floating-point representations conform to the IEEE 754 standard.

The packed SIMD (single-instruction-multiple-data) data types were introduced to the x86 architecture as part of the extensions of the instruction set to optimize performance of multimedia applications. These extensions include MMX (multimedia extensions) and SSE (streaming SIMD extensions). The basic concept is that multiple operands are packed into a single referenced memory item and that these multiple operands are operated on in parallel. The data types are as follows:

- **Packed byte and packed byte integer:** Bytes packed into a 64-bit quadword or 128-bit double quadword, interpreted as a bit field or as an integer
- **Packed word and packed word integer:** 16-bit words packed into a 64-bit quadword or 128-bit double quadword, interpreted as a bit field or as an integer
- **Packed doubleword and packed doubleword integer:** 32-bit doublewords packed into a 64-bit quadword or 128-bit double quadword, interpreted as a bit field or as an integer

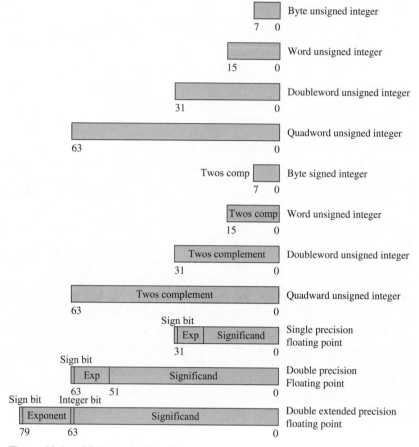

Figure 10.4 x86 Numeric Data Formats

- **Packed quadword and packed qaudword integer:** Two 64-bit quadwords packed into a 128-bit double quadword, interpreted as a bit field or as an integer
- **Packed single-precision floating-point and packed double-precision floating-point:** Four 32-bit floating-point or two 64-bit floating-point values packed into a 128-bit double quadword

ARM Data Types

ARM processors support data types of 8 (byte), 16 (halfword), and 32 (word) bits in length. Normally, halfword access should be halfword aligned and word accesses should be word aligned. For nonaligned access attempts, the architecture supports three alternatives.

- Default case:
  - The address is treated as truncated, with address bits[1:0] treated as zero for word accesses, and address bit[0] treated as zero for halfword accesses.

- Load single word ARM instructions are architecturally defined to rotate right the word-aligned data transferred by a non word-aligned address one, two, or three bytes depending on the value of the two least significant address bits.

- **Alignment checking:** When the appropriate control bit is set, a data abort signal indicates an alignment fault for attempting unaligned access.

- **Unaligned access:** When this option is enabled, the processor uses one or more memory accesses to generate the required transfer of adjacent bytes transparently to the programmer

For all three data types (byte, halfword, and word) an unsigned interpretation is supported, in which the value represents an unsigned, nonnegative integer. All three data types can also be used for twos complement signed integers.

The majority of ARM processor implementations do not provide floating-point hardware, which saves power and area. If floating-point arithmetic is required in such processors, it must be implemented in software. ARM does support an optional floating-point coprocessor that supports the single- and double-precision floating point data types defined in IEEE 754.

ENDIAN SUPPORT A state bit (E-bit) in the system control register is set and cleared under program control using the SETEND instruction. The E-bit defines which endian to load and store data. Figure 10.5 illustrates the functionality associated with the E-bit for a word load or store operation. This mechanism enables efficient dynamic data load/store for system designers who know they need to access data structures in the opposite endianness to their OS/environment. Note that the address of each data byte is fixed in memory. However, the byte lane in a register is different.

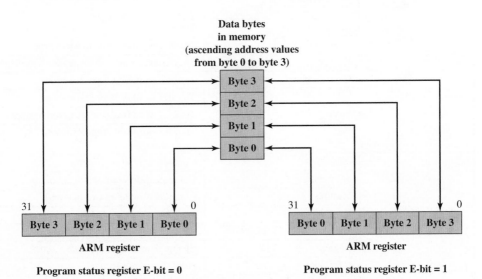

Figure 10.5 ARM Endian Support—Word Load/Store with E-Bit

10.4 TYPES OF OPERATIONS

The number of different opcodes varies widely from machine to machine. However, the same general types of operations are found on all machines. A useful and typical categorization is the following:

- Data transfer
- Arithmetic
- Logical
- Conversion
- I/O
- System control
- Transfer of control

Table 10.3 (based on [HAYE98]) lists common instruction types in each category. This section provides a brief survey of these various types of operations, together with a brief discussion of the actions taken by the processor to execute a particular type of operation (summarized in Table 10.4). The latter topic is examined in more detail in Chapter 12.

Table 10.3 Common Instruction Set Operations

Type	Operation Name	Description
Data Transfer	Move (transfer)	Transfer word or block from source to destination
	Store	Transfer word from processor to memory
	Load (fetch)	Transfer word from memory to processor
	Exchange	Swap contents of source and destination
	Clear (reset)	Transfer word of 0s to destination
	Set	Transfer word of 1s to destination
	Push	Transfer word from source to top of stack
	Pop	Transfer word from top of stack to destination
Arithmetic	Add	Compute sum of two operands
	Subtract	Compute difference of two operands
	Multiply	Compute product of two operands
	Divide	Compute quotient of two operands
	Absolute	Replace operand by its absolute value
	Negate	Change sign of operand
	Increment	Add 1 to operand
	Decrement	Subtract 1 from operand

(continued)

Table 10.3   Continued

Type	Operation Name	Description
Logical	AND	Perform logical AND
	OR	Perform logical OR
	NOT (complement)	Perform logical NOT
	Exclusive-OR	Perform logical XOR
	Test	Test specified condition; set flag(s) based on outcome
	Compare	Make logical or arithmetic comparison of two or more operands; set flag(s) based on outcome
	Set Control Variables	Class of instructions to set controls for protection purposes, interrupt handling, timer control, etc.
	Shift	Left (right) shift operand, introducing constants at end
	Rotate	Left (right) shift operand, with wraparound end
Transfer of Control	Jump (branch)	Unconditional transfer; load PC with specified address
	Jump Conditional	Test specified condition; either load PC with specified address or do nothing, based on condition
	Jump to Subroutine	Place current program control information in known location; jump to specified address
	Return	Replace contents of PC and other register from known location
	Execute	Fetch operand from specified location and execute as instruction; do not modify PC
	Skip	Increment PC to skip next instruction
	Skip Conditional	Test specified condition; either skip or do nothing based on condition
	Halt	Stop program execution
	Wait (hold)	Stop program execution; test specified condition repeatedly; resume execution when condition is satisfied
	No operation	No operation is performed, but program execution is continued
Input/Output	Input (read)	Transfer data from specified I/O port or device to destination (e.g., main memory or processor register)
	Output (write)	Transfer data from specified source to I/O port or device
	Start I/O	Transfer instructions to I/O processor to initiate I/O operation
	Test I/O	Transfer status information from I/O system to specified destination
Conversion	Translate	Translate values in a section of memory based on a table of correspondences
	Convert	Convert the contents of a word from one form to another (e.g., packed decimal to binary)

Table 10.4   Processor Actions for Various Types of Operations

Data Transfer	Transfer data from one location to another
	If memory is involved: Determine memory address Perform virtual-to-actual-memory address transformation Check cache Initiate memory read/write
Arithmetic	May involve data transfer, before and/or after
	Perform function in ALU
	Set condition codes and flags
Logical	Same as arithmetic
Conversion	Similar to arithmetic and logical. May involve special logic to perform conversion
Transfer of Control	Update program counter. For subroutine call/return, manage parameter passing and linkage
I/O	Issue command to I/O module
	If memory-mapped I/O, determine memory-mapped address

Data Transfer

The most fundamental type of machine instruction is the data transfer instruction. The data transfer instruction must specify several things. First, the location of the source and destination operands must be specified. Each location could be memory, a register, or the top of the stack. Second, the length of data to be transferred must be indicated. Third, as with all instructions with operands, the mode of addressing for each operand must be specified. This latter point is discussed in Chapter 11.

The choice of data transfer instructions to include in an instruction set exemplifies the kinds of trade-offs the designer must make. For example, the general location (memory or register) of an operand can be indicated in either the specification of the opcode or the operand. Table 10.5 shows examples of the most common IBM EAS/390 data transfer instructions. Note that there are variants to indicate the amount of data to be transferred (8, 16, 32, or 64 bits). Also, there are different instructions for register to register, register to memory, memory to register, and memory to memory transfers. In contrast, the VAX has a move (MOV) instruction with variants for different amounts of data to be moved, but it specifies whether an operand is register or memory as part of the operand. The VAX approach is somewhat easier for the programmer, who has fewer mnemonics to deal with. However, it is also somewhat less compact than the IBM EAS/390 approach because the location (register versus memory) of each operand must be specified separately in the instruction. We will return to this distinction when we discuss instruction formats, in the next chapter.

In terms of processor action, data transfer operations are perhaps the simplest type. If both source and destination are registers, then the processor simply causes data to be transferred from one register to another; this is an operation internal to

Table 10.5 Examples of IBM EAS/390 Data Transfer Operations

Operation Mnemonic	Name	Number of Bits Transferred	Description
L	Load	32	Transfer from memory to register
LH	Load Halfword	16	Transfer from memory to register
LR	Load	32	Transfer from register to register
LER	Load (Short)	32	Transfer from floating-point register to floating-point register
LE	Load (Short)	32	Transfer from memory to floating-point register
LDR	Load (Long)	64	Transfer from floating-point register to floating-point register
LD	Load (Long)	64	Transfer from memory to floating-point register
ST	Store	32	Transfer from register to memory
STH	Store Halfword	16	Transfer from register to memory
STC	Store Character	8	Transfer from register to memory
STE	Store (Short)	32	Transfer from floating-point register to memory
STD	Store (Long)	64	Transfer from floating-point register to memory

the processor. If one or both operands are in memory, then the processor must perform some or all of the following actions:

1. Calculate the memory address, based on the address mode (discussed in Chapter 11).
2. If the address refers to virtual memory, translate from virtual to real memory address.
3. Determine whether the addressed item is in cache.
4. If not, issue a command to the memory module.

Arithmetic

Most machines provide the basic arithmetic operations of add, subtract, multiply, and divide. These are invariably provided for signed integer (fixed-point) numbers. Often they are also provided for floating-point and packed decimal numbers.

Other possible operations include a variety of single-operand instructions; for example,

- **Absolute:** Take the absolute value of the operand.
- **Negate:** Negate the operand.
- **Increment:** Add 1 to the operand.
- **Decrement:** Subtract 1 from the operand.

Table 10.6 Basic Logical Operations

P	Q	NOT P	P AND Q	P OR Q	P XOR Q	P = Q
0	0	1	0	0	0	1
0	1	1	0	1	1	0
1	0	0	0	1	1	0
1	1	0	1	1	0	1

The execution of an arithmetic instruction may involve data transfer operations to position operands for input to the ALU, and to deliver the output of the ALU. Figure 3.5 illustrates the movements involved in both data transfer and arithmetic operations. In addition, of course, the ALU portion of the processor performs the desired operation.

Logical

Most machines also provide a variety of operations for manipulating individual bits of a word or other addressable units, often referred to as "bit twiddling." They are based upon Boolean operations (see Chapter 20).

Some of the basic logical operations that can be performed on Boolean or binary data are shown in Table 10.6. The NOT operation inverts a bit. AND, OR, and Exclusive-OR (XOR) are the most common logical functions with two operands. EQUAL is a useful binary test.

These logical operations can be applied bitwise to n-bit logical data units. Thus, if two registers contain the data

$$(R1) = 10100101$$
$$(R2) = 00001111$$

then

$$(R1) \text{ AND } (R2) = 00000101$$

where the notation (X) means the contents of location X. Thus, the AND operation can be used as a *mask* that selects certain bits in a word and zeros out the remaining bits. As another example, if two registers contain

$$(R1) = 10100101$$
$$(R2) = 11111111$$

then

$$(R1) \text{ XOR } (R2) = 01011010$$

With one word set to all 1s, the XOR operation inverts all of the bits in the other word (ones complement).

In addition to bitwise logical operations, most machines provide a variety of shifting and rotating functions. The most basic operations are illustrated in Figure 10.6. With a **logical shift**, the bits of a word are shifted left or right. On one end, the bit shifted out is lost. On the other end, a 0 is shifted in. Logical shifts are useful primarily for isolating

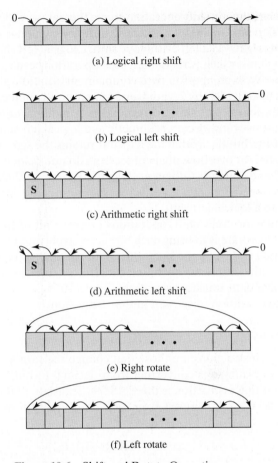

(a) Logical right shift

(b) Logical left shift

(c) Arithmetic right shift

(d) Arithmetic left shift

(e) Right rotate

(f) Left rotate

Figure 10.6 Shift and Rotate Operations

fields within a word. The 0s that are shifted into a word displace unwanted information that is shifted off the other end.

As an example, suppose we wish to transmit characters of data to an I/O device 1 character at a time. If each memory word is 16 bits in length and contains two characters, we must *unpack* the characters before they can be sent. To send the two characters in a word,

1. Load the word into a register.
2. Shift to the right eight times. This shifts the remaining character to the right half of the register.
3. Perform I/O. The I/O module reads the lower-order 8 bits from the data bus.

The preceding steps result in sending the left-hand character. To send the right-hand character,

1. Load the word again into the register.
2. AND with 0000000011111111. This masks out the character on the left.
3. Perform I/O.

The **arithmetic shift** operation treats the data as a signed integer and does not shift the sign bit. On a right arithmetic shift, the sign bit is replicated into the bit position to its right. On a left arithmetic shift, a logical left shift is performed on all bits but the sign bit, which is retained. These operations can speed up certain arithmetic operations. With numbers in twos complement notation, a right arithmetic shift corresponds to a division by 2, with truncation for odd numbers. Both an arithmetic left shift and a logical left shift correspond to a multiplication by 2 when there is no overflow. If overflow occurs, arithmetic and logical left shift operations produce different results, but the arithmetic left shift retains the sign of the number. Because of the potential for overflow, many processors do not include this instruction, including PowerPC and Itanium. Others, such as the IBM EAS/390, do offer the instruction. Curiously, the x86 architecture includes an arithmetic left shift but defines it to be identical to a logical left shift.

Rotate, or cyclic shift, operations preserve all of the bits being operated on. One use of a rotate is to bring each bit successively into the leftmost bit, where it can be identified by testing the sign of the data (treated as a number).

As with arithmetic operations, logical operations involve ALU activity and may involve data transfer operations. Table 10.7 gives examples of all of the shift and rotate operations discussed in this subsection.

Conversion

Conversion instructions are those that change the format or operate on the format of data. An example is converting from decimal to binary. An example of a more complex editing instruction is the EAS/390 Translate (TR) instruction. This instruction can be used to convert from one 8-bit code to another, and it takes three operands:

$$TR \; R1 \; (L), R2$$

The operand R2 contains the address of the start of a table of 8-bit codes. The L bytes starting at the address specified in R1 are translated, each byte being replaced by the contents of a table entry indexed by that byte. For example, to translate from EBCDIC to IRA, we first create a 256-byte table in storage locations, say, 1000-10FF hexadecimal. The table contains the characters of the IRA code in the sequence of the binary representation of the EBCDIC code; that is, the IRA code is placed in the table at the relative location equal to the binary value of the EBCDIC

Table 10.7 Examples of Shift and Rotate Operations

Input	Operation	Result
10100110	Logical right shift (3 bits)	00010100
10100110	Logical left shift (3 bits)	00110000
10100110	Arithmetic right shift (3 bits)	11110100
10100110	Arithmetic left shift (3 bits)	10110000
10100110	Right rotate (3 bits)	11010100
10100110	Left rotate (3 bits)	00110101

code of the same character. Thus, locations 10F0 through 10F9 will contain the values 30 through 39, because F0 is the EBCDIC code for the digit 0, and 30 is the IRA code for the digit 0, and so on through digit 9. Now suppose we have the EBCDIC for the digits 1984 starting at location 2100 and we wish to translate to IRA. Assume the following:

- Locations 2100–2103 contain F1 F9 F8 F4.
- R1 contains 2100.
- R2 contains 1000.

Then, if we execute

TR R1 (4), R2

locations 2100–2103 will contain 31 39 38 34.

Input/Output

Input/output instructions were discussed in some detail in Chapter 7. As we saw, there are a variety of approaches taken, including isolated programmed I/O, memory-mapped programmed I/O, DMA, and the use of an I/O processor. Many implementations provide only a few I/O instructions, with the specific actions specified by parameters, codes, or command words.

System Control

System control instructions are those that can be executed only while the processor is in a certain privileged state or is executing a program in a special privileged area of memory. Typically, these instructions are reserved for the use of the operating system.

Some examples of system control operations are as follows. A system control instruction may read or alter a control register; we discuss control registers in Chapter 12. Another example is an instruction to read or modify a storage protection key, such as is used in the EAS/390 memory system. Another example is access to process control blocks in a multiprogramming system.

Transfer of Control

For all of the operation types discussed so far, the next instruction to be performed is the one that immediately follows, in memory, the current instruction. However, a significant fraction of the instructions in any program have as their function changing the sequence of instruction execution. For these instructions, the operation performed by the processor is to update the program counter to contain the address of some instruction in memory.

There are a number of reasons why transfer-of-control operations are required. Among the most important are the following:

1. In the practical use of computers, it is essential to be able to execute each instruction more than once and perhaps many thousands of times. It may require thousands or perhaps millions of instructions to implement an application.

This would be unthinkable if each instruction had to be written out separately. If a table or a list of items is to be processed, a program loop is needed. One sequence of instructions is executed repeatedly to process all the data.

2. Virtually all programs involve some decision making. We would like the computer to do one thing if one condition holds, and another thing if another condition holds. For example, a sequence of instructions computes the square root of a number. At the start of the sequence, the sign of the number is tested. If the number is negative, the computation is not performed, but an error condition is reported.

3. To compose correctly a large or even medium-size computer program is an exceedingly difficult task. It helps if there are mechanisms for breaking the task up into smaller pieces that can be worked on one at a time.

We now turn to a discussion of the most common transfer-of-control operations found in instruction sets: branch, skip, and procedure call.

BRANCH INSTRUCTIONS A branch instruction, also called a jump instruction, has as one of its operands the address of the next instruction to be executed. Most often, the instruction is a **conditional branch** instruction. That is, the branch is made (update program counter to equal address specified in operand) only if a certain condition is met. Otherwise, the next instruction in sequence is executed (increment program counter as usual). A branch instruction in which the branch is always taken is an **unconditional branch**.

There are two common ways of generating the condition to be tested in a conditional branch instruction. First, most machines provide a 1-bit or multiple-bit condition code that is set as the result of some operations. This code can be thought of as a short user-visible register. As an example, an arithmetic operation (ADD, SUBTRACT, and so on) could set a 2-bit condition code with one of the following four values: 0, positive, negative, overflow. On such a machine, there could be four different conditional branch instructions:

BRP X   Branch to location X if result is positive.

BRN X   Branch to location X if result is negative.

BRZ X   Branch to location X if result is zero.

BRO X   Branch to location X if overflow occurs.

In all of these cases, the result referred to is the result of the most recent operation that set the condition code.

Another approach that can be used with a three-address instruction format is to perform a comparison and specify a branch in the same instruction. For example,

BRE R1, R2, X   Branch to X if contents of R1 = contents of R2.

Figure 10.7 shows examples of these operations. Note that a branch can be either *forward* (an instruction with a higher address) or *backward* (lower address). The example shows how an unconditional and a conditional branch can be used to create a repeating loop of instructions. The instructions in locations 202 through 210 will be executed repeatedly until the result of subtracting Y from X is 0.

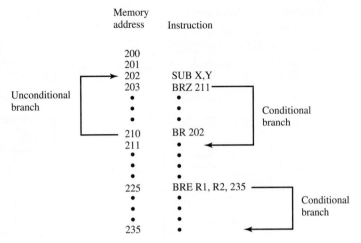

Figure 10.7   Branch Instructions

SKIP INSTRUCTIONS Another form of transfer-of-control instruction is the skip instruction. The skip instruction includes an implied address. Typically, the skip implies that one instruction be skipped; thus, the implied address equals the address of the next instruction plus one instruction length.

Because the skip instruction does not require a destination address field, it is free to do other things. A typical example is the increment-and-skip-if-zero (ISZ) instruction. Consider the following program fragment:

```
301
 .
 .
 .
309    ISZ    R1
310    BR     301
311
```

In this fragment, the two transfer-of-control instructions are used to implement an iterative loop. R1 is set with the negative of the number of iterations to be performed. At the end of the loop, R1 is incremented. If it is not 0, the program branches back to the beginning of the loop. Otherwise, the branch is skipped, and the program continues with the next instruction after the end of the loop.

PROCEDURE CALL INSTRUCTIONS Perhaps the most important innovation in the development of programming languages is the *procedure.* A procedure is a self-contained computer program that is incorporated into a larger program. At any point in the program the procedure may be invoked, or *called.* The processor is instructed to go and execute the entire procedure and then return to the point from which the call took place.

The two principal reasons for the use of procedures are economy and modularity. A procedure allows the same piece of code to be used many times. This is important for economy in programming effort and for making the most efficient use of

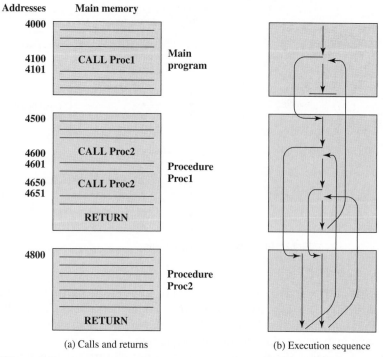

Addresses · Main memory

4000

4100 · **CALL Proc1** · Main program
4101

4500

4600 · **CALL Proc2**
4601 · Procedure
Proc1
4650 · **CALL Proc2**
4651

RETURN

4800

Procedure
Proc2

RETURN

(a) Calls and returns

(b) Execution sequence

Figure 10.8 Nested Procedures

storage space in the system (the program must be stored). Procedures also allow large programming tasks to be subdivided into smaller units. This use of *modularity* greatly eases the programming task.

The procedure mechanism involves two basic instructions: a call instruction that branches from the present location to the procedure, and a return instruction that returns from the procedure to the place from which it was called. Both of these are forms of branching instructions.

Figure 10.8a illustrates the use of procedures to construct a program. In this example, there is a main program starting at location 4000. This program includes a call to procedure PROC1, starting at location 4500. When this call instruction is encountered, the processor suspends execution of the main program and begins execution of PROC1 by fetching the next instruction from location 4500. Within PROC1, there are two calls to PROC2 at location 4800. In each case, the execution of PROC1 is suspended and PROC2 is executed. The RETURN statement causes the processor to go back to the calling program and continue execution at the instruction after the corresponding CALL instruction. This behavior is illustrated in Figure 10.8b.

Three points are worth noting:

1. A procedure can be called from more than one location.

2. A procedure call can appear in a procedure. This allows the *nesting* of procedures to an arbitrary depth.

3. Each procedure call is matched by a return in the called program.

Because we would like to be able to call a procedure from a variety of points, the processor must somehow save the return address so that the return can take place appropriately. There are three common places for storing the return address:

- Register
- Start of called procedure
- Top of stack

Consider a machine-language instruction CALL X, which stands for *call procedure at location X*. If the register approach is used, CALL X causes the following actions:

$$RN \longleftarrow PC + \Delta$$
$$PC \longleftarrow X$$

where RN is a register that is always used for this purpose, PC is the program counter, and Δ is the instruction length. The called procedure can now save the contents of RN to be used for the later return.

A second possibility is to store the return address at the start of the procedure. In this case, CALL X causes

$$X \longleftarrow PC + \Delta$$
$$PC \longleftarrow X + 1$$

This is quite handy. The return address has been stored safely away.

Both of the preceding approaches work and have been used. The only limitation of these approaches is that they complicate the use of *reentrant* procedures. A reentrant procedure is one in which it is possible to have several calls open to it at the same time. A recursive procedure (one that calls itself) is an example of the use of this feature (see Appendix H). If parameters are passed via registers or memory for a reentrant procedure, some code must be responsible for saving the parameters so that the registers or memory space are available for other procedure calls.

A more general and powerful approach is to use a stack (see Appendix 10A for a discussion of stacks). When the processor executes a call, it places the return address on the stack. When it executes a return, it uses the address on the stack. Figure 10.9 illustrates the use of the stack.

In addition to providing a return address, it is also often necessary to pass parameters with a procedure call. These can be passed in registers. Another possibility is to store the parameters in memory just after the CALL instruction. In this case,

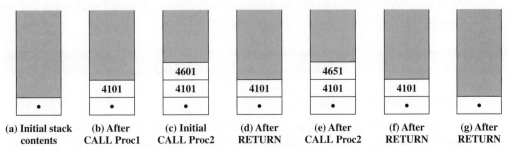

| (a) Initial stack contents | (b) After CALL Proc1 | (c) Initial CALL Proc2 | (d) After RETURN | (e) After CALL Proc2 | (f) After RETURN | (g) After RETURN |

Figure 10.9   Use of Stack to Implement Nested Subroutines of Figure 10.8

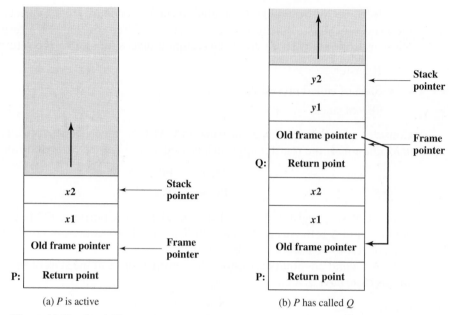

(a) *P* is active   (b) *P* has called *Q*

Figure 10.10   Stack Frame Growth Using Sample Procedures P and Q

the return must be to the location following the parameters. Again, both of these approaches have drawbacks. If registers are used, the called program and the calling program must be written to assure that the registers are used properly. The storing of parameters in memory makes it difficult to exchange a variable number of parameters. Both approaches prevent the use of reentrant procedures.

A more flexible approach to parameter passing is the stack. When the processor executes a call, it not only stacks the return address, it stacks parameters to be passed to the called procedure. The called procedure can access the parameters from the stack. Upon return, return parameters can also be placed on the stack. The entire set of parameters, including return address, that is stored for a procedure invocation is referred to as a *stack frame*.

An example is provided in Figure 10.10. The example refers to procedure P in which the local variables $x1$ and $x2$ are declared, and procedure Q, which P can call and in which the local variables $y1$ and $y2$ are declared. In this figure, the return point for each procedure is the first item stored in the corresponding stack frame. Next is stored a pointer to the beginning of the previous frame. This is needed if the number or length of parameters to be stacked is variable.

10.5 INTEL x86 AND ARM OPERATION TYPES

x86 Operation Types

The x86 provides a complex array of operation types, including a number of specialized instructions. The intent was to provide tools for the compiler writer to produce optimized machine language translation of high-level language programs. Table 10.8

Table 10.8 x86 Operation Types (with Examples of Typical Operations)

Instruction	Description
Data Movement	
MOV	Move operand, between registers or between register and memory.
PUSH	Push operand onto stack.
PUSHA	Push all registers on stack.
MOVSX	Move byte, word, dword, sign extended. Moves a byte to a word or a word to a doubleword with twos-complement sign extension.
LEA	Load effective address. Loads the offset of the source operand, rather than its value to the destination operand.
XLAT	Table lookup translation. Replaces a byte in AL with a byte from a user-coded translation table. When XLAT is executed, AL should have an unsigned index to the table. XLAT changes the contents of AL from the table index to the table entry.
IN, OUT	Input, output operand from I/O space.
Arithmetic	
ADD	Add operands.
SUB	Subtract operands.
MUL	Unsigned integer multiplication, with byte, word, or double word operands, and word, doubleword, or quadword result.
IDIV	Signed divide.
Logical	
AND	AND operands.
BTS	Bit test and set. Operates on a bit field operand. The instruction copies the current value of a bit to flag CF and sets the original bit to 1.
BSF	Bit scan forward. Scans a word or doubleword for a 1-bit and stores the number of the first 1-bit into a register.
SHL/SHR	Shift logical left or right.
SAL/SAR	Shift arithmetic left or right.
ROL/ROR	Rotate left or right.
SETcc	Sets a byte to zero or one depending on any of the 16 conditions defined by status flags.
Control Transfer	
JMP	Unconditional jump.
CALL	Transfer control to another location. Before transfer, the address of the instruction following the CALL is placed on the stack.
JE/JZ	Jump if equal/zero.
LOOPE/LOOPZ	Loops if equal/zero. This is a conditional jump using a value stored in register ECX. The instruction first decrements ECX before testing ECX for the branch condition.
INT/INTO	Interrupt/Interrupt if overflow. Transfer control to an interrupt service routine.

(continued)

Table 10.8 Continued

Instruction	Description
String Operations	
MOVS	Move byte, word, dword string. The instruction operates on one element of a string, indexed by registers ESI and EDI. After each string operation, the registers are automatically incremented or decremented to point to the next element of the string.
LODS	Load byte, word, dword of string.
High-Level Language Support	
ENTER	Creates a stack frame that can be used to implement the rules of a block-structured high-level language.
LEAVE	Reverses the action of the previous ENTER.
BOUND	Check array bounds. Verifies that the value in operand 1 is within lower and upper limits. The limits are in two adjacent memory locations referenced by operand 2. An interrupt occurs if the value is out of bounds. This instruction is used to check an array index.
Flag Control	
STC	Set Carry flag.
LAHF	Load AH register from flags. Copies SF, ZF, AF, PF, and CF bits into A register.
Segment Register	
LDS	Load pointer into DS and another register.
	System Control
HLT	Halt.
LOCK	Asserts a hold on shared memory so that the Pentium has exclusive use of it during the instruction that immediately follows the LOCK.
ESC	Processor extension escape. An escape code that indicates the succeeding instructions are to be executed by a numeric coprocessor that supports high-precision integer and floating-point calculations.
WAIT	Wait until BUSY# negated. Suspends Pentium program execution until the processor detects that the BUSY pin is inactive, indicating that the numeric coprocessor has finished execution.
Protection	
SGDT	Store global descriptor table.
LSL	Load segment limit. Loads a user-specified register with a segment limit.
VERR/VERW	Verify segment for reading/writing.
Cache Management	
INVD	Flushes the internal cache memory.
WBINVD	Flushes the internal cache memory after writing dirty lines to memory.
INVLPG	Invalidates a translation lookaside buffer (TLB) entry.

lists the types and gives examples of each. Most of these are the conventional instructions found in most machine instruction sets, but several types of instructions
are tailored to the x86 architecture and are of particular interest. Appendix A of
[CART06] lists the x86 instructions, together with the operands for each and the effect of the instruction on the condition codes. Appendix B of the NASM assembly
language manual provides a more detailed description of each x86 instruction. Both
documents are available at this book's Web site.

CALL/RETURN INSTRUCTIONS The x86 provides four instructions to support procedure call/return: CALL, ENTER, LEAVE, RETURN. It will be instructive to
look at the support provided by these instructions. Recall from Figure 10.10 that a
common means of implementing the procedure call/return mechanism is via the use
of stack frames. When a new procedure is called, the following must be performed
upon entry to the new procedure:

- Push the return point on the stack.
- Push the current frame pointer on the stack.
- Copy the stack pointer as the new value of the frame pointer.
- Adjust the stack pointer to allocate a frame.

The CALL instruction pushes the current instruction pointer value onto the stack
and causes a jump to the entry point of the procedure by placing the address of the
entry point in the instruction pointer. In the 8088 and 8086 machines, the typical
procedure began with the sequence

PUSH	EBP
MOV	EBP, ESP
SUB	ESP, space_for_locals

where EBP is the frame pointer and ESP is the stack pointer. In the 80286 and later
machines, the ENTER instruction performs all the aforementioned operations in a
single instruction.

The ENTER instruction was added to the instruction set to provide direct support for the compiler. The instruction also includes a feature for support of what are
called nested procedures in languages such as Pascal, COBOL, and Ada (not found
in C or FORTRAN). It turns out that there are better ways of handling nested procedure calls for these languages. Furthermore, although the ENTER instruction
saves a few bytes of memory compared with the PUSH, MOV, SUB sequence
(4 bytes versus 6 bytes), it actually takes longer to execute (10 clock cycles versus
6 clock cycles). Thus, although it may have seemed a good idea to the instruction set
designers to add this feature, it complicates the implementation of the processor
while providing little or no benefit. We will see that, in contrast, a RISC approach to
processor design would avoid complex instructions such as ENTER and might produce a more efficient implementation with a sequence of simpler instructions.

MEMORY MANAGEMENT Another set of specialized instructions deals with memory
segmentation. These are privileged instructions that can only be executed from the operating system. They allow local and global segment tables (called descriptor tables) to
be loaded and read, and for the privilege level of a segment to be checked and altered.

Table 10.9 x86 Status Flags

Status Bit	Name	Description
C	Carry	Indicates carrying or borrowing out of the left-most bit position following an arithmetic operation. Also modified by some of the shift and rotate operations.
P	Parity	Parity of the least-significant byte of the result of an arithmetic or logic operation. 1 indicates even parity; 0 indicates odd parity.
A	Auxiliary Carry	Represents carrying or borrowing between half-bytes of an 8-bit arithmetic or logic operation. Used in binary-coded decimal arithmetic.
Z	Zero	Indicates that the result of an arithmetic or logic operation is 0.
S	Sign	Indicates the sign of the result of an arithmetic or logic operation.
O	Overflow	Indicates an arithmetic overflow after an addition or subtraction for twos complement arithmetic.

The special instructions for dealing with the on-chip cache were discussed in Chapter 4.

STATUS FLAGS AND CONDITION CODES Status flags are bits in special registers that may be set by certain operations and used in conditional branch instructions. The term *condition code* refers to the settings of one or more status flags. In the x86 and many other architectures, status flags are set by arithmetic and compare operations. The compare operation in most languages subtracts two operands, as does a subtract operation. The difference is that a compare operation only sets status flags, whereas a subtract operation also stores the result of the subtraction in the destination operand. Some architectures also set status flags for data transfer instructions.

Table 10.9 lists the status flags used on the x86. Each flag, or combinations of these flags, can be tested for a conditional jump. Table 10.10 shows the condition codes (combinations of status flag values) for which conditional jump opcodes have been defined.

Several interesting observations can be made about this list. First, we may wish to test two operands to determine if one number is bigger than another. But this will depend on whether the numbers are signed or unsigned. For example, the 8-bit number 11111111 is bigger than 00000000 if the two numbers are interpreted as unsigned integers ($255 > 0$) but is less if they are considered as 8-bit twos complement numbers ($-1 < 0$). Many assembly languages therefore introduce two sets of terms to distinguish the two cases: If we are comparing two numbers as signed integers, we use the terms *less than* and *greater than;* if we are comparing them as unsigned integers, we use the terms *below* and *above*.

A second observation concerns the complexity of comparing signed integers. A signed result is greater than or equal to zero if (1) the sign bit is zero and there is no overflow (S = 0 AND O = 0), or (2) the sign bit is one and there is an overflow. A study of Figure 9.4 should convince you that the conditions tested for the various signed operations are appropriate.

x86 SIMD INSTRUCTIONS In 1996, Intel introduced MMX technology into its Pentium product line. MMX is set of highly optimized instructions for multimedia tasks. There are 57 new instructions that treat data in a SIMD (single-instruction, multiple-data) fashion, which makes it possible to perform the same operation, such as addition or multiplication, on multiple data elements at once. Each instruction typically takes a single clock cycle to execute. For the proper application, these fast parallel operations

Table 10.10   x86 Condition Codes for Conditional Jump and SETcc Instructions

Symbol	Condition Tested	Comment
A, NBE	C=0 AND Z=0	Above; Not below or equal (greater than, unsigned)
AE, NB, NC	C=0	Above or equal; Not below (greater than or equal, unsigned); Not carry
B, NAE, C	C=1	Below; Not above or equal (less than, unsigned); Carry set
BE, NA	C=1 OR Z=1	Below or equal; Not above (less than or equal, unsigned)
E, Z	Z=1	Equal; Zero (signed or unsigned)
G, NLE	[(S=1 AND O=1) OR (S=0 and O=0)] AND [Z=0]	Greater than; Not less than or equal (signed)
GE, NL	(S=1 AND O=1) OR (S=0 AND O=0)	Greater than or equal; Not less than (signed)
L, NGE	(S=1 AND O=0) OR (S=0 AND O=1)	Less than; Not greater than or equal (signed)
LE, NG	(S=1 AND O=0) OR (S=0 AND O=1) OR (Z=1)	Less than or equal; Not greater than (signed)
NE, NZ	Z=0	Not equal; Not zero (signed or unsigned)
NO	O=0	No overflow
NS	S=0	Not sign (not negative)
NP, PO	P=0	Not parity; Parity odd
O	O=1	Overflow
P	P=1	Parity; Parity even
S	S=1	Sign (negative)

can yield a speedup of two to eight times over comparable algorithms that do not use the MMX instructions [ATKI96]. With the introduction of 64-bit x86 architecture, Intel has expanded this extension to include double quadword (128 bits) operands and floating-point operations. In this subsection, we describe the MMX features.

The focus of MMX is multimedia programming. Video and audio data are typically composed of large arrays of small data types, such as 8 or 16 bits, whereas conventional instructions are tailored to operate on 32- or 64-bit data. Here are some examples: In graphics and video, a single scene consists of an array of pixels,[2] and there are 8 bits for each pixel or 8 bits for each pixel color component (red, green, blue). Typical audio samples are quantized using 16 bits. For some 3D graphics algorithms, 32 bits are common for basic data types. To provide for parallel operation on these data lengths, three new data types are defined in MMX. Each data type is 64 bits in length and consists of multiple smaller data fields, each of which holds a fixed-point integer. The types are as follows:

- **Packed byte:** Eight bytes packed into one 64-bit quantity
- **Packed word:** Four 16-bit words packed into 64 bits
- **Packed doubleword:** Two 32-bit doublewords packed into 64 bits

---

[2]A pixel, or picture element, is the smallest element of a digital image that can be assigned a gray level. Equivalently, a pixel is an individual dot in a dot-matrix representation of a picture.

Table 10.11   MMX Instruction Set

Category	Instruction	Description
Arithmetic	PADD [B, W, D]	Parallel add of packed eight bytes, four 16-bit words, or two 32-bit doublewords, with wraparound.
	PADDS [B, W]	Add with saturation.
	PADDUS [B, W]	Add unsigned with saturation.
	PSUB [B, W, D]	Subtract with wraparound.
	PSUBS [B, W]	Subtract with saturation.
	PSUBUS [B, W]	Subtract unsigned with saturation.
	PMULHW	Parallel multiply of four signed 16-bit words, with high-order 16 bits of 32-bit result chosen.
	PMULLW	Parallel multiply of four signed 16-bit words, with low-order 16 bits of 32-bit result chosen.
	PMADDWD	Parallel multiply of four signed 16-bit words; add together adjacent pairs of 32-bit results.
Comparison	PCMPEQ [B, W, D]	Parallel compare for equality; result is mask of 1s if true or 0s if false.
	PCMPGT [B, W, D]	Parallel compare for greater than; result is mask of 1s if true or 0s if false.
Conversion	PACKUSWB	Pack words into bytes with unsigned saturation.
	PACKSS [WB, DW]	Pack words into bytes, or doublewords into words, with signed saturation.
	PUNPCKH [BW, WD, DQ]	Parallel unpack (interleaved merge) high-order bytes, words, or doublewords from MMX register.
	PUNPCKL [BW, WD, DQ]	Parallel unpack (interleaved merge) low-order bytes, words, or doublewords from MMX register.
Logical	PAND	64-bit bitwise logical AND
	PNDN	64-bit bitwise logical AND NOT
	POR	64-bit bitwise logical OR
	PXOR	64-bit bitwise logical XOR
Shift	PSLL [W, D, Q]	Parallel logical left shift of packed words, doublewords, or quadword by amount specified in MMX register or immediate value.
	PSRL [W, D, Q]	Parallel logical right shift of packed words, doublewords, or quadword.
	PSRA [W, D]	Parallel arithmetic right shift of packed words, doublewords, or quadword.
Data Transfer	MOV [D, Q]	Move doubleword or quadword to/from MMX register.
State Mgt	EMMS	Empty MMX state (empty FP registers tag bits).

Note: If an instruction supports multiple data types [byte (B), word (W), doubleword (D), quadword (Q)], the data types are indicated in brackets.

Table 10.11 lists the MMX instruction set. Most of the instructions involve parallel operation on bytes, words, or doublewords. For example, the PSLLW instruction performs a left logical shift separately on each of the four words in the packed word operand; the PADDB instruction takes packed byte operands as input and performs parallel additions on each byte position independently to produce a packed byte output.

One unusual feature of the new instruction set is the introduction of **saturation arithmetic** for byte and 16-bit word operands. With ordinary unsigned arithmetic, when an operation overflows (i.e., a carry out of the most significant bit), the extra bit is truncated. This is referred to as wraparound, because the effect of the truncation can be, for example, to produce an addition result that is smaller than the two input operands. Consider the addition of the two words, in hexadecimal, F000h and 3000h. The sum would be expressed as

$$
\begin{array}{rl}
\text{F000h} = & 1111\ 0000\ 0000\ 0000 \\
+\text{3000h} = & \underline{0011\ 0000\ 0000\ 0000} \\
& 10010\ 0000\ 0000\ 0000 = \text{2000h}
\end{array}
$$

If the two numbers represented image intensity, then the result of the addition is to make the combination of two dark shades turn out to be lighter. This is typically not what is intended. With saturation arithmetic, if addition results in overflow or subtraction results in underflow, the result is set to the largest or smallest value representable. For the preceding example, with saturation arithmetic, we have

$$
\begin{array}{rl}
\text{F000h} = & 1111\ 0000\ 0000\ 0000 \\
+\text{3000h} = & \underline{0011\ 0000\ 0000\ 0000} \\
& 10010\ 0000\ 0000\ 0000 \\
& 1111\ 1111\ 1111\ 1111 = \text{FFFFh}
\end{array}
$$

To provide a feel for the use of MMX instructions, we look at an example, taken from [PELE97]. A common video application is the fade-out, fade-in effect, in which one scene gradually dissolves into another. Two images are combined with a weighted average:

$$
\text{Result\_pixel} = \text{A\_pixel} \times \text{fade} + \text{B\_pixel} \times (1 - \text{fade})
$$

This calculation is performed on each pixel position in A and B. If a series of video frames is produced while gradually changing the fade value from 1 to 0 (scaled appropriately for an 8-bit integer), the result is to fade from image A to image B.

Figure 10.11 shows the sequence of steps required for one set of pixels. The 8-bit pixel components are converted to 16-bit elements to accommodate the MMX 16-bit multiply capability. If these images use 640×480 resolution, and the dissolve technique uses all 255 possible values of the fade value, then the total number of instructions executed using MMX is 535 million. The same calculation, performed without the MMX instructions, requires 1.4 billion instruction executions [INTE98].

ARM Operation Types

The ARM architecture provides a large collection of operation types. The following are the principal categories:

- **Load and store instructions:** In the ARM architecture, only load and store instructions access memory locations; arithmetic and logical instructions are performed only on registers and immediate values encoded in the instruction.

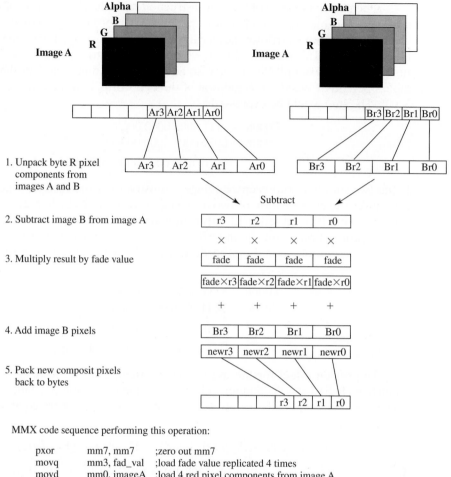

MMX code sequence performing this operation:

```
pxor       mm7, mm7      ;zero out mm7
movq       mm3, fad_val  ;load fade value replicated 4 times
movd       mm0, imageA   ;load 4 red pixel components from image A
movd       mm1, imageB   ;load 4 red pixel components from image B
punpckblw  mm0, mm7      ;unpack 4 pixels to 16 bits
punpckblw  mm1, mm7      ;unpack 4 pixels to 16 bits
psubw      mm0, mm1      ;subtract image B from image A
pmulhw     mm0, mm3      ;multiply the subtract result by fade values
padddw     mm0, mm1      ;add result to image B
packuswb   mm0, mm7      ;pack 16-bit results back to bytes
```

Figure 10.11 Image Compositing on Color Plane Representation

This limitation is characteristic of RISC design and it is explored further in Chapter 13. The ARM architecture supports two broad types of instruction that load or store the value of a single register, or a pair of registers, from or to memory: (1) load or store a 32-bit word or an 8-bit unsigned byte, and (2) load or store a 16-bit unsigned halfword, and load and sign extend a 16-bit halfword or an 8-bit byte

- **Branch instructions:** ARM supports a branch instruction that allows a conditional branch forwards or backwards up to 32 MB. As the program counter is one of the general-purpose registers (R15), a branch or jump can also be generated by writing a value to R15. A subroutine call can be performed by a variant of the standard branch instruction. As well as allowing a branch forward or backward up to 32 MB, the Branch with Link (BL) instruction preserves the address of the instruction after the branch (the return address) in the LR (R14). Branches are determined by a 4-bit condition field in the instruction.

- **Data-processing instructions:** This category includes logical instructions (AND, OR, XOR), add and subtract instructions, and test and compare instructions.

- **Multiply instructions:** The integer multiply instructions operate on word or halfword operands and can produce normal or long results. For example, there is a multiply instruction that takes two 32-bit operands and produces a 64-bit result.

- **Parallel addition and subtraction instructions:** In addition to the normal data processing and multiply instructions, there are a set of parallel addition and subtraction instructions, in which portions of two operands are operated on in parallel. For example, ADD16 adds the top halfwords of two registers to form the top halfword of the result and adds the bottom halfwords of the same two registers to form the bottom halfword of the result. These instructions are useful in image processing applications, similar to the x86 MMX instructions

- **Extend instructions:** There are several instructions for unpacking data by sign or zero extending bytes to halfwords or words, and halfwords to words.

- **Status register access instructions:** ARM provides the ability to read and also to write portions of the status register.

CONDITION CODES The ARM architecture defines four condition flags that are stored in the program status register: N, Z, C, and V (Negative, Zero, Carry and oVerflow), with meanings essentially the same as the S, Z, C, and V flags in the x86 architecture. These four flags constitute a condition code in ARM. Table 10.12 shows the combination of conditions for which conditional execution is defined.

There are two unusual aspects to the use of condition codes in ARM:

1. All instructions, not just branch instructions, include a condition code field, which means that virtually all instructions may be conditionally executed. Any combination of flag settings except 1110 or 1111 in an instruction's condition code field signifies that the instruction will be executed only if the condition is met.

2. All data processing instructions (arithmetic, logical) include an S bit that signifies whether the instruction updates the condition flags.

The use of conditional execution and conditional setting of the condition flags helps in the design of shorter programs that use less memory. On the other hand, all instructions include 4 bits for the condition code, so there is a trade-off in that fewer bits in the 32-bit instruction are available for opcode and operands. Because the

Table 10.12 ARM Conditions for Conditional Instruction Execution

Code	Symbol	Condition Tested	Comment
0000	EQ	Z=1	Equal
0001	NE	Z=0	Not equal
0010	CS/HS	C=1	Carry set/unsigned higher or same
0011	CC/LO	C=0	Carry clear/unsigned lower
0100	MI	N=1	Minus/negative
0101	PL	N=0	Plus/positive or zero
0110	VS	V=1	Overflow
0111	VC	V=0	No overflow
1000	HI	C=1 AND Z=0	Unsigned higher
1001	LS	C=0 OR Z=1	Unsigned lower or same
1010	GE	N=V [(N=1 AND V=1) OR (N=0 AND V=0)	Signed greater than or equal
1011	LT	N≠V [(N=1 AND V=0) OR (N=0 AND V=1)]	Signed less than
1100	GT	(Z=0) AND (N=V)	Signed greater than
1101	LE	(Z=1) OR (N≠V)	Signed less than or equal
1110	AL	—	Always (unconditional)
1111	—	—	This instruction can only be executed unconditionally

ARM is a RISC design that relies heavily on register addressing, this seems to be a reasonable trade-off.

10.6 RECOMMENDED READING

The x86 instruction set is well covered by [BREY09]. The ARM instruction set is covered in [SLOS04] and [KNAG04]. [INTE04b] describes software considerations related to microprocessor Endian architecture and discusses guidelines for developing Endian-neutral code.

BREY09   Brey, B. *The Intel Microprocessors: 8086/8066, 80186/80188, 80286, 80386, 80486, Pentium, Pentium Pro Processor, Pentium II, Pentium III, Pentium 4 and Core2 with 64-bit Extensions.* Upper Saddle River, NJ: Prentice Hall, 2009.

INTE04b   Intel Corp. *Endianness White Paper.* November 15, 2004.

KNAG04   Knaggs, P., and Welsh, S. *ARM: Assembly Language Programming.* Bournemouth University, School of Design, Engineering, and Computing, August 31, 2004. www.freetechbooks.com/arm-assembly-language-programming-t729.html

SLOS04   Sloss, A.; Symes, D.; and Wright, C. *ARM System Developer's Guide.* San Francisco: Morgan Kaufmann, 2004.

10.7 KEY TERMS, REVIEW QUESTIONS, AND PROBLEMS

Key Terms

accumulator	jump	procedure call
address	little endian	procedure return
arithmetic shift	logical shift	push
bi-endian	machine instruction	reentrant procedure
big endian	operand	reverse Polish notation
branch	operation	rotate
conditional branch	packed decimal	skip
instruction set	pop	stack

Review Questions

10.1 What are the typical elements of a machine instruction?

10.2 What types of locations can hold source and destination operands?

10.3 If an instruction contains four addresses, what might be the purpose of each address?

10.4 List and briefly explain five important instruction set design issues.

10.5 What types of operands are typical in machine instruction sets?

10.6 What is the relationship between the IRA character code and the packed decimal representation?

10.7 What is the difference between an arithmetic shift and a logical shift?

10.8 Why are transfer of control instructions needed?

10.9 List and briefly explain two common ways of generating the condition to be tested in a conditional branch instruction.

10.10 What is meant by the term *nesting of procedures*?

10.11 List three possible places for storing the return address for a procedure return.

10.12 What is a reentrant procedure?

10.13 What is reverse Polish notation?

10.14 What is the difference between big endian and little endian?

Problems

10.1 Show in hex notation:
   a. The packed decimal format for 23
   b. The ASCII characters 23

10.2 For each of the following packed decimal numbers, show the decimal value:
   a. 0111 0011 0000 1001
   b. 0101 1000 0010
   c. 0100 1010 0110

10.3 A given microprocessor has words of 1 byte. What is the smallest and largest integer that can be represented in the following representations:
   a. Unsigned
   b. Sign-magnitude
   c. Ones complement
   d. Twos complement
   e. Unsigned packed decimal
   f. Signed packed decimal

10.4 Many processors provide logic for performing arithmetic on packed decimal numbers. Although the rules for decimal arithmetic are similar to those for binary operations, the decimal results may require some corrections to the individual digits if binary logic is used.

Consider the decimal addition of two unsigned numbers. If each number consists of N digits, then there are $4N$ bits in each number. The two numbers are to be added using a binary adder. Suggest a simple rule for correcting the result. Perform addition in this fashion on the numbers 1698 and 1786.

10.5 The tens complement of the decimal number X is defined to be $10^N - X$, where N is the number of decimal digits in the number. Describe the use of ten's complement representation to perform decimal subtraction. Illustrate the procedure by subtracting $(0326)_{10}$ from $(0736)_{10}$.

10.6 Compare zero-, one-, two-, and three-address machines by writing programs to compute

$$X = (A + B \times C)/(D - E \times F)$$

for each of the four machines. The instructions available for use are as follows:

0 Address	1 Address	2 Address	3 Address
PUSH M	LOAD M	MOVE $(X \leftarrow Y)$	MOVE $(X \leftarrow Y)$
POP M	STORE M	ADD $(X \leftarrow X + Y)$	ADD $(X \leftarrow Y + Z)$
ADD	ADD M	SUB $(X \leftarrow X - Y)$	SUB $(X \leftarrow Y - Z)$
SUB	SUB M	MUL $(X \leftarrow X \times Y)$	MUL $(X \leftarrow Y \times Z)$
MUL	MUL M	DIV $(X \leftarrow X/Y)$	DIV $(X \leftarrow Y/Z)$
DIV	DIV M		

10.7 Consider a hypothetical computer with an instruction set of only two n-bit instructions. The first bit specifies the opcode, and the remaining bits specify one of the 2^{n-1} n-bit words of main memory. The two instructions are as follows:

SUBS X   Subtract the contents of location X from the accumulator, and store the result in location X and the accumulator.

JUMP X   Place address X in the program counter.

A word in main memory may contain either an instruction or a binary number in twos complement notation. Demonstrate that this instruction repertoire is reasonably complete by specifying how the following operations can be programmed:
a. Data transfer: Location X to accumulator, accumulator to location X
b. Addition: Add contents of location X to accumulator
c. Conditional branch
d. Logical OR
e. I/O Operations

10.8 Many instruction sets contain the instruction NOOP, meaning no operation, which has no effect on the processor state other than incrementing the program counter. Suggest some uses of this instruction.

10.9 In Section 10.4, it was stated that both an arithmetic left shift and a logical left shift correspond to a multiplication by 2 when there is no overflow, and if overflow occurs, arithmetic and logical left shift operations produce different results, but the arithmetic left shift retains the sign of the number. Demonstrate that these statements are true for 5-bit twos complement integers.

10.10 In what way are numbers rounded using arithmetic right shift (e.g., round toward $+\infty$, round toward $-\infty$, toward zero, away from 0)?

10.11 Suppose a stack is to be used by the processor to manage procedure calls and returns. Can the program counter be eliminated by using the top of the stack as a program counter?

10.12 The x86 architecture includes an instruction called Decimal Adjust after Addition (DAA). DAA performs the following sequence of instructions:

```
if ((AL AND 0FH) >9) OR (AF = 1) then
      AL ← AL + 6;
      AF ← 1;
else
      AF ← 0;
endif;
if   (AL > 9FH) OR (CF = 1) then
      AL ← AL + 60H;
      CF ← 1;
else
      CF ← 0;
endif.
```

"H" indicates hexadecimal. AL is an 8-bit register that holds the result of addition of two unsigned 8-bit integers. AF is a flag set if there is a carry from bit 3 to bit 4 in the result of an addition. CF is a flag set if there is a carry from bit 7 to bit 8. Explain the function performed by the DAA instruction.

10.13 The x86 Compare instruction (CMP) subtracts the source operand from the destination operand; it updates the status flags (C, P, A, Z, S, O) but does not alter either of the operands. The CMP instruction can be used to determine if the destination operand is greater than, equal to, or less than the source operand.
   a. Suppose the two operands are treated as unsigned integers. Show which status flags are relevant to determine the relative size of the two integer and what values of the flags correspond to greater than, equal to, or less than.
   b. Suppose the two operands are treated as twos complement signed integers. Show which status flags are relevant to determine the relative size of the two integer and what values of the flags correspond to greater than, equal to, or less than.
   c. The CMP instruction may be followed by a conditional Jump (Jcc) or Set Condition (SETcc) instruction, where cc refers to one of the 16 conditions listed in Table 10.10. Demonstrate that the conditions tested for a signed number comparison are correct.

10.14 Suppose we wished to apply the x86 CMP instruction to 32-bit operands that contained numbers in a floating-point format. For correct results, what requirements have to be met in the following areas?
   a. The relative position of the significand, sign, and exponent fields.
   b. The representation of the value zero.
   c. The representation of the exponent.
   d. Does the IEEE format meet these requirements? Explain.

10.15 Many microprocessor instruction sets include an instruction that tests a condition and sets a destination operand if the condition is true. Examples include the SETcc on the x86, the Scc on the Motorola MC68000, and the Scond on the National NS32000.
   a. There are a few differences among these instructions:
      • SETcc and Scc operate only on a byte, whereas Scond operates on byte, word, and doubleword operands.
      • SETcc and Scond set the operand to integer one if true and to zero if false. Scc sets the byte to all binary ones if true and all zeros if false.
      What are the relative advantages and disadvantages of these differences?
   b. None of these instructions set any of the condition code flags, and thus an explicit test of the result of the instruction is required to determine its value. Discuss whether condition codes should be set as a result of this instruction.

c. A simple IF statement such as IF a > b THEN can be implemented using a numerical representation method, that is, making the Boolean value manifest, as opposed to a *flow of control* method, which represents the value of a Boolean expression by a point reached in the program. A compiler might implement IF a > b THEN with the following x86 code:

```
        SUB   CX, CX    ;set register CX to 0
        MOV   AX, B     ;move contents of location B to register AX
        CMP   AX, A     ;compare contents of register AX and location A
        JLE   TEST      ;jump if A ≤ B
        INC   CX        ;add 1 to contents of register CX
TEST    JCXZ  OUT       ;jump if contents of CX equal 0
THEN          OUT
```

The result of (A > B) is a Boolean value held in a register and available later on, outside the context of the flow of code just shown. It is convenient to use register CX for this, because many of the branch and loop opcodes have a built-in test for CX.

Show an alternative implementation using the SETcc instruction that saves memory and execution time. (*Hint:* No additional new x86 instructions are needed, other than the SETcc.)

d. Now consider the high-level language statement:

$$A: = (B > C) \text{ OR } (D = F)$$

A compiler might generate the following code:

```
        MOV   EAX, B    ;move contents of location B to register EAX
        CMP   EAX, C    ;compare contents of register EAX and location C
        MOV   BL, 0     ;0 represents false
        JLE   N1        ;jump if B ≤ C
        MOV   BL, 1     ;1 represents false
N1      MOV   EAX, D
        CMP   EAX, F
        MOV   BH, 0
        JNE   N2
        MOV   BH, 1
N2      OR    BL, BH
```

Show an alternative implementation using the SETcc instruction that saves memory and execution time.

10.16 Suppose that two registers contain the following hexadecimal values: AB0890C2, 4598EE50. What is the result of adding them using MMX instructions:
a. for packed byte
b. for packed word

Assume saturation arithmetic is not used.

10.17 Appendix 10A points out that there are no stack-oriented instructions in an instruction set if the stack is to be used only by the processor for such purposes as procedure handling. How can the processor use a stack for any purpose without stack-oriented instructions?

10.18 Convert the following formulas from reverse Polish to infix:
a. AB + C + D ×
b. AB/CD/ +
c. ABCDE +××/
d. ABCDE + F/ + G − H/ ×+

10.19 Convert the following formulas from infix to reverse Polish:
a. A + B + C + D + E
b. (A + B) × (C + D) + E
c. (A × B) + (C × D) + E
d. (A − B) × (((C − D × E)/F)/G) × H

10.20   Convert the expression A + B − C to postfix notation using Dijkstra's algorithm. Show the steps involved. Is the result equivalent to (A + B) − C or A + (B − C)? Does it matter?

10.21   Using the algorithm for converting infix to postfix defined in Appendix 10A, show the steps involved in converting the expression of Figure 10.15 into postfix. Use a presentation similar to Figure 10.17.

10.22   Show the calculation of the expression in Figure 10.17, using a presentation similar to Figure 10.16.

10.23   Redraw the little-endian layout in Figure 10.18 so that the bytes appear as numbered in the big-endian layout. That is, show memory in 64-bit rows, with the bytes listed left to right, top to bottom.

10.24   For the following data structures, draw the big-endian and little-endian layouts, using the format of Figure 10.18, and comment on the results.

        a.   struct {
                double i;   //0x1112131415161718
           } s1;
        b.   struct {
                int i;   //0x11121314
                int j;   //0x15161718
           } s2;
        c.   struct {
                short i;   //0x1112
                short j;   //0x1314
                short k;   //0x1516
                short l;   //0x1718
           } s3;

10.25   The IBM Power architecture specification does not dictate how a processor should implement little-endian mode. It specifies only the view of memory a processor must have when operating in little-endian mode. When converting a data structure from big endian to little endian, processors are free to implement a true byte-swapping mechanism or to use some sort of an address modification mechanism. Current Power processors are all default big-endian machines and use address modification to treat data as little-endian.

    Consider the structure s defined in Figure 10.18. The layout in the lower-right portion of the figure shows the structure s as seen by the processor. In fact, if structure s is compiled in little-endian mode, its layout in memory is shown in Figure 10.12. Explain the mapping that is involved, describe an easy way to implement the mapping, and discuss the effectiveness of this approach.

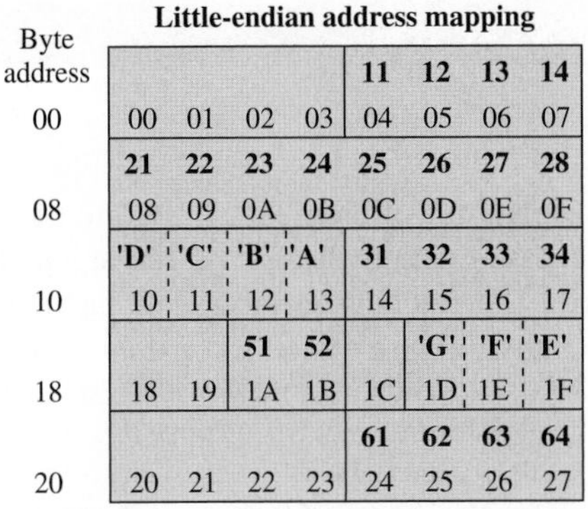

Figure 10.12   Power Architecture
Little-Endian Structure s in Memory

10.26 Write a small program to determine the endianness of machine and report the results. Run the program on a computer available to you and turn in the output.

10.27 The MIPS processor can be set to operate in either big-endian or little-endian mode. Consider the Load Byte Unsigned (LBU) instruction, which loads a byte from memory into the low-order 8 bits of a register and fills the high-order 24 bits of the register with zeros. The description of LBU is given in the MIPS reference manual using a register-transfer language as

$$\text{mem} \leftarrow \text{LoadMemory}(\dots)$$
$$\text{byte} \leftarrow \text{VirtualAddress}_{1..0}$$
if CONDITION **then**
$$\text{GPR}[\text{rt}] \leftarrow 0^{24} || \text{mem}_{31-8 \times \text{byte} .. 24-8 \times \text{byte}}$$
else
$$\text{GPR}[\text{rt}] \leftarrow 0^{24} || \text{mem}_{7+8 \times \text{byte} .. 8 \times \text{byte}}$$
endif

where *byte* refers to the two low-order bits of the effective address and *mem* refers to the value loaded from memory. In the manual, instead of the word CONDITION, one of the following two words is used: BigEndian, LittleEndian. Which word is used?

10.28 Most, but not all, processors use big- or little-endian bit ordering within a byte that is consistent with big- or little-endian ordering of bytes within a multibyte scalar. Let us consider the Motorola 68030, which uses big-endian byte ordering. The documentation of the 68030 concerning formats is confusing. The user's manual explains that the bit ordering of bit fields is the opposite of bit ordering of integers. Most bit field operations operate with one endian ordering, but a few bit field operations require the opposite ordering. The following description from the user's manual describes most of the bit field operations:

A bit operand is specified by a base address that selects one byte in memory (the base byte), and a bit number that selects the one bit in this byte. The most significant bit is bit seven. A bit field operand is specified by: **(1)** a base address that selects one byte in memory; **(2)** a bit field offset that indicates the leftmost (base) bit of the bit field in relation to the most significant bit of the base byte; and **(3)** a bit field width that determines how many bits to the right of the base byte are in the bit field. The most significant bit of the base byte is bit field offset 0, the least significant bit of the base byte is bit field offset 7.

Do these instructions use big-endian or little-endian bit ordering?

APPENDIX 10A STACKS

Stacks

A *stack* is an ordered set of elements, only one of which can be accessed at a time. The point of access is called the *top* of the stack. The number of elements in the stack, or *length* of the stack, is variable. The last element in the stack is the *base* of the stack. Items may only be added to or deleted from the top of the stack. For this reason, a stack is also known as a *pushdown list*[3] or a *last-in-first-out (LIFO) list.*

---

[3]A better term would be *place-on-top-of list* because the existing elements of the list are not moved in memory, but a new element is added at the next available memory address.

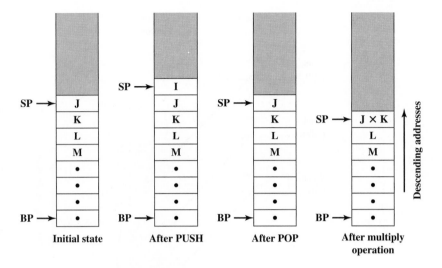

SP = Stack pointer
BP = Base pointer

Figure 10.13   Basic Stack Operation (full/descending)

Figure 10.13 shows the basic stack operations. We begin at some point in time when the stack contains some number of elements. A PUSH operation appends one new item to the top of the stack. A POP operation removes the top item from the stack. In both cases, the top of the stack moves accordingly. Binary operators, which require two operands (e.g., multiply, divide, add, subtract), use the top two stack items as operands, pop both items, and push the result back onto the stack. Unary operations, which require only one operand (e.g., logical NOT), use the item on the top of the stack. All of these operations are summarized in Table 10.13.

Stack Implementation

The stack is a useful structure to provide as part of a processor implementation. One use, discussed in Section 10.4, is to manage procedure calls and returns. Stacks may also be useful to the programmer. An example of this is expression evaluation, discussed later in this section.

The implementation of a stack depends in part on its potential uses. If it is desired to make stack operations available to the programmer, then the instruction set will include stack-oriented operations, including PUSH, POP, and operations that use the top one or two stack elements as operands. Because all of these operations

Table 10.13   Stack-Oriented Operations

PUSH	Append a new element on the top of the stack.
POP	Delete the top element of the stack.
Unary operation	Perform operation on top element of stack. Replace top element with result.
Binary operation	Perform operation on top two elements of stack. Delete top two elements of stack. Place result of operaticn on top of stack.

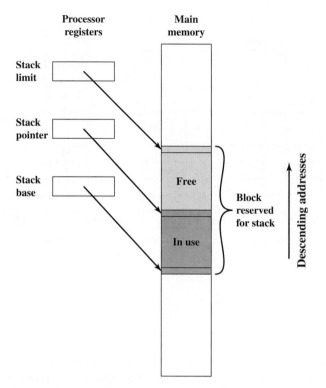

Figure 10.14   Typical Stack Organization (full/descending)

refer to a unique location, namely the top of the stack, the address of the operand or operands is implicit and need not be included in the instruction. These are the zero-address instructions referred to in Section 10.1.

If the stack mechanism is to be used only by the processor, for such purposes as procedure handling, then there will not be explicit stack-oriented instructions in the instruction set. In either case, the implementation of a stack requires that there be some set of locations used to store the stack elements. A typical approach is illustrated in Figure 10.14. A contiguous block of locations is reserved in main memory (or virtual memory) for the stack. Most of the time, the block is partially filled with stack elements and the remainder is available for stack growth.

Three addresses are needed for proper operation, and these are often stored in processor registers:

- **Stack pointer (SP):** Contains the address of the top of the stack. If an item is appended to or deleted from the stack, the pointer is incremented or decremented to contain the address of the new top of the stack.
- **Stack base:** Contains the address of the bottom location in the reserved block. If an attempt is made to POP when the stack is empty, an error is reported.
- **Stack limit:** Contains the address of the other end of the reserved block. If an attempt is made to PUSH when the block is fully utilized for the stack, an error is reported.

Stack implementations have two key attributes:

- **Ascending/descending:** An ascending stack grows in the direction of ascending addresses, starting from a low address and progressing to a higher address. That is, an ascending stack is one in which the SP is incremented when items are pushed and decremented when items are pulled. A descending stack grows in the direction of descending addresses, starting from a high address and progressing to a lower one. Most machines implement descending stacks as a default.

- **Full/empty:** This is a misleading terminology, because is does not refer to whether the stack is completely full or completely empty. Rather, the SP can either point to the top item in the stack (full method), or the next free space on the stack (an empty method). For the full method, when the stack is completely full, the SP points to the upper limit of the stack. For the empty method, when the stack is completely empty, the SP points to the base of the stack.

Figure 10.13 is an example of a descending/full implementation (assuming that numerically lower addresses are depicted higher on the page). The ARM architecture allows the system programmer to specify the use of ascending or descending, empty or full stack operations. The x86 architecture uses a descending/empty convention.

Expression Evaluation

Mathematical formulas are usually expressed in what is known as **infix** notation. In this form, a binary operator appears between the operands (e.g., a + b). For complex expressions, parentheses are used to determine the order of evaluation of expressions. For example, a + (b × c) will yield a different result than (a + b) × c. To minimize the use of parentheses, operations have an implied precedence. Generally, multiplication takes precedence over addition, so that a + b × c is equivalent to a + (b × c).

An alternative technique is known as **reverse Polish**, or **postfix**, notation. In this notation, the operator follows its two operands. For example,

a + b	becomes a b +
a + (b × c)	becomes a b c ×+
(a + b) × c	becomes a b + c×

Note that, regardless of the complexity of an expression, no parentheses are required when using reverse Polish.

The advantage of postfix notation is that an expression in this form is easily evaluated using a stack. An expression in postfix notation is scanned from left to right. For each element of the expression, the following rules are applied:

1. If the element is a variable or constant, push it onto the stack.
2. If the element is an operator, pop the top two items of the stack, perform the operation, and push the result.

After the entire expression has been scanned, the result is on the top of the stack.

The simplicity of this algorithm makes it a convenient one for evaluating expressions. Accordingly, many compilers will take an expression in a high-level

	Stack	General Registers	Single Register
	Push a Push b Subtract Push c Push d Push e Multiply Add Divide Pop f	Load R1, a Subtract R1, b Load R2, d Multiply R2, e Add R2, c Divide R1, R2 Store R1, f	Load d Multiply e Add c Store f Load a Subtract b Divide f Store f
Number of instructions	10	7	8
Memory access	10 op + 6 d	7 op + 6 d	8 op + 8 d

Figure 10.15   Comparison of Three Programs to Calculate
$$f = \frac{a - b}{c + (d \times e)}$$

language, convert it to postfix notation, and then generate the machine instructions from that notation. Figure 10.15 shows the sequence of machine instructions for evaluating $f = (a - b)/(c + d \times e)$ using stack-oriented instructions. The figure also shows the use of one-address and two-address instructions. Note that, even though the stack-oriented rules were not used in the last two cases, the postfix notation served as a guide for generating the machine instructions. The sequence of events for the stack program is shown in Figure 10.16.

The process of converting an infix expression to a postfix expression is itself most easily accomplished using a stack. The following algorithm is due to Dijkstra

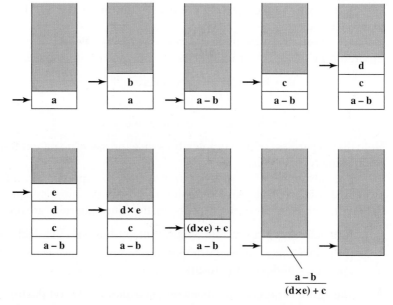

Figure 10.16   Use of Stack to Compute $f = (a - b)/[(d \times e) + c]$

Input	Output	Stack (top on right)
A + B × C + (D + E) × F	empty	empty
+ B × C + (D + E) × F	A	empty
B × C + (D + E) × F	A	+
× C + (D + E) × F	A B	+
C + (D + E) × F	A B	+ ×
+ (D + E) × F	A B C	+ ×
(D + E) × F	A B C × +	+
D + E) × F	A B C × +	+ (
+ E) × F	A B C × + D	+ (
E) × F	A B C × + D	+ (+
) × F	A B C × + D E	+ (+
× F	A B C × + D E +	+
F	A B C × + D E +	+ ×
empty	A B C × + D E + F	+ ×
empty	A B C × + D E + F × +	empty

Figure 10.17   Conversion of an Expression from Infix to Postfix Notation

[DIJK63]. The infix expression is scanned from left to right, and the postfix expression is developed and output during the scan. The steps are as follows:

1. Examine the next element in the input.
2. If it is an operand, output it.
3. If it is an opening parenthesis, push it onto the stack.
4. If it is an operator, then
   - If the top of the stack is an opening parenthesis, then push the operator.
   - If it has higher priority than the top of the stack (multiply and divide have higher priority than add and subtract), then push the operator.
   - Else, pop operation from stack to output, and repeat step 4.
5. If it is a closing parenthesis, pop operators to the output until an opening parenthesis is encountered. Pop and discard the opening parenthesis.
6. If there is more input, go to step 1.
7. If there is no more input, unstack the remaining operands.

Figure 10.17 illustrates the use of this algorithm. This example should give the reader some feel for the power of stack-based algorithms.

APPENDIX 10B LITTLE- , BIG- , AND BI-ENDIAN

An annoying and curious phenomenon relates to how the bytes within a word and the bits within a byte are both referenced and represented. We look first at the problem of byte ordering and then consider that of bits.

Byte Ordering

The concept of endianness was first discussed in the literature by Cohen [COHE81]. With respect to bytes, endianness has to do with the byte ordering of multibyte scalar values. The issue is best introduced with an example. Suppose we have the 32-bit hexadecimal value 12345678 and that it is stored in a 32-bit word in byte-addressable memory at byte location 184. The value consists of 4 bytes, with the least significant byte containing the value 78 and the most significant byte containing the value 12. There are two obvious ways to store this value:

Address	Value		Address	Value
184	12		184	78
185	34		185	56
186	56		186	34
187	78		187	12

The mapping on the left stores the most significant byte in the lowest numerical byte address; this is known as **big endian** and is equivalent to the left-to-right order of writing in Western culture languages. The mapping on the right stores the least significant byte in the lowest numerical byte address; this is known as **little endian** and is reminiscent of the right-to-left order of arithmetic operations in arithmetic units.[4] For a given multibyte scalar value, big endian and little endian are byte-reversed mappings of each other.

The concept of endianness arises when it is necessary to treat a multiple-byte entity as a single data item with a single address, even though it is composed of smaller addressable units. Some machines, such as the Intel 80x86, x86, VAX, and Alpha, are little-endian machines, whereas others, such as the IBM System 370/390, the Motorola 680x0, Sun SPARC, and most RISC machines, are big endian. This presents problems when data are transferred from a machine of one endian type to the other and when a programmer attempts to manipulate individual bytes or bits within a multibyte scalar.

The property of endianness does not extend beyond an individual data unit. In any machine, aggregates such as files, data structures, and arrays are composed of multiple data units, each with endianness. Thus, conversion of a block of memory from one style of endianness to the other requires knowledge of the data structure.

Figure 10.18 illustrates how endianness determines addressing and byte order. The C structure at the top contains a number of data types. The memory layout in

---

[4]The terms *big endian* and *little endian* come from Part I, Chapter 4 of Jonathan Swift's *Gulliver's Travels.* They refer to a religious war between two groups, one that breaks eggs at the big end and the other that breaks eggs at the little end.

```
struct{
    int      a;      //0x1112_1314                      word
    int      pad;    //
    double   b;      //0x2122_2324_2526_2728            doubleword
    char*    c;      //0x3132_3334                       word
    char     d[7];   //'A'.'B','C','D','E','F','G'       byte array
    short    e;      //0x5152                            halfword
    int      f;      //0x6162_6364                       word
} s;
```

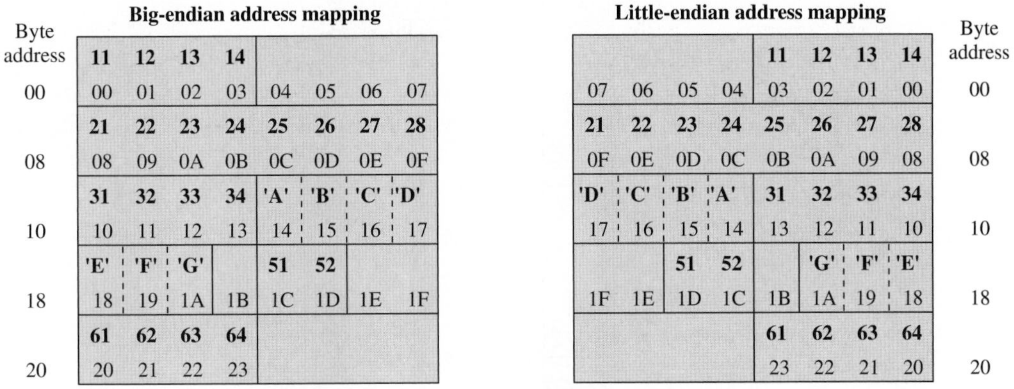

Figure 10.18   Example C Data Structure and its Endian Maps

the lower left results from compilation of that structure for a big-endian machine, and that in the lower right for a little-endian machine. In each case, memory is depicted as a series of 64-bit rows. For the big-endian case, memory typically is viewed left to right, top to bottom, whereas for the little-endian case, memory typically is viewed as right to left, top to bottom. Note that these layouts are arbitrary. Either scheme could use either left to right or right to left within a row; this is a matter of depiction, not memory assignment. In fact, in looking at programmer manuals for a variety of machines, a bewildering collection of depictions is to be found, even within the same manual.

We can make several observations about this data structure:

- Each data item has the same address in both schemes. For example, the address of the doubleword with hexadecimal value 2122232425262728 is 08.
- Within any given multibyte scalar value, the ordering of bytes in the little-endian structure is the reverse of that for the big-endian structure.
- Endianness does not affect the ordering of data items within a structure. Thus, the four-character word c exhibits byte reversal, but the seven-character byte array d does not. Hence, the address of each individual element of d is the same in both structures.

The effect of endianness is perhaps more clearly demonstrated when we view memory as a vertical array of bytes, as shown in Figure 10.19.

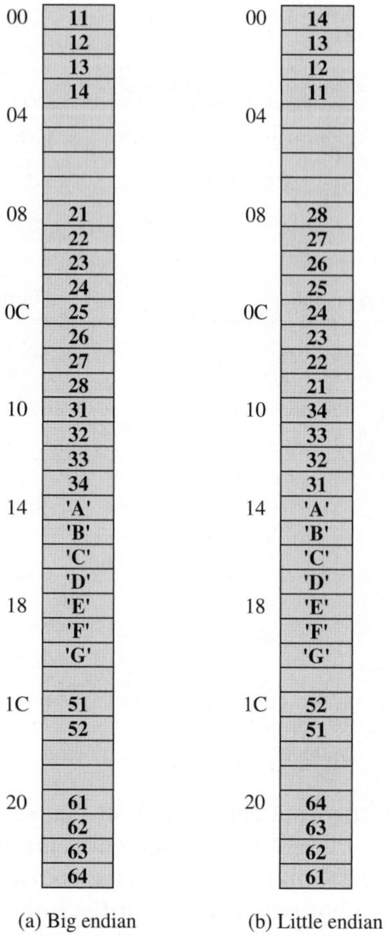

(a) Big endian   (b) Little endian

Figure 10.19 Another View of Figure 10.18

There is no general consensus as to which is the superior style of endianness.[5] The following points favor the big-endian style:

- **Character-string sorting:** A big-endian processor is faster in comparing integer-aligned character strings; the integer ALU can compare multiple bytes in parallel.

- **Decimal/IRA dumps:** All values can be printed left to right without causing confusion.

- **Consistent order:** Big-endian processors store their integers and character strings in the same order (most significant byte comes first).

---

[5]The prophet revered by both groups in the Endian Wars of *Gulliver's Travels* had this to say. "All true Believers shall break their Eggs at the convenient End." Not much help!

The following points favor the little-endian style:

- A big-endian processor has to perform addition when it converts a 32-bit integer address to a 16-bit integer address, to use the least significant bytes.
- It is easier to perform higher-precision arithmetic with the little-endian style; you don't have to find the least-significant byte and move backward.

The differences are minor and the choice of endian style is often more a matter of accommodating previous machines than anything else.

The PowerPC is a bi-endian processor that supports both big-endian and little-endian modes. The bi-endian architecture enables software developers to choose either mode when migrating operating systems and applications from other machines. The operating system establishes the endian mode in which processes execute. Once a mode is selected, all subsequent memory loads and stores are determined by the memory-addressing model of that mode. To support this hardware feature, 2 bits are maintained in the machine state register (MSR) maintained by the operating system as part of the process state. One bit specifies the endian mode in which the kernel runs; the other specifies the processor's current operating mode. Thus, mode can be changed on a per-process basis.

Bit Ordering

In ordering the bits within a byte, we are immediately faced with two questions:

1. Do you count the first bit as bit zero or as bit one?
2. Do you assign the lowest bit number to the byte's least significant bit (little endian) or to the bytes most significant bit (big endian)?

These questions are not answered in the same way on all machines. Indeed, on some machines, the answers are different in different circumstances. Furthermore, the choice of big- or little-endian bit ordering within a byte is not always consistent with big- or little-endian ordering of bytes within a multibyte scalar. The programmer needs to be concerned with these issues when manipulating individual bits.

Another area of concern is when data are transmitted over a bit-serial line. When an individual byte is transmitted, does the system transmit the most significant bit first or the least significant bit first? The designer must make certain that incoming bits are handled properly. For a discussion of this issue, see [JAME90].

CHAPTER 11

INSTRUCTION SETS: ADDRESSING MODES AND FORMATS

KEY POINTS

◆ An operand reference in an instruction either contains the actual value of the operand (immediate) or a reference to the address of the operand. A wide variety of addressing modes is used in various instruction sets. These include direct (operand address is in address field), indirect (address field points to a location that contains the operand address), register, register indirect, and various forms of displacement, in which a register value is added to an address value to produce the operand address.

◆ The instruction format defines the layout fields in the instruction. Instruction format design is a complex undertaking, including such consideration as instruction length, fixed or variable length, number of bits assigned to opcode and each operand reference, and how addressing mode is determined.

In Chapter 10, we focused on *what* an instruction set does. Specifically, we examined the types of operands and operations that may be specified by machine instructions. This chapter turns to the question of *how* to specify the operands and operations of instructions. Two issues arise. First, how is the address of an operand specified, and second, how are the bits of an instruction organized to define the operand addresses and operation of that instruction?

11.1 ADDRESSING

The address field or fields in a typical instruction format are relatively small. We would like to be able to reference a large range of locations in main memory or, for some systems, virtual memory. To achieve this objective, a variety of addressing techniques has been employed. They all involve some trade-off between address range and/or addressing flexibility, on the one hand, and the number of memory references in the instruction and/or the complexity of address calculation, on the other. In this section, we examine the most common addressing techniques:

- Immediate
- Direct
- Indirect
- Register
- Register indirect
- Displacement
- Stack

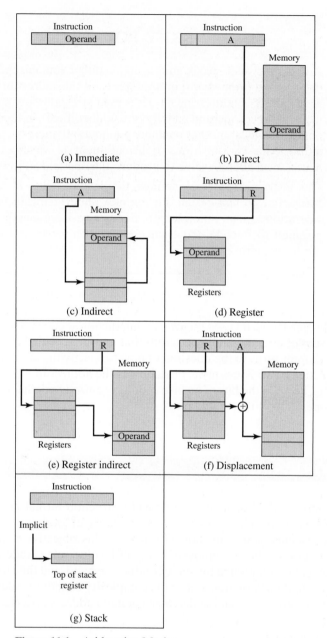

Figure 11.1 Addressing Modes

These modes are illustrated in Figure 11.1. In this section, we use the following notation:

A = contents of an address field in the instruction

R = contents of an address field in the instruction that refers to a register

EA = actual (effective) address of the location containing the referenced operand

(X) = contents of memory location X or register X

Table 11.1   Basic Addressing Modes

Mode	Algorithm	Principal Advantage	Principal Disadvantage
Immediate	Operand = A	No memory reference	Limited operand magnitude
Direct	EA = A	Simple	Limited address space
Indirect	EA = (A)	Large address space	Multiple memory references
Register	EA = R	No memory reference	Limited address space
Register indirect	EA = (R)	Large address space	Extra memory reference
Displacement	EA = A + (R)	Flexibility	Complexity
Stack	EA = top of stack	No memory reference	Limited applicability

Table 11.1 indicates the address calculation performed for each addressing mode.

Before beginning this discussion, two comments need to be made. First, virtually all computer architectures provide more than one of these addressing modes. The question arises as to how the processor can determine which address mode is being used in a particular instruction. Several approaches are taken. Often, different opcodes will use different addressing modes. Also, one or more bits in the instruction format can be used as a *mode field*. The value of the mode field determines which addressing mode is to be used.

The second comment concerns the interpretation of the effective address (EA). In a system without virtual memory, the *effective address* will be either a main memory address or a register. In a virtual memory system, the effective address is a virtual address or a register. The actual mapping to a physical address is a function of the memory management unit (MMU) and is invisible to the programmer.

Immediate Addressing

The simplest form of addressing is immediate addressing, in which the operand value is present in the instruction

$$\text{Operand} = \text{A}$$

This mode can be used to define and use constants or set initial values of variables. Typically, the number will be stored in twos complement form; the leftmost bit of the operand field is used as a sign bit. When the operand is loaded into a data register, the sign bit is extended to the left to the full data word size. In some cases, the immediate binary value is interpreted as an unsigned nonnegative integer.

The advantage of immediate addressing is that no memory reference other than the instruction fetch is required to obtain the operand, thus saving one memory or cache cycle in the instruction cycle. The disadvantage is that the size of the number is restricted to the size of the address field, which, in most instruction sets, is small compared with the word length.

Direct Addressing

A very simple form of addressing is direct addressing, in which the address field contains the effective address of the operand:

$$EA = A$$

The technique was common in earlier generations of computers but is not common on contemporary architectures. It requires only one memory reference and no special calculation. The obvious limitation is that it provides only a limited address space.

Indirect Addressing

With direct addressing, the length of the address field is usually less than the word length, thus limiting the address range. One solution is to have the address field refer to the address of a word in memory, which in turn contains a full-length address of the operand. This is known as *indirect addressing:*

$$EA = (A)$$

As defined earlier, the parentheses are to be interpreted as meaning *contents of.* The obvious advantage of this approach is that for a word length of N, an address space of 2^N is now available. The disadvantage is that instruction execution requires two memory references to fetch the operand: one to get its address and a second to get its value.

Although the number of words that can be addressed is now equal to 2^N, the number of different effective addresses that may be referenced at any one time is limited to 2^K, where K is the length of the address field. Typically, this is not a burdensome restriction, and it can be an asset. In a virtual memory environment, all the effective address locations can be confined to page 0 of any process. Because the address field of an instruction is small, it will naturally produce low-numbered direct addresses, which would appear in page 0. (The only restriction is that the page size must be greater than or equal to 2^K.) When a process is active, there will be repeated references to page 0, causing it to remain in real memory. Thus, an indirect memory reference will involve, at most, one page fault rather than two.

A rarely used variant of indirect addressing is multilevel or cascaded indirect addressing:

$$EA = (\dots(A)\dots)$$

In this case, one bit of a full-word address is an indirect flag (I). If the I bit is 0, then the word contains the EA. If the I bit is 1, then another level of indirection is invoked. There does not appear to be any particular advantage to this approach, and its disadvantage is that three or more memory references could be required to fetch an operand.

Register Addressing

Register addressing is similar to direct addressing. The only difference is that the address field refers to a register rather than a main memory address:

$$EA = R$$

To clarify, if the contents of a register address field in an instruction is 5, then register R5 is the intended address, and the operand value is contained in R5. Typically, an address field that references registers will have from 3 to 5 bits, so that a total of from 8 to 32 general-purpose registers can be referenced.

The advantages of register addressing are that (1) only a small address field is needed in the instruction, and (2) no time-consuming memory references are required. As was discussed in Chapter 4, the memory access time for a register internal to the processor is much less than that for a main memory address. The disadvantage of register addressing is that the address space is very limited.

If register addressing is heavily used in an instruction set, this implies that the processor registers will be heavily used. Because of the severely limited number of registers (compared with main memory locations), their use in this fashion makes sense only if they are employed efficiently. If every operand is brought into a register from main memory, operated on once, and then returned to main memory, then a wasteful intermediate step has been added. If, instead, the operand in a register remains in use for multiple operations, then a real savings is achieved. An example is the intermediate result in a calculation. In particular, suppose that the algorithm for twos complement multiplication were to be implemented in software. The location labeled A in the flowchart (Figure 9.12) is referenced many times and should be implemented in a register rather than a main memory location.

It is up to the programmer or compiler to decide which values should remain in registers and which should be stored in main memory. Most modern processors employ multiple general-purpose registers, placing a burden for efficient execution on the assembly-language programmer (e.g., compiler writer).

Register Indirect Addressing

Just as register addressing is analogous to direct addressing, register indirect addressing is analogous to indirect addressing. In both cases, the only difference is whether the address field refers to a memory location or a register. Thus, for register indirect address,

$$EA = (R)$$

The advantages and limitations of register indirect addressing are basically the same as for indirect addressing. In both cases, the address space limitation (limited range of addresses) of the address field is overcome by having that field refer to a word-length location containing an address. In addition, register indirect addressing uses one less memory reference than indirect addressing.

Displacement Addressing

A very powerful mode of addressing combines the capabilities of direct addressing and register indirect addressing. It is known by a variety of names depending on the context of its use, but the basic mechanism is the same. We will refer to this as *displacement addressing:*

$$EA = A + (R)$$

Displacement addressing requires that the instruction have two address fields, at least one of which is explicit. The value contained in one address field (value = A) is used directly. The other address field, or an implicit reference based on opcode, refers to a register whose contents are added to A to produce the effective address.

We will describe three of the most common uses of displacement addressing:

- Relative addressing
- Base-register addressing
- Indexing

RELATIVE ADDRESSING For relative addressing, also called PC-relative addressing, the implicitly referenced register is the program counter (PC). That is, the next instruction address is added to the address field to produce the EA. Typically, the address field is treated as a twos complement number for this operation. Thus, the effective address is a displacement relative to the address of the instruction.

Relative addressing exploits the concept of locality that was discussed in Chapters 4 and 8. If most memory references are relatively near to the instruction being executed, then the use of relative addressing saves address bits in the instruction.

BASE–REGISTER ADDRESSING For base-register addressing, the interpretation is the following: The referenced register contains a main memory address, and the address field contains a displacement (usually an unsigned integer representation) from that address. The register reference may be explicit or implicit.

Base-register addressing also exploits the locality of memory references. It is a convenient means of implementing segmentation, which was discussed in Chapter 8. In some implementations, a single segment-base register is employed and is used implicitly. In others, the programmer may choose a register to hold the base address of a segment, and the instruction must reference it explicitly. In this latter case, if the length of the address field is K and the number of possible registers is N, then one instruction can reference any one of N areas of 2^K words.

INDEXING For indexing, the interpretation is typically the following: The address field references a main memory address, and the referenced register contains a positive displacement from that address. Note that this usage is just the opposite of the interpretation for base-register addressing. Of course, it is more than just a matter of user interpretation. Because the address field is considered to be a memory address in indexing, it generally contains more bits than an address field in a comparable base-register instruction. Also, we shall see that there are some refinements to indexing that would not be as useful in the base-register context. Nevertheless, the method of calculating the EA is the same for both base-register addressing and indexing, and in both cases the register reference is sometimes explicit and sometimes implicit (for different processor types).

An important use of indexing is to provide an efficient mechanism for performing iterative operations. Consider, for example, a list of numbers stored starting at location A. Suppose that we would like to add 1 to each element on the list. We need to fetch each value, add 1 to it, and store it back. The sequence of effective addresses that we need is $A, A + 1, A + 2, \ldots$, up to the last location on the list. With indexing, this is easily done. The value A is stored in the instruction's address field, and the chosen register, called an *index register*, is initialized to 0. After each operation, the index register is incremented by 1.

Because index registers are commonly used for such iterative tasks, it is typical that there is a need to increment or decrement the index register after each reference to it. Because this is such a common operation, some systems will automatically do this as part of the same instruction cycle. This is known as *autoindexing*. If certain registers are devoted exclusively to indexing, then autoindexing can be invoked implicitly and automatically. If general-purpose registers are used, the autoindex operation may need to be signaled by a bit in the instruction. Autoindexing using increment can be depicted as follows.

$$EA = A + (R)$$
$$(R) \leftarrow (R) + 1$$

In some machines, both indirect addressing and indexing are provided, and it is possible to employ both in the same instruction. There are two possibilities: the indexing is performed either before or after the indirection.

If indexing is performed after the indirection, it is termed *postindexing:*

$$EA = (A) + (R)$$

First, the contents of the address field are used to access a memory location containing a direct address. This address is then indexed by the register value. This technique is useful for accessing one of a number of blocks of data of a fixed format. For example, it was described in Chapter 8 that the operating system needs to employ a process control block for each process. The operations performed are the same regardless of which block is being manipulated. Thus, the addresses in the instructions that reference the block could point to a location (value = A) containing a variable pointer to the start of a process control block. The index register contains the displacement within the block.

With *preindexing*, the indexing is performed before the indirection:

$$EA = (A + (R))$$

An address is calculated as with simple indexing. In this case, however, the calculated address contains not the operand, but the address of the operand. An example of the use of this technique is to construct a multiway branch table. At a particular point in a program, there may be a branch to one of a number of locations depending on conditions. A table of addresses can be set up starting at location A. By indexing into this table, the required location can be found.

Typically, an instruction set will not include both preindexing and postindexing.

Stack Addressing

The final addressing mode that we consider is stack addressing. As defined in Appendix 9A, a stack is a linear array of locations. It is sometimes referred to as a *pushdown list* or *last-in-first-out queue*. The stack is a reserved block of locations. Items are appended to the top of the stack so that, at any given time, the block is partially filled. Associated with the stack is a pointer whose value is the address of the top of the stack. Alternatively, the top two elements of the stack may be in processor registers, in which case the stack pointer references the third element of the stack (Figure 10.14b). The stack pointer is maintained in a register. Thus, references to stack locations in memory are in fact register indirect addresses.

The stack mode of addressing is a form of implied addressing. The machine instructions need not include a memory reference but implicitly operate on the top of the stack.

11.2 x86 AND ARM ADDRESSING MODES

x86 Addressing Modes

Recall from Figure 8.21 that the x86 address translation mechanism produces an address, called a virtual or effective address, that is an offset into a segment. The sum of the starting address of the segment and the effective address produces a linear address. If paging is being used, this linear address must pass through a page-translation mechanism to produce a physical address. In what follows, we ignore this last step because it is transparent to the instruction set and to the programmer.

The x86 is equipped with a variety of addressing modes intended to allow the efficient execution of high-level languages. Figure 11.2 indicates the logic involved. The segment register determines the segment that is the subject of the reference.

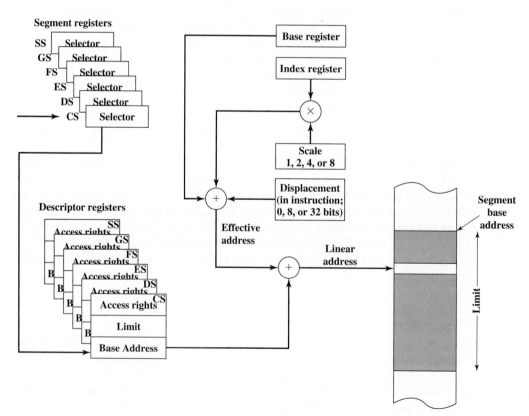

Figure 11.2 x86 Addressing Mode Calculation

There are six segment registers; the one being used for a particular reference depends on the context of execution and the instruction. Each segment register holds an index into the segment descriptor table (Figure 8.20), which holds the starting address of the corresponding segments. Associated with each user-visible segment register is a segment descriptor register (not programmer visible), which records the access rights for the segment as well as the starting address and limit (length) of the segment. In addition, there are two registers that may be used in constructing an address: the base register and the index register.

Table 11.2 lists the x86 addressing modes. Let us consider each of these in turn.

For the **immediate mode**, the operand is included in the instruction. The operand can be a byte, word, or doubleword of data.

For **register operand mode**, the operand is located in a register. For general instructions, such as data transfer, arithmetic, and logical instructions, the operand can be one of the 32-bit general registers (EAX, EBX, ECX, EDX, ESI, EDI, ESP, EBP), one of the 16-bit general registers (AX, BX, CX, DX, SI, DI, SP, BP), or one of the 8-bit general registers (AH, BH, CH, DH, AL, BL, CL, DL). There are also some instructions that reference the segment selector registers (CS, DS, ES, SS, FS, GS).

The remaining addressing modes reference locations in memory. The memory location must be specified in terms of the segment containing the location and the offset from the beginning of the segment. In some cases, a segment is specified explicitly; in others, the segment is specified by simple rules that assign a segment by default.

In the **displacement mode**, the operand's offset (the effective address of Figure 11.2) is contained as part of the instruction as an 8-, 16-, or 32-bit displacement. With segmentation, all addresses in instructions refer merely to an offset in a

Table 11.2   x86 Addressing Modes

Mode	Algorithm
Immediate	Operand = A
Register Operand	LA = R
Displacement	LA = (SR) + A
Base	LA = (SR) + (B)
Base with Displacement	LA = (SR) + (B) + A
Scaled Index with Displacement	LA = (SR) + (I) × S + A
Base with Index and Displacement	LA = (SR) + (B) + (I) + A
Base with Scaled Index and Displacement	LA = (SR) + (I) × S + (B) + A
Relative	LA = (PC) + A

LA = linear address
(X) = contents of X
SR = segment register
PC = program counter
A = contents of an address field in the instruction
R = register
B = base register
I = index register
S = scaling factor

segment. The displacement addressing mode is found on few machines because, as mentioned earlier, it leads to long instructions. In the case of the x86, the displacement value can be as long as 32 bits, making for a 6-byte instruction. Displacement addressing can be useful for referencing global variables.

The remaining addressing modes are indirect, in the sense that the address portion of the instruction tells the processor where to look to find the address. The **base mode** specifies that one of the 8-, 16-, or 32-bit registers contains the effective address. This is equivalent to what we have referred to as register indirect addressing.

In the **base with displacement mode**, the instruction includes a displacement to be added to a base register, which may be any of the general-purpose registers. Examples of uses of this mode are as follows:

- Used by a compiler to point to the start of a local variable area. For example, the base register could point to the beginning of a stack frame, which contains the local variables for the corresponding procedure.
- Used to index into an array when the element size is not 1, 2, 4, or 8 bytes and which therefore cannot be indexed using an index register. In this case, the displacement points to the beginning of the array, and the base register holds the results of a calculation to determine the offset to a specific element within the array.
- Used to access a field of a record. The base register points to the beginning of the record, while the displacement is an offset to the field.

In the **scaled index with displacement mode**, the instruction includes a displacement to be added to a register, in this case called an index register. The index register may be any of the general-purpose registers except the one called ESP, which is generally used for stack processing. In calculating the effective address, the contents of the index register are multiplied by a scaling factor of 1, 2, 4, or 8, and then added to a displacement. This mode is very convenient for indexing arrays. A scaling factor of 2 can be used for an array of 16-bit integers. A scaling factor of 4 can be used for 32-bit integers or floating-point numbers. Finally, a scaling factor of 8 can be used for an array of double-precision floating-point numbers.

The **base with index and displacement mode** sums the contents of the base register, the index register, and a displacement to form the effective address. Again, the base register can be any general-purpose register and the index register can be any general-purpose register except ESP. As an example, this addressing mode could be used for accessing a local array on a stack frame. This mode can also be used to support a two-dimensional array; in this case, the displacement points to the beginning of the array, and each register handles one dimension of the array.

The **based scaled index with displacement mode** sums the contents of the index register multiplied by a scaling factor, the contents of the base register, and the displacement. This is useful if an array is stored in a stack frame; in this case, the array elements would be 2, 4, or 8 bytes each in length. This mode also provides efficient indexing of a two-dimensional array when the array elements are 2, 4, or 8 bytes in length.

Finally, **relative addressing** can be used in transfer-of-control instructions. A displacement is added to the value of the program counter, which points to the next instruction. In this case, the displacement is treated as a signed byte, word, or doubleword value, and that value either increases or decreases the address in the program counter.

ARM Addressing Modes

Typically, a RISC machine, unlike a CISC machine, uses a simple and relatively straightforward set of addressing modes. The ARM architecture departs somewhat from this tradition by providing a relatively rich set of addressing modes. These modes are most conveniently classified with respect to the type of instruction.[1]

LOAD/STORE ADDRESSING Load and store instructions are the only instructions that reference memory. This is always done indirectly through a base register plus offset. There are three alternatives with respect to indexing (Figure 11.3):

- **Offset:** For this addressing method, indexing is not used. An offset value is added to or subtracted from the value in the base register to form the memory address. As an example Figure 11.3a illustrates this method with the assembly language instruction STRB r0, [r1, #12]. This is the store byte instruction. In this case the base address is in register r1 and the displacement is an immediate value of decimal 12. The resulting address (base plus offset) is the location where the least significant byte from r0 is to be stored.
- **Preindex:** The memory address is formed in the same way as for offset addressing. The memory address is also written back to the base register. In other words, the base register value is incremented or decremented by the offset value. Figure 11.3b illustrates this method with the assembly language instruction STRB r0, [r1, #12]!. The exclamation point signifies preindexing.
- **Postindex:** The memory address is the base register value. An offset is added to or subtracted from the base register value and the result is written back to the base register. Figure 11.3c illustrates this method with the assembly language instruction STRB r0, [r1], #12.

Note that what ARM refers to as a base register acts as an index register for preindex and postindex addressing. The offset value can either be an immediate value stored in the instruction or it can be in another register. If the offset value is in a register, another useful feature is available: scaled register addressing. The value in the offset register is scaled by one of the shift operators: Logical Shift Left, Logical Shift Right, Arithmetic Shift Right, Rotate Right, or Rotate Right Extended (which includes the carry bit in the rotation). The amount of the shift is specified as an immediate value in the instruction.

DATA PROCESSING INSTRUCTION ADDRESSING Data processing instructions use either register addressing of a mixture of register and immediate addressing. For register addressing, the value in one of the register operands may be scaled using one of the five shift operators defined in the preceding paragraph.

BRANCH INSTRUCTIONS The only form of addressing for branch instructions is immediate addressing. The branch instruction contains a 24-bit value. For address calculation, this value is shifted left 2 bits, so that the address is on a word boundary. Thus the effective address range is ±32 MB from the program counter.

---

[1]As with our discussion of x86 addressing, we ignore the translation from virtual to physical address in the following discussion.

`STRB r0, [r1, #12]`

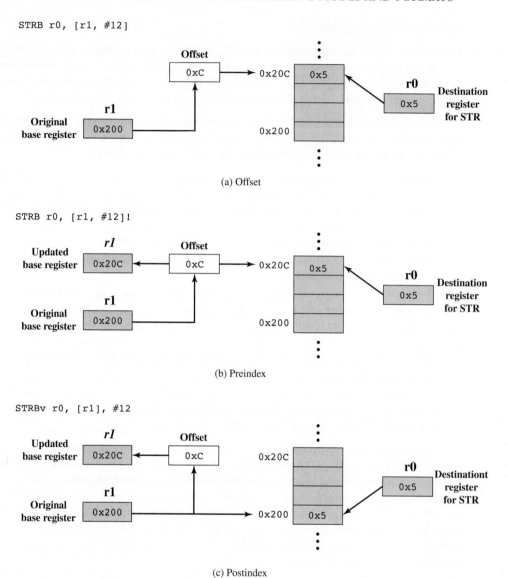

(a) Offset

`STRB r0, [r1, #12]!`

(b) Preindex

`STRBv r0, [r1], #12`

(c) Postindex

Figure 11.3 ARM Indexing Methods

LOAD/STORE MULTIPLE ADDRESSING Load Multiple instructions load a subset (possibly all) of the general-purpose registers from memory. Store Multiple instructions store a subset (possibly all) of the general-purpose registers to memory. The list of registers for the load or store is specified in a 16-bit field in the instruction with each bit corresponding to one of the 16 registers. Load and Store Multiple addressing modes produce a sequential range of memory addresses. The lowest-numbered register is stored at the lowest memory address and the highest-numbered register at the highest memory address. Four addressing modes are used

```
LDMxx r10, {r0, r1, r4}
STMxx r10, {r0, r1, r4}
```

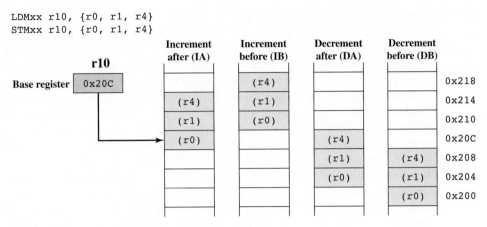

Figure 11.4 ARM Load/Store Multiple Addressing

(Figure 11.4): increment after, increment before, decrement after, and decrement before. A base register specifies a main memory address where register values are stored in or loaded from in ascending (increment) or descending (decrement) word locations. Incrementing or decrementing starts either before or after the first memory access.

These instructions are useful for block loads or stores, stack operations, and procedure exit sequences.

11.3 INSTRUCTION FORMATS

An instruction format defines the layout of the bits of an instruction, in terms of its constituent fields. An instruction format must include an opcode and, implicitly or explicitly, zero or more operands. Each explicit operand is referenced using one of the addressing modes described in Section 11.1. The format must, implicitly or explicitly, indicate the addressing mode for each operand. For most instruction sets, more than one instruction format is used.

The design of an instruction format is a complex art, and an amazing variety of designs have been implemented. We examine the key design issues, looking briefly at some designs to illustrate points, and then we examine the x86 and ARM solutions in detail.

Instruction Length

The most basic design issue to be faced is the instruction format length. This decision affects, and is affected by, memory size, memory organization, bus structure, processor complexity, and processor speed. This decision determines the richness and flexibility of the machine as seen by the assembly-language programmer.

The most obvious trade-off here is between the desire for a powerful instruction repertoire and a need to save space. Programmers want more opcodes, more operands, more addressing modes, and greater address range. More opcodes and more operands make life easier for the programmer, because shorter programs can be written to accomplish given tasks. Similarly, more addressing modes give the programmer greater flexibility in implementing certain functions, such as table manipulations and multiple-way branching. And, of course, with the increase in main memory size and the increasing use of virtual memory, programmers want to be able to address larger memory ranges. All of these things (opcodes, operands, addressing modes, address range) require bits and push in the direction of longer instruction lengths. But longer instruction length may be wasteful. A 64-bit instruction occupies twice the space of a 32-bit instruction but is probably less than twice as useful.

Beyond this basic trade-off, there are other considerations. Either the instruction length should be equal to the memory-transfer length (in a bus system, data-bus length) or one should be a multiple of the other. Otherwise, we will not get an integral number of instructions during a fetch cycle. A related consideration is the memory transfer rate. This rate has not kept up with increases in processor speed. Accordingly, memory can become a bottleneck if the processor can execute instructions faster than it can fetch them. One solution to this problem is to use cache memory (see Section 4.3); another is to use shorter instructions. Thus, 16-bit instructions can be fetched at twice the rate of 32-bit instructions but probably can be executed less than twice as rapidly.

A seemingly mundane but nevertheless important feature is that the instruction length should be a multiple of the character length, which is usually 8 bits, and of the length of fixed-point numbers. To see this, we need to make use of that unfortunately ill-defined word, *word* [FRAI83]. The word length of memory is, in some sense, the "natural" unit of organization. The size of a word usually determines the size of fixed-point numbers (usually the two are equal). Word size is also typically equal to, or at least integrally related to, the memory transfer size. Because a common form of data is character data, we would like a word to store an integral number of characters. Otherwise, there are wasted bits in each word when storing multiple characters, or a character will have to straddle a word boundary. The importance of this point is such that IBM, when it introduced the System/360 and wanted to employ 8-bit characters, made the wrenching decision to move from the 36-bit architecture of the scientific members of the 700/7000 series to a 32-bit architecture.

Allocation of Bits

We've looked at some of the factors that go into deciding the length of the instruction format. An equally difficult issue is how to allocate the bits in that format. The trade-offs here are complex.

For a given instruction length, there is clearly a trade-off between the number of opcodes and the power of the addressing capability. More opcodes obviously mean more bits in the opcode field. For an instruction format of a given length, this reduces the number of bits available for addressing. There is one interesting refinement to this trade-off, and that is the use of variable-length opcodes. In this approach, there is a minimum opcode length but, for some opcodes, additional operations may be specified by using additional bits in the instruction. For a fixed-length instruction, this leaves fewer bits for addressing. Thus, this feature is used for those instructions that require fewer operands and/or less powerful addressing.

The following interrelated factors go into determining the use of the addressing bits.

- **Number of addressing modes:** Sometimes an addressing mode can be indicated implicitly. For example, certain opcodes might always call for indexing. In other cases, the addressing modes must be explicit, and one or more mode bits will be needed.

- **Number of operands:** We have seen that fewer addresses can make for longer, more awkward programs (e.g., Figure 10.3). Typical instructions on today's machines provide for two operands. Each operand address in the instruction might require its own mode indicator, or the use of a mode indicator could be limited to just one of the address fields.

- **Register versus memory:** A machine must have registers so that data can be brought into the processor for processing. With a single user-visible register (usually called the accumulator), one operand address is implicit and consumes no instruction bits. However, single-register programming is awkward and requires many instructions. Even with multiple registers, only a few bits are needed to specify the register. The more that registers can be used for operand references, the fewer bits are needed. A number of studies indicate that a total of 8 to 32 user-visible registers is desirable [LUND77, HUCK83]. Most contemporary architectures have at least 32 registers.

- **Number of register sets:** Most contemporary machines have one set of general-purpose registers, with typically 32 or more registers in the set. These registers can be used to store data and can be used to store addresses for displacement addressing. Some architectures, including that of the x86, have a collection of two or more specialized sets (such as data and displacement). One advantage of this latter approach is that, for a fixed number of registers, a functional split requires fewer bits to be used in the instruction. For example, with two sets of eight registers, only 3 bits are required to identify a register; the opcode or mode register will determine which set of registers is being referenced.

- **Address range:** For addresses that reference memory, the range of addresses that can be referenced is related to the number of address bits. Because this imposes a severe limitation, direct addressing is rarely used. With displacement addressing, the range is opened up to the length of the address register. Even so, it is still convenient to allow rather large displacements from the register address, which requires a relatively large number of address bits in the instruction.

- **Address granularity:** For addresses that reference memory rather than registers, another factor is the granularity of addressing. In a system with 16- or 32-bit words, an address can reference a word or a byte at the designer's choice. Byte addressing is convenient for character manipulation but requires, for a fixed-size memory, more address bits.

Thus, the designer is faced with a host of factors to consider and balance. How critical the various choices are is not clear. As an example, we cite one study [CRAG79] that compared various instruction format approaches, including the use of a stack, general-purpose registers, an accumulator, and only memory-to-register approaches. Using a consistent set of assumptions, no significant difference in code space or execution time was observed.

Let us briefly look at how two historical machine designs balance these various factors.

PDP-8 One of the simplest instruction designs for a general-purpose computer was for the PDP-8 [BELL78b]. The PDP-8 uses 12-bit instructions and operates on 12-bit words. There is a single general-purpose register, the accumulator.

Despite the limitations of this design, the addressing is quite flexible. Each memory reference consists of 7 bits plus two 1-bit modifiers. The memory is divided into fixed-length pages of $2^7 = 128$ words each. Address calculation is based on references to page 0 or the current page (page containing this instruction) as determined by the page bit. The second modifier bit indicates whether direct or indirect addressing is to be used. These two modes can be used in combination, so that an indirect address is a 12-bit address contained in a word of page 0 or the current page. In addition, 8 dedicated words on page 0 are autoindex "registers." When an indirect reference is made to one of these locations, preindexing occurs.

Figure 11.5 shows the PDP-8 instruction format. There are a 3-bit opcode and three types of instructions. For opcodes 0 through 5, the format is a single-address memory reference instruction including a page bit and an indirect bit. Thus, there are only six basic operations. To enlarge the group of operations, opcode 7 defines a register reference or *microinstruction*. In this format, the remaining bits are used to encode additional operations. In general, each bit defines a specific operation (e.g., clear accumulator), and these bits can be combined in a single instruction. The microinstruction strategy was used as far back as the PDP-1 by DEC and is, in a sense,

Memory reference instructions

Opcode		D/I	Z/C	Displacement						
0	2	3	4	5						11

Input/output instructions

1	1	0	Device			Opcode		
0	2	3			8	9		11

Register reference instructions

Group 1 microinstructions

1	1	1	0	CLA	CLL	CMA	CML	RAR	RAL	BSW	IAC
0	1	2	3	4	5	6	7	8	9	10	11

Group 2 microinstructions

1	1	1	0	CLA	SMA	SZA	SNL	RSS	OSR	HLT	0
0	1	2	3	4	5	6	7	8	9	10	11

Group 3 microinstructions

1	1	1	0	CLA	MQA	0	MQL	0	0	0	1
0	1	2	3	4	5	6	7	8	9	10	11

D/I = Direct/Indirect address
Z/C = Page 0 or Current page
CLA = Clear Accumulator
CLL = Clear Link
CMA = CoMplement Accumulator
CML = CoMplement Link
RAR = Rotate Accumulator Right
RAL = Rotate Accumulator Left
BSW = Byte SWap

IAC = Increment ACcumulator
SMA = Skip on Minus Accumulator
SZA = Skip on Zero Accumulator
SNL = Skip on Nonzero Link
RSS = Reverse Skip Sense
OSR = Or with Switch Register
HLT = HaLT
MQA = Multiplier Quotient into Accumulator
MQL = Multiplier Quotient Load

Figure 11.5 PDP-8 Instruction Formats

a forerunner of today's microprogrammed machines, to be discussed in Part Four. Opcode 6 is the I/O operation; 6 bits are used to select one of 64 devices, and 3 bits specify a particular I/O command.

The PDP-8 instruction format is remarkably efficient. It supports indirect addressing, displacement addressing, and indexing. With the use of the opcode extension, it supports a total of approximately 35 instructions. Given the constraints of a 12-bit instruction length, the designers could hardly have done better.

PDP-10 A sharp contrast to the instruction set of the PDP-8 is that of the PDP-10. The PDP-10 was designed to be a large-scale time-shared system, with an emphasis on making the system easy to program, even if additional hardware expense was involved.

Among the design principles employed in designing the instruction set were the following [BELL78c]:

- **Orthogonality:** Orthogonality is a principle by which two variables are independent of each other. In the context of an instruction set, the term indicates that other elements of an instruction are independent of (not determined by) the opcode. The PDP-10 designers use the term to describe the fact that an address is always computed in the same way, independent of the opcode. This is in contrast to many machines, where the address mode sometimes depends implicitly on the operator being used.
- **Completeness:** Each arithmetic data type (integer, fixed-point, floating-point) should have a complete and identical set of operations.
- **Direct addressing:** Base plus displacement addressing, which places a memory organization burden on the programmer, was avoided in favor of direct addressing.

Each of these principles advances the main goal of ease of programming.

The PDP-10 has a 36-bit word length and a 36-bit instruction length. The fixed instruction format is shown in Figure 11.6. The opcode occupies 9 bits, allowing up to 512 operations. In fact, a total of 365 different instructions are defined. Most instructions have two addresses, one of which is one of 16 general-purpose registers. Thus, this operand reference occupies 4 bits. The other operand reference starts with an 18-bit memory address field. This can be used as an immediate operand or a memory address. In the latter usage, both indexing and indirect addressing are allowed. The same general-purpose registers are also used as index registers.

A 36-bit instruction length is true luxury. There is no need to do clever things to get more opcodes; a 9-bit opcode field is more than adequate. Addressing is also straightforward. An 18-bit address field makes direct addressing desirable. For memory sizes greater than 2^{18}, indirection is provided. For the ease of the programmer, indexing is provided for table manipulation and iterative programs. Also, with an 18-bit operand field, immediate addressing becomes attractive.

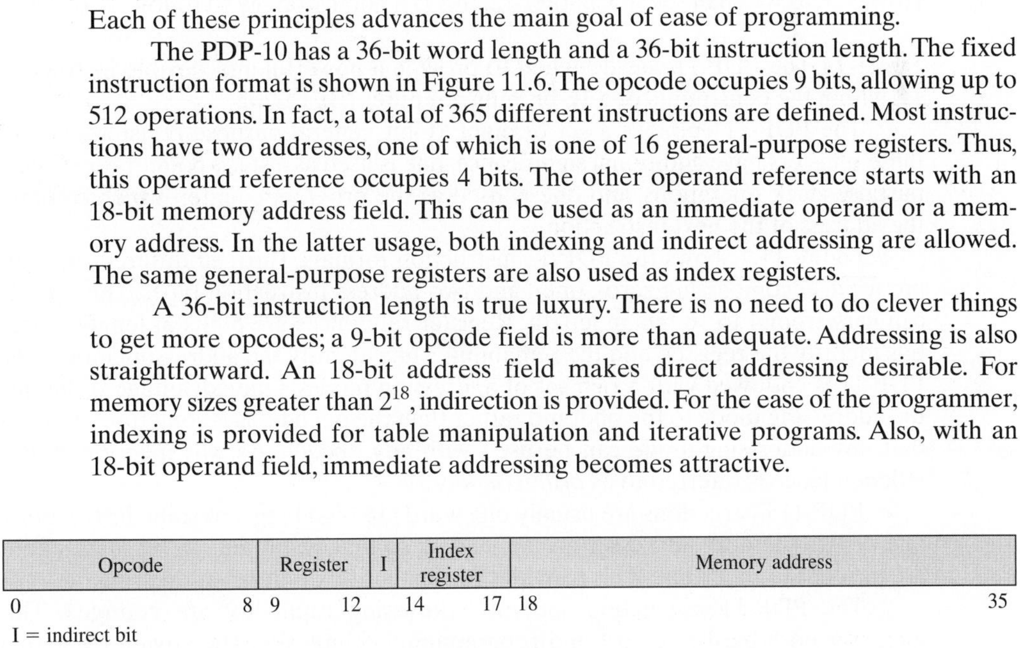

Opcode	Register	I	Index register	Memory address
0	8 9	12 14	17 18	35

I = indirect bit

Figure 11.6 PDP-10 Instruction Format

The PDP-10 instruction set design does accomplish the objectives listed earlier [LUND77]. It eases the task of the programmer or compiler at the expense of an inefficient utilization of space. This was a conscious choice made by the designers and therefore cannot be faulted as poor design.

Variable-Length Instructions

The examples we have looked at so far have used a single fixed instruction length, and we have implicitly discussed trade-offs in that context. But the designer may choose instead to provide a variety of instruction formats of different lengths. This tactic makes it easy to provide a large repertoire of opcodes, with different opcode lengths. Addressing can be more flexible, with various combinations of register and memory references plus addressing modes. With variable-length instructions, these many variations can be provided efficiently and compactly.

The principal price to pay for variable-length instructions is an increase in the complexity of the processor. Falling hardware prices, the use of microprogramming (discussed in Part Four), and a general increase in understanding the principles of processor design have all contributed to making this a small price to pay. However, we will see that RISC and superscalar machines can exploit the use of fixed-length instructions to provide improved performance.

The use of variable-length instructions does not remove the desirability of making all of the instruction lengths integrally related to the word length. Because the processor does not know the length of the next instruction to be fetched, a typical strategy is to fetch a number of bytes or words equal to at least the longest possible instruction. This means that sometimes multiple instructions are fetched. However, as we shall see in Chapter 12, this is a good strategy to follow in any case.

PDP-11 The PDP-11 was designed to provide a powerful and flexible instruction set within the constraints of a 16-bit minicomputer [BELL70].

The PDP-11 employs a set of eight 16-bit general-purpose registers. Two of these registers have additional significance: one is used as a stack pointer for special-purpose stack operations, and one is used as the program counter, which contains the address of the next instruction.

Figure 11.7 shows the PDP-11 instruction formats. Thirteen different formats are used, encompassing zero-, one-, and two-address instruction types. The opcode can vary from 4 to 16 bits in length. Register references are 6 bits in length. Three bits identify the register, and the remaining 3 bits identify the addressing mode. The PDP-11 is endowed with a rich set of addressing modes. One advantage of linking the addressing mode to the operand rather than the opcode, as is sometimes done, is that any addressing mode can be used with any opcode. As was mentioned, this independence is referred to as *orthogonality*.

PDP-11 instructions are usually one word (16 bits) long. For some instructions, one or two memory addresses are appended, so that 32-bit and 48-bit instructions are part of the repertoire. This provides for further flexibility in addressing.

The PDP-11 instruction set and addressing capability are complex. This increases both hardware cost and programming complexity. The advantage is that more efficient or compact programs can be developed.

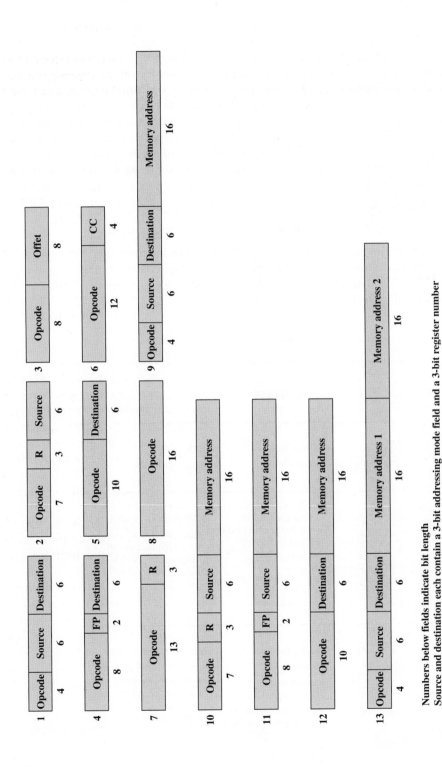

Figure 11.7 Instruction Formats for the PDP-11

Numbers below fields indicate bit length
Source and destination each contain a 3-bit addressing mode field and a 3-bit register number
FP indicates one of four floating-point registers
R indicates one of the general-purpose registers
CC is the condition code field

419

VAX Most architectures provide a relatively small number of fixed instruction formats. This can cause two problems for the programmer. First, addressing mode and opcode are not orthogonal. For example, for a given operation, one operand must come from a register and another from memory, or both from registers, and so on. Second, only a limited number of operands can be accommodated: typically up to two or three. Because some operations inherently require more operands, various strategies must be used to achieve the desired result using two or more instructions.

To avoid these problems, two criteria were used in designing the VAX instruction format [STRE78]:

1. All instructions should have the "natural" number of operands.
2. All operands should have the same generality in specification.

The result is a highly variable instruction format. An instruction consists of a 1- or 2-byte opcode followed by from zero to six operand specifiers, depending on the opcode. The minimal instruction length is 1 byte, and instructions up to 37 bytes can be constructed. Figure 11.8 gives a few examples.

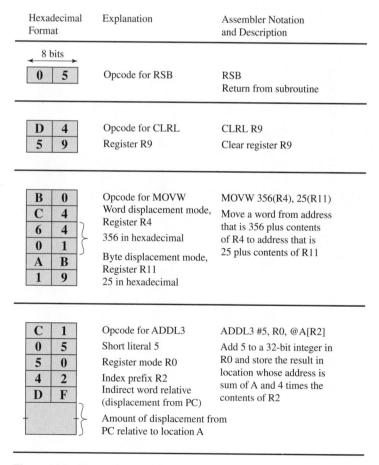

Hexadecimal Format	Explanation	Assembler Notation and Description
8 bits		
0 5	Opcode for RSB	RSB Return from subroutine
D 4 5 9	Opcode for CLRL Register R9	CLRL R9 Clear register R9
B 0 C 4 6 4 0 1 A B 1 9	Opcode for MOVW Word displacement mode, Register R4 356 in hexadecimal Byte displacement mode, Register R11 25 in hexadecimal	MOVW 356(R4), 25(R11) Move a word from address that is 356 plus contents of R4 to address that is 25 plus contents of R11
C 1 0 5 5 0 4 2 D F	Opcode for ADDL3 Short literal 5 Register mode R0 Index prefix R2 Indirect word relative (displacement from PC) Amount of displacement from PC relative to location A	ADDL3 #5, R0, @A[R2] Add 5 to a 32-bit integer in R0 and store the result in location whose address is sum of A and 4 times the contents of R2

Figure 11.8   Example of VAX Instructions

The VAX instruction begins with a 1-byte opcode. This suffices to handle most VAX instructions. However, as there are over 300 different instructions, 8 bits are not enough. The hexadecimal codes FD and FF indicate an extended opcode, with the actual opcode being specified in the second byte.

The remainder of the instruction consists of up to six operand specifiers. An operand specifier is, at minimum, a 1-byte format in which the leftmost 4 bits are the address mode specifier. The only exception to this rule is the literal mode, which is signaled by the pattern 00 in the leftmost 2 bits, leaving space for a 6-bit literal. Because of this exception, a total of 12 different addressing modes can be specified.

An operand specifier often consists of just one byte, with the rightmost 4 bits specifying one of 16 general-purpose registers. The length of the operand specifier can be extended in one of two ways. First, a constant value of one or more bytes may immediately follow the first byte of the operand specifier. An example of this is the displacement mode, in which an 8-, 16-, or 32-bit displacement is used. Second, an index mode of addressing may be used. In this case, the first byte of the operand specifier consists of the 4-bit addressing mode code of 0100 and a 4-bit index register identifier. The remainder of the operand specifier consists of the base address specifier, which may itself be one or more bytes in length.

The reader may be wondering, as the author did, what kind of instruction requires six operands. Surprisingly, the VAX has a number of such instructions. Consider

$$\text{ADDP6 OP1, OP2, OP3, OP4, OP5, OP6}$$

This instruction adds two packed decimal numbers. OP1 and OP2 specify the length and starting address of one decimal string; OP3 and OP4 specify a second string. These two strings are added and the result is stored in the decimal string whose length and starting location are specified by OP5 and OP6.

The VAX instruction set provides for a wide variety of operations and addressing modes. This gives a programmer, such as a compiler writer, a very powerful and flexible tool for developing programs. In theory, this should lead to efficient machine-language compilations of high-level language programs and, in general, to effective and efficient use of processor resources. The penalty to be paid for these benefits is the increased complexity of the processor compared with a processor with a simpler instruction set and format.

We return to these matters in Chapter 13, where we examine the case for very simple instruction sets.

11.4 x86 AND ARM INSTRUCTION FORMATS

x86 Instruction Formats

The x86 is equipped with a variety of instruction formats. Of the elements described in this subsection, only the opcode field is always present. Figure 11.9 illustrates the general instruction format. Instructions are made up of from zero to four optional instruction prefixes, a 1- or 2-byte opcode, an optional address specifier (which

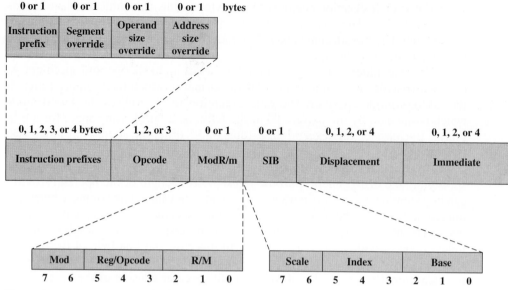

Figure 11.9 x86 Instruction Format

consists of the ModR/m byte and the Scale Index byte) an optional displacement, and an optional immediate field.

Let us first consider the prefix bytes:

- **Instruction prefixes:** The instruction prefix, if present, consists of the LOCK prefix or one of the repeat prefixes. The LOCK prefix is used to ensure exclusive use of shared memory in multiprocessor environments. The repeat prefixes specify repeated operation of a string, which enables the x86 to process strings much faster than with a regular software loop. There are five different repeat prefixes: REP, REPE, REPZ, REPNE, and REPNZ. When the absolute REP prefix is present, the operation specified in the instruction is executed repeatedly on successive elements of the string; the number of repetitions is specified in register CX. The conditional REP prefix causes the instruction to repeat until the count in CX goes to zero or until the condition is met.

- **Segment override:** Explicitly specifies which segment register an instruction should use, overriding the default segment-register selection generated by the x86 for that instruction.

- **Operand size:** An instruction has a default operand size of 16 or 32 bits, and the operand prefix switches between 32-bit and 16-bit operands.

- **Address size:** The processor can address memory using either 16- or 32-bit addresses. The address size determines the displacement size in instructions and the size of address offsets generated during effective address calculation. One of these sizes is designated as default, and the address size prefix switches between 32-bit and 16-bit address generation.

The instruction itself includes the following fields:

- **Opcode:** The opcode field is 1, 2, or 3 bytes in length. The opcode may also include bits that specify if data is byte- or full-size (16 or 32 bits depending on context), direction of data operation (to or from memory), and whether an immediate data field must be sign extended.

- **ModR/m:** This byte, and the next, provide addressing information. The ModR/m byte specifies whether an operand is in a register or in memory; if it is in memory, then fields within the byte specify the addressing mode to be used. The ModR/m byte consists of three fields: The Mod field (2 bits) combines with the r/m field to form 32 possible values: 8 registers and 24 indexing modes; the Reg/Opcode field (3 bits) specifies either a register number or three more bits of opcode information; the r/m field (3 bits) can specify a register as the location of an operand, or it can form part of the addressing-mode encoding in combination with the Mod field.

- **SIB:** Certain encoding of the ModR/m byte specifies the inclusion of the SIB byte to specify fully the addressing mode. The SIB byte consists of three fields: The Scale field (2 bits) specifies the scale factor for scaled indexing; the Index field (3 bits) specifies the index register; the Base field (3 bits) specifies the base register.

- **Displacement:** When the addressing-mode specifier indicates that a displacement is used, an 8-, 16-, or 32-bit signed integer displacement field is added.

- **Immediate:** Provides the value of an 8-, 16-, or 32-bit operand.

Several comparisons may be useful here. In the x86 format, the addressing mode is provided as part of the opcode sequence rather than with each operand. Because only one operand can have address-mode information, only one memory operand can be referenced in an instruction. In contrast, the VAX carries the address-mode information with each operand, allowing memory-to-memory operations. The x86 instructions are therefore more compact. However, if a memory-to-memory operation is required, the VAX can accomplish this in a single instruction.

The x86 format allows the use of not only 1-byte, but also 2-byte and 4-byte offsets for indexing. Although the use of the larger index offsets results in longer instructions, this feature provides needed flexibility. For example, it is useful in addressing large arrays or large stack frames. In contrast, the IBM S/370 instruction format allows offsets no greater than 4K bytes (12 bits of offset information), and the offset must be positive. When a location is not in reach of this offset, the compiler must generate extra code to generate the needed address. This problem is especially apparent in dealing with stack frames that have local variables occupying in excess of 4K bytes. As [DEWA90] puts it, "generating code for the 370 is so painful as a result of that restriction that there have even been compilers for the 370 that simply chose to limit the size of the stack frame to 4K bytes."

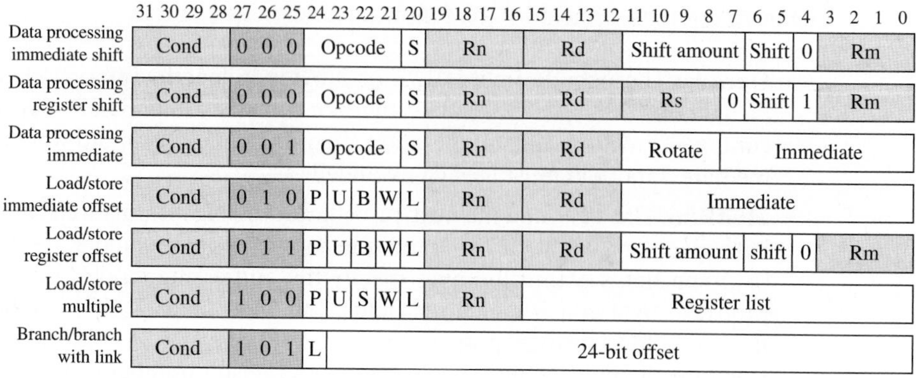

	31 30 29 28	27 26 25	24 23 22 21 20	19 18 17 16	15 14 13 12	11 10 9 8	7	6 5	4	3 2 1 0
Data processing immediate shift	Cond	0 0 0	Opcode S	Rn	Rd	Shift amount		Shift	0	Rm
Data processing register shift	Cond	0 0 0	Opcode S	Rn	Rd	Rs	0	Shift	1	Rm
Data processing immediate	Cond	0 0 1	Opcode S	Rn	Rd	Rotate		Immediate		
Load/store immediate offset	Cond	0 1 0	P U B W L	Rn	Rd	Immediate				
Load/store register offset	Cond	0 1 1	P U B W L	Rn	Rd	Shift amount		shift	0	Rm
Load/store multiple	Cond	1 0 0	P U S W L	Rn	Register list					
Branch/branch with link	Cond	1 0 1 L	24-bit offset							

S = For data processing instructions, signifies that the instruction
   updates the condition codes
S = For load/store multiple instructions, signifies whether instruction
   execution is restricted to supervisor mode
P, U, W = Bits that distinguish between
   different types of addressing_mode
B = Distinguishes between an unsigned
   byte (B==1) and a word (B==0) access
L = For load/store instructions, distinguishes
   between a Load (L==1) and a Store (L==0)
L = For branch instructions, determines whether a
   return address is stored in the link register

Figure 11.10   ARM Instruction Formats

As can be seen, the encoding of the x86 instruction set is very complex. This has to do partly with the need to be backward compatible with the 8086 machine and partly with a desire on the part of the designers to provide every possible assistance to the compiler writer in producing efficient code. It is a matter of some debate whether an instruction set as complex as this is preferable to the opposite extreme of the RISC instruction sets.

ARM Instruction Formats

All instructions in the ARM architecture are 32 bits long and follow a regular format (Figure 11.10). The first four bits of an instruction are the condition code. As discussed in Chapter 10, virtually all ARM instructions can be conditionally executed. The next three bits specify the general type of instruction. For most instructions other than branch instructions, the next five bits constitute an opcode and/or modifier bits for the operation. The remaining 20 bits are for operand addressing. The regular structure of the instruction formats eases the job of the instruction decode units.

IMMEDIATE CONSTANTS To achieve a greater range of immediate values, the data processing immediate format specifies both an immediate value and a rotate value.

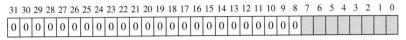

ror #0—range 0 through 0x000000FF—step 0x00000001

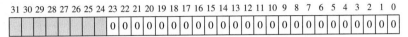

ror #8—range 0 through 0xFF000000—step 0x01000000

ror #30—range 0 through 0x000003FC—step 0x00000004

Figure 11.11   Examples of Use of ARM Immediate Contants

The 8-bit immediate value is expanded to 32 bits and then rotated right by a number of bits equal to twice the 4-bit rotate value. Several examples are shown in Figure 11.11.

THUMB INSTRUCTION SET The Thumb instruction set is a re-encoded subset of the ARM instruction set. Thumb is designed to increase the performance of ARM implementations that use a 16-bit or narrower memory data bus and to allow better code density than provided by the ARM instruction set. The Thumb instruction set contains a subset of the ARM 32-bit instruction set recoded into 16-bit instructions. The savings is achieved in the following way:

1. Thumb instructions are unconditional, so the condition code field is not used. Also, all Thumb arithmetic and logic instructions update the condition flags, so that the update-flag bit is not needed. Savings: 5 bits.
2. Thumb has only a subset of the operations in the full instruction set and uses only a 2-bit opcode field, plus a 3-bit type field. Savings: 2 bits.
3. The remaining savings of 9 bits comes from reductions in the operand specifications. For example, Thumb instructions reference only registers r0 through r7, so only 3 bits are required for register references, rather than 4 bits. Immediate values do not include a 4-bit rotate field.

The ARM processor can execute a program consisting of a mixture of Thumb instructions and 32-bit ARM instructions. A bit in the processor control register determines which type of instruction is currently being executed. Figure 11.12 shows an example. The figure shows both the general format and a specific instance of an instruction in both 16-bit and 32-bit formats.

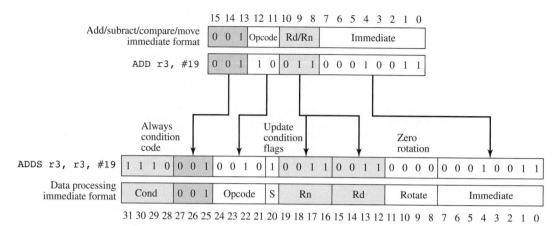

Figure 11.12   Expanding a Thumb ADD Instruction into its ARM Equivalent

11.5 ASSEMBLY LANGUAGE

A processor can understand and execute machine instructions. Such instructions are simply binary numbers stored in the computer. If a programmer wished to program directly in machine language, then it would be necessary to enter the program as binary data.

Consider the simple BASIC statement

$$N = I + J + K$$

Suppose we wished to program this statement in machine language and to initialize I, J, and K to 2, 3, and 4, respectively. This is shown in Figure 11.13a. The program starts in location 101 (hexadecimal). Memory is reserved for the four variables starting at location 201. The program consists of four instructions:

1. Load the contents of location 201 into the AC.
2. Add the contents of location 202 to the AC.
3. Add the contents of location 203 to the AC.
4. Store the contents of the AC in location 204.

This is clearly a tedious and very error-prone process.

A slight improvement is to write the program in hexadecimal rather than binary notation (Figure 10.11b). We could write the program as a series of lines. Each line contains the address of a memory location and the hexadecimal code of the binary value to be stored in that location. Then we need a program that will accept this input, translate each line into a binary number, and store it in the specified location.

For more improvement, we can make use of the symbolic name or mnemonic of each instruction. This results in the *symbolic program* shown in Figure 10.11c. Each line of input still represents one memory location. Each line consists of three fields, separated by spaces. The first field contains the address of a location. For an

Address	Contents			
101	0010	0010	101	2201
102	0001	0010	102	1202
103	0001	0010	103	1203
104	0011	0010	104	3204
201	0000	0000	201	0002
202	0000	0000	202	0003
203	0000	0000	203	0004
204	0000	0000	204	0000

(a) Binary program

Address	Contents
101	2201
102	1202
103	1203
104	3204
201	0002
202	0003
203	0004
204	0000

(b) Hexadecimal program

Address	Instruction	
101	LDA	201
102	ADD	202
103	ADD	203
104	STA	204
201	DAT	2
202	DAT	3
203	DAT	4
204	DAT	0

(c) Symbolic program

Label	Operation	Operand
FORMUL	LDA	I
	ADD	J
	ADD	K
	STA	N
I	DATA	2
J	DATA	3
K	DATA	4
N	DATA	0

(d) Assembly program

Figure 11.13 Computation of the Formula $N = I + J + K$

instruction, the second field contains the three-letter symbol for the opcode. If it is a memory-referencing instruction, then a third field contains the address. To store arbitrary data in a location, we invent a *pseudoinstruction* with the symbol DAT. This is merely an indication that the third field on the line contains a hexadecimal number to be stored in the location specified in the first field.

For this type of input we need a slightly more complex program. The program accepts each line of input, generates a binary number based on the second and third (if present) fields, and stores it in the location specified by the first field.

The use of a symbolic program makes life much easier but is still awkward. In particular, we must give an absolute address for each word. This means that the program and data can be loaded into only one place in memory, and we must know that place ahead of time. Worse, suppose we wish to change the program some day by adding or deleting a line. This will change the addresses of all subsequent words.

A much better system, and one commonly used, is to use symbolic addresses. This is illustrated in Figure 10.11d. Each line still consists of three fields. The first field is still for the address, but a symbol is used instead of an absolute numerical address. Some lines have no address, implying that the address of that line is one more than the address of the previous line. For memory-reference instructions, the third field also contains a symbolic address.

With this last refinement, we have an *assembly language*. Programs written in assembly language (assembly programs) are translated into machine language by an *assembler*. This program must not only do the symbolic translation discussed earlier but also assign some form of memory addresses to symbolic addresses.

The development of assembly language was a major milestone in the evolution of computer technology. It was the first step to the high-level languages in use today. Although few programmers use assembly language, virtually all machines provide one. They are used, if at all, for systems programs such as compilers and I/O routines.

Appendix B provides a more detailed examination of assembly language.

11.6 RECOMMENDED READING

The references cited in Chapter 10 are equally applicable to the material of this chapter. [BLAA97] contains a detailed discussion of instruction formats and addressing modes. In addition, the reader may wish to consult [FLYN85] for a discussion and analysis of instruction set design issues, particularly those relating to formats.

BLAA97   Blaauw, G., and Brooks, F. *Computer Architecture: Concepts and Evolution.* Reading, MA: Addison-Wesley, 1997.

FLYN85   Flynn, M.; Johnson, J.; and Wakefield, S. "On Instruction Sets and Their Formats." *IEEE Transactions on Computers,* March 1985.

11.7 KEY TERMS, REVIEW QUESTIONS, AND PROBLEMS

Key Terms

autoindexing	immediate addressing	preindexing
base-register addressing	indexing	register addressing
direct addressing	indirect addressing	register indirect addressing
displacement addressing	instruction format	relative addressing
effective address	postindexing	word

Review Questions

11.1   Briefly define immediate addressing.
11.2   Briefly define direct addressing.
11.3   Briefly define indirect addressing.
11.4   Briefly define register addressing.
11.5   Briefly define register indirect addressing.
11.6   Briefly define displacement addressing.
11.7   Briefly define relative addressing.
11.8   What is the advantage of autoindexing?
11.9   What is the difference between postindexing and preindexing?
11.10   What facts go into determining the use of the addressing bits of an instruction?
11.11   What are the advantages and disadvantages of using a variable-length instruction format?

Problems

11.1 Given the following memory values and a one-address machine with an accumulator, what values do the following instructions load into the accumulator?
- Word 20 contains 40.
- Word 30 contains 50.
- Word 40 contains 60.
- Word 50 contains 70.
- **a.** LOAD IMMEDIATE 20
- **b.** LOAD DIRECT 20
- **c.** LOAD INDIRECT 20
- **d.** LOAD IMMEDIATE 30
- **e.** LOAD DIRECT 30
- **f.** LOAD INDIRECT 30

11.2 Let the address stored in the program counter be designated by the symbol X1. The instruction stored in X1 has an address part (operand reference) X2. The operand needed to execute the instruction is stored in the memory word with address X3. An index register contains the value X4. What is the relationship between these various quantities if the addressing mode of the instruction is (a) direct; (b) indirect; (c) PC relative; (d) indexed?

11.3 An address field in an instruction contains decimal value 14. Where is the corresponding operand located for
- **a.** immediate addressing?
- **b.** direct addressing?
- **c.** indirect addressing?
- **d.** register addressing?
- **e.** register indirect addressing?

11.4 Consider a 16-bit processor in which the following appears in main memory, starting at location 200:

200	Load to AC	Mode
201	500	
202	Next instruction	

The first part of the first word indicates that this instruction loads a value into an accumulator. The Mode field specifies an addressing mode and, if appropriate, indicates a source register; assume that when used, the source register is R1, which has a value of 400. There is also a base register that contains the value 100. The value of 500 in location 201 may be part of the address calculation. Assume that location 399 contains the value 999, location 400 contains the value 1000, and so on. Determine the effective address and the operand to be loaded for the following address modes:

a. Direct	d. PC relative	g. Register indirect
b. Immediate	e. Displacement	h. Autoindexing with increment, using R1
c. Indirect	f. Register	

11.5 A PC-relative mode branch instruction is 3 bytes long. The address of the instruction, in decimal, is 256028. Determine the branch target address if the signed displacement in the instruction is −31.

11.6 A PC-relative mode branch instruction is stored in memory at address 620_{10}. The branch is made to location 530_{10}. The address field in the instruction is 10 bits long. What is the binary value in the instruction?

11.7   How many times does the processor need to refer to memory when it fetches and executes an indirect-address-mode instruction if the instruction is (a) a computation requiring a single operand; (b) a branch?

11.8   The IBM 370 does not provide indirect addressing. Assume that the address of an operand is in main memory. How would you access the operand?

11.9   In [COOK82], the author proposes that the PC-relative addressing modes be eliminated in favor of other modes, such as the use of a stack. What is the disadvantage of this proposal?

11.10   The x86 includes the following instruction:

$$\text{IMUL op1, op2, immediate}$$

This instruction multiplies op2, which may be either register or memory, by the immediate operand value, and places the result in op1, which must be a register. There is no other three-operand instruction of this sort in the instruction set. What is the possible use of such an instruction? (*Hint:* Consider indexing.)

11.11   Consider a processor that includes a base with indexing addressing mode. Suppose an instruction is encountered that employs this addressing mode and specifies a displacement of 1970, in decimal. Currently the base and index register contain the decimal numbers 48022 and 8, respectively. What is the address of the operand?

11.12   Define: EA = (X)+ is the effective address equal to the contents of location X, with X incremented by one word length after the effective address is calculated; EA = −(X) is the effective address equal to the contents of location X, with X decremented by one word length before the effective address is calculated; EA = (X)− is the effective address equal to the contents of location X, with X decremented by one word length after the effective address is calculated. Consider the following instructions, each in the format (Operation Source Operand, Destination Operand), with the result of the operation placed in the destination operand.
   a.   OP X, (X)
   b.   OP (X), (X)+
   c.   OP (X)+, (X)
   d.   OP −(X), (X)
   e.   OP −(X), (X)+
   f.   OP (X)+, (X)+
   g.   OP (X)−, (X)

Using X as the stack pointer, which of these instructions can pop the top two elements from the stack, perform the designated operation (e.g., ADD source to destination and store in destination), and push the result back on the stack? For each such instruction, does the stack grow toward memory location 0 or in the opposite direction?

11.13   Assume a stack-oriented processor that includes the stack operations PUSH and POP. Arithmetic operations automatically involve the top one or two stack elements. Begin with an empty stack. What stack elements remain after the following instructions are executed?
   PUSH   4
   PUSH   7
   PUSH   8
   ADD
   PUSH   10
   SUB
   MUL

11.14   Justify the assertion that a 32-bit instruction is probably much less than twice as useful as a 16-bit instruction.

11.15   Why was IBM's decision to move from 36 bits to 32 bits per word wrenching, and to whom?

11.16 Assume an instruction set that uses a fixed 16-bit instruction length. Operand specifiers are 6 bits in length. There are K two-operand instructions and L zero-operand instructions. What is the maximum number of one-operand instructions that can be supported?

11.17 Design a variable-length opcode to allow all of the following to be encoded in a 36-bit instruction:
- instructions with two 15-bit addresses and one 3-bit register number
- instructions with one 15-bit address and one 3-bit register number
- instructions with no addresses or registers

11.18 Consider the results of Problem 10.6. Assume that M is a 16-bit memory address and that X, Y, and Z are either 16-bit addresses or 4-bit register numbers. The one-address machine uses an accumulator, and the two- and three-address machines have 16 registers and instructions operating on all combinations of memory locations and registers. Assuming 8-bit opcodes and instruction lengths that are multiples of 4 bits, how many bits does each machine need to compute X?

11.19 Is there any possible justification for an instruction with two opcodes?

11.20 The 16-bit Zilog Z8001 has the following general instruction format:

15	14	13	12	11	10	9	8	7	6	5	4	3	2	1	0
Mode			Opcode					w/b		Operand 2			Operand 1		

The *mode* field specifies how to locate the operands from the *operand* fields. The *w/b* field is used in certain instructions to specify whether the operands are bytes or 16-bit words. The *operand 1* field may (depending on the *mode field* contents) specify one of 16 general-purpose registers. The *operand 2* field may specify any general-purpose registers except register 0. When the *operand 2* field is all zeros, each of the original opcodes takes on a new meaning.

a. How many opcodes are provided on the Z8001?

b. Suggest an efficient way to provide more opcodes and indicate the trade-off involved.

CHAPTER 12

PROCESSOR STRUCTURE AND FUNCTION

KEY POINTS

◆ A processor includes both user-visible registers and control/status registers. The former may be referenced, implicitly or explicitly, in machine instructions. User-visible registers may be general purpose or have a special use, such as fixed-point or floating-point numbers, addresses, indexes, and segment pointers. Control and status registers are used to control the operation of the processor. One obvious example is the program counter. Another important example is a program status word (PSW) that contains a variety of status and condition bits. These include bits to reflect the result of the most recent arithmetic operation, interrupt enable bits, and an indicator of whether the processor is executing in supervisor or user mode.

◆ Processors make use of instruction pipelining to speed up execution. In essence, pipelining involves breaking up the instruction cycle into a number of separate stages that occur in sequence, such as fetch instruction, decode instruction, determine operand addresses, fetch operands, execute instruction, and write operand result. Instructions move through these stages, as on an assembly line, so that in principle, each stage can be working on a different instruction at the same time. The occurrence of branches and dependencies between instructions complicates the design and use of pipelines.

This chapter discusses aspects of the processor not yet covered in Part Three and sets the stage for the discussion of RISC and superscalar architecture in Chapters 13 and 14.

We begin with a summary of processor organization. Registers, which form the internal memory of the processor, are then analyzed. We are then in a position to return to the discussion (begun in Section 3.2) of the instruction cycle. A description of the instruction cycle and a common technique known as instruction pipelining complete our description. The chapter concludes with an examination of some aspects of the x86 and ARM organizations.

12.1 PROCESSOR ORGANIZATION

To understand the organization of the processor, let us consider the requirements placed on the processor, the things that it must do:

- **Fetch instruction:** The processor reads an instruction from memory (register, cache, main memory).
- **Interpret instruction:** The instruction is decoded to determine what action is required.

- **Fetch data:** The execution of an instruction may require reading data from memory or an I/O module.

- **Process data:** The execution of an instruction may require performing some arithmetic or logical operation on data.

- **Write data:** The results of an execution may require writing data to memory or an I/O module.

To do these things, it should be clear that the processor needs to store some data temporarily. It must remember the location of the last instruction so that it can know where to get the next instruction. It needs to store instructions and data temporarily while an instruction is being executed. In other words, the processor needs a small internal memory.

Figure 12.1 is a simplified view of a processor, indicating its connection to the rest of the system via the system bus. A similar interface would be needed for any of the interconnection structures described in Chapter 3. The reader will recall that the major components of the processor are an *arithmetic and logic unit* (ALU) and a *control unit* (CU). The ALU does the actual computation or processing of data. The control unit controls the movement of data and instructions into and out of the processor and controls the operation of the ALU. In addition, the figure shows a minimal internal memory, consisting of a set of storage locations, called *registers*.

Figure 12.2 is a slightly more detailed view of the processor. The data transfer and logic control paths are indicated, including an element labeled *internal processor bus*. This element is needed to transfer data between the various registers and the ALU because the ALU in fact operates only on data in the internal processor memory. The figure also shows typical basic elements of the ALU. Note the similarity between the internal structure of the computer as a whole and the internal structure of the processor. In both cases, there is a small collection of major elements (computer: processor, I/O, memory; processor: control unit, ALU, registers) connected by data paths.

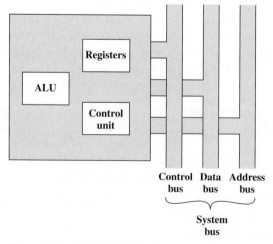

Figure 12.1 The CPU with the System Bus

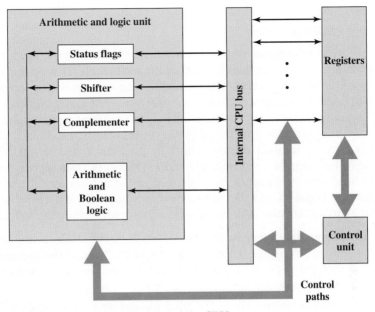

Figure 12.2 Internal Structure of the CPU

12.2 REGISTER ORGANIZATION

As we discussed in Chapter 4, a computer system employs a memory hierarchy. At higher levels of the hierarchy, memory is faster, smaller, and more expensive (per bit). Within the processor, there is a set of registers that function as a level of memory above main memory and cache in the hierarchy. The registers in the processor perform two roles:

- **User-visible registers:** Enable the machine- or assembly language programmer to minimize main memory references by optimizing use of registers.
- **Control and status registers:** Used by the control unit to control the operation of the processor and by privileged, operating system programs to control the execution of programs.

There is not a clean separation of registers into these two categories. For example, on some machines the program counter is user visible (e.g., x86), but on many it is not. For purposes of the following discussion, however, we will use these categories.

User-Visible Registers

A user-visible register is one that may be referenced by means of the machine language that the processor executes. We can characterize these in the following categories:

- General purpose
- Data

- Address
- Condition codes

General-purpose registers can be assigned to a variety of functions by the programmer. Sometimes their use within the instruction set is orthogonal to the operation. That is, any general-purpose register can contain the operand for any opcode. This provides true general-purpose register use. Often, however, there are restrictions. For example, there may be dedicated registers for floating-point and stack operations.

In some cases, general-purpose registers can be used for addressing functions (e.g., register indirect, displacement). In other cases, there is a partial or clean separation between data registers and address registers. **Data registers** may be used only to hold data and cannot be employed in the calculation of an operand address. **Address registers** may themselves be somewhat general purpose, or they may be devoted to a particular addressing mode. Examples include the following:

- **Segment pointers:** In a machine with segmented addressing (see Section 8.3), a segment register holds the address of the base of the segment. There may be multiple registers: for example, one for the operating system and one for the current process.

- **Index registers:** These are used for indexed addressing and may be autoindexed.

- **Stack pointer:** If there is user-visible stack addressing, then typically there is a dedicated register that points to the top of the stack. This allows implicit addressing; that is, push, pop, and other stack instructions need not contain an explicit stack operand.

There are several design issues to be addressed here. An important issue is whether to use completely general-purpose registers or to specialize their use. We have already touched on this issue in the preceding chapter because it affects instruction set design. With the use of specialized registers, it can generally be implicit in the opcode which type of register a certain operand specifier refers to. The operand specifier must only identify one of a set of specialized registers rather than one out of all the registers, thus saving bits. On the other hand, this specialization limits the programmer's flexibility.

Another design issue is the number of registers, either general purpose or data plus address, to be provided. Again, this affects instruction set design because more registers require more operand specifier bits. As we previously discussed, somewhere between 8 and 32 registers appears optimum [LUND77]. Fewer registers result in more memory references; more registers do not noticeably reduce memory references (e.g., see [WILL90]). However, a new approach, which finds advantage in the use of hundreds of registers, is exhibited in some RISC systems and is discussed in Chapter 13.

Finally, there is the issue of register length. Registers that must hold addresses obviously must be at least long enough to hold the largest address. Data registers should be able to hold values of most data types. Some machines allow two contiguous registers to be used as one for holding double-length values.

A final category of registers, which is at least partially visible to the user, holds **condition codes** (also referred to as *flags*). Condition codes are bits set by the processor hardware as the result of operations. For example, an arithmetic operation

Table 12.1 Condition Codes

Advantages	Disadvantages
1. Because condition codes are set by normal arithmetic and data movement instructions, they should reduce the number of COM-PARE and TEST instructions needed. 2. Conditional instructions, such as BRANCH are simplified relative to composite instructions, such as TEST AND BRANCH. 3. Condition codes facilitate multiway branches. For example, a TEST instruction can be followed by two branches, one on less than or equal to zero and one on greater than zero.	1. Condition codes add complexity, both to the hardware and software. Condition code bits are often modified in different ways by different instructions, making life more difficult for both the microprogrammer and compiler writer. 2. Condition codes are irregular; they are typically not part of the main data path, so they require extra hardware connections. 3. Often condition code machines must add special non-condition-code instructions for special situations anyway, such as bit checking, loop control, and atomic semaphore operations. 4. In a pipelined implementation, condition codes require special synchronization to avoid conflicts.

may produce a positive, negative, zero, or overflow result. In addition to the result itself being stored in a register or memory, a condition code is also set. The code may subsequently be tested as part of a conditional branch operation.

Condition code bits are collected into one or more registers. Usually, they form part of a control register. Generally, machine instructions allow these bits to be read by implicit reference, but the programmer cannot alter them.

Many processors, including those based on the IA-64 architecture and the MIPS processors, do not use condition codes at all. Rather, conditional branch instructions specify a comparison to be made and act on the result of the comparison, without storing a condition code. Table 12.1, based on [DERO87], lists key advantages and disadvantages of condition codes.

In some machines, a subroutine call will result in the automatic saving of all user-visible registers, to be restored on return. The processor performs the saving and restoring as part of the execution of call and return instructions. This allows each subroutine to use the user-visible registers independently. On other machines, it is the responsibility of the programmer to save the contents of the relevant user-visible registers prior to a subroutine call, by including instructions for this purpose in the program.

Control and Status Registers

There are a variety of processor registers that are employed to control the operation of the processor. Most of these, on most machines, are not visible to the user. Some of them may be visible to machine instructions executed in a control or operating system mode.

Of course, different machines will have different register organizations and use different terminology. We list here a reasonably complete list of register types, with a brief description.

Four registers are essential to instruction execution:

- **Program counter (PC):** Contains the address of an instruction to be fetched
- **Instruction register (IR):** Contains the instruction most recently fetched
- **Memory address register (MAR):** Contains the address of a location in memory
- **Memory buffer register (MBR):** Contains a word of data to be written to memory or the word most recently read

Not all processors have internal registers designated as MAR and MBR, but some equivalent buffering mechanism is needed whereby the bits to be transferred to the system bus are staged and the bits to be read from the data bus are temporarily stored.

Typically, the processor updates the PC after each instruction fetch so that the PC always points to the next instruction to be executed. A branch or skip instruction will also modify the contents of the PC. The fetched instruction is loaded into an IR, where the opcode and operand specifiers are analyzed. Data are exchanged with memory using the MAR and MBR. In a bus-organized system, the MAR connects directly to the address bus, and the MBR connects directly to the data bus. User-visible registers, in turn, exchange data with the MBR.

The four registers just mentioned are used for the movement of data between the processor and memory. Within the processor, data must be presented to the ALU for processing. The ALU may have direct access to the MBR and user-visible registers. Alternatively, there may be additional buffering registers at the boundary to the ALU; these registers serve as input and output registers for the ALU and exchange data with the MBR and user-visible registers.

Many processor designs include a register or set of registers, often known as the *program status word* (PSW), that contain status information. The PSW typically contains condition codes plus other status information. Common fields or flags include the following:

- **Sign:** Contains the sign bit of the result of the last arithmetic operation.
- **Zero:** Set when the result is 0.
- **Carry:** Set if an operation resulted in a carry (addition) into or borrow (subtraction) out of a high-order bit. Used for multiword arithmetic operations.
- **Equal:** Set if a logical compare result is equality.
- **Overflow:** Used to indicate arithmetic overflow.
- **Interrupt Enable/Disable:** Used to enable or disable interrupts.
- **Supervisor:** Indicates whether the processor is executing in supervisor or user mode. Certain privileged instructions can be executed only in supervisor mode, and certain areas of memory can be accessed only in supervisor mode.

A number of other registers related to status and control might be found in a particular processor design. There may be a pointer to a block of memory containing additional status information (e.g., process control blocks). In machines using vectored interrupts, an interrupt vector register may be provided. If a stack is used to implement certain functions (e.g., subroutine call), then a system stack pointer is needed. A page table pointer is used with a virtual memory system. Finally, registers may be used in the control of I/O operations.

A number of factors go into the design of the control and status register organization. One key issue is operating system support. Certain types of control information are of specific utility to the operating system. If the processor designer has a functional understanding of the operating system to be used, then the register organization can to some extent be tailored to the operating system.

Another key design decision is the allocation of control information between registers and memory. It is common to dedicate the first (lowest) few hundred or thousand words of memory for control purposes. The designer must decide how much control information should be in registers and how much in memory. The usual trade-off of cost versus speed arises.

Example Microprocessor Register Organizations

It is instructive to examine and compare the register organization of comparable systems. In this section, we look at two 16-bit microprocessors that were designed at about the same time: the Motorola MC68000 [STRI79] and the Intel 8086 [MORS78]. Figures 12.3a and b depict the register organization of each; purely internal registers, such as a memory address register, are not shown.

The MC68000 partitions its 32-bit registers into eight data registers and nine address registers. The eight data registers are used primarily for data manipulation and are also used in addressing as index registers. The width of the registers allows 8-, 16-,

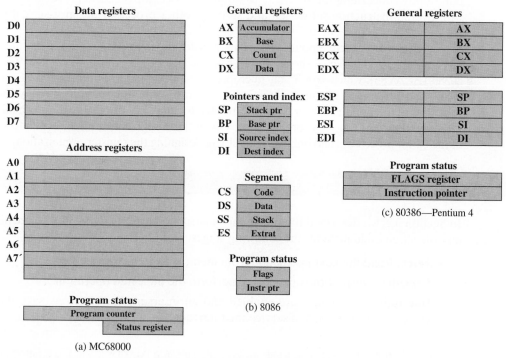

Figure 12.3   Example Microprocessor Register Organizations

and 32-bit data operations, determined by opcode. The address registers contain 32-bit (no segmentation) addresses; two of these registers are also used as stack pointers, one for users and one for the operating system, depending on the current execution mode. Both registers are numbered 7, because only one can be used at a time. The MC68000 also includes a 32-bit program counter and a 16-bit status register.

The Motorola team wanted a very regular instruction set, with no special-purpose registers. A concern for code efficiency led them to divide the registers into two functional components, saving one bit on each register specifier. This seems a reasonable compromise between complete generality and code compaction.

The Intel 8086 takes a different approach to register organization. Every register is special purpose, although some registers are also usable as general purpose. The 8086 contains four 16-bit data registers that are addressable on a byte or 16-bit basis, and four 16-bit pointer and index registers. The data registers can be used as general purpose in some instructions. In others, the registers are used implicitly. For example, a multiply instruction always uses the accumulator. The four pointer registers are also used implicitly in a number of operations; each contains a segment offset. There are also four 16-bit segment registers. Three of the four segment registers are used in a dedicated, implicit fashion, to point to the segment of the current instruction (useful for branch instructions), a segment containing data, and a segment containing a stack, respectively. These dedicated and implicit uses provide for compact encoding at the cost of reduced flexibility. The 8086 also includes an instruction pointer and a set of 1-bit status and control flags.

The point of this comparison should be clear. There is no universally accepted philosophy concerning the best way to organize processor registers [TOON81]. As with overall instruction set design and so many other processor design issues, it is still a matter of judgment and taste.

A second instructive point concerning register organization design is illustrated in Figure 12.3c. This figure shows the user-visible register organization for the Intel 80386 [ELAY85], which is a 32-bit microprocessor designed as an extension of the 8086.[1] The 80386 uses 32-bit registers. However, to provide upward compatibility for programs written on the earlier machine, the 80386 retains the original register organization embedded in the new organization. Given this design constraint, the architects of the 32-bit processors had limited flexibility in designing the register organization.

12.3 INSTRUCTION CYCLE

In Section 3.2, we described the processor's instruction cycle (Figure 3.9). To recall, an instruction cycle includes the following stages:

- **Fetch:** Read the next instruction from memory into the processor.
- **Execute:** Interpret the opcode and perform the indicated operation.
- **Interrupt:** If interrupts are enabled and an interrupt has occurred, save the current process state and service the interrupt.

---

[1]Because the MC68000 already uses 32-bit registers, the MC68020 [MACD84], which is a full 32-bit architecture, uses the same register organization.

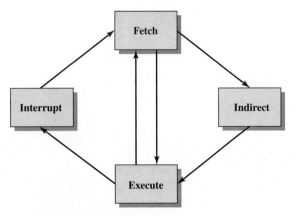

Figure 12.4 The Instruction Cycle

We are now in a position to elaborate somewhat on the instruction cycle. First, we must introduce one additional stage, known as the indirect cycle.

The Indirect Cycle

We have seen, in Chapter 11, that the execution of an instruction may involve one or more operands in memory, each of which requires a memory access. Further, if indirect addressing is used, then additional memory accesses are required.

We can think of the fetching of indirect addresses as one more instruction stages. The result is shown in Figure 12.4. The main line of activity consists of alternating instruction fetch and instruction execution activities. After an instruction is fetched, it is examined to determine if any indirect addressing is involved. If so, the required operands are fetched using indirect addressing. Following execution, an interrupt may be processed before the next instruction fetch.

Another way to view this process is shown in Figure 12.5, which is a revised version of Figure 3.12. This illustrates more correctly the nature of the instruction cycle. Once an instruction is fetched, its operand specifiers must be identified. Each input operand in memory is then fetched, and this process may require indirect addressing. Register-based operands need not be fetched. Once the opcode is executed, a similar process may be needed to store the result in main memory.

Data Flow

The exact sequence of events during an instruction cycle depends on the design of the processor. We can, however, indicate in general terms what must happen. Let us assume that a processor that employs a memory address register (MAR), a memory buffer register (MBR), a program counter (PC), and an instruction register (IR).

During the *fetch cycle,* an instruction is read from memory. Figure 12.6 shows the flow of data during this cycle. The PC contains the address of the next instruction to be fetched. This address is moved to the MAR and placed on the address bus.

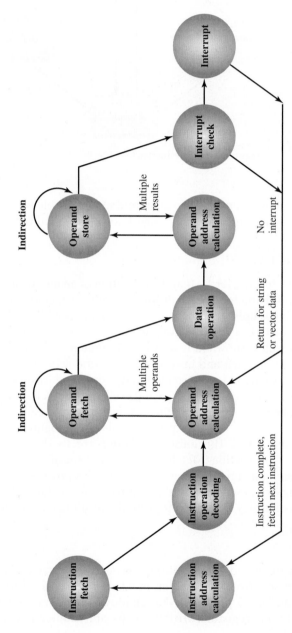

Figure 12.5 Instruction Cycle State Diagram

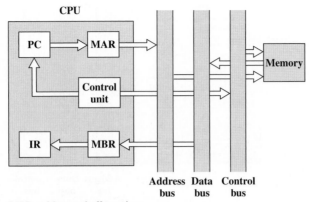

MBR = Memory buffer register
MAR = Memory address register
IR = Instruction register
PC = Program counter

Figure 12.6   Data Flow, Fetch Cycle

The control unit requests a memory read, and the result is placed on the data bus and copied into the MBR and then moved to the IR. Meanwhile, the PC is incremented by 1, preparatory for the next fetch.

Once the fetch cycle is over, the control unit examines the contents of the IR to determine if it contains an operand specifier using indirect addressing. If so, an *indirect cycle* is performed. As shown in Figure 12.7, this is a simple cycle. The rightmost *N* bits of the MBR, which contain the address reference, are transferred to the MAR. Then the control unit requests a memory read, to get the desired address of the operand into the MBR.

The fetch and indirect cycles are simple and predictable. The *execute cycle* takes many forms; the form depends on which of the various machine instructions is in the IR. This cycle may involve transferring data among registers, read or write from memory or I/O, and/or the invocation of the ALU.

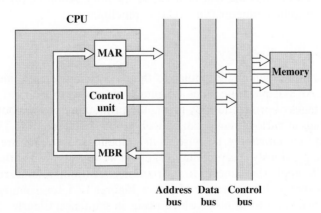

Figure 12.7   Data Flow, Indirect Cycle

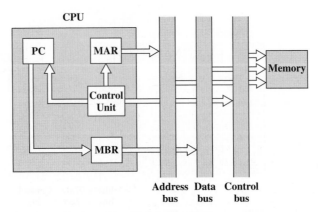

Figure 12.8   Data Flow, Interrupt Cycle

Like the fetch and indirect cycles, the *interrupt cycle* is simple and predictable (Figure 12.8). The current contents of the PC must be saved so that the processor can resume normal activity after the interrupt. Thus, the contents of the PC are transferred to the MBR to be written into memory. The special memory location reserved for this purpose is loaded into the MAR from the control unit. It might, for example, be a stack pointer. The PC is loaded with the address of the interrupt routine. As a result, the next instruction cycle will begin by fetching the appropriate instruction.

12.4 INSTRUCTION PIPELINING

As computer systems evolve, greater performance can be achieved by taking advantage of improvements in technology, such as faster circuitry. In addition, organizational enhancements to the processor can improve performance. We have already seen some examples of this, such as the use of multiple registers rather than a single accumulator, and the use of a cache memory. Another organizational approach, which is quite common, is instruction pipelining.

Pipelining Strategy

Instruction pipelining is similar to the use of an assembly line in a manufacturing plant. An assembly line takes advantage of the fact that a product goes through various stages of production. By laying the production process out in an assembly line, products at various stages can be worked on simultaneously. This process is also referred to as *pipelining,* because, as in a pipeline, new inputs are accepted at one end before previously accepted inputs appear as outputs at the other end.

To apply this concept to instruction execution, we must recognize that, in fact, an instruction has a number of stages. Figures 12.5, for example, breaks the instruction cycle up into 10 tasks, which occur in sequence. Clearly, there should be some opportunity for pipelining.

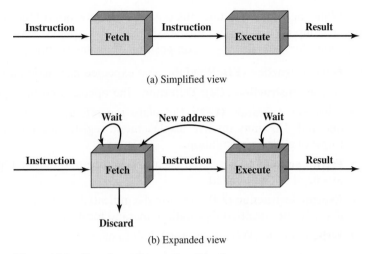

(a) Simplified view

(b) Expanded view

Figure 12.9 Two-Stage Instruction Pipeline

As a simple approach, consider subdividing instruction processing into two stages: fetch instruction and execute instruction. There are times during the execution of an instruction when main memory is not being accessed. This time could be used to fetch the next instruction in parallel with the execution of the current one. Figure 12.9a depicts this approach. The pipeline has two independent stages. The first stage fetches an instruction and buffers it. When the second stage is free, the first stage passes it the buffered instruction. While the second stage is executing the instruction, the first stage takes advantage of any unused memory cycles to fetch and buffer the next instruction. This is called *instruction prefetch* or *fetch overlap*. Note that this approach, which involves instruction buffering, requires more registers. In general, pipelining requires registers to store data between stages.

It should be clear that this process will speed up instruction execution. If the fetch and execute stages were of equal duration, the instruction cycle time would be halved. However, if we look more closely at this pipeline (Figure 12.9b), we will see that this doubling of execution rate is unlikely for two reasons:

1. The execution time will generally be longer than the fetch time. Execution will involve reading and storing operands and the performance of some operation. Thus, the fetch stage may have to wait for some time before it can empty its buffer.

2. A conditional branch instruction makes the address of the next instruction to be fetched unknown. Thus, the fetch stage must wait until it receives the next instruction address from the execute stage. The execute stage may then have to wait while the next instruction is fetched.

Guessing can reduce the time loss from the second reason. A simple rule is the following: When a conditional branch instruction is passed on from the fetch to the execute stage, the fetch stage fetches the next instruction in memory after the branch instruction. Then, if the branch is not taken, no time is lost. If the branch is taken, the fetched instruction must be discarded and a new instruction fetched.

While these factors reduce the potential effectiveness of the two-stage pipeline, some speedup occurs. To gain further speedup, the pipeline must have more stages. Let us consider the following decomposition of the instruction processing.

- **Fetch instruction (FI):** Read the next expected instruction into a buffer.
- **Decode instruction (DI):** Determine the opcode and the operand specifiers.
- **Calculate operands (CO):** Calculate the effective address of each source operand. This may involve displacement, register indirect, indirect, or other forms of address calculation.
- **Fetch operands (FO):** Fetch each operand from memory. Operands in registers need not be fetched.
- **Execute instruction (EI):** Perform the indicated operation and store the result, if any, in the specified destination operand location.
- **Write operand (WO):** Store the result in memory.

With this decomposition, the various stages will be of more nearly equal duration. For the sake of illustration, let us assume equal duration. Using this assumption, Figure 12.10 shows that a six-stage pipeline can reduce the execution time for 9 instructions from 54 time units to 14 time units.

Several comments are in order: The diagram assumes that each instruction goes through all six stages of the pipeline. This will not always be the case. For example, a load instruction does not need the WO stage. However, to simplify the pipeline hardware, the timing is set up assuming that each instruction requires all six stages. Also, the diagram assumes that all of the stages can be performed in parallel. In particular, it is assumed that there are no memory conflicts. For example, the FI,

	Time													
	1	2	3	4	5	6	7	8	9	10	11	12	13	14
Instruction 1	FI	DI	CO	FO	EI	WO								
Instruction 2		FI	DI	CO	FO	EI	WO							
Instruction 3			FI	DI	CO	FO	EI	WO						
Instruction 4				FI	DI	CO	FO	EI	WO					
Instruction 5					FI	DI	CO	FO	EI	WO				
Instruction 6						FI	DI	CO	FO	EI	WO			
Instruction 7							FI	DI	CO	FO	EI	WO		
Instruction 8								FI	DI	CO	FO	EI	WO	
Instruction 9									FI	DI	CO	FO	EI	WO

Figure 12.10 Timing Diagram for Instruction Pipeline Operation

FO, and WO stages involve a memory access. The diagram implies that all these accesses can occur simultaneously. Most memory systems will not permit that. However, the desired value may be in cache, or the FO or WO stage may be null. Thus, much of the time, memory conflicts will not slow down the pipeline.

Several other factors serve to limit the performance enhancement. If the six stages are not of equal duration, there will be some waiting involved at various pipeline stages, as discussed before for the two-stage pipeline. Another difficulty is the conditional branch instruction, which can invalidate several instruction fetches. A similar unpredictable event is an interrupt. Figure 12.11 illustrates the effects of the conditional branch, using the same program as Figure 12.10. Assume that instruction 3 is a conditional branch to instruction 15. Until the instruction is executed, there is no way of knowing which instruction will come next. The pipeline, in this example, simply loads the next instruction in sequence (instruction 4) and proceeds. In Figure 12.10, the branch is not taken, and we get the full performance benefit of the enhancement. In Figure 12.11, the branch is taken. This is not determined until the end of time unit 7. At this point, the pipeline must be cleared of instructions that are not useful. During time unit 8, instruction 15 enters the pipeline. No instructions complete during time units 9 through 12; this is the performance penalty incurred because we could not anticipate the branch. Figure 12.12 indicates the logic needed for pipelining to account for branches and interrupts.

Other problems arise that did not appear in our simple two-stage organization. The CO stage may depend on the contents of a register that could be altered by a previous instruction that is still in the pipeline. Other such register and memory conflicts could occur. The system must contain logic to account for this type of conflict.

To clarify pipeline operation, it might be useful to look at an alternative depiction. Figures 12.10 and 12.11 show the progression of time horizontally across the

	Time							Branch penalty						
	1	2	3	4	5	6	7	8	9	10	11	12	13	14
Instruction 1	FI	DI	CO	FO	EI	WO								
Instruction 2		FI	DI	CO	FO	EI	WO							
Instruction 3			FI	DI	CO	FO	EI	WO						
Instruction 4				FI	DI	CO	FO							
Instruction 5					FI	DI	CO							
Instruction 6						FI	DI							
Instruction 7							FI							
Instruction 15								FI	DI	CO	FO	EI	WO	
Instruction 16									FI	DI	CO	FO	EI	WO

Figure 12.11 The Effect of a Conditional Branch on Instruction Pipeline Operation

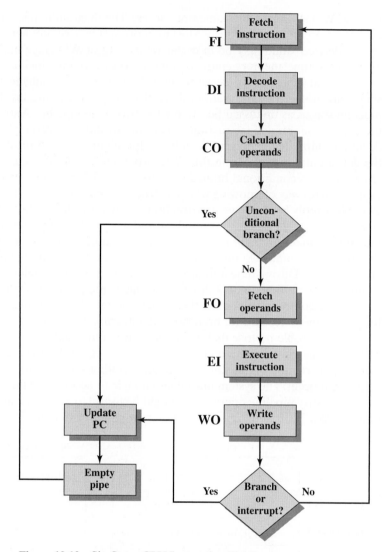

Figure 12.12 Six-Stage CPU Instruction Pipeline

figures, with each row showing the progress of an individual instruction. Figure 12.13 shows same sequence of events, with time progressing vertically down the figure, and each row showing the state of the pipeline at a given point in time. In Figure 12.13a (which corresponds to Figure 12.10), the pipeline is full at time 6, with 6 different instructions in various stages of execution, and remains full through time 9; we assume that instruction I9 is the last instruction to be executed. In Figure 12.13b, (which corresponds to Figure 12.11), the pipeline is full at times 6 and 7. At time 7, instruction 3 is in the execute stage and executes a branch to instruction 15. At this point, instructions I4 through I7 are flushed from the pipeline, so that at time 8, only two instructions are in the pipeline, I3 and I15.

(a) No branches

Time	FI	DI	CO	FO	EI	WO
1	I1					
2	I2	I1				
3	I3	I2	I1			
4	I4	I3	I2	I1		
5	I5	I4	I3	I2	I1	
6	I6	I5	I4	I3	I2	I1
7	I7	I6	I5	I4	I3	I2
8	I8	I7	I6	I5	I4	I3
9	I9	I8	I7	I6	I5	I4
10		I9	I8	I7	I6	I5
11			I9	I8	I7	I6
12				I9	I8	I7
13					I9	I8
14						I9

(b) With conditional branch

Time	FI	DI	CO	FO	EI	WO
1	I1					
2	I2	I1				
3	I3	I2	I1			
4	I4	I3	I2	I1		
5	I5	I4	I3	I2	I1	
6	I6	I5	I4	I3	I2	I1
7	I7	I6	I5	I4	I3	I2
8	I15					I3
9	I16	I15				
10		I16	I15			
11			I16	I15		
12				I16	I15	
13					I16	I15
14						I16

Figure 12.13 An Alternative Pipeline Depiction

From the preceding discussion, it might appear that the greater the number of stages in the pipeline, the faster the execution rate. Some of the IBM S/360 designers pointed out two factors that frustrate this seemingly simple pattern for high-performance design [ANDE67a], and they remain elements that designer must still consider:

1. At each stage of the pipeline, there is some overhead involved in moving data from buffer to buffer and in performing various preparation and delivery functions. This overhead can appreciably lengthen the total execution time of a single instruction. This is significant when sequential instructions are logically dependent, either through heavy use of branching or through memory access dependencies.

2. The amount of control logic required to handle memory and register dependencies and to optimize the use of the pipeline increases enormously with the number of stages. This can lead to a situation where the logic controlling the gating between stages is more complex than the stages being controlled.

Another consideration is latching delay: It takes time for pipeline buffers to operate and this adds to instruction cycle time.

Instruction pipelining is a powerful technique for enhancing performance but requires careful design to achieve optimum results with reasonable complexity.

Pipeline Performance

In this subsection, we develop some simple measures of pipeline performance and relative speedup (based on a discussion in [HWAN93]). The cycle time τ of an instruction pipeline is the time needed to advance a set of instructions one stage through the pipeline; each column in Figures 12.10 and 12.11 represents one cycle time. The cycle time can be determined as

$$\tau = \max_i [\tau_i] + d = \tau_m + d \qquad 1 \le i \le k$$

where

τ_i = time delay of the circuitry in the ith stage of the pipeline

τ_m = maximum stage delay (delay through stage which experiences the largest delay)

k = number of stages in the instruction pipeline

d = time delay of a latch, needed to advance signals and data from one stage to the next

In general, the time delay d is equivalent to a clock pulse and $\tau_m \gg d$. Now suppose that n instructions are processed, with no branches. Let $T_{k,n}$ be the total time required for a pipeline with k stages to execute n instructions. Then

$$T_{k,n} = [k + (n - 1)]\tau \qquad\qquad (12.1)$$

A total of k cycles are required to complete the execution of the first instruction, and the remaining $n - 1$ instructions require $n - 1$ cycles.[2] This equation is easily verified from Figures 12.10. The ninth instruction completes at time cycle 14:

$$14 = [6 + (9 - 1)]$$

Now consider a processor with equivalent functions but no pipeline, and assume that the instruction cycle time is $k\tau$. The speedup factor for the instruction pipeline compared to execution without the pipeline is defined as

$$S_k = \frac{T_{1,n}}{T_{k,n}} = \frac{nk\tau}{[k + (n - 1)]\tau} = \frac{nk}{k + (n - 1)} \qquad (12.2)$$

Figure 12.14a plots the speedup factor as a function of the number of instructions that are executed without a branch. As might be expected, at the limit $(n \rightarrow \infty)$, we have a k-fold speedup. Figure 12.14b shows the speedup factor as a function of the number of stages in the instruction pipeline.[3] In this case, the speedup factor approaches the number of instructions that can be fed into the pipeline without branches. Thus, the larger the number of pipeline stages, the greater the potential for speedup. However, as a practical matter, the potential gains of additional pipeline stages are countered by increases in cost, delays between stages, and the fact that branches will be encountered requiring the flushing of the pipeline.

---

[2]We are being a bit sloppy here. The cycle time will only equal the maximum value of τ when all the stages are full. At the beginning, the cycle time may be less for the first one or few cycles.

[3]Note that the x-axis is logarithmic in Figure 12.14a and linear in Figure 12.14b.

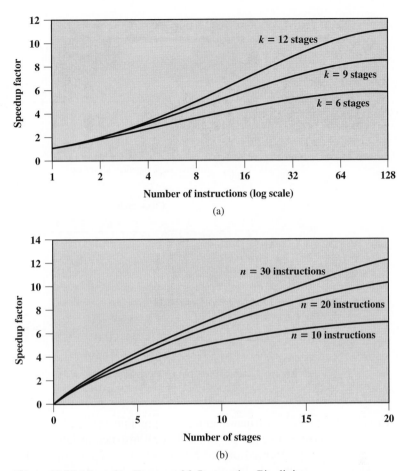

Figure 12.14 Speedup Factors with Instruction Pipelining

Pipeline Hazards

In the previous subsection, we mentioned some of the situations that can result in less than optimal pipeline performance. In this subsection, we examine this issue in a more systematic way. Chapter 14 revisits this issue, in more detail, after we have introduced the complexities found in superscalar pipeline organizations.

A **pipeline hazard** occurs when the pipeline, or some portion of the pipeline, must stall because conditions do not permit continued execution. Such a pipeline stall is also referred to as a *pipeline bubble*. There are three types of hazards: resource, data, and control.

RESOURCE HAZARDS A resource hazard occurs when two (or more) instructions that are already in the pipeline need the same resource. The result is that the instructions must be executed in serial rather than parallel for a portion of the pipeline. A resource hazard is sometime referred to as a *structural hazard*.

Let us consider a simple example of a resource hazard. Assume a simplified five-stage pipeline, in which each stage takes one clock cycle. Figure 12.15a shows the ideal

Clock cycle

	1	2	3	4	5	6	7	8	9
I1	FI	DI	FO	EI	WO				
I2		FI	DI	FO	EI	WO			
I3			FI	DI	FO	EI	WO		
I4				FI	DI	FO	EI	WO	

Instrutcion

(a) Five-stage pipeline, ideal case

Clock cycle

	1	2	3	4	5	6	7	8	9
I1	FI	DI	FO	EI	WO				
I2		FI	DI	FO	EI	WO			
I3			Idle	FI	DI	FO	EI	WO	
I4					FI	DI	FO	EI	WO

Instrutcion

(b) I1 source operand in memory

Figure 12.15   Example of Resource Hazard

case, in which a new instruction enters the pipeline each clock cycle. Now assume that main memory has a single port and that all instruction fetches and data reads and writes must be performed one at a time. Further, ignore the cache. In this case, an operand read to or write from memory cannot be performed in parallel with an instruction fetch. This is illustrated in Figure 12.15b, which assumes that the source operand for instruction I1 is in memory, rather than a register. Therefore, the fetch instruction stage of the pipeline must idle for one cycle before beginning the instruction fetch for instruction I3. The figure assumes that all other operands are in registers.

Another example of a resource conflict is a situation in which multiple instructions are ready to enter the execute instruction phase and there is a single ALU. One solutions to such resource hazards is to increase available resources, such as having multiple ports into main memory and multiple ALU units.

Reservation Table Analyzer

One approach to analyzing resource conflicts and aiding in the design of pipelines is the reservation table. We examine reservation tables in Appendix I.

DATA HAZARDS A data hazard occurs when there is a conflict in the access of an operand location. In general terms, we can state the hazard in this form: Two instructions in a program are to be executed in sequence and both access a particular memory or register operand. If the two instructions are executed in strict sequence, no problem occurs. However, if the instructions are executed in a pipeline, then it is possible for the operand value to be updated in such a way as to produce a different result than would occur with strict sequential execution. In other words, the program produces an incorrect result because of the use of pipelining.

As an example, consider the following x86 machine instruction sequence:

```
ADD EAX, EBX      /* EAX = EAX + EBX
SUB ECX, EAX      /* ECX = ECX - EAX
```

The first instruction adds the contents of the 32-bit registers EAX and EBX and stores the result in EAX. The second instruction subtracts the contents of EAX from ECX and stores the result in ECX. Figure 12.16 shows the pipeline behavior. The ADD instruction does not update register EAX until the end of stage 5, which occurs at clock cycle 5. But the SUB instruction needs that value at the beginning of its stage 2, which occurs at clock cycle 4. To maintain correct operation, the pipeline must stall for two clocks cycles. Thus, in the absence of special hardware and specific avoidance algorithms, such a data hazard results in inefficient pipeline usage.

There are three types of data hazards;

- **Read after write (RAW), or true dependency:** An instruction modifies a register or memory location and a succeeding instruction reads the data in that memory or register location. A hazard occurs if the read takes place before the write operation is complete.
- **Write after read (RAW), or antidependency:** An instruction reads a register or memory location and a succeeding instruction writes to the location. A hazard occurs if the write operation completes before the read operation takes place.
- **Write after write (RAW), or output dependency:** Two instructions both write to the same location. A hazard occurs if the write operations take place in the reverse order of the intended sequence.

The example of Figure 12.16 is a RAW hazard. The other two hazards are best discussed in the context of superscalar organization, discussed in Chapter 14.

Clock cycle

	1	2	3	4	5	6	7	8	9	10
ADD EAX, EBX	FI	DI	FO	EI	WO					
SUB ECX, EAX		FI	DI	Idle		FO	EI	WO		
I3			FI			DI	FO	EI	WO	
I4						FI	DI	FO	EI	WO

Figure 12.16 Example of Data Hazard

CONTROL HAZARDS A control hazard, also known as a *branch hazard,* occurs when the pipeline makes the wrong decision on a branch prediction and therefore brings instructions into the pipeline that must subsequently be discarded. We discuss approaches to dealing with control hazards next.

Dealing with Branches

One of the major problems in designing an instruction pipeline is assuring a steady flow of instructions to the initial stages of the pipeline. The primary impediment, as we have seen, is the conditional branch instruction. Until the instruction is actually executed, it is impossible to determine whether the branch will be taken or not.

A variety of approaches have been taken for dealing with conditional branches:

- Multiple streams
- Prefetch branch target
- Loop buffer
- Branch prediction
- Delayed branch

MULTIPLE STREAMS A simple pipeline suffers a penalty for a branch instruction because it must choose one of two instructions to fetch next and may make the wrong choice. A brute-force approach is to replicate the initial portions of the pipeline and allow the pipeline to fetch both instructions, making use of two streams. There are two problems with this approach:

- With multiple pipelines there are contention delays for access to the registers and to memory.
- Additional branch instructions may enter the pipeline (either stream) before the original branch decision is resolved. Each such instruction needs an additional stream.

Despite these drawbacks, this strategy can improve performance. Examples of machines with two or more pipeline streams are the IBM 370/168 and the IBM 3033.

PREFETCH BRANCH TARGET When a conditional branch is recognized, the target of the branch is prefetched, in addition to the instruction following the branch. This target is then saved until the branch instruction is executed. If the branch is taken, the target has already been prefetched.

The IBM 360/91 uses this approach.

LOOP BUFFER A loop buffer is a small, very-high-speed memory maintained by the instruction fetch stage of the pipeline and containing the *n* most recently fetched instructions, in sequence. If a branch is to be taken, the hardware first checks whether the branch target is within the buffer. If so, the next instruction is fetched from the buffer. The loop buffer has three benefits:

1. With the use of prefetching, the loop buffer will contain some instruction sequentially ahead of the current instruction fetch address. Thus, instructions fetched in sequence will be available without the usual memory access time.

Branch address

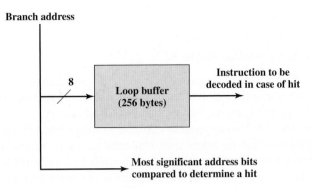

Instruction to be
decoded in case of hit

8

Loop buffer
(256 bytes)

Most significant address bits
compared to determine a hit

Figure 12.17 Loop Buffer

2. If a branch occurs to a target just a few locations ahead of the address of the branch instruction, the target will already be in the buffer. This is useful for the rather common occurrence of IF–THEN and IF–THEN–ELSE sequences.

3. This strategy is particularly well suited to dealing with loops, or iterations; hence the name *loop buffer*. If the loop buffer is large enough to contain all the instructions in a loop, then those instructions need to be fetched from memory only once, for the first iteration. For subsequent iterations, all the needed instructions are already in the buffer.

The loop buffer is similar in principle to a cache dedicated to instructions. The differences are that the loop buffer only retains instructions in sequence and is much smaller in size and hence lower in cost.

Figure 12.17 gives an example of a loop buffer. If the buffer contains 256 bytes, and byte addressing is used, then the least significant 8 bits are used to index the buffer. The remaining most significant bits are checked to determine if the branch target lies within the environment captured by the buffer.

Among the machines using a loop buffer are some of the CDC machines (Star-100, 6600, 7600) and the CRAY-1. A specialized form of loop buffer is available on the Motorola 68010, for executing a three-instruction loop involving the DBcc (decrement and branch on condition) instruction (see Problem 12.14). A three-word buffer is maintained, and the processor executes these instructions repeatedly until the loop condition is satisfied.

**Branch Prediction Simulator
Branch Target Buffer**

BRANCH PREDICTION Various techniques can be used to predict whether a branch will be taken. Among the more common are the following:

- Predict never taken
- Predict always taken

- Predict by opcode
- Taken/not taken switch
- Branch history table

The first three approaches are static: they do not depend on the execution history up to the time of the conditional branch instruction. The latter two approaches are dynamic: They depend on the execution history.

The first two approaches are the simplest. These either always assume that the branch will not be taken and continue to fetch instructions in sequence, or they always assume that the branch will be taken and always fetch from the branch target. The predict-never-taken approach is the most popular of all the branch prediction methods.

Studies analyzing program behavior have shown that conditional branches are taken more than 50% of the time [LILJ88], and so if the cost of prefetching from either path is the same, then always prefetching from the branch target address should give better performance than always prefetching from the sequential path. However, in a paged machine, prefetching the branch target is more likely to cause a page fault than prefetching the next instruction in sequence, and so this performance penalty should be taken into account. An avoidance mechanism may be employed to reduce this penalty.

The final static approach makes the decision based on the opcode of the branch instruction. The processor assumes that the branch will be taken for certain branch opcodes and not for others. [LILJ88] reports success rates of greater than 75% with this strategy.

Dynamic branch strategies attempt to improve the accuracy of prediction by recording the history of conditional branch instructions in a program. For example, one or more bits can be associated with each conditional branch instruction that reflect the recent history of the instruction. These bits are referred to as a taken/not taken switch that directs the processor to make a particular decision the next time the instruction is encountered. Typically, these history bits are not associated with the instruction in main memory. Rather, they are kept in temporary high-speed storage. One possibility is to associate these bits with any conditional branch instruction that is in a cache. When the instruction is replaced in the cache, its history is lost. Another possibility is to maintain a small table for recently executed branch instructions with one or more history bits in each entry. The processor could access the table associatively, like a cache, or by using the low-order bits of the branch instruction's address.

With a single bit, all that can be recorded is whether the last execution of this instruction resulted in a branch or not. A shortcoming of using a single bit appears in the case of a conditional branch instruction that is almost always taken, such as a loop instruction. With only one bit of history, an error in prediction will occur twice for each use of the loop: once on entering the loop, and once on exiting.

If two bits are used, they can be used to record the result of the last two instances of the execution of the associated instruction, or to record a state in some other fashion. Figure 12.18 shows a typical approach (see Problem 12.13 for other possibilities). Assume that the algorithm starts at the upper-left-hand corner of the flowchart. As long as each succeeding conditional branch instruction that is encountered is taken,

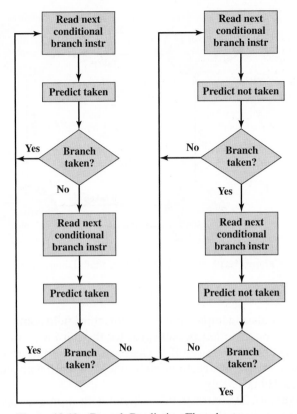

Figure 12.18   Branch Prediction Flowchart

the decision process predicts that the next branch will be taken. If a single prediction is wrong, the algorithm continues to predict that the next branch is taken. Only if two successive branches are not taken does the algorithm shift to the right-hand side of the flowchart. Subsequently, the algorithm will predict that branches are not taken until two branches in a row are taken. Thus, the algorithm requires two consecutive wrong predictions to change the prediction decision.

The decision process can be represented more compactly by a finite-state machine, shown in Figure 12.19. The finite-state machine representation is commonly used in the literature.

The use of history bits, as just described, has one drawback: If the decision is made to take the branch, the target instruction cannot be fetched until the target address, which is an operand in the conditional branch instruction, is decoded. Greater efficiency could be achieved if the instruction fetch could be initiated as soon as the branch decision is made. For this purpose, more information must be saved, in what is known as a branch target buffer, or a branch history table.

The branch history table is a small cache memory associated with the instruction fetch stage of the pipeline. Each entry in the table consists of three elements: the address of a branch instruction, some number of history bits that record the state of use of that instruction, and information about the target instruction. In

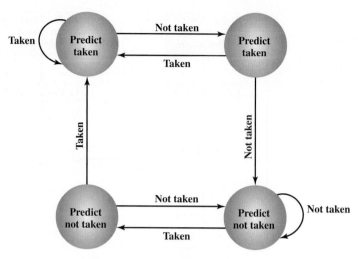

Figure 12.19   Branch Prediction State Diagram

most proposals and implementations, this third field contains the address of the target instruction. Another possibility is for the third field to actually contain the target instruction. The trade-off is clear: Storing the target address yields a smaller table but a greater instruction fetch time compared with storing the target instruction [RECH98].

Figure 12.20 contrasts this scheme with a predict-never-taken strategy. With the former strategy, the instruction fetch stage always fetches the next sequential address. If a branch is taken, some logic in the processor detects this and instructs that the next instruction be fetched from the target address (in addition to flushing the pipeline). The branch history table is treated as a cache. Each prefetch triggers a lookup in the branch history table. If no match is found, the next sequential address is used for the fetch. If a match is found, a prediction is made based on the state of the instruction: Either the next sequential address or the branch target address is fed to the select logic.

When the branch instruction is executed, the execute stage signals the branch history table logic with the result. The state of the instruction is updated to reflect a correct or incorrect prediction. If the prediction is incorrect, the select logic is redirected to the correct address for the next fetch. When a conditional branch instruction is encountered that is not in the table, it is added to the table and one of the existing entries is discarded, using one of the cache replacement algorithms discussed in Chapter 4.

A refined of the branch history approach is referred to as two-level or correlation-based branch history [YEH91]. This approach is based on the assumption that whereas in loop-closing branches, the past history of a particular branch instruction is a good predictor of future behavior, with more complex control-flow structures, the direction of a branch is frequently correlated with the direction of related branches. An example is an if-then-else or case structure. There are a number of strategies possible. Typically, recent global branch history (i.e., the history of the

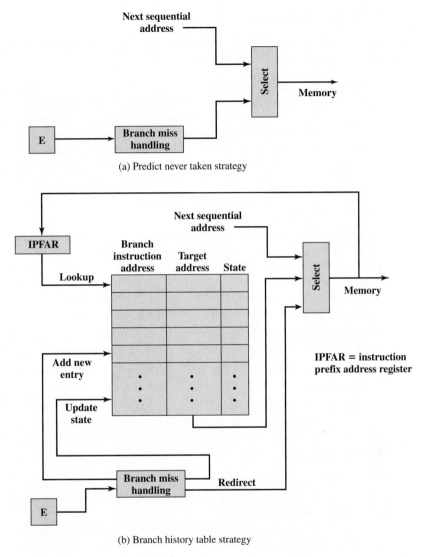

Figure 12.20 Dealing with Branches

most recent branches not just of this branch instruction) is used in addition to the history of the current branch instruction. The general structure is defined as an (m, n) correlator, which uses the behavior of the last m branches to choose from 2^m n-bit branch predictors for the current branch instruction. In other words, an n-bit history is kept for a give branch for each possible combination of branches taken by the most recent m branches.

DELAYED BRANCH It is possible to improve pipeline performance by automatically rearranging instructions within a program, so that branch instructions occur later than actually desired. This intriguing approach is examined in Chapter 13.

Intel 80486 Pipelining

An instructive example of an instruction pipeline is that of the Intel 80486. The 80486 implements a five-stage pipeline:

- **Fetch:** Instructions are fetched from the cache or from external memory and placed into one of the two 16-byte prefetch buffers. The objective of the fetch stage is to fill the prefetch buffers with new data as soon as the old data have been consumed by the instruction decoder. Because instructions are of variable length (from 1 to 11 bytes not counting prefixes), the status of the prefetcher relative to the other pipeline stages varies from instruction to instruction. On average, about five instructions are fetched with each 16-byte load [CRAW90]. The fetch stage operates independently of the other stages to keep the prefetch buffers full.

- **Decode stage 1:** All opcode and addressing-mode information is decoded in the D1 stage. The required information, as well as instruction-length information, is included in at most the first 3 bytes of the instruction. Hence, 3 bytes are passed to the D1 stage from the prefetch buffers. The D1 decoder can then direct the D2 stage to capture the rest of the instruction (displacement and immediate data), which is not involved in the D1 decoding.

- **Decode stage 2:** The D2 stage expands each opcode into control signals for the ALU. It also controls the computation of the more complex addressing modes.

- **Execute:** This stage includes ALU operations, cache access, and register update.

- **Write back:** This stage, if needed, updates registers and status flags modified during the preceding execute stage. If the current instruction updates memory, the computed value is sent to the cache and to the bus-interface write buffers at the same time.

With the use of two decode stages, the pipeline can sustain a throughput of close to one instruction per clock cycle. Complex instructions and conditional branches can slow down this rate.

Figure 12.21 shows examples of the operation of the pipeline. Part a shows that there is no delay introduced into the pipeline when a memory access is required. However, as part b shows, there can be a delay for values used to compute memory addresses. That is, if a value is loaded from memory into a register and that register is then used as a base register in the next instruction, the processor will stall for one cycle. In this example, the processor accesses the cache in the EX stage of the first instruction and stores the value retrieved in the register during the WB stage. However, the next instruction needs this register in its D2 stage. When the D2 stage lines up with the WB stage of the previous instruction, bypass signal paths allow the D2 stage to have access to the same data being used by the WB stage for writing, saving one pipeline stage.

Figure 12.21c illustrates the timing of a branch instruction, assuming that the branch is taken. The compare instruction updates condition codes in the WB stage, and bypass paths make this available to the EX stage of the jump instruction at the same time. In parallel, the processor runs a speculative fetch cycle to the target of

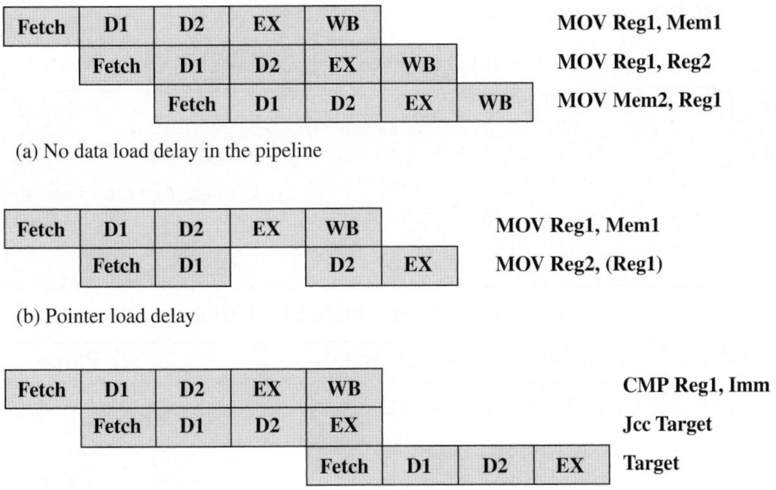

Fetch	D1	D2	EX	WB		MOV Reg1, Mem1
	Fetch	D1	D2	EX	WB	MOV Reg1, Reg2
		Fetch	D1	D2	EX	WB	MOV Mem2, Reg1

(a) No data load delay in the pipeline

| Fetch | D1 | D2 | EX | WB | | | MOV Reg1, Mem1 |
| | Fetch | D1 | | | D2 | EX | MOV Reg2, (Reg1) |

(b) Pointer load delay

Fetch	D1	D2	EX	WB			CMP Reg1, Imm
	Fetch	D1	D2	EX			Jcc Target
		Fetch	D1	D2	EX		Target

(c) Branch instruction timing

Figure 12.21 80486 Instruction Pipeline Examples

the jump during the EX stage of the jump instruction. If the processor determines a false branch condition, it discards this prefetch and continues execution with the next sequential instruction (already fetched and decoded).

12.5 THE x86 PROCESSOR FAMILY

The x86 organization has evolved dramatically over the years. In this section we examine some of the details of the most recent processor organizations, concentrating on common elements in single processors. Chapter 14 looks at superscalar aspects of the x86, and Chapter 18 examines the multicore organization. An overview of the Pentium 4 processor organization is depicted in Figure 4.18.

Register Organization

The register organization includes the following types of registers (Table 12.2):

- **General:** There are eight 32-bit general-purpose registers (see Figure 12.3c). These may be used for all types of x86 instructions; they can also hold operands for address calculations. In addition, some of these registers also serve special purposes. For example, string instructions use the contents of the ECX, ESI, and EDI registers as operands without having to reference these registers explicitly in the instruction. As a result, a number of instructions can be encoded more compactly. In 64-bit mode, there are 16 64-bit general-purpose registers.
- **Segment:** The six 16-bit segment registers contain segment selectors, which index into segment tables, as discussed in Chapter 8. The code segment (CS) register references the segment containing the instruction being executed. The stack segment (SS) register references the segment containing a user-visible

Table 12.2 x86 Processor Registers

(a) Integer Unit in 32-bit Mode

Type	Number	Length (bits)	Purpose
General	8	32	General-purpose user registers
Segment	6	16	Contain segment selectors
EFLAGS	1	32	Status and control bits
Instruction Pointer	1	32	Instruction pointer

(b) Integer Unit in 64-bit Mode

Type	Number	Length (bits)	Purpose
General	16	32	General-purpose user registers
Segment	6	16	Contain segment selectors
RFLAGS	1	64	Status and control bits
Instruction Pointer	1	64	Instruction pointer

(c) Floating-Point Unit

Type	Number	Length (bits)	Purpose
Numeric	8	80	Hold floating-point numbers
Control	1	16	Control bits
Status	1	16	Status bits
Tag Word	1	16	Specifies contents of numeric registers
Instruction Pointer	1	48	Points to instruction interrupted by exception
Data Pointer	1	48	Points to operand interrupted by exception

stack. The remaining segment registers (DS, ES, FS, GS) enable the user to reference up to four separate data segments at a time.

- **Flags:** The 32-bit EFLAGS register contains condition codes and various mode bits. In 64-bit mode, this register is extended to 64 bits and referred to as RFLAGS. In the current architecture definition, the upper 32 bits of RFLAGS are unused.
- **Instruction pointer:** Contains the address of the current instruction.

There are also registers specifically devoted to the floating-point unit:

- **Numeric:** Each register holds an extended-precision 80-bit floating-point number. There are eight registers that function as a stack, with push and pop operations available in the instruction set.
- **Control:** The 16-bit control register contains bits that control the operation of the floating-point unit, including the type of rounding control; single, double, or extended precision; and bits to enable or disable various exception conditions.
- **Status:** The 16-bit status register contains bits that reflect the current state of the floating-point unit, including a 3-bit pointer to the top of the stack; condition codes reporting the outcome of the last operation; and exception flags.

- **Tag word:** This 16-bit register contains a 2-bit tag for each floating-point numeric register, which indicates the nature of the contents of the corresponding register. The four possible values are valid, zero, special (NaN, infinity, denormalized), and empty. These tags enable programs to check the contents of a numeric register without performing complex decoding of the actual data in the register. For example, when a context switch is made, the processor need not save any floating-point registers that are empty.

The use of most of the aforementioned registers is easily understood. Let us elaborate briefly on several of the registers.

EFLAGS REGISTER The EFLAGS register (Figure 12.22) indicates the condition of the processor and helps to control its operation. It includes the six condition codes defined in Table 10.9 (carry, parity, auxiliary, zero, sign, overflow), which report the results of an integer operation. In addition, there are bits in the register that may be referred to as control bits:

- **Trap flag (TF):** When set, causes an interrupt after the execution of each instruction. This is used for debugging.
- **Interrupt enable flag (IF):** When set, the processor will recognize external interrupts.
- **Direction flag (DF):** Determines whether string processing instructions increment or decrement the 16-bit half-registers SI and DI (for 16-bit operations) or the 32-bit registers ESI and EDI (for 32-bit operations).
- **I/O privilege flag (IOPL):** When set, causes the processor to generate an exception on all accesses to I/O devices during protected-mode operation.
- **Resume flag (RF):** Allows the programmer to disable debug exceptions so that the instruction can be restarted after a debug exception without immediately causing another debug exception.
- **Alignment check (AC):** Activates if a word or doubleword is addressed on a nonword or nondoubleword boundary.
- **Identification flag (ID):** If this bit can be set and cleared, then this processor supports the processorID instruction. This instruction provides information about the vendor, family, and model.

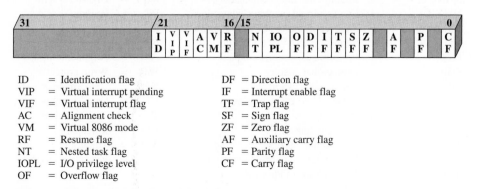

ID	= Identification flag	DF	= Direction flag
VIP	= Virtual interrupt pending	IF	= Interrupt enable flag
VIF	= Virtual interrupt flag	TF	= Trap flag
AC	= Alignment check	SF	= Sign flag
VM	= Virtual 8086 mode	ZF	= Zero flag
RF	= Resume flag	AF	= Auxiliary carry flag
NT	= Nested task flag	PF	= Parity flag
IOPL	= I/O privilege level	CF	= Carry flag
OF	= Overflow flag		

Figure 12.22 Pentium II EFLAGS Register

In addition, there are 4 bits that relate to operating mode. The Nested Task (NT) flag indicates that the current task is nested within another task in protected-mode operation. The Virtual Mode (VM) bit allows the programmer to enable or disable virtual 8086 mode, which determines whether the processor runs as an 8086 machine. The Virtual Interrupt Flag (VIF) and Virtual Interrupt Pending (VIP) flag are used in a multitasking environment.

CONTROL REGISTERS The x86 employs four control registers (register CR1 is unused) to control various aspects of processor operation (Figure 12.23). All of the registers except CR0 are either 32 bits or 64 bits long, depending on whether the implementation supports the x86 64-bit architecture. The CR0 register contains system

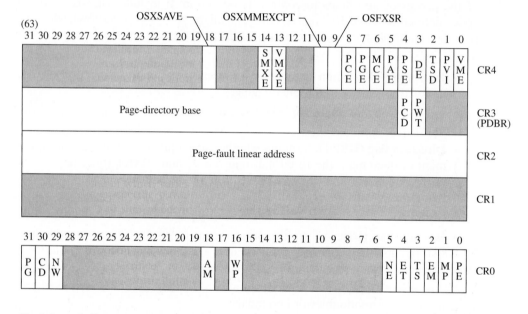

Shaded area indicates reserved bits.

OSXSAVE	=	XSAVE enable bit
SMXE	=	Enable safer mode extensions
VMXE	=	Enable virtual machine extensions
OSXMMEXCPT	=	Support unmasked SIMD FP exceptions
OSFXSR	=	Support FXSAVE, FXSTOR
PCE	=	Performance counter enable
PGE	=	Page global enable
MCE	=	Machine check enable
PAE	=	Physical address extension
PSE	=	Page size extensions
DE	=	Debug extensions
TSD	=	Time stamp disable
PVI	=	Protected mode virtual interrupt
VME	=	Virtual 8086 mode extensions

PCD	=	Page-level cache disable
PWT	=	Page-level writes transparent
PG	=	Paging
CD	=	Cache disable
NW	=	Not write through
AM	=	Alignment mask
WP	=	Write protect
NE	=	Numeric error
ET	=	Extension type
TS	=	Task switched
EM	=	Emulation
MP	=	Monitor coprocessor
PE	=	Protection enable

Figure 12.23 x86 Control Registers

control flags, which control modes or indicate states that apply generally to the processor rather than to the execution of an individual task. The flags are are as follows:

- **Protection Enable (PE):** Enable/disable protected mode of operation.
- **Monitor Coprocessor (MP):** Only of interest when running programs from earlier machines on the x86; it relates to the presence of an arithmetic coprocessor.
- **Emulation (EM):** Set when the processor does not have a floating-point unit, and causes an interrupt when an attempt is made to execute floating-point instructions.
- **Task Switched (TS):** Indicates that the processor has switched tasks.
- **Extension Type (ET):** Not used on the Pentium and later machines; used to indicate support of math coprocessor instructions on earlier machines.
- **Numeric Error (NE):** Enables the standard mechanism for reporting floating-point errors on external bus lines.
- **Write Protect (WP):** When this bit is clear, read-only user-level pages can be written by a supervisor process. This feature is useful for supporting process creation in some operating systems.
- **Alignment Mask (AM):** Enables/disables alignment checking.
- **Not Write Through (NW):** Selects mode of operation of the data cache. When this bit is set, the data cache is inhibited from cache write-through operations.
- **Cache Disable (CD):** Enables/disables the internal cache fill mechanism.
- **Paging (PG):** Enables/disables paging.

When paging is enabled, the CR2 and CR3 registers are valid. The CR2 register holds the 32-bit linear address of the last page accessed before a page fault interrupt. The leftmost 20 bits of CR3 hold the 20 most significant bits of the base address of the page directory; the remainder of the address contains zeros. Two bits of CR3 are used to drive pins that control the operation of an external cache. The page-level cache disable (PCD) enables or disables the external cache, and the page-level writes transparent (PWT) bit controls write through in the external cache.

Nine additional control bits are defined in CR4:

- **Virtual-8086 Mode Extension (VME):** Enables support for the virtual interrupt flag in virtual-8086 mode.
- **Protected-mode Virtual Interrupts (PVI):** Enables support for the virtual interrupt flag in protected mode.
- **Time Stamp Disable (TSD):** Disables the read from time stamp counter (RDTSC) instruction, which is used for debugging purposes.
- **Debugging Extensions (DE):** Enables I/O breakpoints; this allows the processor to interrupt on I/O reads and writes.
- **Page Size Extensions (PSE):** Enables large page sizes (2 or 4-MByte pages) when set; restricts pages to 4 KBytes when clear.
- **Physical Address Extension (PAE):** Enables address lines A35 through A32 whenever a special new addressing mode, controlled by the PSE, is enabled.

- **Machine Check Enable (MCE):** Enables the machine check interrupt, which occurs when a data parity error occurs during a read bus cycle or when a bus cycle is not successfully completed.

- **Page Global Enable (PGE):** Enables the use of global pages. When PGE = 1 and a task switch is performed, all of the TLB entries are flushed with the exception of those marked global.

- **Performance Counter Enable (PCE):** Enables the execution of the RDPMC (read performance counter) instruction at any privilege level. Two performance counters are used to measure the duration of a specific event type and the number of occurrences of a specific event type.

MMX REGISTERS Recall from Section 10.3 that the x86 MMX capability makes use of several 64-bit data types. The MMX instructions make use of 3-bit register address fields, so that eight MMX registers are supported. In fact, the processor does not include specific MMX registers. Rather, the processor uses an aliasing technique (Figure 12.24). The existing floating-point registers are used to store MMX values. Specifically, the low-order 64 bits (mantissa) of each floating-point register are used to form the eight MMX registers. Thus, the older 32-bit x86 architecture is easily extended to support the MMX capability. Some key characteristics of the MMX use of these registers are as follows:

- Recall that the floating-point registers are treated as a stack for floating-point operations. For MMX operations, these same registers are accessed directly.

- The first time that an MMX instruction is executed after any floating-point operations, the FP tag word is marked valid. This reflects the change from stack operation to direct register addressing.

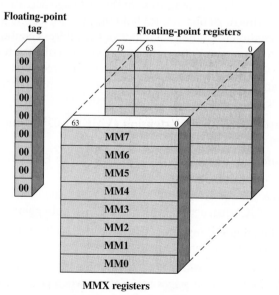

Figure 12.24 Mapping of MMX Registers to Floating-Point Registers

- The EMMS (Empty MMX State) instruction sets bits of the FP tag word to indicate that all registers are empty. It is important that the programmer insert this instruction at the end of an MMX code block so that subsequent floating-point operations function properly.
- When a value is written to an MMX register, bits [79:64] of the corresponding FP register (sign and exponent bits) are set to all ones. This sets the value in the FP register to NaN (not a number) or infinity when viewed as a floating-point value. This ensures that an MMX data value will not look like a valid floating-point value.

Interrupt Processing

Interrupt processing within a processor is a facility provided to support the operating system. It allows an application program to be suspended, in order that a variety of interrupt conditions can be serviced and later resumed.

INTERRUPTS AND EXCEPTIONS Two classes of events cause the x86 to suspend execution of the current instruction stream and respond to the event: interrupts and exceptions. In both cases, the processor saves the context of the current process and transfers to a predefined routine to service the condition. An *interrupt* is generated by a signal from hardware, and it may occur at random times during the execution of a program. An *exception* is generated from software, and it is provoked by the execution of an instruction. There are two sources of interrupts and two sources of exceptions:

1. Interrupts
   - **Maskable interrupts:** Received on the processor's INTR pin. The processor does not recognize a maskable interrupt unless the interrupt enable flag (IF) is set.
   - **Nonmaskable interrupts:** Received on the processor's NMI pin. Recognition of such interrupts cannot be prevented.
2. Exceptions
   - **Processor-detected exceptions:** Results when the processor encounters an error while attempting to execute an instruction.
   - **Programmed exceptions:** These are instructions that generate an exception (e.g., INTO, INT3, INT, and BOUND).

INTERRUPT VECTOR TABLE Interrupt processing on the x86 uses the interrupt vector table. Every type of interrupt is assigned a number, and this number is used to index into the interrupt vector table. This table contains 256 32-bit interrupt vectors, which is the address (segment and offset) of the interrupt service routine for that interrupt number.

Table 12.3 shows the assignment of numbers in the interrupt vector table; shaded entries represent interrupts, while nonshaded entries are exceptions. The NMI hardware interrupt is type 2. INTR hardware interrupts are assigned numbers in the range of 32 to 255; when an INTR interrupt is generated, it must be accompanied on the bus with the interrupt vector number for this interrupt. The remaining vector numbers are used for exceptions.

Table 12.3 x86 Exception and Interrupt Vector Table

Vector Number	Description
0	Divide error; division overflow or division by zero
1	Debug exception; includes various faults and traps related to debugging
2	NMI pin interrupt; signal on NMI pin
3	Breakpoint; caused by INT 3 instruction, which is a 1-byte instruction useful for debugging
4	INTO-detected overflow; occurs when the processor executes INTO with the OF flag set
5	BOUND range exceeded; the BOUND instruction compares a register with boundaries stored in memory and generates an interrupt if the contents of the register is out of bounds.
6	Undefined opcode
7	Device not available; attempt to use ESC or WAIT instruction fails due to lack of external device
8	Double fault; two interrupts occur during the same instruction and cannot be handled serially
9	Reserved
10	Invalid task state segment; segment describing a requested task is not initialized or not valid
11	Segment not present; required segment not present
12	Stack fault; limit of stack segment exceeded or stack segment not present
13	General protection; protection violation that does not cause another exception (e.g., writing to a read-only segment)
14	Page fault
15	Reserved
16	Floating-point error; generated by a floating-point arithmetic instruction
17	Alignment check; access to a word stored at an odd byte address or a doubleword stored at an address not a multiple of 4
18	Machine check; model specific
19–31	Reserved
32–255	User interrupt vectors; provided when INTR signal is activated

Unshaded: exceptions
Shaded: interrupts

If more than one exception or interrupt is pending, the processor services them in a predictable order. The location of vector numbers within the table does not reflect priority. Instead, priority among exceptions and interrupts is organized into five classes. In descending order of priority, these are

- **Class 1:** Traps on the previous instruction (vector number 1)
- **Class 2:** External interrupts (2, 32–255)
- **Class 3:** Faults from fetching next instruction (3, 14)
- **Class 4:** Faults from decoding the next instruction (6, 7)
- **Class 5:** Faults on executing an instruction (0, 4, 5, 8, 10–14, 16, 17)

INTERRUPT HANDLING Just as with a transfer of execution using a CALL instruction, a transfer to an interrupt-handling routine uses the system stack to store the processor state. When an interrupt occurs and is recognized by the processor, a sequence of events takes place:

1. If the transfer involves a change of privilege level, then the current stack segment register and the current extended stack pointer (ESP) register are pushed onto the stack.

2. The current value of the EFLAGS register is pushed onto the stack.

3. Both the interrupt (IF) and trap (TF) flags are cleared. This disables INTR interrupts and the trap or single-step feature.

4. The current code segment (CS) pointer and the current instruction pointer (IP or EIP) are pushed onto the stack.

5. If the interrupt is accompanied by an error code, then the error code is pushed onto the stack.

6. The interrupt vector contents are fetched and loaded into the CS and IP or EIP registers. Execution continues from the interrupt service routine.

To return from an interrupt, the interrupt service routine executes an IRET instruction. This causes all of the values saved on the stack to be restored; execution resumes from the point of the interrupt.

12.6 THE ARM PROCESSOR

In this section, we look at some of the key elements of the ARM architecture and organization. We defer a discussion of more complex aspects of organization and pipelining until Chapter 14. For the discussion in this section and in Chapter 14, it is useful to keep in mind key characteristics of the ARM architecture. ARM is primarily a RISC system with the following notable attributes:

- A moderate array of uniform registers, more than are found on some CISC systems but fewer than are found on many RISC systems.

- A load/store model of data processing, in which operations only perform on operands in registers and not directly in memory. All data must be loaded into registers before an operation can be performed; the result can then be used for further processing or stored into memory.

- A uniform fixed-length instruction of 32 bits for the standard set and 16 bits for the Thumb instruction set.

- To make each data processing instruction more flexible, either a shift or rotation can preprocess one of the source registers. To efficiently support this feature, there are separate arithmetic logic unit (ALU) and shifter units.

- A small number of addressing modes with all load/store addressees determined from registers and instruction fields. Indirect or indexed addressing involving values in memory are not used.

- Auto-increment and auto-decrement addressing modes are used to improve the operation of program loops.

- Conditional execution of instructions minimizes the need for conditional branch instructions, thereby improving pipeline efficiency, because pipeline flushing is reduced.

Processor Organization

The ARM processor organization varies substantially from one implementation to the next, particularly when based on different versions of the ARM architecture. However, it is useful for the discussion in this section to present a simplified, generic ARM organization, which is illustrated in Figure 12.25. In this figure, the arrows indicate the flow of data. Each box represents a functional hardware unit or a storage unit.

Data are exchanged with the processor from external memory through a data bus. The value transferred is either a data item, as a result of a load or store instruction, or an instruction fetch. Fetched instructions pass through an instruction decoder before execution, under control of a control unit. The latter includes pipeline logic and

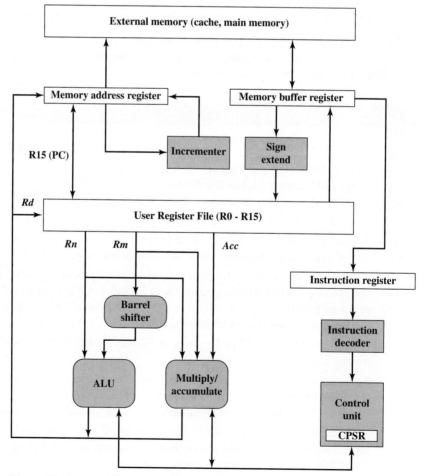

Figure 12.25   Simplified ARM Organization

provides control signals (not shown) to all the hardware elements of the processor. Data items are placed in the register file, consisting of a set of 32-bit registers. Byte or halfword items treated as twos-complement numbers are sign-extended to 32 bits.

ARM data processing instructions typically have two source registers, *Rn* and *Rm*, and a single result or destination register, *Rd*. The source register values feed into the ALU or a separate multiply unit that makes use of an additional register to accumulate partial results. The ARM processor also includes a hardware unit that can shift or rotate the *Rm* value before it enters the ALU. This shift or rotate occurs within the cycle time of the instruction and increases the power and flexibility of many data processing operations.

The results of an operation are fed back to the destination register. Load/store instructions may also use the output of the arithmetic units to generate the memory address for a load or store.

Processor Modes

It is quite common for a processor to support only a small number of processor modes. For example, many operating systems make use of just two modes: a user mode and a kernel mode, with the latter mode used to execute privileged system software. In contrast, the ARM architecture provides a flexible foundation for operating systems to enforce a variety of protection policies.

The ARM architecture supports seven execution modes. Most application programs execute in **user mode**. While the processor is in user mode, the program being executed is unable to access protected system resources or to change mode, other than by causing an exception to occur.

The remaining six execution modes are referred to as privileged modes. These modes are used to run system software. There are two principal advantages to defining so many different privileged modes: (1) The OS can tailor the use of system software to a variety of circumstances, and (2) certain registers are dedicated for use for each of the privileged modes, allows swifter changes in context.

The exception modes have full access to system resources and can change modes freely. Five of these modes are known as exception modes. These are entered when specific exceptions occur. Each of these modes has some dedicated registers that substitute for some of the user mode registers, and which are used to avoid corrupting User mode state information when the exception occurs. The exception modes are as follows:

- **Supervisor mode:** Usually what the OS runs in. It is entered when the processor encounters a software interrupt instruction. Software interrupts are a standard way to invoke operating system services on ARM.

- **Abort mode:** Entered in response to memory faults.

- **Undefined mode:** Entered when the processor attempts to execute an instruction that is supported neither by the main integer core nor by one of the coprocessors.

- **Fast interrupt mode:** Entered whenever the processor receives an interrupt signal from the designated fast interrupt source. A fast interrupt cannot be interrupted, but a fast interrupt may interrupt a normal interrupt.

- **Interrupt mode:** Entered whenever the processor receives an interrupt signal from any other interrupt source (other than fast interrupt). An interrupt may only be interrupted by a fast interrupt.

The remaining privileged mode is the **System mode**. This mode is not entered by any exception and uses the same registers available in User mode. The System mode is used for running certain privileged operating system tasks. System mode tasks may be interrupted by any of the five exception categories.

Register Organization

Figure 12.26 depicts the user-visible registers for the ARM. The ARM processor has a total of 37 32-bit registers, classified as follows:

- Thirty-one registers referred to in the ARM manual as general-purpose registers. In fact, some of these, such as the program counters, have special purposes.
- Six program status registers.

Registers are arranged in partially overlapping banks, with the current processor mode determining which bank is available. At any time, sixteen numbered registers and one or two program status registers are visible, for a total of 17 or 18 software-visible registers. Figure 12.26 is interpreted as follows:

- Registers R0 through R7, register R15 (the program counter) and the current program status register (CPSR) are visible in and shared by all modes.
- Registers R8 through R12 are shared by all modes except fast interrupt, which has its own dedicated registers R8_fiq through R12_fiq.
- All the exception modes have their own versions of registers R13 and R14.
- All the exception modes have a dedicated saved program status register (SPSR)

GENERAL–PURPOSE REGISTERS Register R13 is normally used as a stack pointer and is also known as the SP. Because each exception mode has a separate R13, each exception mode can have its own dedicated program stack. R14 is known as the link register (LR) and is used to hold subroutine return addresses and exception mode returns. Register R15 is the program counter (PC).

PROGRAM STATUS REGISTERS The CPSR is accessible in all processor modes. Each exception mode also has a dedicated SPSR that is used to preserve the value of the CPSR when the associated exception occurs.

The 16 most significant bits of the CPSR contain user flags visible in User mode, and which can be used to affect the operation of a program (Figure 12.27). These are as follows:

- **Condition code flags:** The N, Z, C and V flags, which are discussed in Chapter 10.
- **Q flag:** used to indicate whether overflow and/or saturation has occurred in some SIMD-oriented instructions.
- **J bit:** indicates the use of special 8-bit instructions, known as Jazelle instructions, which are beyond the scope of our discussion.

		Modes				
		Privileged modes				
			Exception modes			
User	**System**	**Supervisor**	**Abort**	**Undefined**	**Interrupt**	**Fast interrupt**
R0	R0	R0	R0	R0	R0	R0
R1	R1	R1	R1	R1	R1	R1
R2	R2	R2	R2	R2	R2	R2
R3	R3	R3	R3	R3	R3	R3
R4	R4	R4	R4	R4	R4	R4
R5	R5	R5	R5	R5	R5	R5
R6	R6	R6	R6	R6	R6	R6
R7	R7	R7	R7	R7	R7	R7
R8	R8	R8	R8	R8	R8	R8_fiq
R9	R9	R9	R9	R9	R9	R9_fiq
R10	R10	R10	R10	R10	R10	R10_fiq
R11	R11	R11	R11	R11	R11	R11_fiq
R12	R12	R12	R12	R12	R12	R12_fiq
R13(SP)	R13(SP)	R13_svc	R13_abt	R13_und	R13_irq	R13_fiq
R14(LR)	R14(LR)	R14_svc	R14_abt	R14_und	R14_irq	R14_fiq
R15(PC)	R15(PC)	R15(PC)	R15(PC)	R15(PC)	R15(PC)	R15(PC)

CPSR	CPSR	CPSR	CPSR	CPSR	CPSR	CPSR
		SPSR_svc	SPSR_abt	SPSR_und	SPSR_irq	SPSR_fiq

Shading indicates that the normal register used by User or System mode has been replaced by an alternative register specific to the exception mode.

SP = stack pointer   CPSR = current program status register
LR = link register   SPSR = saved program status register
PC = program counter

Figure 12.26   ARM Register Organization

- **GE[3:0] bits:** SIMD instructions use bits[19:16] as Greater than or Equal (GE) flags for individual bytes or halfwords of the result.

The 16 least significant bits of the CPSR contain system control flags that can only be altered when the processor is in a privileged mode. The fields are as follows:

- **E bit:** Controls load and store endianness for data; ignored for instruction fetches.
- **Interrupt disable bits:** The A bit disables imprecise data aborts when set; the I bit disables IRQ interrupts when set; and the F bit disables FIQ interrupts when set.
- **T bit:** Indicates whether instructions should be interpreted as normal ARM instructions or Thumb instructions.
- **Mode bits:** Indicates the processor mode

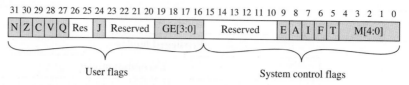

Figure 12.27 Format of ARM CPSR and SPSR

Interrupt Processing

As with any processor, the ARM includes a facility that enables the processor to interrupt the currently executing program to deal with exception conditions. Exceptions are generated by internal and external sources to cause the processor to handle an event. The processor state just before handling the exception is normally preserved so that the original program can be resumed when the exception routine has completed. More than one exception can arise at the same time. The ARM architecture supports seven types of exception. Table 12.4 lists the types of exception and the

Table 12.4 ARM Interrupt Vector

Exception type	Mode	Normal entry address	Description
Reset	Supervisor	0x00000000	Occurs when the system is initialized.
Data abort	Abort	0x00000010	Occurs when an invalid memory address has been accessed, such as if there is no physical memory for an address or the correct access permission is lacking.
FIQ (fast interrupt)	FIQ	0x0000001C	Occurs when an external device asserts the FIQ pin on the processor. An interrupt cannot be interrupted except by an FIQ. FIQ is designed to support a data transfer or channel process, and has sufficient private registers to remove the need for register saving in such applications, therefore minimizing the overhead of context switching. A fast interrupt cannot be interrupted.
IRQ (interrupt)	IRQ	0x00000018	Occurs when an external device asserts the IRQ pin on the processor. An interrupt cannot be interrupted except by an FIQ.
Prefetch abort	Abort	0x0000000C	Occurs when an attempt to fetch an instruction results in a memory fault. The exception is raised when the instruction enters the execute stage of the pipeline.
Undefined instructions	Undefined	0x00000004	Occurs when an instruction not in the instruction set reaches the execute stage of the pipeline.
Software interrupt	Supervisor	0x00000008	Generally used to allow user mode programs to call the OS. The user program executes a SWI instruction with an argument that identifies the function the user wishes to perform.

processor mode that is used to process each type. When an exception occurs, execution is forced from a fixed memory address corresponding to the type of exception. These fixed addresses are called the exception vectors.

If more than one interrupt is outstanding, they are handled in priority order. Table 12.4 lists the exceptions in priority order, highest to lowest.

When an exception occurs, the processor halts execution after the current instruction. The state of the processor is preserved in the SPSR that corresponds to the type of exception, so that the original program can be resumed when the exception routine has completed. The address of the instruction the processor was just about to execute is placed in the link register of the appropriate processor mode. To return after handling the exception, the SPSR is moved into the CPSR and R14 is moved into the PC.

12.7 RECOMMENDED READING

[PATT01] and [MOSH01] provide excellent coverage of the pipelining issues discussed in this chapter. [HENN91] contains a detailed discussions of pipelining. [SOHI90] provides an excellent, detailed discussion of the hardware design issues involved in an instruction pipeline. [RAMA77] is a classic paper on the subject still well worth reading.

[EVER01] examines the evolution of branch prediction strategies. [CRAG92] is a detailed study of branch prediction in instruction pipelines. [DUBE91] and [LILJ88] examine various branch prediction strategies that can be used to enhance the performance of instruction pipelining. [KAEL91] examines the difficulty introduced into branch prediction by instructions whose target address is variable.

[BREY09] provides good coverage of interrupt processing on the x86. [FOG08b] provides a detailed discussion of pipeline architecture for the x86 family.

BREY09   Brey, B. *The Intel Microprocessors: 8086/8066, 80186/80188, 80286, 80386, 80486, Pentium, Pentium Pro Processor, Pentium II, Pentium III, Pentium 4 and Core2 with 64-bit Extensions.* Upper Saddle River, NJ: Prentice Hall, 2009.

CRAG92   Cragon, H. *Branch Strategy Taxonomy and Performance Models.* Los Alamitos, CA: IEEE Computer Society Press, 1992.

DUBE91   Dubey, P., and Flynn, M. "Branch Strategies: Modeling and Optimization." *IEEE Transactions on Computers,* October 1991.

EVER01   Evers, M., and Yeh, T. "Understanding Branches and Designing Branch Predictors for High-Performance Microprocessors." *Proceedings of the IEEE,* November 2001.

FOG08b   Fog, A. *The Microarchitecture of Intel and AMD CPUs.* Copenhagen University College of Engineering, 2008. www.agner.org/optimize/

HENN91   Hennessy, J., and Jouppi, N. "Computer Technology and Architecture: An Evolving Interaction." *Computer,* September 1991.

KAEL91   Kaeli, D., and Emma, P. "Branch History Table Prediction of Moving Target Branches Due to Subroutine Returns." *Proceedings, 18th Annual International Symposium on Computer Architecture,* May 1991.

LILJ88   Lilja, D. "Reducing the Branch Penalty in Pipelined Processors." *Computer,* July 1988.

MOSH01   Moshovos, A., and Sohi, G. "Microarchitectural Innovations: Boosting Microprocessor Performance Beyond Semiconductor Technology Scaling." *Proceedings of the IEEE,* November 2001.

PATT01 Patt, Y. "Requirements, Bottlenecks, and Good Fortune: Agents for Micro-processor Evolution." *Proceedings of the IEEE,* November 2001.

RAMA77 Ramamoorthy, C. "Pipeline Architecture." *Computing Surveys,* March 1977.

SOHI90 Sohi, G. "Instruction Issue Logic for High-Performance Interruptable, Multiple Functional Unit, Pipelined Computers." *IEEE Transactions on Computers,* March 1990.

12.8 KEY TERMS, REVIEW QUESTIONS, AND PROBLEMS

Key Terms

branch prediction	flag	instruction prefetch
condition code	instruction cycle	program status word (PSW)
delayed branch	instruction pipeline	

Review Questions

12.1 What general roles are performed by processor registers?

12.2 What categories of data are commonly supported by user-visible registers?

12.3 What is the function of condition codes?

12.4 What is a program status word?

12.5 Why is a two-stage instruction pipeline unlikely to cut the instruction cycle time in half, compared with the use of no pipeline?

12.6 List and briefly explain various ways in which an instruction pipeline can deal with conditional branch instructions.

12.7 How are history bits used for branch prediction?

Problems

12.1 a. If the last operation performed on a computer with an 8-bit word was an addition in which the two operands were 00000010 and 00000011, what would be the value of the following flags?
  - Carry
  - Zero
  - Overflow
  - Sign
  - Even Parity
  - Half-Carry

  b. Repeat for the addition of −1 (twos complement) and +1.

12.2 Repeat Problem 12.1 for the operation A − B, where A contains 11110000 and B contains 0010100.

12.3 A microprocessor is clocked at a rate of 5 GHz.
  a. How long is a clock cycle?
  b. What is the duration of a particular type of machine instruction consisting of three clock cycles?

12.4 A microprocessor provides an instruction capable of moving a string of bytes from one area of memory to another. The fetching and initial decoding of the instruction

takes 10 clock cycles. Thereafter, it takes 15 clock cycles to transfer each byte. The microprocessor is clocked at a rate of 10 GHz.
  a. Determine the length of the instruction cycle for the case of a string of 64 bytes.
  b. What is the worst-case delay for acknowledging an interrupt if the instruction is noninterruptible?
  c. Repeat part (b) assuming the instruction can be interrupted at the beginning of each byte transfer.

12.5 The Intel 8088 consists of a bus interface unit (BIU) and an execution unit (EU), which form a 2-stage pipeline. The BIU fetches instructions into a 4-byte instruction queue. The BIU also participates in address calculations, fetches operands, and writes results in memory as requested by the EU. If no such requests are outstanding and the bus is free, the BIU fills any vacancies in the instruction queue. When the EU completes execution of an instruction, it passes any results to the BIU (destined for memory or I/O) and proceeds to the next instruction.
  a. Suppose the tasks performed by the BIU and EU take about equal time. By what factor does pipelining improve the performance of the 8088? Ignore the effect of branch instructions.
  b. Repeat the calculation assuming that the EU takes twice as long as the BIU.

12.6 Assume an 8088 is executing a program in which the probability of a program jump is 0.1. For simplicity, assume that all instructions are 2 bytes long.
  a. What fraction of instruction fetch bus cycles is wasted?
  b. Repeat if the instruction queue is 8 bytes long.

12.7 Consider the timing diagram of Figures 12.10. Assume that there is only a two-stage pipeline (fetch, execute). Redraw the diagram to show how many time units are now needed for four instructions.

12.8 Assume a pipeline with four stages: fetch instruction (FI), decode instruction and calculate addresses (DA), fetch operand (FO), and execute (EX). Draw a diagram similar to Figures 12.10 for a sequence of 7 instructions, in which the third instruction is a branch that is taken and in which there are no data dependencies.

12.9 A pipelined processor has a clock rate of 2.5 GHz and executes a program with 1.5 million instructions. The pipeline has five stages, and instructions are issued at a rate of one per clock cycle. Ignore penalties due to branch instructions and out-of-sequence executions.
  a. What is the speedup of this processor for this program compared to a non-pipelined processor, making the same assumptions used in Section 12.4?
  b. What is throughput (in MIPS) of the pipelined processor?

12.10 A nonpipelined processor has a clock rate of 2.5 GHz and an average CPI (cycles per instruction) of 4. An upgrade to the processor introduces a five-stage pipeline. However, due to internal pipeline delays, such as latch delay, the clock rate of the new processor has to be reduced to 2 GHz.
  a. What is the speedup achieved for a typical program?
  b. What is the MIPS rate for each processor?

12.11 Consider an instruction sequence of length n that is streaming through the instruction pipeline. Let p be the probability of encountering a conditional or unconditional branch instruction, and let q be the probability that execution of a branch instruction I causes a jump to a nonconsecutive address. Assume that each such jump requires the pipeline to be cleared, destroying all ongoing instruction processing, when I emerges from the last stage. Revise Equations (12.1) and (12.2) to take these probabilities into account.

12.12 One limitation of the multiple-stream approach to dealing with branches in a pipeline is that additional branches will be encountered before the first branch is resolved. Suggest two additional limitations or drawbacks.

12.13 Consider the state diagrams of Figure 12.28.
  a. Describe the behavior of each.
  b. Compare these with the branch prediction state diagram in Section 12.4. Discuss the relative merits of each of the three approaches to branch prediction.

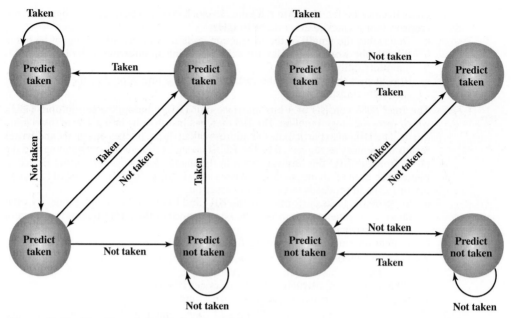

Figure 12.28 Two Branch Prediction State Diagrams

12.14 The Motorola 680x0 machines include the instruction Decrement and Branch According to Condition, which has the following form:

DBcc Dn, displacement

where cc is one of the testable conditions, Dn is a general-purpose register, and displacement specifies the target address relative to the current address. The instruction can be defined as follows:

if (cc = False)
then begin
    Dn := (Dn) − 1;
    if Dn ≠ −1 **then** PC := (PC) + displacement **end**
else PC := (PC) + 2;

When the instruction is executed, the condition is first tested to determine whether the termination condition for the loop is satisfied. If so, no operation is performed and execution continues at the next instruction in sequence. If the condition is false, the specified data register is decremented and checked to see if it is less than zero. If it is less than zero, the loop is terminated and execution continues at the next instruction in sequence. Otherwise, the program branches to the specified location. Now consider the following assembly-language program fragment:

AGAIN   CMPM.L   (A0)+,(A1)+
             DBNE   D1, AGAIN
             NOP

Two strings addressed by A0 and A1 are compared for equality; the string pointers are incremented with each reference. D1 initially contains the number of longwords (4 bytes) to be compared.

a. The initial contents of the registers are A0 = $00004000, A1 = $00005000, and D1 = $000000FF (the $ indicates hexadecimal notation). Memory between $4000 and $6000 is loaded with words $AAAA. If the foregoing program is run, specify

Table 12.5   Branch Behavior in Sample Applications

Occurrence of branch classes:			
Type 1: Branch 72.5%			
Type 2: Loop control 9.8%			
Type 3: Procedure call, return 17.7%			
Type 1 branch: where it goes	**Scientific**	**Commercial**	**Systems**
Unconditional—100% go to target	20%	40%	35%
Conditional—went to target	43.2%	24.3%	32.5%
Conditional—did not go to target (inline)	36.8%	35.7%	32.5%
Type 2 branch (all environments)			
That go to target	91%		
That go inline	9%		
Type 3 branch			
100% go to target			

the number of times the DBNE loop is executed and the contents of the three registers when the NOP instruction is reached.

b. Repeat (a), but now assume that memory between $4000 and $4FEE is loaded with $0000 and between $5000 and $6000 is loaded with $AAA.

12.15   Redraw Figures 12.19c, assuming that the conditional branch is not taken.

12.16   Table 12.5 summarizes statistics from [MACD84] concerning branch behavior for various classes of applications. With the exception of type 1 branch behavior, there is no noticeable difference among the application classes. Determine the fraction of all branches that go to the branch target address for the scientific environment. Repeat for commercial and systems environments.

12.17   Pipelining can be applied within the ALU to speed up floating-point operations. Consider the case of floating-point addition and subtraction. In simplified terms, the pipeline could have four stages: (1) Compare the exponents; (2) Choose the exponent and align the significands; (3) Add or subtract significands; (4) Normalize the results. The pipeline can be considered to have two parallel threads, one handling exponents and one handling significands, and could start out like this:

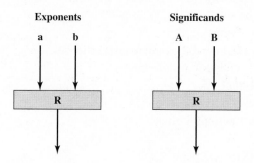

In this figure, the boxes labeled R refer to a set of registers used to hold temporary results. Complete the block diagram that shows at a top level the structure of the pipeline.

CHAPTER 13

REDUCED INSTRUCTION SET COMPUTERS

480

KEY POINTS

◆ Studies of the execution behavior of high-level language programs have provided guidance in designing a new type of processor architecture: the reduced instruction set computer (RISC). Assignment statements predominate, suggesting that the simple movement of data should be optimized. There are also many IF and LOOP instructions, which suggest that the underlying sequence control mechanism needs to be optimized to permit efficient pipelining. Studies of operand reference patterns suggest that it should be possible to enhance performance by keeping a moderate number of operands in registers.

◆ These studies have motivated the key characteristics of RISC machines: (1) a limited instruction set with a fixed format, (2) a large number of registers or the use of a compiler that optimizes register usage, and (3) an emphasis on optimizing the instruction pipeline.

◆ The simple instruction set of a RISC lends itself to efficient pipelining because there are fewer and more predictable operations performed per instruction. A RISC instruction set architecture also lends itself to the delayed branch technique, in which branch instructions are rearranged with other instructions to improve pipeline efficiency.

Since the development of the stored-program computer around 1950, there have been remarkably few true innovations in the areas of computer organization and architecture. The following are some of the major advances since the birth of the computer:

- **The family concept:** Introduced by IBM with its System/360 in 1964, followed shortly thereafter by DEC, with its PDP-8. The family concept decouples the architecture of a machine from its implementation. A set of computers is offered, with different price/performance characteristics, that presents the same architecture to the user. The differences in price and performance are due to different implementations of the same architecture.

- **Microprogrammed control unit:** Suggested by Wilkes in 1951 and introduced by IBM on the S/360 line in 1964. Microprogramming eases the task of designing and implementing the control unit and provides support for the family concept.

- **Cache memory:** First introduced commercially on IBM S/360 Model 85 in 1968. The insertion of this element into the memory hierarchy dramatically improves performance.

- **Pipelining:** A means of introducing parallelism into the essentially sequential nature of a machine-instruction program. Examples are instruction pipelining and vector processing.

- **Multiple processors:** This category covers a number of different organizations and objectives.

- **Reduced instruction set computer (RISC) architecture:** This is the focus of this chapter.

The RISC architecture is a dramatic departure from the historical trend in processor architecture. An analysis of the RISC architecture brings into focus many of the important issues in computer organization and architecture.

Although RISC systems have been defined and designed in a variety of ways by different groups, the key elements shared by most designs are these:

- A large number of general-purpose registers, and/or the use of compiler technology to optimize register usage
- A limited and simple instruction set
- An emphasis on optimizing the instruction pipeline

Table 13.1 compares several RISC and non-RISC systems.

We begin this chapter with a brief survey of some results on instruction sets, and then examine each of the three topics just listed. This is followed by a description of two of the best-documented RISC designs.

13.1 INSTRUCTION EXECUTION CHARACTERISTICS

One of the most visible forms of evolution associated with computers is that of programming languages. As the cost of hardware has dropped, the relative cost of software has risen. Along with that, a chronic shortage of programmers has driven up software costs in absolute terms. Thus, the major cost in the life cycle of a system is software, not hardware. Adding to the cost, and to the inconvenience, is the element of unreliability: it is common for programs, both system and application, to continue to exhibit new bugs after years of operation.

The response from researchers and industry has been to develop ever more powerful and complex high-level programming languages. These high-level languages (HLLs) allow the programmer to express algorithms more concisely, take care of much of the detail, and often support naturally the use of structured programming or object-oriented design.

Alas, this solution gave rise to another problem, known as the *semantic gap*, the difference between the operations provided in HLLs and those provided in computer architecture. Symptoms of this gap are alleged to include execution inefficiency, excessive machine program size, and compiler complexity. Designers responded with architectures intended to close this gap. Key features include large instruction sets, dozens of addressing modes, and various HLL statements implemented in hardware. An example of the latter is the CASE machine instruction on the VAX. Such complex instruction sets are intended to

- Ease the task of the compiler writer.
- Improve execution efficiency, because complex sequences of operations can be implemented in microcode.
- Provide support for even more complex and sophisticated HLLs.

Table 13.1   Characteristics of Some CISCs, RISCs, and Superscalar Processors

Characteristic	Complex Instruction Set (CISC) Computer			Reduced Instruction Set (RISC) Computer			Superscalar	
	IBM 370/168	VAX 11/780	Intel 80486	SPARC	MIPS R4000	PowerPC	Ultra SPARC	MIPS R10000
Year developed	1973	1978	1989	1987	1991	1993	1996	1996
Number of instructions	208	303	235	69	94	225		
Instruction size (bytes)	2–6	2–57	1–11	4	4	4	4	4
Addressing modes	4	22	11	1	1	2	1	1
Number of general-purpose registers	16	16	8	40–520	32	32	40–520	32
Control memory size (Kbits)	420	480	246	–	–	–	–	–
Cache size (KBytes)	64	64	8	32	128	16–32	32	64

483

Meanwhile, a number of studies have been done over the years to determine the characteristics and patterns of execution of machine instructions generated from HLL programs. The results of these studies inspired some researchers to look for a different approach: namely, to make the architecture that supports the HLL simpler, rather than more complex.

To understand the line of reasoning of the RISC advocates, we begin with a brief review of instruction execution characteristics. The aspects of computation of interest are as follows:

- **Operations performed:** These determine the functions to be performed by the processor and its interaction with memory.

- **Operands used:** The types of operands and the frequency of their use determine the memory organization for storing them and the addressing modes for accessing them.

- **Execution sequencing:** This determines the control and pipeline organization.

In the remainder of this section, we summarize the results of a number of studies of high-level-language programs. All of the results are based on dynamic measurements. That is, measurements are collected by executing the program and counting the number of times some feature has appeared or a particular property has held true. In contrast, static measurements merely perform these counts on the source text of a program. They give no useful information on performance, because they are not weighted relative to the number of times each statement is executed.

Operations

A variety of studies have been made to analyze the behavior of HLL programs. Table 4.8, discussed in Chapter 4, includes key results from a number of studies. There is quite good agreement in the results of this mixture of languages and applications. Assignment statements predominate, suggesting that the simple movement of data is of high importance. There is also a preponderance of conditional statements (IF, LOOP). These statements are implemented in machine language with some sort of compare and branch instruction. This suggests that the sequence control mechanism of the instruction set is important.

These results are instructive to the machine instruction set designer, indicating which types of statements occur most often and therefore should be supported in an "optimal" fashion. However, these results do not reveal which statements use the most time in the execution of a typical program. That is, given a compiled machine-language program, which statements in the source language cause the execution of the most machine-language instructions?

To get at this underlying phenomenon, the Patterson programs [PATT82a], described in Appendix 4A, were compiled on the VAX, PDP-11, and Motorola 68000 to determine the average number of machine instructions and memory references per statement type. The second and third columns in Table 13.2 show the relative frequency of occurrence of various HLL instructions in a variety of programs; the data were obtained by observing the occurrences in running programs rather than just the number of times that statements occur in the source code.

Table 13.2   Weighted Relative Dynamic Frequency of HLL Operations [PATT82a]

	Dynamic Occurrence		Machine-Instruction Weighted		Memory-Reference Weighted	
	Pascal	C	Pascal	C	Pascal	C
ASSIGN	45%	38%	13%	13%	14%	15%
LOOP	5%	3%	42%	32%	33%	26%
CALL	15%	12%	31%	33%	44%	45%
IF	29%	43%	11%	21%	7%	13%
GOTO	—	3%	—	—	—	—
OTHER	6%	1%	3%	1%	2%	1%

Hence these are dynamic frequency statistics. To obtain the data in columns four and five (machine-instruction weighted), each value in the second and third columns is multiplied by the number of machine instructions produced by the compiler. These results are then normalized so that columns four and five show the relative frequency of occurrence, weighted by the number of machine instructions per HLL statement. Similarly, the sixth and seventh columns are obtained by multiplying the frequency of occurrence of each statement type by the relative number of memory references caused by each statement. The data in columns four through seven provide surrogate measures of the actual time spent executing the various statement types. The results suggest that the procedure call/return is the most time-consuming operation in typical HLL programs.

The reader should be clear on the significance of Table 13.2. This table indicates the relative significance of various statement types in an HLL, when that HLL is compiled for a typical contemporary instruction set architecture. Some other architecture could conceivably produce different results. However, this study produces results that are representative for contemporary complex instruction set computer (CISC) architectures. Thus, they can provide guidance to those looking for more efficient ways to support HLLs.

Operands

Much less work has been done on the occurrence of types of operands, despite the importance of this topic. There are several aspects that are significant.

The Patterson study already referenced [PATT82a] also looked at the dynamic frequency of occurrence of classes of variables (Table 13.3). The results, consistent between Pascal and C programs, show that the majority of references are to simple

Table 13.3   Dynamic Percentage of Operands

	Pascal	C	Average
Integer Constant	16%	23%	20%
Scalar Variable	58%	53%	55%
Array/Structure	26%	24%	25%

scalar variables. Further, more than 80% of the scalars were local (to the procedure) variables. In addition, references to arrays/structures require a previous reference to their index or pointer, which again is usually a local scalar. Thus, there is a preponderance of references to scalars, and these are highly localized.

The Patterson study examined the dynamic behavior of HLL programs, independent of the underlying architecture. As discussed before, it is necessary to deal with actual architectures to examine program behavior more deeply. One study, [LUND77], examined DEC-10 instructions dynamically and found that each instruction on the average references 0.5 operand in memory and 1.4 registers. Similar results are reported in [HUCK83] for C, Pascal, and FORTRAN programs on S/370, PDP-11, and VAX. Of course, these figures depend highly on both the architecture and the compiler, but they do illustrate the frequency of operand accessing.

These latter studies suggest the importance of an architecture that lends itself to fast operand accessing, because this operation is performed so frequently. The Patterson study suggests that a prime candidate for optimization is the mechanism for storing and accessing local scalar variables.

Procedure Calls

We have seen that procedure calls and returns are an important aspect of HLL programs. The evidence (Table 13.2) suggests that these are the most time-consuming operations in compiled HLL programs. Thus, it will be profitable to consider ways of implementing these operations efficiently. Two aspects are significant: the number of parameters and variables that a procedure deals with, and the depth of nesting.

Tanenbaum's study [TANE78] found that 98% of dynamically called procedures were passed fewer than six arguments and that 92% of them used fewer than six local scalar variables. Similar results were reported by the Berkeley RISC team [KATE83], as shown in Table 13.4. These results show that the number of words required per procedure activation is not large. The studies reported earlier indicated that a high proportion of operand references is to local scalar variables. These studies show that those references are in fact confined to relatively few variables.

The same Berkeley group also looked at the pattern of procedure calls and returns in HLL programs. They found that it is rare to have a long uninterrupted sequence of procedure calls followed by the corresponding sequence of returns.

Table 13.4 Procedure Arguments and Local Scalar Variables

Percentage of Executed Procedure Calls With	Compiler, Interpreter, and Typesetter	Small Nonnumeric Programs
>3 arguments	0–7%	0–5%
>5 arguments	0–3%	0%
>8 words of arguments and local scalars	1–20%	0–6%
>12 words of arguments and local scalars	1–6%	0–3%

Rather, they found that a program remains confined to a rather narrow window of procedure-invocation depth. This is illustrated in Figure 4.21, which was discussed in Chapter 4. These results reinforce the conclusion that operand references are highly localized.

Implications

A number of groups have looked at results such as those just reported and have concluded that the attempt to make the instruction set architecture close to HLLs is not the most effective design strategy. Rather, the HLLs can best be supported by optimizing performance of the most time-consuming features of typical HLL programs.

Generalizing from the work of a number of researchers, three elements emerge that, by and large, characterize RISC architectures. First, use a large number of registers or use a compiler to optimize register usage. This is intended to optimize operand referencing. The studies just discussed show that there are several references per HLL instruction and that there is a high proportion of move (assignment) statements. This, coupled with the locality and predominance of scalar references, suggests that performance can be improved by reducing memory references at the expense of more register references. Because of the locality of these references, an expanded register set seems practical.

Second, careful attention needs to be paid to the design of instruction pipelines. Because of the high proportion of conditional branch and procedure call instructions, a straightforward instruction pipeline will be inefficient. This manifests itself as a high proportion of instructions that are prefetched but never executed.

Finally, a simplified (reduced) instruction set is indicated. This point is not as obvious as the others, but should become clearer in the ensuing discussion.

13.2 THE USE OF A LARGE REGISTER FILE

The results summarized in Section 13.1 point out the desirability of quick access to operands. We have seen that there is a large proportion of assignment statements in HLL programs, and many of these are of the simple form A ← B. Also, there is a significant number of operand accesses per HLL statement. If we couple these results with the fact that most accesses are to local scalars, heavy reliance on register storage is suggested.

The reason that register storage is indicated is that it is the fastest available storage device, faster than both main memory and cache. The register file is physically small, on the same chip as the ALU and control unit, and employs much shorter addresses than addresses for cache and memory. Thus, a strategy is needed that will allow the most frequently accessed operands to be kept in registers and to minimize register-memory operations.

Two basic approaches are possible, one based on software and the other on hardware. The software approach is to rely on the compiler to maximize register usage. The compiler will attempt to allocate registers to those variables that will be used the most in a given time period. This approach requires the use of sophisticated program-analysis algorithms. The hardware approach is simply to use more registers so that more variables can be held in registers for longer periods of time.

In this section, we will discuss the hardware approach. This approach has been pioneered by the Berkeley RISC group [PATT82a]; was used in the first commercial RISC product, the Pyramid [RAGA83]; and is currently used in the popular SPARC architecture.

Register Windows

On the face of it, the use of a large set of registers should decrease the need to access memory. The design task is to organize the registers in such a fashion that this goal is realized.

Because most operand references are to local scalars, the obvious approach is to store these in registers, with perhaps a few registers reserved for global variables. The problem is that the definition of *local* changes with each procedure call and return, operations that occur frequently. On every call, local variables must be saved from the registers into memory, so that the registers can be reused by the called program. Furthermore, parameters must be passed. On return, the variables of the parent program must be restored (loaded back into registers) and results must be passed back to the parent program.

The solution is based on two other results reported in Section 13.1. First, a typical procedure employs only a few passed parameters and local variables (Table 13.4). Second, the depth of procedure activation fluctuates within a relatively narrow range (Figure 4.21). To exploit these properties, multiple small sets of registers are used, each assigned to a different procedure. A procedure call automatically switches the processor to use a different fixed-size window of registers, rather than saving registers in memory. Windows for adjacent procedures are overlapped to allow parameter passing.

The concept is illustrated in Figure 13.1. At any time, only one window of registers is visible and is addressable as if it were the only set of registers (e.g., addresses 0 through $N - 1$). The window is divided into three fixed-size areas. Parameter registers hold parameters passed down from the procedure that called the current procedure and hold results to be passed back up. Local registers are used for local variables, as assigned by the compiler. Temporary registers are used to exchange parameters and results with the next lower level (procedure called by current procedure). The temporary registers at one level are physically the same as the parameter registers at the next

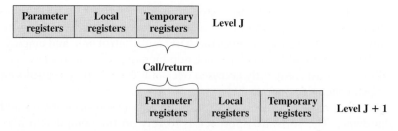

Figure 13.1   Overlapping Register Windows

lower level. This overlap permits parameters to be passed without the actual movement of data. Keep in mind that, except for the overlap, the registers at two different levels are physically distinct. That is, the parameter and local registers at level J are disjoint from the local and temporary registers at level $J + 1$.

To handle any possible pattern of calls and returns, the number of register windows would have to be unbounded. Instead, the register windows can be used to hold the few most recent procedure activations. Older activations must be saved in memory and later restored when the nesting depth decreases. Thus, the actual organization of the register file is as a circular buffer of overlapping windows. Two notable examples of this approach are Sun's SPARC architecture, described in Section 13.7, and the IA-64 architecture used in Intel's Itanium processor, described in Chapter 21.

The circular organization is shown in Figure 13.2, which depicts a circular buffer of six windows. The buffer is filled to a depth of 4 (A called B; B called C; C called D) with procedure D active. The current-window pointer (CWP) points to the window of the currently active procedure. Register references by a machine instruction are offset by this pointer to determine the actual physical register. The saved-window pointer (SWP) identifies the window most recently saved in memory. If procedure D now calls procedure E, arguments for E are placed in D's temporary registers (the overlap between w3 and w4) and the CWP is advanced by one window.

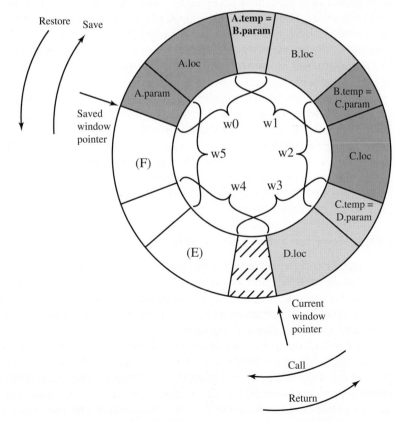

Figure 13.2 Circular-Buffer Organization of Overlapped Windows

If procedure E then makes a call to procedure F, the call cannot be made with the current status of the buffer. This is because F's window overlaps A's window. If F begins to load its temporary registers, preparatory to a call, it will overwrite the parameter registers of A (A.in). Thus, when CWP is incremented (modulo 6) so that it becomes equal to SWP, an interrupt occurs, and A's window is saved. Only the first two portions (A.in and A.loc) need be saved. Then, the SWP is incremented and the call to F proceeds. A similar interrupt can occur on returns. For example, subsequent to the activation of F, when B returns to A, CWP is decremented and becomes equal to SWP. This causes an interrupt that results in the restoration of A's window.

From the preceding, it can be seen that an N-window register file can hold only $N - 1$ procedure activations. The value of N need not be large. As was mentioned in Appendix 4A, one study [TAMI83] found that, with 8 windows, a save or restore is needed on only 1% of the calls or returns. The Berkeley RISC computers use 8 windows of 16 registers each. The Pyramid computer employs 16 windows of 32 registers each.

Global Variables

The window scheme just described provides an efficient organization for storing local scalar variables in registers. However, this scheme does not address the need to store global variables, those accessed by more than one procedure. Two options suggest themselves. First, variables declared as global in an HLL can be assigned memory locations by the compiler, and all machine instructions that reference these variables will use memory-reference operands. This is straightforward, from both the hardware and software (compiler) points of view. However, for frequently accessed global variables, this scheme is inefficient.

An alternative is to incorporate a set of global registers in the processor. These registers would be fixed in number and available to all procedures. A unified numbering scheme can be used to simplify the instruction format. For example, references to registers 0 through 7 could refer to unique global registers, and references to registers 8 through 31 could be offset to refer to physical registers in the current window. There is an increased hardware burden to accommodate the split in register addressing. In addition, the compiler must decide which global variables should be assigned to registers.

Large Register File versus Cache

The register file, organized into windows, acts as a small, fast buffer for holding a subset of all variables that are likely to be used the most heavily. From this point of view, the register file acts much like a cache memory, although a much faster memory. The question therefore arises as to whether it would be simpler and better to use a cache and a small traditional register file.

Table 13.5 compares characteristics of the two approaches. The window-based register file holds all the local scalar variables (except in the rare case of window overflow) of the most recent $N - 1$ procedure activations. The cache holds a selection of recently used scalar variables. The register file should save time, because all local scalar variables are retained. On the other hand, the cache may make more efficient use of space, because it is reacting to the situation dynamically. Furthermore, caches

Table 13.5   Characteristics of Large-Register-File and Cache Organizations

Large Register File	Cache
All local scalars	Recently-used local scalars
Individual variables	Blocks of memory
Compiler-assigned global variables	Recently-used global variables
Save/Restore based on procedure nesting depth	Save/Restore based on cache replacement algorithm
Register addressing	Memory addressing

generally treat all memory references alike, including instructions and other types of data. Thus, savings in these other areas are possible with a cache and not a register file.

A register file may make inefficient use of space, because not all procedures will need the full window space allotted to them. On the other hand, the cache suffers from another sort of inefficiency: Data are read into the cache in blocks. Whereas the register file contains only those variables in use, the cache reads in a block of data, some or much of which will not be used.

The cache is capable of handling global as well as local variables. There are usually many global scalars, but only a few of them are heavily used [KATE83]. A cache will dynamically discover these variables and hold them. If the window-based register file is supplemented with global registers, it too can hold some global scalars. However, it is difficult for a compiler to determine which globals will be heavily used.

With the register file, the movement of data between registers and memory is determined by the procedure nesting depth. Because this depth usually fluctuates within a narrow range, the use of memory is relatively infrequent. Most cache memories are set associative with a small set size. Thus, there is the danger that other data or instructions will overwrite frequently used variables.

Based on the discussion so far, the choice between a large window-based register file and a cache is not clear-cut. There is one characteristic, however, in which the register approach is clearly superior and which suggests that a cache-based system will be noticeably slower. This distinction shows up in the amount of addressing overhead experienced by the two approaches.

Figure 13.3 illustrates the difference. To reference a local scalar in a window-based register file, a "virtual" register number and a window number are used. These can pass through a relatively simple decoder to select one of the physical registers. To reference a memory location in cache, a full-width memory address must be generated. The complexity of this operation depends on the addressing mode. In a set associative cache, a portion of the address is used to read a number of words and tags equal to the set size. Another portion of the address is compared with the tags, and one of the words that were read is selected. It should be clear that even if the cache is as fast as the register file, the access time will be considerably longer. Thus, from the point of view of performance, the window-based register file is superior for local scalars. Further performance improvement could be achieved by the addition of a cache for instructions only.

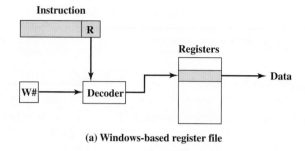

Instruction

(a) Windows-based register file

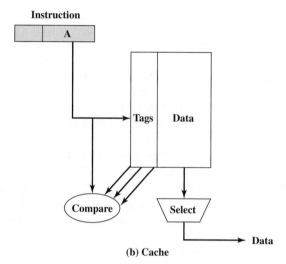

Instruction

(b) Cache

Figure 13.3   Referencing a Scalar

13.3 COMPILER-BASED REGISTER OPTIMIZATION

Let us assume now that only a small number (e.g., 16–32) of registers is available on the target RISC machine. In this case, optimized register usage is the responsibility of the compiler. A program written in a high-level language has, of course, no explicit references to registers. Rather, program quantities are referred to symbolically. The objective of the compiler is to keep the operands for as many computations as possible in registers rather than main memory, and to minimize load-and-store operations.

In general, the approach taken is as follows. Each program quantity that is a candidate for residing in a register is assigned to a symbolic or virtual register. The compiler then maps the unlimited number of symbolic registers into a fixed number of real registers. Symbolic registers whose usage does not overlap can share the same real register. If, in a particular portion of the program, there are more quantities to deal with than real registers, then some of the quantities are assigned to memory locations. Load-and-store instructions are used to position quantities in registers temporarily for computational operations.

The essence of the optimization task is to decide which quantities are to be assigned to registers at any given point in the program. The technique most commonly used in RISC compilers is known as graph coloring, which is a technique borrowed from the discipline of topology [CHAI82, CHOW86, COUT86, CHOW90].

The graph coloring problem is this. Given a graph consisting of nodes and edges, assign colors to nodes such that adjacent nodes have different colors, and do this in such a way as to minimize the number of different colors. This problem is adapted to the compiler problem in the following way. First, the program is analyzed to build a register interference graph. The nodes of the graph are the symbolic registers. If two symbolic registers are "live" during the same program fragment, then they are joined by an edge to depict interference. An attempt is then made to color the graph with n colors, where n is the number of registers. Nodes that share the same color can be assigned to the same register. If this process does not fully succeed, then those nodes that cannot be colored must be placed in memory, and loads and stores must be used to make space for the affected quantities when they are needed.

Figure 13.4 is a simple example of the process. Assume a program with six symbolic registers to be compiled into three actual registers. Figure 13.4a shows the time sequence of active use of each symbolic register. The dashed horizontal lines indicate successive instruction executions. Figure 13.4b shows the register interference graph (shading and cross-hatching are used instead of colors). A possible coloring with three colors is indicated. Because symbolic registers A and D do not interfere, the compile can assign both of these to physical register R1. Similarly, symbolic registers C and E can be assigned to register R3. One symbolic register, F, is left uncolored and must be dealt with using loads and stores.

In general, there is a trade-off between the use of a large set of registers and compiler-based register optimization. For example, [BRAD91a] reports on a study that modeled a RISC architecture with features similar to the Motorola 88000 and the MIPS R2000. The researchers varied the number of registers from 16 to 128, and

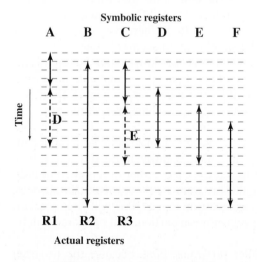

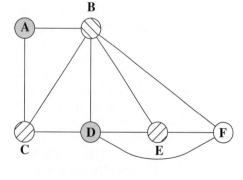

(a) Time sequence of active use of registers   (b) Register interference graph

Figure 13.4   Graph Coloring Approach

they considered both the use of all general-purpose registers and registers split between integer and floating-point use. Their study showed that with even simple register optimization, there is little benefit to the use of more than 64 registers. With reasonably sophisticated register optimization techniques, there is only marginal performance improvement with more than 32 registers. Finally, they noted that with a small number of registers (e.g., 16), a machine with a shared register organization executes faster than one with a split organization. Similar conclusions can be drawn from [HUGU91], which reports on a study that is primarily concerned with optimizing the use of a small number of registers rather than comparing the use of large register sets with optimization efforts.

13.4 REDUCED INSTRUCTION SET ARCHITECTURE

In this section, we look at some of the general characteristics of and the motivation for a reduced instruction set architecture. Specific examples will be seen later in this chapter. We begin with a discussion of motivations for contemporary complex instruction set architectures.

Why CISC

We have noted the trend to richer instruction sets, which include a larger number of instructions and more complex instructions. Two principal reasons have motivated this trend: a desire to simplify compilers and a desire to improve performance. Underlying both of these reasons was the shift to HLLs on the part of programmers; architects attempted to design machines that provided better support for HLLs.

It is not the intent of this chapter to say that the CISC designers took the wrong direction. Indeed, because technology continues to evolve and because architectures exist along a spectrum rather than in two neat categories, a black-and-white assessment is unlikely ever to emerge. Thus, the comments that follow are simply meant to point out some of the potential pitfalls in the CISC approach and to provide some understanding of the motivation of the RISC adherents.

The first of the reasons cited, compiler simplification, seems obvious. The task of the compiler writer is to generate a sequence of machine instructions for each HLL statement. If there are machine instructions that resemble HLL statements, this task is simplified. This reasoning has been disputed by the RISC researchers ([HENN82], [RADI83], [PATT82b]). They have found that complex machine instructions are often hard to exploit because the compiler must find those cases that exactly fit the construct. The task of optimizing the generated code to minimize code size, reduce instruction execution count, and enhance pipelining is much more difficult with a complex instruction set. As evidence of this, studies cited earlier in this chapter indicate that most of the instructions in a compiled program are the relatively simple ones.

The other major reason cited is the expectation that a CISC will yield smaller, faster programs. Let us examine both aspects of this assertion: that programs will be smaller and that they will execute faster.

There are two advantages to smaller programs. First, because the program takes up less memory, there is a savings in that resource. With memory today being so inexpensive, this potential advantage is no longer compelling. More important,

Table 13.6 Code Size Relative to RISC I

	[PATT82a] 11 C Programs	[KATE83] 12 C Programs	[HEAT84] 5 C Programs
RISC I	1.0	1.0	1.0
VAX-11/780	0.8	0.67	
M68000	0.9		0.9
Z8002	1.2		1.12
PDP-11/70	0.9	0.71	

smaller programs should improve performance, and this will happen in two ways. First, fewer instructions means fewer instruction bytes to be fetched. Second, in a paging environment, smaller programs occupy fewer pages, reducing page faults.

The problem with this line of reasoning is that it is far from certain that a CISC program will be smaller than a corresponding RISC program. In many cases, the CISC program, expressed in symbolic machine language, may be *shorter* (i.e., fewer instructions), but the number of bits of memory occupied may not be noticeably *smaller*. Table 13.6 shows results from three studies that compared the size of compiled C programs on a variety of machines, including RISC I, which has a reduced instruction set architecture. Note that there is little or no savings using a CISC over a RISC. It is also interesting to note that the VAX, which has a much more complex instruction set than the PDP-11, achieves very little savings over the latter. These results were confirmed by IBM researchers [RADI83], who found that the IBM 801 (a RISC) produced code that was 0.9 times the size of code on an IBM S/370. The study used a set of PL/I programs.

There are several reasons for these rather surprising results. We have already noted that compilers on CISCs tend to favor simpler instructions, so that the conciseness of the complex instructions seldom comes into play. Also, because there are more instructions on a CISC, longer opcodes are required, producing longer instructions. Finally, RISCs tend to emphasize register rather than memory references, and the former require fewer bits. An example of this last effect is discussed presently.

So the expectation that a CISC will produce smaller programs, with the attendant advantages, may not be realized. The second motivating factor for increasingly complex instruction sets was that instruction execution would be faster. It seems to make sense that a complex HLL operation will execute more quickly as a single machine instruction rather than as a series of more primitive instructions. However, because of the bias toward the use of those simpler instructions, this may not be so. The entire control unit must be made more complex, and/or the microprogram control store must be made larger, to accommodate a richer instruction set. Either factor increases the execution time of the simple instructions.

In fact, some researchers have found that the speedup in the execution of complex functions is due not so much to the power of the complex machine instructions as to their residence in high-speed control store [RADI83]. In effect, the control store acts as an instruction cache. Thus, the hardware architect is in the position of trying to determine which subroutines or functions will be used most frequently and assigning those to the control store by implementing them in microcode. The results have been less than encouraging. On S/390 systems, instructions such as Translate and Extended-Precision-Floating-Point-Divide reside in high-speed storage, while the sequence involved in setting up procedure calls or initiating an interrupt handler are in slower main memory.

Thus, it is far from clear that a trend to increasingly complex instruction sets is appropriate. This has led a number of groups to pursue the opposite path.

Characteristics of Reduced Instruction Set Architectures

Although a variety of different approaches to reduced instruction set architecture have been taken, certain characteristics are common to all of them:

- One instruction per cycle
- Register-to-register operations
- Simple addressing modes
- Simple instruction formats

Here, we provide a brief discussion of these characteristics. Specific examples are explored later in this chapter.

The first characteristic listed is that there is **one machine instruction per machine cycle**. A *machine cycle* is defined to be the time it takes to fetch two operands from registers, perform an ALU operation, and store the result in a register. Thus, RISC machine instructions should be no more complicated than, and execute about as fast as, microinstructions on CISC machines (discussed in Part Four). With simple, one-cycle instructions, there is little or no need for microcode; the machine instructions can be hardwired. Such instructions should execute faster than comparable machine instructions on other machines, because it is not necessary to access a microprogram control store during instruction execution.

A second characteristic is that most operations should be **register to register**, with only simple LOAD and STORE operations accessing memory. This design feature simplifies the instruction set and therefore the control unit. For example, a RISC instruction set may include only one or two ADD instructions (e.g., integer add, add with carry); the VAX has 25 different ADD instructions. Another benefit is that such an architecture encourages the optimization of register use, so that frequently accessed operands remain in high-speed storage.

This emphasis on register-to-register operations is notable for RISC designs. Contemporary CISC machines provide such instructions but also include memory-to-memory and mixed register/memory operations. Attempts to compare these approaches were made in the 1970s, before the appearance of RISCs. Figure 13.5a illustrates the approach taken. Hypothetical architectures were evaluated on program size and the number of bits of memory traffic. Results such as this one led one researcher to suggest that future architectures should contain no registers at all [MYER78]. One wonders what he would have thought, at the time, of the RISC machine once produced by Pyramid, which contained no less than 528 registers!

What was missing from those studies was a recognition of the frequent access to a small number of local scalars and that, with a large bank of registers or an optimizing compiler, most operands could be kept in registers for long periods of time. Thus, Figure 13.5b may be a fairer comparison.

A third characteristic is the use of **simple addressing modes**. Almost all RISC instructions use simple register addressing. Several additional modes, such as dis-

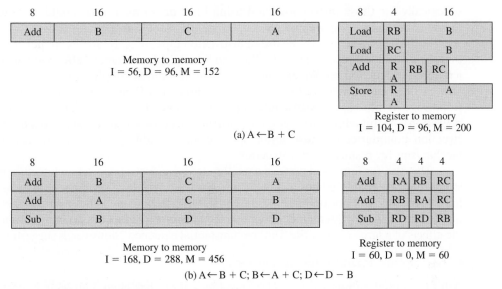

Figure 13.5   Two Comparisons of Register-to-Register and Memory-to-Memory Approaches

placement and PC-relative, may be included. Other, more complex modes can be synthesized in software from the simple ones. Again, this design feature simplifies the instruction set and the control unit.

A final common characteristic is the use of **simple instruction formats**. Generally, only one or a few formats are used. Instruction length is fixed and aligned on word boundaries. Field locations, especially the opcode, are fixed. This design feature has a number of benefits. With fixed fields, opcode decoding and register operand accessing can occur simultaneously. Simplified formats simplify the control unit. Instruction fetching is optimized because word-length units are fetched. Alignment on a word boundary also means that a single instruction does not cross page boundaries.

Taken together, these characteristics can be assessed to determine the potential performance benefits of the RISC approach. A certain amount of "circumstantial evidence" can be presented. First, more effective optimizing compilers can be developed. With more-primitive instructions, there are more opportunities for moving functions out of loops, reorganizing code for efficiency, maximizing register utilization, and so forth. It is even possible to compute parts of complex instructions at compile time. For example, the S/390 Move Characters (MVC) instruction moves a string of characters from one location to another. Each time it is executed, the move will depend on the length of the string, whether and in which direction the locations overlap, and what the alignment characteristics are. In most cases, these will all be known at compile time. Thus, the compiler could produce an optimized sequence of primitive instructions for this function.

A second point, already noted, is that most instructions generated by a compiler are relatively simple anyway. It would seem reasonable that a control unit built specifically for those instructions and using little or no microcode could execute them faster than a comparable CISC.

A third point relates to the use of instruction pipelining. RISC researchers feel that the instruction pipelining technique can be applied much more effectively with a reduced instruction set. We examine this point in some detail presently.

A final, and somewhat less significant, point is that RISC processors are more responsive to interrupts because interrupts are checked between rather elementary operations. Architectures with complex instructions either restrict interrupts to instruction boundaries or must define specific interruptible points and implement mechanisms for restarting an instruction.

The case for improved performance for a reduced instruction set architecture is strong, but one could perhaps still make an argument for CISC. A number of studies have been done but not on machines of comparable technology and power. Further, most studies have not attempted to separate the effects of a reduced instruction set and the effects of a large register file. The "circumstantial evidence," however, is suggestive.

CISC versus RISC Characteristics

After the initial enthusiasm for RISC machines, there has been a growing realization that (1) RISC designs may benefit from the inclusion of some CISC features and that (2) CISC designs may benefit from the inclusion of some RISC features. The result is that the more recent RISC designs, notably the PowerPC, are no longer "pure" RISC and the more recent CISC designs, notably the Pentium II and later Pentium models, do incorporate some RISC characteristics.

An interesting comparison in [MASH95] provides some insight into this issue. Table 13.7 lists a number of processors and compares them across a number of characteristics. For purposes of this comparison, the following are considered typical of a classic RISC:

1. A single instruction size.
2. That size is typically 4 bytes.
3. A small number of data addressing modes, typically less than five. This parameter is difficult to pin down. In the table, register and literal modes are not counted and different formats with different offset sizes are counted separately.
4. No indirect addressing that requires you to make one memory access to get the address of another operand in memory.
5. No operations that combine load/store with arithmetic (e.g., add from memory, add to memory).
6. No more than one memory-addressed operand per instruction.
7. Does not support arbitrary alignment of data for load/store operations.
8. Maximum number of uses of the memory management unit (MMU) for a data address in an instruction.
9. Number of bits for integer register specifier equal to five or more. This means that at least 32 integer registers can be explicitly referenced at a time.
10. Number of bits for floating-point register specifier equal to four or more. This means that at least 16 floating-point registers can be explicitly referenced at a time.

Table 13.7   Characteristics of Some Processors

Processor	Number of instruction sizes	Max instruction size in bytes	Number of addressing modes	Indirect addressing	Load/store combined with arithmetic	Max number of memory operands	Unaligned addressing allowed	Max Number of MMU uses	Number of bits for integer register specifier	Number of bits for FP register specifier
AMD29000	1	4	1	no	no	1	no	1	8	3^a
MIPS R2000	1	4	1	no	no	1	no	1	5	4
SPARC	1	4	2	no	no	1	no	1	5	4
MC88000	1	4	3	no	no	1	no	1	5	4
HP PA	1	4	10^a	no	no	1	no	1	5	4
IBM RT/PC	2^a	4	1	no	no	1	no	1	4^a	3^a
IBM RS/6000	1	4	4	no	no	1	yes	1	5	5
Intel i860	1	4	4	no	no	1	no	1	5	4
IBM 3090	4	8	2^b	no^b	yes	2	yes	4	4	2
Intel 80486	12	12	15	no^b	yes	2	yes	4	3	3
NSC 32016	21	21	23	yes	yes	2	yes	4	3	3
MC68040	11	22	44	yes	yes	2	yes	8	4	3
VAX	56	56	22	yes	yes	6	yes	24	4	0
Clipper	4^a	8^a	9^a	no	no	1	0	2	4^a	3^a
Intel 80960	2^a	8^a	9^a	no	no	1	yes^a	—	5	3^a

[a]RISC that does not conform to this characteristic.
[b]CISC that does not conform to this characteristic.

499

Items 1 through 3 are an indication of instruction decode complexity. Items 4 through 8 suggest the ease or difficulty of pipelining, especially in the presence of virtual memory requirements. Items 9 and 10 are related to the ability to take good advantage of compilers.

In the table, the first eight processors are clearly RISC architectures, the next five are clearly CISC, and the last two are processors often thought of as RISC that in fact have many CISC characteristics.

13.5 RISC PIPELINING

Pipelining with Regular Instructions

As we discussed in Section 12.4, instruction pipelining is often used to enhance performance. Let us reconsider this in the context of a RISC architecture. Most instructions are register to register, and an instruction cycle has the following two stages:

- I: Instruction fetch.
- E: Execute. Performs an ALU operation with register input and output.

For load and store operations, three stages are required:

- I: Instruction fetch.
- E: Execute. Calculates memory address
- D: Memory. Register-to-memory or memory-to-register operation.

Figure 13.6a depicts the timing of a sequence of instructions using no pipelining. Clearly, this is a wasteful process. Even very simple pipelining can substantially improve performance. Figure 13.6b shows a two-stage pipelining scheme, in which the I and E stages of two different instructions are performed simultaneously. The two stages of the pipeline are an instruction fetch stage, and an execute/memory stage that executes the instruction, including register-to-memory and memory-to-register operations. Thus we see that the instruction fetch stage of the second instruction can e performed in parallel with the first part of the execute/memory stage. However, the execute/memory stage of the second instruction must be delayed until the first instruction clears the second stage of the pipeline. This scheme can yield up to twice the execution rate of a serial scheme. Two problems prevent the maximum speedup from being achieved. First, we assume that a single-port memory is used and that only one memory access is possible per stage. This requires the insertion of a wait state in some instructions. Second, a branch instruction interrupts the sequential flow of execution. To accommodate this with minimum circuitry, a NOOP instruction can be inserted into the instruction stream by the compiler or assembler.

Pipelining can be improved further by permitting two memory accesses per stage. This yields the sequence shown in Figure 13.6c. Now, up to three instructions can be overlapped, and the improvement is as much as a factor of 3. Again, branch instructions cause the speedup to fall short of the maximum possible. Also, note that data dependencies have an effect. If an instruction needs an operand that is altered

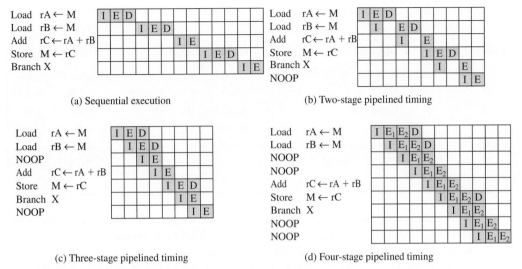

Figure 13.6 The Effects of Pipelining

by the preceding instruction, a delay is required. Again, this can be accomplished by a NOOP.

The pipelining discussed so far works best if the three stages are of approximately equal duration. Because the E stage usually involves an ALU operation, it may be longer. In this case, we can divide into two substages:

- E_1: Register file read
- E_2: ALU operation and register write

Because of the simplicity and regularity of a RISC instruction set, the design of the phasing into three or four stages is easily accomplished. Figure 13.6d shows the result with a four-stage pipeline. Up to four instructions at a time can be under way, and the maximum potential speedup is a factor of 4. Note again the use of NOOPs to account for data and branch delays.

Optimization of Pipelining

Because of the simple and regular nature of RISC instructions, pipelining schemes can be efficiently employed. There are few variations in instruction execution duration, and the pipeline can be tailored to reflect this. However, we have seen that data and branch dependencies reduce the overall execution rate.

DELAYED BRANCH To compensate for these dependencies, code reorganization techniques have been developed. First, let us consider branching instructions. *Delayed branch*, a way of increasing the efficiency of the pipeline, makes use of a branch that does not take effect until after execution of the following instruction (hence the term *delayed*). The instruction location immediately following the branch is referred to as the *delay slot*. This strange procedure is illustrated in Table 13.8. In the column labeled "normal branch," we see a normal symbolic instruction machine-language program.

Table 13.8 Normal and Delayed Branch

Address	Normal Branch		Delayed Branch		Optimized Delayed Branch	
100	LOAD	X, rA	LOAD	X, rA	LOAD	X, rA
101	ADD	1, rA	ADD	1, rA	JUMP	105
102	JUMP	105	JUMP	106	ADD	1, rA
103	ADD	rA, rB	NOOP		ADD	rA, rB
104	SUB	rC, rB	ADD	rA, rB	SUB	rC, rB
105	STORE	rA, Z	SUB	rC, rB	STORE	rA, Z
106			STORE	rA, Z		

After 102 is executed, the next instruction to be executed is 105. To regularize the pipeline, a NOOP is inserted after this branch. However, increased performance is achieved if the instructions at 101 and 102 are interchanged.

Figure 13.7 shows the result. Figure 13.7a shows the traditional approach to pipelining, of the type discussed in Chapter 12 (e.g., see Figures 12.11 and 12.12).

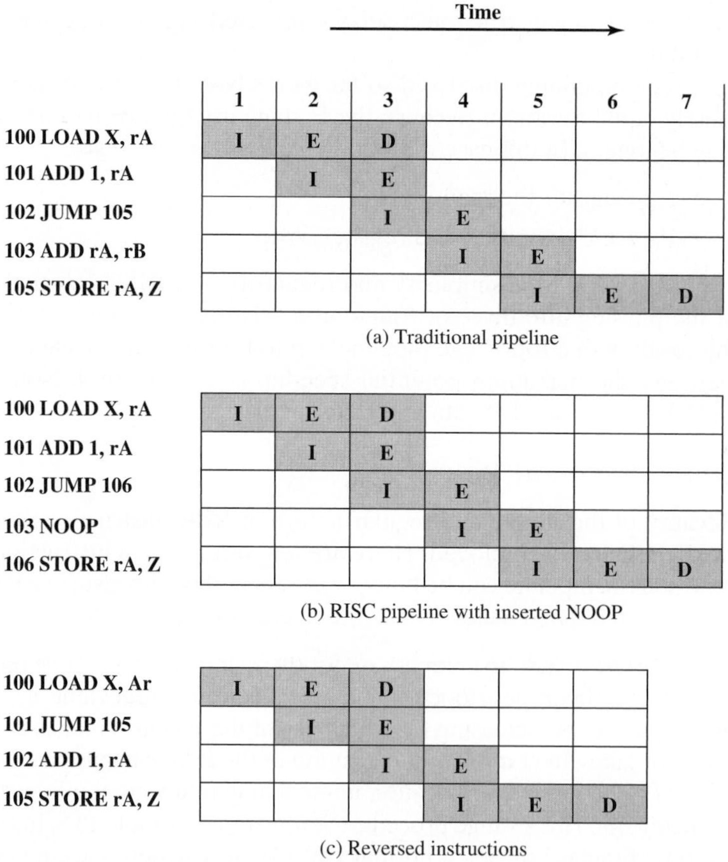

(a) Traditional pipeline

(b) RISC pipeline with inserted NOOP

(c) Reversed instructions

Figure 13.7 Use of the Delayed Branch

The JUMP instruction is fetched at time 3. At time 4, the JUMP instruction is executed at the same time that instruction 103 (ADD instruction) is fetched. Because a JUMP occurs, which updates the program counter, the pipeline must be cleared of instruction 103; at time 5, instruction 105, which is the target of the JUMP, is loaded. Figure 13.7b shows the same pipeline handled by a typical RISC organization. The timing is the same. However, because of the insertion of the NOOP instruction, we do not need special circuitry to clear the pipeline; the NOOP simply executes with no effect. Figure 13.7c shows the use of the delayed branch. The JUMP instruction is fetched at time 2, before the ADD instruction, which is fetched at time 3. Note, however, that the ADD instruction is fetched before the execution of the JUMP instruction has a chance to alter the program counter. Therefore, during time 4, the ADD instruction is executed at the same time that instruction 105 is fetched. Thus, the original semantics of the program are retained but one less clock cycle is required for execution.

This interchange of instructions will work successfully for unconditional branches, calls, and returns. For conditional branches, this procedure cannot be blindly applied. If the condition that is tested for the branch can be altered by the immediately preceding instruction, then the compiler must refrain from doing the interchange and instead insert a NOOP. Otherwise, the compiler can seek to insert a useful instruction after the branch. The experience with both the Berkeley RISC and IBM 801 systems is that the majority of conditional branch instructions can be optimized in this fashion ([PATT82a], [RADI83]).

DELAYED LOAD A similar sort of tactic, called the delayed load, can be used on LOAD instructions. On LOAD instructions, the register that is to be the target of the load is locked by the processor. The processor then continues execution of the instruction stream until it reaches an instruction requiring that register, at which point it idles until the load is complete. If the compiler can rearrange instructions so that useful work can be done while the load is in the pipeline, efficiency is increased.

Loop Unrolling Simulator

LOOP UNROLLING Another compiler technique to improve instruction parallelism is loop unrolling [BACO94]. Unrolling replicates the body of a loop some number of times called the unrolling factor (u) and iterates by step u instead of step 1.

Unrolling can improve the performance by

- reducing loop overhead
- increasing instruction parallelism by improving pipeline performance
- improving register, data cache, or TLB locality

Figure 13.8 illustrates all three of these improvements in an example. Loop overhead is cut in half because two iterations are performed before the test and

```
do i=2, n-1
      a[i] = a[i] + a[i-1] * a[i+1]
end do
```

(a) Original loop

```
do i=2, n-2, 2
      a[i] = a[i] + a[i-1] * a[i+1]
      a[i+1] = a[i+1] + a[i] * a[i+2]
end do

if (mod(n-2, 2) = i)   then
   a[n-1] = a[n-1] + a[n-2] * a[n]
end if
```

(b) Loop unrolled twice

Figure 13.8 Loop unrolling

branch at the end of the loop. Instruction parallelism is increased because the second assignment can be performed while the results of the first are being stored and the loop variables are being updated. If array elements are assigned to registers, register locality will improve because a[i] and a[$i + 1$] are used twice in the loop body, reducing the number of loads per iteration from three to two.

As a final note, we should point out that the design of the instruction pipeline should not be carried out in isolation from other optimization techniques applied to the system. For example, [BRAD91b] shows that the scheduling of instructions for the pipeline and the dynamic allocation of registers should be considered together to achieve the greatest efficiency.

13.6 MIPS R4000

One of the first commercially available RISC chip sets was developed by MIPS Technology Inc. The system was inspired by an experimental system, also using the name MIPS, developed at Stanford [HENN84]. In this section we look at the MIPS R4000. It has substantially the same architecture and instruction set of the earlier MIPS designs: the R2000 and R3000. The most significant difference is that the R4000 uses 64 rather than 32 bits for all internal and external data paths and for addresses, registers, and the ALU.

The use of 64 bits has a number of advantages over a 32-bit architecture. It allows a bigger address space—large enough for an operating system to map more than a terabyte of files directly into virtual memory for easy access. With 1-terabyte and larger disk drives now common, the 4-gigabyte address space of a 32-bit machine becomes limiting. Also, the 64-bit capacity allows the R4000 to process data such as IEEE double-precision floating-point numbers and character strings, up to eight characters in a single action.

The R4000 processor chip is partitioned into two sections, one containing the CPU and the other containing a coprocessor for memory management. The processor has a very simple architecture. The intent was to design a system in which the instruction execution logic was as simple as possible, leaving space available for logic to enhance performance (e.g., the entire memory-management unit).

The processor supports thirty-two 64-bit registers. It also provides for up to 128 Kbytes of high-speed cache, half each for instructions and data. The relatively large cache (the IBM 3090 provides 128 to 256 Kbytes of cache) enables the system to keep large sets of program code and data local to the processor, off-loading the main memory bus and avoiding the need for a large register file with the accompanying windowing logic.

Instruction Set

Table 13.9 lists the basic instruction set for all MIPS R series processors. All processor instructions are encoded in a single 32-bit word format. All data operations are register to register; the only memory references are pure load/store operations.

The R4000 makes no use of condition codes. If an instruction generates a condition, the corresponding flags are stored in a general-purpose register. This avoids the need for special logic to deal with condition codes as they affect the pipelining mechanism and the reordering of instructions by the compiler. Instead, the mechanisms already implemented to deal with register-value dependencies are employed. Further, conditions mapped onto the register files are subject to the same compile-time optimizations in allocation and reuse as other values stored in registers.

As with most RISC-based machines, the MIPS uses a single 32-bit instruction length. This single instruction length simplifies instruction fetch and decode, and it also simplifies the interaction of instruction fetch with the virtual memory management unit (i.e., instructions do not cross word or page boundaries). The three instruction formats (Figure 13.9) share common formatting of opcodes and register references, simplifying instruction decode. The effect of more complex instructions can be synthesized at compile time.

Only the simplest and most frequently used memory-addressing mode is implemented in hardware. All memory references consist of a 16-bit offset from a 32-bit register. For example, the "load word" instruction is of the form

```
lw r2, 128(r3)   /* load word at address 128 offset from
                     register 3 into register 2
```

Each of the 32 general-purpose registers can be used as the base register. One register, r0, always contains 0.

The compiler makes use of multiple machine instructions to synthesize typical addressing modes in conventional machines. Here is an example from [CHOW87], which uses the instruction lui (load upper immediate). This instruction loads the upper half of a register with a 16-bit immediate value, setting the lower

Table 13.9 MIPS R-Series Instruction Set

OP	Description	OP	Description
	Load/Store Instructions	SLLV	Shift Left Logical Variable
LB	Load Byte	SRLV	Shift Right Logical Variable
LBU	Load Byte Unsigned	SRAV	Shift Right Arithmetic Variable
LH	Load Halfword		**Multiply/Divide Instructions**
LHU	Load Halfword Unsigned	MULT	Multiply
LW	Load Word	MULTU	Multiply Unsigned
LWL	Load Word Left	DIV	Divide
LWR	Load Word Right	DIVU	Divide Unsigned
SB	Store Byte	MFHI	Move From HI
SH	Store Halfword	MTHI	Move To HI
SW	Store Word	MFLO	Move From LO
SWL	Store Word Left	MTLO	Move To LO
SWR	Store Word Right		**Jump and Branch Instructions**
	Arithmetic Instructions (ALU Immediate)	J	Jump
ADDI	Add Immediate	JAL	Jump and Link
ADDIU	Add Immediate Unsigned	JR	Jump to Register
SLTI	Set on Less Than Immediate	JALR	Jump and Link Register
SLTIU	Set on Less Than Immediate Unsigned	BEQ	Branch on Equal
		BNE	Branch on Not Equal
ANDI	AND Immediate	BLEZ	Branch on Less Than or Equal to Zero
ORI	OR Immediate	BGTZ	Branch on Greater Than Zero
XORI	Exclusive-OR Immediate	BLTZ	Branch on Less Than Zero
LUI	Load Upper Immediate	BGEZ	Branch on Greater Than or Equal to Zero
	Arithmetic Instructions (3-operand, R-type)	BLTZAL	Branch on Less Than Zero And Link
		BGEZAL	Branch on Greater Than or Equal to Zero And Link
ADD	Add		**Coprocessor Instructions**
ADDU	Add Unsigned		
SUB	Subtract	LWCz	Load Word to Coprocessor
SUBU	Subtract Unsigned	SWCz	Store Word to Coprocessor
SLT	Set on Less Than	MTCz	Move To Coprocessor
SLTU	Set on Less Than Unsigned	MFCz	Move From Coprocessor
AND	AND	CTCz	Move Control To Coprocessor
OR	OR	CFCz	Move Control From Coprocessor
XOR	Exclusive-OR	COPz	Coprocessor Operation
NOR	NOR	BCzT	Branch on Coprocessor z True
	Shift Instructions	BCzF	Branch on Coprocessor z False
SLL	Shift Left Logical		**Special Instructions**
SRL	Shift Right Logical	SYSCALL	System Call
SRA	Shift Right Arithmetic	BREAK	Break

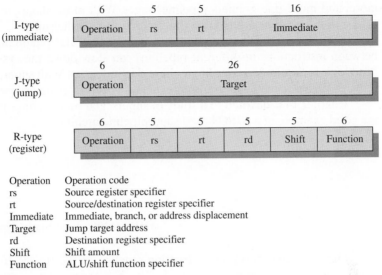

Figure 13.9   MIPS Instruction Formats

half to zero. Consider an assembly-language instruction that uses a 32-bit immediate argument

```
lw r2, #imm(r4)
```
       /* load word at address using a 32-bit immediate offset #imm

       /* offset from register 4 into register 2

This instruction can be compiled into the following MIPS instructions

```
lui r1, #imm-hi
```
       /* where #imm-hi is the high-order 16 bits of #imm

```
addu r1, r1, r4
```
       /* add unsigned #imm-hi to r4 and put in r1

```
lw r2, #imm-lo(r1)
```
       /* where #imm-lo is the low-order 16 bits of #imm

Instruction Pipeline

With its simplified instruction architecture, the MIPS can achieve very efficient pipelining. It is instructive to look at the evolution of the MIPS pipeline, as it illustrates the evolution of RISC pipelining in general.

   The initial experimental RISC systems and the first generation of commercial RISC processors achieve execution speeds that approach one instruction per system clock cycle. To improve on this performance, two classes of processors have evolved to offer execution of multiple instructions per clock cycle: superscalar and superpipelined architectures. In essence, a superscalar architecture replicates each of the pipeline stages so that two or more instructions at the same stage of the pipeline can be processed simultaneously. A superpipelined architecture is one that makes use of more, and more fine-grained, pipeline stages. With more stages, more instructions can be in the pipeline at the same time, increasing parallelism.

Both approaches have limitations. With superscalar pipelining, dependencies between instructions in different pipelines can slow down the system. Also, overhead logic is required to coordinate these dependencies. With superpipelining, there is overhead associated with transferring instructions from one stage to the next.

Chapter 14 is devoted to a study of superscalar architecture. The MIPS R4000 is a good example of a RISC-based superpipeline architecture.

MIPS R3000 Five-Stage Pipeline Simulator

Figure 13.10a shows the instruction pipeline of the R3000. In the R3000, the pipeline advances once per clock cycle. The MIPS compiler is able to reorder instructions to fill delay slots with code 70 to 90% of the time. All instructions follow the same sequence of five pipeline stages:

- Instruction fetch
- Source operand fetch from register file

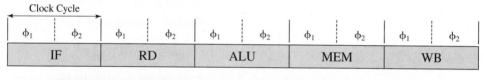

(a) Detailed R3000 pipeline

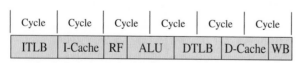

(b) Modified R3000 pipeline with reduced latencies

Cycle	Cycle	Cycle	Cycle	Cycle	Cycle
ITLB	I-Cache	RF	ALU	DTLB	D-Cache	WB

Cycle	Cycle	Cycle	Cycle	Cycle
ITLB	RF	ALU	D-Cache	TC	WB

(c) Optimized R3000 pipeline with parallel TLB and cache accesses

IF	= Instruction fetch
RD	= Read
MEM	= Memory access
WB	= Write back
I-Cache	= Instruction cache access
RF	= Fetch operand from register
D-Cache	= Data cache access
ITLB	= Instruction address translation
IDEC	= Instruction decode
IA	= Compute instruction address
DA	= Calculate data virtual address
DTLB	= Data address translation
TC	= Data cache tag check

Figure 13.10 Enhancing the R3000 Pipeline

- ALU operation or data operand address generation
- Data memory reference
- Write back into register file

As illustrated in Figure 13.10a, there is not only parallelism due to pipelining but also parallelism within the execution of a single instruction. The 60-ns clock cycle is divided into two 30-ns stages. The external instruction and data access operations to the cache each require 60 ns, as do the major internal operations (OP, DA, IA). Instruction decode is a simpler operation, requiring only a single 30-ns stage, overlapped with register fetch in the same instruction. Calculation of an address for a branch instruction also overlaps instruction decode and register fetch, so that a branch at instruction i can address the ICACHE access of instruction $i + 2$. Similarly, a load at instruction i fetches data that are immediately used by the OP of instruction $i + 1$, while an ALU/shift result gets passed directly into instruction $i + 1$ with no delay. This tight coupling between instructions makes for a highly efficient pipeline.

In detail, then, each clock cycle is divided into separate stages, denoted as $\phi1$ and $\phi2$. The functions performed in each stage are summarized in Table 13.10.

The R4000 incorporates a number of technical advances over the R3000. The use of more advanced technology allows the clock cycle time to be cut in half, to 30 ns, and for the access time to the register file to be cut in half. In addition, there is greater density on the chip, which enables the instruction and data caches to be incorporated on the chip. Before looking at the final R4000 pipeline, let us consider how the R3000 pipeline can be modified to improve performance using R4000 technology.

Figure 13.10b shows a first step. Remember that the cycles in this figure are half as long as those in Figure 13.10a. Because they are on the same chip, the instruction

Table 13.10   R3000 Pipeline Stages

Pipeline Stage	Phase	Function
IF	$\phi1$	Using the TLB, translate an instruction virtual address to a physical address (after a branching decision).
IF	$\phi2$	Send the physical address to the instruction address.
RD	$\phi1$	Return instruction from instruction cache.
		Compare tags and validity of fetched instruction.
RD	$\phi2$	Decode instruction.
		Read register file.
		If branch, calculate branch target address.
ALU	$\phi1+\phi2$	If register-to-register operation, the arithmetic or logical operation is performed.
ALU	$\phi1$	If a branch, decide whether the branch is to be taken or not.
		If a memory reference (load or store), calculate data virtual address.
ALU	$\phi2$	If a memory reference, translate data virtual address to physical using TLB.
MEM	$\phi1$	If a memory reference, send physical address to data cache.
MEM	$\phi2$	If a memory reference, return data from data cache, and check tags.
WB	$\phi1$	Write to register file.

and data cache stages take only half as long; so they still occupy only one clock cycle. Again, because of the speedup of the register file access, register read and write still occupy only half of a clock cycle.

Because the R4000 caches are on-chip, the virtual-to-physical address translation can delay the cache access. This delay is reduced by implementing virtually indexed caches and going to a parallel cache access and address translation. Figure 13.10c shows the optimized R3000 pipeline with this improvement. Because of the compression of events, the data cache tag check is performed separately on the next cycle after cache access. This check determines whether the data item is in the cache.

In a superpipelined system, existing hardware is used several times per cycle by inserting pipeline registers to split up each pipe stage. Essentially, each super-pipeline stage operates at a multiple of the base clock frequency, the multiple depending on the degree of superpipelining. The R4000 technology has the speed and density to permit superpipelining of degree 2. Figure 13.11a shows the optimized R3000 pipeline using this superpipelining. Note that this is essentially the same dynamic structure as Figure 13.10c.

Further improvements can be made. For the R4000, a much larger and specialized adder was designed. This makes it possible to execute ALU operations at twice the rate. Other improvements allow the execution of loads and stores at twice the rate. The resulting pipeline is shown in Figure 13.11b.

The R4000 has eight pipeline stages, meaning that as many as eight instructions can be in the pipeline at the same time. The pipeline advances at the rate of two stages per clock cycle. The eight pipeline stages are as follows:

- **Instruction fetch first half:** Virtual address is presented to the instruction cache and the translation lookaside buffer.

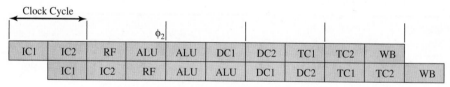

(a) Superpipelined implmentation of the optimized R3000 pipeline

(b) R4000 pipeline

IF	= Instruction fetch first half	DC	= Data cache
IS	= Instruction fetch second half	DF	= Data cache first half
RF	= Fetch operands from register	DS	= Data cache second half
EX	= Instruction execute	TC	= Tag check
IC	= Instruction cache		

Figure 13.11   Theoretical R3000 and Actual R4000 Superpipelines

- **Instruction fetch second half:** Instruction cache outputs the instruction and the TLB generates the physical address.
- **Register file:** Three activities occur in parallel:
  - Instruction is decoded and check made for interlock conditions (i.e., this instruction depends on the result of a preceding instruction).
  - Instruction cache tag check is made.
  - Operands are fetched from the register file.
- **Instruction execute:** One of three activities can occur:
  - If the instruction is a register-to-register operation, the ALU performs the arithmetic or logical operation.
  - If the instruction is a load or store, the data virtual address is calculated.
  - If the instruction is a branch, the branch target virtual address is calculated and branch conditions are checked.
- **Data cache first:** Virtual address is presented to the data cache and TLB.
- **Data cache second:** The TLB generates the physical address, and the data cache outputs the instruction.
- **Tag check:** Cache tag checks are performed for loads and stores.
- **Write back:** Instruction result is written back to register file.

13.7 SPARC

SPARC (Scalable Processor Architecture) refers to an architecture defined by Sun Microsystems. Sun developed its own SPARC implementation but also licenses the architecture to other vendors to produce SPARC-compatible machines. The SPARC architecture is inspired by the Berkeley RISC I machine, and its instruction set and register organization is based closely on the Berkeley RISC model.

SPARC Register Set

As with the Berkeley RISC, the SPARC makes use of register windows. Each window consists of 24 registers, and the total number of windows is implementation dependent and ranges from 2 to 32 windows. Figure 13.12 illustrates an implementation that supports 8 windows, using a total of 136 physical registers; as the discussion in Section 13.2 indicates, this seems a reasonable number of windows. Physical registers 0 through 7 are global registers shared by all procedures. Each process sees logical registers 0 through 31. Logical registers 24 through 31, referred to as *ins,* are shared with the calling (parent) procedure; and logical registers 8 through 15, referred to as *outs*, are shared with any called (child) procedure. These two portions overlap with other windows. Logical registers 16 through 23, referred to as *locals,* are not shared and do not overlap with other windows. Again, as the discussion of Section 12.1 indicates, the availability of 8 registers for parameter passing should be adequate in most cases (e.g., see Table 13.4).

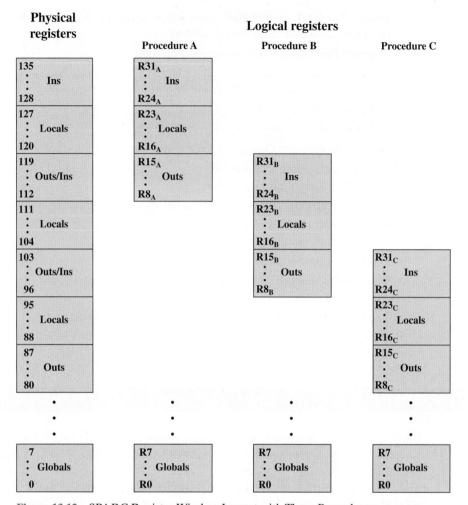

Figure 13.12   SPARC Register Window Layout with Three Procedures

Figure 13.13 is another view of the register overlap. The calling procedure places any parameters to be passed in its *outs* registers; the called procedure treats these same physical registers as it *ins* registers. The processor maintains a current window pointer (CWP), located in the processor status register (PSR), that points to the window of the currently executing procedure. The window invalid mask (WIM), also in the PSR, indicates which windows are invalid.

With the SPARC register architecture, it is usually not necessary to save and restore registers for a procedure call. The compiler is simplified because the compiler need be concerned only with allocating the local registers for a procedure in an efficient manner and need not be concerned with register allocation between procedures.

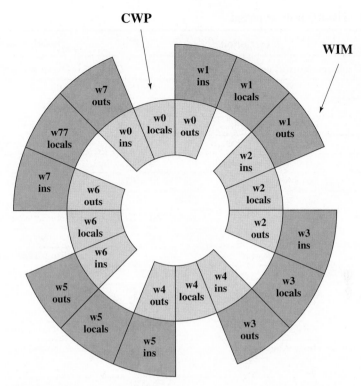

Figure 13.13 Eight Register Windows Forming a Circular Stack in SPARC

Instruction Set

Table 13.11 lists the instructions for the SPARC architecture. Most of the instructions reference only register operands. Register-to-register instructions have three operands and can be expressed in the form

$$R_d \leftarrow R_{S1} \text{ op } S2$$

where R_d and R_{S1} are register references; S2 can refer either to a register or to a 13-bit immediate operand. Register zero (R_0) is hardwired with the value 0. This form is well suited to typical programs, which have a high proportion of local scalars and constants.

The available ALU operations can be grouped as follows:

- Integer addition (with or without carry)
- Integer subtraction (with or without carry)
- Bitwise Boolean AND, OR, XOR and their negations
- Shift left logical, right logical, or right arithmetic

Table 13.11 SPARC Instruction Set

OP	Description	OP	Description
Load/Store Instructions		**Arithmetic Instructions**	
LDSB	Load signed byte	ADD	Add
LDSH	Load signed halfword	ADDCC	Add, set icc
LDUB	Load unsigned byte	ADDX	Add with carry
LDUH	Load unsigned halfword	ADDXCC	Add with carry, set icc
LD	Load word	SUB	Subtract
LDD	Load doubleword	SUBCC	Subtract, set icc
STB	Store byte	SUBX	Subtract with carry
STH	Store halfword	SUBXCC	Subtract with carry, set icc
STD	Store word	MULSCC	Multiply step, set icc
STDD	Store doubleword	**Jump/Branch Instructions**	
Shift Instructions		BCC	Branch on condition
SLL	Shift left logical	FBCC	Branch on floating-point condition
SRL	Shift right logical	CBCC	Branch on coprocessor condition
SRA	Shift right arithmetic	CALL	Call procedure
Boolean Instructions		JMPL	Jump and link
AND	AND	TCC	Trap on condition
ANDCC	AND, set icc	SAVE	Advance register window
ANDN	NAND	RESTORE	Move windows backward
ANDNCC	NAND, set icc	RETT	Return from trap
OR	OR	**Miscellaneous Instructions**	
ORCC	OR, set icc	SETHI	Set high 22 bits
ORN	NOR	UNIMP	Unimplemented instruction (trap)
ORNCC	NOR, set icc	RD	Read a special register
XOR	XOR	WR	Write a special register
XORCC	XOR, set icc	IFLUSH	Instruction cache flush
XNOR	Exclusive NOR		
XNORCC	Exclusive NOR, set icc		

All of these instructions, except the shifts, can optionally set the four condition codes (ZERO, NEGATIVE, OVERFLOW, CARRY). Signed integers are represented in 32-bit twos complement form.

Only simple load and store instructions reference memory. There are separate load and store instructions for word (32 bits), doubleword, halfword, and byte. For the latter two cases, there are instructions for loading these quantities as signed or unsigned numbers. Signed numbers are sign extended to fill out the 32-bit destination register. Unsigned numbers are padded with zeros.

Table 13.12 Synthesizing Other Addressing Modes with SPARC Addressing Modes

Instruction Type	Addressing Mode	Algorithm	SPARC Equivalent
Register-to-register	Immediate	operand = A	S2
Load, store	Direct	EA = A	R_0 + S2
Register-to-register	Register	EA = R	R_{S1}, R_{S2}
Load, store	Register Indirect	EA = (R)	R_{S1} + 0
Load, store	Displacement	EA = (R) + A	R_{S1} + S2

S2 = either a register operand or a 13-bit immediate operand

The only available addressing mode, other than register, is a displacement mode. That is, the effective address (EA) of an operand consists of a displacement from an address contained in a register:

$$EA = (R_{S1}) + S2$$
$$\text{or } EA = (R_{S1}) + (R_{S2})$$

depending on whether the second operand is immediate or a register reference. To perform a load or store, an extra stage is added to the instruction cycle. During the second stage, the memory address is calculated using the ALU; the load or store occurs in a third stage. This single addressing mode is quite versatile and can be used to synthesize other addressing modes, as indicated in Table 13.12.

It is instructive to compare the SPARC addressing capability with that of the MIPS. The MIPS makes use of a 16-bit offset, compared with a 13-bit offset on the SPARC. On the other hand, the MIPS does not permit an address to be constructed from the contents of two registers.

Instruction Format

As with the MIPS R4000, SPARC uses a simple set of 32-bit instruction formats (Figure 13.14). All instructions begin with a 2-bit opcode. For most instructions, this is extended with additional opcode bits elsewhere in the format. For the Call instruction, a 30-bit immediate operand is extended with two zero bits to the right to form a 32-bit PC-relative address in twos complement form. Instructions are aligned on a 32-bit boundary so that this form of addressing suffices.

The Branch instruction includes a 4-bit condition field that corresponds to the four standard condition code bits, so that any combination of conditions can be tested. The 22-bit PC-relative address is extended with two zero bits on the right to form a 24-bit twos complement relative address. An unusual feature of the Branch instruction is the annul bit. When the annul bit is not set, the instruction after the branch is always executed, regardless of whether the branch is taken. This is the typical delayed branch operation found on many RISC machines and described in Section 13.5 (see Figure 13.7). However, when the annul bit is set, the instruction following the branch is executed only if the branch is taken. The processor suppresses the effect of that instruction even though it is already in the pipeline. This annul bit is useful because it makes it easier for the compiler to fill the delay slot following a conditional branch. The instruction that is the target of the branch can always be

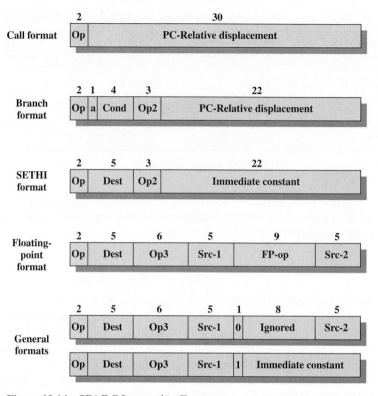

Figure 13.14 SPARC Instruction Formats

put in the delay slot, because if the branch is not taken, the instruction can be annulled. The reason this technique is desirable is that conditional branches are generally taken more than half the time.

The SETHI instruction is a special instruction used to load or store a 32-bit value. This feature is needed to load and store addresses and large constants. The SETHI instruction sets the 22 high-order bits of a register with its 22-bit immediate operand, and zeros out the low-order 10 bits. An immediate constant of up to 13 bits can be specified in one of the general formats, and such an instruction could be used to fill in the remaining 10 bits of the register. A load or store instruction can also be used to achieve a direct addressing mode. To load a value from location K in memory, we could use the following SPARC instructions:

```
sethi    %hi(K), %r8          ;load high-order 22 bits of address of location
                              ;K into register r8
ld       [%r8 + %lo(K)], %r8  ;load contents of location K into r8
```

The macros %hi and %lo are used to define immediate operands consisting of the appropriate address bits of a location. This use of SETHI is similar to the use of the lui instruction on the MIPS.

The floating-point format is used for floating-point operations. Two source and one destination registers are designated.

Finally, all other operations, including loads, stores, arithmetic, and logical operations use one of the last two formats shown in Figure 13.14. One of the formats makes use of two source registers and a destination register, while the other uses one source register, one 13-bit immediate operand, and one destination register.

13.8 RISC VERSUS CISC CONTROVERSY

For many years, the general trend in computer architecture and organization has been toward increasing processor complexity: more instructions, more addressing modes, more specialized registers, and so on. The RISC movement represents a fundamental break with the philosophy behind that trend. Naturally, the appearance of RISC systems, and the publication of papers by its proponents extolling RISC virtues, led to a reaction from those involved in the design of CISC architectures.

The work that has been done on assessing merits of the RISC approach can be grouped into two categories:

- **Quantitative:** Attempts to compare program size and execution speed of programs on RISC and CISC machines that use comparable technology
- **Qualitative:** Examins issues such as high-level language support and optimum use of VLSI real estate

Most of the work on quantitative assessment has been done by those working on RISC systems [PATT82b, HEAT84, PATT84], and it has been, by and large, favorable to the RISC approach. Others have examined the issue and come away unconvinced [COLW85a, FLYN87, DAVI87]. There are several problems with attempting such comparisons [SERL86]:

- There is no pair of RISC and CISC machines that are comparable in life-cycle cost, level of technology, gate complexity, sophistication of compiler, operating system support, and so on.
- No definitive test set of programs exists. Performance varies with the program.
- It is difficult to sort out hardware effects from effects due to skill in compiler writing.
- Most of the comparative analysis on RISC has been done on "toy" machines rather than commercial products. Furthermore, most commercially available machines advertised as RISC possess a mixture of RISC and CISC characteristics. Thus, a fair comparison with a commercial, "pure-play" CISC machine (e.g., VAX, Pentium) is difficult.

The qualitative assessment is, almost by definition, subjective. Several researchers have turned their attention to such an assessment [COLW85a, WALL85], but the results are, at best, ambiguous, and certainly subject to rebuttal [PATT85b] and, of course, counterrebuttal [COLW85b].

In more recent years, the RISC versus CISC controversy has died down to a great extent. This is because there has been a gradual convergence of the technologies.

As chip densities and raw hardware speeds increase, RISC systems have become more complex. At the same time, in an effort to squeeze out maximum performance, CISC designs have focused on issues traditionally associated with RISC, such as an increased number of general-purpose registers and increased emphasis on instruction pipeline design.

13.9 RECOMMENDED READING

Two classic overview papers on RISC are [PATT85a] and [HENN84]. Another survey article is [STAL88]. Accounts of two pioneering RISC efforts are provided by [RADI83] and [PATT82a].

[KANE92] covers the commercial MIPS machine in detail. [MIRA92] provides a good overview of the MIPS R4000. [BASH91] discusses the evolution from the R3000 pipeline to the R4000 superpipeline. The SPARC is covered in some detail in [DEWA90].

BASH91 Bashteen, A.; Lui, I.; and Mullan, J. "A Superpipeline Approach to the MIPS Architecture." *Proceedings, COMPCON Spring '91,* February 1991.

DEWA90 Dewar, R., and Smosna, M. *Microprocessors: A Programmer's View.* New York: McGraw-Hill, 1990.

HENN84 Hennessy, J. "VLSI Processor Architecture." *IEEE Transactions on Computers,* December 1984.

KANE92 Kane, G., and Heinrich, J. *MIPS RISC Architecture.* Englewood Cliffs, NJ: Prentice Hall, 1992.

MIRA92 Mirapuri, S.; Woodacre, M.; and Vasseghi, N. "The MIPS R4000 Processor." *IEEE Micro,* April 1992.

PATT82a Patterson, D., and Sequin, C. "A VLSI RISC." *Computer,* September 1982.

PATT85a Patterson, D. "Reduced Instruction Set Computers." *Communications of the ACM.* January 1985.

RADI83 Radin, G. "The 801 Minicomputer." *IBM Journal of Research and Development,* May 1983.

STAL88 Stallings, W. "Reduced Instruction Set Computer Architecture." *Proceedings of the IEEE,* January 1988.

13.10 KEY TERMS, REVIEW QUESTIONS, AND PROBLEMS

Key Terms

complex instruction set computer (CISC) delayed branch delayed load	high-level language (HLL) reduced instruction set computer (RISC)	register file register window SPARC

Review Questions

13.1 What are some typical distinguishing characteristics of RISC organization?

13.2 Briefly explain the two basic approaches used to minimize register-memory operations on RISC machines.

13.3 If a circular register buffer is used to handle local variables for nested procedures, describe two approaches for handling global variables.

13.4 What are some typical characteristics of a RISC instruction set architecture?

13.5 What is a delayed branch?

Problems

13.1 Considering the call-return pattern in Figure 4.21, how many overflows and underflows (each of which causes a register save/restore) will occur with a window size of
   a. 5?
   b. 8?
   c. 16?

13.2 In the discussion of Figure 13.2, it was stated that only the first two portions of a window are saved or restored. Why is it not necessary to save the temporary registers?

13.3 We wish to determine the execution time for a given program using the various pipelining schemes discussed in Section 13.5. Let

$$N = \text{number of executed instructions}$$
$$D = \text{number of memory accesses}$$
$$J = \text{number of jump instructions}$$

For the simple sequential scheme (Figure 13.6a), the execution time is $2N + D$ stages. Derive formulas for two-stage, three-stage, and four-stage pipelining.

13.4 Reorganize the code sequence in Figure 13.6d to reduce the number of NOOPs.

13.5 Consider the following code fragment in a high-level language:

> **for** I **in** 1...100 **loop**
> $S \leftarrow S + Q(I).\text{VAL}$
> **end loop;**

Assume that Q is an array of 32-byte records and the VAL field is in the first 4 bytes of each record. Using x86 code, we can compile this program fragment as follows:

```
        MOV     ECX,1           ;use register ECX to hold I
LP:     IMUL    EAX, ECX, 32    ;get offset in EAX
        MOV     EBX, Q[EAX]     ;load VAL field
        ADD     S, EBX          ;add to S
        INC     ECX             ;increment I
        CMP     ECX, 101        :compare to 101
        JNE     LP              ;loop until I = 100
```

This program makes use of the IMUL instruction, which multiplies the second operand by the immediate value in the third operand and places the result in the first operand (see Problem 10.13). A RISC advocate would like to demonstrate that a clever compiler can eliminate unnecessarily complex instructions such as IMUL. Provide the demonstration by rewriting the above x86 program without using the IMUL instruction.

13.6 Consider the following loop:

> S := 0;
> **for** K := 1 **to** 100 **do**
>   S : = S − K;

A straightforward translation of this into a generic assembly language would look something like this:

```
            LD      R1, 0           ;keep value of S in R1
            LD      R2, 1           ;keep value of K in R2
    LP      SUB     R1, R1, R2      ;S := S − K
            BEQ     R2, 100, EXIT   ;done if K = 100
            ADD     R2, R2, 1       ;else increment K
            JMP     LP              ;back to start of loop
```

A compiler for a RISC machine will introduce delay slots into this code so that the processor can employ the delayed branch mechanism. The JMP instruction is easy to deal with, because this instruction is always followed by the SUB instruction; therefore, we can simply place a copy of the SUB instruction in the delay slot after the JMP. The BEQ presents a difficulty. We can't leave the code as is, because the ADD instruction would then be executed one too many times. Therefore, a NOP instruction is needed. Show the resulting code.

13.7   A RISC machine may do both a mapping of symbolic registers to actual registers and a rearrangement of instructions for pipeline efficiency. An interesting question arises as to the order in which these two operations should be done. Consider the following program fragment:

```
        LD      SR1, A          ;load A into symbolic register 1
        LD      SR2, B          ;load B into symbolic register 2
        ADD     SR3, SR1, SR2   ;add contents of SR1 and SR2 and store in SR3
        LD      SR4, C
        LD      SR5, D
        ADD     SR6, SR4, SR5
```

   a. First do the register mapping and then any possible instruction reordering. How many machine registers are used? Has there been any pipeline improvement?
   b. Starting with the original program, now do instruction reordering and then any possible mapping. How many machine registers are used? Has there been any pipeline improvement?

13.8   Add entries for the following processors to Table 13.7:
   a. Pentium II
   b. ARM

13.9   In many cases, common machine instructions that are not listed as part of the MIPS instruction set can be synthesized with a single MIPS instruction. Show this for the following:
   a. Register-to-register move
   b. Increment, decrement
   c. Complement
   d. Negate
   e. Clear

13.10   A SPARC implementation has K register windows. What is the number N of physical registers?

13.11   SPARC is lacking a number of instructions commonly found on CISC machines. Some of these are easily simulated using either register R0, which is always set to 0, or a constant operand. These simulated instructions are called pseudoinstructions and are recognized by the SPARC compiler. Show how to simulate the following pseudoinstructions, each with a single SPARC instruction. In all of these, src and dst refer to registers. (*Hint:* A store to R0 has no effect.)

   a. MOV src, dst   d. NOT dst   g. DEC dst
   b. COMPARE src1, src2   e. NEG dst   h. CLR dst
   c. TEST src1   f. INC dst   i. NOP

13.12 Consider the following code fragment:

> **if** K > 10
>> L := K + 1
> **else**
>> L := K − 1;

A straightforward translation of this statement into SPARC assembler could take the following form:

```
         sethi  %hi(K), %r8              ;load high-order 22 bits of address of location
                                         ;K into register r8
         ld     [%r8 + %lo(K)], %r8      ;load contents of location K into r8
         cmp    %r8, 10                  ;compare contents of r8 with 10
         ble    L1                       ;branch if (r8) ≤ 10
         nop
         sethi  %hi(K), %r9
         ld     [%r9 + %lo(K)], %r9      ;load contents of location K into r9
         inc    %r9                      ;add 1 to (r9)
         sethi  %hi(L), %r10
         st     %r9, [%r10 + %lo(L)]     ;store (r9) into location L
         b      L2
         nop
L1:      sethi  %hi(K), %r11
         ld     [%r11 + %lo(K)], %r12    ;load contents of location K into r12
         dec    %r12                     ;subtract 1 from (r12)
         sethi  %hi(L), %r13
         st     %r12, [%r13 + %lo(L)]    ;store (r12) into location L
L2:
```

The code contains a nop after each branch instruction to permit delayed branch operation.

a. Standard compiler optimizations that have nothing to do with RISC machines are generally effective in being able to perform two transformations on the foregoing code. Notice that two of the loads are unnecessary and that the two stores can be merged if the store is moved to a different place in the code. Show the program after making these two changes.

b. It is now possible to perform some optimizations peculiar to SPARC. The nop after the ble can be replaced by moving another instruction into that delay slot and setting the annul bit on the ble instruction (expressed as ble,a L1). Show the program after this change.

c. There are now two unnecessary instructions. Remove these and show the resulting program.

CHAPTER 14

INSTRUCTION-LEVEL PARALLELISM AND SUPERSCALAR PROCESSORS

KEY POINTS

◆ A **superscalar processor** is one in which multiple independent instruction pipelines are used. Each pipeline consists of multiple stages, so that each pipeline can handle multiple instructions at a time. Multiple pipelines introduce a new level of parallelism, enabling multiple streams of instructions to be processed at a time. A superscalar processor exploits what is known as **instruction-level parallelism**, which refers to the degree to which the instructions of a program can be executed in parallel.

◆ A superscalar processor typically fetches multiple instructions at a time and then attempts to find nearby instructions that are independent of one another and can therefore be executed in parallel. If the input to one instruction depends on the output of a preceding instruction, then the latter instruction cannot complete execution at the same time or before the former instruction. Once such dependencies have been identified, the processor may issue and complete instructions in an order that differs from that of the original machine code.

◆ The processor may eliminate some unnecessary dependencies by the use of additional registers and the renaming of register references in the original code.

◆ Whereas pure RISC processors often employ delayed branches to maximize the utilization of the instruction pipeline, this method is less appropriate to a superscalar machine. Instead, most superscalar machines use traditional branch prediction methods to improve efficiency.

A superscalar implementation of a processor architecture is one in which common instructions—integer and floating-point arithmetic, loads, stores, and conditional branches—can be initiated simultaneously and executed independently. Such implementations raise a number of complex design issues related to the instruction pipeline.

Superscalar design arrived on the scene hard on the heels of RISC architecture. Although the simplified instruction set architecture of a RISC machine lends itself readily to superscalar techniques, the superscalar approach can be used on either a RISC or CISC architecture.

Whereas the gestation period for the arrival of commercial RISC machines from the beginning of true RISC research with the IBM 801 and the Berkeley RISC I was seven or eight years, the first superscalar machines became commercially available within just a year or two of the coining of the term *superscalar*. The superscalar approach has now become the standard method for implementing high-performance microprocessors.

In this chapter, we begin with an overview of the superscalar approach, contrasting it with superpipelining. Next, we present the key design issues associated with superscalar implementation. Then we look at several important examples of superscalar architecture.

14.1 OVERVIEW

The term *superscalar,* first coined in 1987 [AGER87], refers to a machine that is designed to improve the performance of the execution of scalar instructions. In most applications, the bulk of the operations are on scalar quantities. Accordingly, the superscalar approach represents the next step in the evolution of high-performance general-purpose processors.

The essence of the superscalar approach is the ability to execute instructions independently and concurrently in different pipelines. The concept can be further exploited by allowing instructions to be executed in an order different from the program order. Figure 14.1 shows, in general terms, the superscalar approach. There are multiple functional units, each of which is implemented as a pipeline, which support parallel execution of several instructions. In this example, two integer, two floating-point, and one memory (either load or store) operations can be executing at the same time.

Many researchers have investigated superscalar-like processors, and their research indicates that some degree of performance improvement is possible. Table 14.1 presents the reported performance advantages. The differences in the results arise from differences both in the hardware of the simulated machine and in the applications being simulated.

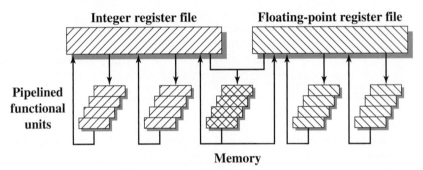

Figure 14.1   General Superscalar Organization

Table 14.1   Reported Speedups of Superscalar-Like Machines

Reference	Speedup
[TJAD70]	1.8
[KUCK77]	8
[WEIS84]	1.58
[ACOS86]	2.7
[SOHI90]	1.8
[SMIT89]	2.3
[JOUP89b]	2.2
[LEE91]	7

Superscalar versus Superpipelined

An alternative approach to achieving greater performance is referred to as super-pipelining, a term first coined in 1988 [JOUP88]. Superpipelining exploits the fact that many pipeline stages perform tasks that require less than half a clock cycle. Thus, a doubled internal clock speed allows the performance of two tasks in one external clock cycle. We have seen one example of this approach with the MIPS R4000.

Figure 14.2 compares the two approaches. The upper part of the diagram illustrates an ordinary pipeline, used as a base for comparison. The base pipeline issues one instruction per clock cycle and can perform one pipeline stage per clock cycle.

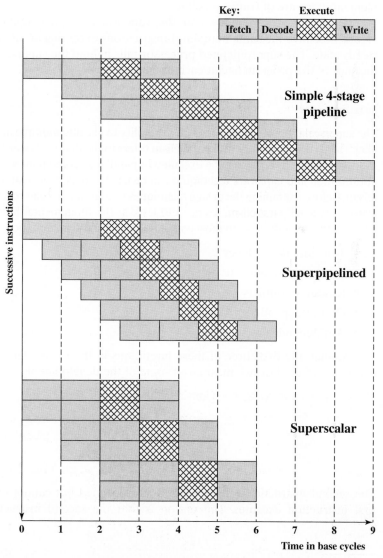

Figure 14.2   Comparison of Superscalar and Superpipeline Approaches

The pipeline has four stages: instruction fetch, operation decode, operation execution, and result write back. The execution stage is crosshatched for clarity. Note that although several instructions are executing concurrently, only one instruction is in its execution stage at any one time.

The next part of the diagram shows a superpipelined implementation that is capable of performing two pipeline stages per clock cycle. An alternative way of looking at this is that the functions performed in each stage can be split into two nonoverlapping parts and each can execute in half a clock cycle. A superpipeline implementation that behaves in this fashion is said to be of degree 2. Finally, the lowest part of the diagram shows a superscalar implementation capable of executing two instances of each stage in parallel. Higher-degree superpipeline and superscalar implementations are of course possible.

Both the superpipeline and the superscalar implementations depicted in Figure 14.2 have the same number of instructions executing at the same time in the steady state. The superpipelined processor falls behind the superscalar processor at the start of the program and at each branch target.

Limitations

The superscalar approach depends on the ability to execute multiple instructions in parallel. The term **instruction-level parallelism** refers to the degree to which, on average, the instructions of a program can be executed in parallel. A combination of compiler-based optimization and hardware techniques can be used to maximize instruction-level parallelism. Before examining the design techniques used in superscalar machines to increase instruction-level parallelism, we need to look at the fundamental limitations to parallelism with which the system must cope. [JOHN91] lists five limitations:

- True data dependency
- Procedural dependency
- Resource conflicts
- Output dependency
- Antidependency

We examine the first three of these limitations in the remainder of this section. A discussion of the last two must await some of the developments in the next section.

TRUE DATA DEPENDENCY Consider the following sequence:[1]

```
ADD  EAX,  ECX  ;load register EAX with the con-
                 tents of ECX plus the contents
                 of EAX
MOV  EBX,  EAX  ;load EBX with the contents of EAX
```

The second instruction can be fetched and decoded but cannot execute until the first instruction executes. The reason is that the second instruction needs data

---

[1]For the Intel x86 assembly language, a semicolon starts a comment field.

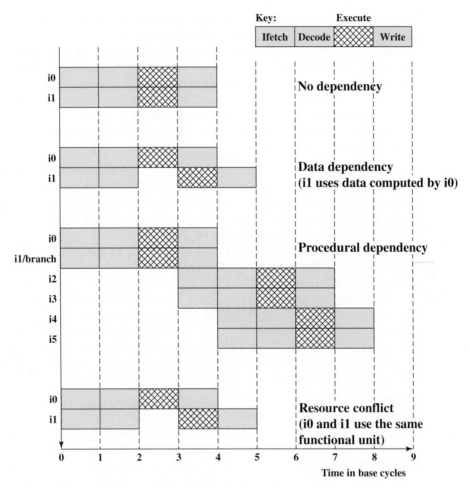

Figure 14.3 Effect of Dependencies

produced by the first instruction. This situation is referred to as a **true data dependency** (also called **flow dependency** or **write after read [WAR] dependency**).

Figure 14.3 illustrates this dependency in a superscalar machine of degree 2. With no dependency, two instructions can be fetched and executed in parallel. If there is a data dependency between the first and second instructions, then the second instruction is delayed as many clock cycles as required to remove the dependency. In general, any instruction must be delayed until all of its input values have been produced.

In a simple pipeline, such as illustrated in the upper part of Figure 14.2, the aforementioned sequence of instructions would cause no delay. However, consider the following, in which one of the loads is from memory rather than from a register:

```
MOV   EAX,   eff   ;load register EAX with the con-
                    tents  of  effective  memory  ad-
                    dress eff
MOV   EBX,   EAX   ;load EBX with the contents of EAX
```

A typical RISC processor takes two or more cycles to perform a load from memory when the load is a cache hit. It can take tens or even hundreds of cycles for a cache miss on all cache levels, because of the delay of an off-chip memory access. One way to compensate for this delay is for the compiler to reorder instructions so that one or more subsequent instructions that do not depend on the memory load can begin flowing through the pipeline. This scheme is less effective in the case of a superscalar pipeline: The independent instructions executed during the load are likely to be executed on the first cycle of the load, leaving the processor with nothing to do until the load completes.

PROCEDURAL DEPENDENCIES As was discussed in Chapter 12, the presence of branches in an instruction sequence complicates the pipeline operation. The instructions following a branch (taken or not taken) have a procedural dependency on the branch and cannot be executed until the branch is executed. Figure 14.3 illustrates the effect of a branch on a superscalar pipeline of degree 2.

As we have seen, this type of procedural dependency also affects a scalar pipeline. The consequence for a superscalar pipeline is more severe, because a greater magnitude of opportunity is lost with each delay.

If variable-length instructions are used, then another sort of procedural dependency arises. Because the length of any particular instruction is not known, it must be at least partially decoded before the following instruction can be fetched. This prevents the simultaneous fetching required in a superscalar pipeline. This is one of the reasons that superscalar techniques are more readily applicable to a RISC or RISC-like architecture, with its fixed instruction length.

RESOURCE CONFLICT A resource conflict is a competition of two or more instructions for the same resource at the same time. Examples of resources include memories, caches, buses, register-file ports, and functional units (e.g., ALU adder).

In terms of the pipeline, a resource conflict exhibits similar behavior to a data dependency (Figure 14.3). There are some differences, however. For one thing, resource conflicts can be overcome by duplication of resources, whereas a true data dependency cannot be eliminated. Also, when an operation takes a long time to complete, resource conflicts can be minimized by pipelining the appropriate functional unit.

14.2 DESIGN ISSUES

Instruction-Level Parallelism and Machine Parallelism

[JOUP89a] makes an important distinction between the two related concepts of instruction-level parallelism and machine parallelism. **Instruction-level parallelism** exists when instructions in a sequence are independent and thus can be executed in parallel by overlapping.

As an example of the concept of instruction-level parallelism, consider the following two code fragments [JOUP89b]:

```
Load R1 ← R2        Add R3 ← R3, "1"
Add R3 ← R3, "1"    Add R4 ← R3, R2
Add R4 ← R4, R2     Store [R4] ← R0
```

The three instructions on the left are independent, and in theory all three could be executed in parallel. In contrast, the three instructions on the right cannot be executed in parallel because the second instruction uses the result of the first, and the third instruction uses the result of the second.

The degree of instruction-level parallelism is determined by the frequency of true data dependencies and procedural dependencies in the code. These factors, in turn, are dependent on the instruction set architecture and on the application. Instruction-level parallelism is also determined by what [JOUP89a] refers to as operation latency: the time until the result of an instruction is available for use as an operand in a subsequent instruction. The latency determines how much of a delay a data or procedural dependency will cause.

Machine parallelism is a measure of the ability of the processor to take advantage of instruction-level parallelism. Machine parallelism is determined by the number of instructions that can be fetched and executed at the same time (the number of parallel pipelines) and by the speed and sophistication of the mechanisms that the processor uses to find independent instructions.

Both instruction-level and machine parallelism are important factors in enhancing performance. A program may not have enough instruction-level parallelism to take full advantage of machine parallelism. The use of a fixed-length instruction set architecture, as in a RISC, enhances instruction-level parallelism. On the other hand, limited machine parallelism will limit performance no matter what the nature of the program.

Instruction Issue Policy

As was mentioned, machine parallelism is not simply a matter of having multiple instances of each pipeline stage. The processor must also be able to identify instruction-level parallelism and orchestrate the fetching, decoding, and execution of instructions in parallel. [JOHN91] uses the term **instruction issue** to refer to the process of initiating instruction execution in the processor's functional units and the term **instruction issue policy** to refer to the protocol used to issue instructions. In general, we can say that instruction issue occurs when instruction moves from the decode stage of the pipeline to the first execute stage of the pipeline.

In essence, the processor is trying to look ahead of the current point of execution to locate instructions that can be brought into the pipeline and executed. Three types of orderings are important in this regard:

- The order in which instructions are fetched
- The order in which instructions are executed
- The order in which instructions update the contents of register and memory locations

The more sophisticated the processor, the less it is bound by a strict relationship between these orderings. To optimize utilization of the various pipeline elements, the processor will need to alter one or more of these orderings with respect to the ordering to be found in a strict sequential execution. The one constraint on the processor is that the result must be correct. Thus, the processor must accommodate the various dependencies and conflicts discussed earlier.

In general terms, we can group superscalar instruction issue policies into the following categories:

- In-order issue with in-order completion
- In-order issue with out-of-order completion
- Out-of-order issue with out-of-order completion

IN-ORDER ISSUE WITH IN-ORDER COMPLETION The simplest instruction issue policy is to issue instructions in the exact order that would be achieved by sequential execution (in-order issue) and to write results in that same order (in-order completion). Not even scalar pipelines follow such a simple-minded policy. However, it is useful to consider this policy as a baseline for comparing more sophisticated approaches.

Figure 14.4a gives an example of this policy. We assume a superscalar pipeline capable of fetching and decoding two instructions at a time, having three separate functional units (e.g., two integer arithmetic and one floating-point arithmetic), and having two instances of the write-back pipeline stage. The example assumes the following constraints on a six-instruction code fragment:

- I1 requires two cycles to execute.
- I3 and I4 conflict for the same functional unit.
- I5 depends on the value produced by I4.
- I5 and I6 conflict for a functional unit.

Instructions are fetched two at a time and passed to the decode unit. Because instructions are fetched in pairs, the next two instructions must wait until the pair of decode pipeline stages has cleared. To guarantee in-order completion, when there is a conflict for a functional unit or when a functional unit requires more than one cycle to generate a result, the issuing of instructions temporarily stalls.

In this example, the elapsed time from decoding the first instruction to writing the last results is eight cycles.

IN-ORDER ISSUE WITH OUT-OF-ORDER COMPLETION Out-of-order completion is used in scalar RISC processors to improve the performance of instructions that require multiple cycles. Figure 14.4b illustrates its use on a superscalar processor. Instruction I2 is allowed to run to completion prior to I1. This allows I3 to be completed earlier, with the net result of a savings of one cycle.

With out-of-order completion, any number of instructions may be in the execution stage at any one time, up to the maximum degree of machine parallelism across all functional units. Instruction issuing is stalled by a resource conflict, a data dependency, or a procedural dependency.

In addition to the aforementioned limitations, a new dependency, which we referred to earlier as an **output dependency** (also called **write after write (WAW) dependency**), arises. The following code fragment illustrates this dependency (*op* represents any operation):

```
I1: R3 ← R3 op R5
I2: R4 ← R3 + 1
I3: R3 ← R5 + 1
I4: R7 ← R3 op R4
```

Decode		Execute				Write		Cycle
I1	I2							1
I3	I4	I1	I2					2
I3	I4	I1						3
	I4				I3	I1	I2	4
I5	I6				I4			5
	I6			I5		I3	I4	6
				I6				7
						I5	I6	8

(a) In-order issue and in-order completion

Decode		Execute				Write		Cycle
I1	I2							1
I3	I4	I1	I2					2
	I4	I1			I3	I2		3
I5	I6				I4	I1	I3	4
	I6			I5		I4		5
				I6		I5		6
						I6		7

(b) In-order issue and out-of-order completion

Decode		Window	Execute			Write		Cycle
I1	I2							1
I3	I4	I1, I2	I1	I2				2
I5	I6	I3, I4	I1		I3	I2		3
		I4, I5, I6		I6	I4	I1	I3	4
		I5		I5		I4	I6	5
						I5		6

(c) Out-of-order issue and out-of-order completion

Figure 14.4 Superscalar Instruction Issue and Completion Policies

Instruction I2 cannot execute before instruction I1, because it needs the result in register R3 produced in I1; this is an example of a true data dependency, as described in Section 14.1. Similarly, I4 must wait for I3, because it uses a result produced by I3. What about the relationship between I1 and I3? There is no data dependency here, as we have defined it. However, if I3 executes to completion prior to I1, then the wrong value of the contents of R3 will be fetched for the execution of I4. Consequently, I3 must complete after I1 to produce the correct output values. To ensure this, the issuing of the third instruction must be stalled if its result might later be overwritten by an older instruction that takes longer to complete.

Out-of-order completion requires more complex instruction issue logic than in-order completion. In addition, it is more difficult to deal with instruction interrupts and exceptions. When an interrupt occurs, instruction execution at the current point is suspended, to be resumed later. The processor must assure that the resumption takes into account that, at the time of interruption, instructions ahead of the instruction that caused the interrupt may already have completed.

OUT-OF-ORDER ISSUE WITH OUT-OF-ORDER COMPLETION With in-order issue, the processor will only decode instructions up to the point of a dependency or conflict. No additional instructions are decoded until the conflict is resolved. As a result, the processor cannot look ahead of the point of conflict to subsequent instructions that may be independent of those already in the pipeline and that may be usefully introduced into the pipeline.

To allow out-of-order issue, it is necessary to decouple the decode and execute stages of the pipeline. This is done with a buffer referred to as an **instruction window**. With this organization, after a processor has finished decoding an instruction, it is placed in the instruction window. As long as this buffer is not full, the processor can continue to fetch and decode new instructions. When a functional unit becomes available in the execute stage, an instruction from the instruction window may be issued to the execute stage. Any instruction may be issued, provided that (1) it needs the particular functional unit that is available, and (2) no conflicts or dependencies block this instruction.

The result of this organization is that the processor has a lookahead capability, allowing it to identify independent instructions that can be brought into the execute stage. Instructions are issued from the instruction window with little regard for their original program order. As before, the only constraint is that the program execution behaves correctly.

Figures 14.4c illustrates this policy. During each of the first three cycles, two instructions are fetched into the decode stage. During each cycle, subject to the constraint of the buffer size, two instructions move from the decode stage to the instruction window. In this example, it is possible to issue instruction I6 ahead of I5 (recall that I5 depends on I4, but I6 does not). Thus, one cycle is saved in both the execute and write-back stages, and the end-to-end savings, compared with Figure 14.4b, is one cycle.

The instruction window is depicted in Figure 14.4c to illustrate its role. However, this window is not an additional pipeline stage. An instruction being in the window simply implies that the processor has sufficient information about that instruction to decide when it can be issued.

The out-of-order issue, out-of-order completion policy is subject to the same constraints described earlier. An instruction cannot be issued if it violates a dependency or conflict. The difference is that more instructions are available for issuing, reducing the probability that a pipeline stage will have to stall. In addition, a new dependency, which we referred to earlier as an **antidependency** (also called **read after write (RAW) dependency**), arises. The code fragment considered earlier illustrates this dependency:

```
I1: R3 ← R3 op R5
I2: R4 ← R3 + 1
I3: R3 ← R5 + 1
I4: R7 ← R3 op R4
```

Instruction I3 cannot complete execution before instruction I2 begins execution and has fetched its operands. This is so because I3 updates register R3, which is a source operand for I2. The term *antidependency* is used because the constraint is similar to that of a true data dependency, but reversed: Instead of the first instruction producing a value that the second instruction uses, the second instruction destroys a value that the first instruction uses.

Reorder Buffer Simulator
Tomasulo's Algorithm Simulator
Alternative Simulation of Tomasulo's Algorithm

One common technique that is used to support out-of-order completion is the reorder buffer. The reorder buffer is temporary storage for results completed out of order that are then committed to the register file in program order. A related concept is Tomasulo's algorithm. Appendix I examines these concepts.

Register Renaming

When out-of-order instruction issuing and/or out-of-order instruction completion are allowed, we have seen that this gives rise to the possibility of WAW dependencies and WAR dependencies. These dependencies differ from RAW data dependencies and resource conflicts, which reflect the flow of data through a program and the sequence of execution. WAW dependencies and WAR dependencies, on the other hand, arise because the values in registers may no longer reflect the sequence of values dictated by the program flow.

When instructions are issued in sequence and complete in sequence, it is possible to specify the contents of each register at each point in the execution. When out-of-order techniques are used, the values in registers cannot be fully known at each point in time just from a consideration of the sequence of instructions dictated by the program. In effect, values are in conflict for the use of registers, and the processor must resolve those conflicts by occasionally stalling a pipeline stage.

Antidependencies and output dependencies are both examples of storage conflicts. Multiple instructions are competing for the use of the same register locations, generating pipeline constraints that retard performance. The problem is made more acute when register optimization techniques are used (as discussed in Chapter 13), because these compiler techniques attempt to maximize the use of registers, hence maximizing the number of storage conflicts.

One method for coping with these types of storage conflicts is based on a traditional resource-conflict solution: duplication of resources. In this context, the technique is referred to as **register renaming**. In essence, registers are allocated dynamically by the processor hardware, and they are associated with the values needed by instructions at various points in time. When a new register value is created (i.e., when an instruction executes that has a register as a destination operand), a new register is allocated for that value. Subsequent instructions that access that value as a source operand in that register must go through a renaming process: the register references in those instructions must be revised to refer to the register containing the needed value. Thus, the same original register reference in several different instructions may refer to different actual registers, if different values are intended.

Let us consider how register renaming could be used on the code fragment we have been examining:

$$I1: R3_b \leftarrow R3_a \text{ op } R5_a$$
$$I2: R4_b \leftarrow R3_b + 1$$
$$I3: R3_c \leftarrow R5_a + 1$$
$$I4: R7_b \leftarrow R3_c \text{ op } R4_b$$

The register reference without the subscript refers to the logical register reference found in the instruction. The register reference with the subscript refers to a hardware register allocated to hold a new value. When a new allocation is made for a particular logical register, subsequent instruction references to that logical register as a source operand are made to refer to the most recently allocated hardware register (recent in terms of the program sequence of instructions).

In this example, the creation of register $R3_c$ in instruction I3 avoids the RAW dependency on the second instruction and the output dependency on the first instruction, and it does not interfere with the correct value being accessed by I4. The result is that I3 can be issued immediately; without renaming, I3 cannot be issued until the first instruction is complete and the second instruction is issued.

Scoreboarding Simulator

An alternative to register renaming is a scoreboarding. In essence, scoreboarding is a bookkeeping technique that allows instructions to execute whenever they are not dependent on previous instructions and no structural hazards are present. See Appendix I for a discussion.

Machine Parallelism

In the preceding, we have looked at three hardware techniques that can be used in a superscalar processor to enhance performance: duplication of resources, out-of-order issue, and renaming. One study that illuminates the relationship among these techniques was reported in [SMIT89]. The study made use of a simulation that modeled a machine with the characteristics of the MIPS R2000, augmented with various superscalar features. A number of different program sequences were simulated.

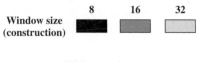

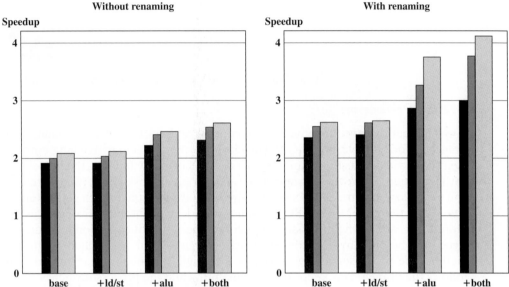

Figure 14.5 Speedups of Various Machine Organizations without Procedural Dependencies

Figure 14.5 shows the results. In each of the graphs, the vertical axis corresponds to the mean speedup of the superscalar machine over the scalar machine. The horizontal axis shows the results for four alternative processor organizations. The base machine does not duplicate any of the functional units, but it can issue instructions out of order. The second configuration duplicates the load/store functional unit that accesses a data cache. The third configuration duplicates the ALU, and the fourth configuration duplicates both load/store and ALU. In each graph, results are shown for instruction window sizes of 8, 16, and 32 instructions, which dictates the amount of lookahead the processor can do. The difference between the two graphs is that, in the second, register renaming is allowed. This is equivalent to saying that the first graph reflects a machine that is limited by all dependencies, whereas the second graph corresponds to a machine that is limited only by true dependencies.

The two graphs, combined, yield some important conclusions. The first is that it is probably not worthwhile to add functional units without register renaming. There is some slight improvement in performance, but at the cost of increased hardware complexity. With register renaming, which eliminates antidependencies and output dependencies, noticeable gains are achieved by adding more functional units. Note, however, that there is a significant difference in the amount of gain achievable between using an instruction window of 8 versus a larger instruction window. This indicates that if the instruction window is too small, data dependencies will prevent effective utilization of the extra functional units; the processor must be able to look quite far ahead to find independent instructions to utilize the hardware more fully.

Pipeline with Static Vs. Dynamic Scheduling—Simulator

Branch Prediction

Any high-performance pipelined machine must address the issue of dealing with branches. For example, the Intel 80486 addressed the problem by fetching both the next sequential instruction after a branch and speculatively fetching the branch target instruction. However, because there are two pipeline stages between prefetch and execution, this strategy incurs a two-cycle delay when the branch gets taken.

With the advent of RISC machines, the delayed branch strategy was explored. This allows the processor to calculate the result of conditional branch instructions before any unusable instructions have been prefetched. With this method, the processor always executes the single instruction that immediately follows the branch. This keeps the pipeline full while the processor fetches a new instruction stream.

With the development of superscalar machines, the delayed branch strategy has less appeal. The reason is that multiple instructions need to execute in the delay slot, raising several problems relating to instruction dependencies. Thus, superscalar machines have returned to pre-RISC techniques of branch prediction. Some, like the PowerPC 601, use a simple static branch prediction technique. More sophisticated processors, such as the PowerPC 620 and the Pentium 4, use dynamic branch prediction based on branch history analysis.

Superscalar Execution

We are now in a position to provide an overview of superscalar execution of programs; this is illustrated in Figure 14.6. The program to be executed consists of a linear sequence of instructions. This is the static program as written by the programmer or generated by the compiler. The instruction fetch process, which includes branch prediction, is used to form a dynamic stream of instructions. This stream is examined for dependencies, and the processor may remove artificial dependencies. The processor then dispatches the instructions into a window of execution. In this window, instructions no longer form a sequential stream but are structured according to their true data dependencies. The processor performs the execution stage of each instruction in an order determined by the true data dependencies and hardware resource availability. Finally, instructions are conceptually put back into sequential order and their results are recorded.

The final step mentioned in the preceding paragraph is referred to as **committing**, or **retiring**, the instruction. This step is needed for the following reason. Because of the use of parallel, multiple pipelines, instructions may complete in an

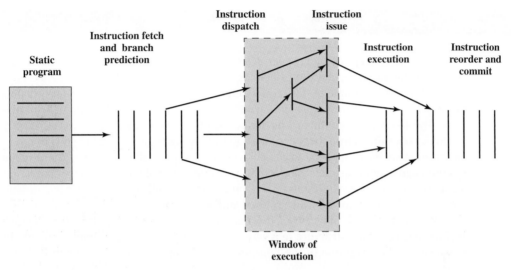

Figure 14.6   Conceptual Depiction of Superscalar Processing

order different from that shown in the static program. Further, the use of branch prediction and speculative execution means that some instructions may complete execution and then must be abandoned because the branch they represent is not taken. Therefore, permanent storage and program-visible registers cannot be updated immediately when instructions complete execution. Results must be held in some sort of temporary storage that is usable by dependent instructions and then made permanent when it is determined that the sequential model would have executed the instruction.

Superscalar Implementation

Based on our discussion so far, we can make some general comments about the processor hardware required for the superscalar approach. [SMIT95] lists the following key elements:

- Instruction fetch strategies that simultaneously fetch multiple instructions, often by predicting the outcomes of, and fetching beyond, conditional branch instructions. These functions require the use of multiple pipeline fetch and decode stages, and branch prediction logic.
- Logic for determining true dependencies involving register values, and mechanisms for communicating these values to where they are needed during execution.
- Mechanisms for initiating, or issuing, multiple instructions in parallel.
- Resources for parallel execution of multiple instructions, including multiple pipelined functional units and memory hierarchies capable of simultaneously servicing multiple memory references.
- Mechanisms for committing the process state in correct order.

14.3 PENTIUM 4

Although the concept of superscalar design is generally associated with the RISC architecture, the same superscalar principles can be applied to a CISC machine. Perhaps the most notable example of this is the Pentium. The evolution of superscalar concepts in the Intel line is interesting to note. The 386 is a traditional CISC nonpipelined machine. The 486 introduced the first pipelined x86 processor, reducing the average latency of integer operations from between two and four cycles to one cycle, but still limited to executing a single instruction each cycle, with no superscalar elements. The original Pentium had a modest superscalar component, consisting of the use of two separate integer execution units. The Pentium Pro introduced a full-blown superscalar design. Subsequent Pentium models have refined and enhanced the superscalar design.

A general block diagram of the Pentium 4 was shown in Figure 4.18. Figure 14.7 depicts the same structure in a way more suitable for the pipeline discussion in this section. The operation of the Pentium 4 can be summarized as follows:

1. The processor fetches instructions from memory in the order of the static program.

2. Each instruction is translated into one or more fixed-length RISC instructions, known as **micro-operations**, or **micro-ops**.

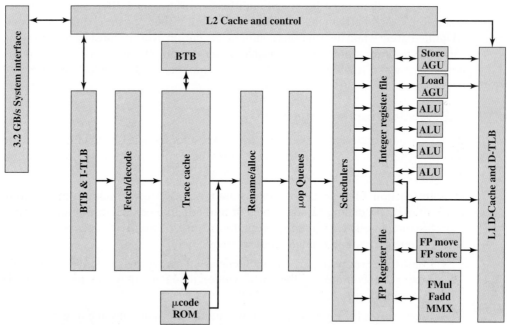

AGU   = address generation unit
BTB   = branch target buffer
D-TLB = data translation lookaside buffer
I-TLB = instruction translation lookaside buffer

Figure 14.7   Pentium 4 Block Diagram

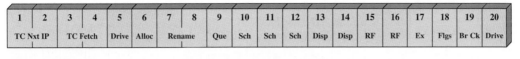

1	2	3	4	5	6	7	8	9	10	11	12	13	14	15	16	17	18	19	20
TC Nxt IP		TC Fetch		Drive	Alloc	Rename		Que	Sch	Sch	Sch	Disp	Disp	RF	RF	Ex	Flgs	Br Ck	Drive

TC Next IP = trace cache next instruction pointer   Rename = register renaming   RF = register file
TC Fetch = trace cache fetch   Que = micro-op queuing   Ex = execute
Alloc = allocate   Sch = micro-op scheduling   Flgs = flags
                                                    Disp = Dispatch   Br Ck = branch check

Figure 14.8   Pentium 4 Pipeline

3. The processor executes the micro-ops on a superscalar pipeline organization, so that the micro-ops may be executed out of order.

4. The processor commits the results of each micro-op execution to the processor's register set in the order of the original program flow.

In effect, the Pentium 4 architecture consists of an outer CISC shell with an inner RISC core. The inner RISC micro-ops pass through a pipeline with at least 20 stages (Figure 14.8); in some cases, the micro-op requires multiple execution stages, resulting in an even longer pipeline. This contrasts with the five-stage pipeline (Figure 12.21) used on the earlier Intel x86 processors and on the Pentium.

We now trace the operation of the Pentium 4 pipeline, using Figure 14.9 to illustrate its operation.

Front End

GENERATION OF MICRO–OPS   The Pentium 4 organization includes an in-order front end (Figure 14.9a) that can be considered outside the scope of the pipeline depicted in Figure 14.8. This front end feeds into an L1 instruction cache, called the trace cache, which is where the pipeline proper begins. Usually, the processor operates from the trace cache; when a trace cache miss occurs, the in-order front end feeds new instructions into the trace cache.

With the aid of the branch target buffer and the instruction lookaside buffer (BTB & I-TLB), the fetch/decode unit fetches Pentium 4 machine instructions from the L2 cache 64 bytes at a time. As a default, instructions are fetched sequentially, so that each L2 cache line fetch includes the next instruction to be fetched. Branch prediction via the BTB & I-TLB unit may alter this sequential fetch operation. The ITLB translates the linear instruction pointer address given it into physical addresses needed to access the L2 cache. Static branch prediction in the front-end BTB is used to determine which instructions to fetch next.

Once instructions are fetched, the fetch/decode unit scans the bytes to determine instruction boundaries; this is a necessary operation because of the variable length of x86 instructions. The decoder translates each machine instruction into from one to four micro-ops, each of which is a 118-bit RISC instruction. Note for comparison that most pure RISC machines have an instruction length of just 32 bits. The longer micro-op length is required to accommodate the more complex Pentium operations. Nevertheless, the micro-ops are easier to manage than the original instructions from which they derive.

The generated micro-ops are stored in the trace cache.

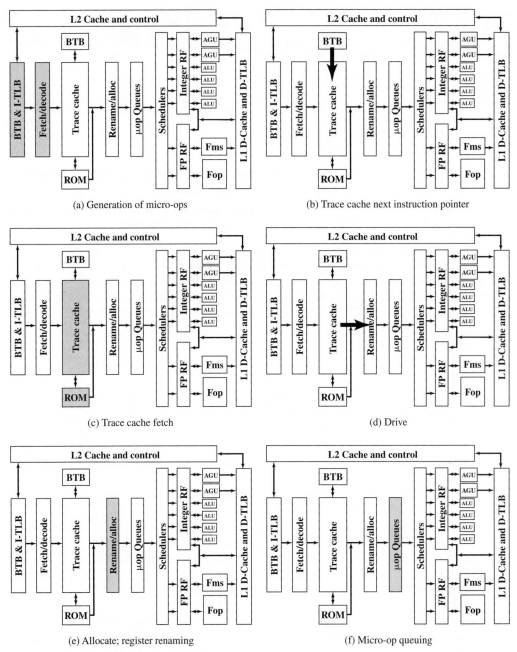

Figure 14.9 Pentium Pipeline Operation

TRACE CACHE NEXT INSTRUCTION POINTER The first two pipeline stages (Figure 14.9b) deal with the selection of instructions in the trace cache and involve a separate branch prediction mechanism from that described in the previous section. The Pentium 4 uses a dynamic branch prediction strategy based on the history of recent executions of branch instructions. A branch target buffer

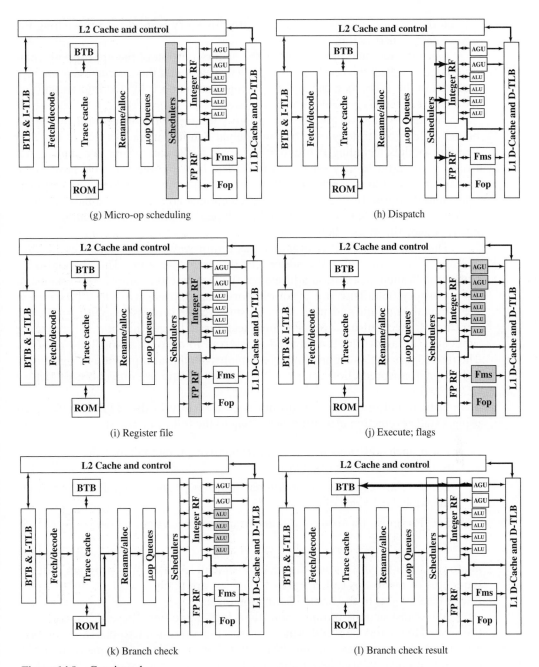

(g) Micro-op scheduling

(h) Dispatch

(i) Register file

(j) Execute; flags

(k) Branch check

(l) Branch check result

Figure 14.9 Continued

(BTB) is maintained that caches information about recently encountered branch instructions. Whenever a branch instruction is encountered in the instruction stream, the BTB is checked. If an entry already exists in the BTB, then the instruction unit is guided by the history information for that entry in determining whether to predict that the branch is taken. If a branch is predicted, then the branch destination address associated with this entry is used for prefetching the branch target instruction.

Once the instruction is executed, the history portion of the appropriate entry is updated to reflect the result of the branch instruction. If this instruction is not represented in the BTB, then the address of this instruction is loaded into an entry in the BTB; if necessary, an older entry is deleted.

The description of the preceding two paragraphs fits, in general terms, the branch prediction strategy used on the original Pentium model, as well as the later Pentium models, including Pentium 4. However, in the case of the Pentium, a relatively simple 2-bit history scheme is used. The later Pentium models have much longer pipelines (20 stages for the Pentium 4 compared with 5 stages for the Pentium) and therefore the penalty for misprediction is greater. Accordingly, the later Pentium models use a more elaborate branch prediction scheme with more history bits to reduce the misprediction rate.

The Pentium 4 BTB is organized as a four-way set-associative cache with 512 lines. Each entry uses the address of the branch as a tag. The entry also includes the branch destination address for the last time this branch was taken and a 4-bit history field. Thus use of four history bits contrasts with the 2 bits used in the original Pentium and used in most superscalar processors. With 4 bits, the Pentium 4 mechanism can take into account a longer history in predicting branches. The algorithm that is used is referred to as Yeh's algorithm [YEH91]. The developers of this algorithm have demonstrated that it provides a significant reduction in misprediction compared to algorithms that use only 2 bits of history [EVER98].

Conditional branches that do not have a history in the BTB are predicted using a static prediction algorithm, according to the following rules:

- For branch addresses that are not IP relative, predict taken if the branch is a return and not taken otherwise.
- For IP-relative backward conditional branches, predict taken. This rule reflects the typical behavior of loops.
- For IP-relative forward conditional branches, predict not taken.

TRACE CACHE FETCH   The trace cache (Figure 14.9c) takes the already-decoded micro-ops from the instruction decoder and assembles them in to program-ordered sequences of micro-ops called traces. Micro-ops are fetched sequentially from the trace cache, subject to the branch prediction logic.

A few instructions require more than four micro-ops. These instructions are transferred to microcode ROM, which contains the series of micro-ops (five or more) associated with a complex machine instruction. For example, a string instruction may translate into a very large (even hundreds), repetitive sequence of micro-ops. Thus, the microcode ROM is a microprogrammed control unit in the sense discussed in Part Four. After the microcode ROM finishes sequencing micro-ops for the current Pentium instruction, fetching resumes from the trace cache.

DRIVE   The fifth stage (Figure 14.9d) of the Pentium 4 pipeline delivers decoded instructions from the trace cache to the rename/allocator module.

Out-of-Order Execution Logic

This part of the processor reorders micro-ops to allow them to execute as quickly as their input operands are ready.

ALLOCATE The allocate stage (Figure 14.9e) allocates resources required for execution. It performs the following functions:

- If a needed resource, such as a register, is unavailable for one of the three micro-ops arriving at the allocator during a clock cycle, the allocator stalls the pipeline.
- The allocator allocates a reorder buffer (ROB) entry, which tracks the completion status of one of the 126 micro-ops that could be in process at any time.[2]
- The allocator allocates one of the 128 integer or floating-point register entries for the result data value of the micro-op, and possibly a load or store buffer used to track one of the 48 loads or 24 stores in the machine pipeline.
- The allocator allocates an entry in one of the two micro-op queues in front of the instruction schedulers.

The ROB is a circular buffer that can hold up to 126 micro-ops and also contains the 128 hardware registers. Each buffer entry consists of the following fields:

- **State:** Indicates whether this micro-op is scheduled for execution, has been dispatched for execution, or has completed execution and is ready for retirement.
- **Memory Address:** The address of the Pentium instruction that generated the micro-op.
- **Micro-op:** The actual operation.
- **Alias Register:** If the micro-op references one of the 16 architectural registers, this entry redirects that reference to one of the 128 hardware registers.

Micro-ops enter the ROB in order. Micro-ops are then dispatched from the ROB to the Dispatch/Execute unit out of order. The criterion for dispatch is that the appropriate execution unit and all necessary data items required for this micro-op are available. Finally, micro-ops are retired from the ROB in order. To accomplish in-order retirement, micro-ops are retired oldest first after each micro-op has been designated as ready for retirement.

REGISTER RENAMING The rename stage (Figure 14.9e) remaps references to the 16 architectural registers (8 floating-point registers, plus EAX, EBX, ECX, EDX, ESI, EDI, EBP, and ESP) into a set of 128 physical registers. The stage removes false dependencies caused by a limited number of architectural registers while preserving the true data dependencies (reads after writes).

---

[2]See Appendix I for a discussion of reorder buffers.

MICRO-OP QUEUING After resource allocation and register renaming, micro-ops are placed in one of two micro-op queues (Figure 14.9f), where they are held until there is room in the schedulers. One of the two queues is for memory operations (loads and stores) and the other for micro-ops that do not involve memory references. Each queue obeys a FIFO (first-in-first-out) discipline, but no order is maintained between queues. That is, a micro-op may be read out of one queue out of order with respect to micro-ops in the other queue. This provides greater flexibility to the schedulers.

MICRO-OP SCHEDULING AND DISPATCHING The schedulers (Figure 14.9g) are responsible for retrieving micro-ops from the micro-op queues and dispatching these for execution. Each scheduler looks for micro-ops in whose status indicates that the micro-op has all of its operands. If the execution unit needed by that micro-op is available, then the scheduler fetches the micro-op and dispatches it to the appropriate execution unit (Figure 14.9h). Up to six micro-ops can be dispatched in one cycle. If more than one micro-op is available for a given execution unit, then the scheduler dispatches them in sequence from the queue. This is a sort of FIFO discipline that favors in-order execution, but by this time the instruction stream has been so rearranged by dependencies and branches that it is substantially out of order.

Four ports attach the schedulers to the execution units. Port 0 is used for both integer and floating-point instructions, with the exception of simple integer operations and the handling of branch mispredictions, which are allocated to Port 1. In addition, MMX execution units are allocated between these two ports. The remaining ports are for memory loads and stores.

Integer and Floating-Point Execution Units

The integer and floating-point register files are the source for pending operations by the execution units (Figure 14.9i). The execution units retrieve values from the register files as well as from the L1 data cache (Figure 14.9j). A separate pipeline stage is used to compute flags (e.g., zero, negative); these are typically the input to a branch instruction.

A subsequent pipeline stage performs branch checking (Figure 14.9k). This function compares the actual branch result with the prediction. If a branch prediction turns out to have been wrong, then there are micro-operations in various stages of processing that must be removed from the pipeline. The proper branch destination is then provided to the Branch Predictor during a drive stage (Figure 14.9l), which restarts the whole pipeline from the new target address.

14.4 ARM CORTEX-A8

Recent implementations of the ARM architecture have seen the introduction of superscalar techniques in the instruction pipeline. In this section, we focus on the ARM Cortex-A8, which provides a good example of a RISC-based superscalar design.

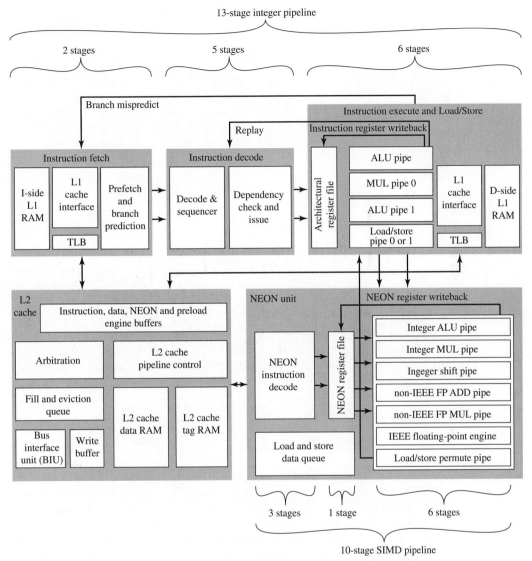

Figure 14.10 Architectural Block Diagram of ARM Cortex-A8

The Cortex-A8 is in the ARM family of processors that ARM refers to as application processors. An ARM application processor is an embedded processor running complex operating systems for wireless, consumer and imaging applications. The Cortex-A8 targets a wide variety of mobile and consumer applications including mobile phones, set-top boxes, gaming consoles and automotive navigation/ entertainment systems.

Figure 14.10 shows a logical view of the Cortex-A8 architecture, emphasizing the flow of instructions among functional units. The main instruction flow is through three functional units that implement a dual, in-order-issue, 13-stage pipeline. The

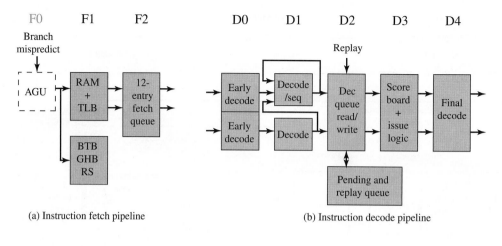

(a) Instruction fetch pipeline   (b) Instruction decode pipeline

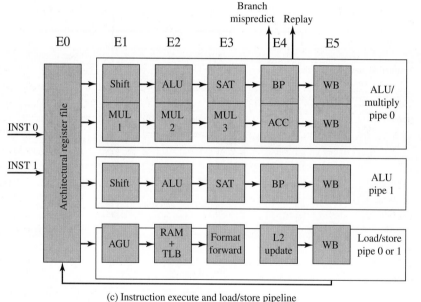

(c) Instruction execute and load/store pipeline

Figure 14.11   ARM Cortex-A8 Integer Pipeline

Cortex designers decided to stay with in-order issue to keep additional power required to a minimum. Out-of-order issue and retire can require extensive amounts of logic consuming extra power.

Figure 14.11 shows the details of the main Cortex-A8 pipeline. There is a separate unit for SIMD (single-instruction-multiple-data) unit that implements a 10-stage pipeline.

Instruction Fetch Unit

The instruction fetch unit predicts the instruction stream, fetches instructions from the L1 instruction cache, and places the fetched instructions into a buffer for consumption by the decode pipeline. The instruction fetch unit also includes the L1 instruction cache. Because there can be several unresolved branches in the pipeline, instruction fetches are speculative, meaning there is no guarantee that they are executed. A branch or exceptional instruction in the code stream can cause a pipeline flush, discarding the currently fetched instructions. The instruction fetch unit can fetch up to four instructions per cycle, and goes through the following stages:

> **F0** The address generation unit (AGU) generates a new virtual address. Normally, this address is the next address sequentially from the preceding fetch address. The address can also be a branch target address provided by a branch prediction for a previous instruction. F0 is not counted as part of the 13-stage pipeline, because ARM processors have traditionally defined instruction cache access as the first stage.

> **F1** The calculated address is used to fetch instructions from the L1 instruction cache. In parallel, the fetch address is used to access the branch prediction arrays to determine if the next fetch address should be based on a branch prediction.

> **F3** Instruction data are placed into the instruction queue. If an instruction results in branch prediction, the new target address is sent to the address generation unit.

To minimize the branch penalties typically associated with a deeper pipeline, the Cortex-A8 processor implements a two-level global history branch predictor, consisting of the branch target buffer (BTB) and the global history buffer (GHB). These data structures are accessed in parallel with instruction fetches. The BTB indicates whether or not the current fetch address will return a branch instruction and its branch target address. It contains 512 entries. On a hit in the BTB a branch is predicted and the GHB is accessed. The GHB consists of 4096 2-bit counters that encode the strength and direction information of branches. The GHB is indexed by 10-bit history of the direction of the last ten branches encountered and 4 bits of the PC. In addition to the dynamic branch predictor, a return stack is used to predict subroutine return addresses. The return stack has eight 32-bit entries that store the link register value in r14 and the ARM or Thumb state of the calling function. When a return-type instruction is predicted taken, the return stack provides the last pushed address and state.

The instruction fetch unit can fetch and queue up to 12 instructions. It issues instructions to the decode unit two at a time. The queue enables the instruction fetch unit to prefetch ahead of the rest of the integer pipeline and build up a backlog of instructions ready for decoding.

Instruction Decode Unit

The instruction decode unit decodes and sequences all ARM and Thumb instructions. It has a dual pipeline structure, called *pipe0* and *pipe1*, so that two instructions can progress through the unit at a time. When two instructions are issued from the instruction decode pipeline, pipe0 will always contain the older instruction in program order. This means that if the instruction in pipe0 cannot issue, then the instruction in pipe1 will not issue. All issued instructions progress in order down the execution pipeline with results written back into the register file at the end of the execution pipeline. This in-order instruction issue and retire prevents WAR hazards and keeps tracking of

WAW hazards and recovery from flush conditions straightforward. Thus, the main concern of the instruction decode pipeline is the prevention of RAW hazards.

Each instruction goes through five stages of processing.

D0 Thumb instructions are decompressed into 32-bit ARM instructions. A preliminary decode function is performed.

D1 The instruction decode function is completed.

D2 This stage writes instructions into and read instructions from the pending/replay queue structure.

D3 This stage contains the instruction scheduling logic. A scoreboard predicts register availability using static scheduling techniques.[3] Hazard checking is also done at this stage.

D4 Performs the final decode for all the control signals required by the integer execute and load/store units.

In the first two stages, the instruction type, the source and destination operands, and resource requirements for the instruction are determined. A few less commonly used instructions are referred to as multicycle instructions. The D1 stage breaks these instructions down into multiple instruction opcodes that are sequenced individually through the execution pipeline.

The pending queue serves two purposes. First, it prevents a stall signal from D3 from rippling any further up the pipeline. Second, by buffering instructions, there should always be two instructions available for the dual pipeline. In the case where only one instruction is issued, the pending queue enables two instructions to proceed down the pipeline together, even if they were originally sent from the fetch unit in different cycles.

The replay operation is designed to deal with the effects of the memory system on instruction timing. Instructions are statically scheduled in the D3 stage based on a prediction of when the source operand will be available. Any stall from the memory system can result in the minimum of an 8-cycle delay. This 8-cycle delay minimum is balanced with the minimum number of possible cycles to receive data from the L2 cache in the case of an L1 load miss. Table 14.2 gives the most common cases that can result in an instruction replay because of a memory system stall.

To deal with these stalls, a recovery mechanism is used to flush all subsequent instructions in the execution pipeline and reissue (replay) them. To support replay, instructions are copied into the replay queue before they are issued and removed as they write back their results and retire. If a replay signal is issued instructions are retrieved from the replay queue and reenter the pipeline.

The decode unit issues two instructions in parallel to the execution unit, unless it encounters an issue restriction. Table 14.3 shows the most common restriction cases.

Integer Execute Unit

The instruction execute unit consists of two symmetric arithmetic logic unit (ALU) pipelines, an address generator for load and store instructions, and the multiply

---

[3]See Appendix I for a discussion of scoreboarding.

Table 14.2   Cortex-A8 Memory System Effects on Instruction Timings

Replay Event	Delay	Description
Load data miss	8 cycles	**1.** A load instruction misses in the L1 data cache. **2.** A request is then made to the L2 data cache. **3.** If a miss also occurs in the L2 data cache, then a second replay occurs. The number of stall cycles depends on the external system memory timing. The minimum time required to receive the critical word for an L2 cache miss is approximately 25 cycles, but can be much longer because of L3 memory latencies.
Data TLB miss	24 cycles	**1.** A table walk because of a miss in the L1 TLB causes a 24-cycle delay, assuming the translation table entries are found in the L2 cache. **2.** If the translation table entries are not present in the L2 cache, the number of stall cycles depends on the external system memory timing.
Store buffer full	8 cycles plus latency to drain fill buffer	**1.** A store instruction miss does not result in any stalls unless the store buffer is full. **2.** In the case of a full store buffer, the delay is at least eight cycles. The delay can be more if it takes longer to drain some entries from the store buffer.
Unaligned load or store request	8 cycles	**1.** If a load instruction address is unaligned and the full access is not contained within a 128-bit boundary, there is a 8-cycle penalty. **2.** If a store instruction address is unaligned and the full access is not contained within a 64-bit boundary, there is a 8-cycle penalty.

pipeline. The execute pipelines also perform register write back. The instruction execute unit:

- Executes all integer ALU and multiply operations, including flag generation
- Generates the virtual addresses for loads and stores and the base write-back value, when required
- Supplies formatted data for stores and forwards data and flags
- Processes branches and other changes of instruction stream and evaluates instruction condition codes

For ALU instructions, either pipeline can be used, consisting of the following stages:

E0 Access register file. Up to six registers can be read from the register file for two instructions.

E1 The barrel shifter (Figure 12.25) performs its function, if needed.

E2 The ALU unit (Figure 12.25) performs its function.

E3 If needed, this stage completes saturation arithmetic used by some ARM data processing instructions.

Table 14.3   Cortex-A8 Dual-Issue Restrictions

Restriction Type	Description	Example	Cycle	Restriction

Load/store resource hazard	There is only one LS pipeline. Only one LS instruction can be issued per cycle. It can be in pipeline 0 or pipeline 1	LDR r5, [r6]
		STR r7, [r8]
		MOV r9, r10
			1
			2
			2
				Wait for LS unit
				Dual issue possible

Multiply resource hazard	There is only one multiply pipeline, and it is only available in pipeline 0.	ADD r1, r2, r3
		MUL r4, r5, r6
		MUL r7, r8, r9
			1
			2
			3
				Wait for pipeline 0
				Wait for multiply unit

Branch resource hazard	There can be only one branch per cycle. It can be in pipeline 0 or pipeline 1. A branch is any instruction that changes the PC.	BX r1 BEQ 0x1000 ADD r1, r2, r3	1 2 2	Wait for branch Dual issue possible

Data output hazard	Instructions with the same destination cannot be issued in the same cycle. This can happen with conditional code.	MOVEQ r1, r2
		MOVNE r1, r3
		
		LDR r5, [r6]
			1
			2
			
			2
				Wait because of output dependency
				Dual issue possible

Data source hazard	Instructions cannot be issued if their data is not available. See the scheduling tables for source requirements and stages results.	ADD r1, r2, r3
		ADD r4, r1, r6
		LDR r7, [r4]
			1
			2
			4
				Wait for r1
				Wait two cycles for r4

Multi-cycle instructions	Multi-cycle instructions must issue in pipeline 0 and can only dual issue in their last iteration.	MOV r1, r2
		LDM r3, {r4-r7}
		LDM (cycle 2)
		LDM (cycle 3)
		
		ADD r8, r9, r10
			1
			2
			3
			4
			
			4
				Wait for pipeline 0, transfer r4
				Transfer r5, r6
				Transfer r7
				Dual issue possible on last transfer

E4 Any change in control flow, including branch misprediction, exceptions, and memory system replays are prioritized and processed.

E5 Results of ARM instructions are written back into the register file.

Instructions that invoke the multiply unit (Figure 12.25) are routed to pipe0; the multiply operation is performed in stages E1 through E3, and the multiply accumulate operation in stage E4.

The load/store pipeline runs parallel to the integer pipeline. The stages are as follows:

E1 The memory address is generated from the base and index register.

E2 The address is applied to the cache arrays.

E3 In the case of a load, data are returned and formatted for forwarding to the ALU or MUL unit. In the case of a store, the data are formatted and ready to be written into the cache.

E4 Performs updates to the L2 cache, if required.

E5 Results of ARM instructions are written back into the register file.

Table 14.4 Cortex-A8 Example Dual Issue Instruction Sequence for Integer Pipeline

Cycle	Program Counter	Instruction	Timing Description
1	0x00000ed0	BX r14	Dual issue pipeline 0
1	0x00000ee4	CMP r0,#0	Dual issue in pipeline 1
2	0x00000ee8	MOV r3,#3	Dual issue pipeline 0
2	0x00000eec	MOV r0,#0	Dual issue in pipeline 1
3	0x00000ef0	STREQ r3,[r1,#0]	Dual issue in pipeline 0, r3 not needed until E3
3	0x00000ef4	CMP r2,#4	Dual issue in pipeline 1
4	0x00000ef8	LDRLS pc,[pc,r2,LSL #2]	Single issue pipeline 0, +1 cycle for load to pc, no extra cycle for shift since LSL #2
5	0x00000f2c	MOV r0,#1	Dual issue with 2nd iteration of load in pipeline 1
6	0x00000f30	B {pc}+8	#0xf38 dual issue pipeline 0
7	0x00000f38	STR r0,[r1,#0]	Dual issue pipeline 1
7	0x00000f3c:	LDR pc,[r13],#4	Single issue pipeline 0, +1 cycle for load to pc
8	0x0000017c	ADD r2,r4,#0xc	Dual issue with 2nd iteration of load in pipeline 1
9	0x00000180	LDR r0,[r6,#4]	Dual issue pipeline 0
9	0x00000184	MOV r1,#0xa	Dual issue pipeline 1
12	0x00000188	LDR r0,[r0,#0]	Single issue pipeline 0: r0 produced in E3, required in E1, so +2 cycle stall
13	0x0000018c	STR r0,[r4,#0]	Single issue pipeline 0 due to LS resource hazard, no extra delay for r0 since produced in E3 and consumed in E3
14	0x00000190	LDR r0,[r4,#0xc]	Single issue pipeline 0 due to LS resource hazard
15	0x00000194	LDMFD r13!,{r4-r6,r14}	Load multiple loads r4 in 1st cycle, r5 and r6 in 2nd cycle, r14 in 3rd cycle, 3 cycles total
17	0x00000198	B {pc}+0xda8	#0xf40 dual issue in pipeline 1 with 3rd cycle of LDM
18	0x00000f40	ADD r0,r0,#2 ARM	Single issue in pipeline 0
19	0x00000f44	ADD r0,r1,r0 ARM	Single issue in pipeline 0, no dual issue due to hazard on r0 produced in E2 and required in E2

Table 14.4 shows a sample code segment and indicates how the processor might schedule it.

SIMD and Floating-Point Pipeline

All SIMD and floating-point instructions pass through the integer pipeline and are processed in a separate 10-stage pipeline (Figure 14.12). This unit, referred to

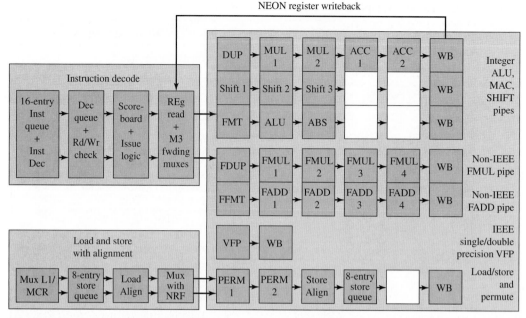

Figure 14.12   ARM Cortex-A8 NEON and Floating-Point Pipeline

as the NEON unit, handles packed SIMD instructions, and provides two types of floating-point support. If implemented, a vector floating-point (VFP) coprocessor performs floating-point operations in compliance with IEEE 754. If the coprocessor is not present, then separate multiply and add pipelines implement the floating-point operations

14.5 RECOMMENDED READING

Two good book-length treatments of superscalar design are [SHEN05] and [OMON99]. Worthwhile survey articles on the subject are [SMIT95] and [SIMA97]. [JOUP89a] examines instruction-level parallelism, looks at various techniques for maximizing parallelism, and compares superscalar and superpipelined approaches using simulation. Recent papers that provide good coverage of superscalar design issues include [SIMA04], [PATT01], and [MOSH01].

[POPE91] provides a detailed look at a proposed superscalar machine. It also provides an excellent tutorial on the design issues related to out-of-order instruction policies. Another look at a proposed system is found in [KUGA91]; this article raises and considers most of the important design issues for superscalar implementation. [LEE91] examines software techniques that can be used to enhance superscalar performance. [WALL91] is an interesting study of the extent to which instruction-level parallelism can be exploited in a superscalar processor.

Volume I of [INTE04a] provides general description of the Pentium 4 pipeline; more detail is provided in [INTE01a] and [INTE01b]. Another detailed treatment is [FOG08b].

[JOHN08] and [ARM08a] provide thorough coverage of the ARM Cortex-A8 pipeline. [RICH07] is a good overview.

ARM08a ARM Limited. *Cortex-A8 Technical Reference Manual.* ARM DDI 0344E, 2008. www.arm.com

FOG08b Fog, A. *The Microarchitecture of Intel and AMD CPUs.* Copenhagen University College of Engineering, 2008. http://www.agner.org/optimize/

HINT01 Hinton, G., et al. "The Microarchitecture of the Pentium 4 Processor." *Intel Technology Journal,* Q1 2001. http://developer.intel.com/technology/itj/

INTE01a Intel Corp. *Intel Pentium 4 Processor Optimization Reference Manual.* Document 248966-04 2001. http://developer.intel.com/design/Pentium4/documentation. htm.

INTE01b Intel Corp. *Desktop Performance and Optimization for Intel Pentium 4 Processor.* Document 248966-04 2001. http://developer.intel.com/design/Pentium4/documentation.htm.

INTE04a Intel Corp. *IA-32 Intel Architecture Software Developer's Manual (4 volumes).* Document 253665 through 253668. 2004. http://developer.intel.com/design/Pentium4/documentation.htm.

JOHN08 John, E., and Rubio, J. *Unique Chips and Systems.* Boca Raton, FL: CRC Press, 2008.

JOUP89a Jouppi, N., and Wall, D. "Available Instruction-Level Parallelism for Superscalar and Superpipelined Machines." *Proceedings, Third International Conference on Architectural Support for Programming Languages and Operating Systems,* April 1989.

KUGA91 Kuga, M.; Murakami, K.; and Tomita, S. "DSNS (Dynamically-hazard resolved, Statically-code-scheduled, Nonuniform Superscalar): Yet Another Superscalar Processor Architecture." *Computer Architecture News,* June 1991.

LEE91 Lee, R.; Kwok, A.; and Briggs, F. "The Floating Point Performance of a Superscalar SPARC Processor." *Proceedings, Fourth International Conference on Architectural Support for Programming Languages and Operating Systems,* April 1991.

MOSH01 Moshovos, A., and Sohi, G. "Microarchitectural Innovations: Boosting Microprocessor Performance Beyond Semiconductor Technology Scaling." *Proceedings of the IEEE,* November 2001.

OMON99 Omondi, A. *The Microarchitecture of Pipelined and Superscalar Computers.* Boston: Kluwer, 1999.

PATT01 Patt, Y. "Requirements, Bottlenecks, and Good Fortune: Agents for Microprocessor Evolution." *Proceedings of the IEEE,* November 2001.

POPE91 Popescu, V., et al. "The Metaflow Architecture." *IEEE Micro,* June 1991.

RICH07 Riches, S., et al. "A Fully Automated High Performance Implementation of ARM Cortex-A8." *IQ Online,* Vol. 6, No. 3, 2007. www.arm.com/iqonline

SHEN05 Shen, J., and Lipasti, M. *Modern Processor Design: Fundamentals of Superscalar Processors.* New York: McGraw-Hill, 2005.

SIMA97 Sima, D. "Superscalar Instruction Issue." *IEEE Micro,* September/October 1997.

SIMA04 Sima, D. "Decisive Aspects in the Evolution of Microprocessors." *Proceedings of the IEEE,* December 2004.

SMIT95 Smith, J., and Sohi, G. "The Microarchitecture of Superscalar Processors." *Proceedings of the IEEE*, December 1995.

WALL91 Wall, D. "Limits of Instruction-Level Parallelism." *Proceedings, Fourth International Conference on Architectural Support for Programming Languages and Operating Systems*, April 1991.

14.6 KEY TERMS, REVIEW QUESTIONS, AND PROBLEMS

Key Terms

antidependency	machine parallelism	register renaming
branch prediction	micro-operations	resource conflict
commit	micro-ops	retire
flow dependency	out-of-order	superpipelined
in-order issue	completion	superscalar
in-order completion	out-of-order issue	true data dependency
instruction issue	output dependency	write-read dependency
instruction-level parallelism	procedural dependency	write-write
instruction window	read-write dependency	dependency

Review Questions

14.1 What is the essential characteristic of the superscalar approach to processor design?

14.2 What is the difference between the superscalar and superpipelined approaches?

14.3 What is instruction-level parallelism?

14.4 Briefly define the following terms:
- True data dependency
- Procedural dependency
- Resource conflicts
- Output dependency
- Antidependency

14.5 What is the distinction between instruction-level parallelism and machine parallelism?

14.6 List and briefly define three types of superscalar instruction issue policies.

14.7 What is the purpose of an instruction window?

14.8 What is register renaming and what is its purpose?

14.9 What are the key elements of a superscalar processor organization?

Problems

14.1 When out-of-order completion is used in a superscalar processor, resumption of execution after interrupt processing is complicated, because the exceptional condition may have been detected as an instruction that produced its result out of order. The program cannot be restarted at the instruction following the exceptional instruction, because subsequent instructions have already completed, and doing so would cause these instructions to be executed twice. Suggest a mechanism or mechanisms for dealing with this situation.

14.2 Consider the following sequence of instructions, where the syntax consists of an op-code followed by the destination register followed by one or two source registers:

```
0    ADD     R3, R1, R2
1    LOAD    R6, [R3]
2    AND     R7, R5, 3
3    ADD     R1, R6, R0
4    SRL     R7, R0, 8
5    OR      R2, R4, R7
6    SUB     R5, R3, R4
7    ADD     R0, R1, R10
8    LOAD    R6, [R5]
9    SUB     R2, R1, R6
10   AND     R3, R7, 15
```

Assume the use of a four-stage pipeline: fetch, decode/issue, execute, write back. Assume that all pipeline stages take one clock cycle except for the execute stage. For simple integer arithmetic and logical instructions, the execute stage takes one cycle, but for a LOAD from memory, five cycles are consumed in the execute stage.

If we have a simple scalar pipeline but allow out-of-order execution, we can construct the following table for the execution of the first seven instructions:

Instruction	Fetch	Decode	Execute	Write Back
0	0	1	2	3
1	1	2	4	9
2	2	3	5	6
3	3	4	10	11
4	4	5	6	7
5	5	6	8	10
6	6	7	9	12

The entries under the four pipeline stages indicate the clock cycle at which each instruction begins each phase. In this program, the second ADD instruction (instruction 3) depends on the LOAD instruction (instruction 1) for one of its operands, r6. Because the LOAD instruction takes five clock cycles, and the issue logic encounters the dependent ADD instruction after two clocks, the issue logic must delay the ADD instruction for three clock cycles. With an out-of-order capability, the processor can stall instruction 3 at clock cycle 4, and then move on to issue the following three independent instructions, which enter execution at clocks 6, 8, and 9. The LOAD finishes execution at clock 9, and so the dependent ADD can be launched into execution on clock 10.

a. Complete the preceding table.
b. Redo the table assuming no out-of-order capability. What is the savings using the capability?
c. Redo the table assuming a superscalar implementation that can handle two instructions at a time at each stage.

14.3 Consider the following assembly language program:

```
I1: Move R3, R7       /R3 ← (R7)/
I2: Load R8, (R3)     /R8 ← Memory (R3)/
I3: Add R3, R3, 4     /R3 ← (R3) + 4/
I4: Load R9, (R3)     /R9 ← Memory (R3)/
I5: BLE R8, R9, L3    /Branch if (R9) > (R8)/
```

This program includes WAW, RAW, and WAR dependencies. Show these.

Decode		Execute				Write		Cycle
I1	I2							1
	I2			I1				2
	I2			I1				3
I3	I4		I2					4
I5	I6		I4	I3		I1	I2	5
I5	I6	I5		I3				6
		I5	I6			I3	I4	7
								8
						I5	I6	9

Figure 14.13 An In-Order Issue, In-Order-Completion Execution Sequence

14.4 **a.** Identify the write-read, write-write, and read-write dependencies in the following instruction sequence:

```
I1:  R1 = 100
I2:  R1 = R2 + R4
I3:  R2 = r4 - 25
I4:  R4 = R1 + R3
I5:  R1 = R1 + 30
```

   b. Rename the registers from part (a) to prevent dependency problems. Identify references to initial register values using the subscript "a" to the register reference.

14.5 Consider the "in-order-issue/in-order-completion" execution sequence shown in Figure 14.13.

   a. Identify the most likely reason why I2 could not enter the execute stage until the fourth cycle. Will "in-order issue/out-of-order completion" or "out-of-order issue/out-of-order completion" fix this? If so, which?

   b. Identify the reason why I6 could not enter the write stage until the nineth cycle. Will "in-order issue/out-of-order completion" or "out-of-order issue/out-of-order completion" fix this? If so, which?

14.6 Figure 14.14 shows an example of a superscalar processor organization. The processor can issue two instructions per cycle if there is no resource conflict and no data dependence problem. There are essentially two pipelines, with four processing stages (fetch, decode, execute, and store). Each pipeline has its own fetch decode and store unit. Four functional units (multiplier, adder, logic unit, and load unit) are available for use in the execute stage and are shared by the two pipelines on a dynamic basis. The two store units can be dynamically used by the two pipelines, depending on availability at a particular cycle. There is a lookahead window with its own fetch and decoding logic. This window is used for instruction lookahead for out-of-order instruction issue.

   Consider the following program to be executed on this processor:

```
I1: Load R1, A      /R1 ← Memory (A)/
I2: Add R2, R1      /R2 ← (R2) + R(1)/
I3: Add R3, R4      /R3 ← (R3) + R(4)/
I4: Mul R4, R5      /R4 ← (R4) + R(5)/
I5: Comp R6         /R6 ← (R6)/
I6: Mul R6, R7      /R3 ← (R3) + R(4)/
```

   a. What dependencies exist in the program?

   b. Show the pipeline activity for this program on the processor of Figure 14.14 using in-order issue with in-order completion policies and using a presentation similar to Figure 14.2.

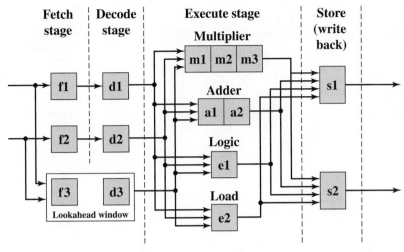

Figure 14.14 A Dual-Pipeline Superscalar Processor

    c. Repeat for in-order issue with out-of-order completion.
    d. Repeat for out-of-order issue with out-of-order completion.

14.7 Figure 14.15 is from a paper on superscalar design. Explain the three parts of the figure, and define w, x, y, and z.

14.8 Yeh's dynamic branch prediction algorithm, used on the Pentium 4, is a two-level branch prediction algorithm. The first level is the history of the last n branches. The second level is the branch behavior of the last s occurrences of that unique pattern of the last n branches. For each conditional branch instruction in a program, there is an entry in a Branch History Table (BHT). Each entry consists of n bits corresponding to the last n executions of the branch instruction, with a 1 if the branch was taken and a

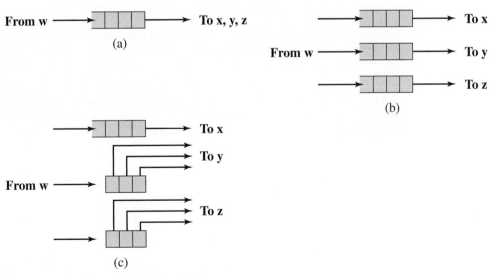

Figure 14.15 Figure for Problem 14.7

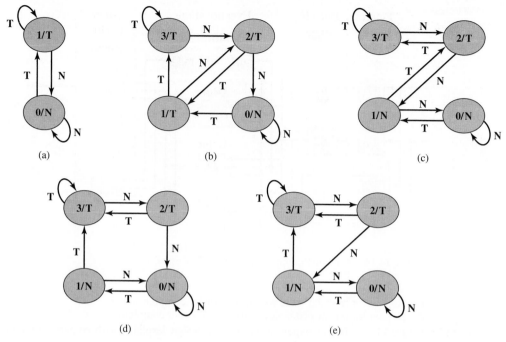

Figure 14.16 Figure for Problem 14.8

0 if the branch was not. Each BHT entry indexes into a Pattern Table (PT) that has $2n$ entries, one for each possible pattern of n bits. Each PT entry consists of s bits that are used in branch prediction, as was described in Chapter 12 (e.g., Figure 12.19). When a conditional branch is encountered during instruction fetch and decode, the address of the instruction is used to retrieve the appropriate BHT entry, which shows the recent history of the instruction. Then, the BHT entry is used to retrieve the appropriate PT entry for branch prediction. After the branch is executed, the BHT entry is updated, and then the appropriate PT entry is updated.

a. In testing the performance of this scheme, Yeh tried five different prediction schemes, illustrated in Figure 14.16. Identify which three of these schemes correspond to those shown in Figures 12.19 and 12.28. Describe the remaining two schemes.

b. With this algorithm, the prediction is not based on just the recent history of this particular branch instruction. Rather, it is based on the recent history of all patterns of branches that match the n-bit pattern in the BHT entry for this instruction. Suggest a rationale for such a strategy.

PART FOUR

The Control Unit

In Part Three, we focused on machine instructions and the operations performed by the processor to execute each instruction. What was left out of this discussion is exactly how each individual operation is caused to happen. This is the job of the control unit.

The control unit is that portion of the processor that actually causes things to happen. The control unit issues control signals external to the processor to cause data exchange with memory and I/O modules. The control unit also issues control signals internal to the processor to move data between registers, to cause the ALU to perform a specified function, and to regulate other internal operations. Input to the control unit consists of the instruction register, flags, and control signals from external sources (e.g., interrupt signals).

ROAD MAP FOR PART FOUR

Chapter 15 Control Unit Operation

In Chapter 15, we turn to a discussion of how processor functions are performed or, more specifically, how the various elements of the processor are controlled to provide these functions, by means of the control unit. It is shown that each instruction cycle is made up of a set of micro-operations that generate control signals. Execution is accomplished by the effect of these control signals, emanating from the control unit to the ALU, registers, and system interconnection structure. Finally, an approach to the implementation of the control unit, referred to as hardwired implementation, is presented.

Chapter 16 Microprogrammed Control

In Chapter 16, we see how the concept of micro-operation leads to an elegant and powerful approach to control unit implementation, known as microprogramming. In essence, a lower-level programming language is developed. Each instruction in the machine language of the processor is translated into a sequence of lower-level control unit instructions. These lower-level instructions are referred to as microinstructions, and the process of translation is referred to as microprogramming. The chapter describes the layout of a control memory containing a microprogram for each machine instruction is described. The structure and function of the microprogrammed control unit can then be explained.

CHAPTER 15

CONTROL UNIT OPERATION

KEY POINTS

◆ The execution of an instruction involves the execution of a sequence of substeps, generally called cycles. For example, an execution may consist of fetch, indirect, execute, and interrupt cycles. Each cycle is in turn made up of a sequence of more fundamental operations, called micro-operations. A single micro-operation generally involves a transfer between registers, a transfer between a register and an external bus, or a simple ALU operation.

◆ The control unit of a processor performs two tasks: (1) It causes the processor to step through a series of micro-operations in the proper sequence, based on the program being executed, and (2) it generates the control signals that cause each micro-operation to be executed.

◆ The control signals generated by the control unit cause the opening and closing of logic gates, resulting in the transfer of data to and from registers and the operation of the ALU.

◆ One technique for implementing a control unit is referred to as hardwired implementation, in which the control unit is a combinatorial circuit. Its input logic signals, governed by the current machine instruction, are transferred into a set of output control signals.

In Chapter 10, we pointed out that a machine instruction set goes a long way toward defining the processor. If we know the machine instruction set, including an understanding of the effect of each opcode and an understanding of the addressing modes, and if we know the set of user-visible registers, then we know the functions that the processor must perform. This is not the complete picture. We must know the external interfaces, usually through a bus, and how interrupts are handled. With this line of reasoning, the following list of those things needed to specify the function of a processor emerges:

1. Operations (opcodes)
2. Addressing modes
3. Registers
4. I/O module interface
5. Memory module interface
6. Interrupts

This list, though general, is rather complete. Items 1 through 3 are defined by the instruction set. Items 4 and 5 are typically defined by specifying the system bus. Item 6 is defined partially by the system bus and partially by the type of support the processor offers to the operating system.

This list of six items might be termed the functional requirements for a processor. They determine what a processor must do. This is what occupied us in Parts Two and

Three. Now, we turn to the question of how these functions are performed or, more specifically, how the various elements of the processor are controlled to provide these functions. Thus, we turn to a discussion of the control unit, which controls the operation of the processor.

15.1 MICRO-OPERATIONS

We have seen that the operation of a computer, in executing a program, consists of a sequence of instruction cycles, with one machine instruction per cycle. Of course, we must remember that this sequence of instruction cycles is not necessarily the same as the *written sequence* of instructions that make up the program, because of the existence of branching instructions. What we are referring to here is the execution *time sequence* of instructions.

We have further seen that each instruction cycle is made up of a number of smaller units. One subdivision that we found convenient is fetch, indirect, execute, and interrupt, with only fetch and execute cycles always occurring.

To design a control unit, however, we need to break down the description further. In our discussion of pipelining in Chapter 12, we began to see that a further decomposition is possible. In fact, we will see that each of the smaller cycles involves a series of steps, each of which involves the processor registers. We will refer to these steps as **micro-operations**. The prefix *micro* refers to the fact that each step is very simple and accomplishes very little. Figure 15.1 depicts the relationship among the various concepts we have been discussing. To summarize, the execution of a program consists of the sequential execution of instructions. Each instruction is executed during an instruction cycle made up of shorter subcycles (e.g., fetch, indirect, execute, interrupt). The execution of each subcycle involves one or more shorter operations, that is, micro-operations.

Micro-operations are the functional, or atomic, operations of a processor. In this section, we will examine micro-operations to gain an understanding of how

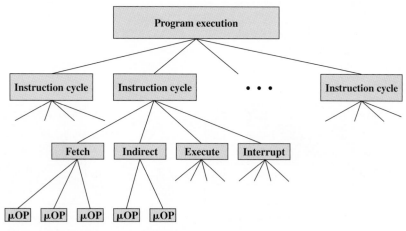

Figure 15.1 Constituent Elements of a Program Execution

the events of any instruction cycle can be described as a sequence of such micro-operations. A simple example will be used. In the remainder of this chapter, we then show how the concept of micro-operations serves as a guide to the design of the control unit.

The Fetch Cycle

We begin by looking at the fetch cycle, which occurs at the beginning of each instruction cycle and causes an instruction to be fetched from memory. For purposes of discussion, we assume the organization depicted in Figure 12.6. Four registers are involved:

- **Memory address register (MAR):** Is connected to the address lines of the system bus. It specifies the address in memory for a read or write operation.
- **Memory buffer register (MBR):** Is connected to the data lines of the system bus. It contains the value to be stored in memory or the last value read from memory.
- **Program counter (PC):** Holds the address of the next instruction to be fetched.
- **Instruction register (IR):** Holds the last instruction fetched.

Let us look at the sequence of events for the fetch cycle from the point of view of its effect on the processor registers. An example appears in Figure 15.2. At the beginning of the fetch cycle, the address of the next instruction to be executed is in the program counter (PC); in this case, the address is 1100100. The first step is to move that address to the memory address register (MAR) because this is the only register connected to the address lines of the system bus. The second step is to bring in the instruction. The desired address (in the MAR) is placed on the address

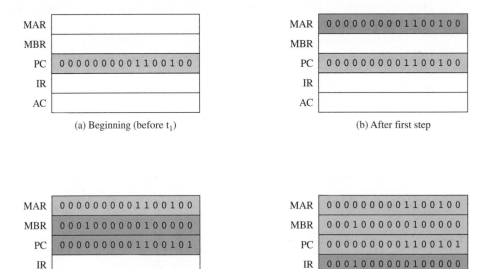

(a) Beginning (before t_1)

(b) After first step

(c) After second step

(d) After third step

Figure 15.2   Sequence of Events, Fetch Cycle

bus, the control unit issues a READ command on the control bus, and the result appears on the data bus and is copied into the memory buffer register (MBR). We also need to increment the PC by the instruction length to get ready for the next instruction. Because these two actions (read word from memory, increment PC) do not interfere with each other, we can do them simultaneously to save time. The third step is to move the contents of the MBR to the instruction register (IR). This frees up the MBR for use during a possible indirect cycle.

Thus, the simple fetch cycle actually consists of three steps and four micro-operations. Each micro-operation involves the movement of data into or out of a register. So long as these movements do not interfere with one another, several of them can take place during one step, saving time. Symbolically, we can write this sequence of events as follows:

$$t_1: \text{MAR} \leftarrow (\text{PC})$$
$$t_2: \text{MBR} \leftarrow \text{Memory}$$
$$\text{PC} \leftarrow (\text{PC}) + I$$
$$t_3: \text{IR} \leftarrow (\text{MBR})$$

where I is the instruction length. We need to make several comments about this sequence. We assume that a clock is available for timing purposes and that it emits regularly spaced clock pulses. Each clock pulse defines a time unit. Thus, all time units are of equal duration. Each micro-operation can be performed within the time of a single time unit. The notation (t_1, t_2, t_3) represents successive time units. In words, we have

- **First time unit:** Move contents of PC to MAR.
- **Second time unit:** Move contents of memory location specified by MAR to MBR. Increment by I the contents of the PC.
- **Third time unit:** Move contents of MBR to IR.

Note that the second and third micro-operations both take place during the second time unit. The third micro-operation could have been grouped with the fourth without affecting the fetch operation:

$$t_1: \text{MAR} \leftarrow (\text{PC})$$
$$t_2: \text{MBR} \leftarrow \text{Memory}$$
$$t_3: \text{PC} \leftarrow (\text{PC}) + I$$
$$\text{IR} \leftarrow (\text{MBR})$$

The groupings of micro-operations must follow two simple rules:

1. The proper sequence of events must be followed. Thus (MAR ← (PC)) must precede (MBR ← Memory) because the memory read operation makes use of the address in the MAR.

2. Conflicts must be avoided. One should not attempt to read to and write from the same register in one time unit, because the results would be unpredictable. For example, the micro-operations (MBR ← Memory) and (IR ← MBR) should not occur during the same time unit.

A final point worth noting is that one of the micro-operations involves an addition. To avoid duplication of circuitry, this addition could be performed by the ALU. The use of the ALU may involve additional micro-operations, depending on the functionality of the ALU and the organization of the processor. We defer a discussion of this point until later in this chapter.

It is useful to compare events described in this and the following subsections to Figure 3.5. Whereas micro-operations are ignored in that figure, this discussion shows the micro-operations needed to perform the subcycles of the instruction cycle.

The Indirect Cycle

Once an instruction is fetched, the next step is to fetch source operands. Continuing our simple example, let us assume a one-address instruction format, with direct and indirect addressing allowed. If the instruction specifies an indirect address, then an indirect cycle must precede the execute cycle. The data flow differs somewhat from that indicated in Figure 12.7 and includes the following micro-operations:

$$t_1: \text{MAR} \leftarrow (\text{IR(Address)})$$
$$t_2: \text{MBR} \leftarrow \text{Memory}$$
$$t_3: \text{IR(Address)} \leftarrow (\text{MBR(Address)})$$

The address field of the instruction is transferred to the MAR. This is then used to fetch the address of the operand. Finally, the address field of the IR is updated from the MBR, so that it now contains a direct rather than an indirect address.

The IR is now in the same state as if indirect addressing had not been used, and it is ready for the execute cycle. We skip that cycle for a moment, to consider the interrupt cycle.

The Interrupt Cycle

At the completion of the execute cycle, a test is made to determine whether any enabled interrupts have occurred. If so, the interrupt cycle occurs. The nature of this cycle varies greatly from one machine to another. We present a very simple sequence of events, as illustrated in Figure 12.8. We have

$$t_1: \text{MBR} \leftarrow (\text{PC})$$
$$t_2: \text{MAR} \leftarrow \text{Save\_Address}$$
$$\text{PC} \leftarrow \text{Routine\_Address}$$
$$t_3: \text{Memory} \leftarrow (\text{MBR})$$

In the first step, the contents of the PC are transferred to the MBR, so that they can be saved for return from the interrupt. Then the MAR is loaded with the address at which the contents of the PC are to be saved, and the PC is loaded with the address of the start of the interrupt-processing routine. These two actions may each be a single micro-operation. However, because most processors provide multiple types and/or levels of interrupts, it may take one or more additional micro-operations to obtain the Save_Address and the Routine_Address before they can be transferred to the MAR and PC, respectively. In any case, once this is done, the final step is to store the MBR, which contains the old value of the PC, into memory. The processor is now ready to begin the next instruction cycle.

The Execute Cycle

The fetch, indirect, and interrupt cycles are simple and predictable. Each involves a small, fixed sequence of micro-operations and, in each case, the same micro-operations are repeated each time around.

This is not true of the execute cycle. Because of the variety opcodes, there are a number of different sequences of micro-operations that can occur. Let us consider several hypothetical examples.

First, consider an add instruction:

```
ADD R1, X
```

which adds the contents of the location X to register R1. The following sequence of micro-operations might occur:

$$t_1: \text{MAR} \leftarrow (\text{IR(address)})$$
$$t_2: \text{MBR} \leftarrow \text{Memory}$$
$$t_3: \text{R1} \leftarrow (\text{R1}) + (\text{MBR})$$

We begin with the IR containing the ADD instruction. In the first step, the address portion of the IR is loaded into the MAR. Then the referenced memory location is read. Finally, the contents of R1 and MBR are added by the ALU. Again, this is a simplified example. Additional micro-operations may be required to extract the register reference from the IR and perhaps to stage the ALU inputs or outputs in some intermediate registers.

Let us look at two more complex examples. A common instruction is increment and skip if zero:

```
ISZ X
```

The content of location X is incremented by 1. If the result is 0, the next instruction is skipped. A possible sequence of micro-operations is

$$t_1: \text{MAR} \leftarrow (\text{IR(address)})$$
$$t_2: \text{MBR} \leftarrow \text{Memory}$$
$$t_3: \text{MBR} \leftarrow (\text{MBR}) + 1$$
$$t_4: \text{Memory} \leftarrow (\text{MBR})$$
$$\text{If } ((\text{MBR}) = 0) \text{ then } (\text{PC} \leftarrow (\text{PC}) + \text{I})$$

The new feature introduced here is the conditional action. The PC is incremented if $(\text{MBR}) = 0$. This test and action can be implemented as one micro-operation. Note also that this micro-operation can be performed during the same time unit during which the updated value in MBR is stored back to memory.

Finally, consider a subroutine call instruction. As an example, consider a branch-and-save-address instruction:

```
BSA X
```

The address of the instruction that follows the BSA instruction is saved in location X, and execution continues at location X + I. The saved address will later be used for return. This is a straightforward technique for providing subroutine calls. The following micro-operations suffice:

$$t_1: \text{MAR} \leftarrow (\text{IR(address)})$$
$$\text{MBR} \leftarrow (\text{PC})$$
$$t_2: \text{PC} \leftarrow (\text{IR(address)})$$
$$\text{Memory} \leftarrow (\text{MBR})$$
$$t_3: \text{PC} \leftarrow (\text{PC}) + \text{I}$$

The address in the PC at the start of the instruction is the address of the next instruction in sequence. This is saved at the address designated in the IR. The latter address is also incremented to provide the address of the instruction for the next instruction cycle.

The Instruction Cycle

We have seen that each phase of the instruction cycle can be decomposed into a sequence of elementary micro-operations. In our example, there is one sequence each for the fetch, indirect, and interrupt cycles, and, for the execute cycle, there is one sequence of micro-operations for each opcode.

To complete the picture, we need to tie sequences of micro-operations together, and this is done in Figure 15.3. We assume a new 2-bit register called the *instruction cycle code* (ICC). The ICC designates the state of the processor in terms of which portion of the cycle it is in:

00: Fetch

01: Indirect

10: Execute

11: Interrupt

At the end of each of the four cycles, the ICC is set appropriately. The indirect cycle is always followed by the execute cycle. The interrupt cycle is always followed by the fetch cycle (see Figure 12.4). For both the fetch and execute cycles, the next cycle depends on the state of the system.

Thus, the flowchart of Figure 15.3 defines the complete sequence of micro-operations, depending only on the instruction sequence and the interrupt pattern. Of course, this is a simplified example. The flowchart for an actual processor would be more complex. In any case, we have reached the point in our discussion in which the operation of the processor is defined as the performance of a sequence of micro-operations. We can now consider how the control unit causes this sequence to occur.

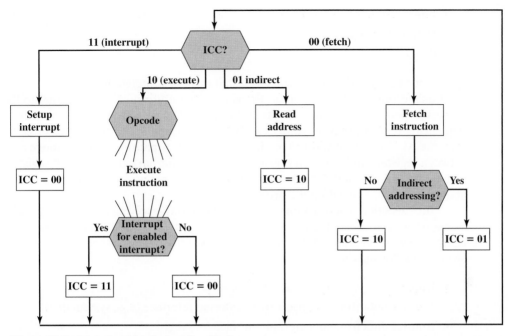

Figure 15.3   Flowchart for Instruction Cycle

15.2 CONTROL OF THE PROCESSOR

Functional Requirements

As a result of our analysis in the preceding section, we have decomposed the behavior or functioning of the processor into elementary operations, called micro-operations. By reducing the operation of the processor to its most fundamental level, we are able to define exactly what it is that the control unit must cause to happen. Thus, we can define the *functional requirements* for the control unit: those functions that the control unit must perform. A definition of these functional requirements is the basis for the design and implementation of the control unit.

With the information at hand, the following three-step process leads to a characterization of the control unit:

1. Define the basic elements of the processor.
2. Describe the micro-operations that the processor performs.
3. Determine the functions that the control unit must perform to cause the micro-operations to be performed.

We have already performed steps 1 and 2. Let us summarize the results. First, the basic functional elements of the processor are the following:

- ALU
- Registers

- Internal data paths
- External data paths
- Control unit

Some thought should convince you that this is a complete list. The ALU is the functional essence of the computer. Registers are used to store data internal to the processor. Some registers contain status information needed to manage instruction sequencing (e.g., a program status word). Others contain data that go to or come from the ALU, memory, and I/O modules. Internal data paths are used to move data between registers and between register and ALU. External data paths link registers to memory and I/O modules, often by means of a system bus. The control unit causes operations to happen within the processor.

The execution of a program consists of operations involving these processor elements. As we have seen, these operations consist of a sequence of micro-operations. Upon review of Section 15.1, the reader should see that all micro-operations fall into one of the following categories:

- Transfer data from one register to another.
- Transfer data from a register to an external interface (e.g., system bus).
- Transfer data from an external interface to a register.
- Perform an arithmetic or logic operation, using registers for input and output.

All of the micro-operations needed to perform one instruction cycle, including all of the micro-operations to execute every instruction in the instruction set, fall into one of these categories.

We can now be somewhat more explicit about the way in which the control unit functions. The control unit performs two basic tasks:

- **Sequencing:** The control unit causes the processor to step through a series of micro-operations in the proper sequence, based on the program being executed.
- **Execution:** The control unit causes each micro-operation to be performed.

The preceding is a functional description of what the control unit does. The key to how the control unit operates is the use of control signals.

Control Signals

We have defined the elements that make up the processor (ALU, registers, data paths) and the micro-operations that are performed. For the control unit to perform its function, it must have inputs that allow it to determine the state of the system and outputs that allow it to control the behavior of the system. These are the external specifications of the control unit. Internally, the control unit must have the logic required to perform its sequencing and execution functions. We defer a discussion of the internal operation of the control unit to Section 15.3 and Chapter 16. The remainder of this section is concerned with the interaction between the control unit and the other elements of the processor.

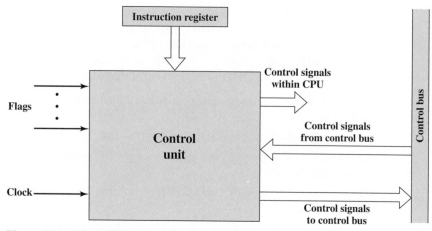

Figure 15.4 Block Diagram of the Control Unit

Figure 15.4 is a general model of the control unit, showing all of its inputs and outputs. The inputs are

- **Clock:** This is how the control unit "keeps time." The control unit causes one micro-operation (or a set of simultaneous micro-operations) to be performed for each clock pulse. This is sometimes referred to as the processor cycle time, or the clock cycle time.
- **Instruction register:** The opcode and addressing mode of the current instruction are used to determine which micro-operations to perform during the execute cycle.
- **Flags:** These are needed by the control unit to determine the status of the processor and the outcome of previous ALU operations. For example, for the increment-and-skip-if-zero (ISZ) instruction, the control unit will increment the PC if the zero flag is set.
- **Control signals from control bus:** The control bus portion of the system bus provides signals to the control unit.

The outputs are as follows:

- **Control signals within the processor:** These are two types: those that cause data to be moved from one register to another, and those that activate specific ALU functions.
- **Control signals to control bus:** These are also of two types: control signals to memory, and control signals to the I/O modules.

Three types of control signals are used: those that activate an ALU function, those that activate a data path, and those that are signals on the external system bus or other external interface. All of these signals are ultimately applied directly as binary inputs to individual logic gates.

Let us consider again the fetch cycle to see how the control unit maintains control. The control unit keeps track of where it is in the instruction cycle. At a given point, it knows that the fetch cycle is to be performed next. The first step is to transfer the contents of the PC to the MAR. The control unit does this by activating the control signal that opens the gates between the bits of the PC and the bits of the MAR. The next step is to read a word from memory into the MBR and increment the PC. The control unit does this by sending the following control signals simultaneously:

- A control signal that opens gates, allowing the contents of the MAR onto the address bus
- A memory read control signal on the control bus
- A control signal that opens the gates, allowing the contents of the data bus to be stored in the MBR
- Control signals to logic that add 1 to the contents of the PC and store the result back to the PC

Following this, the control unit sends a control signal that opens gates between the MBR and the IR.

This completes the fetch cycle except for one thing: The control unit must decide whether to perform an indirect cycle or an execute cycle next. To decide this, it examines the IR to see if an indirect memory reference is made.

The indirect and interrupt cycles work similarly. For the execute cycle, the control unit begins by examining the opcode and, on the basis of that, decides which sequence of micro-operations to perform for the execute cycle.

A Control Signals Example

To illustrate the functioning of the control unit, let us examine a simple example. Figure 15.5 illustrates the example. This is a simple processor with a single accumulator

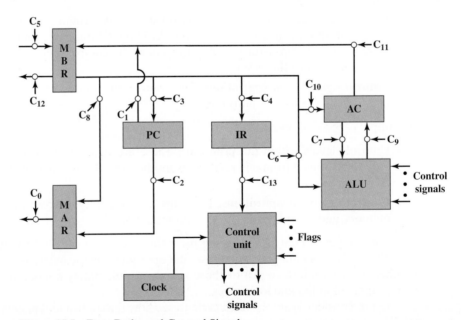

Figure 15.5 Data Paths and Control Signals

(AC). The data paths between elements are indicated. The control paths for signals emanating from the control unit are not shown, but the terminations of control signals are labeled C_i and indicated by a circle. The control unit receives inputs from the clock, the instruction register, and flags. With each clock cycle, the control unit reads all of its inputs and emits a set of control signals. Control signals go to three separate destinations:

- **Data paths:** The control unit controls the internal flow of data. For example, on instruction fetch, the contents of the memory buffer register are transferred to the instruction register. For each path to be controlled, there is a switch (indicated by a circle in the figure). A control signal from the control unit temporarily opens the gate to let data pass.
- **ALU:** The control unit controls the operation of the ALU by a set of control signals. These signals activate various logic circuits and gates within the ALU.
- **System bus:** The control unit sends control signals out onto the control lines of the system bus (e.g., memory READ).

The control unit must maintain knowledge of where it is in the instruction cycle. Using this knowledge, and by reading all of its inputs, the control unit emits a sequence of control signals that causes micro-operations to occur. It uses the clock pulses to time the sequence of events, allowing time between events for signal levels to stabilize. Table 15.1 indicates the control signals that are needed for some of the micro-operation sequences described earlier. For simplicity, the data and control paths for incrementing the PC and for loading the fixed addresses into the PC and MAR are not shown.

Table 15.1   Micro-operations and Control Signals

	Micro-operations	Active Control Signals
Fetch:	t_1: MAR ← (PC)	C_2
	t_2: MBR ← Memory	C_5, C_R
	PC ← (PC) + 1	
	t_3: IR ← (MBR)	C_4
Indirect:	t_1: MAR ← (IR(Address))	C_8
	t_2: MBR ← Memory	C_5, C_R
	t_3: IR(Address) ← (MBR(Address))	C_4
Interrupt:	t_1: MBR ← (PC)	C_1
	t_2: MAR ← Save-address	
	PC ← Routine-address	
	t_3: Memory ← (MBR)	C_{12}, C_W

C_R = Read control signal to system bus.
C_W = Write control signal to system bus.

It is worth pondering the minimal nature of the control unit. The control unit is the engine that runs the entire computer. It does this based only on knowing the instructions to be executed and the nature of the results of arithmetic and logical operations (e.g., positive, overflow, etc.). It never gets to see the data being processed or the actual results produced. And it controls everything with a few control signals to points within the processor and a few control signals to the system bus.

Internal Processor Organization

Figure 15.5 indicates the use of a variety of data paths. The complexity of this type of organization should be clear. More typically, some sort of internal bus arrangement, as was suggested in Figure 12.2, will be used.

Using an internal processor bus, Figure 15.5 can be rearranged as shown in Figure 15.6. A single internal bus connects the ALU and all processor registers.

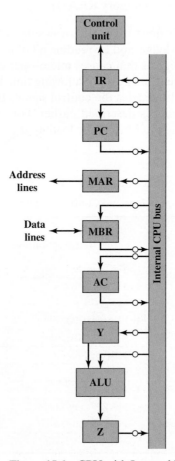

Figure 15.6   CPU with Internal Bus

Gates and control signals are provided for movement of data onto and off the bus from each register. Additional control signals control data transfer to and from the system (external) bus and the operation of the ALU.

Two new registers, labeled Y and Z, have been added to the organization. These are needed for the proper operation of the ALU. When an operation involving two operands is performed, one can be obtained from the internal bus, but the other must be obtained from another source. The AC could be used for this purpose, but this limits the flexibility of the system and would not work with a processor with multiple general-purpose registers. Register Y provides temporary storage for the other input. The ALU is a combinatorial circuit (see Chapter 20) with no internal storage. Thus, when control signals activate an ALU function, the input to the ALU is transformed to the output. Thus, the output of the ALU cannot be directly connected to the bus, because this output would feed back to the input. Register Z provides temporary output storage. With this arrangement, an operation to add a value from memory to the AC would have the following steps:

$$t_1: \text{MAR} \leftarrow (\text{IR(address)})$$
$$t_2: \text{MBR} \leftarrow \text{Memory}$$
$$t_3: \text{Y} \leftarrow (\text{MBR})$$
$$t_4: \text{Z} \leftarrow (\text{AC}) + (\text{Y})$$
$$t_5: \text{AC} \leftarrow (\text{Z})$$

Other organizations are possible, but, in general, some sort of internal bus or set of internal buses is used. The use of common data paths simplifies the interconnection layout and the control of the processor. Another practical reason for the use of an internal bus is to save space.

The Intel 8085

To illustrate some of the concepts introduced thus far in this chapter, let us consider the Intel 8085. Its organization is shown in Figure 15.7. Several key components that may not be self-explanatory are:

- **Incrementer/decrementer address latch:** Logic that can add 1 to or subtract 1 from the contents of the stack pointer or program counter. This saves time by avoiding the use of the ALU for this purpose.
- **Interrupt control:** This module handles multiple levels of interrupt signals.
- **Serial I/O control:** This module interfaces to devices that communicate 1 bit at a time.

Table 15.2 describes the external signals into and out of the 8085. These are linked to the external system bus. These signals are the interface between the 8085 processor and the rest of the system (Figure 15.8).

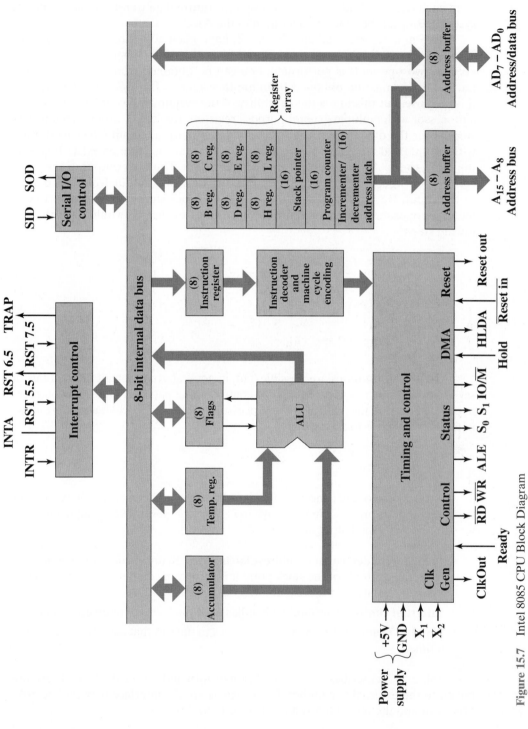

Figure 15.7 Intel 8085 CPU Block Diagram

576

Table 15.2   Intel 8085 External Signals

Address and Data Signals

High Address (A15–A8)
The high-order 8 bits of a 16-bit address.

Address/Data (AD7–AD0)
The lower-order 8 bits of a 16-bit address or 8 bits of data. This multiplexing saves on pins.

Serial Input Data (SID)
A single-bit input to accommodate devices that transmit serially (one bit at a time).

Serial Output Data (SOD)
A single-bit output to accommodate devices that receive serially.

Timing and Control Signals

CLK (OUT)
The system clock. The CLK signal goes to peripheral chips and synchronizes their timing.

X1, X2
These signals come from an external crystal or other device to drive the internal clock generator.

Address Latch Enabled (ALE)
Occurs during the first clock state of a machine cycle and causes peripheral chips to store the address lines. This allows the address module (e.g., memory, I/O) to recognize that it is being addressed.

Status (S0, S1)
Control signals used to indicate whether a read or write operation is taking place.

IO/M
Used to enable either I/O or memory modules for read and write operations.

Read Control (RD)
Indicates that the selected memory or I/O module is to be read and that the data bus is available for data transfer.

Write Control (WR)
Indicates that data on the data bus is to be written into the selected memory or I/O location.

Memory and I/O Initiated Symbols

Hold
Requests the CPU to relinquish control and use of the external system bus. The CPU will complete execution of the instruction presently in the IR and then enter a hold state, during which no signals are inserted by the CPU to the control, address, or data buses. During the hold state, the bus may be used for DMA operations.

Hold Acknowledge (HOLDA)
This control unit output signal acknowledges the HOLD signal and indicates that the bus is now available.

READY
Used to synchronize the CPU with slower memory or I/O devices. When an addressed device asserts READY, the CPU may proceed with an input (DBIN) or output (WR) operation. Otherwise, the CPU enters a wait state until the device is ready.

(Continued)

Table 15.2   Continued

Interrupt-Related Signals

TRAP
   Restart Interrupts (RST 7.5, 6.5, 5.5)

Interrupt Request (INTR)
   These five lines are used by an external device to interrupt the CPU. The CPU will not honor the request if it is in the hold state or if the interrupt is disabled. An interrupt is honored only at the completion of an instruction. The interrupts are in descending order of priority.

Interrupt Acknowledge
   Acknowledges an interrupt.

CPU Initialization

RESET IN
   Causes the contents of the PC to be set to zero. The CPU resumes execution at location zero.

RESET OUT
   Acknowledges that the CPU has been reset. The signal can be used to reset the rest of the system.

Voltage and Ground

VCC
   +5-volt power supply

VSS
   Electrical ground

The control unit is identified as having two components labeled (1) instruction decoder and machine cycle encoding and (2) timing and control. A discussion of the first component is deferred until the next section. The essence of the control unit is the timing and control module. This module includes a clock and accepts as inputs the current instruction and some external control signals. Its output consists of control signals to the other components of the processor plus control signals to the external system bus.

The timing of processor operations is synchronized by the clock and controlled by the control unit with control signals. Each instruction cycle is divided into from one to five *machine cycles;* each machine cycle is in turn divided into from three to five *states*. Each state lasts one clock cycle. During a state, the processor performs one or a set of simultaneous micro-operations as determined by the control signals.

The number of machine cycles is fixed for a given instruction but varies from one instruction to another. Machine cycles are defined to be equivalent to bus accesses. Thus, the number of machine cycles for an instruction depends on the number of times the processor must communicate with external devices. For example, if an instruction consists of two 8-bit portions, then two machine cycles are required to fetch the instruction. If that instruction involves a 1-byte memory or I/O operation, then a third machine cycle is required for execution.

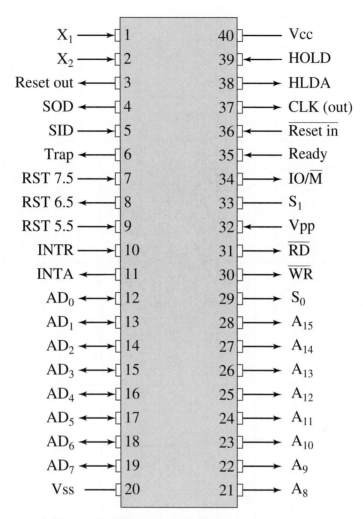

Figure 15.8 Intel 8085 Pin Configuration

Figure 15.9 gives an example of 8085 timing, showing the value of external control signals. Of course, at the same time, the control unit generates internal control signals that control internal data transfers. The diagram shows the instruction cycle for an OUT instruction. Three machine cycles (M_1, M_2, M_3) are needed. During the first, the OUT instruction is fetched. The second machine cycle fetches the second half of the instruction, which contains the number of the I/O device selected for output. During the third cycle, the contents of the AC are written out to the selected device over the data bus.

The Address Latch Enabled (ALE) pulse signals the start of each machine cycle from the control unit. The ALE pulse alerts external circuits. During timing state T_1 of machine cycle M_1, the control unit sets the IO/M signal to indicate that this is a memory operation. Also, the control unit causes the contents of the PC to be placed on the

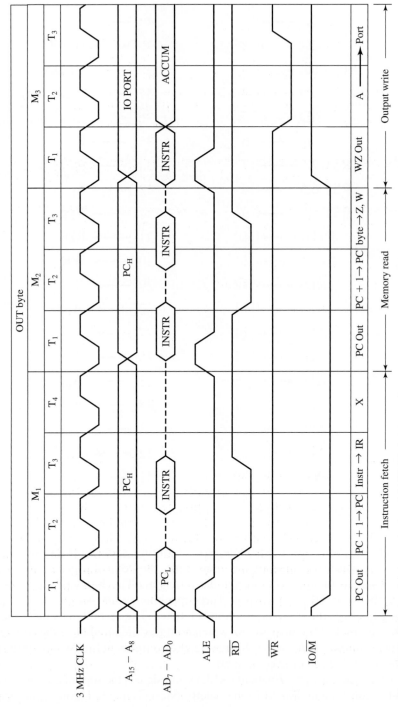

Figure 15.9 Timing Diagram for Intel 8085 OUT Instruction

address bus (A_{15} through A_8) and the address/data bus (AD_7 through AD_0). With the falling edge of the ALE pulse, the other modules on the bus store the address.

During timing state T_2, the addressed memory module places the contents of the addressed memory location on the address/data bus. The control unit sets the Read Control (RD) signal to indicate a read, but it waits until T_3 to copy the data from the bus. This gives the memory module time to put the data on the bus and for the signal levels to stabilize. The final state, T_4, is a *bus idle* state during which the processor decodes the instruction. The remaining machine cycles proceed in a similar fashion.

15.3 HARDWIRED IMPLEMENTATION

We have discussed the control unit in terms of its inputs, output, and functions. We now turn to the topic of control unit implementation. A wide variety of techniques have been used. Most of these fall into one of two categories:

- Hardwired implementation
- Microprogrammed implementation

In a hardwired implementation, the control unit is essentially a state machine circuit. Its input logic signals are transformed into a set of output logic signals, which are the control signals. This approach is examined in this section. Microprogrammed implementation is the subject of Chapter 16.

Control Unit Inputs

Figure 15.4 depicts the control unit as we have so far discussed it. The key inputs are the instruction register, the clock, flags, and control bus signals. In the case of the flags and control bus signals, each individual bit typically has some meaning (e.g., overflow). The other two inputs, however, are not directly useful to the control unit.

First consider the instruction register. The control unit makes use of the opcode and will perform different actions (issue a different combination of control signals) for different instructions. To simplify the control unit logic, there should be a unique logic input for each opcode. This function can be performed by a *decoder,* which takes an encoded input and produces a single output. In general, a decoder will have n binary inputs and 2^n binary outputs. Each of the 2^n different input patterns will activate a single unique output. Table 15.3 is an example for $n = 4$. The decoder for a control unit will typically have to be more complex than that, to account for variable-length opcodes. An example of the digital logic used to implement a decoder is presented in Chapter 20.

The clock portion of the control unit issues a repetitive sequence of pulses. This is useful for measuring the duration of micro-operations. Essentially, the period of the clock pulses must be long enough to allow the propagation of signals along data paths and through processor circuitry. However, as we have seen, the control unit emits different control signals at different time units within a single instruction cycle. Thus, we would like a counter as input to the control unit, with a different control signal being used for T_1, T_2, and so forth. At the end of an instruction cycle, the control unit must feed back to the counter to reinitialize it at T_1.

Table 15.3 A Decoder with Four Inputs and Sixteen Outputs

I1	I2	I3	I4	O1	O2	O3	O4	O5	O6	O7	O8	O9	O10	O11	O12	O13	O14	O15	O16
0	0	0	0	0	0	0	0	0	0	0	0	0	0	0	0	0	0	0	1
0	0	0	1	0	0	0	0	0	0	0	0	0	0	0	0	0	0	1	0
0	0	1	0	0	0	0	0	0	0	0	0	0	0	0	0	0	1	0	0
0	0	1	1	0	0	0	0	0	0	0	0	0	0	0	0	1	0	0	0
0	1	0	0	0	0	0	0	0	0	0	0	0	0	0	1	0	0	0	0
0	1	0	1	0	0	0	0	0	0	0	0	0	0	1	0	0	0	0	0
0	1	1	0	0	0	0	0	0	0	0	0	0	1	0	0	0	0	0	0
0	1	1	1	0	0	0	0	0	0	0	0	1	0	0	0	0	0	0	0
1	0	0	0	0	0	0	0	0	0	0	1	0	0	0	0	0	0	0	0
1	0	0	1	0	0	0	0	0	0	1	0	0	0	0	0	0	0	0	0
1	0	1	0	0	0	0	0	0	1	0	0	0	0	0	0	0	0	0	0
1	0	1	1	0	0	0	0	1	0	0	0	0	0	0	0	0	0	0	0
1	1	0	0	0	0	0	1	0	0	0	0	0	0	0	0	0	0	0	0
1	1	0	1	0	0	1	0	0	0	0	0	0	0	0	0	0	0	0	0
1	1	1	0	0	1	0	0	0	0	0	0	0	0	0	0	0	0	0	0
1	1	1	1	1	0	0	0	0	0	0	0	0	0	0	0	0	0	0	0

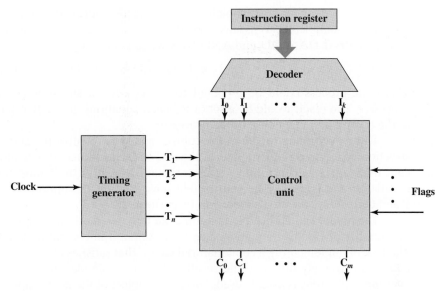

Figure 15.10   Control Unit with Decoded Inputs

With these two refinements, the control unit can be depicted as in Figure 15.10.

Control Unit Logic

To define the hardwired implementation of a control unit, all that remains is to discuss the internal logic of the control unit that produces output control signals as a function of its input signals.

Essentially, what must be done is, for each control signal, to derive a Boolean expression of that signal as a function of the inputs. This is best explained by example. Let us consider again our simple example illustrated in Figure 15.5. We saw in Table 15.1 the micro-operation sequences and control signals needed to control three of the four phases of the instruction cycle.

Let us consider a single control signal, C_5. This signal causes data to be read from the external data bus into the MBR. We can see that it is used twice in Table 15.1. Let us define two new control signals, P and Q, that have the following interpretation:

$$
\begin{array}{ll}
PQ = 00 & \text{Fetch Cycle} \\
PQ = 01 & \text{Indirect Cycle} \\
PQ = 10 & \text{Execute Cycle} \\
PQ = 11 & \text{Interrupt Cycle}
\end{array}
$$

Then the following Boolean expression defines C_5:

$$C_5 = \overline{P} \cdot \overline{Q} \cdot T_2 + \overline{P} \cdot Q \cdot T_2$$

That is, the control signal C_5 will be asserted during the second time unit of both the fetch and indirect cycles.

This expression is not complete. C_5 is also needed during the execute cycle. For our simple example, let us assume that there are only three instructions that read from memory: LDA, ADD, and AND. Now we can define C_5 as

$$C_5 = \overline{P} \cdot \overline{Q} \cdot T_2 + \overline{P} \cdot Q \cdot T_2 + P \cdot \overline{Q} \cdot (LDA + ADD + AND) \cdot T_2$$

This same process could be repeated for every control signal generated by the processor. The result would be a set of Boolean equations that define the behavior of the control unit and hence of the processor.

To tie everything together, the control unit must control the state of the instruction cycle. As was mentioned, at the end of each subcycle (fetch, indirect, execute, interrupt), the control unit issues a signal that causes the timing generator to reinitialize and issue T_1. The control unit must also set the appropriate values of P and Q to define the next subcycle to be performed.

The reader should be able to appreciate that in a modern complex processor, the number of Boolean equations needed to define the control unit is very large. The task of implementing a combinatorial circuit that satisfies all of these equations becomes extremely difficult. The result is that a far simpler approach, known as *microprogramming,* is usually used. This is the subject of the next chapter.

15.4 RECOMMENDED READING

A number of textbooks treat the basic principles of control unit function; two particularly clear treatments are in [FARH04] and [MANO04].

FARH04   Farhat, H. *Digital Design and Computer Organization.* Boca Raton, FL: CRC Press, 2004.

MANO04   Mano, M. *Logic and Computer Design Fundamentals.* Upper Saddle River, NJ: Prentice Hall, 2004.

15.5 KEY TERMS, REVIEW QUESTIONS, AND PROBLEMS

Key Terms

control bus	control signal	hardwired implementation
control path	control unit	microoperations

Review Questions

15.1   Explain the distinction between the written sequence and the time sequence of an instruction.

15.2   What is the relationship between instructions and micro-operations?

15.3   What is the overall function of a processor's control unit?

15.4   Outline a three-step process that leads to a characterization of the control unit.

15.5 What basic tasks does a control unit perform?

15.6 Provide a typical list of the inputs and outputs of a control unit.

15.7 List three types of control signals.

15.8 Briefly explain what is meant by a hardwired implementation of a control unit.

Problems

15.1 Your ALU can add its two input registers, and it can logically complement the bits of either input register, but it cannot subtract. Numbers are to be stored in two's complement representation. List the micro-operations your control unit must perform to cause a subtraction.

15.2 Show the micro-operations and control signals in the same fashion as Table 15.1 for the processor in Figure 15.5 for the following instructions:
- Load Accumulator
- Store Accumulator
- Add to Accumulator
- AND to Accumulator
- Jump
- Jump if AC = 0
- Complement Accumulator

15.3 Assume that propagation delay along the bus and through the ALU of Figure 15.6 are 20 and 100 ns, respectively. The time required for a register to copy data from the bus is 10 ns. What is the time that must be allowed for
   a. transferring data from one register to another?
   b. incrementing the program counter?

15.4 Write the sequence of micro-operations required for the bus structure of Figure 15.6 to add a number to the AC when the number is
   a. an immediate operand
   b. a direct-address operand
   c. an indirect-address operand

15.5 A stack is implemented as shown in Figure 10.14. Show the sequence of micro-operations for
   a. popping
   b. pushing the stack

CHAPTER 16

MICROPROGRAMMED CONTROL

586

KEY POINTS

◆ An alternative to a hardwired control unit is a microprogrammed control unit, in which the logic of the control unit is specified by a microprogram. A microprogram consists of a sequence of instructions in a microprogramming language. These are very simple instructions that specify micro-operations.

◆ A microprogrammed control unit is a relatively simple logic circuit that is capable of (1) sequencing through microinstructions and (2) generating control signals to execute each microinstruction.

◆ As in a hardwired control unit, the control signals generated by a microinstruction are used to cause register transfers and ALU operations.

The term *microprogram* was first coined by M. V. Wilkes in the early 1950s [WILK51]. Wilkes proposed an approach to control unit design that was organized and systematic and avoided the complexities of a hardwired implementation. The idea intrigued many researchers but appeared unworkable because it would require a fast, relatively inexpensive control memory.

The state of the microprogramming art was reviewed by *Datamation* in its February 1964 issue. No microprogrammed system was in wide use at that time, and one of the papers [HILL64] summarized the then-popular view that the future of microprogramming "is somewhat cloudy. None of the major manufacturers has evidenced interest in the technique, although presumably all have examined it."

This situation changed dramatically within a very few months. IBM's System/360 was announced in April, and all but the largest models were microprogrammed. Although the 360 series predated the availability of semiconductor ROM, the advantages of microprogramming were compelling enough for IBM to make this move. Microprogramming became a popular technique for implementing the control unit of CISC processors. In recent years, microprogramming has become less used but remains a tool available to computer designers. For example, as we have seen, on the Pentium 4, machine instructions are converted into a RISC-like format most of which are executed without the use of microprogramming. However, some of the instructions are executed using microprogramming.

16.1 BASIC CONCEPTS

Microinstructions

The control unit seems a reasonably simple device. Nevertheless, to implement a control unit as an interconnection of basic logic elements is no easy task. The design must include logic for sequencing through micro-operations, for executing micro-operations, for interpreting opcodes, and for making decisions based on ALU flags. It is difficult to design and test such a piece of hardware. Furthermore, the design is

Table 16.1 Machine Instruction Set for Wilkes Example

Order	Effect of Order
$A\ n$	$C(Acc) + C(n)$ to Acc_1
$S\ n$	$C(Acc) - C(n)$ to Acc_1
$H\ n$	$C(n)$ to Acc_2
$V\ n$	$C(Acc_2) \times C(n)$ to Acc, where $C(n) \geq 0$
$T\ n$	$C(Acc_1)$ to n, 0 to Acc
$U\ n$	$C(Acc_1)$ to n
$R\ n$	$C(Acc) \times 2^{-(n+1)}$ to Acc
$L\ n$	$C(Acc) \times 2^{n+1}$ to Acc
$G\ n$	IF $C(Acc) < 0$, transfer control to n; if $C(Acc) \geq 0$, ignore (i.e., proceed serially)
$I\ n$	Read next character on input mechanism into n
$O\ n$	Send $C(n)$ to output mechanism

Notation: Acc = accumulator
Acc_1 = most significant half of accumulator
Acc_2 = least significant half of accumulator
n = storage location n
$C(X)$ = contents of X (X = register or storage location)

relatively inflexible. For example, it is difficult to change the design if one wishes to add a new machine instruction.

An alternative, which has been used in many CISC processors, is to implement a microprogrammed control unit.

Consider Table 16.1. In addition to the use of control signals, each micro-operation is described in symbolic notation. This notation looks suspiciously like a programming language. In fact it is a language, known as a **microprogramming language**. Each line describes a set of micro-operations occurring at one time and is known as a **microinstruction**. A sequence of instructions is known as a **microprogram**, or *firmware*. This latter term reflects the fact that a microprogram is midway between hardware and software. It is easier to design in firmware than hardware, but it is more difficult to write a firmware program than a software program.

How can we use the concept of microprogramming to implement a control unit? Consider that for each micro-operation, all that the control unit is allowed to do is generate a set of control signals. Thus, for any micro-operation, each control line emanating from the control unit is either on or off. This condition can, of course, be represented by a binary digit for each control line. So we could construct a *control word* in which each bit represents one control line. Then each micro-operation would be represented by a different pattern of 1s and 0s in the control word.

Suppose we string together a sequence of control words to represent the sequence of micro-operations performed by the control unit. Next, we must recognize that the sequence of micro-operations is not fixed. Sometimes we have an indirect cycle; sometimes we do not. So let us put our control words in a memory, with each word having a unique address. Now add an address field to each control word,

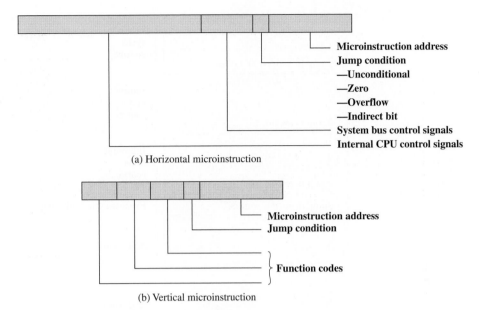

(a) Horizontal microinstruction

     Microinstruction address
     Jump condition
     —Unconditional
     —Zero
     —Overflow
     —Indirect bit
     System bus control signals
     Internal CPU control signals

     Microinstruction address
     Jump condition
     Function codes

(b) Vertical microinstruction

Figure 16.1 Typical Microinstruction Formats

indicating the location of the next control word to be executed if a certain condition is true (e.g., the indirect bit in a memory-reference instruction is 1). Also, add a few bits to specify the condition.

The result is known as a **horizontal microinstruction**, an example of which is shown in Figure 16.1a. The format of the microinstruction or control word is as follows. There is one bit for each internal processor control line and one bit for each system bus control line. There is a condition field indicating the condition under which there should be a branch, and there is a field with the address of the microinstruction to be executed next when a branch is taken. Such a microinstruction is interpreted as follows:

1. To execute this microinstruction, turn on all the control lines indicated by a 1 bit; leave off all control lines indicated by a 0 bit. The resulting control signals will cause one or more micro-operations to be performed.

2. If the condition indicated by the condition bits is false, execute the next microinstruction in sequence.

3. If the condition indicated by the condition bits is true, the next microinstruction to be executed is indicated in the address field.

Figure 16.2 shows how these control words or microinstructions could be arranged in a **control memory**. The microinstructions in each routine are to be executed sequentially. Each routine ends with a branch or jump instruction indicating where to go next. There is a special execute cycle routine whose only purpose is to signify that one of the machine instruction routines (AND, ADD, and so on) is to be executed next, depending on the current opcode.

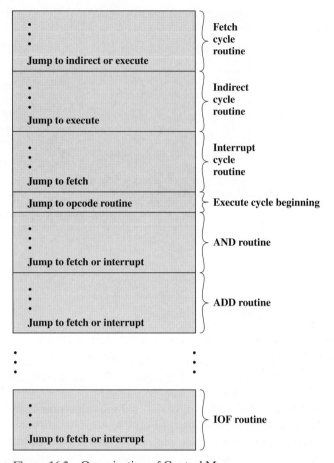

Figure 16.2   Organization of Control Memory

The control memory of Figure 16.2 is a concise description of the complete operation of the control unit. It defines the sequence of micro-operations to be performed during each cycle (fetch, indirect, execute, interrupt), and it specifies the sequencing of these cycles. If nothing else, this notation would be a useful device for documenting the functioning of a control unit for a particular computer. But it is more than that. It is also a way of implementing the control unit.

Microprogrammed Control Unit

The control memory of Figure 16.2 contains a program that describes the behavior of the control unit. It follows that we could implement the control unit by simply executing that program.

Figure 16.3 shows the key elements of such an implementation. The set of microinstructions is stored in the *control memory*. The *control address register* contains the address of the next microinstruction to be read. When a microinstruction is read from the control memory, it is transferred to a *control buffer register*. The left-hand portion of that register (see Figure 16.1a) connects to the control lines emanating

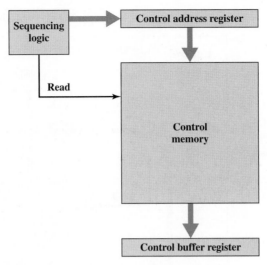

Figure 16.3   Control Unit Microarchitecture

from the control unit. Thus, *reading* a microinstruction from the control memory is the same as *executing* that microinstruction. The third element shown in the figure is a sequencing unit that loads the control address register and issues a read command.

Let us examine this structure in greater detail, as depicted in Figure 16.4. Comparing this with Figure 16.4, we see that the control unit still has the same inputs (IR, ALU flags, clock) and outputs (control signals). The control unit functions as follows:

1. To execute an instruction, the sequencing logic unit issues a READ command to the control memory.
2. The word whose address is specified in the control address register is read into the control buffer register.
3. The content of the control buffer register generates control signals and next-address information for the sequencing logic unit.
4. The sequencing logic unit loads a new address into the control address register based on the next-address information from the control buffer register and the ALU flags.

All this happens during one clock pulse.

The last step just listed needs elaboration. At the conclusion of each microinstruction, the sequencing logic unit loads a new address into the control address register. Depending on the value of the ALU flags and the control buffer register, one of three decisions is made:

- **Get the next instruction:** Add 1 to the control address register.
- **Jump to a new routine based on a jump microinstruction:** Load the address field of the control buffer register into the control address register.
- **Jump to a machine instruction routine:** Load the control address register based on the opcode in the IR.

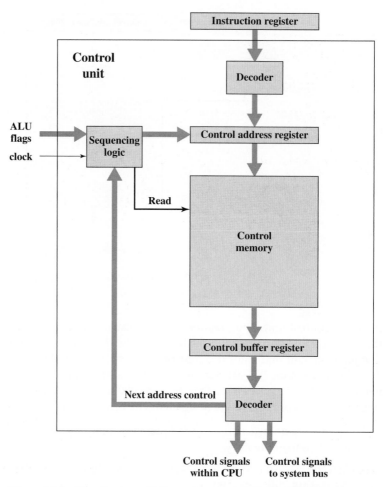

Figure 16.4 Functioning of Microprogrammed Control Unit

Figure 16.4 shows two modules labeled *decoder*. The upper decoder translates the opcode of the IR into a control memory address. The lower decoder is not used for horizontal microinstructions but is used for **vertical microinstructions** (Figure 16.1b). As was mentioned, in a horizontal microinstruction every bit in the control field attaches to a control line. In a vertical microinstruction, a code is used for each action to be performed [e.g., MAR ← (PC)], and the decoder translates this code into individual control signals. The advantage of vertical microinstructions is that they are more compact (fewer bits) than horizontal microinstructions, at the expense of a small additional amount of logic and time delay.

Wilkes Control

As was mentioned, Wilkes first proposed the use of a microprogrammed control unit in 1951 [WILK51]. This proposal was subsequently elaborated into a more detailed design [WILK53]. It is instructive to examine this seminal proposal.

The configuration proposed by Wilkes is depicted in Figure 16.5. The heart of the system is a matrix partially filled with diodes. During a machine cycle, one row of the

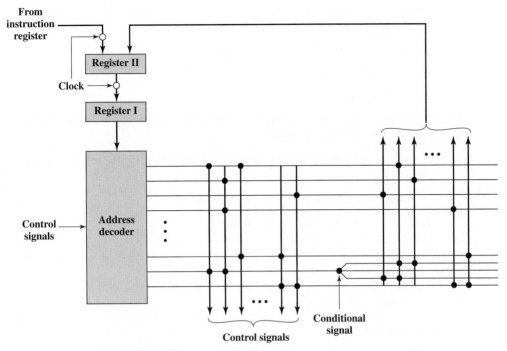

Figure 16.5 Wilkes's Microprogrammed Control Unit

matrix is activated with a pulse. This generates signals at those points where a diode is present (indicated by a dot in the diagram). The first part of the row generates the control signals that control the operation of the processor. The second part generates the address of the row to be pulsed in the next machine cycle. Thus, each row of the matrix is one microinstruction, and the layout of the matrix is the control memory.

At the beginning of the cycle, the address of the row to be pulsed is contained in Register I. This address is the input to the decoder, which, when activated by a clock pulse, activates one row of the matrix. Depending on the control signals, either the opcode in the instruction register or the second part of the pulsed row is passed into Register II during the cycle. Register II is then gated to Register I by a clock pulse. Alternating clock pulses are used to activate a row of the matrix and to transfer from Register II to Register I. The two-register arrangement is needed because the decoder is simply a combinatorial circuit; with only one register, the output would become the input during a cycle, causing an unstable condition.

This scheme is very similar to the horizontal microprogramming approach described earlier (Figure 16.1a). The main difference is this: In the previous description, the control address register could be incremented by one to get the next address. In the Wilkes scheme, the next address is contained in the microinstruction. To permit branching, a row must contain two address parts, controlled by a conditional signal (e.g., flag), as shown in the figure.

Having proposed this scheme, Wilkes provides an example of its use to implement the control unit of a simple machine. This example, the first known design of a microprogrammed processor, is worth repeating here because it illustrates many of the contemporary principles of microprogramming.

The processor of the hypothetical machine includes the following registers:

A   multiplicand
B   accumulator (least significant half)
C   accumulator (most significant half)
D   shift register

In addition, there are three registers and two 1-bit flags accessible only to the control unit. The registers are as follows:

E   serves as both a memory address register (MAR) and temporary storage
F   program counter
G   another temporary register; used for counting

Table 16.1 lists the machine instruction set for this example. Table 16.2 is the complete set of microinstructions, expressed in symbolic form, that implements the control unit. Thus, a total of 38 microinstructions is all that is required to define the system completely.

The first full column gives the address (row number) of each microinstruction. Those addresses corresponding to opcodes are labeled. Thus, when the opcode for the add instruction (A) is encountered, the microinstruction at location 5 is executed. Columns 2 and 3 express the actions to be taken by the ALU and control unit, respectively. Each symbolic expression must be translated into a set of control signals (microinstruction bits). Columns 4 and 5 have to do with the setting and use of the two flags (flip-flops). Column 4 specifies the signal that sets the flag. For example, $(1)C_s$ means that flag number 1 is set by the sign bit of the number in register C. If column 5 contains a flag identifier, then columns 6 and 7 contain the two alternative microinstruction addresses to be used. Otherwise, column 6 specifies the address of the next microinstruction to be fetched.

Instructions 0 through 4 constitute the fetch cycle. Microinstruction 4 presents the opcode to a decoder, which generates the address of a microinstruction corresponding to the machine instruction to be fetched. The reader should be able to deduce the complete functioning of the control unit from a careful study of Table 16.2.

Advantages and Disadvantages

The principal advantage of the use of microprogramming to implement a control unit is that it simplifies the design of the control unit. Thus, it is both cheaper and less error prone to implement. A *hardwired* control unit must contain complex logic for sequencing through the many micro-operations of the instruction cycle. On the other hand, the decoders and sequencing logic unit of a microprogrammed control unit are very simple pieces of logic.

The principal disadvantage of a microprogrammed unit is that it will be somewhat slower than a hardwired unit of comparable technology. Despite this, microprogramming is the dominant technique for implementing control units in pure CISC architectures, due to its ease of implementation. RISC processors, with their simpler instruction format, typically use hardwired control units. We now examine the microprogrammed approach in greater detail.

Table 16.2 Microinstructions for Wilkes Example

Notation: A, B, C, … stand for the various registers in the arithmetical and control register units. *C to D* indicates that the switching circuits connect the output of register *C* to the input register *D*; $(D + A)$ to *C* indicates that the output register of *A* is connected to the one input of the adding unit (the output of *D* is permanently connected to the other input), and the output of the adder to register *C*. A numerical symbol *n* in quotes (e.g., '*n*') stands for the source whose output is the number *n* in units of the least significant digit.

		Arithmetical Unit	Control Register Unit	Conditional Flip-Flop Set	Conditional Flip-Flop Use	Next Micro-instruction 0	Next Micro-instruction 1
	0		F to G and E			1	
	1		(G to '1') to F			2	
	2		Store to G			3	
	3		G to E			4	
	4		E to decoder			—	
A	5	C to D				16	
S	6	C to D				17	
H	7	Store to B				0	
V	8	Store to A				27	
T	9	C to Store				25	
U	10	C to Store				0	
R	11	B to D	E to G			19	
L	12	C to D	E to G			22	
G	13		E to G	$(1)C_5$		18	
I	14	Input to Store				0	
O	15	Store to Output				0	
	16	$(D + $ Store$)$ to C				0	
	17	$(D - $ Store$)$ to C				0	
	18				1	0	1
	19	D to B (R)*	$(G - $ '1'$)$ to E			20	
	20	C to D		$(1)E_5$		21	
	21	D to C (R)			1	11	0
	22	D to C (L)†	$(G - $ '1'$)$ to E			23	
	23	B to D		$(1)E_5$		24	
	24	D to B (L)			1	12	0
	25	'0' to B				26	
	26	B to C				0	
	27	'0' to C	'18' to E			28	
	28	B to D	E to G	$(1)B_1$		29	
	29	D to B (R)	$(G - $ '1'$)$ to E			30	
	30	C to D (R)		$(2)E_5$	1	31	32
	31	D to C			2	28	33

(*Continued*)

Table 16.2 Continued

	Arithmetical Unit	Control Register Unit	Conditional Flip-Flop Set	Use	Next Micro-instruction 0	1
32	$(D + A)$ to C			2	28	33
33	B to D		$(1)B_1$		34	
34	D to B (R)				35	
35	C to D (R)			1	36	37
36	D to C				0	
37	$(D - A)$ to C				0	

*Right shift. The switching circuits in the arithmetic unit are arranged so that the least significant digit of the register C is placed in the most significant place of register B during right shift micro-operations, and the most significant digit of register C (sign digit) is repeated (thus making the correction for negative numbers).

†Left shift. The switching circuits are similarly arranged to pass the most significant digit of register B to the least significant place of register C during left shift micro-operations.

16.2 MICROINSTRUCTION SEQUENCING

The two basic tasks performed by a microprogrammed control unit are as follows:

- **Microinstruction sequencing:** Get the next microinstruction from the control memory.
- **Microinstruction execution:** Generate the control signals needed to execute the microinstruction.

In designing a control unit, these tasks must be considered together, because both affect the format of the microinstruction and the timing of the control unit. In this section, we will focus on sequencing and say as little as possible about format and timing issues. These issues are examined in more detail in the next section.

Design Considerations

Two concerns are involved in the design of a microinstruction sequencing technique: the size of the microinstruction and the address-generation time. The first concern is obvious; minimizing the size of the control memory reduces the cost of that component. The second concern is simply a desire to execute microinstructions as fast as possible.

In executing a microprogram, the address of the next microinstruction to be executed is in one of these categories:

- Determined by instruction register
- Next sequential address
- Branch

The first category occurs only once per instruction cycle, just after an instruction is fetched. The second category is the most common in most designs. However, the design cannot be optimized just for sequential access. Branches, both conditional and unconditional, are a necessary part of a microprogram. Furthermore, microinstruction sequences tend to be short; one out of every three or four microinstructions could be a branch [SIEW82]. Thus, it is important to design compact, time-efficient techniques for microinstruction branching.

Sequencing Techniques

Based on the current microinstruction, condition flags, and the contents of the instruction register, a control memory address must be generated for the next microinstruction. A wide variety of techniques have been used. We can group them into three general categories, as illustrated in Figures 16.6 to 16.8. These categories are based on the format of the address information in the microinstruction:

- Two address fields
- Single address field
- Variable format

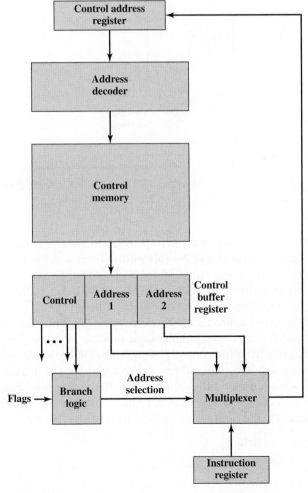

Figure 16.6 Branch Control Logic: Two Address Fields

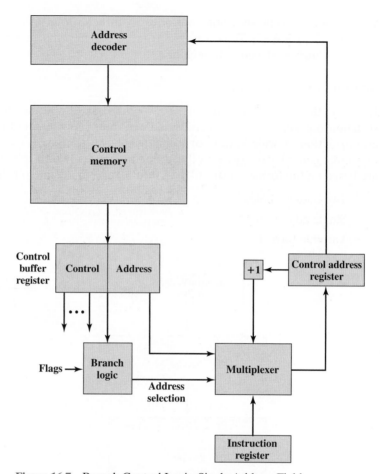

Figure 16.7 Branch Control Logic: Single Address Field

The simplest approach is to provide two address fields in each microinstruction. Figure 16.6 suggests how this information is to be used. A multiplexer is provided that serves as a destination for both address fields plus the instruction register. Based on an address-selection input, the multiplexer transmits either the opcode or one of the two addresses to the control address register (CAR). The CAR is subsequently decoded to produce the next microinstruction address. The address-selection signals are provided by a branch logic module whose input consists of control unit flags plus bits from the control portion of the microinstruction.

Although the two-address approach is simple, it requires more bits in the microinstruction than other approaches. With some additional logic, savings can be achieved. A common approach is to have a single address field (Figure 16.7). With this approach, the options for next address are as follows:

- Address field
- Instruction register code
- Next sequential address

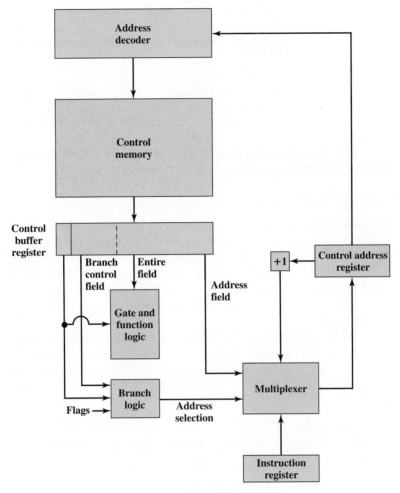

Figure 16.8   Branch Control Logic: Variable Format

The address-selection signals determine which option is selected. This approach reduces the number of address fields to one. Note, however, that the address field often will not be used. Thus, there is some inefficiency in the microinstruction coding scheme.

Another approach is to provide for two entirely different microinstruction formats (Figure 16.8). One bit designates which format is being used. In one format, the remaining bits are used to activate control signals. In the other format, some bits drive the branch logic module, and the remaining bits provide the address. With the first format, the next address is either the next sequential address or an address derived from the instruction register. With the second format, either a conditional or unconditional branch is being specified. One disadvantage of this approach is that one entire cycle is consumed with each branch microinstruction. With the other approaches, address generation occurs as part of the same cycle as control signal generation, minimizing control memory accesses.

Table 16.3 Microinstruction Address Generation Techniques

Explicit	Implicit
Two-field	Mapping
Unconditional branch	Addition
Conditional branch	Residual control

The approaches just described are general. Specific implementations will often involve a variation or combination of these techniques.

Address Generation

We have looked at the sequencing problem from the point of view of format considerations and general logic requirements. Another viewpoint is to consider the various ways in which the next address can be derived or computed.

Table 16.3 lists the various address generation techniques. These can be divided into explicit techniques, in which the address is explicitly available in the microinstruction, and implicit techniques, which require additional logic to generate the address.

We have essentially dealt with the explicit techniques. With a two-field approach, two alternative addresses are available with each microinstruction. Using either a single address field or a variable format, various branch instructions can be implemented. A conditional branch instruction depends on the following types of information:

- ALU flags
- Part of the opcode or address mode fields of the machine instruction
- Parts of a selected register, such as the sign bit
- Status bits within the control unit

Several implicit techniques are also commonly used. One of these, mapping, is required with virtually all designs. The opcode portion of a machine instruction must be mapped into a microinstruction address. This occurs only once per instruction cycle.

A common implicit technique is one that involves combining or adding two portions of an address to form the complete address. This approach was taken for the IBM S/360 family [TUCK67] and used on many of the S/370 models. We will use the IBM 3033 as an example.

The control address register on the IBM 3033 is 13 bits long and is illustrated in Figure 16.9. Two parts of the address can be distinguished. The highest-order 8 bits (00–07) normally do not change from one microinstruction cycle to the next. During the execution of a microinstruction, these 8 bits are copied directly from an 8-bit field of the microinstruction (the BA field) into the highest-order 8 bits of the control address register. This defines a block of 32 microinstructions in control memory. The remaining 5 bits of the control address register are set to specify the specific address of the microinstruction to be fetched next. Each of these bits is

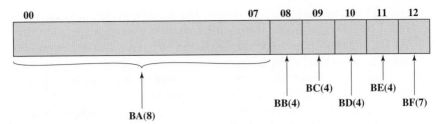

Figure 16.9   IBM 3033 Control Address Register

determined by a 4-bit field (except one is a 7-bit field) in the current microinstruction; the field specifies the condition for setting the corresponding bit. For example, a bit in the control address register might be set to 1 or 0 depending on whether a carry occurred on the last ALU operation.

The final approach listed in Table 16.3 is termed *residual control*. This approach involves the use of a microinstruction address that has previously been saved in temporary storage within the control unit. For example, some microinstruction sets come equipped with a subroutine facility. An internal register or stack of registers is used to hold return addresses. An example of this approach is taken on the LSI-11, which we now examine.

LSI-11 Microinstruction Sequencing

The LSI-11 is a microcomputer version of a PDP-11, with the main components of the system residing on a single board. The LSI-11 is implemented using a microprogrammed control unit [SEBE76].

The LSI-11 makes use of a 22-bit microinstruction and a control memory of 2K 22-bit words. The next microinstruction address is determined in one of five ways:

- **Next sequential address:** In the absence of other instructions, the control unit's control address register is incremented by 1.
- **Opcode mapping:** At the beginning of each instruction cycle, the next microinstruction address is determined by the opcode.
- **Subroutine facility:** Explained presently.
- **Interrupt testing:** Certain microinstructions specify a test for interrupts. If an interrupt has occurred, this determines the next microinstruction address.
- **Branch:** Conditional and unconditional branch microinstructions are used.

A one-level subroutine facility is provided. One bit in every microinstruction is dedicated to this task. When the bit is set, an 11-bit return register is loaded with the updated contents of the control address register. A subsequent microinstruction that specifies a return will cause the control address register to be loaded from the return register.

The return is one form of unconditional branch instruction. Another form of unconditional branch causes the bits of the control address register to be loaded from 11 bits of the microinstruction. The conditional branch instruction makes use of a 4-bit test code within the microinstruction. This code specifies testing of various ALU condition codes to determine the branch decision. If the condition is not true, the next sequential address is selected. If it is true, the 8 lowest-order bits of the control address register are loaded from 8 bits of the microinstruction. This allows branching within a 256-word page of memory.

As can be seen, the LSI-11 includes a powerful address sequencing facility within the control unit. This allows the microprogrammer considerable flexibility and can ease the microprogramming task. On the other hand, this approach requires more control unit logic than do simpler capabilities.

16.3 MICROINSTRUCTION EXECUTION

The microinstruction cycle is the basic event on a microprogrammed processor. Each cycle is made up of two parts: fetch and execute. The fetch portion is determined by the generation of a microinstruction address, and this was dealt with in the preceding section. This section deals with the execution of a microinstruction.

Recall that the effect of the execution of a microinstruction is to generate control signals. Some of these signals control points internal to the processor. The remaining signals go to the external control bus or other external interface. As an incidental function, the address of the next microinstruction is determined.

The preceding description suggests the organization of a control unit shown in Figure 16.10. This slightly revised version of Figure 16.4 emphasizes the focus of this section. The major modules in this diagram should by now be clear. The sequencing logic module contains the logic to perform the functions discussed in the preceding section. It generates the address of the next microinstruction, using as inputs the instruction register, ALU flags, the control address register (for incrementing), and the control buffer register. The last may provide an actual address, control bits, or both. The module is driven by a clock that determines the timing of the microinstruction cycle.

The control logic module generates control signals as a function of some of the bits in the microinstruction. It should be clear that the format and content of the microinstruction will determine the complexity of the control logic module.

A Taxonomy of Microinstructions

Microinstructions can be classified in a variety of ways. Distinctions that are commonly made in the literature include the following:

- Vertical/horizontal
- Packed/unpacked
- Hard/soft microprogramming
- Direct/indirect encoding

All of these bear on the format of the microinstruction. None of these terms has been used in a consistent, precise way in the literature. However, an examination

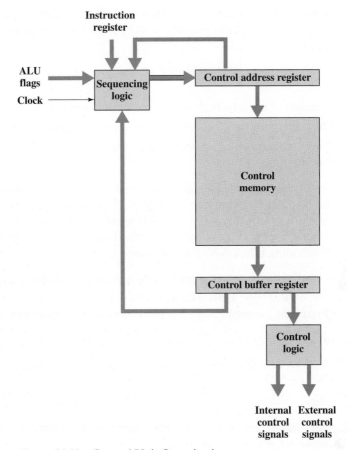

Figure 16.10 Control Unit Organization

of these pairs of qualities serves to illuminate microinstruction design alternatives. In the following paragraphs, we first look at the key design issue underlying all of these pairs of characteristics, and then we look at the concepts suggested by each pair.

In the original proposal by Wilkes [WILK51], each bit of a microinstruction either directly produced a control signal or directly produced one bit of the next address. We have seen, in the preceding section, that more complex address sequencing schemes, using fewer microinstruction bits, are possible. These schemes require a more complex sequencing logic module. A similar sort of trade-off exists for the portion of the microinstruction concerned with control signals. By encoding control information, and subsequently decoding it to produce control signals, control word bits can be saved.

How can this encoding be done? To answer that, consider that there are a total of K different internal and external control signals to be driven by the control unit. In Wilkes's scheme, K bits of the microinstruction would be dedicated to this purpose. This allows all of the 2^K possible combinations of control signals to be generated during any instruction cycle. But we can do better than this if we observe that not all of the possible combinations will be used. Examples include the following:

- Two sources cannot be gated to the same destination (e.g., C_2 and C_8 in Figure 16.5).
- A register cannot be both source and destination (e.g., C_5 and C_{12} in Figure 16.5).
- Only one pattern of control signals can be presented to the ALU at a time.
- Only one pattern of control signals can be presented to the external control bus at a time.

So, for a given processor, all possible allowable combinations of control signals could be listed, giving some number $Q < 2^K$ possibilities. These could be encoded with $\log_2 Q$ bits, with $(\log_2 Q) < K$. This would be the tightest possible form of encoding that preserves all allowable combinations of control signals. In practice, this form of encoding is not used, for two reasons:

- It is as difficult to program as a pure decoded (Wilkes) scheme. This point is discussed further presently.
- It requires a complex and therefore slow control logic module.

Instead, some compromises are made. These are of two kinds:

- More bits than are strictly necessary are used to encode the possible combinations.
- Some combinations that are physically allowable are not possible to encode.

The latter kind of compromise has the effect of reducing the number of bits. The net result, however, is to use more than $\log_2 Q$ bits.

In the next subsection, we will discuss specific encoding techniques. The remainder of this subsection deals with the effects of encoding and the various terms used to describe it.

Based on the preceding, we can see that the control signal portion of the microinstruction format falls on a spectrum. At one extreme, there is one bit for each control signal; at the other extreme, a highly encoded format is used. Table 16.4 shows that other characteristics of a microprogrammed control unit also fall along a spectrum and that these spectra are, by and large, determined by the degree-of-encoding spectrum.

The second pair of items in the table is rather obvious. The pure Wilkes scheme will require the most bits. It should also be apparent that this extreme presents the most detailed view of the hardware. Every control signal is individually controllable by the microprogrammer. Encoding is done in such a way as to aggregate functions or resources, so that the microprogrammer is viewing the processor at a higher, less detailed level. Furthermore, the encoding is designed to ease the microprogramming burden. Again, it should be clear that the task of understanding and orchestrating the use of all the control signals is a difficult one. As was mentioned, one of the consequences of encoding, typically, is to prevent the use of certain otherwise allowable combinations.

Table 16.4   The Microinstruction Spectrum

Characteristics	
Unencoded	Highly encoded
Many bits	Few bits
Detailed view of hardware	Aggregated view of hardware
Difficult to program	Easy to program
Concurrency fully exploited	Concurrency not fully exploited
Little or no control logic	Complex control logic
Fast execution	Slow execution
Optimize performance	Optimize programming
Terminology	
Unpacked	Packed
Horizontal	Vertical
Hard	Soft

The preceding paragraph discusses microinstruction design from the micro-programmer's point of view. But the degree of encoding also can be viewed from its hardware effects. With a pure unencoded format, little or no decode logic is needed; each bit generates a particular control signal. As more compact and more aggregated encoding schemes are used, more complex decode logic is needed. This, in turn, may affect performance. More time is needed to propagate signals through the gates of the more complex control logic module. Thus, the execution of encoded microinstructions takes longer than the execution of unencoded ones.

Thus, all of the characteristics listed in Table 16.4 fall along a spectrum of design strategies. In general, a design that falls toward the left end of the spectrum is intended to optimize the performance of the control unit. Designs toward the right end are more concerned with optimizing the process of microprogramming. Indeed, microinstruction sets near the right end of the spectrum look very much like machine instruction sets. A good example of this is the LSI-11 design, described later in this section. Typically, when the objective is simply to implement a control unit, the design will be near the left end of the spectrum. The IBM 3033 design, discussed presently, is in this category. As we shall discuss later, some systems permit a variety of users to construct different microprograms using the same microinstruction facility. In the latter cases, the design is likely to fall near the right end of the spectrum.

We can now deal with some of the terminology introduced earlier. Table 16.4 indicates how three of these pairs of terms relate to the microinstruction spectrum. In essence, all of these pairs describe the same thing but emphasize different design characteristics.

The degree of packing relates to the degree of identification between a given control task and specific microinstruction bits. As the bits become more *packed,* a given number of bits contains more information. Thus, packing connotes encoding. The terms *horizontal* and *vertical* relate to the relative width of microinstructions.

[SIEW82] suggests as a rule of thumb that vertical microinstructions have lengths in the range of 16 to 40 bits and that horizontal microinstructions have lengths in the range of 40 to 100 bits. The terms *hard* and *soft* microprogramming are used to suggest the degree of closeness to the underlying control signals and hardware layout. Hard microprograms are generally fixed and committed to read-only memory. Soft microprograms are more changeable and are suggestive of user microprogramming.

The other pair of terms mentioned at the beginning of this subsection refers to direct versus indirect encoding, a subject to which we now turn.

Microinstruction Encoding

In practice, microprogrammed control units are not designed using a pure unencoded or horizontal microinstruction format. At least some degree of encoding is used to reduce control memory width and to simplify the task of microprogramming.

The basic technique for encoding is illustrated in Figure 16.11a. The microinstruction is organized as a set of fields. Each field contains a code, which, upon decoding, activates one or more control signals.

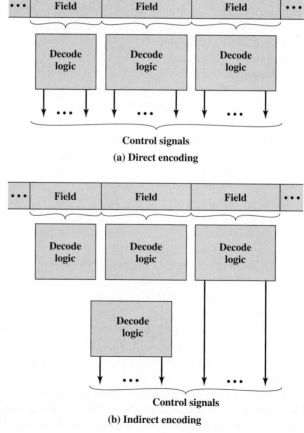

Figure 16.11 Microinstruction Encoding

Let us consider the implications of this layout. When the microinstruction is executed, every field is decoded and generates control signals. Thus, with N fields, N simultaneous actions are specified. Each action results in the activation of one or more control signals. Generally, but not always, we will want to design the format so that each control signal is activated by no more than one field. Clearly, however, it must be possible for each control signal to be activated by at least one field.

Now consider the individual field. A field consisting of L bits can contain one of 2^L codes, each of which can be encoded to a different control signal pattern. Because only one code can appear in a field at a time, the codes are mutually exclusive, and, therefore, the actions they cause are mutually exclusive.

The design of an encoded microinstruction format can now be stated in simple terms:

- Organize the format into independent fields. That is, each field depicts a set of actions (pattern of control signals) such that actions from different fields can occur simultaneously.
- Define each field such that the alternative actions that can be specified by the field are mutually exclusive. That is, only one of the actions specified for a given field could occur at a time.

Two approaches can be taken to organizing the encoded microinstruction into fields: functional and resource. The *functional encoding* method identifies functions within the machine and designates fields by function type. For example, if various sources can be used for transferring data to the accumulator, one field can be designated for this purpose, with each code specifying a different source. *Resource encoding* views the machine as consisting of a set of independent resources and devotes one field to each (e.g., I/O, memory, ALU).

Another aspect of encoding is whether it is direct or indirect (Figure 16.11b). With indirect encoding, one field is used to determine the interpretation of another field. For example, consider an ALU that is capable of performing eight different arithmetic operations and eight different shift operations. A 1-bit field could be used to indicate whether a shift or arithmetic operation is to be used; a 3-bit field would indicate the operation. This technique generally implies two levels of decoding, increasing propagation delays.

Figure 16.12 is a simple example of these concepts. Assume a processor with a single accumulator and several internal registers, such as a program counter and a temporary register for ALU input. Figure 16.12a shows a highly vertical format. The first 3 bits indicate the type of operation, the next 3 encode the operation, and the final 2 select an internal register. Figure 16.12b is a more horizontal approach, although encoding is still used. In this case, different functions appear in different fields.

LSI-11 Microinstruction Execution

The LSI-11 [SEBE76] is a good example of a vertical microinstruction approach. We look first at the organization of the control unit, then at the microinstruction format.

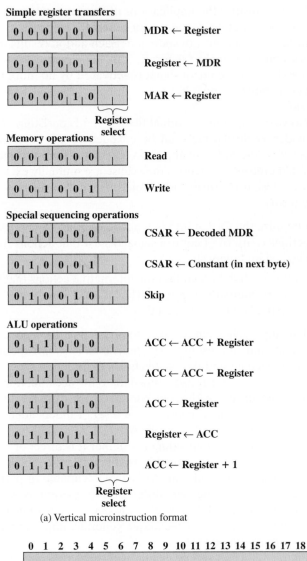

(a) Vertical microinstruction format

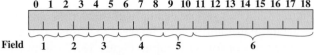

Field definition
1—register transfer   4—ALU operation
2—memory operation   5—register selection
3—sequencing operation   6—Constant

(b) Horizontal microinstruction format

Figure 16.12 Alternative Microinstruction Formats for a Simple Machine

LSI-11 CONTROL UNIT ORGANIZATION The LSI-11 is the first member of the PDP-11 family that was offered as a single-board processor. The board contains three LSI chips, an internal bus known as the *microinstruction bus* (MIB), and some additional interfacing logic.

Figure 16.13 depicts, in simplified form, the organization of the LSI-11 processor. The three chips are the data, control, and control store chips. The data chip contains an 8-bit ALU, twenty-six 8-bit registers, and storage for several condition codes. Sixteen of the registers are used to implement the eight 16-bit general-purpose registers of the PDP-11. Others include a program status word, memory address register (MAR), and memory buffer register. Because the ALU deals with only 8 bits at a time, two passes through the ALU are required to implement a 16-bit PDP-11 arithmetic operation. This is controlled by the microprogram.

The control store chip or chips contain the 22-bit-wide control memory. The control chip contains the logic for sequencing and executing microinstructions. It contains the control address register, the control data register, and a copy of the machine instruction register.

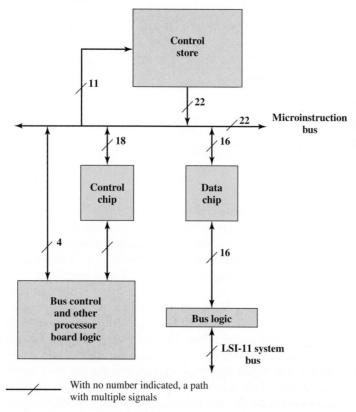

Figure 16.13   Simplified Block Diagram of the LSI-11 Processor

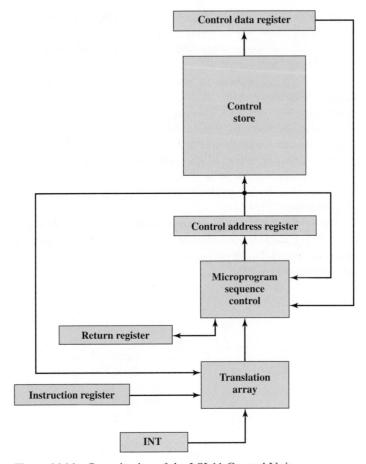

Figure 16.14 Organization of the LSI-11 Control Unit

The MIB ties all the components together. During microinstruction fetch, the control chip generates an 11-bit address onto the MIB. Control store is accessed, producing a 22-bit microinstruction, which is placed on the MIB. The low-order 16 bits go to the data chip, while the low-order 18 bits go to the control chip. The high-order 4 bits control special processor board functions.

Figure 16.14 provides a still simplified but more detailed look at the LSI-11 control unit: The figure ignores individual chip boundaries. The address sequencing scheme described in Section 16.2 is implemented in two modules. Overall sequence control is provided by the microprogram sequence control module, which is capable of incrementing the microinstruction address register and performing unconditional branches. The other forms of address calculation are carried out by a separate translation array. This is a combinatorial circuit that generates an address based on the microinstruction, the machine instruction, the microinstruction program counter, and an interrupt register.

The translation array comes into play on the following occasions:

- The opcode is used to determine the start of a microroutine.
- At appropriate times, address mode bits of the microinstruction are tested to perform appropriate addressing.
- Interrupt conditions are periodically tested.
- Conditional branch microinstructions are evaluated.

LSI-11 MICROINSTRUCTION FORMAT The LSI-11 uses an extremely vertical microinstruction format, which is only 22 bits wide. The microinstruction set strongly resembles the PDP-11 machine instruction set that it implements. This design was intended to optimize the performance of the control unit within the constraint of a vertical, easily programmed design. Table 16.5 lists some of the LSI-11 microinstructions.

Figure 16.15 shows the 22-bit LSI-11 microinstruction format. The high-order 4 bits control special functions on the processor board. The translate bit enables the translation array to check for pending interrupts. The load return register bit is used at the end of a microroutine to cause the next microinstruction address to be loaded from the return register.

Table 16.5 Some LSI-11 Microinstructions

Arithmetic Operations	**General Operations**
Add word (byte, literal)	MOV word (byte)
Test word (byte, literal)	Jump
Increment word (byte) by 1	Return
Increment word (byte) by 2	Conditional jump
Negate word (byte)	Set (reset) flags
Conditionally increment (decrement) byte	Load G low
Conditionally add word (byte)	Conditionally MOV word (byte)
Add word (byte) with carry	
Conditionally add digits	**Input/Output Operations**
Subtract word (byte)	Input word (byte)
Compare word (byte, literal)	Input status word (byte)
Subtract word (byte) with carry	Read
Decrement word (byte) by 1	Write
	Read (write) and increment word (byte) by 1
Logical Operations	Read (write) and increment word (byte) by 2
AND word (byte, literal)	Read (write) acknowledge
Test word (byte)	Output word (byte, status)
OR word (byte)	
Exclusive-OR word (byte)	
Bit clear word (byte)	
Shift word (byte) right (left) with (without) carry	
Complement word (byte)	

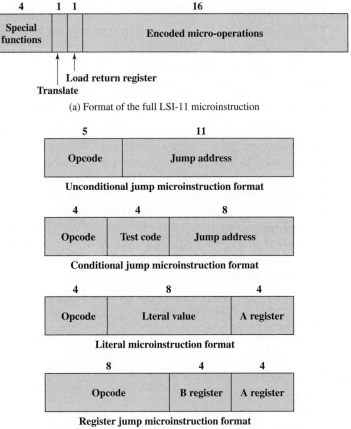

(a) Format of the full LSI-11 microinstruction

Unconditional jump microinstruction format

Conditional jump microinstruction format

Literal microinstruction format

Register jump microinstruction format

(b) Format of the encoded part of the LSI-11 microinstruction

Figure 16.15 LSI-11 Microinstruction Format

The remaining 16 bits are used for highly encoded micro-operations. The format is much like a machine instruction, with a variable-length opcode and one or more operands.

IBM 3033 Microinstruction Execution

The standard IBM 3033 control memory consists of 4K words. The first half of these (0000–07FF) contain 108-bit microinstructions, while the remainder (0800–0FFF) are used to store 126-bit microinstructions. The format is depicted in Figure 16.16. Although this is a rather horizontal format, encoding is still extensively used. The key fields of that format are summarized in Table 16.6.

The ALU operates on inputs from four dedicated, non-user-visible registers, A, B, C, and D. The microinstruction format contains fields for loading these registers from user-visible registers, performing an ALU function, and specifying a user-visible register for storing the result. There are also fields for loading and storing data between registers and memory.

The sequencing mechanism for the IBM 3033 was discussed in Section 16.2.

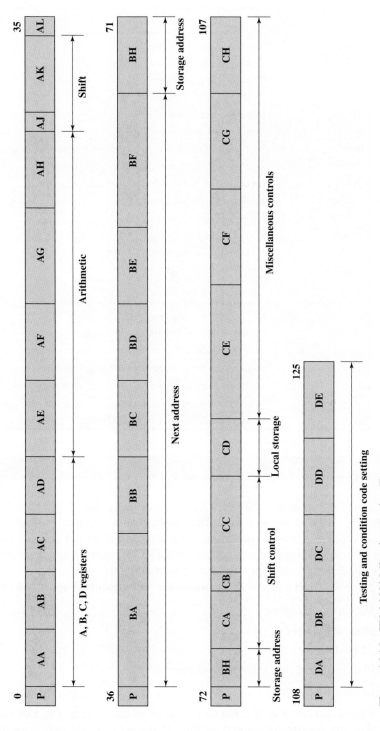

Figure 16.16 IBM 3033 Microinstruction Format

613

Table 16.6   IBM 3033 Microinstruction Control Fields

ALU Control Fields	
AA(3)	Load A register from one of data registers
AB(3)	Load B register from one of data registers
AC(3)	Load C register from one of data registers
AD(3)	Load D register from one of data registers
AE(4)	Route specified A bits to ALU
AF(4)	Route specified B bits to ALU
AG(5)	Specifies ALU arithmetic operation on A input
AH(4)	Specifies ALU arithmetic operation on B input
AJ(1)	Specifies D or B input to ALU on B side
AK(4)	Route arithmetic output to shifter
CA(3)	Load F register
CB(1)	Activate shifter
CC(5)	Specifies logical and carry functions
CE(7)	Specifies shift amount
Sequencing and Branching Fields	
AL(1)	End operation and perform branch
BA(8)	Set high-order bits (00–07) of control address register
BB(4)	Specifies condition for setting bit 8 of control address register
BC(4)	Specifies condition for setting bit 9 of control address register
BD(4)	Specifies condition for setting bit 10 of control address register
BE(4)	Specifies condition for setting bit 11 of control address register
BF(7)	Specifies condition for setting bit 12 of control address register

16.4 TI 8800

The Texas Instruments 8800 Software Development Board (SDB) is a microprogrammable 32-bit computer card. The system has a writable control store, implemented in RAM rather than ROM. Such a system does not achieve the speed or density of a microprogrammed system with a ROM control store. However, it is useful for developing prototypes and for educational purposes.

The 8800 SDB consists of the following components (Figure 16.17):

- Microcode memory
- Microsequencer
- 32-bit ALU
- Floating-point and integer processor
- Local data memory

Two buses link the internal components of the system. The DA bus provides data from the microinstruction data field to the ALU, the floating-point processor,

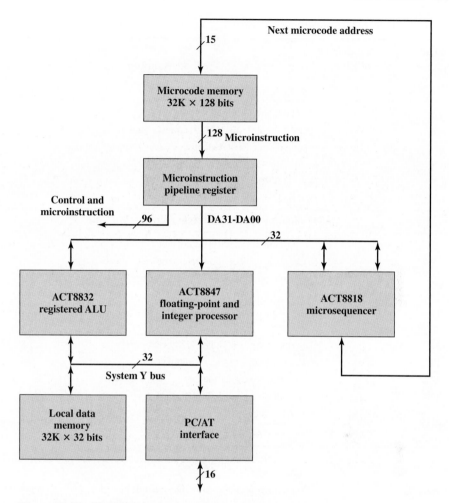

Figure 16.17 TI 8800 Block Diagram

or the microsequencer. In the latter case, the data consists of an address to be used for a branch instruction. The bus can also be used for the ALU or microsequencer to provide data to other components. The System Y bus connects the ALU and floating-point processor to local memory and to external modules via the PC interface.

The board fits into an IBM PC-compatible host computer. The host computer provides a suitable platform for microcode assembly and debug.

Microinstruction Format

The microinstruction format for the 8800 consists of 128 bits broken down into 30 functional fields, as indicated in Table 16.7. Each field consists of one or more bits, and the fields are grouped into five major categories:

- Control of board
- 8847 floating-point and integer processor chip

Table 16.7 TI 8800 Microinstruction Format

Field Number	Number of Bits	Description
		Control of Board
1	5	Select condition code input
2	1	Enable/disable external I/O request signal
3	2	Enable/disable local data memory read/write operations
4	1	Load status/do no load status
5	2	Determine unit driving Y bus
6	2	Determine unit driving DA bus
		8847 Floating Point and Integer Processing Chip
7	1	C register control: clock, do not clock
8	1	Select most significant or least significant bits for Y bus
9	1	C register data source: ALU, multiplexer
10	4	Select IEEE or FAST mode for ALU and MUL
11	8	Select sources for data operands: RA registers, RB registers, P register, 5 register, C register
12	1	RB register control: clock, do not clock
13	1	RA register control: clock, do not clock
14	2	Data source confirmation
15	2	Enable/disable pipeline registers
16	11	8847 ALU function
		8832 Registered ALU
17	2	Write enable/disable data output to selected register: most significant half, least significant half
18	2	Select register file data source: DA bus, DB bus, ALU Y MUX output, system Y bus
19	3	Shift instruction modifier
20	1	Carry in: force, do not force
21	2	Set ALU configuration mode: 32, 16, or 8 bits
22	2	Select input to 5 multiplexer: register file, DB bus, MQ register
23	1	Select input to R multiplexer: register file, DA bus
24	6	Select register in file C for write
25	6	Select register in file B for read
26	6	Select register in file A for write
27	8	ALU function
		8818 Microsequencer
28	12	Control input signals to the 8818
		WCS Data Field
29	16	Most significant bits of writable control store data field
30	16	Least significant bits of writable control store data field

- 8832 registered ALU
- 8818 microsequencer
- WCS data field

As indicated in Figure 16.17, the 32 bits of the WCS data field are fed into the DA bus to be provided as data to the ALU, floating-point processor, or microsequencer. The other 96 bits (fields 1–27) of the microinstruction are control signals that are fed directly to the appropriate module. For simplicity, these other connections are not shown in Figure 16.17.

The first six fields deal with operations that pertain to the control of the board, rather than controlling an individual component. Control operations include the following:

- Selecting condition codes for sequencer control. The first bit of field 1 indicates whether the condition flag is to be set to 1 or 0, and the remaining 4 bits indicate which flag is to be set.
- Sending an I/O request to the PC/AT.
- Enabling local data memory read/write operations.
- Determining the unit driving the system Y bus. One of the four devices attached to the bus (Figure 16.17) is selected.

The last 32 bits are the data field, which contain information specific to a particular microinstruction.

The remaining fields of the microinstruction are best discussed in the context of the device that they control. In the remainder of this section, we discuss the microsequencer and the registered ALU. The floating-point unit introduces no new concepts and is skipped.

Microsequencer

The principal function of the 8818 microsequencer is to generate the next microinstruction address for the microprogram. This 15-bit address is provided to the microcode memory (Figure 16.17).

The next address can be selected from one of five sources:

1. The microprogram counter (MPC) register, used for repeat (reuse same address) and continue (increment address by 1) instructions.
2. The stack, which supports microprogram subroutine calls as well as iterative loops and returns from interrupts.
3. The DRA and DRB ports, which provide two additional paths from external hardware by which microprogram addresses can be generated. These two ports are connected to the most significant and least significant 16 bits of the DA bus, respectively. This allows the microsequencer to obtain the next instruction address from the WCS data field of the current microinstruction or from a result calculated by the ALU.
4. Register counters RCA and RCB, which can be used for additional address storage.
5. An external input onto the bidirectional Y port to support external interrupts.

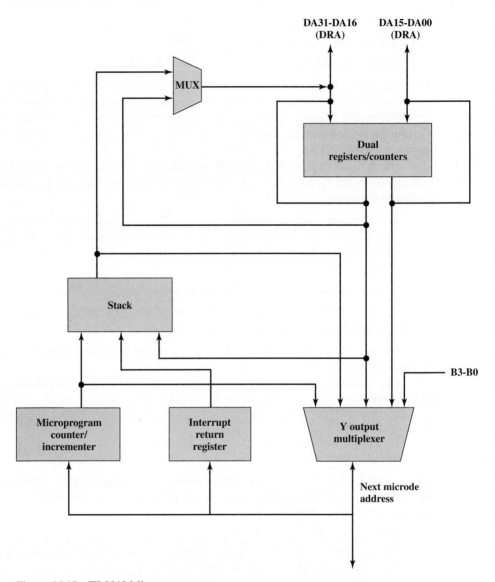

Figure 16.18 TI 8818 Microsequencer

Figure 16.18 is a logical block diagram of the 8818. The device consists of the following principal functional groups:

- A 16-bit microprogram counter (MPC) consisting of a register and an incrementer
- Two register counters, RCA and RCB, for counting loops and iterations, storing branch addresses, or driving external devices
- A 65-word by 16-bit stack, which allows microprogram subroutine calls and interrupts

- An interrupt return register and Y output enable for interrupt processing at the microinstruction level
- A Y output multiplexer by which the next address can be selected from MPC, RCA, RCB, external buses DRA and DRB, or the stack

REGISTERS/COUNTERS The registers RCA and RCB may be loaded from the DA bus, either from the current microinstruction or from the output of the ALU. The values may be used as counters to control the flow of execution and may be automatically decremented when accessed. The values may also be used as microinstruction addresses to be supplied to the Y output multiplexer. Independent control of both registers during a single microinstruction cycle is supported with the exception of simultaneous decrement of both registers.

STACK The stack allows multiple levels of nested calls or interrupts, and it can be used to support branching and looping. Keep in mind that these operations refer to the control unit, not the overall processor, and that the addresses involved are those of microinstructions in the control memory.

Six stack operations are possible:

1. Clear, which sets the stack pointer to zero, emptying the stack
2. Pop, which decrements the stack pointer
3. Push, which puts the contents of the MPC, interrupt return register, or DRA bus onto the stack and increments the stack pointer
4. Read, which makes the address indicated by the read pointer available at the Y output multiplexer
5. Hold, which causes the address of the stack pointer to remain unchanged
6. Load stack pointer, which inputs the seven least significant bits of DRA to the stack pointer

CONTROL OF MICROSEQUENCER The microsequencer is controlled primarily by the 12-bit field of the current microinstruction, field 28 (Table 16.7). This field consists of the following subfields:

- **OSEL (1 bit):** Output select. Determines which value will be placed on the output of the multiplexer that feeds into the DRA bus (upper-left-hand corner of Figure 16.18). The output is selected to come from either the stack or from register RCA. DRA then serves as input to either the Y output multiplexer or to register RCA.
- **SELDR (1 bit):** Select DR bus. If set to 1, this bit selects the external DA bus as input to the DRA/DRB buses. If set to 0, selects the output of the DRA multiplexer to the DRA bus (controlled by OSEL) and the contents of RCB to the DRB bus.
- **ZEROIN (1 bit):** Used to indicate a conditional branch. The behavior of the microsequencer will then depend on the condition code selected in field 1 (Table 16.7).
- **RC2–RC0 (3 bits):** Register controls. These bits determine the change in the contents of registers RCA and RCB. Each register can either remain the same, decrement, or load from the DRA/DRB buses.

- **S2–S0 (3 bits):** Stack controls. These bits determine which stack operation is to be performed.
- **MUX2–MUX0:** Output controls. These bits, together with the condition code if used, control the Y output multiplexer and therefore the next microinstruction address. The multiplexer can select its output from the stack, DRA, DRB, or MPC.

These bits can be set individually by the programmer. However, this is typically not done. Rather, the programmer uses mnemonics that equate to the bit patterns that would normally be required. Table 16.8 lists the 15 mnemonics for field 28. A microcode assembler converts these into the appropriate bit patterns.

As an example, the instruction INC88181 is used to cause the next microinstruction in sequence to be selected, if the currently selected condition code is 1. From Table 16.8, we have

$$INC88181 = 000000111110$$

which decodes directly into

- **OSEL = 0:** Selects RCA as output from DRA output MUX; in this case the selection is irrelevant.
- **SELDR = 0:** As defined previously; again, this is irrelevant for this instruction.
- **ZEROIN = 0:** Combined with the value for MUX, indicates no branch should be taken.
- **R = 000:** Retain current value of RA and RC.
- **S = 111:** Retain current state of stack.
- **MUX = 110:** Choose MPC when condition code = 1, DRA when condition code = 0.

Table 16.8 TI 8818 Microsequencer Microinstruction Bits (Field 28)

Mnemonic	Value	Description
RST8818	000000000110	Reset Instruction
BRA88181	011000111000	Branch to DRA Instruction
BRA88180	010000111110	Branch to DRA Instruction
INC88181	000000111110	Continue Instruction
INC88180	001000001000	Continue Instruction
CAL88181	010000110000	Jump to Subroutine at Address Specified by DRA
CAL88180	010000101110	Jump to Subroutine at Address Specified by DRA
RET8818	000000011010	Return from Subroutine
PUSH8818	000000110111	Push Interrupt Return Address onto Stack
POP8818	100000010000	Return from Interrupt
LOADDRA	000010111110	Load DRA Counter from DA Bus
LOADDRB	000110111110	Load DRB Counter from DA Bus
LOADDRAB	000110111100	Load DRA/DRB
DECRDRA	010001111100	Decrement DRA Counter and Branch If Not Zero
DECRDRB	010101111100	Decrement DRB Counter and Branch If Not Zero

Registered ALU

The 8832 is a 32-bit ALU with 64 registers that can be configured to operate as four 8-bit ALUs, two 16-bit ALUs, or a single 32-bit ALU.

The 8832 is controlled by the 39 bits that make up fields 17 through 27 of the microinstruction (Table 16.7); these are supplied to the ALU as control signals. In addition, as indicated in Figure 16.17, the 8832 has external connections to the 32-bit DA bus and the 32-bit system Y bus. Inputs from the DA can be provided simultaneously as input data to the 64-word register file and to the ALU logic module. Input from the system Y bus is provided to the ALU logic module. Results of the ALU and shift operations are output to the DA bus or the system Y bus. Results can also be fed back to the internal register file.

Three 6-bit address ports allow a two-operand fetch and an operand write to be performed within the register file simultaneously. An MQ shifter and MQ register can also be configured to function independently to implement double-precision 8-bit, 16-bit, and 32-bit shift operations.

Fields 17 through 26 of each microinstruction control the way in which data flows within the 8832 and between the 8832 and the external environment. The fields are as follows:

17. **Write Enable.** These two bits specify write 32 bits, or 16 most significant bits, or 16 least significant bits, or do not write into register file. The destination register is defined by field 24.

18. **Select Register File Data Source.** If a write is to occur to the register file, these two bits specify the source: DA bus, DB bus, ALU output, or system Y bus.

19. **Shift Instruction Modifier.** Specifies options concerning supplying end fill bits and reading bits that are shifted during shift instructions.

20. **Carry In.** This bit indicates whether a bit is carried into the ALU for this operation.

21. **ALU Configuration Mode.** The 8832 can be configured to operate as a single 32-bit ALU, two 16-bit ALUs, or four 8-bit ALUs.

22. **S Input.** The ALU logic module inputs are provided by two internal multiplexers referred to as the S and R multiplexers. This field selects the input to be provided by the S multiplexer: register file, DB bus, or MQ register. The source register is defined by field 25.

23. **R Input.** Selects input to be provided by the R multiplexer: register file or DA bus.

24. **Destination Register.** Address of register in register file to be used for the destination operand.

25. **Source Register.** Address of register in register file to be used for the source operand, provided by the S multiplexer.

26. **Source Register.** Address of register in register file to be used for the source operand, provided by the R multiplexer.

Finally, field 27 is an 8-bit opcode that specifies the arithmetic or logical function to be performed by the ALU. Table 16.9 lists the different operations that can be performed.

Table 16.9   TI 8832 Registered ALU Instruction Field (Field 27)

Group 1		Function
ADD	H#01	R + S + Cn
SUBR	H#02	(NOT R) + S + Cn
SUBS	H#03	R = (NOT S) + Cn
INSC	H#04	S + Cn
INCNS	H#05	(NOT S) + Cn
INCR	H#06	R + Cn
INCNR	H#07	(NOT R) + Cn
XOR	H#09	R XOR S
AND	H#0A	R AND S
OR	H#0B	R OR S
NAND	H#0C	R NAND S
NOR	H#0D	R NOR S
ANDNR	H#0E	(NOT R) AND S
Group 2		**Function**
SRA	H#00	Arithmetic right single precision shift
SRAD	H#10	Arithmetic right double precision shift
SRL	H#20	Logical right single precision shift
SRLD	H#30	Logical right double precision shift
SLA	H#40	Arithmetic left single precision shift
SLAD	H#50	Arithmetic left double precision shift
SLC	H#60	Circular left single precision shift
SLCD	H#70	Circular left double precision shift
SRC	H#80	Circular right single precision shift
SRCD	H#90	Circular right double precision shift
MQSRA	H#A0	Arithmetic right shift MQ register
MQSRL	H#B0	Logical right shift MQ register
MQSLL	H#C0	Logical left shift MQ register
MQSLC	H#D0	Circular left shift MQ register
LOADMQ	H#E0	Load MQ register
PASS	H#F0	Pass ALU to Y (no shift operation)
Group 3		**Function**
SET1	H#08	Set bit 1
Set0	H#18	Set bit 0
TB1	H#28	Test bit 1
TB0	H#38	Test bit 0
ABS	H#48	Absolute value
SMTC	H#58	Sign magnitude/twos-complement
ADDI	H#68	Add immediate
SUBI	H#78	Subtract immediate

Table 16.9 Continued

BADD	H#88	Byte add R to S
BSUBS	H#98	Byte subtract S from R
BSUBR	H#A8	Byte subtract R from S
BINCS	H#B8	Byte increment S
BINCNS	H#C8	Byte increment negative S
BXOR	H#D8	Byte XOR R and S
BAND	H#E8	Byte AND R and S
BOR	H#F8	Byte OR R and S
Group 4		**Function**
CRC	H#00	Cyclic redundancy character accum.
SEL	H#10	Select S or R
SNORM	H#20	Single length normalize
DNORM	H#30	Double length normalize
DIVRF	H#40	Divide remainder fix
SDIVQF	H#50	Signed divide quotient fix
SMULI	H#60	Signed multiply iterate
SMULT	H#70	Signed multiply terminate
SDIVIN	H#80	Signed divide initialize
SDIVIS	H#90	Signed divide start
SDIVI	H#A0	Signed divide iterate
UDIVIS	H#B0	Unsigned divide start
UDIVI	H#C0	Unsigned divide iterate
UMULI	H#D0	Unsigned multiply iterate
SDIVIT	H#E0	Signed divide terminate
UDIVIT	H#F0	Unsigned divide terminate
Group 5		**Function**
LOADFF	H#0F	Load divide/BCD flip-flops
CLR	H#1F	Clear
DUMPFF	H#5F	Output divide/BCD flip-flops
BCDBIN	H#7F	BCD to binary
EX3BC	H#8F	Excess −3 byte correction
EX3C	H#9F	Excess −3 word correction
SDIVO	H#AF	Signed divide overflow test
BINEX3	H#DF	Binary to excess −3
NOP32	H#FF	No operation

As an example of the coding used to specify fields 17 through 27, consider the instruction to add the contents of register 1 to register 2 and place the result in register 3. The symbolic instruction is

CONT11 [17], WELH, SELRYFYMX, [24], R3, R2, R1, PASS + ADD

The assembler will translate this into the appropriate bit pattern. The individual components of the instruction can be described as follows:

- CONT11 is the basic NOP instruction.
- Field [17] is changed to WELH (write enable, low and high), so that a 32-bit register is written into
- Field [18] is changed to SELRFYMX to select the feedback from the ALU Y MUX output.
- Field [24] is changed to designate register R3 for the destination register.
- Field [25] is changed to designate register R2 for one of the source registers.
- Field [26] is changed to designate register R1 for one of the source registers.
- Field [27] is changed to specify an ALU operation of ADD. The ALU shifter instruction is PASS; therefore, the ALU output is not shifted by the shifter.

Several points can be made about the symbolic notation. It is not necessary to specify the field number for consecutive fields. That is,

CONT11 [17], WELH, [18], SELRFYMX

can be written as

CONT11 [17], WELH, SELRFYMX

because SELRFYMX is in field 18.

ALU instructions from Group 1 of Table 16.9 must always be used in conjunction with Group 2. ALU instructions from Groups 3–5 must not be used with Group 2.

16.6 RECOMMENDED READING

There are a number of books devoted to microprogramming. Perhaps the most comprehensive is [LYNC93]. [SEGE91] presents the fundamentals of microcoding and the design of microcoded systems by means of a step-by-step design of a simple 16-bit processor. [CART96] also presents the basic concepts using a sample machine. [PARK89] and [TI90] provide a detailed description of the TI 8800 Software Development Board.

[VASS03] discuss the evolution of microcode use in computer design and its current status.

CART96 Carter, J. *Microprocesser Architecture and Microprogramming.* Upper Saddle River, NJ: Prentice Hall, 1996.

LYNC93 Lynch, M. *Microprogrammed State Machine Design.* Boca Raton, FL: CRC Press, 1993.

PARK89 Parker, A., and Hamblen, J. *An Introduction to Microprogramming with Exercises Designed for the Texas Instruments SN74ACT8800 Software Development Board.* Dallas, TX: Texas Instruments, 1989.

SEGE91 Segee, B., and Field, J. *Microprogramming and Computer Architecture.* New York: Wiley, 1991.

TI90 Texas Instruments Inc. *SN74ACT880 Family Data Manual.* SCSS006C, 1990.

VASS03 Vassiliadis, S.; Wong, S.; and Cotofana, S. "Microcode Processing: Positioning and Directions." *IEEE Micro*, July-August 2003.

16.7 KEY TERMS, REVIEW QUESTIONS, AND PROBLEMS

Key Terms

control memory	microinstruction encoding	microprogrammed control unit
control word	microinstruction execution	microprogramming language
firmware	microinstruction sequencing	soft microprogramming
hard microprogramming	microinstructions	unpacked microinstruction
horizontal microinstruction	microprogram	vertical microinstruction

Review Questions

16.1   What is the difference between a hardwired implementation and a microprogrammed implementation of a control unit?

16.2   How is a horizontal microinstruction interpreted?

16.3   What is the purpose of a control memory?

16.4   What is a typical sequence in the execution of a horizontal microinstruction?

16.5   What is the difference between horizontal and vertical microinstructions?

16.6   What are the basic tasks performed by a microprogrammed control unit?

16.7   What is the difference between packed and unpacked microinstructions?

16.8   What is the difference between hard and soft microprogramming?

16.9   What is the difference between functional and resource encoding?

16.10 List some common applications of microprogramming.

Problems

16.1   Describe the implementation of the multiply instruction in the hypothetical machine designed by Wilkes. Use narrative and a flowchart.

16.2   Assume a microinstruction set that includes a microinstruction with the following symbolic form:

$$\text{IF } (AC_0 = 1) \text{ THEN CAR} \leftarrow (C_{0-6}) \text{ ELSE CAR} \leftarrow (\text{CAR}) + 1$$

where AC_0 is the sign bit of the accumulator and C_{0-6} are the first seven bits of the microinstruction. Using this microinstruction, write a microprogram that implements a Branch Register Minus (BRM) machine instruction, which branches if the AC is negative. Assume that bits C_1 through C_n of the microinstruction specify a parallel set of micro-operations. Express the program symbolically.

16.3   A simple processor has four major phases to its instruction cycle: fetch, indirect, execute, and interrupt. Two 1-bit flags designate the current phase in a hardwired implementation.
   a.   Why are these flags needed?
   b.   Why are they not needed in a microprogrammed control unit?

16.4   Consider the control unit of Figure 16.7. Assume that the control memory is 24 bits wide. The control portion of the microinstruction format is divided into two fields. A micro-operation field of 13 bits specifies the micro-operations to be performed. An address selection field specifies a condition, based on the flags, that will cause a microinstruction branch. There are eight flags.
   a.   How many bits are in the address selection field?
   b.   How many bits are in the address field?
   c.   What is the size of the control memory?

16.5 How can unconditional branching be done under the circumstances of the previous problem? How can branching be avoided; that is, describe a microinstruction that does not specify any branch, conditional or unconditional.

16.6 We wish to provide 8 control words for each machine instruction routine. Machine instruction opcodes have 5 bits, and control memory has 1024 words. Suggest a mapping from the instruction register to the control address register.

16.7 An encoded microinstruction format is to be used. Show how a 9-bit micro-operation field can be divided into subfields to specify 46 different actions.

16.8 A processor has 16 registers, an ALU with 16 logic and 16 arithmetic functions, and a shifter with 8 operations, all connected by an internal processor bus. Design a microinstruction format to specify the various micro-operations for the processor.

PART FIVE

Parallel Organization

P.1 ISSUES FOR PART FIVE

The final part of the book looks at the increasingly important area of parallel organization. In a parallel organization, multiple processing units cooperate to execute applications. Whereas a superscalar processor exploits opportunities for parallel execution at the instruction level, a parallel processing organization looks for a grosser level of parallelism, one that enables work to be done in parallel, and cooperatively, by multiple processors. A number of issues are raised by such organizations. For example, if multiple processors, each with its own cache, share access to the same memory, hardware or software mechanisms must be employed to ensure that both processors share a valid image of main memory; this is known as the cache coherence problem. This design issue, and others, is explored in Part Five.

ROAD MAP FOR PART FIVE

Chapter 17 Parallel Processing

Chapter 17 provides an overview of parallel processing considerations. Then the chapter looks at three approaches to organizing multiple processors: symmetric multiprocessors (SMPs), clusters, and nonuniform memory access (NUMA) machines. SMPs and clusters are the two most common ways of organizing multiple processors to improve performance and availability. NUMA systems are a more recent concept that have not yet achieved widespread commercial success but that show considerable promise. Finally, Chapter 17 looks at the specialized organization known as a vector processor.

Chapter 18 Multicore Computers

A multicore computer is a computer chip that contains more than one processor (core). Multicore chips allow for greater increases in computing power in contrast to a single power continually made to run faster. Chapter 18 looks at some of the fundamental design issues for multicore computers and provides examples from the Intel x86 and ARM architectures.

CHAPTER 17

PARALLEL PROCESSING

628

KEY POINTS

◆ A traditional way to increase system performance is to use multiple processors that can execute in parallel to support a given workload. The two most common multiple-processor organizations are **symmetric multiprocessors** (SMPs) and clusters. More recently, **nonuniform memory access** (NUMA) systems have been introduced commercially.

◆ An SMP consists of multiple similar processors within the same computer, interconnected by a bus or some sort of switching arrangement. The most critical problem to address in an SMP is that of cache coherence. Each processor has its own cache and so it is possible for a given line of data to be present in more than one cache. If such a line is altered in one cache, then both main memory and the other cache have an invalid version of that line. Cache coherence protocols are designed to cope with this problem.

◆ When more than one processor are implemented on a single chip, the configuration is referred to as **chip multiprocessing**. A related design scheme is to replicate some of the components of a single processor so that the processor can execute multiple threads concurrently; this is known as a **multithreaded processor**.

◆ A **cluster** is a group of interconnected, whole computers working together as a unified computing resource that can create the illusion of being one machine. The term *whole computer* means a system that can run on its own, apart from the cluster.

◆ A NUMA system is a shared-memory multiprocessor in which the access time from a given processor to a word in memory varies with the location of the memory word.

◆ A special-purpose type of parallel organization is the vector facility, which is tailored to the processing of vectors or arrays of data.

Traditionally, the computer has been viewed as a sequential machine. Most computer programming languages require the programmer to specify algorithms as sequences of instructions. Processors execute programs by executing machine instructions in a sequence and one at a time. Each instruction is executed in a sequence of operations (fetch instruction, fetch operands, perform operation, store results).

This view of the computer has never been entirely true. At the micro-operation level, multiple control signals are generated at the same time. Instruction pipelining, at least to the extent of overlapping fetch and execute operations, has been around for a long time. Both of these are examples of performing functions in parallel. This approach is taken further with superscalar organization, which exploits instruction-level parallelism. With a superscalar machine, there are multiple execution units within a single processor, and these may execute multiple instructions from the same program in parallel.

As computer technology has evolved, and as the cost of computer hardware has dropped, computer designers have sought more and more opportunities for parallelism, usually to enhance performance and, in some cases, to increase availability. After an overview, this chapter looks at some of the most prominent approaches to parallel organization. First, we examine symmetric multiprocessors (SMPs), one of the earliest and still the most common example of parallel organization. In an SMP organization, multiple processors share a common memory. This organization raises the issue of cache coherence, to which a separate section is devoted. Then we describe clusters, which consist of multiple independent computers organized in a cooperative fashion. Next, the chapter examines multithreaded processors and chip multiprocessors. Clusters have become increasingly common to support workloads that are beyond the capacity of a single SMP. Another approach to the use of multiple processors that we examine is that of nonuniform memory access (NUMA) machines. The NUMA approach is relatively new and not yet proven in the marketplace, but is often considered as an alternative to the SMP or cluster approach. Finally, this chapter looks at hardware organizational approaches to vector computation. These approaches optimize the ALU for processing vectors or arrays of floating-point numbers. They are common on the class of systems known as *supercomputers*.

17.1 MULTIPLE PROCESSOR ORGANIZATIONS

Types of Parallel Processor Systems

A taxonomy first introduced by Flynn [FLYN72] is still the most common way of categorizing systems with parallel processing capability. Flynn proposed the following categories of computer systems:

- **Single instruction, single data (SISD) stream:** A single processor executes a single instruction stream to operate on data stored in a single memory. Uniprocessors fall into this category.
- **Single instruction, multiple data (SIMD) stream:** A single machine instruction controls the simultaneous execution of a number of processing elements on a lockstep basis. Each processing element has an associated data memory, so that each instruction is executed on a different set of data by the different processors. Vector and array processors fall into this category, and are discussed in Section 18.7.
- **Multiple instruction, single data (MISD) stream:** A sequence of data is transmitted to a set of processors, each of which executes a different instruction sequence. This structure is not commercially implemented.
- **Multiple instruction, multiple data (MIMD) stream:** A set of processors simultaneously execute different instruction sequences on different data sets. SMPs, clusters, and NUMA systems fit into this category.

With the MIMD organization, the processors are general purpose; each is able to process all of the instructions necessary to perform the appropriate data transformation. MIMDs can be further subdivided by the means in which the processors communicate (Figure 17.1). If the processors share a common memory, then each processor accesses programs and data stored in the shared memory, and processors

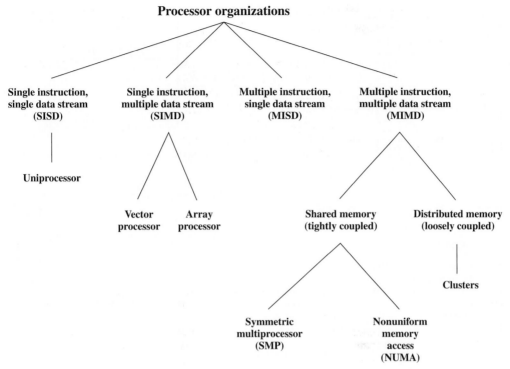

Figure 17.1 A Taxonomy of Parallel Processor Architectures

communicate with each other via that memory. The most common form of such system is known as a **symmetric multiprocessor (SMP)**, which we examine in Section 17.2. In an SMP, multiple processors share a single memory or pool of memory by means of a shared bus or other interconnection mechanism; a distinguishing feature is that the memory access time to any region of memory is approximately the same for each processor. A more recent development is the **nonuniform memory access (NUMA)** organization, which is described in Section 17.5. As the name suggests, the memory access time to different regions of memory may differ for a NUMA processor.

A collection of independent uniprocessors or SMPs may be interconnected to form a **cluster**. Communication among the computers is either via fixed paths or via some network facility.

Parallel Organizations

Figure 17.2 illustrates the general organization of the taxonomy of Figure 17.1. Figure 17.2a shows the structure of an SISD. There is some sort of control unit (CU) that provides an instruction stream (IS) to a processing unit (PU). The processing unit operates on a single data stream (DS) from a memory unit (MU). With an SIMD, there is still a single control unit, now feeding a single instruction stream to multiple PUs. Each PU may have its own dedicated memory (illustrated in Figure 17.2b), or there may be a shared memory. Finally, with the MIMD, there are multiple control units, each feeding a separate instruction stream to its own PU. The MIMD

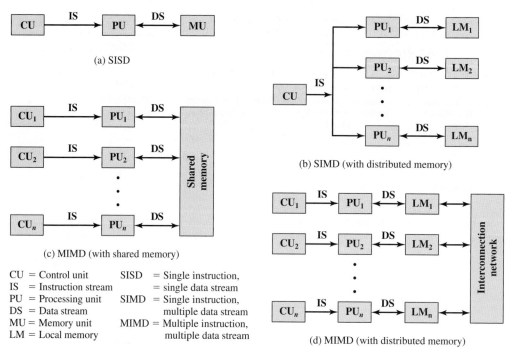

Figure 17.2 Alternative Computer Organizations

may be a shared-memory multiprocessor (Figure 17.2c) or a distributed-memory multicomputer (Figure 17.2d).

The design issues relating to SMPs, clusters, and NUMAs are complex, involving issues relating to physical organization, interconnection structures, interprocessor communication, operating system design, and application software techniques. Our concern here is primarily with organization, although we touch briefly on operating system design issues.

17.2 SYMMETRIC MULTIPROCESSORS

Until fairly recently, virtually all single-user personal computers and most workstations contained a single general-purpose microprocessor. As demands for performance increase and as the cost of microprocessors continues to drop, vendors have introduced systems with an SMP organization. The term *SMP* refers to a computer hardware architecture and also to the operating system behavior that reflects that architecture. An SMP can be defined as a standalone computer system with the following characteristics:

1. There are two or more similar processors of comparable capability.
2. These processors share the same main memory and I/O facilities and are interconnected by a bus or other internal connection scheme, such that memory access time is approximately the same for each processor.

3. All processors share access to I/O devices, either through the same channels or through different channels that provide paths to the same device.

4. All processors can perform the same functions (hence the term *symmetric*).

5. The system is controlled by an integrated operating system that provides interaction between processors and their programs at the job, task, file, and data element levels.

Points 1 to 4 should be self-explanatory. Point 5 illustrates one of the contrasts with a loosely coupled multiprocessing system, such as a cluster. In the latter, the physical unit of interaction is usually a message or complete file. In an SMP, individual data elements can constitute the level of interaction, and there can be a high degree of cooperation between processes.

The operating system of an SMP schedules processes or threads across all of the processors. An SMP organization has a number of potential advantages over a uniprocessor organization, including the following:

- **Performance:** If the work to be done by a computer can be organized so that some portions of the work can be done in parallel, then a system with multiple processors will yield greater performance than one with a single processor of the same type (Figure 17.3).

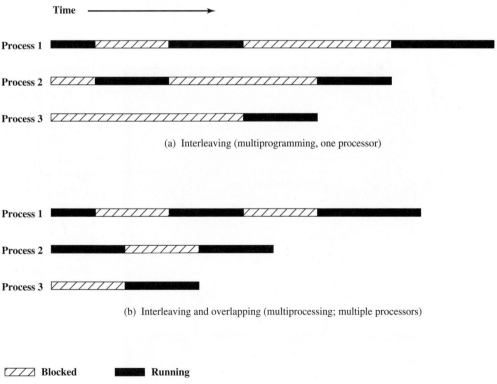

(a) Interleaving (multiprogramming, one processor)

(b) Interleaving and overlapping (multiprocessing; multiple processors)

Blocked   Running

Figure 17.3 Multiprogramming and Multiprocessing

- **Availability:** In a symmetric multiprocessor, because all processors can perform the same functions, the failure of a single processor does not halt the machine. Instead, the system can continue to function at reduced performance.
- **Incremental growth:** A user can enhance the performance of a system by adding an additional processor.
- **Scaling:** Vendors can offer a range of products with different price and performance characteristics based on the number of processors configured in the system.

It is important to note that these are potential, rather than guaranteed, benefits. The operating system must provide tools and functions to exploit the parallelism in an SMP system.

An attractive feature of an SMP is that the existence of multiple processors is transparent to the user. The operating system takes care of scheduling of threads or processes on individual processors and of synchronization among processors.

Organization

Figure 17.4 depicts in general terms the organization of a multiprocessor system. There are two or more processors. Each processor is self-contained, including a control unit, ALU, registers, and, typically, one or more levels of cache. Each processor

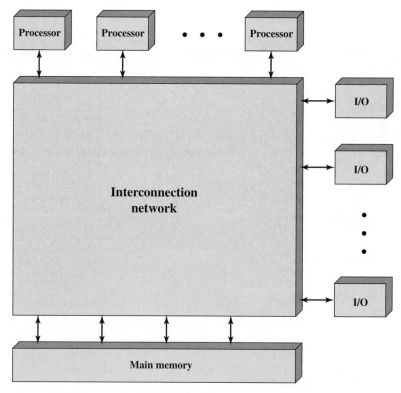

Figure 17.4 Generic Block Diagram of a Tightly Coupled Multiprocessor

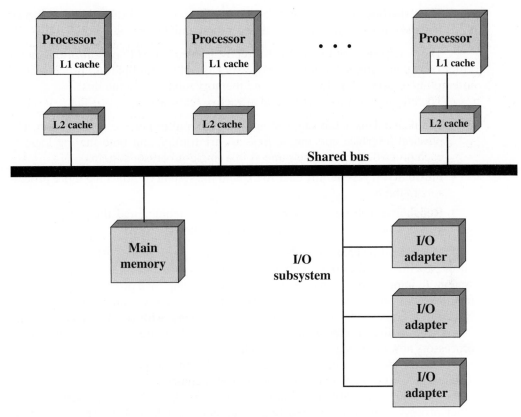

Figure 17.5 Symmetric Multiprocessor Organization

has access to a shared main memory and the I/O devices through some form of interconnection mechanism. The processors can communicate with each other through memory (messages and status information left in common data areas). It may also be possible for processors to exchange signals directly. The memory is often organized so that multiple simultaneous accesses to separate blocks of memory are possible. In some configurations, each processor may also have its own private main memory and I/O channels in addition to the shared resources.

The most common organization for personal computers, workstations, and servers is the time-shared bus. The time-shared bus is the simplest mechanism for constructing a multiprocessor system (Figure 17.5). The structure and interfaces are basically the same as for a single-processor system that uses a bus interconnection. The bus consists of control, address, and data lines. To facilitate DMA transfers from I/O processors, the following features are provided:

- **Addressing:** It must be possible to distinguish modules on the bus to determine the source and destination of data.
- **Arbitration:** Any I/O module can temporarily function as "master." A mechanism is provided to arbitrate competing requests for bus control, using some sort of priority scheme.

- **Time-sharing:** When one module is controlling the bus, other modules are locked out and must, if necessary, suspend operation until bus access is achieved.

These uniprocessor features are directly usable in an SMP organization. In this latter case, there are now multiple processors as well as multiple I/O processors all attempting to gain access to one or more memory modules via the bus.

The bus organization has several attractive features:

- **Simplicity:** This is the simplest approach to multiprocessor organization. The physical interface and the addressing, arbitration, and time-sharing logic of each processor remain the same as in a single-processor system.
- **Flexibility:** It is generally easy to expand the system by attaching more processors to the bus.
- **Reliability:** The bus is essentially a passive medium, and the failure of any attached device should not cause failure of the whole system.

The main drawback to the bus organization is performance. All memory references pass through the common bus. Thus, the bus cycle time limits the speed of the system. To improve performance, it is desirable to equip each processor with a cache memory. This should reduce the number of bus accesses dramatically. Typically, workstation and PC SMPs have two levels of cache, with the L1 cache internal (same chip as the processor) and the L2 cache either internal or external. Some processors now employ a L3 cache as well.

The use of caches introduces some new design considerations. Because each local cache contains an image of a portion of memory, if a word is altered in one cache, it could conceivably invalidate a word in another cache. To prevent this, the other processors must be alerted that an update has taken place. This problem is known as the *cache coherence* problem and is typically addressed in hardware rather than by the operating system. We address this issue in Section 17.4.

Multiprocessor Operating System Design Considerations

An SMP operating system manages processor and other computer resources so that the user perceives a single operating system controlling system resources. In fact, such a configuration should appear as a single-processor multiprogramming system. In both the SMP and uniprocessor cases, multiple jobs or processes may be active at one time, and it is the responsibility of the operating system to schedule their execution and to allocate resources. A user may construct applications that use multiple processes or multiple threads within processes without regard to whether a single processor or multiple processors will be available. Thus a multiprocessor operating system must provide all the functionality of a multiprogramming system plus additional features to accommodate multiple processors. Among the key design issues:

- **Simultaneous concurrent processes:** OS routines need to be reentrant to allow several processors to execute the same IS code simultaneously. With multiple processors executing the same or different parts of the OS, OS tables and management structures must be managed properly to avoid deadlock or invalid operations.

- **Scheduling:** Any processor may perform scheduling, so conflicts must be avoided. The scheduler must assign ready processes to available processors.

- **Synchronization:** With multiple active processes having potential access to shared address spaces or shared I/O resources, care must be taken to provide effective synchronization. Synchronization is a facility that enforces mutual exclusion and event ordering.

- **Memory management:** Memory management on a multiprocessor must deal with all of the issues found on uniprocessor machines, as is discussed in Chapter 8. In addition, the operating system needs to exploit the available hardware parallelism, such as multiported memories, to achieve the best performance. The paging mechanisms on different processors must be coordinated to enforce consistency when several processors share a page or segment and to decide on page replacement.

- **Reliability and fault tolerance:** The operating system should provide graceful degradation in the face of processor failure. The scheduler and other portions of the operating system must recognize the loss of a processor and restructure management tables accordingly.

A Mainframe SMP

Most PC and workstation SMPs use a bus interconnection strategy as depicted in Figure 17.5. It is instructive to look at an alternative approach, which is used for a recent implementation of the IBM zSeries mainframe family [SIEG04, MAK04], called the z990. This family of systems spans a range from a uniprocessor with one main memory card to a high-end system with 48 processors and 8 memory cards. The key components of the configuration are shown in Figure 17.6:

- **Dual-core processor chip:** Each processor chip includes two identical central processors (CPs). The CP is a CISC superscalar microprocessor, in which most of the instructions are hardwired and the rest are executed by vertical microcode. Each CP includes a 256-KB L1 instruction cache and a 256-KB L1 data cache.

- **L2 cache:** Each L2 cache contains 32 MB. The L2 caches are arranged in clusters of five, with each cluster supporting eight processor chips and providing access to the entire main memory space.

- **System control element (SCE):** The SCE arbitrates system communication, and has a central role in maintaining cache coherence.

- **Main store control (MSC):** The MSCs interconnect the L2 caches and the main memory.

- **Memory card:** Each card holds 32 GB of memory. The maximum configurable memory consists of 8 memory cards for a total of 256 GB. Memory cards interconnect to the MSC via synchronous memory interfaces (SMIs).

- **Memory bus adapter (MBA):** The MBA provides an interface to various types of I/O channels. Traffic to/from the channels goes directly to the L2 cache.

The microprocessor in the z990 is relatively uncommon compared with other modern processors because, although it is superscalar, it executes instructions in

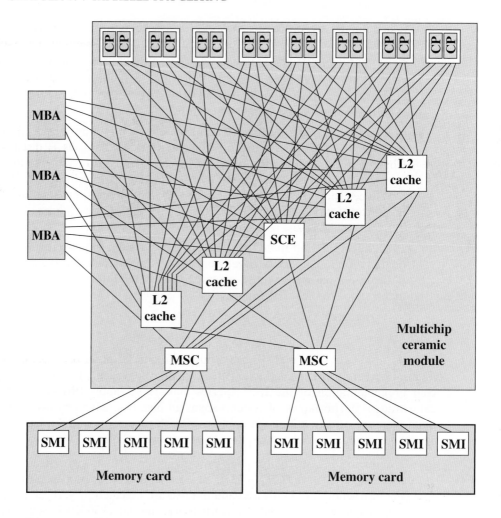

CP = central processor
MBA = memory bus adapter
MSC = main store control
SCE = system control element
SMI = synchronous memory interface

Figure 17.6   IBM z990 Multiprocessor Structure

strict architectural order. However, it makes up for this by having a shorter pipeline and much larger caches and TLBs compared with other processors, along with other performance-enhancing features.

The z990 system comprises one to four **books**. Each book is a pluggable unit containing up to 12 processors with up to 64 GB of memory, I/O adapters, and a system control element (SCE) that connects these other elements. The SCE within each book contains a 32-MB L2 cache, which serves as the central coherency point for that particular book. Both the L2 cache and the main memory are accessible by a processor or I/O adapter within that book or any of the other three books in the system. The SCE and L2 cache chips also connect with corresponding elements on the other books in a ring configuration.

There are a several interesting features in the z990 SMP configuration, which we discuss in turn:

- Switched interconnection
- Shared L2 caches

SWITCHED INTERCONNECTION A single shared bus is a common arrangement on SMPs for PCs and workstations (Figure 17.5). With this arrangement, the single bus becomes a bottleneck affecting the scalability (ability to scale to larger sizes) of the design. The z990 copes with this problem in two ways. First, main memory is split into multiple cards, each with its own storage controller that can handle memory accesses at high speeds. The average traffic load to main memory is cut, because of the independent paths to separate parts of memory. Each book includes two memory cards, for a total of eight cards across a maximum configuration. Second, the connection from processors (actually from L2 caches) to a single memory card is not in the form of a shared bus but rather point-to-point links. Each processor chip has a link to each of the L2 caches on the same book, and each L2 cache has a link, via the MSC, to each of the two memory cards on the same book.

Each L2 cache only connects to the two memory cards on the same book. The system controller provides links (not shown) to the other books in the configuration, so that all of main memory is accessible by all of the processors.

Point-to-point links rather than a bus also provides connections to I/O channels. Each L2 cache on a book connects to each of the MBAs for that book. The MBAs, in turn, connect to the I/O channels.

SHARED L2 CACHES In a typical two-level cache scheme for an SMP, each processor has a dedicated L1 cache and a dedicated L2 cache. In recent years, interest in the concept of a shared L2 cache has been growing. In an earlier version of its mainframe SMP, known as generation 3 (G3), IBM made use of dedicated L2 caches. In its later versions (G4, G5, and z900 series), a shared L2 cache is used. Two considerations dictated this change:

1. In moving from G3 to G4, IBM doubled the speed of the microprocessors. If the G3 organization were retained, a significant increase in bus traffic would occur. At the same time, it was desired to reuse as many G3 components as possible. Without a significant bus upgrade, the BSNs would become a bottleneck.

2. Analysis of typical mainframe workloads revealed a large degree of sharing of instructions and data among processors.

These considerations led the G4 design team to consider the use of one or more L2 caches, each of which was shared by multiple processors (each processor having a dedicated on-chip L1 cache). At first glance, sharing an L2 cache might seem a bad idea. Access to memory from processors should be slower because the processors must now contend for access to a single L2 cache. However, if a sufficient amount of data is in fact shared by multiple processors, then a shared cache can increase throughput rather than retard it. Data that are shared and found in the shared cache are obtained more quickly than if they must be obtained over the bus.

17.3 CACHE COHERENCE AND THE MESI PROTOCOL

In contemporary multiprocessor systems, it is customary to have one or two levels of cache associated with each processor. This organization is essential to achieve reasonable performance. It does, however, create a problem known as the *cache coherence* problem. The essence of the problem is this: Multiple copies of the same data can exist in different caches simultaneously, and if processors are allowed to update their own copies freely, an inconsistent view of memory can result. In Chapter 4 we defined two common write policies:

- **Write back:** Write operations are usually made only to the cache. Main memory is only updated when the corresponding cache line is flushed from the cache.
- **Write through:** All write operations are made to main memory as well as to the cache, ensuring that main memory is always valid.

It is clear that a write-back policy can result in inconsistency. If two caches contain the same line, and the line is updated in one cache, the other cache will unknowingly have an invalid value. Subsequent reads to that invalid line produce invalid results. Even with the write-through policy, inconsistency can occur unless other caches monitor the memory traffic or receive some direct notification of the update.

In this section, we will briefly survey various approaches to the cache coherence problem and then focus on the approach that is most widely used: the MESI (modified/exclusive/shared/invalid) protocol. A version of this protocol is used on both the Pentium 4 and PowerPC implementations.

For any cache coherence protocol, the objective is to let recently used local variables get into the appropriate cache and stay there through numerous reads and write, while using the protocol to maintain consistency of shared variables that might be in multiple caches at the same time. Cache coherence approaches have generally been divided into software and hardware approaches. Some implementations adopt a strategy that involves both software and hardware elements. Nevertheless, the classification into software and hardware approaches is still instructive and is commonly used in surveying cache coherence strategies.

Software Solutions

Software cache coherence schemes attempt to avoid the need for additional hardware circuitry and logic by relying on the compiler and operating system to deal with the problem. Software approaches are attractive because the overhead of detecting potential problems is transferred from run time to compile time, and the design complexity is transferred from hardware to software. On the other hand, compile-time software approaches generally must make conservative decisions, leading to inefficient cache utilization.

Compiler-based coherence mechanisms perform an analysis on the code to determine which data items may become unsafe for caching, and they mark those items accordingly. The operating system or hardware then prevents noncacheable items from being cached.

The simplest approach is to prevent any shared data variables from being cached. This is too conservative, because a shared data structure may be exclusively used during some periods and may be effectively read-only during other periods. It is only during periods when at least one process may update the variable and at least one other process may access the variable that cache coherence is an issue.

More efficient approaches analyze the code to determine safe periods for shared variables. The compiler then inserts instructions into the generated code to enforce cache coherence during the critical periods. A number of techniques have been developed for performing the analysis and for enforcing the results; see [LILJ93] and [STEN90] for surveys.

Hardware Solutions

Hardware-based solutions are generally referred to as cache coherence protocols. These solutions provide dynamic recognition at run time of potential inconsistency conditions. Because the problem is only dealt with when it actually arises, there is more effective use of caches, leading to improved performance over a software approach. In addition, these approaches are transparent to the programmer and the compiler, reducing the software development burden.

Hardware schemes differ in a number of particulars, including where the state information about data lines is held, how that information is organized, where coherence is enforced, and the enforcement mechanisms. In general, hardware schemes can be divided into two categories: directory protocols and snoopy protocols.

DIRECTORY PROTOCOLS Directory protocols collect and maintain information about where copies of lines reside. Typically, there is a centralized controller that is part of the main memory controller, and a directory that is stored in main memory. The directory contains global state information about the contents of the various local caches. When an individual cache controller makes a request, the centralized controller checks and issues necessary commands for data transfer between memory and caches or between caches. It is also responsible for keeping the state information up to date; therefore, every local action that can affect the global state of a line must be reported to the central controller.

Typically, the controller maintains information about which processors have a copy of which lines. Before a processor can write to a local copy of a line, it must request exclusive access to the line from the controller. Before granting this exclusive access, the controller sends a message to all processors with a cached copy of this line, forcing each processor to invalidate its copy. After receiving acknowledgments back from each such processor, the controller grants exclusive access to the requesting processor. When another processor tries to read a line that is exclusively granted to another processor, it will send a miss notification to the controller. The controller then issues a command to the processor holding that line that requires the processor to do a write back to main memory. The line may now be shared for reading by the original processor and the requesting processor.

Directory schemes suffer from the drawbacks of a central bottleneck and the overhead of communication between the various cache controllers and the central controller. However, they are effective in large-scale systems that involve multiple buses or some other complex interconnection scheme.

SNOOPY PROTOCOLS Snoopy protocols distribute the responsibility for maintaining cache coherence among all of the cache controllers in a multiprocessor. A cache must recognize when a line that it holds is shared with other caches. When an update action is performed on a shared cache line, it must be announced to all other caches by a broadcast mechanism. Each cache controller is able to "snoop" on the network to observe these broadcasted notifications, and react accordingly.

Snoopy protocols are ideally suited to a bus-based multiprocessor, because the shared bus provides a simple means for broadcasting and snooping. However, because one of the objectives of the use of local caches is to avoid bus accesses, care must be taken that the increased bus traffic required for broadcasting and snooping does not cancel out the gains from the use of local caches.

Two basic approaches to the snoopy protocol have been explored: write invalidate and write update (or write broadcast). With a write-invalidate protocol, there can be multiple readers but only one writer at a time. Initially, a line may be shared among several caches for reading purposes. When one of the caches wants to perform a write to the line, it first issues a notice that invalidates that line in the other caches, making the line exclusive to the writing cache. Once the line is exclusive, the owning processor can make cheap local writes until some other processor requires the same line.

With a write-update protocol, there can be multiple writers as well as multiple readers. When a processor wishes to update a shared line, the word to be updated is distributed to all others, and caches containing that line can update it.

Neither of these two approaches is superior to the other under all circumstances. Performance depends on the number of local caches and the pattern of memory reads and writes. Some systems implement adaptive protocols that employ both write-invalidate and write-update mechanisms.

The write-invalidate approach is the most widely used in commercial multiprocessor systems, such as the Pentium 4 and PowerPC. It marks the state of every cache line (using two extra bits in the cache tag) as modified, exclusive, shared, or invalid. For this reason, the write-invalidate protocol is called MESI. In the remainder of this section, we will look at its use among local caches across a multiprocessor. For simplicity in the presentation, we do not examine the mechanisms involved in coordinating among both level 1 and level 2 locally as well as at the same time coordinating across the distributed multiprocessor. This would not add any new principles but would greatly complicate the discussion.

The MESI Protocol

To provide cache consistency on an SMP, the data cache often supports a protocol known as MESI. For MESI, the data cache includes two status bits per tag, so that each line can be in one of four states:

- **Modified:** The line in the cache has been modified (different from main memory) and is available only in this cache.

Table 17.1 MESI Cache Line States

	M Modified	E Exclusive	S Shared	I Invalid
This cache line valid?	Yes	Yes	Yes	No
The memory copy is...	out of date	valid	valid	—
Copies exist in other caches?	No	No	Maybe	Maybe
A write to this line...	does not go to bus	does not go to bus	goes to bus and updates cache	goes directly to bus

- **Exclusive:** The line in the cache is the same as that in main memory and is not present in any other cache.
- **Shared:** The line in the cache is the same as that in main memory and may be present in another cache.
- **Invalid:** The line in the cache does not contain valid data.

Table 17.1 summarizes the meaning of the four states. Figure 17.7 displays a state diagram for the MESI protocol. Keep in mind that each line of the cache has

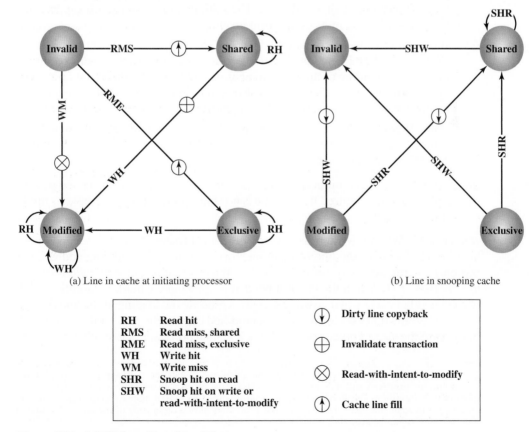

(a) Line in cache at initiating processor   (b) Line in snooping cache

RH	Read hit
RMS	Read miss, shared
RME	Read miss, exclusive
WH	Write hit
WM	Write miss
SHR	Snoop hit on read
SHW	Snoop hit on write or read-with-intent-to-modify

- Dirty line copyback
- Invalidate transaction
- Read-with-intent-to-modify
- Cache line fill

Figure 17.7 MESI State Transition Diagram

its own state bits and therefore its own realization of the state diagram. Figure 17.7a shows the transitions that occur due to actions initiated by the processor attached to this cache. Figure 17.7b shows the transitions that occur due to events that are snooped on the common bus. This presentation of separate state diagrams for processor-initiated and bus-initiated actions helps to clarify the logic of the MESI protocol. At any time a cache line is in a single state. If the next event is from the attached processor, then the transition is dictated by Figure 17.7a and if the next event is from the bus, the transition is dictated by Figure 17.7b. Let us look at these transitions in more detail.

READ MISS When a read miss occurs in the local cache, the processor initiates a memory read to read the line of main memory containing the missing address. The processor inserts a signal on the bus that alerts all other processor/cache units to snoop the transaction. There are a number of possible outcomes:

- If one other cache has a clean (unmodified since read from memory) copy of the line in the exclusive state, it returns a signal indicating that it shares this line. The responding processor then transitions the state of its copy from exclusive to shared, and the initiating processor reads the line from main memory and transitions the line in its cache from invalid to shared.

- If one or more caches have a clean copy of the line in the shared state, each of them signals that it shares the line. The initiating processor reads the line and transitions the line in its cache from invalid to shared.

- If one other cache has a modified copy of the line, then that cache blocks the memory read and provides the line to the requesting cache over the shared bus. The responding cache then changes its line from modified to shared.[1] The line sent to the requesting cache is also received and processed by the memory controller, which stores the block in memory.

- If no other cache has a copy of the line (clean or modified), then no signals are returned. The initiating processor reads the line and transitions the line in its cache from invalid to exclusive.

READ HIT When a read hit occurs on a line currently in the local cache, the processor simply reads the required item. There is no state change: The state remains modified, shared, or exclusive.

WRITE MISS When a write miss occurs in the local cache, the processor initiates a memory read to read the line of main memory containing the missing address. For this purpose, the processor issues a signal on the bus that means *read-with-intent-to-modify* (RWITM). When the line is loaded, it is immediately marked modified. With respect to other caches, two possible scenarios precede the loading of the line of data.

First, some other cache may have a modified copy of this line (state = modify). In this case, the alerted processor signals the initiating processor that another processor

---

[1]In some implementations, the cache with the modified line signals the initiating processor to retry. Meanwhile, the processor with the modified copy seizes the bus, writes the modified line back to main memory, and transitions the line in its cache from modified to shared. Subsequently, the requesting processor tries again and finds that one or more processors have a clean copy of the line in the shared state, as described in the preceding point.

has a modified copy of the line. The initiating processor surrenders the bus and waits. The other processor gains access to the bus, writes the modified cache line back to main memory, and transitions the state of the cache line to invalid (because the initiating processor is going to modify this line). Subsequently, the initiating processor will again issue a signal to the bus of RWITM and then read the line from main memory, modify the line in the cache, and mark the line in the modified state.

The second scenario is that no other cache has a modified copy of the requested line. In this case, no signal is returned, and the initiating processor proceeds to read in the line and modify it. Meanwhile, if one or more caches have a clean copy of the line in the shared state, each cache invalidates its copy of the line, and if one cache has a clean copy of the line in the exclusive state, it invalidates its copy of the line.

WRITE HIT When a write hit occurs on a line currently in the local cache, the effect depends on the current state of that line in the local cache:

- **Shared:** Before performing the update, the processor must gain exclusive ownership of the line. The processor signals its intent on the bus. Each processor that has a shared copy of the line in its cache transitions the sector from shared to invalid. The initiating processor then performs the update and transitions its copy of the line from shared to modified.
- **Exclusive:** The processor already has exclusive control of this line, and so it simply performs the update and transitions its copy of the line from exclusive to modified.
- **Modified:** The processor already has exclusive control of this line and has the line marked as modified, and so it simply performs the update.

L1–L2 CACHE CONSISTENCY We have so far described cache coherency protocols in terms of the cooperate activity among caches connected to the same bus or other SMP interconnection facility. Typically, these caches are L2 caches, and each processor also has an L1 cache that does not connect directly to the bus and that therefore cannot engage in a snoopy protocol. Thus, some scheme is needed to maintain data integrity across both levels of cache and across all caches in the SMP configuration.

The strategy is to extend the MESI protocol (or any cache coherence protocol) to the L1 caches. Thus, each line in the L1 cache includes bits to indicate the state. In essence, the objective is the following: for any line that is present in both an L2 cache and its corresponding L1 cache, the L1 line state should track the state of the L2 line. A simple means of doing this is to adopt the write-through policy in the L1 cache; in this case the write through is to the L2 cache and not to the memory. The L1 write-through policy forces any modification to an L1 line out to the L2 cache and therefore makes it visible to other L2 caches. The use of the L1 write-through policy requires that the L1 content must be a subset of the L2 content. This in turn suggests that the associativity of the L2 cache should be equal to or greater than that of the L1 associativity. The L1 write-through policy is used in the IBM S/390 SMP.

If the L1 cache has a write-back policy, the relationship between the two caches is more complex. There are several approaches to maintaining coherence. For example, the approach used on the Pentium II is described in detail in [SHAN05].

17.4 MULTITHREADING AND CHIP MULTIPROCESSORS

The most important measure of performance for a processor is the rate at which it executes instructions. This can be expressed as

$$\text{MIPS rate} = f \times IPC$$

where f is the processor clock frequency, in MHz, and IPC (instructions per cycle) is the average number of instructions executed per cycle. Accordingly, designers have pursued the goal of increased performance on two fronts: increasing clock frequency and increasing the number of instructions executed or, more properly, the number of instructions that complete during a processor cycle. As we have seen in earlier chapters, designers have increased IPC by using an instruction pipeline and then by using multiple parallel instruction pipelines in a superscalar architecture. With pipelined and multiple-pipeline designs, the principal problem is to maximize the utilization of each pipeline stage. To improve throughput, designers have created ever more complex mechanisms, such as executing some instructions in a different order from the way they occur in the instruction stream and beginning execution of instructions that may never be needed. But as was discussed in Section 2.2, this approach may be reaching a limit due to complexity and power consumption concerns.

An alternative approach, which allows for a high degree of instruction-level parallelism without increasing circuit complexity or power consumption, is called multithreading. In essence, the instruction stream is divided into several smaller streams, known as threads, such that the threads can be executed in parallel.

The variety of specific multithreading designs, realized in both commercial systems and experimental systems, is vast. In this section, we give a brief survey of the major concepts.

Implicit and Explicit Multithreading

The concept of thread used in discussing multithreaded processors may or may not be the same as the concept of software threads in a multiprogrammed operating system. It will be useful to define terms briefly:

- **Process:** An instance of a program running on a computer. A process embodies two key characteristics:
  - **Resource ownership:** A process includes a virtual address space to hold the process image; the process image is the collection of program, data, stack, and attributes that define the process. From time to time, a process may be allocated control or ownership of resources, such as main memory, I/O channels, I/O devices, and files.
  - **Scheduling/execution:** The execution of a process follows an execution path (trace) through one or more programs. This execution may be interleaved with that of other processes. Thus, a process has an execution state (Running, Ready, etc.) and a dispatching priority and is the entity that is scheduled and dispatched by the operating system.

- **Process switch:** An operation that switches the processor from one process to another, by saving all the process control data, registers, and other information for the first and replacing them with the process information for the second.[2]

- **Thread:** A dispatchable unit of work within a process. It includes a processor context (which includes the program counter and stack pointer) and its own data area for a stack (to enable subroutine branching). A thread executes sequentially and is interruptible so that the processor can turn to another thread.

- **Thread switch:** The act of switching processor control from one thread to another within the same process. Typically, this type of switch is much less costly than a process switch.

Thus, a thread is concerned with scheduling and execution, whereas a process is concerned with both scheduling/execution and resource ownership. The multiple threads within a process share the same resources. This is why a thread switch is much less time consuming than a process switch. Traditional operating systems, such as earlier versions of UNIX, did not support threads. Most modern operating systems, such as Linux, other versions of UNIX, and Windows, do support thread. A distinction is made between user-level threads, which are visible to the application program, and kernel-level threads, which are visible only to the operating system. Both of these may be referred to as explicit threads, defined in software.

All of the commercial processors and most of the experimental processors so far have used explicit multithreading. These systems concurrently execute instructions from different explicit threads, either by interleaving instructions from different threads on shared pipelines or by parallel execution on parallel pipelines. Implicit multithreading refers to the concurrent execution of multiple threads extracted from a single sequential program. These implicit threads may be defined either statically by the compiler or dynamically by the hardware. In the remainder of this section we consider explicit multithreading.

Approaches to Explicit Multithreading

At minimum, a multithreaded processor must provide a separate program counter for each thread of execution to be executed concurrently. The designs differ in the amount and type of additional hardware used to support concurrent thread execution. In general, instruction fetching takes place on a thread basis. The processor treats each thread separately and may use a number of techniques for optimizing single-thread execution, including branch prediction, register renaming, and superscalar techniques. What is achieved is thread-level parallelism, which may provide for greatly improved performance when married to instruction-level parallelism.

Broadly speaking, there are four principal approaches to multithreading:

- **Interleaved multithreading:** This is also known as **fine-grained multithreading**. The processor deals with two or more thread contexts at a time, switching from one thread to another at each clock cycle. If a thread is blocked because

---

[2]The term *context switch* is often found in OS literature and textbooks. Unfortunately, although most of the literature uses this term to mean what is here called a process switch, other sources use it to mean a thread switch. To avoid ambiguity, the term is not used in this book.

of data dependencies or memory latencies, that thread is skipped and a ready thread is executed.

- **Blocked multithreading:** This is also known as **coarse-grained multithreading**. The instructions of a thread are executed successively until an event occurs that may cause delay, such as a cache miss. This event induces a switch to another thread. This approach is effective on an in-order processor that would stall the pipeline for a delay event such as a cache miss.

- **Simultaneous multithreading (SMT):** Instructions are simultaneously issued from multiple threads to the execution units of a superscalar processor. This combines the wide superscalar instruction issue capability with the use of multiple thread contexts.

- **Chip multiprocessing:** In this case, the entire processor is replicated on a single chip and each processor handles separate threads. The advantage of this approach is that the available logic area on a chip is used effectively without depending on ever-increasing complexity in pipeline design. This is referred to as multicore; we examine this topic separately in Chapter 18.

For the first two approaches, instructions from different threads are not executed simultaneously. Instead, the processor is able to rapidly switch from one thread to another, using a different set of registers and other context information. This results in a better utilization of the processor's execution resources and avoids a large penalty due to cache misses and other latency events. The SMT approach involves true simultaneous execution of instructions from different threads, using replicated execution resources. Chip multiprocessing also enables simultaneous execution of instructions from different threads.

Figure 17.8, based on one in [UNGE02], illustrates some of the possible pipeline architectures that involve multithreading and contrasts these with approaches that do not use multithreading. Each horizontal row represents the potential issue slot or slots for a single execution cycle; that is, the width of each row corresponds to the maximum number of instructions that can be issued in a single clock cycle.[3] The vertical dimension represents the time sequence of clock cycles. An empty (shaded) slot represents an unused execution slot in one pipeline. A no-op is indicated by N.

The first three illustrations in Figure 17.8 show different approaches with a scalar (i.e., single-issue) processor:

- **Single-threaded scalar:** This is the simple pipeline found in traditional RISC and CISC machines, with no multithreading.

- **Interleaved multithreaded scalar:** This is the easiest multithreading approach to implement. By switching from one thread to another at each clock cycle, the pipeline stages can be kept fully occupied, or close to fully occupied. The hardware must be capable of switching from one thread context to another between cycles.

---

[3]Issue slots are the position from which instructions can be issued in a given clock cycle. Recall from Chapter 14 that instruction issue is the process of initiating instruction execution in the processor's functional units. This occurs when an instruction moves from the decode stage of the pipeline to the first execute stage of the pipeline.

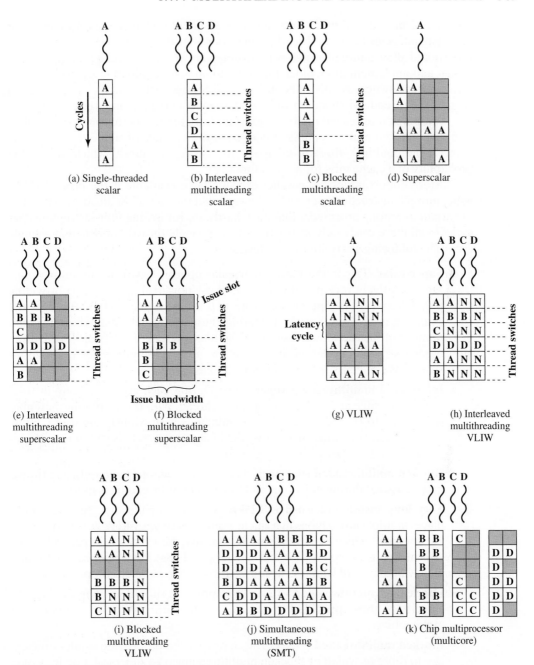

Figure 17.8   Approaches to Executing Multiple Threads

- **Blocked multithreaded scalar:** In this case, a single thread is executed until a latency event occurs that would stop the pipeline, at which time the processor switches to another thread.

Figure 17.8c shows a situation in which the time to perform a thread switch is one cycle, whereas Figure 17.8b shows that thread switching occurs in zero cycles. In the case of interleaved multithreading, it is assumed that there are no control or data dependencies between threads, which simplifies the pipeline design and therefore should allow a thread switch with no delay. However, depending on the specific design and implementation, block multithreading may require a clock cycle to perform a thread switch, as illustrated in Figure 17.8. This is true if a fetched instruction triggers the thread switch and must be discarded from the pipeline [UNGE03].

Although interleaved multithreading appears to offer better processor utilization than blocked multithreading, it does so at the sacrifice of single-thread performance. The multiple threads compete for cache resources, which raises the probability of a cache miss for a given thread.

More opportunities for parallel execution are available if the processor can issue multiple instructions per cycle. Figures 17.8d through 17.8i illustrate a number of variations among processors that have hardware for issuing four instructions per cycle. In all these cases, only instructions from a single thread are issued in a single cycle. The following alternatives are illustrated:

- **Superscalar:** This is the basic superscalar approach with no multithreading. Until relatively recently, this was the most powerful approach to providing parallelism within a processor. Note that during some cycles, not all of the available issue slots are used. During these cycles, less than the maximum number of instructions is issued; this is referred to as *horizontal loss*. During other instruction cycles, no issue slots are used; these are cycles when no instructions can be issued; this is referred to as *vertical loss*.

- **Interleaved multithreading superscalar:** During each cycle, as many instructions as possible are issued from a single thread. With this technique, potential delays due to thread switches are eliminated, as previously discussed. However, the number of instructions issued in any given cycle is still limited by dependencies that exist within any given thread.

- **Blocked multithreaded superscalar:** Again, instructions from only one thread may be issued during any cycle, and blocked multithreading is used.

- **Very long instruction word (VLIW):** A VLIW architecture, such as IA-64, places multiple instructions in a single word. Typically, a VLIW is constructed by the compiler, which places operations that may be executed in parallel in the same word. In a simple VLIW machine (Figure 17.8g), if it is not possible to completely fill the word with instructions to be issued in parallel, no-ops are used.

- **Interleaved multithreading VLIW:** This approach should provide similar efficiencies to those provided by interleaved multithreading on a superscalar architecture.

- **Blocked multithreaded VLIW:** This approach should provide similar efficiencies to those provided by blocked multithreading on a superscalar architecture.

The final two approaches illustrated in Figure 17.8 enable the parallel, simultaneous execution of multiple threads:

- **Simultaneous multithreading:** Figure 17.8i shows a system capable of issuing 8 instructions at a time. If one thread has a high degree of instruction-level parallelism, it may on some cycles be able fill all of the horizontal slots. On other cycles, instructions from two or more threads may be issued. If sufficient threads are active, it should usually be possible to issue the maximum number of instructions on each cycle, providing a high level of efficiency.

- **Chip multiprocessor (multicore):** Figure 17.8k shows a chip containing four processors, each of which has a two-issue superscalar processor. Each processor is assigned a thread, from which it can issue up to two instructions per cycle. We discuss multicore computers in Chapter 18.

Comparing Figures 17.8j and 17.8k, we see that a chip multiprocessor with the same instruction issue capability as an SMT cannot achieve the same degree of instruction-level parallelism. This is because the chip multiprocessor is not able to hide latencies by issuing instructions from other threads. On the other hand, the chip multiprocessor should outperform a superscalar processor with the same instruction issue capability, because the horizontal losses will be greater for the superscalar processor. In addition, it is possible to use multithreading within each of the processors on a chip multiprocessor, and this is done on some contemporary machines.

Example Systems

PENTIUM 4 More recent models of the Pentium 4 use a multithreading technique that the Intel literature refers to as *hyperthreading* [MARR02]. In essence, the Pentium 4 approach is to use SMT with support for two threads. Thus, the single multithreaded processor is logically two processors.

IBM POWER5 The IBM Power5 chip, which is used in high-end PowerPC products, combines chip multiprocessing with SMT [KALL04]. The chip has two separate processors, each of which is a multithreaded processor capable of supporting two threads concurrently using SMT. Interestingly, the designers simulated various alternatives and found that having two two-way SMT processors on a single chip provided superior performance to a single four-way SMT processor. The simulations showed that additional multithreading beyond the support for two threads might decrease performance because of cache thrashing, as data from one thread displaces data needed by another thread.

Figure 17.9 shows the IBM Power5's instruction flow diagram. Only a few of the elements in the processor need to be replicated, with separate elements dedicated to separate threads. Two program counters are used. The processor alternates fetching instructions, up to eight at a time, between the two threads. All the instructions are stored in a common instruction cache and share an instruction translation facility, which does a partial instruction decode. When a conditional branch is encountered, the branch prediction facility predicts the direction of the branch and, if possible, calculates the target address. For predicting the target of a subroutine return, the processor uses a return stack, one for each thread.

Instructions then move into two separate instruction buffers. Then, on the basis of thread priority, a group of instructions is selected and decoded in parallel. Next, instructions flow through a register-renaming facility in program order. Logical registers are mapped to physical registers. The Power5 has 120 physical general-purpose registers and 120 physical floating-point registers. The instructions are then moved into issue queues. From the issue queues, instructions are issued using

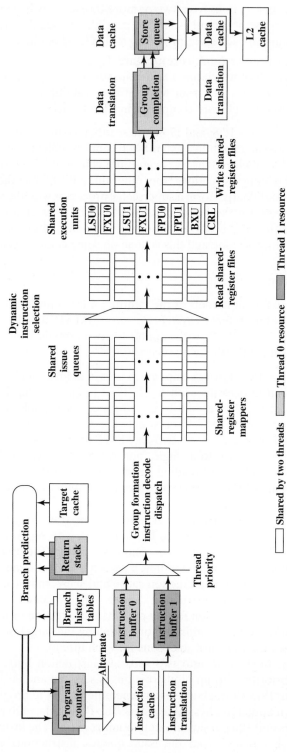

652

BXU = Branch execution unit and
CRL = Condition register logical execution unit
FPU = Floating-point execution unit
FXU = Fixed-point execution unit
LSU = Load/store unit

Figure 17.9 Power5 Instruction Data Flow

symmetric multithreading. That is, the processor has a superscalar architecture and can issue instructions from one or both threads in parallel. At the end of the pipeline, separate thread resources are needed to commit the instructions.

17.5 CLUSTERS

An important and relatively recent development computer system design is clustering. Clustering is an alternative to symmetric multiprocessing as an approach to providing high performance and high availability and is particularly attractive for server applications. We can define a cluster as a group of interconnected, whole computers working together as a unified computing resource that can create the illusion of being one machine. The term *whole computer* means a system that can run on its own, apart from the cluster; in the literature, each computer in a cluster is typically referred to as a *node*.

[BREW97] lists four benefits that can be achieved with clustering. These can also be thought of as objectives or design requirements:

- **Absolute scalability:** It is possible to create large clusters that far surpass the power of even the largest standalone machines. A cluster can have tens, hundreds, or even thousands of machines, each of which is a multiprocessor.
- **Incremental scalability:** A cluster is configured in such a way that it is possible to add new systems to the cluster in small increments. Thus, a user can start out with a modest system and expand it as needs grow, without having to go through a major upgrade in which an existing small system is replaced with a larger system.
- **High availability:** Because each node in a cluster is a standalone computer, the failure of one node does not mean loss of service. In many products, fault tolerance is handled automatically in software.
- **Superior price/performance:** By using commodity building blocks, it is possible to put together a cluster with equal or greater computing power than a single large machine, at much lower cost.

Cluster Configurations

In the literature, clusters are classified in a number of different ways. Perhaps the simplest classification is based on whether the computers in a cluster share access to the same disks. Figure 17.10a shows a two-node cluster in which the only interconnection is by means of a high-speed link that can be used for message exchange to coordinate cluster activity. The link can be a LAN that is shared with other computers that are not part of the cluster or the link can be a dedicated interconnection facility. In the latter case, one or more of the computers in the cluster will have a link to a LAN or WAN so that there is a connection between the server cluster and remote client systems. Note that in the figure, each computer is depicted as being a multiprocessor. This is not necessary but does enhance both performance and availability.

In the simple classification depicted in Figure 17.10, the other alternative is a shared-disk cluster. In this case, there generally is still a message link between

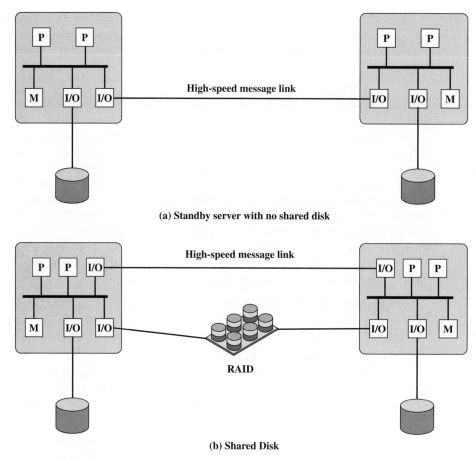

(a) Standby server with no shared disk

(b) Shared Disk

Figure 17.10 Cluster Configurations

nodes. In addition, there is a disk subsystem that is directly linked to multiple computers within the cluster. In this figure, the common disk subsystem is a RAID system. The use of RAID or some similar redundant disk technology is common in clusters so that the high availability achieved by the presence of multiple computers is not compromised by a shared disk that is a single point of failure.

A clearer picture of the range of cluster options can be gained by looking at functional alternatives. Table 17.2 provides a useful classification along functional lines, which we now discuss.

A common, older method, known as **passive standby**, is simply to have one computer handle all of the processing load while the other computer remains inactive, standing by to take over in the event of a failure of the primary. To coordinate the machines, the active, or primary, system periodically sends a "heartbeat" message to the standby machine. Should these messages stop arriving, the standby assumes that the primary server has failed and puts itself into operation. This approach increases availability but does not improve performance. Further, if the only information that is exchanged between the two systems is a heartbeat message, and

Table 17.2   Clustering Methods: Benefits and Limitations

Clustering Method	Description	Benefits	Limitations
Passive Standby	A secondary server takes over in case of primary server failure.	Easy to implement.	High cost because the secondary server is unavailable for other processing tasks.
Active Secondary:	The secondary server is also used for processing tasks.	Reduced cost because secondary servers can be used for processing.	Increased complexity.
Separate Servers	Separate servers have their own disks. Data is continuously copied from primary to secondary server.	High availability.	High network and server overhead due to copying operations.
Servers Connected to Disks	Servers are cabled to the same disks, but each server owns its disks. If one server fails, its disks are taken over by the other server.	Reduced network and server overhead due to elimination of copying operations.	Usually requires disk mirroring or RAID technology to compensate for risk of disk failure.
Servers Share Disks	Multiple servers simultaneously share access to disks.	Low network and server overhead. Reduced risk of downtime caused by disk failure.	Requires lock manager software. Usually used with disk mirroring or RAID technology.

if the two systems do not share common disks, then the standby provides a functional backup but has no access to the databases managed by the primary.

The passive standby is generally not referred to as a cluster. The term *cluster* is reserved for multiple interconnected computers that are all actively doing processing while maintaining the image of a single system to the outside world. The term **active secondary** is often used in referring to this configuration. Three classifications of clustering can be identified: separate servers, shared nothing, and shared memory.

In one approach to clustering, each computer is a **separate server** with its own disks and there are no disks shared between systems (Figure 17.10a). This arrangement provides high performance as well as high availability. In this case, some type of management or scheduling software is needed to assign incoming client requests to servers so that the load is balanced and high utilization is achieved. It is desirable to have a failover capability, which means that if a computer fails while executing an application, another computer in the cluster can pick up and complete the application. For this to happen, data must constantly be copied among systems so that each system has access to the current data of the other systems. The overhead of this data exchange ensures high availability at the cost of a performance penalty.

To reduce the communications overhead, most clusters now consist of servers connected to common disks (Figure 17.10b). In one variation on this approach, called **shared nothing**, the common disks are partitioned into volumes, and each volume is owned by a single computer. If that computer fails, the cluster must be reconfigured so that some other computer has ownership of the volumes of the failed computer.

It is also possible to have multiple computers share the same disks at the same time (called the **shared disk** approach), so that each computer has access to all of the volumes on all of the disks. This approach requires the use of some type of locking facility to ensure that data can only be accessed by one computer at a time.

Operating System Design Issues

Full exploitation of a cluster hardware configuration requires some enhancements to a single-system operating system.

FAILURE MANAGEMENT How failures are managed by a cluster depends on the clustering method used (Table 17.2). In general, two approaches can be taken to dealing with failures: highly available clusters and fault-tolerant clusters. A highly available cluster offers a high probability that all resources will be in service. If a failure occurs, such as a system goes down or a disk volume is lost, then the queries in progress are lost. Any lost query, if retried, will be serviced by a different computer in the cluster. However, the cluster operating system makes no guarantee about the state of partially executed transactions. This would need to be handled at the application level.

A fault-tolerant cluster ensures that all resources are always available. This is achieved by the use of redundant shared disks and mechanisms for backing out uncommitted transactions and committing completed transactions.

The function of switching applications and data resources over from a failed system to an alternative system in the cluster is referred to as **failover**. A related function is the restoration of applications and data resources to the original system once it has been fixed; this is referred to as **failback**. Failback can be automated, but this is desirable only if the problem is truly fixed and unlikely to recur. If not, automatic failback can cause subsequently failed resources to bounce back and forth between computers, resulting in performance and recovery problems.

LOAD BALANCING A cluster requires an effective capability for balancing the load among available computers. This includes the requirement that the cluster be incrementally scalable. When a new computer is added to the cluster, the load-balancing facility should automatically include this computer in scheduling applications. Middleware mechanisms need to recognize that services can appear on different members of the cluster and may migrate from one member to another.

PARALLELIZING COMPUTATION In some cases, effective use of a cluster requires executing software from a single application in parallel. [KAPP00] lists three general approaches to the problem:

- **Parallelizing compiler:** A parallelizing compiler determines, at compile time, which parts of an application can be executed in parallel. These are then split off to be assigned to different computers in the cluster. Performance depends on the nature of the problem and how well the compiler is designed. In general, such compilers are difficult to develop.

- **Parallelized application:** In this approach, the programmer writes the application from the outset to run on a cluster, and uses message passing to move data, as required, between cluster nodes. This places a high burden on the programmer but may be the best approach for exploiting clusters for some applications.

- **Parametric computing:** This approach can be used if the essence of the application is an algorithm or program that must be executed a large number of times, each time with a different set of starting conditions or parameters. A good example is a simulation model, which will run a large number of different scenarios and then develop statistical summaries of the results. For this approach to be effective, parametric processing tools are needed to organize, run, and manage the jobs in an effective manner.

Cluster Computer Architecture

Figure 17.11 shows a typical cluster architecture. The individual computers are connected by some high-speed LAN or switch hardware. Each computer is capable of operating independently. In addition, a middleware layer of software is installed in each computer to enable cluster operation. The cluster middleware provides a unified system image to the user, known as a **single-system image**. The middleware is also responsible for providing high availability, by means of load balancing and responding to failures in individual components. [HWAN99] lists the following as desirable cluster middleware services and functions:

- **Single entry point:** A user logs onto the cluster rather than to an individual computer.
- **Single file hierarchy:** The user sees a single hierarchy of file directories under the same root directory.
- **Single control point:** There is a default workstation used for cluster management and control.
- **Single virtual networking:** Any node can access any other point in the cluster, even though the actual cluster configuration may consist of multiple interconnected networks. There is a single virtual network operation.
- **Single memory space:** Distributed shared memory enables programs to share variables.
- **Single job-management system:** Under a cluster job scheduler, a user can submit a job without specifying the host computer to execute the job.
- **Single user interface:** A common graphic interface supports all users, regardless of the workstation from which they enter the cluster.
- **Single I/O space:** Any node can remotely access any I/O peripheral or disk device without knowledge of its physical location.
- **Single process space:** A uniform process-identification scheme is used. A process on any node can create or communicate with any other process on a remote node.
- **Checkpointing:** This function periodically saves the process state and intermediate computing results, to allow rollback recovery after a failure.
- **Process migration:** This function enables load balancing.

The last four items on the preceding list enhance the availability of the cluster. The remaining items are concerned with providing a single system image.

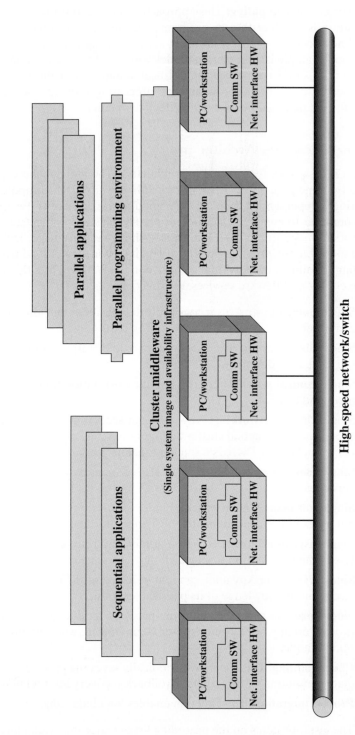

Figure 17.11 Cluster Computer Architecture [BUYY99a]

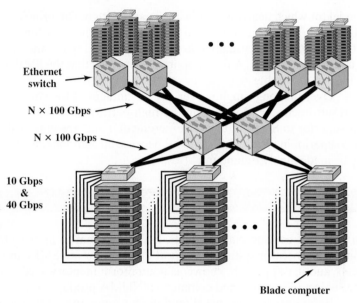

Figure 17.12   Example 100-Gbps Ethernet Configuration for
Massive Blade Server Site

Returning to Figure 17.11, a cluster will also include software tools for enabling the efficient execution of programs that are capable of parallel execution.

Blade Servers

A common implementation of the cluster approach is the blade server. A blade
server is a server architecture that houses multiple server modules ("blades") in a
single chassis. It is widely used in data centers to save space and improve system
management. Either self-standing or rack mounted, the chassis provides the power
supply, and each blade has its own processor, memory, and hard disk.

An example of the application is shown in Figure 17.12, taken from [NOWE07].
The trend at large data centers, with substantial banks of blade servers, is the deployment of 10-Gbps ports on individual servers to handle the massive multimedia traffic
provided by these servers. Such arrangements are stressing the on-site Ethernet
switches needed to interconnect large numbers of servers. A 100-Gbps rate provides
the bandwidth required to handle the increased traffic load. The 100-Gbps Ethernet
switches are deployed in switch uplinks inside the data center as well as providing
interbuilding, intercampus, wide area connections for enterprise networks.

Clusters Compared to SMP

Both clusters and symmetric multiprocessors provide a configuration with multiple
processors to support high-demand applications. Both solutions are commercially
available, although SMP schemes have been around far longer.

The main strength of the SMP approach is that an SMP is easier to manage
and configure than a cluster. The SMP is much closer to the original single-processor

model for which nearly all applications are written. The principal change required in going from a uniprocessor to an SMP is to the scheduler function. Another benefit of the SMP is that it usually takes up less physical space and draws less power than a comparable cluster. A final important benefit is that the SMP products are well established and stable.

Over the long run, however, the advantages of the cluster approach are likely to result in clusters dominating the high-performance server market. Clusters are far superior to SMPs in terms of incremental and absolute scalability. Clusters are also superior in terms of availability, because all components of the system can readily be made highly redundant.

17.6 NONUNIFORM MEMORY ACCESS

In terms of commercial products, the two common approaches to providing a multiple-processor system to support applications are SMPs and clusters. For some years, another approach, known as nonuniform memory access (NUMA), has been the subject of research and commercial NUMA products are now available.

Before proceeding, we should define some terms often found in the NUMA literature.

- **Uniform memory access (UMA):** All processors have access to all parts of main memory using loads and stores. The memory access time of a processor to all regions of memory is the same. The access times experienced by different processors are the same. The SMP organization discussed in Sections 17.2 and 17.3 is UMA.

- **Nonuniform memory access (NUMA):** All processors have access to all parts of main memory using loads and stores. The memory access time of a processor differs depending on which region of main memory is accessed. The last statement is true for all processors; however, for different processors, which memory regions are slower and which are faster differ.

- **Cache-coherent NUMA (CC-NUMA):** A NUMA system in which cache coherence is maintained among the caches of the various processors.

A NUMA system without cache coherence is more or less equivalent to a cluster. The commercial products that have received much attention recently are CC-NUMA systems, which are quite distinct from both SMPs and clusters. Usually, but unfortunately not always, such systems are in fact referred to in the commercial literature as CC-NUMA systems. This section is concerned only with CC-NUMA systems.

Motivation

With an SMP system, there is a practical limit to the number of processors that can be used. An effective cache scheme reduces the bus traffic between any one processor and main memory. As the number of processors increases, this bus traffic also increases. Also, the bus is used to exchange cache-coherence signals, further adding to the burden. At some point, the bus becomes a performance bottleneck. Performance degradation seems to limit the number of processors in an SMP configuration to somewhere between 16 and 64 processors. For example, Silicon Graphics' Power Challenge SMP is limited to 64 R10000 processors in a single system; beyond this number performance degrades substantially.

The processor limit in an SMP is one of the driving motivations behind the development of cluster systems. However, with a cluster, each node has its own private main memory; applications do not see a large global memory. In effect, coherency is maintained in software rather than hardware. This memory granularity affects performance and, to achieve maximum performance, software must be tailored to this environment. One approach to achieving large-scale multiprocessing while retaining the flavor of SMP is NUMA. For example, the Silicon Graphics Origin NUMA system is designed to support up to 1024 MIPS R10000 processors [WHIT97] and the Sequent NUMA-Q system is designed to support up to 252 Pentium II processors [LOVE96].

The objective with NUMA is to maintain a transparent system wide memory while permitting multiple multiprocessor nodes, each with its own bus or other internal interconnect system.

Organization

Figure 17.13 depicts a typical CC-NUMA organization. There are multiple independent nodes, each of which is, in effect, an SMP organization. Thus, each node contains multiple processors, each with its own L1 and L2 caches, plus main memory. The node is the basic building block of the overall CC-NUMA organization. For example, each Silicon Graphics Origin node includes two MIPS R10000 processors; each Sequent NUMA-Q node includes four Pentium II processors. The nodes are interconnected by means of some communications facility, which could be a switching mechanism, a ring, or some other networking facility.

Each node in the CC-NUMA system includes some main memory. From the point of view of the processors, however, there is only a single addressable memory, with each location having a unique system wide address. When a processor initiates a memory access, if the requested memory location is not in that processor's cache, then the L2 cache initiates a fetch operation. If the desired line is in the local portion of the main memory, the line is fetched across the local bus. If the desired line is in a remote portion of the main memory, then an automatic request is sent out to fetch that line across the interconnection network, deliver it to the local bus, and then deliver it to the requesting cache on that bus. All of this activity is automatic and transparent to the processor and its cache.

In this configuration, cache coherence is a central concern. Although implementations differ as to details, in general terms we can say that each node must maintain some sort of directory that gives it an indication of the location of various portions of memory and also cache status information. To see how this scheme works, we give an example taken from [PFIS98]. Suppose that processor 3 on node 2 (P2-3) requests a memory location 798, which is in the memory of node 1. The following sequence occurs:

1. P2-3 issues a read request on the snoopy bus of node 2 for location 798.
2. The directory on node 2 sees the request and recognizes that the location is in node 1.

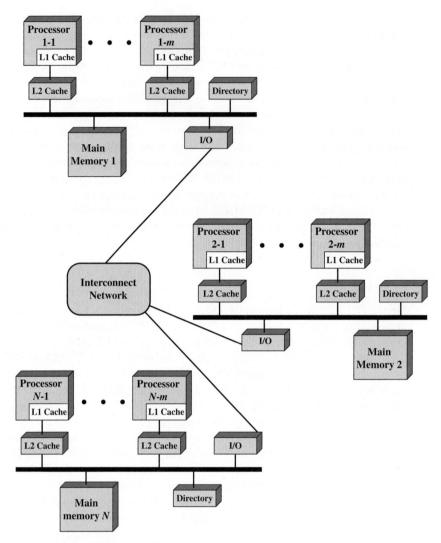

Figure 17.13 CC-NUMA Organization

3. Node 2's directory sends a request to node 1, which is picked up by node 1's directory.

4. Node 1's directory, acting as a surrogate of P2-3, requests the contents of 798, as if it were a processor.

5. Node 1's main memory responds by putting the requested data on the bus.

6. Node 1's directory picks up the data from the bus.

7. The value is transferred back to node 2's directory.

8. Node 2's directory places the data back on node 2's bus, acting as a surrogate for the memory that originally held it.

9. The value is picked up and placed in P2-3's cache and delivered to P2-3.

The preceding sequence explains how data are read from a remote memory using hardware mechanisms that make the transaction transparent to the processor. On top of these mechanisms, some form of cache coherence protocol is needed. Various systems differ on exactly how this is done. We make only a few general remarks here. First, as part of the preceding sequence, node 1's directory keeps a record that some remote cache has a copy of the line containing location 798. Then, there needs to be a cooperative protocol to take care of modifications. For example, if a modification is done in a cache, this fact can be broadcast to other nodes. Each node's directory that receives such a broadcast can then determine if any local cache has that line and, if so, cause it to be purged. If the actual memory location is at the node receiving the broadcast notification, then that node's directory needs to maintain an entry indicating that that line of memory is invalid and remains so until a write back occurs. If another processor (local or remote) requests the invalid line, then the local directory must force a write back to update memory before providing the data.

NUMA Pros and Cons

The main advantage of a CC-NUMA system is that it can deliver effective performance at higher levels of parallelism than SMP, without requiring major software changes. With multiple NUMA nodes, the bus traffic on any individual node is limited to a demand that the bus can handle. However, if many of the memory accesses are to remote nodes, performance begins to break down. There is reason to believe that this performance breakdown can be avoided. First, the use of L1 and L2 caches is designed to minimize all memory accesses, including remote ones. If much of the software has good temporal locality, then remote memory accesses should not be excessive. Second, if the software has good spatial locality, and if virtual memory is in use, then the data needed for an application will reside on a limited number of frequently used pages that can be initially loaded into the memory local to the running application. The Sequent designers report that such spatial locality does appear in representative applications [LOVE96]. Finally, the virtual memory scheme can be enhanced by including in the operating system a page migration mechanism that will move a virtual memory page to a node that is frequently using it; the Silicon Graphics designers report success with this approach [WHIT97].

Even if the performance breakdown due to remote access is addressed, there are two other disadvantages for the CC-NUMA approach. Two in particular are discussed in detail in [PFIS98]. First, a CC-NUMA does not transparently look like an SMP; software changes will be required to move an operating system and applications from an SMP to a CC-NUMA system. These include page allocation, already mentioned, process allocation, and load balancing by the operating system. A second concern is that of availability. This is a rather complex issue and depends on the exact implementation of the CC-NUMA system; the interested reader is referred to [PFIS98].

Vector Processor Simulator

17.7 VECTOR COMPUTATION

Although the performance of mainframe general-purpose computers continues to improve relentlessly, there continue to be applications that are beyond the reach of the contemporary mainframe. There is a need for computers to solve mathematical problems of physical processes, such as occur in disciplines including aerodynamics, seismology, meteorology, and atomic, nuclear, and plasma physics.

Typically, these problems are characterized by the need for high precision and a program that repetitively performs floating-point arithmetic operations on large arrays of numbers. Most of these problems fall into the category known as *continuous-field simulation.* In essence, a physical situation can be described by a surface or region in three dimensions (e.g., the flow of air adjacent to the surface of a rocket). This surface is approximated by a grid of points. A set of differential equations defines the physical behavior of the surface at each point. The equations are represented as an array of values and coefficients, and the solution involves repeated arithmetic operations on the arrays of data.

Supercomputers were developed to handle these types of problems. These machines are typically capable of billions of floating-point operations per second. In contrast to mainframes, which are designed for multiprogramming and intensive I/O, the supercomputer is optimized for the type of numerical calculation just described.

The supercomputer has limited use and, because of its price tag, a limited market. Comparatively few of these machines are operational, mostly at research centers and some government agencies with scientific or engineering functions. As with other areas of computer technology, there is a constant demand to increase the performance of the supercomputer. Thus, the technology and performance of the supercomputer continues to evolve.

There is another type of system that has been designed to address the need for vector computation, referred to as the *array processor.* Although a supercomputer is optimized for vector computation, it is a general-purpose computer, capable of handling scalar processing and general data processing tasks. Array processors do not include scalar processing; they are configured as peripheral devices by both mainframe and minicomputer users to run the vectorized portions of programs.

Approaches to Vector Computation

The key to the design of a supercomputer or array processor is to recognize that the main task is to perform arithmetic operations on arrays or vectors of floating-point numbers. In a general-purpose computer, this will require iteration through each element of the array. For example, consider two vectors (one-dimensional arrays) of numbers, A and B. We would like to add these and place the result in C. In the example of Figure 17.14, this requires six separate additions. How could we speed up this computation? The answer is to introduce some form of parallelism.

Several approaches have been taken to achieving parallelism in vector computation. We illustrate this with an example. Consider the vector multiplication $C = A \times B$, where A, B, and C are $N \times N$ matrices. The formula for each element of C is

$$c_{i,j} = \sum_{k=1}^{N} a_{i,k} \times b_{k,j}$$

$$
\begin{bmatrix} 1.5 \\ 7.1 \\ 6.9 \\ 100.5 \\ 0 \\ 59.7 \end{bmatrix} + \begin{bmatrix} 2.0 \\ 39.7 \\ 1000.003 \\ 11 \\ 21.1 \\ 19.7 \end{bmatrix} = \begin{bmatrix} 3.5 \\ 46.8 \\ 1006.093 \\ 111.5 \\ 21.1 \\ 79.4 \end{bmatrix}
$$

$$A \quad + \quad B \quad = \quad C$$

Figure 17.14   Example of Vector Addition

where A, B, and C have elements $a_{i,j}$, $b_{i,j}$, and $c_{i,j}$, respectively. Figure 17.15a shows a FORTRAN program for this computation that can be run on an ordinary scalar processor.

One approach to improving performance can be referred to as *vector processing*. This assumes that it is possible to operate on a one-dimensional vector of data. Figure 17.15b is a FORTRAN program with a new form of instruction that allows

```
      DO 100 I = 1, N

      DO 100 J = 1, N

      C(I, J) = 0.0

      DO 100 K = 1, N

      C(I, J) = C(I, J) + A(I, K) + B(K, J)

100   CONTINUE
```

(a) Scalar processing

```
      DO 100 I = 1, N
      C(I, J) = 0.0 (J = 1, N)
      DO 100 K = 1, N
      C(I, J) = C(I, J) + A(I, K) + B(K, J) (J = 1, N)
100   CONTINUE
```

(b) Vector processing

```
      DO 50 J = 1, N − 1
      FORK 100
50    CONTINUE
      J = N
100   DO 200 I = 1, N
      C(I, J) = 0.0
      DO 200 K = 1, N
      C(I, J) = C(I, J) + A(I, K) + B(K, J)
200   CONTINUE
```

(c) Parallel processing

Figure 17.15   Matrix Multiplication (C = A × B)

vector computation to be specified. The notation $(J = 1, N)$ indicates that operations on all indices J in the given interval are to be carried out as a single operation. How this can be achieved is addressed shortly.

The program in Figure 17.15b indicates that all the elements of the ith row are to be computed in parallel. Each element in the row is a summation, and the summations (across K) are done serially rather than in parallel. Even so, only N^2 vector multiplications are required for this algorithm as compared with N^3 scalar multiplications for the scalar algorithm.

Another approach, *parallel processing,* is illustrated in Figure 17.15c. This approach assumes that we have N independent processors that can function in parallel. To utilize processors effectively, we must somehow parcel out the computation to the various processors. Two primitives are used. The primitive FORK n causes an independent process to be started at location n. In the meantime, the original process continues execution at the instruction immediately following the FORK. Every execution of a FORK spawns a new process. The JOIN instruction is essentially the inverse of the FORK. The statement JOIN N causes N independent processes to be merged into one that continues execution at the instruction following the JOIN. The operating system must coordinate this merger, and so the execution does not continue until all N processes have reached the JOIN instruction.

The program in Figure 17.15c is written to mimic the behavior of the vector-processing program. In the parallel processing program, each column of C is computed by a separate process. Thus, the elements in a given row of C are computed in parallel.

The preceding discussion describes approaches to vector computation in logical or architectural terms. Let us turn now to a consideration of types of processor organization that can be used to implement these approaches. A wide variety of organizations have been and are being pursued. Three main categories stand out:

- Pipelined ALU
- Parallel ALUs
- Parallel processors

Figure 17.16 illustrates the first two of these approaches. We have already discussed pipelining in Chapter 12. Here the concept is extended to the operation of the ALU. Because floating-point operations are rather complex, there is opportunity for decomposing a floating-point operation into stages, so that different stages can operate on different sets of data concurrently. This is illustrated in Figure 17.17a. Floating-point addition is broken up into four stages (see Figure 9.22): compare, shift, add, and normalize. A vector of numbers is presented sequentially to the first stage. As the processing proceeds, four different sets of numbers will be operated on concurrently in the pipeline.

It should be clear that this organization is suitable for vector processing. To see this, consider the instruction pipelining described in Chapter 12. The processor goes through a repetitive cycle of fetching and processing instructions. In the absence of branches, the processor is continuously fetching instructions from sequential locations. Consequently, the pipeline is kept full and a savings in time is achieved. Similarly, a pipelined ALU will save time only if it is fed a stream of data from sequential

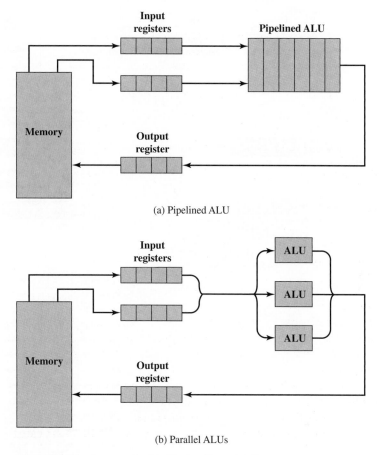

(a) Pipelined ALU

(b) Parallel ALUs

Figure 17.16 Approaches to Vector Computation

locations. A single, isolated floating-point operation is not speeded up by a pipeline. The speedup is achieved when a vector of operands is presented to the ALU. The control unit cycles the data through the ALU until the entire vector is processed.

The pipeline operation can be further enhanced if the vector elements are available in registers rather than from main memory. This is in fact suggested by Figure 17.16a. The elements of each vector operand are loaded as a block into a vector register, which is simply a large bank of identical registers. The result is also placed in a vector register. Thus, most operations involve only the use of registers, and only load and store operations and the beginning and end of a vector operation require access to memory.

The mechanism illustrated in Figure 17.17 could be referred to as *pipelining within an operation*. That is, we have a single arithmetic operation (e.g., $C = A + B$) that is to be applied to vector operands, and pipelining allows multiple vector elements to be processed in parallel. This mechanism can be augmented with *pipelining across operations*. In this latter case, there is a sequence of arithmetic vector operations, and instruction pipelining is used to speed up processing. One approach to

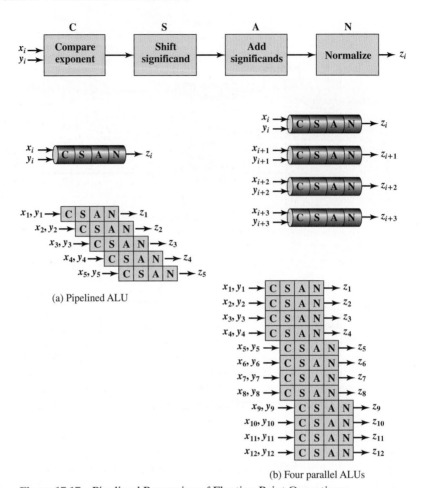

Figure 17.17 Pipelined Processing of Floating-Point Operations

this, referred to as **chaining**, is found on the Cray supercomputers. The basic rule for chaining is this: A vector operation may start as soon as the first element of the operand vector(s) is available and the functional unit (e.g., add, subtract, multiply, divide) is free. Essentially, chaining causes results issuing from one functional unit to be fed immediately into another functional unit and so on. If vector registers are used, intermediate results do not have to be stored into memory and can be used even before the vector operation that created them runs to completion.

For example, when computing $C = (s \times A) + B$, where $A, B,$ and C are vectors and s is a scalar, the Cray may execute three instructions at once. Elements fetched for a load immediately enter a pipelined multiplier, the products are sent to a pipelined adder, and the sums are placed in a vector register as soon as the adder completes them:

1. Vector load $A \rightarrow$ Vector Register (VR1)
2. Vector load $B \rightarrow$ VR2

3. Vector multiply   s × VR1 → VR3

4. Vector add   VR3 + VR2 → VR4

5. Vector store   VR4 → C

Instructions 2 and 3 can be chained (pipelined) because they involve different memory locations and registers. Instruction 4 needs the results of instructions 2 and 3, but it can be chained with them as well. As soon as the first elements of vector registers 2 and 3 are available, the operation in instruction 4 can begin.

Another way to achieve vector processing is by the use of multiple ALUs in a single processor, under the control of a single control unit. In this case, the control unit routes data to ALUs so that they can function in parallel. It is also possible to use pipelining on each of the parallel ALUs. This is illustrated in Figure 17.17b. The example shows a case in which four ALUs operate in parallel.

As with pipelined organization, a parallel ALU organization is suitable for vector processing. The control unit routes vector elements to ALUs in a round-robin fashion until all elements are processed. This type of organization is more complex than a single-ALU CPI.

Finally, vector processing can be achieved by using multiple parallel processors. In this case, it is necessary to break the task up into multiple processes to be executed in parallel. This organization is effective only if the software and hardware for effective coordination of parallel processors is available.

We can expand our taxonomy of Section 17.1 to reflect these new structures, as shown in Figure 17.18. Computer organizations can be distinguished by the presence of one or more control units. Multiple control units imply multiple processors. Following our previous discussion, if the multiple processors can function cooperatively on a given task, they are termed *parallel processors*.

The reader should be aware of some unfortunate terminology likely to be encountered in the literature. The term *vector processor* is often equated with a pipelined ALU organization, although a parallel ALU organization is also designed for vector processing, and, as we have discussed, a parallel processor organization may also be designed for vector processing. *Array processing* is sometimes used to refer to a parallel ALU, although, again, any of the three organizations is optimized for the processing of arrays. To make matters worse, *array processor* usually refers to an auxiliary processor attached to a general-purpose processor and used to perform vector computation. An array processor may use either the pipelined or parallel ALU approach.

At present, the pipelined ALU organization dominates the marketplace. Pipelined systems are less complex than the other two approaches. Their control

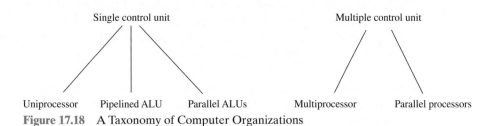

Figure 17.18   A Taxonomy of Computer Organizations

unit and operating system design are well developed to achieve efficient resource allocation and high performance. The remainder of this section is devoted to a more detailed examination of this approach, using a specific example.

IBM 3090 Vector Facility

A good example of a pipelined ALU organization for vector processing is the vector facility developed for the IBM 370 architecture and implemented on the high-end 3090 series [PADE88, TUCK87]. This facility is an optional add-on to the basic system but is highly integrated with it. It resembles vector facilities found on supercomputers, such as the Cray family.

The IBM facility makes use of a number of vector registers. Each register is actually a bank of scalar registers. To compute the vector sum $C = A + B$, the vectors A and B are loaded into two vector registers. The data from these registers are passed through the ALU as fast as possible, and the results are stored in a third vector register. The computation overlap, and the loading of the input data into the registers in a block, results in a significant speeding up over an ordinary ALU operation.

ORGANIZATION The IBM vector architecture, and similar pipelined vector ALUs, provides increased performance over loops of scalar arithmetic instructions in three ways:

- The fixed and predetermined structure of vector data permits housekeeping instructions inside the loop to be replaced by faster internal (hardware or microcoded) machine operations.
- Data-access and arithmetic operations on several successive vector elements can proceed concurrently by overlapping such operations in a pipelined design or by performing multiple-element operations in parallel.
- The use of vector registers for intermediate results avoids additional storage reference.

Figure 17.19 shows the general organization of the vector facility. Although the vector facility is seen to be a physically separate add-on to the processor, its architecture is an extension of the System/370 architecture and is compatible with it. The vector facility is integrated into the System/370 architecture in the following ways:

- Existing System/370 instructions are used for all scalar operations.
- Arithmetic operations on individual vector elements produce exactly the same result as do corresponding System/370 scalar instructions. For example, one design decision concerned the definition of the result in a floating-point DIVIDE operation. Should the result be exact, as it is for scalar floating-point division, or should an approximation be allowed that would permit higher-speed implementation but could sometimes introduce an error in one or more low-order bit positions? The decision was made to uphold complete compatibility with the System/370 architecture at the expense of a minor performance degradation.
- Vector instructions are interruptible, and their execution can be resumed from the point of interruption after appropriate action has been taken, in a manner compatible with the System/370 program-interruption scheme.

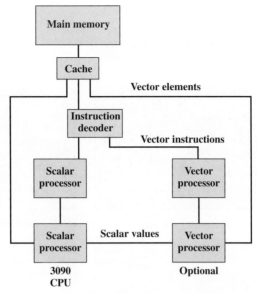

Figure 17.19 IBM 3090 with Vector Facility

- Arithmetic exceptions are the same as, or extensions of, exceptions for the scalar arithmetic instructions of the System/370, and similar fix-up routines can be used. To accommodate this, a vector interruption index is employed that indicates the location in a vector register that is affected by an exception (e.g., overflow). Thus, when execution of the vector instruction resumes, the proper place in a vector register is accessed.
- Vector data reside in virtual storage, with page faults being handled in a standard manner.

This level of integration provides a number of benefits. Existing operating systems can support the vector facility with minor extensions. Existing application programs, language compilers, and other software can be run unchanged. Software that could take advantage of the vector facility can be modified as desired.

REGISTERS A key issue in the design of a vector facility is whether operands are located in registers or memory. The IBM organization is referred to as *register to register,* because the vector operands, both input and output, can be staged in vector registers. This approach is also used on the Cray supercomputer. An alternative approach, used on Control Data machines, is to obtain operands directly from memory. The main disadvantage of the use of vector registers is that the programmer or compiler must take them into account for good performance. For example, suppose that the length of the vector registers is K and the length of the vectors to be processed is $N > K$. In this case, a vector loop must be performed, in which the operation is performed on K elements at a time and the loop is repeated N/K times. The main advantage of the vector register approach is that the operation is decoupled from slower main memory and instead takes place primarily with registers.

FORTRAN ROUTINE:

```
        DO 100 J = 1, 50
        CR(J) = AR(J) * BR(J) − AI(J) * BI(J)
100     CI(J) = AR(J) * BI(J) + AI(J) * BR(J)
```

Operation	Cycles
AR(J) * BR(J) → T1(J)	3
AI(J) * BI(J) → T2(J)	3
T1(J) − T2(J) → CR(J)	3
AR(J) * BI(J) → T3(J)	3
AI(J) * BR(J) → T4(J)	3
T3(J) + T4(J) → CI(J)	3
TOTAL	18

(a) Storage to storage

Operation	Cycles
AR(J) → V1(J)	1
V1(J) * BR(J) → V2(J)	1
AI(J) → V3(J)	1
V3(J) * BI(J) → V4(J)	1
V2(J) − V4(J) → V5(J)	1
V5(J) → CR(J)	1
V1(J) * BI(J) → V6(J)	1
V4(J) * BR(J) → V7(J)	1
V6(J) + V7(J) → V8(J)	1
V8(J) → CI(J)	
TOTAL	10

(c) Storage to register

Vi = Vector registers
AR, BR, AI, BI = Operands in memory
Ti = Temporary locations in memory

Operation	Cycles
AR(J) → V1(J)	1
BR(J) → V2(J)	1
V1(J) * V2(J) → V3(J)	1
AI(J) → V4(J)	1
BI(J) → V5(J)	1
V4(J) * V5(J) → V6(J)	1
V3(J) − V6(J) → V7(J)	1
V7(J) → CR(J)	1
V1(J) * V5(J) → V8(J)	1
V4(J) * V2(J) → V9(J)	1
V8(J) + V9(J) → V0(J)	1
V0(J) → CI(J)	1
TOTAL	12

(b) Register to register

Operation	Cycles
AR(J) → V1(J)	1
V1(J) * BR(J) → V2(J)	1
AI(J) → V3(J)	1
V2(J) − V3(J) * BI(J) → V2(J)	1
V2(J) → CR(J)	1
V1(J) * BI(J) → V4(J)	1
V4(J) + V3(J) * BR(J) → V5(J)	1
V5(J) → CI(J)	
TOTAL	8

(d) Compound instruction

Figure 17.20 Alternative Programs for Vector Calculation

The speedup that can be achieved using registers is demonstrated in Figure 17.20. The FORTRAN routine multiplies vector A by vector B to produce vector C, where each vector has a real part (AR, BR, CR) and an imaginary part (AI, BI, CI). The 3090 can perform one main-storage access per processor, or clock, cycle (either read or write); has registers that can sustain two accesses for reading and one for writing per cycle; and produces one result per cycle in its arithmetic unit. Let us assume the use of instructions that can specify two source operands and a result.[4] Part a of the figure shows that, with memory-to-memory instructions, each iteration of the computation requires a total of 18 cycles. With a pure register-to-

---

[4]For the 370/390 architecture, the only three-operand instructions (register and storage instructions, RS) specify two operands in registers and one in memory. In part a of the example, we assume the existence of three-operand instructions in which all operands are in main memory. This is done for purposes of comparison and, in fact, such an instruction format could have been chosen for the vector architecture.

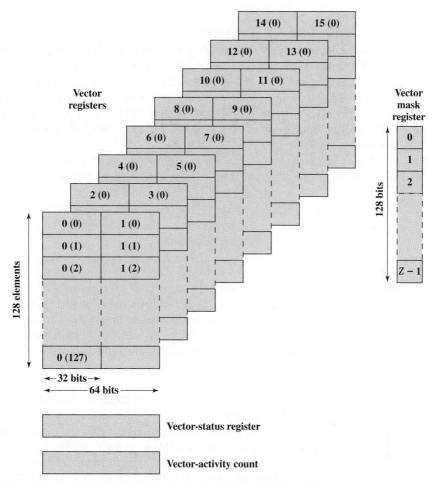

Figure 17.21   Registers for the IBM 3090 Vector Facility

register architecture (part b), this time is reduced to 12 cycles. Of course, with register-to-register operation, the vector quantities must be loaded into the vector registers prior to computation and stored in memory afterward. For large vectors, this fixed penalty is relatively small. Figure 17.20c shows that the ability to specify both storage and register operands in one instruction further reduces the time to 10 cycles per iteration. This latter type of instruction is included in the vector architecture.[5]

Figure 17.21 illustrates the registers that are part of the IBM 3090 vector facility. There are sixteen 32-bit vector registers. The vector registers can also be coupled to form eight 64-bit vector registers. Any register element can hold an integer or floating-point value. Thus, the vector registers may be used for 32-bit and 64-bit integer values, and 32-bit and 64-bit floating-point values.

---

[5]Compound instructions, discussed subsequently, afford a further reduction.

The architecture specifies that each register contains from 8 to 512 scalar elements. The choice of actual length involves a design trade-off. The time to do a vector operation consists essentially of the overhead for pipeline startup and register filling plus one cycle per vector element. Thus, the use of a large number of register elements reduces the relative startup time for a computation. However, this efficiency must be balanced against the added time required for saving and restoring vector registers on a process switch and the practical cost and space limits. These considerations led to the use of 128 elements per register in the current 3090 implementation.

Three additional registers are needed by the vector facility. The vector-mask register contains mask bits that may be used to select which elements in the vector registers are to be processed for a particular operation. The vector-status register contains control fields, such as the vector count, that determine how many elements in the vector registers are to be processed. The vector-activity count keeps track of the time spent executing vector instructions.

COMPOUND INSTRUCTIONS As was discussed previously, instruction execution can be overlapped using chaining to improve performance. The designers of the IBM vector facility chose not to include this capability for several reasons. The System/370 architecture would have to be extended to handle complex interruptions (including their effect on virtual memory management), and corresponding changes would be needed in the software. A more basic issue was the cost of including the additional controls and register access paths in the vector facility for generalized chaining.

Instead, three operations are provided that combine into one instruction (one opcode) the most common sequences in vector computation, namely multiplication followed by addition, subtraction, or summation. The storage-to-register MULTIPLY-AND-ADD instruction, for example, fetches a vector from storage, multiplies it by a vector from a register, and adds the product to a third vector in a register. By use of the compound instructions MULTIPLY-AND-ADD and MULTIPLY-AND-SUBTRACT in the example of Figure 17.20, the total time for the iteration is reduced from 10 to 8 cycles.

Unlike chaining, compound instructions do not require the use of additional registers for temporary storage of intermediate results, and they require one less register access. For example, consider the following chain:

$$A \rightarrow VR1$$
$$VR1 + VR2 \rightarrow VR1$$

In this case, two stores to the vector register VR1 are required. In the IBM architecture there is a storage-to-register ADD instruction. With this instruction, only the sum is placed in VR1. The compound instruction also avoids the need to reflect in the machine-state description the concurrent execution of a number of instructions, which simplifies status saving and restoring by the operating system and the handling of interrupts.

THE INSTRUCTION SET Table 17.3 summarizes the arithmetic and logical operations that are defined for the vector architecture. In addition, there are memory-to-

Table 17.3 IBM 3090 Vector Facility: Arithmetic and Logical Instructions

Operation	Floating-Point Long	Floating-Point Short	Binary or Logical	Operand Locations			
Add	FL	FS	BI	V + V → V	V + S → V	Q + V → V	Q + S → V
Subtract	FL	FS	BI	V − V → V	V − S → V	Q − V → V	Q − S → V
Multiply	FL	FS	BI	V × V → V	V × V → V	Q × V → V	Q × S → V
Divide	FL	FS	—	V/V → V	V/S → V	Q/V → V	Q/S → V
Compare	FL	FS	BI	V · V → V	V · S → V	Q · V → V	Q · S → V
Multiply and Add	FL	FS	—	V + V × V → V	V + V × S → V	V + Q × V → V	V + Q × S → V
Multiply and Subtract	FL	FS	—	V − V × V → V	V − V × S → V	V − Q × V → V	V − Q × S → V
Multiply and Accumulate	FL	FS	—	P + · V → V	P + · S → V		
Complement	FL	FS	BI	− V → V			
Positive Absolute	FL	FS	BI	|V| → V			
Negative Absolute	FL	FS	BI	−|V| → V			
Maximum	FL	FS	—	· V → V		Q · V → Q	
Maximum Absolute	FL	FS	—	· V → V		Q · V → Q	
Minimum	FL	FS	—			Q · V → Q	
Shift Left Logical	—	—	LO	· V → V			
Shift Right Logical	—	—	LO	· V → V			
And	—	—	LO	V & V → V	V & S → V	Q & V → V	Q & S → V
OR	—	—	LO	V|V → V	V|S → V	Q|V → V	Q|S → V
Exclusive-OR	—	—	LO	V ⊕ V → V	V ⊕ S → V	Q ⊕ V → V	Q ⊕ S → V

Explanation:

Data Types
FL Long floating point
FS Short floating point
BI Binary integer
LO Logical

Operand Locations
V Vector register
S Storage
Q Scalar (general or floating-point register)
P Partial sums in vector register
· Special operation

675

register load and register-to-memory store instructions. Note that many of the instructions use a three-operand format. Also, many instructions have a number of variants, depending on the location of the operands. A source operand may be a vector register (V), storage (S), or a scalar register (Q). The target is always a vector register, except for comparison, the result of which goes into the vector-mask register. With all these variants, the total number of opcodes (distinct instructions) is 171. This rather large number, however, is not as expensive to implement as might be imagined. Once the machine provides the arithmetic units and the data paths to feed operands from storage, scalar registers, and vector registers to the vector pipelines, the major hardware cost has been incurred. The architecture can, with little difference in cost, provide a rich set of variants on the use of those registers and pipelines.

Most of the instructions in Table 17.3 are self-explanatory. The two summation instructions warrant further explanation. The accumulate operation adds together the elements of a single vector (ACCUMULATE) or the elements of the product of two vectors (MULTIPLY-AND-ACCUMULATE). These instructions present an interesting design problem. We would like to perform this operation as rapidly as possible, taking full advantage of the ALU pipeline. The difficulty is that the sum of two numbers put into the pipeline is not available until several cycles later. Thus, the third element in the vector cannot be added to the sum of the first two elements until those two elements have gone through the entire pipeline. To overcome this problem, the elements of the vector are added in such a way as to produce four partial sums. In particular, elements 0, 4, 8, 12, . . ., 124 are added in that order to produce partial sum 0; elements 1, 5, 9, 13, . . ., 125 to partial sum 1; elements 2, 6, 10, 14, . . ., 126 to partial sum 2; and elements 3, 7, 11, 15, . . ., 127 to partial sum 4. Each of these partial sums can proceed through the pipeline at top speed, because the delay in the pipeline is roughly four cycles. A separate vector register is used to hold the partial sums. When all elements of the original vector have been processed, the four partial sums are added together to produce the final result. The performance of this second phase is not critical, because only four vector elements are involved.

17.8 RECOMMENDED READING AND WEB SITE

[CATA94] surveys the principles of multiprocessors and examines SPARC-based SMPs in detail. SMPs are also covered in some detail in [STON93] and [HWAN93].

[MILE00] is an overview of cache coherence algorithms and techniques for multiprocessors, with an emphasis on performance issues. Another survey of the issues relating to cache coherence in multiprocessors is [LILJ93]. [TOMA93] contains reprints of many of the key papers on the subject.

[UNGE02] is an excellent survey of the concepts of multithreaded processors and chip multiprocessors. [UNGE03] is a lengthy survey of both proposed and current multithreaded processors that use explicit multithreading.

A thorough treatment of clusters can be found in [BUYY99a] and [BUYY99b]. [WEYG01] is a less technical survey of clusters, with good commentary on various commercial products. [DESA05] describes IBM's blade server architecture.

Good discussions of vector computation can be found in [STON93] and [HWAN93].

BUYY99a   Buyya, R. *High-Performance Cluster Computing: Architectures and Systems.* Upper Saddle River, NJ: Prentice Hall, 1999.

BUYY99b   Buyya, R. *High-Performance Cluster Computing: Programming and Applications.* Upper Saddle River, NJ: Prentice Hall, 1999.

CATA94   Catanzaro, B. *Multiprocessor System Architectures.* Mountain View, CA: Sunsoft Press, 1994.

DESA05   Desai, D., et al. "BladeCenter System Overview." *IBM Journal of Research and Development,* November 2005.

HWAN93   Hwang, K. *Advanced Computer Architecture.* New York: McGraw-Hill, 1993.

LILJ93   Lilja, D. "Cache Coherence in Large-Scale Shared-Memory Multiprocessors: Issues and Comparisons." *ACM Computing Surveys,* September 1993.

MILE00   Milenkovic, A. "Achieving High Performance in Bus-Based Shared-Memory Multiprocessors." *IEEE Concurrency,* July-September 2000.

STON93   Stone, H. *High-Performance Computer Architecture.* Reading, MA: Addison-Wesley, 1993.

TOMA93   Tomasevic, M., and Milutinovic, V. *The Cache Coherence Problem in Shared-Memory Multiprocessors: Hardware Solutions.* Los Alamitos, CA: IEEE Computer Society Press, 1993.

UNGE02   Ungerer, T.; Rubic, B.; and Silc, J. "Multithreaded Processors." *The Computer Journal,* No. 3, 2002.

UNGE03   Ungerer, T.; Rubic, B.; and Silc, J. " A Survey of Processors with Explicit Multithreading." *ACM Computing Surveys,* March, 2003.

WEYG01   Weygant, P. *Clusters for High Availability.* Upper Saddle River, NJ: Prentice Hall, 2001.

Recommended Web site:

- **IEEE Computer Society Task Force on Cluster Computing:** An international forum to promote cluster computing research and education.

17.9 KEY TERMS, REVIEW QUESTIONS, AND PROBLEMS

Key Terms

active standby	MESI protocol	symmetric multiprocessor
cache coherence	multiprocessor	(SMP)
cluster	nonuniform memory access	uniform memory access
directory protocol	(NUMA)	(UMA)
failback	passive standby	uniprocessor
failover	snoopy protocol	vector facility

Review Questions

17.1 List and briefly define three types of computer system organization.

17.2 What are the chief characteristics of an SMP?

17.3 What are some of the potential advantages of an SMP compared with a uniprocessor?

17.4 What are some of the key OS design issues for an SMP?

17.5 What is the difference between software and hardware cache coherent schemes?

17.6 What is the meaning of each of the four states in the MESI protocol?

17.7 What are some of the key benefits of clustering?

17.8 What is the difference between failover and failback?

17.9 What are the differences among UMA, NUMA, and CC-NUMA?

Problems

17.1 Let α be the percentage of program code that can be executed simultaneously by n processors in a computer system. Assume that the remaining code must be executed sequentially by a single processor. Each processor has an execution rate of x MIPS.

    a. Derive an expression for the effective MIPS rate when using the system for exclusive execution of this program, in terms of n, α, and x.

    b. If $n = 16$ and $x = 4$ MIPS, determine the value of α that will yield a system performance of 40 MIPS.

17.2 A multiprocessor with eight processors has 20 attached tape drives. There are a large number of jobs submitted to the system that each require a maximum of four tape drives to complete execution. Assume that each job starts running with only three tape drives for a long period before requiring the fourth tape drive for a short period toward the end of its operation. Also assume an endless supply of such jobs.

    a. Assume the scheduler in the OS will not start a job unless there are four tape drives available. When a job is started, four drives are assigned immediately and are not released until the job finishes. What is the maximum number of jobs that can be in progress at once? What are the maximum and minimum number of tape drives that may be left idle as a result of this policy?

    b. Suggest an alternative policy to improve tape drive utilization and at the same time avoid system deadlock. What is the maximum number of jobs that can be in progress at once? What are the bounds on the number of idling tape drives?

17.3 Can you foresee any problem with the write-once cache approach on bus-based multiprocessors? If so, suggest a solution.

17.4 Consider a situation in which two processors in an SMP configuration, over time, require access to the same line of data from main memory. Both processors have a cache and use the MESI protocol. Initially, both caches have an invalid copy of the line. Figure 17.22 depicts the consequence of a read of line x by Processor P1. If this is the start of a sequence of accesses, draw the subsequent figures for the following sequence:

    1. P2 reads x.

    2. P1 writes to x (for clarity, label the line in P1's cache x').

    3. P1 writes to x (label the line in P1's cache x'').

    4. P2 reads x.

17.5 Figure 17.23 shows the state diagrams of two possible cache coherence protocols. Deduce and explain each protocol, and compare each to MESI.

17.6 Consider an SMP with both L1 and L2 caches using the MESI protocol. As explained in Section 17.3, one of four states is associated with each line in the L2 cache. Are all four states also needed for each line in the L1 cache? If so, why? If not, explain which state or states can be eliminated.

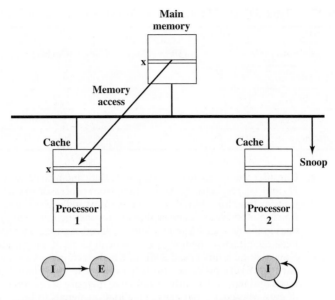

Figure 17.22 MESI Example: Processor 1 Reads Line x

17.7 An earlier version of the IBM mainframe, the S/390 G4, used three levels of cache. As with the z990, only the first level was on the processor chip [called the processor unit (PU)]. The L2 cache was also similar to the z990. An L3 cache was on a separate chip that acted as a memory controller, and was interposed between the L2 caches and the memory cards. Table 17.4 shows the performance of a three-level cache arrangement for the IBM S/390. The purpose of this problem is to determine whether the inclusion of the third level of cache seems worthwhile. Determine the access penalty (average number of PU cycles) for a system with only an L1 cache, and normalize that value to 1.0. Then determine the normalized access penalty when both an L1 and L2 cache are used, and the access penalty when all three caches are used. Note the amount of improvement in each case and state your opinion on the value of the L3 cache.

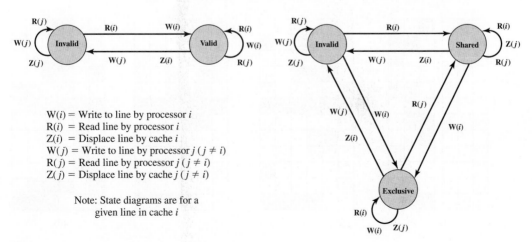

$W(i)$ = Write to line by processor i
$R(i)$ = Read line by processor i
$Z(i)$ = Displace line by cache i
$W(j)$ = Write to line by processor j ($j \neq i$)
$R(j)$ = Read line by processor j ($j \neq i$)
$Z(j)$ = Displace line by cache j ($j \neq i$)

Note: State diagrams are for a
given line in cache i

Figure 17.23 Two Cache Coherence Protocols

Table 17.4 Typical Cache Hit Rate on S/390 SMP Configuration [MAK97]

Memory Subsystem	Access Penalty (PU cycles)	Cache Size	Hit Rate (%)
L1 cache	1	32 KB	89
L2 cache	5	256 KB	5
L3 cache	14	2 MB	3
Memory	32	8 GB	3

17.8 **a.** Consider a uniprocessor with separate data and instruction caches, with hit ratios of H_d and H_i, respectively. Access time from processor to cache is c clock cycles, and transfer time for a block between memory and cache is b clock cycles. Let f_i be the fraction of memory accesses that are for instructions, and f_d is the fraction of dirty lines in the data cache among lines replaced. Assume a write-back policy and determine the effective memory access time in terms of the parameters just defined.

   b. Now assume a bus-based SMP in which each processor has the characteristics of part (a). Every processor must handle cache invalidation in addition to memory reads and writes. This affects effective memory access time. Let f_{inv} be the fraction of data references that cause invalidation signals to be sent to other data caches. The processor sending the signal requires t clock cycles to complete the invalidation operation. Other processors are not involved in the invalidation operation. Determine the effective memory access time.

17.9 What organizational alternative is suggested by each of the illustrations in Figure 17.24?

17.10 In Figure 17.8, some of the diagrams show horizontal rows that are partially filled. In other cases, there are rows that are completely blank. These represent two different types of loss of efficiency. Explain.

17.11 Consider the pipeline depiction in Figure 12.13b, which is redrawn in Figure 17.25a, with the fetch and decode stages ignored, to represent the execution of thread A. Figure 17.25b illustrates the execution of a separate thread B. In both cases, a simple pipelined processor is used.

   a. Show an instruction issue diagram, similar to Figure 17.8a, for each of the two threads.

   b. Assume that the two threads are to be executed in parallel on a chip multiprocessor, with each of the two processors on the chip using a simple pipeline. Show an

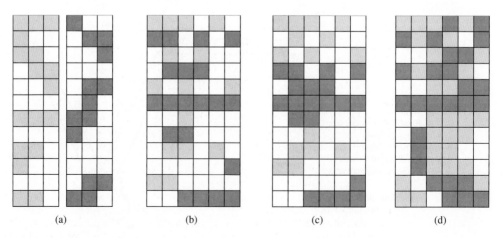

(a)   (b)   (c)   (d)

Figure 17.24 Diagram for Problem 18.9

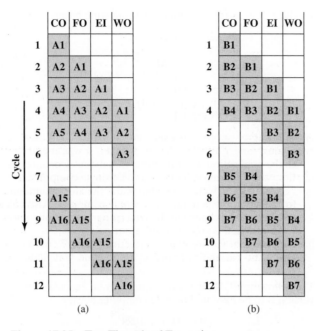

Figure 17.25 Two Threads of Execution

instruction issue diagram similar to Figure 17.8k. Also show a pipeline execution diagram in the style of Figure 17.25.

c. Assume a two-issue superscalar architecture. Repeat part (b) for an interleaved multithreading superscalar implementation, assuming no data dependencies. *Note:* There is no unique answer; you need to make assumptions about latency and priority.

d. Repeat part c for a blocked multithreading superscalar implementation.

e. Repeat for a four-issue SMT architecture.

17.12 The following code segment needs to be executed 64 times for the evaluation of the vector arithmetic expression: $D(I) = A(I) + B(I) \times C(I)$ for $0 \le I \le 63$.

$$
\begin{array}{ll}
\text{Load R1, B(I)} & /R1 \leftarrow \text{Memory}(\alpha + I)/ \\
\text{Load R2, C(I)} & /R2 \leftarrow \text{Memory}(\beta + I)/ \\
\text{Multiply R1, R2} & /R1 \leftarrow (R1) \times (R2)/ \\
\text{Load R3, A(I)} & /R3 \leftarrow \text{Memory}(\gamma + I)/ \\
\text{Add R3, R1} & /R3 \leftarrow (R3) + (R1)/ \\
\text{Load D1, R3} & /\text{Memory}(\theta + I) \leftarrow (R3)/
\end{array}
$$

where R1, R2, and R3 are processor registers, and $\alpha, \beta, \gamma, \theta$ are the starting main memory addresses of arrays B(I), C(I), A(I), and D(I), respectively. Assume four clock cycles for each Load or Store, two cycles for the Add, and eight cycles for the Multiplier on either a uniprocessor or a single processor in an SIMD machine.

a. Calculate the total number of processor cycles needed to execute this code segment repeatedly 64 times on a SISD uniprocessor computer sequentially, ignoring all other time delays.

b. Consider the use of an SIMD computer with 64 processing elements to execute the vector operations in six synchronized vector instructions over 64-component vector data and both driven by the same-speed clock. Calculate the total execution time on the SIMD machine, ignoring instruction broadcast and other delays.

c. What is the speedup gain of the SIMD computer over the SISD computer?

17.13 Produce a vectorized version of the following program:

$$
\begin{aligned}
&\textbf{DO } 20 \text{ I} = 1, \text{N} \\
&\text{B(I, 1)} = 0 \\
&\textbf{DO } 10 \text{ J} = 1, \text{M} \\
&\quad \text{A(I)} = \text{A(I)} + \text{B(I, J)} \times \text{C(I, J)} \\
&10 \quad \textbf{CONTINUE} \\
&\quad \text{D(I)} = \text{E(I)} + \text{A(I)} \\
&20 \quad \textbf{CONTINUE}
\end{aligned}
$$

17.14 An application program is executed on a nine-computer cluster. A benchmark program took time T on this cluster. Further, it was found that 25% of T was time in which the application was running simultaneously on all nine computers. The remaining time, the application had to run on a single computer.
   a. Calculate the effective speedup under the aforementioned condition as compared to executing the program on a single computer. Also calculate α, the percentage of code that has been parallelized (programmed or compiled so as to use the cluster mode) in the preceding program.
   b. Suppose that we are able to effectively use 17 computers rather than 9 computers on the parallelized portion of the code. Calculate the effective speedup that is achieved.

17.15 The following FORTRAN program is to be executed on a computer, and a parallel version is to be executed on a 32-computer cluster.

```
L1:      DO 10 I = 1, 1024
L2:          SUM(I) = 0
L3:          DO 20 J = 1, I
L4:  20          SUM(I) = SUM(I) + I
L5:  10  CONTINUE
```

Suppose lines 2 and 4 each take two machine cycle times, including all processor and memory-access activities. Ignore the overhead caused by the software loop control statements (lines 1, 3, 5) and all other system overhead and resource conflicts.
   a. What is the total execution time (in machine cycle times) of the program on a single computer?
   b. Divide the I-loop iterations among the 32 computers as follows: Computer 1 executes the first 32 iterations (I = 1 to 32), processor 2 executes the next 32 iterations, and so on. What are the execution time and speedup factor compared with part (a)? (Note that the computational workload, dictated by the J-loop, is unbalanced among the computers.)
   c. Explain how to modify the parallelizing to facilitate a balanced parallel execution of all the computational workload over 32 computers. By a balanced load is meant an equal number of additions assigned to each computer with respect to both loops.
   d. What is the minimum execution time resulting from the parallel execution on 32 computers? What is the resulting speedup over a single computer?

17.16 Consider the following two versions of a program to add two vectors:

```L1: DO 10 I = 1, N```	```DOALL K = 1, M```
```L2: A(I) = B(I) + C(I)```	``` DO 10 I = L(K−1) + 1, KL```
```L3: 10 CONTINUE```	``` A(I) = B(I) + C(I)```
```L4: SUM = 0```	```10 CONTINUE```
```L5: DO 20 J = 1, N```	``` SUM(K) = 0```
```L6: SUM = SUM + A(J)```	``` DO 20 J = 1, L```
```L7: 20 CONTINUE```	``` SUM(K) = SUM(K) + A(L(K−1) + J)```
	```20 CONTINUE```
	``` ENDALL```

a. The program on the left executes on a uniprocessor. Suppose each line of code L2, L4, and L6 takes one processor clock cycle to execute. For simplicity, ignore the time required for the other lines of code. Initially all arrays are already loaded in main memory and the short program fragment is in the instruction cache. How many clock cycles are required to execute this program?

b. The program on the right is written to execute on a multiprocessor with M processors. We partition the looping operations into M sections with $L = N/M$ elements per section. DOALL declares that all M sections are executed in parallel. The result of this program is to produce M partial sums. Assume that k clock cycles are needed for each interprocessor communication operation via the shared memory and that therefore the addition of each partial sum requires k cycles. An l-level binary adder tree can merge all the partial sums, where $l = \log_2 M$. How many cycles are needed to produce the final sum?

c. Suppose $N = 2^{20}$ elements in the array and $M = 256$. What is the speedup achieved by using the multiprocessor? Assume $k = 200$. What percentage is this of the theoretical speedup of a factor of 256?

CHAPTER 18

MULTICORE COMPUTERS

684

KEY POINTS

♦ A multicore computer, or chip multiprocessor, combines two or more processors on a single computer chip.

♦ The use of ever more complex single-processor chips has reached a limit due to hardware performance issues, including limits in instruction-level parallelism and power limitations.

♦ On the other hand, the multicore architecture poses challenges to software developers to exploit the capability for multithreading across multiple cores.

♦ The main variables in a multicore organization are the number of processors on the chip, the number of levels of cache memory, and the extent to which cache memory is shared.

♦ Another organizational design decision in a multicore system is whether the individual cores will be superscalar or will implement simultaneous multithreading (SMT).

A **multicore** computer, also known as a **chip multiprocessor**, combines two or more processors (called cores) on a single piece of silicon (called a die). Typically, each core consists of all of the components of an independent processor, such as registers, ALU, pipeline hardware, and control unit, plus L1 instruction and data caches. In addition to the multiple cores, contemporary multicore chips also include L2 cache and, in some cases, L3 cache.

This chapter provides an overview of multicore systems. When begin with a look at the hardware performance factors that led to the development of multicore computers and the software challenges of exploiting the power of a multicore system. Next, we look at multicore organization. Finally, we examine two examples of multicore products, those of Intel and ARM.

18.1 HARDWARE PERFORMANCE ISSUES

As we discuss in Chapter 2, microprocessor systems have experienced a steady, exponential increase in execution performance for decades. Figure 2.12 shows that this increase is due partly to refinements in the organization of the processor on the chip, and partly to the increase in the clock frequency.

Increase in Parallelism

The organizational changes in processor design have primarily been focused on increasing instruction-level parallelism, so that more work could be done in each clock cycle. These changes include, in chronological order (Figure 18.1):

• **Pipelining:** Individual instructions are executed through a pipeline of stages so that while one instruction is executing in one stage of the pipeline, another instruction is executing in another stage of the pipeline.

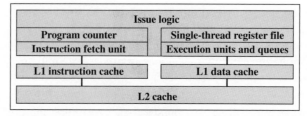

(a) Superscalar

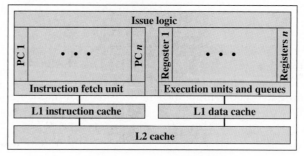

(b) Simultaneous multithreading

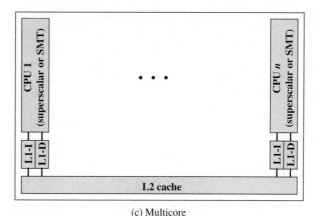

(c) Multicore

Figure 18.1 Alternative Chip Organizations

- **Superscalar:** Multiple pipelines are constructed by replicating execution resources. This enables parallel execution of instructions in parallel pipelines, so long as hazards are avoided.

- **Simultaneous multithreading (SMT):** Register banks are replicated so that multiple threads can share the use of pipeline resources.

For each of these innovations, designers have over the years attempted to increase the performance of the system by adding complexity. In the case of pipelining, simple three-stage pipelines were replaced by pipelines with five stages, and then many more stages, with some implementations having over a dozen stages. There is a practical limit to how far this trend can be taken, because with more stages, there is the need for more logic, more interconnections, and more control signals. With superscalar organization, performance increases can be achieved by increasing the number of parallel pipelines. Again, there are diminishing returns as the number of pipelines increases. More logic is required to manage hazards and to stage instruction resources. Eventually, a single thread of execution reaches the point where hazards and resource dependencies prevent the full use of the multiple pipelines available. This same point of diminishing returns is reached with SMT, as the complexity of managing multiple threads over a set of pipelines limits the number of threads and number of pipelines that can be effectively utilized.

Figure 18.2, from [OLUK05], is instructive in this context. The upper graph shows the exponential increase in Intel processor performance over the years.[1] The middle graph is calculated by combining Intel's published SPEC CPU figures and processor clock frequencies to give a measure of the extent to which performance improvement is due to increased exploitation of instruction-level parallelism. There is a flat region in the late 1980s before parallelism was exploited extensively. This is followed by a steep rise as designers were able to increasingly exploit pipelining, superscalar techniques, and SMT. But, beginning about 2000, a new flat region of the curve appears, as the limits of effective exploitation of instruction-level parallelism are reached.

There is a related set of problems dealing with the design and fabrication of the computer chip. The increase in complexity to deal with all of the logical issues related to very long pipelines, multiple superscalar pipelines, and multiple SMT register banks means that increasing amounts of the chip area is occupied with coordinating and signal transfer logic. This increases the difficulty of designing, fabricating, and debugging the chips. The increasingly difficult engineering challenge related to processor logic is one of the reasons that an increasing fraction of the processor chip is devoted to the simpler memory logic. Power issues, discussed next, provide another reason.

Power Consumption

To maintain the trend of higher performance as the number of transistors per chip rise, designers have resorted to more elaborate processor designs (pipelining, superscalar, SMT) and to high clock frequencies. Unfortunately, power requirements have grown exponentially as chip density and clock frequency have risen. This is shown in the lowest graph in Figure 18.2.

One way to control power density is to use more of the chip area for cache memory. Memory transistors are smaller and have a power density an order of magnitude lower than that of logic (see Figure 18.3a). As Figure 18.3b, from [BORK03], shows, the percentage of the chip area devoted to memory has grown to exceed 50% as the chip transistor density has increased.

---

[1]The data are based on published SPEC CPU figures from Intel, normalized across varying suites.

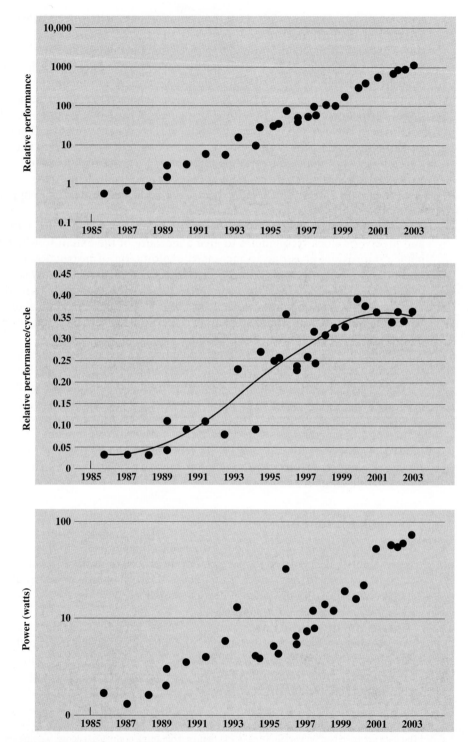

Figure 18.2 Some Intel Hardware Trends

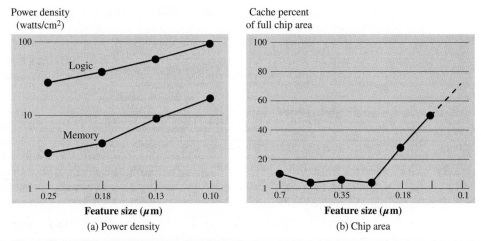

Power density (watts/cm²)

Cache percent of full chip area

Feature size (μm)

(a) Power density

Feature size (μm)

(b) Chip area

Figure 18.3   Power and Memory Considerations

Figure 18.4, from [BORK07], shows where the power consumption trend is leading. By 2015, we can expect to see microprocessor chips with about 100 billion transistors on a 300 mm² die. Assuming about 50–60% of the chip area is devoted to memory, the chip will support cache memory of about 100 MB and leave over 1 billion transistors available for logic.

How to use all those logic transistors is a key design issue. As discussed earlier in this section, there are limits to the effective use of such techniques as superscalar and SMT. In general terms, the experience of recent decades has been

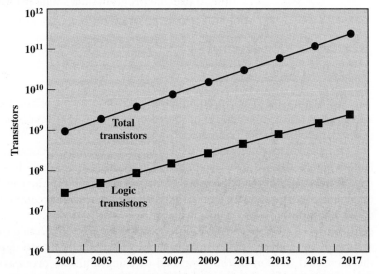

Figure 18.4   Chip Utilization of Transistors

encapsulated in a rule of thumb known as **Pollack's rule** [POLL99], which states that performance increase is roughly proportional to square root of increase in complexity. In other words, if you double the logic in a processor core, then it delivers only 40% more performance. In principle, the use of multiple cores has the potential to provide near-linear performance improvement with the increase in the number of cores.

Power considerations provide another motive for moving toward a multicore organization. Because the chip has such a huge amount of cache memory, it becomes unlikely that any one thread of execution can effectively use all that memory. Even with SMT, you are multithreading in a relatively limited fashion and cannot therefore fully exploit a gigantic cache, whereas a number of relatively independent threads or processes has a greater opportunity to take full advantage of the cache memory.

18.2 SOFTWARE PERFORMANCE ISSUES

A detailed examination of the software performance issues related to multicore organization is beyond our scope. In this section, we first provide an overview of these issues, and then look at an example of an application designed to exploit multicore capabilities.

Software on Multicore

The potential performance benefits of a multicore organization depend on the ability to effectively exploit the parallel resources available to the application. Let us focus first on a single application running on a multicore system. Recall from Chapter 2 that Amdahl's law states that:

$$\text{Speedup} = \frac{\text{time to execute program on a single processor}}{\text{time to execute program on } N \text{ parallel processors}}$$

$$= \frac{1}{(1-f) + \dfrac{f}{N}} \tag{18.1}$$

The law assumes a program in which a fraction $(1 - f)$ of the execution time involves code that is inherently serial and a fraction f that involves code that is infinitely parallelizable with no scheduling overhead.

This law appears to make the prospect of a multicore organization attractive. But as Figure 18.5a shows, even a small amount of serial code has a noticeable impact. If only 10% of the code is inherently serial ($f = 0.9$), the running the program on a multicore system with 8 processors yields a performance gain of only a factor of 4.7. In addition, software typically incurs overhead as a result of communication and distribution of work to multiple processors and cache coherence overhead. This results in a curve where performance peaks than then begins to degrade because of the increased burden of the overhead of using multiple processors. Figure 18.5b, from [MCDO05], is a representative example.

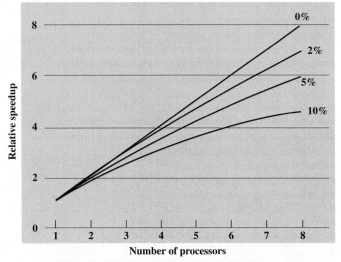

(a) Speedup with 0%, 2%, 5%, and 10% sequential portions

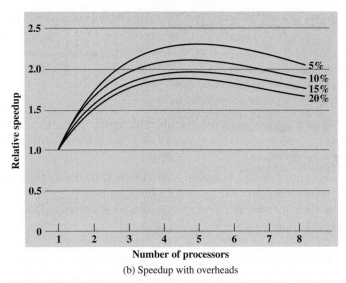

(b) Speedup with overheads

Figure 18.5   Performance Effect of Multiple Cores

However, software engineers have been addressing this problem and there are numerous applications in which it is possible to effectively exploit a multicore system. [MCDO05] reports on a set of database applications, in which great attention was paid to reducing the serial fraction within hardware architectures, operating systems, middleware, and the database application software. Figure 18.6 shows the result. As this example shows, database management systems and database applications are one area in which multicore systems can be used effectively. Many kinds of servers can also effectively use the parallel multicore organization, because servers typically handle numerous relatively independent transactions in parallel.

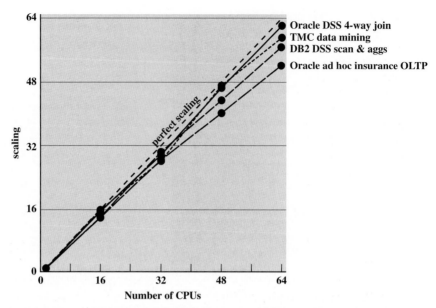

Figure 18.6   Scaling of Database Workloads on Multiple-Processor Hardware

In addition to general-purpose server software, a number of classes of applications benefit directly from the ability to scale throughput with the number of cores. [MCDO06] lists the following examples:

- **Multithreaded native applications:** Multithreaded applications are characterized by having a small number of highly threaded processes. Examples of threaded applications include Lotus Domino or Siebel CRM (Customer Relationship Manager).

- **Multiprocess applications:** Multiprocess applications are characterized by the presence of many single-threaded processes. Examples of multi-process applications include the Oracle database, SAP, and PeopleSoft.

- **Java applications:** Java applications embrace threading in a fundamental way. Not only does the Java language greatly facilitate multithreaded applications, but the Java Virtual Machine is a multithreaded process that provides scheduling and memory management for Java applications. Java applications that can benefit directly from multicore resources include application servers such as Sun's Java Application Server, BEA's Weblogic, IBM's Websphere, and the open-source Tomcat application server. All applications that use a Java 2 Platform, Enterprise Edition (J2EE platform) application server can immediately benefit from multicore technology.

- **Multiinstance applications:** Even if an individual application does not scale to take advantage of a large number of threads, it is still possible to gain from multicore architecture by running multiple instances of the application in parallel. If multiple application instances require some degree of isolation, virtualization technology (for the hardware of the operating system) can be used to provide each of them with its own separate and secure environment.

Application Example: Valve Game Software

Valve is an entertainment and technology company that has developed a number of popular games, as well as the Source engine, one of the most widely played game engines available. Source is an animation engine used by Valve for its games and licensed for other game developers.

In recent years, Valve has reprogrammed the Source engine software to use multithreading to exploit the power of multicore processor chips from Intel and AMD [REIM06]. The revised Source engine code provides more powerful support for Valve games such as Half Life 2.

From Valve's perspective, threading granularity options are defined as follows [HARR06]:

- **Coarse threading:** Individual modules, called systems, are assigned to individual processors. In the Source engine case, this would mean putting rendering on one processor, AI (artificial intelligence) on another, physics on another, and so on. This is straightforward. In essence, each major module is single threaded and the principal coordination involves synchronizing all the threads with a timeline thread.

- **Fine-grained threading:** Many similar or identical tasks are spread across multiple processors. For example, a loop that iterates over an array of data can be split up into a number of smaller parallel loops in individual threads that can be scheduled in parallel.

- **Hybrid threading:** This involves the selective use of fine-grain threading for some systems and single threading for other systems.

Valve found that through coarse threading, it could achieve up to twice the performance across two processors compared to executing on a single processor. But this performance gain could only be achieved with contrived cases. For real-world gameplay, the improvement was on the order of a factor of 1.2. Valve also found that effective use of fine-grain threading was difficult. The time per work unit can be variable, and managing the timeline of outcomes and consequences involved complex programming.

Valve found that a hybrid threading approach was the most promising and would scale the best as multicore systems with eight or sixteen processors became available. Valve identified systems that operate very effectively being permanently assigned to a single processor. An example is sound mixing, which has little user interaction, is not constrained by the frame configuration of windows, and works on its own set of data. Other modules, such as scene rendering, can be organized into a number of threads so that the module can execute on a single processor but achieve greater performance as it is spread out over more and more processors.

Figure 18.7 illustrates the thread structure for the rendering module. In this hierarchical structure, higher-level threads spawn lower-level threads as needed. The rendering module relies on a critical part of the Source engine, the world list, which is a database representation of the visual elements in the game's world. The first task is to determine what are the areas of the world that need to be rendered. The next task is to determine what objects are in the scene as viewed from multiple angles. Then comes the processor-intensive work. The rendering module has to work out the rendering of each object from multiple points of view, such as the player's view, the view of TV monitors, and the point of view of reflections in water.

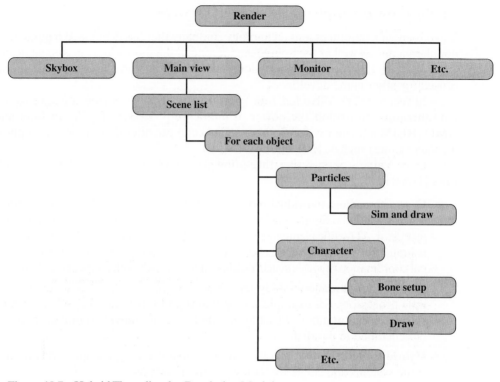

Figure 18.7   Hybrid Threading for Rendering Module

Some of the key elements of the threading strategy for the rendering module are listed in [LEON07] and include the following:

- Construct scene-rendering lists for multiple scenes in parallel (e.g., the world and its reflection in water).
- Overlap graphics simulation.
- Compute character bone transformations for all characters in all scenes in parallel.
- Allow multiple threads to draw in parallel.

The designers found that simply locking key databases, such as the world list, for a thread was too inefficient. Over 95% of the time, a thread is trying to read from a data set, and only 5% of the time at most is spent in writing to a data set. Thus, a concurrency mechanism known as the single-writer-multiple-readers model works effectively.

18.3 MULTICORE ORGANIZATION

At a top level of description, the main variables in a multicore organization are as follows:

- The number of core processors on the chip
- The number of levels of cache memory
- The amount of cache memory that is shared

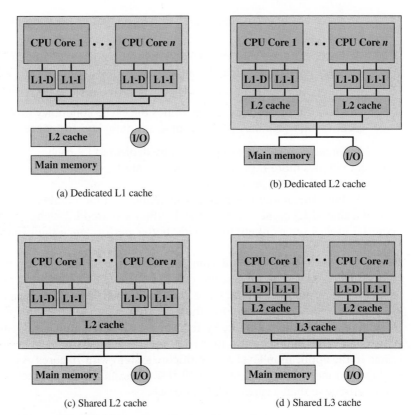

Figure 18.8 Multicore Organization Alternatives

Figure 18.8 shows four general organizations for multicore systems. Figure 18.8a is an organization found in some of the earlier multicore computer chips and is still seen in embedded chips. In this organization, the only on-chip cache is L1 cache, with each core having its own dedicated L1 cache. Almost invariably, the L1 cache is divided into instruction and data caches. An example of this organization is the ARM11 MPCore.

The organization of Figure 18.8b is also one in which there is no on-chip cache sharing. In this, there is enough area available on the chip to allow for L2 cache. An example of this organization is the AMD Opteron. Figure 18.8c shows a similar allocation of chip space to memory, but with the use of a shared L2 cache. The Intel Core Duo has this organization. Finally, as the amount of cache memory available on the chip continues to grow, performance considerations dictate splitting off a separate, shared L3 cache, with dedicated L1 and L2 caches for each core processor. The Intel Core i7 is an example of this organization.

The use of a shared L2 cache on the chip has several advantages over exclusive reliance on dedicated caches:

1. Constructive interference can reduce overall miss rates. That is, if a thread on one core accesses a main memory location, this brings the frame containing the referenced location into the shared cache. If a thread on another core soon thereafter accesses the same memory block, the memory locations will already be available in the shared on-chip cache.

2. A related advantage is that data shared by multiple cores is not replicated at the shared cache level.

3. With proper frame replacement algorithms, the amount of shared cache allocated to each core is dynamic, so that threads that have a less locality can employ more cache.

4. Interprocessor communication is easy to implement, via shared memory locations.

5. The use of a shared L2 cache confines the cache coherency problem to the L1 cache level, which may provide some additional performance advantage.

A potential advantage to having only dedicated L2 caches on the chip is that each core enjoys more rapid access to its private L2 cache. This is advantageous for threads that exhibit strong locality.

As both the amount of memory available and the number of cores grow, the use of a shared L3 cache combined with either a shared L2 cache or dedicated per-core L2 caches seems likely to provide better performance than simply a massive shared L2 cache.

Another organizational design decision in a multicore system is whether the individual cores will be superscalar or will implement simultaneous multithreading (SMT). For example, the Intel Core Duo uses superscalar cores, whereas the Intel Core i7 uses SMT cores. SMT has the effect of scaling up the number of hardware-level threads that the multicore system supports. Thus, a multicore system with four cores and SMT that supports four simultaneous threads in each core appears the same to the application level as a multicore system with 16 cores. As software is developed to more fully exploit parallel resources, an SMT approach appears to be more attractive than a superscalar approach.

18.4 INTEL x86 MULTICORE ORGANIZATION

Intel has introduced a number of multicore products in recent years. In this section, we look at two examples: the Intel Core Duo and the Intel Core i7.

Intel Core Duo

The Intel Core Duo, introduced in 2006, implements two x86 superscalar processors with a shared L2 cache (Figure 18.8c).

The general structure of the Intel Core Duo is shown in Figure 18.9. Let us consider the key elements starting from the top of the figure. As is common in multicore systems, each core has its own dedicated **L1 cache**. In this case, each core has a 32-KB instruction cache and a 32-KB data cache.

Each core has an independent **thermal control unit**. With the high transistor density of today's chips, thermal management is a fundamental capability, especially for laptop and mobile systems. The Core Duo thermal control unit is designed to manage chip heat dissipation to maximize processor performance within thermal constraints. Thermal management also improves ergonomics with a cooler system and lower fan acoustic noise. In essence, the thermal management unit monitors digital sensors for high-accuracy die temperature measurements. Each core can be defined as in independent thermal zone. The maximum temperature for each thermal

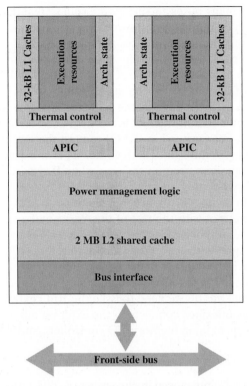

Figure 18.9   Intel Core Duo Block Diagram

zone is reported separately via dedicated registers that can be polled by software. If the temperature in a core exceeds a threshold, the thermal control unit reduces the clock rate for that core to reduce heat generation.

The next key element of the Core Duo organization is the **Advanced Programmable Interrupt Controller** (APIC). The APIC performs a number of functions, including the following:

1. The APIC can provide interprocessor interrupts, which allow any process to interrupt any other processor or set of processors. In the case of the Core Duo, a thread in one core can generate an interrupt, which is accepted by the local APIC, routed to the APIC of the other core, and communicated as an interrupt to the other core.

2. The APIC accepts I/O interrupts and routes these to the appropriate core.

3. Each APIC includes a timer, which can be set by the OS to generate an interrupt to the local core.

The **power management logic** is responsible for reducing power consumption when possible, thus increasing battery life for mobile platforms, such as laptops. In essence, the power management logic monitors thermal conditions and CPU activity and adjusts voltage levels and power consumption appropriately. It includes an advanced power-gating capability that allows for an ultra fine-grained logic control that turns on individual processor logic subsystems only if and when they are needed.

Additionally, many buses and arrays are split so that data required in some modes of operation can be put in a low power state when not needed.

The Core Duo chip includes a shared 2-MB **L2 cache**. The cache logic allows for a dynamic allocation of cache space based on current core needs, so that one core can be assigned up to 100% of the L2 cache. The L2 cache includes logic to support the MESI protocol for the attached L1 caches. The key point to consider is when a cache write is done at the L1 level. A cache line gets the M state when a processor writes to it; if the line is not in E or M-state prior to writing it, the cache sends a Read-For-Ownership (RFO) request that ensures that the line exists in the L1 cache and is in the I state in the other L1 cache. The Intel Core Duo extends this protocol to take into account the case when there are multiple Core Duo chips organized as a symmetric multiprocessor (SMP) system. The L2 cache controller allow the system to distinguish between a situation in which data are shared by the two local cores, but not with the rest of the world, and a situation in which the data are shared by one or more caches on the die as well as by an agent on the external bus (can be another processor). When a core issues an RFO, if the line is shared only by the other cache within the local die, we can resolve the RFO internally very fast, without going to the external bus at all. Only if the line is shared with another agent on the external bus do we need to issue the RFO externally.

The **bus interface** connects to the external bus, known as the Front Side Bus, which connects to main memory, I/O controllers, and other processor chips.

Intel Core i7

The Intel Core i7, introduced in November of 2008, implements four x86 SMT processors, each with a dedicated L2 cache, and with a shared L3 cache (Figure 18.8d).

The general structure of the Intel Core i7 is shown in Figure 18.10. Each core has its own **dedicated L2 cache** and the four cores share an 8-MB **L3 cache**. One mechanism Intel uses to make its caches more effective is prefetching, in which

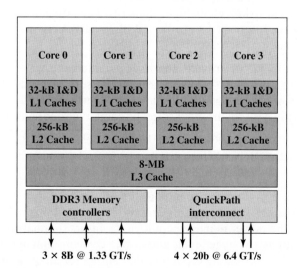

Figure 18.10 Intel Core i7 Block Diagram

Table 18.1 Cache Latency (in clock cycles)

CPU	Clock Frequency	L1 Cache	L2 Cache	L3 Cache
Core 2 Quad	2.66 GHz	3 cycles	15 cycles	—
Core i7	2.66 GHz	4 cycles	11 cycles	39 cycles

the hardware examines memory access patterns and attempts to fill the caches speculatively with data that's likely to be requested soon. It is interesting to compare the performance of this three-level on chip cache organization with a comparable two-level organization from Intel. Table 18.1 shows the cache access latency, in terms of clock cycles for two Intel multicore systems running at the same clock frequency. The Core 2 Quad has a shared L2 cache, similar to the Core Duo. The Core i7 improves on L2 cache performance with the use of the dedicated L2 caches, and provides a relatively high-speed access to the L3 cache.

The Core i7 chip supports two forms of external communications to other chips. The **DDR3 memory controller** brings the memory controller for the DDR main memory[2] onto the chip. The interface supports three channels that are 8 bytes wide for a total bus width of 192 bits, for an aggregate data rate of up to 32 GB/s. With the memory controller on the chip, the Front Side Bus is eliminated.

The **QuickPath Interconnect** (QPI) is a cache-coherent, point-to-point link based electrical interconnect specification for Intel processors and chipsets. It enables high-speed communications among connected processor chips. The QPI link operates at 6.4 GT/s (transfers per second). At 16 bits per transfer, that adds up to 12.8 GB/s, and since QPI links involve dedicated bidirectional pairs, the total bandwidth is 25.6 GB/s.

18.5 ARM11 MPCore

The ARM11 MPCore is a multicore product based on the ARM11 processor family. The ARM11 MPCore can be configured with up to four processors, each with its own L1 instruction and data caches, per chip. Table 18.1 lists the configurable options for the system, including the default values.

Figure 18.11 presents a block diagram of the ARM11 MPCore. The key elements of the system are as follows:

- **Distributed interrupt controller (DIC):** Handles interrupt detection and interrupt prioritization. The DIC distributes interrupts to individual processors.
- **Timer:** Each CPU has its own private timer that can generate interrupts.
- **Watchdog:** Issues warning alerts in the event of software failures. If the watchdog is enabled, it is set to a predetermined value and counts down to 0. It is periodically reset. If the watchdog value reaches zero, an alert is issued.
- **CPU interface:** Handles interrupt acknowledgement, interrupt masking, and interrupt completion acknowledgement.

---

[2]The DDR synchronous RAM memory is discussed in Chapter 5.

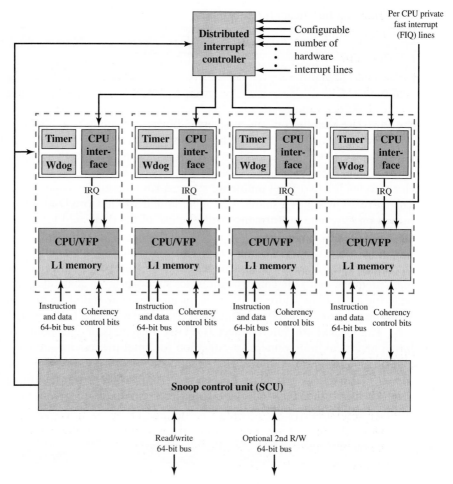

Figure 18.11 ARM11 MPCore Processor Block Diagram

- **CPU:** A single ARM11 processor. Individual CPUs are referred to as **MP11 CPUs**.
- **Vector floating-point (VFP) unit:** A coprocessor that implements floating-point operations in hardware.
- **L1 cache:** Each CPU has its own dedicated L1 data cache and L1 instruction cache.
- **Snoop control unit (SCU):** Responsible for maintaining coherency among L1 data caches.

Interrupt Handling

The Distributed Interrupt Controller (DIC) collates interrupts from a large number of sources. It provides

- Masking of interrupts
- Prioritization of the interrupts
- Distribution of the interrupts to the target MP11 CPUs

18.5 / ARM11 MPCore **701**

- Tracking the status of interrupts
- Generation of interrupts by software

The DIC is a single functional unit that is placed in the system alongside MP11 CPUs. This enables the number of interrupts supported in the system to be independent of the MP11 CPU design. The DIC is memory mapped; that is, control registers for the DIC are defined relative to a main memory base address. The DIC is accessed by the MP11 CPUs using a private interface through the SCU.

The DIC is designed to satisfy two functional requirements:

- Provide a means of routing an interrupt request to a single CPU or multiple CPUs, as required.
- Provide a means of interprocessor communication so that a thread on one CPU can cause activity by a thread on another CPU.

As an example that makes use of both requirements, consider a multithreaded application that has threads running on multiple processors. Suppose the application allocates some virtual memory. To maintain consistency, the operating system must update memory translation tables on all processors. The OS could update the tables on the processor where the virtual memory allocation took place, and then issue an interrupt to all the other processors running this application. The other processors could then use this interrupt's ID to determine that they need to update their memory translation tables.

The DIC can route an interrupt to one or more CPUs in the following three ways:

- An interrupt can be directed to a specific processor only.
- An interrupt can be directed to a defined group of processors. The MPCore views the first processor to accept the interrupt, typically the least loaded, as being best positioned to handle the interrupt.
- An interrupt can be directed to all processors.

From the point of view of software running on a particular CPU, the OS can generate an interrupt to all but self, to self, or to specific other CPUs. For communication between threads running on different CPUs, the interrupt mechanism is typically combined with shared memory for message passing. Thus, when a thread is interrupted by an interprocessor communication interrupt, it reads from the appropriate block of shared memory to retrieve a message from the thread that triggered the interrupt. A total of 16 interrupt IDs per CPU are available for interprocessor communication.

From the point of view of an MP11 CPU, an interrupt can be

- **Inactive:** An Inactive interrupt is one that is nonasserted, or which in a multiprocessing environment has been completely processed by that CPU but can still be either Pending or Active in some of the CPUs to which it is targeted, and so might not have been cleared at the interrupt source.
- **Pending:** A Pending interrupt is one that has been asserted, and for which processing has not started on that CPU.
- **Active:** An Active interrupt is one that has been started on that CPU, but processing is not complete. An Active interrupt can be pre-empted when a new interrupt of higher priority interrupts MP11 CPU interrupt processing.

Interrupts come from the following sources:

- **Interprocessor interrupts (IPIs):** Each CPU has private interrupts, ID0-ID15, that can only be triggered by software. The priority of an IPI depends on the receiving CPU, not the sending CPU.

- **Private timer and/or watchdog interrupts:** These use interrupt IDs 29 and 30.

- **Legacy FIQ line:** In legacy IRQ mode, the legacy FIQ pin, on a per CPU basis, bypasses the Interrupt Distributor logic and directly drives interrupt requests into the CPU.

- **Hardware interrupts:** Hardware interrupts are triggered by programmable events on associated interrupt input lines. CPUs can support up to 224 interrupt input lines. Hardware interrupts start at ID32.

Figure 18.12 is a block diagram of the DIC. The DIC is configurable to support between 0 and 255 hardware interrupt inputs. The DIC maintains a list of interrupts, showing their priority and status. The Interrupt Distributor transmits to each CPU Interface the highest Pending interrupt for that interface. It receives back the information that the interrupt has been acknowledged, and can then change the status of the corresponding interrupt. The CPU Interface also transmits End of Interrupt

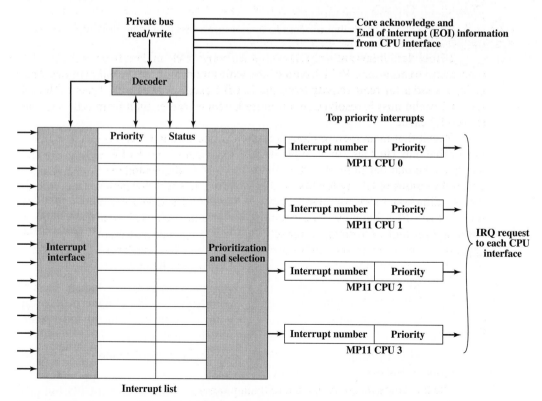

Figure 18.12 Interrupt Distributor Block Diagram

Table 18.2   ARM11 MPCore Configurable Options

Feature	Range of Options	Default Value
Processors	1 to 4	4
Instruction cache size per processor	16 KB, 32 KB, or 64 KB	32 KB
Data cache size per processor	16 KB, 32 KB, or 64 KB	32 KB
Master ports	1 or 2	2
Width of interrupt bus	0 to 224 by increments of 32 pins	32 pins
Vector floating point (VFP) coprocessor per processor	Included or not	Included

Information (EOI), which enables the Interrupt Distributor to update the status of this interrupt from Active to Inactive.

Cache Coherency

The MPCore's Snoop Control Unit (SCU) is designed to resolve most of the traditional bottlenecks related to access to shared data and the scalability limitation introduced by coherence traffic.

The L1 cache coherency scheme is based on the MESI protocol described in Chapter 17. The SCU monitors operations shared data to optimize MESI state migration. The SCU introduces three types of optimization: direct data intervention, duplicated tag RAMs, and migratory lines.

Direct data intervention (DDI) enables copying clean data from one CPU L1 data cache to another CPU L1 data cache without accessing external memory. This reduces read after read activity from the Level 1 cache to the Level 2 cache. Thus, a local L1 cache miss is resolved in a remote L1 cache rather than from access to the shared L2 cache.

Recall that main memory location of each line within a cache is identified by a tag for that line. The tags can be implemented as a separate block of RAM of the same length as the number of lines in the cache. In the SCU, **duplicated tag RAMs** are duplicated versions of L1 tag RAMs used by the SCU to check for data availability before sending coherency commands to the relevant CPUs. Coherency commands are sent only to CPUs that must update their coherent data cache. This reduces the power consumption and performance impact from snooping into and manipulating each processor's cache on each memory update. Having tag data available locally lets the SCU limit cache manipulations to processors that have cache lines in common.

The **migratory lines** feature enables moving dirty data from one CPU to another without writing to L2 and reading the data back in from external memory. The operation can be described as follows. In a typical MESI protocol, one processor has a modified line and another processor attempts to read that line, the following actions occur:

1. The line contents are transferred from the modified line to the processor that initiated the read.

2. The line contents are read back to main memory.

3. The line is put in the shared state in both caches.

The MPCore SCU handles this situation differently. The SCU monitors the system for a migratory line. If one processor has a modified line, and another processor reads then writes to it, the SCU assumes such a location will experience this same operation in the future. As this operation starts again, the SCU will automatically move the cache line directly to an invalid state rather than expending energy moving it first into the shared state. This optimization also causes the processor to transfer the cache line directly to the other processor without intervening external memory operations.

18.6 RECOMMENDED READING AND WEB SITE

Two books that provide good coverage of the issues in this chapter are [OLUK07] and [JERR05]. [GOCH06] and [MEND06] describe the Intel Core Duo. [FOG08b] provides a detailed description of the Core Duo pipeline architecture.

[ARM08b] provides thorough coverage of the ARM Cortex-A8 pipeline. [HIRA07] and [GOOD05] are good overview articles.

ARM08b ARM Limited. *ARM11 MPCore Processor Technical Reference Manual.* ARM DDI 0360E, 2008. www.arm.com

FOG08b Fog, A. *The Microarchitecture of Intel and AMD CPUs.* Copenhagen University College of Engineering, 2008. http://www.agner.org/optimize/

GOCH06 Gochman, S., et al. "Introduction to Intel Core Duo Processor Architecture." *Intel Technology Journal,* May 2006.

GOOD05 Goodacre, J., and Sloss, A. "Parallelism and the ARM Instruction Set Architecture." *Computer,* July 2005.

HIRA07 Hirata, K., and Goodacre, J. "ARM MPCore: The Streamlined and Scalable ARM11 processor core." *Proceedings, 2007 Conference on Asia South Pacific Design Automation,* 2007.

JERR05 Jerraya, A., and Wolf, W., eds. *Multiprocessor Systems-on-Chips.* San Francisco: Morgan Kaufmann, 2005.

MEND06 Mendelson, A., et al. "CMP Implementation in Systems Based on the Intel Core Duo Processor." *Intel Technology Journal,* May 2006.

OLUK07 Olukotun, K.; Hammond, L.; and Laudon, J. *Chip Multiprocessor Architecture: Techniques to Improve Throughput and Latency.* San Rafael, CA: Morgan & Claypool, 2007.

Recommended Web site:

- **Multicore Association:** Vendor organization promoting the development of and use of multicore technology.

18.7 KEY TERMS, REVIEW QUESTIONS, AND PROBLEMS

Key Terms

Amdahl's law	multicore	superscalar
chip multiprocessor	simultaneous multithreading (SMT)	

Review Questions

18.1 Summarize the differences among simple instruction pipelining, superscalar, and simultaneous multithreading.

18.2 Give several reasons for the choice by designers to move to a multicore organization rather than increase parallelism within a single processor.

18.3 Why is there a trend toward given an increasing fraction of chip area to cache memory?

18.4 List some examples of applications that benefit directly from the ability to scale throughput with the number of cores.

18.5 At a top level, what are the main design variables in a multicore organization?

18.6 List some advantages of a shared L2 cache among cores compared to separate dedicated L2 caches for each core.

Problems

18.1 Consider the following problem. A designer has available a chip and decided what fraction of the chip will be devoted to cache memory (L1, L2, L3). The remainder of the chip can be devoted to a single complex superscalar and/or SMT core or multiple somewhat simpler cores. Define the following parameters:

n = maximum number of cores that can be contained on the chip

k = actual number of cores implemented ($1 \leq k \leq n$, where $r = n/k$ is an integer)

$perf(r)$ = sequential performance gain by using the resources equivalent to r cores to form a single processor, where $perf(1) = 1$.

f = fraction of software that is parallelizable across multiple cores.

Thus, if we construct a chip with n cores, we expect each core to provide sequential performance of 1 and for the n cores to be able to exploit parallelism up to a degree of n parallel threads. Similarly, if the chip has k cores, then each core should exhibit a performance of $perf(r)$ and the chip is able to exploit parallelism up to a degree of k parallel threads. We can modify Amdhal's law (Equation 18.1) to reflect this situation as follows:

$$\text{Speedup} = \frac{1}{\dfrac{1 - f}{perf(r)} + \dfrac{f \times r}{perf(r) \times n}}$$

a. Justify this modification of Amdahl's law.

b. Using Pollack's rule, we set $perf(r) = \sqrt{r}$. Let $n = 16$. We want to plot speedup as a function of r for $f = 0.5; f = 0.9; f = 0.975; f = 0.99; f = 0.999$. The results are available in a document at this book's Web site (multicore-performance.pdf). What conclusions can you draw?

c. Repeat part (b) for $n = 256$.

18.2 The technical reference manual for the ARM11 MPCore says that the Distributed Interrupt Controller is memory mapped. That is, the core processors use memory mapped I/O to communicate with the DIC. Recall from Chapter 7 that with memory-mapped I/O, there is a single address space for memory locations and I/O devices. The processor treats the status and data registers of I/O modules as memory locations and uses the same machine instructions to access both memory and I/O devices. Based on this information, what path through the block diagram of Figure 18.11 is used for the core processors to communicate with the DIC?

APPENDIX A

PROJECTS FOR TEACHING COMPUTER ORGANIZATION AND ARCHITECTURE

A.1 Interactive Simulations

A.2 Research Projects

A.3 Simulation Projects

> SimpleScalar
> SMPCache

A.4 Assembly Language Projects

A.5 Reading/Report Assignments

A.6 Writing Assignments

A.7 Test Bank

Many instructors believe that research or implementation projects are crucial to the clear understanding of the concepts of computer organization and architecture. Without projects, it may be difficult for students to grasp some of the basic concepts and interactions among components. Projects reinforce the concepts introduced in the book, give students a greater appreciation of the inner workings of processors and computer systems, and can motivate students and give them confidence that they have mastered the material.

In this text, I have tried to present the concepts of computer organization and architecture as clearly as possible and have provided numerous homework problems to reinforce those concepts. Many instructors will wish to supplement this material with projects. This appendix provides some guidance in that regard and describes support material available in the instructor's manual. The support material covers six types of projects and other student exercises:

- Interactive simulations
- Research projects
- Simulation projects
- Assembly language projects
- Reading/report assignments
- Writing assignments
- Test bank

A.1 INTERACTIVE SIMULATIONS

New to this edition is the incorporation of interactive simulations. These simulations provide a powerful tool for understanding the complex design features of a modern computer system. Today's students want to be able to visualize the various complex computer systems mechanisms on their own computer screen. A total of 20 simulations are used to illustrate key functions and algorithms in computer organization and architecture design. Table A.1 lists the simulations by chapter. At the relevant point in the book, an icon indicates that a relevant interactive simulation is available online for student use.

Because the simulations enable the user to set initial conditions, they can serve as the basis for student assignments. The **Instructor's Resource Center** (IRC) for this book includes a set of assignments, one set for each of the interactive simulations. Each assignment includes a several specific problems that can be assigned to students.

The interactive simulations were developed under the direction of Professor Israel Koren, at the University of Massachusetts Department of Electrical and Computer Engineering. Aswin Sreedhar of the University of Massachusetts developed the interactive simulation assignments.

A.2 RESEARCH PROJECTS

An effective way of reinforcing basic concepts from the course and for teaching students research skills is to assign a research project. Such a project could involve a literature search as well as a Web search of vendor products, research lab activities, and standardization efforts. Projects could be assigned to teams or, for smaller projects, to

Table A.1 Computer Organization and Architecture—Interactive Simulations by Chapter

Chapter 4—Cache Memory	
Cache Simulator	Emulates small sized caches based on a user-input cache model and displays the cache contents at the end of the simulation cycle based on an input sequence which is entered by the user, or randomly generated if so selected.
Cache Time Analysis	Demonstrates Average Memory Access Time analysis for the cache parameters you specify.
Multitask Cache Demonstrator	Models cache on a system that supports multitasking.
Selective Victim Cache Simulator	Compares three different cache policies.
Chapter 5—Internal Memory	
Interleaved Memory Simulator	Demonstrates the effect of interleaving memory.
Chapter 6—External Memory	
RAID	Determine storage efficiency and reliability.
Chapter 7—Input/Output	
I/O System Design Tool	Evaluates comparative cost and performance of different I/O systems.
Chapter 8—OS Support	
Page Replacement Algorithms	Compares LRU, FIFO, and Optimal.
More Page Replacement Algorithms	Compares a number of policies.
Chapter 12—CPU Structure and Function	
Reservation Table Analyzer	Evaluates reservation tables. which are a way of representing the task flow pattern of a pipelined system.
Branch Prediction	Demonstrates three different branch prediction schemes.
Branch Target Buffer	Combined branch predictor/branch target buffer simulator.
Chapter 13—Reduced Instruction Set Computers	
MIPS 5-Stage Pipeline	Simulates the pipeline.
Loop Unrolling	Simulates the loop unrolling software technique for exploiting instruction-level parallelism.
Chapter 14—Instruction-Level Parallelism and Superscalar Processors	
Pipeline with Static vs. Dynamic Scheduling	A more complex simulation of the MIPS pipeline.
Reorder Buffer Simulator	Simulates instruction reordering in a RISC pipeline.
Scoreboarding Technique for Dynamic Scheduling	Simulation of an instruction scheduling technique used in a number of processors.
Tomasulo's Algorithm	Simulation of another instruction scheduling technique.
Alternative Simulation of Tomasulo's Algorithm	Another simulation of Tomasulo's algorithm.
Chapter 17—Parallel Processing	
Vector Processor Simulation	Demonstrates execution of vector processing instructions.

individuals. In any case, it is best to require some sort of project proposal early in the term, giving the instructor time to evaluate the proposal for appropriate topic and appropriate level of effort. Student handouts for research projects should include

- A format for the proposal
- A format for the final report

- A schedule with intermediate and final deadlines
- A list of possible project topics

The students can select one of the listed topics or devise their own comparable project. The IRC includes a suggested format for the proposal and final report as well as a list of possible research topics.

A.3 SIMULATION PROJECTS

An excellent way to obtain a grasp of the internal operation of a processor and to study and appreciate some of the design trade-offs and performance implications is by simulating key elements of the processor. Two useful tools that are useful for this purpose are SimpleScalar and SMPCache.

Compared with actual hardware implementation, simulation provides two advantages for both research and educational use:

- With simulation, it is easy to modify various elements of an organization, to vary the performance characteristics of various components, and then to analyze the effects of such modifications.
- Simulation provides for detailed performance statistics collection, which can be used to understand performance trade-offs.

SimpleScalar

SimpleScalar [BURG97, MANJ01a, MANJ01b] is a set of tools that can be used to simulate real programs on a range of modern processors and systems. The tool set includes compiler, assembler, linker, and simulation and visualization tools. SimpleScalar provides processor simulators that range from an extremely fast functional simulator to a detailed out-of-order issue, superscalar processor simulator that supports nonblocking caches and speculative execution. The instruction set architecture and organizational parameters may be modified to create a variety of experiments.

The IRC for this book includes a concise introduction to SimpleScalar for students, with instructions on how to load and get started with SimpleScalar. The manual also includes some suggested project assignments.

SimpleScalar is a portable software package the runs on most UNIX platforms. The SimpleScalar software can be downloaded from the SimpleScalar Web site. It is available at no cost for noncommercial use.

SMPCache

SMPCache is a trace-driven simulator for the analysis and teaching of cache memory systems on symmetric multiprocessors [RODR01]. The simulation is based on a model built according to the architectural basic principles of these systems. The simulator has a full graphic and friendly interface. Some of the parameters that they can be studied with the simulator are: program locality; influence of the number of processors, cache coherence protocols, schemes for bus arbitration, mapping, replacement policies, cache size (blocks in cache), number of cache sets (for set associative caches), number of words by block (memory block size).

The IRC for this book includes a concise introduction to SMPCache for students, with instructions on how to load and get started with SMPCache. The manual also includes some suggested project assignments.

SMPCache is a portable software package the runs on PC systems with Windows. The SMPCache software can be downloaded from the SMPCache Web site. It is available at no cost for noncommercial use.

A.4 ASSEMBLY LANGUAGE PROJECTS

Assembly language programming is often used to teach students low-level hardware components and computer architecture basics. CodeBlue is a simplified assembly language program developed at the U. S. Air Force Academy. The goal of the work was to develop and teach assembly language concepts using a visual simulator that students can learn in a single class. The developers also wanted students to find the language motivational and fun to use. The CodeBlue language is much simpler than most simplified architecture instruction sets such as the SC123. Still it allows students to develop interesting assembly level programs that compete in tournaments, similar to the far more complex SPIMbot simulator. Most important, through CodeBlue programming, students learn fundamental computer architecture concepts such as instructions and data co-residence in memory, control structure implementation, and addressing modes.

To provide a basis for projects, the developers have built a visual development environment that allows students to create a program, see its representation in memory, step through the program's execution, and simulate a battle of competing programs in a visual memory environment.

Projects can be built around the concept of a Core War tournament. Core War is a programming game introduced to the public in the early 1980s, which was popular for a period of 15 years or so. Core War has four main components: a memory array of 8000 addresses, a simplified assembly language Redcode, an executive program called MARS (an acronym for Memory Array Redcode Simulator) and the set of contending battle programs. Two battle programs are entered into the memory array at randomly chosen positions; neither program knows where the other one is. MARS executes the programs in a simple version of time-sharing. The two programs take turns: a single instruction of the first program is executed, then a single instruction of the second, and so on. What a battle program does during the execution cycles allotted to it is entirely up to the programmer. The aim is to destroy the other program by ruining its instructions. The CodeBlue environment substitutes CodeBlue for Redcode and provides its own interactive execution interface.

The IRC includes the CodeBlue environment, a user's manual for students, other supporting material, and suggested assignments.

A.5 READING/REPORT ASSIGNMENTS

Another excellent way to reinforce concepts from the course and to give students research experience is to assign papers from the literature to be read and analyzed. The IRC site includes a suggested list of papers to be assigned, organized by chapter.

The IRC provides a copy of each of the papers. The IRC also includes a suggested assignment wording.

A.6 WRITING ASSIGNMENTS

Writing assignments can have a powerful multiplier effect in the learning process in a technical discipline such as data communications and networking. Adherents of the Writing Across the Curriculum (WAC) movement (**http://wac.colostate.edu/**) report substantial benefits of writing assignments in facilitating learning. Writing assignments lead to more detailed and complete thinking about a particular topic. In addition, writing assignments help to overcome the tendency of students to pursue a subject with a minimum of personal engagement, just learning facts and problem-solving techniques without obtaining a deep understanding of the subject matter.

The IRC contains a number of suggested writing assignments, organized by chapter. Instructors may ultimately find that this is the most important part of their approach to teaching the material. I would greatly appreciate any feedback on this area and any suggestions for additional writing assignments.

A.7 TEST BANK

A test bank for the book is available at the IRC site for this book. For each chapter, the test bank includes true/false, multiple choice, and fill-in-the-blank questions. The test bank is an effective way to assess student comprehension of the material.

APPENDIX B

ASSEMBLY LANGUAGE AND RELATED TOPICS

KEY POINTS

◆ An assembly language is a symbolic representation of the machine language of a specific processor, augmented by additional types of statements that facilitate program writing and that provide instructions to the assembler.

◆ An assembler is a program that translates assembly language into machine code.

◆ The first step in the creation of an active process is to load a program into main memory and create a process image.

◆ A linker is used to resolve any references between loaded modules.

The topic of assembly language was briefly introduced in Chapter 11. This appendix provides more detail and also covers a number of related topics. There are a number of reasons why it is worthwhile to study assembly language programming (as compared with programming in a higher-level language), including the following:

1. It clarifies the execution of instructions.

2. It shows how data is represented in memory.

3. It shows how a program interacts with the operating system, processor, and the I/O system.

4. It clarifies how a program accesses external devices.

5. Understanding assembly language programmers makes students better high-level language (HLL) programmers, by giving them a better idea of the target language that the HLL must be translated into.

We begin this chapter with a study of the basic elements of an assembly language, using the x86 architecture for our examples.[1] Next, we look at the operation of the assembler. This is followed by a discussion of linkers and loaders.

Table B.1 defines some of the key terms used in this appendix.

B.1 ASSEMBLY LANGUAGE

Assembly language is a programming language that is one step away from machine language. Typically, each assembly language instruction is translated into one machine instruction by the assembler. Assembly language is hardware dependent, with a different assembly language for each type of processor. In particular, assembly language instructions can make reference to specific registers in the processor, include all of the opcodes of the processor, and reflect the bit length of the various

---

[1]There are a number of assemblers for the x86 architecture. Our examples use NASM (Netwide Assembler), an open source assembler. A copy of the NASM manual is at this book's Web site.

Table B.1   Key Terms for this Appendix

Assembler

A program that translates assembly language into machine code.

Assembly Language

A symbolic representation of the machine language of a specific processor, augmented by additional types of statements that facilitate program writing and that provide instructions to the assembler.

Compiler

A program that converts another program from some source language (or programming language) to machine language (object code). Some compilers output assembly language which is then converted to machine language by a separate assembler. A compiler is distinguished from an assembler by the fact that each input statement does not, in general, correspond to a single machine instruction or fixed sequence of instructions. A compiler may support such features as automatic allocation of variables, arbitrary arithmetic expressions, control structures such as FOR and WHILE loops, variable scope, input/ouput operations, higher-order functions and portability of source code.

Executable Code

The machine code generated by a source code language processor such as an assembler or compiler. This is software in a form that can be run in the computer.

Instruction Set

The collection of all possible instructions for a particular computer; that is, the collection of machine language instructions that a particular processor understands.

Linker

A utility program that combines one or more files containing object code from separately compiled program modules into a single file containing loadable or executable code.

Loader

A program routine that copies an executable program into memory for execution.

Machine Language, or Machine Code

The binary representation of a computer program which is actually read and interpreted by the computer. A program in machine code consists of a sequence of machine instructions (possibly interspersed with data). Instructions are binary strings which may be either all the same size (e.g., one 32-bit word for many modern RISC microprocessors) or of different sizes.

Object Code

The machine language representation of programming source code. Object code is created by a compiler or assembler and is then turned into executable code by the linker.

registers of the processor and operands of the machine language. An assembly language programmer must therefore understand the computer's architecture.

Programmers rarely use assembly language for applications or even systems programs. HLLs provide an expressive power and conciseness that greatly eases the programmer's tasks. The disadvantages of using an assembly language rather than an HLL include the following [FOG08a]:

1. **Development time.** Writing code in assembly language takes much longer than writing in a high-level language.

2. **Reliability and security.** It is easy to make errors in assembly code. The assembler is not checking if the calling conventions and register save conventions are obeyed. Nobody is checking for you if the number of PUSH and POP instructions

is the same in all possible branches and paths. There are so many possibilities for hidden errors in assembly code that it affects the reliability and security of the project unless you have a very systematic approach to testing and verifying.

3. **Debugging and verifying.** Assembly code is more difficult to debug and verify because there are more possibilities for errors than in high-level code.

4. **Maintainability.** Assembly code is more difficult to modify and maintain because the language allows unstructured spaghetti code and all kinds of tricks that are difficult for others to understand. Thorough documentation and a consistent programming style are needed.

5. **Portability.** Assembly code is platform-specific. Porting to a different platform is difficult.

6. **System code can use intrinsic functions instead of assembly.** The best modern C++ compilers have intrinsic functions for accessing system control registers and other system instructions. Assembly code is no longer needed for device drivers and other system code when intrinsic functions are available.

7. **Application code can use intrinsic functions or vector classes instead of assembly.** The best modern C++ compilers have intrinsic functions for vector operations and other special instructions that previously required assembly programming.

8. **Compilers have been improved a lot in recent years.** The best compilers are now quite good. It takes a lot of expertise and experience to optimize better than the best C++ compiler.

Yet there are still some advantages to the occasional use of assembly language, including the following [FOG08a]:

1. **Debugging and verifying.** Looking at compiler-generated assembly code or the disassembly window in a debugger is useful for finding errors and for checking how well a compiler optimizes a particular piece of code.

2. **Making compilers.** Understanding assembly coding techniques is necessary for making compilers, debuggers and other development tools.

3. **Embedded systems.** Small embedded systems have fewer resources than PCs and mainframes. Assembly programming can be necessary for optimizing code for speed or size in small embedded systems.

4. **Hardware drivers and system code.** Accessing hardware, system control registers etc. may sometimes be difficult or impossible with high level code.

5. **Accessing instructions that are not accessible from high-level language.** Certain assembly instructions have no high-level language equivalent.

6. **Self-modifying code.** Self-modifying code is generally not profitable because it interferes with efficient code caching. It may, however, be advantageous, for example, to include a small compiler in math programs where a user-defined function has to be calculated many times.

7. **Optimizing code for size.** Storage space and memory is so cheap nowadays that it is not worth the effort to use assembly language for reducing code size. However, cache size is still such a critical resource that it may be useful in some cases to optimize a critical piece of code for size in order to make it fit into the code cache.

8. **Optimizing code for speed.** Modern C++ compilers generally optimize code quite well in most cases. But there are still cases where compilers perform poorly and where dramatic increases in speed can be achieved by careful assembly programming.

9. **Function libraries.** The total benefit of optimizing code is higher in function libraries that are used by many programmers.

10. **Making function libraries compatible with multiple compilers and operating systems.** It is possible to make library functions with multiple entries that are compatible with different compilers and different operating systems. This requires assembly programming.

The terms *assembly language* and *machine language* are sometimes, erroneously, used synonymously. Machine language consists of instructions directly executable by the processor. Each machine language instruction is a binary string containing an opcode, operand references, and perhaps other bits related to execution, such as flags. For convenience, instead of writing an instruction as a bit string, it can be written symbolically, with names for opcodes and registers. An assembly language makes much greater use of symbolic names, including assigning names to specific main memory locations and specific instruction locations. Assembly language also includes statements that are not directly executable but serve as instructions to the assembler that produces machine code from an assembly language program.

Assembly Language Elements

A statement in a typical assembly language has the form shown in Figure B.1. It consists of four elements: label, mnemonic, operand, and comment.

LABEL If a label is present, the assembler defines the label as equivalent to the address into which the first byte of the object code generated for that instruction will be loaded. The programmer may subsequently use the label as an address or as data in another instruction's address field. The assembler replaces the label with the assigned value when creating an object program. Labels are most frequently used in branch instructions.

As an example, here is a program fragment:

```
L2:  SUB   EAX,   EDX  ; subtract contents of register EDX from
                       ; contents of EAX and store result in EAX
     JG    L2          ; jump to L2 if result of subtraction is
                       ; positive
```

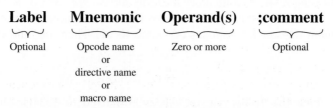

Figure B.1   Assembly-Language Statement Structure

The program will continue to loop back to location L2 until the result is zero or negative. Thus, when the jg instruction is executed, if the result is positive, the processor places the address equivalent to the label L2 in the program counter.

Reasons for using a label include the following;

1. A label makes a program location easier to find and remember.

2. The label can easily be moved to correct a program. The assembler will automatically change the address in all instructions that use the label when the program is reassembled.

3. The programmer does not have to calculate relative or absolute memory addresses, but just uses labels as needed.

MNEMONIC The mnemonic is the name of the operation or function of the assembly language statement. As discussed subsequently, a statement can correspond to a machine instruction, an assembler directive, or a macro. In the case of a machine instruction, a mnemonic is the symbolic name associated with a particular opcode.

Table 10.8 lists the mnemonic, or instruction name, of many of the x86 instructions. Appendix A of [CART06] lists the x86 instructions, together with the operands for each and the effect of the instruction on the condition codes. Appendix B of the NASM manual provides a more detailed description of each x86 instruction. Both documents are available at this book's Web site.

OPERAND(S) An assembly language statement includes zero or more operands. Each operand identifies an immediate value, a register value, or a memory location. Typically, the assembly language provides conventions for distinguishing among the three types of operand references, as well as conventions for indicating addressing mode.

For the x86 architecture, an assembly language statement may refer to a register operand by name. Figure B.2 illustrates the general-purpose x86 registers, with their symbolic name and their bit encoding. The assembler will translate the symbolic name into the binary identifier for the register.

As discussed in Section 11.2, the x86 architecture has a rich set of addressing modes, each of which must be expressed symbolically in the assembly language. Here we cite a few of the common examples. For **register addressing**, the name of the register is used in the instruction. For example, MOV ECX, EBX copies the contents of register EBX into register ECX. Immediate addressing indicates that the value is encoded in the instruction. For example, MOV EAX, 100H copies the hexadecimal value 100 into register EAX. The immediate value can be expressed as a binary number with the suffix B or a decimal number with no suffix. Thus, equivalent statements to the preceding one are MOV EAX, 100000000B and MOV EAX, 256. **Direct addressing** refers to a memory location and is expressed as a displacement from the DS segment register. This is best explained by example. Assume that the 16-bit data segment register DS contains the value 1000H. Then the following sequence occurs:

```
MOV AX, 1234H
MOV [3518H], AX
```

First the 16-bit register AX is initialized to 1234H. Then, in line two, the contents of AX are moved to the logical address DS:3518H. This address is formed

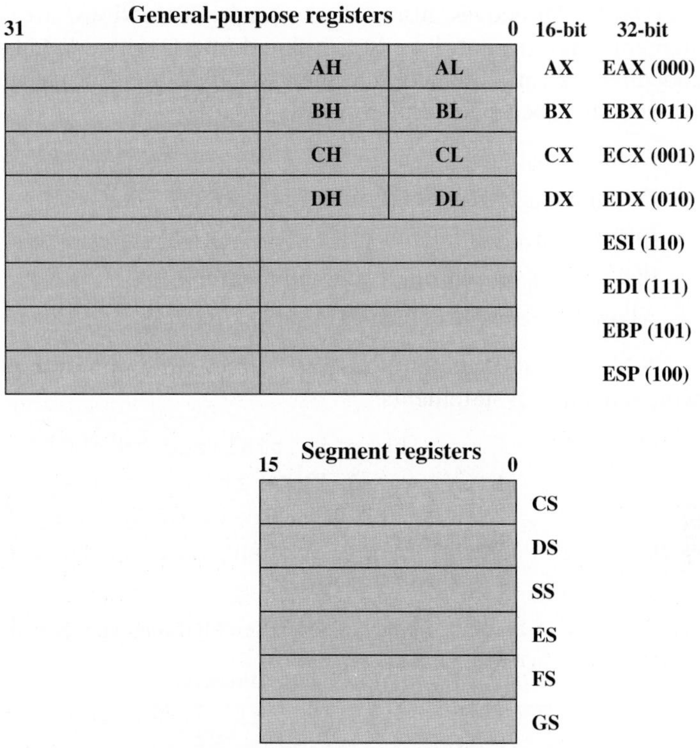

General-purpose registers

			16-bit	32-bit
	AH	AL	AX	EAX (000)
	BH	BL	BX	EBX (011)
	CH	CL	CX	ECX (001)
	DH	DL	DX	EDX (010)
				ESI (110)
				EDI (111)
				EBP (101)
				ESP (100)

Segment registers

	CS
	DS
	SS
	ES
	FS
	GS

Figure B.2   Intel x86 Program Execution Registers

by shifting the contents of DS left 4 bits and adding 3518H to form the 32-bit logical address 13518H.

COMMENT All assembly languages allow the placement of comments in the program. A comment can either occur at the right-hand end of an assembly statement or can occupy an entire text line. In either case, the comment begins with a special character that signals to the assembler that the rest of the line is a comment and is to be ignored by the assembler. Typically, assembly languages for the x86 architecture use a semicolon (;) for the special character.

Type of Assembly Language Statements

Assembly language statements are one of four types: instruction, directive, macro definition, and comment. A comment statement is simply a statement that consists entirely of a comment. The remaining types are briefly described in this section.

INSTRUCTIONS The bulk of the noncomment statements in an assembly language program are symbolic representations of machine language instructions. Almost invariably, there is a one-to-one relationship between an assembly language instruction and a machine instruction. The assembler resolves any symbolic references and translates the assembly language instruction into the binary string that comprises the machine instruction.

DIRECTIVES Directives, also called **pseudo-instructions**, are assembly language statements that are not directly translated into machine language instructions. Instead, directives are instruction to the assembler to perform specified actions doing the assembly process. Examples include the following:

- Define constants
- Designate areas of memory for data storage
- Initialize areas of memory
- Place tables or other fixed data in memory
- Allow references to other programs

Table B.2 lists some of the NASM directives. As an example, consider the following sequence of statements:

```
L2  DB   "A"       ; byte initialized to ASCII code for A (65)
    MOV  AL, [L1]  ; copy byte at L1 into AL
    MOV  EAX, L1   ; store address of byte at L1 in EAX
    MOV  [L1], AH  ; copy contents of AH into byte at L1
```

Table B.2   Some NASM Assembly-Language Directives

(a) Letters for RES*x* and D*x* Directives

Unit	Letter
byte	B
word (2 bytes)	W
double word (4 bytes)	D
quad word (8 bytes)	Q
ten bytes	T

(b) Directives

Name	Description	Example
DB, DW, DD, DQ, DT	Initalize locations	L6 DD 1A92H ; doubleword at L6 initialized to 1A92H
RESB, RESW, RESD, RESQ, REST	Reserve uniitialized locations	BUFFER RESB 64 ; reserve 64 bytes starting at BUFFER
INCBIN	Include binary file in output	INCBIN "file.dat" ; include this file
EQU	Define a symbol to a given constant value	MSGLEN EQU 25 ; the constant MSGLEN equals decimal 25
TIMES	Repeat instruction multiple times	ZEROBUF TIMES 64 DB 0 ; initialize 64-byte buffer to all zeros

If a plain label is used, it is interpreted as the address (or offset) of the data. If the label is placed inside square brackets, it is interpreted as the data at the address.

MACRO DEFINITIONS A macro definition is similar to a subroutine in several ways. A subroutine is a section of a program that is written once, and can be used multiple times by calling the subroutine from any point in the program. When a program is compiled or assembled, the subroutine is loaded only once. A call to the subroutine transfers control to the subroutine and a return instruction in the subroutine returns control to the point of the call. Similarly, a macro definition is a section of code that the programmer writes once, and then can use many times. The main difference is that when the assembler encounters a macro call, it replaces the macro call with the macro itself. This process is called **macro expansion**. So, if a macro is defined in an assembly language program and invoked 10 times, then 10 instances of the macro will appear in the assembled code. In essence, subroutines are handled by the hardware at run time, whereas macros are handled by the assembler at assembly time. Macros provide the same advantage as subroutines in terms of modular programming, but without the runtime overhead of a subroutine call and return. The tradeoff is that the macro approach uses more space in the object code.

In NASM and many other assemblers, a distinction is made between a single-line macro and a multi-line macro. In NASM, single-line macros are defined using the %DEFINE directive. Here is an example in which multiple single-line macros are expanded. First, we define two macros:

$$\%\text{DEFINE B(X)} = 2*X$$
$$\%\text{DEFINE A(X)} = 1 + B(X)$$

At some point in the assembly language program, the following statement appears:

```
MOV AX, A(8)
```

The assembler expands this statement to:

```
MOV AX, 1+2*8
```

which assembles to a machine instruction to move the immediate value 17 to register AX.

Multiline macros are defined using the mnemonic &MACRO. Here is an example of a multiline macro definition:

```
%MACRO PROLOGUE 1
        PUSH EBP        ; push contents of EBP onto stack
                        ; pointed to by ESP and
                        ; decrement contents of ESP by 4
        MOV EBP, ESP    ; copy contents of ESP to EBP
        SUB ESP, %1     ; subtract first parameter value from ESP
```

The number 1 after the macro name in the %MACRO line defines the number of parameters the macro expects to receive. The use of %1 inside the macro definition refers to the first parameter to the macro call.

The macro call

```
MYFUNC:   PROLOGUE 12
```

expands to the following lines of code:

```
MYFUNC:   PUSH    EBP
          MOV     EBP,    ESP
          SUB     ESP,    12
```

Example: Greatest Common Divisor Program

As an example of the use of assembly language, we look at a program to compute the greatest common divisor of two integers. We define the greatest common divisor of the integers a and b as follows:

$$\gcd(a, b) = \max[k, \text{ such that } k \text{ divides } a \text{ and } k \text{ divides } b]$$

where we say that k divides a if there is no remainder. Euclid's algorithm for the greatest common divisor is based on the following theorem. For any nonnegative integers a and integer b,

$$\gcd(a, b) = \gcd(b, a \bmod b)$$

Here is a C language program that implements Euclid's algorithm:

```
unsigned int gcd (unsigned int a, unsigned int b)
{
    if (a == 0 && b == 0)
        b = 1;
    else if (b == 0)
        b = a;
    else if (a != 0)
        while (a != b)
            if (a <b)
                b -= a;
            else
                a -= b;
    return b;
}
```

Figure B.3 shows two assembly language versions of the preceding program. The program on the left was done by a C compiler; the program on the right was programmed by hand. The latter program uses a number of programmer's tricks to produce a tighter, more efficient implementation.

gcd:	mov	ebx,eax
	mov	eax,edx
	test	ebx,ebx
	jne	L1
	test	edx,edx
	jne	L1
	mov	eax,1
	ret	
L1:	test	eax,eax
	jne	L2
	mov	eax,ebx
	ret	
L2:	test	ebx,ebx
	je	L5
L3;	cmp	ebx,eax
	je	L5
	jae	L4
	sub	eax,ebx
	jmp	L3
L4:	sub	ebx,eax
	jmp	L3
L5:	ret	

gcd:	neg	eax
	je	L3
L1:	neg	eax
	xchg	eax,edx
L2:	sub	eax,edx
	jg	L2
	jne	L1
L3:	add	eax,edx
	jne	L4
	inc	eax
L4:	ret	

(a) Compiled program   (b) Written directly in assembly language

Figure B.3 Assembly Programs for Greatest Common Divisor

B.2 ASSEMBLERS

The assembler is a software utility that takes an assembly program as input and produces object code as output. The object code is a binary file. The assembler views this file as a block of memory starting at relative location 0.

There are two general approaches to assemblers: the two-pass assembler and the one-pass assembler.

Two-Pass Assembler

We look first at the two-pass assembler, which is more common and somewhat easier to understand. The assembler makes two passes through the source code (Figure B.4):

FIRST PASS In the first pass, the assembler is only concerned with label definitions. The first pass is used to construct a **symbol table** that contains a list of all labels and their associated **location counter** (LC) values. The first byte of the object code will have the LC value of 0. The first pass examines each assembly statement. Although the assembler is not yet ready to translate instructions, it must examine each instruction sufficiently to

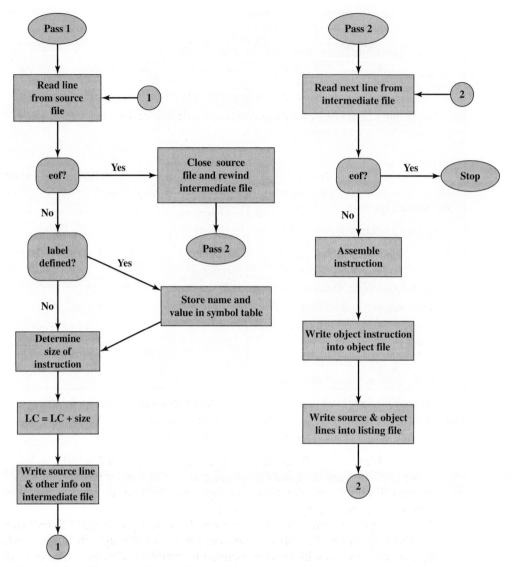

Figure B.4 Flowchart of Two-Pass Assembler

determine the length of the corresponding machine instruction and therefore how much to increment the LC. This may require not only examining the opcode but also looking at the operands and the addressing modes.

Directives such as DQ and REST (see Table B.2) cause the location counter to be adjusted according to how much storage is specified.

When assembler encounters a statement with a label, it places the label into the symbol table, along with the current LC value. The assembler continues until it has read all of the assembly language statements.

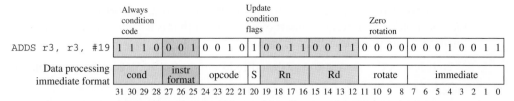

Figure B.5 Translating an ARM Assembly Instruction into a Binary Machine Instruction

SECOND PASS The second pass reads the program again from the beginning. Each instruction is translated into the appropriate binary machine code. Translation includes the following operations:

1. Translate the mnemonic into a binary opcode.
2. Use the opcode to determine the format of the instruction and the location and length of the various fields in the instruction.
3. Translate each operand name into the appropriate register or memory code.
4. Translate each immediate value into a binary string.
5. Translate any references to labels into the appropriate LC value using the symbol table.
6. Set any other bits in the instruction that are needed, including addressing mode indicators, condition code bits, and so on.

A simple example, using the ARM assembly language, is shown in Figure B.5. The ARM assembly language instruction ADDS r3, r3, #19 is translated in to the binary machine instruction 1110 0010 0101 0011 0011 0000 0001 0011.

ZEROTH PASS Most assembly language includes the ability to define macros. When macros are present there is an additional pass that the assembler must make before the first pass. Typically, the assembly language requires that all macro definitions must appear at the beginning of the program.

The assembler begins this "zeroth pass" by reading all macro definitions. Once all the macros are recognized, the assembler goes through the source code and expands the macros with their associated parameters whenever a macro call is encountered. The macro processing pass generates a new version of the source code with all of the macro expansions in place and all of the macro definitions removed.

One-Pass Assembler

It is possible to implement an assembler that makes only a single pass through the source code (not counting the macro processing pass). The main difficulty in trying to assemble a program in one pass involves forward references to labels. Instruction operands may be symbols that have not yet been defined in the source program. Therefore, the assembler does not know what relative address to insert in the translated instruction.

In essence, the process of resolving forward references works as follows. When the assembler encounters an instruction operand that is a symbol that is not yet defined, the assembler does the following:

1. It leaves the instruction operand field empty (all zeros) in the assembled binary instruction.

2. The symbol used as an operand is entered in the symbol table. The table entry is flagged to indicate that the symbol is undefined.

3. The address of the operand field in the instruction that refers to the undefined symbol is added to a list of forward references associated with the symbol table entry.

When the symbol definition is encountered so that a LC value can be associated with it, the assembler inserts the LC value in the appropriate entry in the symbol table. If there is a forward reference list associated with the symbol, then the assembler inserts the proper address into any instruction previously generated that is on the forward reference list.

Example: Prime Number Program

We now look at an example that includes directives. This example looks at a program that finds prime numbers. Recall that prime numbers are evenly divisible by only 1 and themselves. There is no formula for doing this. The basic method this program uses is to find the factors of all odd numbers below a given limit. If no factor can be found for an odd number, it is prime. Figure B.6 shows the basic algorithm written in C. Figure B.7 shows the same algorithm written in NASM assembly language.

```c
unsigned guess;                        /* current guess for prime */
unsigned factor;                       /* possible factor of guess */
unsigned limit;                        /* find primes up to this value */

printf ("Find primes up to : ");
scanf("%u", &limit);
printf ("2\n");                        /* treat first two primes as */
printf ("3\n");                        /* special case */
guess = 5;                             /* initial guess */
while (guess < = limit) {              /* look for a factor of guess */
    factor = 3;
    while (factor * factor < guess && guess% factor != 0)
    factor + = 2;
    if (guess % factor != 0)
        printf ("%d\n", guess);
    guess += 2;                        /* only look at odd numbers */
}
```

Figure B.6 C Program for Testing Primality

```
%include "asm_io.inc"
segment .data
Message db "Find primes up to: ", 0

segment .bss
Limit resd 1                            ; find primes up to this limit
Guess resd 1                            ; the current guess for prime

segment .text
    global _asm_main
_asm_main:
    enter 0,0                           ; setup routine
    pusha

    mov eax, Message
    call print_string
    call read_int                       ; scanf("%u", & limit);
    mov [Limit], eax
    mov eax, 2                          ; printf("2\n");
    call print_int
    call print_nl
    mov eax, 3                          ; printf("3\n");
    call print_int
    call print_nl

    mov dword [Guess], 5                ; Guess = 5;
while_limit:                            ; while (Guess <= Limit)
    mov eax, [Guess]
    cmp eax, [Limit]
    jnbe end_while_limit                ; use jnbe since numbers are unsigned

    mov ebx, 3                          ; ebx is factor = 3;
while_factor:
    mov eax,ebx
    mul eax                             ; edx:eax = eax*eax
    jo end_while_factor                 ; if answer won't fit in eax alone
    cmp eax, [Guess]
    jnb end_while_factor                ; if !(factor*factor < guess)
    mov eax,[Guess]
    mov edx,0
    div ebx                             ; edx = edx:eax% ebx
    cmp edx, 0
    je end_while_factor                 ; if !(guess% factor != 0)

    add ebx,2; factor += 2;
    jmp while_factor
end_while_factor:
    je end_if                           ; if !(guess% factor != 0)
    mov eax,[Guess]                     ; printf("%u\n")
    call print_int
    call print_nl
end_if:
    add dword [Guess], 2                ; guess += 2
    jmp while_limit
end_while_limit:

    popa
    mov eax, 0                          ; return back to C
    leave
    ret
```

Figure B.7   Assembly Program for Testing Primality

B.3 LOADING AND LINKING

The first step in the creation of an active process is to load a program into main memory and create a process image (Figure B.8). Figure B.9 depicts a scenario typical for most systems. The application consists of a number of compiled or assembled modules in object-code form. These are linked to resolve any references between modules. At the same time, references to library routines are resolved. The library routines themselves may be incorporated into the program or referenced as shared code that must be supplied by the operating system at run time. In this section, we summarize the key features of linkers and loaders. First, we discuss the concept of relocation. Then, for clarity in the presentation, we describe the loading task when a single program module is involved; no linking is required. We can then look at the linking and loading functions as a whole.

Relocation

In a multiprogramming system, the available main memory is generally shared among a number of processes. Typically, it is not possible for the programmer to know in advance which other programs will be resident in main memory at the time of execution of his or her program. In addition, we would like to be able to swap active processes in and out of main memory to maximize processor utilization by providing a large pool of ready processes to execute. Once a program has been swapped out to disk, it would be quite limiting to declare that when it is next swapped back in, it must be placed in the same main memory region as before. Instead, we may need to **relocate** the process to a different area of memory.

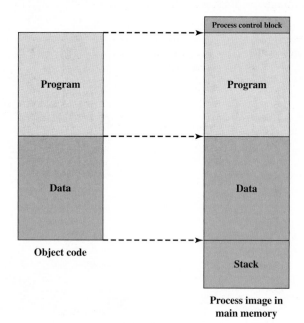

Figure B.8   The Loading Function

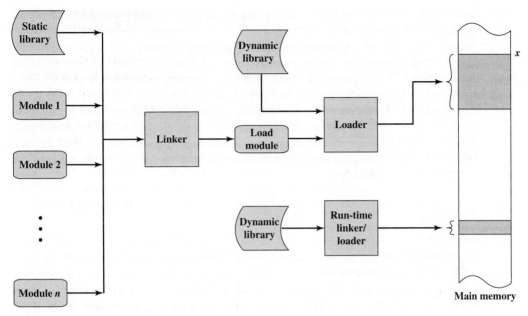

Figure B.9   A Linking and Loading Scenario

Thus, we cannot know ahead of time where a program will be placed, and we must allow that the program may be moved about in main memory due to swapping. These facts raise some technical concerns related to addressing, as illustrated in Figure B.10. The figure depicts a process image. For simplicity, let us assume that the process image occupies a contiguous region of main memory. Clearly, the operating

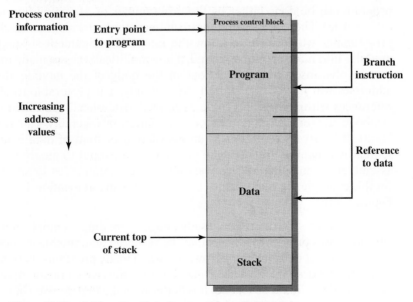

Figure B.10   Addressing Requirements for a Process

system will need to know the location of process control information and of the execution stack, as well as the entry point to begin execution of the program for this process. Because the operating system is managing memory and is responsible for bringing this process into main memory, these addresses are easy to come by. In addition, however, the processor must deal with memory references within the program. Branch instructions contain an address to reference the instruction to be executed next. Data reference instructions contain the address of the byte or word of data referenced. Somehow, the processor hardware and operating system software must be able to translate the memory references found in the code of the program into actual physical memory addresses, reflecting the current location of the program in main memory.

Loading

In Figure B.9, the loader places the load module in main memory starting at location x. In loading the program, the addressing requirement illustrated in Figure B.10 must be satisfied. In general, three approaches can be taken:

- Absolute loading
- Relocatable loading
- Dynamic run-time loading

ABSOLUTE LOADING An absolute loader requires that a given load module always be loaded into the same location in main memory. Thus, in the load module presented to the loader, all address references must be to specific, or absolute, main memory addresses. For example, if x in Figure B.9 is location 1024, then the first word in a load module destined for that region of memory has address 1024.

The assignment of specific address values to memory references within a program can be done either by the programmer or at compile or assembly time (Table B.3a). There are several disadvantages to the former approach. First, every programmer would have to know the intended assignment strategy for placing modules into main memory. Second, if any modifications are made to the program that involve insertions or deletions in the body of the module, then all of the addresses will have to be altered. Accordingly, it is preferable to allow memory references within programs to be expressed symbolically and then resolve those symbolic references at the time of compilation or assembly. This is illustrated in Figure B.11. Every reference to an instruction or item of data is initially represented by a symbol. In preparing the module for input to an absolute loader, the assembler or compiler will convert all of these references to specific addresses (in this example, for a module to be loaded starting at location 1024), as shown in Figure B.11b.

RELOCATABLE LOADING The disadvantage of binding memory references to specific addresses prior to loading is that the resulting load module can only be placed in one region of main memory. However, when many programs share main memory, it may not be desirable to decide ahead of time into which region of memory a particular module should be loaded. It is better to make that decision at load time. Thus we need a load module that can be located anywhere in main memory.

Table B.3 Address Binding

(a) Loader

Binding Time	Function
Programming time	All actual physical addresses are directly specified by the programmer in the program itself.
Compile or assembly time	The program contains symbolic address references, and these are converted to actual physical addresses by the compiler or assembler.
Load time	The compiler or assembler produces relative addresses. The loader translates these to absolute addresses at the time of program loading.
Run time	The loaded program retains relative addresses. These are converted dynamically to absolute addresses by processor hardware.

(b) Linker

Linkage Time	Function
Programming time	No external program or data references are allowed. The programmer must place into the program the source code for all subprograms that are referenced.
Compile or assembly time	The assembler must fetch the source code of every subroutine that is referenced and assemble them as a unit.
Load module creation	All object modules have been assembled using relative addresses. These modules are linked together and all references are restated relative to the origin of the final load module.
Load time	External references are not resolved until the load module is to be loaded into main memory. At that time, referenced dynamic link modules are appended to the load module, and the entire package is loaded into main or virtual memory.
Run time	External references are not resolved until the external call is executed by the processor. At that time, the process is interrupted and the desired module is linked to the calling program.

To satisfy this new requirement, the assembler or compiler produces not actual main memory addresses (absolute addresses) but addresses that are relative to some known point, such as the start of the program. This technique is illustrated in Figure B.11c. The start of the load module is assigned the relative address 0, and all other memory references within the module are expressed relative to the beginning of the module.

With all memory references expressed in relative format, it becomes a simple task for the loader to place the module in the desired location. If the module is to be loaded beginning at location x, then the loader must simply add x to each memory reference as it loads the module into memory. To assist in this task, the load module must include information that tells the loader where the address references are and how they are to be interpreted (usually relative to the program origin, but also possibly relative to some other point in the program, such as the current location). This set of information is prepared by the compiler or assembler and is usually referred to as the relocation dictionary.

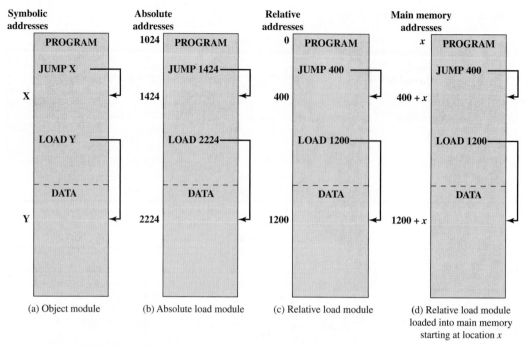

Figure B.11   Absolute and Relocatable Load Modules

DYNAMIC RUN–TIME LOADING Relocatable loaders are common and provide obvious benefits relative to absolute loaders. However, in a multiprogramming environment, even one that does not depend on virtual memory, the relocatable loading
scheme is inadequate. We have referred to the need to swap process images in and
out of main memory to maximize the utilization of the processor. To maximize main
memory utilization, we would like to be able to swap the process image back into different locations at different times. Thus, a program, once loaded, may be swapped out
to disk and then swapped back in at a different location. This would be impossible if
memory references had been bound to absolute addresses at the initial load time.

The alternative is to defer the calculation of an absolute address until it is actually needed at run time. For this purpose, the load module is loaded into main
memory with all memory references in relative form (Figure B.11c). It is not until an
instruction is actually executed that the absolute address is calculated. To assure that
this function does not degrade performance, it must be done by special processor
hardware rather than software. This hardware is described in Chapter 8.

Dynamic address calculation provides complete flexibility. A program can be
loaded into any region of main memory. Subsequently, the execution of the program
can be interrupted and the program can be swapped out of main memory, to be later
swapped back in at a different location.

Linking

The function of a linker is to take as input a collection of object modules and produce a load module, consisting of an integrated set of program and data modules, to

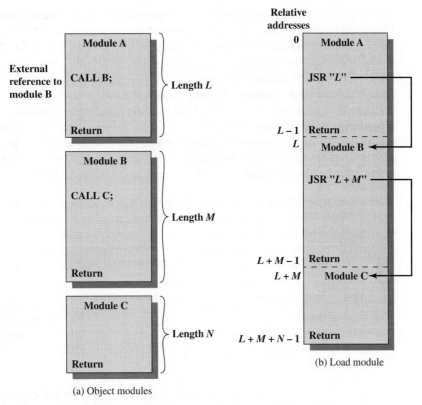

Figure B.12   The Linking Function

be passed to the loader. In each object module, there may be address references to locations in other modules. Each such reference can only be expressed symbolically in an unlinked object module. The linker creates a single load module that is the contiguous joining of all of the object modules. Each intramodule reference must be changed from a symbolic address to a reference to a location within the overall load module. For example, module A in Figure B.12a contains a procedure invocation of module B. When these modules are combined in the load module, this symbolic reference to module B is changed to a specific reference to the location of the entry point of B within the load module.

LINKAGE EDITOR The nature of this address linkage will depend on the type of load module to be created and when the linkage occurs (Table B.3b). If, as is usually the case, a relocatable load module is desired, then linkage is usually done in the following fashion. Each compiled or assembled object module is created with references relative to the beginning of the object module. All of these modules are put together into a single relocatable load module with all references relative to the origin of the load module. This module can be used as input for relocatable loading or dynamic run-time loading.

A linker that produces a relocatable load module is often referred to as a linkage editor. Figure B.12 illustrates the linkage editor function.

DYNAMIC LINKER As with loading, it is possible to defer some linkage functions. The term *dynamic linking* is used to refer to the practice of deferring the linkage of some external modules until after the load module has been created. Thus, the load module contains unresolved references to other programs. These references can be resolved either at load time or run time.

For **load-time dynamic linking** (involving upper dynamic library in Figure B.9), the following steps occur. The load module (application module) to be loaded is read into memory. Any reference to an external module (target module) causes the loader to find the target module, load it, and alter the reference to a relative address in memory from the beginning of the application module. There are several advantages to this approach over what might be called static linking:

- It becomes easier to incorporate changed or upgraded versions of the target module, which may be an operating system utility or some other general-purpose routine. With static linking, a change to such a supporting module would require the relinking of the entire application module. Not only is this inefficient, but it may be impossible in some circumstances. For example, in the personal computer field, most commercial software is released in load module form; source and object versions are not released.

- Having target code in a dynamic link file paves the way for automatic code sharing. The operating system can recognize that more than one application is using the same target code because it loaded and linked that code. It can use that information to load a single copy of the target code and link it to both applications, rather than having to load one copy for each application.

- It becomes easier for independent software developers to extend the functionality of a widely used operating system such as Linux. A developer can come up with a new function that may be useful to a variety of applications and package it as a dynamic link module.

With **run-time dynamic linking** (involving lower dynamic library in Figure B.9), some of the linking is postponed until execution time. External references to target modules remain in the loaded program. When a call is made to the absent module, the operating system locates the module, loads it, and links it to the calling module. Such modules are typically shareable. In the Windows environment, these are call dynamic-link libraries (DLLs) Thus, if one process is already making use of a dynamically-linked shared module, then that module is in main memory and a new process can simply link to the already-loaded module.

The use of DLLs can lead to a problem commonly referred to as **DLL hell**. DLL occurs if two or more processes are sharing a DLL module but expect different versions of the module. For example, an application or system function might be re-installed and bring in with it an older version of a DLL file.

We have seen that dynamic loading allows an entire load module to be moved around; however, the structure of the module is static, being unchanged throughout the execution of the process and from one execution to the next. However, in some cases, it is not possible to determine prior to execution which object modules will be required. This situation is typified by transaction-processing applications, such as an airline reservation system or a banking application. The nature of the transaction dictates which program modules are required, and they are loaded as appropriate and linked with the main program. The advantage of the use of such a dynamic linker is that it is not necessary to allocate memory for program units unless those units are referenced. This capability is used in support of segmentation systems.

One additional refinement is possible: An application need not know the names of all the modules or entry points that may be called. For example, a charting program may be written to work with a variety of plotters, each of which is driven by a different driver package. The application can learn the name of the plotter that is currently installed on the system from another process or by looking it up in a configuration file. This allows the user of the application to install a new plotter that did not exist at the time the application was written.

B.4 RECOMMENDED READING AND WEB SITES

[SALO93] covers the design and implementation of assemblers and loaders.

The topics of linking and loading are covered in many books on program development, computer architecture, and operating systems. A particularly detailed treatment is [BECK97]. [CLAR98] also contains a good discussion. A thorough practical discussion of this topic, with numerous OS examples, is [LEVI00].

[BART03] is an excellent treatment for learning assembly language for x86 processors; suitable for self-study. [CART06] covers assembly language for x86 machines. For the serious x86 programmer, [FOG08a] is highly useful. [KNAG04] is a thorough treatment of ARM assembly language.

BART03   Bartlett, J. *Programming from the Ground Up.* 2003. Available at this book's Web site.

BECK97   Beck, L. *System Software.* Reading, MA: Addison-Wesley, 1997.

CART06   Carter, P. *PC Assembly Language.* July 23, 2006. Available at this book's Web site.

CLAR98   Clarke, D., and Merusi, D. *System Software Programming: The Way Things Work.* Upper Saddle River, NJ: Prentice Hall, 1998.

FOG08a   Fog, A. *Optimizing Subroutines in Assembly Language: An Optimization Guide for x86 Platforms.* Copenhagen University College of Engineering, 2008. http://www.agner.org/optimize/

KNAG04   Knaggs, P., and Welsh, S. *ARM: Assembly Language Programming.* Bournemouth University School of Design, Engineering & Computing. August 31, 2004. Available at this book's Web site.

LEVI00   Levine, J. *Linkers and Loaders.* San Francisco: Morgan Kaufmann, 2000.

SALO93   Salomon, D. *Assemblers and Loaders.* Ellis Horwood Ltd, 1993. Available at this book's Web site.

Recommended Web sites:

- **Gavin's Guide to 80x86 Assembly**: A good, concise overview of x86 assembler language.
- **The Art of Assembly Language Programming**: A 1500-page online mega-book on the subject. Should be enough for any student of the subject.

B.5 KEY TERMS, REVIEW QUESTIONS, AND PROBLEMS

Key Terms

assembler	label	mnemonic
assembly language	linkage editor	one-pass assembler
comment	linking	operand
directive	load-time dynamic linking	relocation
dynamic linker	loading	run-time dynamic linking
instruction	macro	two-pass assembler

Review Questions

B.1 List some reasons why it is worthwhile to study assembly language programming.

B.2 What is an assembly language?

B.3 List some disadvantages of assembly language compared to high-level languages.

B.4 List some advantages of assembly language compared to high-level languages.

B.5 What are the typical elements of an assembly language statement.

B.6 List and briefly define four different kinds of assembly language statements.

B.7 What is the difference between a one-pass assembler and a two-pass assembler?

Problems

B.1 Core War is a programming game introduced to the public in the early 1980s [DEWD84], which was popular for a period of 15 years or so. Core War has four main components: a memory array of 8000 addresses, a simplified assembly language Redcode, an executive program called MARS (an acronym for Memory Array Redcode Simulator) and the set of contending battle programs. Two battle programs are entered into the memory array at randomly chosen positions; neither program knows where the other one is. MARS executes the programs in a simple version of time-sharing. The two programs take turns: a single instruction of the first program is executed, then a single instruction of the second, and so on. What a battle program does during the execution cycles allotted to it is entirely up to the programmer. The aim is to destroy the other program by ruining its instructions. In this problem and the next several, we use an even simpler language, called CodeBlue, to explore some Core War concepts.

CodeBlue contains only five assembly language statements and uses three addressing modes (Table B.4). Addresses wrap around, so that for the last location in memory, the relative address of +1 refers to the first location in memory. For example, ADD #4, 6 adds 4 to the contents of relative location 6 and stores the results in location 6; JUMP @5 transfers execution to the memory address contained in the location five slots past the location of the current JUMP instruction.

a. The program Imp is the single instruction COPY 0, 1. What does it do?

b. The program Dwarf is the following sequence of instructions:

```
ADD #4, 3
COPY 2, @2
JUMP -2
DATA 0
```

What does it do?

Table B.4   CodeBlue Assembly Language

(a) Instruction Set

Format		Meaning
DATA	<value>	<value> set at current location
COPY	A, B	copies source A to destination B
ADD	A, B	adds A to B, putting result in B
JUMP	A	transfer execution to A
JUMPZ	A, B	if B = 0, transfer to A

(b) Addressing Modes

Mode	Format	Meaning
Literal	# followed by value	This is an immediate mode, the operand value is in the instruction.
Relative	Value	The value represents an offset from the current location, which contains the operand.
Indirect	@ followed by value	The value represents an offset from the current location; the offset location contains the relative address of the location that contains the operand.

   c. Rewrite Dwarf using symbols, so that it looks more like a typical assembly langauge program.

B.2 What happens if we pit Imp against Dwarf?

B.3 Write a "carpet bombing" program in CodeBlue that zeros out all of memory (with the possible exception of the program locations).

B.4 How would the following program fare against Imp?

```
Loop   COPY #0, -1
       JUMP -1
```

Hint: Remember that instruction execution alternates between the two opposing programs.

B.5 **a.** What is the value of the C status flag after the following sequence:

```
mov al,  3
add al,  4
```

   b. What is the value of the C status flag after the following sequence:

```
mov al,  3
sub al,  4
```

B.6 Consider the following NAMS instruction:

```
cmp vleft, vright
```

For signed integers, there are three status flags that are relevant. If vleft = vright, then ZF is set. If vleft > vright, ZF is unset (set to 0) and SF = OF. If vleft < vright, ZF is unset and SF ≠ OF. Why does SF = OF if vleft > vright?

B.7 Consider the following NASM code fragment:

```
mov al, 0
cmp al, al
je  next
```

Write an equivalent program consisting of a single instruction.

B.8 Consider the following C program:

```
/* a simple C program to average 3 integers */
main ()
{ int avg;
  int i1 = 20;
  int i2 = 13;
  int i3 = 82;
  avg = (i1 + i2 + i3)/3;
}
```

Write an NASM version of this program.

B.9 Consider the following C code fragment:

```
if (EAX == 0) EBX = 1;
else EBX = 2;
```

Write an equivalent NASM code fragment.

B.10 The initialize data directives can be used to initialize multiple locations. For example,

```
db  0x55,0x56,0x57
```

reserves three bytes and initializes their values.

NASM supports the special token $ to allow calculations to involve the current assembly position. That is, $ evalutes to the assembly position at the beginning of the line containing the expression. With the preceding two facts in mind, consider the following sequence of directives:

```
message db 'hello, world'
msglen equ $-message
```

What value is assigned to the symbol msglen?

B.11 Assume the three symbolic variables V1, V2, V3 contain integer values. Write an NASM code fragment that moves the smallest value into integer ax. Use only the instructions mov, cmp, and jbe.

B.12 Describe the effect of this instruction: cmp eax, 1

Assume that the immediately preceding instruction updated the contents of eax.

B.13 The xchg instruction can be used to exchange the contents of two registers. Suppose that the x86 instruction set did not support this instruction.
   a. Implement xchg ax, bx using only push and pop instructions.
   b. Implement xchg ax, bx using only the xor instruction (do not involve other registers).

B.14 In the following program, assume that a, b, x, y are symbols for main memory locations. What does the program do? You can answer the question by writing the equivalent logic in C.

```
mov    eax,a
mov    ebx,b
xor    eax,x
```

```
        xor    ebx,y
        or     eax,ebx
        jnz    L2
   L1:                    ; sequence of instructions...
        jmp    L3
   L2:                    ; another sequence of instructions...
   L3:
```

B.15   Section B.1 includes a C program that calculates the greatest common divisor of two integers.
   a. Describe the algorithm in words and show how the program does implement the Euclid algorithm approach to calculating the greatest common divisor.
   b. Add comments to the assembly program of Figure B.3a to clarify that it implements the same logic as the C program.
   c. Repeat part (b) for the program of Figure B.3b.

B.16   **a.** A 2-pass assembler can handle future symbols and an instruction can therefore use a future symbol as an operand. This is not always true for directives. The EQU directive, for example, cannot use a future symbol. The directive 'A EQU B+1' is easy to execute if B is previously defined, but impossible if B is a future symbol. What's the reason for this?
   b. Suggest a way for the assembler to eliminate this limitation such that any source line could use future symbols.

B.17   Consider a symbol directive MAX of the following form:

symbol MAX list of expressions

The label is mandatory and is assigned the value of the largest expression in the operand field. Example:

```
        MSGLEN MAX A, B, C ; where A, B, C are defined
                             symbols
```

How is MAX executed by the Assembler and in what pass?

GLOSSARY

absolute address   An address in a computer language that identifies a storage location or a device without the use of any intermediate reference.

accumulator   The name of the CPU register in a single-address instruction format. The accumulator, or AC, is implicitly one of the two operands for the instruction.

address bus   That portion of a system bus used for the transfer of an address. Typically, the address identifies a main memory location or an I/O device.

address space   The range of addresses (memory, I/O) that can be referenced.

arithmetic and logic unit (ALU)   A part of a computer that performs arithmetic operations, logic operations, and related operations.

ASCII   American Standard Code for Information Interchange. ASCII is a 7-bit code used to represent numeric, alphabetic, and special printable characters. It also includes codes for *control characters*, which are not printed or displayed but specify some control function.

assembly language   A computer-oriented language whose instructions are usually in one-to-one correspondence with computer instructions and that may provide facilities such as the use of macroinstructions. Synonymous with *computer-dependent language*.

associative memory   A memory whose storage locations are identified by their contents, or by a part of their contents, rather than by their names or positions.

asynchronous timing   A technique in which the occurrence of one event on a bus follows and depends on the occurrence of a previous event.

autoindexing   A form of indexed addressing in which the index register is automatically incremented or decremented with each memory reference.

base   In the numeration system commonly used in scientific papers, the number that is raised to the power denoted by the exponent and then multiplied by the mantissa to determine the real number represented (e.g., the number 10 in the expression $2.7' \ 10^2 = 270$).

base address   A numeric value that is used as a reference in the calculation of addresses in the execution of a computer program.

binary operator   An operator that represents an operation on two and only two operands.

bit   In the pure binary numeration system, either of the digits 0 and 1.

block multiplexor channel   A multiplexer channel that interleaves blocks of data. See also *byte multiplexor channel*. Contrast with *selector channel*.

branch prediction   A mechanism used by the processor to predict the outcome of a program branch prior to its execution.

buffer   Storage used to compensate for a difference in rate of flow of data, or time of occurrence of events, when transferring data from one device to another.

bus   A shared communications path consisting of one or a collection of lines. In some computer systems, CPU, memory, and I/O components are connected by a common bus. Since the lines are shared by all components, only one component at a time can successfully transmit.

bus arbitration   The process of determining which competing bus master will be permitted access to the bus.

bus master   A device attached to a bus that is capable of initiating and controlling communication on the bus.

byte   A sequence of eight bits. Also referred to as an *octet.*

byte multiplexor channel   A multiplexer channel that interleaves bytes of data. See also *block multiplexor channel.* Contrast with *selector channel.*

cache   A relatively small fast memory interposed between a larger, slower memory and the logic that accesses the larger memory. The cache holds recently accessed data, and is designed to speed up subsequent access to the same data.

cache coherence protocol   A mechanism to maintain data validity among multiple caches so that every data access will always acquire the most recent version of the contents of a main memory word.

cache line   A block of data associated with a cache tag and the unit of transfer between cache and memory.

cache memory   A special buffer storage, smaller and faster than main storage, that is used to hold a copy of instructions and data in main storage that are likely to be needed next by the processor and that have been obtained automatically from main storage.

CD-ROM   Compact Disk Read-Only Memory. A nonerasable disk used for storing computer data. The standard system uses 12-cm disks and can hold more than 550 Mbytes.

central processing unit (CPU)   That portion of a computer that fetches and executes instructions. It consists of an Arithmetic and Logic Unit (ALU), a control unit, and registers. Often simply referred to as a *processor.*

cluster   A group of interconnected, whole computers working together as a unified computing resource that can create the illusion of being one machine. The term *whole computer* means a system that can run on its own, apart from the cluster.

combinational circuit   A logic device whose output values, at any given instant, depend only upon the input values at that time. A combinational circuit is a special case of a sequential circuit that does not have a storage capability. Synonymous with *combinatorial circuit.*

compact disk (CD)   A nonerasable disk that stores digitized audio information.

computer architecture   Those attributes of a system visible to a programmer or, put another way, those attributes that have a direct impact on the logical execution of a program. Examples of architectural attributes include the instruction set, the number of bits used to represent various data types (e.g., numbers, characters), I/O mechanisms, and techniques for addressing memory.

computer instruction   An instruction that can be recognized by the processing unit of the computer for which it is designed. Synonymous with *machine instruction.*

computer instruction set   A complete set of the operators of the instructions of a computer together with a description of the types of meanings that can be attributed to their operands. Synonymous with *machine instruction set.*

computer organization   Refers to the operational units and their interconnections that realize the architectural specifications. Organizational attributes include those hardware details transparent to the programmer, such as control signals; interfaces between the computer and peripherals; and the memory technology used.

conditional jump   A jump that takes place only when the instruction that specifies it is executed and specified conditions are satisfied. Contrast with *unconditional jump.*

condition code   A code that reflects the result of a previous operation (e.g., arithmetic). A CPU may include one or more condition codes, which may be stored separately within the CPU or as part of a larger control register. Also known as a *flag.*

control bus   That portion of a system bus used for the transfer of control signals.

control registers   CPU registers employed to control CPU operation. Most of these registers are not user visible.

control storage   A portion of storage that contains microcode.

control unit   That part of the CPU that controls CPU operations, including ALU operations, the movement of data within the CPU, and the exchange of data and control signals across external interfaces (e.g., the system bus).

daisy chain   A method of device interconnection for determining interrupt priority by connecting the interrupt sources serially.

data bus   That portion of a system bus used for the transfer of data.

data communication   Data transfer between devices. The term generally excludes I/O.

decoder   A device that has a number of input lines of which any number may carry signals and a number of output lines of which not more than one may carry a signal, there being a one-to-one correspondence between the outputs and the combinations of input signals.

demand paging   The transfer of a page from auxiliary storage to real storage at the moment of need.

direct access   The capability to obtain data from a storage device or to enter data into a storage device in a sequence independent of their relative position, by means of addresses that indicate the physical location of the data.

direct address   An address that designates the storage location of an item of data to be treated as operand. Synonymous with *one-level address.*

direct memory access (DMA)   A form of I/O in which a special module, called a *DMA module,* controls the exchange of data between main memory and an I/O module. The CPU sends a request for the transfer of a block of data to the DMA module and is interrupted only after the entire block has been transferred.

disabled interrupt   A condition, usually created by the CPU, during which the CPU will ignore interrupt request signals of a specified class.

diskette A flexible magnetic disk enclosed in a protective container. Synonymous with *flexible disk.*

disk pack An assembly of magnetic disks that can be removed as a whole from a disk drive, together with a container from which the assembly must be separated when operating.

disk stripping A type of disk array mapping in which logically contiguous blocks of data, or strips, are mapped round-robin to consecutive array members. A set of logically consecutive strips that maps exactly one strip to each array member is referred to as a stripe.

dynamic RAM A RAM whose cells are implemented using capacitors. A dynamic RAM will gradually lose its data unless it is periodically refreshed.

emulation The imitation of all or part of one system by another, primarily by hardware, so that the imitating system accepts the same data, executes the same programs, and achieves the same results as the imitated system.

enabled interrupt A condition, usually created by the CPU, during which the CPU will respond to interrupt request signals of a specified class.

erasable optical disk A disk that uses optical technology but that can be easily erased and rewritten. Both 3.25-inch and 5.25-inch disks are in use. A typical capacity is 650 Mbytes.

error-correcting code A code in which each character or signal conforms to specific rules of construction so that deviations from these rules indicate the presence of an error and in which some or all of the detected errors can be corrected automatically.

error-detecting code A code in which each character or signal conforms to specific rules of construction so that deviations from these rules indicate the presence of an error.

execute cycle That portion of the instruction cycle during which the CPU performs the operation specified by the instruction opcode.

fetch cycle That portion of the instruction cycle during which the CPU fetches from memory the instruction to be executed.

firmware Microcode stored in read-only memory.

fixed-point representation system A radix numeration system in which the radix point is implicitly fixed in the series of digit places by some convention upon which agreement has been reached.

flip-flop A circuit or device containing active elements, capable of assuming either one of two stable states at a given time. Synonymous with *bistable circuit, toggle.*

floating-point representation system A numeration system in which a real number is represented by a pair of distinct numerals, the real number being the product of the fixed-point part, one of the numerals, and a value obtained by raising the implicit floating-point base to a power denoted by the exponent in the floating-point representation, indicated by the second numeral.

G Prefix meaning 2^{30}.

gate An electronic circuit that produces an output signal that is a simple Boolean operation on its input signals.

general-purpose register A register, usually explicitly addressable, within a set of registers, that can be used for different purposes, for example, as an accumulator, as an index register, or as a special handler of data.

global variable A variable defined in one portion of a computer program and used in at least one other portion of that computer program.

high-performance computing (HPC) A research area dealing with supercomputers and the software that runs on supercomputers. The emphasis is on scientific applications, which may involve heavy use of vector and matrix computation, and parallel algorithms.

immediate address The contents of an address part that contains the value of an operand rather than an address. Synonymous with *zero-level address*.

indexed address An address that is modified by the content of an index register prior to or during the execution of a computer instruction.

indexing A technique of address modification by means of index registers.

index register A register whose contents can be used to modify an operand address during the execution of computer instructions; it can also be used as a counter. An index register may be used to control the execution of a loop, to control the use of an array, as a switch, for table lookup, or as a pointer.

indirect address An address of a storage location that contains an address.

indirect cycle That portion of the instruction cycle during which the CPU performs a memory access to convert an indirect address into a direct address.

input-output (I/O) Pertaining to either input or output, or both. Refers to the movement of data between a computer and a directly attached peripheral.

instruction address register A special-purpose register used to hold the address of the next instruction to be executed.

instruction cycle The processing performed by a CPU to execute a single instruction.

instruction format The layout of a computer instruction as a sequence of bits. The format divides the instruction into fields, corresponding to the constituent elements of the instruction (e.g., opcode, operands).

instruction issue The process of initiating instruction execution in the processor's functional units. This occurs when an instruction moves from the decode stage of the pipeline to the first execute stage of the pipeline

instruction register A register that is used to hold an instruction for interpretation.

integrated circuit (IC) A tiny piece of solid material, such as silicon, upon which is etched or imprinted a collection of electronic components and their interconnections.

interrupt A suspension of a process, such as the execution of a computer program, caused by an event external to that process, and performed in such a way that the process can be resumed. Synonymous with *interruption*.

interrupt cycle That portion of the instruction cycle during which the CPU checks for interrupts. If an enabled interrupt is pending, the CPU saves the current program state and resumes processing at an interrupt-handler routine.

interrupt-driven I/O A form of I/O. The CPU issues an I/O command, continues to execute subsequent instructions, and is interrupted by the I/O module when the latter has completed its work.

I/O channel   A relatively complex I/O module that relieves the CPU of the details of I/O operations. An I/O channel will execute a sequence of I/O commands from main memory without the need for CPU involvement.

I/O controller   A relatively simple I/O module that requires detailed control from the CPU or an I/O channel. Synonymous with *device controller*.

I/O module   One of the major component types of a computer. It is responsible for the control of one or more external devices (peripherals) and for the exchange of data between those devices and main memory and/or CPU registers.

I/O processor   An I/O module with its own processor, capable of executing its own specialized I/O instructions or, in some cases, general-purpose machine instructions.

isolated I/O   A method of addressing I/O modules and external devices. The I/O address space is treated separately from main memory address space. Specific I/O machine instructions must be used. Compare *memory-mapped* I/O.

k   Prefix meaning $2^{10} = 1024$. Thus, 2 kb = 2048 bits.

local variable   A variable that is defined and used only in one specified portion of a computer program.

locality of reference   The tendency of a processor to access the same set of memory locations repetitively over a short period of time.

M   Prefix meaning $2^{20} = 1,048,576$. Thus, 2 Mb = 2,097,152 bits.

magnetic disk   A flat circular plate with a magnetizable surface layer, on one or both sides of which data can be stored.

magnetic tape   A tape with a magnetizable surface layer on which data can be stored by magnetic recording.

mainframe   A term originally referring to the cabinet containing the central processor unit or "main frame" of a large batch machine. After the emergence of smaller minicomputer designs in the early 1970s, the traditional larger machines were described as mainframe computers, mainframes. Typical characteristics of a mainframe are that it supports a large database, has elaborate I/O hardware, and is used in a central data processing facility.

main memory   Program-addressable storage from which instructions and other data can be loaded directly into registers for subsequent execution or processing.

memory address register (MAR)   A register, in a processing unit, that contains the address of the storage location being accessed.

memory buffer register (MBR)   A register that contains data read from memory or data to be written to memory.

memory cycle time   The inverse of the rate at which memory can be accessed. It is the minimum time between the response to one access request (read or write) and the response to the next access request.

memory-mapped I/O   A method of addressing I/O modules and external devices. A single address space is used for both main memory and I/O addresses, and the same machine instructions are used both for memory read/write and for I/O.

microcomputer A computer system whose processing unit is a microprocessor. A basic microcomputer includes a microprocessor, storage, and an input/output facility, which may or may not be on one chip.

microinstruction An instruction that controls data flow and sequencing in a processor at a more fundamental level than machine instructions. Individual machine instructions and perhaps other functions may be implemented by microprograms.

micro-operation An elementary CPU operation, performed during one clock pulse.

microprocessor A processor whose elements have been miniaturized into one or a few integrated circuits.

microprogram A sequence of microinstructions that are in special storage where they can be dynamically accessed to perform various functions.

microprogrammed CPU A CPU whose control unit is implemented using microprogramming.

microprogramming language An instruction set used to specify microprograms.

multiplexer A combinational circuit that connects multiple inputs to a single output. At any time, only one of the inputs is selected to be passed to the output.

multiplexor channel A channel designed to operate with a number of I/O devices simultaneously. Several I/O devices can transfer records at the same time by interleaving items of data. See also *byte multiplexor channel, block multiplexor channel.*

multiprocessor A computer that has two or more processors that have common access to a main storage.

multiprogramming A mode of operation that provides for the interleaved execution of two or more computer programs by a single processor.

multitasking A mode of operation that provides for the concurrent performance or interleaved execution of two or more computer tasks. The same as multiprogramming, using different terminology.

nonuniform memory access (NUMA) multiprocessor A shared-memory multiprocessor in which the access time from a given processor to a word in memory varies with the location of the memory word.

nonvolatile memory Memory whose contents are stable and do not require a constant power source.

nucleus That portion of an operating system that contains its basic and most frequently used functions. Often, the nucleus remains resident in main memory.

ones complement representation Used to represent binary integers. A positive integer is represented as in sign magnitude. A negative integer is represented by reversing each bit in the representation of a positive integer of the same magnitude.

opcode Abbreviated form for *operation code.*

operand An entity on which an operation is performed.

operating system Software that controls the execution of programs and that provides services such as resource allocation, scheduling, input/output control, and data management.

operation code A code used to represent the operations of a computer. Usually abbreviated to opcode.

orthogonality   A principle by which two variables or dimensions are independent of one another. In the context of an instruction set, the term is generally used to indicate that other elements of an instruction (address mode, number of operands, length of operand) are independent of (not determined by) opcode.

page   In a virtual storage system, a fixed-length block that has a virtual address and that is transferred as a unit between real storage and auxiliary storage.

page fault   Occurs when the page containing a referenced word is not in main memory. This causes an interrupt and requires the operating system to bring in the needed page.

page frame   An area of main storage used to hold a page.

parity Bit   A binary digit appended to a group of binary digits to make the sum of all the digits either always odd (odd parity) or always even (even parity).

peripheral equipment   In a computer system, with respect to a particular processing unit, any equipment that provides the processing unit with outside communication. Synonymous with *peripheral device*.

pipeline   A processor organization in which the processor consists of a number of stages, allowing multiple instructions to be executed concurrently.

predicated execution   A mechanism that supports the conditional execution of individual instructions. This makes it possible to execute speculatively both branches of a branch instruction and retain the results of the branch that is ultimately taken.

process   A program in execution. A process is controlled and scheduled by the operating system.

process control block   The manifestation of a process in an operating system. It is a data structure containing information about the characteristics and state of the process.

processor   In a computer, a functional unit that interprets and executes instructions. A processor consists of at least an instruction control unit and an arithmetic unit.

processor cycle time   The time required for the shortest well-defined CPU micro-operation. It is the basic unit of time for measuring all CPU actions. Synonymous with *machine cycle time*.

program counter   Instruction address register.

programmable logic array (PLA)   An array of gates whose interconnections can be programmed to perform a specific logical function.

programmable read-only memory (PROM)   Semiconductor memory whose contents may be set only once. The writing process is performed electrically and may be performed by the user at a time later than original chip fabrication.

programmed I/O   A form of I/O in which the CPU issues an I/O command to an I/O module and must then wait for the operation to be complete before proceeding.

program status word (PSW)   An area in storage used to indicate the order in which instructions are executed, and to hold and indicate the status of the computer system. Synonymous with *processor status word*.

random-access memory (RAM)   Memory in which each addressable location has a unique addressing mechanism. The time to access a given location is independent of the sequence of prior access.

read-only memory (ROM)   Semiconductor memory whose contents cannot be altered, except by destroying the storage unit. Nonerasable memory.

redundant array of independent disks (RAID)   A disk array in which part of the physical storage capacity is used to store redundant information about user data stored on the remainder of the storage capacity. The redundant information enables regeneration of user data in the event that one of the array's member disks or the access path to it fails.

registers   High-speed memory internal to the CPU. Some registers are user visible; that is, available to the programmer via the machine instruction set. Other registers are used only by the CPU, for control purposes.

scalar   A quantity characterized by a single value.

secondary memory   Memory located outside the computer system itself; that is, it cannot be processed directly by the processor. It must first be copied into main memory. Examples include disk and tape.

selector channel   An I/O channel designed to operate with only one I/O device at a time. Once the I/O device is selected, a complete record is transferred one byte at a time. Contrast with *block multiplexor channel, multiplexor channel.*

semiconductor   A solid crystalline substance, such as silicon or germanium, whose electrical conductivity is intermediate between insulators and good conductors. Used to fabricate transistors and solid-state components.

sequential circuit   A digital logic circuit whose output depends on the current input plus the state of the circuit. Sequential circuits thus possess the attribute of memory.

sign–magnitude representation   Used to represent binary integers. In an N-bit word, the leftmost bit is the sign ($0 = $ positive, $1 = $ negative) and the remaining $N - 1$ bits comprise the magnitude of the number.

solid-state component   A component whose operation depends on the control of electric or magnetic phenomena in solids (e.g., transistor crystal diode, ferrite core).

speculative execution   The execution of instructions along one path of a branch. If it later turns out that this branch was not taken, then the results of the speculative execution are discarded.

stack   An ordered list in which items are appended to and deleted from the same end of the list, known as the top. That is, the next item appended to the list is put on the top, and the next item to be removed from the list is the item that has been in the list the shortest time. This method is characterized as last-in-first-out.

static RAM   A RAM whose cells are implemented using flip-flops. A static RAM will hold its data as long as power is supplied to it; no periodic refresh is required.

superpipelined processor   A processor design in which the instruction pipeline consists of many very small stages, so that more than one pipeline stage can be executed during one clock cycle and so that a large number of instructions may be in the pipeline at the same time.

superscalar processor   A processor design that includes multiple-instruction pipelines, so that more than one instruction can be executing in the same pipeline stage simultaneously.

symmetric multiprocessing (SMP)   A form of multiprocessing that allows the operating system to execute on any available processor or on several available processors simultaneously.

synchronous timing   A technique in which the occurrence of events on a bus is determined by a clock. The clock defines equal-width time slots, and events begin only at the beginning of a time slot.

system bus   A bus used to interconnect major computer components (CPU, memory, I/O).

truth table   A table that describes a logic function by listing all possible combinations of input values and indicating, for each combination, the output value.

twos complement representation   Used to represent binary integers. A positive integer is represented as in sign magnitude. A negative number is represented by taking the Boolean complement of each bit of the corresponding positive number, then adding 1 to the resulting bit pattern viewed as an unsigned integer.

unary operator   An operator that represents an operation on one and only one operand.

unconditional jump   A jump that takes place whenever the instruction that specified it is executed.

uniprocessing   Sequential execution of instructions by a processing unit, or independent use of a processing unit in a multiprocessing system.

user-visible registers   CPU registers that may be referenced by the programmer. The instruction-set format allows one or more registers to be specified as operands or addresses of operands.

vector   A quantity usually characterized by an ordered set of scalars.

very long instruction word (VLIW)   Refers to the use of instructions that contain multiple operations. In effect, multiple instructions are contained in a single word. Typically, a VLIW is constructed by the compiler, which places operations that may be executed in parallel in the same word.

virtual storage   The storage space that may be regarded as addressable main storage by the user of a computer system in which virtual addresses are mapped into real addresses. The size of virtual storage is limited by the addressing scheme of the computer system and by the amount of auxiliary storage available, and not by the actual number of main storage locations.

volatile memory   A memory in which a constant electrical power source is required to maintain the contents of memory. If the power is switched off, the stored information is lost.

word   An ordered set of bytes or bits that is the normal unit in which information may be stored, transmitted, or operated on within a given computer. Typically, if a processor has a fixed-length instruction set, then the instruction length equals the word length.

REFERENCES

ABBREVIATIONS

ACM   Association for Computing Machinery
IBM   International Business Machines Corporation
IEEE   Institute of Electrical and Electronics Engineers

ABBO04   Abbot, D. *PCI Bus Demystified.* New York: Elsevier, 2004.

ACOS86   Acosta, R.; Kjelstrup, J.; and Torng, H. "An Instruction Issuing Approach to Enhancing Performance in Multiple Functional Unit Processors." *IEEE Transactions on Computers,* September 1986.

ADAM91   Adamek, J. *Foundations of Coding.* New York: Wiley, 1991.

AGAR89   Agarwal, A. *Analysis of Cache Performance for Operating Systems and Multiprogramming.* Boston: Kluwer Academic Publishers, 1989.

AGER87   Agerwala, T., and Cocke, J. *High Performance Reduced Instruction Set Processors.* Technical Report RC12434 (#55845). Yorktown, NY: IBM Thomas J. Watson Research Center, January 1987.

AMDA67   Amdahl, G. "Validity of the Single-Processor Approach to Achieving Large-Scale Computing Capability." *Proceedings, of the AFIPS Conference,* 1967.

ANDE67a   Anderson, D.; Sparacio, F.; and Tomasulo, F. "The IBM System/360 Model 91: Machine Philosophy and Instruction Handling." *IBM Journal of Research and Development,* January 1967.

ANDE67b   Anderson, S., et al. "The IBM System/360 Model 91: Floating-Point Execution Unit." *IBM Journal of Research and Development,* January 1967. Reprinted in [SWAR90, Volume 1].

ANDE03   Anderson, D. "You Don't Know Jack About Disks." *ACM Queue,* June 2003.

ANDE98   Anderson, D. *FireWire System Architecture.* Reading, MA: Addison-Wesley, 1998.

ANTH08   Anthes, G. "What's Next for the x86?" *ComputerWorld,* June 16, 2008.

ARM08a   ARM Limited. *Cortex-A8 Technical Reference Manual.* ARM DDI 0344E, 2008. www.arm.com

ARM08b   ARM Limited. *ARM11 MPCore Processor Technical Reference Manual.* ARM DDI 0360E, 2008. www.arm.com

ASH90   Ash, R. *Information Theory.* New York: Dover, 1990.

ATKI96   Atkins, M. "PC Software Performance Tuning." *IEEE Computer,* August 1996.

AZIM92   Azimi, M.; Prasad, B.; and Bhat, K. "Two Level Cache Architectures." *Proceedings COMPCON '92,* February 1992.

BACO94   Bacon, F.; Graham, S.; and Sharp, O. " Compiler Transformations for High-Performance Computing." *ACM Computing Surveys,* December 1994.

BAIL93   Bailey, D. "RISC Microprocessors and Scientific Computing." *Proceedings, Supercomputing '93,* 1993.

BART03   Bartlett, J. *Programming from the Ground Up.* 2003. Available at this book's Web site.

BASH81   Bashe, C.; Bucholtz, W.; Hawkins, G.; Ingram, J.; and Rochester, N. "The Architecture of IBM's Early Computers." *IBM Journal of Research and Development,* September 1981.

BASH91   Bashteen, A.; Lui, I.; and Mullan, J. "A Superpipeline Approach to the MIPS Architecture." *Proceedings, COMPCON Spring '91,* February 1991.

BECK97   Beck, L. *System Software.* Reading, MA: Addison-Wesley, 1997.

BELL70   Bell, C.; Cady, R.; McFarland, H.; Delagi, B.; O'Loughlin, J.; and Noonan, R. "A New Architecture for Minicomputers—The DEC PDP-11." *Proceedings, Spring Joint Computer Conference,* 1970.

BELL71   Bell, C., and Newell, A. *Computer Structures: Readings and Examples.* New York: McGraw-Hill, 1971.

BELL74   Bell, J.; Casasent, D.; and Bell, C. "An Investigation into Alternative Cache Organizations." *IEEE Transactions on Computers,* April 1974. http://research.microsoft.com/users/GBell/gbvita.htm

BELL78a   Bell, C.; Mudge, J.; and McNamara, J. *Computer Engineering: A DEC View of Hardware Systems Design.* Bedford, MA: Digital Press, 1978.

BELL78b   Bell, C.; Newell, A.; and Siewiorek, D. "Structural Levels of the PDP-8." In [BELL78a].

BELL78c   Bell, C.; Kotok, A.; Hastings, T.; and Hill, R. "The Evolution of the DEC System-10." *Communications of the ACM,* January 1978.

BENH92   Benham, J. "A Geometric Approach to Presenting Computer Representations of Integers." *SIGCSE Bulletin,* December 1992.

BETK97   Betker, M.; Fernando, J.; and Whalen, S. "The History of the Microprocessor." *Bell Labs Technical Journal,* Autumn 1997.

BEZ03   Bez, R.; et al. Introduction to Flash Memory. *Proceedings of the IEEE*, April 2003.

BHAR00   Bharandwaj, J., et al. "The Intel IA-64 Compiler Code Generator." *IEEE Micro,* September/October 2000.

BLAA97   Blaauw, G., and Brooks, F. *Computer Architecture: Concepts and Evolution.* Reading, MA: Addison-Wesley, 1997.

BLAH83   Blahut, R. *Theory and Practice of Error Control Codes.* Reading, MA: Addison-Wesley, 1983.

BOHR98   Bohr, M. "Silicon Trends and Limits for Advanced Microprocessors." *Communications of the ACM,* March 1998.

BOHR03   Bohr, M. " High Performance Logic Technology and Reliability Challenges." *International Reliability Physics Symposium,* March 2003. http://www.irps.org/03-41st

BORK03   Borkar, S. "Getting Gigascale Chips: Challenges and Opportunities in Continuing Moore's Law." *ACM Queue,* October 2003.

BORK07   Borkar, S. "Thousand Core Chips—A Technology Perspective." *Proceedings, ACM/IEEE Design Automation Conference,* 2007.

BRAD91a   Bradlee, D.; Eggers, S.; and Henry, R. "The Effect on RISC Performance of Register Set Size and Structure Versus Code Generation Strategy." *Proceedings, 18th Annual International Symposium on Computer Architecture,* May 1991.

BRAD91b   Bradlee, D.; Eggers, S.; and Henry, R. "Integrating Register Allocation and Instruction Scheduling for RISCs." *Proceedings, Fourth International Conference on Architectural Support for Programming Languages and Operating Systems,* April 1991.

BREW97   Brewer, E. "Clustering: Multiply and Conquer." *Data Communications,* July 1997.

BREY09   Brey, B. *The Intel Microprocessors: 8086/8066, 80186/80188, 80286, 80386, 80486, Pentium, Pentium Pro Processor, Pentium II, Pentium III, Pentium 4 and Core2 with 64-bit Extensions.* Upper Saddle River, NJ: Prentice Hall, 2009.

BROW96   Brown, S., and Rose, S. "Architecture of FPGAs and CPLDs: A Tutorial." *IEEE Design and Test of Computers,* Vol. 13, No. 2, 1996.

BURG97   Burger, D., and Austin, T. "The SimpleScalar Tool Set, Version 2.0." *Computer Architecture News,* June 1997.

BURK46   Burks, A.; Goldstine, H.; and von Neumann, J. *Preliminary Discussion of the Logical Design of an Electronic Computer Instrument.* Report prepared for U.S. Army Ordnance Dept., 1946, reprinted in [BELL71].

BUYY99a   Buyya, R. *High Performance Cluster Computing: Architectures and Systems.* Upper Saddle River, NJ: Prentice Hall, 1999.

BUYY99b   Buyya, R. *High Performance Cluster Computing: Programming and Applications.* Upper Saddle River, NJ: Prentice Hall, 1999.

CANT01   Cantin, J., and Hill, H. "Cache Performance for Selected SPEC CPU2000 Benchmarks." *Computer Architecture News,* September 2001.

CART96   Carter, J. *Microprocesser Architecture and Microprogramming.* Upper Saddle River, NJ: Prentice Hall, 1996.

CART06   Carter, P. *PC Assembly Language.* July 23, 2006. Available at this book's Web site.

CATA94   Catanzaro, B. *Multiprocessor System Architectures.* Mountain View, CA: Sunsoft Press, 1994.

CEKL97   Cekleov, M., and Dubois, M. "Virtual-Address Caches, Part 1: Problems and Solutions in Uniprocessors." *IEEE Micro,* September/October 1997.

CHAI82   Chaitin, G. "Register Allocation and Spilling via Graph Coloring." *Proceedings, SIGPLAN Symposium on Compiler Construction,* June 1982.

CHAS00   Chasin, A. "Predication, Speculation, and Modern CPUs." *Dr. Dobb's Journal,* May 2000.

CHEN94   Chen, P.; Lee, E.; Gibson, G.; Katz, R.; and Patterson, D. "RAID: High-Performance, Reliable Secondary Storage." *ACM Computing Surveys,* June 1994.

CHEN96   Chen, S., and Towsley, D. "A Performance Evaluation of RAID Architectures." *IEEE Transactions on Computers,* October 1996.

CHOW86   Chow, F.; Himmelstein, M.; Killian, E.; and Weber, L. "Engineering a RISC Compiler System." *Proceedings, COMPCON Spring '86,* March 1986.

CHOW87   Chow, F.; Correll, S.; Himmelstein, M.; Killian, E.; and Weber, L. "How Many Addressing Modes Are Enough?" *Proceedings, Second International Conference on Architectural Support for Programming Languages and Operating Systems,* October 1987.

CHOW90   Chow, F., and Hennessy, J. "The Priority-Based Coloring Approach to Register Allocation." *ACM Transactions on Programming Languages,* October 1990.

CLAR85   Clark, D., and Emer, J. "Performance of the VAX-11/780 Translation Buffer: Simulation and Measurement." *ACM Transactions on Computer Systems,* February 1985.

CLAR98   Clarke, D., and Merusi, D. *System Software Programming: The Way Things Work.* Upper Saddle River, NJ: Prentice Hall, 1998.

CLEM00   Clements, A. "The Undergraduate Curriculum in Computer Architecture." *IEEE Micro,* May/June 2000.

COHE81   Cohen, D. "On Holy Wars and a Plea for Peace." *Computer,* October 1981.

COLW85a   Colwell, R.; Hitchcock, C.; Jensen, E.; Brinkley-Sprunt, H.; and Kollar, C. "Computers, Complexity, and Controversy." *Computer,* September 1985.

COLW85b   Colwell, R.; Hitchcock, C.; Jensen, E.; and Sprunt, H. "More Controversy About 'Computers, Complexity, and Controversy.'" *Computer,* December 1985.

COME00   Comerford, R. "Magnetic Storage: The Medium that Wouldn't Die." *IEEE Spectrum,* December 2000.

COOK82   Cook, R., and Dande, N. "An Experiment to Improve Operand Addressing." *Proceedings, Symposium on Architecture Support for Programming Languages and Operating Systems,* March 1982.

COON81   Coonen J. "Underflow and Denormalized Numbers." *IEEE Computer,* March 1981.

COUT86   Coutant, D.; Hammond, C.; and Kelley, J. "Compilers for the New Generation of Hewlett-Packard Computers." *Proceedings, COMPCON Spring '86,* March 1986.

CRAG79   Cragon, H. "An Evaluation of Code Space Requirements and Performance of Various Architectures." *Computer Architecture News,* February 1979.

CRAG92   Cragon, H. *Branch Strategy Taxonomy and Performance Models.* Los Alamitos, CA: IEEE Computer Society Press, 1992.

CRAW90   Crawford, J. "The i486 CPU: Executing Instructions in One Clock Cycle." *IEEE Micro,* February 1990.

CRIS97   Crisp, R. "Direct RAMBUS Technology: The New Main Memory Standard." *IEEE Micro,* November/December 1997.

CUPP01   Cuppu, V., et al. "High Performance DRAMS in Workstation Environments." *IEEE Transactions on Computers,* November 2001.

DATT93   Dattatreya, G. "A Systematic Approach to Teaching Binary Arithmetic in a First Course." *IEEE Transactions on Education,* February 1993.

DAVI87   Davidson, J., and Vaughan, R. "The Effect of Instruction Set Complexity on Program Size and Memory Performance." *Proceedings, Second International Conference on Architectural Support for Programming Languages and Operating Systems,* October 1987.

DENN68   Denning, P. "The Working Set Model for Program Behavior." *Communications of the ACM,* May 1968.

DERO87   DeRosa, J., and Levy, H. "An Evaluation of Branch Architectures." *Proceedings, Fourteenth Annual International Symposium on Computer Architecture,* 1987.

DESA05   Desai, D., et al. "BladeCenter System Overview." IBM Journal of Research and Development." November 2005.

DEWA90   Dewar, R., and Smosna, M. *Microprocessors: A Programmer's View.* New York: McGraw-Hill, 1990.

DEWD84   Dewdney, A. "In the Game Called Core War Hostile Programs Engage in a Battle of Bits." *Scientific American,* May 1984.

DIJK63   Dijkstra, E. "Making an ALGOL Translator for the X1." In *Annual Review of Automatic Programming, Volume 4.* Pergamon, 1963.

DOWD98   Dowd, K., and Severance, C. *High Performance Computing.* Sebastopol, CA: O'Reilly, 1998.

DUBE91   Dubey, P., and Flynn, M. "Branch Strategies: Modeling and Optimization." *IEEE Transactions on Computers,* October 1991.

DULO98   Dulong, C. "The IA-64 Architecture at Work." *Computer,* July 1998.

ECKE90   Eckert, R. "Communication Between Computers and Peripheral Devices—An Analogy." *ACM SIGCSE Bulletin,* September 1990.

ELAY85   El-Ayat, K., and Agarwal, R. "The Intel 80386—Architecture and Implementation." *IEEE Micro,* December 1985.

ERCE04   Ercegovac, M., and Lang, T. *Digital Arithmetic.* San Francisco: Morgan Kaufmann, 2004.

EISC07   Eischen, C. "RAID 6 Covers More Bases." *Network World,* April 9, 2007.

EVAN03   Evans, J., and Trimper, G. *Itanium Architecture for Programmers.* Upper Saddle River, NJ: Prentice Hall, 2003.

EVEN00a   Even, G., and Paul, W. "On the Design of IEEE Compliant Floating-Point Units." *IEEE Transactions on Computers,* May 2000.

EVEN00b   Even, G., and Seidel, P. "A Comparison of Three Rounding Algorithms for IEEE Floating-Point Multiplication." *IEEE Transactions on Computers,* July 2000.

EVER98   Evers, M., et al. "An Analysis of Correlation and Predictability: What Makes Two-Level Branch Predictors Work." *Proceedings, 25th Annual International Symposium on Microarchitecture,* July 1998.

EVER01   Evers, M., and Yeh, T. "Understanding Branches and Designing Branch Predictors for High-Performance Microprocessors." *Proceedings of the IEEE,* November 2001.

FARH04   Farhat, H. *Digital Design and Computer Organization.* Boca Raton, FL: CRC Press, 2004.

FARM92   Farmwald, M., and Mooring, D. "A Fast Path to One Memory." *IEEE Spectrum,* October 1992.

FLEM86   Fleming, P., and Wallace, J. "How Not to Lie with Statistics: The Correct Way to Summarize Benchmark Results." *Communications of the ACM,* March 1986.

FLYN72   Flynn, M. "Some Computer Organizations and Their Effectiveness." *IEEE Transactions on Computers,* September 1972.

FLYN85   Flynn, M.; Johnson, J.; and Wakefield, S. "On Instruction Sets and Their Formats." *IEEE Transactions on Computers,* March 1985.

FLYN87   Flynn, M.; Mitchell, C.; and Mulder, J. "And Now a Case for More Complex Instruction Sets." *Computer,* September 1987.

FLYN01   Flynn, M., and Oberman, S. *Advanced Computer Arithmetic Design.* New York: Wiley, 2001.

FOG08a   Fog, A. *Optimizing Subroutines in Assembly Language: An Optimization Guide for x86 Platforms.* Copenhagen University College of Engineering, 2008. http://www.agner.org/optimize/

FOG08b   Fog, A. *The Microarchitecture of Intel and AMD CPUs.* Copenhagen University College of Engineering, 2008. http://www.agner.org/optimize/

FRAI83   Frailey, D. "Word Length of a Computer Architecture: Definitions and Applications." *Computer Architecture News,* June 1983.

FRIE96   Friedman, M. "RAID Keeps Going and Going and …" *IEEE Spectrum,* April 1996.

FURB00   Furber, S. *ARM System-On-Chip Architecture.* Reading, MA: Addison-Wesley, 2000.

FURH87   Furht, B., and Milutinovic, V. "A Survey of Microprocessor Architectures for Memory Management." *Computer,* March 1987.

FUTR01   Futral, W. *InfiniBand Architecture: Development and Deployment.* Hillsboro, OR: Intel Press, 2001.

GENU04   Genu, P. *A Cache Primer.* Application Note AN2663. Freescale Semiconductor, Inc., 2004. www.freescale.com/files/32bit/doc/app_note/AN2663.pdf

GHAI98   Ghai, S.; Joyner, J.; and John, L. *Investigating the Effectiveness of a Third Level Cache.* Technical Report TR-980501-01, Laboratory for Computer Architecture, University of Texas at Austin. http://lca.ece.utexas.edu/pubs-by-type.html

GIBB04   Gibbs, W. "A Split at the Core." *Scientific American*, November 2004.

GIFF87   Gifford, D., and Spector, A. "Case Study: IBM's System/360-370 Architecture." *Communications of the ACM,* April 1987.

GOCH06   Gochman, S., et al. "Introduction to Intel Core Duo Processor Architecture." *Intel Technology Journal*, May 2006.

GOLD91   Goldberg, D. "What Every Computer Scientist Should Know About Floating-Point Arithmetic." *ACM Computing Surveys,* March 1991.

GOOD83   Goodman, J. "Using Cache Memory to Reduce Processor-Memory Bandwidth." *Proceedings, 10th Annual International Symposium on Computer Architecture,* 1983. Reprinted in [HILL00].

GOOD05   Goodacre, J., and Sloss, A. "Parallelism and the ARM Instruction Set Architecture." *Computer,* July 2005.

GREG98   Gregg, J. *Ones and Zeros: Understanding Boolean Algebra, Digital Circuits, and the Logic of Sets.* New York: Wiley, 1998.

GRIM05   Grimheden, M., and Torngren, M. "What is Embedded Systems and How Should It Be Taught?—Results from a Didactic Analysis." *ACM Transactions on Embedded Computing Systems,* August 2005.

GUST88   Gustafson, J. "Reevaluating Amdahl's Law." *Communications of the ACM,* May 1988.

HALF97   Halfhill, T. "Beyond Pentium II." *Byte,* December 1997.

HAMM97   Hammond, L.; Nayfay, B.; and Olukotun, K. "A Single-Chip Multiprocessor." *Computer,* September 1997.

HAND98   Handy, J. *The Cache Memory Book.* San Diego: Academic Press, 1993.

HARR06   Harris, W. "Multi-core in the Source Engine." bit-tech.net technical paper, November 2, 2006. bit-tech.net/gaming/2006/11/02/Multi_core_in_the_Source_Engin/1

HAUE07   Haeusser, B., et al. *IBM System Storage Tape Library Guide for Open Systems.* IBM Redbook SG24-5946-05, October 2007. ibm.com/redbooks

HAYE98   Hayes, J. *Computer Architecture and Organization.* New York: McGraw-Hill, 1998.

HEAT84   Heath, J. "Re-Evaluation of RISC 1." *Computer Architecture News*, March 1984.

HENN82   Hennessy, J., et al. "Hardware/Software Tradeoffs for Increased Performance." *Proceedings, Symposium on Architectural Support for Programming Languages and Operating Systems,* March 1982.

HENN84   Hennessy, J. "VLSI Processor Architecture." *IEEE Transactions on Computers,* December 1984.

HENN91 Hennessy, J., and Jouppi, N. "Computer Technology and Architecture: An Evolving Interaction." *Computer,* September 1991.

HENN06 Henning, J. "SPEC CPU2006 Benchmark Descriptions." *Computer Architecture News,* September 2006.

HENN07 Henning, J. "SPEC CPU Suite Growth: An Historical Perspective." *Computer Architecture News,* March 2007.

HIDA90 Hidaka, H.; Matsuda, Y.; Asakura, M.; and Kazuyasu, F. "The Cache DRAM Architecture: A DRAM with an On-Chip Cache Memory." *IEEE Micro,* April 1990.

HIGB90 Higbie, L. "Quick and Easy Cache Performance Analysis." *Computer Architecture News,* June 1990.

HILL64 Hill, R. "Stored Logic Programming and Applications." *Datamation,* February 1964.

HILL89 Hill, M. "Evaluating Associativity in CPU Caches." *IEEE Transactions on Computers,* December 1989.

HILL00 Hill, M.; Jouppi, N.; and Sohi, G. *Readings in Computer Architecture.* San Francisco: Morgan Kaufmann, 2000.

HINT01 Hinton, G., et al. "The Microarchitecture of the Pentium 4 Processor." *Intel Technology Journal,* Q1 2001. http://developer.intel.com/technology/itj/

HIRA07 Hirata, K., and Goodacre, J. "ARM MPCore: The Streamlined and Scalable ARM11 processor core." *Proceedings, 2007 Conference on Asia South Pacific Design Automation,* 2007.

HUCK83 Huck, T. *Comparative Analysis of Computer Architectures.* Stanford University Technical Report No. 83-243, May 1983.

HUCK00 Huck, J., et al. "Introducing the IA-64 Architecture." *IEEE Micro,* September/October 2000.

HUGU91 Huguet, M., and Lang, T. "Architectural Support for Reduced Register Saving/Restoring in Single-Window Register Files." *ACM Transactions on Computer Systems,* February 1991.

HUTC96 Hutcheson, G., and Hutcheson, J. "Technology and Economics in the Semiconductor Industry." *Scientific American,* January 1996.

HWAN93 Hwang, K. *Advanced Computer Architecture.* New York: McGraw-Hill, 1993.

HWAN99 Hwang, K, et al. "Designing SSI Clusters with Hierarchical Checkpointing and Single I/O Space." *IEEE Concurrency,* January–March 1999.

HWU98 Hwu, W. "Introduction to Predicated Execution." *Computer,* January 1998.

HWU01 Hwu, W.; August, D.; and Sias, J. "Program Decision Logic Optimization Using Predication and Control Speculation." *Proceedings of the IEEE,* November 2001.

IBM01 International Business Machines, Inc. *64 Mb Synchronous DRAM.* IBM Data Sheet 364164, January 2001.

INTE98 Intel Corp. *Pentium Pro and Pentium II Processors and Related Products.* Aurora, CO, 1998.

INTE00a Intel Corp. *Intel IA-64 Architecture Software Developer's Manual (4 volumes).* Document 245317 through 245320. Aurora, CO, 2000.

INTE00b Intel Corp. *Itanium Processor Microarchitecture Reference for Software Optimization.* Aurora, CO, Document 245473. August 2000.

INTE01a Intel Corp. *Intel Pentium 4 Processor Optimization Reference Manual.* Document 248966-04 2001. http://developer.intel.com/design/Pentium4/documentation.htm

INTE01b Intel Corp. *Desktop Performance and Optimization for Intel Pentium 4 Processor.* Document 248966-04 2001 http://developer.intel.com/design/Pentium4/documentation.htm

INTE04a Intel Corp. *IA-32 Intel Architecture Software Developer's Manual (4 volumes).* Document 253665 through 253668. 2004. http://developer.intel.com/design/Pentium4/documentation.htm

INTE04b Intel Research and Development. *Architecting the Era of Tera.* Intel White Paper, February 2004. http://www.intel.com/labs/teraera/index.htm

INTE04b   Intel Corp. *Endianness White Paper.* November 15, 2004.

INTE08   Intel Corp. Intel ® 64 and *IA-32 Intel Architectures Software Developer's Manual (3 volumes).* Denver, CO, 2008. intel.com/products/processor/manuals

JACO08   Jacob, B.; Ng, S.; and Wang, D. *Memory Systems: Cache, DRAM, Disk.* Boston: Morgan Kaufmann, 2008.

JAME90   James, D. "Multiplexed Buses: The Endian Wars Continue." *IEEE Micro,* September 1983.

JARP01   Jarp, S. "Optimizing IA-64 Performance." *Dr. Dobb's Journal,* July 2001.

JERR05   Jerraya, A., and Wolf, W., eds. *Multiprocessor Systems-on-Chips.* San Francisco: Morgan Kaufmann, 2005.

JOHN91   Johnson, M. *Superscalar Microprocessor Design.* Englewood Cliffs, NJ: Prentice Hall, 1991.

JOHN08   John, E., and Rubio, J. *Unique Chips and Systems.* Boca Raton, FL: CRC Press, 2008.

JOUP88   Jouppi, N. "Superscalar versus Superpipelined Machines." *Computer Architecture News,* June 1988.

JOUP89a   Jouppi, N., and Wall, D. "Available Instruction-Level Parallelism for Superscalar and Superpipelined Machines." *Proceedings, Third International Conference on Architectural Support for Programming Languages and Operating Systems,* April 1989.

JOUP89b   Jouppi, N. "The Nonuniform Distribution of Instruction-Level and Machine Parallelism and Its Effect on Performance." *IEEE Transactions on Computers,* December 1989.

KAEL91   Kaeli, D., and Emma, P. "Branch History Table Prediction of Moving Target Branches Due to Subroutine Returns." *Proceedings, 18th Annual International Symposium on Computer Architecture,* May 1991.

KAGA01   Kagan, M. "InfiniBand: Thinking Outside the Box Design." *Communications System Design,* September 2001. www.csdmag.com

KALL04   Kalla, R.; Sinharoy, B.; and Tendler, J. "IBM Power5 Chip: A Dual-Core Multithreaded Processor." *IEEE Micro,* March–April 2004.

KANE92   Kane, G., and Heinrich, J. *MIPS RISC Architecture.* Englewood Cliffs, NJ: Prentice Hall, 1992.

KAPP00   Kapp, C. "Managing Cluster Computers." *Dr. Dobb's Journal,* July 2000.

KATE83   Katevenis, M. *Reduced Instruction Set Computer Architectures for VLSI.* PhD dissertation, Computer Science Department, University of California at Berkeley, October 1983. Reprinted by MIT Press, Cambridge, MA, 1985.

KATH01   Kathail. B.; Schlansker, M.; and Rau, B. "Compiling for EPIC Architectures." *Proceedings of the IEEE,* November 2001.

KATZ89   Katz, R.; Gibson, G.; and Patterson, D. "Disk System Architecture for High Performance Computing." *Proceedings of the IEEE,* December 1989.

KEET01   Keeth, B., and Baker, R. *DRAM Circuit Design: A Tutorial.* Piscataway, NJ: IEEE Press, 2001.

KHUR01   Khurshudov, A. *The Essential Guide to Computer Data Storage.* Upper Saddle River, NJ: Prentice Hall, 2001.

KNAG04   Knaggs, P., and Welsh, S. *ARM: Assembly Language Programming.* Bournemouth University, School of Design, Engineering, and Computing, August 31, 2004. www.freetechbooks .com/arm-assembly-language-programming-t729.html

KNUT71   Knuth, D. "An Empirical Study of FORTRAN Programs." *Software Practice and Experience,* vol. 1, 1971.

KNUT98   Knuth, D. *The Art of Computer Programming, Volume 2: Seminumerical Algorithms.* Reading, MA: Addison-Wesley, 1998.

KOOP96   Koopman, P. "Embedded System Design Issues (the Rest of the Story). *Proceedings, 1996 International Conference on Computer Design,* 1996.

KUCK77   Kuck, D.; Parker, D.; and Sameh, A. "An Analysis of Rounding Methods in Floating-Point Arithmetic." *IEEE Transactions on Computers.* July 1977.

KUGA91   Kuga, M.; Murakami, K.; and Tomita, S. "DSNS (Dynamically-hazard resolved, Statically-code-scheduled, Nonuniform Superscalar): Yet Another Superscalar Processor Architecture." *Computer Architecture News,* June 1991.

LEE91   Lee, R.; Kwok, A.; and Briggs, F. "The Floating Point Performance of a Superscalar SPARC Processor." *Proceedings, Fourth International Conference on Architectural Support for Programming Languages and Operating Systems,* April 1991.

LEON07   Leonard, T. "Dragged Kicking and Screaming: Source Multicore." *Proceedings, Game Developers Conference 2007,* March 2007.

LEON08   Leong, p. "Recent Trends in FPGA Architectures and Applications." *Proceedings, 4th IEEE International symposium on Electronic Design, Test, and Applications,* 2008.

LEVI00   Levine, J. *Linkers and Loaders.* San Francisco: Morgan Kaufmann, 2000.

LILJ88   Lilja, D. "Reducing the Branch Penalty in Pipelined Processors." *Computer,* July 1988.

LILJ93   Lilja, D. "Cache Coherence in Large-Scale Shared-Memory Multiprocessors: Issues and Comparisons." *ACM Computing Surveys,* September 1993.

LOVE96   Lovett, T., and Clapp, R. "Implementation and Performance of a CC-NUMA System." *Proceedings, 23rd Annual International Symposium on Computer Architecture,* May 1996.

LUND77   Lunde, A. "Empirical Evaluation of Some Features of Instruction Set Processor Architectures." *Communications of the ACM,* March 1977.

LYNC93   Lynch, M. *Microprogrammed State Machine Design.* Boca Raton, FL: CRC Press, 1993.

MACD84   MacDougall, M. "Instruction-level Program and Process Modeling." *IEEE Computer,* July 1984.

MAHL94   Mahlke, S., et al. "Characterizing the Impact of Predicated Execution on Branch Prediction." *Proceedings, 27th International Symposium on Microarchitecture,* December 1994.

MAHL95   Mahlke, S., et al. "A Comparison of Full and Partial Predicated Execution Support for ILP Processors." *Proceedings, 22nd International Symposium on Computer Architecture,* June 1995.

MAK04   Mak, P., et al. "Processor Subsystem Interconnect for a Large Symmetric Multiprocessing System." *IBM Journal of Research and Development,* May/July 2004.

MANJ01a   Manjikian, N. "More Enhancements of the SimpleScalar Tool Set." *Computer Architecture News,* September 2001.

MANJ01b   Manjikian, N. "Multiprocessor Enhancements of the SimpleScalar Tool Set." *Computer Architecture News,* March 2001.

MANO04   Mano, M. *Logic and Computer Design Fundamentals.* Upper Saddle River, NJ: Prentice Hall, 2004.

MANS97   Mansuripur, M., and Sincerbox, G. "Principles and Techniques of Optical Data Storage." *Proceedings of the IEEE,* November 1997.

MARC90   Marchant, A. *Optical Recording.* Reading, MA: Addison-Wesley, 1990.

MARK00   Markstein, P. *IA-64 and Elementary Functions.* Upper Saddle River, NJ: Prentice Hall PTR, 2000.

MARR02   Marr, D.; et al. "Hyper-Threading Technology Architecture and Microarchitecture." *Intel Technology Journal,* First Quarter, 2002.

MASH95   Mashey, J. "CISC vs. RISC (or what is RISC really)." *USENET comp.arch newsgroup, article 46782,* February 1995.

MAYB84   Mayberry, W., and Efland, G. "Cache Boosts Multiprocessor Performance." *Computer Design,* November 1984.

MAZI03   Mazidi, M., and Mazidi, J. *The 80x86 IBM PC and Compatible Computers: Assembly Language, Design and Interfacing.* Upper Saddle River, NJ: Prentice Hall, 2003.

MCDO05   McDougall, R. "Extreme Software Scaling." *ACM Queue,* September 2005.

MCDO06   McDougall, R., and Laudon, J. "Multi-Core Microprocessors are Here." *;login,* October 2006.

MCEL85   McEliece, R. "The Reliability of Computer Memories." *Scientific American,* January 1985.

MCNA03   McNairy, C., and Soltis, D. "Itanium 2 Processor Microarchitecture." *IEEE Micro,* March-April 2003.

MEE96a   Mee, C., and Daniel, E. eds. *Magnetic Recording Technology.* New York: McGraw-Hill, 1996.

MEE96b   Mee, C., and Daniel, E. eds. *Magnetic Storage Handbook.* New York: McGraw-Hill, 1996.

MEND06   Mendelson, A., et al. "CMP Implementation in Systems Based on the Intel Core Duo Processor." *Intel Technology Journal,* May 2006.

MILE00   Milenkovic, A. "Achieving High Performance in Bus-Based Shared-Memory Multiprocessors." *IEEE Concurrency,* July-September 2000.

MIRA92   Mirapuri, S.; Woodacre, M.; and Vasseghi, N. "The MIPS R4000 Processor." *IEEE Micro,* April 1992.

MOOR65   Moore, G. "Cramming More Components Onto Integrated Circuits." *Electronics Magazine,* April 19, 1965.

MORS78   Morse, S.; Pohlman, W.; and Ravenel, B. "The Intel 8086 Microprocessor: A 16-bit Evolution of the 8080." *Computer,* June 1978.

MOSH01   Moshovos, A., and Sohi, G. "Microarchitectural Innovations: Boosting Microprocessor Performance Beyond Semiconductor Technology Scaling." *Proceedings of the IEEE,* November 2001.

MYER78   Myers, G. "The Evaluation of Expressions in a Storage-to-Storage Architecture." *Computer Architecture News,* June 1978.

NAFF02   Naffziger, S., et al. "The Implementation of the Itanium 2 Microprocessor." *IEEE Journal of Solid-State Circuits,* November 2002.

NOER05   Noergarrd, T. *Embedded Systems Architecture: A Comprehensive Guide for Engineers and Programmers.* New York: Elsevier, 2005.

NOVI93   Novitsky, J.; Azimi, M.; and Ghaznavi, R. "Optimizing Systems Performance Based on Pentium Processors." *Proceedings COMPCON '92,* February 1993.

NOWE07   Nowell, M.; Vusirikala, V.; and Hays, R. "Overview of Requirements and Applications for 40 Gigabit and 100 Gigabit Ethernet." *Ethernet Alliance White Paper,* August 2007.

OBER97a   Oberman, S., and Flynn, M. "Design Issues in Division and Other Floating-Point Operations." *IEEE Transactions on Computers,* February 1997.

OBER97b   Oberman, S., and Flynn, M. "Division Algorithms and Implementations." *IEEE Transactions on Computers,* August 1997.

OLUK96   Olukotun, K., et al. "The Case for a Single-Chip Multiprocessor." *Proceedings, Seventh International Conference on Architectural Support for Programming Languages and Operating Systems,* 1996.

OLUK05   Olukotun, K., and Hammond, L. "The Future of Microprocessors." *ACM Queue,* September 2005.

OLUK07   Olukotun, K.; Hammond, L.; and Laudon, J. *Chip Multiprocessor Architecture: Techniques to Improve Throughput and Latency.* San Rafael, CA: Morgan & Claypool, 2007.

OMON99   Omondi, A. *The Microarchitecture of Pipelined and Superscalar Computers.* Boston: Kluwer, 1999.

OVER01   Overton, M. *Numerical Computing with IEEE Floating Point Arithmetic.* Philadelphia, PA: Society for Industrial and Applied Mathematics, 2001.

PADE81   Padegs, A. "System/360 and Beyond." *IBM Journal of Research and Development,* September 1981.

PADE88   Padegs, A.; Moore, B.; Smith, R.; and Buchholz, W. "The IBM System/370 Vector Architecture: Design Considerations." *IEEE Transactions on Communications,* May 1988.

PARH00   Parhami, B. *Computer Arithmetic: Algorithms and Hardware Design.* Oxford: Oxford University Press, 2000.

PARK89   Parker, A., and Hamblen, J. *An Introduction to Microprogramming with Exercises Designed for the Texas Instruments SN74ACT8800 Software Development Board.* Dallas, TX: Texas Instruments, 1989.

PATT82a   Patterson, D., and Sequin, C. "A VLSI RISC." *Computer,* September 1982.

PATT82b   Patterson, D., and Piepho, R. "Assessing RISCs in High-Level Language Support." *IEEE Micro,* November 1982.

PATT84   Patterson, D. "RISC Watch." *Computer Architecture News,* March 1984.

PATT85a   Patterson, D. "Reduced Instruction Set Computers." *Communications of the ACM.* January 1985.

PATT85b   Patterson, D., and Hennessy, J. "Response to 'Computers, Complexity, and Controversy.'" *Computer,* November 1985.

PATT88   Patterson, D.; Gibson, G.; and Katz, R. "A Case for Redundant Arrays of Inexpensive Disks (RAID)." *Proceedings, ACM SIGMOD Conference of Management of Data,* June 1988.

PATT01   Patt, Y. "Requirements, Bottlenecks, and Good Fortune: Agents for Microprocessor Evolution." *Proceedings of the IEEE,* November 2001.

PEIR99   Peir, J.; Hsu, W.; and Smith, A. "Functional Implementation Techniques for CPU Cache Memories." *IEEE Transactions on Computers,* February 1999.

PELE97   Peleg, A.; Wilkie, S.; and Weiser, U. "Intel MMX for Multimedia PCs." *Communications of the ACM,* January 1997.

PFIS98   Pfister, G. *In Search of Clusters.* Upper Saddle River, NJ: Prentice Hall, 1998.

POLL99   Pollack, F. "New Microarchitecture Challenges in the Coming Generations of CMOS Process Technologies (keynote address)." *Proceedings of the 32nd annual ACM/IEEE International Symposium on Microarchitecture,* 1999.

POPE91   Popescu, V., et al. "The Metaflow Architecture." *IEEE Micro,* June 1991.

PRES01   Pressel, D. "Fundamental Limitations on the Use of Prefetching and Stream Buffers for Scientific Applications." *Proceedings, ACM Symposium on Applied Computing,* March 2001.

PRIN97   Prince, B. *Semiconductor Memories.* New York: Wiley, 1997.

PRIN02   Prince, B. *Emerging Memories: Technologies and Trends.* Norwell, MA: Kluwer, 2002.

PRZY88   Przybylski, S.; Horowitz, M.; and Hennessy, J. "Performance Trade-offs in Cache Design." *Proceedings, Fifteenth Annual International Symposium on Computer Architecture,* June 1988.

PRZY90   Przybylski, S. "The Performance Impact of Block Size and Fetch Strategies." *Proceedings, 17th Annual International Symposium on Computer Architecture,* May 1990.

RADD08   Radding, A. "Small Disks, Big Specs." *Storage Magazine,* September 2008.

RADI83   Radin, G. "The 801 Minicomputer." *IBM Journal of Research and Development,* May 1983.

RAGA83   Ragan-Kelley, R., and Clark, R. "Applying RISC Theory to a Large Computer." *Computer Design,* November 1983.

RAMA77   Ramamoorthy, C. "Pipeline Architecture." *Computing Surveys,* March 1977.

RECH98   Reches, S., and Weiss, S. "Implementation and Analysis of Path History in Dynamic Branch Prediction Schemes." *IEEE Transactions on Computers,* August 1998.

REDD76   Reddi, S., and Feustel, E. "A Conceptual Framework for Computer Architecture." *Computing Surveys,* June 1976.

REIM06   Reimer, J. "Valve Goes Multicore." ars technica, November 5, 2006. arstechnica.com/articles/paedia/cpu/valve-multicore.ars

RICH07   Riches, S., et al. "A Fully Automated High Performance Implementation of ARM Cortex-A8." *IQ Online,* Vol. 6, No. 3, 2007. www.arm.com/iqonline

RODR01   Rodriguez, M.; Perez, J.; and Pulido, J. "An Educational Tool for Testing Caches on Symmetric Multiprocessors." *Microprocessors and Microsystems,* June 2001.

ROSC03   Rosch, W. *Winn L. Rosch Hardware Bible.* Indianapolis, IN: Que Publishing, 2003.

SAKA02   Sakai, S. "CMP on SoC: architect's view." *Proceedings. 15th International Symposium on System Synthesis,* 2002.

SALO93   Salomon, D. *Assemblers and Loaders.* Ellis Horwood Ltd, 1993. Available at this book's Web site.

SATY81   Satyanarayanan, M., and Bhandarkar, D. "Design Trade-Offs in VAX-11 Translation Buffer Organization." *Computer,* December 1981.

SCHA97   Schaller, R. "Moore's Law: Past, Present, and Future." *IEEE Spectrum,* June 1997.

SCHL00a   Schlansker, M.; and Rau, B. "EPIC: Explicitly Parallel Instruction Computing." *Computer,* February 2000.

SCHL00b   Schlansker, M.; and Rau, B. *EPIC: An Architecture for Instruction-Level Parallel Processors.* HPL Technical Report HPL-1999-111, Hewlett-Packard Laboratories (www.hpl.hp.com), February 2000.

SCHW99   Schwarz, E., and Krygowski, C. "The S/390 G5 Floating-Point Unit." *IBM Journal of Research and Development,* September/November 1999.

SEAL00   Seal, D., ed. *ARM Architecture Reference Manual.* Reading, MA: Addison-Wesley, 2000.

SEBE76   Sebern, M. "A Minicomputer-compatible Microcomputer System: The DEC LSI-11." *Proceedings of the IEEE,* June 1976.

SEGA95   Segars, S.; Clarke, K.; and Goudge, L. "Embedded Control Problems, Thumb, and the ARM7TDMI." *IEEE Micro,* October 1995.

SEGE91   Segee, B., and Field, J. *Microprogramming and Computer Architecture.* New York: Wiley, 1991.

SERL86   Serlin, O. "MIPS, Dhrystones, and Other Tales." *Datamation,* June 1, 1986.

SHAN38   Shannon, C. "Symbolic Analysis of Relay and Switching Circuits." *AIEE Transactions,* vol. 57, 1938.

SHAN99   Shanley, T., and Anderson, D. *PCI Systems Architecture.* Richardson, TX: Mindshare Press, 1999.

SHAN03   Shanley, T. *InfinBand Network Architecture.* Reading, MA: Addison-Wesley, 2003.

SHAN05   Shanley, T. *Unabridged Pentium 4, The: IA32 Processor Genealogy.* Reading, MA: Addison-Wesley, 2005.

SHAR97   Sharma, A. *Semiconductor Memories: Technology, Testing, and Reliability.* New York: IEEE Press, 1997.

SHAR00   Sharangpani, H., and Arona, K. "Itanium Processor Microarchitecture." *IEEE Micro,* September/October 2000.

SHAR03   Sharma, A. *Advanced Semiconductor Memories: Architectures, Designs, and Applications.* New York: IEEE Press, 2003.

SHEN05   Shen, J., and Lipasti, M. *Modern Processor Design: Fundamentals of Superscalar Processors.* New York: McGraw-Hill, 2005.

SIEG04   Siegel, T.; Pfeffer, E.; and Magee, A. "The IBM z990 Microprocessor." *IBM Journal of Research and Development,* May/July 2004.

SIEW82   Siewiorek, D.; Bell, C.; and Newell, A. *Computer Structures: Principles and Examples.* New York: McGraw-Hill, 1982.

SIMA97   Sima, D. "Superscalar Instruction Issue." *IEEE Micro,* September/October 1997.

SIMA04   Sima, D. "Decisive Aspects in the Evolution of Microprocessors." *Proceedings of the IEEE,* December 2004.

SIMO96   Simon, H. *The Sciences of the Artificial.* Cambridge, MA: MIT Press, 1996.

SLOS04   Sloss, A.; Symes, D.; and Wright, C. *ARM System Developer's Guide.* San Francisco: Morgan Kaufmann, 2004.

SMIT82   Smith, A. "Cache Memories." *ACM Computing Surveys,* September 1992.

SMIT95   Smith, J., and Sohi, G. "The Microarchitecture of Superscalar Processors." *Proceedings of the IEEE,* December 1995.

SMIT87   Smith, A. "Line (Block) Size Choice for CPU Cache Memories." *IEEE Transactions on Communications,* September 1987.

SMIT88   Smith, J. "Characterizing Computer Performance with a Single Number." *Communications of the ACM,* October 1988.

SMIT89   Smith, M.; Johnson, M.; and Horowitz, M. "Limits on Multiple Instruction Issue." *Proceedings, Third International Conference on Architectural Support for Programming Languages and Operating Systems,* April 1989.

SMIT08   Smith, B. "ARM and Intel Battle over the Mobile Chip's Future." *Computer,* May 2008.

SODE96   Soderquist, P., and Leeser, M. "Area and Performance Tradeoffs in Floating-Point Divide and Square-Root Implementations." *ACM Computing Surveys,* September 1996.

SOHI90   Sohi, G. "Instruction Issue Logic for High-Performance Interruptable, Multiple Functional Unit, Pipelined Computers." *IEEE Transactions on Computers,* March 1990.

STAL88   Stallings, W. "Reduced Instruction Set Computer Architecture." *Proceedings of the IEEE,* January 1988.

STAL07   Stallings, W. *Data and Computer Communications, Eighth Edition.* Upper Saddle River, NJ: Prentice Hall, 2007.

STAL09   Stallings, W. *Operating Systems, Internals and Design Principles, Sixth Edition.* Upper Saddle River, NJ: Prentice Hall, 2009.

STEN90   Stenstrom, P. "A Survey of Cache Coherence Schemes of Multiprocessors." *Computer,* June 1990.

STEV64   Stevens, W. "The Structure of System/360, Part II: System Implementation." *IBM Systems Journal,* Vol. 3, No. 2, 1964. Reprinted in [SIEW82].

STON93   Stone, H. *High-Performance Computer Architecture.* Reading, MA: Addison-Wesley, 1993.

STON96   Stonham, T. *Digital Logic Techniques.* London: Chapman & Hall, 1996.

STRE78   Strecker, W. "VAX-11/780: A Virtual Address Extension to the DEC PDP-11 Family." *Proceedings, National Computer Conference,* 1978.

STRE83   Strecker, W. "Transient Behavior of Cache Memories." *ACM Transactions on Computer Systems,* November 1983.

STRI79   Stritter, E., and Gunter, T. "A Microprocessor Architecture for a Changing World: The Motorola 68000." *Computer,* February 1979.

SWAR90   Swartzlander, E., editor. *Computer Arithmetic, Volumes I and II.* Los Alamitos, CA: IEEE Computer Society Press, 1990.

TAMI83   Tamir, Y., and Sequin, C. "Strategies for Managing the Register File in RISC." *IEEE Transactions on Computers,* November 1983.

TANE78   Tanenbaum, A. "Implications of Structured Programming for Machine Architecture." *Communications of the ACM,* March 1978.

TANE97   Tanenbaum, A., and Woodhull, A. *Operating Systems: Design and Implementation.* Upper Saddle River, NJ: Prentice Hall, 1997.

THOM00   Thompson, D. "IEEE 1394: Changing the Way We Do Multimedia Communications." *IEEE Multimedia,* April–June 2000.

TI90   Texas Instruments Inc. *SN74ACT880 Family Data Manual.* SCSS006C, 1990.

TJAD70   Tjaden, G., and Flynn, M. "Detection and Parallel Execution of Independent Instructions." *IEEE Transactions on Computers,* October 1970.

TOMA93   Tomasevic, M., and Milutinovic, V. *The Cache Coherence Problem in Shared-Memory Multiprocessors: Hardware Solutions.* Los Alamitos, CA: IEEE Computer Society Press, 1993.

TOON81   Toong, H., and Gupta, A. "An Architectural Comparison of Contemporary 16-Bit Microprocessors." *IEEE Micro,* May 1981.

TRIE01   Triebel, W. *Itanium Architecture for Software Developers.* Intel Press, 2001.

TUCK67   Tucker, S. "Microprogram Control for System/360." *IBM Systems Journal,* No. 4, 1967.

TUCK87   Tucker, S. "The IBM 3090 System Design with Emphasis on the Vector Facility." *Proceedings, COMPCON Spring '87,* February 1987.

UNGE02 Ungerer, T.; Rubic, B.; and Silc, J. "Multithreaded Processors." *The Computer Journal,* No. 3, 2002.

UNGE03 Ungerer, T.; Rubic, B.; and Silc, J. "A Survey of Processors with Explicit Multithreading." *ACM Computing Surveys,* March 2003.

VASS03 Vassiliadis, S.; Wong, S.; and Cotofana, S. "Microcode Processing: Positioning and Directions." *IEEE Micro,* July–August 2003.

VOEL88 Voelker, J. "The PDP-8." *IEEE Spectrum,* November 1988.

VOGL94 Vogley, B. "800 Megabyte Per Second Systems Via Use of Synchronous DRAM." *Proceedings, COMPCON '94,* March 1994.

VONN45 Von Neumann, J. *First Draft of a Report on the EDVAC.* Moore School, University of Pennsylvania, 1945. Reprinted in *IEEE Annals on the History of Computing,* No. 4, 1993.

VRAN80 Vranesic, Z., and Thurber, K. "Teaching Computer Structures." *Computer,* June 1980.

WALL85 Wallich, P. "Toward Simpler, Faster Computers." *IEEE Spectrum,* August 1985.

WALL91 Wall, D. "Limits of Instruction-Level Parallelism." *Proceedings, Fourth International Conference on Architectural Support for Programming Languages and Operating Systems,* April 1991.

WANG99 Wang, G., and Tafti, D. "Performance Enhancement on Microprocessors with Hierarchical Memory Systems for Solving Large Sparse Linear Systems." *International Journal of Supercomputing Applications,* vol. 13, 1999.

WEIC90 Weicker, R. "An Overview of Common Benchmarks." *Computer,* December 1990.

WEIN75 Weinberg, G. *An Introduction to General Systems Thinking.* New York: Wiley, 1975.

WEIS84 Weiss, S., and Smith, J. "Instruction Issue Logic in Pipelined Supercomputers." *IEEE Transactions on Computers,* November 1984.

WEYG01 Weygant, P. *Clusters for High Availability.* Upper Saddle River, NJ: Prentice Hall, 2001.

WHIT97 Whitney, S., et al. "The SGI Origin Software Environment and Application Performance." *Proceedings, COMPCON Spring '97,* February 1997.

WICK97 Wickelgren, I. "The Facts About FireWire." *IEEE Spectrum,* April 1997.

WILK51 Wilkes, M. "The Best Way to Design an Automatic Calculating Machine." *Proceedings, Manchester University Computer Inaugural Conference,* July 1951.

WILK53 Wilkes, M., and Stringer, J. "Microprogramming and the Design of the Control Circuits in an Electronic Digital Computer." *Proceedings of the Cambridge Philosophical Society,* April 1953. Reprinted in [SIEW82].

WILK65 Wilkes, M. "Slave memories and dynamic storage allocation," *IEEE Transactions on Electronic Computers,* April 1965. Reprinted in [HILL00].

WILL90 Williams, F., and Steven, G. "Address and Data Register Separation on the M68000 Family." *Computer Architecture News,* June 1990.

YEH91 Yeh, T., and Patt, N. "Two-Level Adapting Training Branch Prediction." *Proceedings, 24th Annual International Symposium on Microarchitecture,* 1991.

ZHAN01 Zhang, Z.; Zhu, Z.; and Zhang, X. "Cached DRAM for ILP Processor Memory Access Latency Reduction." *IEEE Micro,* July–August 2001.

INDEX